Y0-BEC-379

ARCHITECTURAL HANDBOOK

ARCHITECTURAL HANDBOOK

ENVIRONMENTAL ANALYSIS, ARCHITECTURAL PROGRAMMING, DESIGN AND TECHNOLOGY, AND CONSTRUCTION

ALFRED M. KEMPER

Foreword by George J. Hasslein

with material by

Howard N. Helfman
Jack P. Hoag
Roy Irving
Frank J. Moreaux
Ajit S. Randhava

Special Projects by the Offices of

Lee Harris Pomeroy Associates
Albert C. Martin & Associates
Turnbull Associates

A WILEY-INTERSCIENCE PUBLICATION

JOHN WILEY & SONS
New York • Chichester • Brisbane • Toronto

Library of Congress Cataloging in Publication Data:

Kemper, Alfred M 1933–
Architectural handbook.

"A Wiley-Interscience publication."
Bibliography: p.
Includes index.
1. Architecture—Handbooks, manuals, etc.
I. Title.

NA2540.K37 720 78-15257
ISBN 0-471-02697-2

Printed in the United States of America

10 9 8 7 6 5 4 3 2 1

To the memory of my father

DIPLOMINGENIEUR ALPHONSE KEMPER

FOREWORD

The "beret and smock" image of an architect as an artist still lingers in the memory of some who practice architecture today. The architect's craft was once patronized only by the rich and the nobility—those who could afford "quality life." The architect's plaint thus has always been about the elective and dispensable nature of his or her services, and the resulting minimal, even though important, involvement in the constructed environment.

Dramatic social and technological changes in the past few decades have forced us to understand our dependency on and unity with natural systems. A tough lesson is still being learned—that "quality of life" is of the universal human condition and is not specially awarded. Since architecture is existential in nature and tends to reflect the culture, architects must be educated to respond and must practice by responding. As never before, the architect is now sought out for skill in moving the building process through the complex network of requirements for public safety, community responsibility, and societal aspirations. This new assignment may not be possible; time will tell. No other profession, however, is yet as well prepared to take the current labyrinthian trip that can deliver the physical environment. Architectural practice is in some ways beginning to resemble the practice of law: though anyone may present his or her own case, experience has taught that one survives best with wise and experienced counsel. The value and worth of such services are obviously intrinsic, rather than legislated or created by sales techniques.

The marketplace value of the architect increases as he or she masters an increasing rational body of information and principles, yet how well we know that this important work is not totally based on the eternal verities of the sciences. The architect is still the creator of the sensate visual environment—symbols, spaces, and objects. Furthermore, the architect must still adapt to changing principles and values, and converge technology, sociology, and economics into that ineffable "life richness." Consider the direction that the architect's work would take had the hydrogen atom been harnessed (as it surely will) for energy, instead of our facing the specter of finite fossil fuels. One learns something from our semantics, which has devised two separate words for science and art that can connote an adversary relationship. Why haven't we been able to develop a word in our language conveying an activity or body of skills that is both science and art, such as the work of an architect? This is significant of the dilemma.

Alfred Kemper's *Architectural Handbook* is indeed an ambitious undertaking. It includes topics ranging from the fundamentals of earthquake design to the psychology of experiencing buildings. More than any other book to date, it displays the multitude of factors that impinge on the creation of the human habitat. To do this the author has drawn assistance from many specialists and consultants, all of whom contribute the bits and pieces that must somehow be assembled to create a single habitat or multiplied into an environmental fabric. The range of topics is awesome and intimidating, which will be further compounded by changing values and technologies. This is a handbook for architects in their ever continuing education.

GEORGE J. HASSLEIN, FAIA
Dean, School of Architecture and Environmental Design
California Polytechnic State University

San Luis Obispo, California

PREFACE

In about 1900 William R. Ware wrote in his *The American Vignola*, The Five Orders:

A building is a shelter from rain, sun and wind. This implies a roof and walls support it. If the walls entirely enclose the space within, there are doorways for access and windows for light. Roofs and walls, door and windows are the essential features of buildings. . . .

Besides being valuable as a shelter, a building may be in itself a noble and delightful object; architects are builders who, by giving a building good proportions and fine details, and by employing beautiful materials, make it valuable on its own account, independently of its uses.

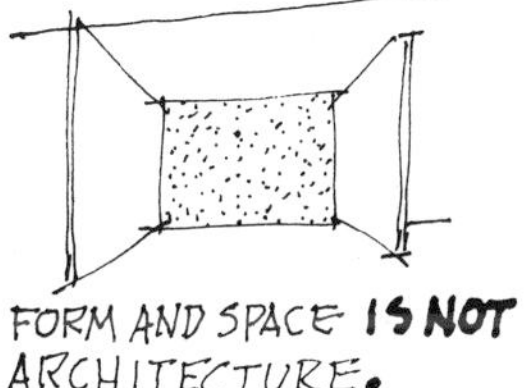

William Wayne Caudill, *Architecture by Team*, Van Nostrand Reinhold, 1971.

That, I venture to say, is what architecture must be. The principle has changed little since then. Architecture has become part of an enormous building industry, however. It now constructs not only shelter from rain, sun, and wind, but also bridges and subways, as well as moving structures to house other moving structures, which eventually will bring us to other planets to live and build again and again.

Each physical structure—whether planned for our planet or for other planets, or whether to be built into the ground or into the ocean—must be in harmony with the environment for which it is intended. Primitive people were shaped by the environment. Like other animals, they remained in equilibrium with the environment until they developed culture. The equilibrium was then shattered, and we have exerted an increasing influence on our environment ever since. In fact, rampant technology has placed us under the direct selective influence of another exciting environment of our own making: the "city." Moreover, architecture is now affected by a variety of aspects, rather than a singular and specific environment.

This book reflects the comprehensive nature of modern architecture. It aims to serve as an overall handbook for architects, various building design engineers, planners, contractors, and other professionals active in building design. It is basically an introduction to the more specialized fields involved in creating what we call contemporary architecture. The ideas in this book have been taken from many sources and then condensed and reorganized. They are all based on the studies and work of various contemporary educators and architects, whom I quote on matters that are important for the future of architecture.

Contemporary architects must be familiar not only with roofs, walls, and windows, but also with history, building materials, engineering techniques, human behavior, social structures, politics, environmental impact, law, and so on. Even though they can make use of specialists in every area, firsthand knowledge is to the architect's advantage.

In reviewing Irwin Allen's motion picture "The Towering Inferno" (1975), the *Los Angeles Times* architecture critic John Pastier wrote:

[Paul] Newman [the architect in the movie] knows the location of every pipe shaft, duct run and panel box in the building. He understands its wiring and electrical circuits better than the journeymen hardhats who installed them in the first place. He knows fire door thicknesses better than a retiring specification writer, is an elevator expert and also manages to find time to rescue more people than anyone except Steve McQueen. . . .

Though Pastier's incredulity may be understandable, the irony is misplaced: the motion picture portrays an event—fire in a highrise building—that has actually occurred several times since the movie was made. Architects should indeed know all the things that the film's architect supposedly knew, but—and here I agree with John Pastier—they should be aware of fire safety problems *before* the building goes up. As a result, I included additional information on the fire safety of buildings and some interesting sections by Richard E. Steven, NFPA Director of Engineering Services, and A. Elwood Willey, NFPA Fire Record Department, as well as good examples described by B. H. Bocook from the Office of Albert C. Hoover & Associates. In fact, the motion picture by Irwin Allen has created great awareness of public safety, hence led to the removal of existing fire hazards as well as brought about legislation to prevent such fire hazards in the future. Fire safety is certainly part of the architect's function, no less than keeping out the rain, cold, and wind.

Earthquakes present a much greater problem and have more serious consequences. They have killed more human beings than any other natural disaster. The motion picture "Earthquake" depicts the horrors of an earthquake, but, being a piece of entertainment, does not clearly show the few simple precautions that can be taken during an earthquake. Again, this led to the inclusion here of a special section on the most recent knowledge about earthquakes, written by Ajit S. Randhava.

This book, I hope, will bridge the communication gap between the various disciplines of the construction industry and create mutual respect among those who shape architecture. In school as well as in practice, the architect tends to get lost among the trees of technical knowledge, losing sight of the broad overall perspectives of the many new technical influences. Increasingly, the question should be asked: to build or not to build? Our professional priorities must fit the times. Medical doctors tend to study "diseases" rather than health from the first day of medical school throughout their professional lives. So do architects, in that they learn "to build" for the client from the first day of architectural school, and continue to do so throughout the years of architectural practice. Too often both the users of the building and the building's environments (physical and/or social) are ignored. The architect is bombarded with monthly research publications and reports slickly and expensively packaged, with very little said about the impact of the new technical products on the economic and social aspects of our society. Only recently has the American Institute of Architects (AIA) initiated a program to evaluate structures *after* a period of use. This should prompt our profession to consider the human elements involved in designing.

Many colleges and universities have encouraged their students to work in an architect's office (during the summer at least) so as to become aware of the complexities of the profession. Such an experience can be lively and vital, but also very traumatic. The profession of architecture is indeed a very complex profession, and the teaching of it grows more difficult as we become more aware of the magnitude of human-environment problems and of our tremendous impact on the natural world.

Although there are scores of books on the individual aspects of the human-environment field, there was no balanced text for architecture that pulled the various elements together until the National Council of Architectural Registration Boards (NCARB) established a new system for the national registration of architects. The NCARB examination handbook, prepared by a large team of architectural professionals and educators, establishes an overall picture of the involvement and influence of various specialties in the design of buildings. The tremendously enlarged scope of environmental problems has required more broadly based solutions, involving federal, state, and local governmental agencies. As a result, many problems that used to seem intractable or unavoidable are now dealt with and reduced to manageable proportions. California's Proposition 20 on coastal protection is an example.

This book will serve as a basis for further studies for the specialist. It will also be understood by any college student or general reader interested in the science of building and its engineering, construction, and legal complexities. Consequently, although basic principles are mentioned wherever necessary, no attempt is made to present them systematically. To do so would have doubled the book's length and also changed its focus. Instead, I follow the basic NCARB examination outline and discuss each category in relation to contemporary architecture. Historical aspects are mentioned wherever necessary. A fuller treatment of specific principles can be found in the books listed in the bibliography.

Some section titles were modified somewhat from the NCARB examination handbook based on my experience in the field both as a practicing architect and as a teacher. Each section can be read separately, but, like architecture itself, the sections are interdependent—everything is influenced by and connected with everything else. Many areas overlap. Thus, logically, the orientation of a building is important not only for the general urban design, but also for the mechanical engineer and for the structural engineer.

The techniques and principles discussed in this book are based on present technology and the most important present social acceptance. As technology and society change, so must our attitude toward planning and designing. Some values will shift slowly; others will change drastically. For instance, the energy crisis affected the design of buildings more suddenly than anything else that architects have experienced before (even though we should have been prepared for it).

Architects now know, too, that all designs will sooner or later undergo a long series of modifications, which sometimes, but not always, are beyond their control. The architect should try to foresee these changes, if possible, or provide for adaptation both for the building and its immediate surroundings. Every building site and its microenvironment has not only its present possibilities or limitations, but also a capacity or incapacity for adaptation to meet future demands. After all, architecture is the organization of various physical spaces and psychological environments to accommodate a variety of human behavior. Since human behavior is subject to constant changes, architecture and especially the design process must alter as necessary to create an environment that fits human purpose. For design has two basic considerations: one is oriented toward human purpose and the other toward the physical environment as a constant, ongoing system.

In preparing this book, I have relied on specialists, as does an architect in actual practice. The structural engineering portion was written by Ajit S. Randhava, the mechanical engineering section by Howard N. Helfman, and the electrical engineering material by Frank Moreaux. I am grateful for the contribution of these professionals to this book, as well as to the field of architecture in general.

A section on solar energy, written by Roy Irving, is included, since architects can strongly affect energy usage by way of their designs. Solar energy can go a long way toward solving our energy problems. It eliminates environmental intrusions, and generates no waste to be disposed of either into the air or into the ground. In his book *Designing and Building a Solar House* architect Donald Watson writes: "A solar house in its relation to the land and the surrounding . . . community can embody our most professional feelings about living with nature and with society."

To make solar energy economically feasible, a special professional effort is needed. Collectors, heat storage hardware, and controls must be perfected, and so must the overall design concept: the passive tools of energy conservation. Solar energy is not a new tool that will overpower our basic design mistakes, as we have learned to do with all mechanical systems. Contemporary architects rely entirely on the mechanical engineer for heating and ventilation of their designs. Once we have learned the passive application of energy conservation, a solar energy system that is carefully designed to fit the design, and vice versa, will make a major contribution to our lives.

The legal aspects of harnessing sunlight as an energy source are probably more important than is the mechanical equipment. However, as more people turn to the sun for energy, legal experts as well as land planners and zoning officials must turn to the law books to try to head off problems that literally cloud future uses of solar power. The focal point is "sun rights." Once solar energy becomes marketable and the demand for it competitive, people will wish to ensure access to sunlight. One case of drawn-out legal tangles over denied access to sunlight could scare not only homeowners but developers away from solar heating and cooling applications. I know already of cases where dearly bought solar collectors are shaded by a new highrise building and a neighbor's maturing trees. Little legal protection exists at this time. United States law, as far as I know, has little to say about a person's "right" to sunlight. This is not the case in other countries. In England, the ancient lights doctrine gives a homeowner who, for example, has received sunlight for 27 years without interference the right to continue receiving that light. United States law protects only the right to get sunlight directly from above, even though most of the sun's rays reach homes at an angle and are therefore susceptible to being cut off by neighboring buildings or trees. We must, therefore, rewrite our zoning ordinances to include protection for solar equipment. This may be accomplished by "purchasing" easement rights over neighboring property. Our water laws may be used as a legal precedent. Water, like sunlight, is a renewable resource and has "directionality," passing at an angle over adjoining parcels. Eventually, of course, these problems will be solved, including those of aesthetics and of the nuisance created by light reflected off the various collectors.

Walter F. Wagner, Jr., editor of *Architectural Records*, writes as follows (June 1977):

> "And so—I hope those involved in solar-energy design and . . . manufacturing do not announce a revolution; but press with all responsible speed for an important evolution."

I think our entire construction industry is ready for an important "evolution," while architecture or architectural education is prepared for a "revolution." We should listen more to the "people" using our designs: that is,

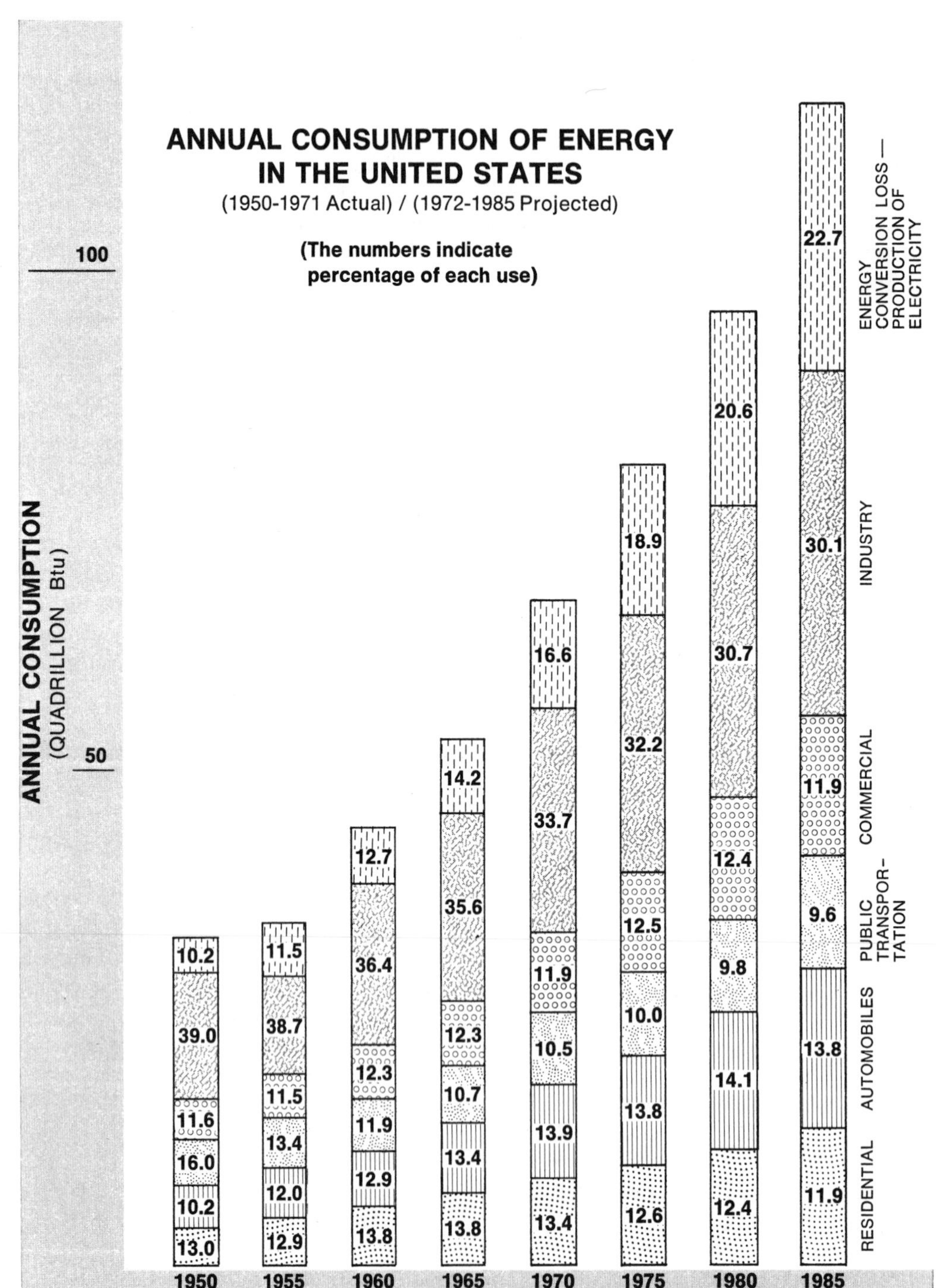

U.S. Government

we should consider more the ''effects'' of our environment on human beings. Most architects and engineers are crudely concerned with the physical creation and the mechanical ''control'' of the environment. Some do bridge the gap between the ''pure'' engineered environment and people, but our present training does not really prepare us for such a step. So far neither *Graphic Standards* nor *Time-Saver Standards* has material on ''architectural psychology,'' such as checklists of ''form sensation'' or ''sensual levels,'' ''meanings of perceptions,'' ''scale,'' ''symbols,'' and so on.

I have the privilege of including some excellent examples of parts of an environmental study, ''Manitou Station,'' a proposed residential community in Philipstown, New York, by the office of Lee Harris Pomeroy Associates. The Biloxi Library and Cultural Center project, City of Biloxi, Mississippi, by the offices of Turnbull Associates, is an example of design programming. Various environmental impact evaluations and feasibility studies for different building types—all new areas of services for the contemporary architect—are also included. An article by Jack P. Hoag outlines the complexity of this new field. Since these are very important new services for our profession, I included an article about the procedure for evaluating environmental impact reports, written by Luna B. Leopold, Frank E. Clarke, Bruce B. Hanshaw, and James R. Balsley for the Department of the Interior in 1971.

I also adopted portions of a special 1974 study, ''The Cost of Sprawl,'' by the Real Estate Research Corporation for the Department of Housing and Urban Development. This study shows clearly the tremendous impact of various design solutions on our physical environment, as well as on our pocketbooks. The future architect will face ever increasing responsibilities that will demand a professionalism far beyond that required when I went to school. But the available tools and especially the professional consultants are also becoming much more sophisticated and learned. The computer as a design tool is one example. ''Envelope: Energy Program: A Simulation Process for Building Design'' by the office of Albert C. Martin & Associates shows the design sophistication achieved with the help of the computer. Architects have performed similar studies in the past, some centuries ago, but only by way of very expensive, time-consuming, and laborious procedures. The modern architect has better tools and experience available to serve his or her client. I hope that architects will continue the trend of changing for and advancing toward a better environment in the future.

Throughout the book the various building codes, the new OSHA regulations, and the metric system are discussed. The book concludes with a section entitled ''Building Value: Energy Design Guidelines for Buildings,'' which is adopted from the guidelines for state buildings by the California State Architect, Sim van Der Ryn & Bender de Moll.

I thank all my fellow architects, both American and Canadian, who have supplied the excellent photographs that make this book more stimulating to read, inspiring the young architect-to-be to pursue the excellence of design that our profession has set out to achieve.

ALFRED M. KEMPER, AIA

Los Angeles, California
January 1979

ACKNOWLEDGMENTS

I express my gratitude to all who have generously assisted in the preparation of this book. I thank Alean Lichtman and Elizabeth Lee Farnsworth for general research and editing; Architekt Bernt Capra for the feasibility studies and environmental impact reports undertaken by my office; architect Fran P. Hosken for ideas from her books and her general review of the text; architect-to-be Jeff Lee for his drawings; my former partners from Architectural License Seminar, engineers Roy T. Beck and Robert Marks and architects Lester Wertheimer and Harry Wood, for their help with the research. For all the statistics, I thank such governmental agencies as the Department of Housing and Urban Development, Environmental Protection Agency, Council on Environmental Quality, Department of the Interior, and the National Commission on Urban Problems.

My appreciation goes to the manuscript editor, Brenda B. Griffing, for her laborious work in checking and correcting such a varied technical text and to the designer of the book, Aline Walton.

My special gratitude is due to architect Harold D. Hauf, FAIA, who suggested that I write this book and gave encouragement as well as detailed help in writing and completing it; and to architect William Dudley Hunt, Jr., FAIA, author of *Total Design* and the architecture editor of the publisher, who made it possible for me to place the book.

A. M. K.

CONTENTS

ARCHITECTURAL HANDBOOK

FLORIDA STATE MUSEUM
Gainesville, Florida
Architect: William Morgan P.A.
Photo: Office

ONE ENVIRONMENTAL ANALYSIS

Environmental analysis encompasses the interrelationship of land use with the environment, involving physical, functional, legal-political, economic, and social relationships. Indeed, the earliest professional decisions that affect the adequacy of the physical environment cannot be made in the absence of such analysis. In general, the architect may participate in four different processes or in a combination of them. The first possibility, *site analysis,* calls for the architect to study the feasibility of a project on several different sites. In *use analysis* the architect assesses the feasibility and compatibility of the project for a specific site. *Impact analysis,* the third possibility, entails the assessment of the impact on the environment of proposed uses in a proposed location(s) given specific land uses and location(s). This option usually emphasizes social and political impacts; large-scale urban design programs, for example, are most applicable. The fourth possibility, the reverse of the impact analysis, is called *land use programming*. Here the architect assesses the most appropriate land use strategy for achieving a *desired* environmental impact and goals. Thus we find that environmental analysis refers to the architect's ability in four areas.

1. Understanding the interrelationship of land use and the environment
2. Assessing the feasibility of a given use on various sites
3. Assessing the feasibility of alternate uses for a specific site
4. Evaluating the environmental criteria relevant to (*a*) programming, and (*b*) design of selected uses on specific sites.

1 PHYSICAL FACTORS

This section discusses the factors involved in site analysis; however they are not all tangible factors, which can be measured accurately. To get a feel for these intangibles (sound, light, wind conditions, etc.), the architect should inspect the site more than once, at different times of the day, as well as on different weekdays. Aerial surveys are necessary on larger sites; the data are obtained from aerial photographs as well as from geological survey maps. The accompanying table indicates the major approaches to the classification of data on physical factors.

Climate

Historically, architectural forms have largely resulted from man's struggle with adverse climate conditions. Today, in our technological age, we have been able to make any area of the planet habitable. Since interior climate control is achieved mainly by ways of mechanical heating and cooling, this advance in construction technology has contributed to the worldwide uniformity

ENVIRONMENTAL ANALYSIS

	PHYSICAL	FUNCTIONAL	SOCIAL	LEGAL	ECONOMICS
	Location Surroundings Ecology Landform	Areas Proximity Utilities Services Catchment Circulation	Perception Psychological Historic Symbolic	Real estate law Codes Zoning Jurisdictions	Real estate econmics Markets Financing
GOALS	Physical Landform Physical impact Surroundings Location	Floor area Utilities Services Proximity User	Effects Impact	Ownership Political associations Zoning limits Political strategies	Profit Equity Market limits Rent Sales Funding Budget Impact
FACTS Organize Analyze	Roads Slopes Views Vegetation Geology Soil Climate	Area parameters Catchment statistics Vehicles Pedestrian	Statistics Social structure Behavior Perception History	Surveys Codes Zoning Deed Easements Jurisdictions	Interest Capitalization Taxes Land cost Rent-sales Transportation Economics Financing Utilities
CONCEPTS Test	Ecological stability Microclimate Ecological impact	Connectivity Catchment Land use	Life-style Behavior setting	Cooperatives Condominiums Air rights Advocacy Leasehold Joint venture Eminent domain	Economic return Leverage Best use Cost sensitivity Absorption rate
NEEDS Determine	Buildable area Limitations Ecological analysis	Area requirements Traffic capacity Parking Catchment Utilty and service capacities Access	Sociological Psychological Perceptual	Political feasibility Legal feasibility Ownership Rulings and variances	Market analysis Population projection Economic impact Traffic projections Cash flow

Figure 1.1 *Source*. U.S. Government.

Figure 1.2 (*a*) The motion of the earth around the sun. (*b*) Seasonal relations between the sun and the earth. *Source*. Jim Leckie, Gil Masters, Harry Whitehouse, and Lily Young, *Other Homes and Garbage*, Sierra Club Books, 1975.

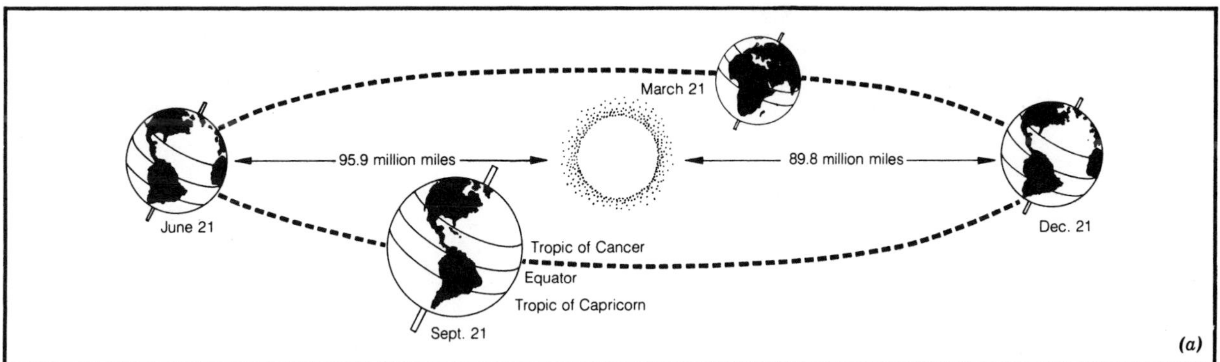

of architecture and to the disappearance of distinct regional types of housing. Because climate is a necessary stimulus to human life, housing that no longer relates to the natural cycles of the local climate is not desirable.

General Climate. The general climate of any area is mainly a function of latitude (distance from the equator), altitude above sea level, distance from the ocean, and conditions of the ocean. Climate can be measured in terms of temperature, humidity, and air movement. A description of the general climate must contain observations of these data for the entire annual cycle and sometimes for more than one decade.

The angle which solar radiation penetrates the atmosphere determines the amount of solar energy received at the various climatic zones on the planet; this angle, for any place on earth, can be found if the latitude is known.

The oceans function as moderating elements in the daily and annual temperature cycles. They store the solar heat of the day and release it at night. Since large water bodies have much less heat loss during the winter than does land, they create mild winters in coastal areas,

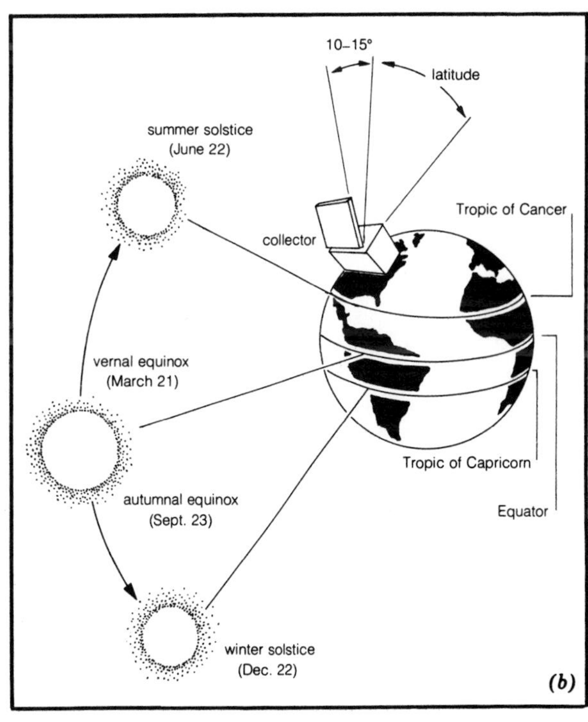

NORTHERN ELECTRIC COMPANY LTD, TORONTO BRANCH LABORATORY
Bramalea, Ontario
Architects: Adamson Associates
Photo: N. & H. Studio

whereas in the summer the water temperature is lower than that of the land, and the cool ocean breeze prevents excessive heat.

The density of the atmosphere changes with altitude, and since the thinner air in high altitudes is less capable of conducting and storing solar heat, the temperature drops as the elevation increases.

Wind, clouds, rain, and snow are functions of the above-mentioned factors, but they are also influenced by the shape, direction, and formation of mountain ranges. The general climatic conditions within the United States can be summarized in four major climate zones:

1 Cool.
2 Temperate.
3 Hot arid.
4 Hot humid.

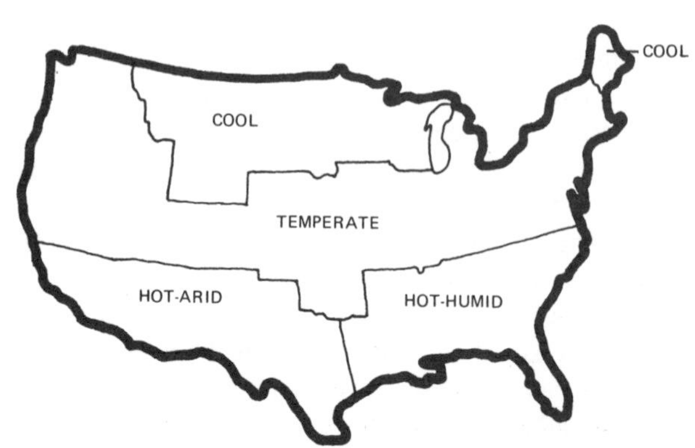

Figure 1.3 Climate regions in the United States. *Source*. U.S. Government.

WOODLAND MEMORIAL HOSPITAL
Woodland, California
Architects: Rex Allen-Drever-Lechowski
Photo: G. Ratto

The main source of information on general climate conditions in the United States is the National Weather Service.

Microclimate. Local changes in the general climate, big enough to require consideration by the architect, can occur at any site. Wind conditions, for instance, may change significantly within a few yards in an urban environment. In addition to man-made features, there are again the factors of elevation, topography, and water bodies, which, on a smaller scale, affect the microclimate. Conditions are modified by the type of ground surface and vegetation present, as well. The effect of elevation on temperatures was mentioned earlier. Expressed in quantitative terms, a 300 to 400 foot rise in altitude decreases the temperature by one degree Fahrenheit.

The directions of slopes in temperate zones may greatly modify the microclimate. South sloping sites may be much warmer than slopes facing north and may have a much longer growth period for vegetation. Similarly, there is usually more rain falling on the leeward side of a mountain, and wind turbulence is the lowest at the bottom of the hill, while the highest wind speed occurs at the top.

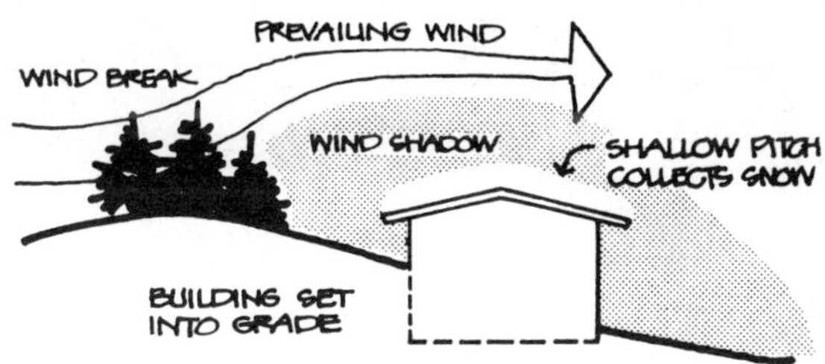

Figure 1.4 Wind patterns modified by ground contours. *Source. Solar Dwelling Design Concepts for Living*, Air Research Corporation for the U.S. Department of Housing and Urban Development, 1976.

The ground surface affects on the temperature because it either reflects or absorbs the solar heat. Paved surfaces thus increase temperatures, while grasses have a high absorption capacity, thus cooling the site. Trees, too, are great natural climate control elements. They provide shade, filter the air, and reduce noise. Moreover, deciduous trees do not block off the desired winter sun. Wooded areas can also control excess wind speeds.

The man-made environment, in particular the urban areas, usually makes undesirable modifications to the microclimate. The cities are usually warmer and noisier than the surrounding countryside, they are burdened with the problem of air pollution, and they are more tiring to the eye because of the glare produced by paved surfaces and by buildings. Also, the highrise buildings in downtown areas tend to create their own wind patterns because of temperature differences between the sunny sides and the surfaces in the shade. The resulting air currents, then, are often increased by the funnel effect created between two buildings.

The architect may find official sources of information regarding data on the general climate, but he or she will need to rely on personal observations as far as the microclimate is concerned. The people who have lived in the particular area for a long time, however, may provide valuable information on local microclimates.

Figure 1.5 Wind pattern over barrier (blown smoke). *Source.* Eugene Eccli, *Low-Cost Energy Efficient Shelter*, Rodale Press, 1976.

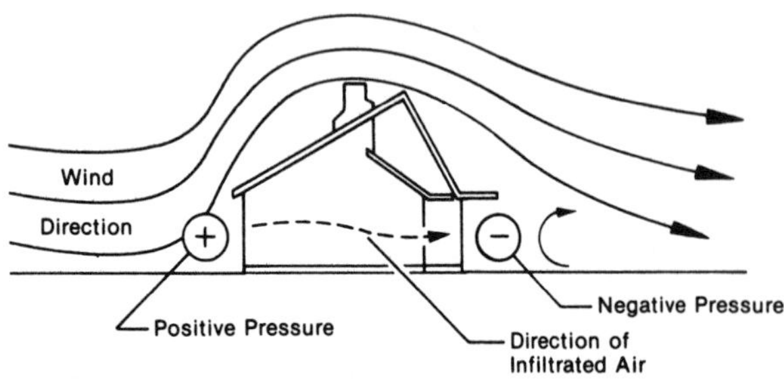

Figure 1.6 Wind flow patterns over house. *Source.* Eugene Eccli, *Low-Cost Energy Efficient Shelter*, Rodale Press, 1976.

Human Comfort. A healthy human body maintains a constant inner body temperature of around 98°F. In temperatures below this level, the body stores the heat that is released in the process of metabolism. If the outside temperature rises, the blood dissipates excessive heat through the blood in the skin's capillaries, and perspiration creates an additional cooling effect by means of evaporation. Although the body can be trained to maintain its temperature in extreme climatic conditions, most people feel discomfort in temperatures below 60° and above 85°F. High humidity adds to the discomfort in hot weather as well as in the cold, as Figure 1.7 illustrates.

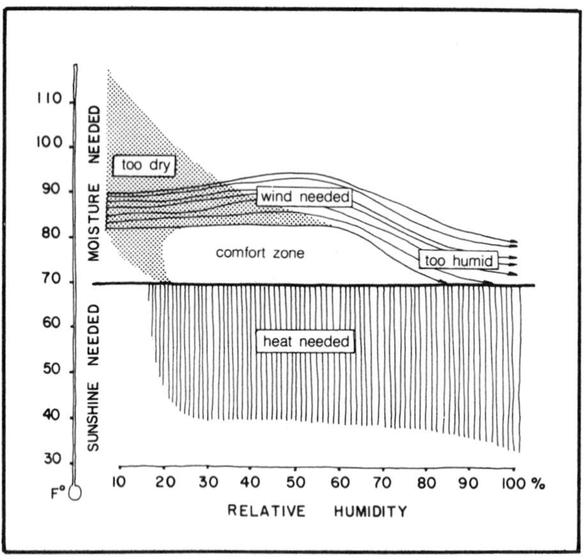

Figure 1.7 Bioclimatic chart. *Source.* Jim Leckie, Gil Masters, Harry Whitehouse, and Lily Young, *Other Homes and Garbage*, Sierra Club Books, 1975.

Naturally sensitivity to temperature and humidity varies slightly from person to person. People's comfort zones also vary with the different climatic zones on the planet. In temperatures below the comfort zone people seek the sunshine, although winds are desired when temperatures outside are high. Wind velocities between 50 and 200 feet per minute are experienced as pleasant; above this speed, the wind adds discomfort. Architecture tries to create an inside climate within the comfort zone by mechanically regulating the effect of solar radiation and by setting up sources of natural ventilation.

Air Pollution. Our cities emit large quantities of smoke and noxious gases, the majority of which are products of vehicular and industrial combustion. In some metropolitan areas the phenomenon of temperature in-

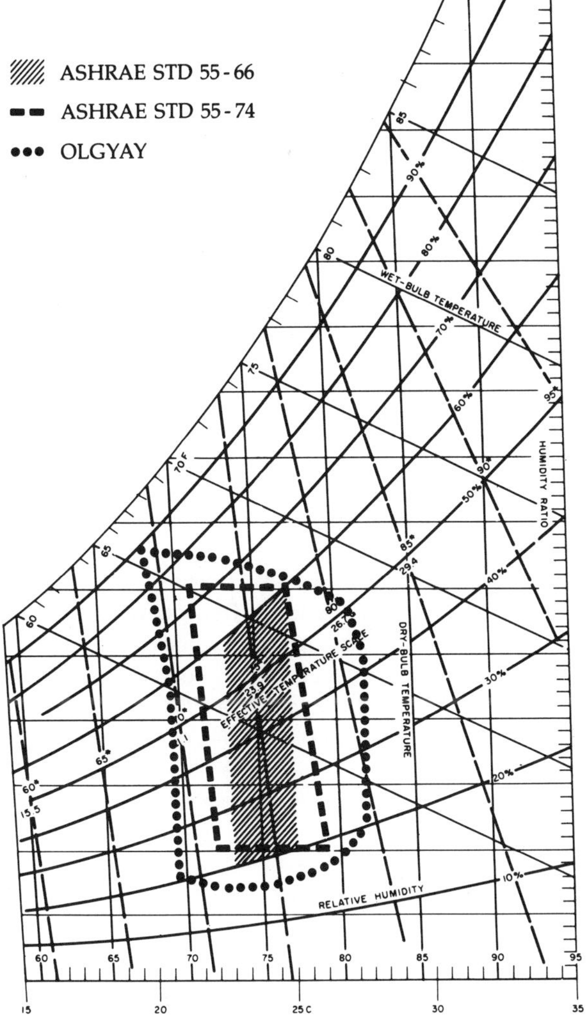

Figure 1.8 Comfort zone comparison. *Source*. State of California.

version adds to the smog problem. Since temperature usually drops by 1°F with every 300 to 400 feet of rise in elevation, the air close to the ground is warmer than the air above, and as it rises it leaves a vacuum that is in turn filled by fresh air descending from cooler areas. This natural air movement helps to dissipate the smog. In some cities, however, the lower layers of air tend to be colder, therefore heavier than the air above, and they do not rise but keep the gaseous pollutants close to the ground. This situation often prevails in cities like Los Angeles and Tokyo.

Ecology

By "ecology" we mean the totality of relationships that exist between organisms and their environment. The term is also used to designate the branch of science dealing with these relationships.

Ecosystems. If a community of plants and animals in one particular environment is observed, the area of study is called an ecology system or ecosystem. Such ecosystems can be natural, like a forest, or man-made, like a fish tank.

Ecosystems are in a state of dynamic balance, collaborating and competing with one another for sun, space, and food. In man-made ecosystems this balance is usually maintained by man's continuous interaction, such as the feeding of fish in an aquarium, or the mowing of a meadow which would otherwise turn into a forest. Some man-made ecosystems may later turn into natural ones. This happens, for instance, when harvested woods are reforested.

The dynamic balance of an ecosystem can have varying degrees of stability. Generally speaking, the stability of the system increases with its diversity, and uniform ecosystems, such as the man-made ecosystems of modern agriculture, tend to be very vulnerable.

Photosynthesis. The energy for all organic life on earth comes from the sun. But whereas animals and human beings can assimilate very little energy directly from solar radiation, plants are equipped to feed themselves directly from sunlight through photosynthesis. The actual process of conversion is still a mystery to us, but we know, for instance, that chlorophyll is essential. Solar energy may enter the human body in one more step of transformation (i.e., if we eat a plant) or through a series of intermediate steps—for instance, if we eat fish which feed on other fish, or if we eat one fish which feeds on plankton, which feeds on light. This cycle is called a food chain. Figure 1.9 depicts the relationship between the quantities of energy produced by plants (producers) and taken in by animals and people (consumers).

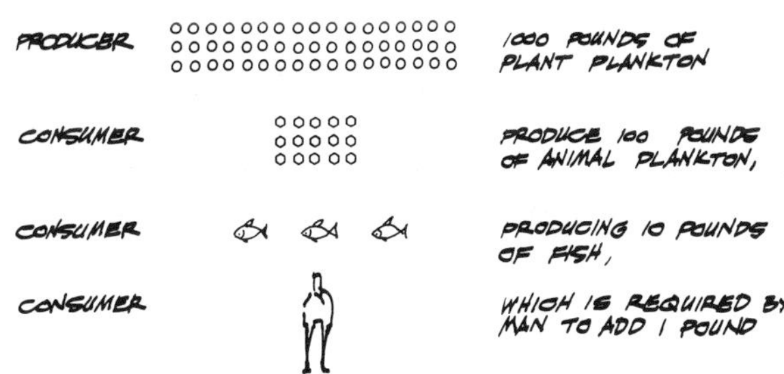

Figure 1.9 The food chain. *Source*. Richard Chan, Architectural License Seminars.

A food chain very rarely has more than five links. Photosynthesis not only produces primary food for man, it also regenerates the atmosphere, since plants extract carbon dioxide from the air and release oxygen, the exact reverse of human or animal breathing.

The Biosphere. Biosphere is the term used to denote the part of the planet's surface in which life can exist. It reaches approximately 500 feet into the ocean and extends into the zone of permanent ice on our mountains. The biosphere provides a special niche for each animal, with living conditions suited best for the particular species. Since all organisms are interacting, the extinction of one species, which leaves one environmental niche empty, may also endanger the existence of various other species.

Damages to the Ecosystem. The science of ecology provides an increasing amount of information regarding the long-range changes in ecosystems caused by the activities of human beings. Agriculture has been responsible for a great variety of ecological changes. Agricultural land produces much more sediment material in rivers than the natural ecology. This buildup alters stream ecosystems and lowers water quality. In addition, the water is polluted with insecticides and fertilizers, which can reach harmful levels in some consumers of the food chain.

Agriculture, as well as cattle raising, has turned grassy brushland into dry prairies. The lowering of ground water tables has had the same effect in many areas. The rising of water temperatures in our streams, due to industrial cooling, has made certain waters uninhabitable for many species. Mistakes in forestry, too, are well known and happened as early as pre-Roman times. For example, erosions and floods were frequent results of the loss of woods in the mountains in the Lebanon, when cedars were removed. Today, as we become aware of such ecological transformations, we must incorporate into the planning process a new set of factors relating to the preservation and balance of our natural resourses.

Land Use Patterns. Although economic factors determined to a great extent the land use patterns of the past, the economics of ecosystems were not readily understood. Today it is apparent that the supply of open land is limited, and new guidelines for future land use are being developed, including the following:

1 Restrictions on private use of waterfronts.
2 Tight control over proposals to convert good agricultural land to other uses.
3 Limited construction over courses of underground water.
4 Preservation of the natural ecosystems in all undeveloped spaces.

Topography

The topography, that is, the shape of the land, is a prime determinant of land use and circulation patterns. On an urban scale the topography influences the shape of cities, but topographical considerations are also a major part in any individual design program. The architect uses topographical maps to study the character of the site. These maps show slopes, hills, valleys, streams, wooded areas, and all man-made features such as roads and structures. Easements, property lines, and utilities are also indicated.

The contour lines on the map connect all points of equal elevation above sea level. Depending on the scale of the map, the contour intervals (vertical distances) are usually 1, 2, 5, and 10 feet. Evenly spaced contour lines indicate a uniform slope, and the closer they are, the steeper is the slope, and vice versa. Sometimes it is

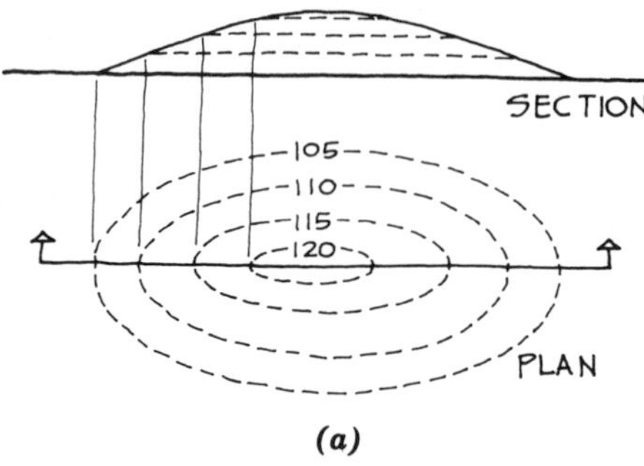

(a)

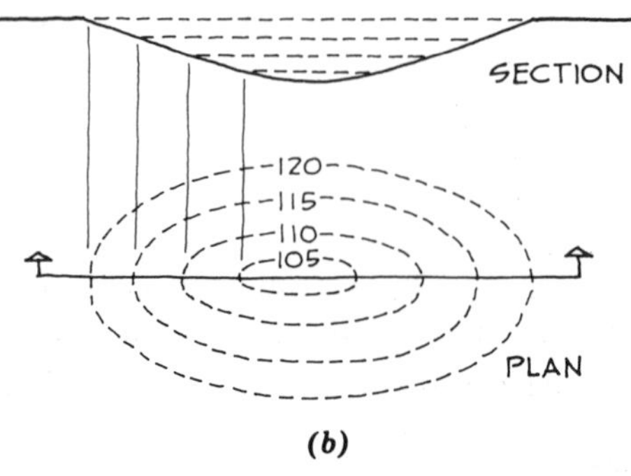

(b)

Figure 1.10 Contours showing (*a*) a peak and (*b*) a depression. *Source*. Albert J. Rutledge, *Anatomy of a Park*, McGraw-Hill Book Company, 1971.

CHAPEL OF THE HOLY CROSS
Sedona, Arizona
Architects: Anshen & Allen
Photo: J. Shulman

difficult to distinguish between valleys and ridges on topography maps. In this case it should be remembered that contour lines point in the direction of the higher numbers in valleys and toward the lower ones on ridges.

The U.S. Department of Geological Survey provides contour maps of all areas in the scale of 1–24,000; that is, 1 inch equals 2000 feet. Contour intervals on these maps are 10 to 20 feet. For more detailed maps, the services of surveyors and civil engineers are usually needed.

The slopes of a site determine to a large extent its development potential. Slopes under 4% are considered level. From 4 to 10% they are called easy grades and can be used for almost all types of construction. Over 10% they are considered steep, and construction becomes more expensive. If there is no slope, a site may have drainage problems, and slopes of 50% or more are subject to erosion. Maximum slopes for some other types of land use are as follows:

Grassy recreation areas	3%
Walkways	4%
Parking areas	5%
Driveways	8%

Natural and man-made drainage networks must be identified on the topography map. If the network is to be replaced or altered by the development, the new system should have at least the same drainage capacity.

The architect must also identify the views available from different points of the site. It is well to use a contour map to make notes regarding the exposure to sun and wind on different slopes.

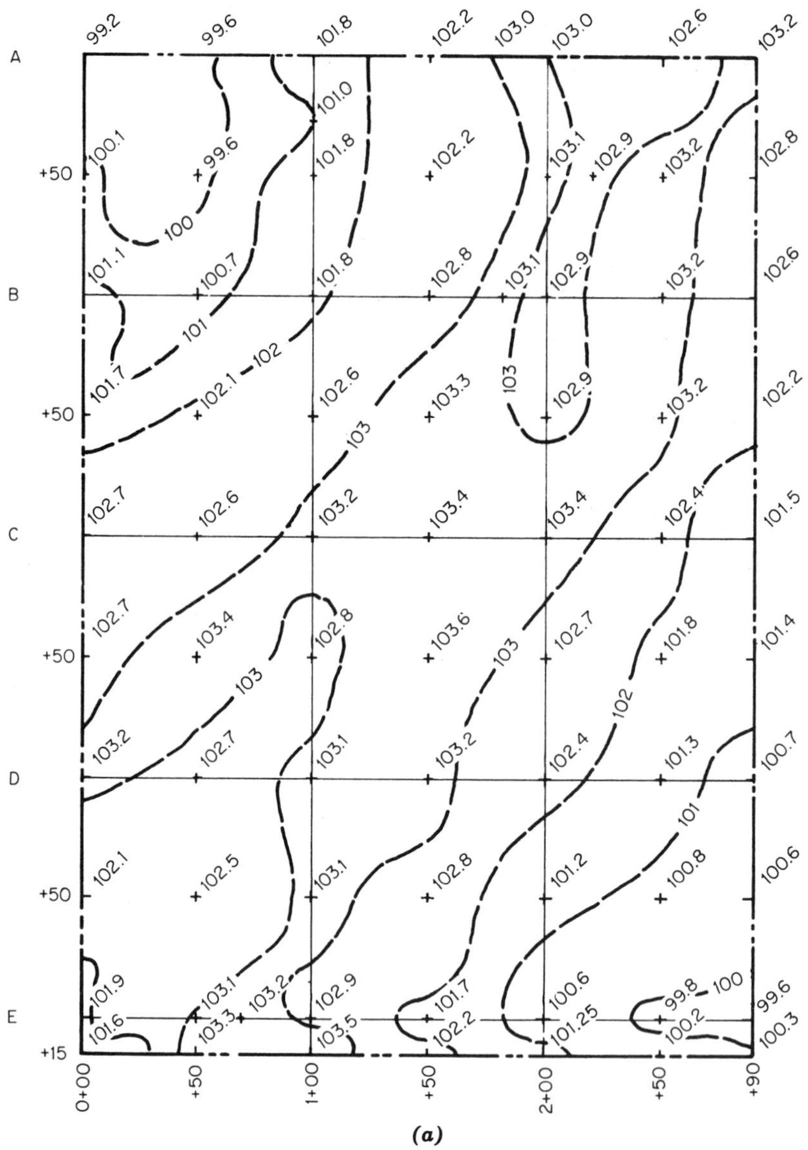

Figure 1.11 (*a*) Topographic map from grid survey. *Source.* Albe E. Munson, *Construction Design for Landscape Architects*, McGraw-Hill Book Company, 1971.

Geology and Soil

Geology distinguishes three basic types of rock according to their process of formation:

1 Sedimentary rocks.
2 Igneous rocks.
3 Metamorphic rocks.

Sedimentary Rocks. Sedimentary rocks are composed of sand and gravel, which were carried along by rivers, oceans, or glaciers, or by the wind. These sediments were deposited in distinct beds, or layers, which can be observed in places of erosion like the Grand Canyon, which is composed entirely of sedimentary rocks. The conversion of loose sand into rock is known as lithification. According to the type of sediment contained, sedimentary rocks are classified as sandstone, shale, mudstone, or limestone.

Sandstone has a high loading capacity and good drainage. A sandstone area typically shows a rugged topography and a thin layer of soil over bedrock. A uniform forest is the typical ground cover of a sandstone area.

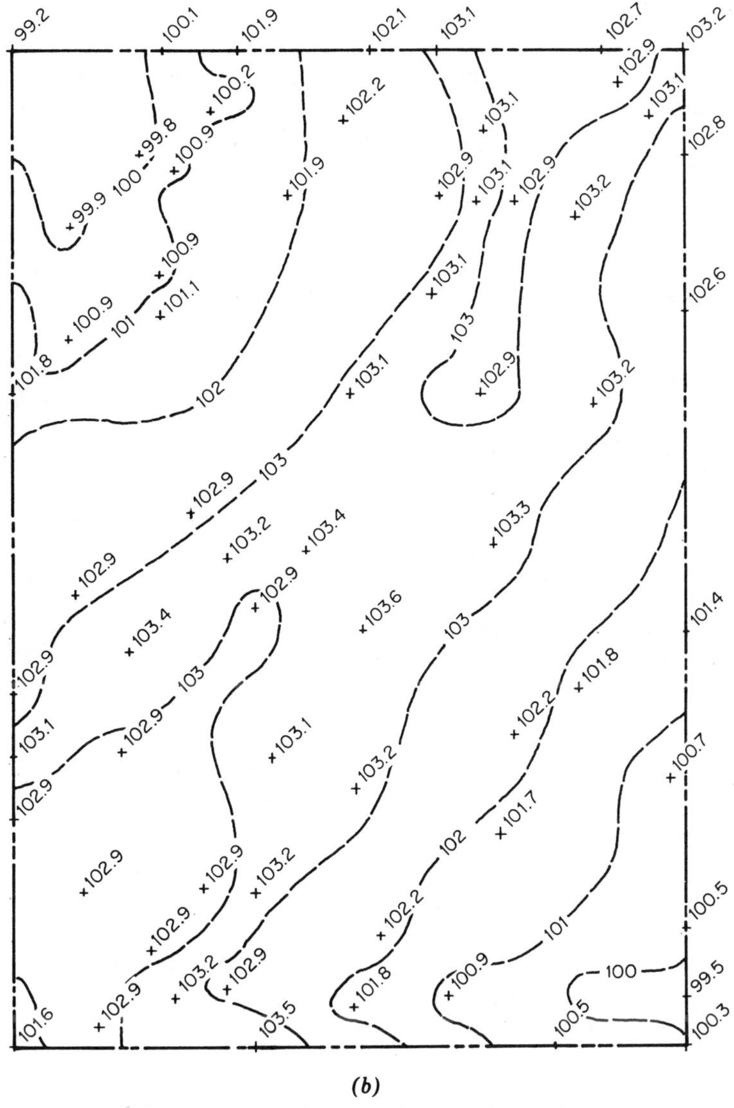

(b)

Figure 1.11 (*b*) Topographic map from stadia survey. *Source*. Albe E. Munson, *Construction Design for Landscape Architects*, McGraw-Hill Book Company, 1971.

Usually the water table is located below the soil layer, within the bedrock.

The most widely found type of sedimentary rock is *shale,* which is formed of clay, silt, or mud, and forms a gentle topography suited for agriculture. Shale has a good bearing capacity but slow internal drainage.

Limestone consists of sediments from the ocean, such as shells and corals, and is subject to erosion by rain, as well as through underground streams and rivers. The rocks, therefore, form very impressive mountain shapes that often contain underground caves and grottoes. The water table in limestone areas typically lies 15 to 20 feet deep, and drainage is usually very good.

Igneous Rocks. Igneous rocks are crystallizations out of molten and liquid minerals that either erupted to the surface of the earth or cooled off slowly below the surface. Granite, the best known representative of this group of rocks, has the highest load-bearing capacity. It is usually covered by only a thin layer of soil, however, which can make drainage problematic.

Metamorphic Rocks. Metamorphic rocks were formed out of sedimentary or igneous rocks during periods of movement within the crust of the earth. These movements were accompanied by great pressure and heat, which changed the crystalline structure of the rock.

If the minerals were pressed into layers, the rock is called foliated. Gneiss, slate, and schist are foliated metamorphic rocks; the unfoliated ones include marble and quartzite. Gneiss is metamorphosed granite; therefore it has the same load-bearing and drainage characteristics. Slate is the metamorphosed shale, but unlike the original rock, it forms a rugged topography and has a higher loading capacity. The soil is usually not more than 4 feet deep, and drainage is good. Schist, the most closely foliated of the three rocks, has good drainage; the bedrock is usually covered with up to 15 feet of soil.

Weathering. The weathering of bedrock is a continuous process on the surface of our planet. Rocks are being destroyed through disintegration, which is a result of the mechanical effects of frost and expansion and contraction through rapid temperature change, and so on, and through decomposition, which includes the chemical changes caused by acid-carrying water and bacteria. Disintegrated rock is eventually washed into rivers and deposited again in a new location in the form of gravel, sand, or clay. Decomposed rock forms the basis for fertile topsoil, where it is mixed with decaying organic material.

Erosion. Erosion is caused by the action of surface water and ice, which carry the weathered rock to a lower level. Thus the effect of erosion is much stronger in areas with high precipitation levels than in arid zones. Erosion can take the following forms: rapid mass movements (including catastrophic events such as landslides, mudslides, and earthflows) and slow mass movements (including solifluction or creep, as well as the action of glaciers).

Hydrologic Cycle. Most of the earth's water (97%) is contained in the oceans, and it is continuously being evaporated into the atmosphere. A small amount of evaporation is also contributed by plants, and this effect is significant enough to create certain microclimates. Precipitation returns the water to the surface, and much rain and snow again fall on the ocean. Most of the precipitation falling on land evaporates again. The remainder either infiltrates the soil or runs directly into the rivers as surface runoff. That which infiltrates the soil either evaporates through plants or reaches the rivers, surfacing again through springs.

Rivers. Rivers and streams can have laminar flow (flow lines run parallel to the banks) or turbulent flow with swirls and eddies, which causes greater erosion on transport material and channel walls. As the velocity of a river decreases, the transport material is gradually deposited. The coarse material is dropped first, and the finest muds are carried the longest. The deposits in a river channel form the so-called flood plain. A flood plain may eventually fill an entire wide valley, where the river often changes its course and must be controlled by dams. The water table is extremely close to the surface, and the soil is very suitable for agriculture. Bedrock is found only in great depth, and the soil is not ideal for high foundation loads. The entire area that is drained by one particular river is called the *drainage basin.*

An *alluvial fan* is a thick deposit of soil that built up at the point where a river changed its speed abruptly from fast to slow. This formation is often found in arid southern areas. As a river enters the ocean, it also loses velocity very rapidly and drops all transport material, which then forms a *delta.*

Soils. All weathered material above the bedrock is called soil. Geologists distinguish three basic levels of soil: the "A" horizon, consisting of the topsoil, which is a mixture of organic and mineral material and feeds the roots of the plants; the "B" horizon, which is made up of minerals; and the "C" horizon, which consists of the partially weathered top zone of the bedrock.

For engineering purposes, soil is classified according to the size of its particles:

Particle size 2 mm$^+$	=	gravel
0.02–2 mm	=	sand
0.002–0.02 mm	=	silt
under 0.002 mm	=	clay

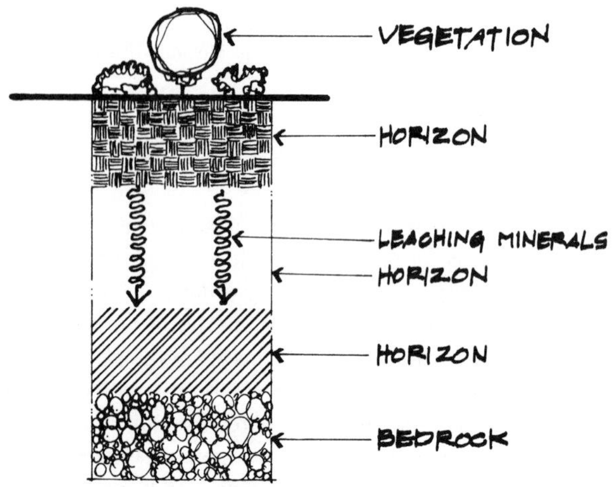

Figure 1.12 Typical soil zones. Drawing by Jeff Lee, Kemper & Associates.

A more detailed classification is provided by the Unified Soil Classification System:

Coarse-grained soils:	
Well-graded gravels	GW
Poorly graded gravels	GP
Silty gravels	GM
Clayey gravels	GC
Well-graded sands	SW
Poorly graded sands	SP
Silty sands	SM
Clayey sands	SC
Fine-grained soils:	
Nonplastic silts	ML
Plastic silts	MH
Organic silts	OL
Nonplastic clays	CL
Plastic clays	CH
Organic clays	OH
Highly organic soils:	
Peat and muck	PT

Apart from the size and shape of particles, the engineer defines soil in terms of mechanical composition, specific gravity, moisture content, unit weight, porosity, consistency, and color. For example, a property important for the planning of septic tanks (leaching fields) is soil permeability.

Volume changes of the soil, which may limit its load-bearing capacity, may be caused by changes in the water table, by frost, or by compression. Swelling and shrinking due to changes in moisture is typical for clays.

The shear strength of a soil, an important property in earthquake-prone areas, can be measured in laboratories through a triaxial compression test on a sample probe. The best soils for construction purposes are sands and gravels, which drain well and have a high load-bearing capacity. Silts and clays are unstable when wet and should not be used for fills.

Underground Water. The permeable material, through which the precipitation water sinks into the ground, is called *aquifer*. In this aquifer, two zones of underground water are distinguished: The zone of *aeration,* which is the one closer to the surface, where both water and air are found between the soil particles; and the zone of *saturation,* which is below, where all voids are filled with water. The line between the two zones is called the *ground water table*.

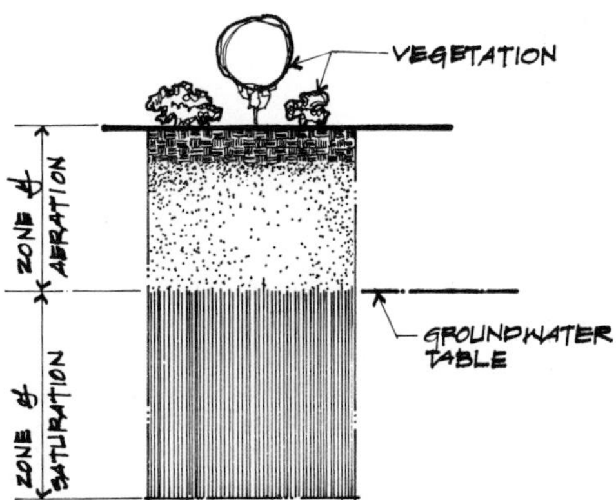

Figure 1.13 Typical underground water zones. Drawing by Jeff Lee, Kemper & Associates.

Soil Tests. Geological information relevant to an architectural site analysis includes the following:

1 Surface drainage patterns.
2 Erosion, sliding, subsidence, inundation.
3 Depth to bedrock.
4 Depth to water table.
5 Load-bearing capacity.

Some of these data can be obtained only from subsurface tests. Preliminary tests may employ sonic, electrical, or seismic techniques. But for more accurate data, test borings are necessary. The methods most frequently used for sampling are rotary-, wash-, or auger-borings. Preliminary borings may be spaced 100 feet apart, but the final tests require borings at least every 25 feet. The borings must penetrate the unstable strata of soil and should extend for at least 20 more feet into the firm strata, which has the required load-bearing capacity.

Laboratory tests give information regarding the settlement of the soil under building loads, its shear strength, and its resistance to earthquakes. The suitability for septic tanks is determined in a percolation test.

Septic Tanks. The following site conditions are required for a septic tank leaching field:

1 A maximum grade of 12%.
2 Depth to water table at least 4 feet.
3 Minimum percolation rate of 1 inch per hour
4 No wells closer than 100 feet.

Sewage that infiltrates the ground water table is a very serious health hazard, and contaminated drinking water has been identified as the primary cause of infant mortality in many countries.

PLATNER RESIDENCE
San Francisco, California
Architect: Warren Platner
Photo: E. Stoller, ESTO

Vegetation

The natural vegetation of a site can give the architect valuable information regarding the soil and the local microclimate. If the site is poorly drained, its trees and shrubs will differ from those on a site that is dry and rocky. The amount of vegetation on hillsides of differing orientation also indicates the different amounts of precipitation to which these areas are exposed.

Existing plants indicate also the types of new planting likely to grow well on the site. Existing large trees should be preserved wherever possible. Not only are they beautiful to look at and complementary to a building, they also control the microclimate with respect to wind, temperature, noise, glare, and humidity. This aspect of design is explored further in Chapter 3.

Manitou Station: A Proposed Residential Community

Manitou Station Development Group
Lee Harris Pomeroy Associates, Architects

"Manitou Station" is a proposed new residential community conceived in response to several stated parameters:

- The need to provide homes for an increasing number of people over the next 10 to 15 years.
- The desire to preserve large natural and ecologically significant countryside.
- The wish to take advantage of the unique qualities of a large and very special site with extensive Hudson River and Route 9D frontage, major wetlands, other valuable natural resources, and a Penn Central Railroad stop on the property.

We believe the design of this project to be consistent with the highest standards of environmentally sound planning and the best interests of the people of the Town of Philipstown. Its construction would provide the best possible use for this property and would fulfill the intent and objectives of the Philipstown Zoning Law as stated in the Planned Development District Regulations.

This is an opportunity to bring to Philipstown a unique community with appropriate shopping, recreation, and commuter services, as well as open space advantages that can be shared by all the residents of the town. With realization of this plan, 4/5 mile of otherwise private Hudson River frontage becomes accessible to the people of the town forever. Every effort has been made to plan an ecologically sound, balanced community, which will preserve the existing values and traditions of the town and its people and reinforce the natural qualities of the river, the land, and its resources.

Growth. Growth is inevitable. What is important is that any change necessary to accommodate it respect the natural environment, as well as the existing community values and living patterns. This can be ensured only through clear vision, sound planning, and thoughtful community action.

The Future of Putnam County. Since the end of World War II, the United States has reached a point of development without precedent or parallel. Population grew almost 50% in between 1945 and 1970, or by 65 million. Official projections point to a further increase of almost 100 million by the year 2000.

During the same period, the nation's productivity grew by almost 300%, and experts believe that this economic growth—like the population—will continue at an even greater rate through the year 2000. The New York metropolitan region, one of the largest and most complex urban areas in the world, contains 10% of the country's population, in an area of about 9000 square miles—larger than several of the states. It includes 28 counties and planning subregions, with more than 18 million inhabitants. By 1985, this region will have 25 million people. In other words, it must absorb two cities the size of Chicago in a very short time. By the year 2000, forecasts indicate a population of 30 million!

Pressure from the South. Regional planners believe that New York City will continue to serve as a regional job magnet. Of the 7.8 million people employed in the region [in 1970], 28% work in the Manhattan central business district. The Manhattan office building concentration brings to the region a huge assemblage of managerial, business, and professional talent and the impact from this extends throughout the metropolitan area. By 1985, more than 2.5 million nonagricultural jobs will have been added to the regional employment market.

Growth between 1945 and 1970 has taken place primarily in the inner suburbs of New York City. But these suburbs are beginning to reach saturation, and a new tier of developable land must absorb the ever-expanding population. The Tri-State Regional Planning Commission, the official regional planning agency in the New York metropolitan area, whose members represent New York, New Jersey, and Connecticut points out that continued urbanization will have caused about half of the 8000 square miles within the region to be fully developed by 1985. By far the greater amount of this growth and urbanization will take place in areas from 20 to 60 miles out from Manhattan, where much of the presently vacant land will be developed. Putnam County, New York, lies well within that range.

Putnam County has already been growing, but pressures are increasing. Population growing in outer parts of New York City and the surrounding counties will be complemented by a continuing rise in industrial development and new commercial subcenters in these areas. This has important implications in terms of housing, employment, and transportation as the job opportunities move closer and closer to the county. But Manhattan is not the only direction from which Putnam is experiencing growth pressure.

Pressure from the West. Other factors will increase pressure for development in the Highlands also. Rock-

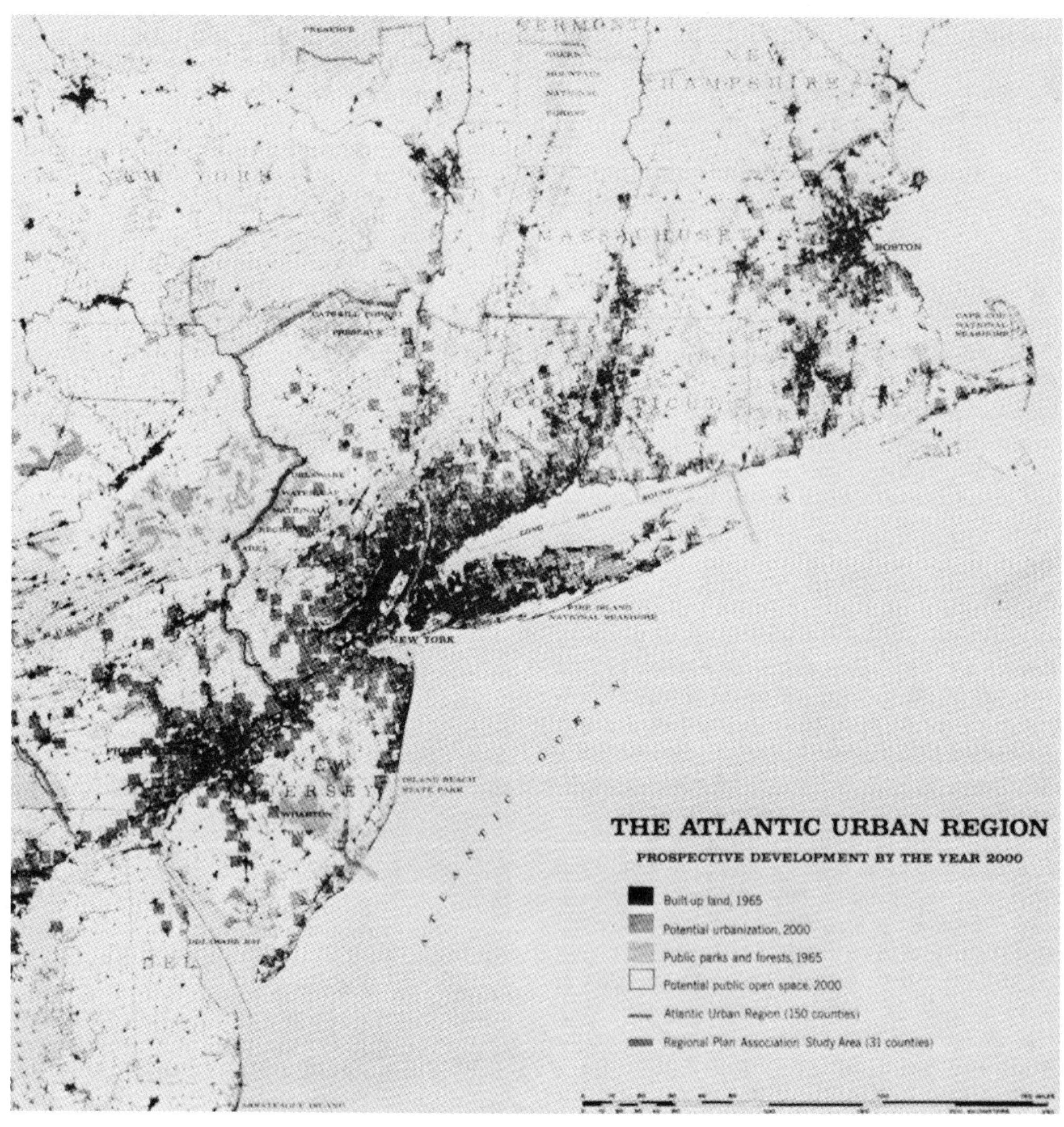

Figure 1.14

land County, to the southwest, is now virtually all developed in its easterly portions, and development is moving beyond the permanent open spaces of the Harriman State Park to Orange County. U.S. Route 6, recently reconstructed to connect the Bear Mountain Bridge with the Palisades Interstate Parkway, as well as the New York Thruway and Route 17 (the "Quickway"), have brought the Highlands into easy reach from the west. Rail improvements and major regional facilities such as Stewart Jetport, can only accelerate growth and increase pressure for development in Putnam.

Pressure from the North. The Putnam County Planning Department reports that the county is also becoming more popular as a residential area because of the rapid industrial and commercial development in the Beacon/Newburgh area of the Interstate 84 highway corridor immediately to the north. The County Planning Depart-

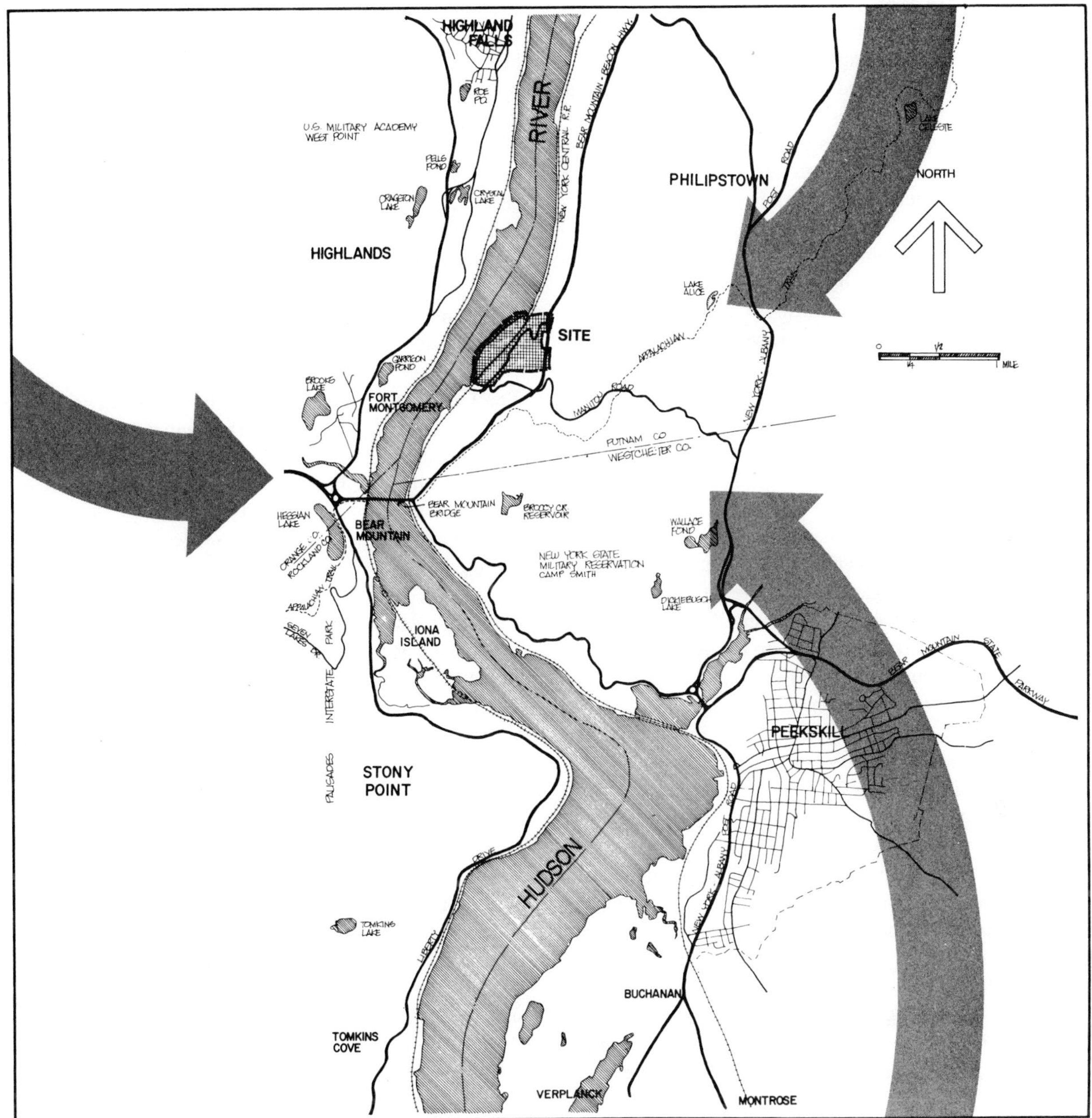

Figure 1.15

ment notes that Putnam "finds itself located between the outward population expansion of both the New York Region to the south and the mid-Hudson area to the north, which unique situation has resulted in substantial in-migration from both directions and which has sustained a growth rate which is presently considered to be the highest of all counties in New York State." County planners estimate that Putnam will have doubled its population by 1990.

The Need: Homes Must Be Provided. The most direct result of population growth is a rising demand for the basic necessities of life—food, clothing, and shelter. National planners foresee a need for more than 2 million new dwelling units every year, to accommodate the rising population and to replace housing that is lost.

In the seven-county mid-Hudson area, which includes Putnam County, Pattern for Progress and the Regional Plan Association see a need for 13,000 new dwellings every year, until 1980 or 1990. By contrast, an average of only about 5000 units were built during each year in the late 1960s. The Putnam County Planning Board estimated a countywide need of about 7800 units during the 1970s.

The preceding decade has seen a tremendous increase in multifamily housing construction in the nation at large and an even greater increase in this region. Multifamily dwellings accounted for more than half of new residential construction in some of the suburban counties. This remarkable increase has been due to several factors.

1 Most significant is income versus housing costs. Many families, especially the young ones, simply cannot afford a single-family house. The skyrocketing costs of land and construction have led to a dramatic and continuing rise in the prices of one-family houses.
2 Older people constitute a large and increasing part of the population. Many elderly couples, whose children have grown up and left home, no longer need a large single-family home and often consider the maintenance of it a burden.
3 Household size contributes to the demand for multifamily housing. Single people and childless couples generally neither need nor want a large house, and the Census revealed a marked increase in one- and two-person households during the 1960s. According to the Regional Plan Association, such households will increase by 84% between 1965 and 2000 in the New York Region, compared with an increase of only 46% for households of three or more persons. (The number of people born during the postwar "baby boom," who were in their early and mid-twenties during the 1960s, obviously has a lot to do with this.)
4 The increasing mobility of our population also creates demand for multifamily housing. Census figures show that the average family moves once every 5 years, and frequent moves by executives in major business concerns are an accepted part of life. Such mobility increases the need for rental housing, which often means multifamily housing.
5 Preference is an increasingly important factor. In the past, people thought of the multifamily dwelling as a stopgap or way station for the young, the old, and the transient. But the facts no longer bear out this assumption. To be sure, economics plays an important part in the demand for multifamily housing. But the increasing popularity of cooperatives and condominiums, luxury apartments, and town houses indicates that many people prefer living in multifamily housing.

In areas of great natural beauty, such as the Highlands, multifamily or clustered housing clearly provides the best opportunity to preserve natural resources, since it minimizes the covering of land with buildings, driveways, and roads. Then, too, most forms of multifamily housing produce more local taxes than other kinds of housing; income from apartments normally exceeds all expenses to a community.

Multifamily housing can be an all-around benefit to the community, providing maximum tax return, open space preservation, resource conservation, and minimum community burden—while helping to meet the pressing need for new housing.

The Challenge. The challenge then is to accommodate the pressures of growth and urbanization while preserving the natural resources and scenic beauty of the Hudson River and the Manitou Station site. Putnam County and Philipstown can grow while sustaining a regional "greenbelt" and a beautiful living environment for their citizens.

The River and Its Shoreline Must Be Preserved. It is the Hudson River that makes the challenge of environmental planning so significant in Philipstown. Any use and development of this majestic river and its shorelines must be aimed at preserving its natural resources. Major problems of pollution, urban blight, inaccessibility, and extravagant, misdirected land use policies must be overcome.

Manitou Station is blessed with some of the cleanest, most productive, most beautiful Hudson River frontage in the entire 60 miles of Hudson Highlands. Conservationists consider the Highlands among the most beautiful river scenery in America, and they point out that the "Highlands stretch" is perhaps the most spectacular instance of a broad, major river breaking through a major chain of the Appalachians.

The river cuts through the mountains at sea level, creating an estuarial—almost fjordlike—environment, permitting tidal currents and tempered ocean breezes to penetrate nearly 100 miles into the heartland of New York State. This felicitous combination of relatively warmer climate and varying river water salinity is a rare natural gift to the New York region and provides a unique environment for its flora and fauna.

Open Space Must Be Conserved. Inevitably, new housing must be built to accommodate the expanding population. But at the same time, open spaces must be preserved and natural resources conserved.

In the New York region in 1970 there were 400,000 acres of open space lands: parks, water bodies, and

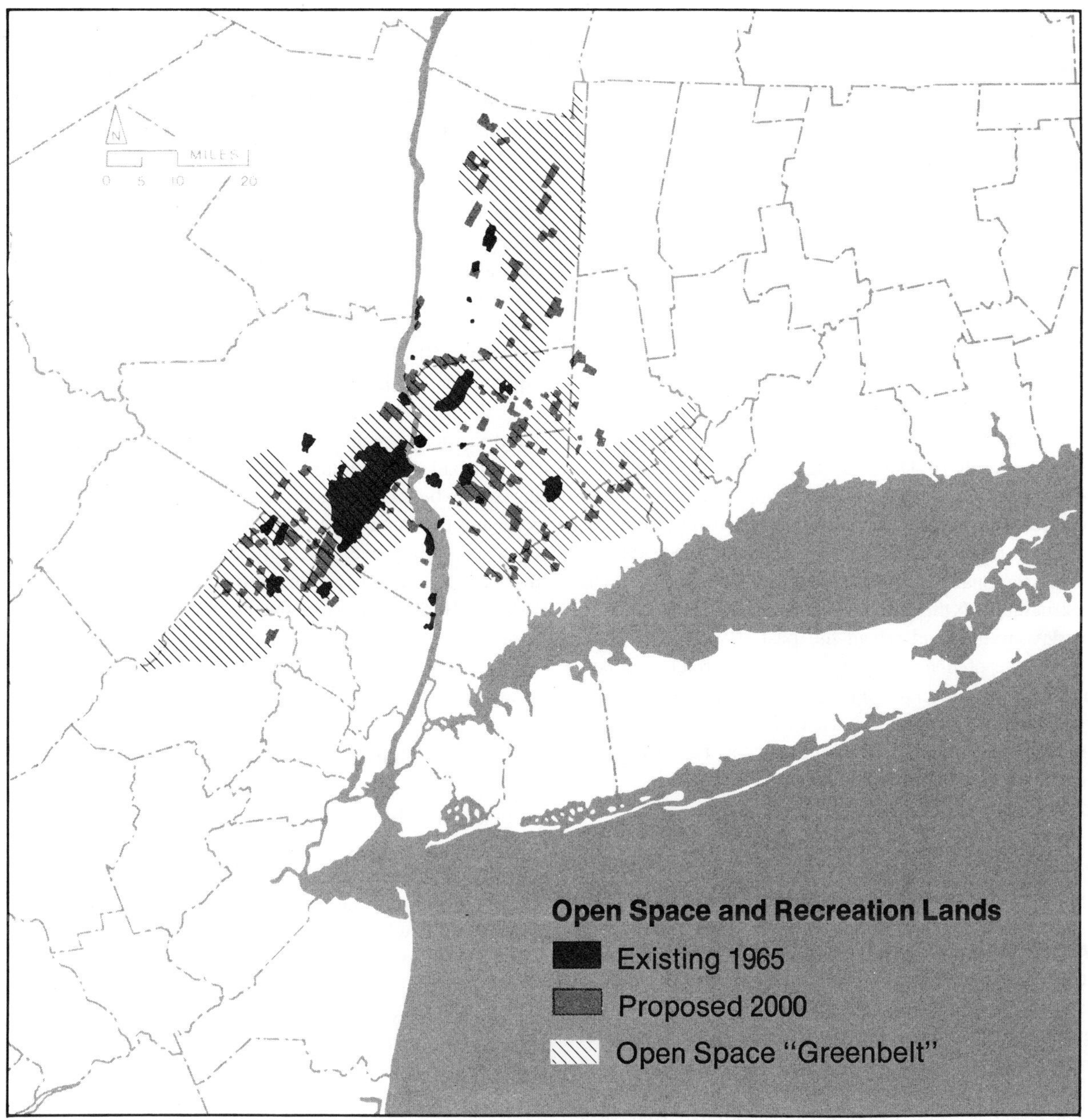

Figure 1.16

forests. At least 200,000 more acres, both public and private, will be needed to satisfy recreation demands just to 1985. Putnam County represents perhaps the greatest treasure of such potential open spaces in the region. Regional planners advocate the permanent establishment of additional recreation land in Putnam County and, particularly, in Philipstown, as an extension of Harriman and Fahnestock state parks.

Across the Hudson in Rockland and Orange counties, vast federal and state land holdings have tended to preserve the magnificence of the river valley. Major land acquisitions by New York State have ensured the preservation of the northern portion of the Hudson Highlands in Philipstown and Fishkill. At West Point and other places where these agencies have undertaken development, work has tended to complement the river and its embracing mountains in style and in magnitude. Yet in far too many areas such as Annsville, Fort Montgomery, and Highland Falls, private developers have been permitted to desecrate the scenery.

Regional planners see Philipstown (and most of northwest Putnam) as a continuation of an extensive open space greenbelt, stretching from the Kitatinny and Ramapo mountains in northern New Jersey through Rockland and Orange counties, incorporating Bear Mountain and Harriman state parks, West Point, Storm King Park, and Camp Smith Reservation east and west of the Hudson in the Highlands, and on to the northeast through Fahnestock State Park, the New York City watershed lands, to the Connecticut State forests and the Berkshires. Because of its beauty and rugged terrain, this greenbelt would contain the major recreation and semiwilderness areas in easy reach of the growing metropolitan and mid-Hudson population.

Urbanization would continue to spread northward up the Hudson Valley, through the rolling and easily developable lands of Dutchess and Orange counties. To meet the demands of an expanding population, this massive greenbelt will necessarily contain housing, villages, and small urban centers, many of which already exist.

The Regional Plan Association urges that this growth be structured so that new building and development will not devour the land, as in the past. By concentrating growth, the planners feel that substantial tracts of open space can be preserved and the region's major natural resources protected. By the use of multifamily and cluster dwellings, additional population can be accommodated without "spoiling" large areas or rendering them inaccessible.

New housing will come, but it can work for—rather than against—the preservation of open spaces and the ideal of the greenbelt.

The Site's Natural Resources Must Be Protected. The site selected for Manitou Station is one of outstanding beauty and significance to the Hudson Highlands. Its remarkable combination of size, shape, location, and unique natural resources virtually demands that it be treated with the sensitivity necessary to enhance its unique features and to ensure its continued role as a magnificent landscape element in the Highlands.

The site incorporates such varied natural elements as a reservoir, waterfalls, a fast-flowing stream, a large freshwater marsh, forested valley walls and floor, and a magnificent rock bluff facing the Hudson River. Manmade elements include the Penn Central Railroad, an entrance drive from the Bear Mountain–Beacon Highway (Route 9D) that terminates at the existing Livingston Mansion, an arched stone bridge, a brick ice house at the reservoir, and brick stables and barns. Views are excellent from almost any vantage point but particularly good from the river bluff and from the valley looking north and south.

With the exception of the marsh, the site is extremely rugged, with slopes ranging from 15 to 35%. Since, in addition, the area consists almost entirely of bedrock with a thin soil layer, typical house and lot construction is inappropriate.

The topography is relatively level for the first few hundred feet paralleling Route 9D, then drops precipitously into the valley of Copper Mine Creek. This steep valley and its stream define the major rock fault and upland aquifer on Manitou Station. It is a major natural resource and feature of beauty to be preserved. Farther west the land rises steeply again to a forested plateau between 140 and 160 feet above the river and roughly equivalent to the height of Route 9D. Beyond the plateau, to the north and west, the land tumbles downward in rocky, steep hillsides to its lowest elevations at the railroad and Manitou Marsh. The marsh extends to the south beyond the site, across Manitou Road. This road and the Penn Central Railroad were constructed by extensive filling over a century ago. Beyond the railroad the site rises again to a magnificent 100-foot bluff, affording Hudson River vistas to the north and south, spoiled only by views of trailer parks directly across the river. Finally, the land plunges into the Hudson along almost a mile of rocky river frontage.

Vegetation Analysis. The entire site is forested, except for Manitou Marsh. Hemlock, with its streamside association of ferns and mosses, predominates along the rocky stream channel and high ridge. Oak, maple, ash, tulip, and an understory of dogwood, blueberry, and laurel, make up the valley walls and plateaus. The freshwater lowland association of beech, birch, wild cherry, red maple, a shrub layer of blueberry and a ground layer of ferns, Virginia creeper, and poison ivy, cover the valley floor. Though treeless, Manitou Marsh exhibits a variety of aquatic plantlife including cattails, arrowhead, and reeds.

Ecology Profile. The site is part of the Hudson Highlands, which extends 15 miles south of Newburgh, New York. Having a forest classification of Oak-Hickory-Chestnut, the site basically consists of a thin layer of stony soil covering basalt and granite bedrock from which there are many rock outcroppings and faults.

The Hudson River itself is fresh to brackish, with a mean tidal range of 3.9 feet. The riverbed is composed of glacial boulders, sand and gravel, and silt and clay over basalt bedrock. The river edge is subjected to tidal inundations of brackish water and winter ice flows, which has resulted in a rocky, steep ledge lacking vegetation, with steep wooded slopes above. Lying behind this first rocky hill, Manitou Marsh is part of a large marsh that extends south to the Bear Mountain Bridge.

The site is an ecological network of related parts. The marsh provides a breeding ground for marine life, which supplies food to terrestrial animals, which in turn find shelter in the wooded slopes, which protect the marsh, and so on.

Alternative Development: Can These Choices Meet the Challenge? Various uses for the property have been studied in an attempt to realistically determine the best site utilization. Land conservation objectives, a respect for the Hudson, the need for new housing in Putnam County, and the long-range interests of the people of Philipstown as well as the owners of the land have been considered.

Can the property remain as it is?

Should it become a county, state or federal park, as some planners have suggested?

Should it be left to be developed for single-family homes on individual lots in typical subdivision fashion?

Can it be developed with clustered houses along Route 9D or on relatively limited flatlands on the site?

Is commercial development of the site desirable for the town, or economically possible?

Is there another alternative that recognizes the social and economic necessities while respecting the quality of life in Manitou and offering local conservation as well as economic and recreation advantages?

As a Private Estate. Conceivably, the site could remain as is. Yet the high cost of taxes and property maintenance make this option virtually impossible to accept. In the heyday of river mansions, the wealthy were able to preserve the openness of the Highlands and at the same time provide jobs for the local economy. Now, high maintenance costs, taxes, vandalism. and changing life patterns have all but eliminated the choice of maintaining large estates and their manor houses in the style for which they were designed. Improvised uses or sheer neglect remain the likely prospect, while land speculators continue to eye such properties for ultimate and often thoughtless exploitation.

As a State Park. Acquisition of the site as part of a major state or regional park might conserve natural resources, but the town would lose a significant source of revenue, and Philipstown would have little control over the recreational use of the land. By opening up the site to the general public, which State Park designation would do, local traffic would be increased and the town would be exposed to public pressures. Moreover, more than 40% of all property in Philipstown is currently off the tax roles.

As Zoned—A Subdivision. The site could be developed under the existing R-80 zoning district and the town's zoning regulations. Such use would severely disturb the natural terrain and the qualities of the land. Furthermore, use of almost a mile of Hudson River frontage would be forever restricted to the exclusive use of a few single-family homeowners.

Since development costs would be high, most houses would have to be large, many-bedroom units, which would attract large families. This generates school and town expenses larger than the taxes these houses would pay. Then, too, the town would have additional headaches of subdivision roads and utilities to maintain and service.

The value of the marshland and other natural resources would also be placed in jeopardy as land costs increased and pressures for development grew. The marsh would be particularly difficult to protect under conventional subdivision techniques, since effective maintenance by homeowners' groups, local public agencies, or conservation groups is harder to achieve under such circumstances.

As a "Clustered" Development. The conventional "clustering" of single-family houses or town houses on buildable portions of the site is an option. But such concentration is practical only on the relatively flat land along Route 9D, small selected areas in the site, or in the marsh area. Development of these areas would tend to make visible encroachments along the highway and to create potential septic and pollution problems. Such development might not be able to support a high-quality treatment plant.

Therefore, conventionally clustered houses located on the most likely areas of the site, with related town roads and services, would be built at the inevitable expense of significant natural resources. Such development would also create a tax liability similar to that associated with the average single-family home.

As a Commercial Development. The site could be used for commercial or light industrial development. Indeed, commercially zoned property exists to the north and east, and nonconforming residential property lies on the south, perhaps someday to place additional pressure on the town for such rezoning. Large office or commercial buildings and related parking facilities would vastly change the nature of the site. Also, considerable peak-hour traffic would be generated as employees arrived at and left the building(s). Considering the market for such uses and the potential trade area of the site, it is unlikely that a major company could be attracted. Other commercial uses often invite poor quality development and may downgrade nearby residential areas.

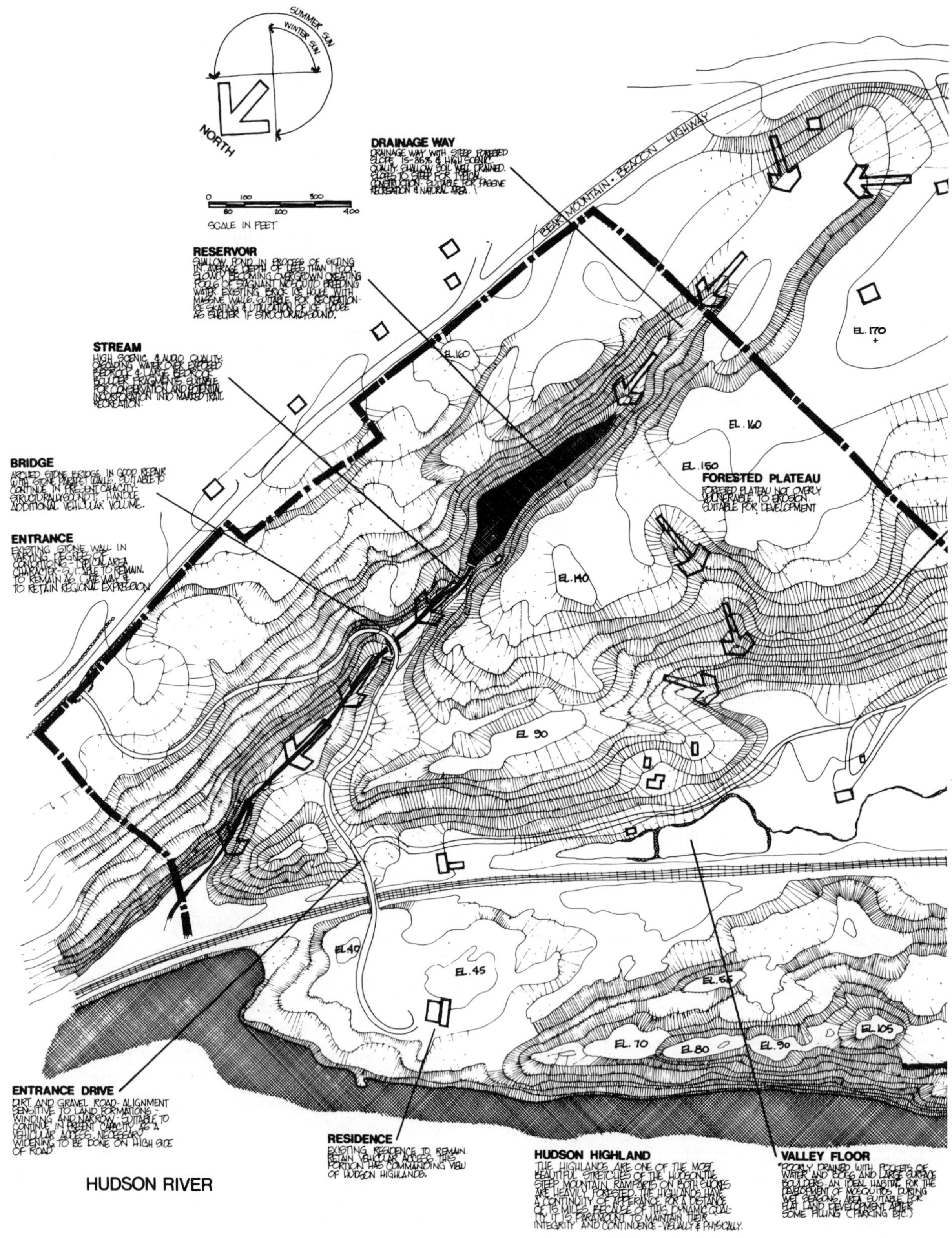
SUMMER SUN
WINTER SUN
NORTH
0 100 300
50 200 400
SCALE IN FEET
BEAR MOUNTAIN - BEACON HIGHWAY
DRAINAGE WAY
DRAINAGE WAY WITH STEEP FORESTED SLOPE 15-35% & HIGH SCENIC QUALITY. SHALLOW SOIL WELL DRAINED. SLOPES TO STEEP FOR TYPICAL CONSTRUCTION. SUITABLE FOR PASSIVE RECREATION & NATURAL AREA.
RESERVOIR
SHALLOW POND IN PROCESS OF SILTING IN. AVERAGE DEPTH OF LESS THAN 1 FOOT. SLOWLY BECOMING OVERGROWN CREATING POOLS OF STAGNANT MOSQUITO BREEDING WATER. EXISTING BRICK ICE HOUSE WITH MASSIVE WALLS. SUITABLE FOR RECREATION- ICE SKATING & UTILIZATION OF ICE HOUSE AS SHELTER IF STRUCTURALLY SOUND.
STREAM
HIGH SCENIC & AUDIO QUALITY. CASCADING WATER OVER EXPOSED BEDROCK & LARGE BEDROCK BOULDER FRAGMENTS. SUITABLE FOR CONSERVATION AND POTENTIAL INCORPORATION INTO MARKED TRAIL RECREATION.
BRIDGE
ARCHED STONE BRIDGE IN GOOD REPAIR WITH STONE PARAPET WALLS. SUITABLE TO CONTINUE IN PRESENT CAPACITY- STRUCTURALLY SOUND TO HANDLE ADDITIONAL VEHICULAR VOLUME.
ENTRANCE
EXISTING STONE WALL IN VARYING DEGREES OF CONDITIONS- TYPICAL AREA CHARACTER- SUITABLE TO REMAIN. TO REMAIN AS GATEWAY & TO RETAIN REGIONAL EXPRESSION
EL. 170
EL. 160
EL. 160
EL. 150
FORESTED PLATEAU
FORESTED PLATEAU NOT OVERLY VULNERABLE TO EROSION. SUITABLE FOR DEVELOPMENT
EL. 140
EL. 90
EL. 40
EL. 45
EL. 55
EL. 70
EL. 80
EL. 90
EL. 105
ENTRANCE DRIVE
DIRT AND GRAVEL ROAD- ALIGNMENT SENSITIVE TO LAND FORMATIONS - WINDING AND NARROW - SUITABLE TO CONTINUE IN PRESENT CAPACITY AS A VEHICULAR ACCESS. NECESSARY WIDENING TO BE DONE ON HIGH SIDE OF ROAD.
RESIDENCE
EXISTING RESIDENCE TO REMAIN. RETAIN VEHICULAR ACCESS. THIS PORTION HAS COMMANDING VIEW OF HUDSON HIGHLANDS.
HUDSON HIGHLAND
THE HIGHLANDS ARE ONE OF THE MOST BEAUTIFUL STRETCHES OF THE HUDSON. THE STEEP MOUNTAIN RAMPARTS ON BOTH SHORES ARE HEAVILY FORESTED. THE HIGHLANDS HAVE A CONTINUITY OF APPERANCE FOR A DISTANCE OF 15 MILES. BECAUSE OF THIS DYNAMIC QUALITY IT IS PARAMOUNT TO MAINTAIN THEIR INTEGRITY AND CONTINUENCE - VISUALLY & PHYSICALLY.
VALLEY FLOOR
POORLY DRAINED WITH POCKETS OF WATER AND BOGS AND LARGE SURFACE BOULDERS. AN IDEAL HABITAT FOR THE DEVELOPMENT OF MOSQUITOS DURING WET SEASONS. AREA SUITABLE FOR FLAT LAND DEVELOPMENT AFTER SOME FILLING (PARKING ETC.)
HUDSON RIVER

Figure 1.17

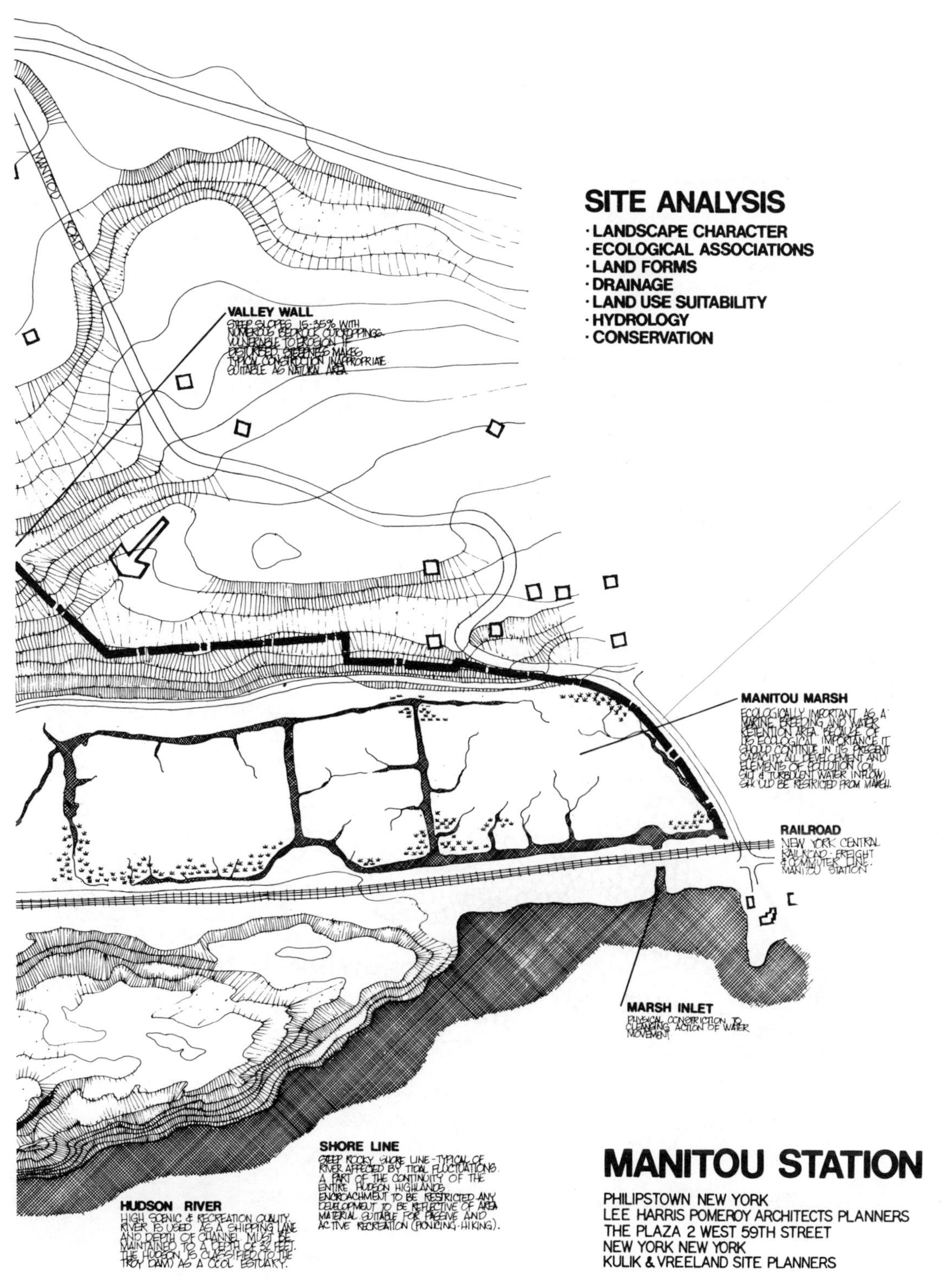
SITE ANALYSIS
· LANDSCAPE CHARACTER
· ECOLOGICAL ASSOCIATIONS
· LAND FORMS
· DRAINAGE
· LAND USE SUITABILITY
· HYDROLOGY
· CONSERVATION
MANITOU ROAD
VALLEY WALL
STEEP SLOPES 15-35% WITH NUMEROUS BEDROCK OUTCROPPINGS. VULNERABLE TO EROSION IF DISTURBED. STEEPNESS MAKES TYPICAL CONSTRUCTION INAPPROPRIATE. SUITABLE AS NATURAL AREA.
MANITOU MARSH
ECOLOGICALLY IMPORTANT AS A MARINE BREEDING AND WATER RETENTION AREA. BECAUSE OF ITS ECOLOGICAL IMPORTANCE IT SHOULD CONTINUE IN ITS PRESENT CAPACITY. ALL DEVELOPMENT AND ELEMENTS OF POLLUTION (OIL, SILT & TURBULENT WATER INFLOW) SHOULD BE RESTRICTED FROM MARSH.
RAILROAD
NEW YORK CENTRAL RAILROAD - FREIGHT & COMMUTER LINE. MANITOU STATION.
MARSH INLET
PHYSICAL CONSTRICTION TO CLEANSING ACTION OF WATER MOVEMENT
SHORE LINE
STEEP ROCKY SHORE LINE - TYPICAL OF RIVER AFFECTED BY TIDAL FLUCTUATIONS. A PART OF THE CONTINUITY OF THE ENTIRE HUDSON HIGHLANDS. ENCROACHMENT TO BE RESTRICTED. ANY DEVELOPMENT TO BE REFLECTIVE OF AREA MATERIAL. SUITABLE FOR PASSIVE AND ACTIVE RECREATION (PICNICING-HIKING).
HUDSON RIVER
HIGH SCENIC & RECREATION QUALITY. RIVER IS USED AS A SHIPPING LANE AND DEPTH OF CHANNEL MUST BE MAINTAINED TO A DEPTH OF 32 FEET. THE HUDSON IS CLASSIFIED (TO THE TROY DAM) AS A COOL ESTUARY.
MANITOU STATION
PHILIPSTOWN NEW YORK
LEE HARRIS POMEROY ARCHITECTS PLANNERS
THE PLAZA 2 WEST 59TH STREET
NEW YORK NEW YORK
KULIK & VREELAND SITE PLANNERS

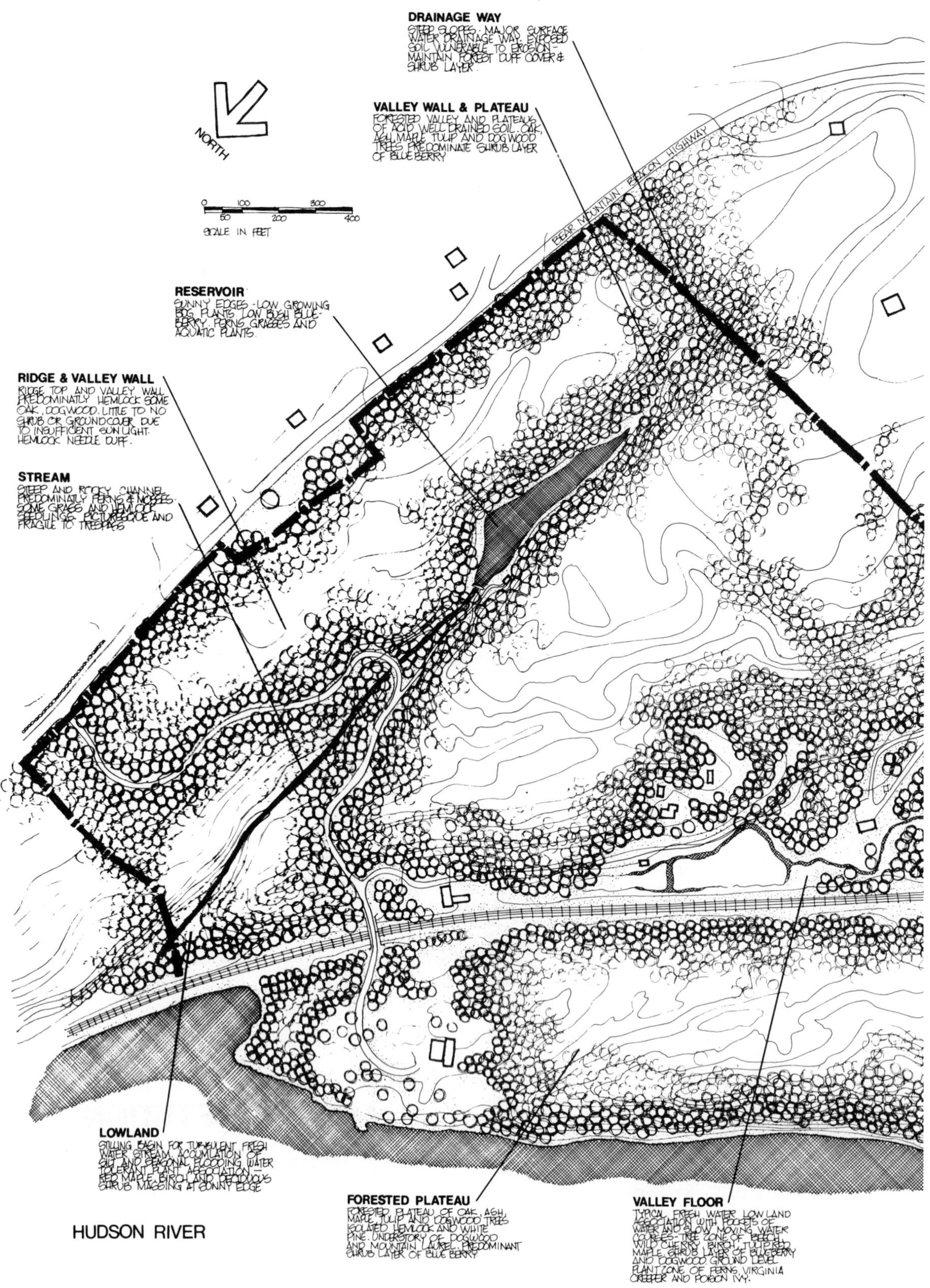
DRAINAGE WAY
STEEP SLOPES. MAJOR SURFACE WATER DRAINAGE WAY. EXPOSED SOIL VULNERABLE TO EROSION - MAINTAIN FOREST DUFF COVER & SHRUB LAYER.
VALLEY WALL & PLATEAU
FORESTED VALLEY AND PLATEAUS OF ACID WELL DRAINED SOIL. OAK, ASH, MAPLE TULIP AND DOGWOOD TREES PREDOMINATE SHRUB LAYER OF BLUEBERRY
NORTH
0 100 300
50 200 400
SCALE IN FEET
BEAR MOUNTAIN - BEACON HIGHWAY
RESERVOIR
SUNNY EDGES - LOW GROWING BOG PLANTS LOW BUSH BLUEBERRY. FERNS GRASSES AND AQUATIC PLANTS.
RIDGE & VALLEY WALL
RIDGE TOP AND VALLEY WALL PREDOMINATLY HEMLOCK SOME OAK, DOGWOOD. LITTLE TO NO SHRUB OR GROUNDCOVER DUE TO INSUFFICIENT SUNLIGHT. HEMLOCK NEEDLE DUFF.
STREAM
STEEP AND ROCKY CHANNEL PREDOMINATLY FERNS & MOSSES. SOME GRASS AND HEMLOCK SEEDLINGS. PICTURESQUE AND FRAGILE TO TRESPASS
LOWLAND
STILLING BASIN FOR TURBULENT FRESH WATER STREAM. ACCUMULATION OF SILT AND SEASONAL FLOODING. WATER TOLERANT PLANT ASSOCIATION - RED MAPLE, BIRCH AND DECIDUOUS SHRUB MASSING AT SUNNY EDGE
HUDSON RIVER
FORESTED PLATEAU
FORESTED PLATEAU OF OAK, ASH, MAPLE, TULIP AND DOGWOOD TREES ISOLATED HEMLOCK AND WHITE PINE. UNDERSTORY OF DOGWOOD AND MOUNTAIN LAUREL. PREDOMINANT SHRUB LAYER OF BLUE BERRY.
VALLEY FLOOR
TYPICAL FRESH WATER LOWLAND ASSOCIATION WITH POCKETS OF WATER AND SLOW MOVING WATER COURSES - TREE ZONE OF BEECH, WILD CHERRY, BIRCH, TULIP RED MAPLE. SHRUB LAYER OF BLUEBERRY AND DOGWOOD. GROUND LEVEL PLANT ZONE OF FERNS, VIRGINIA CREEPER AND POISON IVY.

Figure 1.18

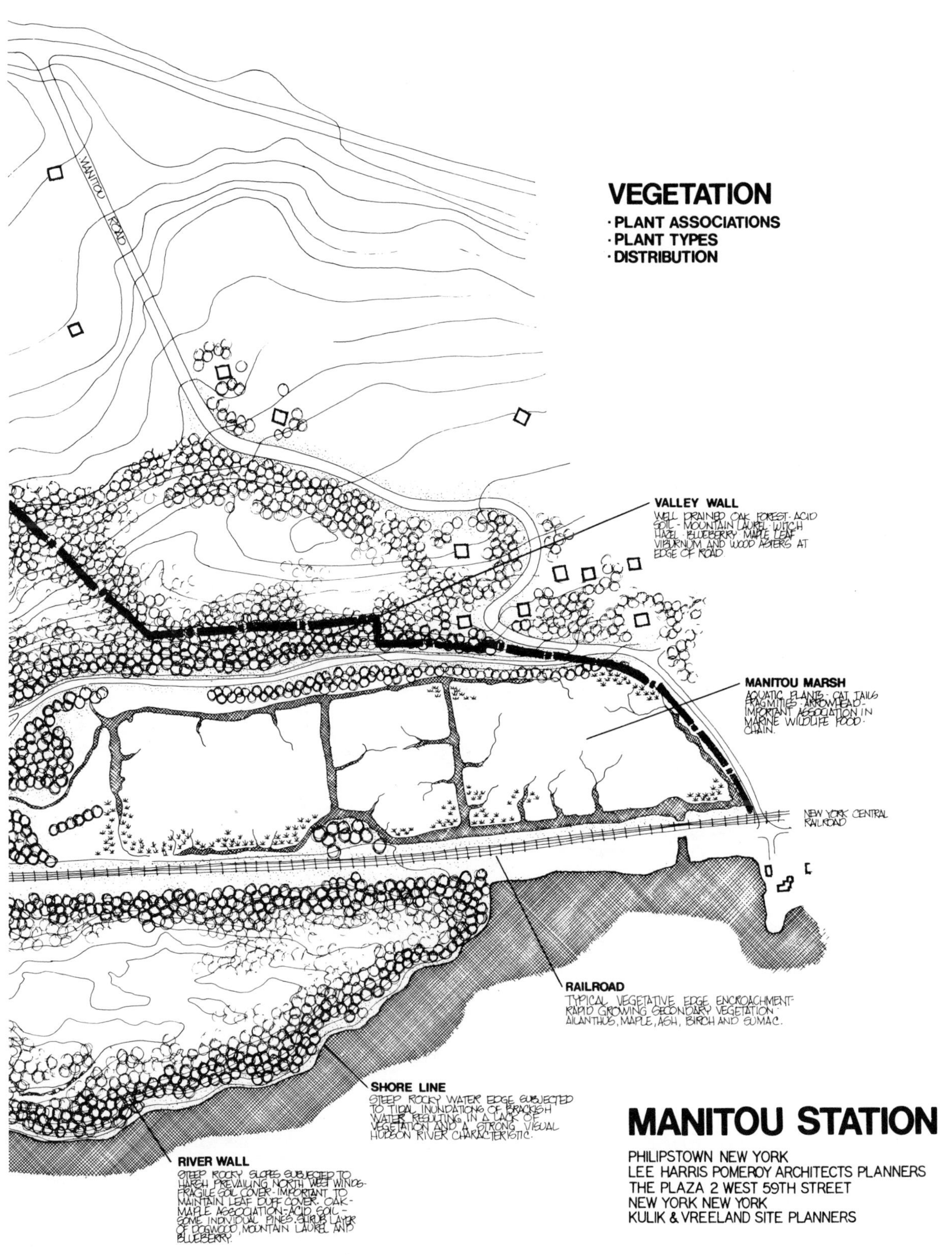
MANITOU ROAD
VEGETATION
·PLANT ASSOCIATIONS
·PLANT TYPES
·DISTRIBUTION
VALLEY WALL
WELL DRAINED OAK FOREST·ACID SOIL - MOUNTAIN LAUREL·WITCH HAZEL·BLUEBERRY·MAPLE LEAF VIBURNUM AND WOOD ASTERS AT EDGE OF ROAD.
MANITOU MARSH
AQUATIC PLANTS - CAT TAILS FRAGMITIES - ARROWHEAD - IMPORTANT ASSOCIATION IN MARINE WILDLIFE FOOD-CHAIN.
NEW YORK CENTRAL RAILROAD
RAILROAD
TYPICAL VEGETATIVE EDGE ENCROACHMENT-RAPID GROWING SECONDARY VEGETATION AILANTHUS, MAPLE, ASH, BIRCH AND SUMAC.
SHORE LINE
STEEP ROCKY WATER EDGE SUBJECTED TO TIDAL INUNDATIONS OF BRACKISH WATER RESULTING IN A LACK OF VEGETATION AND A STRONG VISUAL HUDSON RIVER CHARACTERISTIC.
RIVER WALL
STEEP ROCKY SLOPES SUBJECTED TO HARSH PREVAILING NORTH WEST WINDS-FRAGILE SOIL COVER - IMPORTANT TO MAINTAIN LEAF DUFF COVER. OAK-MAPLE ASSOCIATION-ACID SOIL - SOME INDIVIDUAL PINES. SHRUB LAYER OF DOGWOOD, MOUNTAIN LAUREL AND BLUEBERRY.
MANITOU STATION
PHILIPSTOWN NEW YORK
LEE HARRIS POMEROY ARCHITECTS PLANNERS
THE PLAZA 2 WEST 59TH STREET
NEW YORK NEW YORK
KULIK & VREELAND SITE PLANNERS

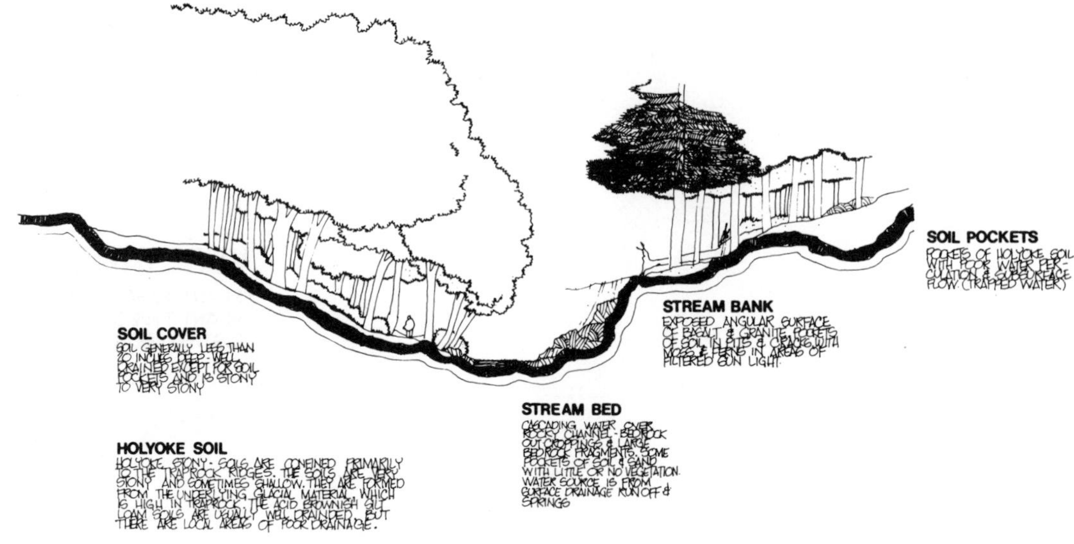
SOIL POCKETS
POCKETS OF HOLYOKE SOIL WITH POOR WATER PERCULATION & SUBSURFACE FLOW (TRAPPED WATER)
STREAM BANK
EXPOSED ANGULAR SURFACE OF BASALT & GRANITE. POCKETS OF SOIL IN PITS & CRACKS WITH MOSS & FERNS IN AREAS OF FILTERED SUN LIGHT.
SOIL COVER
SOIL GENERALLY LESS THAN 20 INCHES DEEP-WELL DRAINED EXCEPT FOR SOIL POCKETS AND IS STONY TO VERY STONY
STREAM BED
CASCADING WATER OVER ROCKY CHANNEL-BEDROCK OUTCROPPINGS & LARGE BEDROCK FRAGMENTS. SOME POCKETS OF SOIL & SAND WITH LITTLE OR NO VEGETATION. WATER SOURCE IS FROM SURFACE DRAINAGE RUN OFF & SPRINGS
HOLYOKE SOIL
HOLYOKE STONY-SOILS ARE CONFINED PRIMARILY TO THE TRAPROCK RIDGES. THE SOILS ARE VERY STONY AND SOMETIMES SHALLOW. THEY ARE FORMED FROM THE UNDERLYING GLACIAL MATERIAL, WHICH IS HIGH IN TRAPROCK. THE ACID BROWNISH SILT LOAM SOILS ARE USUALLY WELL DRAINDED, BUT THERE ARE LOCAL AREAS OF POOR DRAINAGE.

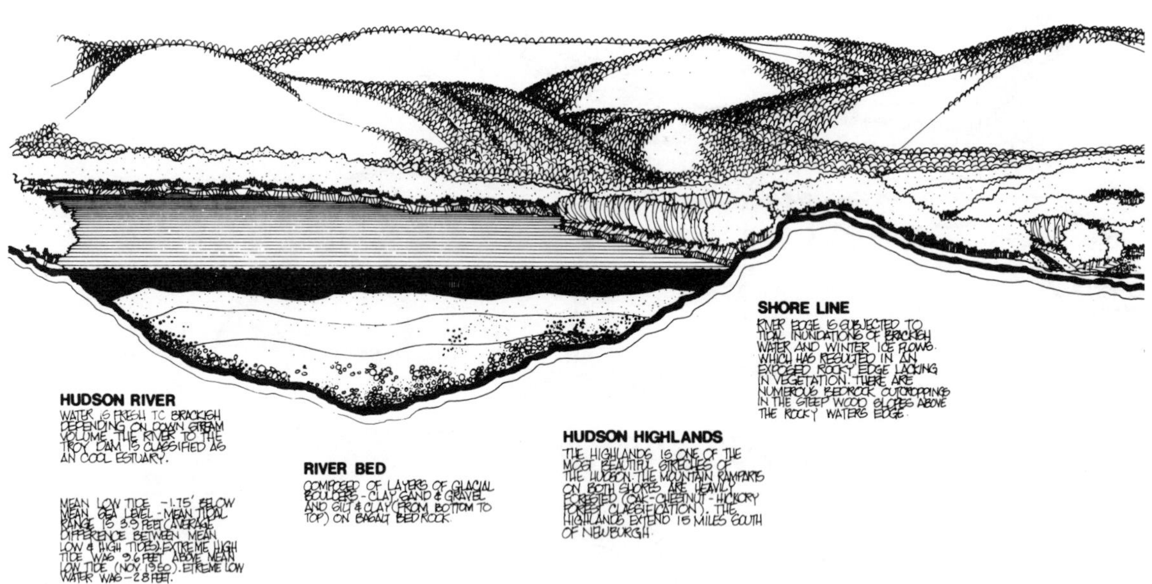
SHORE LINE
RIVER EDGE IS SUBJECTED TO TIDAL INUNDATIONS OF BRACKISH WATER AND WINTER ICE FLOWS. WHICH HAS RESULTED IN AN EXPOSED ROCKY EDGE LACKING IN VEGETATION. THERE ARE NUMEROUS BEDROCK OUTCROPPINGS IN THE STEEP WOOD SLOPES ABOVE THE ROCKY WATERS EDGE.
HUDSON RIVER
WATER IS FRESH TC BRACKISH DEPENDING ON DOWN STREAM VOLUME. THE RIVER TO THE TROY DAM IS CLASSIFIED AS AN COOL ESTUARY.
MEAN LOW TIDE -1.75' BELOW MEAN SEA LEVEL-MEAN TIDAL RANGE IS 3.9 FEET (AVERAGE DIFFERENCE BETWEEN MEAN LOW & HIGH TIDES). EXTREME HIGH TIDE WAS 9.6 FEET ABOVE MEAN LOW TIDE (NOV 1950). EXTREME LOW WATER WAS -2.8 FEET.
RIVER BED
COMPOSED OF LAYERS OF GLACIAL BOULDERS-CLAY SAND & GRAVEL AND SILT & CLAY (FROM BOTTOM TO TOP) ON BASALT BEDROCK.
HUDSON HIGHLANDS
THE HIGHLANDS IS ONE OF THE MOST BEAUTIFUL STRECHES OF THE HUDSON. THE MOUNTAIN RAMPARTS ON BOTH SHORES ARE HEAVILY FORESTED (OAK-CHESTNUT-HICKORY FOREST CLASSIFICATION). THE HIGHLANDS EXTEND 15 MILES SOUTH OF NEWBURGH.

Figure 1.19

ECOLOGY PROFILE

- ECOLOGICAL ASSOCIATIONS
- CHARACTER
- GEOLOGY
- SOILS
- VEGETATION

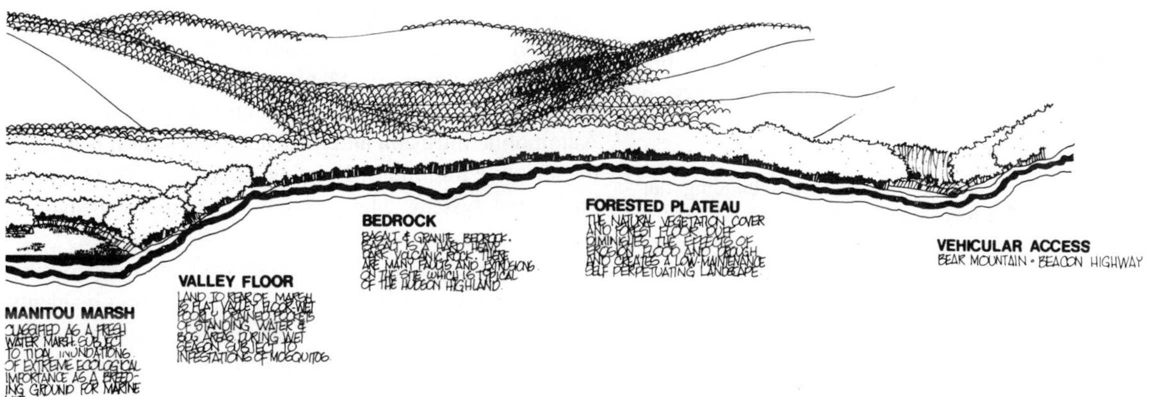

MANITOU STATION

PHILIPSTOWN NEW YORK
LEE HARRIS POMEROY ARCHITECTS PLANNERS
THE PLAZA 2 WEST 59TH STREET
NEW YORK NEW YORK
KULIK & VREELAND SITE PLANNERS

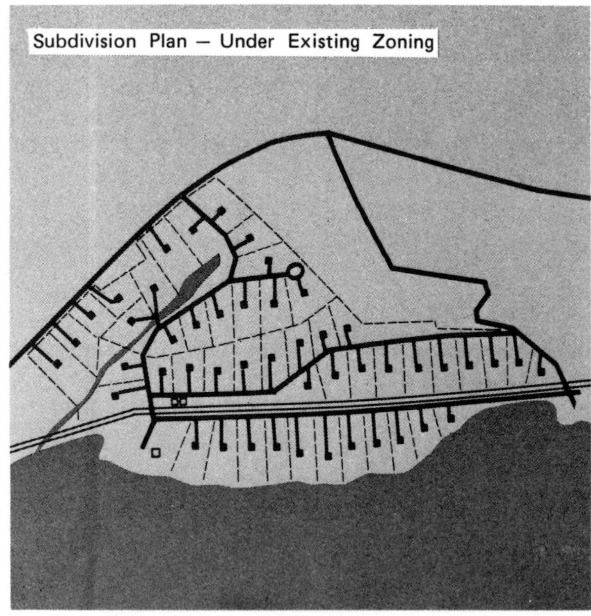

Figure 1.20

None of These Alternatives Does Honor to the Site. As the Tri-State Regional Planning Commission states:

> Doing our work with skill and purpose means building our Region with all the competence that can be marshalled. At the least it calls for the reduction of noise, ugliness, and pollution. At the next level it implies preservation of unique imprints of nature and history. At a more ambitious scale it suggests creation of beauty and interest.

It is our sincere belief that a highly desirable, sensitive alternative to ordinary and often destructive development schemes exists and is embodied in the proposal for Manitou Station.

The Response. A place for people to live and play with grace and amenity, where natural beauty abounds and delicate ecosystems are maintained: Manitou Station, Philipstown, New York.

Building Concept. The utilization of existing landforms, plus an awareness of the importance of ecology both to the environment and to the success of the plan, can help to achieve a harmonious relationship between man and the land.

The major structure at Manitou Station is planned as a V-shaped building, located deep within the site, spanning the railroad and the valley floor north of the marsh. This structure itself would nestle in the valley like a wall or dam, below the tree line of the riverfront hill, leaving the Hudson River shoreline visually free.

The structure contains 630 single-family, owner-occupied dwellings. Of this number, 25% are studio and 1-bedroom units; 50% are 2-bedroom units, and 25% are 3-bedroom units. The dwellings in each leg of the V-shaped structure are designed to provide outstanding vistas either downriver toward the Bear Mountain Bridge, or upriver toward West Point.

The outer perimeter of the "V" will have direct and unobstructed contact with the Hudson Highlands and all its beauty. Homeowners will be able to walk from their dwellings onto the grounds. Each floor of the multilevel structure has direct contact with the hillside at both ends.

In contrast to this natural setting, a small commercial area containing convenience shopping, services, professional offices, and community facilities is located within the confines of the "V." The Manitou Railroad Station would be moved to this area of the building and, along with a multilevel arcade and pedestrian paths, would provide a villagelike atmosphere for both the residents and the townspeople.

To a large degree the building concept is generated by the desire to minimize coverage of the land with extensive parking areas. At Manitou Station no unnecessary intrusion of the auto onto the land will be permitted. Automobile intrusion and its resultant pollution is held to the absolute minimum. Existing roads are utilized for the basic road system, which avoids substantial upheaval of natural areas.

Also, to minimize site coverage, landscaped and screened parking primarily for Manitou Station residents is located on the roof and inside the structure itself. Additional landscaped parking is located at ground level on the land area within the "V" for town house residents and townspeople using the railroad station, the commercial area, and the club. The development is highly concentrated, thus providing areas of undeveloped open space, which become legitimate parks and conservation areas.

Manitou Station is conceived as a direct response to the goal of creating "a region that is rich in natural and man-made environs, offering a variety of forms to match the diversity of individual preferences and personalities."

Along the River's Edge: A Comparison of Forms. Obvious and tempting as it was, we considered but rejected building a "lowrise" along the river's edge as well as a "highrise" structure on the hilltop crest. The lower Hudson shoreline, and the Palisades, are fraught with examples of buildings competing with the natural beauty of the shoreline.

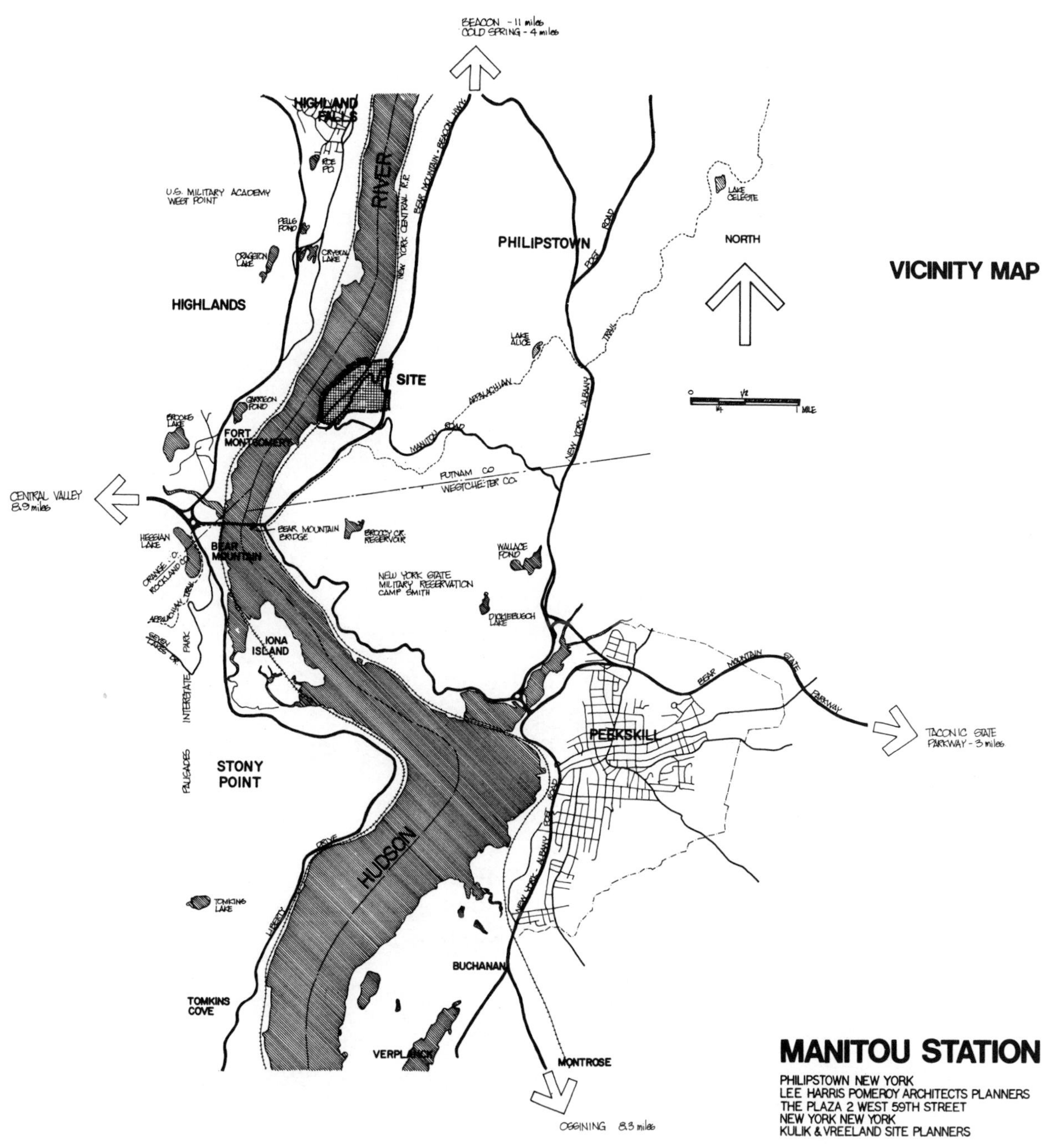
BEACON - 11 miles
COLD SPRING - 4 miles
HIGHLAND FALLS
RIVER
U.S. MILITARY ACADEMY WEST POINT
PHILIPSTOWN
NORTH
VICINITY MAP
HIGHLANDS
SITE
FORT MONTGOMERY
PUTNAM CO
WESTCHESTER CO.
CENTRAL VALLEY 8.9 miles
BEAR MOUNTAIN BRIDGE
BEAR MOUNTAIN
NEW YORK STATE MILITARY RESERVATION CAMP SMITH
IONA ISLAND
PEEKSKILL
TACONIC STATE PARKWAY - 3 miles
STONY POINT
HUDSON
BUCHANAN
TOMKINS COVE
VERPLANCK
MONTROSE
OSSINING 8.3 miles
MANITOU STATION
PHILIPSTOWN NEW YORK
LEE HARRIS POMEROY ARCHITECTS PLANNERS
THE PLAZA 2 WEST 59TH STREET
NEW YORK NEW YORK
KULIK & VREELAND SITE PLANNERS

Figure 1.21

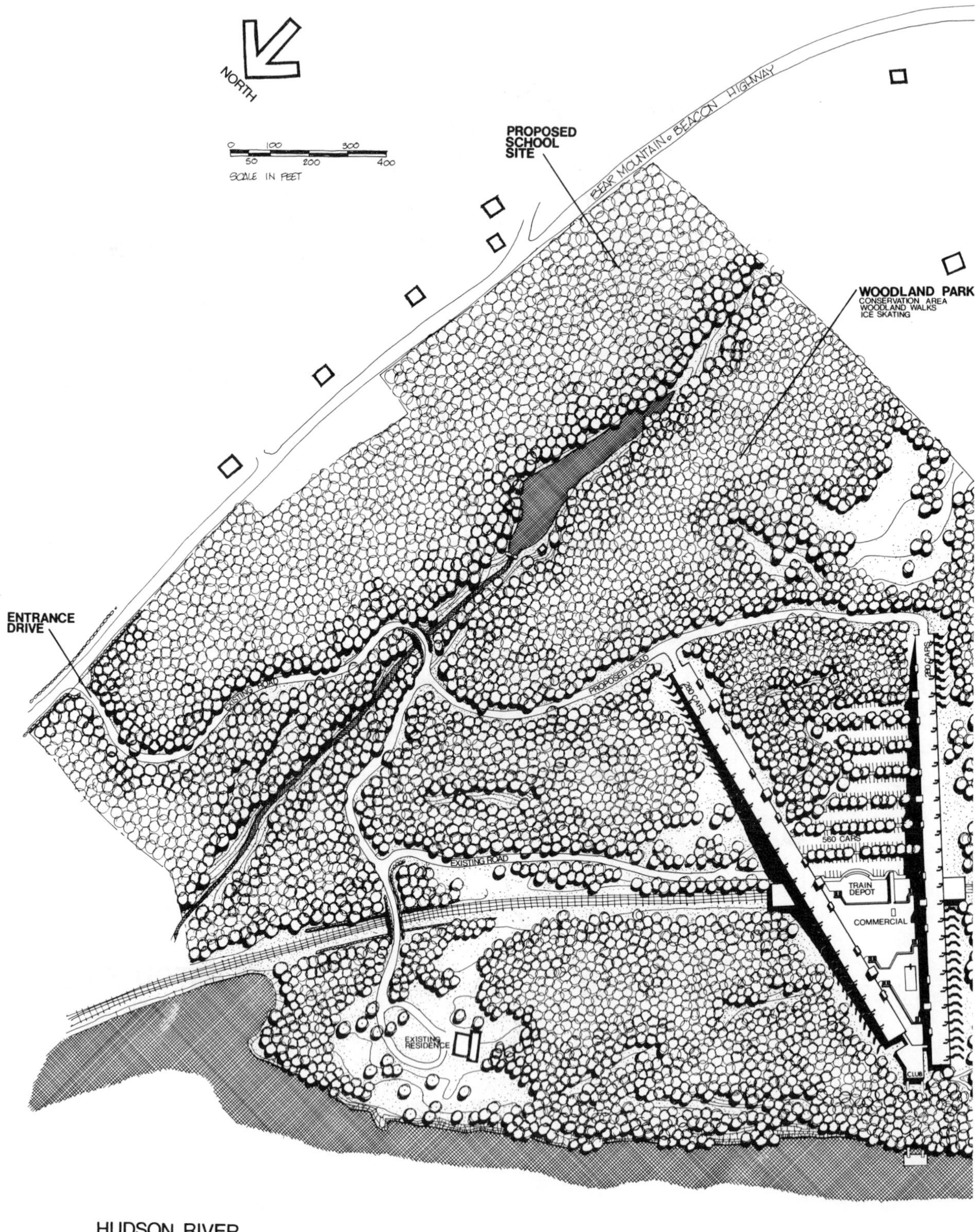
NORTH
0 100 300
50 200 400
SCALE IN FEET
BEAR MOUNTAIN • BEACON HIGHWAY
PROPOSED
SCHOOL
SITE
WOODLAND PARK
CONSERVATION AREA
WOODLAND WALKS
ICE SKATING
ENTRANCE
DRIVE
PROPOSED ROAD
560 CARS
EXISTING ROAD
TRAIN
DEPOT
COMMERCIAL
EXISTING
RESIDENCE
CLUB
HUDSON RIVER

Figure 1.22

SITE PLAN

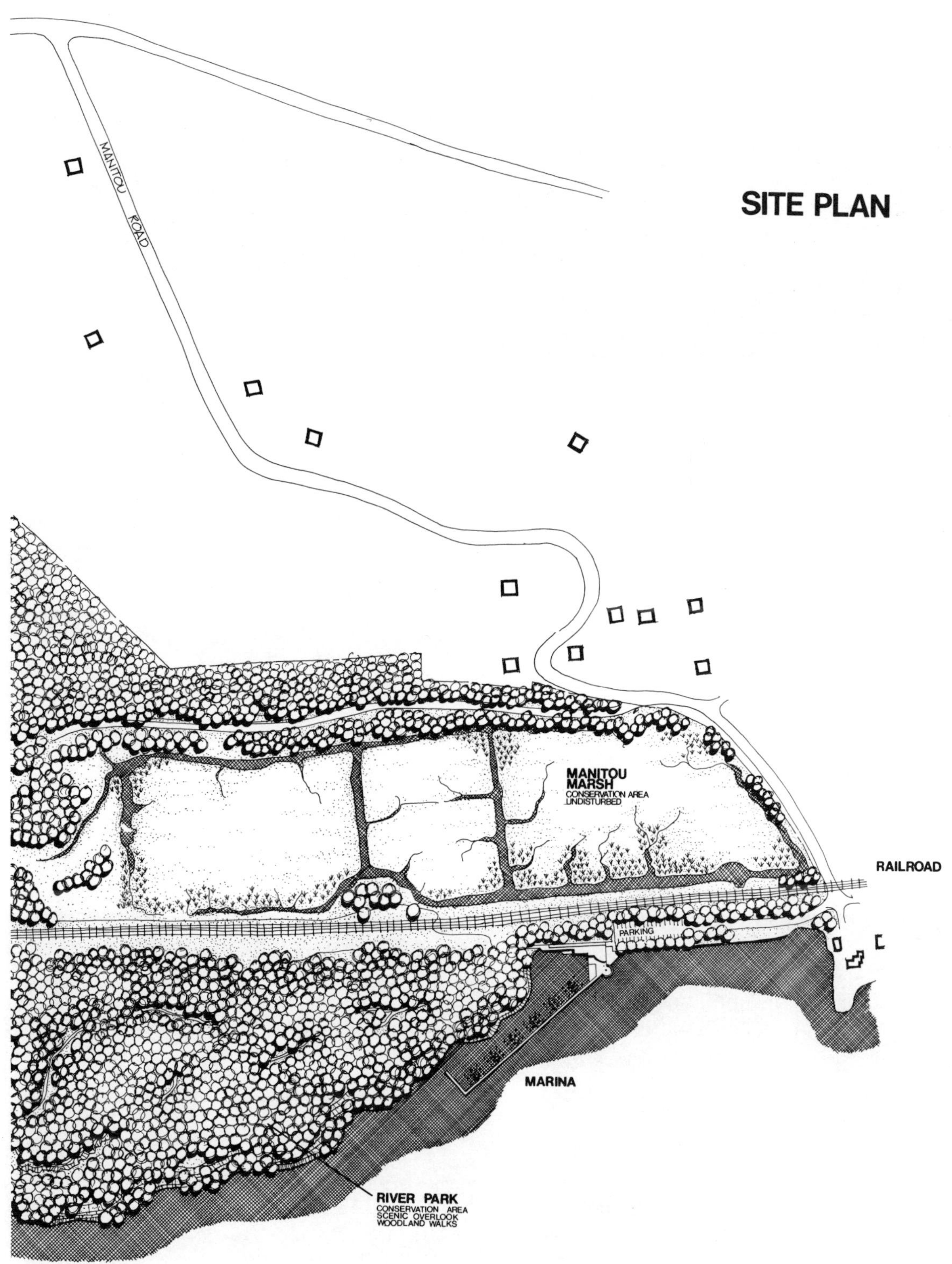
MANITOU ROAD
MANITOU MARSH
CONSERVATION AREA
UNDISTURBED
RAILROAD
PARKING
MARINA
RIVER PARK
CONSERVATION AREA
SCENIC OVERLOOK
WOODLAND WALKS

Figure 1.23 Major construction competing with the natural qualities of a river's edge: lowrise buildings.

Figure 1.24 A highrise building located on a river bank.

(a) *(b)*

Figure 1.25 The proposed site of "Manitou Station." (*a*) View from the Hudson River. (*b*) View from above Route 9D. At normal eye level, the building would not be visible from the road.

As development of the Hudson Valley proceeds northward, the danger of destruction increases. Any building solution that permits man-made forms to dominate the valley should be rejected. Lowrise buildings (structures with major horizontal axes) destroy the integrity of the river's edge and might seriously endanger adjacent marsh areas.

A highrise building solution on the bank of the river is also inappropriate because it would permit man-made development to dominate the landscape and would be in conflict with the rural character of Philipstown.

Manitou Station provides a guarantee that almost a mile of river frontage in the uniquely beautiful Highlands will be preserved in its natural state. The design of Manitou Station embraces this strong design for conservation by setting the building where it will not be seen from the highway and will be only slightly visible from the river. Table 1.1 shows the building program envisaged.

Table 1.1 The Building Program

Total Acreage:	125.94 acres
Total Ground Coverage for Building:	206,775 sq. ft. or 4.755 acres
Parking, Roads and Service Buildings:	4.5 acres approximately
Building Coverage at Grade:	less than 5% of total site
Density:	5 units/acre
Open Space: Area to remain for nature conservation and recreational use.	113+ acres (over 90% of site)

Program

Development to be staged over a period of five or more years.

Stage I	
South Building	330 Dwellings
Stage II	
North Building	300 Dwellings
Related Facilities	30,000 sq. ft.
Professional Offices	
Convenience Shopping, Services and Club	
Recreational Facilities	
Railroad Station	
Marina	
Utilities, Sewage and Water Systems	

Proposed Apartment Distribution

25%—1 bedroom
50%—2 bedroom
No greater than 25%—3 bedroom

Parking

Residential Rooftop Parking	560 spaces
Residential on Grade Parking	385 spaces
Total Residential Spaces (1.5 cars/family)	945 spaces
Additional parking for railroad station and visitors	175 spaces

Minimum Setbacks

From Route 9D	1,020 feet
From South East Boundary	340 feet

Height of Buildings

Average Height:	5 stories
Height at side closest to road:	0 stories
Height near Hudson River:	2 stories

Building drops down between hills to 11 stories at center.

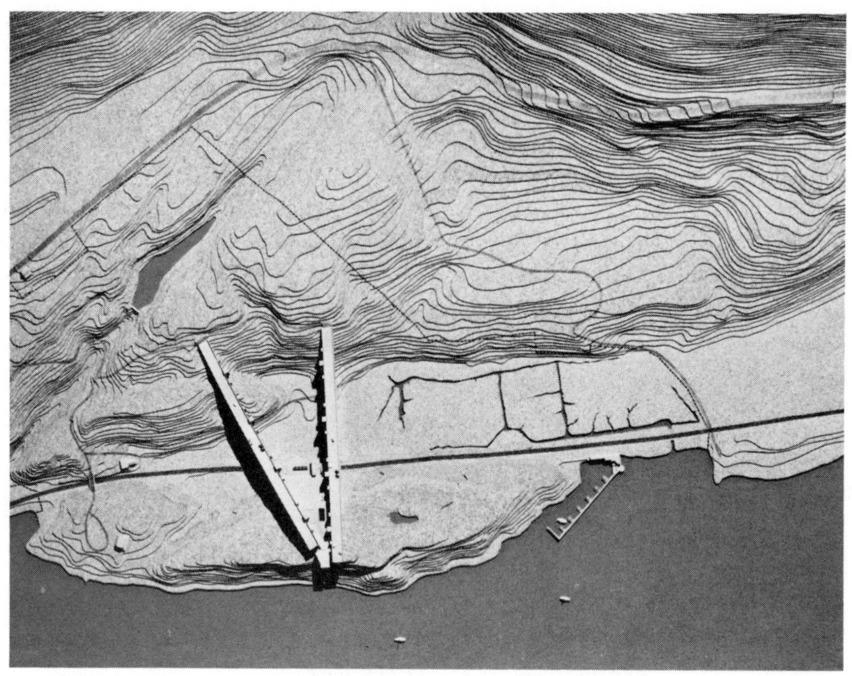

Figure 1.26

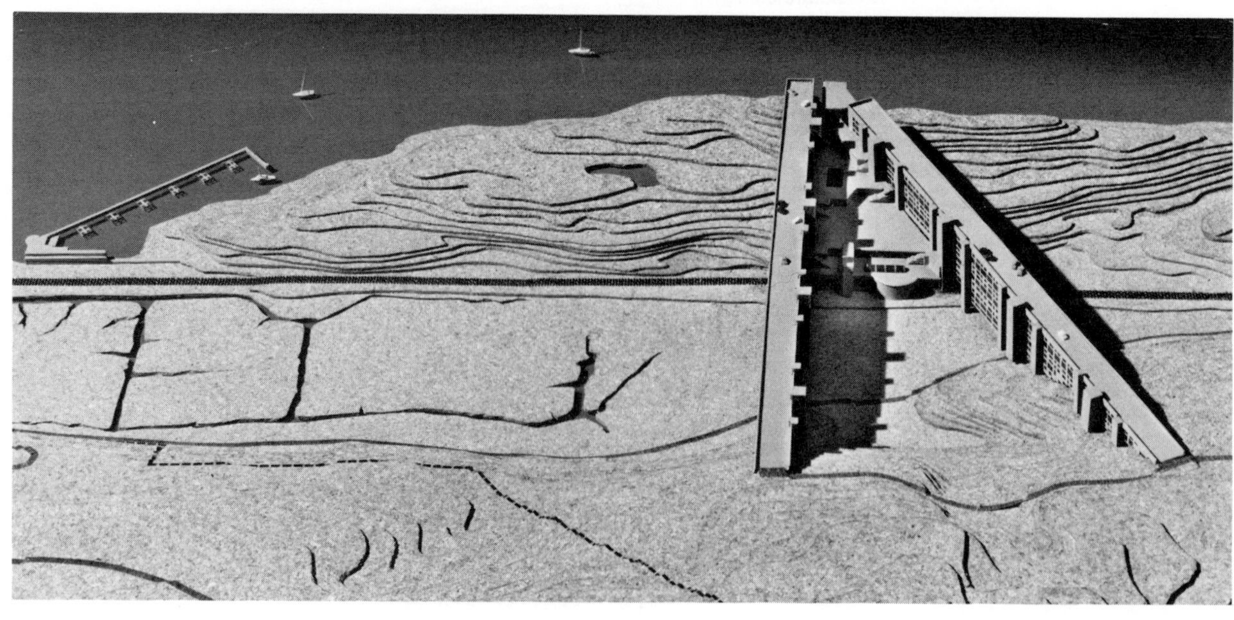

Figure 1.27

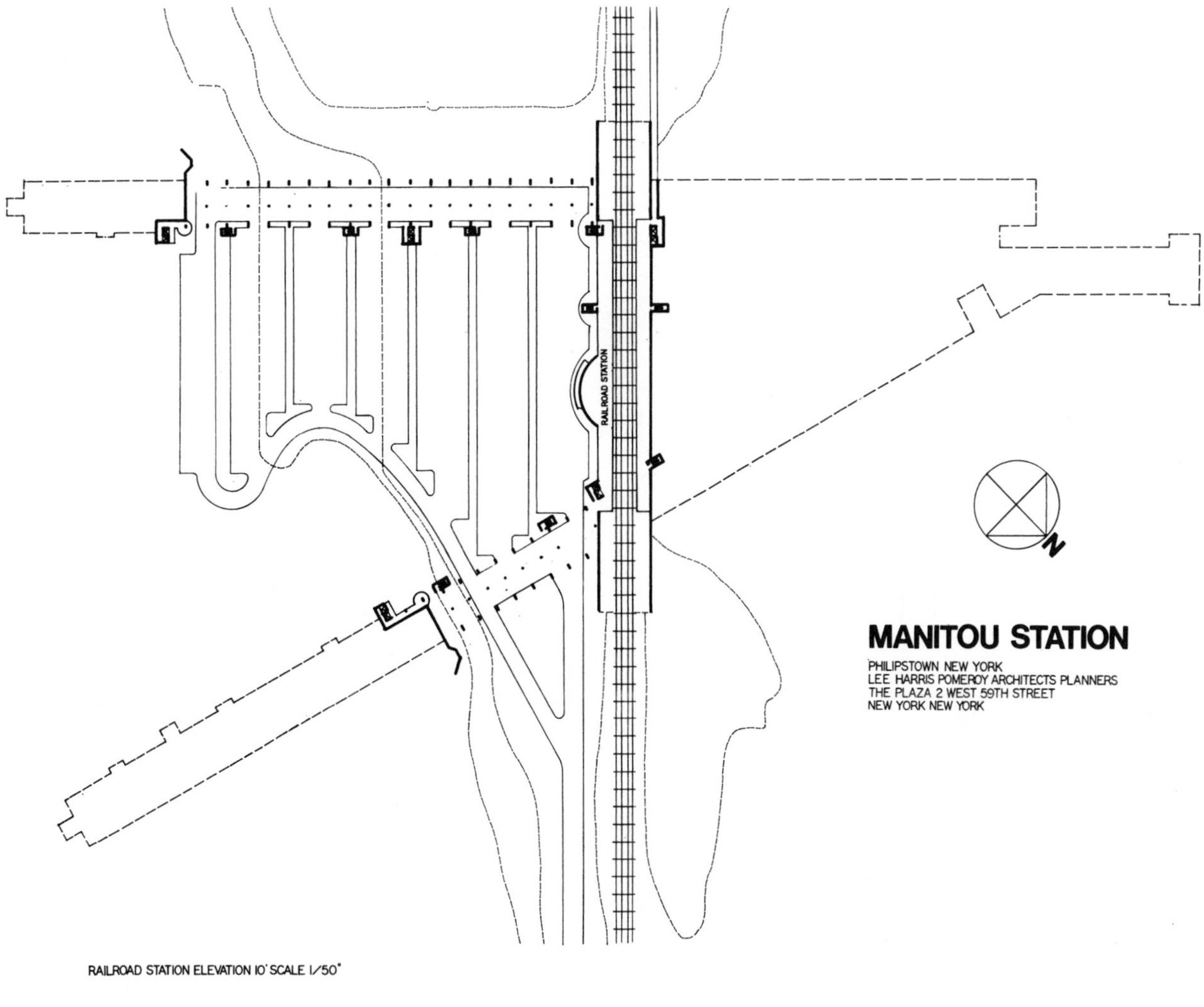

RAILROAD STATION

N

MANITOU STATION

PHILIPSTOWN NEW YORK
LEE HARRIS POMEROY ARCHITECTS PLANNERS
THE PLAZA 2 WEST 59TH STREET
NEW YORK NEW YORK

RAILROAD STATION ELEVATION 10' SCALE 1/50"

Figure 1.28

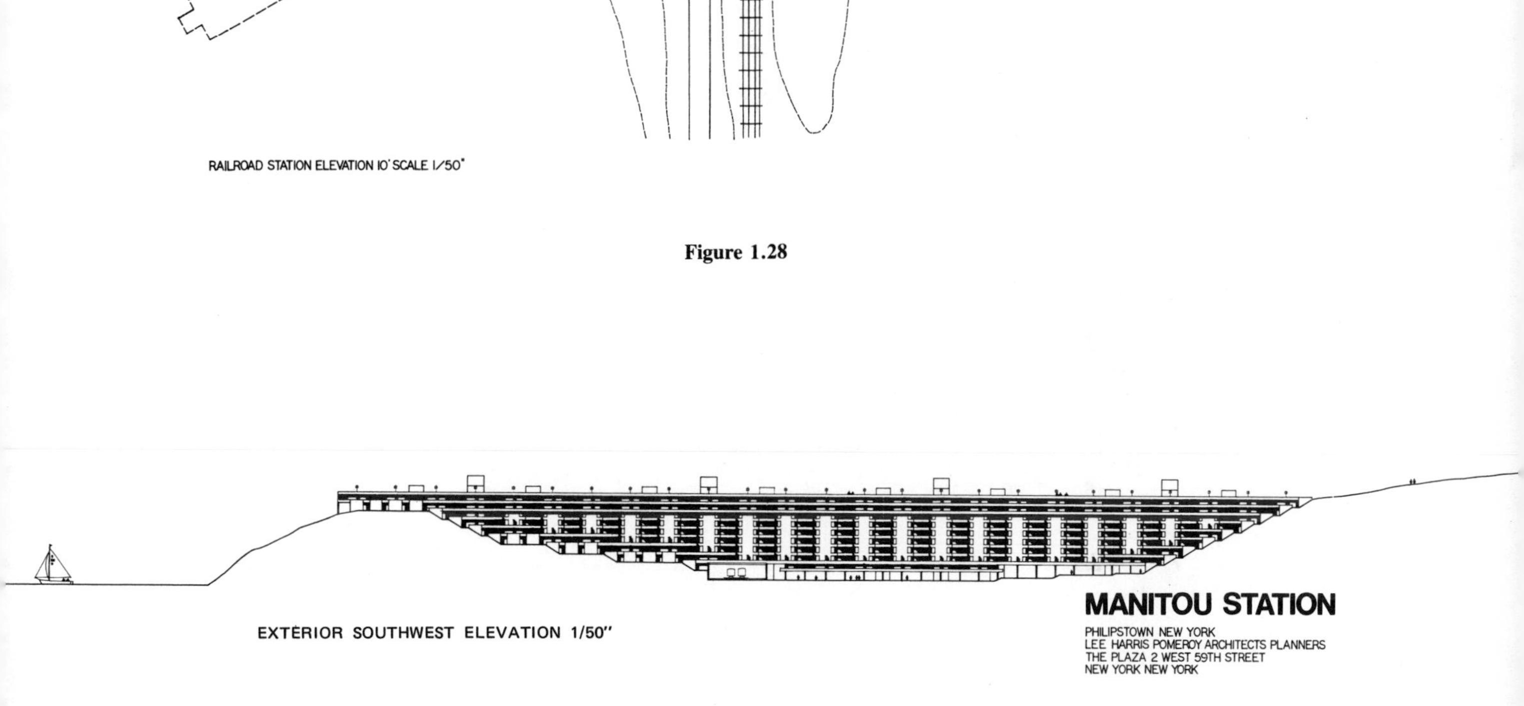

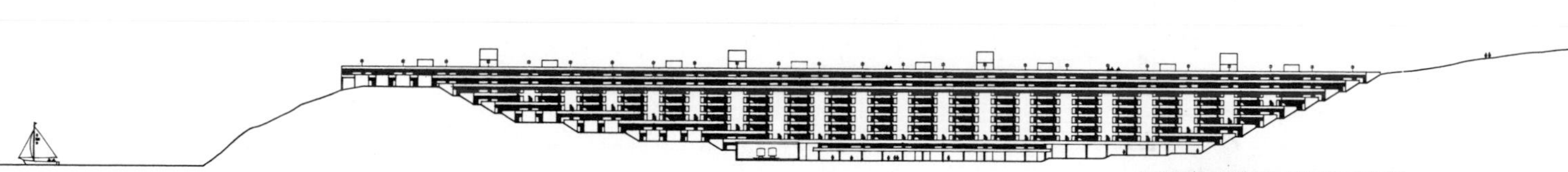

MANITOU STATION

EXTERIOR SOUTHWEST ELEVATION 1/50"

PHILIPSTOWN NEW YORK
LEE HARRIS POMEROY ARCHITECTS PLANNERS
THE PLAZA 2 WEST 59TH STREET
NEW YORK NEW YORK

Figure 1.29

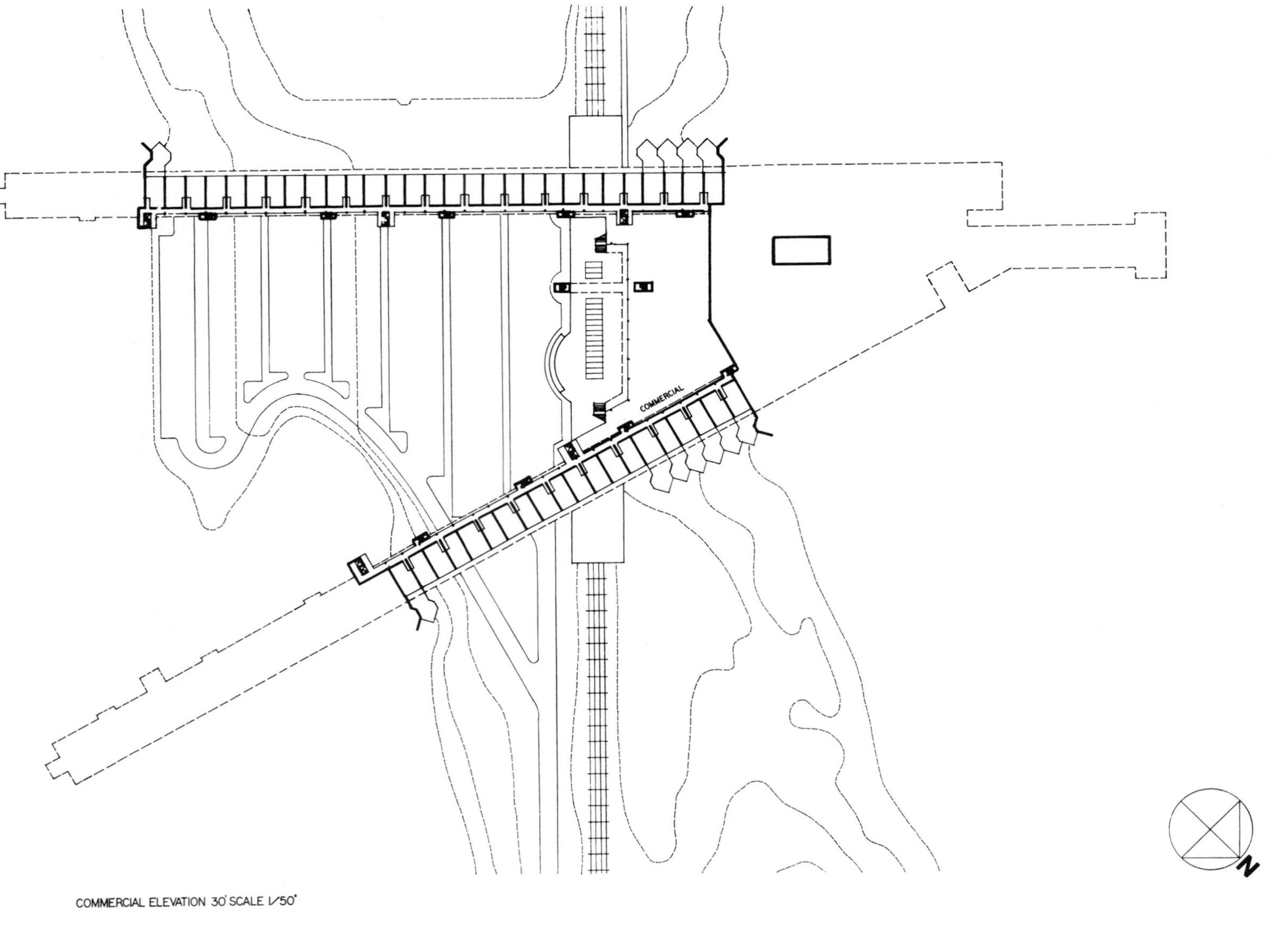
COMMERCIAL
COMMERCIAL ELEVATION 30' SCALE 1/50'
N
MANITOU STATION
PHILIPSTOWN NEW YORK
LEE HARRIS POMEROY ARCHITECTS PLANNERS
THE PLAZA 2 WEST 59TH STREET
NEW YORK NEW YORK

Figure 1.30

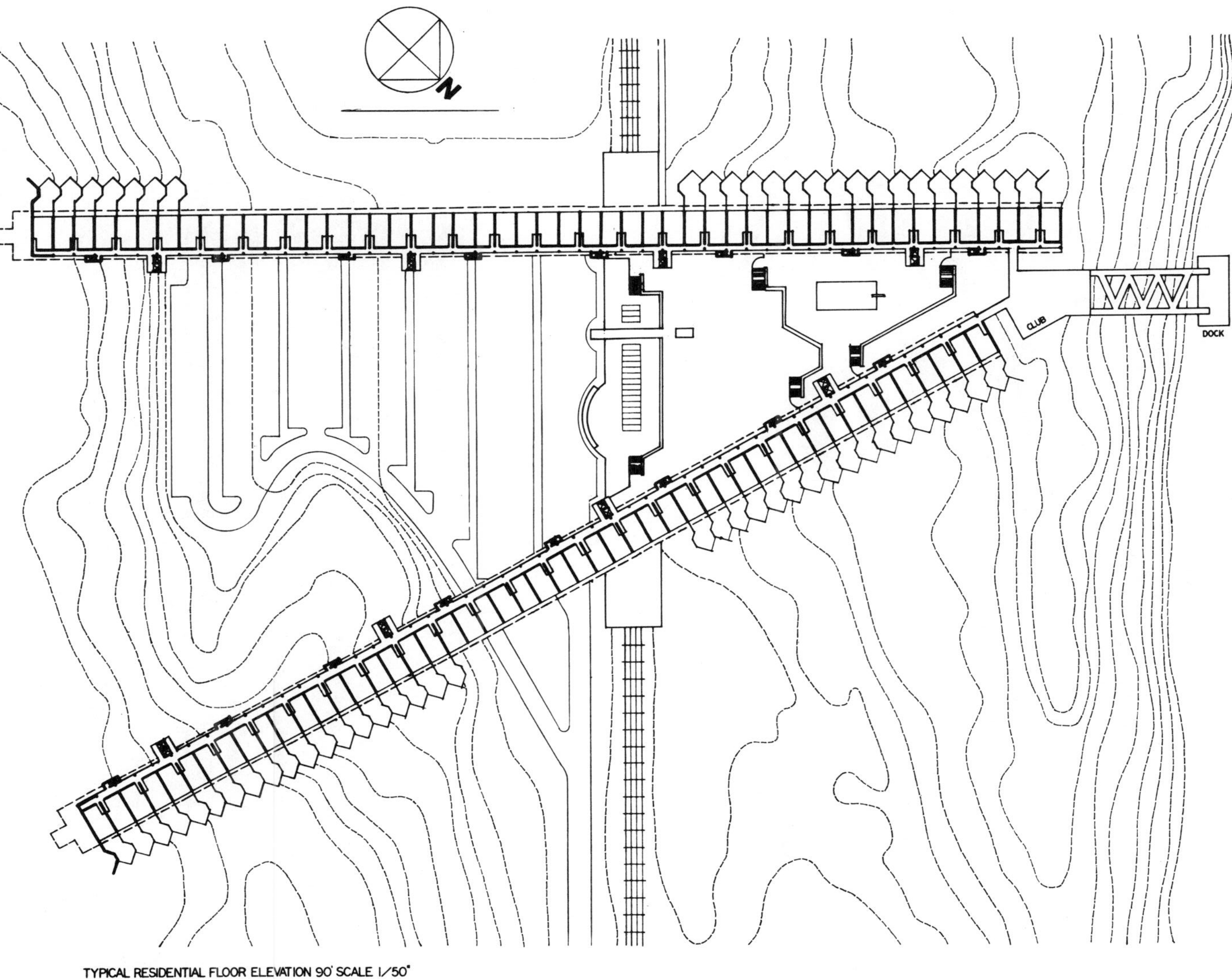

MANITOU STATION

Figure 1.31

Figure 1.32

Figure 1.33

Figure 1.34

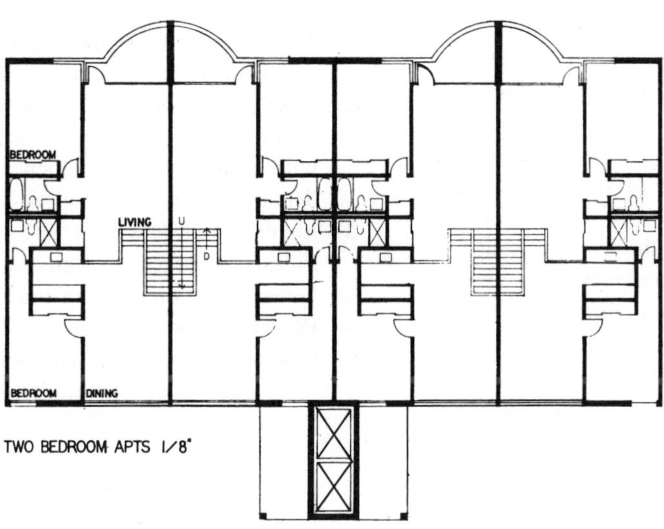

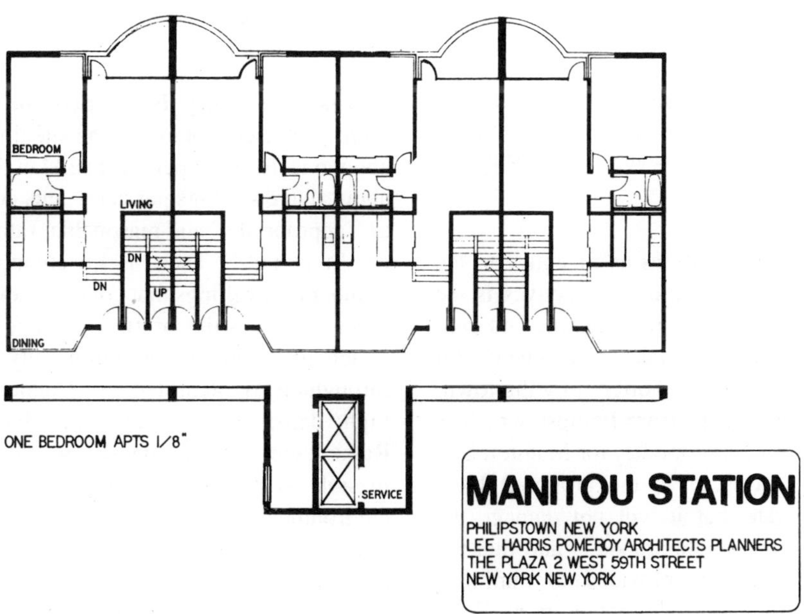

Figure 1.35

The Effect on Philipstown. In addition to housing needs and natural resource preservation, there are important considerations of the possible physical, economic, and social impact of Manitou Station on the community.

Philipstown has a major responsibility—within the region and to local government in general—to illustrate how it can use its power of planning and zoning to protect its natural environment and to accommodate man-made growth. Higher levels of government have effectively protected the Highlands on some of the west side of the Hudson River, but by and large local governments there have not matched these accomplishments. The development of trailer parks and other unsightly uses may very well be the responses of a community forced to grasp for tax returns and "ratables" when placed in a desperate situation by the removal of vast areas of land from the tax rolls by higher levels of government. A lesson may be learned from across the river, for state and federal acquisition of open space land may tend to be too high a price to pay for preservation of open space for the region.

Philipstown has begun to respond to its unique challenge by adopting a zoning ordinance that states that it is designed to permit and encourage the "appropriate and orderly development of the Town and the neighborhood [by permitting the] modifications of the strict application [of the town's zoning] for the following purposes. . .":

1 To permit tracts . . . of considerable size to be developed . . . (a) harmonious units.
2 To permit the establishment of uses . . . not otherwise permitted . . . when . . . beneficial to the Town.
3 To permit the design . . . of buildings, structures, and facilities . . . which by virtue of their location, orientation, texture, materials, landscaping, or other features, demonstrate design merit.

The concept of zoning flexibility as an incentive to the attainment of the town's development objectives is the essence of good and responsive town planning and zoning. The burden of proof rests with the entrepreneur. But the opportunity for achievement is offered by the town. To receive zoning endorsement from Philipstown, it is necessary and, we submit, appropriate, for Manitou Station to illustrate its "need . . . in the proposed location," . . . to demonstrate that it will not damage the "existing character of the neighborhood"; and that the proposal includes "safeguards provided to minimize possible detrimental effects on adjacent property." . . . [W]e have submitted a "statement" for approval of the Manitou Station proposal as a "Planned Development District" under Article IV, Sections 41 and 43, of Local Law No. 2-1968-Zoning Law No. 2-1968—Zoning Law—Town of Philipstown. We submit that Manitou Station meets the town demand for high-quality development, while fully recognizing all important regional concerns.

Who Will Live at Manitou Station? It is expected that residents of Manitou Station will be drawn from various groups and will live there for several reasons.

1 It will be ideal for people who commute to New York City or Westchester and Dutchess counties, to jobs at IBM and other major corporations.
2 It will suit people who want the comfort of living near convenient shopping and recreation facilities, without the adverse elements of city life and the demands of home and ground maintenance.
3 Manitou Station will attract families with homes in Florida and other southern areas who want a second home in a cooler part of the country.
4 People who love the river will naturally be drawn to Manitou Station, as will those who enjoy hiking, water sports, and natural beauty.
5 Present residents of Philipstown and its immediate surroundings who no longer wish to maintain large single-family houses, or cannot afford to, yet want to stay where their friends are, amid familiar surroundings.
6 Finally, Manitou Station will be desirable for families of officers, retired West Point personnel, and others associated with the academy.

Increased Density Is Needed for Quality Development. Present zoning on the site limits gross density to about one dwelling per 2 acres; Manitou Station proposes about five dwellings per acre. This density is considered as "appropriate" and reasonable, rather than "minimal" or "maximal." There is no attempt to maximize the number of dwellings that could be constructed on the site to suggest densities of 10 to 15 dwelling units per acre, which are common in multifamily zoning ordinances throughout Westchester and Connecticut—or the even high densities of many mid-Hudson communities. Rather, the proposed density would make it financially feasible to develop the property and still preserve the environmental qualities of the land.

Provision of high-quality utility and service systems, and construction of a first-class solid waste disposal plant and drainage facilities that would ensure protection of the vegetation, marsh, and natural land characteristics are important considerations. Such facilities are also expensive. The goal of the sponsors is to balance these objectives with sound business practices resulting in an economically viable, model residential community that will attract the desired inhabitants, offer Philipstown convenient recreational facilities, a new railroad station, a significant nature conservation area, perpetual access to the river, and a very substantial tax asset.

We believe that the size and character of the proposed project will permit such advantages for the residents of Philipstown and will provide the sponsors with a fair return on their long-range investment.

The Effect of Manitou Station on Education and Taxes

Education. The Manitou Station property is located in the Manitou Common School District (Table 1.2). Presently, it is a district with no school; the only school having been closed because it did not conform to New York State educational standards.

The children of Manitou are unable to attend school in the adjacent school district, Garrison Union Free, because Garrison children attend school by contract in a school district across the Hudson River in Orange County. Garrison children pass through Manitou on their way to and from school. The Manitou children attend the Haldane Central School District in Cold Spring and pass through Garrison on their way to and from school.

This unique situation inspired an attempt to recentralize the three districts: Haldane, Garrison, and Manitou. The proposition suffered a narrow defeat and "cross-busing," and education-by-contract continues. A major concern of the proponents of the recentralization, which included a steering committee appointed by all three boards of education, was that the Town of Philipstown was fragmented and was being denied its goal of a total and natural community.

The Manitou Station concept, including its enormous tax advantage to the town, will potentially improve education for the children of Manitou and also for the children in the surrounding area (Table 1.3). Whether to recentralize is the prerogative of the voters of Philipstown; but in either event Manitou Station will be a substantial friend to education (Tables 1.4 and 1.5).

Table 1.2 Manitou Common School District

	Number of Pupils	Approximate Educational Cost/Pupil**	Total Cost
Present District	80	$1,000.00	$ 80,000.00
'Manitou Station' Proposal*	150	$1,000.00	$150,000.00
Estimated Cost to Manitou Residents after Completion of 'Manitou Station'	230	$1,000.00	$230,000.00

*New pupils at the rate of 25 per year for six years.

**By contract with Haldane District, excluding State contribution.

Table 1.3 School Tax Rates: Manitou Common School District

	Assessed Valuation (approximate)	Estimated Cost of Education	School Tax Rate (per thousand assessed valuation; approximate)
Present District	$ 2,200,000.00	$ 80,000.00	$38.50
'Manitou Station' Proposal	$10,000,000.00	$150,000.00	—
After Completion of 'Manitou Station'	$12,200,000.00	$230,000.00	$20.00*

*This tax rate reflects a savings of $18.50 per thousand of assessed valuation. This could mean a savings of $400.00 per year to a homeowner in Manitou District with a home valued at $40,000.00.

Table 1.4 Comparative Costs of a Manitou Station Townhouse and a Single-Family Detached House

	Cost to Taxpayers	Tax Revenue Paid	Result
Detached House with 1.5 pupils	$1,500 00	$750.00	$750.00 loss per year*
Townhouse with 0.2 pupils	$ 200.00	$500.00	$300.00 gain per year

*This means for every new detached house built, the remaining taxpayers must share the loss of $750.00 each year added to their school tax.

Table 1.5 Tax Advantage to the Town (including Nelsonville and Cold Spring)

	Assessed Valuation (approximate)	Total Tax Revenue (approximate)
Town of Philipstown	—	$1,400,000.00*
'Manitou Station Proposal (1)	$10,000,000.00**	$ 385,000.00***

*Directory and Tax Levy of Putnam County, 1972.

**Based upon 55% equalization rate multiplied by estimated true value.

***Based upon existing Town tax rate of approximately $38.50 per assessed valuation.

(1) At the current tax rate, 'Manitou Station' would contribute over 25% of the present tax. More likely, this will effectuate a tax savings. Since 'Manitou Station' would provide many of its own services, including sewerage systems and road maintenance, the vast percentage of this tax revenue would constitute a net gain to the Town.

A planned community such as Manitou Station can be expected to have about one child of school age for every four or five homes. Therefore, it can be reasonably forecast that there will be no more than 150 students, or about 25 new students per year for 6 years. Under present circumstances, these children would attend the Haldane school, and the taxpayers of Manitou would continue to pay their share of the cost of education. Haldane has a record of above-average academic performance over the years and is planning a new 28-room elementary school. The Haldane District is changing for many reasons, including old buildings and the possibility that the local Catholic school will close. The additional children from Manitou Station would not be so numerous as to cause a problem, but there would be enough of them to assist in amortizing the new building already planned. The residents of Manitou, who now enjoy the lowest school tax rate among the three districts, would receive an even lower tax rate—and more important, would be able to offset the inevitable higher cost of tuition with the increased ratables from $20 million in real estate values. Otherwise, in the event of a successful recentralization, all three districts would share the tax revenue directly. Manitou residents would benefit to a greater extent than they would under the recentralization proposed in 1967.

Taxes. The current assessed valuation in the Town of Philipstown is about $33 million, which represents a true market value of just under $60 million. Manitou Station would provide an additional $20 million in real value and more than $10 million in assessed valuation—almost one-third the existing total ratables in the entire town.

The Town of Philipstown has only two choices for the future: either to keep raising the taxes of existing residents, or to find good taxpayers to help out existing residents. There is no better or more realistic taxpayer than a well-planned condominium development. It is unlikely that major corporations or large shopping centers will locate in Philipstown, and it is quite doubtful that they would provide the same net tax dollars as Manitou Station.

Each new single-family house that is built in Philipstown creates a tax loss to the town and the school district that must be absorbed by all the taxpayers. These losses, plus the ever-increasing general costs, mean higher taxes for everyone. Older families with fixed incomes, young families with future potential but small incomes, and middle-class families with their wages subject to a national freeze, will be driven out of their own homes, and only wealthier families will enjoy the benefits of living in Philipstown.

Based on existing tax formulas, Manitou Station could provide \$0.75 million each year to the town and the school district. The cost to the town would be minimal, and the large resulting surplus would greatly ease the inevitable future tax burden. A study of 3000 apartments and condominiums in Westchester County and Fairfield County, Connecticut, showed that they contributed substantially more revenue than cost. Cooperatives and condominiums similar to Manitou Station actually provided an average of 500% more revenue than cost.

Vehicular Access. Manitou Station is accessible from almost all directions. The Palisades Interstate Parkway, just a few minutes to the south across the Bear Mountain Bridge, makes it possible to reach mid-Manhattan in little more than an hour. The New York State Thruway and Interstate 84 are each within 15 minutes drive of the site. Major shopping and health facilities in northern Westchester and southern Dutchess counties can be reached within 20 minutes.

Recently reconstructed west of the bridge, U.S. Route 6 provides high-speed access to the Thruway and major points in the Hudson Valley. This new road is the first link in a major highway reconstruction program across the region midway between the Cross Westchester–Tappan Zee Bridge corridor to the south and Interstate 84 to the north. This new regional route will link the Thruway and the Quickway (Route 17) with the Bear Mountain Parkway near Westchester in the general vicinity of the Route 202-35 highway corridor. Key link in this high-speed road will be construction of the proposed connection from the Route 9–Route 6–Bear Mountain Mountain Bridge. This link, which must pass through rugged terrain, is nonetheless given high priority by the Tri-State Planning Commission and the New York State Department of Transportation. In many respects it will be similar to the Route 6 reconstruction completed just a few years ago in similar terrain a few miles to the west in the Harriman State Park. According to the highway planners, construction of this high-speed connector will include an interchange at Route 9D just a short distance south of Manitou Station.

Site Access. By building site access and internal circulation roads primarily on existing drives, it will be possible to minimize any massive scarring of the land. The major vehicular access to the site will be by way of the existing drive from Route 9D. Improvements will be made to Route 9D to permit safe acceleration and deceleration on that road from and to the entrance drive. Traffic engineering studies by Wilbur Smith and Associates show that the daily and peak-hour traffic volumes that may be generated by Manitou Station would have an almost insignificant effect on Route 9D capacity and certainly would not overload it. The existing drive, widened as necessary, would continue to the rooftop parking areas and down to the surface parking area, train station, and shops within the confines of the building.

To conserve energy, a second existing drive along the east side of the marsh would be improved to continue to give access to the lower portion of Manitou Road. Also, for safety and convenience, the existing drive to the former Livingston Mansion would be continued southwesterly to give access to the westerly end of the V-shaped structure.

The Railroad. The property is unique in that it contains on site an existing railroad stop—Manitou Station. This presents a special opportunity and advantage for future residents of the proposed development and people of Philipstown. Rail travel provides a convenient alternative to auto and water transportation. It also offers the promise of a more self-sufficient residential community.

The Hudson Division of the Penn Central line is electrified to Croton-on-Hudson in Westchester County. The number of rail commuters in the Putnam-Dutchess area is significant and growing, and proposals by the Metropolitan Transportation Authority to improve commuter service as far north as Poughkeepsie are envisioned.

Relocation of the local station to a position under the main building is proposed as a means for providing an improved railroad station with additional daily train service, and appropriate parking and accessibility for Philipstown rail commuters.

Recreation. Major recreation facilities are proposed along the Hudson River and Copper Mine Creek. A small boat marina will be located at the southerly end of the property, to be reached from within the site by walking trails and a service drive. The facility will include floating docks and boat slips, a small boat launching ramp, an area for minor repairs, and lockers, eating facilities, and parking.

The pond on Copper Mine Creek will be improved for ice skating. The old ice house, a structure of some character, will be renovated as a warming hut for skaters.

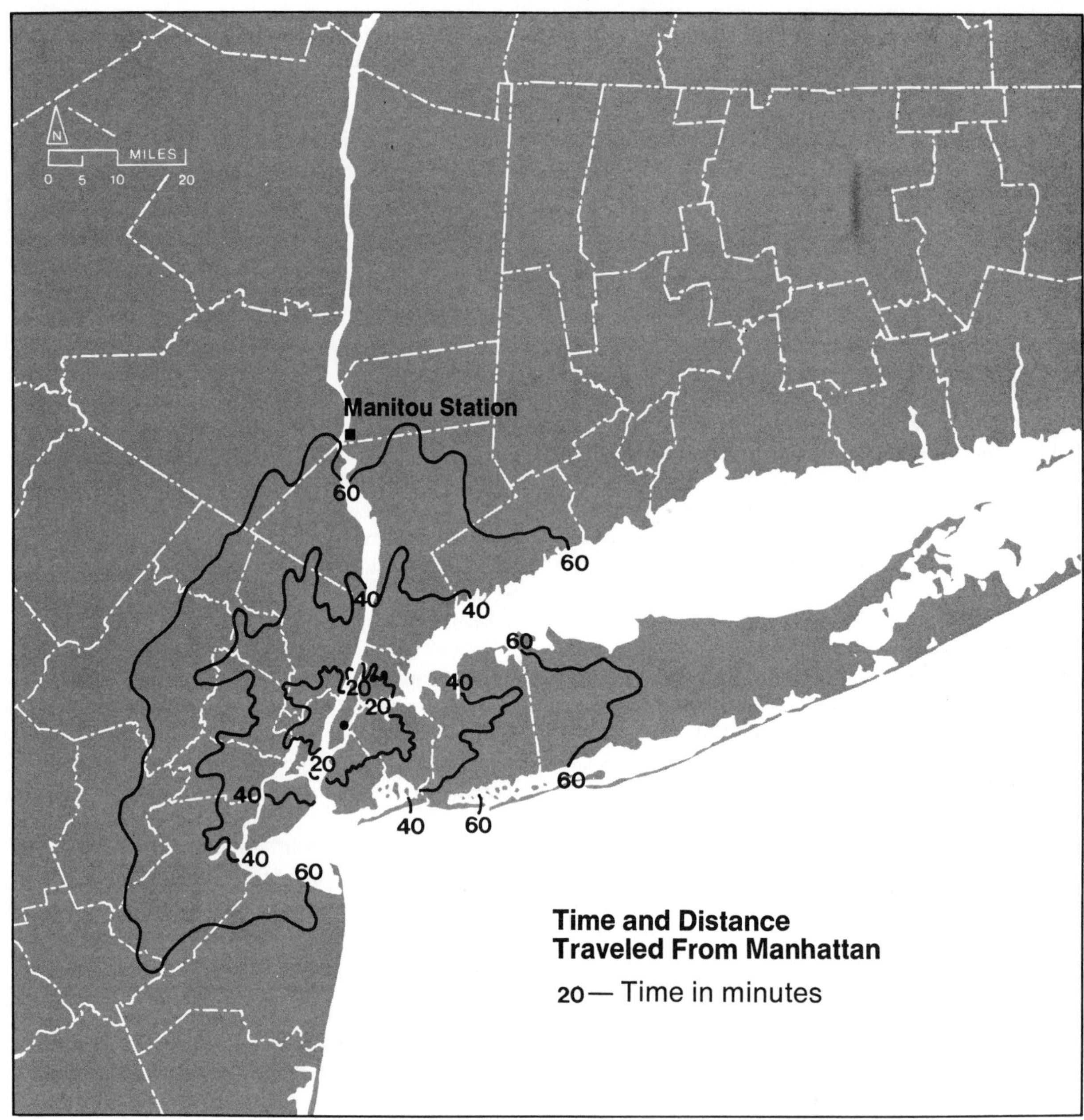

N
MILES
0 5 10 20
Manitou Station
60
60
40
40
60
40
20
20
20
40
40
60
40
60
60
Time and Distance
Traveled From Manhattan
20— Time in minutes

Figure 1.36

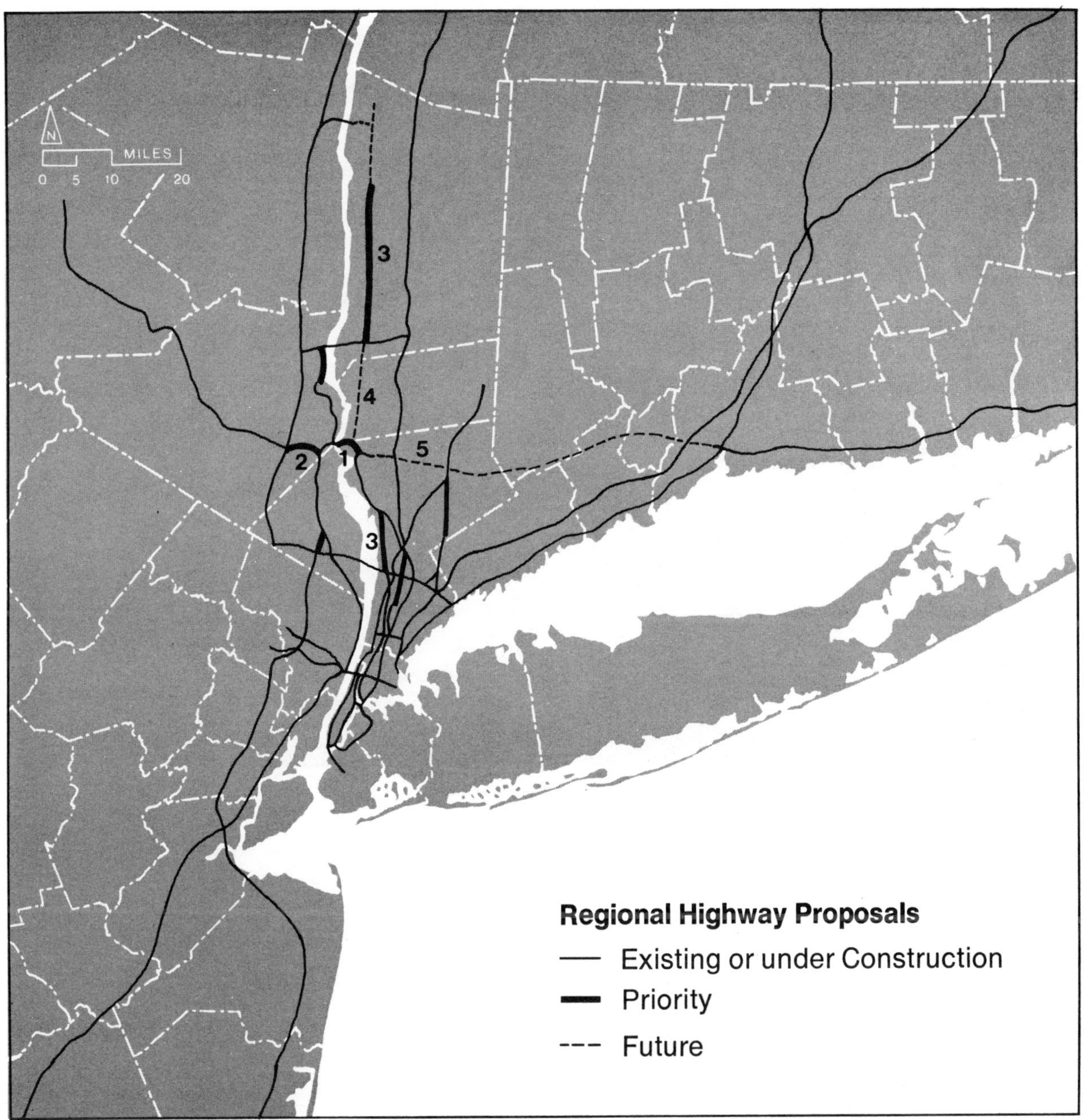

Figure 1.37 Tri-State Transportation Commission's highway proposal. *1, 2, Long Mountain Parkway* (recently completed section of Route 6); east-west route through Orange County; extends Quickway (N.Y. 17) to Palisades Parkway and Bear Mountain Bridge. *3, U.S. 9 Expressway:* north-south route in Westchester County and in western Dutchess County; connects Poughkeepsie urban area to interstate route; serves fast-growing suburban and industrial areas. *4, U.S. 9 Expressway:* north-south route through Putnam and Dutchess counties; serves commercial traffic needs east of the Hudson River. *5, N.Y. 35 Expressway:* east-west route through northern Westchester County; serves rapidly developing suburban area; fills need for peripheral route, including approach to Bear Mountain Bridge from the east. *Source. Tri-State Transportation 1985: An Interim Plan,* May 1966.

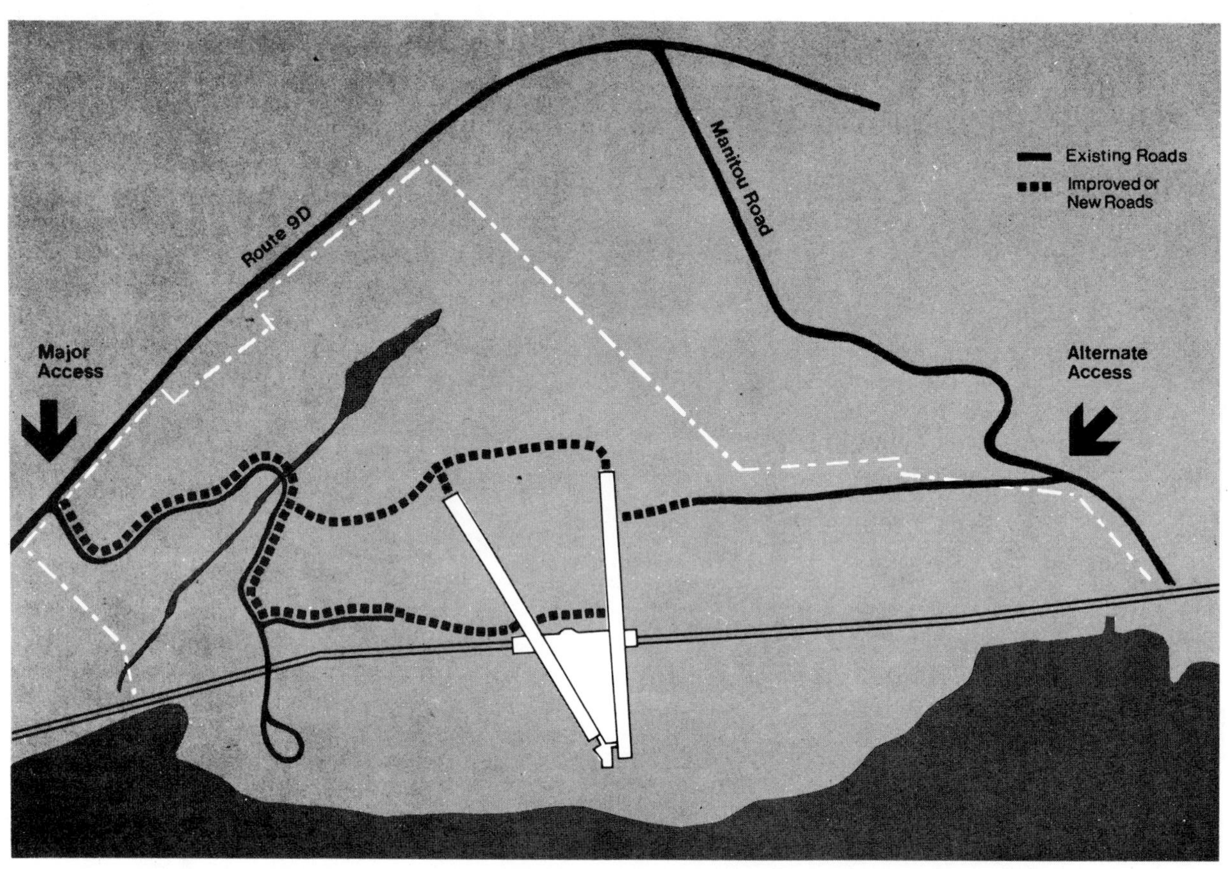
Route 9D
Manitou Road
Existing Roads
Improved or
New Roads
Major
Access
Alternate
Access

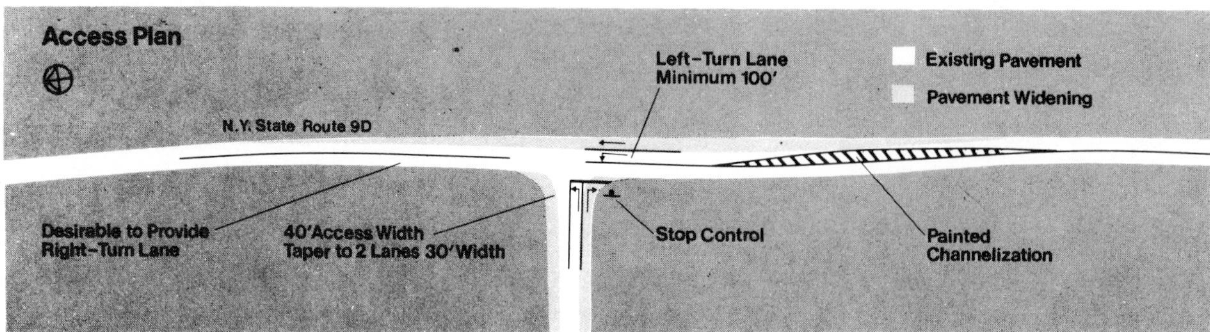
Access Plan
Left-Turn Lane
Minimum 100′
Existing Pavement
Pavement Widening
N.Y. State Route 9D
Desirable to Provide
Right-Turn Lane
40′Access Width
Taper to 2 Lanes 30′Width
Stop Control
Painted
Channelization

Figure 1.38

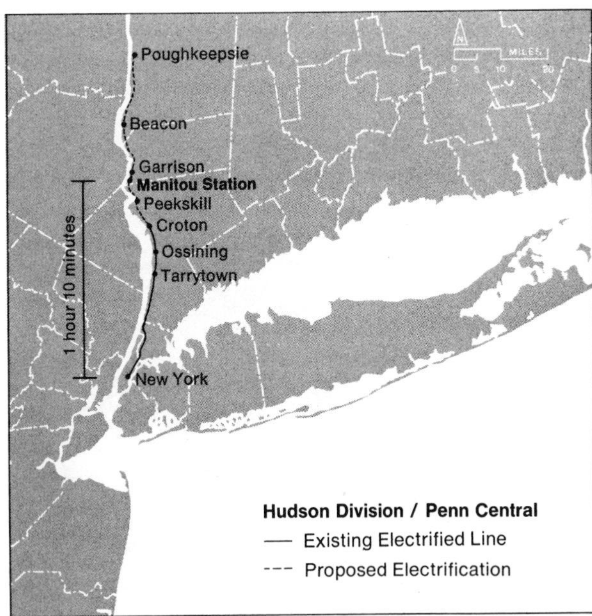

Figure 1.39

The entire site would be available for hiking and nature study. There would be access to the river for fishing and boating, and provision for a restaurant and private swim and tennis club for occupants of Manitou Station and Philipstown residents.

Services and Utilities

Water Supply. Preliminary engineering analysis indicates a design need for 188,000 gallons of water per day, or an average water demand of 131 gallons per minute. The potable water part of this demand would be provided from on-site wells (about 80 gallons per minute), and the remainder is available from the Hudson River for supply of nonpotable requirements (about 53 gallons per minute).

Engineering work underway by Roy F. Weston & Company, environmental scientists, and Lehr Associates, consulting engineers, and an analysis of the geology of the site and buildings indicate that sufficient water would be available to support the potable water demands of Manitou Station without unduly taxing available water supplies in the town.

Figure 1.40

Figure 1.41

By utilizing the Hudson River water for sewage treatment, fire safety, and building and grounds maintenance, it would be possible to return water to the river and into the site in a purer condition that it was obtained, thereby furthering the aim of gradually eliminating river pollution.

Waste Disposal. A high-quality waste disposal system would be constructed on the site. Sewage generated by Manitou Station would be treated in strict conformity to state and county standards and the recommendations of recognized ecology groups concerned with the quality of water in the Hudson. Preliminary discussion with the New York State Department of Environmental Conservation indicates that there would be no problem in disposing of sewage effluent into the river with a treatment plant designed to operate in accordance with state standards. Because of increasingly stringent requirements of water effluent quality anticipated in the coming years, such a plant would be constructed in an advanced design so that it could continue to meet all future requirements as well. Solid waste collection and disposal would be the responsibility of Manitou Station. Garbage and trash would be removed from the site and deposited in authorized and approved disposal areas.

Fire Protection. Given the location of the building next to the river and its proposed construction of masonry and fireproof materials, coupled with a specific design that permits access to every floor directly from adjacent land, the structure would be especially easy to protect against fire.

In addition, on-site fire control equipment satisfactory to the local Garrison Fire Protection District 1 would be provided. An early warning system, in-house training of personnel in fire prevention programs, and the ability to reach all parts of the building from not only the ground but directly from the rooftop roadway system, would speed fire department response time and increase their ability to provide necessary fire protection.

Fire Underwriters Standards for On-Site High Pressure Pumping Systems and early warning controls add further to this protection and ensure that Manitou Station would be among the safest of structures from a standpoint of fire protection.

Health Care and Related Facilities. Manitou Station would provide office space for at least one resident doctor and one dentist, to make available immediate treatment facilities for emergencies. Both the Butterfield Memorial Hospital in Cold Spring and the Peekskill

Hospital serve the Manitou Station area. Volunteer ambulance service from these hospitals would be available to Manitou Station residents. We propose, subject to the approval of the ambulance service, to provide space and/or an ambulance vehicle at the site for use by the inhabitants of this part of the town.

Miscellaneous Emergency and Maintenance Services. Emergency, maintenance, and service vehicles would be housed in an existing building on the site. In addition to providing for fire needs and ambulance service, this equipment would be used for road maintenance, snow plowing, emergency vehicle towing, buildings and grounds maintenance, bus service to Cold Spring and Peekskill, and other miscellaneous activities.

Conclusions

1 Manitou Station is conceived in the belief that growth must be accommodated and that carefully planned access to, and use of, the Hudson River by people is the surest way to meet social responsibility, future conservation goals, and ensure long-range protection of the Highlands.

2 The project provides for 630 dwelling units clustered in two structures, convenience shopping, club and recreation facilities, and a new railroad station, coupled with distinct conservation zones.

3 Four-fifths of a mile of otherwise private Hudson River frontage would be left visually free of man-made structures and accessible to building residents and to the people of Philipstown.

4 The buildings would be set into the sloping contours of the site, fully screened from Route 9D and the town.

5 The buildings and site would act as a transition from higher intensity development in the mid-Hudson area and to the south.

6 The project represents an economically viable alternative to frequently destructive development practices along the river's edge.

7 More than 90% of the site (100+ acres), including ecologically important marshland, will remain forever protected for land conservation purposes, walking, and natural use by the residents and people of Philipstown.

8 Combining conservation and recreational facilities (marina, club, ice skating, fishing, and tennis), Manitou Station establishes a vital activity center and new amenities for Philipstown.

9 An adequate tax base is provided, in contrast to traditional one-family housing. Manitou Station will substantially increase the taxable valuation of Philipstown and provide more than $0.75 million to the town and school district, giving funds to the town for needed public improvements and significantly reducing the present tax rate.

10 This proposal is consistent with the stated objectives and requirements of Article IV, Sections 41 and 43, of the Town of Philipstown "Planned Development District" Zoning Law.

11 The applicant is a well-established, financially sound development group with concern for the environment and a firm conviction that the practice of building fine residential facilities and respecting the land on which they are built, is not only good for the residents and community but good business as well.

2 FUNCTIONAL REQUIREMENTS

Environmental analysis with regard to functional requirements deals with the economic feasibility of proposed land usage, examining a project in terms of a real estate investment, and investigating the interfaces of the site with other parts of the community, especially in the area of transportation.

On larger developments, economic and market research activities are usually the responsibility of special consultants, but in many cases the architect is asked to make decisions regarding site selection, highest and best use of a site, or the feasibility of the construction of a predetermined type of structure on a particular site. He or she therefore must be familiar with the functional and economic implication of certain commercial and public facilities, and with their impact on traffic patterns.

Floor Area

A market demand study based on the catchment of a proposed development indicates the maximum floor area

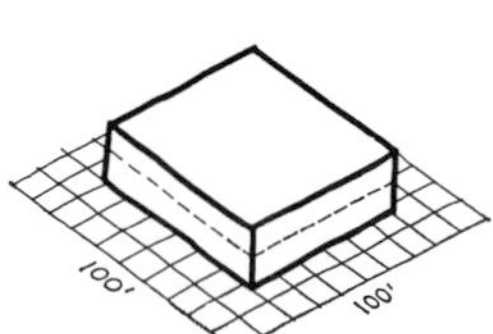

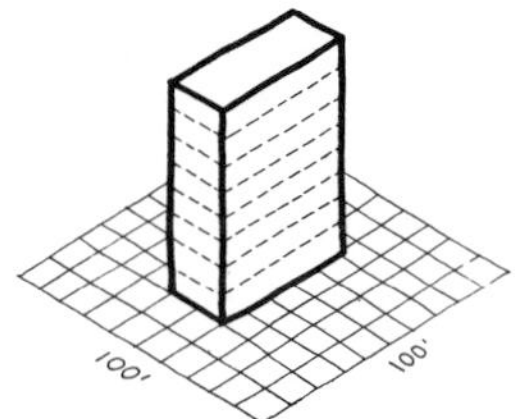

Floor area ratio (FAR). *This ratio indicates how much gross floor area may be built over a specific lot area in any given zoning district. Both diagrams above show buildings with a FAR of 80—yet, obviously, their shapes differ radically. The building at left, above, has two 4,000 sq. ft. floors; the building at right has eight 1,000 sq. ft. floors. The lot area is 10,000 sq. ft. The FAR is the total floor area (8,000 sq. ft. in each case) multiplied by 100, and divided by the lot area (10,000 sq ft.). Result: a FAR of 80, for both buildings. For midtown Manhattan a FAR of about 1,000 is proposed. This is the FAR of the new Seagram Building (*FORUM*, July '58).*

Figure 1.42 The floor area ratio approach to controlling bulk. *Source. Architectural Record*, April 1959, "Zoning: New York Tries Again," Architects Voorhees, Walker & Smith, Haines.

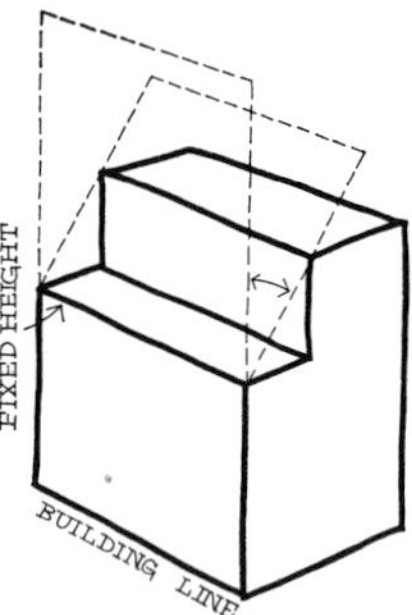

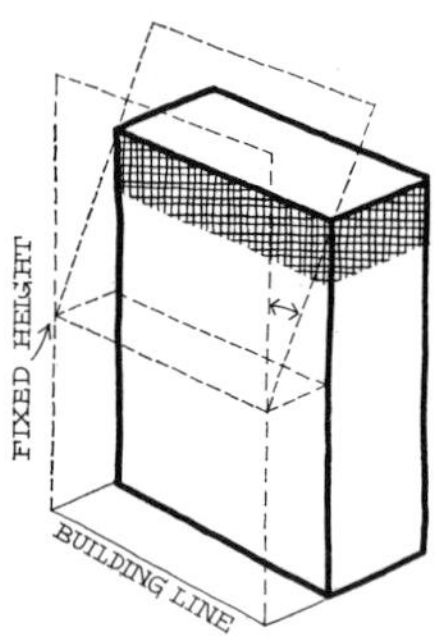

Sky exposure plane (SEP). *This device is designed to control the heights of buildings on a given street. The zoning proposal suggests two different standards—one for narrow streets, the other for wide streets. There would be a fixed height to which any structure may rise directly from the building line; after reaching that height, the building must be set back. The depth of setback and height of any additional floors will be determined by the slope of a plane which is assumed to start slanting back and away from the street once the fixed height has been reached. No part of the building, except for the tower, may penetrate this theoretical plane (diagram above, left). However, if a builder agrees to set back his building from the building line, he gets a bonus in terms of added building height. This bonus is determined by making the angle of the SEP a little steeper, so that the building can go farther up before hitting the plane (diagram above, right).*

Figure 1.43 The sky exposure plane approach to controlling bulk. *Source. Architectural Record*, April 1959, "Zoning: New York Tries Again," Architects Voorhees, Walker & Smith, Haines.

that is economically feasible on a given site. Other factors determining the floor area are usually represented by the zoning and building codes applicable to the site, and by the functional and economic requirements of the development itself. The experienced developer is well informed about optimal floor areas for certain functions. Reference books are available for the architect on this subject.

Catchments

The term "catchment" denotes the total geographic area from which people are drawn by a given center of activity, such as a factory or a shopping center. Naturally, each location in an urban environment is covered by several catchments, and the boundaries of any particular catchment are not always clearly defined. A supermar-

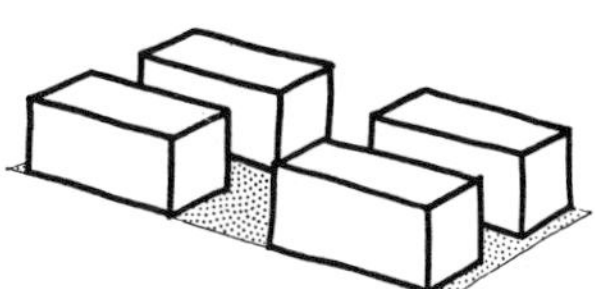

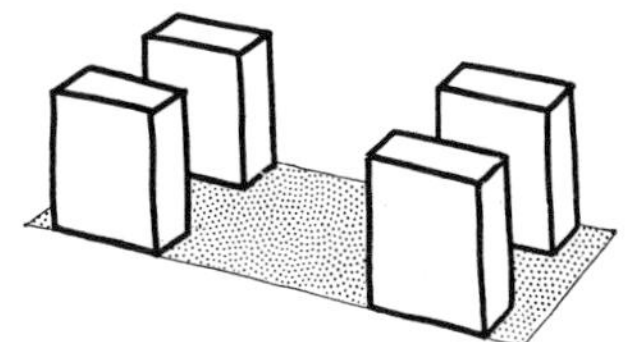

Open space ratio (OSR). *This ratio indicates how much communal park space is available in any given apartment project. The drawings above show two kinds of apartments—low and high—both conforming to the same FAR. However, the taller development has a much higher OSR, because it has opened up a much more generous park area to communal use. The OSR is figured by multiplying the area of open space by 100, then dividing by the total area contained within the buildings on the property in question. If the required OSR in a specific district is 50, then an apartment development containing 100,000 sq. ft. of floor area must provide at least 50,000 sq. ft. of open space. Where a builder goes beyond the required minimum, the proposal offers him a bonus of an increased FAR and slightly higher densities.*

Figure 1.44 The open space ratio approach to controlling bulk. *Source. Architectural Record*, April 1959, "Zoning: New York Tries Again," Architects Voorhees, Walker & Smith, Haines.

ket, for instance, may have a primary catchment area responsible for 80% of its business, and a secondary catchment, covering a much larger geographic area, contributing another 15%.

Most often the catchment is determined by the accessibility factor. In the case of a supermarket, it may be defined as the area within 7 minutes of driving distance. Thus a traffic barrier such as a river or a freeway may become a catchment boundary. Sometimes, however, boundaries result from cultural preferences—for example, in the case of the catchment of a soul food restaurant.

In economic research, catchments for income property are referred to as "market areas"; for commercial facilities they are often called "trade areas," and "tributary areas" is the name applied to catchments for manufacturing facilities. Catchment areas fluctuate over the years, depending on changes in all or some of the following variables:

1 Accessibility (new freeways, etc.).
2 Population growth.
3 Income levels.
4 Competition.
5 Economic obsolescence (railroad station, etc.).

Catchments are not always based on patterns of circulation or on preferences of people. On occasion they are determined by an administrative act, as in school districts, or by areas covered by municipal services or in distribution of utilities.

In most cases the definition and determination of catchment boundaries is based on demographic data contained in the federal census. Statistical averages, computed from census information, are also available

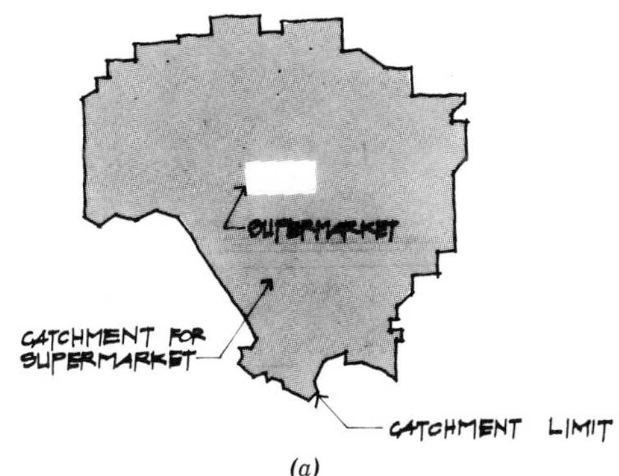

(*a*)

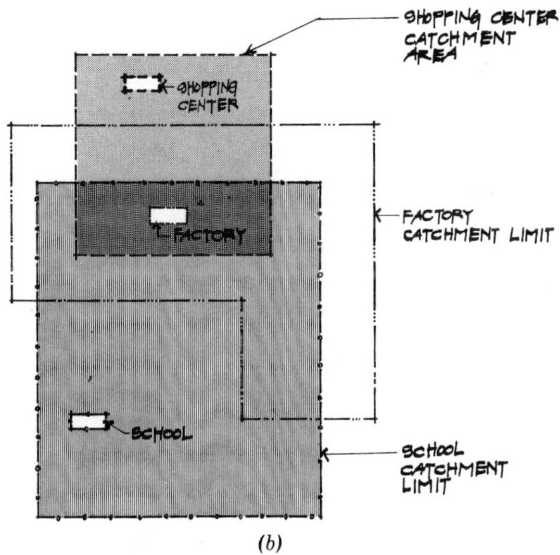

(*b*)

Figure 1.45 (*a*) Supermarket catchment. (*b*) Overlapping catchment areas. Drawings by Jeff Lee, Kemper & Associates.

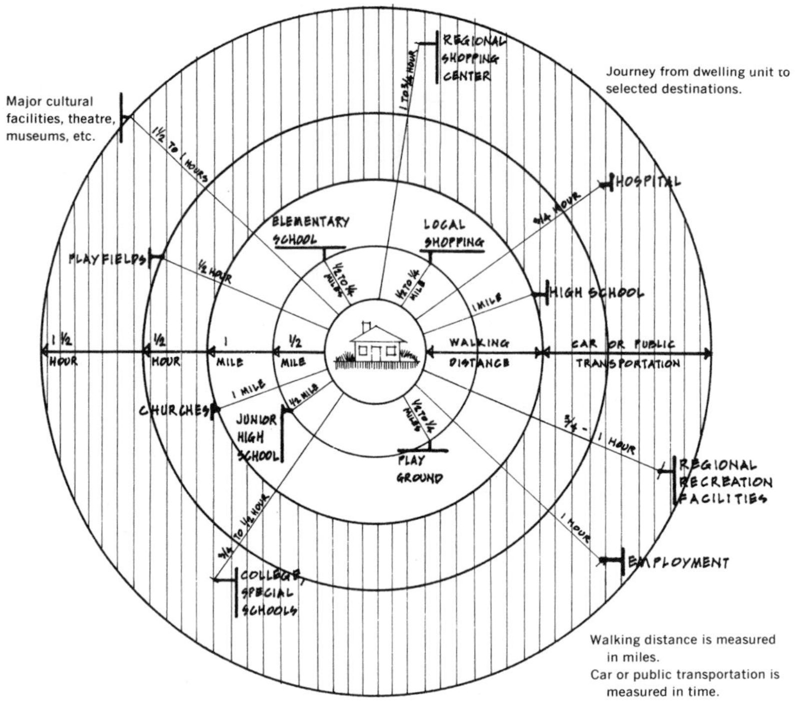

Major cultural facilities, theatre, museums, etc.

Journey from dwelling unit to selected destinations.

Walking distance is measured in miles.
Car or public transportation is measured in time.

Figure 1.46 Recommended distances for community facilities. *Source*. Joseph de Chiara and Lee Koppelman, *Planning Design Criteria*, Van Nostrand Reinhold, 1968.

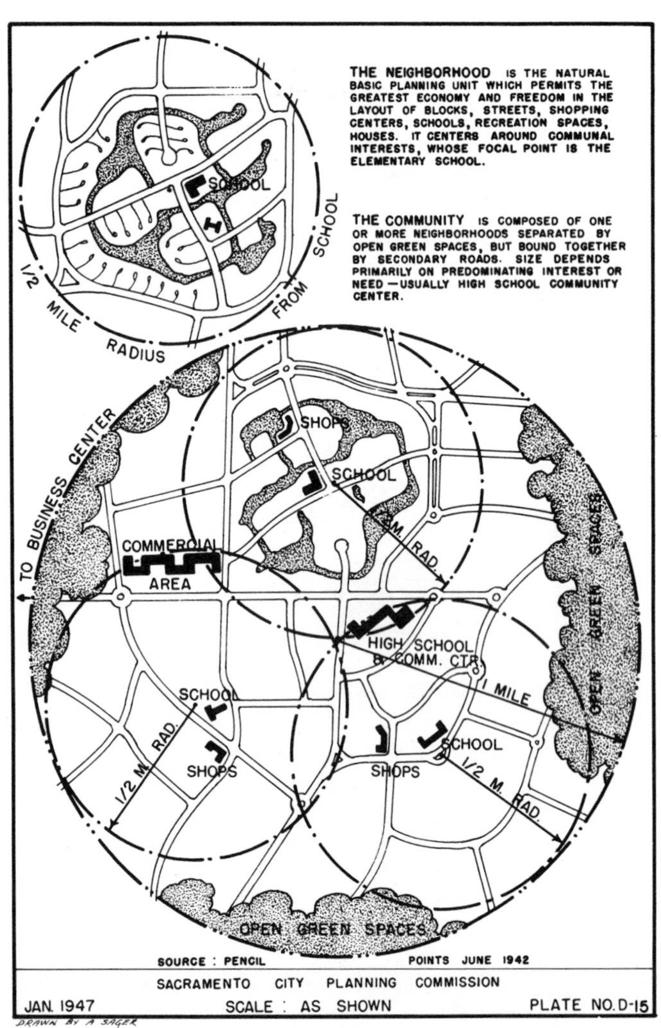

Figure 1.47 The neighborhood unit conception of Clarence Stein. *Source*. Sacramento City Planning Commission, Sacramento, California.

(Opposite page)
Figure 1.48 The neighborhood. *Source*. Heikki von Hertzen and Paul D. Spreiregen, *Building a New Town: Tapiola*, MIT Press, 1973.

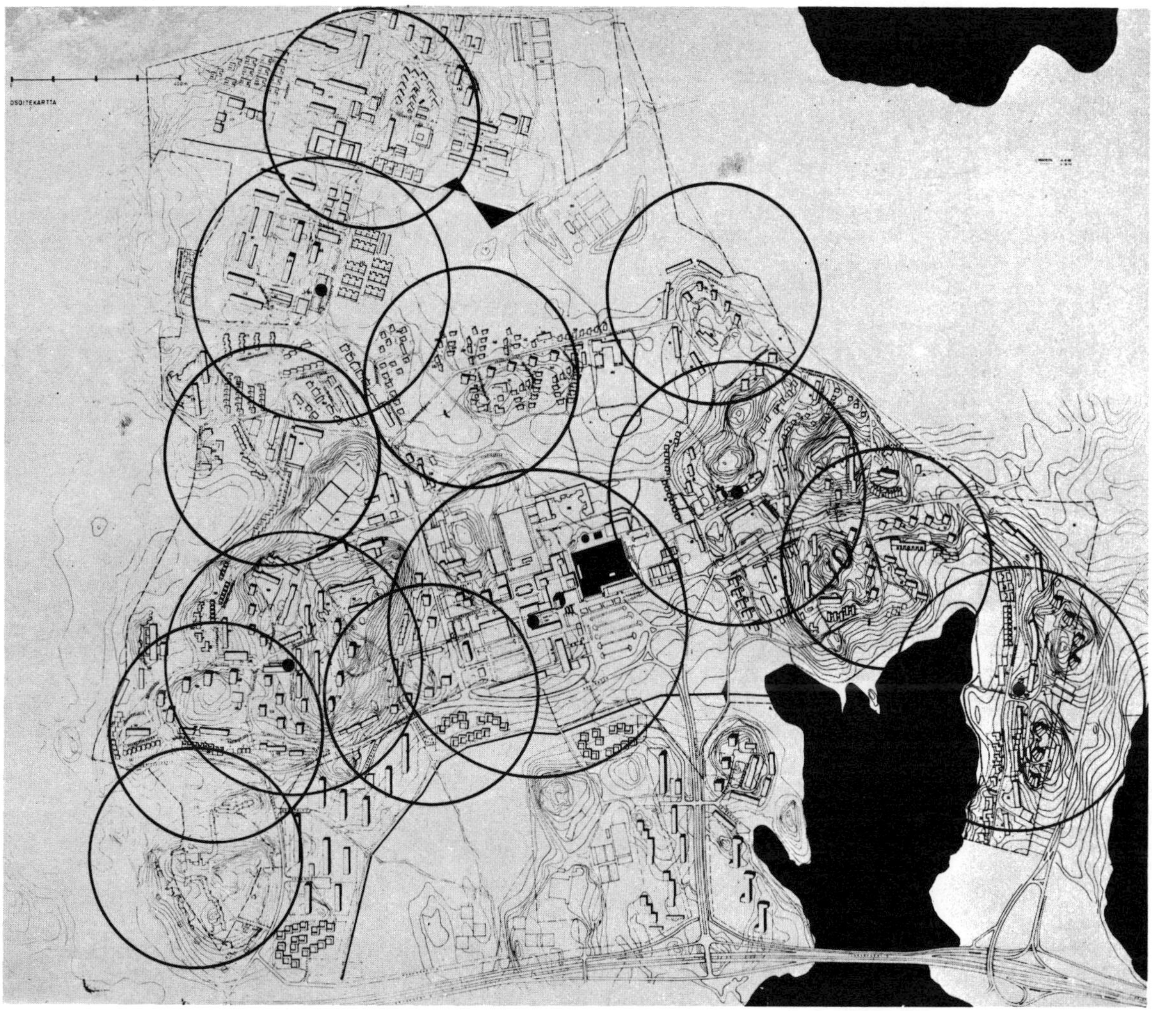

through government sources, such as the Bureau of Labor Statistics of the U.S. Department of Labor. These data make market demand evaluations possible, as illustrated in the simplified example that follows.

A certain site is being considered for the construction of a supermarket. A local survey indicates that most shoppers will not travel further than 1 mile, or 5 minutes, to make a purchase. This information determines the catchment as an area of 1-mile radius. Census data are used to find the number of households within this radius, and these are classified according to four groups of income levels.

Labor statistics are now utilized to determine how much money an average household in each of the four income brackets will spend on the type of goods supplied by the proposed shopping facility. These average figures, multiplied by the actual number of households in the catchment, give the potential annual sales revenue that can be expected for the project. From various statistics on shopping centers, it is then ascertained how many square feet of building space are needed to accommodate the projected sales volume. This will lead to an estimate of the floor area feasible at the subject location. Developers and planners can then decide whether the type of facility originally proposed is economically feasible or whether the catchment will be unable to support such a development.

The allocation of community facilities is also based on catchment areas determined by accessibility factors; however a different set of demographic data is used for each type of development. Figure 1.46 illustrates maximum distances of access recommended for different facilities.

An example of a planning commission's application of these guidelines appears in Figure 1.47. Figure 1.48 gives another example.

FLUOR SOUTHERN CALIFORNIA DIVISION, FACILITY
Irvine, California
Architects: Welton Becket Associates
Photo: Fluor

Circulation and Movement

Most of our cities, like living organisms, are growing continuously. Although none of the world metropolitan areas has stopped growing, each, after reaching a certain parameter, exhibits a noticeable decrease in growth rate. This tendency seems to be partly connected with the decreasing quality of living conditions brought about by a growth beyond that parameter. Traditionally, the factors limiting growth involved food, water supply, and sanitation. Today, however, the factor contributing most to the deterioration of urban environment is the problem of circulation. Therefore cities seem to grow at a normal rate only as long as the quality of circulation remains adequate; beyond that point the existing circulation systems must be improved if additional growth is to occur.

The opposite situation has also been experienced recently. Proposed improvements in the circulation systems were voted down by communities, in order to curb growth. Examples of such cases can be found in the Greater Los Angeles area, where construction of many proposed freeways, such as those of Beverly Hills and Malibu, was stopped for that reason.

Urban land value is largely a function of accessibility; that is, value depends on an area's accessibility or travel distance to the city's employment centers and to its universities, hospitals, labor markets, and recreational areas. Thus a change in accessibility patterns as represented by the construction of a new freeway or a new subway system, will greatly increase land values along that route. Enforcement of zoning laws often serves to slow this rapid price increase and the change in land use patterns associated with it by not permitting the highest possible economic use.

In the past, the growth of cities was largely induced by the construction of railroad, tram, and subway lines; more recently, however, the automobile has determined growth patterns. The disadvantages of a circulation system relying heavily on private cars are obvious to all planners: excessive space requirements (40%) of roads, freeways, and parking structures, high mileage cost (8 to 15 cents), and increasing problems of air pollution and noise. The advantages are to be found, in part, in the realm of personal satisfaction. The car is perceived as an extension and magnification of the driver's physical powers. In terms of individualized routes and immediate response, the car is seen as the key component in tapping the great flexibility and adaptability of the system.

The partial change from the automobile to rapid transit therefore meets resistance, as long as the individual car owner only pays for the direct cost of driving. However if a system could be devised that would hold the driver responsible for the indirect cost of auto traffic, such as medical expenses due to the effects of pollution, or an inflated city budget because of the wide spread of suburbia, the concept of mass transit would compare more favorably to dependence on the automobile. Then mass transit would become economically feasible in areas like Los Angeles, where low population densities seem to prohibit its implementation today.

Urban designers are always challenged by the problems resulting from the overlap of vehicular and pedestrian traffic patterns, but there is also a problem of scale involved in the mix of the two systems. If commercial facilities along a street are designed to be reached by means of private cars, they tend to be spaced too far apart to encourage walking. The parking lot, or the subterranean garage, thus becomes the main building access, and the intimate scale, which related to walking speed and to the perception of a pedestrian, is abandoned. The result is often experienced as monotony and a "plastic" feeling of the environment.

Pedestrian. Inside structures, people are pedestrians. Their undisturbed domain extends along the sidewalks and, increasingly, to the new pedestrian malls and to recreation areas. However pedestrian circulation always intersects the patterns of vehicular access. At these points cars are in competition with walkers for the use of space.

A total separation of the two circulation patterns has been successful only in special areas, such as airports or high-density downtown locations. People-mover systems have been introduced in these areas, to make pedestrian circulation more efficient and to increase the distance within which individuals will walk rather than take a private car or call a taxi.

Vehicular. In most areas the same streets and roads are used by private cars, taxis, buses, and trucks. During rush-hour traffic all these vehicles are competing for circulation space. The more vehicles are on the road, the more slowly the traffic moves. Freeway studies have shown that maximum capacity (i.e., the maximum number of cars per hour) is reached at a speed of about 35 miles per hour. If the traffic flow speed is higher, greater spacing of vehicles necessarily reduces the total volume of cars passing through in a given unit of time. If the speed drops below this high value, the decrease in distance between cars no longer makes up for the slower flow.

A separation of truck traffic from cars can improve a circulation system. Most new zoning codes, for instance, require loading docks for business, thereby eliminating curbside loading and delivery, which block the flow of car circulation. Truck traffic can also be restricted to certain routes, a practice implemented in most cities, or to certain hours, as in some European countries, where truck traffic over the weekend either is generally prohibited or is restricted to the night hours. Newer attempts to improve rush-hour traffic include the reservation of one freeway lane for buses, or for vehicles carrying two or more passengers. These regulations are implemented to encourage the use of mass transit, as well as the creation of car pools.

Much of the congestion occurring in inner cities is attributable to vehicles circulating in search of parking spaces. Adequate parking facilities, then, help to reduce the total traffic volume. Unfortunately, however, in the economics of urban land use, space is the most scarce, therefore the most expensive, where parking is needed most. Therefore inner city parking structures need to produce an income high enough to be competitive with the alternative land use of, say, an office building.

Traffic Capacities. Vehicular flow rates can be measured in vehicles per hour per lane. Typical maximum flow rates for the above mentioned four roadways are as follows:

Freeway	1800 vehicles per lane-hour
Arterial street	1000 vehicles per lane-hr
Collector street	500 vehicles per lane-hr
Local access street	50 vehicles per lane-hr

The number of people carried at these vehicular flows depends on the average number of passengers in one car. Although most cars have five seats, the average rush-hour car carries only 1.5 passengers, which corresponds to a maximum freeway flow of 2700 people per lane-hour.

In comparison, a bus service with 50 passengers per bus leaving at 1-minute intervals (headway) has a traffic flow of 3000 persons per hour. A rush-hour subway with eight cars, each carrying 50 passengers, with a headway of 2 ½ minutes, can haul 9600 people per hour.

The capacity of roadways varies with the improvements in traffic controls. For instance, the more the traffic lights correspond to actual flow rates in a street system, the greater will be the traffic capacity. Another advantage of smoother traffic flow is less air pollution contributed by idling cars.

Most downtown areas today consist of a system of one-way streets. This increases traffic flow as well as safety, since left-hand turns are avoided. Prohibition of curb parking during rush hour can provide an additional traffic lane, thus increasing the flow.

Inner city freeways always form a barrier that greatly changes the patterns of community cohesion, business, and land use. This circulation barrier can be reduced either by elevating the freeway, thus enabling surface traffic to continue, or by suppressing the tract by constructing bridges for the arterial streets. The first solution still creates a strong visual barrier, and the second permits only partial continuity of surface traffic.

A third solution is to use the air space above a suppressed freeway for construction of apartment houses or administration centers. An example of the latter is the East River Drive in New York below the UN headquarters. Naturally, this solution involves very costly construction and is found only in areas where urban land is extremely valuable.

Roadway Classifications. A metropolitan area has four distinct patterns of roads, each with its own properties in terms of traffic capacity, speed of traffic flow, spacing of nodes, and so on.

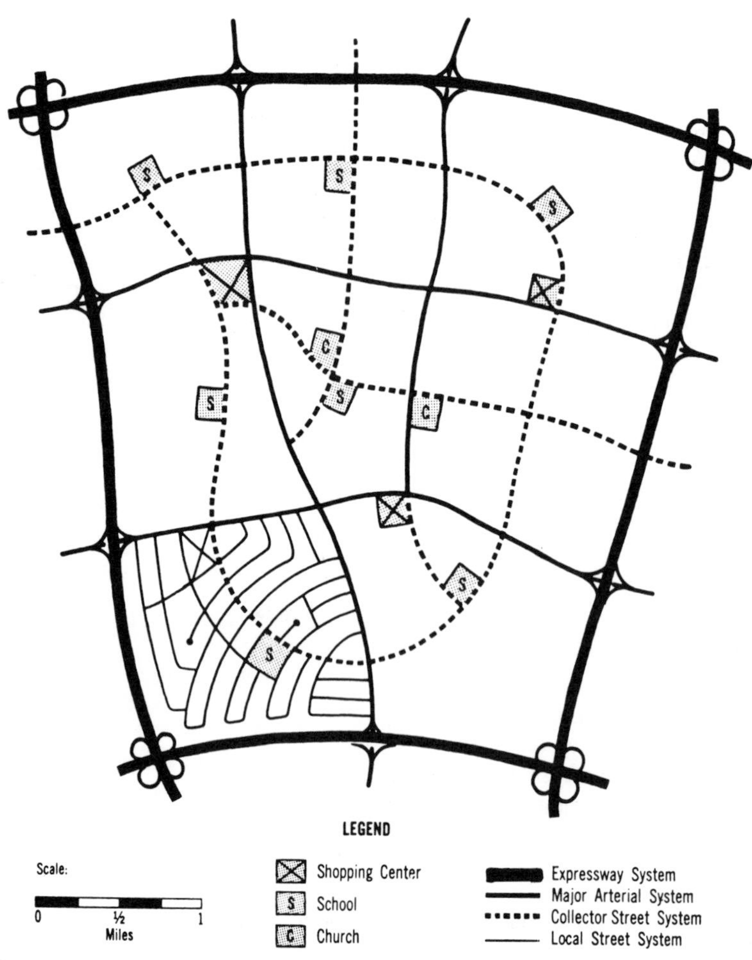

SOURCE: Standards for Street Facilities and Services, Procedure Manual 7A, National Committee on Urban Transportation, Public Administration Service, Chicago, Ill.—1958

Figure 1.49 Street classification.

Freeways (Expressways, Turnpikes). There are no grade crossings. Access and egress within the city are limited to an average spacing of 1 mile. The pattern of surface streets and pedestrian ways is interrupted by the freeway, except for certain routes that cross the freeway with bridges or tunnels. Maximum speed today is 55 miles per hour. Initially freeway patterns were linear or radial, with urban centers located at the nodes. Rings around downtown areas were often added to the pattern. Freeway grids were planned for new urban areas, but this development became stalled because of environmental concerns. The beginnings of a grid pattern can be observed in the Los Angeles freeway system.

Arterial Streets (Highways). This pattern is interconnected with the network of freeways at the access and egress ramps. Crossings are at grade with signal controls. Parking is generally banned from arteries. Access to roadside business and residential areas is often through the side streets. Standard speed limit is 40 miles per hour. Arterial streets in old cities developed along radial patterns, which were later connected by rings that help to keep a portion of the traffic volume outside the centers. Arterial grids are found in master-planned urban environments. The spacing of nodes is usually 1 mile, and residential or commercial patterns develop within these 1-mile squares.

Collector Streets. There is no connection with freeways. Crossings with arteries have signal controls and those with local access streets have stop signs. Parking is restricted to non-rush-hour times.

Local Access Streets. These can be through streets or cul-de-sacs with low speeds and usually no parking restrictions. The pattern of local access streets is most commonly that of a grid. Irregular patterns—sometimes a result of hilly topography or the product of a conscious design effort—should increase the visual interest of the neighborhood and discourage through traffic.

Safety. In the planning of pedestrian circulation, it is important that the data on which the functional requirements are based not be taken solely from the healthy adult; the limited capacities of children, the aged, and the handicapped also must be considered. The American National Standards Institute has developed very useful guidelines to remind designers that to many people, elements like high curbs, revolving doors, and long flights of stairs, are insurmountable obstacles.

Pedestrian safety in the area outside the structure often does not receive adequate consideration in the design of highrise buildings. The access to public transportation, in particular, needs to be considered in the very first steps of the design. Many office towers in downtown areas now considered to be overbuilt were constructed before their impact on traffic problems was fully realized.

If all employees of an office building were to be provided with indoor parking spaces (300 ft^2/car, including driveways), the floor area of the parking structure would equal the office space floor area. This would necessitate either exorbitant parking fees or higher leasing rates. Since neither alternative is feasible, many employees are obliged either to walk to work or to use public transport. In some cities, commuters drive their cars from the suburbs to the parking lot of a subway station and continue by train.

The Commuter

The average time employees are willing to spend on commuting varies with the city and country. In the United States, the maximum commuting time is found to be around 1 hour, and the majority of commuters will not spend more than 45 minutes travel time each way.

The distance covered in these average time spans varies greatly with circulation conditions. In an automobile, a distance of 30 miles can be covered in 45 minutes, if the average speed is 40 mph. At 55 miles per hour the distance increases to 41¼ miles. Thus if the catchment area of an employment center is defined as the area within 45 minutes of reach, it will not look like a circle, but will be extended along freeways and contracted in areas of poor accessibility.

City Streets and Rural Roads: Key Dimensions, Key Changes

Our interstate highway system and mile after mile of rural roads are designed to handle high-volume, high-speed vehicle traffic with minimum delay and maximum safety.

Inflation and funding shortages are limiting new construction of highways. Energy issues are likely to grow in intensity in the 1980s and 1990s. Add to this the possibility of materials shortages, and the result is concern over the nation's future highways and especially tomorrow's vehicles. Evaluating trends already set into motion may help us to examine some possible influences on highway operation and vehicle design in the future.

By 1990, according to the Federal Highway Administration, total highway mileage should be slightly greater than the present 3.8 million miles. The proportion of

WORLDWAY POSTAL CENTER
Los Angeles, California
Architects: Daniel, Mann, Johnson & Mendenhall
Photo: M. Rand

highways with hard surfaces will continue to increase, reaching 60% by 1990. More than 90% of all vehicle travel should be on hard surfaces. At present some 20% of travel is on freeways, and only a slight increase is projected by 1990. A larger proportion of all travel will continue to be on two-lane rural highways and on city streets.

Spending Share to Change. Expenditures for highways will keep mounting because of inflation, but will decline as a percentage of gross national product.

Highway fuel consumption has nearly doubled the past 15 years, and the rising vehicle population will bring further increases by 1990. The number of persons per vehicle of driving age, now 1.2, should reach unity by 1990. The proportion of trucks also should rise steadily, although most will be pickups and panel trucks. Tractor trailers, accounting for 2% of all vehicles today, may go to 2.5% by 1990.

Vehicle-miles of travel are projected to go up substantially, but at a lower rate than previously. Trucks and combinations now account for 4.3% of all travel, and this figure may increase to 4.8% by 1990. This small percentage of total travel is important, however, because it accounts for 18% of intercity ton-miles of freight hauled by all modes of transport.

Speeds soared steadily over the past several decades as automotive power increased and highways improved, reaching a peak in 1973, after which the 55-mile-per-hour limit resulted in a substantial reduction in average speeds. Current speeds should prevail into 1990.

Safety Improves. Highway fatalities reached a peak of 56,000 in 1972, then fell to 46,000 in 1974 and 1975, primarily as a result of the lower speed limit, but also because of reduced travel, changes in types of travel, and other factors.

Further improvement in highways and vehicles helped achieve an all-time low fatality rate in 1975. Although the rate should drop even more in coming years, the cost of highway accidents is expected to increase, mainly because of inflation.

One consideration that may affect highway and vehicle design is whether the 55 mile-per-hour speed limit is retained or abandoned. If the limit is retained indefinitely, it may be possible to put less stringent design requirements on vehicles. Once the Interstate (highway) system is complete, moreover, few additional urban freeways will be built, with only a modest increase in suburban and rural freeways. Given this trend, vehicle design must continue to take account of the need for most travel on city streets and rural highways.

If current efforts to encourage people to use mass transit and car pools succeed, congestion may be reduced and growth in travel slowed. However it is unlikely that the design of vehicles will be changed as a result. But if electric cars are successfully developed and marketed, there might be a radical switch in the mix of vehicles in urban areas, with important design and operating implications for vehicles and highways. Traffic signals might have to be retimed for slower speeds and less acceleration. Special lanes on city streets might have to be reserved for electric vehicles. Conventional cars and trucks may be used for high-speed travel for a greater part of their useful life. There also is the possibility of electrified and automated freeways, as well as the use of taxes or fees to reduce vehicle use in congested areas and to discourage vehicular travel during certain hours or days.

Rapid Transit

Given the dominance of the automobile, rapid transit systems have often become the mode of transportation for low-income people—traditionally, the very young, the very old, and members of minority groups. Rates for fares have been controlled by municipalities, and most systems were subsidized. Because of this economic situation, rapid transit systems did not expand at the same pace as the road and freeway network; and most of the new areas of urban growth became accessible only by automobile. Consequently, the low-income group had to stay in the cities' centers. This is the common situation today in most metropolitan areas.

As mentioned earlier, urban economics seems to favor the automobile over rapid transit only if the large proportion of social cost originating from the use of private cars is not taken into account. Social costs include those caused by such factors as pollution, disruption of neighborhoods, and elimination of walking areas.

Rapid transit systems include subways, suburban trains, streetcars, trolley buses, and buses. Train and subway systems have very high initial costs, but they are

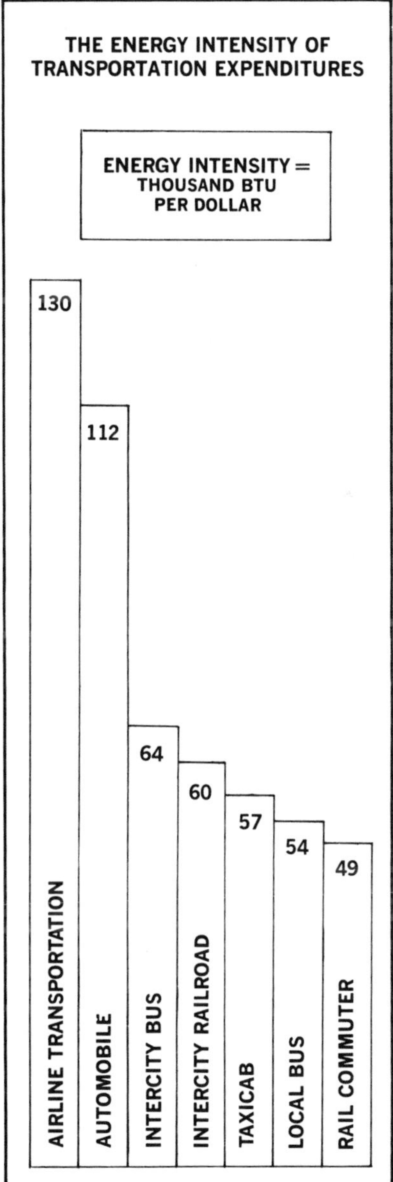

Figure 1.50 *Source.* Gil Bailey, "California's Tomorrow, Cry California," *Transportation in California,* Summer 1976.

NISSAN MOTORS BUILDING
Carson, California
Architects: Hayahiko Takase, Kajima Associates
Photo: Office

the only means of transportation that does not compete with cars for traffic space, and there is a significant improvement in street circulation. Since interurban trains and subways have fixed routes, they are, like freeways, structures that determine the shape of the city and the mix of its land use.

Trolleys have an advantage over buses in that they are powered not by internal combustion engines, with their associated gaseous pollutants, but by electric motors. Since electricity is the most expensive form of energy, however, the trolley car may not be economically efficient in the future. Streetcars are outdated, mainly because their tracks are incompatible with the heavy vehicular traffic that uses the same street space. Wherever streetcars are still in use, it is more for their nostalgic value than for functional reasons—for instance, in New Orleans and San Francisco. It could be argued that open-air transit systems such as trolleys are more appealing, perhaps less frightening, because they are part of the city proper and not submerged or otherwise estranged from the safe, known street environment.

New systems developed for rapid transit include several monorail designs and people-mover systems that incorporate elevated routes and small, individual vehicles with semiautomatic controls. It is usually proposed to construct the elevated tracks in the air space above rivers or freeways. So far, the subway is the only fixed system used for the construction of new rapid transit developments. It is currently being introduced or expanded in San Francisco, Montreal, Milan, Vienna, and Munich.

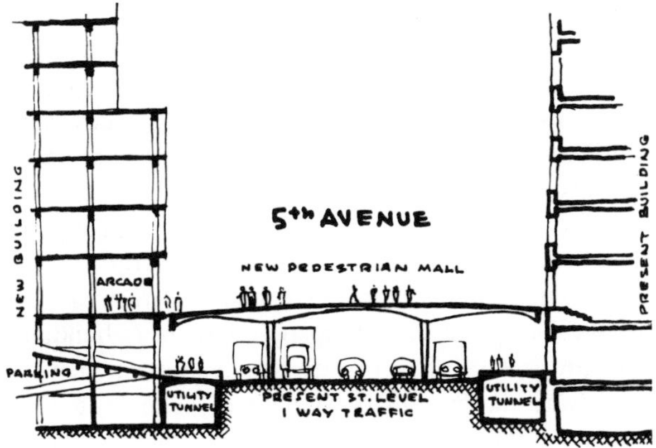

Figure 1.51 *Source.* Paul and Percival Goodman, *Communitas,* 2nd edition, Revised. Vintage Books, 1960.

Parking

Vehicular traffic consists of two parts: circulation and parking. Although cars are designed for transportation, their parked time always exceeds the time they are actually moving. Typically, a privately owned car is driven for an average of 5000 hours per year, which means that it is stored for remaining 8260 hours. This ratio of use to disuse indicates one aspect of inefficiency in today's traffic systems.

The space required for parking is a fraction of the space needed for circulation in residential areas, yet this relationship differs in central business districts, where a great number of vehicular trips end. Parking stalls measuring 10 feet by 20 feet have 200 square feet of space; with the addition of adequate space for circulation, this amounts to a requirement for 300 to 400 square feet per vehicle. In comparison, an office employee may occupy an average of 200 square feet of floor space, and although no office building design attempts to provide as much parking as one stall per occupant, the amount of space needed for parking is always a major concern.

The amount of parking space needed per car can be reduced with double or triple parking, which, in most cases, requires the services of parking attendants. This solution, however, still may be less costly than the construction and maintenance cost of 350 square feet per vehicle. Mechanical parking systems have been used to reduce space, but they generally lack flexibility and responsiveness to the desires of the users and are not very successful.

Most zoning ordinances specify the number of parking stalls required per unit of floor area. Typical parking requirements for office buildings are one stall per 300 to 500 net square feet of floor area; for shopping centers it may be one to 1000; and for multiple dwelling units the number of garage spaces required per apartment often corresponds to the number of bedrooms. In every case, the parking ratio has a significant influence on total building cost and sometimes on the financial feasibility of the project.

The distance a person is willing to walk between parking space and destination often depends on the quality of the walking route. At a shopping center, for instance, where the walk consists of the crossing of an immense parking lot, 300 feet may be the maximum distance tolerated by the customer. In a lively downtown area, on the other hand, with a route of great visual interest, including window shopping and other attractions, 1000 feet may be acceptable.

3 LEGAL AND POLITICAL CONSTRAINTS

Real estate ownership today is a legal status that carries a set of restrictions and obligations as well as a set of rights. The rights are guaranteed only as long as the owner continues to pay real estate taxes; therefore the difference between simple ownership and various forms of leasehold seems only to be one of gradations.

The rights of ownership usually include the right to possess and use the land with all improvements, trees, and plants, and to sell, lease, rent, or will it to others. Often limited are the use of airspace above the property, the right to extract oil and minerals, the use of river or spring water (which is regulated by special riparian rights), and, in general, any use of the property that is against the general welfare or creates excessive nuisance to neighbors. The concern for public welfare has also created the law of eminent domain, under which an owner can be forced to sell his or her property if it is needed for public use, such as a freeway. In cities, the use of property is largely regulated by zoning laws, building codes, and sometimes by owners' associations.

Legal Documents

The general term for the legal document used to convey real property is *deed,* and every such instrument contains a description of the property. A deed must be signed by the grantor (seller) and delivered to the grantee (buyer). To be legally recognized, the deed must be recorded in the public land records, which provide the so-called title information (names of all successive owners of the property, as well as all the particulars of any mortgages, liens, easements, or other restrictions of use). There are various forms of deeds, to cover specific situations. Most common are grant deeds, trust deeds, and quitclaim deeds.

The parties to a *trust deed* sale are the buyer, the seller, the lender, and the trustee. The buyer, who makes only a down payment on the property, borrows the rest of the money from a lender and gives a trust deed to the trustee, who will deed the property to the lender in the event that the buyer is unable to pay off the loan. If the buyer decides to sell the property before the balance of the loan is paid off, the trust deed either is assumed by the new owner or is paid off in cash or by means of refinancing. Terms of these transactions are spelled out in detail in the respective legal documents. Very often the lender will charge a prepayment penalty if the loan is being paid off before its term.

The older form of real estate financing is by means of a *mortgage*. The main differences between a mortgage and a trust deed are (*a*) the absence of a trustee in the former and (*b*) the need of a foreclosure action in case of default on a mortgage. Because of the costly and time-consuming court actions involved in foreclosure proceedings, the trust deed is often preferred today over the mortgage.

A property owner may secure additional financing by means of a second mortgage or trust deed on the same property. Since the first mortgage holder takes priority in the event of foreclosure, and since property with two mortgage loans represents a higher risk, the term of a second mortgage or trust deed is always shorter, and the interest rate is higher than that of the first.

In a mortgage foreclosure, the lender (mortgagee) obtains a court order mandating the (forced) sale of the property. The proceeds are to be used to pay back principal plus interest to the mortgagee, plus all court and legal costs. The remainder of the money goes to the defaulted owner. In some cases the mortgagee can obtain title to the property without a forced sale if an owner was unable to make repayment, as ordered by a court, within a specified time. Legal practices regarding foreclosures vary from state to state.

Restrictions on Real Property

Although the architect's main concern is with the restrictions specified in the building and zoning codes, some additional areas of restrictions may influence design and land use of a property.

An *easement* is the right of one party to make use of another party's land in a specific way. This right may be permanent or temporary. For example, a *light and air easement* may prevent a property owner from building a structure right at the property line if this action would take away the customary amount of natural light and fresh air from the neighboring building. Such easements are common and are usually the result of agreements among adjacent owners; compensation for the restriction is often part of the bargain.

Air right easements are found in areas with very high land values, such as Manhattan island, where it becomes feasible to build a structure into the airspace above another building. The owner of the existing property thus grants to a developer the right to use the airspace above his or her land. Since the new structure needs to be connected with the land for foundations, utilities, and access, this form of easement can be a very complex legal contract.

A *covenant* or deed restriction may modify the use of a property much in the way a zoning ordinance would restrict development activity, by specifying acceptable densities, building heights, architectural styles, and so on. In contrast to the zoning laws, a covenant is not created by city or county administrations but by a private party, usually the original owner of the property. In new land subdivisions, the developer usually submits a legal document called "conditions, covenants, and restrictions" (C, C, & R), which are implemented to protect the character, quality, and value of the new community.

Right-of-way restrictions obligate property owners to let certain neighbors pass over their land (private right-of-way), or to keep such access open to the public (public right-of-way). This right is needed in the case of landlocked property. Sometimes a public right-of-way is granted based on the long and continuous use of a certain access way or path by the public. In this situation, a property owner may be forbidden to prevent the public to pass over the land if such use has been tolerated for many years.

Riparian rights are concerned with the use of rivers for domestic, industrial, transportation, and agricultural purposes. They regulate the diversion of water, the construction of dams, and navigation. If the water body is a lake or ocean, rather than a river, the correct term is *littoral rights*.

MARINA TOWERS
Chicago, Illinois
Architect: Bertrand Goldberg
Photo: Suter, Hedrich-Blessing

Mineral rights may grant to a party other than the owner of the land the right to extract mineral deposits or oil and natural gas. Sometimes a previous owner of a piece of land retains the mineral rights to it. Any use made of such rights by a previous owner may represent a substantial restriction to the present owner's use of the land.

Solar rights are a new form of restriction made necessary as we begin to use direct solar radiation for the climate control of structures. Similar to a light and air easement, a solar easement may be used to protect a building that uses solar energy from being cut off from direct sunshine through new construction on adjacent parcels.

Types of Ownership

During the different political and economic periods of the past, a variety of ownership forms have been used and abandoned, each one in correspondence with the specific social hierarchy. Today the most common forms of ownership are the following:

1 Fee simple.
2 Condominium.
3 Cooperative.
4 Leasehold
5 Sale-leaseback, a special form of real estate transaction.

In many cases, the form of ownership chosen depends on the income and tax structure of both the buyer and the seller. Some property, such as land along seashores and rivers, is owned by the government but leased to individual parties on terms corresponding to the economic life of improvements, after which time a renewal of the lease may be denied and the land converted to public use.

Fee simple represents the least restricted form of ownership. Most single-family residences are owned this way, but the full ownership is realized only when the property is owned "free and clear"—that is, not mortgaged or liened. The individual owner has full ownership of the entire site including the airspace above.

In *condominium* ownership the individual party has full ownership of one particular space of the property plus ownership by tenancy in common or as an undivided interest for the remaining property. In the case of a housing project, for instance, the individual would own the airspace of his or her apartment, as defined by its inside walls, and a share in the rest of the structure (including hallways, stairs, roofs, etc.), as well as a share in the land, with all recreational facilities.

The condominium principle is not limited to residential property; it can be applied equally to offices, industrial parks, or retail space. Ownership entitles one to sell, rent, mortgage, or bequeath the property, but restrictions may be imposed on individual use through the tenants' association—a nonprofit organization of owners, sometimes also referred to as tenant council or homeowners' association, which serves to protect the common interest of tenants and to maintain the property owned by tenancy in common. For the latter purpose, the association charges a monthly fee to its members. Part of the building's utilities may also be paid by the association. Property taxes are usually paid by the individual owners.

Cooperatives are nonprofit organizations created for a variety of purposes. A housing cooperative owns the entire project, and each individual tenant owns a share in the corporation without holding title to any particular space of the property. The size of each share corresponds to the value of the space the owner is entitled to occupy. In addition, each shareholder makes periodic payments to the corporation, to cover such costs as mortgage payments, taxes, maintenance, insurance, and the company's overhead. Each resale of shares usually needs approval from the board of directors, but ownership can be bequeathed without restriction.

Leaseholds are agreements whereby ownership and rights to possess and use are divided between two parties, the lessor (owner) and the lessee (user). The agreement, or *lease,* states the amount of rent to be paid by the tenant, and the term of the lease. Most commonly, the lease is written for a definite term, but there are alternatives, such as a term for the lifetime of the lessee or for "the pleasure of parties," meaning that the lease can be terminated by either party at will. Leaseholds granted by governments often have long terms, up to 99 years. This enables the lessee to erect on the property structures that have an economic life shorter than the term of the lease and therefore are amortized long before the lease has expired. At the end of the term, however, all property improvements belong to the lessor. In most leases, the owner/lessor retains the right to sell the property without the approval of the lessee/tenant.

Sale and leaseback transactions allow tax advantages to both parties. A corporation, for instance, may decide to build a plant and sell it during construction and then, simultaneously, to lease it back from the buyer. This way, the company recaptures its construction capital, makes it available for other investments, and can deduct from its income all lease payments made to the buyer. For the buyer/lessor, the transaction means the acquisition of a low-risk investment, an income property with guaranteed full occupancy.

Types of Owner

In the case of a real estate cooperative, the legal owner is a *corporation*. Thus each stockholder has a share of the company's assets, liabilities, profits, or losses in proportion to the value of his or her share. Further expressing their joint ownership, the stockholders elect a number of decision makers who become the corporate board of directors.

Joint tenancy is another very common type of ownership, used mostly between husband and wife but also by groups of unrelated individuals. Each partner has an undivided, equal share in the property, and when one joint tenant dies, his or her interest is passed on to the others without any probate action. A tenant may sell his or her share of ownership without terminating the joint tenancy. The signatures of all tenants are required, before title to the property can be sold.

Tenancy by the entirety and *tenancy in common* are forms of ownership reserved to married couples. Both partners must agree on any transaction planned, and details of the various possible arrangements are contained in the community property laws of each state.

A partnership of two or more persons may own or lease real estate. In a general partnership, all members are involved in the control of the property. More common, however, is the limited partnership, which consists of one or more general partners and a number of limited partners who are not involved in the control and management of the partnership. Unlike a corporation, partner-

COOPERATIVE HOUSES, HARPER SQUARE
Chicago, Illinois
Architects: George Fred Keck, William Keck
Photo: Airpix

ship ceases to exist if one of the partners dies; it is also dissolved automatically if a partner steps out of the agreement.

Land owned by the government, which is not under private ownership, is called *public land.* The government body managing such land is the Bureau of Land Management, U.S. Department of the Interior.

Property Description

A property description, often also referred to as a legal description, or land measurement, is found in the official records of the county recorder's office and is inserted in the deed when property is transferred.

Recorded Maps. All city lots are recorded on subdivision maps filed in the recorder's office and can be identified from these maps, as the following typical description illustrates:

Lot 8, Block 25, Tract 2200, in the City of San Francisco, as per Map recorded in Book 4, page 113, Records of San Francisco County.

To locate this lot at the recorder's office, one would ask for Book 4 and would find the full legal description on page 113. Instead of a number (2200), the tract often has a name, such as Whitaker Tract.

Townships. In 1785 the United States government started a survey that created a rectangular subdivision system composed of *base* and *meridian* lines. The base lines run east and west, and the meridian lines run north and south. This system of base and meridian lines serves as reference and origin for the numbering of the townships, which represent the next smaller unit in the network of the government survey. A township is a square of 6 miles by 6 miles. The base and meridian lines have names relating to their location, such as Mount Diablo base and meridian line for the district of San Francisco.

The location of a specific township, in reference to the origin of the district's base and meridian lines, is identified by two code numbers. The top number tells how many rows to the south or north of the base line the township is located. The bottom code number refers to the number of ranges east or west of the meridian line. Thus a township marked T2N, R3E would be located two rows north of the origin and three ranges east.

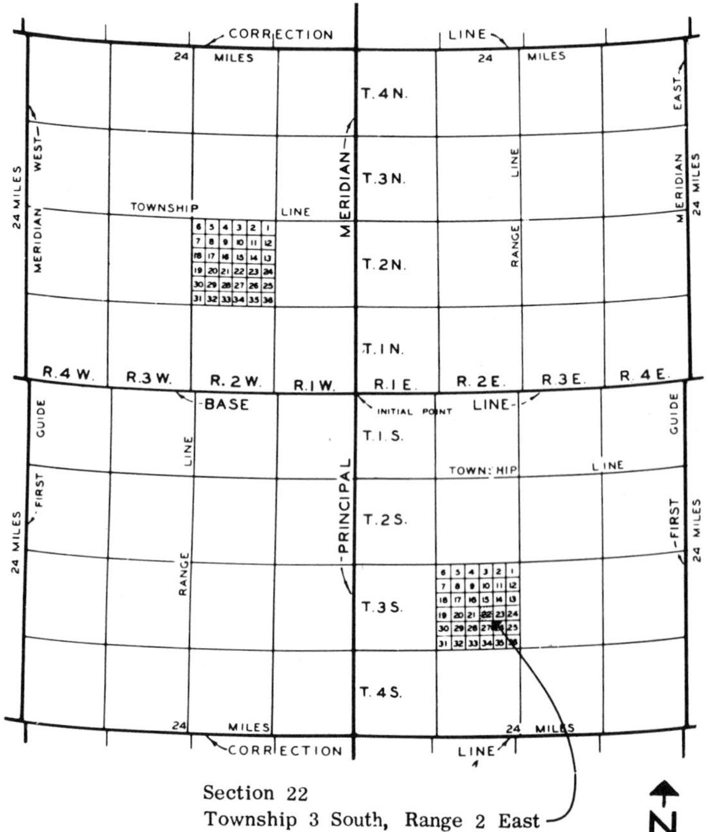

Figure 1.52 Division of land by rectangular survey system. *Source.* John L. Schmidt, Harold Bennett Olin, and Walter H. Lewis, *Construction Principles, Materials, and Methods*, 2nd edition, American Savings and Loan Institute, 1972.

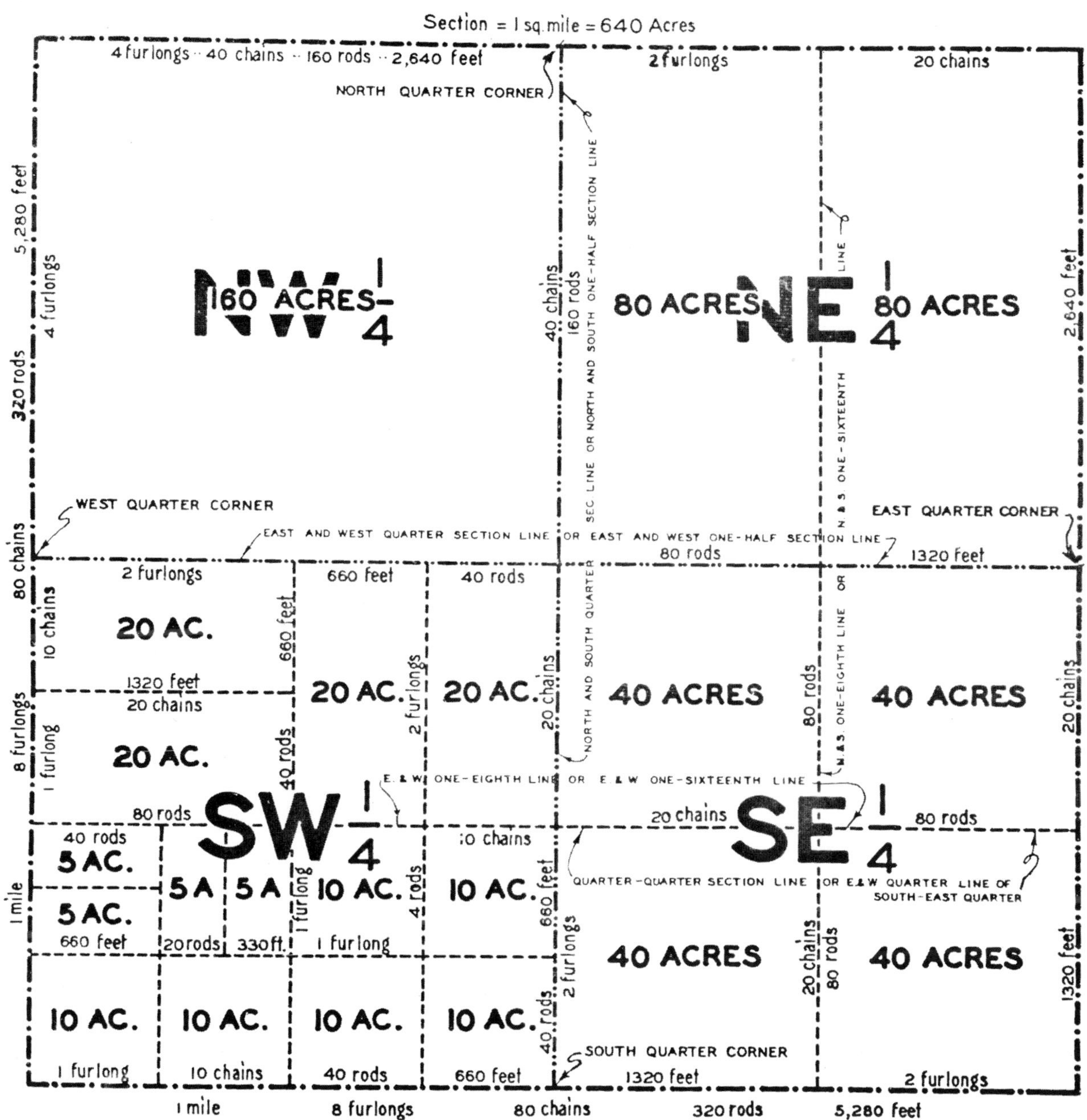

Figure 1.53 *Source*. John L. Schmidt, Harold Bennett Olin, and Walter H. Lewis, *Construction Principles, Materials, and Methods*, 2nd edition, American Savings and Loan Institute, 1972.

Sections. A township contains 36 sections, that is, 36 squares of 1 square mile each. Township sections are always numbered the same way (see Figure 1.52).

Sections are further broken down into fractional sections, which are measured in acres. Since a section contains 640 acres, a half-section has 320 acres, a quarter-section has 160, and so on. The legal description of a typical parcel in a fractional section would read as follows:

The southwest quarter (SW ¼) of the northeast quarter (NE ¼) of section 20. Since there are 640 acres in a section, this parcel, being a quarter of a quarter, would therefore cover 40 acres.

Metes and Bounds. Parcels that are not exact fractions of a section are described in terms of metes and bounds. This system defines the property by measuring the length and direction of its boundary line segments. If the boun-

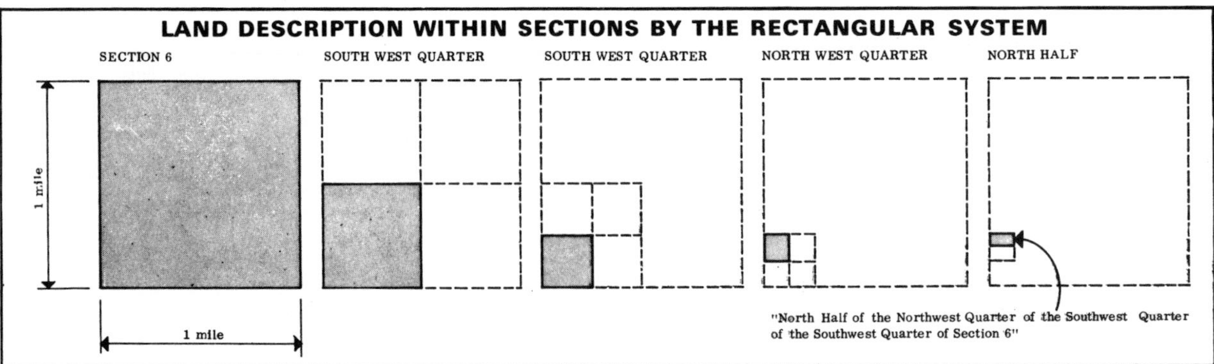

Figure 1.54 *Source*. John L. Schmidt, Harold Bennett Olin, and Walter H. Lewis, *Construction Principles, Materials, and Methods*, 2nd edition, American Savings and Loan Institute, 1972.

daries consist of straight lines, the description is of the straight line type. The irregular type involves curves of varying degrees.

Older descriptions by metes and bounds also use such linear measurements as rods, links, and chains. A rod measures 16 ½ feet; a link is 7.92 inches; and a chain consists of 100 links, or 66 feet. More important figures to remember are the following:

1 acre	= 43,560 ft^2
1 mile	= 5,280 ft
1 section	= 1 mi^2 = 640 acres
1 township	= 6 × 6 miles = 36 sections

If an error is found in a land description, the field notes of the surveyor are used as a record. These notes are bound and contain enough data to permit another surveyor to rerun the job. In the case of a court proceeding, the following general rules are applied to settle the dispute:

1 Boundaries take precedence over areas if the two sets of data do not correspond.
2 An obvious error does not void a deed if the plain intent of the description as a whole can be determined.
3 If a land is bounded by a road, the deed includes ownership to the centerline of the road, unless stated otherwise.
4 If corners are identified by visible, immovable objects, these objects are accepted as evidence of the intentions of the original parties.
5 In case of ambiguity, the interpretation should be in favor of the purchaser.

Zoning

Zoning laws are enacted by local legislative bodies, such as the board of supervisors for a county or the city council for a city. These ordinances serve to divide the land into zones of similar land use and structural design. The purpose of zoning restrictions is to coordinate the development activities of all individual areas to secure the interest of the city as a whole, in terms of public health, safety, and welfare, and to guarantee minimum standards in the working and living spaces of individuals.

The general classifications of zones are:

- R Residential.
- C Commercial (offices, stores).
- M Manufacturing (industrial).
- A Agricultural.

These basic zones are usually further subdivided. A residential area, for instance, may consist of R-1, R-2, R-3, and R-4 zones, each corresponding to a distinct type of housing, from single-family dwelling to highrise apartments. The exact definition of each of these zones and its specific restrictions vary from city to city: one R-3 zone limits building heights to 3 stories, whereas the R-3 zone of another area may permit highrise construction.

Figure 1.55 gives an example of municipal zoning regulations. Zoning laws define the maximum economic use of the property, and lesser use is generally permitted. For instance, it is possible to build a walkup apartment building in an area zoned for maximum residential density, but the economics of real estate development often make only the highest land use feasible.

The original zoning in most cities was based on a master plan that often followed the principle of strict

ZONING REGULATIONS (1) CITY OF GLENDALE

USE ZONE		SETBACK AND YARD REQ'S.				LOT REQUIREMENTS				BLDG. REQ'S.	PARKING REQ'S.			
	ZONE DESIGNATION	MINIMUM FRONT SETBACK	MINIMUM SIDE SETBACK	MINIMUM SIDE YARD	MINIMUM REAR YARD	MINIMUM SITE AREA	MINIMUM SITE AREA/DWELLING (8)	MAXIMUM LOT COVERAGE	MAXIMUM HEIGHT LIMIT	MINIMUM FLOOR AREA-SQ.FT.	PARKING SPACES	GUEST PARKING SPACES	LOADING SPACES	OUTSIDE STORAGE
RESTRICTED ONE-FAMILY ZONE SINGLE FAMILY UNITS, GUEST HOUSE AND ACCESSORY BLDGS.	RIR	25'	5'	3'	10'	—	—	—	3 STORIES	1400	2 COVERED	—	—	NO
ONE-FAMILY ZONE SINGLE FAMILY UNITS, GUEST HOUSE, FOSTER HOME & ACCESSORY BLDGS.	RI	25'	5'	3'	10'	—	—	—	3 STORIES	—	2 COVERED	—	—	NO
THREE-FAMILY ZONE R1 USES AND A MAXIMUM OF THREE DWELLING UNITS	R2	25'	5'	3'	10'	—	2000 SQ.FT PER DU	—	3 STORIES	—	1 B.R.-1 1/2 2 BR-1 3/4 3 B.R.-2 COVERED	—	—	NO
LIMITED MULTIPLE DWELLING ZONE R2 USES, MULTIPLE DWELLINGS	R3	25'	5'	3'	10'	—	1250 SQ.FT PER DU	—	4 STORIES	—	1 BR-1 1/2 2 BR-1 3/4 3 BR-2 COVERED	—	—	NO
RESTRICTED LIMITED MULTIPLE DWELLING ZONE MULTIPLE DWELLINGS (2)	R3R	55' FROM ℄ OR 25 MIN.	10% 15' MAX.	6'	10'	12,000 SQ.FT.	—	60%	3 STORIES	1 B.R.-850 2 BR 1000 3 BR-1200 AVG-1000	2 PER DU COVERED	1 PER 10 D.U 2 MIN.	—	NO
MULTIPLE DWELLING ZONE R3 USES, HOTELS, MULTIPLE DWELLINGS, DORMITORIES, SCHOOLS, CHURCHES	R4	45' FROM ℄ OR 15' MIN	5'	5'	10'	—	750 SQ FT	60%	3 STORIES	1 BR-600 2 B.R.-800 3 BR-1000	1 BR-1 1/2 2 BR-1 3/4 3 BR-2 COVERED	—	—	NO
RESTRICTED MULTIPLE DWELLING ZONE R4 USES	R4L	25'	5'	3'	10'	—	—	—	4 STORIES	—	1 BR-1 1/2 2 BR-1 3/4 3 BR-2 COVERED	—	—	NO
HIGH DENSITY MULTIPLE DWELLING ZONE R4 USES AND LIMITED C USES	R5	VARIES MIN 40' FROM ℄	10'	10'	10'	—	—	75%	—	—	—	—	—	NO
HORSE ZONE (OVERLAY) RESIDENTIAL USES, INCLUDING HORSES	H	VARIES	5'	VARIES	10'	3000 SQ.FT PER HORSE 4 MAX	—	—	—	—	—	—	—	—
PLANNED RESIDENTIAL CLUSTER ZONE RESIDENTIAL	PRC	8'	5'	5'	8'	40,000 SQ.FT. PER DEVELOP	1500 SQFT PER DU	60%	35 FT	1 BR-750 2 B.R.-1000 3 B.R.-1200 4 B.R.-1450	2 PER D.U. COVERED	—	—	NO
PLANNED UNIT DEVELOPMENT ZONE (OVERLAY) RESIDENTIAL & COMMERCIAL	PUD	15'	10'	10'	20'	20 AC. PER DEVELOP.	VARIES	25 % OF TOT. PUD SITE	—	VARIES	2 PER D.U 1/400 SQ.FT FLOOR AREA	—	—	NO
AUTOMOBILE PARKING ZONE (OVERLAY) "R" USES AND PARKING AREAS DEVELOPED ACCORDING TO SECTION 407.	P	60% OF BLDG SETBACK	5' (7)	0' (7)	0' (7)	—	—	—	—	—	—	—	—	NO
RESTRICTED COMMERCIAL ZONE R4 USES, PROF. OFFICES, RESTAURANTS, BANKS, BARBERS, NURSERIES, CLOTHING (3) (9)	CI	15'	0'	0'	20'	—	—	50%	35 FT.	—	1/500 SQ.FT FLOOR AREA	—	—	NO
LIMITED COMMERCIAL ZONE C1 USES, OFFICES, STORES, CLUBS, SERVICE STATIONS, COCKTAIL LOUNGES (6) (9)	C2	0'	0'	0'	0'	—	—	—	—	—	1/400 SQ.FT. FLOOR AREA	—	—	NO
COMMERCIAL ZONE C2 USES, WHOLESALE OR RETAIL BUSINESS, AUTO REPAIR SHOPS (6) (9)	C3	0'	0'	0'	0'	—	—	—	—	—	1/500 SQ.FT. FLOOR AREA	—	—	MERCH. YES IF OPAQUE FENCING
COMMERCIAL MANUFACTURING ZONE C3 USES, MANUFACTURING, PROCESSING PLANTS, SUPER SERVICE STATIONS (6) (9)	CM	0'	0'	0'	0'	—	—	—	—	—	1/500 SQ.FT. FLOOR AREA	—	—	INCIDENTAL REAR 1/2, 3000 SQ.FT MAXIMUM
COMMERCIAL AGRICULTURAL ZONE ANIMAL HOSPITALS, AQUARIUMS, PET SHOPS, PUBLIC STABLES	CA	25'	5'	0'	0'	—	—	—	—	—	1 PER 4 HORSES 1/500 SQ.FT. FLOOR AREA	—	—	INCIDENTAL
SPECIAL RESTRICTED INDUSTRIAL ZONE CM USES, AUTO BODY SHOPS, ELECT. MANUFACTURE, WAREHOUSES (4) (6)	MIA	10'	0'	0'	0'	—	—	—	2 1/2 STORIES OR 35FT.	—	1 PER 1000 SQ.FT	—	1 PER (5) 50 FT OF BLDG. WIDTH	WITHIN WALLED AREA
RESTRICTED INDUSTRIAL ZONE M1A USES, LUMBER YARDS, STORAGE, PACKAGING, FABRICATING (4) (6)	MI	0'	0'	0'	0'	—	—	—	—	—	1 PER 1000 SQ FT	—	1 PER (5) 50 FT OF BLDG. WIDTH	WITHIN WALLED AREA
INDUSTRIAL ZONE M1 USES, MACHINE SHOPS, TRAILER PARKS, PLANING MILL (4) (6)	M2	0'	0'	0'	0'	—	—	—	—	—	1 PER 1000 SQ.FT.	—	1 PER (5) 50 FT. OF BLDG WIDTH	—
HEAVY INDUSTRIAL ZONE M2 USES, AUTO WRECKING, USED PARTS STORAGE, JUNK DEALERS (4) (6)	M3	0'	0'	0'	0'	—	—	—	—	—	1 PER 1000 SQ.FT.	—	1 PER (5) 50 FT OF BLDG WIDTH	—
SPECIAL RECREATION ZONE PUBLIC, SEMI-PUBLIC OR PRIVATE PARKS, PLAYFIELDS & RECREATION AREAS	SR	—	—	—	10'	—	—	—	—	—	—	—	—	—
CEMETERY ZONE (OVERLAY) MAUSOLEUMS, FUNERAL PARLORS, CEMETERY USES	CEM	(OVERLAY ZONE FOR CEMETARY PURPOSES)												

1 THE FOLLOWING IS ONLY A GENERAL GUIDE OF THE ZONING REGULATIONS OF THE CITY OF GLENDALE. THE REQUIREMENTS ARE NOT ALL INCLUSIVE AND FOR FURTHER INFORMATION PLEASE CONSULT THE GLENDALE MUNICIPAL CODE, OR PHONE 956-2115.

2 SINGLE FAMILY RESIDENCES NOT PERMITTED: 60 FEET MINIMUM FRONTAGE REQUIRED.

3 NO USED OR SECONDHAND EQUIPMENT OFFERED FOR SALE.

4 RESIDENCES, HOTELS, BOARDINGHOUSES AND LODGINGHOUSES ARE PROHIBITED. NO LOT OR PARCEL OF LAND SHALL BE USED FOR ANY USE PERMITTED IN ANY CM OR M ZONE UNLESS ALL RESIDENTIAL STRUCTURES AND ACCESSORY BUILDINGS THERETO ARE REMOVED.

5 ADDITIONAL SPACES ARE REQUIRED IF AREA OF BUILDING EXCEEDS 37,500 SQ. FT.

6 SPECIAL REQUIREMENTS RELATING TO SITE IMPROVEMENT ARE SET FORTH FOR SERVICE STATIONS, TIRE STORES, & AUTO LAUNDRIES.

7 PARKING AREAS ONLY.

8 LOTS LOCATED IN MOUNTAINOUS TERRAIN, 7,500 SQ. FT. MINIMUM; AVERAGE 10,000 SQ. FT. MINIMUM

9 SPECIFIC PARKING REQUIREMENTS FOR SELECT USES (SEE SECTIONS).

PLANNING DIVISION CITY OF GLENDALE
633 EAST BROADWAY
AUGUST 1976
PLANNING DIRECTOR
ZONING ADMINISTRATOR
956-2115

Figure 1.55

The Lawyer

"For the lawyers, they write according to the states in which they live, what is received law, and not what ought to be law."

Bacon

JOHN Delafons offers this inscrutable British comment about the origins of zoning in the United States: "All the great luminaries of the early days of zoning were lawyers—Edward Bassett, Alfred Bettman, James Metzenbaum, F. B. Williams. Given the nature of American institutions and attitudes, it may have been inevitable that lawyers rather than architects or professional planners should have been the successful pioneers of land-use controls."

Whatever may be meant by the "nature of American institutions," it is true that lawyers dominated the early days of zoning. This preeminence of the lawyer in the early days was not, however, as significant to the course of zoning law in America as was the legal profession's notable lack of interest during the following three decades. It was as though the bar regarded the initial victories for zoning in the United States Supreme Court and the state courts in the twenties as an intellectual exercise. Having demonstrated their facility at the game, the lawyers tossed the cards to onlookers to play with as they chose. From 1930 to 1950 the bar—and in that I include municipal attorneys—regard zoning as a piddling bother. This indifference of the bar was matched by the indifference of most law schools toward the legal and social implications of land-use planning.

Source. Richard F. Babcock. *The Zoning Game.* University of Wisconsin Press, 1973.

separation of land usage. Today this principle is often relaxed in favor of more lively neighborhoods, for in many cases a certain mix of densities and of residential and commercial land uses is preferred.

The three main purposes of restrictions in residential zones are to limit population densities, often defined in dwelling units per acre; to provide sufficient open space between structures (setbacks, lot coverage, etc.); and to control the bulk of buildings (maximum ratio of floor area to site area).

Since each zoning law created by a local government applies over quite a large area, such laws are inherently rigid and inflexible. To compensate for this shortcoming, governmental procedures were created to make exceptions possible. Four types are most frequently used.

Variances, which do not change the actual zoning but relax certain requirements such as setbacks or densities. The basis for granting a variance is the owner's claim of undue hardship caused by a certain aspect of the ordinance. A petition for variance must be submitted to the planning commission. If it is refused, a property owner can appeal to the local legislative body. If it is again refused, the person has recourse to a court of law where he or she can claim that the zoning law is unfairly discriminatory.

A *conditional use* permit makes a change in land use possible. It is granted to make the construction of public facilities possible in residential areas. Such facilities may include hospitals, schools, airports, cemeteries, and public utilities. A conditional use always requires public hearings. It does not change the existing zoning but permits an exceptional land use that was found to be in the public interest.

An *urban renewal zone* suspends all previous zoning in areas where the development of a new master plan is desired. Once this master plan is approved, the area is rezoned and becomes subject to the general zoning laws.

A *nonconforming* use exists where structures had been erected long before the zoning laws pertaining to the area were created. The maintenance of such antedating structures may be permitted either for a limited time or for an infinite future time. However buildings existing under this exception cannot be altered or enlarged.

Zoning laws are established to protect the interest of the community as well as the interest of the individual. By restricting development activity in areas subject to special hazards such as brush fires, floods, or landslides, a good zoning law can serve to protect the innocent buyer.

The energy crisis, together with the increasing interest in environmental protection, has led many governmental authorities to reevaluate existing master plans, which were based on certain expectations of population growth. The results of this new research have led many cities and counties to set new goals of desired growth rates and total community size—often much below the previously established figures. This planning activity in turn led to a process often referred to as *downzoning,* whereby the limits for maximum residential densities were lowered, and agricultural areas that had been rezoned for residential development were converted to their original status.

Codes

Building codes exist for all types of construction activity. They regulate design, construction technology, and maintenance of all building types, to assure maximum safety (during construction as well as for the users) and adequate living and working conditions. Building codes, like the Uniform Building Code or the National Plumbing Code, have been established on a national basis. Whether these codes are adopted in a specific city is decided by the local authorities.

Building codes can be very detailed, actually specifying materials, dimensions, and construction processes that are acceptable under given conditions. This system somewhat limits space for innovative design. New solutions may be accepted, however, if they can be evaluated in terms of performance. A recognized agency can conduct tests on alternate design and construction elements that in turn will be approved by the authorities if the results are satisfactory. Naturally, this procedure requires more time than the standard building inspection; innovations, therefore, must promise real benefits to warrant the resulting extra cost.

Building regulations, like zoning codes, also tend to create a certain uniformity and homogeneity within a particular zone by specifying minimum floor areas, room sizes, garage spaces, and so on. This perhaps negative aspect of building regulations comes about because the minimum standards in space, construction, and lot size relate to a very narrow margin of minimum housing costs, which may exclude many families who could afford housing in the area if smaller units were available or if less stringent requirements were made for secondary space such as bathrooms, closets, and garages.

The increased requirements of existing building codes, which have been introduced based on new experiences, technological progress, or changes in living standards, raise the question of how close to the new standards existing structures must be brought. More stringent requirements in the areas of fire and earthquake standards are often made retroactive, but a certain sensible time limit will be granted for the upgrade work necessary. In many cases it is necessary to improve the existing structure to comply only if the building is being extended or extensively remodeled.

New codes for the handicapped provide guidelines for making most new and remodeled buildings accessible to and usable by handicapped people—those in wheelchairs, on crutches, with leg braces, individuals with

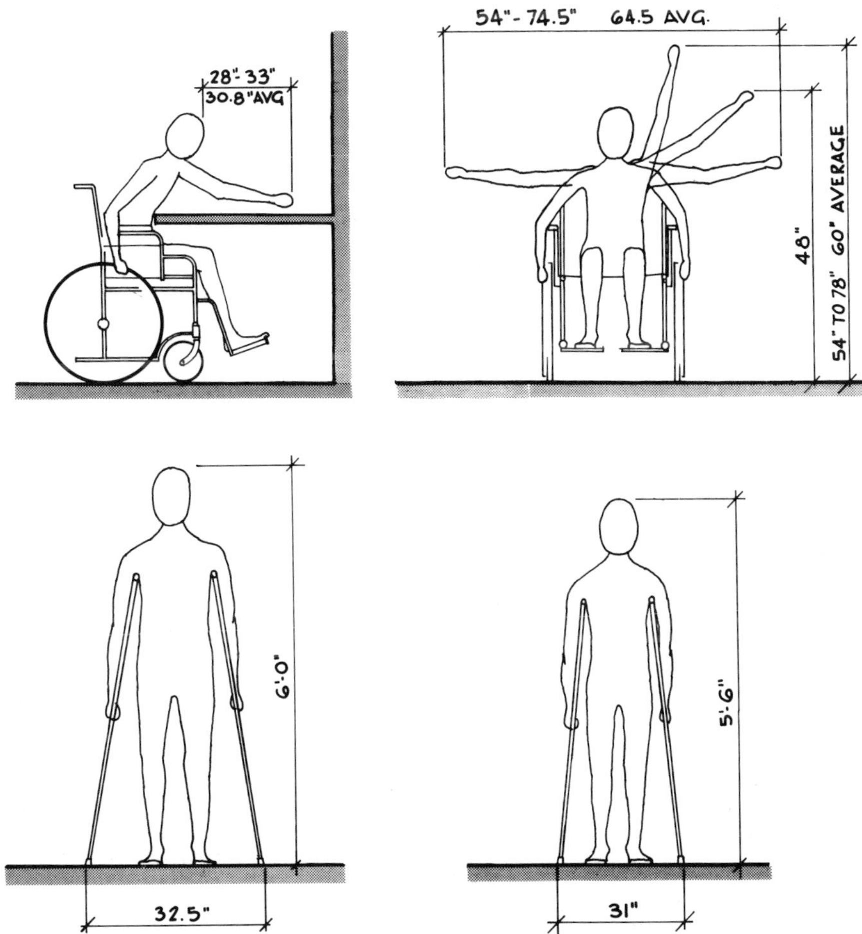

Figure 1.56 *Source*. North Carolina State Building Code.

sight, hearing, or coordination defects, or those who move with difficulty because of aging, accident, or disease. It is the spirit and intent of the code requirements to provide for these people full and free use of all buildings and facilities so that they may have the education, employment, living, and recreation opportunities necessary to allow them to be as self-sufficient as possible.

Governmental Jurisdictions

Figure 1.57 graphically represents the position of the architect in the hierarchy that exists in relation to the building of a school, and Figures 1.58 and 1.59 illustrate in flow chart form how laws and zoning variances come into being. Besides counties and municipalities, there exist some other small political units, the most common being the districts and the authorities.

A *district* is formed by the vote of landowners and/or residents within its boundaries. It is administered by an elected board and has taxing authority. The area of a district may cross several city or county border lines according to its purpose. Districts are created to administer public services not provided by municipalities. Examples are school districts, flood control districts, and rural fire protection districts.

An *authority* is similar to a district, but it usually covers a larger area, such as harbors and airports in more than one state. The Port of New York Authority is an example of this type of political unit.

City and county codes regarding zoning and building are enforceable through police power. Also enforceable is the power of *eminent domain,* which enables political authorities to build the infrastructure of a city by purchasing private property, regardless of whether the owner wants to sell. The owner, however, is entitled to a just compensation. As mentioned earlier, land acquisitions for freeways, airports, power lines, sewers, and so on, are made under the power of eminent domain.

Urban Renewal

Housing is deteriorating in the downtown areas in all our large cities. The middle class is moving into the suburbs. Low-income groups are limited to the central areas by their lack of mobility, and since they cannot afford the rents in areas of low population density, their housing

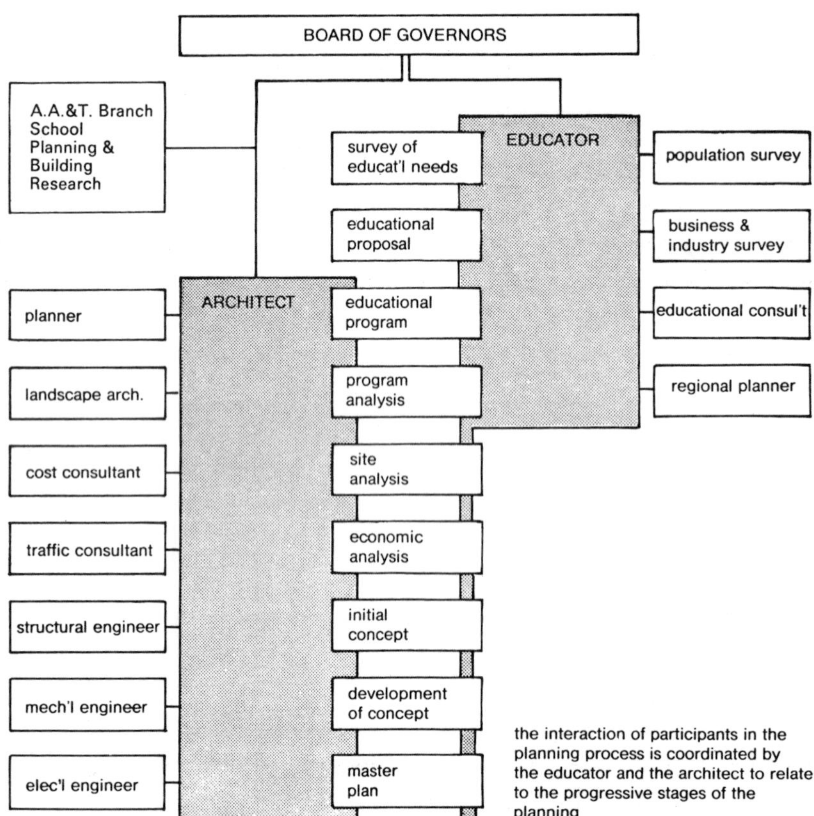

Figure 1.57 Interaction of participants.

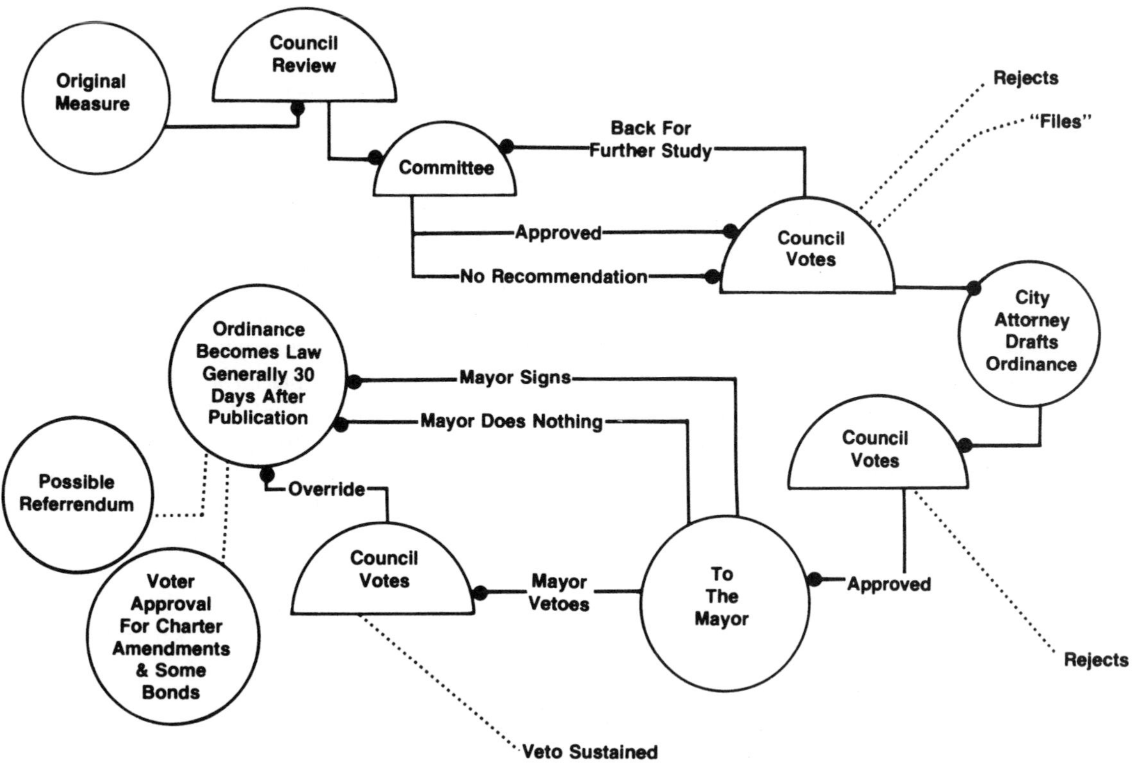

Figure 1.58 How a legislative proposal becomes law.

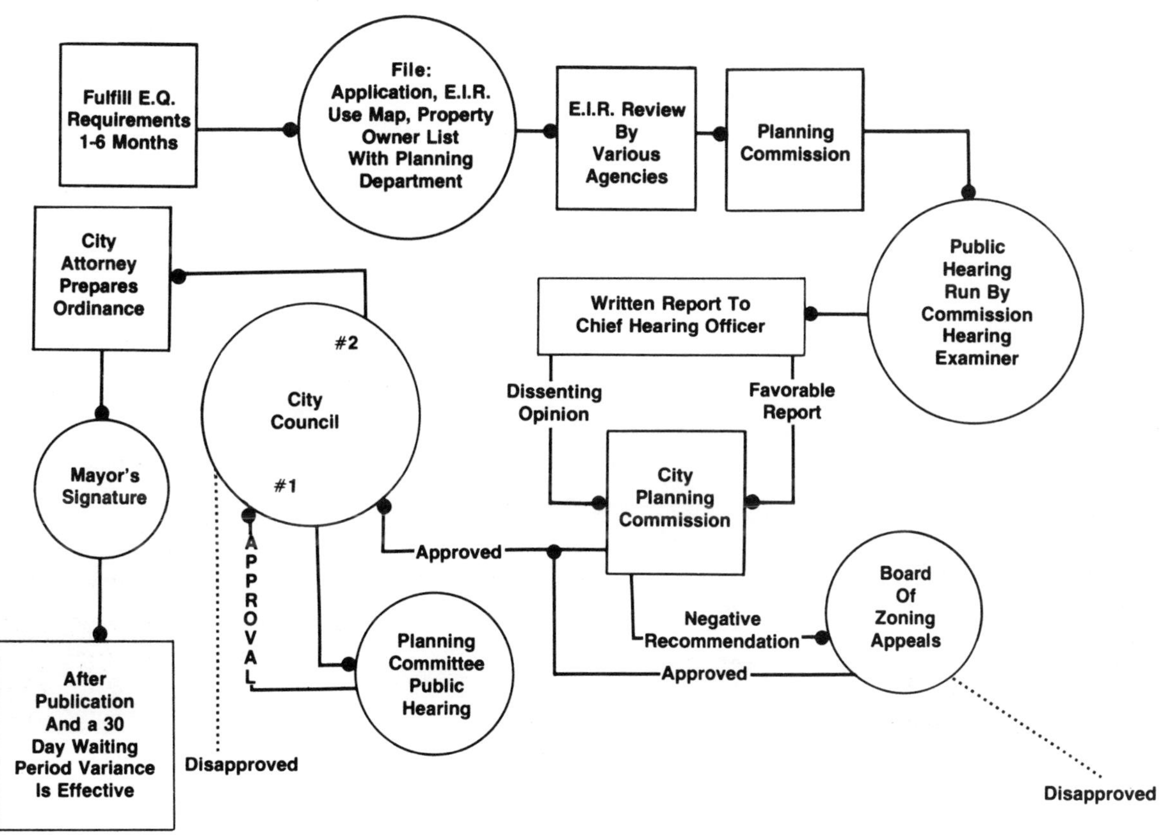

Figure 1.59 Flow chart of zoning variance process.

conditions are crowded and often below the acceptable standards.

The urban renewal concept was created to reverse the trend of middle-class flight from the cities and to improve the housing standards of low-income communities. The implementation of this concept proceeds through the following steps:

1 The state government passes a law granting to a city the authority to start an urban renewal project.
2 The city council creates a renewal agency consisting of urban planners who define the area. Usually an urban renewal zone classification is assigned to this area, to facilitate the master planning process.
3 The city council authorizes a contribution of local tax money to match the federal funding in a ratio of one-third to two-thirds or, if the population of the city is less than 50,000, in a ratio of one-quarter to three-quarters.
4 The renewal agency purchases the land in the renewal zone, relocates the residents, demolishes the old structures, and sells the land to private developers. In the land acquisition phase, the agency has the power of eminent domain as granted by a 1949 Supreme Court decision.
5 The private developers build out the area in accordance with the renewal agency's master plan.

Besides the goals of creating central area, middle-income housing opportunities and improving substandard housing, the city also expects a substantial tax increase to result from the upgrading of the area.

There are, however, many risks involved in an urban renewal project. Unfortunately, too, most of the negative aspects affect the displaced low-income residents. For example, by law the displaced residents are guaranteed assistance from the urban renewal agency in relocating, but they often have no choice but to move into another slum because not enough subsidized housing is available. In addition, the total number of dwelling units is usually smaller after redevelopment.

For many projects proposed in the master plan, moreover, there is no immediate market demand, and since private developers are involved, large areas often remain undeveloped for years after they have been cleared of the old structures.

Urban renewal always involves the breaking up of a closely knit community. This can be especially tragic for older people, because they are often unable to rebuild all the intimate relationships that made their lives enjoyable.

CONCOURSE VILLAGE
Bronx, New York
Architects: Francis X. Gina & Partners
Photo: B. Rothschild

Political Action Groups

Political action groups attempt to influence voters in their ballot decisions and to engage in lobbying (i.e., bringing a specific area of concern to the attention of legislators for the purpose of winning their support). The many election and reelection committees formed in support of political candidates are examples of the first kind of group, and minority organizations, lobbyists, and labor unions are part of the second.

The architect should be aware of political action groups concerned with environmental protection and with the protection and preservation of existing low-income communities. If such a group is influential in an area proposed for development, and the development team ignores its existence and interest, the whole project may be delayed indefinitely, and great amounts of resources may be wasted.

Proximity

Zoning and building ordinances and official master plans do not necessarily determine the highest and best use of a particular site. Whether a particular development is appropriate and feasible depends greatly on the support that can be expected from surrounding land uses. Much of this support belongs in the area of economics and is not of direct concern to the architect. However the relationships in terms of space, environmental quality, and circulation that are associated with typical developments lie in the architect's area of responsibility.

Today the most urgent environmental requirement for urban *residential areas* is protection from excessive noise. This means separation from freeways, railroad stations, airports, major thoroughfares, and commercial and industrial establishments that produce excessive noise. Supportive land uses required by residential areas include shopping centers, schools, hospitals, parks, and restaurants. The degree of accessibility of such supporting facilities greatly determines the desirability and market acceptance of new housing, and also the mix of residents (age groups represented, complete vs. incomplete households, etc.).

Schools and *hospitals* should be located in areas with low crime rates, low noise levels, and good air. Proximity to earthquake faults can make a site undesirable for

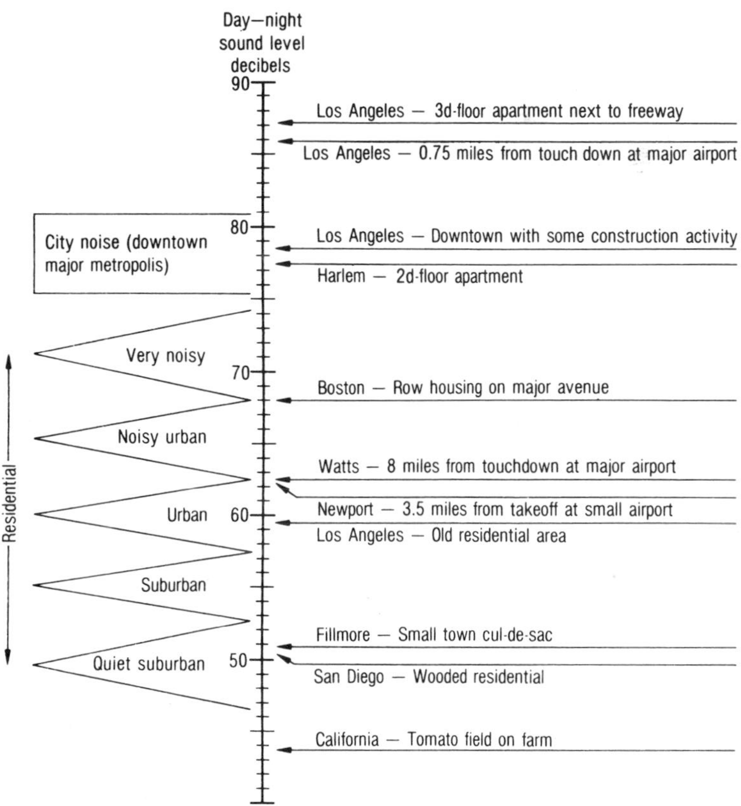

Figure 1.60 Outdoor sound levels at various locations.

Source: Environmental Protection Agency, *Information on Levels of Environmental Noise Requisite to Protect Public Health and Welfare with an Adequate Margin of Safety* (Washington, D.C.: Government Printing Office, 1974), p. 14.

school buildings. Elementary and high schools should be easily accessible to residences with a minimum of dangerous traffic crossings.

Colleges, which generally have a large proportion of out-of-town or out-of-state students, are not dependent on local catchment. However since on-campus housing often covers only a small percentage of the total student housing needed, there must be moderate-income rental housing available in the vicinity. In addition, certain colleges depend on facilities and resources other than housing; medical schools require hospitals, and agricultural colleges need farming areas.

Civic centers consist of the city hall, police department, municipal court, and jail house. However many supporting branch offices of state, federal, or county governments are needed in the proximity of these facilities. Thus a substantial amount of general office space is needed in the civic center vicinity. Accessibility by means of freeways and rapid transit, and convenient parking facilities, of course, are vitally important.

Site suitability for *shopping centers* is largely a function of the potential market demand for such a facility. Accessibility, however, including the convenience of the type of parking provided, will determine the extent of the center's catchment area, thus the total size of the potential market. Next to the availability of space, accessibility is the most important factor in planning for many *industrial* land uses. Truck traffic, railroads, and proximity to airports is of greater importance to industrial parks than is accessibility by individual cars.

Utilities and Services

The availability of utilities and services provided by the community an extremely important factor in the land use question. The main concern here is with water supply and the sewer system—two elements required in every type of real estate development.

Water supply is readily available in cities and is usually provided by a municipally controlled utility company. However in redevelopment situations, which sometimes involve the replacement of low-density areas by highrise structures, the new demand may be beyond the capacity of the old system.

The municipal service area may not extend into certain suburban areas, and alternatives must be found. These may include the drilling of wells for small developments, the creation of a reservoir for precipitation and runoff water, or the utilization of a nearby river. Treatment plants may be required in these cases to assure that the supply does not become contaminated. Agreements to share water supply systems with nearby communities or developments may provide other feasible alternatives. Among the factors determining the most feasible solution are initial and maintenance costs, capacity for growth, and risk of water shortage.

Sewer service is usually supplied by a branch of the municipal authorities. Some cities make a single charge for the service, others charge on a continuing basis, and still others use both approaches. The fee may be computed by street frontage, zoning, number of bathrooms, and other methods.

As a rule, the sewer system operates by gravity flow. The architect, then, has to relate the level of the lowest fixture to existing sewer levels. The use of sewage lift stations is to be avoided wherever possible because of higher costs, maintenance problems, and possibility of mechanical failure. Fixtures inside a building located below the level of the building drain require the installation of a sewage ejector, which poses similar problems.

Any municipal sewer system must operate primary and secondary treatment plants. Only treated effluent can be recirculated into oceans, lakes, rivers, or fields. In local septic tanks, the effluent must be treated more extensively if it is run back into a body of surface water than if it is disposed of in a leaching field. (Leaching fields must be located a safe distance away from any wells used for domestic water.)

Garbage disposal is not dependent on any fixed system and can therefore be arranged in many ways. Landfills were once the most popular method for disposing of all solid waste, but the principle of recycling is now applied more and more, with garbage being separated into reusable materials and combustibles for thermic power plants and similar facilities.

If a site is not presently served by *electrical and telephone utilities* the owner/developer will have to pay in advance for the extension of services to the site. The contract with the utility company usually specifies that the owner is being paid back his or her investment over a certain period of time. In many areas today underground utility wires are required.

Although *natural gas* has been the most economical fuel for heating and cooking in many countries, the supply today is limited; in many cities the gas companies do not extend their service network. The availability of this utility therefore depends on the general energy situation.

Except for some factories that have their own firemen, *fire protection* is always part of the municipal or county services. The developer may be concerned with the services available because their quality often determines insurance rates, thus influences the maintenance budget.

Energy conservation and diversification of energy supply are major issues today. In comparison to other countries with high standards of living, the United States is far ahead in per capita energy consumption. Switzerland, for instance, uses only one-fourth the amount of our per capita average, and even progressive Sweden uses only half as much, in spite of a great demand for year-round heating.

The true cost of energy is quite apparent today, and energy consciousness must be reflected in new energy-saving design concepts. In fact, many states are in the process of legislating restrictions for the building industry with the goal of conserving energy. In an effort to become less dependent on petroleum, the utilization of resources is emphasized. Such alternatives include the use of coal, oil shale, and solid waste for fuels, and the intensive exploitation of the power of running water for electricity, construction of nuclear power plants, and the use of solar and geothermal energy for domestic heating and hot water supply.

4 SOCIOLOGICAL INFLUENCES

The rapid advance of technology has increased tremendously the possibility of creating a physical environment that efficiently provides for our tangible needs. Climate control, transportation, communication, and waste disposal are developed to an extent that makes virtually every space on earth habitable. We do know, however, that habitability also depends on factors that lie in the realm of emotional and spiritual experience, of which we have little scientifically measurable knowledge. Yet when breakthroughs have been achieved in technology, very little consideration has been given to the emotional or spiritual impact of the resulting innovations.

Now as in the past, the great civilizations are associated with urban life. Yet experts disagree as to why the majority of people choose to live in cities. This question becomes even more mysterious today in light of the obvious hardship and stress imposed on people by city life.

The main reasons, though, may very well be the ones outlined in architect Fran P. Hosken's book, *The Language of Cities:* "One of the basic and continuing functions of the city is its economic function, both as producer and marketplace." These urban functions are linked with transportation, however, since transportation has always determined the location of cities. In the past, the market city drew on its immediate surroundings, accelerating the division of labor and encouraging specialization among residents. Now these effects are often spread over a whole country or continent.

Another prime function of the city throughout history has been to serve as a center of worship and government. Education is a continuing function of the city. The cultural function of the city is and has been related to the educational one.

Providing housing has always been the largest single function of the city; indeed, from a social and quantitative point of view, it dominates the scene. Housing patterns today in every American city most of all reflect racial and economic discrimination between people and separation of functions such as residential, industrial, and recreational.

Cities are made by people, and the man-made environment marks our species. Cities reflect our joint aspirations, our manipulation of the natural surroundings for communal goals. That the man-made environment cannot be successful if it is built for the wrong reasons—to achieve profit for a few rather than to establish a prospering community for the many who live there—is evident if we look around us here and now. We know that there is a richness and needed stimulus associated with urban life that makes it worthwhile for people to suffer pollution, stress, traffic, lack of privacy, separation from nature, and other discomforts, but we are far from identifying all the elements that produce this richness.

Interpersonal relationships seem to be more important to most people than physical qualities of their environment. This is clearly evident from the experience with urban renewal projects. Slum dwellers who are moved into new housing in a different area often are deeply dissatisfied with their new habitats; all the physical amenities cannot compensate for the loss of personal relationships that existed in the old neighborhoods. In such cases it becomes apparent that the people who are making the decisions about the shape of our cities often have a perception of the environment very different from that of the people for whom they decide. To avoid mistakes resulting from this lack of identical experiences, planners must base their decisions less on personal judgment and much more on real-life evidence.

Biological Considerations

The latest findings in anthropology seem to indicate that the genetic endowment of human beings has not changed significantly over the thousands of years of our exis-

ST. FRANCIS SQUARE
San Francisco, California
Architects: Marquis & Stoller
Photo: K. H. Riek

tence. Although achievements such as space walks and experimental living in suboceanic dwellings appear to reveal a great adaptability to life outside our normal biosphere, the basic necessities of people have remained unchanged. Many of our bodily functions, for instance, controlled by our inborn biological time clock, are tuned, in turn, to the cycle of night and day. The condition known as jet lag is an example of the limits of our biological adaptability.

Our fundamental needs always include privacy, open space, contact with the natural environment, and a margin of independence in our personal activities. Yet many people live in urban environments that do not provide enough of these needed conditions, and some seem to have developed tolerances for the adverse influences to which they are continually exposed. We also have learned that long-range effects of dense city life on physical and mental health manifest themselves in the form of chronic disease, heart failure, or high suicide rates.

In the future planning of our cities, we will have to abandon certain innovative designs of spaces, which are convincing only on a mathematical or logical level, in favor of a physical environment that will not be too different from successful forms of urban living in the past.

Psychological Considerations

All human beings need *intimate contacts* with others. To have intimate contact means to be able to show one's weaknesses, fears, and passions to another person. Much of the magnetism common to cities stems from the potential of contacts offered. However this great number of actual or possible contacts often makes individual interactions more superficial and less satisfying, and loneliness and alienation are associated more with big urban centers than with life in a rural community.

Intimate contact serves as a shield against shocks and disappointments. It is a natural way to repair psychic damage, and it should be provided by the three primary groups of society: the family, the children's play group, and the neighborhood group. The military life represents for many men an extension of the children's play group, which explains why men often talk so fondly about their war experiences. Adults, however, live and work in a type of society in which almost all contacts center on material concerns and do not reach the needed level of intimacy. Some people are even unable to find this unselfish type of relationship in their marriages or with their own children, and often the assistance of a psychiatrist is required before this basic need can be fulfilled. The conclusion that deprivation of intimate human contact is closely related to mental disorder is supported by the results of many studies showing that the highest rates of schizophrenia occur among people who live an isolated life in hotels, in rooming houses, or otherwise separated from their original neighborhood. The frequency of psychiatric problems was always found to be directly related to the number of friends reported by the individual. Higher crime rates were also found among people living in social isolation.

A mentally depressed person tends to withdraw, avoiding contact with other people. However our common sense, as well as all evidence from psychiatric research, tells us that someone suffering depression should do the exact opposite to overcome this destructive state; that is, he or she should actively seek the comfort of intimate human contact.

Similarly, the typical suburban life-style, which often eliminates the neighborhood primary group, may be a dangerously wrong response to the stress people experience in their daily professional activities. Sometimes suburban living even interferes with the formation of a children's play group, which is much richer in intimate contacts if it is formed naturally in the streets of a neighborhood than if it is organized in schools and community centers.

The physical design of suburban communities, with individual houses having only unusable lawns and driveways in the front and a carefully fenced and walled-in yard in the back, marks this tendency to avoid opportunities of intimate contact. In contrast, the traditional village scene, with people gathering after work on their front porch to participate in street life, is now believed to represent a more healthy psychological environment. The best response to the stress of our cities is now thought to be the individual's exposure to the urban experience, not the creation of situations that facilitate withdrawal.

Spatial Aspects

Sociological research in the field of territoriality has provided architects with new factors regarding the minimum and optimum spaces for certain human activities. Originally, the term "territoriality" referred to the pattern of behavior associated with the defense of a male animal's territory. Today it is used to describe the spatial attitudes of a species, which serve to protect the group from enemies, to express the hierarchical order within the group, and to regulate density, thus ensuring the food supply.

From the many observations of territorial behavior among animals, sociologists have drawn parallels to human behavioral responses regarding privacy, property, and critical distance. Architects today need to be familiar with the basic psychological space requirements as learned from this research. Four concepts of distance in territoriality have been proposed, based on the work of Edward T. Hall, author of *The Hidden Dimension* and *The Silent Language*.

1 *Personal Distance.* The distance maintained among members of one group. This distance varies with the individual, according to his or her hierarchical ranking. "Personal distance" is the term originally used by Martin Heidegger to designate the distance consistently separating the members of noncontact species. It might be thought of as a small protective sphere or bubble that an organism maintains between itself and others. Hall describes two types of "personal distance": close phase and far phase. In the *close phase* (distance of 1½-2½ ft) the kinesthetic sense of closeness derives in part from the possibilities regarding what each participant can do to the other with his or her extremities. At this distance, one can hold or grasp the other person. The other's features are not visually distorted, however, there is noticeable feedback from the muscles that control the eyes. In the *far phase* (distance of 2 ½–4 ft) we are able to "keep someone at arm's length." This phase of personal distance extends from a point that is just outside easy touching distance by one person to a point where two people can touch fingers if they extend both arms. This is the limit of physical domination in a very real sense.
2 *Social Distance.* A maximum distance between the individual and the group, beyond which the individual is not considered to be a part of the group any more and becomes subject to outside aggression. This is the boundary line between the far phase of personal distance and the close phase of social distance; it marks, in the words of one subject, the "limit of domination."
3 *Critical Distance.* The distance at which an animal might attack an approaching stranger.
4 *Flight Distance.* The distance at which an animal might take flight from an approaching stranger.

Regarding human reactions the distance concepts used by sociologists are, ranking from small to large:

1 Intimate distance.
2 Personal distance.
3 Social distance.
4 Public distance.

Figure 1.61 Critical distance for an animal. *Source.* Edward T. Hall, *The Hidden Dimension*, Doubleday Anchor Books, 1966.

These psychological distances have not yet entered the standard publications on human spatial requirements, in which the field of observation is always limited to physical activities. However in situations of stress and overcrowding, it may well be these psychological space requirements that determine the minimum safe amount of space. A situation of panic, for instance, illustrates how the psychological space requirement may be well above that allocated for the physical function of circulation. In an urban environment where overcrowding is a daily experience, this safety margin for primal behavioral responses becomes increasingly important.

Studies on overcrowding have revealed a very clear correlation between the space available for housing and physical and mental health. Below a certain minimum space per household, health problems were found to increase very rapidly. But this critical margin was also found to vary greatly with the social and cultural groups under observation. People from northern countries, such as Scandinavians and Britains, appear to need more personal space than, say, Mediterraneans.

Disorientation is another potential source of fear in an urban environment. People generally derive a sense of

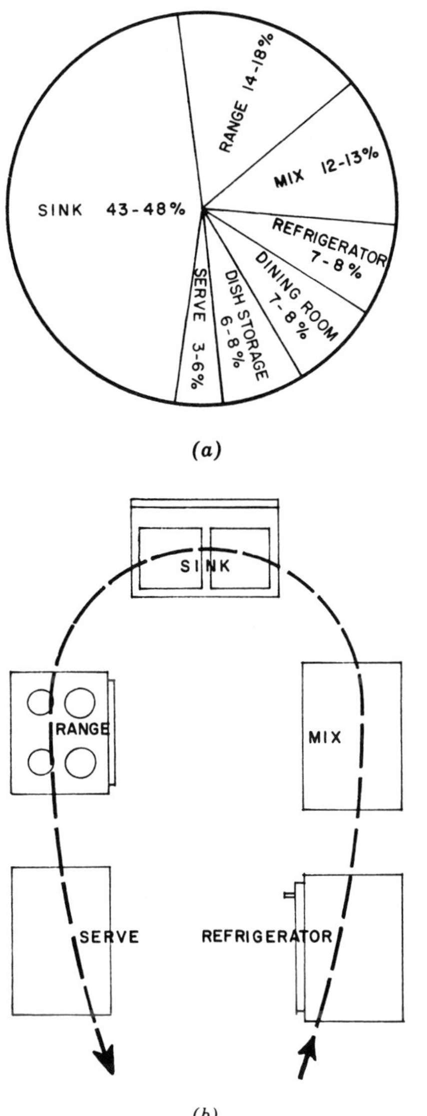

Figure 1.62 (*a*) Percentage distribution of trips in food preparation. (*b*) Flow of work in food preparation. *Source.* Joseph de Chiara and Joseph Hancock Callender, *Time-Saver Standards for Building Types* McGraw-Hill Book Company, 1974.

comfort from an environment having an organization that is familiar to them, and the inability to orient oneself in space is often associated with a feeling of mental disorder. An organized environment is referred to as a fixed feature space. Most structures represent a fixed feature space, where separate spaces are designated to each principal activity, as illustrated in Figure 1.62 on the scale of a single room in a house. Yet all the spaces in a single dwelling must fit together as a unit, in relation to the house itself and to the community, as Figure 1.63 suggests.

The two principal urban fixed-feature patterns are the grid and the star. Both are ancient, and both make orientation easy once some dominant points are identified. The pattern of the radiating star is assumed to be sociopetal, which means it tends to bring people together, whereas the grid pattern is known as sociofugal because it tends to separate people. Examples of these properties on a small scale would be the arrangement of chairs around a table (sociopetal) versus the back-to-back seating arrangement in an airport waiting area (sociofugal).

Demographic Considerations

Demography is concerned with quantitative information regarding size, distribution, density, and vital statistics. Throughout history there is evidence of population counts or censuses, and of efforts to balance the number and mix of people with the environment. The term "census" dates back to Roman times; it refers to taxation, the original purpose of such counts. The science of demography originated in the seventeenth century, when John Graunt in England developed life expectancy statistics out of the study of mortality tables.

Today population data are available through the work of the U.S. Bureau of the Census. The census is an enumeration taking place every 10 years, which also elicits detailed information on living conditions, economic characteristics, and educational levels. The first census in the United States was taken in 1850. Many government programs now depend on census information.

Whyte, who studied the social notes from two newspapers in Chicago's middle-class bedroom community of Park Forest, found that the guests at social gatherings usually came from a small geographic area, whereas special-interest groups like gourmet societies drew their membership from a much broader area. Whyte also discovered that Park Forest residents rarely made friends with neighbors whose properties adjoined back to back, but were more likely to be friendly with those who lived on either side.

In England, architect Peter Ellis detected a definite relationship between the arrangement of houses in the suburbs and social contacts. "We should accept the fact that architects can be social engineers in the same way as parents, educationists, and teachers," said Ellis. "At the same time, relationships between people are two-way; people do things to buildings as well as buildings doing things to people."

Ellis focused on new houses in Chalvedon, a housing development in Basildon New Town, 30 miles from London. He concluded that social contacts there were

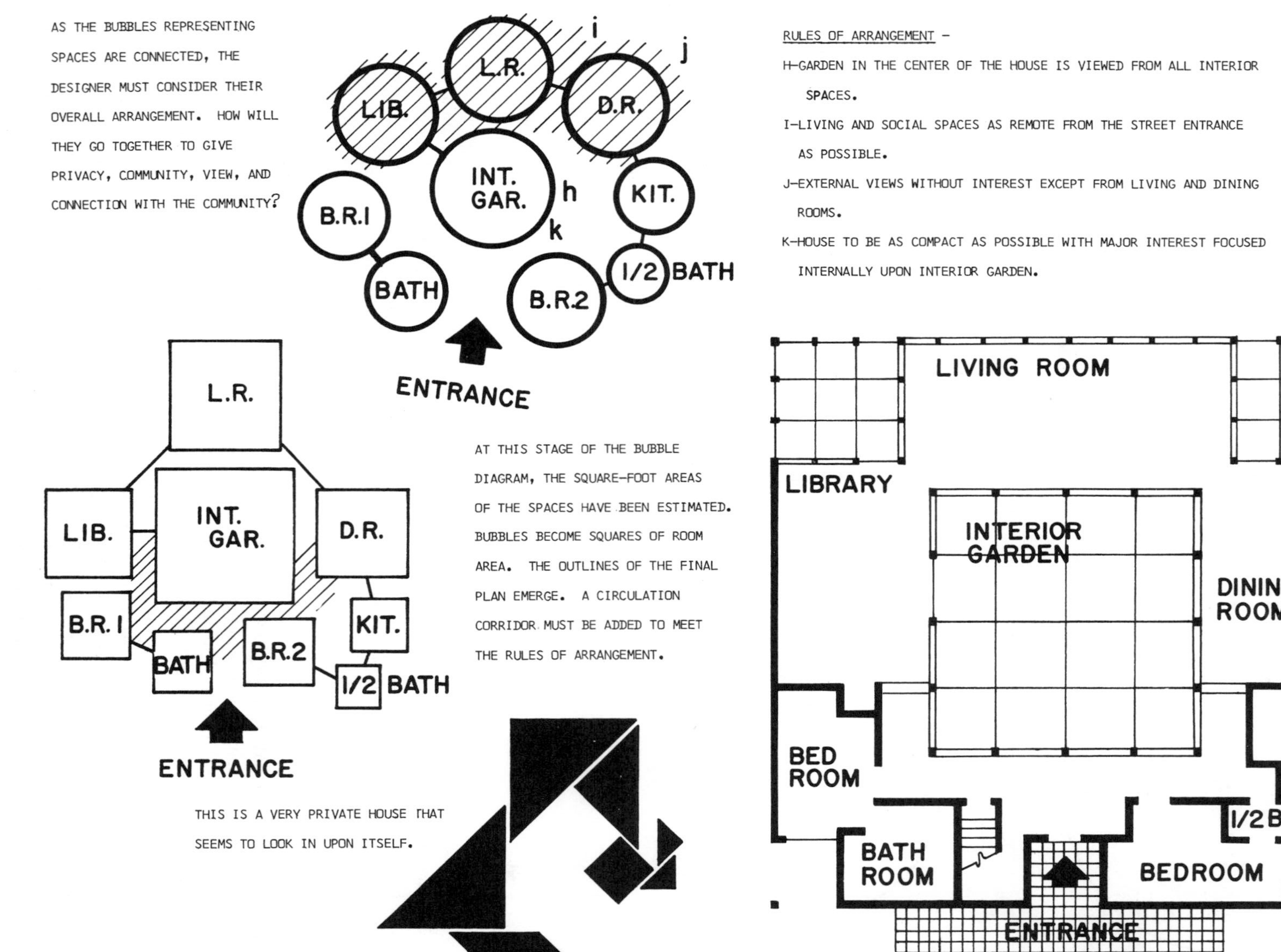

Figure 1.63 From bubble diagram to house plan. *Source*. Forrest Wilson, *Graphic Guide to Interior Design*, Van Nostrand Reinhold, 1977.

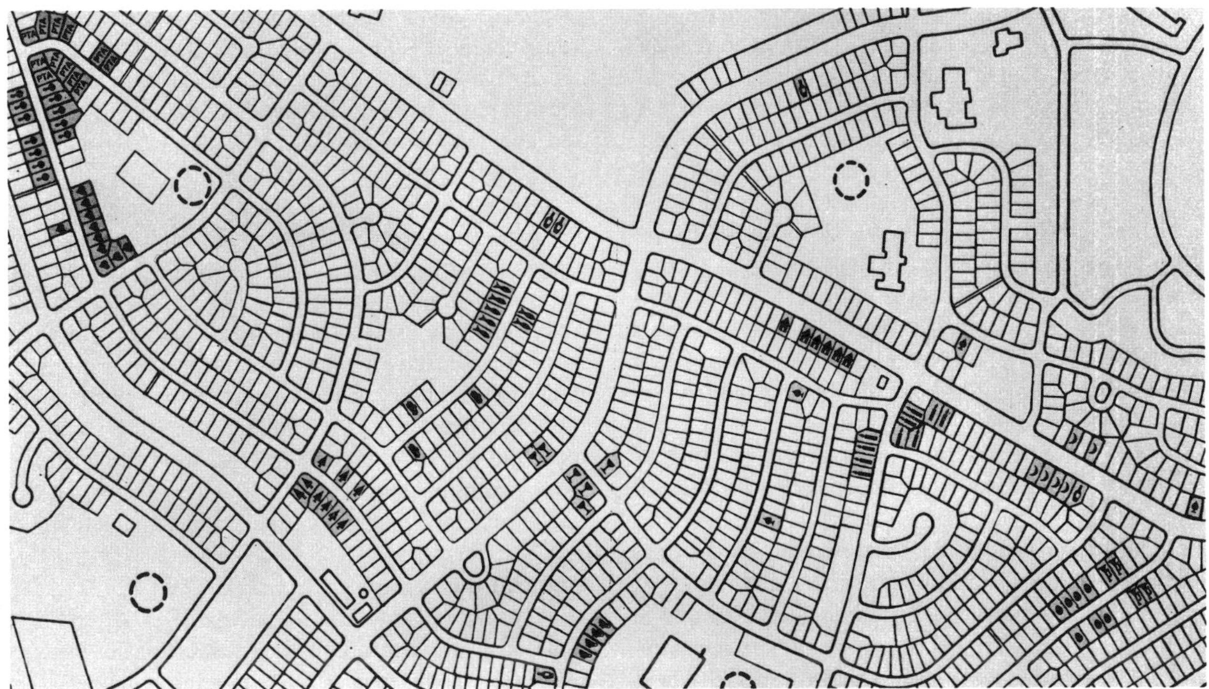

On a map of Park Forest, Illinois, parties and club meetings over a six-month period are plotted with symbols identified at left below.

Who knows whom in Park Forest

- Come-as-you-are birthday party
- Saturday-night bridge group
- New Year's Eve party
- Saturday-night party
- Eggnog before Poinsettia Ball
- Fishhouse punch party
- Picnic at Sauk Trail Forest Preserve
- Hosts at joint dinner party
- St. Valentine's Day costume party
- Surprise baby party
- PTA P.T.A. party
- Meeting of the Homemakers
- Post-dance breakfast
- Pre-dance cocktails
- Gourmet Society

Figure 1.64 *Source. The Community*, by the Editors of Time-Life Books, 1976.

strongly influenced by the positioning of mailboxes. Chalvedon consisted of row houses with gardens behind them. Some houses were separated by only a walk, others by a garden and a walk. The houses were much alike, and the architects had designed them in such a way that either the garden side or the walk side might have been the front. But since the post office department did not want the mailmen to have to walk through the gardens and be challenged by dogs, the mailboxes were put up on the walk sides of the houses, and this official identification of a main entry made residents accept the walk-mailbox sides as the fronts of their houses. This recognition of the front had a marked effect on visiting habits. Residents preferred that people call at the front door where the mailbox was. The result was that the people whose houses were separated by walks got to know each other more easily than those who were separated by both a garden and a walk.

Population growth is one aspect of demography of which the public is most aware. It is only in very recent times that a high rate of population increase has ceased to be considered desirable. Economic and strategic power in the past were always associated with an expanding population. Today, however, the consensus is that environmental deterioration and limited natural resources almost outweigh the economic power generated by the greater number of people, and the concept of zero population growth is supported by many.

A constant universal growth rate of 1% corresponds to a population growth following an exponential function, which means that the actual population growth increases over the years. Expressed in numerical terms, if today's population were to continue to grow at the rate of 1% for 370 years, the population would multiply by 1000, thus would total 5200 billion, enough to cover the entire surface of the planet (oceans included) with a density equal to that of Manhattan. In reference to population growth it is necessary to define the terms "density," "agglomeration," and "crowding."

Density measures the number of people per unit of area. Since density is a ratio, it is possible for a small village to have a much higher density than a large city, and indeed this is usually the case, because less space is allocated to infrastructures such as roads and freeways. *Agglomeration* designates the total number of people in an area, without specifying their density. *Crowding* refers to a negative psychological reaction caused by high density. The degree of density perceived as crowding varies very much with the situation and with the local conditioning of people. A half-filled sports stadium will not evoke a feeling of crowding, but a picnic area with the same density may be perceived as overcrowded. Likewise, a residential quarter in California may cause reactions to overcrowding at half the density of a Tokyo housing area, perceived in Japan as spacious.

Thus population density is not always related directly to the quality of urban life. High densities become most disturbing in a monotonous environment and in one that lacks a close relationship to the human scale. If a big-scale environment is broken down into distinct areas small enough to permit individuals to identify with them on a visual as well as on a social level, high density may produce the kind of energies a city is appreciated for.

Effects of Density

Even though a variety of outstanding efforts in the arts and in communications are a function of the high-density conditions in the center of a metropolitan area, there is very clear statistical evidence that density causes stress, and that stress is related to many pathological states, physical, mental, and social.

One study on this subject was performed in Philadelphia, where data on major diseases of all types were gathered for small subareas covering the whole city and correlated to data regarding densities, economic levels, pollution, and so on. The results were presented graphically, in the form of shaded areas on the city map. The emerging picture revealed very clearly that the incidence of most major diseases increased significantly with density, and the concomitant deterioration of physical and economic environment. The core of the city also proved to be the center of disease.

Naturally such health problems are not entirely the result of density itself, but they are caused by density-related variables, such as lack of privacy, malnutrition, noise, and economic insecurity. Again, the example of Tokyo demonstrates that a city with a higher density than New York can have a much lower crime rate, as well as a much lower rate of suicides, than any American metropolitan area. In looking for the specific factors that make this situation possible, we will find some answers in the realms of cultural and racial homogeneity, a condition completely contrary to the American situation.

Cultural Background

Individuals differ greatly in their perceptions of the environment. The differences stem, to a minor degree, from variations in the sensitivity and balance of our senses. But for the most part they are a result of the filtering process of sensory impressions, according to what each personality considers important for its own way of life. Since these life-styles are largely patterned by cultural heritage, it is important for planners to be familiar with the values and preferences of a given cultural group, to understand the particular sensory world of its members. Unfortunately, an antagonistic approach often has been taken in urban renewal projects. With the major focus on better utilization of space and improved sanitary conditions, lively neighborhoods were transformed into blocks of mid- or highrise apartments whose physical design made it impossible to reestablish the original social patterns. The failure of such developments as the West End Renewal Project in Boston clearly indicates that to ensure the vitality and health of a community, the possibility for intimate contact need be considered at least as much as the standards regarding occupancy rates and plumbing facilities. These opportunities for intimate contact existed amply in the old neighborhood, in the form of streets, little stores, churches, and hallways, all of which were eliminated by the design of the new elevator highrises.

Perceptual Structure

Besides adequate nutrition and clean air, human beings need the energy of thought to encourage harmonious development. Thoughts, to keep from becoming repetitive

HENRY STREET STUDIOS
Brooklyn Heights, New York (restoration)
Architects: Pomeroy, Lebduska Associates
Photo: D. Hirsch

and purely functional, must be stimulated by a great variety of sensory impressions.

In the education of our infants we try to create a stimulating sensory environment, and we know that deprivation of appropriate stimuli retards the growth of children. However this continuous need for new impressions prevails throughout life. Every day we can observe many cases of people who, in choosing between alternatives, intuitively select the one that offers more visual interest and variety. The patterns of pedestrian routes in cities, for example, indicates that routes along short city blocks are preferred to long unbroken routes.

Besides fulfilling the need for visual stimulus, people must satisfy a sense of adventure, which is charged by an environment of continuously changing scenes and many unexpected elements. This joy from encounters with unexpected impressions is not only typical of young people. Tourism shows that people of all ages are recharged with energy through travels in unfamiliar areas.

Environmental planners have coined the term *urban legibility* to describe a pattern that permits an individual to recognize the basic structures of a city from any point of observation. That is, people can point out the direction of major traffic arteries and know the approximate location of major centers in reference to their point of observation. City scapes that are generally agreed to be beautiful and friendly, like San Francisco and New Orleans, have this legibility to a high degree. Urban legibility also projects to people a rich mental image of a city, formed of both sensory and emotional qualities, which allows us to talk about cities as distinct personalities.

The principal spatial elements that form the image of a city include the following:

1 *Activity Centers*. Often referred to as *nodes*. Traditionally these consist of a village square or a market place. Today a civic center or a whole downtown area represents a node.
2 *Districts*. Sometimes only created for the purpose of administration, but sometimes definable as areas with common identifying characters.
3 *Streets*. Paths like Broadway in New York, remembered not only as a path of circulation but also as an axis connected with a variety of experiences.

In his examination of the form of the city, Professor Lynch found that people use five basic elements to construct their mental image of a city.

1 *Pathways*. These are the major and minor routes of circulation. A city has a network of major routes and a neighborhood network of minor routes. A building has several main routes that people use to get to it and from it. An urban highway network is a network of pathways for a whole city. The footpaths of a college campus are pathways for the campus.
2 *Districts*. A city is composed of component neighborhoods or districts: its center, uptown, midtown, its in-town residential areas, train yards, factory areas, suburbs, college campuses, and so on. Sometimes the districts are distinct in form and extent—like the Wall Street area of Manhattan. Sometimes they are considerably mixed in character and do not have distinct limits—like the midtown area of Manhattan.
3 *Edges*. The termination of a district is its edge. Some districts have no distinct edges at all but gradually taper off and blend into another district. When two districts are joined at an edge they form a seam. In Manhattan, for example, Fifth Avenue is the eastern edge of Central Park. A narrow park may be a joining seam for two urban neighborhoods.
4 *Landmarks*. The prominent visual features of the city are its landmarks. Some landmarks, such as the Empire State Building or a radio mast, can be seen at great distances. Some landmarks are very small and can be seen only close up—a street clock, a fountain, or a small statue in a park. Landmarks are an important element of urban form because they help people to orient themselves in the city and help identify an area. A good landmark is a distinct but harmonious element in its urban setting.
5 *Nodes*. A node is a center of activity. Actually it is a type of landmark, distinguished from a proper landmark by virtue of its active function. Whereas a landmark is a distinct visual object, a node is a distinct hub of activity. Times Square in mid-Manhattan is both a landmark and a node.

These five elements of urban form alone are sufficient to make a useful visual survey of the form of a city. They are important because people think of a city's form in terms of these basic elements.

The quality of images common to a city depends on the presence and uniqueness of the elements above. The shape of Manhattan, for instance, is easily imaginable because of its waterfront (edge). Likewise, Paris has an abundance of landmarks—the Eiffel Tower, the Arc de Triomphe, the Cathedral of Notre Dame—which serve as reference points in actual circulation, as well as in the mental image. Examples of new cities like Brasilia or

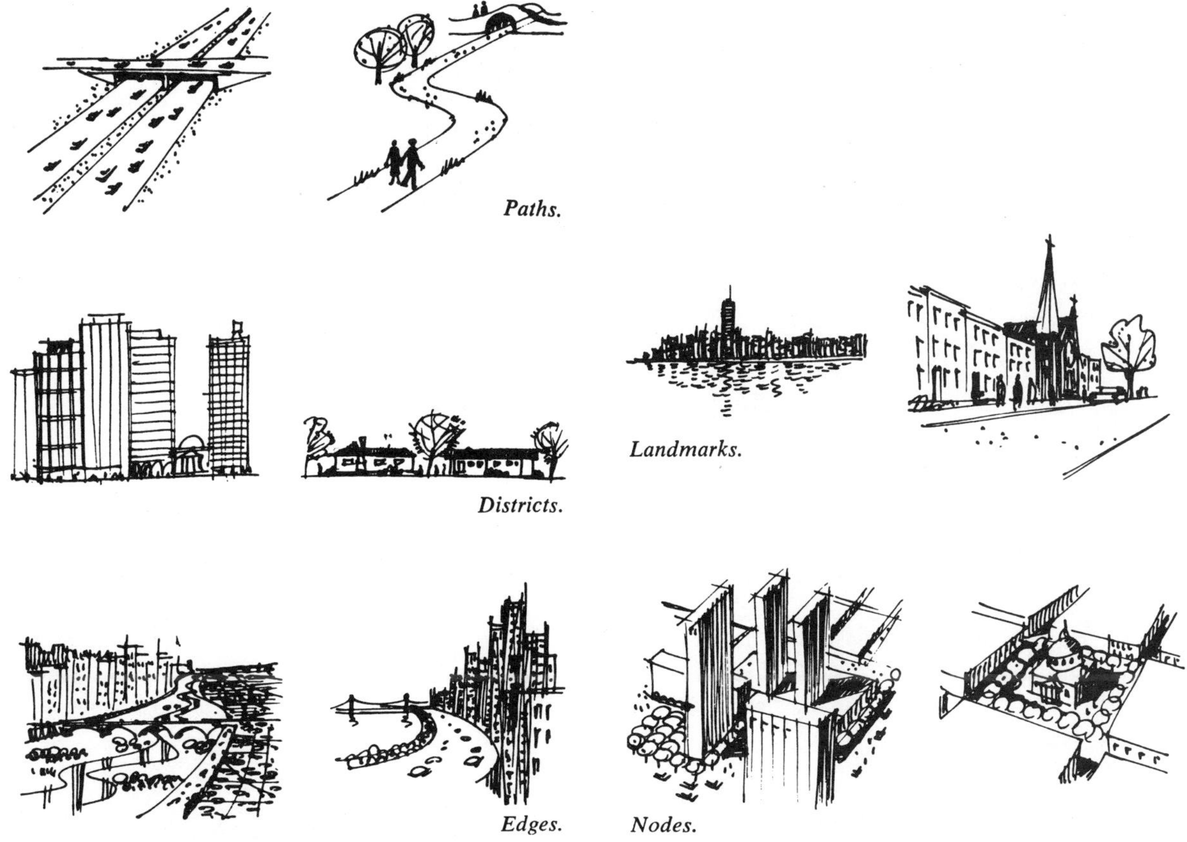

Figure 1.65 *Source*. Paul D. Spreiregen, *Urban Design: The Architecture of Towns and Cities,* McGraw-Hill Book Company, 1965.

Chandigarh show us how the designer's attempts to create an urban image on the drafting board can lead to an environment that conveys feelings of authoritativeness and artificiality, rather than humaneness. The need for an image, however, is real.

The main difference between a new town being constructed over a time span not longer than one decade, and a city that has taken more than a century to grow, seems to be the much greater number of individual structures, systems, and groups composing the latter, and the much more complex pattern of interaction that has developed among them. It seems impossible for a single group of planners, sometimes all belonging to the same social and ethnic group and period of history, to creat this variety with all its overlap and spontaneity. For one thing, the system would be too complex to be visualized. For another, the group simply does not have the broad basis of human experience that is manifested in a city created by numerous generations through various cultures and social orders.

At the turn of the century, as the art of city planning developed, the awakening of functionalism inspired the first ideas. Separation of functions, one of the essential principles, had great merit where housing was separated from heavy manufacturing and so on. But the general separation of housing and business is often abandoned today for the sake of greater interaction and vitality of urban areas. Similarly, the strict separation of pedestrian and vehicular traffic is no longer considered to be an ideal solution, in spite of the safety merits associated with adherence to this principle.

It is believed today that the approach of strict separation of different functions, as suggested in early examples like Tony Garnier's Cité Industrielle, mainly stems from the natural tendency of the human mind to reduce the complexity of a problem by means of grouping and categorizing. The rigidity and lifelessness of urban design, then, is often the result of a direct implementation of the mental model, which should have served only as an intermediate step in the process of identification of the

CONSTITUTION PLAZA
Hartford, Connecticut
Architect: Charles Du Bose
Photo: J. W. Molitor

problem. One deplorable example of this preference for compartmentalization is the design of retirement communities. The elderly are separated from the active life of the community and housed in a system that was designed to serve only their immediate physical needs.

Although it is certainly impossible to design an urban environment that matches the richness and variety of an old city, it can still be the goal of the planners to strive for a maximum in complexity and stimulus. With this goal in mind, they will probably have to limit their design decisions to the city's infrastructure and to certain centers of administration, leaving design and development decisions for major areas open to the greatest possible varity of interest groups and individuals.

Citizen Participation

New communities and towns are planned and partly built before any of the inhabitants are on the scene, thus it is most difficult to organize a viable framework for citizen participation in planning and governing.

One possible approach is to arrange for community groups to work as consultants with the developers. Another is to conduct opinion polls among the citizens' groups of roughly the same economic and social composition as those anticipated to move into the new communities. The sample should include people from all income groups, and the interviews should be conducted by social research organizations that have experience in the field. One difficulty with polls, however, is that most people's opinions are based on what they know from the past, and few are able to visualize what will be, especially concerning their environment.

As soon as the inhabitants are beginning to settle in their new environment, a framework for participation in the decision-making process should be organized. The experience of the first new town inhabitants, in this country and abroad, will be helpful for future residents. Social research consultants should be part of the new town planning from the start.

Little work has been done to ensure and facilitate citizen participation in relation to the innovations of the governmental and institutional framework of new communities, and indeed this represents a difficult problem. Yet an administrative framework that safeguards the existence of participatory democracy for future residents, must be set up first.

In the few new communities that have been built in the United States, there has been virtually no innovation. The new town administration is organized within the existing local and county governments, for instance, in Columbia, Maryland, or Reston, Virginia. Experience around the world has shown that the opportunity to innovate and to create more responsive systems of participatory democracy has been entirely ignored.

The model cities legislation in the United States, for instance, in Boston, has resulted in broadly based citizen participation; its methods should be studied and applied in new communities.

Functionalism and Response

If we refer to a part of a city as depressing or creepy or sterile, we have experienced a distinct emotional response to the physical environment. Many urban forms provoke the same feeling in people from all walks of life. This indicates that to some degree human emotional reactions to certain aspects of the physical environment can be anticipated and incorporated in the planning factors considered. Unfortunately the functionalist approach of past years has tended to ignore these factors, and environmental planning, yet undeveloped, must advance a great deal before the basic emotional needs of people can be integrated scientifically in the planning process.

The emotional stress caused by monotony is a psychological effect known to all, and the emotional problems brought about by repetitious work were observed long ago. During the Industrial Revolution the production processes were designed without consideration for the emotional side of human nature. Only in our age of great individual freedom, the manufacturing industry is trying to create working conditions conducive to emotional satisfaction and intellectual vigor, even at the cost of failure to maximize short-term productivity. A monotonous housing environment has been found to be equally harmful to the emotional balance of residents. Speculative mass housing projects everywhere, which were designed with only the most obvious economic factors in mind, give evidence of the serious problems that occur when people are deprived of variety and sensory stimuli.

The environment shapes the personality of its inhabitants, not only by the negative aspects mentioned previously, but also in a multitude of positive ways. Without citing any scientific evidence, we can state the basic differences in personality between city people and country folks and can even distinguish the personalities associated with different cities (thus referring to a certain person as a typical New Yorker, etc.). Although it would be beyond the scope of the task of environmental planners to design a city by defining the type of personality it should be conducive to, their perceptual considerations should have some general goals, such as stimulus, variety, peacefulness, and intimacy.

5 ECONOMIC INFLUENCES

Location Theory

Land Characteristics. Immobility, indestructibility, and scarcity are the main qualities of land that determine its character as an economic commodity. The buyer of land actually acquires two economic commodities: physical space and location. The value assigned to the land always reflects the combination of the two goods. For the same price the buyer could acquire more land in a less valuable location or could trade quantity for a better location. The value of location varies for different land uses. Any land use restriction usually lowers the value of the property. Conversely, a zoning change permitting a higher land use always increases the property value.

Agricultural Land Use. The nineteenth-century economist von Thynen developed a model to illustrate the relation between location and land use. It is assumed that farmers are grouped around a market where they sell their products. They all try to maximize their profits, that is, the selling price less production and transportation costs. Since the selling price and production cost do not change, the profit margin depends on the distance to the market, thus on the transportation cost. Therefore, assuming that all land is rented, and each farmer produces one product, farmers will bid for locations according to the profitability of their respective products. The resultant land use distribution will be that land-intensive production, which requires daily trips to the market and is therefore very sensitive to transportation cost, will locate close to the center, whereas land-extensive production, which requires only occasional trips to the marketplace, will locate at the periphery. Thus in von Thynen's agricultural model, vegetables would be grown close to the market, wheat would be further away, and cattle ranches would locate at an even greater distance.

Location of Business. The urban business executive's decisions are guided by the factor that is most likely ensure maximum profit. Therefore he or she will be indifferent to location when areas that are equally profitable are available.

The profit of a business may be defined as the remainder after operating costs and land costs have been deducted from the volume of business. Since operating costs are closely connected with the volume of production, the market demand, and the supply of production, resources at any given location become important factors, and the simple model of agricultural land use is no longer valid.

General conditions determining the location of business include the following:

1 Location of markets for the product (catchment).
2 Quantity and quality of manpower available.
3 Accessibility of raw materials (transportation cost).
4 Favorable governmental policies.
5 Competition from other businesses.
6 Availability of supplementary businesses.
7 Availability and value of land.

Each business and industry has a different economic structure in terms of these factors. Business structures emphasizing accessibility to clients, such as banks, department stores, and corporate headquarters, usually prefer a downtown location. Industrial plants, in contrast, need accessibility to airports and harbors; since they need space and are sensitive to high cost of floor areas, they locate along freeways and railroads outside the city.

Location of Housing. Housing differs from business and agriculture in that the goal is maximum satisfaction, not maximum profit. A household with a given budget and specific life-style will try to balance the cost and strain of commuting against the advantages of lower housing cost and more space, which improve with the distance. The optimal location will depend on a satisfactory balance of these factors.

A model similar to the location theory of agriculture can be used to explain housing patterns. People with good incomes put great value in the privacy of a big lot and the comfort of a big house. They are also very mobile, having more than one car per household, and they are not too sensitive to transportation cost. Therefore they will move to a suburban location where they can buy property large enough to suit them, and where

HOUSE
Rye, New York
Architects: Ulrich Franzen & Associates
Photo: E. Stoller Associates

commuting will not be too difficult. The poor, however, cannot buy or rent much property at any location. And since they can afford only a small quantity of land, changes in land values are not as important to them as the cost and problems of commuting. Thus the poor tend to live in central locations with high land values, and the rich tend to live in the suburbs with lower land values.

In summary, accessibility is the main factor determining land use and, consequently, the rent or sales value of any urban property. Depending on the economics of a business or the budget and desires of a household, a distinct location will maximize profit and satisfaction. This leads to the general urban land use pattern in which offices, banks, corporate headquarters, and low-income housing are found in the center, industrial parks lie outside the central business district; and medium- to high-income housing is located in the suburbs.

Market Analysis

The Real Estate Markets. The *market* for a certain type of real estate is an area within which all properties of the same type are in direct competition and are linked by a continuous chain of substitution. In a housing market, a family may substitute a condominium for an apartment and a duplex for the condominium, a single-family residence for the condominium, and so on. Ideally, buyers and sellers in this market area are in such free communication that the same commodity demands exactly the same price. Real estate markets, however, are far from exhibiting this perfect communication, and the incomplete knowledge of buyers and sellers makes the market respond erratically to certain economic factors. Property values and rent levels, therefore, reflect the interplay of supply and demand with a degree of imperfection.

HICKORY CLUSTER
Reston, Virginia
Architects: Charles M. Goodman Associates
Photo: Office

Supply and Demand Factors

Housing. Generally speaking, the for-sale housing market responds to changes in demand and supply much faster than does the rental market. Factors influencing the demand for both commodities include the following:

1 *Population Growth*. Generally, the city's growth due to migration is much greater than the natural growth.
2 *Employment Rates*. Housing demand is directly related to employment figures.
3 *Income Levels*. In a constant population, the increase in family income will create demand for new housing units, since more people can afford separate living accommodations.
4 *Household Formation*. A population with more nonfamily households (roommates, singles, couples without children) will demand more housing units than a population consisting mainly of complete families. A trend toward incomplete and nonfamily households will therefore increase the demand, even without actual population increase.

Increasing demand stimulates the supply of housing. Housing developers, however, also respond to other economic factors.

1 *Vacancy Rates*. Landlords, in an effort to maximize profit, will raise the rents to a level at which a certain percentage of apartments is always vacant. If they attempt to fill all units by cutting

rents, income will decrease. Vacancy rates in a strong market are between 2 and 5%, which indicates a demand for new units. If vacancies rise above 10%, there is a temporary oversupply of units, and developers will hesitate to build in the area.

2 *Construction Cost.* Since the costs of labor and material in the housing industry often rise faster than sales values and rent levels, developers are sometimes obliged to wait until rent increases and for-sale prices have caught up with the escalation in construction cost.

3 *Skilled Labor.* In new housing markets, there are not always enough subcontractors available to make volume construction possible. This lack of skilled labor may cause the supply to lag behind the demand of the area.

Commercial (Retail) Space. Retail space is found in three general urban formations: the department stores of the central business area, the shopping streets in the neighborhoods, and the master planned shopping centers in the suburbs and new towns.

The quality and type of goods that can be sold in each of these formations is directly related to the total mass of the shopping area. *Convenience goods*—that is, goods purchased daily—are sold in neighborhood stores and markets. *Shopping goods,* items for which the customer shops for quality and bargains, are sold only in centers that offer a choice of stores, such as downtown areas. The sale of *specialty goods* is largely the result of unplanned (impulse) purchasing. Specialty stores are therefore most successful in locations that attract people because of their atmosphere, the beauty of their environment, or the opportunity that is afforded for social contacts.

Vehicular access (parking) is an important success factor for retail businesses. A new shopping center that provides easy access and ample parking space can draw a substantial percentage of business from older stores in the same market area that have little or no off-street parking.

GLENDALE GALLERIA
Glendale, California
Architects: Charles Kober Associates
Photo: W. Simon

Office Space. Most of the office space in cities is supplied by highrise buildings in downtown locations. Demand for this type of business space is due mainly to interaction with other businesses and the economic value attached to a prestige location. Most cities have a chronic oversupply of office space, evident in the high vacancy rates found in highrise office buildings. The reason for this gap between supply and demand lies partly in the corporate developer's fiscal structure—a structure that makes high vacancies and sometimes even unoccupied buildings feasible.

A new type of office building, the garden office, has recently created a special market demand. This product consists of a low- to midrise structure offering first-class office space that includes amenities such as patios, interior courts, balconies, private bathrooms with showers, rich landscaping, and sometimes tennis courts or swimming pools. Such office buildings are usually located in an uncongested area outside the central business district. These features of habitability, atmosphere, and individuality make the garden office competitive with conventional highrise business space. New developments of this type have been found to be successful in areas with an oversupply of standard office space.

Industrial Space. The availability of warehouse and manufacturing space depends to a great extent on the zoning of a city that has led to the formation of industrial

COMMERCE CLEARING HOUSE
San Rafael, California
Architects: Marquis & Stoller
Photo: B. Parker, ESTO

parks. Demand is generally tied in with the economic growth of an area and with the national economy as well. Since transportation cost and production and storage cost are major factors in the profit structure of a company, the demand at any given location will be very sensitive to differences in accessibility and rents or sales prices per square foot.

Absorption Rates. A complete market analysis ends with the projection of absorption rates believed to be achievable by the proposed development. These rates express the estimated time to sell or rent all units of a given development, that is, the time the market needs to absorb the new supply. Absorption rates are expressed in different ways: in number of units sold per week for condominium projects, in number of square feet leased per month for office buildings, and so forth. This absorption rate bears heavily on the profit margin, since the daily costs of unsold inventory are a major factor in the economics of every development.

Development Economics: Investment Theories

Characteristics of Real Estate Investments. Today's building industry emphasizes economic and tangible factors and de-emphasizes the factors that traditionally belong to the architect's area of competence (i.e., harmony, style, feeling, and expression). To maintain their share of power and influence in the development process, architects are forced to expand their competence into the areas of economics and finance. A basic knowledge of the mechanics of real estate investment contributes to this goal.

Real estate is the largest single category of investment in the national economy, and investments are so diverse that a classification of types of is difficult. Housing always takes the largest share. Since there is a nationwide trend away from the single-family home toward multiple-dwelling structures, the share of investment capital versus homeowner's capital is growing significantly. Most real estate investments are made with a large share of borrowed money, which usually comes from financial institutions. As a result, banks and other mortgage lenders exert a great deal of influence on what is built. Savings and loan associations, commercial banks, life insurance companies, and pension funds account for most of the mortgage lending.

Equity investors in real estate can be divided into two major groups: short-term and long-term investors. Individuals, syndications, and real estate investment trusts are primarily interested in short and medium terms. Life insurance companies, business corporations, and pension funds are typical long-term investors.

Some common characteristics make real estate investments distinctly different from other investment alternatives such as stocks, bonds, and securities. These characteristics can be summarized as follows:

1 The individuality of each parcel of real estate.
2 The immobility of real property.
3 The large size and volume of most real estate.
4 The great complexity of the market in terms of laws, financing, and physical forms.

These factors result in a great segregation of submarkets within which a limited group of investors has a detailed knowledge of the property and connected technicalities. The large dollar value of real estate, coupled with its immobility, makes this investment suited for a high degree of leverage (low owner's equity and high share of borrowed capital). Since the property will always be there and its value is not likely to drop, mortgage lenders consider it an ideal medium.

Tax Advantages. Implicit in the immobility of real estate is the impossibility of hiding it from tax authorities. Thus owners of real estate cannot escape periodic increases in property taxes. The real estate investor, however, can profit from a number of favorable federal tax regulations that offer a tax shelter and inflation hedge. The principal tax incentives for real estate investments are as follows:

1 Deductibility of interest payments.
2 Methods of accelerated depreciation (deducted from taxable income).
3 Low capital gains tax on the income resulting from sale of real estate.

These tax advantages must be considered in evaluating an investment, and the after tax rate of return becomes an important indicator.

Rates of Return. The rates of return provide the most important tool for evaluating investments. The rate of return considered to be high enough for a particular investment depends on the term, the amount of risk involved, and the amount of management effort needed. Taking the net returns, typical rates of return for different real estate investments are as follows:

Average apartment house	5%
Prime controlled apartments	8%
Prime commercial buildings	9%
Hotels and motels	11%
Shopping centers	13%

Different methods are used for calculating the rate of return. The most widely used is as follows:

$$\frac{\text{net income before interest and depreciation, first year}}{\text{purchase price}}$$

The reciprocal value of this return gives the net income multiplier used in the quick evaluation of income property (rate of return of 8% = multiplier of 1/0.08 = 12.5). The same method can also be expressed as:

$$\frac{\text{annual cash spendable income, first year}}{\text{cash down payment}}$$

Or in another variation:

$$\frac{\text{annual cash spendable income} \atop \text{loan payment, first-year interest}}{\text{cash down payment}}$$

To reflect the increasing amount of owner's equity due to the amortization of the loan, this annual "equity build-up" is sometimes added to the income. As mentioned earlier, tax savings also may be added to the income to reflect the true earnings of the investor.

Syndication. Real estate syndication enables individuals to invest in a large income-producing property through multiple ownership. In its simplest form, real estate syndication exists when two or more unrelated individuals join together and own some form of real es-

Table 1.6 Project Cost Analysis for 250 Dwelling Units: Density = 30

					Monthly Rent			
					Unfurnished		Furnished	
Percentage	Number	Type[a]	Rentable Area, Each (ft³)	Rentable Area, Total (ft³)	Each	Total	Each	Total
30%	75	Single, all F	450	33,750	$125	$ 9,375	$300	$ 22,500
43%	107	1 Bd–1 Ba, 80F	650	69,550	170	18,190	350	28,000
2%	6	2 Bd–1 Ba, U	800	6,800	200	1,200		
25%	62	2 Bd–2 Ba, 10F	950	58,900	225	13,950	400	4,000
				169,000		$ 42,715		$ 54,500
(a)	*Annual Rent*					$512,580		$654,000
	Less utilities (10/unit/mo)					(30,000)		
	Annual rental income (ARI)					482,580		
	Miscellaneous Income							
	Extra garages					2,400		
	Laundry					9,000		
(b)	*Gross annual income (GAI)*					493,980		
	Less vacancy and collection loss							
	5% × GAI					(24,699)		(3,270)
	34.5% × ARI					(166,490)		(22,563)
(c)	*Net annual income (NAI)*					302,791		39,500
	Less debt service					(223,639)		
	Spendable return on investment					79,152		
	Furniture income					39,567		
(d)	*Spendable return on investment at 95% occupancy*					118,719		
(e)	*First trust deed determination (1 TD)*							
	1 4.9 × GAI					2,360,500		
	2 0.80 × GAI less operating expenses loan constant					2,311,400		
	3 NAI capitalized at 9.5 × 0.75					2,390,400		
Assumed first trust deed						2,354,100		

[a]Key = Bd, bedroom; Ba, bathroom; U, unfurnished; F, furnished.

tate. Syndicates can range from the small, privately held groups with 10 or fewer investors to major syndications such as the Empire State Building, with hundreds of individual investors. Legally speaking, a real estate syndication generally takes the form of a limited partnership with the general partner being the syndicator and/or realtor, or an accounting firm, and the limited partners consisting of professional people who are not involved in the management of the property. Because of tax advantages, participation in real estate syndicates has become very popular among professionals in high income brackets, and huge complexes of apartments in resort areas have been built to satisfy this demand for tax shelter.

Financial Feasibility Studies

After a market demand study has been made, a financial feasibility study is necessary to determine whether a project will yield enough return on the investment, given the for-sale prices or rent levels projected in the market study. The following outline summarizes a typical financial feasibility study done for a 250-unit apartment building. Tables 1.6 to 1.8 give appropriate figures.

1 The projections for optimal apartment sizes and rents per square foot from the market study are used to calculate the *annual rent (a).*

2 Adjustments for utilities paid by the owner and for additional income from laundromats and garages lead to the *gross annual income (b).*

3 Loss through vacancies and a statistical average percentage for operating expenses (34.5%) are deducted, thus determining the *net annual income (c).*

4 From this amount the annual mortgage payment (principal + interest) is deducted, and additional income realized through the rental of furniture is added to determine the *spendable return on investment (d).*

5 The figure used for the annual mortgage payment is taken from amortization tables, assuming the current interest rate and the usual term of 25 or 30 years. Before this can be done, however, we must estimate the amount of the mortgage loan, by taking the average of the products of the three estimating formulas listed under *first trust deed (TD) determination (e).*

6 Next, the construction cost is estimated, as summarized in Table 1.7, and the figure for *total construction cost* is entered *(f).*

7 The cost of the cleared land, ready to build, is entered, including off-site utility cost *(g).*

8 All other development costs are added, including architectural, engineering, and financing costs *(h)* based on the assumed first TD in *(e)* and on a 6-month construction period. Adding the cost of furniture, this leads to the figure of *total development cost (i).*

Table 1.7 Construction Costs of 250 Dwelling Units

Cost		Area (ft²)	Cost per Square Foot	At $9.25/ft²	At $10/ft²
Basic cost per rentable square foot		169,000		$1,563,250	$1,690,000
Added costs per rentable square foot					
Concrete garage or parking structure					
Detached garages (200 ft² × 345 spaces)		69,000	$ 2.50	187,500	same
Open parking and driveways (150 × 345)		51,750	0.25	14,062	same
Recreational structures		2,000	20.00	40,000	same
Laundries		1,000	10.00	10,000	same
On-site utilities (200/unit)				50,000	same
Exterior common areas					
Land and acres	485,600				
Less building	(99,400)				
Recreation building	(1,500)				
Parking	(75,000)				
Driveways	(56,250)				
Green area	116,400	116,400	1.25	145,512	same
				2,010,324	2,137,074
General Contractor fee: general conditions, overhead and profit, 8%				174,810	185,832
(f) Total construction cost				$2,185,134	$2,322,906

Table 1.8 Project Cost Analysis for 250 Dwelling Units

	Cost	Low Range	High Range
(g)	*Land, including offsite costs*	$ 578,476	$ 578,476
	Construction, see Table 1.7	2,185,134	2,322,906
	Architecture and engineering, 3%	65,554	69,687
	Advertising and promotion	42,715	42,715
	Fees and contingencies, 3%	65,554	69,687
(h)	*Financing costs*		
	Loan fees: assume 2.5 points	58,852	58,852
	Interest during construction	61,204	61,204
	Furniture for 165 units	144,500	144,500
(i)	*Total development cost*	3,201,989	3,348,027
	Developer's profit, 10%	355,777	372,003
		3,557,776	3,720,030
	Sales commission, 2.5%	91,224	95,385
(j)	*Total project value*	3,648,990	3,815,410
	Feasibility tests		
(k)	Debt service ratio, 559,380/223,639 = 1.5 = (total annual cash revenues − annual mortgage payment)		
(l)	Break-even occupancy, 73.5%		
(m)	Gross income multiplier: *j/b*	7.1	7.4
(n)	Overall capitalization rate: *c/j*	8.3	7.9

9 Adding to the development cost a 10% profit margin for the developer, plus a sales commission that will accrue if the project is offered for sale on the market, the *total project value* is determined *(j)*. In the example selected, a low and a high range were assumed for each item in the development cost schedule.

10 The ratios used in the feasibility tests determine whether the rate of return is satisfactory for this kind of investment, whether there is a safe margin between cash receipts and the payment to be made on the mortgage *(k)*, and the minimum rate of occupancy at which the income will offset the project expenses *(l)*.

An additional analysis can be made to incorporate the tax benefits in the total rate of return. Taxable income in this case would be a loss in the first year, since the additional cost figures for depreciation and for the interest portion of the mortgage payment can be deducted from net annual income. According to the tax bracket of the investor, this tax loss can be deducted from the individual's taxable income, which results in a certain figure of tax savings. These savings are now added to the spendable return on investment *(d)*. For further accuracy, the equity portion of the annual mortgage payment can also be added to the spendable return, since the owner's equity in the property increases with every payment. Thus the total rate of return is calculated as follows:

$$\frac{\text{Spendable return} + \text{tax savings} + \text{equity buildup}}{\text{cash down payment}}$$

Tables 1.6 to 1.8 illustrate these principles with data for a typical project.

Mortgage Payments. Most real estate loans are repaid in equal monthly installments payable over the term of the loan. Some loans, however, are due before the end of the term. The last payment, which includes the entire outstanding balance, is called a *balloon payment*.

The equal monthly mortgage payment consists of two shares. One is accounted toward the amortization of the loan balance (principal), and the other represents the cost of the borrowed money (interest). At the beginning of the loan the interest share is very large, since it depends on the amount of outstanding loan balance. As the interest portion becomes smaller with each consecutive payment, the principal portion increases. Toward the end of the term, the monthly installments consist almost entirely of the principal part, and the loan balance is therefore amortized at an accelerated rate.

Monthly payments on a mortgage loan of a given amount, term, and interest rate can be found in amortization tables. The breakdown into principal and interest requires complex calculations. However convenient computer programs are available to quickly determine this ratio.

Municipal and Government Financing: Funding Techniques

The main form of revenue of municipal budgets is general property taxes. This constant inflow of cash stands against a great variation in expenditures, caused by the periodic need for large-scale constructions such as freeways, sewer systems, and new civic centers. To meet these extra cash requirements, the city must borrow additional funds, which it does by issuing municipal bonds of four types.

General obligation bonds, which are secured by a pledge that the full faith and credit of the municipality are used to pay them off. The property tax money is used to pay back these bonds, and since the risk factor is low, this type of paper bears a low interest rate.

Mortgage bonds are secured by a mortgage on the project financed. They are most commonly used to buy or build utilities, and their interest rate is higher than that of general obligation bonds.

Revenue bonds are paid back out of the revenues produced by the project financed. Typically, these projects include toll bridges, expressways, and parking structures. As security, the municipality agrees to set charges high enough to pay back the bond issue, and because of these guaranteed provisions, this type of bond has a good reputation.

Special assessment bonds are also not paid back out of tax funds but through a special charge to the people who benefit from the improvement financed. If, for instance, neighborhood streets are paved and storm drains are installed, a special assessment is made on all properties along the streets affected, because it is assumed that these residents will receive most of the benefits.

Interest rates on municipal bonds are regulated by the federal government, which applies a system of credit ratings to every city. The government also subsidizes these bond issues indirectly by granting to the buyers of municipal bonds tax exemption for the income derived from interest earned.

Taxes. The basic source of tax money is either the annual income of individuals and organizations or their wealth, the greatest taxable portion of which consists of real estate. The two principles used to guarantee the citizens' equal and fair share of the tax burden are their degree of ability to pay and their share in the benefits from things financed with tax money. Highway taxes exemplify the application of the latter principle.

The taxation policies of municipalities are regulated and controlled by state governments, which restrict them as to the types of tax levied, tax increases, conditions, and so on. About 80% of municipal tax revenues comes out of *property taxation*. Another form of municipal tax is the *sales tax*. Foods and necessities are usually exempted in the cities charging sales taxes because low-income people spend a much larger amount of their income on these goods.

A special form of income tax, often called *payroll tax,* can be charged by the municipality. This tax consists of a percentage of the amount shown on the payroll rather than of a percentage of net income. In contrast to the sales tax, the payroll tax forces people working in the city but living in the suburbs outside city boundaries to contribute to the city budget.

Business taxes, charged by the city to businesses that require health and safety inspections, are used mainly to pay for these inspections. Taxes on restaurant licenses are an example of a business tax. Other less frequent business taxes may include cigarette taxes, hotel room taxes, and admission fee taxes.

Attempts to reform tax systems and to create new forms of taxation are made periodically. The proposal most often mentioned in this context is the elimination of property taxation, which is always a matter of general controversy. So far, however, no substitute for property taxation has been found that satisfies everyone.

6 ENVIRONMENTAL PLANNING

History and Theory

The earliest known systems of urban design were based on patterns related to one of three areas: agriculture, defense, and religion. Forms developed out of the geometry of field irrigation patterns became the gridiron systems used by Egyptians, Greeks, and Romans alike. Defense systems generated radiocentric patterns, such as the ones found in most medieval towns in Europe. Religious considerations led to geometrical patterns aligned with the cardinal directions, which usually incorporated a main axis used for ceremonial purposes. Cities in pre-Columbian America, such as Monte Alban in Mexico, are examples of this pattern.

The size of early cities was usually limited by restrictions on supplies of food and water and by santiary considerations. The Romans were the first to make significant advances in urban technology by introducing aqueducts, which made cities independent of local sources of water. This, and the development of sewer systems, made possible the growth of Imperial Rome, which reached a population of exceeding 250,000.

Later the typical town expressed a major concern with defense, and each one was vital in the patchwork of small sovereignties engaged in the periodic warfare that was endemic in medieval Europe. The towns, constructed around a castle or a monastery, were designed for a certain size (usually not more than 50,000 inhabitants). The surrounding defense systems made further

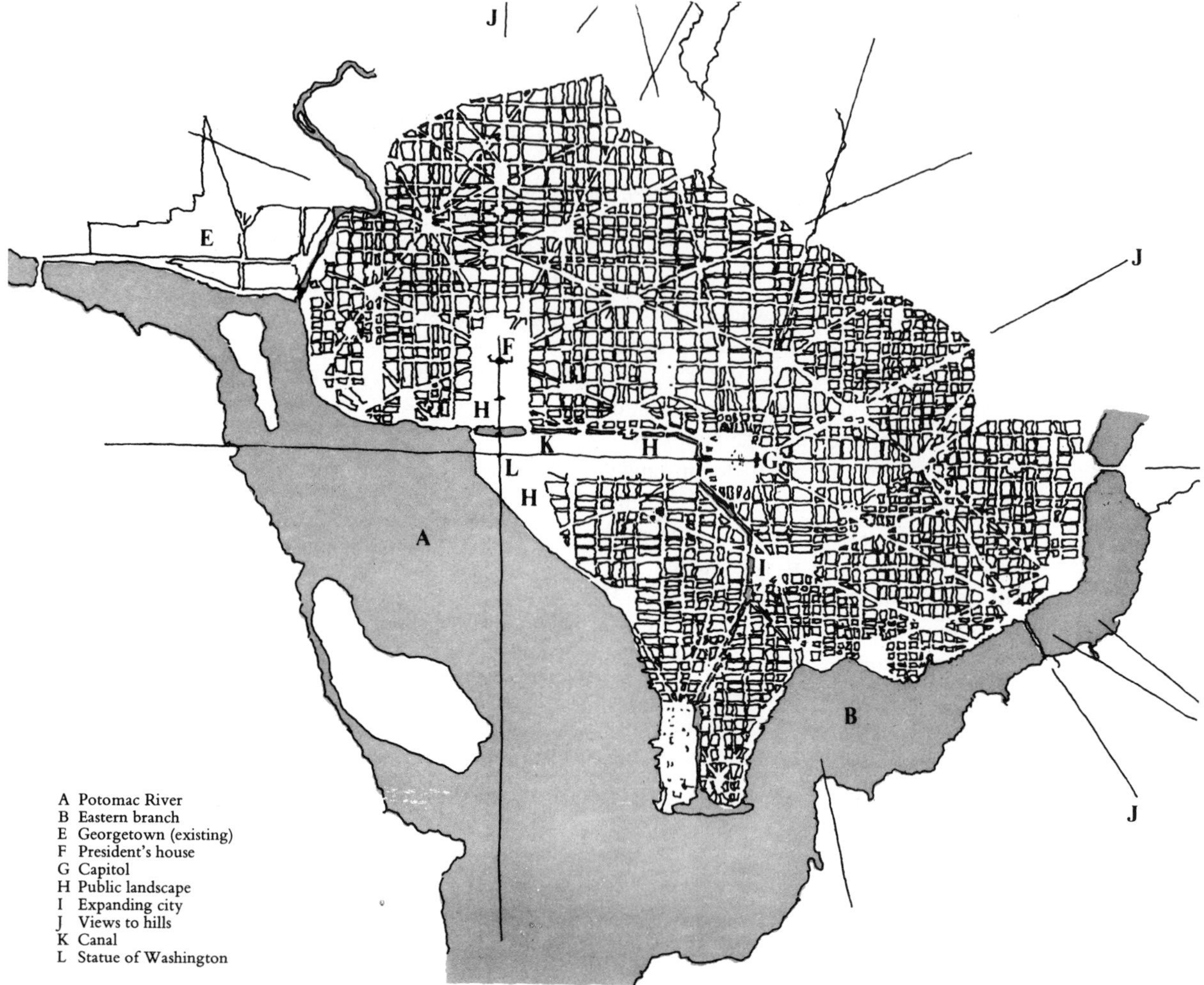

Figure 1.66 L'Enfant's plan for Washington, D.C. *Source*. Geoffrey and Susan Jellicoe, *The Landscape of Man*, Viking Press-Studio Book, 1975.

growth impossible, and for surplus population new towns had to be founded.

The revival of the sciences during the Renaissance brought new theoretical interest into urban design. Concepts for ideal cities were developed by Leon Alberti and Leonardo da Vinci based on radiating stars. Leonardo's plans showed elaborate systems for sanitation, circulation, and defense. Some of these ideas developed in the Renaissance were executed in the following age of the Baroque. Paris is full of examples with its radiating squares, such as the Concorde and the Étoile, and its great boulevards, which were created as axes of symmetry.

The Industrial Revolution, which changed every aspect of social life in the Western world in the nineteenth century, also found its expression in new urban concepts. Urban living conditions declined greatly in the beginning because of the migration of farm workers to the new centers of production. The British were the first to design new living quarters for factory workers. The group known as the "Utopians," who identified with Robert Owen, designed new model neighborhoods incorporating public parks and private gardens into the system of attached housing. Port Sunlight, near Liverpool, is an example of this work.

Early in the twentieth century, a number of theoretical city models were developed. Among them were Sant' Elia's New City, a remarkable work of graphic art, the Linear City, proposed in Spain by Soria y Mata, and the Cité Industrielle of Tony Garnier.

The oldest large-scale urban design in the United States was the plan for the federal capital, which had its roots in the baroque architecture of Paris. Designed by Pierre Charles l'Enfant, it evinces, like its model, a gridiron system of streets broken up through radial boulevards, which meet at the centers of the city. In

---

The earliest traces of cities are found to date from about five thousand years ago, a period representing only $\frac{1}{2}$ to 1 per cent of man's time on Earth. Still, five thousand years is a goodly stretch, and during it, a powerful urban mystique has been developed. The City is the birthplace of culture ; the City is the cross roads of commerce ; the City is adventure, excitement, variety, opportunity, stimulation. For five thousand years this has been the urban image,—for the most part a true one. And for five thousand years the peasant, the farmer, the hunter and the plainsman have gravitated towards the city, with its bright lights, its full coffers and its siren daughters.

It is only in the last fifty years or so that the image has turned untrue, first as a disillusionment and now as an outright fraud. One by one the attractions of the city have gone bad, until each has begun to resemble its opposite more than itself. The big city sophisticate, the quick-witted denizen of penthouses, cafés and cocktail parties, is now more likely to be a member of the dull-eyed hordes shuffling their way into the subway or standing in long lines to see a movie. Diamond Jim, the big spender, is now more often an out-of-town buyer being entertained by an eager salesman on an expense account, while the really, *really* rich are off on their ranches in Venezuela, their villas in Venice or their hideaways in Las Vegas. And of course the richest of them all lives nowhere at all, or rather anywhere : he has a palatial yacht, with its own airplane on deck. The real glamor image is one step ahead of the jet set. The city slicker is badly out-of-date.

Source. Eugene Raskin, *Sequel to Cities*, Bloch Publishing Company, 1969.

contrast to Paris, however, the generously planned open spaces are lacking human scale. They create a feeling of monumentality, but they are not designed to be used by citizens for play and relaxation.

At the Columbian exhibition of 1893 in Chicago, the architect Daniel Burnham started a new school of city planning known as the City Beautiful Era. A sense of classic grandeur was characteristic of the movement, and many domed city halls stem from this period.

Great European theoreticians in urban design at the turn of the century included Camillo Sitte in Vienna and Patrick Geddes in Scotland. The most influential of all, however, was Ebenezer Howard of England with his concept of the Garden City. Howard was an economist, and his great merit was to define in precise models the interrelationship of location and land use based on the variables of transportation cost and intensity of land utilization. To eliminate speculation and to assure the best possible land use pattern (i.e., to combine the advantages of town and country living) his model implied that all land was owned by the community. Garden City consisted of a radial plan with the center reserved for the administrative function. Next were rings of commercial facilities, housing, manufacturing at the outskirts, and a belt of agricultural land beyond that, large enough to supply the city with food.

Howard published his ideas in 1898, in his book *Tomorrow*. Two new towns, both located outside London, were actually built after his Garden City model—Letchworth in 1902, and Welwyn in 1920. These two projects demonstrated the weakest point of his concept. Designed according to Howard's plan for a population of 30,000, these towns were not big enough centers of gravity to develop their own economic and social base. They became satellites to London, serving mainly as bedroom cities.

In 1929 a new concept was developed in the United States: the "superblock" of Radburn, New Jersey. Designed by Clarence Stein and Henry Wright, this plan was an attempt to combine the Garden City idea with a circulation system based exclusively on the automobile. Radburn might have been America's first modern "new town" had its development not been arrested by the Depression. Radburn is the world's first community designed for the motor age. You see its influence in every new settlement where it is possible to allow children to play outdoors without fear that they will be run over by an automobile. Although incomplete, Radburn remains a happy community, an island of tranquility in a sea of chaotic urban sprawl.

The essence of Radburn's livability is not only that combustion engines are separated from human flesh, that there are motorways and walkways. Nor is it the common green and private yards that make Radburn a "garden city" despite its relative compactness. It has a density of about 20 persons per acre, and there is never a long walk to school, to the store, or to community affairs. In every detail of Radburn's design, the aim is to make the most economical use not of the land, but of people—protecting them from the abrasive effects of noise, poisoned air, needless tensions, fears, and alienation. Stein's ingenious plan proved that this goal can be achieved without any sacrifice of technically advanced living. Cars are parked in front of every house. There are electric refrigerators, dehumidifiers, knife sharpeners, and television sets. And yet machines do not dominate. The place is, as Lewis Mumford said, "deeply human."

Stein's designs grew out of an approach to urbanization—indeed, a concept of people's place on earth—that was diametrically opposed to the design philosophy of what is known as the Modern movement, the architecture and urban design of the Bauhaus and of Le Corbusier.

GARDEN CITY

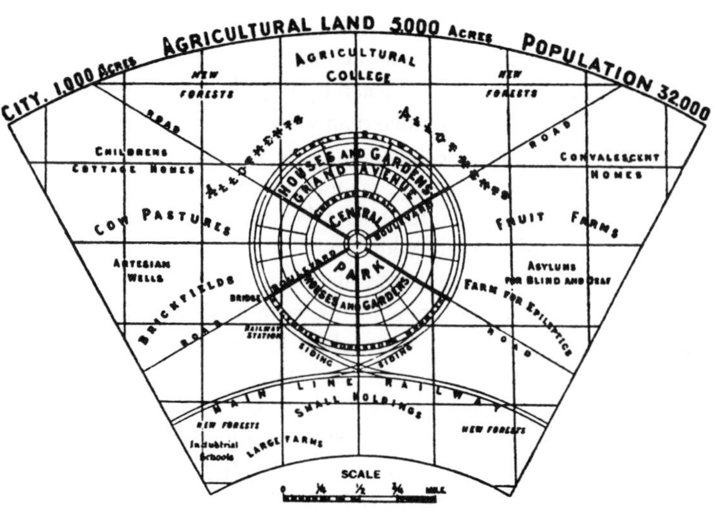

GARDEN CITY AND RURAL BELT

Figure 1.67 Ebenezer Howard's Garden City. *Source*. Joseph de Chiara and Lee Koppelman, *Planning Design Criteria*, Van Nostrand Reinhold, 1968.

Ebenezer Howard put forth his concept of a garden city in a book entitled **Tomorrow: A Peaceful Path to Real Reform** in 1898. The basic goal was to combine the advantages of town life with that of the country. He advocated the building of "towns designed for healthy living and industry; of a size that makes possible a full measure of social life, but not larger; surrounded by a rural belt; the whole of the land being in public ownership, or held in trust for the community."

SOURCE: Ebenezer Howard, Garden Cities of Tomorrow—1946, Faber & Faber—London

Figure 1.68 Radburn, New Jersey, 1928. *Source*. Joseph de Chiara and Lee Koppelman, *Planning Design Criteria*, Van Nostrand Reinhold, 1968.

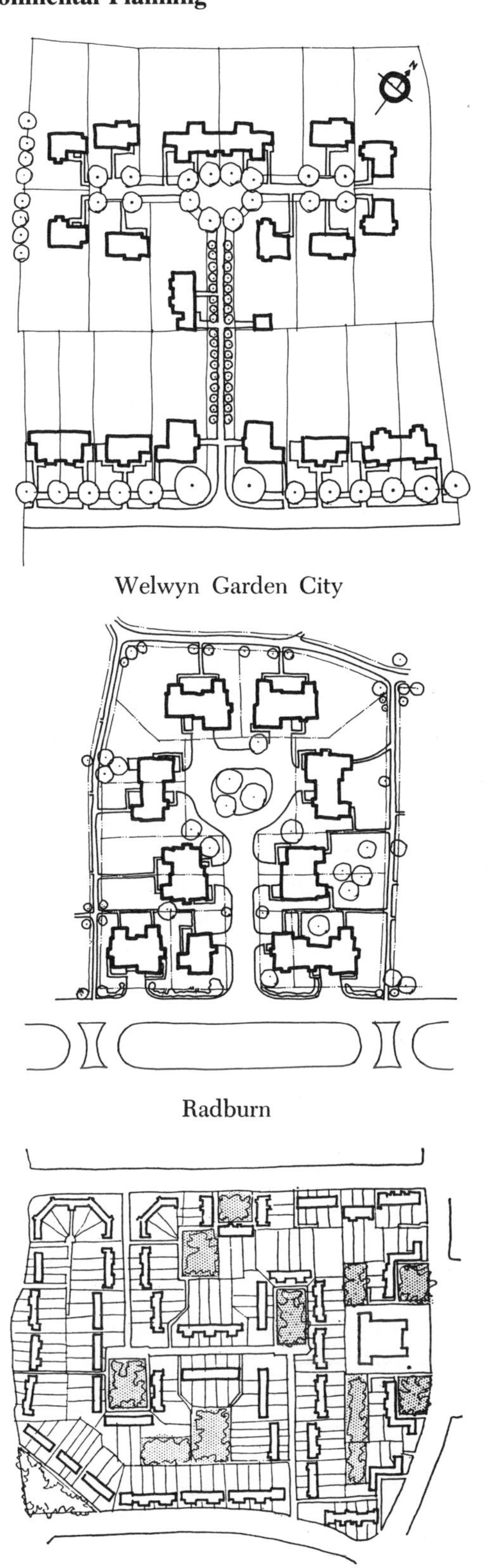

Figure 1.69 Three cul-de-sac arrangements. *Source*. Joseph de Chiara and Lee Koppelman, *Planning Design Criteria*, Van Nostrand Reinhold, 1968.

Le Corbusier produced many models of urban design, such as the Plan Voisin for Paris, several proposals for Algiers, his theoretical concepts of the Radiant City, and the Contemporary Town. His executed plans for Chandigarh, India, amplified all these ideas and found their greatest echo in the South American urban design of Brasilia (Oscar Niemeyer).

Frank Lloyd Wright's contribution to the theory of city planning consisted of two extreme projects: the Broadacre City, which proposed 1 acre of land for every household; and his vertical city in the form of a mile-high skyscraper.

Recent development concepts in residential housing include "planned unit development" (PUD), which is in a sense a progression from the Radburn idea. Individual homes are clustered along access roads, which eliminate the front and side yards. Private backyards usually are reduced to a patio, and the open space between the building clusters is used and owned jointly by the community. This space often includes parks and facilities for active recreation that would be inaccessible to most individuals in a conventional housing subdivision.

The PUD principle was used in the design of two American new towns already mentioned: Reston and Columbia. Both new towns are considered to be successful ventures today, financially as well as sociologically.

Reston was begun in 1962 and has today a population of 25,000, with an independent economic base consisting of 100 primary industries employing 2500 persons and a great variety of service industries. Columbia was begun in 1964. It features a spatial village organization with neighborhoods, which are organized in housing clusters. The planning process represented a truly multidisciplinary approach, which was headed by architect James Rouse.

What Is Proper Housing?

Despite worldwide concern about housing, we lack a definition of "proper housing." There are two basic causes of this confusion. The first involves the notion of proper standards, their significance, and the laws that would impose them.

Obviously, we must both stress the need for standards and clarify what the standards are. Our obligation, however, is to help people who are struggling to reach these standards, and if they cannot reach them overnight we must help them reach the goals in stages. Our policies should not be aimed primarily at determining what should be stopped, as often happens. Rather, we should define the goals and establish ways of achieving them.

The second source of confusion involves the definition of the complete house. There is a tendency to limit the term to the area covered by the house itself; this may be correct theoretically, but it is usually incorrect practically. The house is one spatial unit, but it is not independent, since its function and quality depend on the house group of which it is a part as well as on its neighborhood and city.

New Towns. The so-called new town concept may have passed its zenith. Land has become too scarce and development costs too expensive to make the creation of new towns feasible, therefore attractive enough for investment by private builders. An ideal new town covers approximately 5000 acres, houses about 60,000 people, and is within a half-hour of a major metropolitan area. There are a limited number of places available that could accommodate these conditions, especially since about 1000 houses a year would have to be sold to break even, according to today's economics of large community developers.

In other countries most new towns are developed as political and social institutions and most people are forced to relocate. In America, most federal projects have failed because of improper marketing and unrealistic financing. However several private developments were successful; Rancho Bernardo in San Diego, Irvine and Laguna Miguel in Orange County, California, and, of course, Reston and Columbia, among others. In principle, new towns have to be sold as a village-life concept to attract city dwellers, and every attempt should be made to avoid a city atmosphere. At this point we must ask the question that Constantinos Doxiadis asked in his book *Action—for Human Settlements*: What is proper housing?

The Neighborhood. One of the basic concepts in urban design, the neighborhood, consists of a collection of households with common interests, goals, and needs. These common denominators, which brought people together to form a particular neighborhood, were often based on national and racial backgrounds, which led to the development of so-called ethnic neighborhoods. But in some neighborhoods, the unifying element is the common economic level or social status of its residents (class distinction); this is particularly true for the upper middle class.

The first theoretical work on the concept of neighborhood was published by Clarence A. Perry in 1929. The size of the neighborhood in the Perry plan is defined by the elementary school, which requires a certain number of families and leads to the following standard figures:

Capacity of elementary school	1000–1200 pupils
Population of neighborhood	5000–6000
Average density	10 single-family houses per acre
Acreage covered	160 acres
Maximum distance to elementary school	1/4 mile
Amount of recreational land	10%

The elementary school in the Perry plan not only determined the size of the neighborhood, it was also thought to be a community center where neighbors assembled to decide on joint efforts of mutual concern.

Basic principles defined in the Perry plan have been applied in many urban planning projects. The original plan, however, is a very rigid concept that ignores the numerous spatial relationships that a family may develop outside the neighborhood. Thus it serves best as a theoretical model for understanding the planning elements involved in a neighborhood. If implemented, it demonstrates the same shortcomings exhibited by other designs based on new theories, such as the Radburn superblock, or Le Corbusier's housing unit in Marseilles.

Housing Patterns

The basic demographic unit in housing is the household, which conventionally consists of one family, although it may also be formed by a single individual, by single parents, childless couples, or by two or more roommates. Households other than families are often referred to as "incomplete households." In certain central urban districts, the "incompletes" outnumber the family households.

The physical unit that accommodates a household is referred to as a dwelling unit. Dwelling units can be assembled in a variety of building types, each corresponding to certain conditions relating to density, land values, and socioeconomic factors. The following building types are found most frequently:

1 *Single-Family House.* Once the most common housing form in America, now often replaced by apartments and condominiums to achieve economies of space and maintenance.
2 *Duplex, Triplex, Fourplex.* The next step to increase economy by retaining as much privacy as possible.
3 *Clusters.* A group of five to ten attached dwelling units, most often found in planned unit developments with joint ownership of recreational facilities.
4 *Row House.* A historic concept developed mainly in post-industrial England, which leads to a certain monotony. Row house patterns sometimes look pleasant from a distance, as in the south of San

Francisco (Daly City), but the uniformity of homes and backyards deprives residents of the needed environmental stimulus.

5 *Walkup Apartment*. Popular and economical form of medium-density living. Contact with the ground and intimate scale are still maintained. This building type, if used for higher densities, lacks privacy and unobstructed views. Midrise and highrise apartments: privacy, views, and maximum security are the advantages of this building type. It has the highest construction cost and is feasible only in areas with maximum land values. Loss of contact with the ground and with the outside climate are disadvantages.

Single-family houses or low-density condominiums can be arranged in different patterns of vehicular access:

1 *Street Front Pattern*. The most commonly used form. Pedestrian and vehicular access from the same street. Formerly chosen because of its simplicity and because it allows residents to participate in street life this form is often undesirable, given today's traffic.

2 *Finger Pattern*. Short rows along side streets placed in a 90° angle to main street. This reduces the length of the big access street and keeps traffic further away from residents, offering the possibility of separate pedestrian ways between backyards.

3 *Court Pattern*. Popular in historic England. The common space between a group of homes encouraged intimate contact. Today, if homes have individual garages, the concept's intimate quality is lost.

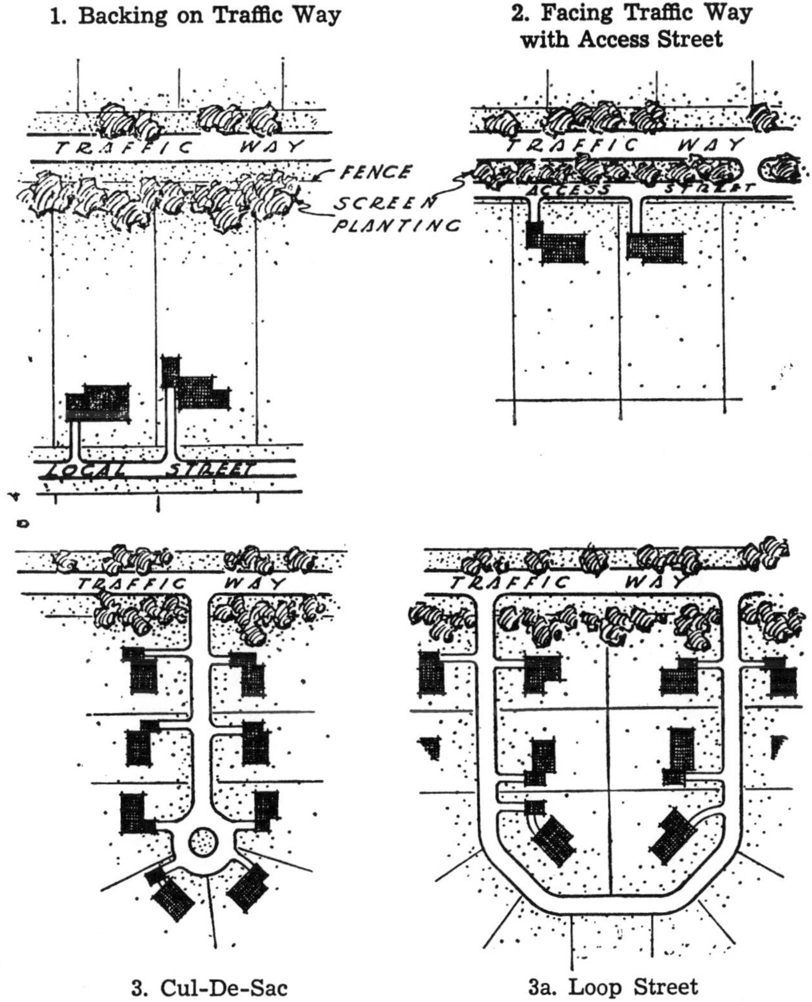

Figure 1.70 Housing patterns. *Source*. *The Community Builders' Handbook*, 1954 Members' Edition, Urban Land Institute.

4 *Cluster Pattern*. A concept not clearly defined in terms of access. A group of attached or semidetached houses with private open space as well as common green. Clusters may be grouped around cul-de-sacs or along winding roads; either individual garages or community parking structures may be featured.
5 *Point Pattern*. Used in ranch-type subdivisions with large individual parcels or for highrise apartment buildings in northern hemispheres, where the low angle of solar radiation demands ample spacing of towers.

The basic patterns always must be modified according to topography, views, surrounding structures, trees, solar and wind orientation, and similar factors. A larger housing community usually works best with a combination of these concepts.

Urban Development

Analogous to housing patterns, the organization of traffic also defines urban patterns on a large scale. Basic forms of growth can be identified in every city. Such forms include the following:

1 *Sheet*. Few major centers or axes can be identified; Los Angeles is a good example.
2 *Linear*. A string of communities along one major thoroughfare, like the cities along the eastern seaboard.
3 *Ring*. A traffic pattern, like the one that developed around San Francisco Bay.
4 *Grid*. Refers to patterns on a smaller scale; this is the organizing principle of most cities in the United States.
5 *Core*. A pattern found in every metropolitan area. Business and social activities are concentrated in a downtown area of maximum density.
6 *Star*. Develops when major thoroughfares radiate from the central business district.
7 *Constellation*. A number of cores, connected by an asymmetric net of linear arteries, is the typical form of this pattern. Heavily industrialized areas usually show this type of development.
8 *Satellite*. One center in a constellation is the city, and the others are suburbs or bedroom towns with no independent industries.

Often the type of transportation system available was the main determinant for the pattern of urban growth. Both the grid and the sheet, for example, are related to the automobile, whereas cities with a circulation of predominantly mass transit systems are more likely to develop massive core and satellite patterns. Since the latter forms are so closely related to transportation, they are often not conducive to a change in the circulation system. Los Angeles, for instance, with its sheet pattern, seems to make any form of efficient mass transit impossible. On the other hand, it seems to be equally difficult to accommodate the ever-increasing vehicular traffic in cities with a dominant core pattern, which developed in the days of railroads and tramways.

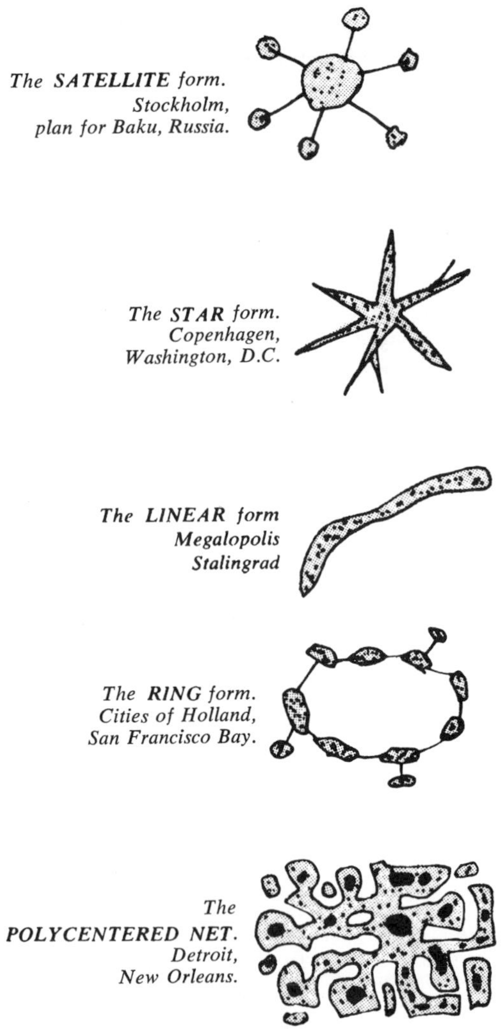

Figure 1.71 *Source*. Paul D. Spreiregen, *Urban Design: The Architecture of Towns and Cities*, McGraw-Hill Book Company, 1965.

The Cost of Sprawl

Local officials are facing increasingly difficult decisions about how land should be used and how much and what type of development should be allowed. They are receiving proposals for new and sometimes unfamiliar types of development: clustered single-family housing, town houses, walkup apartments, and highrise apartments are appearing in cities, even out to the urban fringe. At the same time, there is increased attention to the impacts of new development on the community. This concern has focused mainly on the economic effects of developments—whether the added tax base would compensate for the added costs imposed on the community by the new residents. In recent years these economic considerations have been joined by environmental and other concerns. What will the development do to air pollution, water pollution, wildlife, and open space? What is the impact of development on energy consumption? On water consumption? How will the development affect the lives of the people who live in it? Those who live near it?

There has been no recent effort to assess all the economic costs associated with different types of development; nor until now has there been a document that attempted to integrate the various economic, environmental, natural resource, and social costs of these developments. *The Costs of Sprawl,* a detailed cost analysis prepared in 1974 by the Real Estate Research Corporation (RERC) for several governmental agencies, (Council on Environmental Quality, Housing and Urban Development, Environmental Protection Agency) seeks to help fill this information void that has made local decision making so difficult. The study attempts to summarize what is known about the different costs as they apply to different neighborhood types and to different community development patterns, and it indicates whether the costs are incurred publicly or privately. Table 1.9 lists the types of cost that have been included. These are not the only costs associated with residential development, but they are among the most important ones.

Table 1.9 Types of Cost Analyzed

Economic Costs (capital and operating)	Environmental Effects
Residential (capital only)	Air pollution
Open space/recreation	Water pollution, erosion
Schools	Noise
Streets and roads	Vegetation and wildlife
Utilities (sewer, water, storm drainage, gas, electric, telephone)	Visual effects
	Water and energy consumption
Public facilities and services	**Personal Effects**
Police, fire, solid waste, collection, library, health care, churches, general government	Use of discretionary time
	Psychic costs
	Travel time
	Traffice accidents
Land	Crime

Source. The Cost of Sprawl, Real Estate Research Corporation, 1974.

The Study Method. The study is an analysis of prototype development patterns, not of actual developments, although many of the data were obtained from empirical studies undertaken by others. The investigators assumed typical site conditions and an absence of any existing infrastructure (roads, sewers, etc.) at the site; then, using standard unit cost figures, they estimated the costs of building alternative types of development.

The various costs were first estimated for different neighborhood types, each neighborhood being composed of 1000 dwelling units of one of the following types:

- Single-family homes, conventionally located.
- Single-family homes, clustered.
- Town houses.
- Walkup apartments (2 stories).
- Highrise apartments (6 stories).

Because many environmental and some economic costs cannot be clearly identified on such a small scale, neighborhoods were aggregated into different communities, containing 10,000 dwelling units apiece (corresponding to a population of 33,000). Six community types were analyzed, and each had a mixture of the five principal neighborhood housing types but differed in the amount of community "planning" (used here to mean a general compactness of development) and in the average development density.

Whereas different neighborhood types were assumed to require different amounts of land for the 1000 dwelling units, all six communities were assumed to contain the same amount of land—6000 acres, with a mix of neighborhood types. The neighborhoods also differed slightly in population, depending on the housing type, whereas all the communities were assumed to contain the same population. The assumption of constant population underlying the community analyses was made to emphasize the differences among community development patterns. The actual populations, of course, could differ quite substantially from those assumed, with corresponding impacts on costs. Table 1.10 at the end of this section summarizes the specific land use, housing, and population characteristics of the different neighborhood types and community development patterns.

The results of the study depend strongly on some of the assumptions underlying these basic cost analyses.

Thus for certain critical parameters (population, acreage developed, etc.), additional analyses were carried out to illustrate the sensitivity of the results to the assumption that was made.

Results of the Analyses. In so complicated a study, it is difficult to summarize the results briefly and in a readily comprehensible form. To provide an overview here, we must avoid most of the details.

Community Analysis. This summary refers to three of the community types analyzed: the "low-density sprawl," the "combination mix," and the "high-density planned" communities. They can be defined as follows:

- *Low-Density Sprawl.* The entire community is made up of single-family homes, 75% sited in a traditional grid pattern and the rest clustered. Neighborhoods are sited in a "leapfrog" pattern with little contiguity. This represents the typical pattern of suburban development.
- *Combination Mix.* This community consists of a housing mix of 20% of each of the five types of dwellings, half located in planned unit developments, half in traditional subdivisions.
- *High-Density Planned.* In this community, housing is composed of 40% highrise apartments, 30% walkup apartments, 20% town houses, and 10% clustered single-family homes. All the dwelling units are clustered together into contiguous neighborhoods, much in the pattern of a high-density "new community."

The following briefly summarizes the study's findings in terms of land use, economic costs, environmental costs, energy and water consumption, and some personal costs.

1 *Land Use.* Although all the communities cover the same area, more than half the land in the high-density planned community remains completely undeveloped, whereas all the land is at least partially developed in the low-density sprawl community. On the other hand, the low-density sprawl community has more land that is improved but vacant, an indication of the amount of leapfrogging that occurs there. "Improved" here means that the land has been provided with at least some infrastructure such as streets and sewers.

Figure 1.72 shows how these communities differ in land use. Although four times as much land is used for residential purposes in the low-density sprawl community as in the high-density planned community, only two-thirds as much is dedicated to public open space. However if backyards, which are also a form of open space, are included, the low-density community has twice the public and private land dedicated to open space as the high-density community; it must be remembered, however, that in the high-density planned community, more than half the land is not developed.

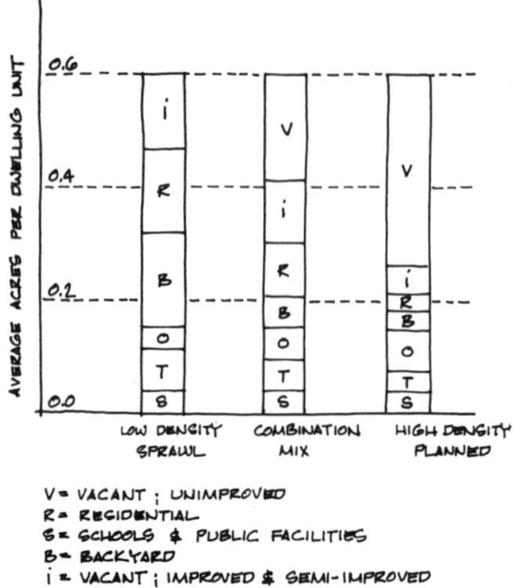

Figure 1.72 Land use.

2 *Economic Costs.* In terms of total investment costs, the high-density planned community is distinctly lower: 21% below the combination mix community and 44% below the low-density sprawl community. Most of these savings result from differences in development density—savings of about 3% of total development costs result from better "planning," whereas savings from increased density amount to 41%. Throughout this study "planning" is used in a very limited sense to mean increased clustering or compactness of development. Good planning, which includes much more than clustering, may result in more significant cost savings than those cited here. The largest cost savings are in construction of residential dwellings, although important savings are attributable to reduced costs for roads and utilities, which are about 55% lower in the high-density than in the low-density community.

Figures 1.73 and 1.74 summarize the abovementioned investment and operating costs for the three communities. The total investment costs do not include costs of the land; these are indicated separately in Figure 1.73. The operating and maintenance costs do not include the cost of maintaining the residential structures (although the operating costs for utilities comprise a substantial portion of this cost), the financing costs for the capital investments that have been made, or the costs of operating automobiles.

Figure 1.73 also shows the difference in investment costs that are borne privately (initially by the developer)

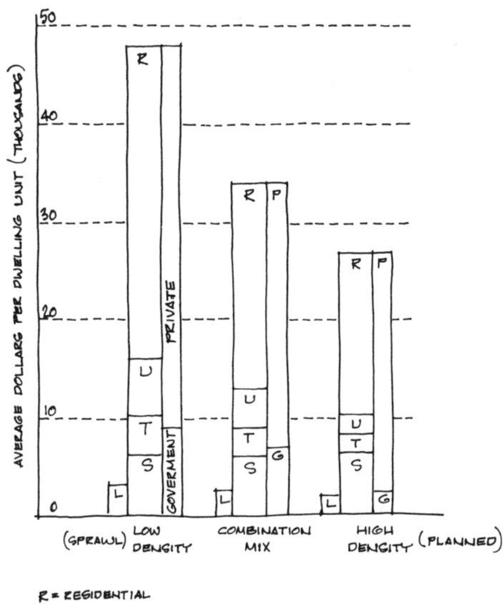

Figure 1.73 Costs of the land.

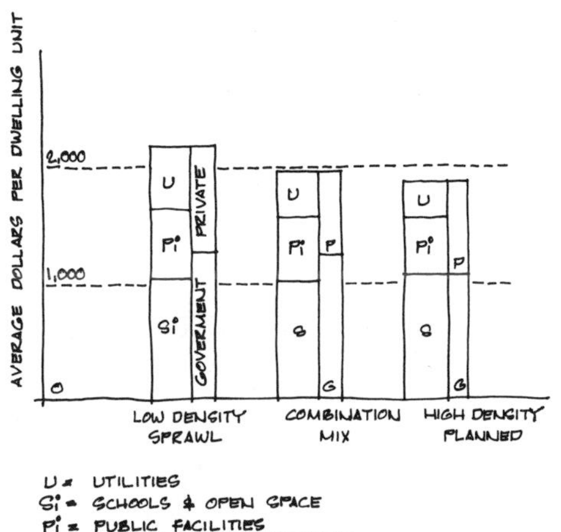

Figure 1.74 Annual operating and maintenance costs.

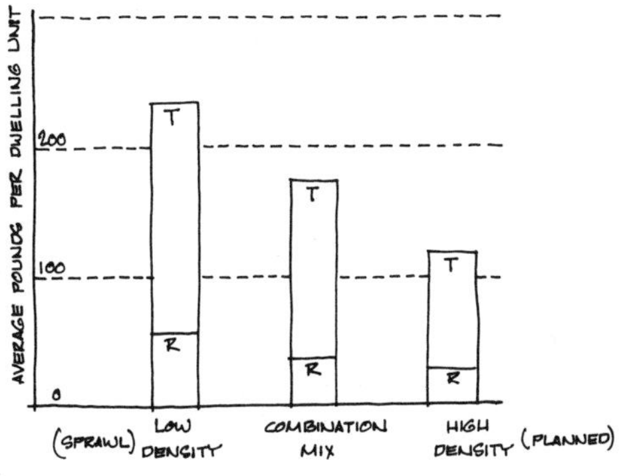

Figure 1.75 Annual air-polluting emissions.

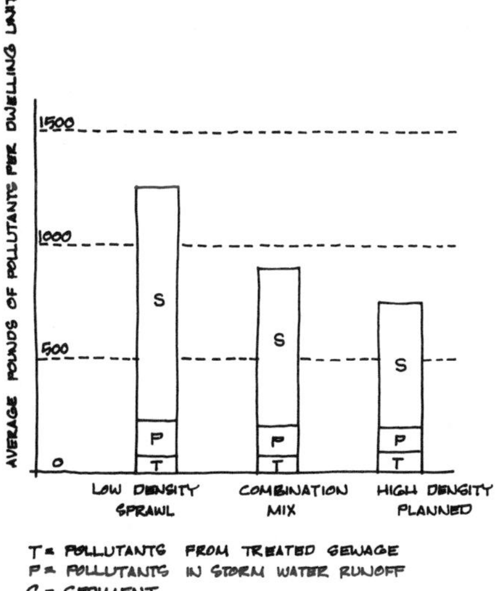

Figure 1.76 Annual water pollution generation.

and publicly. Not only does the high-density planned community cost less to construct, but a lower proportion of the costs is likely to be borne by government.

The difference in operating and maintenance costs is less noticeable than the difference in investment costs because these costs are related more to the population being served than to the pattern of development. However the higher density communities are again somewhat less costly in terms of the total operating and maintenance costs and in the costs paid by government.

3 *Environmental Costs.* Air pollution has two major sources: automobiles and residential heating. Higher density developments require less energy for heating, and higher density and better "planned" communities stimulate less automobile use. Thus the high-density planned community generates about 45% less air pollution than the low-density sprawl community. Although "planning" has no effect on the amount of pollution resulting from residential heating, it can reduce the amount from automobiles by 20 to 30%. Figure 1.75 gives the amounts of air pollution generated by the different communities.

Figure 1.76 indicates a similar pattern of water pollution generated by the different development patterns. Type of development has no effect on the amount of sanitary sewage generated because this is a function of population alone. Sanitary sewage pollutants indicated are those remaining after tertiary treatment of the sewage. With only secondary treatment, which is more common, the volume of pollutants would be increased 5 to 10 times. However development type does affect the important problems of storm water pollution and sediment. The less paved area there is, the less storm water runoff there will be. This is important not only with respect to water pollution problems but also in relation to downstream flooding. More clustered communities have somewhat less pavement than sprawl communities, but again the significant savings come from increasing density.

For both air and water pollution, it is important to note that although the higher density community generates less pollution, its activity is confined to a smaller area, resulting in a higher amount of pollution generated per acre developed.

Planning is the key to eliminating noise problems, preserving valuable wildlife and vegetation, and creating a visually attractive development. For a given developed area, increased density allows the planner greater flexibility in accomplishing these goals. However the increased density does concentrate noise-generating activities and puts added demands on the designer to create aesthetically pleasing developments.

4 *Energy and Water Use.* Energy consumption is determined primarily by residential heating and air conditioning requirements and by automobile use. Heating and air conditioning requirements are related primarily to the type of dwelling unit—denser developments have lower demands than do single-family units. Transportation demands are affected both by the degree of clustering and community planning and by density. "Planning" alone can save nearly 14% of total energy consumed, but "planning" combined with increased density can save up to 44%.

Water consumed in cooking, drinking, bathing, and other indoor activities, is not affected by either planning or density. However water for lawn watering is affected by both. Clustering alone can save 6% of total water consumption, but the high-density planned development can save 35% more than low-density sprawl development. Figures 1.77 and 1.78 indicate the variations in consumption of these two valuable natural resources.

5 *Personal Costs.* Some personal costs were also assessed in the study. These are more difficult to estimate. In general, "planning" and increased density reduce the amount of time that family members spend traveling to work, school, and other destinations, and higher density developments typically take less of the residents' time to clean and maintain. There are likely to be fewer traffic accidents with better planning, but crime

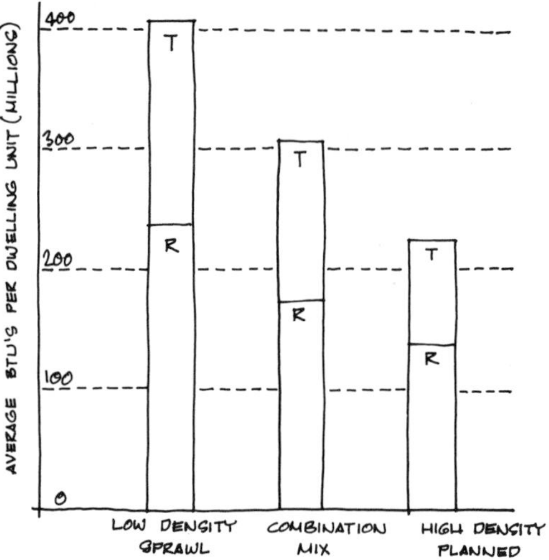

Figure 1.77 Annual energy consumption.

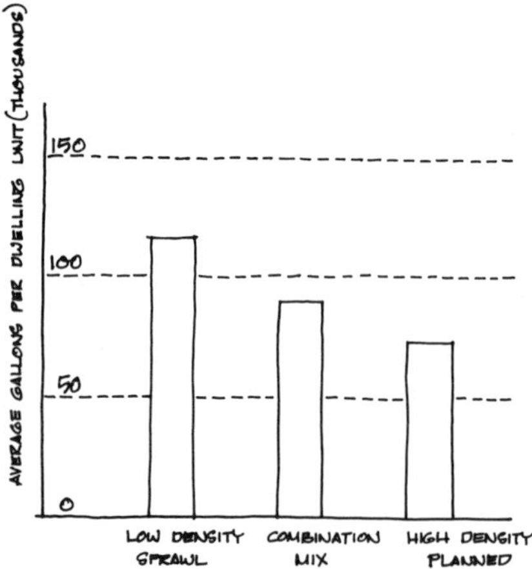

Figure 1.78 Annual water consumption.

may increase with higher densities, as will various psychic costs that are particularly dependent on design and planning details.

These are the costs estimated for the different community development patterns. More details may be found in the summary Tables 1.10 through 1.15, presented in the concluding section.

Neighborhood Analysis. Few officials face a decision about the kind of development pattern that is best for a community of 33,000. Rather, the decisions regard individual subdivision proposals. For these decisions, the neighborhood cost analyses, which pertain to only 1000 units, may be more useful than the community analysis.

Most of the neighborhood costs are similar to the community costs, and the same conclusions—that better "planning" and higher density result in lower economic, environmental, natural resource, and to some extent, personal and social costs—apply to the neighborhood also. Some of these costs, however, are more difficult to identify on the neighborhood level, and some depend to a greater extent on how the neighborhood is integrated with the community. Nevertheless, it is helpful to review the results of some of the neighborhood analyses. Figures 1.79 and 1.80 indicate the investment and operating costs per dwelling unit for the five neighborhood types analyzed. As in the community cost analysis, increased density is less expensive in terms of total costs and even more so in terms of the portion of total costs typically borne by government. Walkup apartments are the least costly type of dwelling unit to construct (considering residential costs only). For streets and roads, utilities, and particularly schools, however, the highrise apartment is less expensive, and these cost savings more than compensate for the higher residential costs. The cost savings associated with higher densities are reduced if the higher density units are assumed to have the same living area or to contain the same population as the lower density units.

Site Analysis. All the results above pertain to the costs of providing a given number of dwelling units. The study also broke down the costs of developing a given parcel of land. In this analysis, the number of dwelling units constructed on the site was found to increase with the higher density neighborhood types. Because there are more dwelling units, total costs associated with development of the site tend to increase with the higher density development patterns, even though the cost per dwelling unit increases.

Total capital costs are highest for highrise apartments, and capital costs borne by government are highest for highrise and town house developments. Operating and maintenance costs are highest for walkup apartments, both in total and with respect to the portion borne by government. (Figures 1.81 and 1.82). The air and water pollution emissions from a given site are also higher for higher density developments.

Conclusion. The results of the study, presented in more detail in Tables 1.10 to 1.15, show a surprising consistency: "planning" to some degree, but higher densities to a much greater extent, result in lower economic costs, environmental costs, natural resource consumption, and some personal costs for a given number of dwelling units. These results do not necessarily hold for the development of a given land parcel. The results are not directly applicable to any specific development, existing or proposed. The features of a particular site or community substantially affect the magnitude of any of

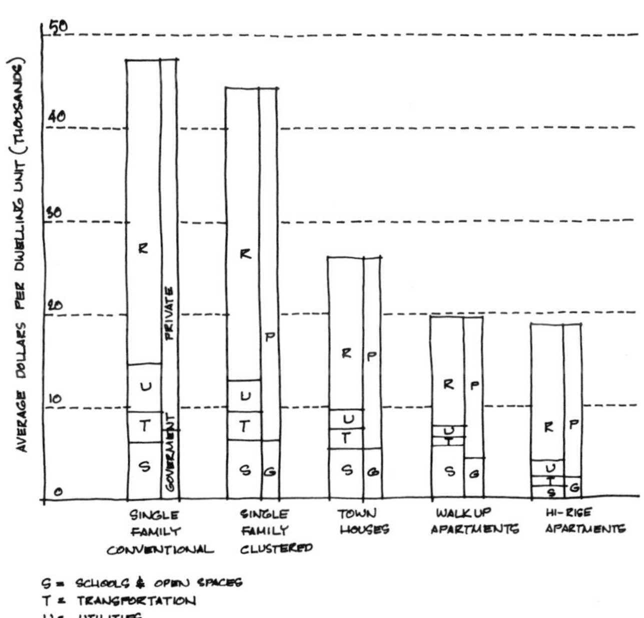

Figure 1.79 Capital costs.

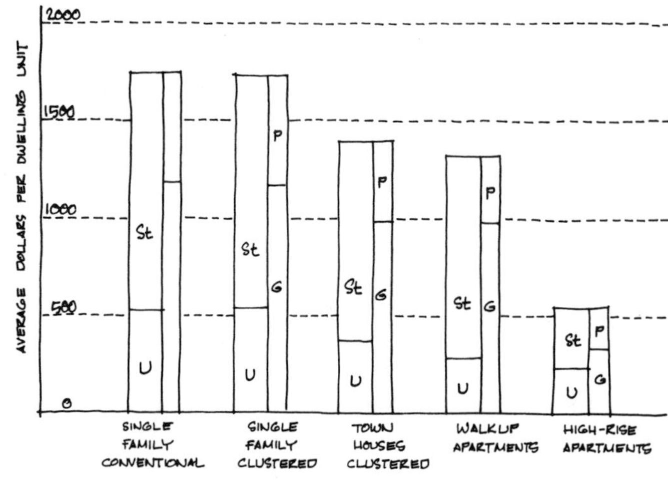

Figure 1.80 Annual operating and maintenance costs.

the costs. Nor should the results be interpreted as recommending one type of development over another: too many costs and benefits have not been included, particularly those associated with questions of personal preferences and the revenues generated by different development types.

However the analyses should provide a better information base relating to the impacts of different development patterns.

Most concerned architects have developed ideas along this line. I studied a system in 1963, and numerous other architects have done the same. The technical problems all can be solved feasibly except for the initial expenses. Several schemes have vitality and great possibilities if further developed and worked out in detail. I shall not repeat the most famous experiments, since they are discussed in books about well-known architects. The most successful solutions are still the contemporary highrise structures, and as Clovis Heimsath mentions in his book *Behavioral Architecture*: "The logic of vertical buildings is based on the simplicity of bypass." All far-out attempts have not been satisfactory physically, and consequently financially. Most have the same flaw—the extreme case would be Soleri's proposals and I agree with John Lobel, of the Pratt Institute, whose opinion, quoted earlier by Heimsath, appears here.

Having learned these lessons, many humanists are now turning to Soleri's cities as solutions. But Soleri's cities compound every problem we know of. These gigantic, concentric, beehive structures will require rigid programmed conformity from their inhabitants in order to function safely. They will require a complexity of technology which may not even be possible, and the level of dependence on technology will imply a rule by the technocrats. A power failure would mean chaos for tens of thousands of trapped residents. Strikes and other antisocial actions and attitudes would have to be strictly outlawed, for they too could quickly lead to mass disruption.

These giant cities are complete and closed systems. For example, there is no room to introduce a new transportation system if an existing one proves obsolete or unworkable. Worst of all is the symmetrical centrality of these designs. Once the center is occupied by an institution (government media, education, etc.), there is no way to replace that institution once it grows old and unresponsive. . . .

I do not doubt the sincerity of Soleri and his supporters. I simply see something very different from what they see when I look at his architecture.

Source. Clovis Heimsath, *Behavioral Architecture*, McGraw-Hill Book Company, 1977.

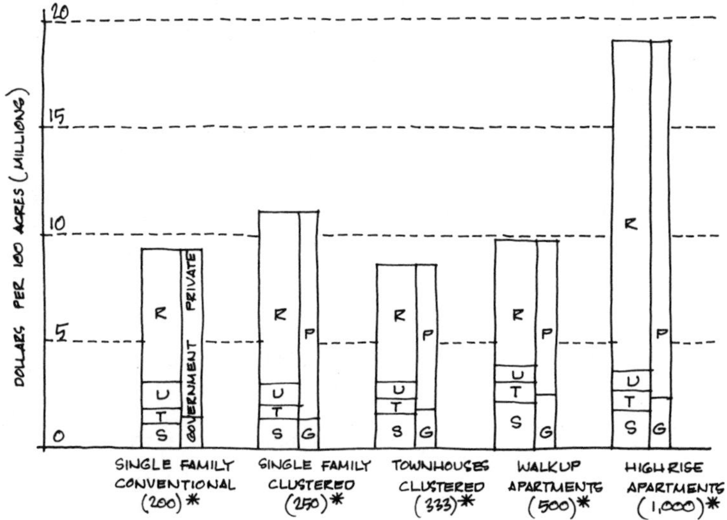

Figure 1.81 Capital costs.

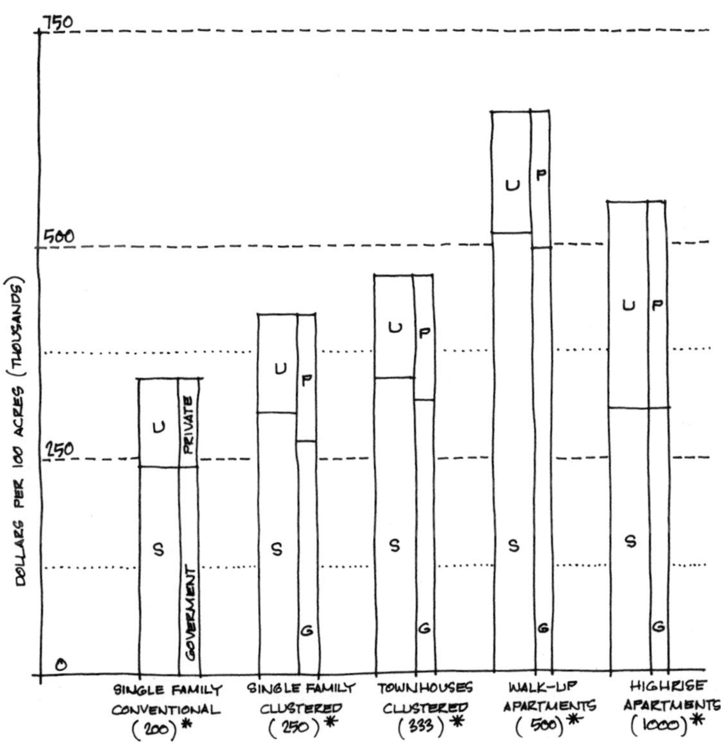

Figure 1.82 Annual operating and maintenance costs.

Table 1.10 Neighborhood and Community Characteristics

NEIGHBORHOOD AND COMMUNITY COST ANALYSIS

	Neighborhood Housing Types					
	A Single-Family Conventional	B Single-Family Clustered	C Townhouses Clustered	D Walk-Up Apartments	E High-Rise Apartments	F Housing Mix (20% Each A-E)
Dwelling Units	1,000	1,000	1,000	1,000	1,000	1,000
Average Floor Area Per Unit (square foot)	1,600	1,600	1,200	1,000	900	1,260
Total Population	3,520	3,520	3,330	3,330	2,825	3,300
Persons per Unit	3.5	3.5	3.3	3.3	2.8	3.3
School Children	1,300	1,300	1,100	1,100	300	1,100
Total Acreage	500	400	300	200	100	300
Residential	330	200	100	66	33	145
Open Space/Recreation	45	90	90	73	32	66
Schools	29	29	26	26	15	26
Churches	5	5	5	5	5	5
Streets and Roads	75	60	45	30	15	45
Vacant	16	16	34	0	0	13
Residential Density						
Units per Gross Acre	2	2.5	3.3	5	10	3.3
Units per Net Residential Acre	3	5.0	10.0	15	30	6.9

	Community Development Patterns					
	I Planned Mix	II Combination Mix (50% PUD, 50% Sprawl)	III Sprawl Mix	IV Low Density Planned	V Low Density Sprawl	VI High Density Planned
Dwelling Units	10,000	10,000	10,000	10,000	10,000	10,000
Housing Types[1/]	20% - Type A 20% - Type B 20% - Type C 20% - Type D 20% - Type E	Same as I.	Same as I.	75% - Type B 25% - Type A	75% - Type A 25% - Type B	10% - Type B 20% - Type C 30% - Type D 40% - Type E
Total Population	33,000	33,000	33,000	33,000	33,000	33,000
School Children	11,000	11,000	11,000	11,000	11,000	11,000
Total Acreage	6,000	6,000	6,000	6,000	6,000	6,000
Residential	1,450	1,450	1,450	2,333	3,000	733
Open Space/Recreation	660	530	400	660	400	660
Schools	260	260	260	260	260	260
Other Public Facilities	140	140	140	140	140	140
Streets and Roads	530	530	530	720	790	380
Vacant, Improved [2/]	152	213	278	206	459	109
Vacant, Semi-Improved [3/]	456	922	1,390	617	951	326
Vacant, Unimproved	2,352	1,955	1,522	1,064	0	3,392

Notes: 1/ Type A - single-family, conventional; Type B - single-family, clustered; Type C - townhouses, clustered; Type D - walk-up apartments; Type E - high-rise apartments.

2/ Includes all roads and utilities.

3/ Includes only arterial roads and trunk utility lines.

Source. The Cost of Sprawl, Real Estate Research Corporation, 1974.

Table 1.11 Community Cost Analysis: Capital Costs

	Community Development Pattern (10,000 Units)											
	I		II		III		IV		V		VI	
	Planned Mix		Combination Mix 50 Percent PUD, 50 Percent Sprawl		Sprawl Mix		Low Density Planned		Low Density Sprawl		High Density Planned	
COST CATEGORY	Cost	Percent of Total Cost	Cost	Percent of Total Cost	Cost	Percent of Total Cost	Cost	Percent of Total Cost	Cost	Percent of Total Cost	Cost	Percent of Total Cost
					(in thousands)							
Open Space/Recreation	$ 2,968 (111% of III)	1%	$ 2,826 (105% of III)	1%	$ 2,684	1%	$ 2,968 (111% of V)	1%	$ 2,684	1%	$ 2,968 (111% of V)	1%
Schools	$ 45,382 (100% of III)	13%	$ 45,382 (100% of III)	12%	$ 45,382	12%	$ 45,382 (100% of V)	9%	$ 45,382	9%	$ 45,382 (100% of V)	16%
Public Facilities	$ 16,216 (99% of III)	5%	$ 16,441 (100% of III)	4%	$ 16,453	4%	$ 16,259 (98% of V)	3%	$ 16,615	3%	$ 16,304 (98% of V)	6%
Transportation - Streets and Roads	$ 27,077 (84% of III)	8%	$ 29,768 (92% of III)	8%	$ 32,353	9%	$ 33,770 (89% of V)	7%	$ 37,965	7%	$ 22,862 (60% of V)	8%
Utilities	$ 33,227 (86% of III)	9%	$ 36,042 (93% of III)	10%	$ 38,684	10%	$ 47,444 (77% of V)	10%	$ 61,974	12%	$ 22,432 (36% of V)	8%
Subtotal	$124,870 (92% of III)	35%	$130,459 (96% of III)	35%	$135,556	36%	$145,823 (89% of V)	30%	$164,620	32%	$109,943 (68% of V)	38%
Residential	$214,172 (100% of III)	60%	$214,172 (100% of III)	58%	$214,172	57%	$318,291 (99% of V)	65%	$320,400	62%	$160,300 (50% of V)	56%
Total Exclusive of Land	$339,042 (97% of III)	95%	$344,631 (99% of III)	94%	$349,728	94%	$464,114 (97% of V)	95%	$485,020	94%	$270,248 (56% of V)	94%
Land (Developed Area and Vacant Improved)	$ 18,491 (80% of III)	5%	$ 23,531 (102% of III)	6%	$ 23,105	6%	$ 25,692 (87% of V)	5%	$ 29,539	6%	$ 16,814 (57% of V)	6%
Total Capital Cost	$357,533 (96% of III)	100%	$368,162 (99% of III)	100%	$372,833	100%	$489,806 (95% of V)	100%	$514,559	100%	$287,062 (56% of V)	100%
Present Value (exclusive of land)												
Present Value at 5%	$270,173		$272,183		$277,261		$367,557		$377,325		$216,502	
Present Value at 10%	$221,431		$221,191		$226,088		$299,528		$302,391		$178,311	
(Comparison of Results at 10%)	(98% of III)		(98% of III)				(99% of V)				(59% of V)	
Incidence of Cost												
Government/Private (%/%)	16%/84%		21%/79%		24%/76%		12%/88%		19%/81%		18%/82%	
Cost to the Household												
Capital Cost/Service Charges/Taxes (%/%/%)	47%/38%/15%		43%/37%/20%		41%/37%/22%		81%/ 7%/12%		75%/ 6%/19%		26%/56%/18%	

Source: Real Estate Research Corporation.

Source. *The Cost of Sprawl*, Real Estate Research Corporation, 1974.

Table 1.12 Community Cost Analysis: Environmental and Personal Effects

	Community Development Pattern (10,000 Units)					
	I Planned Mix	II Combination Mix 50 Percent PUD, 50 Percent Sprawl	III Sprawl Mix	IV Low Density Planned	V Low Density Sprawl	VI High Density Planned
ENVIRONMENTAL EFFECTS						
Air Pollution						
Pollutants from Private Automobiles (CO, HC, NO_x)	70% of emission levels in Community III; differences result from variation in auto use among development patterns.	83% of emission levels in Community III.	CO: 3,628 pounds per day HC: 437 pounds per day NO_x: 427 pounds per day	81% of emission levels in Community V.	CO: 4,040 pounds per day HC: 487 pounds per day NO_x: 475 pounds per day	50% of emission levels in Community V.
Pollutants from Residential Natural Gas Consumption (Particulates, SO_x, CO, HC, NO_x)	100% of emission levels in Community III; differences are a function of housing type, not development pattern.	100% of emission levels in Community III.	Particulates: 104 pounds per day SO_x: 4 pounds per day CO: 2 pounds per day HC: 231 pounds per day NO_x: 693 pounds per day	100% of emission levels in Community V.	Particulates: 143 pounds per day SO_x: 5 pounds per day CO: 3 pounds per day HC: 317 pounds per day NO_x: 951 pounds per day	57% of emission levels in Community V; differences reflect housing mix and variation in energy use by housing type.
Water Pollution and Erosion						
Volume of Sediment from Erosion (average annual)	Slightly greater than III due to land budget variation in developed acreage.	Virtually 100% of III.	4,431 tons per year.	89% of V; difference results from variation in developed acreage.	6,170 tons per year.	60% of V; difference results from variation in developed acreage.
Pollutants from Sewage Effluent (BOD, COD, N, P, S.S., FCB)	No variation by housing type or development pattern. Sewage volume is a function of population, and its resulting pollutants a function of treatment level. Sewage volume is approximately 4.5 billion liters per year.	Same as I.	Same as I.	Same as I.	Same as I.	Same as I.
Pollutants from Storm Run-Off (BOD, COD, N, P, S.S., FCB)	99% of III; small difference results from more paved area (road length) in III.	Same as I.	Total run-off volume is approximately 7.8 billion liters per year.	93% of V; difference results from variation in amount of paved area.	Run-off volume is approximately 9 billion liters per year.	Run-off and its resulting pollutants are the lowest in this community. Volume is approximately 7.1 billion liters per year.
Pollutants from Sanitary Landfill Leachate (BOD, N, P, FCB)	No variation by housing type or development pattern. Solid waste volume disposed of in landfills is a function of population; amount of pollutants is largely a function of soil characteristics and quality of operation.	Same as I.	Same as I.	Same as I.	Same as I.	Same as I.
Noise	Where open space buffer strips separate highways from residential areas and where careful planning locates dwellings only along minor streets, noise impact will be significantly less than in sprawl alternatives.	A less efficient traffic pattern is likely here as compared with I; some buffering of noise can be expected, although some homes may be located along busy arterials.	Where buffers and setbacks are absent, high level of noise irritation is likely.	Lower density means more auto use and hence more auto noise than in I. However, noise impacts are spread over a larger area.	Buffers more likely to be lacking than in III. Much higher total auto use than I means greater transportation noise, although spread over a larger area.	High density causes concentrated traffic flows which must be compensated for with buffers and setbacks.
Vegetation and Wildlife	Less species disruption where significant tracts of land are preserved as permanent open space. Degree of adverse effect depends on ability of species to adapt to human proximity.	Greater disruption than in I, as few large open areas can be retained.	Similar to I.. Leapfrog development pattern leaves only small pockets of undisturbed area.	Low density development decreases the amount of open land preserved in its natural condition. Careful planning can protect areas of special significance as species habitats - i.e., woodlands, swamps.	Virtually no land will be left totally undisturbed, thus eliminating habitats and causing a disruption in ecological balance.	Least adverse effect through careful planning to conserve special habitats and through high density development which preserves large tracts of undisturbed land.

Note: Abbreviations as follows: CO (carbon monoxide), HC (hydrocarbons), NO_x (nitrogen oxides), SO_x (sulfur oxides), B.O.D. (biological oxygen demand), COD (chemical oxygen demand), N (nitrogen compounds), P (phosphorus compounds), S.S. (suspended solids), FCB (fecal coliform bacteria).

	Community Development Pattern (10,000 Units)					
	I	II	III	IV	V	VI
	Planned Mix	Combination Mix 50 Percent PUD, 50 Percent Sprawl	Sprawl Mix	Low Density Planned	Low Density Sprawl	High Density Planned
Visual Effects	Development controls for retention of visually pleasing natural features and careful building design are likely to occur.	Individual developments may be well designed; however, lack of overall control will result in the haphazard spreading of urban uses in a manner which lowers the visual quality of the community.	Similar to II.	Similar to I.	Similar to II.	Similar to I.
Water and Energy Consumption						
Water Use (gallons per year)	Same as III. Water consumption is largely a function of household size, housing type, and lawn sprinkling demand.	Same as III.	Approximately 91 million gallons per year.	94% of V; difference reflects varying needs for lawn sprinkling.	Approximately 117 million gallons per year - greater sprinkling and household use than in III.	65% of V; difference reflects variations in residential consumption and sprinkling uses by housing type.
Energy Use (billion BTUs per year)	86% of III; difference reflects variation in gasoline used for auto travel. Natural gas and electricity consumption a function of housing type, with apartment units consuming less than single-family homes.	92% of III; difference reflects variation in gasoline used for auto travel.	Approximately 3,281 billion BTUs per year.	92% of V; difference reflects variation in gasoline used for auto travel.	Approximately 4,060 billion BTUs per year.	56% of V; difference reflects variations in residential power consumption by housing type and decrease in auto use in high density planned areas.
PERSONAL EFFECTS						
Travel Time	Auto travel time is estimated at 62% of III. Greater time spent in bicycle travel or walking. Time saved is largely a function of better planning and location of facilities and services.	Auto travel time is estimated at 81% of time consumed in III.	Estimate of almost 3 hours per day spent in auto travel by the average household. Park and travel time need results from "leapfrog" development pattern which increases travel distances.	Time spent in auto travel is 33% greater than in I due to lower density but is 20% less than in V due to better planning of facility and service locations.	Similar to III, with slightly greater travel time due to longer travel distances and greater likelihood of auto use.	Auto travel time is 52% of V, due to decreased auto use, more walking. Somewhat less than I due to greater density of development and increased proximity of facilities and services.
Traffic Accidents (per year, both fatal and non-fatal, intersection and non-intersection)	64% of III; difference results from variation in total vehicle miles traveled, lengths of road, street widths.	82% of III.	694 accidents per year.	80% of V; 33% greater than I due to increased auto use and road length.	743 accidents per year, 7% more than in III due to greater auto use and road length.	47% of V; difference reflects decreased auto use, shorter road length, wider road widths in high-density areas.
Crime	Same as III; no variation by development pattern. Differences are a function of housing type.	Same as III.	1,460 crimes per year, 5% of which are crimes to persons.	Same as V; no variation by development pattern. Differences are a function of housing type.	1,300 crimes per year, 5% of which are crimes to persons.	20% more crime than in V, due to higher density.
Psychic Costs (Design, natural features, leisure facilities and services, socio-economic status, investment)	More varied design, safer vehicular circulation pattern; emphasis on preserving open space; wide variety of community activities encouraging group participation. Residents are willing to bear the cost of higher quality services, many of which are provided by community associations. Likely to have a wide range of housing prices and a heterogeneous population.	Residents of planned unit developments will reap psychic benefits in design, preservation of open space, availability of leisure activities. In other ways, costs and benefits will be similar to III.	Housing shows little design variation; land development reflects a desire to economize on direct costs; public services are not likely to be extensive. Leisure activities oriented around home and family. Likely to be homogeneous with regard to race, income, education.	Same as I.	Same as III.	Same as I.

Source: Real Estate Research Corporation.

Source. *The Cost of Sprawl*, Real Estate Research Corporation, 1974.

Table 1.13 Community Cost Analysis: Operating and Maintenance Costs

	Community Development Pattern (10,000 Units)											
	I		II		III		IV		V		VI	
	Planned Mix		Combination Mix 50 Percent PUD, 50 Percent Sprawl		Sprawl Mix		Low Density Planned		Low Density Sprawl		High Density Planned	
	Cost	Percent of Total Cost	Cost	Percent of Total Cost	Cost	Percent of Total Cost	Cost	Percent of Total Cost	Cost	Percent of Total Cost	Cost	Percent of Total Cost
COST CATEGORY					(in thousands)							
Open Space/Recreation	$ 380 (146% of III)	2%	$ 320 (123% of III)	2%	$ 260	1%	$ 380 (146% of V)	2%	$ 260	1%	$ 380 (146% of V)	2%
Schools	$ 9,643 (99% of III)	50%	$ 9,652 (99% of III)	49%	$ 9,737	50%	$ 9,643 (99% of V)	47%	$ 9,737	46%	$ 9,643 (99% of V)	51%
Public Services	$ 5,103 (94% of III)	26%	$ 5,296 (98% of III)	27%	$ 5,405	28%	$ 5,165 (95% of V)	25%	$ 5,575	26%	$ 5,164 (93% of V)	28%
Transportation - Streets and Roads	$ 260 (100% of III)	1%	$ 260 (100% of III)	1%	$ 261	1%	$ 354 (89% of V)	2%	$ 396	2%	$ 209 (53% of V)	1%
Utilities	$ 3,987 (100% of III)	21%	$ 3,988 (100% of III)	20%	$ 3,989	20%	$ 5,130 (100% of V)	25%	$ 5,141	24%	$ 3,335 (65% of V)	18%
Total Year Ten Operating Costs	$ 19,373 (99% of III)	100%	$ 19,516 (99% of III)	100%	$ 19,652	100%	$ 20,672 (98% of V)	100%	$ 21,109	100%	$ 18,731 (89% of V)	100%
Cumulative Ten Year Operating Costs	$125,265		$117,299		$109,489		$133,186		$116,827		$120,919	
Present Value												
Present Value at 5%	$ 95,526		$ 88,860		$ 82,377		$101,567		$ 87,804		$ 92,212	
Present Value at 10%	$ 74,913		$ 69,210		$ 63,710		$ 79,651		$ 67,822		$ 72,315	
(Comparison of Results at 10%)	(118% of III)		(109% of III)				(118% of V)				(107% of V)	
Incidence of Cost - Year Ten Government/Private (%/%)	55%/45%		60%/40%		61%/39%		51%/49%		57%/43%		55%/45%	
Cost to the Household - Year Ten Service Charges/Taxes (%/%)	49%/51%		44%/56%		43%/57%		52%/48%		46%/54%		48%/52%	

Note: Residential operating and maintenance costs are not estimated.

Source: Real Estate Research Corporation.

Source. The Cost of Sprawl, Real Estate Research Corporation, 1974.

Table 1.14 Neighborhood Cost Analysis: Capital Costs

	Housing Pattern (1,000 Units)											
	A		B		C		D		E		F	
	Single-Family Conventional		Single-Family Clustered		Townhouse Clustered		Walk-Up Apartment		High-Rise Apartment		Housing Mix (20 Percent Each A - E)	
	Cost	Percent of Total Cost	Cost	Percent of Total Cost	Cost	Percent of Total Cost	Cost	Percent of Total Cost	Cost	Percent of Total Cost	Cost	Percent of Total Cost
COST CATEGORY					(in thousands)							
Open Space/Recreation	$ 220	0%	$ 274	1%	$ 274	1%	$ 252	1%	$ 203	1%	$ 245	1%
Percent of A	-		125%		125%		115%		92%		111%	
Schools	$ 5,354	11%	$ 5,354	12%	$ 4,538	17%	$ 4,538	21%	$ 1,646	8%	$ 4,538	14%
Percent of A	-		100%		85%		85%		31%		85%	
Transportation - Streets and Roads	$ 3,080	6%	$ 2,661	6%	$ 2,111	8%	$ 1,464	7%	$ 801	4%	$ 2,064	6%
Percent of A	-		86%		69%		48%		26%		67%	
Utilities	$ 5,483	11%	$ 3,649	8%	$ 2,369	9%	$ 1,579	7%	$ 958	5%	$ 2,782	8%
Percent of A	-		67%		43%		29%		17%		51%	
Subtotal	$ 14,137	29%	$ 11,938	26%	$ 9,292	34%	$ 7,833	37%	$ 3,628	18%	$ 9,629	29%
Percent of A	-		84%		66%		55%		26%		68%	
Residential	$ 32,146	66%	$ 31,724	69%	$ 16,263	60%	$ 11,766	55%	$ 15,188	73%	$ 21,417	65%
Percent of A	-		99%		51%		37%		47%		67%	
Total Exclusive of Land	$ 46,283	95%	$ 43,662	94%	$ 25,555	94%	$ 19,599	92%	$ 18,796	91%	$ 31,046	94%
Percent of A	-		94%		55%		42%		41%		67%	
Land	$ 2,628	5%	$ 2,596	6%	$ 1,704	6%	$ 1,683	8%	$ 1,900	9%	$ 2,042	6%
Percent of A	-		99%		65%		64%		72%		78%	
Total Capital Costs	$ 48,911	100%	$ 46,258	100%	$ 27,259	100%	$ 21,282	100%	$ 20,696	100%	$ 33,088	100%
Percent of A	-		95%		56%		44%		42%		68%	
Incidence of Cost												
Government/Private	15%/85%		15%/85%		20%/80%		25%/75%		13%/87%		18%/82%	
Cost to the Households												
Capital Cost/Service Charges/Taxes	83%/ 3%/14%		38%/43%/19%		38%/43%/19%		13%/62%/25%		16%/71%/13%		46%/37%/17%	

Source: Real Estate Research Corporation.

Source. *The Cost of Sprawl*, Real Estate Research Corporation, 1974.

Table 1.15 Neighborhood Cost Analysis: Operating and Maintenance Cost

	Housing Pattern (1,000 Units)											
	A		B		C		D		E		F	
	Single-Family Conventional		Single-Family Clustered		Townhouse Clustered		Walk-Up Apartment		High-Rise Apartment		Housing Mix (20 Percent Each A - E)	
COST CATEGORY	Cost	Percent of Total Cost	Cost	Percent of Total Cost	Cost	Percent of Total Cost	Cost	Percent of Total Cost	Cost	Percent of Total Cost	Cost	Percent of Total Cost
						(in thousands)						
Open Space/Recreation	$ 30	2%	$ 41	2%	$ 41	3%	$ 41	3%	$ 30	5%	$ 37	3%
Percent of A	-		137%		137%		137%		100%		123%	
Schools	$1,168	68%	$1,168	68%	$ 989	71%	$ 989	75%	$ 270	49%	$ 989	70%
Percent of A	-		100%		85%		85%		23%		85%	
Transportation - Streets and Roads	$ 37	2%	$ 28	2%	$ 18	1%	$ 11	1%	$ 6	1%	$ 19	1%
Percent of A	-		76%		49%		30%		16%		51%	
Utilities	$ 484	28%	$ 483	28%	$ 340	25%	$ 278	21%	$ 243	45%	$ 365	27%
Percent of A	-		100%		70%		57%		50%		75%	
Total Operating Costs	$1,721	100%	$1,720	100%	$1,388	100%	$1,319	100%	$ 548	100%	$1,410	100%
Percent of A	-		100%		81%		77%		32%		82%	
Incidence of Cost												
Government/Private	67%/33%		67%/33%		72%/28%		74%/26%		57%/43%		71%/29%	
Cost to the Household												
Service Charges/Taxes	35%/65%		36%/64%		33%/67%		30%/70%		52%/48%		34%/66%	

Note: Residential operating and maintenance costs are not estimated.

Source: Real Estate Research Corporation.

Source. The Cost of Sprawl, Real Estate Research Corporation, 1974.

7 ENVIRONMENTAL IMPACT EVALUATIONS

Procedure for Evaluating Environmental Impact

The following section is adopted from a report containing a procedure that was prepared by Luna B. Leopold, Frank E. Clarke, Bruce B. Hanshaw, and James R. Balsley to develop a uniform environmental impact statement for the Department of the Interior and the Council on Environmental Quality.

The heart of the system is a matrix that is general enough to be used as a reference checklist or a reminder of the full range of actions and impacts on the environment that may relate to proposed actions. The marked matrix also serves as an abstract of the text of the environmental assessment, to enable the numerous reviewers of impact reports to determine quickly what are considered to be the significant effects and their relative importance as evaluated by the originators of the impact report.

Many exhaustive studies of the use of matrices for environmental studies are now being undertaken. This comparatively simple system is intended as a guide for those who must evaluate and prepare environmental impact reports. At present, however, there is no uniformity in approach, nor agreement on the objectives of an impact analysis.

The procedure does not limit the development of detail in any specific aspect of the environment; a separate expanded matrix for any environmental aspect can easily be developed within the framework provided in this section. A proposal for construction or development usually includes an analysis of the need for the development and the relationship between its monetary costs and monetary benefits. This is good practice from the standpoints of engineering and economics. More recently, society has recognized that in addition to these customary economic analyses and discussions of need, there should be a detailed assessment of the effect of a proposed development on the environment, thus its ecological benefits and costs separate from the monetary aspects. Put together, these assessments comprise an Environmental Impact Statement. The preparation of such a statement or report should be done by a team of physical and social scientists and engineers; likewise, reviews of statements generally require an interdisciplinary team effort.

The Environmental Policy Act of 1969 directs all agencies of the federal government to "identify and develop methods and procedures which will insure that presently unquantified environmental amenities and values are given appropriate consideration in decision-making along with economic and technical considerations." In furtherance of Section 102 of the act, the Council on Environmental Quality has set forth guidelines for the preparation of the required environmental statements. It is recommended in these guidelines that the second item to be included in the statement is "the probable impact of the proposed action on the environment."

The guidelines suggest an approach to accomplish that specific requirement by providing a system for the analysis and numerical weighting of probable impacts. This type of analysis does not produce an overall quantitative rating but portrays many value judgments. It can also serve as a guide in preparing the statement called for under the act. A primary purpose is to ensure that the impacts of alternative actions are evaluated and considered in project planning.

Development of an Action Program: Generalized Procedure

Evaluating the environmental impact of an action program or proposal is a late step in the series of events discussed in this section. Figure 1.84 is a flow chart of the recommended sequence of events resulting in an environmental impact statement. The sequence is outlined briefly below, and the portion that deals with impact assessment is covered in more detail later.

- A The major objective sought by the proposed project is stated.
- B The technologic possibilities of achieving the objective are analyzed.
- C One or more actions are proposed for achieving the stated objective. The alternative plans that were considered as practicable ways of reaching the objective are spelled out in the proposal.

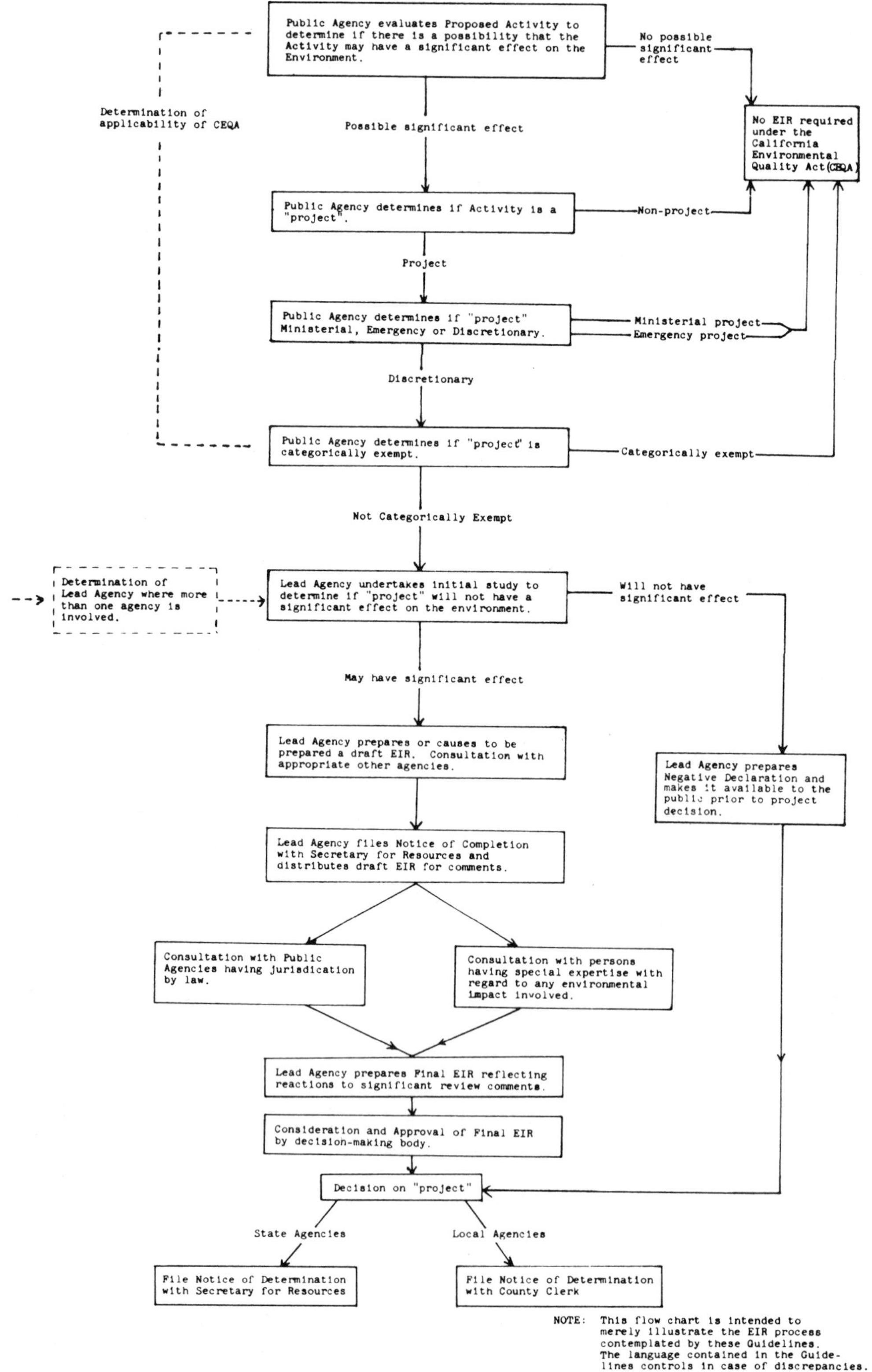

Figure 1.83 Illustrative flow chart. *Source*. U.S. Department of the Interior.

D A report detailing the characteristics and conditions of the existing environment prior to the proposed action is prepared. In some cases this report is incorporated in the engineering proposal.

E The principal engineering proposals are put into final form as a report or series of separate reports, one for each plan. The plans ordinarily contain analyses of monetary benefits and costs.

F The proposed plan of action, usually the engineering report, together with the report characterizing the present environment, set the stage for evaluating the environmental impact of the proposal. If alternative ways of reaching the objective are proposed in part C, and if alternative engineering plans are detailed in the engineering report, separate environmental impact analyses must deal with each alternative. If only one proposal is made in the engineering report, it is still necessary to evaluate environmental impacts.

The environmental impact analyses require the definition of the magnitude of the impact on specific sectors of the environment. The term "magnitude" is used in the sense of degree, extensiveness, or scale. For example, highway development will alter or affect the existing drainage pattern, thus may have a large *magnitude* of impact on the drainage. Next it is necessary to weigh the degree of "importance" (i.e., significance) of the particular action on the environmental factor in the specific instance under analysis. Thus the overall *importance* of impact of a highway on a particular drainage pattern may be small because the highway is planned to be very short or because it will not interfere significantly with the drainage. Depending on the thoroughness and scope of the report that inventories existing environmental conditions, the analysis of *magnitude* of impact, though subjective in some details, can nevertheless be factual and unbiased. It should not include weights that express preference or bias.

The *importance* of each specific environmental impact must include consideration of the consequences on other factors in the environment of changing the particular condition. Again, the adequacy of the report under part D would affect the objectivity in the assignment of the values for specific environmental conditions. Unlike *magnitude* of impact, which can be more readily evaluated on the basis of facts, evaluation of the *importance* of impact is generally based on the value judgment of the evaluator. The numerical values of magnitude and importance of impact reflect the best estimates of pertinence of each action.

G The text of the environmental impact report should be an assessment of the impacts on various facets of the environment of the separate actions that comprise the project, thus justification is provided for the determinations presented in part F. Each plan of action should be analyzed independently.

H The statement should end with a summation and recommendations. The conclusion should deal with the relative merits of the various proposed actions and alternative engineering plans and should explain the rationale behind the final choice of action and the plan for achieving the stated objective.

TEMPE MUNICIPAL BUILDING
Tempe, Arizona
Architects: Michael & Kemper Goodwin
Photo: C. R. Conley

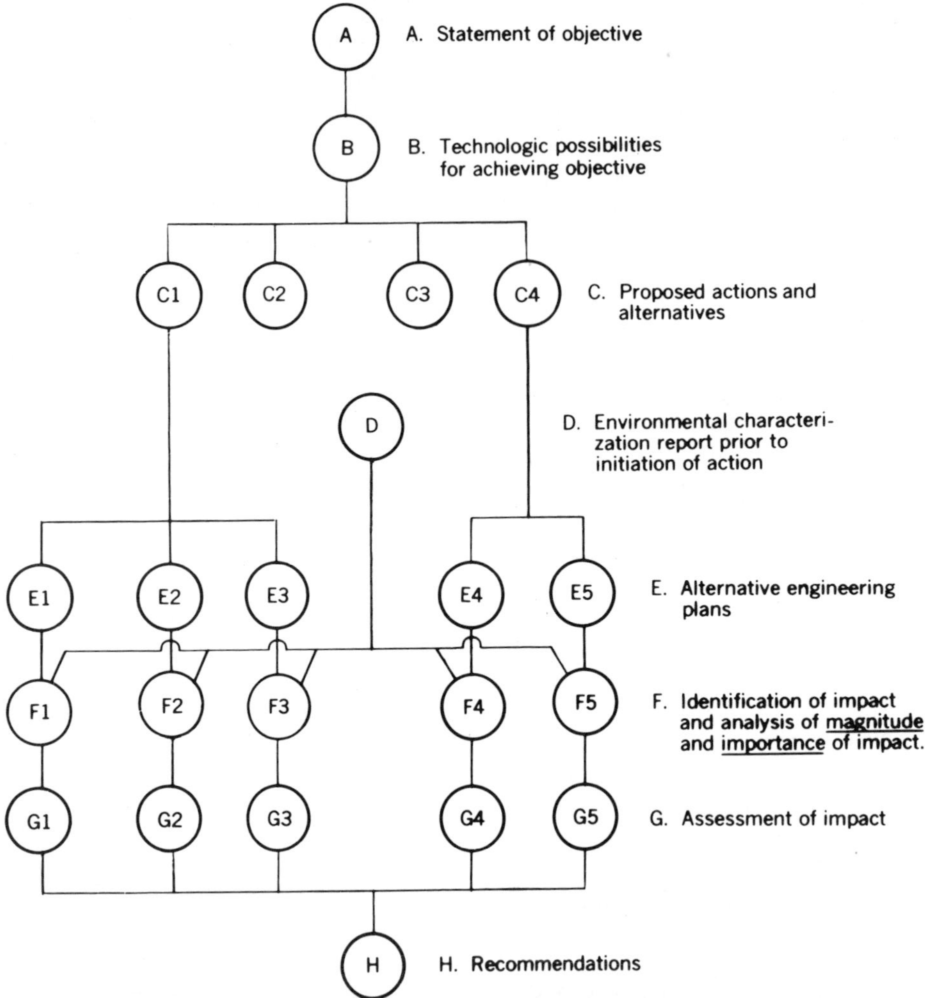

Figure 1.84 Flow chart for development of action programs. *Source*. U.S. Department of the Interior.

The Environmental Impact Statement

An environmental impact statement consists of four basic items:

1 A complete analysis of the need for the proposed action. This would include parts A, B, and C of the generalized procedure above.

2 An informative description of the environment to be involved, including a careful consideration of the boundaries of a project. For example, because of erosion, every drainage crossed by a highway may be affected downstream as well, and these effects beyond the right-of-way should be described in part D of the generalized procedure.

3 A discussion of the pertinent details of the proposed action—part E.

4 An assessment of the probable impacts of the variety of specific aspects of the proposed action on the variety of existing environmental elements and factors (parts F and G) and a summary or recommendation (part H), which includes the rationale supporting the selected plan of action.

The analysis of need, item 1, should consider the full range of values to be derived, not simply the usual cost-benefit analysis. It should include a discussion of the overall objectives and possible alternatives to meet them.

The characterization of the existing environment, item 2, should be a detailed description of present environmental elements and factors, with special emphasis on the rare or unique aspects, both good and bad, that might not be common to other similar areas. It should provide sufficient information to permit an objective evaluation of the environmental factors that together make up the ecosystem of the area. The vertical margin of the matrix can be used as a checklist in preparing this section.

The details of proposed action, item 3, should include discussion of possible alternative engineering methods or approaches to accomplish the proposed development (item 1). There should be enough detail to permit checking all actions that may have impact on the environment (item 2). The horizontal margin of the matrix can be used as a checklist in preparing this section.

The environmental impact assessment, item 4, should consist of three basic elements: (*a*) a listing of the effects on the environment that would be caused by the proposed development, and an estimate of the *magnitude* of each; (*b*) an evaluation of the *importance* of each of these effects; (*c*) the combining of *magnitude* and *importance* estimates in a summary evaluation.

We shall not deal at length with items 1 through 3, and it is assumed that generalized procedures for their preparation are commonly followed, since these items have been incorporated in many engineering feasibility studies and benefit-cost analyses of past projects. Rather, we focus on the new requirement, addressing primarily the preparation of item 4—the environmental impact assessment.

Environmental Impact Assessment

Matrix. The analysis embodied in subitems *a, b,* and *c* is made with a matrix on one axis are located the actions that cause environmental impact, and on the other we put existing environmental conditions that might be affected. This provides a format for comprehensive review to remind the investigators of the variety of interactions that might be involved. It also helps the planners to identify alternatives that might lessen impact. There are 100 actions listed horizontally in this sample matrix, and the vertical list of environmental characteristics contains 88, for a total of 8800 possible interactions. Within such a matrix, only a few of the interactions would be likely to involve impacts of such *magnitude* and *importance* that they deserve comprehensive treatment. Although the items listed represent most of the basic actions and environmental factors likely to be involved in the full range of developments that require impact reporting, not all would apply to every project proposal. Even this large matrix may not contain all elements necessary to make a full analysis of every project proposal encountered. However the coding and the format are designed for easy expansion to include additional items. Preliminary trials suggest that the number of applicable interactions for a typical project analysis will be between 25 and 50.

The most efficient way to use the matrix is to check each action (top horizontal list) that is likely to be involved significantly in the proposed project. Generally, only about a dozen actions are important. Each action thus checked is evaluated in terms of *magnitude* of effect on environmental characteristics on the vertical axis, and a slash is placed diagonally from upper right to lower left across each block that represents significant interaction. In marking the matrix, it is important to remember that an action may have a major short-term (for a year or so) impact that is ameliorated in a few years, thus is of minor or negligible importance in a long time frame. Conversely, other actions resulting in lesser initial impact may produce more significant and persistent secondary effects, therefore may have major impact in a long time frame. In the discussion of the matrix included in the report, it should be indicated whether one is assessing short-term or long-term impact. As an example, oil drilling rigs are commonly considered to be noisy and nonaesthetic, but they are on location for short periods of time—generally 1 to 6 months per site, whereas untreated spoil banks may silt and acidify streams for many years after completion of a project.

In marking the boxes, unnecessary replication can be avoided by concentrating on first-order effects of specific actions. For example, "mineral processing" would not be marked as affecting "aquatic life" even if the waste products are toxic in aquatic environments. The aquatic impact would be covered under "emplacement of tailing," "spills and leaks," or other processing operations that may lead to degradation of aquatic habitat.

After all the boxes representing possible impact have been marked with a diagonal line, the most important ones are evaluated individually. In each box representing a significant interaction between an action and an environmental factor, place a number from 1 to 10 in the upper left-hand corner to indicate the relative *magnitude* of impact; 10 represents the greatest magnitude; 1, the least. In the lower right-hand corner of the box, evaluate the relative *importance* of the impact, again using a scale of 1 to 10, with 10 the greatest.

As an example, assume that a particular engineering proposal recommends construction of highways and bridges. The proposed action is item II.B.d on the matrix of Figure 1.85. "Highways and bridges" might have environmental impacts through effect on "erosion" and related "deposition and sedimentation," among other things. "Erosion" and "deposition-sedimentation" occur under the main heading "Physical and Chemical Characteristics of the Environment" on the left-hand side (ordinate) of the matrix and in the horizontal rows I.A.4.b and I.A.4.c, respectively.

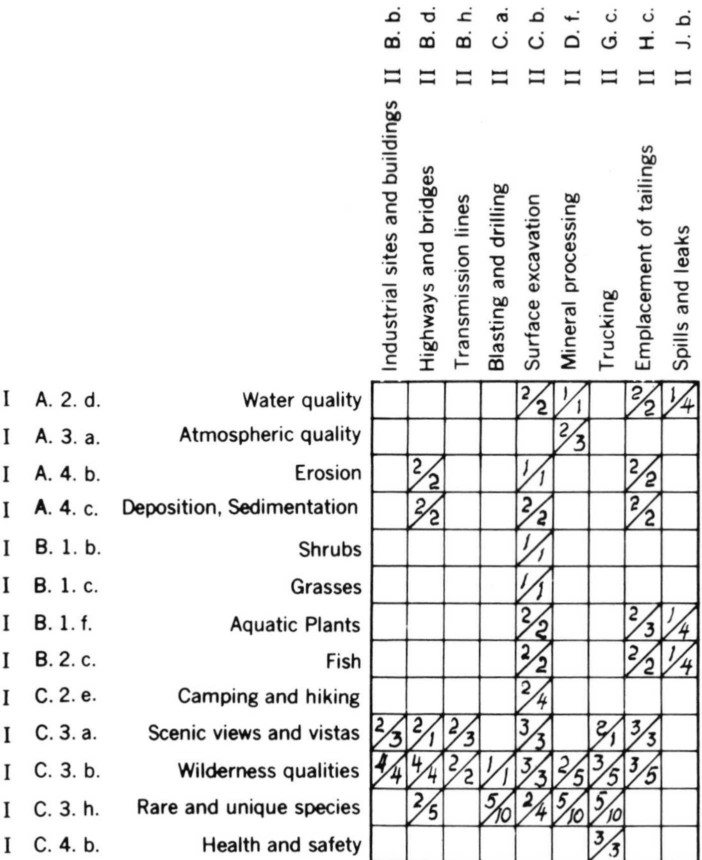

			Industrial sites and buildings II B. b.	Highways and bridges II B. d.	Transmission lines II B. h.	Blasting and drilling II C. a.	Surface excavation II C. b.	Mineral processing II D. f.	Trucking II G. c.	Emplacement of tailings II H. c.	Spills and leaks II J. b.
I	A. 2. d.	Water quality					2/2	1/1		2/2	1/4
I	A. 3. a.	Atmospheric quality						2/3			
I	A. 4. b.	Erosion		2/2			1/1			2/2	
I	A. 4. c.	Deposition, Sedimentation		2/2			2/2			2/2	
I	B. 1. b.	Shrubs					1/1				
I	B. 1. c.	Grasses					1/1				
I	B. 1. f.	Aquatic Plants					2/2			2/3	1/4
I	B. 2. c.	Fish					2/2			2/2	1/4
I	C. 2. e.	Camping and hiking					2/4				
I	C. 3. a.	Scenic views and vistas	2/3	2/1	2/3		3/3		2/1	3/3	
I	C. 3. b.	Wilderness qualities	4/4	4/4	2/2	1/1	3/3	2/5	3/5	3/5	
I	C. 3. h.	Rare and unique species		2/5		5/10	2/4	5/10	5/10		
I	C. 4. b.	Health and safety							3/3		

Figure 1.85 Reduced matrix for a phosphate mining lease. *Source*. U.S. Department of the Interior.

Perhaps in this example bridges would cause an important amount of bank erosion because geologic materials in the area are poorly consolidated. This might lead the investigator to mark the *magnitude* of impact on erosion of highways and bridges as 6 or more. If, however, the streams involved already have high sediment loads and appear to be capable of carrying such loads without objectionable secondary effects, the effective *importance* of bridges through increased erosion and sedimentation might be considered to be relatively small, perhaps being marked 1 or 2 in the lower right-hand corner of the block. This would mean that while *magnitude* of impact is relatively high, the *importance* of impact is not great.

In the assessment of accidents (II, J) such as "spills and leaks," it would be desirable to have some guide for determining the probability and effect of accidents. In this matter, the inclusion of controls that would reduce the probability of an accident would lower the matrix entry of *magnitude,* but it would have no influence on the evaluation of *importance* of impact.

The next step is to evaluate the numbers in the slashed boxes. It is convenient to construct a simplified or reduced matrix that consists of only the actions and environmental characteristics that have been identified as interacting. Boxes with exceptionally high individual numbers may be specially noted—for example, by circling them. When comparing alternatives in an action program, a convenient convention (not used here) is to identify the beneficial impacts with +, because alternate action plans may have different degrees of both beneficial and possibly detrimental impacts. However in most cases the preparer would consider all impacts to be potentially deleterious because all the + factors had been covered in the engineering report. Other investigators may wish to devise their own numerical rating methods; hence the marginal boxes may be simply titled as "computations."

It must be emphasized that no two boxes on any one matrix are precisely equivalent. Rather, the significance of high or low numbers for any one box indicates only the degree of impact one type of action may have on one part of the environment. If alternative actions are under consideration, and a separate matrix is prepared for each action, identical boxes in the two matrices will provide a numerical comparison of the environmental impact for the alternatives considered.

As far as possible, assignment of numerical weights to the *magnitude* and *importance* of impacts should be based on factual data rather than preference. Thus the use of a rating scheme such as the one suggested here discourages purely subjective opinion and requires authors of environmental impact statements to attempt to quantify their judgment of probable impacts. The overall rating allows the reviewers to follow the originators' line of reasoning and will aid in identifying points of agreement and disagreement. The matrix is in fact the abstract for the text of the environmental assessment.

Text. The text of an environmental impact assessment should be a discussion of the individual boxes that were given the larger numerical values for *magnitude* and *importance*. Additionally, columns that cause a large number of actions to be marked, regardless of their numerical values, should be discussed in detail. Likewise, the elements of the environment (rows) that have relatively large numbers of boxes marked should be addressed.

The discussion of those items should cover the following points as put forth in the Council on Environmental Quality's guidelines published in the *Federal Register* (1971):

1 A description of the proposed action including information and technical data adequate to permit careful assessment of impact. (This has been covered as items C and F in Figure 1.84).
2 The probable impact of the proposed action on the environment.
3 Any probable adverse environmental effects that cannot be avoided.
4 Alternatives to the proposed action.
5 The relationship between local short-term uses of the environment and the maintenance and enhancement of long-term productivity.
6 Any irreversible and irretrievable commitments of resources that would be involved in the proposed action, should it be implemented.
7 Where appropriate, a discussion of problems and objections raised by other federal, state, and local agencies and by private organizations and individuals in the review process and the disposition of the issues involved. This section may be added at the end of the review process in the final text of the environmental statement.

INTERNATIONAL BUSINESS MACHINES
Toronto, Ontario, Canada
Architects: John B. Parkin Associates
Photo: Office

TRUE DAVIDSON ACRES: NEGRO HOME FOR THE AGED
East York, Ontario
Architect: Jerome Markson
Photo: Roger Jowett

All these points can be covered as part of a discussion of the matrix. The text that accompanies the completed matrix should deal primarily with the reasoning behind the assignment of numerical values for the *magnitude* of impact effects and their relative *importance*. The text should discuss the actions that have significant impact and should not be diluted by trivial side issues.

To be fully understandable, the discussion of the *magnitude* and *importance* of applicable impacts and responses will require some coverage of the principal physical and ecological characteristics of the environment itself and some of the important characteristics of the proposed action that govern its environmental impact. The environmental impact assessment thus relies on and refers to the data incorporated in items 1, 2, and 3 (p. 127)—the full description of the geography, physical setting, vegetation, climate, and other facts about the environment and the physical and engineering aspects of the proposed development. The environmental impact assessment need not be burdened and should not be padded with descriptions of the project and the environment per se. It should include only such details as are needed for evaluating the environmental impact. The completed environmental impact assessment, together with items 1, 2, and 3, comprises the finished environmental impact statement; all four items are required for review purposes.

Concluding Statement. Although it is obvious that no scheme of impact assessment will be universally applicable, greatest need is not for a single and universally applicable assessment method, but rather for a simple way of summarizing which impacts the people making the assessment consider to be of greatest moment. Assessors seldom come to identical conclusions, but it is useful to know the bases for the differences.

A matrix is helpful because it can serve as a checklist or reminder of the full range of actions and impacts. The proposed manner of using the matrix is aimed at separating as far as possible factual information on *magnitude* of each type impact from the more subjective evaluation of the *importance* of the impact, the latter involving preference or bias to some degree. This separation of fact from preference is highly desirable.

Appendix: Impact Assessment of a Phosphate Mining Lease by Matrix Analysis. A phosphate deposit estimated to include 80 million tons of crude ore of an average content of 8.7% phosphate (P_2O_5) is located in Los Padres National Forest, Ventura County, California. The ore consists of sand-size pellets of phosphorite occurring in a sequence of sandstones and siltstones of Late Miocene age. The beds crop out on hillslopes along a strike length of about 5 miles. The beds dip approximately 30° north. The minable beds are 90 feet thick with an overburden varying from 0 to 200 feet.

Application for a prospecting permit was made in February 1964, and a permit was granted in November 1964. A 3-year extension of the permit was approved in October 1966. The company made an application for a preference right phosphate lease in April 1969. The background material needed for the present analysis is contained in the company's report, parts of which are abstracted below.

The Regional Environment. The deposit occurs in a semiarid region receiving 23 inches of annual precipitation, mostly between November and April. The principal drainage system in the area is Sespe Creek; its headwaters are about 5 miles west of the lease application. In its upper reaches, Sespe is an ephemeral stream. The proposed mining operation would be 2 miles north of the Sespe. Vegetation, which ranges from sparse to medium heavy, is of a chaparral type including oak, manzanita, and mountain mahogany; there is a low-density ground cover of grass.

Access to the area is by means of California State Highway 33, a black-topped paved road that runs from Ventura north to Bakersfield. The prospect is within 1 to 2 miles of this highway; present access is over a temporary unpaved road. To develop the property, about $1^1/_2$ miles of permanent paved road would have to be built.

The region is sparsely settled. In a 5-mile radius of the proposed mine, there are six year-round residents and 10 summer residences. The nearest towns are Meiners Oaks and Ojai, 25 miles to the south, and New Cuyama about 35 miles to the north.

General Mining Plans. The ore crops out as a narrow band about 5 miles long. Test core drilling indicated that the rock is too unstable to support underground workings, and the company proposes to develop the mine by open-pit methods. The strike is approximately perpendicular to the local stream channels that drain toward Sespe Creek. The small canyons cut across the ore zone every 2000 to 3000 feet along the strike. To prevent damage to the watershed, the company envisions a mining operation that would not dam or interrupt these channels. Therefore, over the life of the mining operation a series of open pits would be dug parallel to the strike and would be terminated short of the tributary valleys that cross the ore body. The dimensions of the proposed open pits would be determined by the interval between adjacent canyons. Pit width would be a function of the amount of overburden that could be removed economically. In the downdip direction, mining would not extend past the point of economic removal of overburden.

The planned open-pit geometry is V-shaped. One limb would follow the foot wall of the ore zone at approximately 30° from the horizontal. The high wall would be cut at 45° to the horizontal. Such a pit would be worked in a series of benches, 20 feet high, running parallel to the strike.

Ore Processing. An ore-processing plant would be constructed at the mine site to crush the ore. After crushing, the phosphate would be leached out with acid. The resultant pregnant liquor would be neutralized with quicklime to precipitate dicalcium phosphate in granular form.

The tailings from the leaching process is quartz sand, which would be washed, dewatered, and stored in the open-pit areas where mining had been completed.

The phosphate, in either granular solid or liquid form, would be transported to market by truck. The major raw materials required to be brought in are quicklime and sulfur, the latter being converted to sulfuric acid at the mine site. Water required for the processing is to be supplied by a 1000-foot deep well already drilled; relatively little is needed.

Watershed and Environmental Values. Two principal environmental values call for consideration in this area: (1) the effect on the California condor, a rare and endangered species present in the general region, and (2) location of the mine lease close to the center of a large block of National Forest land. (The total lease, 2434 acres, is small by comparison with the total forest.) Since the site is 15 miles east-southeast along the mountain ridge from the edge of the San Rafael Wilderness, no designated wilderness lands are involved. However the need for recreational use of undeveloped public lands in California to relieve population pressure is relatively great, and any commercial operation in an undeveloped area would have an effect on such use.

The Sespe Condor Sanctuary, located in the National Forest, lies 15 miles east of the mining area. From this sanctuary, the condors are said to range along the crestline to the northwest, across the center of the whole National Forest area. The ordinary flight or soaring patterns for condors would pass through the general region of the proposed mine site. One condor nest, apparently now abandoned, has been noted a few miles west of the mining site. The other known condor nests all lie within the sanctuary.

A few of the many subsidiary environmental impacts that might be caused by the mining operation are mentioned briefly below; they are discussed in more detail in connection with the impact matrix.

The possibility of water pollution from the phosphate itself is minimized by the relative insolubility of the phosphate ore, as shown by water quality analyses on surface water in the area. The mining operation would not increase the soluble phosphate content of the water resource. The effectiveness of erosion control measures applied within the mining area will determine the quantity of particulate phosphate mineral and other sediments added to Sespe Creek. The liquid chemicals handled at the plant are to be confined within dikes. Except for possible leakage from these dikes, or in case of spills on the highway, water pollution from processing chemicals and products should not occur.

Increased soil erosion and related sediment load to stream channels will depend on the manner in which the stream channels crossing the ore body are protected from the open-pit mining operation.

Some level of air pollution is possible from noxious gases emanating from the plant in the form of fluorine from the ore, sulfur dioxide gas from the manufacture of sulfuric acid, and fuel combustion products. Blasting, drilling, and equipment noise could have some environmental impact. Noise from the diesel-powered mining equipment is to be controlled by the use of conventional mufflers.

The power requirements of the plant are estimated to be 5000 V·A. The mine would require the construction of 14 miles of transmission lines, to be erected on wooden poles on the right-of-way of State Highway 33. Natural gas would be taken from a pipeline already in the area which passes within 3 miles of the proposed plant site, using either overhead or buried lines.

Over the life of the mine, only 400 acres would be subjected to actual mining, thus mitigating the impact on vegetation and wildlife. The mining operation would involve an annual excavation of 4 to 5 acres, with reclamation following soon afterward in the mined-out areas. A total of about 40 acres would be disturbed at any given time.

This brief summary shows the main aspects of the planned mining operation for which environmental impact is being evaluated. The mining company issued a report presenting more details on these and other aspects of the area and the project plan.

Using material contained in the company's report, an information matrix analysis would be completed in the manner described previously. The outcome of the analysis is recapitulated in reduced form as Figure 1.85. The explanations that follow indicate the reasoning used in this example.

Since the mining plan calls for a small "alternation of drainage," effects on "erosion" and "sedimentation" should be minor compared with the effect of "highways and bridges" and "emplacement of tailings." "Modification of habitat" and "alteration of ground cover" are not likely to be important impacts because the total mined area is relatively small. "Industrial buildings" and "construction of highways" are considered to be among the more important impacts. The short-term "blasting and drilling" under "construction" not shown in Figure 1.85) will have limited impact, but "drilling and blasting" for "resource extraction" will continue sporadically over the life of the project and is therefore relatively important. "Surface excavation" and "mineral processing" appear to have relatively important impact potential. On detailed consideration, "product storage" and "erosion control" are viewed as less important than some of the construction and resource extraction items noted above. Changes in traffic owing to the increase in "trucking" rather than to an increase in "automobile traffic" are considered to be capable of producing important impact. The "emplacement of tailings" would occur throughout the life of the project and could have significant effects if poorly controlled. "Liquid effluent discharge," which would be small during all phases of the project, would be relatively unimportant by comparison. "Spills and leaks" due to accidents could be important in the mining operation area, depending on the effectiveness of diking. Accidents would be especially significant on the highways over which new materials and finished products must be hauled.

With such consideration, the number of proposed actions considered enough for discussion was reduced to 9. Under each of these items in the vertical column, existing characteristics and conditions of the environment were inspected individually. Where the interaction was deemed sufficiently important, the impact was numerically evaluated in terms of *magnitude* and *importance*. The resulting codification appears in the completed matrix (Figure 1.86). The types of impact are discussed below in order of the items listed on the left-hand side of Figure 1.85.

1 *Water Quality (I.A.2.d).* Water quality could be affected by the "surface excavation," by "emplacement of tailings," and by "accidental spills and leaks." Since the planned "surface excavation" is off-channel, the *magnitude* 2 was assigned. Because the streams are ephemeral, the *importance* of the excavation in affecting water quality was rated 2 also.

The same reasoning applies to the "emplacement of tailings," which are off channel and not noxious. "Spills and leaks" were predicted to be sufficiently rare to merit *magnitude* 1, but *if* they occurred they would be moderately *important,* therefore receiving a value of 4.

In practice, any of the identified impacts can be expanded to produce secondary matrices that can cover greater detail than is possible in Figure 1.85 if the analyst or reviewer feels the need to do so. As an example, expanding the matrix items related to "water quality" may show the relative *magnitude* and *importance* of different specific actions more clearly than would be done by merely using the main headings in the matrix. An example (Figure 1.86) indicates how expansion may show details pertinent to the individual situation. Additionally, water quality could also be expanded into subcategories such as pH, dissolved oxygen, and turbidity.

2 *Atmospheric Quality (I.A.3.a).* "Mineral processing" would be the principal source of degradation in atmospheric quality. Its *magnitude* was rated 2 owing to the small size of the plant and the absence of other industrial operations. Its *importance,* however, was rated 3 because the gases produced would be sulfuric.

3 *Erosion (I.A.4.b) and Deposition (I.A.4.c).* Some "erosion," thus some channel "deposition," would be caused by the construction of "highways and bridges" and by the "emplacement of tailings." The sandy washes in the area, producing naturally high sediment loads, give both the "erosion" and the "deposition" caused by the project a relatively low importance. The *magnitude* and the *importance* of each was relatively low because the mining operation would involve the construction of less than 2 miles of new roads, and protection against erosion is included in the design of the mining operation.

4 *Shrubs (I.B.1.b) and Grasses (I.B.1.c).* The disturbance of native "shrubs" and "grasses" is important only on the area that is going to be physically disturbed by the mining. Because vegetation change would occur only on parts of the 2434-acre lease over the life of the project and revegetation is part of the scheduled project, both the *magnitude* and *importance* are rated low.

5 *Aquatic Plants (I.B.1.f).* "Aquatic plants" do not occur in the ephemeral streams near the plant site, but they do occur in the portion of the main stream some miles down valley where Sespe Creek is perennial. Any effect on "aquatic plants" reaching that far downstream would come from "excavation" and from "emplacement of tailings." The distance to the perennial stream indicated low values for *magnitude,* but a moderate value for *importance* in the case of "spills."

6 *Fish (I.B.2.c).* The same reasoning that governed the assessment of impact on "aquatic plants" applies also to "fish," which persist only some miles downstream where Sespe Creek is perennial and the probable impacts are rated low.

7 *Camping and Hiking (I.C.2.e).* The only alteration involving "camping and hiking" would be caused by "surface excavation." Given the small area to be affected, its *magnitude* is rated 2, but its *importance* was

	Industrial sites and buildings				Highways and bridges		Transmission lines		Surface excavation			Mineral processing		Trucking	Emplacement of tailings			Spills and leaks			
	Waste water	Sewage	Washing	Runoff from paving	Runoff during construction	Runoff from finished road	Sediment from cleared zone	Construction sediment	Sediment from fill	Effects of ore exposures	Effects of deep seepage	Sulfuric acid use	Acidity of yard runoff	Spilled sulfur compounds	Erosion of fill	Deep seepage	Acidity of seepage	Highway truck spills	Tailings pond leak	Tailings dams washout	Plant spills of acid
Water quality	3/3	3/3	1/1	1/2	1/1	1/2	1/1	1/1	2/2	1/1	1/1	1/1	1/3	1/4	3/3	1/2	1/2	1/3	1/3	1/1	1/1

Figure 1.86 Expanded matrix showing actions that would have an impact on water quality. *Source.* U.S. Department of the Interior.

considered to be moderate and was rated 4 because any environmental change that interrupts recreational use of public land in a highly populated state is relatively important.

8 *Scenic Views and Vistas (I.C.3.a).* This is one of the characteristics that would suffer the most serious impact from the proposed development. "Scenic views" would be impaired in quality by "industrial buildings," "highways and bridges," "transmission lines," "surface excavation," "trucking," and "emplacement of tailings." All these have a low to moderate value of *magnitude* and generally a somewhat higher figure for *importance*. Compared with any of the preceding items, the actions affecting "scenic views and vistas" are more numerous.

9 *Wilderness qualities (I.C.3.b).* The item "wilderness and open space" as a land use is not important in this area because it is not designated wilderness; accordingly, it was not rated. However the aesthetic and human interest item—"wilderness qualities"—is important. Thus a distinction is made between wilderness as a "land use," not important in this area, and the "quality" of wild land, which is highly important in the area. Impact on "wilderness qualities" under the proposed project would come primarily from "industrial buildings," "highways and bridges," "surface excavation," "trucking," and "emplacement of tailings." The influence of each of these factors on "wilderness qualities" may be considered to be a potentially important impact of the proposed development.

10 *Rare and Unique Species (I.C.3.h).* Possibly the most important environmental impact of the proposed development is its potential effect on the condor. A distinction is made between the biological conditions of fauna, "endangered species" (not shown), and the item under "aesthetics and human interest," "rare and unique species." The condor could be covered under either of these two, but should not be under both. Arbitrarily, then, the condor problem is specified under the item of "aesthetics and human interest."

The main nesting area for the condors is some miles to the southeast, and a naval training camp involving much heavy equipment is already operating near that nesting area. It is believed that the main effects on condors would come from the "blasting" and from the increase in "truck traffic." For both these actions, the *magnitude* is considered to be moderate and is rated 5, but the *importance* of the survival of condors was considered to be great; thus any impact is of high importance. Therefore those two items were given an *importance* score of 10. Also the sulfur fumes from "mineral processing" might be an important deterrent to the use of this part of the range by condors. The effect on the birds is unknown, but it is conceivable that air pollution would keep them from landing to catch prey wherever the smell and smoke occurred. The *magnitude* of impact of this action was assessed as 5 and *importance* as 10.

11 *Health and Safety (I.C.4.b).* "Health and safety" would be affected primarily by the increase in "trucking" on the highway as a result of mine operation.

Summary. Inspection of Figure 1.85 immediately gives the essence of the matrix analysis: the proposed actions having the most environmental impacts are the construction of "highways and bridges," the "blasting," "surface excavation," "mineral processing," "trucking," and the "emplacement of tailings." The environmental characteristics most frequently affected are those of "scenic views and vistas," "wilderness qualities," and "rare and unique species."

As an outcome of this matrix analysis, if the potential impact were deemed sufficiently great, the reviewers could ask the petitioners for the phosphate project, "What actions can you take to reduce these possible impacts to lower levels?" For example, assume that the company, in light of the comparative values shown in the simplified matrix, decided to substitute for daytime trucking, a nighttime-only schedule for moving supplies and products. If it were known that condors soar only during the day and would not be affected by nighttime traffic, that *magnitude-importance* impact might be significantly reduced. Assume also that as another step to reduce impact, the company decided to mat the ground surface prior to any rock blasting. If this step were deemed effective, the matrix entry of 5/10 of blasting on rare and unique species might be reduced the entry to 1/10. These changes may appear to be minor, but in fact they would cause a significant reduction in impact on the specific environmental factor shown to be most affected.

Environmental Impact Evaluation Example: Proposed Housing Tract

This sample is based on an actual case study, but all data (dates and names) are fictitious. It was prepared by LANCO. Maps referred to were omitted, since all city data and maps change constantly and are obvious supplementary supports for any official report.

This report is an analysis of Tentative Tract No. 26507 and the impact of the project in regard to property in the immediate area and the entire City of Torrance, California.

The major objective of the proposed project is the conversion of a partly vacant land area and operating open-pit sand extraction operation to a planned residential neighborhood. The current use of the 125-acre property is a major blighting influence on the surrounding residential environment, and its conversion to more compatible neighborhood-oriented uses is the primary objective of the development concept. Various environmental factors that would be modified, examined in detail in this impact study, can be summarized as follows:

1 Land use patterns proposed for change:
(*a*) Approximately 80 acres of open-pit mining (sand extraction) would be converted to planned residential (single-family detached, single-family attached, and neighborhood-oriented recreation–open space areas).
(*b*) Approximately 45 acres of vacant land (some of which provides heavy equipment access to the sand extraction areas) would be converted to single-family detached and attached dwellings and to a small neighborhood-oriented convenience commercial service area and recreation-open space for both public and private residential use.
2 Traffic and circulation patterns would change from heavy equipment operations to residential-oriented vehicular and service activities.
3 General environmental conditions would change from a noisy, dust-producing, heavy industrial condition to a quiet, passive residential neighborhood status. In addition, an uncontrolled recreational vehicle activity, which currently creates poor environmental relationships with peripheral residential areas, would be eliminated.

Technologic Possibilities of Achieving the Objective. Preliminary investigations of technical factors have been conducted on the property, the experts believe that the land is suitable for development as a planned residential neighborhood.

The reports of the preliminary investigations are:

1 *Soils.*
(*a*) Preliminary site investigation, dated October 13, 1971.
(*b*) Buttress calculations and seismic considerations, dated February 22, 1972.
(*c*) Settlement studies, dated February 23, 1972.
2 *Geology.*
(*a*) Engineering geologic report, dated October 11, 1971.
(*b*) Seismic report, dated February 5, 1972.
3 *Domestic Water:* Preliminary engineering report, dated October 20, 1971.

Other improvements listed below are adjacent to the project and are of sufficient capacity to accommodate the service requirements from the property:

1 Streets.
2 Sewer.
3 Storm drain.
4 Electric.
5 Natural gas.
6 Telephone.

Proposed Actions and Alternatives. Plans for high-density residential development have been submitted to the City of Torrance by other developers. The previous proposals (one for construction of 3600 dwellings) met with considerable opposition from the adjacent homeowners' group and the city staff. This design for a planned residential neighborhood, consisting of about 750 homes, was conceived to conform to the present land use of the adjoining areas and various recommendations made by the city staff. The proposed improvements would be constructed in conformity to the ordinances, requirements, codes, and recommendations of the City of Torrance, the County of Los Angeles, and the State of California.

Characteristics and Conditions of the Existing Environment. The proposed neighborhood development is located in the City of Torrance at its southerly limit, between Crenshaw Boulevard and Hawthorne Boulevard. The project encompasses approximately 125 acres.

The majority of the property is now under mining lease to Chandler's Sand and Gravel Company. They are extracting sand at the rate of approximately 500,000 cubic yards per year. The southerly third of the property has been stripped from previous mining operations, leaving some near-vertical banks ranging up to 100 feet high. This area is sparsely covered with chaparral-type vegetation, some grasses, and numerous roads and trails from motorcycles and off-road recreational vehicles. Approximately 10 acres of the southerly third of the property had been used as a disposal site for waste products from oil drilling (to the depth of 40 feet in some areas).

The Los Angeles County Sanitation District is presently conducting a sanitary landfill operation on property in the City of Rolling Hills Estates, adjacent to the southerly line of the proposed project. The landfill encompasses approximately 185 acres. On completion of the landfill, an 18-hole golf course and a regional park would be constructed by the county. Completion of the landfill is tentatively scheduled for 1976 or 1977, and the regional park complex about one year thereafter.

The Los Angeles County Sanitation District has stated that provisions for control of escaping gas, polluted water, and erosion control are a part of their improvement plans. If polluted water is found to be escaping from the project, it will be conducted to a sanitary sewer by the County of Los Angeles.

The property is now subject to considerable erosion because of steep slopes and the absence of ground cover. However the major portion of eroded material flows to the open mine pits and does not materially affect adjacent properties. Nevertheless, a considerable amount of eroded material enters the Los Angeles County Flood Control District storm drain at the northwest corner of the project.

The adjacent area to the north, east, and west in the City of Torrance is composed of single-family homes on lots ranging from 5000 to 6000 square feet. There is considerable commercial and high-density residential development in this area. South of the project, in the City of Rolling Hills Estates, is the future 185-acre park, as well as single-family residential units on lots of approximately 20,000 square feet. The residential area is significantly separated from the City of Torrance and the proposed development by changes in elevation and existing topography.

Hawthorne Boulevard, adjacent to the proposed development, is now a 4-lane divided highway, and Crenshaw Boulevard on the east is scheduled for improvement to 4-lane divided-highway status this year. Construction of the Crenshaw Boulevard improvement will be done by the Los Angeles County Road Department using state gasoline tax funds.

The City of Torrance presently has a 10,000-gallon underground concrete water reservoir at Crenshaw Boulevard and Rolling Hills Road. However the adjacent areas suffer from the lack of water pressure and adequate fire fighting volume. This situation arose when many multiple-family and commercial developments were constructed in this area.

The proposed project is served by the Torrance Unified School District for kindergarten through twelfth grade. Grades K-8 are served by Walteria and Hillside Schools, which are both approximately 1/2 mile from the center of the project. Grades 9 through 12 are served by South High School, which is approximately 1 mile away.

The City of Torrance is part of the community college district served by El Camino College located at the northwest corner of the city, approximately 5 miles distant.

Alternate Engineering Plans. This report is based on Plan C-180, however changes in the map will be made after final conditions and recommendations are obtained from the city. As stated earlier, plans had been submitted previously to the City of Torrance and were denied. This information is included so that this report will conform to guidelines outlined in "A Procedure for Evaluating Environmental Impact," Geological Survey Circular No. 45, U.S. Department of the Interior, published 1971. The circular was provided by the City of Torrance to assist in the preparation of this report.

Identification of Impact and Analysis of Its Magnitude to Adjacent Area and to the City of Torrance. The identification of impact was achieved using a matrix (not given here). Existing characteristics and conditions in the area were listed on the left vertical side of the page. The proposed actions or improvements were listed at the top horizontally, permitting the investigator to make a comprehensive review of the possible interactions between the existing environment and the proposed actions.

The impact, when identified, was assigned a number between 1 and 10; 10 represents the greatest magnitude or impact, and 1, the least. A plus sign preceding the assessment number in a given interaction indicates that the interaction is beneficial. The impact was rated on the magnitude to the adjacent area and the city at large by separate number values in each interaction box.

Effects of Grading, Alteration of Drainage, Erosion Control: Items A–C, Table 1.16

1 *Mineral Resources.* Construction of the project would eliminate the present mining operation, which has been in operation since the 1920s. The product is a fine to coarse sand used for asphalt road-paving plants. Numerous other sources are available within the Los Angeles area at approximately the same price to the consumer. The operation is extracting approximately 500,000 cubic yards per year.

When the subdivision receives tentative approval by the city, the owner will proceed to negotiate the purchase of the mining lease. If lease is purchased and grading is started in the next 6 to 12 months, adequate material will be available on the project to bring grades to planned elevations.

2 *Landform.* Grading of the project would eliminate the unsightly stripped hills visible from most of Torrance on the southerly portion of the property, and the existing mining pits, in excess of 100 feet deep, would be transformed into usable building sites. Slopes and other open spaces would be planted and irrigated to

Table 1.16 Identification of Impact and Analysis of Magnitude

IMPACT ON ADJACENT AREAS #/# IMPACT ON CITY
(short term) (long term)

Numbers 1-10 = Magnitude of Impact
Symbol Plus = Impact is Beneficial

	A	B	C	D	E	F	G	H	I	J	K	L	M	N	O
1. Mineral Resources	1/1														
2. Land Form	+10/+3	2/1	+5/+2										10/+2	10/2	10/10
3. Underground Water		1/1													
4. Climate	4/1								+5/+3	+7/2	+5/+1	+2/+1	+10/+2	+10/+2	+10/+10
5. Erosion	+5/+2	+5/+2	+5/+2										+5/+2		+5/+10
6. Stability (slides and slumps)	+9/+2		+9/+2										+4/+2		
7. Stress & Strain (earthquake)	+5/+9														
8. Plant Life	10/5		+10/+5										+10/+5	+5/+2	+10/+3
9. Mining	10/5														
10. Waste Disposal	10/5														+8/+4
11. Scout Clubhouse	5/2												+5/+2	+5/+2	+8/+3
12. Health & Safety	4/2	+4/+2	+4/+2	+4/+2	+5/+2				+4/+1				+5/+2	+10/+4	
13. Truck Traffic	+4/+2								+2/+1			2/1			+8/+3
14. Auto Traffic	+5/+2								+5/+2	3/1	2/1	1/1			6/2
15. Utilities A. Telephone								2/1							8/4
16. B. Electric							2/1								3/4
17. C. Gas						2/1									
18. Domestic Water	+8/+2				+8/+2										
19. Sewer				2/1											
20. Storm Drain	+2/+1	2/1	+2/+1	+2/+1											
21. Density										3/1	2/1				
22. Schools										4/2	3/2	+2/+1			
23. Parks									10/4	4/2	3/1				
24. City Income										5/5	5/5	5/5			
25. City Expense										3/3	3/3	3/3			
26. Economy										3/3	7/3	2/3			

A = Grading
B = Alteration of Drainage
C = Erosion Control
D = Sewer & Storm Drain
E = Domestic Water
F = Gas
G = Electrical
H = Telephone
I = Streets
J = R-1
K = R.T.H
L = Commercial
M = Landscape
N = Parks
O = Visual Impact

Source. U.S. Department of Interior.

control erosion and to harmonize with the surrounding residential areas.

3 *Underground Water*. The underground water supply would not be appreciably affected by grading. However a minor amount of runoff presently collected in mine pits would be diverted into storm drains. Water level is approximately sea level, and the finished elevations of the project range from 200 to 315 feet above sea level.

4 *Climate*. The project would not affect the general climate in the area. However it is important to note that oxygen-producing plant materials installed as part of the residential environment will replace the sparsely foliated slopes and dust-producing open-pit mines. The grading operation anticipated as part of constructing the new neighborhood would be confined to a relatively short period and would result in the elimination of the dust-producing activity.

5 *Erosion.* Erosion would be eliminated; however most of the existing eroded material is deposited in the mining pits on the property.

6 *Stability.* Slides and slumps would be eliminated because the near-vertical slopes ranging in height up to 100 feet would be graded down. Grading would be accomplished adhering to all prevailing governmental requirements and would be certified by the supervising soils engineer and geologist.

7 *Earthquake.* There are numerous faults or shear zones in the South Bay area. The nearest fault that appears on a published map is commonly called the Palos Verdes Fault; it lies about 1 mile to the northwest and it trends northwest-southeast. Geologic testing in Tract 26507 uncovered direct and indirect evidence of a northwest-southeast trending shear zone cutting through the longitudinal axis of the property. It is referred to as an inferred shear zone in the geologic report. A fault trace approximately 1100 feet north and parallel to the inferred shear zone on the property is shown on the California Division of Oil and Gas Map in "Summary of Operations" (Vol. 42, No. 2, July–December, 1956). None of the abovementioned fault or shear zones have undergone movement in recent geologic times and are therefore assumed to be inactive, as stated in the geologist's report.

8 *Plant Life.* The sparse indigenous plant life would be replaced by considerably more vegetation both in community open space areas (public and private) and in individual yard areas proposed for the project. In addition, existing plant materials are highly flammable and threaten the safety of the surrounding residential areas. All vegetation proposed for the project area would be watered or irrigated to reduce the potential for fire damage. There are no specimen materials whose loss would constitute a problem from either historic or visual standpoints.

9 *Waste Disposal.* The large amounts of waste oil material dumped on the property will be processed and used in the fill or hauled away from the property. The decision will be made by the supervising soils engineer during grading.

10 *Walteria Businessmen's Club Clubhouse.* The Walteria Businessmen's Club presently maintains a clubhouse on property owned by the developer at the northwest corner of the project. The clubhouse is used by the Boy Scouts and various other civic and service groups. At his own expense, the developer plans to relocate the clubhouse to an area adjacent to or within proposed public park in Tract 26507.

11 *Health and Safety.* Grading would eliminate a large dangerous area now used by many operators of motorcycles and off-road vehicles. Many injuries have occurred in the past, although there is no record of fatalities. The property is presently fenced and is patrolled 18 hours a day in response to numerous complaints from nearby homeowners. However the fence has been cut a number of times and it has been impossible to keep all trespassers off the property.

A large silt disposal pond now used by the mining operation would be eliminated. This area is now fenced; however the material inside the fence is highly water saturated and reacts much like quicksand to any weight exerted from the surface or from persons attempting to walk across the pond.

The adjacent areas have certainly been affected by dust and noise from mining operations, trucks, and motorcycles, as well as by dust from large exposed ground areas during prevailing afternoon winds. Many other items relating to health and safety are discussed in this section.

12 *Truck Traffic.* Grading of the project would eliminate the mining and support operations including trucks, which account for more than 5% of the total daytime traffic on Crenshaw Boulevard.

13 *Automobile Traffic.* The filling of the mine pits and grading for Bluff Road would allow for completion of Bluff Road, which has been in the planning stages by the City of Torrance and the Los Angeles County Road Department for many years.

14 *Storm Drain.* Grading property to plan elevations would allow for construction of approximately 480 feet of 10 × 10 foot reinforced concrete box storm drain at the northwest corner of the development. This section is now an open ditch. Completion of this drain would also prevent eroded material from entering the drain, thereby lowering maintenance costs.

The existing drains at each end of the unimproved section are now accessible to pedestrian traffic through openings in the existing trash protectors. Completion of the storm drain surely would have a beneficial impact on the adjacent homeowners by denying this hazard to the children in the area.

Sewer and Storm Drain Item D, Table 1.16. The City of Torrance and the Los Angeles County Flood Control District have existing facilities adjacent to or within the project, and these authorities state that the facilities are of sufficient size and capacity to accommodate the additional loading from Tract 26507. In-tract storm drains could accept all runoff from project and channel water into existing storm drains.

Domestic Water Item E, Table 1.16. The City of Torrance has commissioned Wildan Engineering Associates to design a water system that would eliminate the deficient water pressure and fire flow requirements in the area up to 2 miles from the proposed project. This would considerably lower potential fire losses to existing improved residential and commercial development throughout the water improvement district, increasing water pressure to the existing residents in the higher adjacent areas, as well.

Grading would allow for construction of the 12-inch water main now proposed by the city to correct the water pressure deficiency in the entire area as mentioned previously. The water main is proposed to be installed in Winlock Road, north of the project for a distance of approximately 4000 feet. This street is composed of single-family residences, and water main installation would create numerous hazards and inconveniences for residents. If the project is approved, construction of the 12 inch main would be routed through the project in stages before completion of residential development in that stage, thus eliminating the danger and inconvenience to the nearby residents.

The solution to the problem as proposed in the Wildan report could be more economically achieved in conjunction with improvements in Tract 26507.

Assuming that construction on Tract 26507 is started in the near future, better financing arrangements could be negotiated with the developer as opposed to the 1911 Act Assessment District as recommended in the Wildan report.

Water mains within Tract 26507 and connections to existing water mains would upgrade circulation and fire flow throughout the system.

Gas, Electric, and Telephone: Items F–H, Table 1.16. The following utilities have adjacent to the project facilities of sufficient size and capacity to accommodate the additional loading from the project.

1 *Sewer:* Los Angeles County Sanitation District.
2 *Storm Drain:* City of Torrance and Los Angeles County Flood Control District.
3 *Telephone:* Pacific Telephone Company.
4 *Gas:* Southern California Gas Company.
5 *Electric:* Southern California Edison Company.

It should be noted that all utilities to be installed in the project would be placed underground.

Streets: Item I, Table 1.16. Street improvements within the project, including Bluff Road, could provide for increased circulation throughout the area and would tend to balance the traffic count on Hawthorne Boulevard and Crenshaw Boulevard. The Bluff Road improvement would also relieve some of the east-west traffic from Palos Verdes Drive North and Pacific Coast Highway. The extension of Madison Avenue to Bluff Road would relieve approximately 6% of the Hawthorne Boulevard traffic generated from the project.

Streets within the project would provide access by residents of the adjacent areas to public park facilities within the project. The cost of signaling Bluff Road at the revisions of the existing 3-way intersections at Hawthorne and Crenshaw will be paid by the developer.

Effects of R-1, R.T.H., and Commercial Development Zoning: Items J–L, Table 1.16

Climate. Development and landscaping of proposed homes and nighborhood-type commercial establishments would eliminate the hazards of dust and noise as discussed earlier.

Traffic. The project would generate traffic that is estimated to increase the count on Crenshaw Boulevard approximately 13.25% and on Hawthorne Boulevard approximately 13.92%, based on a traffic count dated October 9, 1970 by the City of Torrance. These percentages do not reflect the following:

1 The 1972 count on Crenshaw and Hawthorne Boulevards has increased approximately 4% from 1970. Therefore previously stated percentage increases would be lower each year.
2 The Madison Avenue extention to Bluff Road would lower the Hawthorne Boulevard count from the project approximately 9%.
3 Trucks from existing mining, which accounts for approximately 5% of Crenshaw traffic count, would cease to operate in the area when grading was completed.
4 Truck traffic to and from sanitary landfill would stop when landfill was complete (1976–1977).
5 Traffic generated from the project should have no effect on the 1990 traffic projection by the Los Angeles County Regional Planning Commission because the projection was based on all property in the area at the highest use. Therefore impact on traffic count in the area would be a reasonably short-term effect.
6 In addition, it should be noted that traffic comparisons are made primarily on a statistical basis. The character of the traffic currently generated from the property and its interference with other movements should be explained. Currently, heavy, slow truck traffic exerts a very hazardous influence on the surrounding area (see Table 1.17). Both Hawthorne and Crenshaw are rela-

Table 1.17 Traffic Impact

	Traffic	Traffic	1	2	3	4	5	6	7
Crenshaw	20,400	28,600							
Trips per Unit			540	504	512	516	352	140	140
Culm. Total			540	1044	1556	2072	2424	2564	2704
% Increase	13.25%	9.45%	2.65	5.12	7.63	10.16	11.88	12.57	13.21
Hawthorne	24,600	31,400							
Trips per Unit			540	624	632	636	472	260	260
Culm. Total			540	1164	1796	2432	2904	3164	3424
% Increase	13.92%	10.90%	2.20	4.73	7.30	9.89	11.80	12.86	13.92

Const. Units	Start Date	Finish Date	R-1 No. Lots	R.T.H. No. Lots	Total	Culm. Total
1	3/73	9/73	135		135	135
2	9/73	3/74	91	50	141	276
3	3/74	9/74	93	50	143	419
4	9/74	3/75	94	50	144	563
5	3/75	9/75	53	50	103	666
6	9/75	3/76		50	50	716
7	3/76	9/76		50	50	766

(4) TRUCK TRAFFIC VS. DAYTIME TOTAL TRAFFIC

STREET	MINING	LAND FILL
Crenshaw Blvd.	5%	18%
Hawthorne Blvd.	-	10%

Source. U.S. Department of the Interior.

tively high-speed arterials serving the Palos Verdes Peninsula. Daily interference (uncontrolled) creates constant friction and safety problems. Street design proposed for the project is intended to minimize this condition with proper controls and a compatible type of traffic.

Density. The density in the proposed project is less per usable acre than in previously developed adjacent areas. The following information was obtained by dividing the lot areas in the adjoining area by the number of residential electric meter services for that area (as supplied by Southern California Edison).

These calculations have been devised on the net basis, so that the closest comparison of existing development and the proposed project can be made. The areas measured included residential land uses and excluded tributary streets.

Area	Total Lot Area (acres)	Residential Electric Meters	Dwelling Units per Acre
1	23.305	437	18.75
2	115.7	1328	11.47
3	94.884	586	6.24
Tract 26507	85.9	766	8.92

Area 3 is composed of single-family residences on minimum lots of 5000 square feet. The development is in hilly terrain, and numerous slopes increase the square footage considerably. However many lots have less than 5000 square feet of usable flat pad area.

Schools. Pupil generation from R-1 and R.T.H. development can be readily absorbed into the existing facilities from kindergarten through twelfth grade. When

Table 1.18 Zoning Impact Data for the Torrance School District (February 16, 1972)

Impact on Schools

Source	Grades (K-8)	Grades (9-12)
R-1	0.7	0.08
R.T.H.	0.14	0.06

Pupil Generation and Construction Units

	R-1					Pupils 6 Generated			R.T.H.	
Unit #	Start Date	Complet. Date	Lower Lots	View Lots	Totals	Grades Unit Total	K-8 Cum. Tot.	Grades 9-12	Dwell. Units	Grades 9-12
1	3-73	9-73	94	41	135	95	95	11		
2	9-73	3-74	41	50	91	64	159	7	50	3
3	3-74	9-74	41	52	93	65	224	7	50	3
4	9-74	3-75	42	52	94	66	290	8	50	3
5	3-75	9-75		53	53	37	327	4	50	3
6	9-75	3-76							50	3
7	3-76	9-76							50	3
TOTALS			218	248	466	327	327	37	300	18

Grand Totals at Completion of Project

Grades	R-1	R.T.H.	Totals
K-8	327	0	327
9-12	37	18	55

1969-1973 Enrollment Figures from Torrance School District

Amounts Based on Enrollment

School Year	Hillside School K-8	Walteria School K-8	Totals	South High School
1969-70	507	618	1,125	
1970-71	489	611	1,100	
1971-72	367	696	1,063	
1972-73	347	693	1,040	2,755
Capacity	576	800	1,376	3,000

Source. U.S. Department of the Interior.

the project is completed, the schools will be about 4.2% below optimum capacity at the grammar school level, and about 6.3% below at the high school level.

Since the R.T.H. development is to be restricted to families with children older than 14 years of age, it would not generate pupils of grammar school age.

The school enrollment at the two grammar schools appears to be declining at a rate of between 3 and 5% per year; therefore the project should not have a long-term impact on the school system. Table 1.18 gives pupil generation figures and school service areas.

The proposed project would not overload the existing school facilities as Figure 1.87 demonstrates. Moreover, very little additional vacant land is available for residential development in the school service area. Thus it is highly unlikely that existing school plants could ever achieve full capacity usage.

Parks: Item N, Table 1.16. The City of Torrance requires that park space be provided as a condition of approving any residential development in the community. The city utilizes a formula of dollar value park land required per dwelling unit. Instead, contributions of land may be required as a condition of approval of some subdivisions by the city.

Parks for this project would be provided by the developer in the form of land at fair market value up to amount of fees. Park fees in the City of Torrance, presently $350 per dwelling unit, and would increase by $50 each year on July 1, until they reach a maximum of $550 on July 1, 1975 (see Table 1.19).

The area is now served by the 4.46-acre Walteria Park and by the Alta Loma Park (about 7 acres). Walteria Park is west of Hawthorne Boulevard at Pacific Coast Highway, and Alta Loma Park is east of Crenshaw Boulevard and south of Pacific Coast Highway. Approximately 4600 residents of the Walteria area between Hawthorne and Crenshaw must now cross the 4-lane highways to reach either park.

The developer of Tract 26507 will dedicate at least 5

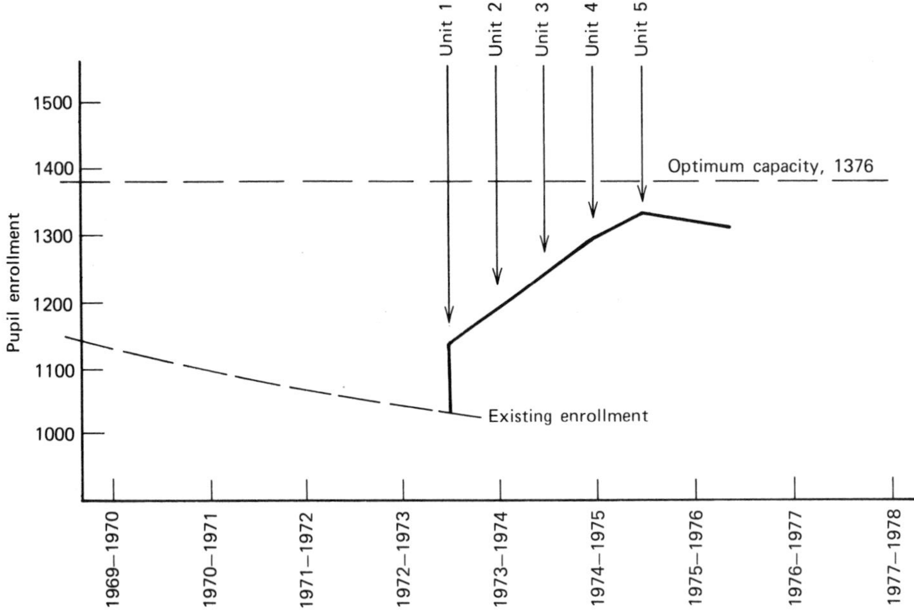

Figure 1.87 Enrollment chart. *Source*. U.S. Department of the Interior.

Table 1.19 Projected Park Fees Generated from Tract 26507

Release	Start Date	Dwelling Units	Fees per Dwelling Unit	Sub Total
1	6/73	135	$400.00	$54,000.00
2	9/73	141	$450.00	$63,450.00
3	3/74	143	$450.00	$64,350.00
4	9/74	144	$500.00	$72,000.00
5	3/75	103	$500.00	$51,500.00
6	9/75	50	$550.00	$27,500.00
7	3/76	50	$550.00	$27,500.00
			Total Park Fees	$359,300.00

Source. U.S. Department of the Interior.

acres of park land to the City of Torrance. The park would be placed adjacent to the north tract line to allow use by residents of the adjacent improved area who must now cross the highways to reach a park. The numerous other parks and recreational facilities to be improved in the immediate area are listed in Table 1.20.

The improvement of the regional park and Rolling Hills Estates Rural Youth Center are conditioned on completion of the existing sanitary landfill, tentatively scheduled for 1977.

The public tennis facilities planned for the Walteria Reservoir are to be privately operated on a lease-back arrangement with the City of Torrance.

This total is revenue generated in the form of taxes directly applicable to project residents; it does not include benefits to the economy and indirect revenue generated from a combined estimated annual income of $11,490,000 for all residents in the project, as shown on page 142.

Table 1.20 Parks

Name	Agency	Acres	Use	Tent. Compl. Date
Regional Park	L.A. Co. Parks & Rec.	185 + or −	25A Gen. 160 A Golf	1978–79
Walteria Reservoir	City of Torrance	10 + or −	Tennis Courts & Pro Shop	Not Available
Rolling Hills Est. Rural Youth Center	City of Rolling Hills Estates	34.84	Equestrian Oriented	1978–80

Source. U.S. Department of the Interior.

Table 1.21 City Income from Project

CITY INCOME FROM PROJECT

(Tax rates and sources from City of Torrance, William Dundore, Director of Finance, April 3, 1972. Projections by writer)

Tract No. 26507 would generate annual revenue to the City of Torrance as follows:

A. Property Tax

1. Market Value

R-1	466 units @ 51,400 each	=	23,946,000
R.T.H.	300 units @ 40,000 each	=	12,000,000
Commercial	10 acres @ 700,000	=	7,000,000
			$42,946,000

2. Assessed valuation
42,946,000 X 25% = $10,736,500

3. Tax Rate

Torrance	$1.1380 per hundred
County Schools	.0328 per hundred
Unified Schools	5.0921 per hundred
Total	$6.2629 per hundred

4. Tax Generated 107.736 X 62629 = $674,739

B. State Disbursement to City

$18.00 per capita
766 units X 3.47 people = 2658 people
2658 X $18.00 = $47,844

Note: Legislation is pending for Federal Fund Sharing which would increase disbursement by $12.00 per capita.

C. 1% City Sales Tax

766 units @ $15,000 combined annual income
766 X $40.00 per year = $30,640

D. 5% Utility Users Tax

1. Estimated utility cost, per month, per unit

Gas	$15.00
Water & Trash	10.00
Telephone	15.00
Electric	15.00
Total	$55.00

766 units x $55 x 12 months = $505,160

$505,160 x 5% = $25,258

Total annual revenue from project $778,481

Source. U.S. Department of the Interior.

1	Total residential units	766
2	Estimated annual income per dwelling unit	$15,000
3	$15,000 × 766	$11,490,000

Revenues from water, trash and building permits, and so on, are not included because these functions are self-supporting and do not create appreciable net revenue accruing to the city.

The sources of revenue for the entire City of Torrance are as follows:

1	Property tax	26%
2	Sales tax	20%
3	Utility user's tax	7%
4	Revenue from other agencies	10%
5	Other taxes	8%
6	Charges for current services	5%
7	Airport, bus, and water	15%
8	Licenses and permits	1%
9	All other	8%
	Total	100%

Direct annual revenue as projected above includes only 63% (sources 1, 2, 3, and 4) of the total sources of revenue for the entire city.

City Expenses from Project

Schools (*Source*. Robert J. Ellsworth, Child Welfare and Attendance, Torrance Unified School District, April 7, 1972).

1	Average annual cost per pupil, grades K–12	$789.26
2	Total pupils from project	382
3	Additional cost to school district from project, 382 × $789.26	$301,497

Fire Protection (*Source*. Fire Marshal Agapito, Torrance Fire Department, April 6, 1975).

1	1 additional man per 1000 population	
2	766 units × 3.47	2658 people
3	3 additional men, plus miscellaneous expense	
4	Additional cost to fire department from project	$60,000

Police Protection (*Source*. Sgt. Dunn, Research Division, Torrance Police Department April 5, 1972).

1	1.3 police per 1000 people	
2	766 units × 3.47	2658 people
3	3 police additional and 1 additional record clerk	
4	Additional cost to police department from project	$90,000

Street and Sewer Maintenance (*Source*. Glen Kirkruff, Torrance Street Maintenance Department April 7, 1972). Costs are based on the first 20-year period.

1	Parkway trees, 700 × $11.00 each	$7,700
2	Street cleaning, $5 per curb mile: 38,000 lin. ft of curb = 7.2 miles, 7.2 × $5 =	$36
3	Street and sidewalk maintenance	$1,800
4	Sewer maintenance: $0.04 per lin. ft of main line sewer, $0.04 × 19,000 lin. ft =	$760
5	Additional cost to street maintenance from project	$10,296

Parks and Recreation (*Source*. Harry Van Bellehem and John Hoffman, Torrance Park Department April 7, 1972). Costs are based on a 5-acre park.

1	Maintenance of improvements	$10,000
2	Staffing at park	$15,000–$25,000

Extra costs for police and fire protection are based on population only and do not reflect service requirements for commercial and industrial facilities; assuming that such nonresidential facilities account for 50% of fire and police calls, the actual service requirement for residential development can be assumed to be 50% of the "per capita" cost derived from relating fire protection budgets solely to population.

Total of all additional annual city expense from project	$486,793
Total annual revenues from project	$778,481
Surplus revenue to city	$291,688

Economy. Tract 26507 will create 766 dwelling units plus 10 acres of commercial property. Assuming a total value of $42,946,000 for the project upon completion, it is reasonable to conclude that a major portion of this amount will be spent on improvements to the land over a period of 3½ years. The personnel and materials to construct the improvements will be supplied by local firms.

Money spent for construction of the project could have an immediate beneficial impact on the area economy; the annual income from residents of the project would have a continuing impact on the economy for years to come.

Conclusion. Construction of Tract 26507 would eliminate the mining operation with all its offensive side effects (e.g., the scarred hillside visible from most of Torrance), help correct a deficient water system, create additional park lands to update the existing park system in the area, and provide for better traffic circulation and safety in the adjacent improved area. Other favorable considerations are as follows:

1 The mix of R-1, R.T.H., and commercial zoning would be compatible with land use in the adjacent areas.
2 The proposed improvements would materially appreciate the value of the homes in adjacent areas. The increased valuation should be approximately 10% for each $25,000 to $30,000 home.
3 The project would generate considerable surplus funds for the City of Torrance as shown in city costs versus city expenses, and there would be a generous cash flow into the area.
4 The visual impact of landscaping on lots, slopes, parks, parkways, new homes, and streets in this planned development would be a drastic change from the blighted property today.
5 The project would be visible to travelers on Hawthorne and Crenshaw Boulevards, aircraft approaching Torrance Municipal Airport, and residents in the lower elevation areas of the city.

It is the opinion of the writer after thoroughly analyzing the effects on the environment of this project that the positive impact on the environment far outweighs the negative impact and that the development of this project would be of great benefit to the area.

LAFAYETTE SQUARE
Washington, D.C.
Architects: John Carl Warnecke & Associates
Photo: J. Alexander

TWO ARCHITECTURAL PROGRAMMING

Webster's Dictionary defines programming as a process leading to the statement of an architectural problem and the requirements to be met in offering a solution. In this chapter we are concerned with programming a specific architectural solution on a specific site. Programming is basically a problem-seeking process. It defines the *problem* that the design must *solve*. An architect can become involved with architectural programming in many ways. For instance, an architect must recognize and analyze major influences that may give form to, hence directly determine, the physical design. It is the architect's responsibility to convert raw data and the client's wishes into negotiable information. He or she must also be aware of missing information, must evaluate the implications of various data, and must distinguish between pertinent facts and irrelevant details.

A major aspect of programming is to establish realistic *requirements* and explore *alternatives* in order to find the

ARCHITECTURAL PROGRAMMING

	FORM	FUNCTION	ECONOMY	TIME
	Site	People	Initial budget	Present
	Environment	Activities	Operating	Future
	Quality	Relationship	Long term	
GOALS	Site elements	Human values	Limit of funds	Growth
Decide	Psychological environment	Relationships	Quality	Occupancy
	Quality space	Efficiency	Time	Change
	Neighbors	Identity	Limits	Limits
	Projected image	Relationship		
		Activities		
FACTS	Site analysis	Statistical data	Economic data	Schedule
Organize	Codes	User characteristics	Budget	Economic
Analyze	Psychological implications	Community considerations	Market analysis	projections
		Area parameters	Feasibility	
		Space limits		
CONCEPT	Orientation	Priority	Multifunction	Convertibility
Uncover	Place concept	Flow	Flexibility	Expansibility
Develop	Psychological influence	Affinities		Phasing
		Security		
NEEDS	Environment	Area requirement	Budget analysis	Phasing growth
Determine	Site	Parking	Initial cost	Escalation
	Cost influence	Efficiency ratio		Change implications
	Form-giving image	Alternatives		
		Performance requirements		

uniqueness of a building project. Once the simplest, clearest, and most definitive form of the building's problems is stated, design can begin.

To summarize, *architectural programming* refers to the architect's ability to do the following:

1 Turn raw data into negotiable, useful information.
2 Evaluate data for design and analyze their influences on major design elements.
3 Compare alternatives and establish requirements.
4 Abstract all program requirements to find the project's "uniqueness."

1 PROGRAMMING AND SPACE DETERMINATIONS

Sophisticated architectural programming and efficient utilization of space are essential today. One reason is the very complex organization of our industry, commerce, administration, teaching, communal living, and so on, which requires buildings with an equally complex organization of space. Furthermore, the costs of construction and space are now so high that the complex functions just enumerated must be accommodated in a minimum of space and structure.

Space Needs

The allocation of the right amount of space to every activity and function in a program greatly determines the quality and efficiency of a design. The architect, at this point of the programming process, needs to translate the owner/user's ideas into square-foot areas of net usable space as well as into square feet of space required for service and circulation. This is accomplished by following the standard figures of space requirements that have been established over the years for almost every function of concern.

In a restaurant for 150 persons, for instance, the size of the dining room can be estimated by assuming a space need of 15 square feet per person, a standard figure based on the space needed for seating as well as for circulation. The space required for kitchen and services can be estimated in the same manner.

The share of floor area needed for services and circulation in a building determines its efficiency. This factor is a ratio derived by dividing the square feet of net usable area by the square feet of gross building area. In an apartment building the net usable area would correspond to the inside floor spaces of each apartment, and the gross area would be measured to the exterior face of the building's perimeter walls. This efficiency factor varies greatly with the type of structure, but it usually lies somewhere between 60 and 80%.

The estimate of square foot floor areas is not always derived from the individual's space needs, as in the example of the restaurant. Sometimes objects determine the dimensions; for example, the size of the automobile determines the floor area of a garage. An arbitrary and/or conventional set of rules can also be the determinant, as in the case of the conventional sizes of playing areas of sports facilities.

Finally, safety standards specified in the applicable building code are determinants of square foot areas. Corridors and stair wells, for instance, require certain minimum dimensions to secure safe egress for the number of occupants they serve.

GATHERING, ANALYSIS, EVALUATION AND ORGANIZATION OF FACTS. These form the core of programming in architecture. They are essentially concerned with insuring that as many of the important consequences of the building design as possible are anticipated and planned for so that the building is successful in these critical respects.

RESPONSE TO FACTS IN DESIGN. The planning of the building is based upon the establishment of the desired building effects or consequences in programming and the creation of the physical product which will most effectively bring about those consequences. The more comprehensive the designer's program the more knowledgeably he can plan his product.

BUILDING. The physical product of the design process is not the designer's final concern. The consequences of the building are in the last analysis the critical issue in design.

BUILDING CONSEQUENCES. Buildings will have their effects whether planned for or not. Because a fact has not been considered in programming or design will not prohibit it from having its consequences.

EVALUATION. This is an effective method for expanding our awareness of consequences of individual design decisions and building features. In effect, evaluation is a form of research and serves as a feedback mechanism to facts, programming and design. Evaluation and feedback loops also occur between every event in the sequence.

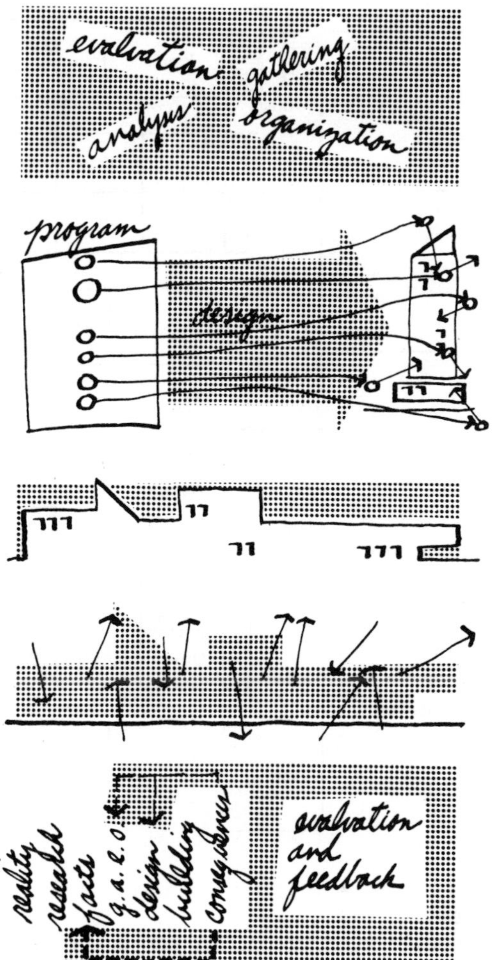

Figure 2.1 *Source.* Edward T. White, *Introduction to Architectural Programming*, Architectural Media, 1972.

Estimating Space Needs

The numeric method expresses quantitatively the space and time required for all the potential individual activities of future users. This method is most widely used for detailed estimates. For a factory, these values relate to the production process inside the structure; but in the case of a shopping center, they may be taken from census data of the catchment area. To illustrate the process of the numeric method, this chapter analyzes a few facilities.

Colleges

Libraries. The type of space needed can be divided into three categories: stack space, reader space, and service space.

The *stack space,* or collection space, is usually planned large enough to have every book shelf only three-quarters filled. A standard figure for space need is 0.1 square foot for each book. There is a space economy, however, and this figure varies with the total number of volumes collected as follows:

Up to 150,000 books	=	0.1 net ft^2 per book
Additional 150,000 books	=	0.09 net ft^2 per book
Additional 300,000 books	=	0.08 net ft^2 per book
All other additional books	=	0.07 net ft^2 per book

For materials other than books, space requirements are determined by using the following equivalence data:

15 classified pamphlets	=	1 book
15 music scores	=	1 book
6 records	=	1 book
4 microfilm cassettes	=	1 book
9 maps	=	1 book

Reading space requirements depend on the type of library, since research work takes up much more space than general reading. In a college library, then, the

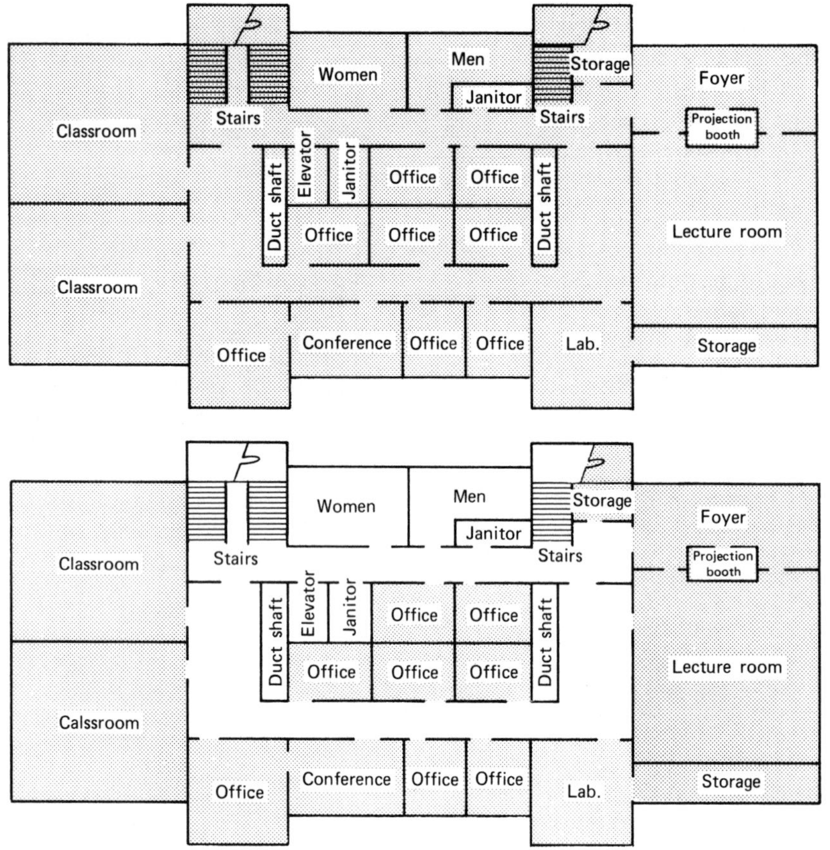

Figure 2.2 Gross area (*top*) and net area (*bottom*). *Source*. Architectural License Seminar.

number of square feet needed per station varies with the status of the reader as follows:

Undergraduate and intermediate graduate student	7.5 ft²
Advanced graduate student, and faculty with low research level	15 ft²
Faculty with high research level	30 ft²

As a rule of thumb, the total number of reading stations should be 25% of the total number of students.

Service space is usually estimated as a percentage of reading space, and 25%, which includes space for offices, reference desks, the general catalog, and archives, is considered standard.

Based on the data given above, the space for a college library could be estimated as follows:

Stack space

150,000 books	× 0.1	=	15,000 net ft²
100,000 books	× 0.09	=	9,000 net ft²
100,000 classified pamphlets	× 0.006	=	600 net ft²
			30,000 net ft²

Reading space:

2000 undergraduates	× 7.5	=	15,000 net ft²
1000 graduates	× 15	=	15,000 net ft²
100 faculty members	× 30	=	3,000 net ft²
			33,000 net ft²

Service space: 33,000 × 0.25	=	8,250 net ft²
Total net area needed	=	71,250 ft²
Total gross building area (70% efficiency)	=	101,800 ft²

Lecture Halls. The total space required for classrooms depends on the following factors:

- The total number of students enrolled in the department.
- The number of classes per week (in weekly hours).
- The average percentage of attendance.
- The amount of square feet required per student.

A standard frequency of use of a classroom is 30 hours per week, an average attendance figure is 65%, and the average amount of space per student station is 15 square feet. These factors are combined in an index figure, which from these givens would be as follows:

$$\text{index} = \frac{15}{30 \times 0.65} = 0.769$$

Thus if we know that the department has 500 students, and they attend 8 hours of lectures every week, the space would be:

$$500 \times 8 \times 0.769 = 3070 \text{ ft}^2$$

This space can be broken down into classrooms in several ways, depending on other variables. The total building area, however, can be estimated immediately by assuming an efficiency factor of 60%:

$$\text{total building area} = \frac{3070}{0.6} = 5100 \text{ ft}^2$$

Laboratories. The method of calculating space needs for institutional laboratories is the same as that used with lecture halls. Standard figures for a chemical laboratory, for instance, are:

- 25 hours per week frequency.
- 80% utilization (attendance).
- 70 ft^2 station space per student.

Thus the index factor for this situation is

$$\frac{70}{25 \times 0.8} = 3.5$$

Shopping Centers. Depending on their size and on the size of catchment area they are supporting, shopping centers can be classified into neighborhood, community, and regional centers. Their characteristics can be expressed in the following figures:

Major tenant	Supermarket, drugstore	Variety store, junior department store	Major department store
Other tenants	Foods, drugs, sundries	Wearing apparel, hardware, appliances	Furniture
Population needed	7500–20,000	20,000–100,000	100,000–250,000
Building Area (ft^2)	30,000–75,000	100,000–300,000	300,000–1,500,000
Site Area (acres)	4–10	10–30	30–150

The type and size of shopping center that a given area can support must be determined in market demand and financial feasibility studies, which are based on statistics on the amount of sales dollars required per square foot per year for each type and for various areas in the United States. Since the number of dollars spent per year per person on each retail category is also known through census data, the number of people needed in each income bracket to support the center can be estimated. The size of the catchment area in which these people are living then depends on population densities and on the availability of competitive facilities. Population growth, future facilities planned, and similar factors are also considered in these calculations. Because of the size of the investment involved, and because of all the projections of economic and demographic growth factors included in the feasibility studies, their scope extends much beyond the architectural practice. However the architect must be familiar with the problem and with the basic method of solving it.

Traffic Count

Although knowledge of the volume and character of passing traffic is always useful, a traffic survey does not always make a difference. If other selection factors are so significant that the outcome of a traffic study will have relatively little bearing on the decision, such a study is unnecessary. But once it is determined that a traffic count is needed, the general objective is to count the passing traffic—both pedestrian and vehicular—that would constitute potential customers for a particular type of store. In the central business district, land values and rents are frequently based on traffic counts. The site in the central business district that produces the highest traffic count with regard to the type of traffic desired by a particular store is considered to be its 100% location. However a 100% location for one type of store may not be 100% for other types. For example, a site that rates 100% for a drugstore may be only 80% for a men's clothing shop and 60% for an appliance store.

Data from a traffic count should show not only how many people pass by but should indicate generally what kind of people they are. Analysis of the characteristics of

CENTURY BANK BUILDING
Los Angeles, California
Architects: Daniel, Mann, Johnson & Mendenhall
Photo: D. Lang

the passing traffic frequently reveals patterns and variations not readily apparent from casual observation.

For counting purposes, the passing traffic is divided into different classifications according to the characteristics of the customers who would be likely to patronize a certain type of business. Whereas a drugstore is interested in the total volume of passing traffic, a men's clothing store is obviously more concerned with the male traffic, especially men who are between the ages of 16 and 65.

It is also important to classify passing traffic by its reasons for passing. A woman on the way to a beauty salon is probably a poor prospect for a paint store, but she may be a good prospect for a drugstore. The hours at which individuals go by are often an indication of their purpose. In the early morning hours people are generally on their way to work. In the late afternoon the same people are usually returning from work. When one chain organization estimates the number of potential women customers, it considers women passing a site between 10 A.M. and 5 P.M. to be the serious shoppers. Evaluation of the financial bracket of passersby is also significant. Out of 100 women passing a prospective location for an exclusive dress shop, only 10 may appear to have the income necessary to patronize the shop. Of course the more experience one has had in a particular retail trade, the more accurately one can estimate the number of potential customers.

In summary, the qualitative information gathered about the passing traffic should include a count of the individuals who seem to possess the characteristics appropriate to the desired clientele, a judgment of the individuals' reasons for using that route, and a calculation of their ability to buy.

Pedestrian Traffic Count. In making a pedestrian count one must decide who is to be counted, where the count should take place, and when the count should be made. Before the study begins, one should consider *who*—that is, what types of people—should be included. If the directions on whom to include are not completely clear, the counters will be inconsistent and the total figure may be either too high or too low.

As previously indicated, it is frequently desirable to divide the pedestrian traffic into classes. Quite often separate counts of men and women and certain age categories are wanted. A trial run will indicate the existence of any difficulties in identifying those to be counted or in placing them into various groupings. Next one determines the specific place *where* the count is to be taken, deciding whether all the traffic near the site should be counted or only the traffic passing directly in front of the site.

If all the pedestrians passing through an area are counted, there is the possibility of double counting. Since a person must both enter and leave an area, it is important that each individual be counted only once—either when entering or when leaving. Therefore, it is essential that each counter consistently count at the same location. To determine what proportion of the passing traffic represents potential shoppers, some of the pedestrians should be interviewed about the origin of their trip, their destination, and the stores in which they plan to shop. Information of this type can provide a better estimate of the number of potential customers.

The season, month, week, day, and hour all affect traffic surveys. For example, during the summer there is generally an increased flow of traffic on the shady side of the street. During a holiday period (e.g., the month before Christmas or the week before Easter), traffic is denser than it is regularly. The patronage of a store varies by day of the week, too. Store traffic usually increases during the latter part of a week. Certain locations in some communities experience heavier-than-normal traffic on factory paydays and on days when social security checks are received.

The day of the week and the time of day should represent a normal period for traffic flow. Pedestrian flow accelerates around noon as office workers go out for lunch. Generally more customers enter a downtown store between 10 A.M. and noon and between 1 P.M. and 3 P.M. than at any other time. Local custom or other factors, however, may cause a variation in these expected traffic patterns.

After one has chosen the day that has normal traffic flow, the day should be divided into half-hour and hourly intervals. Traffic should be counted and recorded for each half-hour period of a store's customary operating hours. If it is not feasible to count the traffic for each half-hour interval, the traffic flow can be sampled. Traffic in representative half-hour periods in the morning, noon, afternoon, and evening can be counted.

Estimate of Store Sales. Data from a pedestrian traffic survey can give information on whether the site would generate a profitable volume for a certain store. A retailer with some past experience in the merchandise line for which a store is planned can make a reasonable estimate of sales volume if the following information is available (in lieu of past personal experience, the trade association for certain types of businesses may be of help):

PORTLAND PLAZA
Portland, Oregon
Architects: Daniel, Mann, Johnson & Mendenhall
Photo: D. W. Edmundson

- Characteristics of individuals who are most likely to be store customers (from pedestrian interviews).
- Number of such individuals passing the site during store hours (from traffic counts).
- Proportion of passersby who will enter the store (from pedestrian interviews).
- Proportion of those entering who will become purchasers (from pedestrian interviews).
- Amount of the average transaction (from past experience, trade associations, and trade publications).

One retailer divides the people who pass a given site into three categories: those who enter a store, those who inspect the window displays and may become customers, and those who pass without entering or looking. His prior experience enables this retailer to estimate from the percentage falling into each classification not only the number who will make purchases but also the amount of the average purchase. If, out of 1000 passersby each day, 5% enter and each person spends an average of $8, a store at that site open 300 days a year will have an annual sales volume of $120,000.

Types of Consumer Goods. Another factor that affects site selection is the customers' view of the goods sold by a store. Consumers tend to group products into three major categories: convenience, shopping, and specialty.

1 *Convenience* usually applies to items of low unit price that are purchased frequently, often are bought by habit, and are sold in numerous outlets; little selling effort is entailed. Examples are candy bars, cigarettes, and milk.
2 *Shopping* usually applies to goods of high unit price that are purchased infrequently; more intensive selling effort is usually required on the part of the store owner; price and features are compared, and the items are sold in selectively franchised outlets. Examples are men's suits, automobiles, and furniture.
3 *Specialty* usually applies to goods of high unit price (although price is not a purchase consideration); sold exclusively in franchised outlets; these items are bought infrequently, requiring a special effort by the customer to make the purchase, and no substitutes are considered. Examples are jewelry, perfume, cameras, and so on, of specific brands.

For stores handling *convenience goods,* the quantity of pedestrian traffic is most important. The corner of an intersection that offers two distinct traffic streams and a large window display area is usually a better site than the middle of a block. Downtown convenience goods stores, such as low-priced, read-to-wear stores and drugstores, have a limited ability to generate their own traffic. Therefore they must be situated in or near what is (for them) the 100% block. In merchandising convenience goods, it is easier to build the store within the traffic than to route the traffic to the store. Convenience goods are often purchased on impulse in easily accessible stores.

For stores handling *shopping goods,* the quality of the traffic is more important. Whereas convenience goods are purchased by nearly everyone, certain kinds of shopping goods are purchased by only certain segments of shoppers. Moreover, it is sometimes the character of the retail establishment rather than the type of goods offered that governs the selection of a site. For example, a conventional men's wear store should be in a downtown location close to a traffic generator like a department store. On the other hand, a discount store handling men's wear would be better placed in an accessible highway location. Stores that generate their own traffic through extensive promotional effort can locate away from the 100% location.

Buyers of shopping goods often like to compare the items in several stores by traveling a minimum distance. As a result, stores offering complementary items tend to locate close together. An excellent site is next to a department store or between two large department stores where traffic flows from one to the other. Another good site is one between a major parking area and a department store.

Specialty goods are frequently sought by consumers who are already "sold" on the product, the brand, or both. Stores catering to this type of consumer may use isolated locations because they generate their own consumer traffic. Stores carrying specialty goods that are complementary to certain other kinds of shopping goods may desire to locate close to the shopping goods stores. In general, the specialty goods retailer should locate in neighborhood where the adjacent stores and other establishments are compatible to his operation.

Automobile Traffic Count. A growing number of retail firms depend on drive-in traffic for their sales. Both the quantity and the quality of automotive traffic can be analyzed in the same way as pedestrian traffic. Data on traffic flow for the major streets in urban areas may come from the city engineer, the planning commission, the state highway department, or an outdoor advertising company. However it may be necessary to modify this information to suit special needs. For example, one data relating to total count of vehicles passing the site should be supplemented with actual observation, to permit evaluation of such influences on traffic as commercial vehicles, changing of shifts at nearby factories, through highway traffic, and increased flow caused by special events or activities.

Types of Trip. Automobile traffic may be classified according to the reason for the trip, that is, the work trip, the shopping trip, and the pleasure trip. Knowledge of the type of trip can assist one in making the correct site decision. Careful observation of the character of the traffic and even a few short interviews with drivers who have stopped for a traffic signal will reveal the nature of their trips.

Different retailers seek different locations, although they are serving the same type of customer. For example, to serve a *work trip* customer, a drycleaner and a convenience foodstore usually desire to be located on different sides of the street. The drycleaner wants to locate on the going-to-work side of the street, and the convenience foodstore wants to be on the going-home side.

A good location for a retailer seeking the customer on a *planned shopping trip* is along the right-hand side of the main street leading into a shopping district and adjacent to other streets carrying traffic into, out of, or across

MORRIS A. MECHANIC THEATER
Baltimore, Maryland
Architects: Johansen & Bhavnani
Photo: M. E. Warren

BRIGHTON WAY BUILDING
Beverly Hills, California
Architects: Kahn, Kappe, Lotery, Boccato
Photo: J. Lagman

town. The beginning or end of a row of stores is preferable to a site across the street from the stores. The side on which the older, established stores are located provides a clue to the best side of the street. But it is essential to find out whether these stores are still on the rise or are on the decline.

In smaller communities, where the major streets lead to and from the downtown area, the traffic pattern can be readily identified. In larger cities, where there are suburban shopping center locations, the traffic moves in many different directions. Since shopping centers tend to generate traffic, an analysis of the traffic flow to centers and between centers may reveal that a particular store location is outstanding.

The person on a *pleasure or recreational trip* is in the market for services such as those offered by motels, restaurants, and service stations. The probability of attracting this type of customer increases if the facility is located alongside a well-traveled highway and adjacent to a major entrance to the community.

Types of Consumer Goods. Understanding the business of people passing a site in cars also depends on the same analysis of consumer behavior used in classifying pedestrians. There are the same three categories of goods or products to consider: convenience, shopping, and specialty.

In general, the greater the automobile traffic, the greater the sales of *convenience goods* for catering to the drive-in traffic. For the drive-in store selling low-priced convenience goods, the volume of traffic passing the site is a most important factor in making a site decision. Consumers purchase convenience goods frequently and want them to be readily available. In addition, when passing a convenience goods store they are reminded of needs for particular items.

If consumers must make special trips to purchase such convenience staple goods as food and drug items, they want the store to be close to home. One study of foodstore purchases in the central city area revealed that nearly 70% of the women patronized stores within 1 to 5 blocks of their homes. Another study of foodstores indicated that for suburban locations the majority of customers lived within 3 miles of the stores, and the maximum trading area was 5 miles. For rural locations, the majority of consumers lived within a 10-minute drive to the store, with the maximum trading area within a 20-minute drive. A West Coast supermarket chain will not consider any location that does not have a minimum of 3500 homes within a 1½-mile radius of a shopping center. Re-

AGRONOMY BUILDING, CORNELL UNIVERSITY
Ithaca, New York
Architect: Ulrich Franzen & Associates
Photo: G. Cserna

NEW BOSTON CITY HALL
Boston, Massachusetts
Architects: Kallmann & McKinnell
Photo: C. Robinson

search indicated that 80% of the customers of pizza carryouts lived within a mile of the establishments.

On the other hand, a retailer dealing in *shopping goods* can have a much wider trading area. Lacking a heavily trafficked location—but with the help of adequate promotion—this more expensive type of store can generate its own traffic, and a location with low traffic density but easy accessibility from a residential area is a satisfactory site. Consumers buy shopping goods infrequently; they deliberately plan their purchases, and they will travel some distance to make shopping comparisons. A merchant who offers shopping goods, however, should not locate too far away from potential customers. One study of a discount department store showed that 79.6% of the shoppers lived within 5 miles of the store and another 16.1% lived within a 10-mile radius. The magnitude of the trading area for a shopping goods store can be determined by a customer survey, automobile license checks, sales slips, charge account records, store deliveries, and the extent of local newspaper circulation.

The same principles of location that are applicable to the walk-in *specialty goods* stores are appropriate for the drive-in facility. Because retailers of this type generate their own traffic, they can locate away from the major traffic arteries.

Market Analysis for Shopping Center Development: A Case Study

By Jack P. Hoag

A market study is a major factor in guiding the development of a successful shopping center. It is a prime step in determining the economic feasibility of a proposed project. Projected income, based on the study, can be compared with estimated operating expenses, building costs, financial costs and potential appreciation in land value to determine the project's economic prospects. Intensive analysis should produce a better center than one built with a limited or erroneous understanding of the market.

Simplification of an actual case study reflects the premises, problems, and projections inherent in any market analysis for retail development. In our example, the subject site is approximately 6 miles north of the central business district of a relatively large Arizona city. Approximate size of the proposed project is 210,000 square feet, with about 62,000 square feet of maximum building space. This is a parking ratio of more than 3 square feet to each square foot of building space. Major market segments to which the center must appeal were tentatively determined: (1) residents residing within 1 to

MANUFACTURERS BANK BUILDING
Los Angeles, California
Architects: Daniel, Mann, Johnson & Mendenhall
Photo: D. Lang

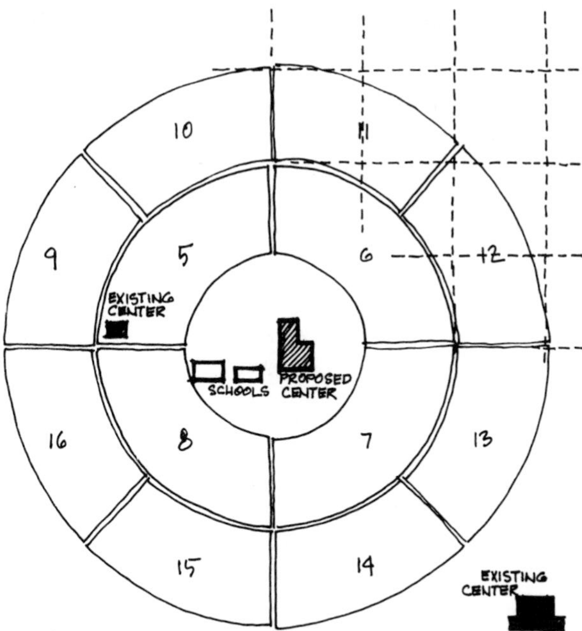

Figure 2.3 Drawing by author.

$1^1/_2$ miles of the center, (2) large volumes of automobile traffic moving by the proposed center site, (3) the large student market enrolled at a high school and junior high school, both located directly southwest of the proposed center.

It is of particular interest that all secondary data relating to the market were obtained from several general sources, including: (1) the 1960 U.S. Census of Population, (2) the U.S. Census of Housing, (3) the subject city's traffic department, planning and zoning commission, and major utility firms, and (4) general statistical handbooks. The only secondary data used but not generally available were extracted from several market studies conducted by private research firms. (Such studies are relatively easy to obtain by anyone contemplating a center development.) The only primary data gathered, reflecting the shopping behavior of area residents, were obtained from a random survey of residents in the assumed trade area and a convenience sample of customers at the major competing centers.

Population Size and Buying Patterns of the Market Area. The initial step was to ascertain the current and projected 5-year populations for each of 16 geographic market segments. Estimates were based on three independent population projections; one by the subject city's planning and zoning commission, a second by its street department, and a third by its school system.

Projections indicated that the population within a half-mile radius of the subject property will continue to be sparse. Only about 2300 individuals comprising 830 families live within this area. Populations within the succeeding two half-mile radii are much denser, however, consisting of approximately 9800 and 13,400 individuals, respectively. Thus about 12,100 people live within a 1-mile radius of the subject site, and about 25,500 individuals reside within a $1^1/_2$-mile radius.

Since population within a half-mile radius is the backbone of the center's long-run market, sparse population immediately adjacent to the subject site is one major limitation of the proposed project. If this area's current or expected population is too sparse, the center becomes extremely vulnerable to nearby competition. The study showed that areas to the north of the subject site, especially in the northwest quadrant, were likely to have the largest population expansion. The area to the south was already fully developed, and there was relatively little vacant land suitable for residential development.

Table 2.1 gives major population and housing characteristics for the subject city and the relevant subject area. Residents of the trade area are primarily middle-income Caucasian families. Most own a car and approximately half own their own home.

Table 2.1 Population and Housing Characteristics for Subject City and Area[a]

Category	Subject City	Subject Area
Average family income	$5,703	$5,300
Average family size	3.1	2.8
Average age (male)	26.2	28.5
Percent Caucasian	95.6	99.7
Average years of education	12.1	11.0
Percent owner occupied	61.3	55.4
Percent of homes vacant	8.3	9.0
Percent of homes sound	88.1	91.7
Average value of owned home	$11,600	$10,400
Average rent	$74	$70
Percent owning automobile	88.7	90.8

[a] Family size data derived from subject city planning and zoning commission data and the 1960 U.S. Census of Population.

Once the number and composition of the families and average family income have been determined for each segment, it is relatively simple to estimate total consumer expenditures in each segment by product type.

Table 2.2 Average Family Expenditure Pattern for Families Typical of the Subject Area[a]

Type of Store	Average Annual Expenditures
Supermarket	$1400
Beauty salon	30
Barber shop	34
Dry cleaning	38
Shoe repair	6
Bakery	22
Variety	85
Hardware	60
Florist	18
Jewelry	22
Mens' and boys' clothes	170
Ladies' and girls' clothes	210
Childrens' clothes	13
Shoes	83
Yard goods	20
Toy and hobby	44
Restaurant	100

[a] Based primarily on Bureau of Labor Statistics data.

Table 2.3 Estimate of Potential Supermarket Sales for Proposed Center: Average $1400 for Groceries per Family

Area[a]	Number of Families	Total Food Expenditures	Percentage of Pull	Potential Sales
1	327	$ 457,000	60	$ 274,680
2	344	481,600	55	264,880
3	163	228,200	50	114,100
4	0	0	0	0
5	826	1,156,400	30	346,920
6	716	1,002,400	25	250,600
7	1,433	2,006,200	15	300,930
8	329	460,600	20	92,120
9	356	498,400	15	74,760
10	338	473,200	25	118,300
11	175	245,000	35	85,750
12	667	933,800	5	46,900
13	748	1,047,200	5	52,360
14	988	1,383,200	5	69,160
15	500	700,000	10	70,000
16	765	1,071,000	15	160,650
Totals	8,675	$12,145,000		$2,322,110
Sales from outside area (15%)				348,316
Total expected sales				$2,670,426

Sources. Number of families, 1960 U.S. Census of Population; average food expenditures for specific groups, Bureau of Labor Statistics data; percentage of pull, analysis of traffic, accessibility, competition, buying behavior, and so on, as determined by the study.

[a] See map, Figure 2.3.

There are many sources of information on the expenditure behavior of family groups of specific types and specific sizes and in different areas of the United States. The U. S. Bureau of Labor Statistics provided the basic data regarding consumer expenditure patterns for this case (Table 2.2). Separate expenditure patterns can be established for each market segment. However characteristics of the population in the 16 market segments were so similar that a single expenditure pattern was adopted. The average family expenditure pattern in each of the 16 geographic market segments was then multiplied by the number of families in each of the market segments to arrive at the total consumer expenditures by product for each of the 16 separate markets. Table 2.3 presents this procedure for food sales.

Pulling Power of the Center. Once the available personal consumption expenditures by retail classification were known for each segment, we evaluated the center's potential influence on each of these population segments, keeping in mind the basic principles of retail location analysis. Accessibility to the potential market is one of the most important location factors for a convenience center. Accessibility can be viewed in several ways. Shoppers generally follow the "natural flow of traffic." Thus a location that intersects traveling patterns of shoppers or potential shoppers is an accessible site. But future traffic patterns and street construction should also be considered. Large volumes of passing traffic are not as important to a convenience center as is accessibility to that traffic. The subject site was found to be readily accessible to residents in the trade area, students in the nearby schools, and large volumes of passing traffic on the adjacent major north-south street.

Any estimate of a center's ability to attract customers is also dependent on competing facilities. The general market area studied already contained two large, successful, well-entrenched neighborhood centers regarded as the strong competition for the proposed center. One center was located 1 mile west of the subject site; the other center was approximately 3 miles southeast of the subject site (see map; Figure 2.3). Though successful, neither of the two existing centers was well planned, attractively designed or effectively promoted. In today's competitive economy such centers tend to age quickly, becoming highly susceptible to new competition. Thus apparent success of the two existing centers would not necessarily forestall the development of a new and well-planned center in the same area. Consumer surveys taken in the trade area and at the two competing shopping centers helped to determine the proposed center's trading area and the strength of these two established shopping centers.

Any convenience shopping center development should attempt to locate in an area with reasonable protection against the encroachment of new competition from new centers or satellite stores. In this case no land was available for development of either new centers or satellite stores within 1 mile of the subject site. A successful center, particularly if it has no room for expansion, tends to encourage growth of competing facilities. Since a new center is often more attractive, more complete, and better attuned to the current market, it can create tremendous competition for an existing center. Ability of the proposed center to "pull" the consumer depends, of course, on many additional factors. The center's architecture, the mixture of retail tenants, promotion, and management are very important also.

Specific "percents of pull" were established by keeping in mind all the preceding factors concerning the potential pull of the center and its tenants, as well as the experience of centers in similar situations. Because of the relatively high depth of penetration by convenience goods retailers in this case, the "percent of pull" for all 16 geographic segments for each of the convenience goods categories and services was established. Because of the relatively low market penetration achieved by shopping goods retailers, however, the "percent pull" for shopping goods was developed for octants only.

Potential Sales of the Proposed Center. When the "percent of pull" was determined, it was applied to the consumer expenditures for each of the 16 areas as estimated earlier. An amount was then added that represented the estimated potential sales volume from those living outside the subject area. This amount, which varied between 10 and 15% of the projected sales within the area, was determined by an analysis of consumer buying behavior (via survey techniques) in the subject area as well as at the two competing centers. Other studies contributed also. Table 2.4 summarizes the results of this procedure for selected retail stores and services. These are "potential" sales only. Restrictions of the size of the proposed center are considered next.

Tenant Size and Mixture. The next step in the market analysis was to determine the composition of the proposed center's retail outlets and the size of each one. Selection of specific tenants depends on many factors already discussed in addition to the availability of desirable tenants. Center developers must strive for relatively complete merchandise coverage to create a "shopping atmosphere." Thus initial suggestions for tenants were kept in mind so that the ultimate tenant mixture did not vary greatly from the original concept nor adversely affect the center's ability to attract and satisfy its potential market.

Once the size of a shopping center has been determined, there are various sources to help the developer plan the tenant mix; including data on the average sales

Table 2.4 Estimate of First Year Income for Proposed Center

		Rental Rates				
Tenant	Floor Area	Square Foot Rate	Percentage of Sales Rate	Minimum Income	Estimated Sales	Expected Income
Supermarket	19,500	$1.50	1.25	$ 31,700	$2,400,000	$ 31,700
Beauty shop	1,000	2.50	7	2,500	32,000	2,500
Barber shop	1,000	2.50	7	2,500	40,451	2,830
Shoe repair	500	2.50	7	1,200	14,000	1,200
Bakery	1,000	2.50	8	2,500	37,765	3,020
Drugstore	9,000	1.50	2.5	13,500	540,000	13,500
Ice cream parlor	750	3.00	8	2,250	250,000	2,250
Florist	750	2.50	7	1,875	28,732	2,010
Jewelry	500	2.50	6	1,250	20,665	1,250
Toy and hobby	1,500	2.50	6	3,750	64,048	3,840
Restaurant	2,000	2.50	6	5,000	97,584	5,850
Variety	5,000	1.75	5	8,750	157,500	8,750
Clothing and shoes	15,000	2.00	5	30,000	607,500	30,375
Hardware	3,960	2.00	5	7,920	140,000	7,920
Total	61,460			$114,445	$4,180,245	$117,495

per square foot for similar centers in similar situations, especially in the same geographic area. Thus a rough estimate of the maximum size of a prospective tenant's operation was projected by dividing potential sales by the sales per square foot. In general, the total size is based on the market, regardless of whether the market demand is substantial enough to suggest a larger shopping center than the site can physically accommodate, or whether smaller center is indicated.

A shopping center's long-run success is ensured, and its susceptibility to future competition decreased, by selecting tenants based on satisfaction of the potential market within the constraints of size. Tenants and store sizes chosen for a proposed center must maximize its total pulling power. Potential tenants were eliminated if it appeared that they would detract from or fail to add to the center's pulling power and ability to satisfy the market. Also, each store was kept small enough to better guarantee "overages" and increase the number of stores available to serve the market. Although deviations from initial suggestions are necessary in most cases, it is essential to preserve the concept of the center. The effect of future competition can be minimized in this way.

This approach to tenant selection is, of course, more complex, more time-consuming, and different from the "any tenant is all right" or "just fill the space" attitude of many of those responsible for leasing space in shopping centers. The often unfavorable competitive and financial conditions of such centers are evident.

Estimating Shopping Center Income. To determine expected center income, a rental schedule was established (Table 2.4), based on the desirability of the proposed center relative to competing centers. (Rental schedules of competing centers are normally available.) Maximum income from minimum rental rates is calculated by adding minimum rates for each retail store. An amount is then subtracted from this potential "minimum" income to allow for vacancies. It is this income estimate that particularly concerns financial institutions and developers. Since we have previously estimated sales volume for each of the retail outlets, we can readily find total income expected from the minimum rental and from "overages" resulting from the percentage leases. Table 2.4 shows these two estimates for the first year. The latter "percentage" lease is also projected for a 5 year period (Table 2.5). An allowance is made for unleased space, and the resulting income estimates become the final product of the market study.

Development of a successful shopping center, or indeed any retail operation, entails much coordinated planning. No single step is solely responsible for success.

Table 2.5 Projected 5-Year Income for Proposed Center Based on Percentage of Sales Rental Rate

Year	Estimated Income
1	$117,495
2	123,185
3	128,767
4	133,655
5	137,572

Conversely, however, omission of any of the necessary steps could make a liabilty of a financial adventure that might otherwise have been rewarding.

Feasibility Study: A 27-Condominium Residential Unit

KEMPER & ASSOCIATES, ARCHITECTS

General Information

Location: 10480-10486-10490-10496 Eastborne Avenue, in Westwood, Los Angeles, California.

Site area: 0.64 acre; 208-foot frontage on Eastborne Avenue, 133-foot frontage on Thayer Avenue.

Zoning: R-3-1-0

Gross floor area:

Garages	20,500 ft^2
Gross living area	60,500 ft^2
	81,000 ft^2

Unit mix:

17 2 Bd–1 3/4 Ba; average size:	1,640 ft^2
6 3 Bd–2 1/2 Ba; average size:	1,830 ft^2
4 3 Bd–2 3/4 Ba; average size:	1,920 ft^2
27 units, total net square feet:	46,650 ft^2

Accessories:

Pool, Jacuzzi, gym, sauna
Shuffleboard courts
Large sundeck with brick paving
View from all units
Patios, balconies, roof gardens
Step-down living rooms with fireplaces

Accessories: Luxury master baths with sunken bathtubs
Built-in oven, range, air conditioning, dishwasher, disposal, trash compactor
Carpeting and drapes
Elevator, full securities

Parking: Concrete garage for 54 cars

Land value: $289,441

Sponsor developer: Bryant L. Morris Development Company

Mortgage Loan Application

Loan requirement: Request for a loan commitment for the aggregate amount of $1,492,800, being 80% of the gross sales price. Commitment amount is premised on the eligibility of purchasers for first trust deeds with loan-to-value ratios of 90% for owner-occupied units, and of 80% for non-owner-occupied sales.

Required terms and conditions of loan:

1 *Term.* Not less than 29 years
2 *Interest Rate.* To be established at time of closing of each individual apartment mortgage.
3 *Points and Service Fee.* To be negotiated. It is requested that service fee allocable to developer be netted from the final escrow draw at time of delivery of unit.

Funding: Request is made for $260,500 in advance for land purchase.

Upon demolition and grading start, escrow agent will be requested to make monthly disbursements to pay for construction cost in proportion to the valuation of work completed as certified by the architect or the superintendent.

The balance of mortage loan proceeds for each individual apartment shall be disbursed by lender to escrow agent when the following have occurred:

1 Apartment has been substantially completed and is ready for occupancy.
2 Bryant L. Morris Development Company advises the lender that it has notified the purchaser that the apartment is ready for occupancy.
3 Bryant L. Morris Development Company produces evidence satisfactory to the lender that the owner has accepted the apartment.

Project Description. The Thayer-Eastborne condominiums will be located at the southeast side of Westwood in a low-density residential area with average home values exceeding $50,000.

This location provides for ideal accessibility to some of the most attractive centers of activity in the Los Angeles area. Just minutes away are the new business districts of Century City and Westwood, the UCLA campus, the Los Angeles Country Club, the center of Beverly Hills, and the San Diego Freeway.

The proposed development will offer 27 large and luxurious apartments priced from $50,300 for a 2-bedroom unit, to $85,000 for a 3-bedroom penthouse. All apartments have views and include such amenities as wood-burning fireplaces and sunken living rooms.

The market study summarized in Tables 2.6 through 2.9 indicates that for this market area new condominiums of wood-frame and stucco construction are selling at average prices between $35 and $42 per square foot. The subject development is designed as a brick building with concrete floors, and it is anticipated that at the proposed selling price of $40 per square foot, the 27 units will be sold within 7 months of start of construction.

An Architectural View of the Project. The project will consist of 27 condominium residential units. All units have 2 bedrooms with the exception of the upper ones, which, in addition, will feature a mezzanine and roof terrace. The $3^{1}/_{2}$-story structure above a subterranean garage is served by an elevator.

The proposed structure is classified by the City of Los Angeles Building Department as a Type III structure in construction, which is essentially a Type I structure in material use. The structural elements are load-bearing masonry for the division walls between units and precast concrete planks for all floors.

The choice of using high-quality material in lieu of the standard Type V construction (wood and stucco) was based on a market evaluation with regard to resale and reflects a desire to achieve an absolutely soundproof and fireproof structure. The basic design concept provides every unit with a view. There are no units that face a side yard or a rear yard (or alley), as is commonly found in standard design solutions where the owner builds to the maximum zoning limit.

The unusual stepped-back design allows the lower units more sunlight for all rooms and creates a more open and spacious feeling at the exterior recreation areas.

The shape and contours of the site provide for a natural division of building and subterranean garages—that is, two buildings and two garages, rather than a standard solution of one building and one garage.

Table 2.6 Financial Analysis

Costs	Footages (ft²)	Breakdown	Extension	
Construction Cost				
1 *Condominiums*				
Net floor area	42,980	$18.00	$773,658	
Mezzanines	3,670	10.00	36,700	
Balconies	550	9.00	4,950	
Roof gardens	3,275	6.00	19,650	
Total condominiums				$834,960
2 *Garages*	20,570	7.00		143,990
3 *Recreation*				
Swimming pool	7,000		7,000	
Jacuzzi		10.00	2,500	
Gym and sauna	350	10.00	3,500	
Sun deck	3,600	2.50	9,000	
Total recreation				22,000
4 *Site Work*				
Demolition			4,000	
Landscaping	6,500	2.50	16,250	
Total site work				20,250
		Total Construction Cost =		$1,021,200
Development Fees				
1 *Builder's overhead and profit (8% of construction costs)*				$81,696
2 *Preliminary studies*				2,225
3 *Architecture and engineering*				35,000
4 *Civil engineer (surveyor)*				
Tentative map			$ 400	
Formal subdivision map			1000	
Condominium plan		($125/Unit)	3375	
Total civil engineer				4,775
5 *Attorney*				2,800
6 *Title company*				8,991
7 *Filing fees*				
Tentative subdivision map			78	
Final subdivision map			260	
Public report			381	
Plan check fee			2800	
Total filing fees				3,519
8 *Utility cost*				
Sewer connection fee			6142	
Water meter			717	
Curb and street lights			1200	
Total utility cost				8,059
9 *Park and recreation fee*				5,400
		Total Development Fees =		$152,465
		Subtotal =		$1,173,665
Cost of Land				289,441
		Subtotal =		$1,463,106
Financing Cost				
1 *Loan commitment (3 points)*			$42,800.00	
2 *Interest during construction*			70,000.00	
		Total Financing Cost =		112,800
		Total Project Cost =		$1,575,906

Table 2.6 Financial Analysis (*continued*)

Summary and Pro Forma Profit	
Income from sales	$1,866,000
Cost of sales (2.5%)	46,650
	$1,819,350
	$1,575,906
Total project cost	$1,575,906
Developer's profit	$ 243,444

Table 2.7 Pro Forma Cash Flow Schedule of Project Expenses

Item	Costs to Date	Preconstruction Cost	First Month	Second Month	Third Month	Fourth Month	Fifth Month	Sixth Month	Seventh Month	Budget
Land	$28,941	$260,500								$289,441
Demolition		4,000								4,000
Utilities			$6,142	$717	$1,200					8,059
Landscaping							$8,750	$4,000	$4,000	16,250
Loan commitment		18,000					12,400	12,400		42,800
Construction (including profit)			125,000	225,000	180,000	$180,000	180,000	84,381		974,381
Retentions (10%)			14,000	25,000	20,000	20,000	20,000	9,265		103,265
Architect	5,000	20,000	10,000							35,000
Preliminary studies	2,225									2,225
Surveyor	400	1,000	3,375							4,775
Attorney		2,800								2,800
Title company			1,998	665	1,332	1,332	1,332	1,332	1,000	8,991
Filing fees		3,519								3,519
Park and recreation fees		5,400								5,400
Sales and advertising		6,150	9,000	3,000	6,000	6,000	6,000	6,000	4,500	46,600
Expenses before interest	36,566	321,369	169,515	254,382	208,532	207,332	227,982	117,378	9,500	1,552,556
Interest										70,000
Total project cost										1,622,556
Sales ($69,100 average)			414,600	138,200	276,400	276,400	276,400	276,400	207,600	1,866,000
Profit from project										243,444
Schedule of Events			Grading	Construction Start		Roof		Landscaping	Occupancy	
Construction			6	2	4	4	4	4	3	
Sales per month, cumulative			6	8	12	16	20	24	27	

Table 2.8 Sales Prices

Level	Unit Number	Space (ft^2)	Price/ft^2	Unit Price
First	1	1,910.	$38.40	$72,900
	2	1,375.	36.60	50,300
	3	1,460.	36.60	53,400
	4	1,535.	37.00	56,800
	5	1,490.	37.70	56,100
Second	6	1,375.	37.00	50,900
	7	1,460.	37.50	54,800
	8	1,535.	37.00	56,800
	9	1,490.	36.10	53,800
	10	1,880.	36.60	68,800
	11	1,880.	36.60	68,800
	12	1,880.	36.60	68,800
	13	1,750.	37.50	65,600
	14	1,750.	37.50	65,600
Third	15	1,710.	41.50	70,900
	16	1,780.	41.30	73,600
	17	1,780.	41.30	73,600
	18	1,780.	40.10	71,400
	19	1,685.	40.20	67,800
	20	1,690.	42.70	72,200
	21	1,890.	43.10	81,400
	22	1,850.	42.80	79,200
Fourth	23	1,985.	43.00	85,300
	24	1,900.	43.60	82,800
	25	1,900.	43.60	82,800
	26	1,900.	43.60	82,800
	27	1,820.	43.50	79,200
Total square feet =		50,400		
Average price per square foot =			$40.00	
Total sales value =				$1,931,600

Table 2.9 Estimated Monthly Maintenance Budget

Management		$150
Janitor		150
Insurance		100
Pool		50
Repairs (miscellaneous)		45
Gardener		75
Elevator		45
Rubbish		36
Lights and water		145
Fire extinguisher service		10
Reserves		
Roof	$24.00	
Painting	30.00	
Elevator	20.00	
Security system	15.00	
		89

Total monthly cost = $885
Monthly cost per unit = $32.80

Careful design consideration had been given to the natural cross-ventilation and minimum traffic within the garages. Each street has its own entry, thereby minimizing traffic hazards at the street level. Living units vary in size, spatial configuration, exposure to the exterior, and so on. Each was designed on the basis of a comparison matrix.

Recreational Amenities

1 A very large brick-paved sun deck in addition to the pool area is the main attraction in this unusually large open area.
2 The heated swimming pool and Jacuzzi pool have been designed to form a waterfall, which makes this recreation area especially attractive.
3 Mature trees have been carefully placed in the pool area to give a parklike atmosphere.
4 All other trees are placed to give unit consideration in terms of view and sun exposure.
5 An indoor gym is located below the sun deck area next to the men's and women's saunas. The gym is openable to the exterior and may be converted into a recreation or meeting room.

Exterior Design Concepts. Site planning and exterior design concepts include the following:

1 Spacious living with a visually controlled environment.
2 Special consideration to view and sun exposure for all units and all rooms.
3 Total soundproofing between each pair of units; brick walls separating each unit from the next, and 10-inch concrete floors between all units.
4 Liberal use of quality material; exposed burned brick and laminated woods.
5 Large areas of glass.
6 Balconies and patios.
7 Freedom from exterior maintenance for lasting project beauty.
8 Natural cross-ventilation of all units; all casement windows.
9 Reduced heating and cooling costs through thick masonry walls and concrete floors.
10 Sky roof walkway covers.
11 Solid railings at all balconies.
12 Integrated landscaping.

Interior Design Features. All units have been designed from the inside out. Intimacy and scale are maintained by careful consideration of height and detailing of skywindow-fronts; sunken living areas and fireplace conversation areas give the units a sense of comfort.

The quality construction previously mentioned minimizes interior maintenance while enhancing the wide range of luxury features.

1 Full security.
2 Elevator to all levels.
3 Exposed brick walls in all rooms.
4 Acoustical ceiling sprayed on Spancrete.
5 Freedom to alter interior partitions—Spancrete plans span entire living units.
6 Tile floors on all patios and balconies.
7 Luminous ceilings in kitchens, master baths, and walk-in closets.
8 Fireplaces with conversation areas.
9 All casement windows.
10 Deluxe dishwashers.
11 Built-in ovens and ranges with vented hoods.
12 Individual washers and dryers.
13 Built-in disposals and compactors to ease waste disposal.
14 Carpeting and quality resilient floor finishes throughout.
15 Walk-in closets and generous storage areas.
16 Full mirrored sliding doors.
17 Walk-in Roman bathtubs.
18 Decorator-selected hardware and lighting fixtures.
19 Coordinated interior colors and finishes.
20 Prewiring for telephone and television.
21 Well-placed electrical outlets.
22 Guest closets.
23 Enclosed parking.
24 Drapes.
25 Air conditioning.
26 Bay windows.
27 Wet bars.

Market Analysis. According to our agreement dated November 2, 1972, we have conducted a market survey and financial analysis for the proposed condominium development in West Los Angeles, on Thayer and Eastborne Avenues.

We have concluded that based on the current R3-1-0 zoning regulations, a 27-unit 3 1/2-story condominium development of about 50,000 square feet of total for-sale area, would be the highest and best use of the property, and that selling prices between $35 and $40 per square foot of net living space can be anticipated. The following report summarizes our findings in market research and economic feasibility.

Site Characteristics. It is our understanding that the property consists of Lots 8, 9, 10, and 11, in Block 52 of Tract 4677, covering a total area of 29,133.83 square feet. Since this location is equally close to Century City, Westwood, and Beverly Hills, condominiums on this site will be very marketable and compatible with similar developments in Westwood and in Beverly Hills. Having 340 feet of frontage on both Thayer and Eastborne Avenues will make it possible to give a view to the majority of apartments, an amenity that will make the units very competitive. The strip of commercial structures between the site and Santa Monica Boulevard brings retail facilities and restaurants within walking distance.

Zoning Regulations. The entire block is zoned R3-1-0; therefore the following land use restrictions are applicable:

1 *Maximum Number of Stories:* 3
2 *Maximum Height:* 45 feet from highest point of sidewalk; 60 feet from lowest point of sidewalk.
3 *Maximum Number of Units:* 26 to 39, depending size:
   1-bedroom units require 800 ft^2 of land area.
   2-bedroom units require 1000 ft^2 of land area.
   3-bedroom units requre 1200 ft^2 of land area.
   For zoning purposes the property extends halfway into the alley, which increases the total area to 31,498 square feet. Our recommended mix, 19 2-bedroom plus 10 3-bedroom units, requires a land area of 31,000 square feet.
4 *Setback Requirements:*
   Eastborne Avenue (front): 15 feet
   All other sides: 6 feet
5 *Parking Requirements:*
   1 1/2 spaces for each 1-bedroom unit.
   2 spaces for each 2- or more bedroom unit.

Market Area. The market area, within which condominium projects will be in competition with the subject development, consists mainly of Westwood and Beverly Hills. Residential densities and land values are similar in both communities, and market data out of these two areas are our main indicators for the depth of demand and for established selling price levels of condominiums.

STEPHEN S. WISE TEMPLE
Los Angeles, California
Architect: Daniel Dworsky
Photo: J. Lagman

Our survey, however, also includes projects in Santa Monica, Bel Air, and Culver City, to relate the subject development to the surrounding condominium market areas.

Competitive Condominium Developments. The *El Camino Townhouse* is at present the only new condominium development in the subject area that has been completed and sold. Five more projects are under construction and will be completed in December, or early next year; their total number of units is 104. In addition to those already under construction, 10 more developments are planned for this immediate area; however building permits have been issued for only four.

All these new projects are addressing the same type of tenant and are similar in design. Therefore a structure with higher aesthetic appeal and features such as superior soundproofing would have a competitive advantage in this location.

The number of highrise condominium units proposed and planned for this market area is much greater at present than that of lowrise, Type 5 construction units. Plans for approximately 1000 new for-sale highrise apartments have recently been submitted for developments along Wilshire Boulevard and Century City. The conversion of *Glen Towers,* and *Century Towers* from rental apartments to condominiums will add 360 more units to this figure. The activity in highrise development, however, will have little effect on the marketing of the subject condominium units, first because highrises have a 20 to 30% higher price level, therefore their own distinct audience, and second, because if the developer decides to move ahead immediately, the subject condominiums will be completed and sold before most of the highrise developments get under way.

Two projects that are now the most comparable to the subject development are the *Summerset House,* and the *Beverly Lencrest*. Both are located a few blocks away from the subject site, in areas with comparable property values. However the *Summerset* condominiums are poorly designed and have no swimming pool, and at the high square-foot price of $39, they have sold three units in 5 months. The units at *Lencrest* are designed better, and they sell at $37.30 per square foot. Deposits had been made on all 24 condominiums within 4 weeks; however six sales were canceled, mainly because the developers were unable to maintain their promised date of occupancy. The *El Camino* project sold well at top prices, which probably include a premium for the Beverly Hills address. *Raintree* and *Renaissance* are located in areas with lower land values, and they feature square-foot rents around $28. Their preselling program is very successful, and prices will be raised considerably for the second phase of each development.

Profile of Prospective Tenants (Audience). The primary market support for the subject development will be derived from former homeowners around 45 years of age and older who lived in the surrounding residential neighborhoods and wish to remain in this area; their children no longer live at home, and consequently less living space is needed. This market group appreciates a maintenance-free, security-type condominium. The subject condominiums can also be expected to draw prospec-

DEPARTMENT OF WATER AND POWER BUILDING
Los Angeles, California
Architects: Albert C. Martin & Associates
Photo: J. Shulman

MALIN RESIDENCE
Hollywood, California
Architect: John Lautner
Photo: J. Shulman

tive buyers from nearby apartment buildings, including semi-retired people who would prefer ownership but are tired of maintenance problems, and, to a lesser extent, young couples without children, who have never owned a home before and are attracted by the tax advantages offered by a condominium.

Recommended Product. The foregoing analysis of competitive projects and their typical audience, as well as the prevailing zoning regulations, lead us to believe that condominiums of the following mix, average size, and average selling price will represent the highest and best use of the subject property:

17	2 Bd-2 Ba, level	1600 ft²	\$59,200	\$37/ft²
10	2 Bd-Den-Loft-2 1/2 Ba	1900 ft²	\$70,300	\$37/ ft²

All figures are considered to be *average values:* unit sizes may change according to design criteria, and prices may vary with the view and other amenities of each individual unit. The zoning regulations permit only 3 full stories of living area, but we recommend taking advantage of the possibility to create additional for-sale floor area and amenities by building units with 2-story living rooms and lofts on the third level.

Financial Analysis. The recommended price level refers to a Type V construction building, as outlined in alternative A of the construction cost schedule (see Table 2.12, below). We have also tested the feasibility of a construction with load-bearing masonry walls and concrete slabs, since we believe that buyers will be willing to pay a premium for the higher resale values and better sound insulation of such a condominium unit (alternative

B). Total construction costs of this alternative are estimated to be 14% higher.

Alternative A, based on a selling price of $37 per square foot, yields a profit of $298,400, or $10,290 per unit, to the developer. Adding to this the contractor's profit, the total profit to a builder-developer amounts to $372,100, or $12,831 per unit.

Alternative B, based on a selling price of $40 per square foot, yields a developer's profit of $9369 per unit, or $12,317 including the profit of the contractor.

Tables 2.10 to 2.14 survey competitive condominium developments and compare various aspects of alternatives A and B.

Table 2.10 Summary of Status of Competitive Condominium Developments

Project	Number of Units	Units per Acre	Developer
Condominiums Completed			
El Camino Townhouses 9501 West Olympic Boulevard Beverly Hills	10	26	Norris/Gorman Beverly Hills
Raintree 4909 St. Louis Court Culver City	61	20	Levitt & Sons Los Angeles
Bel Air Condominiums 2345 Roscomare Road Bel Air	24	45	Julian Weinstock
Condominiums Under Construction			
Summerset House 1710 Malcolm Avenue Westwood	15	50	George Zahler
Beverly Lencrest 2276 South Beverly Glen Rancho Park	24	48	Lawrence Stevens, Inc.
Rancho Lencrest 2324 South Beverly Glen Rancho Park	24	48	Lawrence Stevens, Inc.
Rochester/Kelton Westwood	36	70	Donald Sterling Beverly Hills
440 North Oakhurst Drive Beverly Hills	8	46	Don-Ja-Ran Construction Co.
The Woods 2502 Arizona Avenue Santa Monica	39	24	Shareholders, Inc. Century City
The Renaissance Jefferson/Overland Culver City	240	35	Urbanetics Co. Beverly Hills
Building Permits Issued			
441 North Oakhurst Drive Beverly Hills	36	69	Urbanetics Co.
321 North Oakhurst Drive Beverly Hills	36	69	Urbanetics Co.

Table 2.10 Summary of Status of Competitive Condominium Developments *(continued)*

Tract Number	Project	Number of Units	Units per Acre	Developer
Building Permits Issued				
	141 South Palm Drive Beverly Hills	24	88	Urbanetics Co.
	438 North Palm Drive Beverly Hills	5	29	Louis Yolles
Condominiums Proposed				
29555	1828 Holmby Avenue West Los Angeles	12	39	Irving Seidner
29886	10650 Holman Avenue Westwood	35	45	E. W. Moulton Co.
30391	1261-81 South Beverly Glen, Westwood	28	45	Lawrence Stevens
28742	Beverly Glen/La Grange West Los Angeles	12	46	A. P. Katzman
31222	Santa Monica/Beverly Glen Westwood	—	—	
31215	Beverly Boulevard/Oakhurst Beverly Hills	15	45	Lincoln Properties
30520	Wilshire/Beverly Glen Westwood	120	150	Lincoln Properties
28668	Wilshire/Warner Avenue Westwood	154	150	Equity Funding
29841	Avenue of the Stars/Pico Century City	600	48	West Lear Co.
—	Wilshire/Linden Drive Beverly Hills	120	100	U.S. Financial
Apartments Converted into Condominiums				
26279	Glen Towers 1333 South Beverly Glen Westwood	50	50	U.S. Condominium Company
26242	Century Towers 2220 Avenue of the Stars Century City	310	76	Alcoa
	Villa Canyon 434 South Canyon Drive Beverly Hills	10	40	—
	Raintree 4909 St. Louis Court Culver City	354	40	Levitt & Sons

Table 2.11 Unit Data on Select Competitive Condominiums

Project and Units	Space per Unit (ft^2)	Price per Unit	Price/ft^2
El Camino			
10 2 Bd-den-2½ Ba	1900	$79,500	$42.00
Description	Split-level townhouses with individual double garages; no pool.		
Occupancy	September 1972.		
Sold	All.		
Raintree			
2 Bd-2 Ba	1400	$45,500–$ 47,500	$33.20
2 Bd-den-3 Ba	1600	48,000– 51,000	30.60
3 Bd-2½ Ba	1800	51,000– 53,000	28.30
3 Bd-2½ Ba	1750	50,000– 51,500	29.00
3 Bd-den-3 Ba	2000	53,000– 55,500	27.30
61 units in phase 1; 210 units total			
Description	Townhouses with individual garages; part of planned community with 564 units, lake, tennis, pools, and so on.		
Occupancy	December 1972.		
Sold	80 units.		
Bel Air			
12 1 Bd-den-1½ Ba	1000	$50,950	$40.00
12 2 Bd-2 Ba	1300	52,000	41.00
24 units			
Description	3-story building; small pool, gym, sauna.		
Occupancy	March 1972.		
Sold	23 units.		
Summerset			
15 2 Bd-2 Ba	1400	$52,500–$ 58,500	$39.00
Description	3-story building, all units are level; no pool, but sauna and party room.		
Occupancy	January 1973.		
Sold	3 units.		
The Renaissance			
2 Bd-2 Ba level	1090	$31,950	$29.30
2 Bd-2 Ba plus loft	1334	34,500	25.90
3 Bd-2 Ba level	1272	38,000	30.00
3 Bd-2 Ba plus loft	1437	40,500	28.20
3 Bd-2 Ba studio	1583	42,000	26.50
3 Bd-2½ Ba studio	1736	43,500	25.00
4 Bd-2½ Ba studio	1880	47,500	25.30
144 units under construction; 96 units planned for phase 2			
Description	3-story buildings with 12 units each, and 24 subterranean parking stalls; pools, and complete health club.		
Occupancy	March 1973.		
Sold	Deposits for 120 units.		
Beverly Lencrest			
1 Bd-den-2 Ba	1500	$52,500	$35.00
2 Bd-2 Ba	1400	55,500	39.00
1 Bd-den-Loft-1 Ba	1800	69,500	38.00
24 units.			
Description	3 stories plus lofts on 4th; pool, Jacuzzi, sauna, party room.		
Occupancy	April 1973.		
Sold	18 units.		
Rochester/Kelton			
12 1 Bd-1 Ba	900	$37,800	$42.00
12 1 Bd-1½ Ba	990	41,600	42.00
12 2 Bd-2 Ba	1200	50,400	42.00
36 units			
Description	5-story building, originally designed for rental apartments, prices are not final; pool, sauna, party room.		
Occupancy	April 1973.		
Sold	None, no permit yet.		
Oakhurst			
2 Bd-den-2½ Ba	2400	$89,500– $94,500	$38.30
2 Bd-2½ Ba	3200	130,000	40.60
1 Bd-den-2½ Ba	2100	104,500	49.80
2 Bd-den-2½ Ba	2400	114,500	47.70
8 units			
Description	3 stories above security garage; pool, Jacuzzi.		
Occupancy	March 1973.		
Sold	3 units.		
The Woods			
2 Bd-2 Ba studio	1154	$33,500–$ 35,500	$29.90
2 Bd-2 Ba studio	1172	34,800– 36,800	30.54
3 Bd-2½ Ba studio	1225	36,500– 38,500	30.61
3 Bd-2½ Ba studio	1467	38,500– 40,500	27.00
Description	2½-story townhouse-type units, individual parking (1 garage, 1 carport), pool, Jacuzzi, party room.		
Occupancy	January 1973.		
Sold	Reservations for all units.		
Glen Towers			
17 1 Bd plus 1½ Ba	1800	$73,000–$105,500	$49.58
33 2 Bd plus 2 Ba	2400	106,000– 136,000	50.42
50 units			
10-story building, 10 years old, real luxury design and finish.			
Escrow opens December 1972.			
Reservations for 25 units.			

Table 2.12 Construction Cost Schedule

	Space (ft²)	Cost/ft²	Total
Alternative A: Wood-frame and stucco construction			
Basic cost per net rentable square foot	49,400	$15	$741,000
Concrete garages: 58 spaces, at 350 ft²	20,300	7	142,100
Pool and recreation facilities	10,000	20	20,000
On-site utilities: $100 per unit			3,000
Landscaping	5,000	3	15,000
Contractor's profit (8%)			73,700
Total construction cost			$994,800
Alternative B: Concrete-masonry construction			
Basic cost	49,400	$18	$889,200
Garages	20,300	7	142,100
Pool and recreation	10,000	20	20,000
On-site utilities			3,000
Landscaping	5,000	3	15,000
Contractor's profit (8%)			85,500
Total construction cost			$1,154,800

Table 2.13 Project Sales Basis

Item	Alternate A	Alternate B
Improved land	$ 300,000	$ 300,000
Construction cost	994,800	1,154,800
Architecture and engineering	12,000	12,000
Loan fee (3½ points)	48,000	50,000
Interest during construction (8 months)	72,000	75,000
Park and recreation fee ($200/unit)	6,000	6,000
Other fees	10,000	10,000
Subtotal	$1,442,800	$1,607,800
Sales commission (6%)	86,600	96,500
Total development cost	$1,529,400	$1,704,300
Developer's profit	298,400	271,700
Total market value	$1,827,800	$1,976,000
Projected Sales Revenues	$37/ft²	$40/ft²
Total net area for sale 49,400 ft²	$1,827,800	$1,976,000

Table 2.14 Development Cost per Condominium Unit

Item	Alternate A		Alternate B	
Improved land	$10,345	16.4%	$10,345	15.2%
Construction cost	34,303	54.5	39,820	58.4
Architect and engineer	414	0.6	414	0.6
Loan fee	1,655	2.6	1,724	2.5
Interest during construction	2,438	4.0	2,586	3.8
Park and recreation fee	207	0.3	207	0.3
Other fees	345	0.6	345	0.5
Subtotal	$49,752	79.0%	$55,441	81.3%
Sales and marketing	2,986	4.7	3,328	4.9
Total development cost	$52,738	83.7%	$58,769	86.2%
Developer's profit	10,290	16.3	9,369	13.8
Total market value	$63,028	100.0%	$68,138	100.0%

Market Survey and Financial Analysis: A Single-Family Residence

KEMPER & ASSOCIATES, ARCHITECTS

Intent: To build a single residence for lease until overall development in this community builds a market strong enough to make sale of the property feasible.

Market Area. The primary market area for this project is the Victor Valley, a high desert area north of the Cajon Pass in San Bernardino County; it consists of the cities of Victorville and Adelanto and the unincorporated areas of Hesperia and Apple Valley.

The economic base of the area is generated mainly by the activities of George Air Force Base, tourism, and manufacturing. Table 2.15 illustrates the present employment distribution of the Victor Valley area. This survey was done in 1972. The actual number of employees living in the Victor Valley area is higher than 9900 because the people commuting to San Bernardino are not included in this figure. Exact data on commuters are not available, but traffic counts at the Cajon Pass show an increase of traffic by 300% during rush hours.

The Housing Market. The Victor Valley area has experienced a rapid growth in the past two decades. Table 2.16 shows an increase in the number of dwelling units from 2111 in 1950 to 12,077 units in 1970. These data also reflect the development of the city of Victorville into the regional business and shopping center and the shift of residential growth to the surrounding neighborhoods.

The rapid pace in growth and development can be inferred from the increase of assessed property valuation.

Table 2.15 Distribution of Jobs in the Victor Valley Area

Job Category	Number Employed	Percentage of Work Force
Agriculture, mining	275	2.8%
Construction	550	5.6%
Manufacturing	1,265	12.8%
Transportation, communications utilities	1,100	11.1%
Trade	1,595	16.1%
Finance, insurance, real estate	330	3.3%
Service	2,035	20.6%
Government	2,750	27.8%
Total civilian employment	9,900	100.0%

Source. Chamber of Commerce, San Bernardino.

Between 1971 and 1972 the total of assessed property values in the Victor Valley area rose from $20.7 million to $27.0 million. This 29% increase was the highest anywhere in San Bernardino County.

Rental Apartments. Out of the total number of dwelling units in this market area, 14% are apartments, most of them located on the George Air Force Base. Victorville has mostly small, moderate-income apartments, which are 10 or more years old. Recently some new apartments have been constructed in Apple Valley. These projects are usually leased out during construction; their monthly rents exceed $200. Table 2.17 lists recent apartment projects in this area, all located within 7 miles of Spring Valley Lake. In addition to the apartment units

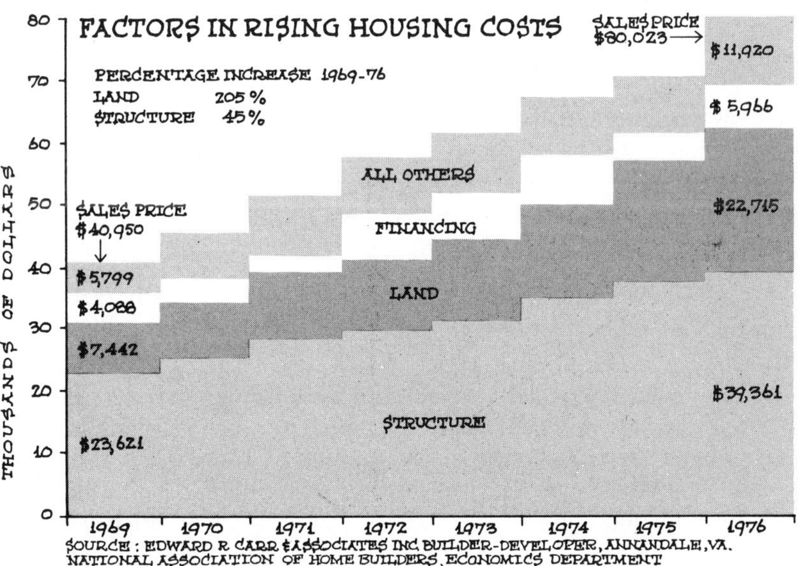

Figure 2.4 *Source. Time*, September 12, 1977.

Table 2.16 Growth of Residential Areas in the Victor Valley

Sector	Number of Dwelling Units 1950	Number of Dwelling Units 1960	Percentage Increase	Number of Dwelling Units, 1970	Percentage Increase
George Air Force Base	214	698	225	1310	87
Apple Valley	779	2898	270	3838	33
Victorville[a]	889	1378	55	1466	7
South Victorville, Spring Valley Lake	171	1428	735	2339	68
Hesperia	356	1744	380	3124	80

Source. Census computations for Planning District 18, San Bernardino County Planning Department.
[a]The City of Victorville has developed into the business and shopping center of the area despite little residential growth (7% in 10 years). People working in Victorville prefer to live in the surrounding unincorporated areas.

Table 2.17 Recent Apartment Projects Near Spring Valley Lake

Project	Years Open	Number of Units	Unit Type	Monthly Rent[a]
Brenn's Garden Apartments Highway 18, Apple Valley	1	10	2 Bd-2 Ba	$250–$270
Executive Apartments Desert Knolls	2	1 9	1 Bd-2 Ba 2 Bd-2 Ba	$175 $200
Hillcrest Apartments Highway 18, Apple Valley	2	12	2 Bd-2 Ba	$225–$240
McCarter Apartments Apple Valley Road	1	4 16	3 Bd-2 Ba 2 Bd-2 Ba	$225 $210
Green Tree Townhouses Valley Hi, Victorville	6	21 4	2 Bd-2 Ba 3 Bd-2 Ba	$200 $225

Source. Field survey by Capra Associates, September 2, 1972.
[a]All rents are for unfurnished units.

in this area, a small percentage of single-family dwellings is rented out. The Apple Valley Rancho Realty has a listing service for these homes, which are usually absorbed very quickly. Rents for 2- and 3-bedroom houses are between $250 and $375.

Spring Valley Lake. In 1969 the Boise Cascade Corporation purchased the Kelin Ranch, a 2000-acre estate between Apple Valley and Bear Valley Roads, 5 miles south of the city of Victorville. This property was developed into a recreation-oriented neighborhood of 4078 single-family residential lots. The recreational facilities consist of the following:

- A 200-acre man-made lake (completed March 1970).
- A championship par 72 golf course (completed May 1971).
- A 30,300 square foot country club (opened August 1971).
- A $250,000 equestrian center (under construction).

The main asset of the development, the almost unlimited water supply from the Mojave underground river, makes possible a continuous renewal of the lake water and perfect upkeep of the golf course.

Lot sales started in September 1969; today 80 of the original 4078 lots are unsold. Original lot prices were:

- $ 7000 to $15,000 off lake.
- $16,600 to $27,000 on the water.

The off-site improvements provided by the developer include asphalt streets with concrete curbs and sidewalks, and gas, water, power, telephone, and a sewer system connected to the net of Victorville. Construction on these improvements is today about 95% completed.

Since August 1, 1972, building permits have been available for all lots, and thus far 12 houses have been constructed in this subdivision. Three are model homes erected by Boise Cascade, priced from $22,700 to $27,100, land not included. The nine private homes are valued between $25,000 and $65,000, including the lot price. An $80,000 home is presently under construction on the lake.

Prospective Tenants. Low vacancies, together with high rent schedules of existing apartments and homes, indicate a shortage for this commodity in the market area. The demand is generated mainly by three centers of activity:

1 George Air Force Base, a training center for Allied fighter pilots. Officers in higher ranks, committed to 18-month terms on this base, need adequate homes for themselves and their families and are qualified for high monthly rents.
2 Branches of major chain stores, supermarkets, and banks in Victorville. Executives go out to these towns on 6- to 12-month terms.
3 Homes on the lake could provide for ideal faculty housing to serve the Victor Valley College, whose campus is adjacent to the Spring Valley Lake. Built 3 years ago, the college has a current enrollment of 1800 and is still expanding.

Conclusions. Tenants of a waterfront home at the subject site will have unrestricted use of the lake for boating and fishing; they will have an excellent golf course across the street, and a country club with tennis courts and other facilities within a 5-minute walk. These amenities are unsurpassed by any other location in the Victor Valley area. Given the present shortage in first-quality housing, with rents on homes lacking all the advantages just listed reaching $375 per month, we conclude that a 4-bedroom house valued at about $35,000 can be rented for more than $400 a month without vacancy problems. We project the following rental income:

1973	Monthly rent:	$400
	Annual rent (5 months):	$2000
1974	Monthly rent:	$400
	Annual rent:	$4800
1975	Monthly rent:	$450
	Annual rent:	$5400
1976	Monthly rent:	$450
	Annual rent:	$5400
1977	Monthly rent:	$500
	Annual rent:	$6000

Tables 2.18 and 2.19 give cash requirements and projected income and cash flow, respectively. The economic model is based on financing terms offered by United California Bank of Victorville, the primary financial institution involved in construction lending at Spring Valley Lake.

Table 2.18 Cash Requirements

Property	4-bedroom house at Spring Valley Lake, Lot 241, Tract 8099, San Bernardino County	
Construction Start	December 15, 1972	
Completion	May 15, 1973	
Requirements	Land	$24,600
	Construction costs	27,400
	Builder's profit	3,400
	Processing fees	2,200
	Interest during construction	1,320
	Financing fees	660
	Title and recording	300
	Insurance	120
	Total cash requirements	$60,000
Sources	Mortgage proceeds	$44,000
	Note	10,000
	Equity in land	4,100
	Retained fees	1,900
	Total cash sources	$60,000

Table 2.19 Projection of income and cash flow

Item	1973	1974	1975	1976	1977
1 Annual rental income	$2000	$4800	$5400	$5400	$6000
Less					
Payment on first trust deed[a]	4163	3726	3726	3726	3726
Payment on note[b]	2491	2491	2491	2491	2491
Taxes[c]	650	1600	1650	1700	1750
Operating expenses[d]	440	295	310	325	340
Insurance	120	120	120	120	120
2 Total expenses	7864	8232	8297	8362	8427
3 Net cash flow (deficit) (1 − 2)	(5864)	(3432)	(2897)	(2962)	(2472)
Less					
Principal on first trust deed	252	475	512	552	595
Principal on note	1658	1813	1984	2170	2373
4 Total payments on principal	1910	2288	2496	2722	2968
5 Net income (loss) (3 + 4)	(3954)	(1144)	(401)	(240)	541
6 Depreciation	750	1675	1580	1500	1420
7 Net taxable income (loss) (5 − 6)	(4704)	(2819)	(1981)	(1740)	(879)
8 Tax savings (40% bracket)	1882	1128	792	696	352
9 Income (loss) after taxes (5 + 8)	(2172)	(16)	391	456	893
Equity Buildup	$7910	$10,198	$12,694	$15,416	$18,384

Source. Delphi Computer Sciences Company, Santa Monica.
[a]Face amount, $44,000; terms, 29 years; interest, 7½%.
[b]Face amount, $10,000; term, 5 years; interest, 9%.
[c]Current tax rate for Victor Valley is $12.50 per $100 of assessed valuation.
[d]Includes maintenance and association fees.

Economic Base Profile and Housing Market Analysis: Residential (Victor Valley Area*)

KEMPER & ASSOCIATES, ARCHITECTS

This study constitutes a test of the local housing market for the feasibility of new apartment house construction. It was done in 1974.

Abstract. These data indicate that the basic economic activities are generated by the George Air Force Base, tourism, and manufacturing.

Over the past few years the population of the area has been increasing at an annual rate of about 15%. Recently property values increased by almost 30% per year. An analysis of the housing market shows high rent schedules for the relatively few existing apartment structures (in San Bernardino County, only Lake Arrowhead shows rents above those of Apple Valley). Vacancy rates have been very low (below 3%), as indicated by Federal Housing Administration studies and surveys of the Victorville City Hall. The apartment structure analyzed in the case study shows an estimated annual return of 14% on the investment.

*Consists of the towns of Adelanto and Victorville, and the unincorporated areas of Apple Valley and Hesperia.

Conclusions. A shortage in both houses and apartments can be deduced from the census data available. With rent schedules comparable to those of new structures in Orange County or San Fernando Valley, with land prices still much lower than in the metropolitan area, and with continuing low vacancy rates due to economic pressure and population growth, construction of new multiple dwelling units can be a very profitable venture in the subject area now.

George Air Force Base has the single largest share of the total of 9000 jobs. Activities at the base are geared mainly to the training of Allied fighter pilots and were not affected by recent fluctuations in funding for government defense programs.

Tourism is the second largest economic activity of the area, and the jobs created there are mainly reflected in the figures of "service" and "transportation." A substantial increase of tourist traffic is expected with the completion of Lake Silverwood and its surrounding recreational areas.

Manufacturing has a share of 13% in the labor market. Light industries find a number of amenities in the Victor Valley: open space is available at low cost; excellent accessibility is provided by the Barstow Freeway, two railroads, and the Apple Valley Airport; the Mojave River plus the California Aqueduct can supply all the water needed; and the dry climate allows inexpensive outdoor storage.

Commuters to other areas are not included in the figure of 9000 employees attributed to George Air Force Base. The employment centers of San Bernardino, Riverside, and Fontana are all within 30 to 40 minutes of commuting time. Actual figures on commuters are not available, but traffic counts taken at the Cajon Pass by the Department of Highways show a peak at 8:00 A.M. of 2700 cars per hour, compared to the daily average of 900 cars per hour.

Related Tables. For specific data on the growth of the residential areas in the Victor Valley, refer again to Table 2.16. These data also show the continuous growth of the George Air Force Base, the main employment center of the area. Table 2.20 reveals that in 1971–1972

Table 2.20 Assessed Property Values in San Bernardino County

City	Value × 10^6		Percentage Increase
	1970–1971	1971–1972	
San Bernardino	179.9	192.3	7
Barstow	22.9	25.2	11
Ontario	102.2	120.6	18
Fontana	30.1	36.6	21.5
Victorville	20.7	26.5	28.5

Sources. Office of the County Assessor of San Bernardino County; John Bevis.

Victorville showed the greatest increase in property values in San Bernardino County. About 16% of the $5.8 million increase was due to new construction, but the increase in land values accounts for 84% of this amount. Table 2.21 summarizes the distribution of rental units, including mobile homes, in nine price ranges for four area communities.

Table 2.22 gives vacancy rates for Apple Valley, Hesperia, and Victorville. The Planning Department of the City of Victorville has the following vacancy figures, based on idle electricity meters for the Edison District which approximates the Joint Union High School District.

Table 2.21 Rental Unit Types and Price Ranges in Four Areas[a]

PLACE	VICTORVILLE		HESPERIA		GEORGE A.F.B.		APPLE VALLEY	
TOTAL POPULATION	10,845		4,592		7,404		6,702	
DATA ITEM:	COUNT	PERCENT	COUNT	PERCENT	COUNT	PERCENT	COUNT	PERCENT
1-UNIT STRUCTURES	2881	80.6%	1705	90.4%	521	39.8%	1873	80.4%
2 OR MORE UNIT ST.	475	13.3%	105	5.6%	789	60.2%	344	14.8%
MOBILE HOMES	220	6.2%	77	4.1%	0	0.0	114	4.9%
TOTAL DWELLING UNITS	3581		1888		1310		2331	
RENT OF RENTER OCCUPIED UNITS:								
0-40 $ PER MONTH	67		15		2		13	
40-59	131		8		0		5	
60-79	298		48		0		47	
80-99	354		76		0		101	
100-119	205		103		741		109	
120-149	210		66		291		177	
150-199	141		23		28		144	
200-299	46		7		2		37	
300-+	4		0		0		7	
MEDIAN	93		105		114		127	

[a]The average monthly rent in San Bernardino County is $92; Apple Valley, with an average of $127, shows the highest rent schedule of the county.

Source. Census data, 1970; first summary report, San Bernardino County Planning Department.

Table 2.22 Apartment and Home Vacancy Rates in the Victor Valley

	Apartments			Homes		
Town	Total Number of Units	Units Vacant	Vacancy Rate	Total Number of Units	Units Vacant	Vacancy Rate
Apple Valley	343	12	3.5%	2648	116	4.4%
Hesperia	10	—	0.0%	2241	37	1.6%
Victorville	1844	37	2.0%	3549	93	2.6%

Source. The vacancy survey for 1970, conducted by the FHA, in collaboration with local post offices.

Table 2.23 Rental Data on Comparable Buildings in the Victor Valley

Building Name	Manager	Location	Age (years)	Number of Units	Type	Monthly Rent
Earl Apartments	Apple Valley Ranchos	Apple Valley	10	10	2 Bd-1 Ba-U(nfurnished)	$150
Executive Apartments	Apple Valley Ranchos	Desert Knolls, Apple Valley	1	10	1 Bd-2 Ba-U 2 Bd-2 Ba-U	$175 $200
Hillcrest Apartments	Apple Valley Ranchos	Highway 18, Apple Valley	1	12	2 Bd-2 Ba-U	$225
Horrell Apartments	Mr. Horrell, resident	Kiowa Street, Apple Valley	—	6	2 Bd-1 Ba-U	$175
Green Tree Town Houses	Green Tree Inn	Victorvillle	6	25	2 Bd-2 Ba-U 3 Bd-2 Ba-U	$200 $225
Valley View Garden Apartments	Mr. Kiggins, owner	Bear Valley Road, Hesperia	1	5	1 Bd-1 Ba-U	$125

Residential meters idle:
2.83%, end of 1969
2.57%, yearly average, 1970
December 1970
Total meters = 3585
Meters idle = 102 (2.85%)
Residential meters = 2967
Meters idle = 76 (2.45%)
Mobile homes vacancies = 2.48%

Comparable rental data for several locations in the Victor Valley appear in Table 2.23. None of the apartment buildings listed had any vacancies in 1971; the Hillcrest Apartments were all leased before construction started, the Executive Apartments have a waiting list.

Income and Investment Analysis for Executive Apartments. The estimated value of improvements of this building (item 2, Table 2.23) is based on a construction cost of $14 per square foot. The land was acquired at a price of 66¢ per square foot. The project was financed with a conventional loan for 75% of the total cost; the term was 25 years, at an interest rate of 8.5%.

Based on these conservative figures, the price of the project is $165,000, the down payment is $41,300, and an annual cash flow is as follows:

Gross rental income	$22,600
Less	
Operating expenses	6,360
Interest payments	10,400
	16,760
Total return	$ 5,840

The annual return on the down payment is 14%, tax savings have not been added to these figures. Tables 2.24, 2.25, and 2.26 give a property analysis, and income property statement, and a depreciation schedule, respectively.

Table 2.24 Property Analysis for Executive Apartments

Feasability Study 7-9-71		
Executive Apartments		
Desert Knolls, Apple Valley		
Apartments - 10 Units		
List Price: $165,000		
Loans: $123,700		
List Price Equity: $41,300		
Existing Financing: $123,700 over 25 years		
$11,800 Annual Payment		
8 1/2% Interest		
Scheduled Gross Income:		$23,300.00
Less: Vacancy & Credit losses 3%		700.00
Gross Operating Income:		22,600.00
Less Operating Expenses		
Taxes	1 3/4%	2,600.00
Insurance		300.00
Utilities		400.00
Licenses, Permits, Ads		150.00
Management		1,000.00
Payroll		50.00
Supplies		60.00
Services		600.00
Maintenance		1,200.00
TOTAL EXPENSES		$6,360.00
INCOME		$16,240.00

Income Approach	
10,000 sq. ft. @ Apts. 14.00 per sq. ft.	$140,000.00
2,000 sq. ft. @ Carports 2.50 per sq. ft.	5,000.00
Total	$145,000.00
Pool Site Improvement, Asphalt	5,000.00
Land: 24,500 sq. ft. @ 0.60	15,000.00
Estimate of Market Value by Cost Approach	$165,000.00
Income Adjusted to Financing	
Income	$16,240.00
Interest . . . . $10,400 1st Loan	
Principal . . . 1,400	
Total Payment	11,800.00
Dependable Income	4,440.00
Principal Payment	1,400.00
Equity Income (Rate 14)	5,840.00
Depreciation (1st Year)	15,000.00
Loss	9,150.00

Source. Capra & Associates, Los Angeles.

Table 2.25 Income Property Statement for Executive Apartments

Executive Apartments
Desert Knolls, Apple Valley
Special Features: Contemporary Architecture, View, Pool
Lot Size: 140 x 175 = 24,500 sq. ft.
Zone: R3
Age: 1 Year
Construction: F+S
Parking: Cpts
Stories: 2
Sewer: No
Heat: Yes
A/C: Yes
Financing: 1st: $123,700; Payments: $11,800
Interest: $10,400; Original No. Years 25, to go 24

Scheduled Income:

# Unit	Description	Rent
1	1 bedr. unf.	$175
2	2 bedr. unf.	200
3	2 " 2 bath unf.	200
4	2 " " "	200
5	2 " " "	200
6	2 " " "	200
7	2 " " "	200
8	2 " " "	200
9	2 " " "	200
10	2 " " "	200
	TOTAL	$1,975

INVESTMENT INFORMATION

Price	$165,000
Loan	123,700
Down	41,300
Income	23,300
Vacancy Fact. 3%	7,700
Gross Operat. Income	22,600
Operating Expense	6,360
Net Operating Income	16,240
Loan Payment	11,800
Gross Spendable	4,440
Carpet	800
Adjusted Gross Spendable	3,640
Paid on Principal	1,400
Total Return	4,040

Earns 2.5% on Sale Price
Spendable of 14% on Down Payment
Earns 10% on Down Payment
Purchase Price is 7.3 Times Gross

Source. Capra & Associates, Los Angeles.

Table 2.26 Depreciation Schedule, 200% Double Declining Balance, for Executive Apartments

			1970	1971	1972	1973	1974
Appliances, Carpets, Drapes etc,	5 Years	12,800	5,100	3,100	1,840	1,100	1,100
Air Conditioning, Plumbing, Heating, Roofing, Landscaping, Etc.,	15 Years	37,200	4,900	4,200	3,700	3,200	2,800
Building	40 Years	100,000	5,000		4,500	4,200	4,000
	Total	150,000	15,000	12,050	10,040	8,500	7,900
	less Income		5,850	5,850	5,850	5,850	5,850
	Taxable Income (Loss)		(9,150)	(6,200)	(4,190)	(2,650)	(2,050)

Source. Capra & Associates, Los Angeles.

Programming

Programming establishes the uniqueness of a design problem by identifying the task and explaining its task. Since this work is partly based on the evaluation of quantitative information, computers can be very helpful in the process. Many factors, however, cannot be expressed readily in numbers, and this limits the scope of computers in this field.

Before the architect concentrates on particular assignment, he or she will research similar building types and organizations, to obtain an idea of the problems involved. The development of the specific program will be the effort of a team, which usually includes the architect, the owner, future occupants and users of the building proposed, and specialists and consultants. The main responsibility for communication among team members will lie with the architect. In using graphic tools such as diagrams and renderings for this task, however, the architect must be aware that the average individual's capacity for understanding and visualizing a graphic presentation is not as developed as that of the professional.

The Process of Programming

Generally speaking the safest and most efficient approach to programming is to work from the broad concepts and big blocks of information toward more detailed and specific points. Thus it is best to begin by establishing a schematic or conceptual program, which is graphically expressed in a schematic design. If this schematic program satisfies the major criteria, the architect can proceed with a more detailed preliminary program, which leads to the design development phase. In this way the architect avoids the danger of losing the overview of a problem by becoming overly concerned with one detail. Both stages of programming follow the same process, which can be structured in five steps.

1 *Definition of the Client's Objectives.* The architect evaluates the client's goals in terms of the building program and the space, time, and money available. This leads to a series of discussions with the client that permits the clear establishment of his or her goals.

2 *Collection, Organization, and Analysis of Facts.* All information gathered is classified in terms of its relevance to the specific problem and the basic functions of the project. The data should cover the building's future use and obsolescence, and the relationship of the project to the surrounding environment. A major organizing factor in this process is the characteristics of the site—its physical as well as legal and community-related aspects. Money, of course, is the prime organizer in every business enterprise, and budgetary considerations are omnipresent in every step of programming.

3 *Evaluation of Alternative Concepts.* Such concepts include centralization versus decentralization, compartmentation versus open-space plans, and flexibility versus explicit functionality. These alternatives must be tested in their performance against the needs and preferences of the users.

4 *Determination of Space Requirements.* When the minimum space required and the optimum amount of space for each function of the project have been determined, the efficiency of the building can be tested with ratios such as the net usable space divided by the gross building space. Whether the building program is in line with the preliminary budget is also ascertained in this

MUTUAL BENEFIT LIFE INSURANCE COMPANY BUILDING
Los Angeles, California
Architects: William L. Pereira Associates
Photo: W. Thom

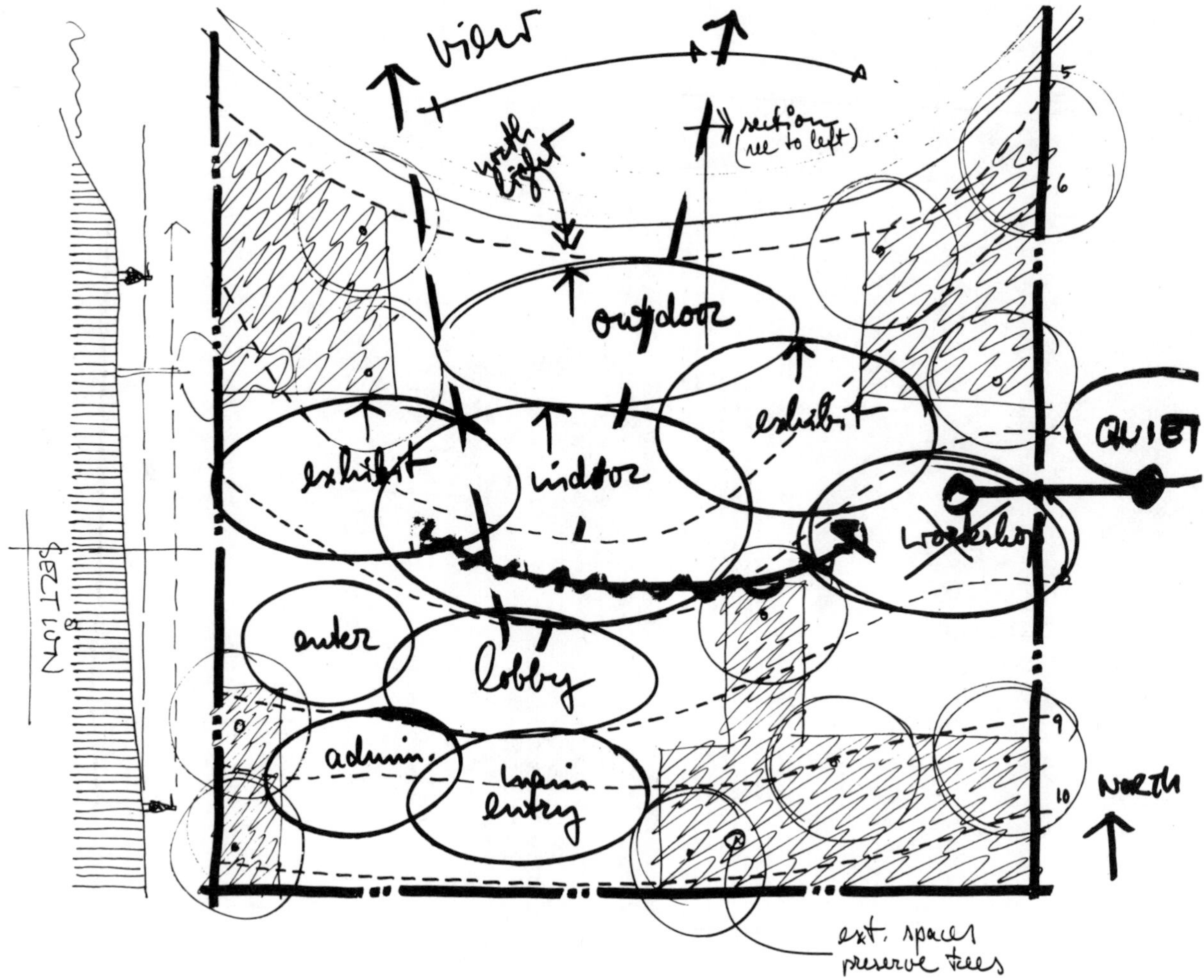

Figure 2.5 Relationship bubble diagram. Drawing by author.

phase; the amount of space allowances above the minimum largely depends on these financial evaluations.

5 *Statement of the Problem.* In the conceptual program this statement should be quite broad. It should not specify the individual forms of buildings but rather their functions and performances. Detailed information concerning the site, cost, time, and specific design solutions should be kept to a minimum in favor of a clear overall picture of all factors involved.

Throughout this process the architect should incorporate the feedback from the owner and user in every step, to ensure that the program clearly reflects their intentions. If this is done, the program itself can be used as a basis for arbitration if disagreements occur later between parties. A good program will reduce the amount of future changes, thus reducing predevelopment and construction cost.

The term ''program guide'' refers to a format outline for the preparation of a master plan program on big projects. It is intended to help owner/users express their concepts, and it classifies information into three general categories:

- Goals and objectives.
- Functional needs.
- Basic space requirements.

According to the program instrument, the project must be defined starting from the general and moving toward more detailed considerations. Thus the first step is the development of the master plan for the ''total complex,'' including data regarding access, circulation, parking, servicing of the project, fire protection, and similar matters.

Next to be developed is the ''total building'' program. It focuses on a single building in the project and defines all its functions, their interrelationship, their space requirements, and the environmental qualities needed.

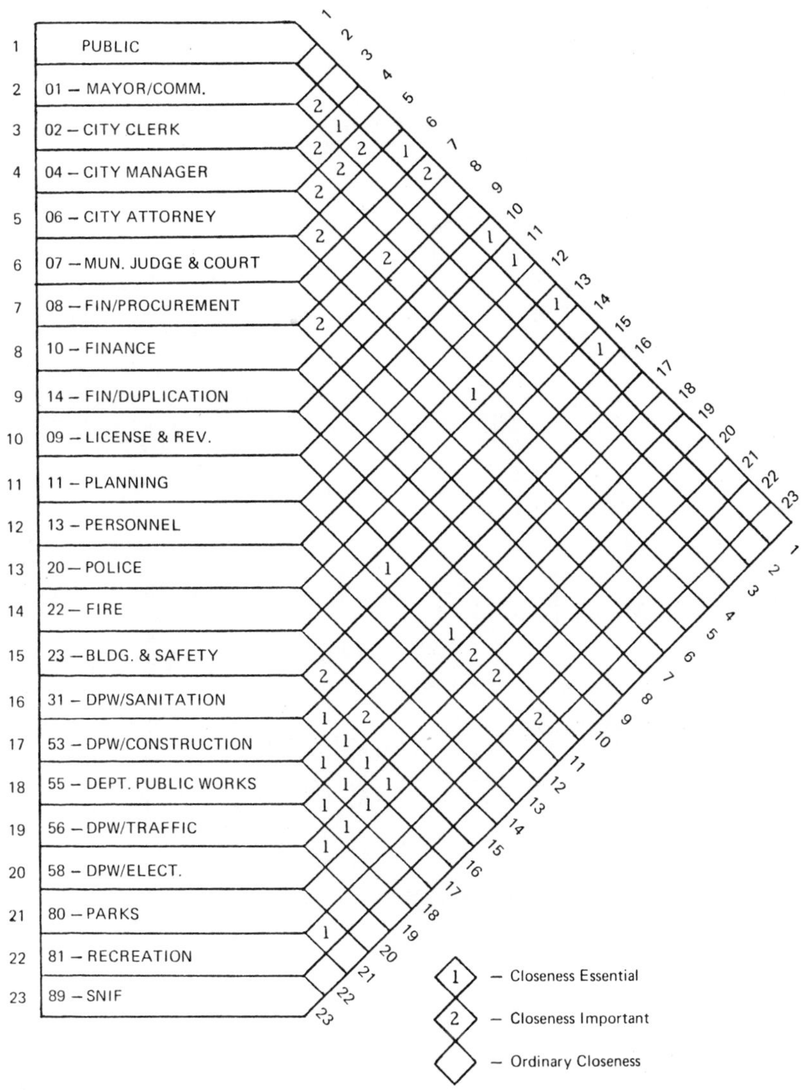

Figure 2.6 Relationship matrix showing functional relationships among city departments in the Las Vegas City Hall complex. *Source*. Daniel, Mann, Johnson & Mendenhall, Architects.

The next smaller program unit is the "activity center"; this includes several rooms and related spaces that are all supposed to serve the same general activity. In a hospital, for instance, an outpatient clinic would be such an activity center, and the program would include a list of its staff and their activities.

The smallest unit of the program is called "individual space." In this part, the data are detailed enough to include the exact amount of square feet of floor space, as well as furniture, fixtures, and so on.

When the completed program instrument is revised and approved by both architect and owner, it can serve the designer as a guideline throughout the job, and it is indispensable in arriving at realistic cost estimates.

Biloxi Library/Cultural Center, Biloxi, Mississippi

MLTW/TURNBULL ASSOCIATES, ARCHITECTS

Project Description. The old and historic city of Biloxi, Mississippi, has elected to erect a new library and cultural center as their bicentennial gesture in 1976.

The plan was announced as a 1-week teaching and design charette, and several professionals from all over the United States were invited to participate. The process of physically working in the community made one aware of the problems confronting the Library Board and of the numerous points of view proposed as a response to the program, the budget, and local building techniques.

ST. PETER'S LUTHERAN CHURCH
Edina, Minnesota
Architect: Ralph Rapson, Douglas Baird Associate
Photo: Office

The solution envisages a walled garden opening up the street across from the old City Hall and providing a landscaped foreground to this important public structure. The small original Creole Library was relocated in the garden as a historic object, providing temporal continuity in land usage. The walls of the garden are symbolically the walls of the bookcases, which form, under one expansive roof, an intimate reading layer for the user to enjoy next to the exterior foliage. Between the Cultural Center and the Library is a large skylit rotunda containing the circulation and information desks. The cultural facility is marked in the rear by a tower, recalling the old Gulf Coast lighthouse, and entry is through a foyer 65 feet high. Grand stairs, in the traditional southern manner, lead to the second floor meeting space, and adjacent areas will be given over to cultural display purposes.

The 33,000-square-foot building is constructed with the emphasis on the enclosing roof form (with its historic overtones), and white reflecting stucco walls recall the surrounding older residential buildings.

Interior furnishings will be in oak, and paint colors are soft and muted blues and lavenders, which offer refreshing qualities appropriate to this hot and humid environment. Live oak trees are planted adjacent to the new structure and the old Creole Library, and in time, the building and the landscape will come together as a special public realm. Construction is scheduled for completion in July 1977.

Purpose. To provide a Library/Cultural Center that will inspire and enhance the education of all citizens of Biloxi through its resource collections and its services.

The Center will provide space and facilities for a full-service library, local art and craft displays, and educational programs of cultural and historical interest with special emphasis on local folklore and ethnic communities in the city.

Objectives. The Library/Cultural Center will ensure efficient operation, provide flexibility of space, be direct and easily understood in arrangement, and provide an environment that is friendly, intimate, and pleasant. The facility will be a live, vital place in which the discovery of ideas becomes exciting.

The six main areas of the Library/Cultural Center are outlined below. Table 2.27 gives the square footage required by each.

Table 2.27 Square Footage Summary of Major Areas of Library/Cultural Center

Type of Area	Size (ft^2)
Public Service Area	
1 Main entrance/lobby (including coat room, public telephones, men's and women's restrooms)	2,000
2 Main circulation desk and card catalog	1,200
3 Reference area (including reference librarian's office, multimedia area)	1,900
4 Popular reading and browsing	2,400
5 Adult stacks, reading and browsing	8,700
6 Children's stacks, reading and browsing	2,000
Special Service Areas	
1 Conference room (seating for 20)	350
2 Assembly/exhibit (seating for 110, including storage)	1,850
3 Museum/exhibit (including storage)	3,600
Administrative Areas	
1 Head librarian's office	150
2 Offices/study	250
3 Staff room with kitchen unit	250
4 Storage	100
Work Area	
Technical process area (including receiving and mailing, catalog, serials, circulation and storage)	950
Mechanical Area	
1 Mechanical rooms	1,300
2 Janitor's room and storage	150
Observation Tower	1,000
Total net square footage	28,000
Nonassignable space, 15%	4,000
Gross square footage	32,000
Volume capacity without future mezzanine	68,000 volumes

Library/Cultural Center Areas

Public Service Areas

Main Entrance

1 The lobby should serve to introduce and welcome people to the library, capture their interest by displays and special exhibits, help in directing them toward specific destinations, and generally set the tone and atmosphere of the building. There should be enough space to house basic operational functions, and a small lounge or seating area may be included. Other activities and facilities that should be part of, or adjacent to, this area are (*a*) outside book return mechanism, (*b*) display of new books (recent acquisitions), and (*c*) special exhibits and notices.

2 The following facilities will be adjacent to the main entrance but will be located so as to discourage off-street use: (*a*) coat room, (*b*) public telephones, and (*c*) men's and women's restrooms.

Main Circulation Desk, Card Catalog

1 The circulation desk should be visible from the lobby and should be located to serve as a control point for people entering and leaving the library. The circulation desk should also be located in the proximity of the card catalog and the reference or bibliography collection. The desk will require space for charging records and a cash drawer. Library users will check out and return books to this desk. Returned books will be stored temporarily before being trucked to various locations and reshelved. The circulation desk may also serve as an information desk. Other activities that will take place at the circulation desk are issuance of library cards, payment of library fines, and keeping of general book circulation records. The circulation desk will be staffed by a maximum of two persons during busy hours.

2 The card catalog should be visible from the lobby and adjacent to the circulation desk, the reference center, and the technical process department. Since the card catalog will grow as the book collection expands, it should be located in a position that will allow for expansion. The card catalog cabinets should have built-in telephone jacks so that staff working with the catalog can communicate with staff members in the technical process

TEMPLE EMANU-EL AND SCHOOL
Livingston, New Jersey
Architects: James Baker & Peter Blake
Photo: Office

department. The card catalog area should have adjacent seating tables for those making prolonged study of the cards.

Reference Area. Reference services will include facilities for a reference librarian, a reference desk, and a collection of reference books, periodical indexes, and a periodical directory. The reference section may also include a bibliographical collection grouped together in this area rather than dispersed by subject. Atlas and map collections, photographs, public documents, and special reference collections may also be included in this section of the library. Although most of the reference materials will be on open stacks, some materials, such as unbound past periodicals and newspapers and special reference volumes, will be shelved on closed stacks and/or controlled by the reference librarian. Adjacent to the reference materials, a reference reading-study area should be provided with a combination of individual carrels, table seating, and some lounge-type seating to accommodate approximately 20 persons. The reference section will contain a microfilm reader-printer and will accommodate the Mississippi collection and genealogy. The reference section will contain approximately 2500 reference volumes when the library opens.

Popular Reading and Browsing (including current newspapers and periodicals). This area of the library may include new fiction, best sellers, and current newspapers and periodicals, plus books of special interest. The stacks will be open, visually and physically accessible to the library user. This area will include a general reading area with group table and seating and lounge-type seating. The popular reading and browsing area will contain approximately 2500 volumes plus current periodicals and newspapers when the library opens.

Adult Stacks, Reading and Browsing. The adult area will include open stacks that house the general book collection. The reading area will be adjacent to the stacks. It should be a pleasant and comfortable area in which people can sit quietly and read. A variety of seating accommodations will be provided: lounge type seating, group table seating, and a limited number of carrels. The adult library area will contain approximately 42,000 volumes when the library opens.

Children's Stacks, Reading and Browsing. This area will have facilities for a children's librarian. It should be a pleasant place for children to come and read and look through books. The children's area will include an area for story telling and group seating. The children's area will contain approximately 9000 volumes when the library opens.

Public Service Area Summary

1 The library will accommodate 55,000 volumes at the time of opening. The capacity of the library will be expandable to approximately 68,000 volumes without any structural changes in the building. Subsequent addition of a mezzanine level to the building will increase the capacity to approximately 85,000 volumes.
2 The books will be housed on open stacks, although special collections and rare books may be housed on closed stacks, controlled by the library staff.
3 All public facilities will be accessible to the handicapped.

Special Service Areas

Multimedia Collection. The multimedia collection will include phonograph records and tapes, film strips, microfilm, and slides. The housing of these materials will require special shelving and storage units. Adjacent to this area, booths for listening and viewing will be provided. The multimedia collection will initially be very limited but will be added to periodically.

ADLAI E. STEVENSON COLLEGE, UNIVERSITY OF CALIFORNIA
Santa Cruz, California
Architects: Esherick Homsey Dodge & Davis
Photo: R. Partridge

WASHINGTON & LEE HIGH SCHOOL GYMNASIUM
Montross, Virginia
Architects: Stevenson Flemer, Eason Cross, Harry Adreon
Photo: J. Alexander

Area for Blind and Handicapped Persons. This room or area should be easily accessible in the library, preferably near the front entrance and near staff stations in the building so that staff personnel will be available to assist the handicapped users. This area may be combined with the reference area. Most of the materials for the blind and handicapped are usually used at home.

Conference Room. The conference room will be used by both the library staff and the public. It should be located near the head librarian's office but also should be accessible to the public for small group meetings and conferences. This room will be planned to accommodate 20 people.

Auditorium/Exhibit. The auditorium will be planned for film showing, other audiovisual services,and large group meetings (110 maximum), with space allocated for exhibits. This room will have a level floor to permit flexibility of use, since it may also be used as an exhibit area. Space for chair storage will be provided. The auditorium is to be usable when other parts of the library are closed.

Museum and Exhibit. The museum will provide space for local art and craft displays and will include special presentations of filmed and oral history of the Biloxi environs. Exhibits will include materials relating to the ethnic communities in the city, and the folklore of the fishermen and other pioneers of the area. The museum will have permanent special collections and may accommodate rotating or traveling exhibits. The museum is to be accessible when other parts of the library are closed.

Administrative Areas. Administrative areas of the library include the individual offices or stations for staff directly involved in the administration and supervision of the library.

1 The head librarian's office should be accessible to the public through a secretary and should be convenient to the other staff and work areas of the library.
2 The reference librarian's office will be located in the reference area to provide supervision and control. The office will be provided with backup work

C. Y. STEPHENS AUDITORIUM, IOWA STATE UNIVERSITY
Ames, Iowa
Architects in joint venture: Crites, McConnell, Steveley, Anderson and Brooks, Borg & Skiles
Photo: J. Shulman

area and should be located adjacent to the library work area.

3 The desk of the children's librarian will be located in the children's area to facilitate supervision and control. The children's librarian will organize children's programs and activities.
4 The staff room will provide a place for staff members to prepare simple meals during coffee and lunch breaks. It should be a pleasant place for the staff to relax.

Work Area (Technical Process). This department will be responsible for the planning and development of resources as well as their maintenance and bibliographical control. The area will include the following services:

1 *Receiving and Mailing*. In this area all incoming material is unpacked and sent to the acquisitions area. Packages are wrapped and mail is sent out. All incoming materials are sorted here and forwarded to their respective departments.

2 *Acquisitions*. This department orders all library materials and checks all incoming materials against orders and invoices. Card files, shelves for bibliographies; and dealers' catalogs are usually required.
3 *Catalog Department*. In this area of the library, books are catalogued and classified. This area will be adjacent to the catalog department and the reference department.
4 *Serials*. The serials area is where unbound library materials are collated and organized before distribution to respective locations in the library.

Mechanical and Maintenance Areas Mechanical Room. The mechanical room will accommodate the equipment necessary to air condition and heat the building, as well as other equipment associated with the building utilities. The mechanical room should be acoustically isolated from the library.

Janitor's Quarters and Storage. The janitor's quarters will have a service sink, as well as storage facilities to house maintenance equipment and materials.

Observation Tower. The observation tower will provide a high vantage point in the downtown area to view and survey the Biloxi area. It will attract visitors and tourists and will have telescopes directed to local points of interest, as well as tape recordings of local history.

Mechanical Facilities and Comfort Requirements

Lighting. The quality of light in the library is a basic consideration; it should be appropriate to the space and comfortable for the purpose to which it is being used. Quality of light is not easily measured because it depends on several factors, particularly the light source, the fixtures used, and the lighting intensity.

Natural illumination is a good source of light if it is properly controlled and used in conjunction with artificial light sources. It should be noted, however, that books are damaged by direct sunlight because of ultraviolet rays, which fade bindings and hasten paper deterioration.

The intensity of artificial lighting will vary according to its particular use. Different intensities will be required for reading areas, stack spaces, offices, work areas, and auditorium and museum spaces. The quality of light in the reading areas should be comfortable and attractive, designed to reduce glare and strong contrast. The choice of fluorescent, incandescent, or a combination of both should be made with the consideration of the cost of installation, maintenance, and operation, but attractiveness and the comfort of the users and staff is of prime importance.

All lighting should be panel switched in public areas except for individual movable fixtures.

Table 2.28 Outline Specifications: Biloxi Library/Cultural Center (May 28, 1975)

STRUCTURAL ASSEMBLIES AND RELATED FINISHES

Site Preparation

1 Clear, grub, and strip topsoil.
2 Foundation excavation and backfill.
3 Fill and grade to required elevations.

Foundations. Reinforced concrete spread footings.

Exterior Walls

1 *Structure*. Reinforced concrete and reinforced, grouted concrete block.
2 *Exterior Finish*. Textured waterproof coating, fiberglass-reinforced polyester resin.
3 *Insulation*. Fiberglass batts (3½ in).
4 *Interior Finish*. Gypsum wallboard, painted.

Interior Masonry Walls

1 *Structure*. Reinforced, grouted concrete block.
2 *Finish*. Plaster, painted.

Ground Floor

1 *Structure*. Reinforced concrete slab on grade.
2 *Finishes*. As noted on drawings and specified below.

Upper Floors

1 *Structure*. Wood joists and glued laminated beams with plywood deck.
2 *Floor Finish*. As noted on drawings and specified below.
3 *Ceiling Finish*. Gypsum wallboard, painted.

Roof

1 *Structure*. Wood joists and glued laminated beams with plywood deck.
2 *Exterior Finish*. Standing seam aluminum roof with integral color and finish.
3 *Insulation*. Fiberglass batts (6 in).
4 *Ceiling Finish*. Gypsum wallboard, painted.

Interior Partitions (bearing and nonbearing)

1 *Structure*. Wood stud.
2 *Finish*. Gypsum wallboard, painted.

Special Structural Conditions

1 Reinforced concrete beams and lintels at openings in masonry walls.
2 Miscellaneous steel connections and bracing at skylight openings.

FINISHES, ASSEMBLIES NOT INCLUDED WITH STRUCTURE

Windows. Fixed glass in anodized aluminum frames, commercial grade.

Exterior Doors

1 *Public Entrances.* Narrow stile aluminum and glass (anodized), institutional grade hardware.

2 *Service and Emergency Exit Doors.* Wood, solid core, in hollow metal frames, with institutional grade hardware.

Skylights: Clear wire glass in aluminum frames.

Stairs

1 *Interior.* Wood frame with finish to match adjacent floor surfaces.

2 *Spiral (to mezzanine).* Prefabricated steel.

3 *Observation Tower.* Reinforced concrete and steel pan with concrete fill.

Floor Finishes

1 *Carpet.* Tufted, level loop acrylic-modacrylic at library public areas, except for circulation desk rotunda, and second floor exhibit assembly and lobby areas (72 oz).

2 *Hardwood.* Oak strip, at first floor exhibit areas, lobby, and circulation desk rotunda.

3 *Ceramic Tile.* At toilet rooms.

4 *Resilient.* Vinyl asbestos tile, at offices, conference room, work and utility areas.

5 *Exposed Concrete.* At first floor mechanical rooms.

Suspended Ceilings and Soffits

1 *Interior.* Gypsum wallboard, painted, on steel suspension system.

2 *Exterior.* Cement plaster, sand finish, painted.

Interior Doors. Wood, solid core, in hollow metal frames, with institutional grade hardware, fire ratings as required.

Miscellaneous Millwork

1 *Cabinetwork and Shelving.* wood; AWI custom grade, in public and staff areas; AWI economy grade in utility areas.

2 *Miscellaneous Trim.* AWI custom grade throughout.

Miscellaneous Metal Work: Railings, miscellaneous access ladders; steel painted.

Accessories

1 *Entry Mats.* Rubber.

2 *Toilet Partitions.* Steel, baked enamel finish.

3 *Toilet Accessories.* Stainless steel, institutional grade.

Library Shelving: Open, standard mounted, steel library shelving with baked enamel finish.

SERVICES

Heating, Ventilating, and Air Conditioning

1 *Scope.* Furnish all labor, materials, equipment, and services required to install complete and properly operating heating, ventilating, and air conditioning systems. Work includes, but is not limited to the following:

(*a*) Ducted forced-air heating and cooling systems for all areas. Reading and book areas will have high limit humidity control.

(*b*) Water chiller, hot water boiler, circulating pumps, cooling tower, expansion tanks, trim, and accessories.

(*c*) Chilled and hot water piping distribution system with valves, supports, insulation, trim, and accessories.

(*d*) Mechanical exhaust for

(i) Toilets.

(ii) Staff.

(iii) Observation tower.

2 *Heating, Ventilating, and Air Conditioning Systems*

(*a*) Each air heating and cooling system will consist of air handling units with cooling and reheat coils, filters, vibration isolators, controls, and mixing box to allow 10% fresh air at all times (fixed mix).

(*b*) Supply air will be ducted with insulated galvanized steel ducts to the rooms through diffuser and registers. Return air will be ducted from return air registers back to the fan units, where it will be mixed with a fixed amount of outside air, filtered, and heated and/or cooled.

3 *Mechanical Exhaust Systems.* The exhaust fans for toilets, staff, and observation tower will be of the roof-mounted mushroom type, and galvanized steel exhaust ducts and exhaust grilles.

4 *Piping.* The heating and chilled water piping will be schedule 40, ASTM A-120 black steel with 150 psi malleable or cast iron fittings. Weld fittings will be used on pipe sizes 3 inches and larger. Buried chilled and condensing water piping will be asbestos-cement pressure pipe with ring-tight joints, 150 psi class. Aboveground condensing water piping will be schedule 40, ASTM A-120, galvanized steel pipe with victaulic type fittings.

5 *Insulation*

(*a*) *Piping, Above Ground.* The heating and chilled water piping insulation will be 1 1/2-inch thick fiberglass with self-sealing jacket. For chilled water piping, vapor barrier jacket will be used. Buried heating hot water piping will be protected in accordance with manufacturer's recommendations.

(*b*) *Duct*

(i) *Concealed.* Heating and cooling system ductwork will be insulated on the exterior with 1-inch thick; 1-pound density rigid board insulation covered with vapor barrier aluminum foil jacket.

(ii) *For sound control.* Internally lined with 1-inch

acoustical duct liner, duct size will be increased to allow for insulation.

6 *Ductwork.* Installed in accordance with the requirements of the Sheet Metal and Air Conditioning Contractors' National Association, Inc. (SMACNA), manual for "A Code of Trade Practice for Ventilating and Air Conditioning Work," low velocity section.

7 *Code Requirements.* All work shall conform with the Southern Standard Mechanical Code, all state and local codes, and all applicable governing rules and regulations of agencies having jurisdiction over this project.

8 *Temperature Control System*

(*a*) Temperature control system will be pneumatic type, with wall-mounted thermostats for zone control and humidistats for high-limit humidity control in some areas.

(*b*) Automatic control functions will be initiated by local time clocks and integrated with the control system, with interface as required.

9 Special precautions will be taken for sound and vibration control.

10 High-limit humidity control will be provided in book areas only.

11 In all areas 45% (minimum) efficient filters will be used.

12 Maintenance instructions will be provided by the contractor for personnel on mechanical systems and equipment. Bound volumes of vendor-supplied parts and maintenance and operating data will be furnished to the owner on completion of the contract.

Plumbing

1 *Scope.* Furnish all labor, materials, equipment, and services required to install a complete and properly operating plumbing and fire protection system. Work includes but is not limited to the following:

(*a*) Toilet rooms, staff room, and janitor closets; plumbing fixtures and trim including electric water coolers in public areas.

(*b*) Rough in, provide necessary time, and make final connections to equipment furnished under other sections of the work.

(*c*) Domestic electric hot water heater and related accessories and controls.

(*d*) Extension of sanitary sewer and domestic water services to the building from street mains.

(*e*) Sanitary soil, waste, and venting piping systems.

(*f*) Rainwater piping system.

(*g*) Domestic cold water and insulated hot water piping systems.

(*h*) Natural gas piping system.

2 *Plumbing Fixtures and Trim*

(*a*) Unless otherwise designated, fixtures will be American Standard, Kohler, Crane, or equivalent.

(*b*) *Water Closets.* Wall hung, vitreous china, siphon jet, flush valves, sealless cover, chair carrier.

(*c*) *Urinals.* Wall hung, vitreous china, top spud, flush valves, carrier.

(*d*) *Lavatories.* Vitreous china, front overflow, antisplash rim, splash back, fitting to receive soap dispenser, two-valve, single-spout faucet, loose key stops and escutcheons, cast brass P-trap, and steel support backing plate.

(*e*) *Service Sinks.* Floor-mounted terrazzo receptor, faucet with integral stops, hose end, pain hook, and vacuum breaker; 3-inch P-trap with strainer, U-type stainless steel rim guard.

(*f*) *Electric Water Cooler.* Semirecessed, stainless steel cabinet, mounting frame and fan-cooled condensing unit.

(*g*) *Staff Room Sink.* Stainless steel, two-valve, single-spout faucet, loose key stops, cast brass P-trap, disposal, and mounting frame.

(*h*) *Hose Bibb.* Wall hydrant type adjacent to building entries and interior courts. Chrome-plated, keyless units for toilets and public areas. Rough bronze for nonpublic areas.

3 *Domestic Water Heater.* Electric storage type, automatic, copper lined, 100% safety shutoff, ASME temperature and pressure relief valve.

4 *Floor, Roof and Area Drains.* Wade, Josam, Zurn or equivalent.

5 *Sanitary Soil, Waste, and Venting Piping*

(*a*) Soil, waste, and vent piping above ground, 3 inches and larger, will be service-weight, cast iron soil pipe and fittings, ASTM A-72-42. All sizes underground will be cast iron soil pipe and fittings. Joints will be oakum and lead, compression fittings, or NO-HUB system.

(*b*) Soil, waste, and venting piping above ground, 2 1/2 inches and smaller, will be screwed, galvanized Schedule 40 steel piping, ASTM A-120. Fittings will be galvanized cast iron drainage screwed fittings; ASA B16.12 or NO-HUB cast iron pipe and fittings system will be used.

6 *Rainwater Lead Piping.* Rainwater piping above ground, all sizes, will be service weight cast iron soil pipe and fittings ASTM N. A-74-42. All sizes underground will be cast iron pipe and fittings. Joints will be oakum and lead, compression fittings, or NO-HUB system. Exposed rainwater leaders will be galvanized steel pipe with drainage fittings.

7 *Domestic Cold and Hot Water Piping*

(*a*) Domestic cold water piping required to the city water main will be of the same materials as the main, with compatible fittings, or as below.

(*b*) Domestic water piping underground will be type L copper tubing, ASTM B-88, with wrought copper fittings. Piping will be protected with a double coat of approved Vitumastic paint, 95-5 solder.

(*c*) Domestic cold and hot water piping above ground

will be type L copper tubing, ASTM B-88, with wrought copper fittings, 50-50 solder.

(*d*) Domestic hot water piping will be insulated with 3/4-inch inorganic glass fiber pipe insulation, self-sealing lap type, Owens/Corning Fiberglas or equivalent.

(*e*) A pressure-regulating valve assembly and check valve will be installed in the incoming domestic water supply if required.

8 *Gas Piping*. Piping will comply with the Southern Standard Gas Code. Gas piping above ground will be Schedule 40 steel pipe with galvanized 150-pound malleable iron screwed fittings for 1 1/2-inch and smaller pipe and welding fittings for 2-inch and larger pipe. Pipe will be black except for piping and fittings exposed to the weather, which will be galvanized. All pipes underground will be Schedule 40 black steel pipe with welding fittings and wrapped with Standard Pipe protection "X-TRU-COAT."

9 *Code Requirements*. All work will conform with the Southern Standard Plumbing Code, all state and local codes, and all applicable governing rules and regulations of agencies having jurisdiction over this project.

Electrical Distribution Systems

1 *Scope*. Incoming services at 120/208 volts, 3 phase, 4 wire, from the utility company transformer. The main switchboard will contain the utility company meter, the main breaker, and the distribution section for the feeders to panelboards throughout the building.
Equipment will be served at the following voltages:
Lighting. 120 volts.
Duplex Receptacles. 120 volts.
Motors, 0.5 Horsepower and Less. 120 volts.
Motors, 0.75 Horsepower and Larger. 208 volts, 3 phase.
Emergency Standby Power. 12 volt d.c. battery units connected to illuminated exit fixtures lighting paths of egress.

2 Materials

(*a*) *Main Switchboard*. Indoor, metal enclosed, class I construction with convertible distribution section.

(*b*) *Panelboards*

(i) All breakers bolted to busses.

(ii) 120- and 208-volt breakers, type TQ.

(iii) Assembly to conform to type NLAB construction.

3 *Standards*. Install in accordance with manufacturer's shop drawings. Fabricate to meet UL standards and NEMA requirements.

Lighting: Fixtures and Lamps

1 *Scope*. Provide complete lighting systems as follows:

(*a*) *Stack Areas*. Shielded fluorescent mounted from stacks, 25 footcandles.

(*b*) *Main Reading Rooms*. Portable lamps.

(*c*) *Children's Reading Area*. Recessed incandescent.

(*d*) *Reference and Work Rooms*. Surface fluorescent, 80 footcandles.

(*e*) *Assembly*. Surface fluorescent and system of light track.
Light Track on Dimmer System. 80 footcandles.

(*f*) *Exhibit Room*. System of light track and incandescent floods.

2 *Materials*

(*a*) *Ballasts*. Class "O", UL. CMB labeled with self-resetting thermal protectors.

(*b*) *Lamps*. Fluorescent lamps warm white, incandescent lamps rated 130 volts.

3 *Standards*. Install in accordance with manufacturer's shop drawings.

Fire Alarm Systems

1 *Scope*. Provide master-coded, supervised, zone-annunciated fire alarm system. Smoke detectors and manual station provide for alarm. Horns sound alert for building evacuation.

2 *Materials*. All equipment will be installed and wired in accordance with manufacturer's specifications. Equipment listed by Underwriters' Laboratory, Inc.

3 *Standards*. National Board of Fire Underwriters' pamphlets 13 and 72 and all applicable local ordinances.

Telephone System

1 *Scope*. Provide empty raceway and outlet system for installation of public telephone system.

2 *Materials*. Empty raceway and outlet boxes.

Elevator. Oil hydraulic passenger elevator, 1 stop, 5 × 5 foot cab.

SITEWORK

Concrete Curb, Gutter, Sidewalk. New curb, gutter, sidewalk, and patching of those existing, in accordance with City of Biloxi standard.

Asphalt Concrete Paving: In accordance with City of Biloxi standard.

Landscaping.

Table 2.29 Biloxi Library/Cultural Center Area Tabulation (May 28, 1975)

	First Floor	Library (ft²)	Cultural Center (ft²)
1	Main entrance lobby (including coat room, public telephone, toilet rooms)	970	970
2	Circulation desk and card catalogue	1050	
3	Reference area (including multimedia area)	1360 (5000 volumes)	
4	Popular reading	2700 (5000 volumes)	
5	Adult reading	7800 (48,050 volumes)	
6	Children's reading	2080 (10,000 volumes)	
7	Technical process area and storage	980	
8	Staff room	250	
9	Exhibit, lobby		2180
10	Mechanical (two areas)	500	500
	Second Floor	**Library (ft²)**	**Cultural Center (ft²)**
21	Assembly		1620
22	Catering/storage		200
23	Museum/exhibit		1350
24	Exhibit storage		80
25	Exhibit office		170
26	Head librarian's office	130	
27	Study rooms		180
28	Conference		240
29	Mezzanine and bridge	1200	
30	Mechanical (second level)	1040	
31	Mechanical (third level)		600
Observation tower			400
	Assigned area	20,060	8490
	Gross enclosed area	23,500	9900
	Covered unenclosed area	1,200	400
	Volume capacity without future mezzanine	68,000 volumes	

Heating, Ventilation, and Air Conditioning. Constant and consistent temperature and humidity levels are absolute requirements for the preservation of library materials such as books, tapes, and films. The building will be completely air conditioned, and heating, ventilation, and air conditioning decisions will be determined based on the local climatic conditions, the projected amount of use, the incidence of pollution and dust in the air, and the relative costs and efficiencies of the various types of installation available for use. Maximum and minimum desired temperatures and relative humidity during the winter and summer will be requirements in the design of the system. The following are some considerations unique to libraries:

1. Books tend to last longer at cooler temperatures.
2. Low relative humidity tends to deteriorate bindings and paper.
3. Air filtering systems should be of top quality, since dust deteriorates books.
4. Particular attention should be paid to the requirement that ventilation equipment and plumbing services function quietly.

Specifications for the proposed Library/Cultural Center are outlined in Table 2.28. Table 2.29 gives the square footage. Figures 2.7 to 2.16 present details of the project, as well as models, plans, and possible interior arrangements.

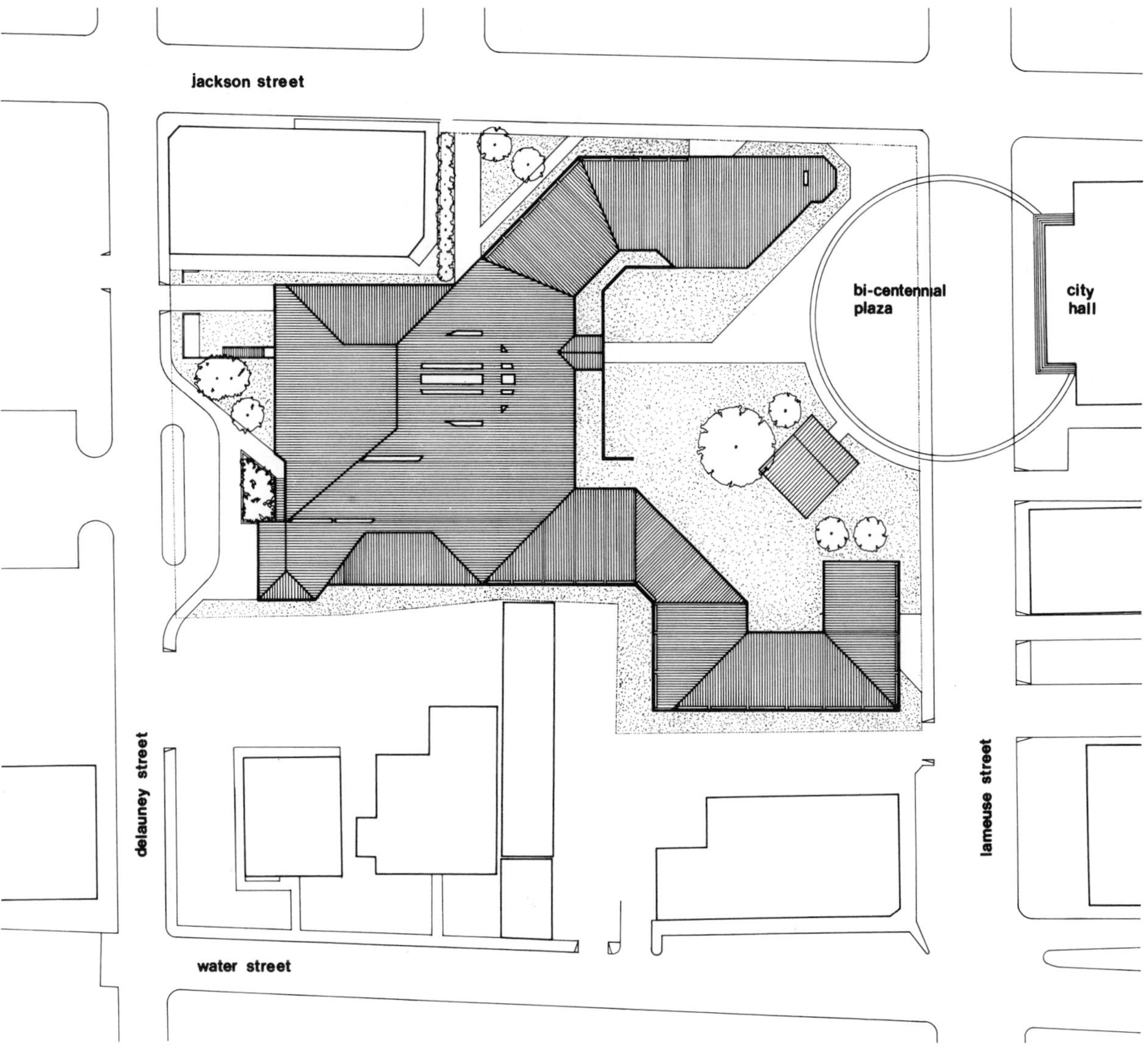

SITE PLAN

Figure 2.7

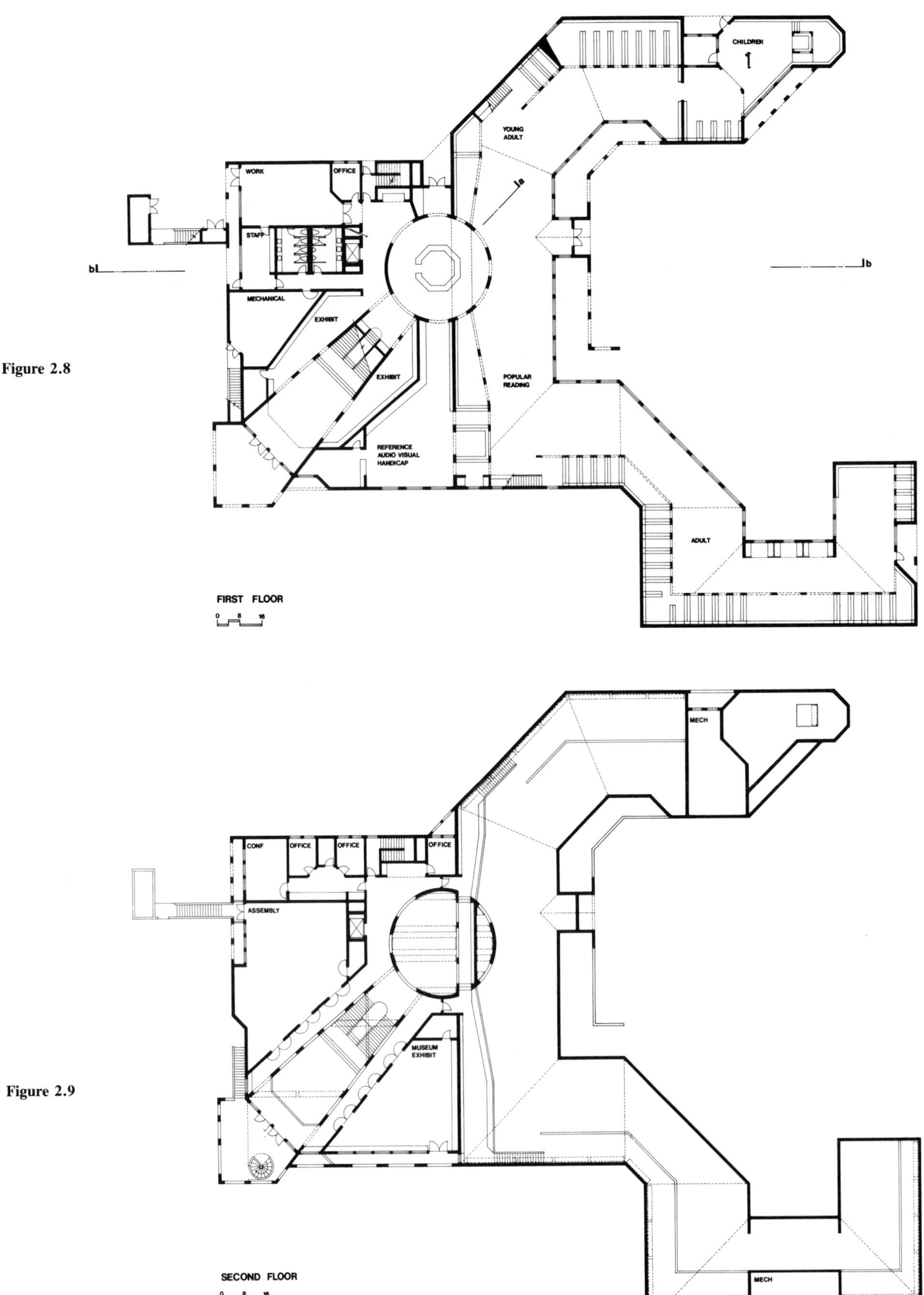

Figure 2.8

Figure 2.9

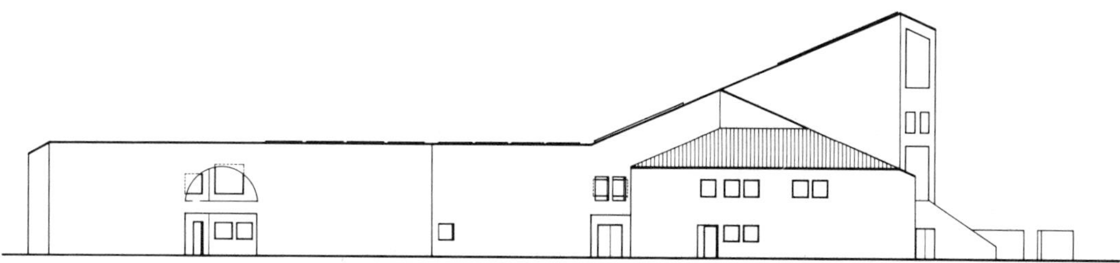

NORTH

0 8 16

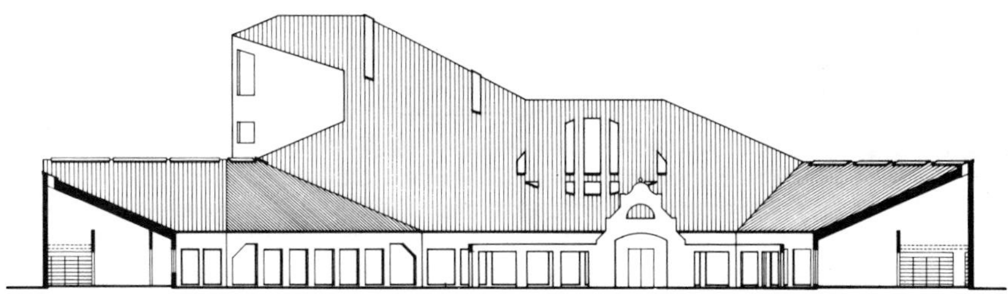

EAST

0 8 16

Figure 2.10

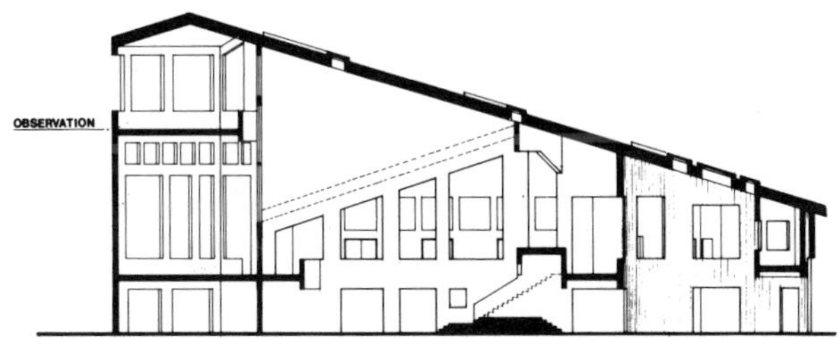

SECTION a

0 8 16

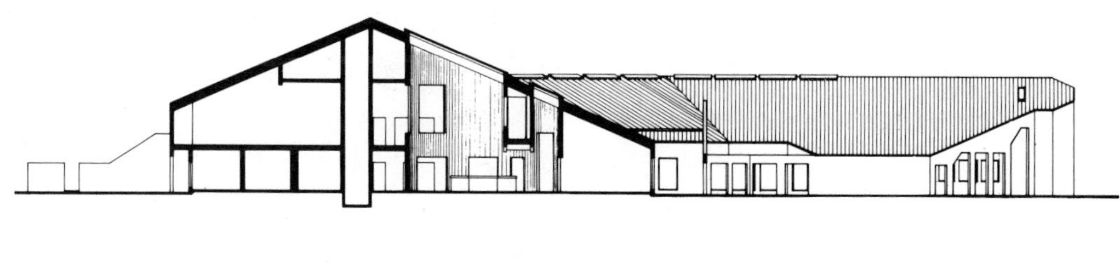

SECTION b

0 8 16

Figure 2.11

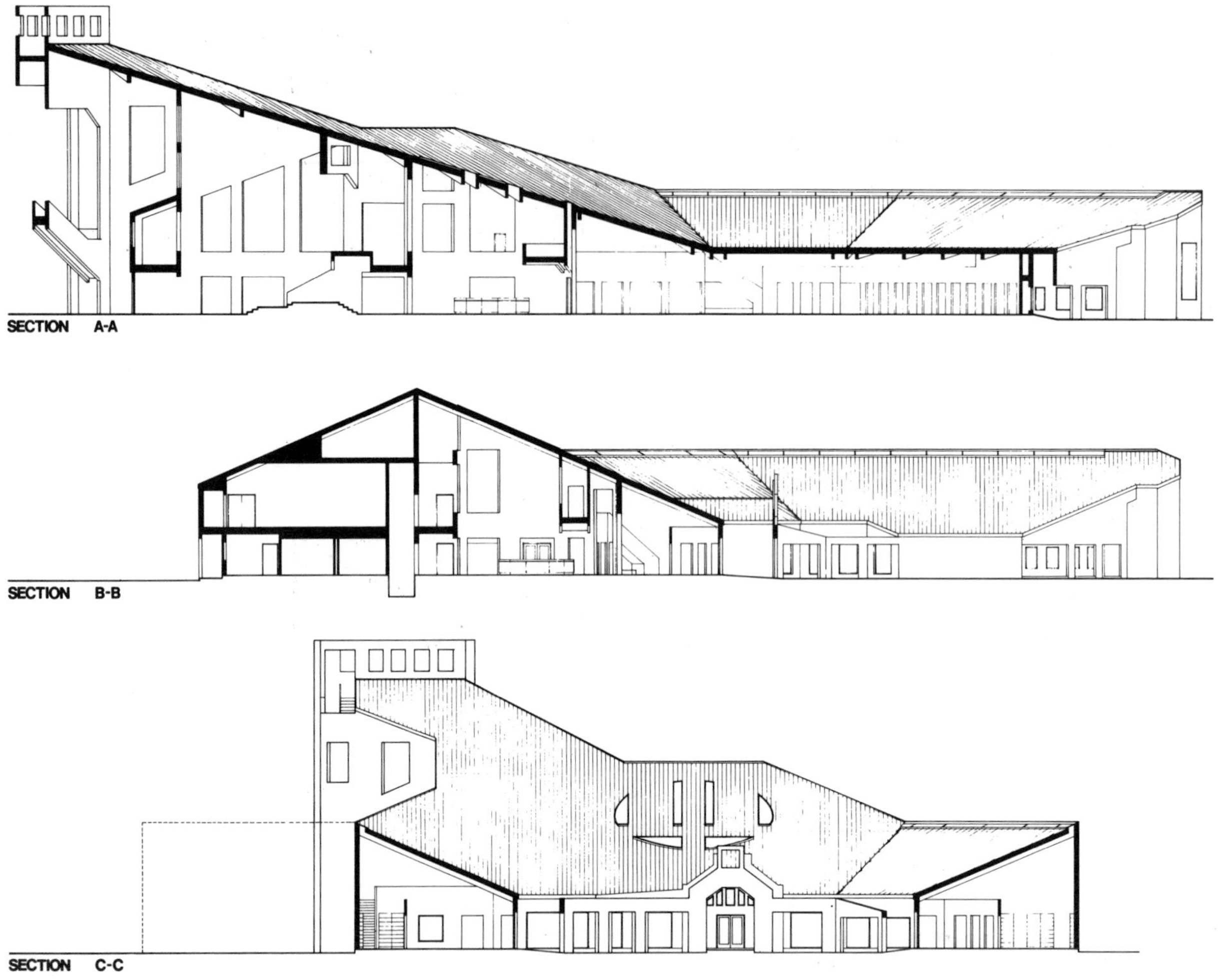

SECTION A-A

SECTION B-B

SECTION C-C

Figure 2.12

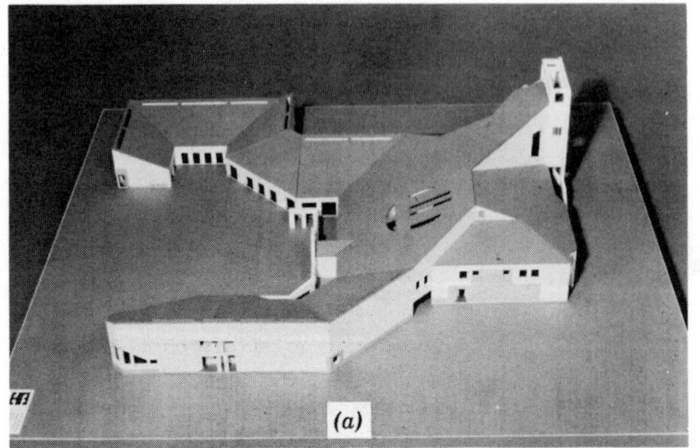

(a)

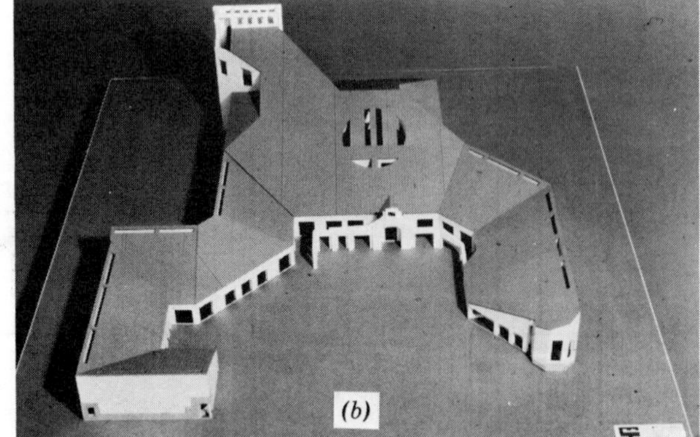

(b)

Figure 2.13

Figure 2.14

Figure 2.15

BANK OF AMERICA BUILDING
Beverly Hills, California
Architects: The Landau Partnership Inc.
Photo: Office

2 CODES AND LAND USE RESTRICTIONS

Since most design projects are for urban land, the utilization of space is restricted by building codes, zoning ordinances, easements, or other regulations pertaining to the common interest. All these requirements are important in the selection of design alternatives because they limit the number of building forms that are feasible on the particular site.

Architects must study all these regulations and deed restrictions very carefully; in fact, this is how we usually begin the conceptual design phase, because any overlooking of these restrictions or requirements may lead to major revisions later or may render a design completely unfeasible.

Zoning Ordinances

A zoning ordinance is a law created to preserve and promote the health, safety, and general welfare of the citizens, and to preserve or increase aesthetic values and property values of an area. The law must be obeyed by everyone unless the local government with appropriate jurisdiction grants a variance or exception. In some areas,the term "zoning code" or "zoning law" is used; the meaning is identical.

Variances and Conditional Uses. If the literal terms of a zoning law create for an owner a particular hardship that was not intended or foreseen by the lawmakers, a *variance* may be granted by the zoning board or commission. Such decisions are made after public hearings before the Board of Adjustment or the Board of Appeals.

A *conditional use,* granted with the welfare and convenience of the public in mind, applies to the construction of such facilities as schools and hospitals; the types of use considered under this provision are usually listed in the ordinance.

Nonconforming Use. Buildings that were erected before the local zoning code was created may not be in compliance with the present code. Such a structure represents a nonconforming use: if it meets the safety requirements pertaining to the area, its continued use is usually permitted, but additions or alterations are prohibited.

Features of Zoning Codes. Zoning laws have a great influence on the architectural forms of a city. Luckily, each city creates its own code of zoning, for the absence of a standardized zoning code, equivalent to the Uniform Building Code, ensures the existence of the great variety of architectural expression among our cities.

All zoning ordinances deal with the segregation of land uses, the control of densities, setback and building height requirements, and vehicular access and parking. The permitted land use is established on zoning maps, which form a part of the code. The maps reflect the intention to separate land uses that seem to be incompatible and to create homogeneous areas of similar land values. Restrictions of population densities are created to assure healthy living conditions, reduce crime rates, and maintain a good balance between the community and the infrastructure that serves it.

The building form is subject to a great number of regulations, including the total volume, height, number of stores, setbacks, lot sizes, lot coverage, minimum unit sizes, number of units per acre, number of parking stalls

SHRINERS HOSPITAL FOR CRIPPLED CHILDREN
San Francisco, California
Architect: Milton T. Pflueger
Photo: J. Freiwald

and type of parking access, and advertising signs. Setback requirements and regulations concerning maximum lot coverage, which restrict the maximum land use of the property in favor of wider streets, more open space, and more privacy, are important in multiple residential areas. Setbacks may also be necessary to guarantee access to structures by firefighting equipment and to accommodate intended future street widening.

To avoid canyonlike streets in downtown areas, the bulk of a building is sometimes limited by a formula containing a ratio between the number of stories and the percentage of permitted lot coverage. This ensures that taller buildings have more surrounding open space than less intrusive structures. Another concern of height limitations involves safety in the event of fires and earthquakes. Figure 2.26, at the end of the section on legal restrictions, illustrates some additional areas of restrictions concerning lot sizes and land uses.

Building Codes

The first building codes were concerned exclusively with the preservation of human life in case of fire. Today other hazards are considered as well, including earthquakes, wind storms, panic in large crowds, and power failure. The building codes now also reflect the concern for healthy living and working conditions, as expressed in regulations for lighting, ventilation, and plumbing.

Only large cities, such as New York and Los Angeles, have issued their own building codes. Most cities or counties have adopted one of the standard building codes, such as those mentioned in the section Codes and Code Groups. Usually a particular edition of one of these codes is adopted, and the code may also be modified by additions, deletions, and alterations.

Building codes embody one of two basic principles. In one, the construction technology is specified; in the other, specifications refer to the functional requirements of a structure. Although specifications based on the first principle are easy to follow, this type of code tends to make innovations very difficult. New construction technology and new design ideas can be introduced more easily with a building code based on the second principle: the administration of such a code, however, is much more complicated.

Features of Building Codes. To determine which requirements of the code apply to a proposed building, the structure must first be classified by means of:

- Location of structure on the property.
- Allowable floor area.
- Height and number of stories.
- Occupancy group.
- Occupancy load.
- Building type or type of construction.
- Fire zone or district.

Fire Zones. According to the potential fire hazard—a function of density, building height, accessibility, and the efficiency of the fire department—urban areas are divided into three classes. The code is more restrictive in areas of greater fire hazards and requires less protective features in others.

Occupancy Load. Sports arenas and theaters represent an increased risk of panic and require high standards of fire protection. Another factor that receives increasing weight is the disability of some people to move fast and

PHILADELPHIA VETERANS STADIUM
Philadelphia, Pennsylvania
Architects: Hugh Stubbins & Associates
Photo: J. Green

logically, as in the case of hospital patients, especially children, residents of homes for the aged, and patients in psychiatric clinics.

Occupancy Group. The type of use of a structure also influences significantly the level of fire hazard. Therefore the occupancy group classification divides buildings into types (schools, hotels, manufacturing, etc.) and further classifies manufacturing uses according to the materials handled or stored. Materials such as flammable gases or explosive dust for milling always require a higher fire rating. If the use of the building is changed at a later time, the building must be improved to comply with the newly applicable fire protection requirements.

Types of Construction. Types of construction are classified according to their fire resistance, usually ranging from Type I for a highrise structure to Type V for a wood-frame and stucco residence. The type of construction to be selected for a particular project depends on the fire zone district and the intended use. For each type there are specific regulations concerning height, number of floors, materials permitted, and so on.

Location of Structure on Property. Since one aspect of fire protection is the restriction of the spread of conflagrations from one building to the other, the location of a structure on property is important. Alleys and setbacks serve as firebreaks, thus determining to some extent the degree of fire resistance required and the openings permitted in exterior walls.

Floor Areas. The maximum floor area permitted in a given fire zone, and for a given use, can be increased by installing an automatic sprinkler system or by subdividing the structure with fire-resistive walls. In the latter

HOTEL, WALT DISNEY WORLD
Orlando, Florida
Architects: Welton Becket Associates
Photo: Office

ALCOA BUILDING
San Francisco, California
Architects: Skidmore Owings & Merrill
Photo: P. L. Molten

case, each area between two separation walls is considered to be a separate building. The walls must go through the whole height of the building, and automatic fire doors must be installed at all openings.

Height. The same criterion that applies to floor areas also determines the height permitted for a structure. If the building is sprinklered, the height permitted may be greater than it would be for a building of the same type but without sprinklers. Building codes do not usually set height limits for highrise buildings of Type I construction.

Fire Resistance. In the case of a big fire, a structure is supposed to resist long enough for the occupants to evacuate the building and for the firemen to extinguish the fire before the structure collapses. Fire resistance of construction elements is expressed in hours, and specific ratings are required for the structural frame, floors, ceilings, walls, roofs, and windows. The range of ratings usually extends from 45 minutes to 4 hours.

No construction material is fireproof; even concrete cracks in excessive heat, but the use of vermiculite plaster, gypsum, and similar materials, increases the number of hours the structure can withstand flames. Asbestos was once widely applied in Type I steel construction, but in the light of evidence that it may cause cancer in those who work with it, its use has been limited of late.

Flame and Smoke Ratings. Flame and smoke ratings are measures concerning the propagation of flames through certain materials and the amount of smoke the burning materials are expected to create. These ratings apply mainly to carpets and surface finishing materials and are usually included in the written specifications. Of major concern regarding fire and smoke are the furnishings of buildings, since most of the plastic materials composing today's furnishings are flammable and produce a great amount of smoke and fumes.

The Various Building Codes. The various local, state, and national building codes pose the architect's biggest headache. A drastic technical overhaul is overdue, and the intergovernmental aspect, too, must be dealt with. The problems faced by producers of materials, builders, engineers, and architects are alarming and in most instances not justified. We must create a climate in which American industry and American craftsmen can use their inventive genius for new products, innovative processes, and improved building practices to achieve the goal of a decent home in a suitable living environment and at a reasonable price for all Americans.

Goal of All Codes. We should seek to establish machinery whereby new products and innovations can be properly tested and judged on their merits in the competitive marketplace, unhindered either by needless physical restrictions or by the whims of local officials. Standards should be set and judgments made objectively, by broadly based bodies that include not only building officials but representatives of the building industry, professional groups, and the general public. Decisions should be made not only on more objectively but much faster. A far larger role should be played by metropolitan areas or regions, and by the states—especially in attaining uniformity of standards and fair appeal procedures.

In short, we need a system that frees the building industry from unnecessarily constraining private and governmental restrictions at all levels—one that unleashes our innovative and entrepreneurial genius.

Codes and Code Groups. A building code is a series of standards and specifications designed to establish minimum safeguards in the erection and construction of buildings, to protect the people who live and work in them from fire and other hazards, and to establish regulations to further protect the health and safety of the public. Formulated and enforced through the police powers of state governments, building codes are ordinarily administered by local governments, usually municipalities. In one form or another, codes go back to the earliest days of civilized society, and they serve an essential purpose.

Various organizations in modern America have promulgated a plethora of codes. In the building construction field alone there are four major groups known as the model code groups. The Building Officials' Conference of America (BOCA) is most prominent in the east and north central areas of the country but also has membership elsewhere. Its code is called the Basic Building Code.

The International Conference of Building Officials (ICBO) is the most influential code group in the western states, but like BOCA it is not limited exclusively to a single region. Its code is known as the Uniform Building Code (UBC). In the south, the Southern Standard Building Code is the major code, although again, it does not have exclusive jurisdiction.

The National Building Code, the code published by the American Insurance Association, is estimated to have been adopted in about 1600 communities. The BOCA, ICBO, and National codes overlap it in many areas.

In addition to codes confined strictly to building, there are mechanical codes, mainly plumbing and electrical but also including codes for elevators and boilers, and the special codes, usually promulgated by states, for hospitals, schools, theaters, factories, nursing homes, and other special categories.

Of the mechanical codes, the two best known are the National Electrical Code (NEC) and the National Plumbing Code (NPC). Recently the model code groups have adopted their own plumbing codes as well.

Problems. Complaints about building codes, building code organizations, and local officials are widespread. It is alleged that unneeded provisions and restrictions in locally adopted codes add significantly to the cost of housing for the following reasons: (1) they delay construction, (2) they prevent the use of the most up-to-date and modern materials, (3) they inhibit creative design, (4) their provisions are antiquated and outdated, and (5) the procedures for modernizing and amending them are slow, laborious, lacking in objective standards, and dominated by a very small group in the industry—namely, building code officials and officials of the trade associations in the building materials field. It is charged that other directly interested parties, including qualified building, producing, and professional groups, are excluded from the decision-making bodies, and that the

DESIGN RESEARCH CENTER
Cambridge, Massachusetts
Architect: Benjamin Thompson Associates
Photo: E. Stoller ESTO

general public and the public interest are represented inadequately, if at all.

There are more than half a dozen additional complaints against building codes and their administration, including the following:

1. Lack of uniformity of both provisions and administration at the local level and in metropolitan areas in which there are numerous independent cities, towns, and counties.
2. Inadequacies of training and absence of stringent qualifications for local building officials.
3. Lack of proper appeal procedures.
4. Excessive difficulties associated with marketing of mobile homes and prefabricated housing.
5. Prevention by conventional builders of large-scale building and selling, which could achieve economies of mass production and the standardization of production.
6. Abandonment by the states to the localities of responsibilities and functions that should be exercised at the state level.
7. Diverse standards and regulations of various federal agencies responsible for building construction, with confusion and added costs as results.

Exit Requirements

Exits. The number of exits required is mainly a function of the number of occupants of the structure. Exits should always be placed in such a way that it will be unlikely for one fire to block them all at the same time.

The code specifies minimum widths of corridors, stairways, and doors along exit passageways by relating to the number of occupants. In some building codes, the total number of occupants to be served is divided by a constant (e.g., 50) to obtain the required width in feet. Others specify one "unit" of exit width (usually 22 feet)

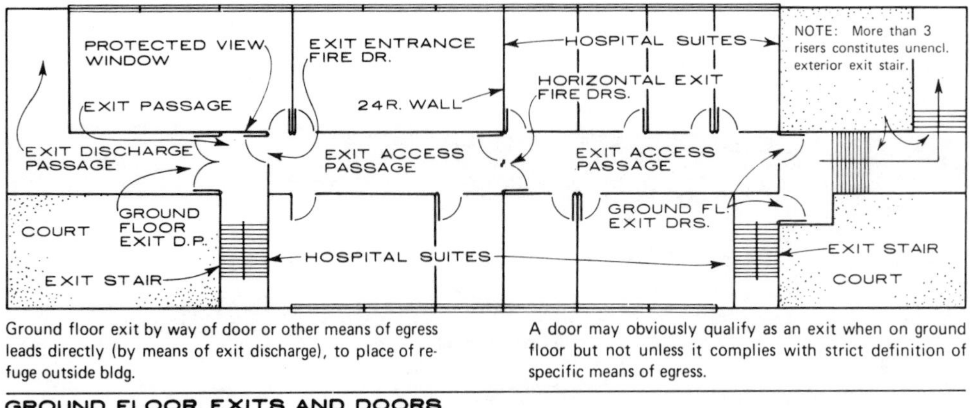

Figure 2.16 Reprinted from C. G. Ramsey and H. R. Sleeper, *Architectural Graphic Standards,* 6th ed., American Institute of Architects, John Wiley & Sons, 1970.

per every 50 or 100 people. If sprinklers are installed, the number of occupants per exit can often be increased.

Further specifications concerning the escape routes refer to length, fire resistance, lighting, ventilation, and directional signs. Also limited is the total distance any occupant must traverse to reach the nearest exterior exit door or enclosed stairway. This distance is 150 feet for unsprinklered buildings, 200 feet if the structure is sprinklered.

Stairways. If the stairway serves as part of the required exit passageway, it is subject to very detailed regulations regarding width, rise and run of steps, size and placement of landings, headroom, handrails, fire resistance of materials, and other aspects. One of the stairwells in a highrise building 75 feet high or higher must be a smokeproof tower (fire tower), connected to the interior of the building by way of balconies and open air vestibules or mechanically ventilated vestibules that prevent smoke from entering the stairwell, allowing people to escape without panic. Mechanical ventilation usually entails special requirements to secure a reliable power supply.

For the control of smoke during a fire, the ventilation system may be designed to switch from recirculation to exhaust only, since there is a potential danger that the smoke created by a fire in one area may be blown into other parts of the building through air conditioning ducts. Another preventive means is the installation of separate circulation systems for each of the building's fire areas.

Panic. A major cause of panic is the inability of the occupants of a burning building to see the escape route, as a result of heavy smoke, power failure, or both. Therefore special attention is given to the specifications of exit signs: they must be illuminated at all times, and their power supply must have a higher reliability rating than that of the lighting circuits. Separate power sources such as emergency generators or batteries are sometimes required; in other cases the code simply calls for a separate circuit for signs, connected ahead of the main breaker.

Vertical Transportation. Elevators are a very unreliable means of vertical transportation during a fire and are never classified as fire escape routes. Not only are they subject to stall because of power failure, but all their electronic controls, including call buttons and photocells for opening and closing automatic doors, are very sensitive to flames, smoke, and high temperature. However some codes specify that one or more elevators must be available for firemen during an emergency. Elevators can greatly assist firemen in transporting heavy equipment to higher floors, in spite of the risk that the occupants will be trapped.

If floors are connected by escalators, there is increased danger that flames and smoke will find a free vertical passway over several stories. Thus the building code may require the installation of automatic rolling shutters to close off the floor opening, or the escalators may have to be installed in an enclosed structure with fire-rated doors, similar to that of a stairwell. Or sprinkler systems may be required.

Other Exitways. Moving sidewalks and escalators are generally not permitted as part of the fire escape route. Ramps may be classified as fire exitways if they conform to the code. Sometimes permitted are revolving doors with collapsing wings (i.e., wings that fold flat against each other if people press hard against them).

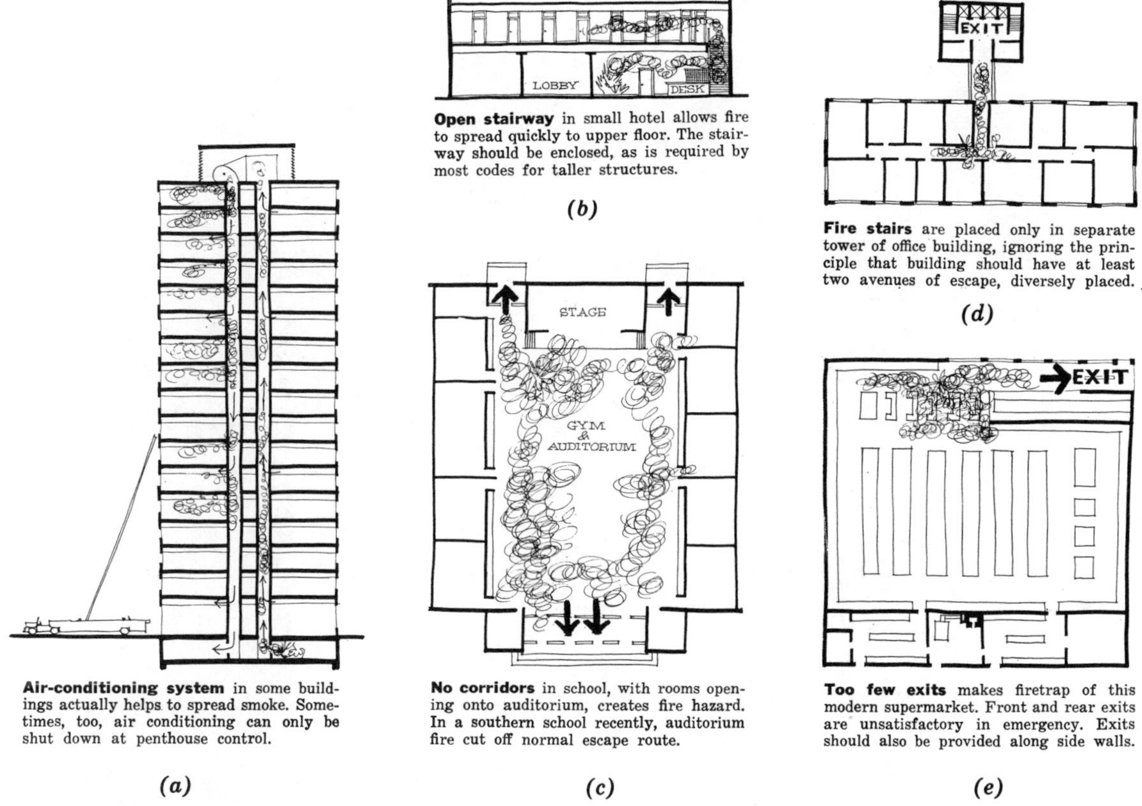

Figure 2.17 (*a*) Ventilation hazard that may be created by an air conditioning system. (*b*) to (*e*) Four common exit hazards that may trap occupants in burning buildings. *Source*. Sketches by John C. Thornton, AIA, text by D. Allison, *Architectural Forum*, February 1959.

Places of Refuge. Places of refuge are areas in highrise buildings that are separated from the general floor area by means of construction elements with high fire rating. They are located along the escape route, and they must be big enough to accommodate all occupants of the respective floor areas. Places of refuge provide a haven for people while escape routes are overcrowded or while others are waiting to be rescued.

Fireproofing Requirements

Standpipes. Most codes require standpipes for buildings of three or more stories. A wet standpipe system is always filled with pressurized water; it supplies cabinets with fire hoses located on every floor and distributed in a such way that every area can be reached by at least one hose. This system is designed for use by the occupants.

The dry standpipe system, installed for use by firemen only, is designed to be supplied with water from the fire truck. Since these pipes are not subject to freezing, they can be located outside, but usually they are placed in the smokeproof tower. There is also a system of combination standpipes, consisting of a wet system that can be used by both firemen and occupants.

Most codes also specify the needed water supply. A wet standpipe, for instance, may be required to provide a water pressure of 30 psi simultaneously on two outlets, for a duration of 25 minutes. If the public supply is insufficient, these requirements may necessitate the installation of electrical firepumps. When standpipes are part of the fire protection system during construction, they are made operational immediately for each new floor erected. A roof tank may also serve as a source of water.

Sprinklers. Automatic fire extinguishing systems have proved to be very effective in many emergencies, but the high cost of installation generally limits their use to areas in which they are required by building codes (storage spaces of flammable material, certain parts of theaters, subterranean garages, etc.). Many codes permit higher occupancy rates and require fewer fire-rated walls and fewer exits if sprinklers are installed. These tradeoffs should always be considered. The reduced insurance

WITTINGTON TOWER
Toronto, Ontario
Architect: Leslie Rebanks
Photo: Office

rates for fully sprinklered buildings represent another big incentive, and the developer should weigh higher initial cost against a lower maintenance budget.

Fire-Rated Doors. Doors in separation walls between different fire areas must be fire rated. In some cases the doors may be kept open under normal conditions, but in separation walls they must be equipped with a device that closes them automatically in the event of fire. The closing device can be released either by a fusible link or by electronic sensors reacting to heat, smoke, or sprinkler water. The device can also be connected to the alarm system. Air ducts penetrating fire walls need to be equipped with fire dampers, which are open in normal operation and close automatically in a fire. The controls activating fire dampers are of the same kind as the ones used on fire doors.

Fire Alarms. The building code may require fire alarm systems for certain buildings with high occupancy rates, such as schools, hotels, and highrise apartment buildings. Some acoustical alarms serve to alert occupants of the building only, others also activate a bell in the fire department. Most are equipped with automatic controls using the following types of sensor: smoke detectors, which react to the obscuring of a light beam; products-of-combustion detectors operating with ionization chambers; and temperature detectors, which may be adjusted either to a fixed temperature or to the marginal rate of rising temperature.

ROSE F. KENNEDY RESEARCH CENTER
Bronx, New York
Architects: Pomerance & Breines
Photo: J. Horner-Pennyroyal

Fire Safety

ICBO Requirements for Highrise Buildings

By Richard E. Steven

The International Conference of Building Officials (ICBO), which publishes the Uniform Building Code, recently adopted new fire protection requirements for highrise buildings. The requirements will appear in Section 1807 of the code "Special Provisions for High Rise Group H Occupancies and Group F, Division 2, Office Buildings." Group H occupancies are hotels and apartment buildings. For the purposes of that section, highrise buildings are defined as "such buildings having floors used for human occupancy located more than 75 feet above the lowest level of fire department vehicle access."

Compartmentation. Areas of refuge can be provided either by dividing each story with horizontal exits into areas not exceeding 30,000 square feet or by subdividing the building into 5-story compartments by (1) interrupting stair shafts with smoke barriers every fifth floor, (2) using smokeproof enclosures for all stairways, or (3) using any other means to prevent smoke from spreading between compartments. When openings in exterior walls are located vertically, one above the other, compartmentation is also required between stories by either horizontal or vertical flame barriers at the exterior walls.

Control Station and Communication System. A central control station for fire department operations, where signals are received from much of the control equipment, is mandatory. The control station must also contain two voice communication systems, one for fire department use and the other for communication with building occupants in locations designed by the section. Where approved, one system may serve both functions.

Fire Alarm Boxes. In specified locations there must be manual fire alarm boxes that are connected to the central control station and to the voice communication system.

Fire Detectors. Every mechanical equipment room and the return air portion of any air conditioning system or mechanical ventilation system that serves floors other than the floor on which it is located must have fire detectors that respond to products of combustion other than heat. These detectors must activate the voice communication system and must be connected to the central control station.

Smoke Control. The new section calls for either mechanical or natural venting of the products of combustion. The following means of compliance may be used:

1 Panels, openable windows, or windows glazed with tempered glass of size and location specified in the section.
2 In a sprinklered building, the return and exhaust portion of the mechanical air-handling system.
3 A mechanically vented shaft that will provide 60 air changes per hour in the largest compartment served.
4 Any other means that will provide equivalent results.

Elevators. At least one elevator in each bank must provide fire department access to any floor of the building. The elevator must open into a lobby that is separated from the remainder of the building.

Standby Power and Light. The section requires a standby electrical generating system that operates automatically and can be controlled at the central control station. The system must pick up the load within 1 minute and must be able to provide the full load for not less than 2 hours. The system must serve (*a*) the fire alarm system, (*b*) the exit and emergency lighting, (*c*) the fire protection equipment, (*d*) the required mechanical ventilation, (*e*) the fire department elevator, and (*f*) the voice communication system.

Sprinkler System Alternative. As an alternative to compartmentation, a sprinkler system may be provided. The requirements for the system are based on Chapter 8 of NFPA Standard 13, Standard for the Installation of Sprinkler Systems, but special provisions deal with such matters as the design of the system, fire pumps, and the water supply. The system must be connected to the voice communication system.

If the sprinkler system is installed, code requirements pertaining to the fire-resistance ratings for certain structural components, walls, and partitions may be lowered; standpipe hose for occupant use is not required; the travel distance to exits may be increased to 300 feet; the requirement for smokeproof enclosures may be waived, although the stairway must be pressurized; and the requirement to prevent the spread of fire from floor to floor by way of exterior openings may be waived.

Other Provisions. There are some special requirements for anchorage in Seismic Zones 2 and 3 for certain equipment specified by this section. The section also states that stairway doors that are locked from the stair side must have electric strikes operable from the central control station.

SHERATON HOTEL
Philadelphia, Pennsylvania
Architects: Perry, Dean, Stahl & Rogers, Inc.
Photo: J. Stelman

BAYCREST TERRACE AND DAY CENTRE
Toronto, Ontario
Architects: Boigon & Armstrong
Photo: Applied Photography, Ltd.

What's Above the Ceiling?

Recent fire experience indicates that more attention should be given to the material installed above suspended ceilings. Electrical wiring, communications wiring, ducts, duct connectors, duct coverings, conduit, piping, and catwalks are some of the more common potential fuel sources added to the space above the suspended ceiling. Some NFPA standards set limits of combustibility and smoke production for a few of the items mentioned. For example, the NFPA Standard for the Installation of Air Conditioning and Ventilating Systems (90 A), recommends that duct material be iron, steel, aluminum, or other approved metal, or materials such as clay or asbestos cement. It also permits ducts made of Class 1 materials as tested in accordance with Underwriters' Laboratories, Inc., Standard for Air Ducts (UL 181). That standard sets limits of flame spread (25) and smoke development (50) for Class 1 duct materials. It also contains recommendations on flexible duct connectors, depending on their diameter, and limits their length. In accordance with the standard, duct connectors must be tested by UL Standard 181, and they must be Class 2 if less than 8 inches in diameter or Class 1 if greater than 8 inches in diameter. If a duct connector is located in a concealed space consisting partly of combustible materials, the connector must pass the 15-minute flame penetration test for Class 2 ducts in the UL standard, which limits the flame spread rating for duct coverings and linings to 25 and the smoke-developed rating to 50. The ratings are determined from the NFPA Standard Method of Test of Surface Burning Characteristics of Building Materials (255).

The National Electrical Code (NFPA Standard 70) requires that any rigid nonmetallic conduct used above ground be flame retardant. If UL-listed conduit is used, the degree of flame retardance is determined by UL in accordance with its Standard 651, Rigid Nonmetallic Conduit. Smoke development characteristics are not determined by that standard. The code permits use of approved rigid nonmetallic conduit in concealed spaces, such as between a suspended ceiling and the floor above, except where the space is used for air handling and in certain occupancies (e.g., places of assembly).

Similarly, the code permits nonmetallic sheathed cable to be installed in the concealed space with the same exceptions as for nonmetallic conduit. Wiring for communications systems is exempt from the provisions of the code pertaining to the flame retardancy of the insulation or the outer covering and from the provisions pertaining to its location in concealed spaces.

Duct systems for the removal of flammable vapors or dust or for conveying stock or refuse are dealt with in the NFPA Standard for the Installation of Blower and Exhaust Systems for Dust, Stock, and Vapor Removal or Conveying (91), which requires that ducts be constructed of sheet metal or other noncombustible material. NFPA standards do not cover waste pipe or duct systems for hoods in chemical laboratories.

A considerable amount of potential fuel may lie in the concealed space above a suspended ceiling, and when pyrolized, some of that fuel can produce prodigious quantities of smoke. It has been calculated, for example, that each linear foot of 1-inch polyvinyl chloride rigid nonmetallic conduit that catches fire has the potential of a lethal concentration of hydrogen chloride through approximately 1650 feet and a heavy, obscuring smoke through approximately 3500 cubic feet. As has been pointed out, the only NFPA standard setting limits on smoke development from the kinds of materials used in these concealed spaces is 90A, which sets limits on ducts, duct connectors, linings, and coverings. Another important consideration is the effect during fire exposure of these materials on the fire resistance rating of a floor-ceiling assembly in which they are installed. Even materials that are flame retardant or have a low flame spread rating are combustible to some extent. To this writer's knowledge, of the materials that may add fuel to the concealed space, only some air conditioning duct materials have been included in floor-ceiling assemblies during fire tests.

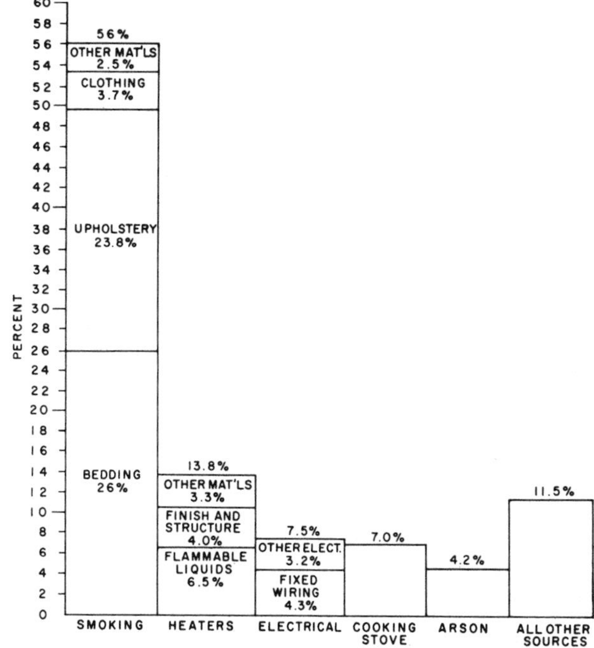

Figure 2.19 *Source. Fire Protection Handbook,* 14th ed., National Fire Protection Association, 1976.

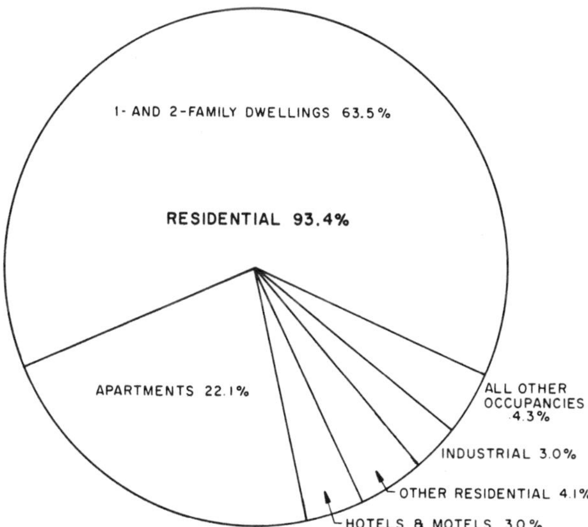

Figure 2.18 Locations of deaths by fire in buildings, expressed as percentages of occupancies. *Source. Fire Protection Handbook,* 14th ed., National Fire Protection Association, 1976.

Violations of Codes and Code Requirements: Security Versus Life Safety. Security is uppermost in the minds of the owners and operators of many properties. Store managers report large losses from theft, as do operators and managers of hotels and office buildings. School administrators are concerned about the safety of dormitory occupants. Industrial and warehouse properties report losses from theft, vandalism, and arson.

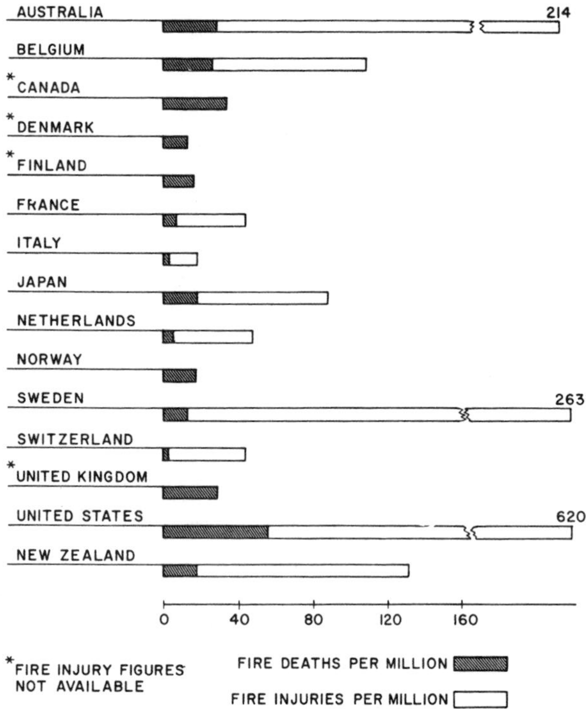

Figure 2.20 Fire casualty figures for 15 nations. *Source. Fire Protection Handbook*, 14th ed., National Fire Protection Association, 1976.

Even hospitals suffer losses from fires accidentally set by vagrants seeking shelter.

Hardly any physical property is immune from damage due to malicious and accidental acts, and the result is a demand for more effective means to secure property from unauthorized entry and for continual surveillance of property to detect illicit entry. Designers and builders must consider this increasingly costly problem in safeguarding people and property. Unfortunately, the answers provided by designers and builders are not always compatible with good fire prevention practices and recommendations to protect people and property from fire.

Some Common Solutions. Too frequently, proposals for securing buildings involve locking exit doors, barring windows or covering them with security screens, and constructing buildings with no openings except those necessary for minimum accessibility during operating hours.

On 1-story buildings, roof vents that would allow firemen to vent a fire are avoided because they might furnish a means of unauthorized access. Glass is replaced with tough transparent plastic to prevent breakage and hinder access. Yet windows have traditionally been the means enabling firemen to vent fire and rescue people. They also allow trapped occupants to obtain fresh air while awaiting rescue. Windows low enough to the ground may be the means by which occupants flee from the building. Fixed sashes, unbreakable lites, bars, or security screens, and complete lack of windows eliminate the firefighting—and sometimes life-saving—advantages of windows.

Equipping exit doors with hardware that cannot be opened from inside the building except with a key or by some special effort known only to certain occupants is not an uncommon solution to the security problem. However this approach violates the principles of escape from fire. An alternative proposal is to use electric locks on the exit doors, which would be automatically unlocked if a manual fire alarm box were actuated elsewhere in the building or at a central station in the building. Fire experience has shown that occupants too often fail to think of pulling an alarm box in a fire emergency, and when a central office in a building is notified of a fire, someone is dispatched to determine whether there really is a fire before any other action is taken.

Designers are urged to place exits discharging at the street-floor level and leading out of the street floor, so that the exits can be surveyed continuously to detect unauthorized entry and subsequent theft. This can result in a building whose exits' are not sufficiently remote from each other to assure that an adequate number would be available for use if fire were to make other exits inaccessible.

Many more examples could be cited of current and proposed solutions to the security problem that violate principles of life safety from fire and code provisions. One may hope that typical examples are enough to remind the designer and builder that security is only one of the considerations that are important in safeguarding people.

Some Code Violations. The following extracts from NFPA Standard 101, the Life *Safety Code,* may be helpful to the architect in considering measures to provide security for a building and safety from fire.

General Requirements

2-1114. In every building or structure, exits shall be so arranged and maintained as to provide free and unobstructed egress from all parts of the building or structure at all times when it is occupied. No lock or fastening to prevent free escape from the inside of any building shall be installed except in mental, penal, or corrective institutions where supervisory personnel are continually on duty and effective provisions are made to remove occupants in case of fire or other emergency.

Maintenance of Means of Egress

2-3111. Every required exit, way of approach thereto, and way of travel from the exit into the street or open space, shall be continuously maintained free of all obstructions or impediments to full instant use in the case of fire or other emergency.

Hardware on Exit Doors

5-2131. An exit door shall be so arranged as to be readily opened from the side from which egress is to be made at all times when the building served thereby is occupied. Locks, if provided, shall not require the use of a key for operation from the inside of the building.

5-2132. A latch or other fastening device on an exit door shall be provided with a knob, handle, panic bar, or other simple type of releasing device, the method of operation of which is obvious, even in darkness.

Windows in Schools

9-1511. Except in buildings with complete sprinkler protection in accordance with Section 6-4, every room or space used for classroom or other educational purposes or normally subject to student occupancy, unless it has a door leading directly to the outside of the building, shall have at least one outside window which can readily be used for emergency rescue or ventilation purposes, and which meets all the following provisions:

1 Is readily openable from the inside without the use of tools.
2 Provides a clear opening with a minimum dimension of approximately 28 inches and is approximately 784 square inches in area.
3 Bottom of window opening is not more than 32 inches above the floor.
4 Where storm windows, screens, or burglar guards are used, these shall be provided with quick-opening devices so that they may be readily opened from the inside for emergency egress, and shall be so arranged that when opened they will not drop to the ground.

Windows in Dwellings

11-6212. Every sleeping room, unless it has two doors providing separate ways of escape or a door leading outside the building directly, shall have at least one outside window that can be opened from the inside without the use of tools to provide a clear opening of not less than 16 inches in least dimension and 400 square inches in area, with the bottom of the opening not more than 4 feet above the floor.

Access Panels for Windowless Buildings

16-4311. Every windowless building shall be provided with outside access panels on each floor level, designed for fire department access from ladders for purposes of ventilation and rescue of trapped occupants.

Building codes and other documents regulating the design and maintenance of buildings have similar requirements that should be considered when security measures are contemplated.

Compatible Solutions Possible. The need for adequate security measures for property cannot be underestimated, and everyone concerned with the problem must deal with it. Surely design and construction to provide security can be compatible with recommendations for life safety from fire and fire department needs to effect fire suppression at minimum hazard to fire fighters.

Designers, builders, building owners and managers, hardware manufacturers, designers of security systems, and all others involved in meeting the problems of making property secure are urged to work with enforcing authorities (fire department and building officials) to be certain that the measures for security and fire protection are compatible. Only such cooperative effort will prevent future fire tragedies.

In November 1970 I addressed the NFPA Fall Conference, held in Nashville, Tennessee. The address was delivered by Edward J. Reilly, Director of Information, National Automatic Sprinkler and Fire Control Association, Inc.

In summarizing the important myths and facts about sprinkler protection, we thought that the consumer should first be made aware of the principal advantages of sprinkler systems.

What are those advantages?

Sprinklers offer the highest assurance of safety to life from fire.

Sprinklers can reduce construction cost as much as 60% when they are installed throughout a building in compliance with most modern building codes.

Fire insurance premiums can be reduced from 40 to 85%.

Sprinklers protect "intangible" but vital assets that are not insurable under any conditions. How can a value be placed on the holograph copy of a speech by Abraham Lincoln if it is destroyed by fire?

Sprinklers prevent costly "down time" and assure continuity of business operations.

Sprinklers protect the jobs of workers.

Sprinklers safeguard business income.

Sprinklers prevent loss of customers who might go to another source of supply after a fire.

Sprinklers permit greater design freedom and building flexibility.

Sprinklers conserve water.

What are the most common myths about sprinkler protection?

When a fire breaks out in a building, all the sprinklers begin to operate and flood the building.

Not true. Each sprinkler fuses (opens) when heat from the fire causes the individual unit to open. Sprinklers open only when there is sufficient heat to require water.

According to the Automatic Sprinkler Performance Tables, more than 70% of the fires in sprinklered buildings are extinguished or controlled by three or fewer sprinklers. These statistics, based on a small sample of all fires in sprinklered properties, come from reports submitted by insurance authorities and occasionally by fire chiefs. Hundreds of thousands of small

KNIGHTS OF COLUMBUS HEADQUARTERS
New Haven, Connecticut
Architect: Kevin Roche, John Dinkeloo & Associates
Photo: C. Alexander

fires are extinguished every year, however, at losses so small that no insurance claims are made. Moreover, high-limit deductible insurance coverage, common today, shuts off a source of information on most one- and two-head extinguishments.

Probably 90% of all fires are extinguished by one sprinkler. Why doesn't the sprinkler industry develop a high-speed sprinkler capable of more rapid activation at lower temperatures?

"Thermal lag," or the resistance of the mass of the fusible element to fuse as a result of a rise in temperature, is intentionally built into every sprinkler. If this were not done, sprinklers would fuse too rapidly, causing needless water damage when extinguishing small fires.

Underwriters' Laboratories, Inc., and the Factory Mutual Laboratories, made a judgment based on insurance industry experience with loss control in sprinklered buildings to build this thermal inertia into sprinklers, and the UL and FM standards specify just how much delay is required for approval of each sprinkler head. There is no mechanical or engineering reason for not developing sprinklers to fuse faster or at lower temperatures. Sprinklers are designed to open only when the built-in programmed element determines that a fire has reached a level that threatens life or property, or both.

Another myth is that sprinklers open because of mechanical defects, flooding buildings and damaging contents.

Records from a leading fire insurance laboratory, however, indicate that one sprinkler in 3,335,000 discharges because of structural defects in manufacturing. Automatic sprinklers undergo extremely careful examination by inspectors at the time of manufacture to assure that they will fuse at the temperature for which they were designed, will not break down because of structural defects, and will not leak and cause unnecessary water damage. Sprinklers can be discharged by a physical blow, such as might come from a fork-lift truck, but this is unlikely in most buildings.

Myth number three: sprinklers increase the cost of buildings.

Not necessarily. Modern building codes, intelligently applied, enable architects to design completely sprinklered buildings at lower costs than those that apply to unsprinklered buildings. Most codes permit reduction or elimination of "fireproofing" around structural members and interior assemblies when buildings are sprinklered. Larger areas—sometimes unlimited areas—are permitted for most sprinklered occupancies. Sprinklers often enable architects to specify less fire-resistive types of construction for sprinklered buildings; an unprotected steel building can usually be built for 20 to 40% less than a fire-resistive unsprinklered building.

Finally, it is sometimes alleged that "fireproof" buildings do not need sprinkler protection.

The NFPA has been keeping fire loss records for about 70 years. Actual loss experience has proved that building occupants die of smoke inhalation long before the fire reaches them, and death invariably occurs before the structure itself becomes involved. Two years of fire testing by the Los Angeles Fire Department proved that without exception, untenable smoke and heat conditions develop before buildings become enveloped by fire. Therefore construction is not a factor insofar as life safety is concerned. A "fireproof" building is like a stove; it contains and confines heat and prevents fire spread, but its contents are consumed by fire. Given sufficient heat and time, the most fire-resistive building in the world can be reduced to rubble.

The principal reason for the destruction of buildings by fire is burning contents. No building, regardless of construction, can sustain prolonged exposure to high temperatures. With sprinkler systems the temperature is immediately brought under control, thus permitting use of less fire-resistive construction and reducing building cost.

Why do fire protection engineers insist on complete sprinkler protection? (1) No one knows where fires begin. (2) Fires originating in unsprinklered areas can overpower sprinklers in adjoining sprinklered areas. (3) Smoke is the real killer. The sooner the cause is eliminated, the safer are the occupants.

New Systems: A Bar Joist that is Part Sprinkler Pipe. A unique new structural bar joist that incorporates steel sprinkler pipe as its lower chord could dramatically cut installation costs for sprinkler protection—perhaps by as much as 50%—according to its inventor, Morton Hirsch, president of Active Fire Sprinkler Corporation, a Brooklyn sprinkler contracting firm. Outlets for sprinklers are located on uniform modular centers, rather than on a specific sprinkler-design spacing. The 4-foot centers are most desirable, considering web spacing, architectural layouts, and typical sprinkler-head multiples. The uniform centers facilitate the design of sprinkler systems and the design and production of bar joists. Unused outlets are plugged.

The outlets may be aimed up or down, depending on whether the joists will be left exposed or a finished ceiling and pendant heads will be used.

Obviously not all joists need by hydraulic. The designer might use a hydraulic joist every sixth or seventh one for floor construction where framing is on 2-foot centers, or every third or fourth one for roof construction, with framing on 4-foot centers.

The modularity of the system allows a sprinkler system to be installed before the type of occupancy is known, and it can be adapted to future architectural and occupancy changes. In addition to the sprinkler-head connection, two other mechanical connections are required. One is the end connection that joins two hydraulic joists in a straight line. The other is the cross-main connection that connects two parallel hydraulic joists.

The lower chord of a bar joist is essentially a tension member, but it also must have stiffness between panel points to allow hanging of lighting fixtures, pipes, and so on. The inventor's structural consultant, Milton Alpern, points out that a pipe section is stiffer than the customary

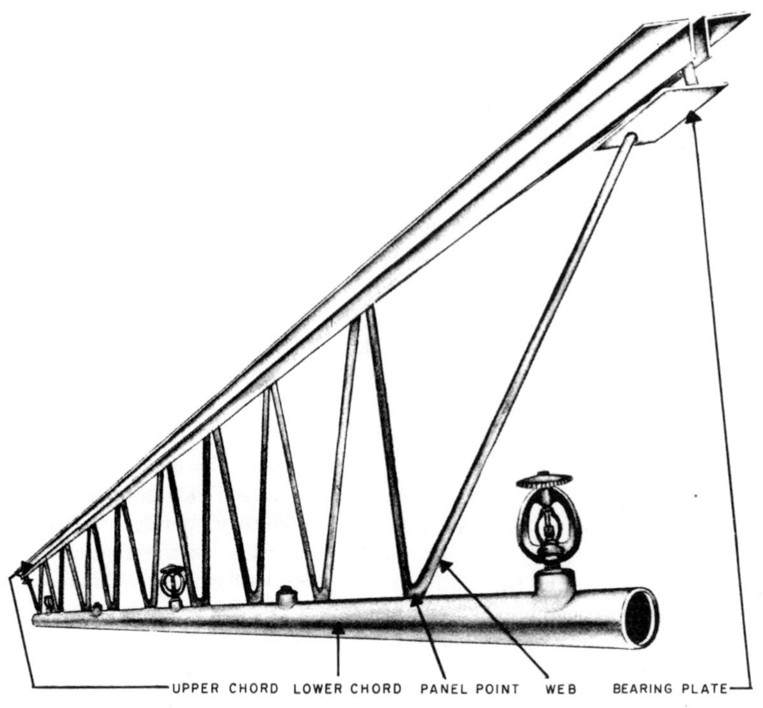

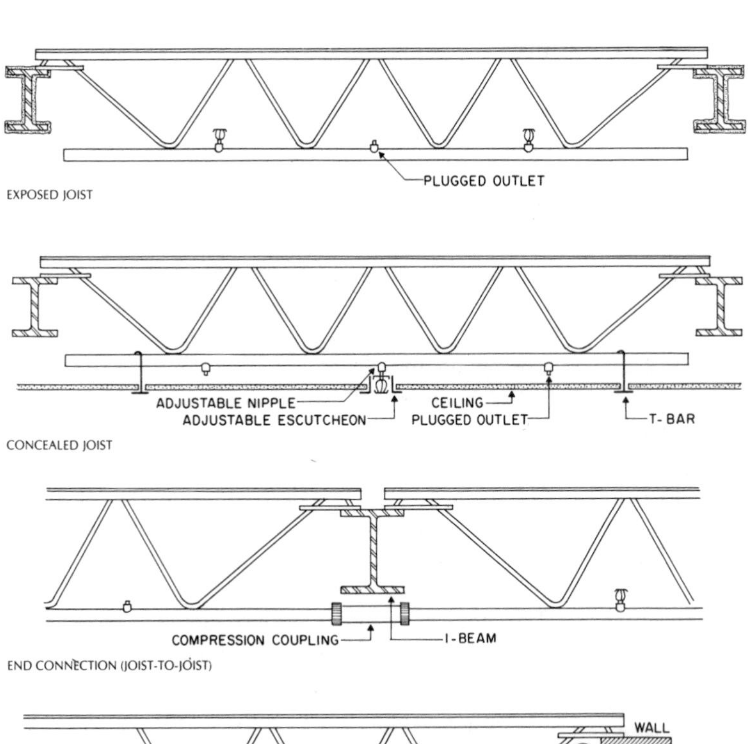

Figure 2.21 *Source. Architectural Record,* July 1977.

bars of bar joists, and because there are welded outlets on the holes, the material cross-sectional area of the pipe can be compared directly to the cross-sectional area of the lower chord of any standard bar joists. The hydraulic bar joists can use either 1 1/4, 1 1/2- or 2-inch pipe, depending on the design load, joist spacing and span.

A Tragic Example: Baptist Towers Housing for the Elderly, Atlanta, Georgia

A. ELWOOD WILLEY

On November 30, 1972, the day after a fatal highrise fire in New Orleans, there was a fire at the Baptist Towers Home for Senior Citizens in Atlanta, Georgia. Ten people died as a result of this fire in an 11-story, fire-resistive apartment building designed to house the elderly. The victims included eight residents and a guard on the floor of origin, the seventh floor; one resident from the tenth floor died 6 days later (Table 2.30). Since the fire occurred in a modern fire-resistive structure that was designed essentially in accordance with local and federal codes, this presents a highly relevant example of a fire causing multiple fatalities in a residential occupancy.

The fire at the Baptist Towers, which originated from the ignition of combustible contents in a seventh-floor apartment, exposed the adjacent corridor and 29 other

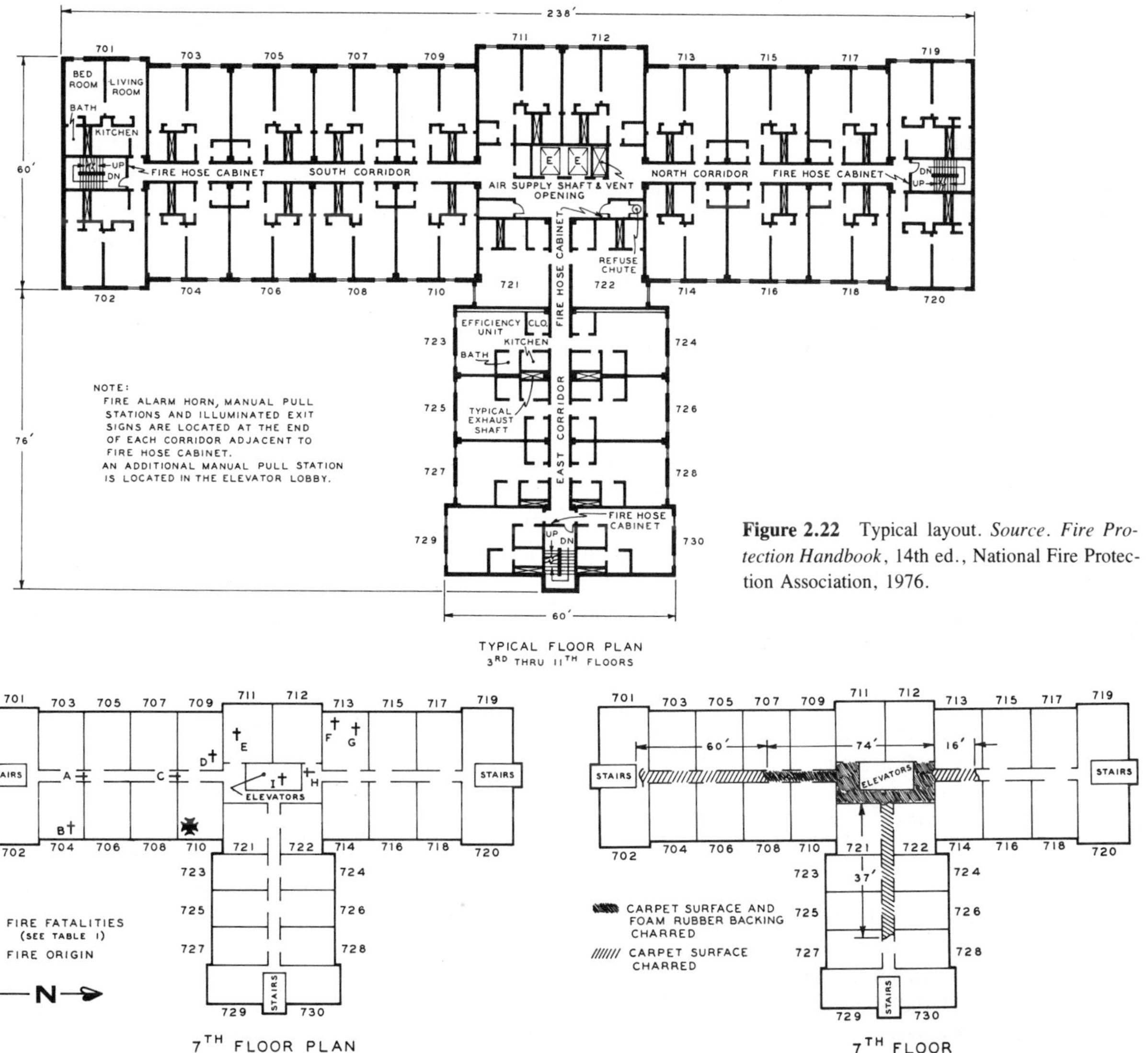

Figure 2.22 Typical layout. *Source. Fire Protection Handbook*, 14th ed., National Fire Protection Association, 1976.

Figure 2.23 Layout of seventh floor, showing locations of victims. *Source. Fire Protection Handbook*, 14th ed., National Fire Protection Association, 1976.

Figure 2.24 Corridor carpet char patterns. *Source. Fire Protection Handbook*, 14th ed., National Fire Protection Association, 1976.

Table 2.30 Occupants Who Died

Occupant	*Age*	*Sex*	*Apt. No.*	*Per Cent Carbon Monoxide*	*Cause of Death*	*Remarks*
A	78	Male	704	20%	Carbon monoxide intoxication and thermal burns	Laboratory reported blood sample unsatisfactory (diluted).
B	60	Female	704	55%	Carbon monoxide intoxication and thermal burns	
C	61	Female	710	80%	Carbon monoxide intoxication	Suffered from Parkinsonism; walked with cane; heavy smoker.
D	75	Female	709	68%	Carbon monoxide intoxication	
E	71	Female	711	45%	Carbon monoxide intoxication	
F	82	Male	713	Less than 5%	Carbon monoxide intoxication	Laboratory reported blood sample unsatisfactory (diluted).
G	75	Female	713	62%	Carbon monoxide intoxication	
H	91	Male	721	50%	Thermal burns	
I	64	Male	guard	40%	Thermal burns	Lived on tenth floor; died on seventh floor in elevator.
J	67	Female	1007		Smoke inhalation	Died after six days' hospitalization; no laboratory work done (victim from tenth floor).

Source. Fire Protection Handbook, 14th ed., National Fire Protection Association, 1976.

apartments. A combination of factors contributed to the fire exposure: delayed alarm; open door to the apartment of origin; use of corridor to supply makeup air, presence of corridor carpeting with fire hazard characteristics beyond what is considered acceptable for the location; and the location of the apartment of origin, on the windward side of the building. Smoke that spread through the elevator shaft was also a threat to occupants on five other floors.

An Example of Good Design: Life Safety in the Santa Clara County Office Building

By B. H. Bocook, *Albert A. Hoover & Associates, Architects*

Recent tragedies involving fatalities in highrise buildings have caused building officials around the world to reexamine the design criteria for these structures. Higher land costs and improved building technology have contributed to the popularity of highrise buildings. At the same time, however, new buildings are continually being constructed without the incorporation of many life safety features, simply because codes and regulations have not yet caught up with recommendations by public officials. Interestingly enough, the Uniform Building Code has no requirement for smoke detectors, emergency-keyed elevator service, or emergency power for buildings having more than seven stories.

In April 1973, construction began on the new 13-story office building in Santa Clara County, California. Early in the planning stages the architects and their consultants, in conjunction with the County Department of Public Works and the County Fire Marshal, wanted to ensure the safety of personnel and were gravely concerned with the possibility of a major fire or earthquake, which could result in death to occupants and in excessively high property losses. All the parties involved in the crucial development stage undertook an intensive investigation and review of proposed methods and procedures for providing the new building with the safest, most effective, and yet most practical life safety features available.

Although safety was a main consideration, the architects and engineers felt that design and engineering flexibility had to be maintained. The County Fire Marshal's department was extremely helpful in its review and interpretation of codes, and in cooperating to maintain flexibility as well as safety. By taking advantage of certain tradeoffs available in construction procedure, the design team felt that incorporation of all the safety features in the project was economically justified in the overall design costs. The life safety features proposed for the building fall into five categories: seismic protection, fire sprinklers, smoke control, elevators, and emergency electrical facilities.

Recent earthquakes in Alaska, Caracas, and San Fernando have shown that even buildings that meet UBC requirements can suffer great damage from seismic disturbances. At the request of the county, structural design criteria exceeding code requirements were developed, resulting in a recommendation that a seismic criterion of 8.25 be utilized for the structural frame. This additional strength would increase life safety and minimize physical damage. The resulting 2-hour steel structure, encased in sprayed fireproofing, added some 600 extra tons of steel in excess of the basic UBC requirements.

The square building concentrates regularly spaced columns on the exterior and interior of the building. This column bracing arrangement, along with provision of a concrete slab over a metal deck floor diaphragm, will best take the initial shock of earthquakes and will immediately transfer the horizontal forces to the frame. The building will be evacuated by means of two exterior stair cores symmetrically located at the outside building corners, with direct fire department access from West Hedding and North First Streets.

An amount of soil weighing as much as the building will be excavated and removed from the site to provide a subleval plaza around the structure, so that there will be minimal disturbances to the underlying soil. Soils experts and structural engineers recommended this approach to stabilizing the building by relieving the tendency to heave or settle.

In addition to sprayed-on fireproofing, the main structural members will receive a plaster finish. A seismic deflection of 1 1/2 inches has been designed into the frame as well as into the exterior curtain wall. This movement potential will enable the building to absorb the energy generated by earthquakes. Four devices to record strong seismic motion will be distributed throughout the building to furnish precise readings of earth movement during an earthquake.

Fire Sprinklers. The new office building, including the new chambers room, the remodeled link, and the existing chambers room, will have automatic sprinklers. The system will be served by risers that also serve as a fire department standpipe system. Valved hose connections will be located on each floor. Flow switches, once activated, will automatically signal the county's Monitoring Automatic Control (MAC) and simultaneously will sound the building fire alarm. Fire personnel will have direct access to the building at the exterior stairs. Tempered glass sash located adjacent to these exit shafts will provide knockout ventilation for each floor. Additionally, hand fire extinguishers will be distributed throughout the building according to fire code standards.

By providing a fully supervised sprinkler system, which is not required by the UBC, it was possible to achieve the following tradeoffs in fire requirements to offset construction costs:

1 Use of nonrated exit corridors.
2 Elimination of wet standpipes and cabinets.
3 Elimination of separate dry standpipes.
4 Reduction of fire-resistance requirements by 1 hour, except for the structural frame and shaft protection.
5 Waiver of smokeproof entrance enclosures to exit stairs.

All valves controlling water supply are supervised by the MAC. The fire sprinkler riser is designed to deliver 500 gallons of water per minute at the most remote portion of the top floor. On each floor of light-hazard occupancy, the sprinkler system is designed to deliver 250 gallons per minute to the most remote portion of the floor at a design density of 0.11 gallon of water per square foot of floor area. On each floor of ordinary-hazard occupancy, the sprinkler system is designed to deliver 500 gallons per minute to the most remote portion of the floor at a design density of 0.17 gallon of water per square foot of floor area.

Additionally, it was found that if the main fire line connection could be made at 70 West Hedding (the existing office building) instead of taking a new line underground to West Hedding at the new building, there would be no added costs to sprinkler the existing chamber link. Thus if a sprinkler system is desired in the future for 70 West Hedding, it could be installed at much lower cost than would be required for an entirely new system.

Smoke Control. Because control of smoke travel and safe ventilation of both smoke and heat are of great importance in fire emergencies, smoke detectors in the return air part of the heating, ventilating, and air conditioning (HVAC) system, once activated, will channel all return air to the outside through fire-rated shafts. At the same time, dampers will be activated to prevent smoke from entering other areas. When the detectors sense smoke, 100% fresh air will enter the HVAC system and, simultaneously, an automatic signal will sound the building fire alarm system.

If products of combustion are detected in the fresh air supply, the system will immediately shut down. The MAC tie-in gives added flexibility to the HVAC system. If the fire marshal elects to do so, he can override the smoke detectors by working through the MAC, thus adding to his fire-fighting capabilities. Also, through the MAC, the fire marshal has complete control of the HVAC and fresh air system.

Elevators. Recent instances of evacuation of buildings under panic and fire emergency conditions have shown that exit stairs alone cannot safely do the job. Experience with smoke and overcrowding in stairways, especially in highrise buildings, has caused safety personnel to reexamine use of elevators in emergencies. New safety features are now being considered for future codes and regulations.

The elevator specifications, drafted under the guidance of the elevator consultant, introduce many of the newer safety features and provided the county with the safest system available. Complete fire service will include the following elements.

1 A key switch at the lobby that will simultaneously commandeer all elevators, bringing them down to the lobby level, where they will remain.
2 Smoke detectors that, like the key switch, will activate automatic recall of elevators.
3 To avoid exposing elevator passengers to a floor containing fire or smoke, elevators returning to the lobby level (as described in items 1 and 2) will not stop at intermediate floors.

All present safety codes are silent on the issue of seismic protection for elevators. However after the San Fernando quake of 1971, during which 700 counterweights were thrown out of their guide rails and 1000 out of 9000 elevator systems suffered damage, the industry is seriously considering the adoption of a new set of safety standards for earthquake conditions. The elevators for the new office building will include the following full-scale earthquake-protective features:

1 Sensing devices on counterweights. If counterweights leave the rails, the elevator will stop.
2 Guideshoe and counterweight frame retainers located on all counterweights.
3 Extra-heavy bracketing and guide rails for counterweights (12 lb/ft per foot, in lieu of 8lb/ft).
4 Guards for all outstanding brackets, to prevent the hoist or compensating cables from becoming entangled and twisted.
5 Extra-heavy guards on all sheaves, to prevent cables from jumping.
6 All generators and controllers anchored against 2 g acceleration.
7 All machine beams arranged against tilting (4 g).
8 Compensating and governor tension sheaves tied down to prevent jumpout.

The emergency power arrangements are as follows:

1 Under emergency power, all cabs will immediately return to the lobby level, one at a time, at half-speed.
2 One elevator will be available, on emergency power, to county personnel.
3 The MAC will have the ability to monitor all abnormal operations.

Emergency Electrical Facilities. An emergency control center (ECC), which is located in the link, contains the essential items for the building systems and is extremely valuable for fire control and emergencies. It will include the following components.

1 A public address system for paging throughout the building, which can be used by trained personnel during emergencies.
2 Controls and supervisory equipment for door security monitoring.
3 A fire alarm control panel with break-glass station for sounding the alarm signal throughout the building, in accordance with NFPA Standard 73 (Standard for the Installation, Maintenance and Use of Public Fire Service Communications).
4 Emergency power shutoff for the entire building.
5 HVAC control switch, through the MAC service connection.

An emergency fire alarm system, consisting of three red telephones on each floor, is connected directly to the ECC. If for any reason the ECC is unmanned, calls will be transferred automatically to the fire department. Also, if the phone is merely lifted off the hook, the fire department will be signaled. Firemen will also communicate by these red telephones during emergencies.

A building alarm for evacuation can be activated from the ECC or remotely by the MAC. Water flowing in the sprinkler system or smoke in the HVAC system will automatically activate the building evacuation alarm.

A nightwatch station, to be located adjacent to the ECC, will be staffed to provide information and a security check 24 hours a day. The station will include:

1 Monitors for television surveillance sets.
2 Security check for 45 doors.
3 Red telephone.
4 General information and telephones for staff use.

Safety to life, decreased property losses, and reduced insurance rates provided incentives in the program stage for incorporation of safety features that often exceed code requirements in the design of this 13-story office building. In many instances the added features were incorporated at little or no extra cost, thanks to tradeoffs achieved by working with the county fire marshal. The latest research by the General Services Administration, the NFPA, regional fire departments, and other safety organizations described current thinking and techniques that were incorporated to achieve maximum protection at minimum cost and minimum disturbance to the county personnel occupying the building.

Construction Types. For buildings of most types the floor loads to be used in the structural calculations are specified in the applicable code. Live loads have a range between 40 and 300 pounds per square foot according to specific uses. Homes have the lowest requirements, and structures used for heavy storage are ranked highest. Also specified are roof loads, which depend on local weather conditions, since they are based on the impact of wind, rain, and snow.

Next to live loads, two wind loads and earthquake loads determine the required strength of the structural system. Wind loads are specified according to the geographic location and according to the height of the building. Seismic loading is also determined by location, and the required values are taken from a seismic map that indicates the potential earthquake activity for a given location. The code usually also specifies the design systems permitted for certain types of building. These specifi-

PARADISE PARK DAY USE CENTER
Mount Rainier, Washington
Architects: Wimberly, Whisenand, Allison, Tong & Goo
Photo: R. Springgate

cations are based on past experiences as well as on results of experiments with simulation models. The goal of structural regulations concerning earthquakes is to preserve human life by building structures strong enough to withstand earthquakes without collapsing and without blocking the safe exit of occupants.

Other Code Restrictions. The majority of the regulations contained in the building code deal with the prevention of life safety hazards that may stem from insufficient structural design or from catastrophes. A number of requirements specified in the code, however, refer to the areas of sanitation, illumination, and ventilation.

Separate bathrooms for each sex are generally required in buildings open to the public and in places of business of more than a specified number of employees. Public water fountains are also required by code. Toilet facilities are subject to detailed ventilation and lighting regulations. The size and capacity of school toilets is specified according to the maximum number of students.

Specifications for ventilation are expressed in air changes per hour and in cubic feet per minute per person. There are special modifications for toilets, kitchens, and other rooms with strong odors that require the exhaustion of air instead of recirculation.

Other Standards. Developments financed with loans guaranteed by the Federal Housing Administration (FHA) are subject to regulations set forth in the following publications:

- Minimum Property Standards for One and Two Living Units, FHA 300.
- Minimum Standards for Multifamily Housing, FHA 2600.

The requirements are often more detailed than those of the building code. The Occupational Safety and Health Act, containing new federal standards of safety and health requirements for employees, became law in 1970. Areas of concern included in this code are:

1 Fire protection.
2 Scaffolding.
3 Electrical installations.
4 Ventilation.
5 Exposure to air contaminants.
6 Noise.
7 Radiation hazards.

For industrial and commercial developments, these standards are applicable during construction as well as for the lifetime of the structure. For residential developments they are applicable only during construction. Parts of the act consist of existing building codes such as the National Electrical Code, which was integrated into the new standard. Other parts contain newly written material. All requirements are enforceable by federal and state officials, who may inspect facilities on their own account or by request. Although the regulations contained in this law pertain more to the work of the contractor and to the management of future users, the architect must be familiar with this code and its applicability.

Legal Restrictions

Easements. Easements are rights of neighbors or other parties to use part of a property for a special purpose—for example, to gain access to a closed-in parcel across the neighbor's land or to install public utility lines or storm drains. An easement restricts the owner's use of the land because it usually prohibits construction in the area concerned, but it still permits other, nonconflicting uses.

Scenic easements are a newer type of land use restriction. They were created by local governments to preserve public vistas along scenic routes by means of purchase or condemnation.

The agreement for an easement must be documented in a grant deed and must also be recorded in the public records.

Deed Restrictions. A grant deed may contain several clauses that restrict or modify the use of the property sold. A covenant in a new land subdivision, for instance, may specify certain aesthetic standards of construction to ensure the creation of a neighborhood of a certain character, and these may be enforced later by a homeowners' association. A clause that binds the buyer to perform certain services, such as maintaining a sidewalk, is called an *affirmative covenant.* Owners' association fees assessed to condominium owners may also be expressed in the legal form of an active covenant.

A condition is a restrictive clause specifying that the title to a property will revert to the original grantor or his or her heirs if the buyer fails to abide by the restriction. Some restrictions are no longer enforceable today, such as clauses pertaining to race or religion or forbidding the use of alcohol and tobacco. Some conditions have an expiration date, but others do not and can be changed only by the ruling of a court.

Air rights, a special form of easement concerning the air space above a property, are important in areas with very high land values. The construction of a bridge or similar structure above ground may be restricted by such air rights.

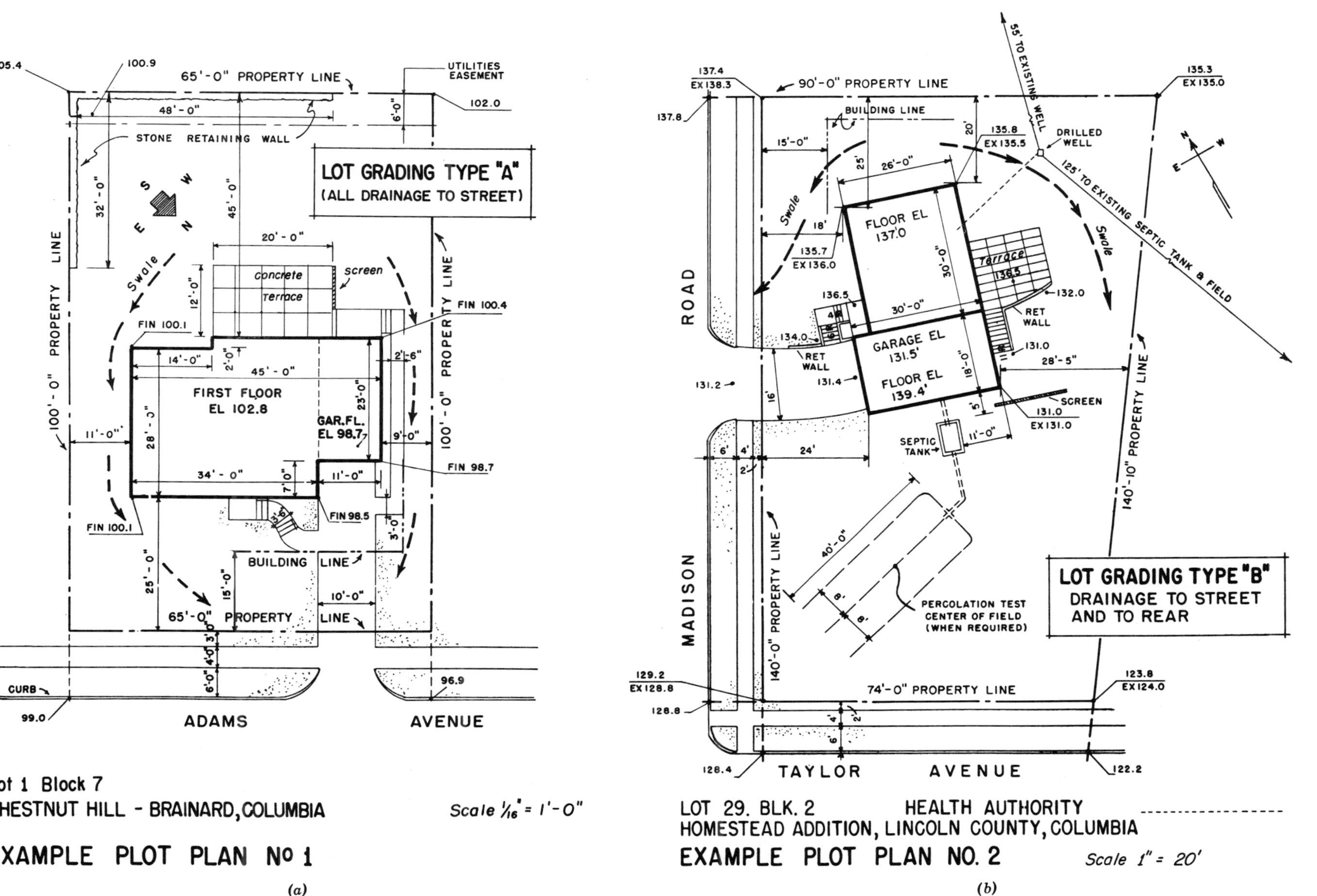

Figure 2.25 *Source*. Federal Housing Administration Standards.

SUMMARY OF ZONING REGULATIONS
CITY OF LOS ANGELES

CLASSIFICATION	ZONE	USE	MAXIMUM HEIGHT STORIES	MAXIMUM HEIGHT FEET	REQUIRED YARDS FRONT	REQUIRED YARDS SIDE	REQUIRED YARDS REAR	MINIMUM AREA PER LOT	MINIMUM AREA PER DWELLING UNIT	MINIMUM LOT WIDTH	PARKING SPACE	EAGLE PRISMACOLOR PENCIL CHART
AGRICULTURAL	A1	AGRICULTURAL ONE-FAMILY DWELLINGS - PARKS - PLAYGROUNDS - COMMUNITY CENTERS GOLF COURSES - TRUCK GARDENING - EXTENSIVE AGRICULTURAL USES	3	45 FT.	25 FT.	25 FT. MAXIMUM 10% LOT WIDTH 3 FT. MINIMUM	25 FT.	5 ACRES	2 ½ ACRES	300 FT.	TWO SPACES PER DWELLING UNIT	909 GRASS GREEN
AGRICULTURAL	A2	AGRICULTURAL A1 USES	3	45 FT.	25 FT.	25 FT. MAXIMUM 10% LOT WIDTH 3 FT. MINIMUM	25 FT.	2 ACRES	1 ACRE	150 FT.	TWO SPACES PER DWELLING UNIT	912 APPLE GREEN
AGRICULTURAL	RA	SUBURBAN LIMITED AGRICULTURAL USES	3	45 FT.	25 FT.	10'-1 & 2 STORIES 11'-3 STORIES	25 FT.	✱ 17,500 SQ. FT.	✱ 17,500 SQ. FT.	✱ 70 FT.	TWO GARAGE SPACES PER DWELLING UNIT	910 TRUE GREEN
ONE FAMILY RESIDENTIAL	RE40	RESIDENTIAL ESTATE ONE-FAMILY DWELLINGS PARKS PLAYGROUNDS COMMUNITY CENTERS TRUCK GARDENING	3	45 FT.	25 FT.	10 FT	25 FT.	✱ 40,000 SQ. FT.	✱ 40,000 SQ. FT.	✱ 80 FT.	TWO GARAGE SPACES PER DWELLING UNIT	950 GOLD
ONE FAMILY RESIDENTIAL	RE20				25 FT.	10 FT.	25 FT.	✱ 20,000 SQ. FT.	✱ 20,000 SQ. FT.	✱ 80 FT.		
ONE FAMILY RESIDENTIAL	RE15				25 FT.	10 FT. MAXIMUM 10% LOT WIDTH 5 FT. MINIMUM	25 FT.	✱ 15,000 SQ. FT.	✱ 15,000 SQ. FT.	✱ 80 FT.		
ONE FAMILY RESIDENTIAL	RE11				25 FT.	5'-1 & 2 STORIES 6'-3 STORIES	25 FT.	✱ 11,000 SQ. FT.	✱ 11,000 SQ. FT.	✱ 70 FT.		
ONE FAMILY RESIDENTIAL	RE9				25 FT.	5 FT. MAXIMUM 10% LOT WIDTH 3 FT. MINIMUM	25 FT.	✱ 9,000 SQ. FT.	✱ 9,000 SQ. FT.	✱ 65 FT.		
ONE FAMILY RESIDENTIAL	RS	SUBURBAN ONE-FAMILY DWELLINGS - PARKS PLAYGROUNDS - TRUCK GARDENING	3	45 FT.	25 FT.	5'-1 & 2 STORIES 6'-3 STORIES	20 FT.	7,500 SQ. FT.	7,500 SQ. FT.	60 FT.	TWO GARAGE SPACES PER DWELLING UNIT	911 OLIVE GREEN
ONE FAMILY RESIDENTIAL	R1	ONE-FAMILY DWELLING RS USES	3	45 FT.	20 FT.	5'-1 & 2 STORIES 6'-3 STORIES	15 FT.	5,000 SQ. FT.	5,000 SQ. FT.	50 FT.	TWO GARAGE SPACES PER DWELLING UNIT	916 CANARY YELLOW
ONE FAMILY RESIDENTIAL	RW1	ONE-FAMILY RESIDENTIAL WATERWAYS ZONE	3	45 FT.	10 FT.	● 4' PLUS 1' EACH STORY ABOVE 2ND 10% LOT WIDTH	15 FT.	2,300 SQ. FT.	2,300 SQ. FT.	28 FT.	TWO GARAGE SPACES PER DWELLING UNIT	914 CREAM
	RW2	TWO-FAMILY RESIDENTIAL WATERWAYS ZONE							1,150 SQ. FT.			
	R2	TWO-FAMILY DWELLING R1 USES TWO-FAMILY DWELLINGS	3	45 FT.	20 FT.	5'-1 & 2 STORIES 6'-3 STORIES	15 FT.	5,000 SQ. FT.	2,500 SQ. FT.	50 FT.	TWO SPACES ONE IN A GARAGE	917 YELLOW ORANGE

MULTIPLE RESIDENTIAL

RD1.5			20 FT.	6 FT.	20 FT.	6,000 SQ. FT.	1,500 SQ. FT.	60 FT.		
RD2						8,000 SQ. FT.	2,000 SQ. FT.	60 FT.		
RD3							3,000 SQ. FT.			
RD4	RESTRICTED DENSITY MULTIPLE DWELLING ZONE TWO-FAMILY DWELLING APARTMENT HOUSES MULTIPLE DWELLINGS	HEIGHT DISTRICT NO. 1 3 STORIES 45 FT. HEIGHT DISTRICT NOS. 2,3 OR 4 6 STORIES 75 FT.	20 FT.	10 FT.	25 FT.	12,000 SQ. FT.	4,000 SQ. FT.	70 FT	ONE SPACE EACH DWELLING UNIT OF LESS THAN THREE ROOMS ONE AND ONE HALF SPACES EACH DWELLING UNIT OF THREE ROOMS TWO SPACES EACH DWELLING UNIT OF MORE THEN THREE ROOMS ONE SPACE EACH GUEST ROOM (FIRST THIRTY)	940 SAND
RD5							5,000 SQ. FT.			
RD6							6,000 SQ. FT.			
R3	MULTIPLE DWELLING R2 USES APARTMENT HOUSES MULTIPLE DWELLINGS		15 FT.	5'-1 & 2 STORIE 6'-3 STORIES	15 FT.	5,000 SQ. FT.	800 TO 1,200 SQ. FT.	50 FT.		918 ORANGE
R4	MULTIPLE DWELLING R3 USES CHURCHES HOTELS-SCHOOLS	UNLIMITED ✱	15 FT.	5' PLUS 1' EACH STORY ABOVE 2ND. 16 FT. MAX.	15' PLUS 1' EACH STORY ABOVE 3RD. 20 FT. MAX.	5,000 SQ. FT.	400 TO 800 SQ. FT.	50 FT.		943 BURNT OCHRE
R5	MULTIPLE DWELLING R4 USES CLUBS-HOSPITALS LODGES-SANITARIUMS	UNLIMITED ✱	15 FT.	5' PLUS 1' EACH STORY ABOVE 2ND. 16 FT. MAX.	15' PLUS 1' EACH STORY ABOVE 3RD. 20 FT. MAX.	5,000 SQ. FT.	200 TO 400 SQ. FT.	50 FT.		946 DARK BROWN

✱ SEE HEIGHT DISTRICTS AT THE BOTTOM OF PAGE 2

● FOR TWO OR MORE LOTS THE INTERIOR SIDE YARDS MAY BE ELIMINATED, BUT 4 FT. IS REQUIRED ON EACH SIDE OF THE GROUPED LOTS.

✱ "H" HILLSIDE OR MOUNTAINOUS AREA DESIGNATION MAY ALTER THESE REQUIREMENTS IN THE RA-H OR RE-H ZONES, SUBDIVISIONS MAY BE APPROVED WITH SMALLER LOTS, PROVIDING LARGER LOTS ARE ALSO INCLUDED. EACH LOT MAY BE USED FOR ONLY ONE SINGLE-FAMILY DWELLING. SEE MINIMUM WIDTH & AREA REQUIREMENTS BELOW.

ZONE COMBINATION	MINIMUM TO WHICH NET AREA MAY BE REDUCED	MINIMUM TO WHICH LOT WIDTH MAY BE REDUCED
RA-H	14,000 SQ. FT.	63 FT.
RE 9 -H	7,200 SQ. FT.	60 FT.
RE 11 -H,	8,800 SQ. FT.	63 FT.
RE 15 -H	12,000 SQ. FT.	72 FT.
RE 20 -H	16,000 SQ. FT.	72 FT.
RE 40 -H	32,000 SQ. FT.	NO REDUCTION

SHEET 1 OF 2

PREPARED BY CITY PLANNING DEPARTMENT

CP FORM 10
JANUARY 1976

Figure 2.26 *Source*. Los Angeles City Standards.

SUMMARY OF ZONING REGULATIONS

CITY OF LOS ANGELES

CLASSIFICATION	ZONE	USE	MAXIMUM HEIGHT		REQUIRED YARDS			MINIMUM AREA PER LOT AND UNIT	MINIMUM LOT WIDTH	LOADING SPACE	PARKING SPACE	EAGLE PRISMACOLOR PENCIL CHART
			STORIES	FEET	FRONT	SIDE	REAR					
COMMERCIAL — RESIDENTIAL USES (EXCEPT HOTELS) PROHIBITED UNLESS CONDITIONAL USE IS APPROVED BY ZONING ADMINISTRATOR	CR	LIMITED COMMERCIAL BANKS, CLUBS, HOTELS, CHURCHES, SCHOOLS, BUSINESS & PROFESSIONAL OFFICES, PARKING AREAS	6	75 FT.	10 FEET	5'-10' CORNER LOT, RESIDENTIAL USE OR ADJOINING AN "A" OR "R" ZONE SAME AS R4 ZONE	15' PLUS 1' EACH STORY ABOVE 3rd	SAME AS R4 FOR DWELLINGS OTHERWISE NONE	50 FEET FOR RESIDENCE USE OTHERWISE NONE	HOSPITALS, HOTELS INSTITUTIONS, AND WITH EVERY BUILDING WHERE LOT ABUTS ALLEY ➡ MINIMUM LOADING SPACE 400 SQUARE FEET ADDITIONAL SPACE REQUIRED FOR BUILDINGS CONTAINING MORE THAN 50,000 SQUARE FEET OF FLOOR AREA NONE REQUIRED FOR APARTMENT BUILDINGS 20 UNITS OR LESS	ONE SPACE FOR EACH 500 SQ. FT. OF FLOOR AREA	939 FLESH
	C1	LIMITED COMMERCIAL LOCAL RETAIL STORES, OFFICES OR BUSINESSES, HOTELS, LIMITED HOSPITALS AND/OR CLINICS, PARKING AREAS	UNLIMITED *			3'-5' CORNER LOT OR ADJOINING AN "A" OR "R" ZONE RESIDENTIAL USE SAME AS R4 ZONE	15' PLUS 1' EACH STORY ABOVE 3rd RESIDENTIAL USE OR ABUTTING AN "A" OR "R" ZONE OTHERWISE NONE	SAME AS R3 FOR DWELLINGS EXCEPT 5000 SQ. FT. PER UNIT IN C1-H ZONES — OTHERWISE NONE			ONE SPACE FOR EACH 500 SQUARE FEET OF FLOOR AREA IN ALL BUILDINGS ON ANY LOT MUST BE LOCATED WITHIN 750 FEET OF BUILDING	929 PINK
	C1.5	LIMITED COMMERCIAL C1 USES — DEPARTMENT STORES, THEATRES, BROADCASTING STUDIOS, PARKING BUILDINGS, PARKS & PLAYGROUNDS						SAME AS R4 FOR DWELLINGS OTHERWISE NONE				928 BLUSH
	C2	COMMERCIAL C1.5 USES — RETAIL BUSINESSES WITH LIMITED MANUFACTURING, AUTO SERVICE STATION & GARAGE, RETAIL CONTRACTORS BUSINESSES, CHURCHES, SCHOOLS			NONE	NONE FOR COMMERCIAL BUILDINGS RESIDENTIAL USES - SAME AS IN R4 ZONE	NONE FOR COMMERCIAL BUILDINGS RESIDENTIAL USES - SAME AS IN R4 ZONE					922 SCARLET RED
	C4	COMMERCIAL C2 USES — (WITH EXCEPTIONS, SUCH AS AUTO SERVICE STATIONS, AMUSEMENT ENTERPRISES, CONTRACTORS BUSINESSES, SECOND-HAND BUSINESSES)										924 CRIMSON RED
	C5	COMMERCIAL C2 USES — LIMITED FLOOR AREAS FOR LIGHT MANUFACTURING OF THE CM-ZONE TYPE									SEE CODE FOR ASSEMBLY AREAS, HOSPITALS AND CLINICS	925 CRIMSON LAKE
	CM	COMM'L MANUFACTURING WHOLESALE BUSINESSES, STORAGE BUILDINGS, CLINICS, LIMITED MANUFACTURING, C2 USES - EXCEPT HOSPITALS, SCHOOLS, CHURCHES				NONE FOR INDUSTRIAL OR COMMERCIAL BUILDINGS RESIDENTIAL USES - SAME AS IN R4 ZONE	NONE FOR INDUSTRIAL OR COMMERCIAL BUILDINGS RESIDENTIAL USES - SAME AS IN R4 ZONE	SAME AS R3 FOR DWELLINGS OTHERWISE NONE				905 AQUA-MARINE
INDUSTRIAL — RESIDENTIAL USES PROHIBITED IN ALL INDUSTRIAL ZONES	MR1	RESTRICTED INDUSTRIAL CM USES — LIMITED COMMERCIAL & MANUFACTURING USES, HOSPITALS, CLINICS, SANITARIUMS, LIMITED MACHINE SHOPS	UNLIMITED *		15 FT.			SAME AS R4 FOR DWELLINGS OTHERWISE NONE	50 FEET FOR RESIDENCE USE OTHERWISE NONE	HOSPITALS, HOTELS INSTITUTIONS, AND WITH EVERY BUILDING WHERE LOT ABUTS ALLEY ➡ MINIMUM LOADING SPACE 400 SQUARE FEET ADDITIONAL SPACE REQUIRED FOR BUILDINGS CONTAINING MORE THAN 50,000 SQUARE FEET OF FLOOR AREA NONE REQUIRED FOR APARTMENT BUILDINGS 20 UNITS OR LESS	ONE SPACE FOR EACH 500 SQUARE FEET OF FLOOR AREA IN ALL BUILDINGS ON ANY LOT MUST BE LOCATED WITHIN 750 FEET OF BUILDING	901 INDIGO BLUE
	MR2	RESTRICTED LIGHT INDUSTRIAL MR1 USES — ADDITION INDUSTRIAL USES, MORTUARIES, AGRICULTURE										906 COPEN-HAGEN BLUE
	M1	LIMITED INDUSTRIAL CM USES — LIMITED INDUSTRIAL & MANUFACTURING USES — NO "R" ZONE USES, NO HOSPITALS, SCHOOLS OR CHURCHES			NONE							904 LIGHT BLUE
	M2	LIGHT INDUSTRIAL M1 USES — ADDITIONAL INDUSTRIAL USES, STORAGE YARDS OF ALL KINDS, ANIMAL KEEPING — NO "R" ZONE USES									SEE CODE FOR ASSEMBLY AREAS, HOSPITALS AND CLINICS	902 ULTRA-MARINE
	M3	HEAVY INDUSTRIAL M2 USES — ANY INDUSTRIAL USES — NUISANCE TYPE - 500 FT. FROM ANY OTHER ZONE — NO "R" ZONE USES				NONE	NONE	NONE — NOTE — "R" ZONE USES PROHIBITED	NONE			931 PURPLE

PARKING	P	AUTOMOBILE PARKING – SURFACE & UNDERGROUND PROPERTY IN A "P" ZONE MAY ALSO BE IN AN "A" OR "R" ZONE PARKING PERMITTED IN LIEU OF AGRICULTURAL OR RESIDENTIAL USES						NONE UNLESS ALSO IN AN "A" OR "R" ZONE	NONE UNLESS ALSO IN AN "A" OR "R" ZONE	—	—	967 COLD GREY LIGHT
	PB	PARKING BUILDING AUTOMOBILE PARKING WITHIN OR WITHOUT A BUILDING	* *	—	0', 5', OR 10' DEPENDING ON ZONING IN BLOCK AND ACROSS STREET	5' PLUS 1' EACH STORY ABOVE 2nd IF ABUTTING OR ACROSS STREET FROM 'A' OR 'R' ZONE	5' PLUS 1' EACH STORY ABOVE 2nd IF ABUTTING AN "A" OR "R" ZONE, TO A 16' MAXIMUM	NONE	NONE	—	—	936 SLATE GREY
SPECIAL	SL	SUBMERGED LAND ZONE COMMERCIAL SHIPPING NAVIGATION FISHING RECREATION										919 SKY BLUE
	(T)	TENTATIVE CLASSIFICATION USED IN COMBINATION WITH ZONE CHANGE ONLY - DELAYS ISSUANCE OF BUILDING PERMIT UNTIL SUBDIVISION OR PARCEL MAP RECORDED										
	(F)	FUNDED IMPROVEMENT CLASSIFICATION AN ALTERNATE MEANS OF EFFECTING ZONE CHANGES AND SECURING IMPROVEMENTS (WHEN NO SUBDIVISION OR DEDICATIONS ARE INVOLVED)										
	(Q)	QUALIFIED CLASSIFICATION USED IN COMBINATION WITH ZONE CHANGES ONLY EXCEPT WITH RA, RE, RS OR R1 ZONES - RESTRICTS USES OF PROPERTY AND ASSURES DEVELOPMENT COMPATIBLE WITH THE SURROUNDING PROPERTY										

SUPPLEMENTAL USE DISTRICTS: G ROCK AND GRAVEL • O OIL DRILLING • S ANIMAL SLAUGHTERING • RPD RESIDENTIAL PLANNED DEVELOPMENT
K HORSE - KEEPING • CA COMMERCIAL AND ARTCRAFT

(ESTABLISHED IN CONJUNCTION WITH ZONES)

* HEIGHT DISTRICT		
	Nº 1	FLOOR AREA OF MAIN BUILDING MAY NOT EXCEED THREE TIMES THE BUILDING AREA OF THE LOT
	Nº 1L	SAME AS Nº 1 AND MAXIMUM HEIGHT - 6 STORIES OR 75 FT.
	Nº 1-VL	SAME AS Nº 1 AND MAXIMUM HEIGHT - 3 STORIES OR 45 FT.
	Nº 2	FLOOR AREA OF MAIN BUILDING MAY NOT EXCEED SIX TIMES THE BUILDABLE AREA OF THE LOT
	Nº 3	FLOOR AREA OF MAIN BUILDING MAY NOT EXCEED TEN TIMES THE BUILDABLE AREA OF THE LOT
	Nº 4	FLOOR AREA OF MAIN BUILDING MAY NOT EXCEED THIRTEEN TIMES THE BUILDABLE AREA OF THE LOT

* * MAXIMUM PB ZONE HEIGHTS		
	Nº 1	2 STORIES AND ROOF
	Nº 2	6 STORIES
	Nº 3	10 STORIES
	Nº 4	13 STORIES

NOTE: ALL INFORMATION GENERAL - FOR SPECIFIC DETAILS CHECK WITH DEPARTMENT OF BUILDING AND SAFETY

SHEET 2 OF 2

PREPARED BY CITY PLANNING DEPARTMENT — JANUARY 1976

Figure 2.26 *Continued.*

If two adjacent buildings share a party wall, the owners involved must sign an agreement stating that neither owner can tear down or alter the party wall; the recorded agreement gives each party an easement over the other's property to the extent of half of the thickness of the wall. Since party walls are always fire walls, they must comply to all pertaining regulations specified in the building code.

3 FUNCTIONAL CONSIDERATIONS OF BUILDING TYPES

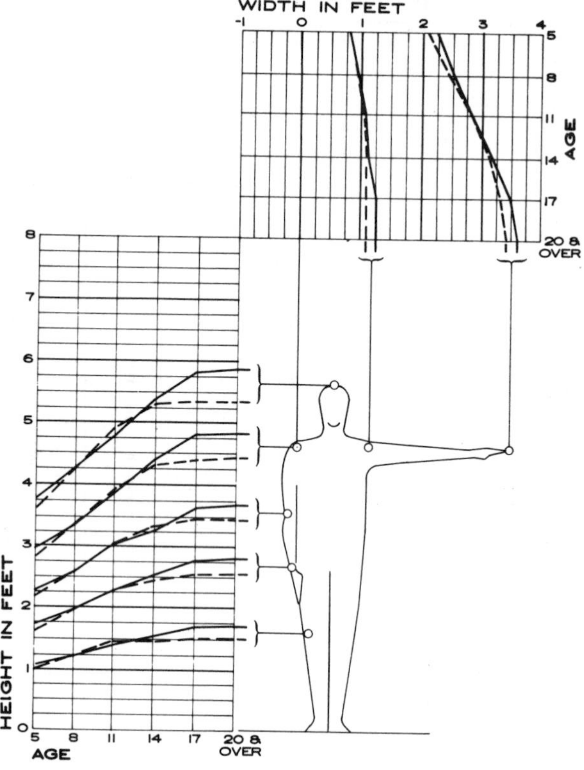

Figure 2.27 *Source.* Reprinted from C. G. Ramsey and H. R. Sleeper, *Architectural Graphic Standards*, 6th ed., American Institute of Architects, John Wiley & Sons, 1970.

Artichectural programming is the development of a spatial organization, given the limitations of a specific situation, that represents an optimal environment for the activities of people. This process is based on the space requirements of the human body, thus on its dimensions and proportions. Therefore buildings and spaces that show little relationship to the human scale are known to cause stress and other discomfort. Figure 2.27 gives the most important dimensions of the growing male and female bodies. Most of our standardized building elements, like stairs and doors, are based on these measurements.

The specific quality of an architectural design can always be related to the elements of its principal use. The task of the architect consists of collecting and processing information about this use, and defining the resulting functions of the building. To avoid reinventing the wheel with every new project, the architect must be familiar with the inventory of general building types and their functional characteristics.

Schools

Schools are for learning, which involves much more than the passing on of information from teachers to students. In schools, children learn how to live in groups other than families, and their introduction into social life should happen in a human, warm, and natural environment. Many schools that are organized efficiently in terms of teaching, show few of the qualities above.

The architect must define the program in collaboration with the school board and also with various community groups, because many schools have adult evening classes, public performances, and meetings, and school recreational facilities may serve the whole community. In addition to the conventional approach, many schools use team teaching and other alternatives, which all require increased space and greater flexibility.

The optimum classroom capacity depends on the grade and the subject, ranging from 20 pupils in first grade to an art class in high school with over 50 students. Typical floor areas of classrooms are between 700 and 1100 square feet. Noise aversion is a major factor in the arrangement of classrooms, but the single most important consideration in school design is life safety. A school building requires higher safety standards than do most other projects.

LONGVIEW SCHOOL
Davis, California
Architects: Hirshen, Gammill, Trumbo & Cook
Photo: Office

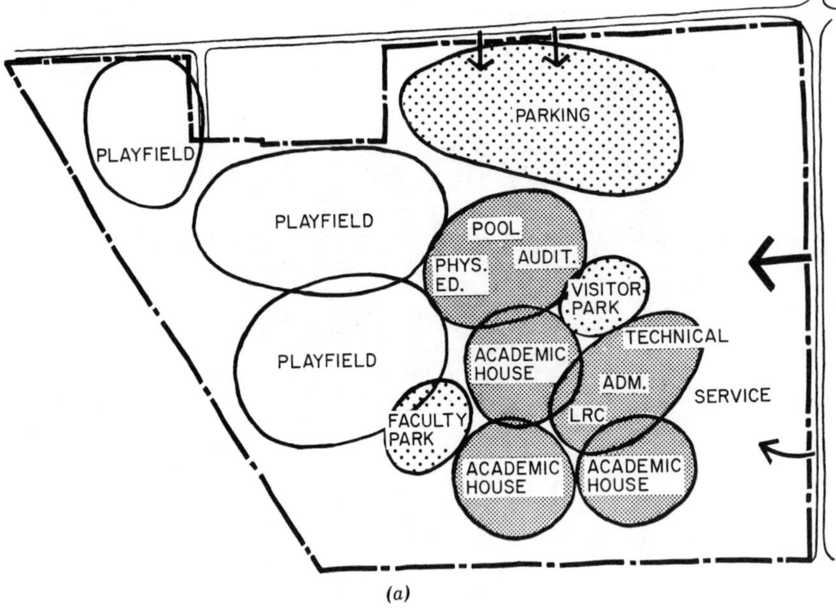

(a)

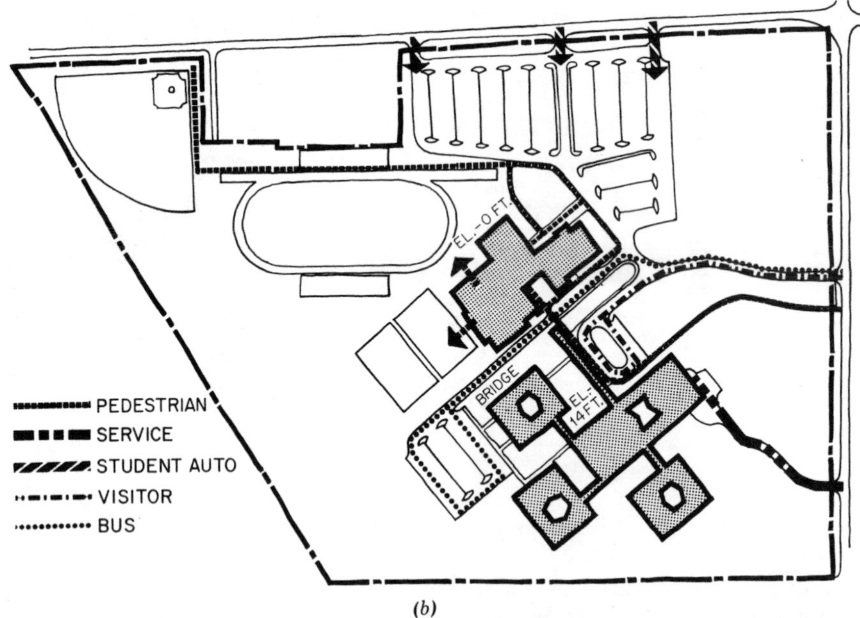

(b)

Figure 2.28 (*a*) Land use diagram for elementary and secondary schools. (*b*) Site circulation plan. *Source.* Joseph de Chiara and John Hancock Callender, *Time-Saver Standards for Building Types,* McGraw-Hill Book Company, 1974.

Since most schools today are experimenting with new ways of teaching and with creative play activities, flexibility has become a very important design factor. The typical classroom unit often gives way to organization patterns of small groups that change according to the activities of the class.

Churches

Many religious organizations are now reforming their practices of worship and community leadership; thus temples and churches representing traditional building types are often replaced by new forms.

A church usually incorporates more than a space for worship, as Figure 2.29 illustrates. The total project often includes a church school, a social hall, and a courtyard used for weddings and outdoor services; support facilities (lobby, sacristy, choir room, dressing room, toilets, offices, storage rooms, etc.) are needed as well.

The central space of worship can be based on a variety of plans that are either traditional, such as the rectangle, the cross, or the central form, or new, as exemplified by many multiform and multifocus concepts. However they all share some basic characteristics according to the activities common in every form of worship. An open

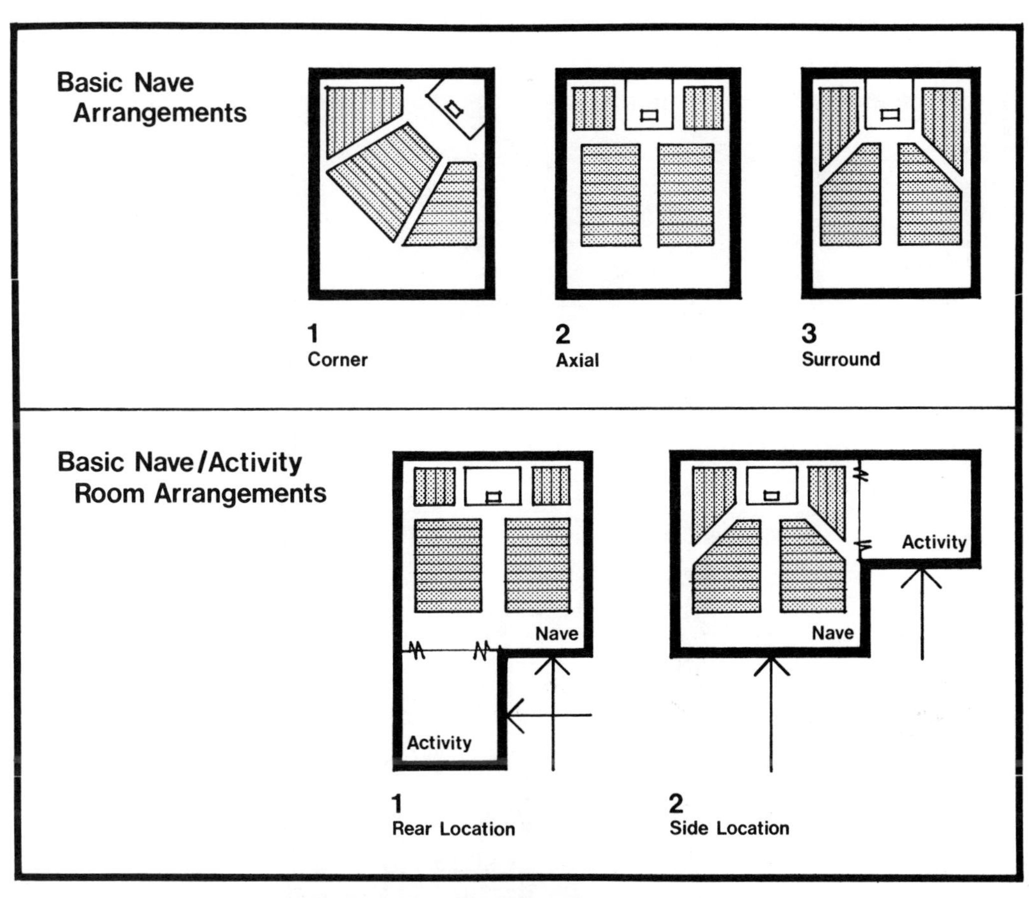

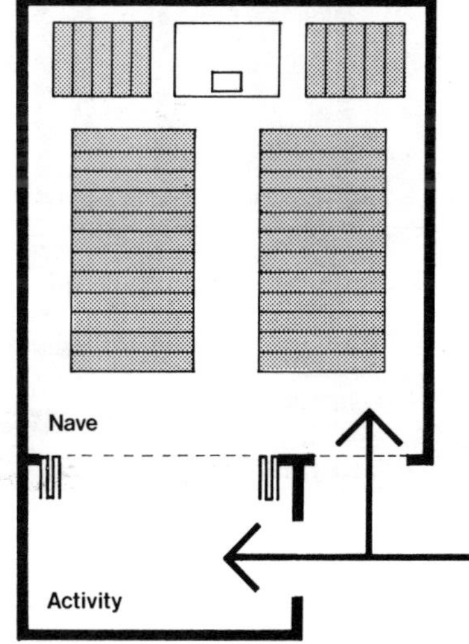

Figure 2.29 Nave arrangements: in a church there are a limited number of possible arrangements; the constraint is geometric. *Source*. Clovis Heimsath, *Behavioral Architecture*, McGraw-Hill Book Company, 1977.

space without columns is needed for assembly, and pastor and congregation should always be able to maintain eye contact. The focus of this space is the altar. Acoustics or electronic equipment must make the word of the pastor understandable throughout the congregation and should support singing and instrumental music. Seating is always required; it can be of the fixed pew type, or it can consist of individual chairs, which allows for greater flexibility but requires storage space.

The program of religious schools often covers a variety of activities, including the screening of films, theatrical performances, crafts classes, and exercising. Usually one classroom is enough. Its size can be estimated by assuming that each student needs 15 to 20 square feet of space. Churches may become active centers of the community during the week, and the factors of accessibility, traffic flow, and parking requirements are important elements of the program.

ST. BASIL'S CHURCH
Los Angeles, California
Architects: Albert C. Martin & Associates
Photo: W. Thom

FIRST PRESBYTERIAN CHURCH
Stamford, Connecticut
Architects: Harrison & Abramovitz
Photo: J. W. Molitor

Housing

The volume of residential construction is always greater than the total volume of all other building types combined. Dwelling units have taken an endless variety of shapes, from tepees to highrise apartments; yet their functional problems are so complex that each design poses a new challenge to the architect.

The conventional house organizes the main functions into separate rooms, but since the activities of a household follow the general pattern only vaguely, great flexibility is required. Children, for instance, use bedrooms for a great many functions as they grow up, and even a bathroom, which seems to have a clear functional definition, may be used for such activities as laundering and exercising, or even serving as a darkroom.

The functional questions to be addressed in planning a dwelling unit are, how much space do people need, and how can spaces be arranged for optimal circulation patterns? Certain relationships have become conventional standards. Bedrooms, for instance, should have direct access to bathrooms, dining areas and kitchens need to be together, the outdoors should be accessible from the living room, and so on (Figure 2.30).

Furniture types and combinations are greatly standardized in our society, as are the tolerances for spacing them. Although people are not aware of the actual dimensions, we tend to feel uncomfortable in a dining area that has less than 2 feet of table space per person or less than 2 feet of clearance between the chairs and the wall.

Multifamily living, in apartments or condominiums, is becoming the dominant form of housing in our cities.

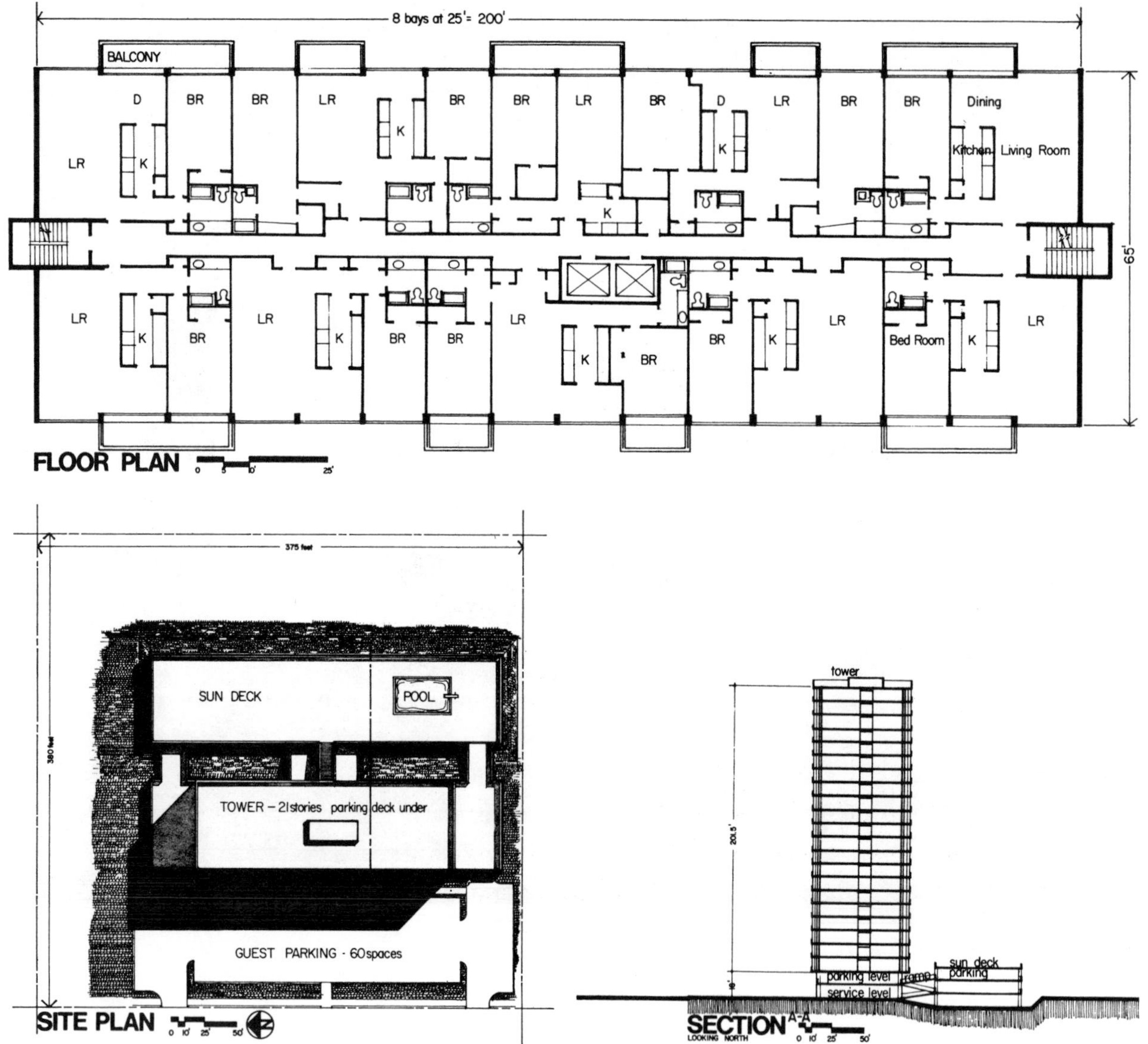

Figure 2.30 *Source.* Clovis Heimsath, *Behavioral Architecture,* McGraw-Hill Book Company, 1977.

Multifamily units are a result of the need for greater economy, which can be served by using repetitive modules, simple unit outlines that minimize party walls, and a high ratio of interior volume to exterior wall area. Access and circulation are more complex in multiple dwelling projects, and there is a need for such additional areas as corridors, lobbies, recreation rooms, and service facilities. Economy of circulation can be achieved by placing small units with greater night traffic close to access points and large family units at the corners of the structure. This arrangement also reduces the length of hallways and increases the window area of large units. Bathroom and kitchen units will need less in the way of mechanical services if they can be placed back to back.

In highrise apartment buildings the ground floor serves a multitude of functions, becoming the central area of the project and the element that links the indoors to the outdoor space.

Hospitals

The programming and design of hospitals requires a great deal of special knowledge. Hospitals vary greatly in their organization of staff hierarchies, administration, and the relation between outpatient and inpatient sectors, and in terms of their specialization in certain areas of medicine. In every case, however, the bedroom tract with the nursing wards accounts for the greatest part of

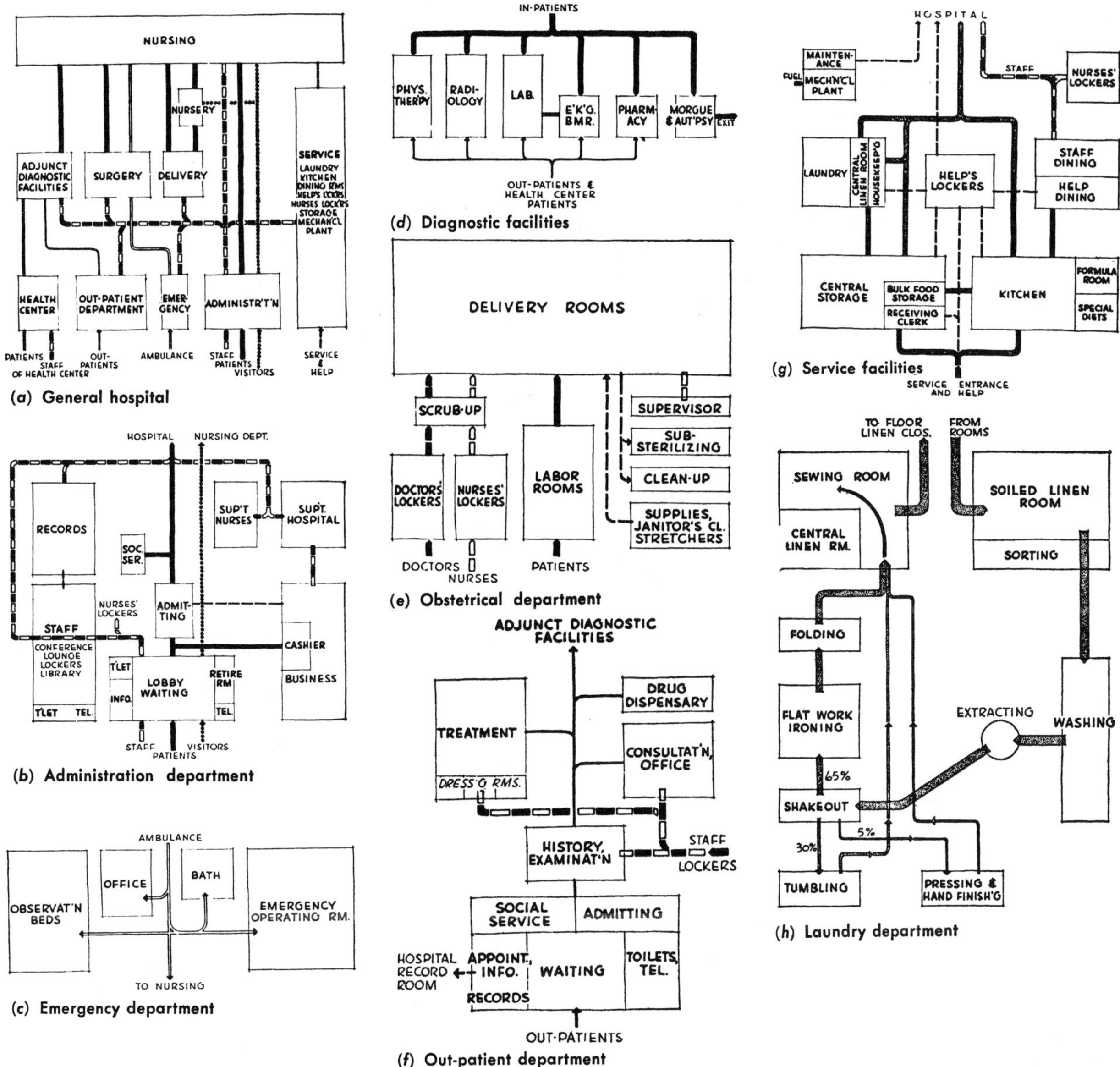

From Design and Construction of General Hospitals by Public Health Service, U.S. Department of Health, Education and Welfare (1953).

Figure 2.31 Flow charts for hospitals. Reprinted from Joseph de Chiara and John Hancock Callender, *Time-Saver Standards for Building Types*, McGraw-Hill Book Company, 1974.

space volume. Other, very detailed components generally include surgical suites, pediatric units, X-ray units, therapy rooms, intensive-care wards, emergency units, and the clinics for the treatment of outpatients. Since the programming of most of these units is largely the responsibility of medical experts, the architect must concentrate on the elements of outer and inner circulation of staff, patients, visitors, and supply, on the administrative facilities, and on the design of the nursing units.

The most common type of nursing unit today has two corridors, with supply and staff rooms in the middle. A single room typically has 150 square feet, a 2-bed room has 200, and a 4-bed room has 400. Three-bed room arrangements are usually avoided. The room should be between 10 and 14 feet wide and between 15 and 22 feet deep. Four-bed rooms are twice the width of 2-bed rooms. Today an individual bath for every room is a standard arrangement, as are wardrobes.

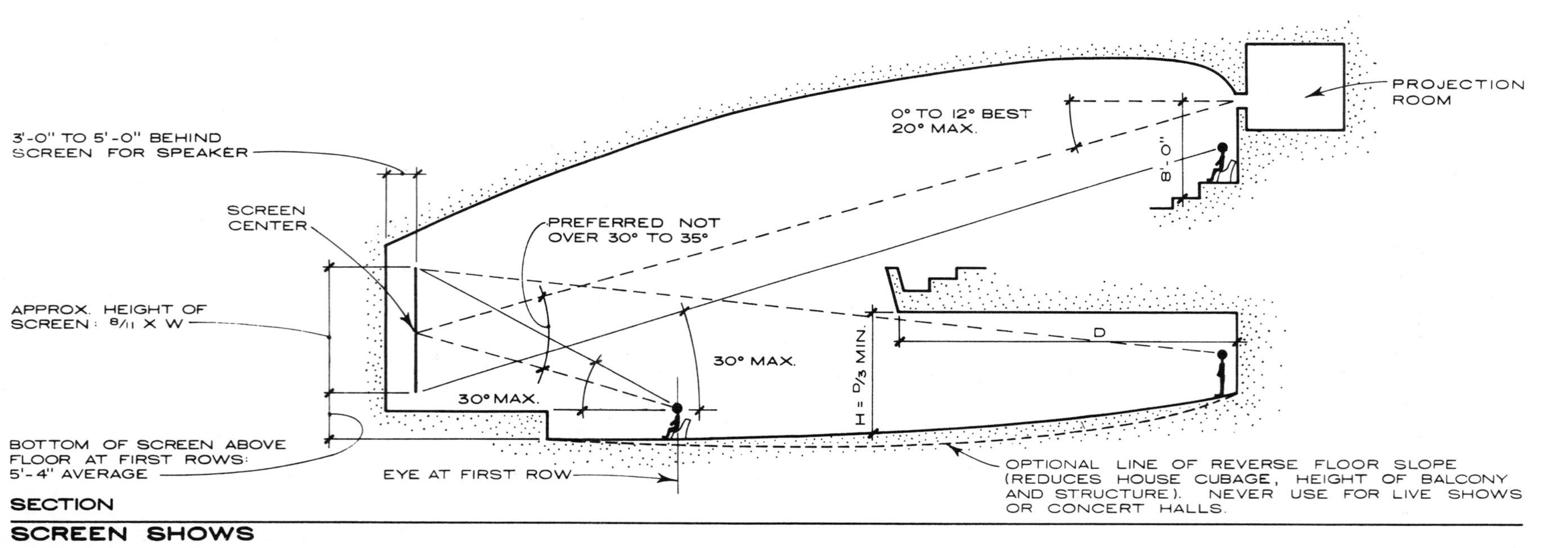

Figure 2.32 Reprinted from C. G. Ramsey and H. R. Sleeper, *Architectural Graphic Standards*, 6th ed., American Institute of Architects, John Wiley & Sons, 1970.

In the design of windows, it should be remembered that visual contact with the outside world serves as a stimulus to recovery and a source of energy to the patients. Electric lighting conditions are also important in creating a comfortable environment. The mechanical installations of a hospital are voluminous and complex; a very frequent approach to organization is to have one mechanical floor sandwiched between two floors of wards or clinics.

Theaters

Like a hotel, a theater has a front area that accommodates the audience (guests and visitors) and a backstage part, which is limited to the performers and all supporting staff and facilities (hotel personnel). Figure 2.32 shows a typical organization of these elements. Most important for the design is the relationship of space between audience and stage. A good solution (see, e.g., Figure 2.33) can apply only to a limited number of uses, since each type of performance has specific functional requirements. The big multipurpose auditoriums therefore are not very suitable for theater performances. An auditorium for plays without music can be very small, whereas the reverberation time of musical notes determines the minimum size for concert halls.

The size of the stage is also closely related to the dimensions of the auditorium. For best visibility, the depth of the house should be approximately 5 times the width of the stage, and the width of the house should be about 3 times the width of the stage. A good proportion for the auditorium is

$$\text{depth} = \text{width} \times 2$$

In real numbers, the depth of the theater auditorium should not exceed 75 feet, although today performances are given in much bigger auditoriums where seats are as far as 200 feet away from the stage. At this distance, however, the visibility of the actors is greatly reduced for many spectators.

The same visibility considerations that influence the seating arrangements also apply in the design of parking facilities, as are illustrated in the section that follows, where the maximum vertical angle for the spectator's field of vision is found to be limited to 30°. On the horizontal plane these factors determine the curvature of rows and the staggering of seats.

Fire laws make aisles necessary, but they take away valuable viewing space, especially if the size of the auditorium requires a center aisle. An alternative is the so-called continental seating arrangement, where wide spaces between continuous rows permit fast clearing in the transverse direction.

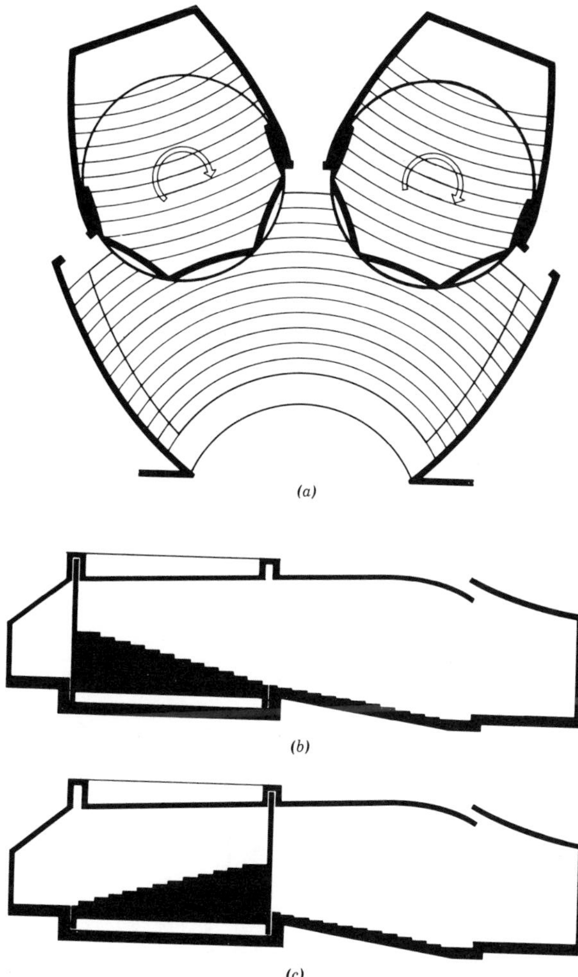

Figure 2.33 (*a*) A typical TDA floor plan. Simplified section views of the TDA section turned toward the stage to form one auditorium with maximum seating capacity (*b*) and turned away from the stage to form a separate lecture hall (*c*). *Source*. Macton Corporation.

Parking Facilities

In some of the building types described in this section the largest portion of structural volume may be required for the storage of cars. Whether ground level parking is chosen, as opposed to multilevel garage structures, is mainly a function of the availability and cost of land. In downtown areas the underground garage may be the only feasible alternative, although it represents the most expensive type of parking structure. The main design consideration for any parking facility is to minimize the driving time to the stall and the walking distance to the entrance. Three hundred feet is considered a maximum walking distance, and larger garages require escalators or elevators.

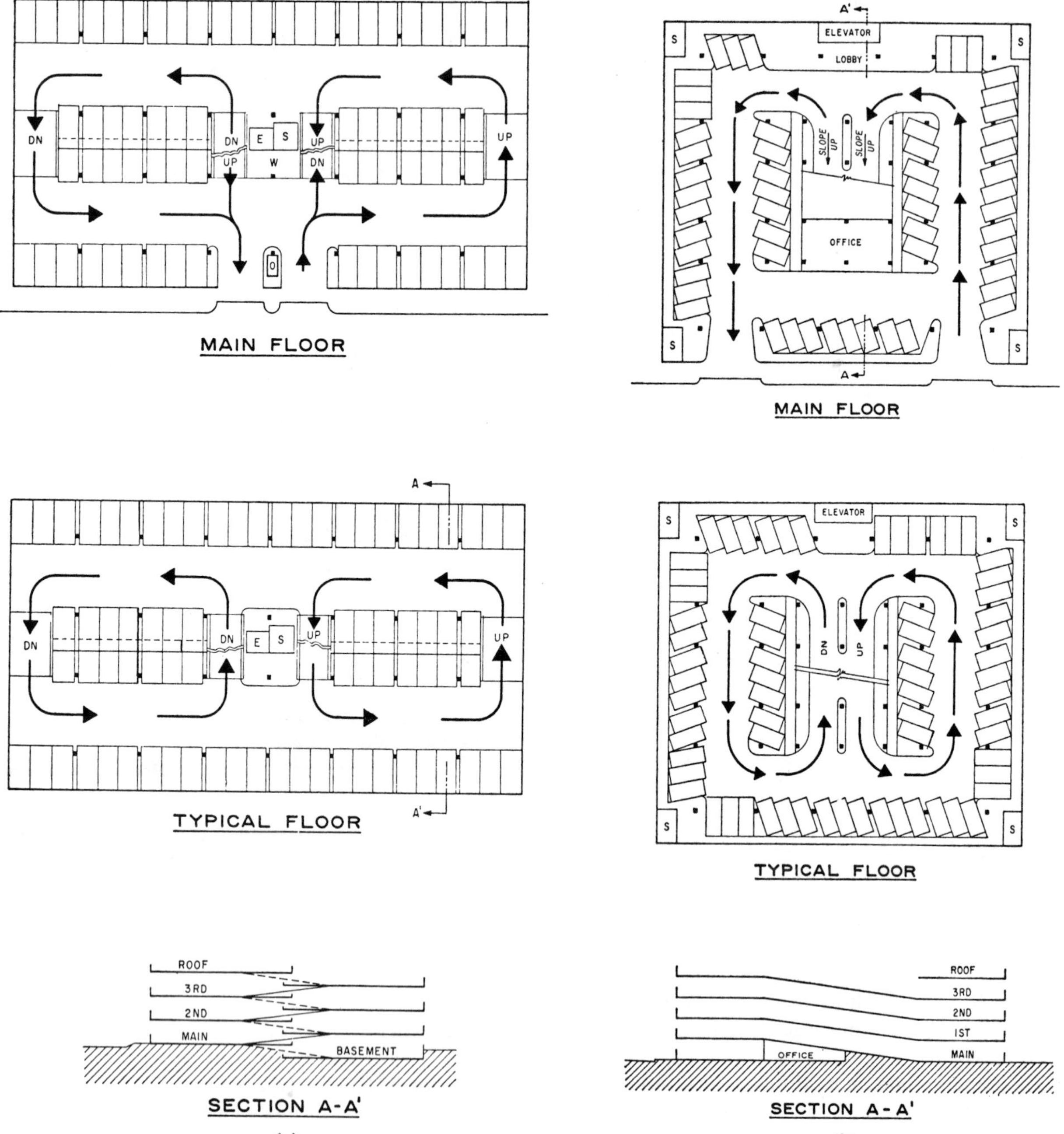

Figure 2.34 Functional plans for parking garages. (*a*) Staggered-floor garage. (*b*) Straight ramp garage. *Source*. American Institute of Steel Construction.

The parking layout depends on whether self-parking or attendant parking is used. The basic dimension of the parking stall, however, remains the same in both cases: namely, a minimum of 9 by 19 feet. End stalls should be at least 10 feet wide, and there may be a number of special stalls for small cars.

The 90° parking scheme uses space most efficiently and is also flexible in terms of driving directions. Ramps connecting parking levels can be straight or can consist of a single or double spiral; the latter is used to separate up- and down-flowing traffic. Ramp grades should not exceed 12% or 7°.

A variety of critical dimensions and angles must enter into the design of a safe and convenient parking structure. These measurements include width of driveways, the radius of ramps, and the ramp approach and departure angles. Additional space is needed to accommodate cars waiting in line, to repair or tow stalled cars, and for the installation of control and fee collection facilities.

The selection of building types given in this section does not include all structures encountered in the field of design, but this sampling should illustrate the process of architectural programming, which always consists of the same basic steps: from the collection of information to the definition of the specific functions of the structure, whereupon the functions are accommodated into the organization of space in an efficient, aesthetic, and economically feasible way.

Hotels and Motels

The three basic types of contemporary hotels are the transient hotel, as it is found in the downtown areas of our cities; the resort hotel, which caters mainly to vacationers away from the cities; and the motor inn or motel, usually located along highways and at the peripheries of cities. Each type serves a different segment of the hospitality industry, and all three have different standards and facilities.

A motel provides the guest with a bedroom, a bathroom, and a parking space. It may or may not have a restaurant or coffee shop. Service areas are reduced to an office, a laundry, and a supply room.

A hotel has an area in front that is accessible to the guests and a back part containing all the supporting

SUNRIVER LODGE
Bend, Oregon
Architects: Rockrise, Odermatt, Mountjoy, Amis
Photo: E. Lee

facilities, of which the guest should be minimally aware. Dining rooms, lounges, bars, beauty parlors, and stores belong to the front; administration, supply kitchen, laundry, housekeeping, storage, and maintenance are functions organized in the back of the hotel.

In the programming of the front part, the architect tries to make everything easily accessible to the guests. The location of such facilities as reception desk, elevators, bar, and restaurant should be apparent even to new arrivals, to avoid confusion and disorientation. Corridors are usually 6 feet wide, and their length should not exceed 100 feet.

Guest rooms vary greatly in size and amenities, from a minimum-size motel room to a suite in a luxury hotel. In an average situation, the dimensions are determined by the number and sizes of beds. A standard width is 12 ½ feet, corresponding to a length between 14 and 20 feet. A single bed measures 3 × 6 ½ feet, a king size bed is 6 × 7 feet. Bathroom sizes and closet space also vary with the type of hotel and should be designed for the specific needs of the patrons expected. Each floor of guest rooms is connected with the back part of the hotel by means of a service elevator, which is accessible only through the supply and service room, thus helping to separate the circulation patterns of guests and hotel staff.

Housing for the Elderly

Many elderly Americans are poorly prepared for retirement and have no means for producing incomes other than Social Security payments of $400 a month, or $4800 a year. About 3.3 million Americans live on incomes below the individual poverty level of $2730 a year. Such deprivation of financial stability, as well as loss of role status as a producing worker in the larger society, often creates a passive, dependent nature closed to seeking personal opportunities. This serves to perpetuate social opinions that alienate and segregate the elderly from the mainstream of society.

It is also true that out of 23 million Americans, 12 million are physically handicapped with chronic ailments that leave them confined to nursing homes, requiring constant attention. More than 1 million are complete invalids who have no comprehension of their environment. To experience losses with respect to one's health—the senses of sound, sight, touch, and taste, and the loss of loved ones and friends—can compound feelings of confusion, uncertainty, and isolation. Facing this stage in life creates abruptly an entirely new structure of life's processes, mostly misunderstood and frightening to the individual.

Given these data indicating the financially and physically restrictive facts of life for the over-65 age group, the establishment of housing requirements calls for a sense of social inquiry as well as design and environmental aesthetics. Ideally, the elderly would remain as an integral part of the family and the community. This is often the case in ethnic or older established villages, where there is a large network of familial relations and extended families. The elderly are a recognized segment, even the elite of some cultures, and financial and health limitations are absorbed within this framework of society.

Since World War II, the population has increased threefold, and medical and technological advances have created a longer life expectancy. The American family has been mobilized into cross-country moves; better jobs, greater opportunities, and more money have destroyed the stability of the extended family. The elderly who tend to remain in their home towns with their religious and friendship ties can find familiar resources needed to make the transition easily into a contented and productive old age. Those who do follow their families on interstate moves generally find fewer friends with common mutual interests. They desire a fixed location where they can rebuild friendship patterns and reestablish family relations that are independent in spirit and action.

There is a shortage of housing for the elderly resident, and the programming and design process must display social awareness as well as adaptations for the physically handicapped. As a group, the elderly wish to choose their surroundings for as long as possible, and it is for their ease of adjustment, as well as for their sociability, safety, and comfort, that the effort to accommodate this population is being made by builders and developers. Obviously there are differences in incomes, and the funding for housing comes from several sources, private or governmental.

During site selection, whether the target area be urban (see Table 2.31), suburban, or a small town neighborhood, special attention should be paid to availability of services, pedestrian walkways, lighting and security systems, transportation, and scale (building mass and height relationships).

In an urban community the crime rate may have to be considered when designing additional features to implement a housing project, such as security precautions or proximity to full-service shopping. Health care and services would be more readily available in this type of community, as would clusters of elderly populations already present. Opportunities for community involvements would already be available in existing facilities such as museums and historical societies, libraries, churches, community park systems, and adult education programs.

Table 2.31 Open Space–Density Recommendations

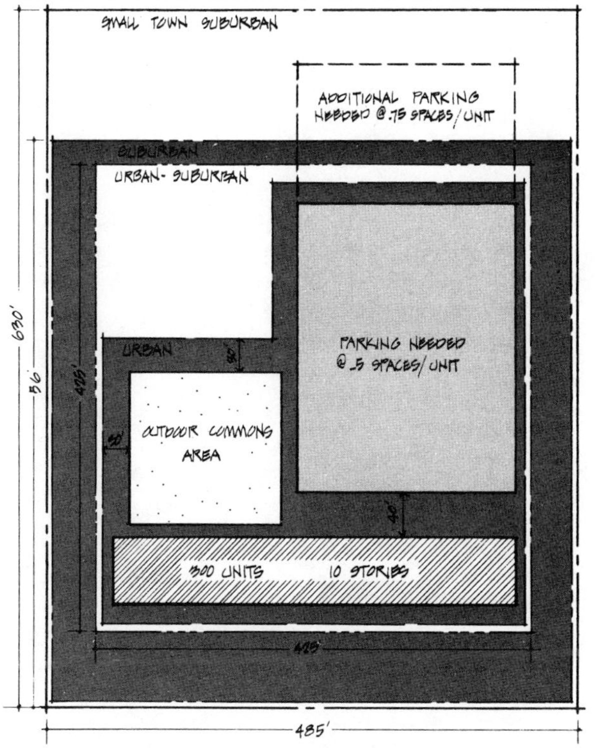

GRAPHIC OPEN SPACE/DENSITY COMPARISON

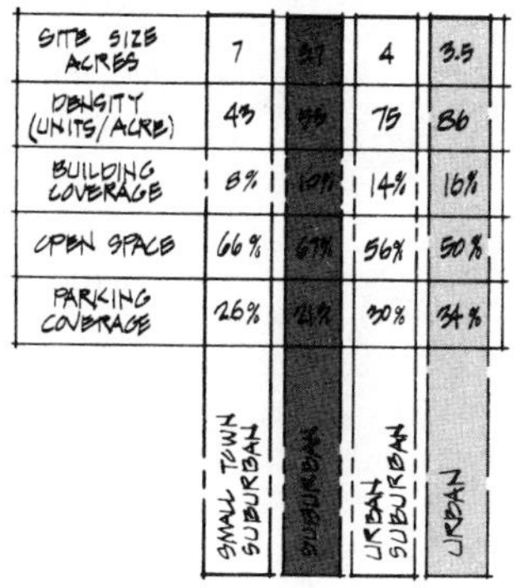

NUMERICAL OPEN SPACE/DENSITY COMPARISON

	SMALL TOWN		SUBURBAN		URBAN-SUBURBAN		URBAN	
100 UNITS	4 Stories	8 Stories	4 Stories	8 Stories	4 Stories	8 Stories	4 Stories	8 Stories
Site size (acres)	7	7	5.7	5.7	4	4	2	2
Density (units/acre)	14	14	18	18	25	25	50	50
Building coverage	6%	3%	8%	4%	11%	6%	22%	12%
Open space	83%	86%	81%	85%	74%	79%	58%	69%
Parking coverage	11%*	11%*	11% †	11% †	15% †	15% †	20% ††	20% ††
200 UNITS	6 Stories	10 Stories	6 Stories	10 Stories	6 Stories	10 Stories	6 Stories	10 Stories
Site size (acres)	7	7	5.7	5.7	4	4	3	3
Density (units/acre)	29	29	35	35	50	50	67	67
Building coverage	9%	5%	11%	6%	15%	9%	20%	12%
Open space	68%	72%	68%	73%	55%	61%	53%	61%
Parking coverage	23%*	23%*	21% †	21% †	30% †	30% †	27% ††	27% ††
300 UNITS	8 Stories	12 Stories	8 Stories	12 Stories	8 Stories	12 Stories	8 Stories	12 Stories
Site size (acres)	7	7	5.7	5.7	4	4	3.5	3.5
Density (units/acre)	43	43	53	53	75	75	86	86
Building coverage	10%	6%	12%	8%	17%	11%	19%	13%
Open space	56%	60%	56%	60%	38%	44%	47%	53%
Parking coverage	34%*	34%*	32% †	32% †	45% †	45% †	34% ††	34% ††

*1.0 spaces/unit † .75 spaces/unit †† .50 spaces/unit

Source. Isaac Green, Bernard E. Fedewa, Charles A. Johnston, William M. Jackson, and Howard L. Deardorff, *Housing for the Elderly*, Van Nostrand Reinhold Company, 1974.

HOUSING FOR THE ELDERLY
Winthrop, Massachusetts
Architect: Joan E. Goody, Goody, Clancy & Associates
Photo: Steve Rosenthal

Suburban neighborhood sites usually fall in residential districts on the outer edges of a large town. In this case the closeness of service centers depends more on the public transportation system and the management and administrative abilities of the housing development.

Sites located in small towns need to fit quietly into the existing neighborhood, and they must have a sufficient market demand to ensure funding feasibility. The elderly tenants need a special kind of small town background in order to keep occupied in a slower paced environment that does not seek to entertain its citizens quite as much as would an urban setting.

Given the foregoing general types of regional community setting for site selection, we can begin to define particular housing facilities. Note that nursing homes and institutions are omitted here and should be investigated further by medical services architects. Keep in mind the idea that there is still room for the architect and the city planner to devise other types and methods for housing the elderly; creative attempts at realizing different life-

HOUSING FOR THE ELDERLY
Winthrop, Massachusetts
Architect: Joan E. Goody, Goody, Clancy & Associates
Photo: Steve Rosenthal

styles and sociological needs in this age group are still evolving.

Living spaces for the elderly should not be much different from those provided for any other age group, and indeed they should have cross-sectional marketability. Adequate resident and visitor parking space must be incorporated into the design. Special attention must be paid to hardware and other designs that facilitate movement accessibility and adaptability for the physically handicapped, as in ramps for wheelchairs and support bars in bathrooms.

Tenants must be given choices in living situations and a given community should have a range of housing types; within a given development, a range of unit types should be available. The following housing categories are defined:

1 *Housing for the Independent Elderly.* This category includes those who are independent physically, able to provide food for themselves, and generally self-sufficient in life-style. Housing tends to be in self-contained units, such as houses or highrise apartments, with a possibility for a community center for social activities. Mixed in with this group can be family housing, giving some age integration. Almost as a rule, the elderly in this group have the means for maintaining an automobile and are able to drive. Some minimal independent living supportive systems might be planned on—for example, proximity to postal systems, laundry facilities, public toilets, trash facility, public telephones, food shopping centers, medical care, and tenant storage.

2 *Mixed Housing for the Independent/Dependent Elderly*. Provisions must be made for congregate facilities and services for persons who desire independent residential accommodations as well as those who require some measure of assistance in their everyday activities. Minimally, supportive services include a common dining area, plus separate kitchenettes, housekeeping aids, personal health services, and other services as described later in connection with recreational and social activities.
3 *Housing for the Dependent Elderly*. The occupants depend on minimal support systems, short of nursing home care. Facilities are in congregate form and are available in on-site locations. The basic services are a central food service, social services and referral consultations, medical outpatient clinic, housekeeping assistance, central laundry service, and management office space.

The overall spatial requirements of the site should allow enough room to accommodate a common indoor/outdoor facility that supports recreational and social activities if one is not already available in the immediate community. On a sociological perceptual level, this facility is one of the most important of those noted here. The elderly individual needs a means for overcoming loneliness, the ability to express personal feelings and knowledge, and involvement in community action. A facility that answers these needs is extremely dependent on an ongoing, effective management system that reflects awareness of varied cultural habits and traditions of the housing population.

The selection of activities that fill an elderly person's life include such mass activities as dances, movies, entertainment programs, information meetings, plays, bands, instrumental music groups, and chorus groups. Medium-sized and smaller groups are involved in crafts such as painting, sewing, sculpture, ceramics, woodwork, and shop hobbies.

Poetry reading sessions, discussion groups, and educational study groups tend to be popular, as well as mandatory for socialization. Table games include cards, backgammon, crossword puzzles, jigsaw puzzles, checkers, chess, and pool. Libraries and exercise lounges are a must in the design development as well as on-site commercial beauty and barber shops.

Outside recreational areas need to be large and flexible enough to provide active sports like shuffleboard or bocce ball, exercise classes for dance or yoga, and sedentary activities that call for a comfortable, shaded place where there is some element of privacy.

Mobile Parks: The New Way of Living

Mobile homes and parks fill a need for people who want to take their house with them when they move about. For some, the movement is connected with occupations, such as construction work. In other cases, the movement is for recreational purposes.

In the mobile homes and parks business, some small firms supply products and services to manufacturers of mobile home vehicles or to mobile home park operators and residents. In addition, more than 7000 dealers sell mobile homes, and other people operate park sites for these homes on wheels.

Some of the parks are for mobile homes—used for permanent, year-round residences, ranging from 10 to 24 feet in width and from 32 to 70 feet in length. Other parks cater to recreational vehicles, which provide portable housing for vacation or temporary dwellings; these vehicles are usually less than 32 feet long and no more than 8 feet wide.

Recreational vehicles are produced in a wide variety of types, sizes, and styles. Thus buyers can select the vehicle—a travel trailer, a pickup coach, a motorized home, or a camping trailer—that suits their pocketbooks and traveling needs. Then a trip can be planned, routed to park sites best suited to serve the particular recreational vehicle.

Mobile homes, the other type of home-built-on-wheels, are the larger, more elaborate units. They are designed on a chassis without a permanent foundation, to be transported to a permanent dwelling site. When the mobile home is placed on supporting foundations at a park site and connected to utility facilities, it becomes a permanent home. Often a mobile home is towed by a commercial carrier to the park site. The movement of mobile homes, whether over highways or on railroad flatcars, is controlled by state highway regulations. More than 53% of the mobile homes in use are longer than 60 feet, and 85% are 12 feet wide. Mobile homes offer the buyer a wide choice of sizes, self-contained equipment, storage space, and built-in furniture, in many different materials.

Originally mobile homes were purchased by people in construction work, military service, and other occupations that call for frequent moves. More recently, however, young married couples and retirees, attracted by the relatively low cost of completely furnished and equipped housing accommodations, have become the two largest groups of owners of mobile homes. Mobile homes represent about 86% of all single-family homes sold in the low-cost housing market throughout the nation. This expanding market is demanding the development of an increased number of mobile home parks.

Parks for Mobile Homes

Not only more but better mobile home park communities are needed. Some of the existing parks should be remodeled to accommodate the newer and larger units. A recent survey indicated that the lack of convenient parks with adequate parking space is, for many, the biggest drawback to ownership of a mobile home.

Some of the newer mobile home parks are solely for senior citizens. Other parks are divided into special-interest areas—for example, one for retirees and another for families with children.

Type of Park

The type of park is determined largely by the residents it serves. The park facilities perform two basic functions: (1) housing, mainly for employed people who want convenient access to work areas, and (2) community service, often serving retired, semiretired, or elderly residents in locations that offer relaxed living.

Park developers need to ascertain why mobile home owners locate in various places. In a recent survey, most of the owners said they rented space in parks that were convenient to work, to schools, to shopping areas, or to recreation areas. Others claimed that park services were the most important factor for choosing the park, and some owners settled their mobile homes in areas where they found people with similar interests. Still others gave privacy and economy as their reasons for renting park spaces.

Location

Mobile home parks are located in areas suited to multiple housing developments rather than commercial zones. Although normally parks are located on flat lands, some hilly land can be developed into satisfactory park areas. Land areas subject to excessive noise, smoke, odors, poor drainage, or flood threats should be avoided as park sites.

Before beginning to develop a new park site or to remodel an existing park, the surrounding community should be studied carefully. What kind of access roads are available? Is the terrain of the park site land capable of being developed economically? Are adequate community service facilities available?

Some other location factors to be considered are (1) the number, type, and condition of present mobile home parks in the area, including number of parking spaces; (2) local occupancy and rental rates in these parks; (3) businesses and residential areas in the community; (4) number of sales and registrations of mobile homes in the surrounding city or county; (5) present standards for streets and future highway planning; (6) public attitude, zoning laws, and tax rates; (7) public utilities and rates; and (8) pattern of community development. In addition, overall economical factors should be studied to determine the feasibility of a proposed park.

Parking Spaces and Services

Parking spaces should be large enough to accommodate mobile home units of a variety of sizes and shapes. For homes that range from 60 to 70 feet long and from 10 to 24 feet wide, experts say that a minimum of 3200 square feet is needed per space site. Older parks contained 14 to 16 sites per acre, but new parks are averaging only 6 to 8 sites per acre. Also, local ordinances may prescribe minimum space requirements.

As a rule, a park should have not less than 50 spaces for the following reasons:

1 Construction cost per space is usually less when 50 or more sites are developed. Parks of 100 to 200 parking spaces are preferable. A greater number of spaces also permits a greater per-space annual revenue. If an FHA loan is contemplated for park development, at least 50 spaces are required.
2 Mobile home owners want recreational facilities such as swimming pools, clubhouses, and children's playgrounds.
3 Sound business management is essential to a park's success, and the larger the park, the more readily owners can afford competent personnel.

Health Facilities

Facilities such as sewage disposal, provision of garbage receptacles and collection, private police protection, clubhouses, toilets and showers, and laundry facilities are installed under the auspices of state or local inspection agencies. Most states have regulations to provide continuing health control. Before starting construction, park developers should learn the local health department's regulations on construction specifications and park operation. Some standards are set by federal regulating agencies; others are found in local ordinances, such as building and zoning codes. The prospective park owner may contact the state or regional mobile home association for further information about the various regulations.

Management

Managing a mobile home park is a full-time job that requires sound business practices. Parks of 100 spaces or less can generally be run by a husband and wife team. Parks with more than 100 spaces often require special management personnel and a maintenance man.

Shopping Centers

Throughout history villages and towns have had market squares, and streets with a concentration of stores and other retail facilities. Such an area was called *agora* in Greece, *bazaar* in Turkey, and *casbah* in Morocco. The shape of today's shopping center reflects the intention to give retailers maximum accessibility to private cars. This led to clusters of stores, surrounded by parking that covers 3 to 5 times more ground than the buildings. Recently the advantages of pedestrian circulation within the center were rediscovered, and the "new" concept of malls and courts is reminiscent of the medieval marketplaces.

According to the extension of its catchment area, a shopping center is classified as a regional, community, or neighborhood facility. The tenant mix (i.e., the proportions in which stores for apparel, food, gifts, etc., are mixed with restaurants and coffee shops) determines its character as either a general or a specialty shopping center. A specialty shopping center should offer a stimulating atmosphere that invites people who did not plan to buy anything to browse and stroll, tempting them to make so-called impulse purchases. In the specialty type, then, the tenant mix favors gift and import stores.

A shopping mall may have one or more levels. Some malls are open, but most shopping centers constructed today feature some climate control or are completely enclosed and heated or air conditioned. A mall is between 30 and 40 feet wide; the length seldom exceeds 800 feet. Store fronts are 20 to 30 feet wide, and depths are most commonly between 120 and 140 feet, unless an L-shaped store wraps around a little shop in the front. The ceiling height generally used today is 12 feet. Parking ratios now required are five to six parking stalls for 1000 square feet of retail area. In downtown areas serviced by mass transit, this ratio can be lowered 3 : 1000.

Vehicular traffic should be completely separate from the pedestrian circulation on the mall. This sometimes requires either separate service areas for pickup, deliveries, trash collection, and maintenance trucks, or service roads and tunnels, if below-grade parking is featured.

THE BROADWAY
Riverside, California
Architects: Charles Luckman Associates
Photo: B. Korab

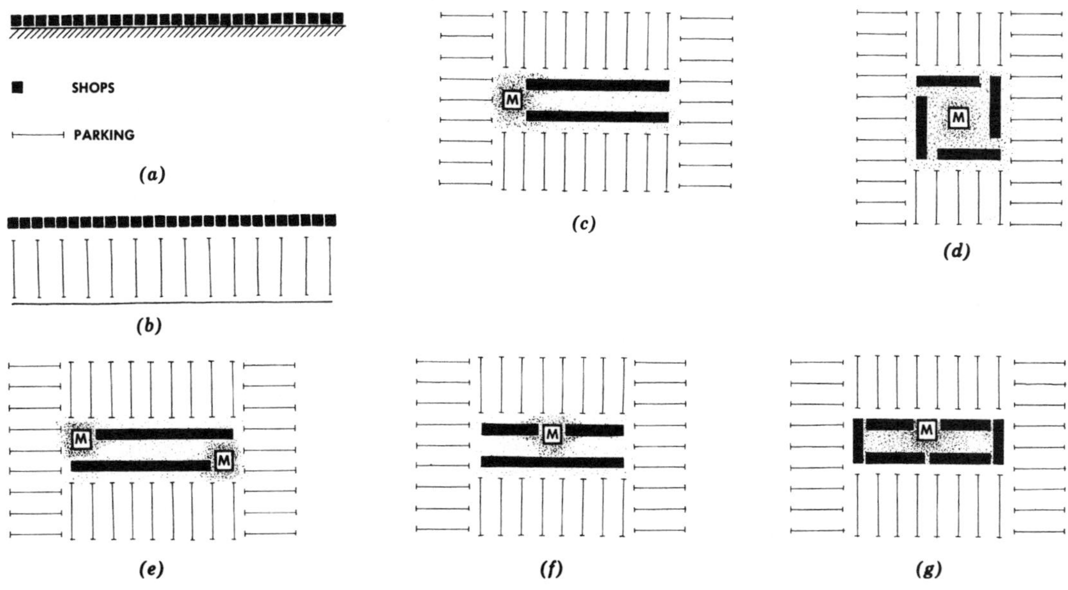

Figure 2.35 Regional shopping center types. (*a*) Strip center with curb parking. (*b*) Strip center with off-street parking. (*c*) Mall center with only one magnet. (*d*) Cluster-type center. (*e*) Double-strip center with off-street parking. (*f*) Mall center with magnet centrally placed. (*g*) "Introverted" center. *Source*. Joseph de Chiara and John Hancock Callender, *Time-Saver Standards for Building Types*, McGraw-Hill Book Company, 1974.

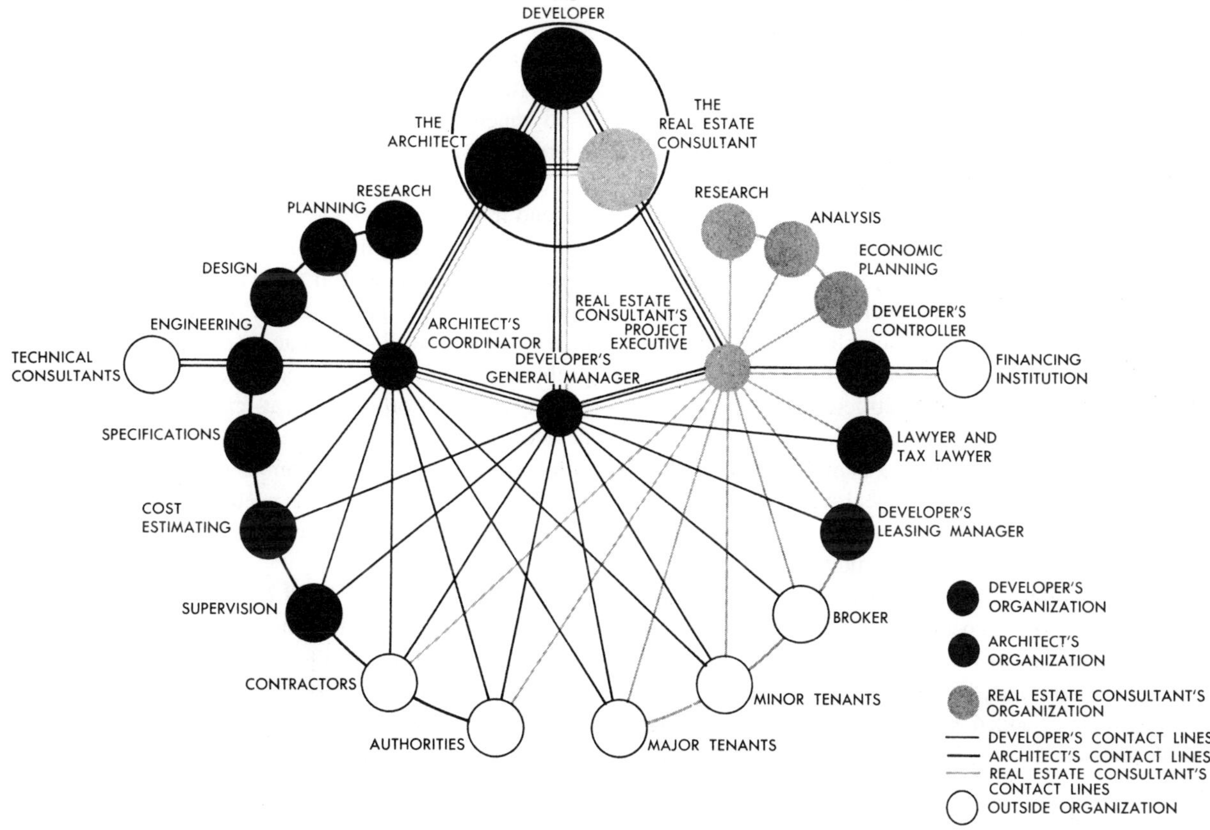

Figure 2.36 The planning team. *Source*. Joseph de Chiara and John Hancock Callender, *Time-Saver Standards for Building Types*, McGraw-Hill Book Company, 1974.

4 INFLUENCE OF SITE CONDITIONS

Since the physical conditions of the site, such as climate, topography and drainage, geology and soil conditions, all have an impact on design and building costs, they are evaluated directly after a site has been selected.

Climate

For every location, it is possible to distinguish between the general climate of the area and the microclimate of a specific site. The characteristics of the general climate can be derived from statistics giving, for example, range and distribution of temperatures, hours and direction of sunshine, wind orientation and velocity, and data on precipitation and humidity. The microclimate is a local variant of these conditions that results from the effects of specific topography, existing structures, rivers, lakes, ground cover, and from the site's elevation.

The range of temperature and humidity within which people in Western civilizations feel comfortable is relatively narrow. It is generally assumed to be between 70 and 80°F and 30 to 50% humidity. Ventilation or mechanical cooling will be needed if higher temperatures prevail, and if the temperature drops below this range, we resort to heating or we seek additional solar radiation. If the relative humidity lies outside the "comfort" range, moisture must be added or removed from the air to maintain desired conditions. It is the goal of the architect to create this zone of comfort, not only by mechanical means of heating and cooling systems, but by means of building orientation, surface materials and window modification, landscaping, and controlled sun exposure and shading.

Orientation. Rooms and glass areas in structures should be oriented to avoid excessive solar radiation in the summer and to maximize winter solar radiation. In the Northern Hemisphere this is best achieved with an orientation slightly east of south, since the south side receives more sun in the winter than during summer. East and west sides should be without major glass areas, since low morning and afternoon sun in the summer can create excessive heat gain and glare. Such unwanted radiation is magnified near the highly reflective surface of the ocean or of a lake. Fenestration for artists' studios, galleries, and so on, should be facing north, since this side of the building receives a minimum of radiation.

The architect's decisions on building orientation and fenestration in the final design, however, reflect consideration of many more factors, including the views, traffic patterns, and the aesthetic form of inner and outer building space.

Fenestration. Windows modify the relation of inside spaces to the outside in terms of light, view, solar heat, and ventilation. A visual connection with the outside is very desirable for both living and working spaces, and most people will feel less psychological strain and discomfort in rooms with windows. For air circulation, most mid- and highrise buildings today rely on mechanical systems only. Openable windows, however, may be used much more in the future as the conservation of energy becomes a more highly weighted factor.

The heat gain and loss characteristics of a building depend mainly on its window areas. Solar energy entering a building through glass surfaces can become a major natural heating element in the winter. However the low insulating factor of glass—about 20 times lower than that of an insulated wall—also causes a rapid heat loss. This problem can be met with modifications such as multiple glazing, heat-absorbing or heat-reflecting glass, shading devices, and window areas that can be opened for ventilation. In terms of the economics of a structure, the desirable features of glass areas need to be weighed against their high initial and maintenance costs.

The Sun's Path. For a full consideration of the effect on a structure of the sun, the architect must know the sun's specific annual path for the subject location. Figure 2.37, taken at the latitude of Chicago, shows the four characteristic days of the year (i.e., winter solstice, vernal equinox, autumnal equinox, and summer solstice). The inclination of the sun's path in this diagram is the most important variable. Not only does it vary with the seasons, but also with latitudes. In addition, because of the sun's lower average position in the northern sky and its higher path in the south, the heat transmission of walls

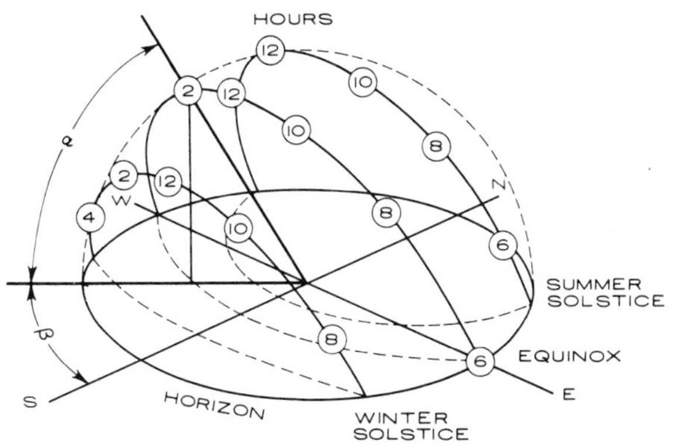

Figure 2.37 *Source*. Reprinted from C. G. Ramsey and H. R. Sleeper, *Architectural Graphic Standards*, 6th ed., American Institute of Architects, John Wiley & Sons, 1970.

is most important in the north, whereas in the south the architect is concerned with the heat transmission of roofs.

Sun Controls. The building elements most widely used for sun control are overhangs, fins, and louvers. If designed properly, they block the worst of the sun's heat and glare without obstructing the view or making the rooms much darker. They may be part of the building's structure, such as cantilevered decks and roofs, or they may consist of fixed or adjustable elements attached to the structure. Either horizontal or vertical members may be used, or both may be combined in a grid of sunbreakers. Sun shading elements should control the sun's effect in the summer, yet admit full solar radiation during the winter months. All shields and louvers are more effective if used on the building's exterior than if used for absorption and reflection of sun rays inside. Outside, however, all sun controls are on a larger scale and may have a considerable effect on the aesthetics of the building.

Sun shading elements can reduce heat gain very drastically, thus cut down the initial and operating costs of air conditioning systems by 15% and more. They are very rarely used on highrise buildings today, however, because of the high installation cost, maintenance problems, and adverse past experiences with inadequately designed devices.

Figure 2.38 illustrates how vertical fins and baffles work. Vertical fins are mainly used to block out east and west radiation; vertical baffles, that is, elements parallel to the walls of the building, are effective for southern exposure as well. Over the years, standardized and conventional sun shading elements have always proved to be more effective than unusual mechanical devices.

Interior sun shading devices have the advantage of easy maintenance, but shades, blinds, and curtains always take away more light and view, yet are less effective as exterior devices in reducing heat gains.

Deciduous trees can be very effective in shading low buildings, since their leaves block the unwanted summer sun, and in winter the bare branches let in desirable solar radiation. If placed properly, they can also protect the structure from winter winds without stopping the cooling (usually differently prevailing) summer breezes. Apart from their function as sun- and wind-controlling elements, trees can also block out excessive noise, create spaces of privacy, purify the air, and enhance the aesthetics of a building.

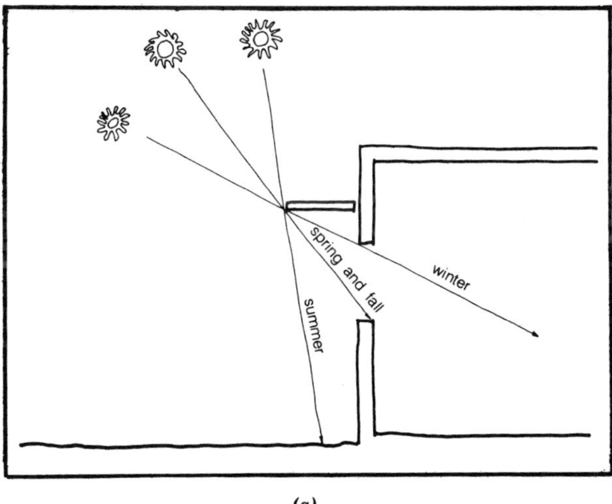

(*a*)

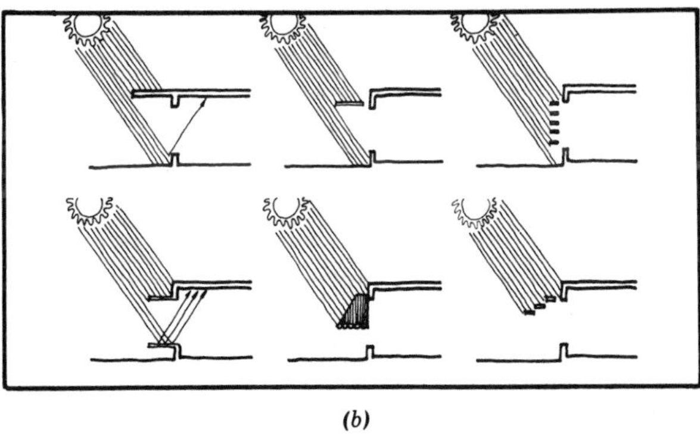

(*b*)

Figure 2.38 (*a*) The sizing of a fixed shading device. (*b*) Horizontal shading devices. *Source*. Jim Leckie, Gil Masters, Harry Whitehouse, and Lily Young, *Other Homes and Garbage*, Sierra Club Books, 1975.

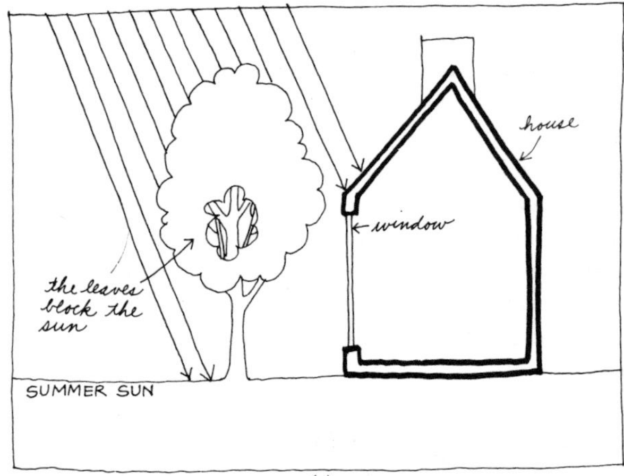

(a)

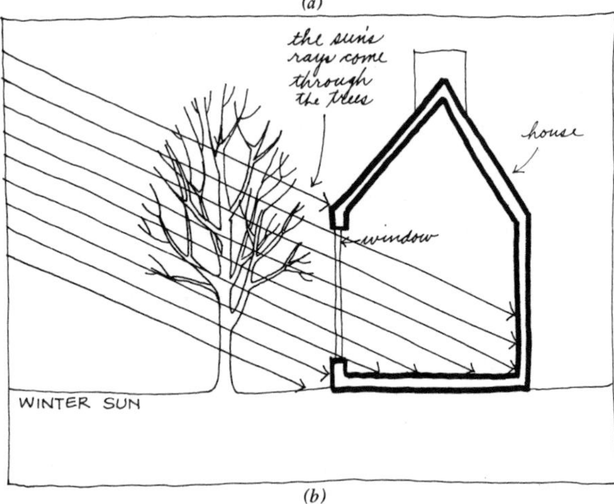

(b)

Figure 2.39 *Source*. Les Walker and Jeff Milstein, *Designing Houses*, Overlook Press, 1976.

Materials. Insulation of walls and roofs reduces both heat gains in summer and heat losses in winter. In zones with high temperature variations from night to day, concrete or masonry walls will preserve the coolness of the night into the middle of the day and at night will radiate the heat stored in the afternoon. Therefore the use of heavy walls creates a more balanced condition and is very effective in hot and dry places like Phoenix. In areas like Miami, on the other hand, where the temperatures do not vary much between night and day, and the air is hot and humid, no heat storage is required. But materials with good light insulation are very important. An area with temperate climate, such as New York City, needs only a moderate amount of insulation in walls, except for the west side of buildings, where heavy insulation should be installed to avert heat gains from the afternoon sun. Heavy insulation in all walls gives the best performance in cool areas like Montana.

Slabs are usually not insulated in warm to moderate areas, but in temperate to cool areas rigid insulation material should be used at the edges of all slabs above grade to prevent heat transmission from inside.

Each climate zone has special material deterioration problems, For example, wood should be exposed to air in hot and humid areas to avoid mold and fungi, but it must be protected from extreme dryness in desert areas, where splits and checks are common in exposed lumber. Metals corrode quickly by the sea; thus use of metal outside should be minimized near the ocean.

Mechanical Equipment. Even with a design that maximizes solar heat gain and minimizes heat loss, a heating system will be needed in all cool and temperate areas. To find out how extensive the system will have to be, ascertain the prevailing outdoor winter design temperature, which is an assumed average of temperature lows: in Miami, 40°C; in Los Angeles, 20°C; and in Boston, 0°C.

The indoor design temperature varies with the outdoor temperature (higher in the summer, lower in the winter), but in estimating temperature requirements, the amount of physical activity of the occupants must also be taken into account. Requirements are assumed to be the lowest in gymnasiums and the highest in hospitals. An average value, however, is 75°F.

According to the climate zone in which the building is to be located, the critical function of mechanical equipment is heating, cooling, or dehumidifying. Outside design temperatures that require cooling vary from 85° in Massachusetts to 110° in California.

Solar Heating and Cooling. Systems of heating and cooling with solar energy are still in an experimental state. Many solar heating systems are operational today, although the cooling part is still problematic; a satisfactory solution for a complete system can be expected for the near future, however, and eventually even the supply of electrical energy in buildings may be partially generated from solar radiation.

Winds. Wind patterns and wind loads are of paramount concern to both architect and structural engineer. Data on wind pressures are available for all areas of the United States. The wind pressure increases with the square of the wind velocity. Thus a wind velocity of 30 miles per hour causes a pressure of 4 pounds per square foot. If the velocity doubles to 60 miles, the pressure reaches 16 pounds per square foot.

Our knowledge of wind movements is very limited. Only in recent years have we discovered the design inadequacies of many tall buildings in terms of wind effects. For example, wind patterns divide the wind that passes such buildings into an upward and a downward flow. The flow that goes down on the face of the building creates a vortex of high velocity at the ground level, which can make many plaza designs useless for relaxation. If the ground story is open, it creates a wind tunnel with multiplied velocities.

The change in wind patterns is difficult to anticipate in calculations. Accurate projections are possible only on the basis of simulation tests made in wind tunnels. The architect, however, should research local wind conditions thoroughly in the planning stage, because protection from unwanted winter winds and the use of winds for air circulation in the summer can greatly increase the comfort and economy of the design.

Apart from their influence on climate and comfort, local wind conditions represent one of the major variables in structural engineering. The architect must be aware that the cost of the structural system of a building in an area with high wind loads may be substantially greater than that for a comparable building in another area.

Topography and Drainage

A careful analysis of site topography determines how much of its natural shape can be utilized for the design of structures and traffic patterns. If regrading is required, it should be done in harmony with the surrounding landscape. Cuts and fills should be balanced as far as possible to minimize the movement of soil.

Planned improvements often change the drainage patterns of the site. The new pattern then must be designed to tie in with the natural drainage system of the specific area. The improvements must not block this system, and, if they increase the flow, the system's capacity must be increased as well.

The drainage system must be designed to carry the amount of runoff a site will generate in a storm, that is, the water that does not seep into the ground. Thus runoff is a function of the duration and intensity of a storm, the size of the site, and its porosity, slope, and cover. To determine a value for storm water, the most severe storm of the last 5, 10, 25, or 50 years is taken as an example. For a low-value structure, the 5-year history may be used, but for expensive improvements, such as a new civic center, a 50-year history of storms should be considered.

A slope of at least 0.5 to 1% on the site creates a surface sheet flow. Near the structures, this slope should be at least 2%. The slope of drainage ditches should be between 2 and 10%, and the maximum slope of a grass grade should be 25%, but a ground cover such as ivy makes slopes up to 50% possible. Runoff causes erosion on steeper slopes, and undrained depressions should always be avoided.

The surface sheet flow is often collected in grass swales or paved gutters to protect slopes from erosion. These channels are then connected with underground storm drains or natural drainage systems.

The minimum slope required for underground drainage pipes is 0.3%. Above this grade, the lines remain self-cleansing. In cold areas the lines must be in frostfree depth, which is about 3 to 4 feet. Scouring action may be a problem on very steep slopes, and the architect must investigate to determine whether special designs are needed. A cost-competitive drainage layout uses surface drainage over underground pipes, minimizes grading, and specifies the shortest lines and fewest manholes possible to minimize excavation and material.

To drain a site from underground water, the use of subsurface tile lines with perforations and open joints is most common. Minimum slope requirements are similar to those of storm drains. The capacity of the system depends on the diameter, the perforation, and the joint spacing of the pipes, as well as the permeability of the soil and the depth of the lines. Some maximum slope values are as follows: recreational greens, 3%; walkways next to buildings, 4%; parking areas, 5%; streets, 8%. Site slopes under 4% are called "level"; between 4 and 10% lie the "easy" grades, and the "steep" grades exceed 10%. Foundations and utility connections are more expensive on steep grades. The architect, however, should take advantage of the slope of the site to achieve a design that is harmonious with the topography in terms of split levels and views.

Geology and Soils

Soil Report. The soil report should be prepared by a soils engineer during the architect's first conceptual design studies. Conclusions about the mechanics of the soil are derived from laboratory tests of soil samples, which can be acquired only through test borings. The number of borings needed is sometimes specified in the local building codes for the type of structure planned as well as for the uniformity of the soil. Preliminary borings may be 100 to 400 feet apart. The final borings for a big structure are usually only 50 feet apart in both directions. The borings must reach a firm stratum suitable for funding and must extend into this layer for a minimum of 20 feet.

The test report contains a plot plan indicating the location of each boring. The type of soil in each test probe is recorded in a separate log for each boring. In these logs the soil is classified in the terms of the Unified Soil

Classification System, which contains the following categories:

1 Well graded (a good mix of a variety of grain sizes).
2 Poorly graded (all particles have a uniform size).
3 Highly organic.
4 Fine grained.
5 Coarse grained.

These classes contain the range of particle sizes from gravel to sand and silt, to clay with a grain of less than 0.002 mm in diameter.

The results of the laboratory tests are used to determine the bearing capacity of the soil, the amount of settlement under load, and the impact of earthquakes. Particle size distribution, moisture, and density are the variables that influence the inner cohesion and friction of the probe. A triaxial compression test together with cyclic loading to stimulate earthquakes is used to estimate the shear strength of the soil. The final soil report, which also recommends the foundation systems possible under the prevailing conditions and their safe bearing capacity and minimum foundation depths, summarizes the test results.

Bearing Capacity. The ultimate bearing capacity (BC), as estimated in the laboratory, is the maximum stress to which a soil may be subjected without permitting detrimental settling of the structure. The structural engineers are concerned with the safe bearing capacity, which is the ultimate BC divided by a safety factor of 2 to 4. Good values of safe bearing capacities, as found in well-drained gravels and sands, are between 3000 and 12,000 pounds per square foot. In silts and clays, average values range from 1000 to 4000 pounds, whereas bedrock has a safe bearing capacity as high as 100,000 pounds per square foot.

The safe bearing capacity also determines the area of a spread footing (footing that delivers the load in direct bearing to the supporting stratum). This area is derived by dividing the load by the safe bearing capacity. For example:

$$\text{load} = 400 \text{ kilopounds}$$

$$\text{safe bearing capacity} = 2 \text{ kilopounds per square foot}$$

$$\frac{400}{2} = 200 \text{ square feet}$$

Table 2.32 gives allowable soil bearing pressures. Table 2.33 describes various soils and classifies them in terms of their value as foundation materials.

Expansive Soils. A change in moisture content of soils such as silts and clays can cause shrinking and swelling; the resulting upward forces can damage foundations and ground floor slabs. Soils exhibiting these characteristics are called expansive soils. Where such conditions prevail, the perimeter footing must be extended into strata with constant moisture. Damages can also be averted with special treatment of foundation excavations. Sometimes the footings require special reinforcement.

Table 2.32 Allowable Soil Bearing Pressures

Soil material	Tons per sq ft	Notes
Hard sound rock	60	No unusual seam structure
Medium hard rock	40	
Intermediate rock	20	
Soft rock	8	
Hardpan	12	Well cemented
Hardpan	8	Poorly cemented
Gravel soils	10	Compact, well graded
Gravel soils	8	Compact with more than 10% gravel
Gravel soils	6	Loose, poorly graded
Gravel soils	4	Loose, mostly sand
Sand soils	3 to 6	10% of blow count on sampling spoon per ft penetration
Fine sand	2 to 4	
Clay soils	5	Hard
Clay soils	2	Medium
Silt soils	3	Dense
Silt soils	1½	Medium
Fills and soft soils	....	By load test only

Source. Frederick S. Merritt, *Building Construction Handbook*, McGraw-Hill Book Company.

Table 2.33 Soil Types and Various Properties of Each

DIVISION	SYMBOLS			SOIL DESCRIPTION	VALUE AS A FOUNDATION MATERIAL	FROST ACTION	DRAINAGE
	LETTER	HATCHING	COLOR				
GRAVEL AND GRAVELLY SOILS	GW		Red	Well graded Gravel, or Gravel-Sand mixture, little or no Fines	Excellent	None	Excellent
	GP		Red	Poorly graded Gravel, or Gravel-Sand mixtures, little or no Fines	Good	None	Excellent
	GM		Yellow	Silty Gravels, Gravel-Sand-Silt mixtures	Good	Slight	Poor
	GC		Yellow	Clayey-Gravels, Gravel-Clay-Sand Mixtures	Good	Slight	Poor
SAND AND SANDY SOILS	SW		Red	Well-graded Sands, or Gravelly Sands, little or no Fines	Good	None	Excellent
	SP		Red	Poorly Graded Sands, or Gravelly Sands, little or no Fines	Fair	None	Excellent
	SM		Yellow	Silty Sands, Sand-Silt mixtures	Fair	Slight	Fair
	SC		Yellow	Clayey Sands, Sand-Clay mixtures	Fair	Medium	Poor
SILTS AND CLAYS LL < 50	ML		Green	Inorganic Silts & Very Fine Sands, Rock Flour, Silty or Clayey Fine Sands, or Clayey Silts with slight plasticity	Fair	Very High	Poor
	CL		Green	Inorganic Silts of low to medium plasticity, Gravelly Sands, Silty Clays, Lean Clays	Fair	Very High	Impervious
	OL		Green	Organic Silt-Clays of low plasticity	Poor	High	Impervious
SILTS AND CLAYS LL > 50	MH		Blue	Inorganic Silts, Micaceous or Diatomaceous Fine Sandy or Silty Soils, Elastic Silts	Poor	Very High	Poor
	CH		Blue	Inorganic Clays of high plasticity, Fat Clays	Very Poor	Medium	Impervious
	OH		Blue	Organic Clays of medium to high plasticity, Organic Silts	Very Poor	Medium	Impervious
HIGHLY ORGANIC SOILS	Pt		Orange	Peat & Other Highly Organic Soils	Not Suitable	Slight	Poor

1. Consult soil engineers and local building codes for allowable soil bearing capacities.
2. L. L. indicates liquid limit.

Smith, Hinchman & Grylls Associates, Inc.; Detroit, Michigan

Reprinted from Frederick S. Merritt, *Building Construction Handbook,* McGraw-Hill Book Company, 1975.

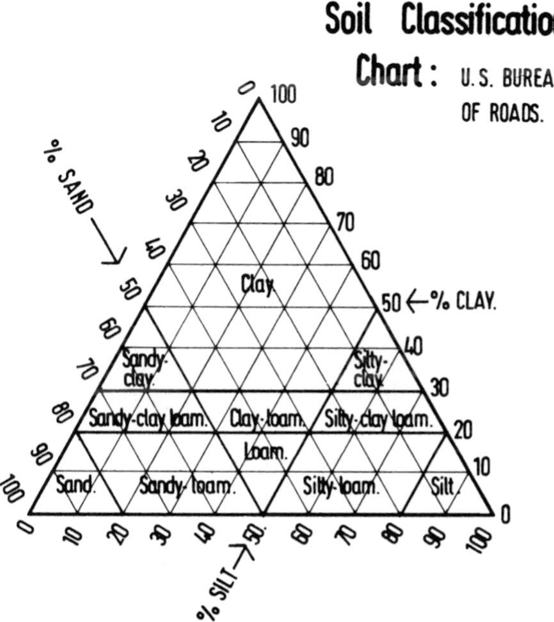

Figure 2.40 *Source*. Peter Harper and Godfrey Boyle, *Radical Technology*, Pantheon Books, 1976.

Compaction. Compaction of soft soil and fill is done with mechanical equipment, usually in 6-inch layers. This permits the use of fill for building foundations up to a bearing capacity of 3000 pounds per square foot. Sands and gravels are better for compaction than silts and clays. Sometimes the excavated soil is suitable, but sometimes it is necessary to import more suitable soil, which either is used exclusively or is blended with the excavated soil.

Rock. Footings founded on rock can be much smaller than those on soil because of the high bearing capacity of the material. This can reduce the cost of a foundation, but any construction below grade is much more expensive in rock because the cost of excavation is 2 to 3 times higher for rock than for soil. In addition, the unit cost for rock excavation of a small site is much higher than that of a large one, and these tradeoffs must be considered when planning basements and subterranean parking.

Small footings may be excavated with jackhammers, but hard rock must be blasted for any mass excavation. The cost of hard rock excavation depends on the following variables:

1 *Proximity of Buildings and Utility Lines.* Vibrations must be minimized and blasting modified to control flying debris.
2 *The Water Level.* This determines the requirements for draining and pumping installations.
3 *Presence of Vertical Banks.* Sheeting and bracing are needed with rock bolts that extend into the unexcavated rock or with steel or wood braces.

Pile Foundations. If there are no satisfactory soil strata beneath the proposed structure, steel, lumber, or concrete piles must be driven by hammer through the weak soil into the supporting strata. The piles transmit their load either into a good stratum at their tip (*end-bearing piles*) or into the strata in between by means of friction between the pile surface and the soil (*friction piles*). The load-bearing capacity of a pile can be limited either by the structural strength of the pile or by the strength of the soil. In the latter case, this bearing capacity can be measured in a dynamic or a static load test. In the dynamic test, the capacity is derived from the energy of the hammer in the last few blows and from the amount of penetration from each blow, as for instance, in the *ENR-News* formula. In static load tests, a static load is placed on the pile and the bearing capacity is derived from the weight of the load and the settlement resulting from it. Pile foundations are generally much more expensive than spread footings. The architect, however, has some control over the cost: the number of interior columns can be minimized (thus the number of piles and driving hammer setups), and the overall weight of the structure can be reduced through the utilization of curtain walls, lightweight concrete, and steel frame instead of concrete frame structures.

For a lightweight structure on soft ground it may be sufficient to drill a hole and fill it with concrete. This type of friction pile is called a *drilled, cast-in-place concrete pier*. It can also work as an end-bearing pile, if the hole is drilled until a firm stratum is reached. To increase the bearing area, these piles are usually belled or splayed out at the end. Such *belled caissons* are costly, and the bottom of the shaft must be cleaned out manually rather than by mechanical equipment.

Mat Foundations. An expensive alternative to piles is to construct a mat foundation by spreading the footing over the entire base of the structure. These mat foundations are reinforced concrete slabs with inverted loads; that is, the uniform load is at the bottom and the single loads (columns, walls) are on top.

Cost Factors. As a rule of thumb, the cost of foundation can be assumed to be 5% of the total building cost. This percentage, however, varies with the size of structure, soil conditions, ground water level, accessibility of the site, and so on. The spread footing, the most conventional and least expensive foundation, can be used wherever the soil has a loading capacity of at least 3000 pounds per square foot. Driven piles are the most expensive type of foundation; they usually cost 2 to 3 times more than spread footings.

A high groundwater level can make the design of below-grade levels of construction altogether unfeasible because of requirements for costly additional installations. For example, if excavation is not braced for hydrostatic pressure and kept dry by pumping, the bearing capacity of foundation strata will be reduced. Sometimes underground tanks are necessary to compensate the uplift, and all basements must be waterproofed and reinforced against hydrostatic stress. The ground water table is usually determined when test borings are made.

Earthquakes

A seismic risk map of the United States, which outlines the areas with high earthquake probability, is part of the Uniform Building Code. In a high risk area, like California, every important building is expected to be subject to at least one major earthquake during its existence. California's 1974 Report on Seismic Safety suggests that "all [buildings] should therefore be located, designed, and built to withstand future shaking; to minimize possible death or injury, and avoid unnecessary or unacceptable damage." According to the regulations set forth in the UBC, no structure should collapse in a major earthquake, although it may suffer structural damages; no structural damages should occur in moderate earthquakes, and minor earthquakes should cause no damage at all. However the code can provide no protection for catastrophes such as landslides, subsidence, or faulting of the ground next to the structure, which may occur in connection with earthquakes.

High-occupancy buildings, such as theaters and schools and structures that are vital following a catastrophe (fire and police stations, hospitals, etc.) should be designed for additional earthquake resistance. The cost for normal earthquake resistance construction is between 1 and 2% of total construction cost, but additional earthquake resistance costs are between 5 and 15% of the total building cost.

In areas of high earthquake activity, a geotechnical consultant is asked to evaluate the site in terms of the probabilities of any of the following earthquake hazards; active faults on the site, the probability of liquefaction of the foundation soils, and landslides. The presence of any one of these conditions may render a given site unfeasible for construction. If no landsliding, faulting, or subsiding is expected for the site, the seismic report may give recommendations concerning the acceleration for which the structures should be designed.

5 COST ESTIMATING AND BUDGET ANALYSIS

Budget Analysis

Development budgets may be established by adding up the estimated cost for each item in a planning program. An alternative approach is to begin by determining the market value of a proposed development, and from this amount to find the maximum budget feasible, based on the projections for per-square-foot sales prices or rental rates.

In the first instance there is no danger of sacrificing quality or scope of project in favor of a lower budget; but in the latter case, it is the responsibility of the architect to explain to the developer the scope of project that is possible under the fixed budget proposed and to ensure that adequate quality can be maintained. If the client is a public agency, the architect is often presented with a planning program that includes a total development budget. Sometimes maximum funding for this budget has already been approved by an act of legislation. It is then necessary for the architect to analyze both the architectural program and the cost figures to ensure their completeness and realism.

Often the architect discovers that factors that would increase the proposed budget substantially (e.g., soil problems, special earthquake requirements, or off-site utility construction) have been overlooked. Also, the inflation factor may have been ignored; of course it must not be—this unstable factor should be built into all projections. If preparation has been inadequate, it may be necessary to modify the quality or scope of the building program, to maintain the fixed budget's feasibility.

It is best to involve the architect at the beginning of preliminary budgeting and to develop both the budget and the architectural program at the same time.

The Project Development Budget. Although construction cost always represents the largest percentage of the development budget, if such other items as predevelopment cost and cost of financing are not considered properly, the whole project may be found to be unfeasible after a substantial amount of money has been spent on planning and land acquisition. To ensure the inclusion of all items pertaining to a given development, it is advisable to follow a budget format that has been established earlier for similar projects. Some public bodies have developed their own forms of project budgets, which must be followed by the architect.

A difficult aspect of every construction budget is rising construction costs. Cost projections should be made for the specific period of construction. This can be done by estimating the rates of price increase by means of statistics and index data and by calculating the future construction cost for the midpoint date of construction.

Budget Breakdown. Let us analyze a sample budget of a condominium development. The project consists of 30 units with a total net floor area of 45,000 square feet. The gross floor area of 60,000 square feet, which gives the building an efficiency factor of 75%, does not include the subterranean garage, which covers an additional floor area of 20,000 square feet. Also included in the project is a recreation area that covers most of the remaining area of the lot.

The architect was asked by the project developer to prepare a preliminary budget for the entire project that could serve as the basis for the developer's mortgage loan application. Since this preliminary budget was established in the conceptual design phase, it does not represent a construction cost estimate. This was developed as a later stage. In establishing the development budget, the architect used the budget outline form given in Table 2.34, which entails the following development costs:

A1 Based on a previous market study, the net floor area desired was assumed to be 45,000 square feet (see Table 2.35). A typical efficiency ratio of 75% added 15,000 square feet of nonrentable floor area. The architect then used various sources of cost data to arrive at a realistic cost per square foot. To supplement personal experience, the architect might have consulted the *Dodge Building Cost Calculator and Valuation Guide,* which provides values in dollars per square foot for various building types. Another

Table 2.34 Architect's Budget Outline Form

Name of Project ______________________

Date of Budget ______________________

Anticipated Construction Start ______________________

Net area (ft²) ______________________

Gross area (ft²) ______________________

A Construction Cost

1 Building
2 Garages
3 Recreation
4 On-site Work

B Development Fees

1 Builder's overhead and profit
2 Preliminary studies
3 Architecture and engineering
4 Surveying
5 Attorney
6 Title company
7 Filing fees
8 Utility cost
9 Park and recreation fee
10 Contingencies

C Cost of Land

D Financing Cost

possibility would be collaboration with a contractor to establish current levels of hard cost of construction. All these standard figures, however, should be modified with premiums and discounts according to the special features proposed in the market study for the particular building.

A2 Cost of garages depends on whether the levels are below or above grade and whether they are equipped with an automatic sprinkler system. The cost of $7 per square foot was for an unsprinklered garage above grade.

A3 In the sample project, the entire open area was used for recreational facilities. In some cities where a park and recreation fee is assessed for every new residential construction, the fee is reduced according to the amount of open space dedicated to "active recreation."

A4 This heading often includes all improvement within the property lines other than the building. Thus parking areas, roads, landscaping, pools, and lighting can be listed here. In the sample project, however, garage and recreational facilities were listed separately. This heading included the cost of demolition of existing structures on the site (three old residences), the cost of utility lines from the lot line to within 5 feet of the building, and the cost of landscaping.

B1 In the sample case, the builder's overhead and profit were not included in the construction cost, since the developer considered acting as general contractor himself and wanted only the "hard" cost presented under this heading.

B2 This item included the cost of a market demand study authorized by the developer to determine the highest and best use of the site. It also covered the cost of soil tests and a preliminary soil report.

B3 Architecture and engineering included all services, from the first inspection of the site to the administration of the construction contract. This figure must also reflect all costs of consulting engineers (civil, structural, electrical, and mechanical) and, if needed, such specialists as lighting and acoustical consultants.

B4 In the case of a condominium building, the civil engineer not only does the site survey, but also produces the condominium plan, often also referred to as the vertical subdivision map, which outlines the exact air space to be owned by every buyer. This cost is usually established on a per-unit basis.

B5 The attorney was needed to file the preliminary and final public reports with the real estate commissioner of the state, a requirement pertaining to all land subdivisions, including condominiums.

B6 The title company is instrumental in the recording of sales contracts between the developer and each individual condominium buyer, and their fees are a substantial part of the development budget.

B7 Often overlooked in preliminary budgets are the various filing fees charged by all local governments that approve the maps and reports. The biggest single item under this heading is always the plan check fee charged by the building department.

B8 Utility companies may charge connection fees, which are included here. The city may also require the installation of additional street lighting or additional fire hydrants, a cost that often is borne by the developer.

B9 In many cities the department of recreation charges for each new construction a fee that is determined mainly by the density of occupancy of the proposed development. The philosophy of the department is that new parks and recreation areas must be created when the population density of any area is increased, and the fees charged should be used for the acquisition and development of new recreational land.

B10 Contingencies should be included in every budget to create a reserve for unexpected costs that may accrue in various areas of the development project. Since the bidding climate cannot be known when the preliminary budget is established, a bidding contingency is important. If the budget is based on the present value of dollars, it is necessary to include a contingency for inflation that can be used to adjust for the construction cost increases expected for the midpoint date of construction. The construction cost contingency is a safety hedge against additional costs incurred through delays, changes, or unforeseen site and building conditions.

C This figure includes the sales price of the land as well as all commissions and legal fees involved.

D Since the cost of permanent financing for a condominium project is borne by the buyers, this heading includes only the fee charged for the lender's commitment to interim financing and the interest to be paid during construction and during the sales period of the project.

Table 2.35 shows this sample budget with actual dollar values as it was prepared by the architect. The summary at the end is a projection of the developer's profit, which is derived by subtracting development cost and cost of sales from the expected sales income.

Table 2.35 Preliminary Development Budget

Name of Project Beverly Wilshire Condominiums

Date of Budget September 1974

Anticipate Construction Start March 1975

Net Area 45,000 ft²

Gross Area 60,000 ft²

Cost and Fees	Area (ft²)	Cost/ft²	Subtotal	Total
A Construction cost				
1 *Condominiums*				
Net floor area	45,000	$20	$900,000	
Balconies	1,000	10	10,000	
Roof gardens	1,000	5	5,000	
Total condominiums				$915,000
2 *Garages*	20,000	$10		200,000
3 *Recreation*				
Pool			7,000	
Jacuzzi			3,000	
Gym and Sauna			3,500	
Sun deck	4,000	$3	12,000	
Total recreation				25,500
4 *Site work*				
Demolition			4,000	
On-site utilities			8,000	
Landscaping	6,000	$3	18,000	
Total site work				30,000
Total construction cost = $1,170,500				

Table 2.35 Preliminary Development Budget *(continued)*

Cost and Fees	Subtotal	Total
B Development Fees		
1 *Builder's overhead and profit (8%)*		93,600
2 *Preliminary studies and tests*		12,000
3 *Architecture and engineering*		35,000
4 *Civil engineering*		
Tentative map	400	
Subdivision map	1,000	
Condominium plan	4,000	
Total civil engineering		5,400
5 *Attorney*		2,600
6 *Title company*		10,300
7 *Filing fees*		
Tentative subdivision map	100	
Final subdivision map	300	
Public report	350	
Plan check fee	2,650	
Total filing fees		3,400
8 *Utility Cost*		
Sewer connection fee	6,400	
Water meter	800	
Fire hydrant	1,200	
Total utility cost		8,400
9 *Park and recreation fee*		9,800
10 *Contingencies*		
Bidding contingency	50,000	
Inflation contingency	110,000	
Construction contingency	60,000	
Total contingencies		220,000
Total development fees = $400,000		
C Cost of Land		
D Financing Cost		
1 *Loan commitment*	60,800	
2 *Interest during construction*	85,000	
Total financing cost		125,800
Total project cost = $1,946,800		

Summary and Pro Forma Profit

Income from sales	$2,320,000
Cost of sales (3%)	(70,000)
Total project cost	(1,946,800)
Developer's profit	$ 303,200

Estimating Construction Cost

One of the characteristics of a good design is efficient use of material and manpower. Buckminster Fuller expressed it this way: "to achieve more with less." With this goal in mind, the architect must continuously evaluate his or her ideas in terms of construction cost, from the preplanning stage to the end of the production phase. Even if estimating firms are employed, the architect still must know the methodology used, and consequently, the critical information needed. Most of all, it is necessary to determine the distinct phases of the development process that require accurate estimates. In the *preplanning and proposal phase,* the first budget estimates are based mostly on standards for single unit costs, such as the cost per square foot of net rentable space or the cost per student. With the help of established ratios relating net floor areas and supporting circulation and service spaces, the cost of gross building area can be established.

In the *programming phase* the costs per square foot of floor area are broken down into functional activities, such as space for kitchens and bathrooms versus bedroom and living room space. An initial determination of the level of amenities and conveniences feasible for the project can be made in this phase.

Cost comparisons are a major basis in evaluating structural alternatives and type of construction during the *schematic design phase*. At this point the design also reflects efforts to maximize the efficiency of plumbing and heating systems, and so on; such attempts can succeed only if the architect is aware of the costs associated with each alternative.

The *design development phase* necessitates cost estimates for smaller units of construction, as more components and subsystems are specified. The architect usually calls for a meeting with the client to align all the figures with the development budget and to decide on the feasible alternatives in critical areas.

Information on unit rates of all components, assemblies, and systems used is assembled in the *construction contract documents phase*. Now specifications on all materials are written, which makes possible a very detailed cost estimate. The architect's familiarity with the unit rates also enables him or her to later check the cost breakdowns furnished by the contractor during construction on which payment advances are based. To facilitate the work of the architect, detailed unit price levels are published nationally by companies like Marshall Stevens and the Construction Publishing Company, and by local publishers in the construction industry. But often prices change very fast, and some information is already outdated by the time it becomes available. Moreover, the information contained in such publications is too detailed to be useful in the initial stages of conceptual planning. In this phase the most valuable data are those which the architect personally has accumulated from previous projects.

The cost figures available from contractors are usually categorized by trades of subcontractors. Since this order has little to do with the functional logic of a building, however, the information is of limited use to designers. A better system of classification, published by the Ministry of Universities and Colleges, Province of Ontario, is based on the function of each part or subsystem, These publications, available in the form of "subsystem categories," are designed to facilitate the comparison between different elements that fulfill the same function, thus enabling the architect to control the cost budget through proper selection.

These elemental-type breakdowns have the advantage of using the same architectural vocabulary for projects of all types. Thus it is possible to compare cost figures of a certain element—for example, a structural system for identical spans—even if the units occurred in different building types. The most difficult facet of the use of this classification is the conversion of the conventional breakdown in construction trend costs into subcategory form. It should be remembered, however, that cost comparisons make sense only if the figures are accompanied with detailed specifications regarding the special qualities of each element and its exact dimensions.

P/A Building Cost File

For the scope of architectural practice, a building cost file developed along the above mentioned principles will be much more useful than estimating by means of price books, which in many cases make separate estimations of labor cost and cost of heavy equipment. One of the most useful listings of elemental categories of construction costs is found in the *Progressive Architecture* Building Cost File (Tables 2.36 and 2.37). It arranges costs in two main categories: building costs (100–600), and site development costs (900).

Building costs are broken down into the following elemental categories:

1 Foundations (100).
2 Building shell (200).
3 Interiors (300).
4 Conveying systems (400), mechanical transportation.
5 Mechanical and electrical (500).
6 General conditions and profit (600), the contractor's overhead and profit.

Table 2.36 Building Cost File

Building type: University Laboratory Building

Classification No. 721

Project: Graduate Chemistry Building

Location: Stony Brook, New York

Architect: Smith, Hinchman & Grylls Assoc., Inc.
Owner: State University of New York
General Contractor: 16 separate contract packages

Tender date/completion: Sept. 1970–Oct. 1972
Market conditions: Average 3 to 4 bids
Cost index: per package

Elemental category	Element cost		Element amount		Cost per sq ft		%
	Quantity	Unit Rate	Sub	Group	Sub	Group	
100 Foundations	**25,846 sq ft**	**26.12**		**675,054**		**2.20**	**3.62**
110 Normal foundations	25,846 sq ft	16.79	433,955		1.42		
120 Basement excavation	374,767 cu ft	0.08	30,000		0.09		
130 Special foundations	25,846 sq ft	8.16	211,099		0.69		
200 Building shell	**532,096 sq ft**	**8.52**	—	**4,535,370**		**14.79**	**24.31**
210 Structure	**322,771 sq ft**	**7.17**	**2,313,467**		**7.55**		
211 *Lowest floor construction*	26,294 sq ft	2.52	66,250		0.22		
212 *Upper floors construction*	280,263 sq ft	6.74	1,890,213		6.16		
213 *Roof construction*	42,508 sq ft	8.40	358,004		1.17		
220 Roof finishes	**42,508 sq ft**	**2.49**	**104,934**		**0.34**		
230 Exterior cladding	**173,031 sq ft**	**10.98**	**1,900,712**		**6.20**		
231 *Basement walls*	13,785 sq ft	9.29	128,135		0.42		
232 *Exterior walls above grade*	126,211 sq ft	12.39	1,563,697		5.10		
233 *Windows*	32,395 sq ft	5.77	186,920		0.61		
234 *Entrances & storefront*	640 sq ft	34.41	21,960		0.07		
240 Stairs	**470 lin ft**	**460.12**	**216,257**		**0.70**		
300 Interiors	—	—	—	**4,537,064**		**14.92**	**24.52**
310 Partitions and doors	**317,656 sq ft**	**4.39**	**1,395,891**		**4.55**		
320 Interior finishes	—	—	**1,305,018**		**4.27**		
321 *Floor finishes*	303,467 sq ft	0.49	149,040		0.49		
322 *Ceiling finishes*	306,557 sq ft	3.05	934,782		3.05		
323 *Wall finishes*	746,514 sq ft	0.30	221,196		0.73		
330 Specialties & Equipment	—	—	**1,872,155**		**6.10**		
331 *Specialties & fittings*	—	—	89,872		0.29		
332 *Equipment*	—	—	1,782,283		5.81		
400 Conveying systems	—	—	—	**352,800**		**1.15**	**1.89**
410 Elevators	25 stops	14,112.00	352,800				
420 Moving stairs and walks	—	—	—				
500 Mechanical & Electrical	—	—	—	**7,660,865**		**24.99**	**41.07**
510 Mechanical	—	—	**4,876,994**		**15.91**		
511 *Plumbing and drainage*	—	—	1,459,081		4.76		
512 *Fire protection*	—	—	97,800		0.32		
513 *HVAC*	4,753,436 cu ft	0.70	3,320,113		10.83		
520 Electrical	—	—	**2,783,871**		**9.08**		
521 *Distribution*	—	—	2,394,310		7.81		
522 *Lighting*	—	—	293,561		0.96		
523 *Special systems*	—	—	96,000		0.31		
600 General conditions & profit	—	—	—	—	—	—	—
Net building cost: $				**17,797,153**	**$**	**58.05**	
900 Site development	**80,456 sq ft**	**10.61**		**854,038**		**2.79**	**4.59**
Total cost: $				**18,651,191**	**$**	**60.84**	

Performance & Specification Data

Areas and volumes

Gross floor area (GFA):	306,557 sq ft
Net floor area:	151,884 sq ft
Volume:	4,753,436 cu ft
Exterior wall area:	173,031 sq ft
Roof area:	42,508 sq ft
No. of stories above grade:	8
No. of basement levels	1

Ratios

Net floor area/GFA	— 0.50:1
Volume/GFA	— 15.51:1
Exterior wall area/GFA	— 0.56:1
Roof area/GFA	— 0.14:1
Lin. ft. partitions/GFA	— 0.08:1

Capacities

Percent exterior wall glazed: 19.1%
Soil characteristics: sandy
Density plumbing fixtures: 1/3035 sq ft
Heating capacity: 141/BTU/hr/sq ft
Cooling capacity: 110 sq ft/ton
Ventilation capacity: 1.34 DFM/sq ft
Lighting intensity: 70 ft candle general, 100 ft candle labs.

Outline specifications

Analysis based on final costs

110 3000 psi concrete in spread footings and column bases.
120 Excavated material off site.
130 Sheet steel piling.
211 4000 psi concrete in slab on grade.
212 Structural steel framing with metal deck and concrete infill suspended slabs.
213 Metal deck.
220 4 Ply built-up roofing with aggregate surface and rigid insulation.
232 4" brick veneer, 2" cavity and 4" block inner skin with parging.
233 Aluminum framed bronze tinted insulating glass.
234 Aluminum framed entrance with plate glass doors.
240 Metal pan stairs with concrete infill, cast abrasive stair nosing, pipe handrails and complete stair structure.
310 Mainly movable metal partitions with hollow metal and wood doors and frames, toilet and shower cubicles.
321 Resilient flooring with some brick paving.
322 Suspended acoustic tile and painted plaster on metal lathing.
323 Painted conc. (Bsmt.) gypsum board, lath plaster and ceramic tile.
331 Millwork, toilet accessories, lockers and mirrors.
332 Laboratory casework.
410 Two passenger elevators having gearless traction 3000 lb capacity, and 350 fpm speed. One passenger elevator having gearless traction, 6000 lb capacity and 5000 fpm speed. One dock elevator having geared traction, 9000 lb capacity and 50 fpm speed.
511 Building sanitary drainage, storm drainage, domestic hot and cold water, distilled water, natural gas, laboratory acid waste, plumbing fixtures and liquid soap dispensers.
512 Fire hose cabinets and risers.
513 Cold room refrigeration system, supply and return air, heating hot water steam, vibration elimination, chilled water, acoustical insulation, temperature controls, emergency gas generator mechanical sources and balancing.
521 Electrical services fed underground from main transformer.
522 Generally incandescent and high intensity mercury vapor.
523 Fire alarm.
600 Site overhead costs included in individual contract packages and distributed in foregoing elements. Construction management fee is excluded.
900 Grading site clearance, fencing, paving, landscaping, retaining walls and steps, lighting, loading dock, volatile storage and utility tunnel.

Cost per cu ft: $3.74 (Building only)

Based on data supplied by Smith, Hinchman & Grylls Associates, Inc.
Cost and performance analysis prepared by HANSCOMB ROY Associates Inc.

Table 2.37 Elemental Categories and Units of Measurement

Element Content	Exclusions	Unit of measurement for cost analysis
100 Foundations		
110 Normal foundations		
Excavation or fill to reduce or raise levels	Slab on grade (211) Excavation for basements (120) Basement walls (231) Caissons and piles (130) Excavation and backfill for mechanical and electrical services (511 and 521)	Sq ft—gross area on plan measured to outside face of perimeter walls or to outer extent of foundations
Excavation, backfill, concrete and masonry for wall footings, columns bases and caps, grade beams, pile caps		
Foundation walls up to level of slab on grade		
Drainage tile		
120 Basement excavation		
Additional excavation and backfill required for construction of basement	Basement walls (231)	Cu ft—Volume of basement below grade measured to outside face of perimeter walls and underside of grade slab
130 Special foundations		
Caissons and piles	Pile caps (110)	According to special conditions (e.g. piles in Lin. ft)
Extra cost of excavation in rock		
Special shoring		
Special dewatering		
Any other special foundation conditions		
200 Building shell		
210 Structure		
211 Lowest floor construction	**Final finish to slab (321)**	
Slab on grade		Sq ft total area of 211, 212, 213, 230
Suspended slabs over crawl space		Sq ft total area of 212 and 213
Fill below slabs		Sq ft—Gross area of slab measured to outside face of perimeter walls
Waterproofing, skim coat, vapor barriers		
Small sump pits and trenches, machinery and equipment bases		
Construction and expansion joints		
Construction and expansion joints		
Curtain walls and window wall systems		
Balcony railings and upstands		
Exterior finishes to overhangs and projections		
Exterior sunshades		
233 Windows		
Window frames including mullions and transoms	Curtain walls (232) Window working equipment (322)	Sq ft—Area of windows
Glazing		
Hardware		
Lintels, sills, stools and special surrounds		
Fly screens, storm windows		
Louvers		
Damp-proof courses and caulking		
Painting and finishing		
234 Entrances and storefronts		
Exterior doors and entrances		Sq ft—Area of entrance openings, screens and storefronts
Glazing		
Overhead doors and shutters		
Storefronts and entrance screens		
Revolving doors		
Hardware and operating devices		
Lintels, sills and special surrounds		
Damp-proof courses and caulking		
Painting and finishing		
240 Stairs		

Table 2.37 Elemental Categories and Units of Measurement *(continued)*

212 Upper floor construction		
Columns and interior load-bearing walls	Floor finishes (321)	Sq ft—Gross area of suspended floor construction measured to outside face of perimeter walls
Beams and joists	Applied and suspended ceiling finishes (322)	
Sub-floors, slabs and decks	Roof construction (213)	
Fireproofing	Exterior load-bearing walls (231 and 232)	
Base plates and anchor bolts	Ramps (240)	
Balcony floor construction		
213 Roof construction		
Columns and interior load-bearing walls	Roof finish (220)	Sq ft—Gross area of roof measured flat on plan
Beams, joists, rafters, purlins, trusses	Insulation, cants, flashings (220)	
Slabs, decks, boarding	Roof drains, eavestroughs, rainwater leaders (511)	
Canopy construction	Exterior load-bearing walls (232)	
220 Roof finishes		
Roof finish, insulation, vapor barrier	Parapet walls and copings (232)	Sq ft—Area of roof and terrace finishes
Cant strips, flashings, curbs		
Fascias, eaves, barge boards		
Roof-and sky-lights		
Waterproof membranes, patio and terrace paving, traffic toppings		
Roof finish to canopies and overhangs		
230 Exterior cladding		
231 Basement walls		
Enclosing walls below grade level to basements	Finishes to interior face of wall (323)	Sq ft—Total area of 231, 232, 233, 234
Water- and damp-proofing, insulation	Exterior wall construction above grade (232)	Sq ft—Area of basement wall below grade level and above slab on grade
	Foundation walls below slab on grade (110)	
232 Exterior walls above grade		
Exterior wall construction Facing materials Exterior applied finishes Back-up construction and framing Insulation and vapor barrier	Finishes to interior face of wall (323)	Sq ft—Area of exterior wall above grade level
	Balcony floor construction (212)	
	Balcony finishes (321 and 322)	
Parapet walls and copings		
Damp-proof courses	Chimneys and flues (513)	
Treads and risers	Enclosing walls (230 and 310)	Lin. ft—Total rise of all staircases and steps (exclude ladders)
Landings		
Stringers and supporting framework		
Balustrades and handrails		
Finishes to treads, risers, landings and soffits		
Painting		
Steps and ladders		
Ramps		
300 Interiors		
310 Partitions and doors		
Interior partitions and non-load-bearing walls	Load-bearing walls (212 and 213)	Sq ft—Gross area of partitions and walls measured over doors and openings
Interior glazed partitions and borrowed lights	Applied finishes (323)	
Movable partitions		
Folding and demountable partitions		
Toilet and shower partitions		
Interior doors and frames, including glazing, hardware, painting and finishing		
320 Interior finishes		
321 Floor finishes		
Toppings	Access flooring (331)	Sq ft—Gross floor area of finished spaces
Floor finishes (applied and integral)		
Bases		
Mat sinkages, frames and mats, floor grilles		
Expansion joint cover plates		
322 Ceiling finishes		
Applied and suspended ceiling finishes	Special illuminated ceilings (522)	Sq ft—Gross area of finished ceilings
Bulkheads		
Cornices		
323 Wall finishes		
Applied interior finishes to walls and partitions	Exterior wall finishes (232) Self-finished partitions (310)	Sq ft—Gross area of finished walls and partitions (measured both sides)
330 Specialties and equipment		

Element Content	Exclusions	Unit of measurement for cost analysis
331 Specialties and fittings Toilet and bath accessories	Items of equipment (332)	Record costs only on a gross building floor area basis
Cupboards, counters, shelving and cabinet work		
Mirrors		
Chalkboards, tackboards, directory boards		
Access flooring		
Lockers		
Mail chutes and boxes, linen chutes		
Auditorium seating and bleachers		
Telephone enclosures		
Blinds		
332 Equipment All items of equipment not included in 331, such as: kitchen, laundry, library, stage, parking, laboratory, athletic, checkroom, darkroom, vault, window washing, security (non-electronic), etc.	Electronic security equipment (523)	Record costs only on a gross building floor area basis
400 Conveying systems		
410 Elevators Passenger and freight elevators	Hoisting enclosure (212, 213 and 310)	Stops.—Total number of stops and floors served
Dumbwaiters	Power supply (521)	
420 Moving stairs and walks Escalators	Power supply (521)	No.—Number of continuous lifts
Moving walks		Lin. ft—Length of walk
500 Mechanical and electrical		
510 Mechanical		
511 Plumbing and drainage Water supply and treatment	Fire protection systems (512)	Fixtures—Total number of plumbing fixtures

Element Content	Exclusions	Unit of measurement for cost analysis
Controls and instrumentation		
Insulation		
Chimneys and flues		
520 Electrical		
521 Distribution and power Power transmission	Service connections (900)	Record costs only on a gross building floor area basis
Service and distribution		
Emergency power generation		
Controls		
522 Lighting Lighting fixtures and branch circuits		Record costs only on a gross floor area basis
523 Special systems Communications		Record costs only on a gross building floor area basis
Electric heating		
600 General Conditions and profit		
Indirect and site overheads and expenses supervision, site accommodation, site protection, temporary facilities and services, insurance and bonds, permits, site equipment, clean-up, winter conditions, etc.	Subcontractor's overheads and profit to be included in appropriate subdivision	Record costs only on a gross building area basis and percentage of total cost
General contractor's head office overhead and profit, or construction manager's fee		
700 and 800 — Vacant		
Use these open categories to record speical items, such as demolition, alterations, renovations		
900 Site development		
Roads, walks, parking lots, curbs, gutters	Floodlighting of building (522)	Sq ft—Gross site area less area occupied by building

Table 2.37 Elemental Categories and Units of Measurement *(continued)*

Waste water disposal and treatment	Service connection (900)		Grading	
Plumbing fixtures			Seeding, sodding and landscaping	
Insulation			Paved areas, steps	
512 Fire protection			Retaining walls	
Sprinkler equipment	Service connections and fire hydrant systems (900)	Sq ft—Record costs only on a gross building floor area basis	Pools, fountains and decorative site elements	
Extinguishing equipment			Site furniture and signs, flagpoles	
Standpipe and fire hose equipment			Fencing and gates, walls, barriers	
Fire extinguisher cabinets			Service connections and distribution	
Hood and duct fire protection				
513 HVAC				
Heat generation equipment and piping	Machine and equipment bases (211)	Cu ft—Volume of building	Exterior lighting	
Refrigeration equipment and piping	Service connections and exterior distribution (900)		Site drainage	
Heat transfer units and equipment			Irrigation systems	
Air distribution			Fire hydrant systems	

In the further breakdown of each of these categories, the units of measurement for the quantities of each element are specified. Thus if floor areas and building volumes are calculated according to the same standards for every building, the architect can compare the efficiency of various design alternatives and of different floor-to-floor heights.

For purposes of each cross reference, the file should also have a classification code for building types, such as the one proposed by Brian Bowen, the creator of the P/A Building Cost File system. With an analysis like this, the whole project is expressed in terms of statistical data, including various ratios, which permit evaluation of the project's efficiency and performance. These data serve as the basic pricing input during the phases of programming and planning.

ENR/Cost File

Parameter Costs of Buildings. Another system for the estimation and control of building costs was developed by *Engineering News Record* (ENR). The parameters used are the measures of the building, on which the unit cost of each trade is based. Heating, ventilating, and air conditioning, for instance, are measured by tons of air, and the parameter used to calculate the unit cost of the structural frame (steel, formed concrete), is the "area supported." All together, 15 parameters are used for the different trades; all cost data come from contractor reports on actual projects. The ENR parameter cost files reflect the range of unit costs, and the data are always updated according to the ENR Building Cost Index.

The parameter method is entirely satisfactory for preliminary estimates, since a rough building outline is sufficient as a basis; it also makes cost-cutting procedures easier if the total cost turns out to be too high. If the parameter cost data of one project are to be used on a building in a different geographical area, the 20-Cities Building Cost Index series, also published by ENR, can be used for adjustment to local price levels.

Comparative Cost Value Engineering. The parameter method can be extended to establish cost budgets for each separate design discipline in the preliminary stages, by indicating which trades represent the major cost shares. To control total cost, alternative engineering possibilities should be analyzed in these areas—this is the essence of comparative cost value engineering.

For example if the structural system chosen in a particular budget were steel frame, at a budget of $270,000, a value engineering analysis could determine whether other structural systems would have a lower cost budget. In such a sample situation the analysis might reveal that reinforced concrete would cost less, but the budgets for prefabricated concrete (prestressed modules) or for laminated timber would be higher than that for steel.

Initial cost is not always the only cost factor considered in the preliminary budget. In a budget for a hotel project, for instance, maintenance costs would be a dominant concern. The item of toilet partitions can illustrate this point. If the alternative materials available were wood, porcelain enamel, metal, stainless steel, and marble, wood would have had the lowest unit cost (e.g., $70), but the material chosen might have been metal (unit cost, e.g., $200) because performance and aesthetic appeal were of greater importance than price alone.

Variable Cost Influences

Availability of Labor and Materials. The conditions of the construction market vary substantially among different geographical locations, and, in general, between urban and rural areas. The following statements can be made regarding these variations:

- Centers of greater population densities have higher construction costs than rural areas; but if one moves too far from cities, costs rise very fast again because supply and transportation costs increase.
- The construction industry of the cities supplies the rural or semiurban areas, and their accessibility is an important factor.
- Because of changing labor market and delivery conditions, rural areas tend to have more volatile construction cost values than metropolitan areas.

Generally speaking, the differences of construction costs are caused by the basic conditions of supply and demand and by the cost of transportation. The recent oil shortage, for instance, has increased the cost of all petroleum-based products, and if temporary shortages in the supply of structural steel are caused by strikes, there will be substantial cost fluctuations. The government involvement in the construction industry as represented by price controls and subsidies is another influential factor.

The cyclical changes of construction volumes are directly related to the changes in interest rates; many price changes follow these patterns. Lumber prices, for instance, are high in a very active construction period, but they tend to decrease if the industry slows down and the demand declines.

Labor costs are mainly determined by the conditions negotiated through the labor unions in new contracts. The demands made follow the rate of inflation, but they also reflect increases in productivity and corporate earnings. If the whole industry is slow, the interests of the unions will shift from wage increases to the control of unemployment rates.

Construction Overhead and Profit. The contractor distinguishes between two basic types of overhead cost.

1 *General Overhead Costs.* These include fixed expenses such as office rent and costs that cannot be charged to any particular job. The following items fall into this category:

Rent	Salaries and wages for
Furniture	Estimators
Telephone	Secretaries
Heat and light	Bookkeepers
Stationery and supplies	Clerks
Insurance	Draftsmen
Advertising	
Entertainment	Consulting fees
Automobile and travel	Legal expenses

2 *Project Overhead Costs.* These include all costs related to a particular project that are not accounted for under materials, labor, and equipment. This covers the following items:

Temporary buildings	Permits
Equipment storage	Insurance
Temporary walks, stairs, and bridges	Interest
	Bonds
Sanitary facilities	Taxes
Project office and furniture	Transportation
	Clean-up
Utilities and telephone	Trash removal
Police and fire protection	

Permits may be required for the extension of sidewalks, offices over sidewalks, other temporary structures, storage of combustible material, mobile toilets, temporary utilities, wide loads, or heavy loads on trucks.

Bonds required may include labor and material payment bonds, performance bonds, bid bonds, and surety bonds.

Insurance costs that are accounted for under project overhead generally include some of the following types:

Workmen's Compensation	Social Security
Workmen's Liability	Unemployment
Public Liability	Old age
Fire	Owner's contingencies
Structure	Automobile
Property damage	Vehicle
Wind	Glass
Rain	Elevator
Flood	Occupancy
Earthquake	Theft

The share of general overhead costs that must be added to the budget of each of the contractor's projects can be determined either by the time duration of each job or by its total budget. Some contractors do not account separately for general and project overhead; instead, they find the sum of both as a percentage of cost of labor or cost of material, labor, and equipment.

The item "taxes" usually covers property taxes on structures under construction, if they are not paid by the owner. Payroll taxes belong in the labor cost category.

The contractor's profit, projected as a percentage of the total of estimated costs, varies with the type of project and with the special risks involved. Thus smaller projects, and more hazardous ones, have a larger percentage of profit. The contractor's profit margin also depends on how competitive the field is at the time and on the contractor's particular need to keep staff and equipment busy. Generally the following percentage rates apply:

Very large project	5–10%
Large project	10–15%
Medium-sized project	15–20%
Small project	20–25%

Construction Cost Escalation. One of the most difficult tasks of cost estimating is the projection of construction costs into the future. Although cost increases in the building industry generally follow inflation rates, there are so many external influences that projections cannot be based on inflation alone.

The ENR Building Cost Index, which appears weekly in *Engineering News Record,* is one of the main sources of data used to project construction cost trends. It includes indexes on construction cost, common labor, skilled labor, and materials. The indexes are based on the analysis of data from between 20 and 50 major urban areas in the United States.

When the ENR Building Cost Index was created in 1938, it was designed to analyze the relationship between construction cost and the cost of skilled labor. For construction cost levels, the materials selected that related most closely to the national economy were steel, cement, and lumber. Similarly, cost of skilled labor was based on the average of wages among carpenters, structural steel workers, and bricklayers. As a basis of comparison, ENR assumed a hypothetical construction block valued at $100 in 1913 dollars. Each of the materials included in the Building Cost Index is weighted accord-

Table 2.38 Building Costs

INDEXES: April 1977		Current Indexes				1941=100.00 (except as noted)
Metropolitan area	Cost differential	non-res.	residential	masonry	steel	% change last 12 months
Major U.S. City Average	8.7	587.6	551.2	580.1	566.0	+09.4
Atlanta	7.8	710.6	669.9	697.8	687.6	+16.4
Baltimore	8.2	616.6	579.6	601.0	590.5	−00.6
Birmingham	7.9	551.4	512.8	544.5	532.5	+16.1
Boston	9.1	575.6	543.8	578.1	561.0	+05.9
Buffalo	9.0	619.4	581.6	609.1	592.8	+07.5
Chicago	8.8	672.1	632.4	661.9	648.8	+18.1
Cincinnati	8.9	624.2	587.2	612.4	597.4	+02.1
Cleveland	9.3	628.6	591.5	618.3	602.8	+07.0
Columbus, Ohio	8.6	614.9	577.4	611.5	595.4	+17.4
Dallas	7.7	565.7	547.7	563.2	548.6	+10.6
Denver	9.0	664.1	624.7	655.1	642.3	+13.0
Detroit	9.7	641.8	611.3	640.4	625.1	+03.1
Houston	7.6	536.9	504.1	529.8	517.9	+06.1
Indianapolis	8.6	567.3	532.7	554.9	544.2	+18.1
Kansas City	8.9	576.1	544.3	568.4	555.1	+08.4
Los Angeles	9.4	725.5	663.1	708.3	693.3	+18.3
Louisville	8.0	587.8	551.9	581.6	568.7	+14.7
Memphis	7.6	543.1	509.9	526.1	515.4	−00.4
Miami	8.3	612.4	583.4	608.6	596.6	+02.8
Milwaukee	9.3	702.9	660.0	699.8	678.1	+13.9
Minneapolis	8.8	600.1	564.5	593.2	578.2	+08.1
Newark	8.4	526.4	494.3	527.4	509.9	+05.4
New Orleans	8.0	588.3	555.2	582.8	567.7	+10.9
New York	10.0	622.2	578.5	611.3	597.3	+12.6
Philadelphia	9.0	623.1	593.6	619.9	603.0	+05.8
Phoenix (1947 = 100)	8.4	342.4	321.5	340.2	330.3	+08.5
Pittsburgh	8.9	556.0	523.1	547.7	537.6	+08.0
St. Louis	9.1	614.2	579.7	611.5	598.7	+11.6
San Antonio (1960 = 100)	7.6	218.8	205.4	214.4	209.5	+02.1
San Diego (1960 = 100)	9.4	260.5	244.6	257.3	250.6	+04.2
San Francisco	10.5	925.3	845.7	915.4	882.6	+14.4
Seattle	9.4	619.9	554.8	605.7	585.1	+14.7
Washington, D.C.	8.3	556.6	522.6	547.1	533.4	+06.1

Cost differentials compare current local costs, not indexes, on a scale of 10 based on New York

Tables compiled by Dodge Building Cost Services, McGraw-Hill Information Systems Company

Reprinted from *Architectural Record*, April 1977.

ing to the annual national production level and the number of skilled labor hours involved in the production. Only rarely are these weights adjusted.

The ENR Construction Cost Index, based on the component of unskilled labor, today diverges quite substantially from the ENR Building Cost Index, which reflects skilled labor costs. In general, today, the Building Cost Index is better suited for use in projecting construction cost escalation. Other sources of cost data are contained in indexes published by the following companies:

1 American Appraisal Company, Inc.
2 Austin Company.
3 Bureau of Reclamation.
4 H. F. Campbell Construction Company.
5 Dodge Building Cost.
6 Fruin-Colnon Contracting Company.
7 Handy Whitman Company.
8 Marshall & Swift Publication Company.
9 Nelson Indexes.
10 The Port Authority of New York and New Jersey.
11 Preliminary Cost Guide (AIA, Pasadena).
12 Smith, Hinchman & Grylls, Inc.
13 Turner Construction Company.
14 U.S. Department of Commerce Composite Cost Index.

If any of these specialized indexes are chosen in preference to a general construction cost index, the user must know the components and geographical areas reflected most closely by each index. Table 2.38 shows the difference in rates of cost increase plotted by some of the indexes listed above. Table 2.38 indicates how much difference exists between cost increases of various geographical areas. Yet despite the availability of all these data on historic cost figures and rates of increase, the forecasting of future cost increases remains a very difficult task, and we have no simple methodology to ensure accuracy in cost projections.

6 ORGANIZATIONAL CONCEPTS

The development of organizational patterns for a design program begins with the observation of the characteristic activity patterns of the users. This will reveal a hierarchy of activities for which the program must offer a solution. One rung in such a hierarchy is frequency of use. This organizing principle places the main library in the center of a university and recreational facilities in peripheral, less accessible locations. In spatial terms this means center and periphery orientation for horizontally organized projects and ground floor versus higher levels in vertically organized structures.

The physical design is generally the result of a combination of three concepts used by the architect:

1 The characteristics of the construction site (its shape, the surrounding environment, views, etc.) will lead to a specific form of design.
2 The physical form is a direct result of the optimal organization of activities in space.
3 The architect attempts to accommodate the program in a predetermined spatial form.

Although it seems obvious that the best organizational solution will be a product of all of these concepts, most architects employ their own distinct alphabet of archetypal forms within which they have developed their special skill of visualization and design. Some of these models are the grid, the linear axis, the constellation, the star, and the ring. Each of these basic forms favors a special form of organization that is flexible or rigid, open ended or finite, centralized or decentralized, and so on. The final form selected, however, will reflect considerations of economic feasibility and the aesthetic preferences of the client, as well as the concepts above.

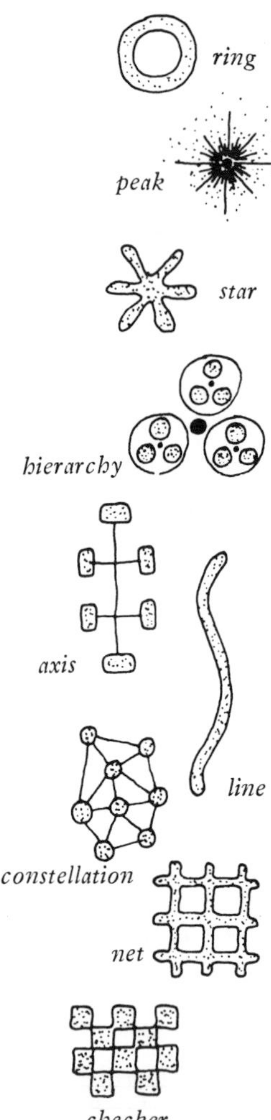

Figure 2.41 Formal prototypes. *Source*. Kevin Lynch, *Site Planning*, 2nd ed., MIT Press, 1971.

Organizational Values

The efficiency of an organizational scheme can be evaluated in terms of five major aspects.

1 *Circulation*. The objective is to minimize the total length of circulation as well as to reduce friction. For certain activities the design should encourage social contacts by means of common entrances and ample opportunities for visual communication; for others, occasions for interaction should be avoided to ensure privacy. Circulation is usually facilitated by a harmonious flow of space without abrupt changes and having a sufficiency of connecting elements.

THE OLYMPIC VILLAGE
Montreal, Quebec
Architects: D'Astous & Durand
Photo: J. P. Beaudin

2 *Behavior Characteristics*. Does the space organization allow people to do things the way they want to do them? Whether the structure will support or restrict the behavior of its occupants can be projected only by architects familiar with the occupants' needs.

3 *Health*. Hazards to physical health such as bad lighting, noise, and sources of accidents are usually recognized, but the effects on human emotions are often neglected. The stress caused by adverse spatial and organizational conditions is not always detectable, since people adjust quickly and often are not consciously aware of the negative effects.

4 *Adaptability*. The activities within a structure are likely to grow and change during the lifespan of a building, and the organizational patterns must be evaluated in terms of their potential for future development. Growth and reorganization should be possible without interrupting the project's major functions.

5 *Cost*. The economy of space and construction often suggests forms that are the opposite of those developed in accordance with the other organizing principles. A compact form of great regularity with a high density often represents the most economical solution; but when such long-term costs as maintenance and loss of productivity are included in the financial evaluation, a higher initial construction cost may seem to be feasible.

Organization and Design

The creation of an original design involves the definition of a project's basic functions and the visualization of a spatial form best serves the functions. In practice, however, the architect very rarely has the opportunity to follow this approach. Both the conceptual design and the production phase are often greatly facilitated if the architect uses a stereotype solution developed in the past that has a good record of performance in similar situations.

Stereotypes are valid also because they ensure a smooth and cost-saving process of construction. The architect needs to be familiar with them to be able to evaluate the possibility of adapting a particular stereotype to fit a specific design problem. Under certain unique site characteristics and climatic conditions, however, use of a standard design may be impossible. The stereotype design for an elementary school in a warm climate may be a spread-out solution, but this form is not transferable to a cold climate zone, where the need to economize on energy mandates a compact solution. Very complex design projects are usually divided into units or modules of a size that can be comprehended and visualized in terms of individual functions and parts.

Organizational Factors

Design factors that are determined not by the internal function of a project but by its construction site and its relation to the surrounding community, are called design factors. All factors relating to the site, such as topography, soil, boundaries, and climate, may eliminate many alternatives of spatial organizations and will influence selection of a feasible solution. The weather conditions, for instance, will determine how much outside space will be usable, and the space limits will influence the concept of growth and flexibility.

The way in which the project is to be linked to the movement patterns of the surrounding communities is another important organizational factor. In the organization of an airport, factors such as vehicular access, connection to mass transportation, and the movement and control of pedestrians, will be dominant in the design program. Pedestrian movement is even more significant in the organization of theaters and sports arenas.

Another link with the community consists of public utilities and services. These factors may make compact and centralized schemes more feasible than spread-out, constellation-type organizations. Factors of change may include not only the number of occupants or users, and the type of user activities, but also the need for replacement caused by normal wear and tear, and social and economic obsolescence caused by discoveries in science and innovations in technology. All these factors call for a scheme of great flexibility.

Organizational Patterns

The nine conventional types of organization illustrated in Figure 2.41 are related to the archetypal forms of design mentioned previously. The grid or net or checker pattern offers the greatest flexibility. Its modular structure can be extended and changed without interrupting the whole organization. It also makes it easy to solve. A very complex organization responds well to this pattern, but it may lead to monotony and a lack of identity in the project. The opposite of the grid, the radial or star or peak pattern, is appropriate if all functions and activities have their origin or destination in the central core. Instead of flexibility, radial design offers simplicity in organization and encourages interactions of all kind.

The precinctual plan avoids a central core, and organization and spatial composition are achieved by establishing a harmonious balance among all parts. This pattern has no direction of growth and is not as rigid as the radial pattern. It is the most frequently used of all conventional types.

A linear pattern has a single spine along which all elements are organized and which determines the direction of growth. If land is available, new segments can be added easily, but eventually the spine may become overloaded. If a secondary spine is added at a right angle to the linear type, the pattern is called *axial*. This gives more of a focus than the linear pattern, and it can be developed in phases. Most urban design projects follow the axial pattern.

7 SOCIOLOGICAL AND PSYCHOLOGICAL ASPECTS

In a conventional building program the sociological and psychological needs of the future users receive very little consideration. This leads to shortcomings in the design that become obvious when people fail to use spaces in the manner conceived by the architect. Architects are frequently blamed for the design of spaces that make it impossible for people to live and work in comfort. One reason for this situation is certainly our lack of scientific knowledge about the effect of the total environment on human well-being and behavior.

It is usually the client who furnishes the architect with the data that compose the architectural program of a project. This information, expressed in terms of the number of people to be accommodated and business-related goals of the project, very rarely includes data about desirable human qualities, which ultimately may be more important to the inhabitants than economic efficiency. As a result, our urban environment is no longer desirable for anyone.

Although architects try to design structures for the life-styles of specific users, unconsciously they are guided by the standards they consider to be adequate for themselves. Yet the qualities of privacy, comfort, sociability, and community living should be defined in accordance with the specific culture of the users of each project; when this is not done, results are unsatisfactory.

We know that there exists a relationship between the physical environment and the social and interpersonal behavior of people. But although we can measure human tolerance levels regarding noise, pollution, isolation, overcrowding, and so on, we cannot say with accuracy which designs will bring people together and which plans are likely to keep them apart. Indeed, recent case studies of housing projects make it doubtful whether the influencing of human behavior through design should even be attempted. The example of the Pruitt-Igoe public housing project in Chicago demonstrated that a structure designed to encourage social mixing can lead to fears among neighbors so severe that security comes to be valued more than all planned facilities for socializing, which initially were thought to be the chief attraction of the development.

Another case of friendship versus privacy values became apparent when the design of washrooms for dormitories was studied. It was shown that more friendships were made in dorms with common bathrooms than in those with private ones. Can architects consider all these unintentional effects of design in their programming?

Even if the architect knows about the effects of lack of mobility and greater neighborhood orientation and dependence of poor families, he or she will not have the time or the means to translate all data into an effective building program. Perhaps this is the function of a planner-sociologist, in collaboration with both client and designer. Since most people are unable to articulate feelings about their environment precisely and rationally, the sociologist would also be needed to help define how people experience different environments.

Visual and spatial terms cannot be related directly to elements of human behavior that are described with the same words. The architect, for instance, may say that the physical environment is "flexible," "free," "harmonious," or "open," but it would be an erroneous oversimplification to assume that a "free" floor plan will make people feel free or that a fence on the property line will discourage neighborly contacts. The difficulties in predicting the direction in which physical design will influence human behavior are illustrated by the case of plazas. Since open spaces between buildings are associated historically with communal activities in politics, religion, or commerce, planners today intend to use the plaza design to create a sense of community. In most cases, though, this concept does not come alive because the designers have neglected the specific patterns developed by the public in their contemporary leisure activities.

A recent study on the visual impact of buildings suggested that the architect's perception of the aesthetic quality of buildings is apparently very different from that of nonarchitects. The very examples picked by the architects as good, beautiful, and interesting were found to be bad, ugly, and boring by nonarchitects. In a different follow-up study of a housing project, a very low percentage of the people interviewed were aware at all of nonpractical, aesthetic qualities. These examples confirm the suspicion that the architect may be out of touch with the human experiences and needs of the users.

Having developed their own terms and concepts in communicating, architects are sometimes unaware that their language of ideas of space and design is not readily understood by clients. The architect may often wish that a client's visual awareness were greater, but it is incumbent on him or her to arrive at an understanding of a nonarchitect's way of conceiving space, form, and style.

Too many architects assume that by simply changing our environment it is possible to change human behavior. This concept spawned the myth that a move from a slum to a new housing estate will automatically bring improvements in health, morals, and patterns of living. This deterministic attitude is too simple; the actual success of housing is determined not only by the reaction of the actual user to the planned physical environment, but also by a highly complex interaction between the physical environment, natural or man-made, and the user's social organization and values.

For example, with his housing estate at Pessac (1926), Le Corbusier intended to change the image of a modern home held by already industrialized, "modern," lower-middle-class workers. As Le Corbusier reported it, M. Fruges, the instigator-patron of the project, viewed Pessac as a test of modern design. "I authorize you to put your theories into practice and to carry them to their most extreme conclusions. . . . Pessac must be regarded as a laboratory. I authorize you to break with all conventions and abandon traditional methods. . . ." And Le Corbusier did just that. Based on standardization, his "machine-to-live-in" used many of the design elements that are now almost synonymous with modern architecture: cubist forms, flat roofs, terraces, wide windows, free flowing plan. Yet today Pessac is virtually unrecognizable, and its condition is attributable to more than the effects of time and dilapidation; it is the result of a very real conflict between the architect's vision and the users' desires.

Without repeated support from important officials in the French government, the project at Pessac probably would never have been completed. Even after it was built, the municipality refused to allow the water pipes to be laid for 3 years, during which time, despite architectural reviews that were not negative and often were rather uncomprehendingly positive, the reputation of the project suffered from the implication some grave fault was preventing its completion. These problems only added to the difficulties of finding purchasers for the houses. Because of the flat, cubist forms of the houses and the terraces, the district was called disparagingly the Moroccan District and the Algerian District.

Not only were the physical forms of the houses un-French, Le Corbusier and Fruges had decided to paint the facades in bright, strange colors: horizon blue, golden yellow, jade green, off white, and maroon. But the inhabitants of the project at Pessac did not mold themselves to fit Le Corbusier's design; they began to modify the design to fit their needs. If the colors were strange and hostile, the house could always be repainted. The "oriental" terraces were used as storage for old things, or if the owner was rich enough, they were roofed over with a traditional pitched roof, making the house look more "proper" and providing additional space for the family. More than half the original wide windows were converted to the traditional narrow type. In fact, almost all the exterior changes that were made reflected a desire to return to the traditional French house style, the "lean-to."

The opposition of the people of Bordeaux was far stronger than the backers of the project had anticipated. The buyers' attachment to the traditional lean-to house led them to make changes both in the exterior appearance and in the interior arrangement of the houses that ruined the architectural style but made the structures into homes for their inhabitants. Having added pitched roofs, converted the windows, and repainted the façades, they took advantage of the freedom inherent in Le Corbusier's open floor plan by reinstating the basic plan of the lean-to house, a central corridor giving access to rooms on either side.

The modifications made by the inhabitants of Pessac on their individual homes have radically changed, even destroyed, the atmosphere of the original plan. Le Corbusier's environment was intended to "teach" its inhabitants, to create new "average" people to fit the architect's plan. This was great arrogance, and the result in relation to traditional architectural standards was disastrous. The question still remains whether Pessac, as a living environment, changed, modified, and used by its inhabitants, is a great success.

Territoriality and Dominance

The terms "territoriality" and "dominance" were first used by ethologists who studied the behavior of animals. Territoriality relates to an order in space, whereby an animal lays claim to an area and defends it against intruders. Dominance refers to a social hierarchy, which animals usually establish by means of aggression. In recent years we have become aware of the applicability of these principles to human behavior and the terms are now widely used by sociologists.

Territoriality. In its broadest sense this term covers the relationship of an individual to space. It applies to classifications such as nations, states, cities, and neighborhoods, and to the private sphere and the intimate, personal, and so on distances required by individuals under different conditions. The theories developed around territoriality still reflect their origin from the study of animal behavior and should be used with caution when defining human needs of space. Some of these conflicting views are as follows:

1 Every human being needs a certain minimum of space, without which a normal and harmonious life is impossible.
2 The territorial behavior of human beings is biologically determined, thus lies in the realm of instinct.
3 To varying degrees the territorial instinct is always associated with aggression and conflict, since it implies the defending of the individual's own space.

Some see territoriality as a basic means of avoiding food shortages that could endanger the species or a group, by controlling the relationship of population density to food supply. Aggression is often seen as the principal biological instrument of maintaining territorial order. In the animal world as well as in political geography, however, aggression often assumes only a ritual character, and relative peace is maintained among neighboring groups. Such intergroup ritual manifestations of aggression and defense can be observed in competitive sports between rival schools or countries, in the open display of aggression between political parties at election time, or in the negotiations between unions and management at the bargaining table.

Dominance. In each social organism certain individuals and groups control the activity of others. This expresses the principle of dominance, which leads to hierarchical orders. In any society the individual is part of a number of interacting hierarchical orders, which are related to his or her occupation, family, friends, or religious activities. The interplay of orders of dominance often limits the authority of the individual, as in the case of the police officer who stops someone for a traffic violation, then recognizes a prominent public figure.

In most social encounters, the hierarchical order is established through the submission of some, rather than through aggression by one or a few. Use of respectful titles such as professor, president, or doctor, and differentiated responses to the wearers of uniforms are manifestations of submissive behavior.

Territorial Groups. Identification with a precisely defined territory is important to groups as well as to individuals. The claim of a territory makes it possible for groups to distinguish clearly between people who belong to it, and those who do not. Naturally, everybody belongs to several territorial groups—school districts, home towns, nations, and so on. The boundaries between areas of group territoriality serve as a form of accommodation among groups and reduce conflict. This effect can be observed on a neighborhood level as well as in international relations.

The territory helps an individual or a group to define its identity. People associate with their territory a common history and a common fate, and they are drawn together as a group in the cooperation that is required for survival. The negative aspect of this principle lies in the competition arising between groups of different territorial identity, which in its most extreme manifestation leads to open warfare.

Status. Like chickens adhering to a pecking order, we associate a particular status with various members of our society. This status represents a certain social standing that each person has relative to everyone else. The status of a member of society is easily recognizable, and we are so accustomed to identifying it in terms of the individual's behavior and physical possessions that we call them "status symbols." In private life certain locations and types of residences, cars, and social and cultural participations become status symbols, whereas the status of a member of a public body is amplified intentionally—for example, by seating the judge above all others in court.

Every social system seems to be concerned with a status hierarchy of one kind or another. Not only privileges but also restrictions define a person's status. In any organization a superior will find it difficult to enter the "territories" of people of much lower status, because his or her presence will be perceived as threat or as a sign of unusual events. The amount of respect shown by employees for the personal territory represented by another's office can also be an indicator of status. Employees of equal status tend to knock and enter quickly, whereas subordinates will knock and wait. The seating order at a conference table is another physical expression of status.

Space Relationships

Space Needs. Before the space requirements in a design program can be determined, the amount of space needed by each individual must be known. This figure will greatly vary with each person's activity. It used to be assumed that a person in a crowd needs a minimum space of 2 square feet. However recent studies of big crowds at political campaigns indicate that one person in a dense crowd occupies between 6 and 8 square feet, and the average for a loose crowd with a constant flux of people was found to be closer to 10 square feet.

The minimum space a person needs is often determined by the psychological effects of crowding rather than purely physical action. This personal space or "breathing room" is a function of the psychological distance required by the individual, who will feel threatened if people breach these invisible boundaries. Personal space is sometimes referred to as portable territory, since it surrounds people as they move around. Personal space does not extend equally into all directions, however, since some people are less sensitive to the closeness of a person on their side than to someone standing right in front of them. Personal space requirements also influence individual distancing, a concept related to the distribution of persons, population density, and territorial behavior.

In housing, the occupant's preference of space is rarely satisfied, and families typically find that the new house is just one room too small. Thus the amount of money available determines the amount of space provided for a household, and the degree of satisfaction of spatial needs greatly depends on the people's expectations. People do not generally perceive their housing space requirements in terms of square feet; rather we are concerned with the number of rooms, their arrangement, and their capacity to accommodate the furniture. Therefore a design that is closely related to the particular activities of a household can meet the need for space even if the floor area is relatively small.

Spatial Distancing. Distancing is another term that was first used by ethologists. It was found that as young animals grow up, they learn to maintain certain distances with respect to different members of the species. Getting too close evokes aggressive behavior, while staying too far away excludes the individual from the group.

Distancing patterns can be observed in every household. They follow invisible boundaries, known by all. An outsider, for instance, can easily enter the living room, but only close friends will settle in the kitchen. Bedrooms are restricted to friends with an even more intimate affiliation. Only a special gesture of hospitality can encourage people to break these patterns.

The distance required by an individual varies with personality type. Extroverted people, for instance, tend to keep much closer to their conversation partners than introverted types. The mood of a crowd also has an effect on distancing, thus on space requirements; members of an agitated, emotional crowd usually stay much closer together than people in a reserved and critical mood.

The distances that people maintain can also be linked to their cultures and nationalities: for example, Latin peoples do not feel uncomfortable being very close to one another, whereas Britons and Scandinavians keep relatively far apart.

Spatial Invasion. The discomfort associated with the invasion of personal space is most strongly felt by persons in a vulnerable position; patients in a hospital are prime examples. Such are very sensitive to the numerous violations of their privacy by nurses, doctors, and visitors. Generally, we can distinguish among three forms of trespassing:

1 *Violation.* The unauthorized use of space (e.g., a parking violation).
2 *Invasion.* The presence of an individual in restricted territory (e.g., a man in a ladies' room).
3 *Contamination.* Polluting a territory by using it contrary to its designation (e.g., riding a dirt bike in a park).

Observations in public places confirm that people usually react very predictably to spatial invasion. In libraries, for example, people space themselves as far apart as possible. If a newcomer to the reading room sits closer to someone than is necessary, the first occupant will shift his or her chair away or move to another table. The way people place themselves apart from one another on a long bench in a waiting room is another example of respect for personal space. On the other hand, a janitor entering an executive's office to remove some wastepaper is able to trespass on personal space without being considered to be an invader. The janitor is perceived as part of the environment, not as a person; thus does not attract attention or cause discomfort.

Privacy. Everyone needs to withdraw periodically, to spend some time alone and undisturbed. In public areas this "right" of privacy is not very well protected, except for regulations concerning unlawful search or arrest by the police. The privacy of a home is protected by laws against trespassing and disturbing the peace, but even in the home, privacy is violated by unwanted visits from salesmen and field agents in public service. Privacy is additionally violated by telephone calls, since the installation of a phone makes the subscriber vulnerable to intrusions from the outside world.

Crowding. If overcrowding occurs in the animal world, social systems and behaviors usually start to disintegrate. Human beings can adjust to extreme situations, but in slum environments, for example, overcrowding causes some major problems. Lack of privacy means no place for the children to do their homework and no place for the parents to have a moment of peace. If overcrowding prevails over a large area, people sometimes adjust to the situation by withdrawing from social contacts and by showing indifference to one another. This is why urban dwellers appear to be cold and unconcerned, and these characteristics are also sometimes associated with the British, who have built a highly structured, orderly society on a small and crowded island.

Spatial Defense. People defend their private space with a wide range of generally understood symbolic gestures and actions involving position, posture, and gesture. Some of these reactions belong to the realm of unintentional reflexes and are manifested when the invisible boundaries of instinctive territories are violated. For example, a person's *position* in a room can indicate his or her readiness for defensive action; *posture,* or the mode of standing, can indicate the extent to which space is occupied in a working position; and *gesture* includes a wide range of nonverbal body expressions that convey messages of welcome or hostility.

Territories that people feel defensive about can be classified in four types: public territory, such as streets; home territory, such as a club house; interactional territory, such as a private home; and body territory, which refers to personal space.

Spatial defense can be offensive or defensive. A person choosing a seat in an empty train compartment, for instance, can display offensive behavior by taking the middle seat to discourage other passengers from entering. A passenger with a defensive attitude, on the other hand, would choose a corner seat, showing a way to retreat from contact. The defensive attitude is more frequently observed in restaurants, where diners, not wanting to risk encroachment by newcomers, seem to seek remote corner tables or booths.

Territorial markers are commonly used and respected as means of securing private space in public places. A coat placed on a seat in an airplane or movie theater, for instance, functions effectively as such a marker.

Group Behavior

Group Types. It is of great importance to the designer to know where certain groups are formed, their duration, their size, and whether there are ideal group sizes for certain human activities. Sociologists define a group as an aggregation of individuals who have a common purpose for being together. Early studies of groups have revealed that people work more efficiently in groups. If the work requires a high degree of concentration, however, competition among fellow workers or distraction from spectators may cause a decline in output.

Newer studies are concerned with the statistical and optimum sizes of various groups, and the results of one investigation of a number of informal groups were most revealing. The groups studied were those formed for such everyday activities as walking, playing, conversation, and shopping. It was learned that 70% of the groups consisted of only two people, 20% of three, and 7% of four; only 3% had five or more members.

The finding that most groups consist of couples, and that very few are larger than five, has important implications for the design of social areas, especially since it can be assumed that in general the average group size will be greatly overestimated. Social scientists who have traced a continuous reduction of group sizes in the history of our civilization cite dancing as an example: its transformation from a communal village event to the kind of solo activity popular today.

Seating behavior at tables is a frequently studied phenomenon. Findings on optimal arrangements for casual conversation indicate that a couple will prefer opposite seats if the table is less than 5 1/2 feet wide and side-by-side seating if the table is wider. Couples also tend to sit closer together as room size increases and, naturally, as the noise level is raised. For cooperative work the side-by-side position is preferred; competing pairs will sit opposite one another, and two people working separately at one table will choose a catty-corner arrangement.

Studies of benches at bus stops and other locations demonstrate that long benches are undesirable because the first two people will place themselves at opposite ends, and newcomers will often stand rather than take a seat in the middle.

The overwhelming implication of all these studies of group behavior is that designers can anticipate spacing patterns that will be experienced as comfortable in the

PERCENTAGE OF Ss CHOOSING THIS ARRANGEMENT

Seating Arrangement	Condition 1 (conversing)	Condition 2 (cooperating)	Condition 3 (co-acting)	Condition 4 (competing)
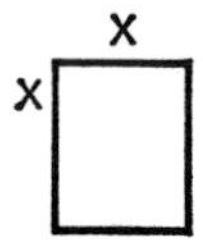 Corner (X top, X left side)	42	19	3	7
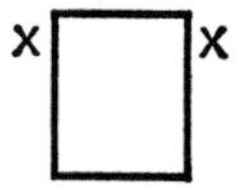 Opposite sides (X left, X right)	46	25	32	41
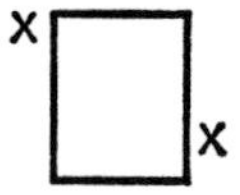 Diagonal (X left top, X right bottom)	1	5	43	20
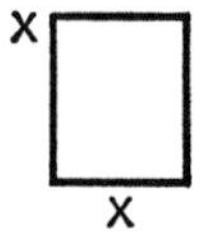 Diagonal (X left top, X bottom end)	0	0	3	5
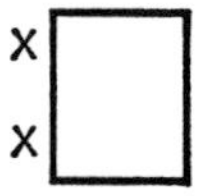 Side by side (X, X same side)	11	51	7	8
 Ends (X top, X bottom)	0	0	13	18
TOTAL	100	100	100	99

Figure 2.42 Seating preferences at rectangular tables. *Source*. Robert Sommer, *Personal Space*, Prentice-Hall, 1969.

appropriate set of activities if they consider variables relating to environment, culture, personality type, and the task or function of the group. With this knowledge a library can be designed as a sociofugal place—that is, a space that discourages people from making social contacts. It is also possible to increase the capacity of rooms by encouraging arrangements that minimize violations of private territory. The important thing is always to let the values of the user be the yardstick, not the designer's personal principles of aesthetic handling of space.

Roles. The theory of roles helps to anticipate the behavior of an individual in a specific situation by relating it to the person's status or social position. The various roles that people assume, which lead them to somewhat standardized behavior, can be summarized in three major groups:

1 *Personal Roles*. This concept implies that individuals do not act to satisfy their own needs and desires as they become aware of them; instead, they play roles suggested to them by parents, teachers, superiors, or by society as a whole. Thus behavior becomes a social stereotype. However the individual who assumes such a personal role with all its habits and mannerisms, can be confident that his or her authority and competence in that particular area will not be questioned. This was demonstrated in experiments in which actors posing as renowned scientists delivered nonsense lectures on highly abstract subjects. Yet their

"contributions" were accepted as valuable by audiences consisting of professional people.

2 *Group Roles.* In a group an individual assumes a certain role to satisfy the common interest of the unit and to conform to the needs and wishes of its members. Groups can take a wide variety of forms, from street gangs to religious organizations. Since we all belong to more than one group, the pattern of our membership roles is the product of a combination of influences with varying degrees of group identity. A professional man, for instance, may be fully identified in his role as a doctor, to a lesser extent as a member of the white upper-middle class, and only very marginally with his religious background, which may be that of a Protestant.

3 *Societal Roles.* This classification covers all the functions and professions that individuals assume in a society. People shape their roles according to the conventions and ethical codes of their society, which generally leads to the projection of a very idealized image of the chosen profession. The image, however, will generate a feeling of security in the individual, who identifies his or her own role with a larger-than-life institution.

People can drop their roles in privacy, and the schoolteacher whose language is impeccable in class may be found telling dirty jokes to drinking pals. However a politician who publicly moves out of his role may cause a scandal that jeopardizes his career. To the architect, the theory of role playing is of interest insofar as it helps to explain and predict the behavior of individuals and groups who will be accommodated in the structures he or she designs.

Human Perception

It is important for architects, who are generally visually oriented, to realize that visual information is only one of many bits of information that are necessary for a person to accurately perceive a spatial environment. Perception changes with experience, and throughout life people learn how to see things differently. Things that were once imperceptible can be recognized in subsequent encounters because past experience tells us what to look for.

More than visual information is necessary whenever spaces become too big to be perceived through the searching eye. The experience of space, then, is brought about through the process of cognition in which we complement the visual perception with our imagination, remembrance, evaluation, and other faculties. Thus elements that are outside our field of vision become integrated into our experience of the spatial environment. This is called "cognitive mapping."

Like a road map, cognitive mapping helps the individual to determine where certain things are and how to get to them. In terms of cybernetics, the process involves the acquiring, coding, storing, recalling, and decoding of information. Cognitive maps are synthesized out of visual images perceived in the past. Individuals who enter an entirely new spatial environment soon become aware of their lack of a cognitive map that would help orientation. Such disorientation was experienced by the astronauts who made the Apollo 14 moonwalk. They had to return to the spacecraft without reaching their target location because they were unable to place themselves in an environment whose forms looked completely new from a close distance. Later they discovered that they had been as close as 75 feet to their target area.

The architect must recognize that words used in reference to certain spatial areas are interpreted differently by every individual. Terms like "suburb," "city," and "ghetto" cover different territory for different people according to past experience, background, and bias. Therefore we can never be certain that our perceptions of reality are shared by everybody else.

Often designs do not reflect our capacity to perceive the environment with all our senses. The experience of a harbor area, for example, might consist of a composition of sights, sounds of ships and fog horns, the smell of the ocean, and the kinesthetic sensation of the rolling movements of boats and docks. Characteristic smells will often bring back visual memories, demonstrating the significance of our olfactory sense in the acquisition of spatial knowledge.

Architects, with their natural tendency to overemphasize the visual, often deceive their clients and themselves by their strictly visual presentations. Their models and drawings of proposed environments do not contain any information regarding air pollution, wind conditions, noise levels, and so on, and often even lack any reference to surrounding structures. The executed project may be a failure if important environmental factors are eliminated from the planning process.

These aspects of sociological behavior and spatial perception mentioned in this section indicate clearly (1) that the physical design of our environment has a great influence on the behavior of its inhabitants and users, and (2) that we still lack precise scientific knowledge regarding many aspects of the relations between people and their spatial environment. If architects integrate into their programming process only some of the fragments of knowledge now available in this field, however, many of the mistakes of the past can be avoided.

8 DESIGN AND CONSTRUCTION SCHEDULING

Scheduling for Design

Setting Up the Schedule. One of the criteria by which a client judges the performance of an architect is his or her ability to deliver every one of the promised services on time. To set up an accurate time schedule requires experience; but there is a method that makes this important part of architectural performance easier. The process of scheduling begins with breaking down the services rendered into four basic phases: schematic design, design development, construction documents, and bidding or negotiations.

Schematic Design. In this phase the concept of the project is developed. Schematic drawings show the general organization and dimensioning of space and the basic structural system; a preliminary cost estimate is also drawn up. This initial work can be done by one or two designers alone. The time required depends on many factors, including the following:

- The experience and inspiration of the architect. An expert in school design, for instance, will need little time to convert a familiar problem into a conceptual design. A very inspired solution, on the other hand, may readily win the approval of a development team, thereby creating momentum on its own.
- The complexity and size of the problem. A very complex job requires much more time for thorough comprehension of the spatial needs than does a project that can be visualized easily.
- The client's ability to specify needs and to clarify budgetary constraints at the beginning. An experienced developer will furnish the architect with detailed data regarding the functions and performance of the project, thus saving time that otherwise would be spent attending meetings and waiting for approvals.
- The decision-making ability of the development team. This depends on the number of decision makers involved and their corporate and legal relationship.

Because of this great number of variables, there is no standard time span for the first phase, and a project can remain between a month and a year in schematic design.

Design Development. The preliminary drawings produced in this phase outline the form, size, and materials of a project, as well as the structural, mechanical, and electrical systems used. Included also is a preliminary cost estimate. The availability of manpower is of major importance in this phase, and the number of personnel assigned must be related to the size and scope of the project. The time required also depends on the efficient scheduling of the collaboration with consulting engineers. A standard time span for this phase is 2 to 4 months.

Construction Documents. This phase requires from 3 to 7 months, and it includes the production of a final cost estimate as well as the preparation of a complete set of working drawings and specifications, ready for plan checking.

Bidding or Negotiation. In this phase proposals and bids from contractors are analyzed, and addenda are prepared. This takes between 3 and 6 weeks, regardless of the size of the project.

At the conclusion of each phase, some time should be scheduled for securing the client's approval; this usually amounts to a total of 1 week, ranging up to 1 month. However such external factors as the need to wait for a financial commitment from a lender or for approval by a governmental body, may lengthen this period substantially.

Another time factor over which the architect has little control is the time required for plan checking. The length of this period varies greatly with the complexity of the project and with the number of agencies involved. An average time span for plan checking is 2 months. A bar graph (Figure 2.43) is often used as a visual representation of the design schedule. It can serve as a guideline throughout the design process, reminding the architect to make adjustments to subsequent phases, should one phase extend beyond the scheduled completion date.

Contingencies. All unexpected problems that may delay the work in any of the design phases are covered by the term "contingencies." A consultant may need more time, the building department may change one of its

PROJECT TIME SCHEDULE

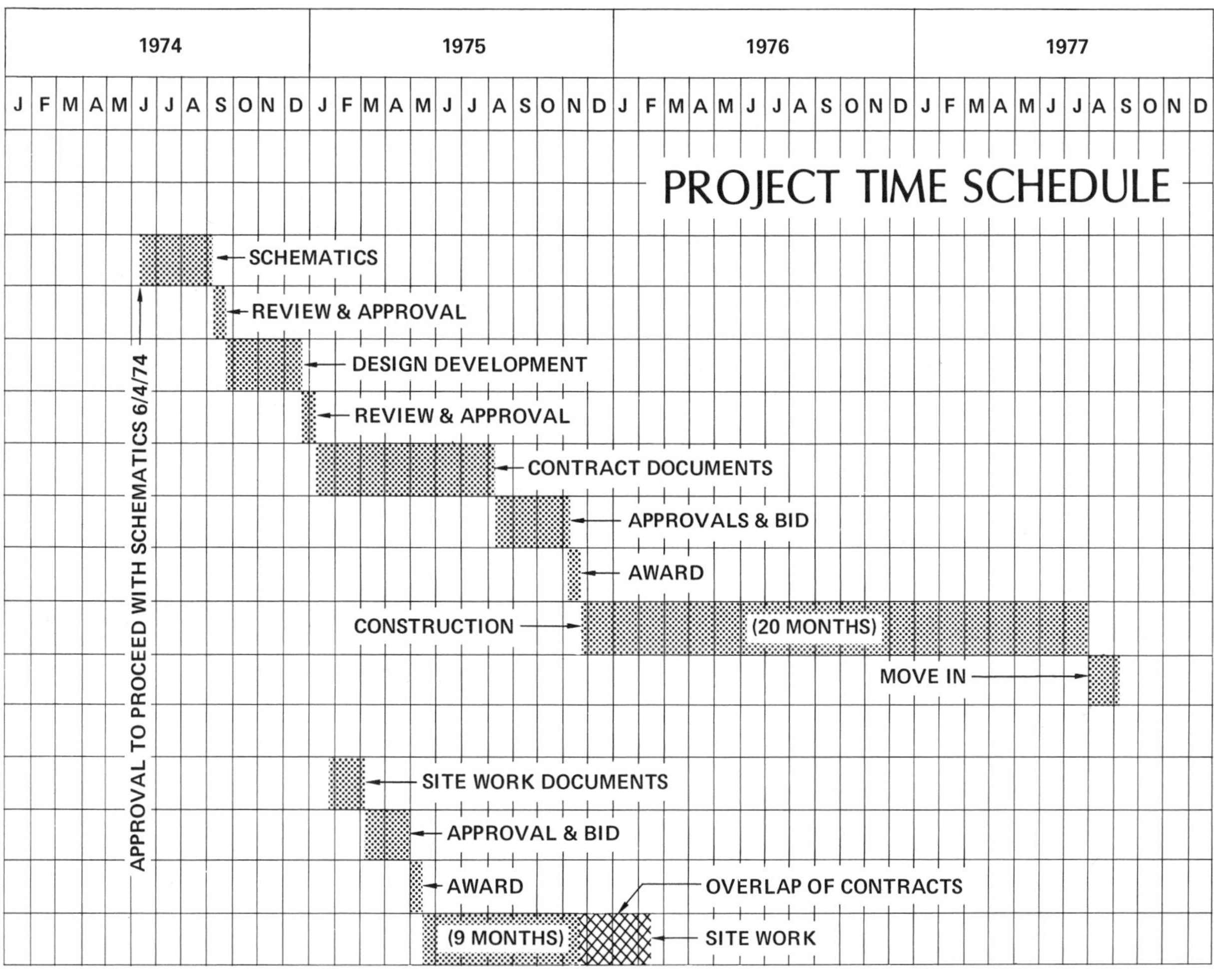

Figure 2.43 *Source*. Daniel, Mann, Johnson & Mendenhall, Architects.

policies, or other causes for delay may be encountered. Therefore the architect should add an extra 3 weeks or so to the total time scheduled.

Working with a Contractor. In the conventional design process, the contractor enters the picture at the end of the construction documents phase, and the architect hopes that his or her cost estimates will be close to the bid or the negotiated proposal of the contractor. Recently, however, the cost of construction materials has been fluctuating so widely that the architect is often unable to come up with an accurate cost figure. Thus the contractor is consulted as early as in the conceptual design phase, and alternative designs are evaluated in terms of construction cost before the design development phase. This sometimes allows the contractor to guarantee a firm maximum cost of construction by the end of the design development.

Working with the contractor changes the typical design schedule. More time is spent on conceptual design and on design development, but the working drawings can be produced faster, and the time allocated for bidding and negotiation is also shortened. The total scheduled time is about the same as in the conventional working process.

Expanding the Schedule. For every project there exists an optimum time schedule, and most often a realistic deadline helps to keep up the momentum of the project going. Thus a deadline is preferable to an open-ended time budget.

Apart from the effect on quality and performance of the design team, certain economic factors make expansions of design schedules undesirable. The owner may need to pay interest on money borrowed to buy the land or for predevelopment cost in general, or a loan commitment may expire. The rate of inflation can make delays expensive for the developer, since construction cost has been increasing by a monthly rate of almost 1%.

Compressing the Schedule. Financial considerations may lead the owner to seek a compression of design schedule. In this case it is the duty of the architect to explain the possible consequences of such a speed-up on cost of construction and on the quality of the project.

The architect has the following alternative means to reduce production time: hiring more people, having the original team work overtime, or electing to spend less time on certain areas of work. The negative effects of these options include higher project design cost, the incorporation of fewer aesthetic considerations in the design, and (probably) higher cost of construction—since the working drawings and specifications will be less detailed and will not always reflect the most efficient solution.

Scheduling for Construction

Preparing the Schedule. A good construction schedule enables the contractor to utilize manpower and equipment in the most efficient way. If the construction process is planned in all details at the beginning, each operation will follow the last without any waiting period, and the cost of labor and equipment will be minimized.

On very complex projects contractors are using modern management techniques to achieve this goal; the most important is the critical path method (CPM).

The Critical Path Method. In the CPM approach, all activities of a particular construction process are represented in a network diagram, and the total project time is determined by following the "critical path" (i.e., the route requiring the longest total time) through this network. The CPM diagram represents each job by an arrow called *activity*. The start and the finish of each activity are marked by circles, called events or nodes. These events represent the points in time at which one activity has been completed and the next one is ready to start. This derived network or arrow diagram shows the order in which the activities must be carried out. It has no gaps or discontinuities.

Figure 2.44 indicates that some activities can proceed simultaneously, but others cannot start until the preceding activity has been completed. Each event occurs only once in the network and is numbered according to its occurrence in time. Thus to read the diagram one starts with event 1 and finishes with the event bearing the highest number.

If two parts of a project are planned in separate parts and diagrams, there may be "interface events"—that is, events common to both, such as the connection of utilities between two buildings.

CPM Scheduling. The network diagram discussed so far represents a model of the construction job and illustrates the logic of the process in an optimal way. The contractor now estimates the time required for each activity and enters this information, expressed in working days, in the diagram. The number below each arrow (Figure 2.45*a*) now gives the number of days needed for this activity.

Critical Path. Figure 2.45*b* shows several alternate paths between start and finish. To determine the critical path, we add the number of working days along each path. The critical path, the one with the largest number of days, represents the total project time. All activities along this path are called *critical activities,* and expansion of any of them will delay the completion of construction. Thus the critical activities need maximum attention and control.

Float Values. *Float* is the difference in time between the longest (critical) path and another path between the same events. If, for instance, the time between event 1 and event 6 is 15 days along the critical path and 12 days along another, the second path has a float value of 3. This means that the work performed in connection with that path can be delayed by 3 days without endangering the completion date. Therefore all secondary paths are also referred to as float paths.

Project Calendar. After the critical path diagram has been established, the time schedule must be converted to actual dates on the calendar. The duration of construction can be found by multiplying the total number of days of the critical path by 7/5, which corresponds to the 7-day week with 5 working days. The dates of all events are then marked on the calendar; critical activities are usually indicated in red.

Contingencies. Before the final dates are established on the construction calendar, the contractor adds certain time reserves for potential delays. Among the usual delaying factors are adverse weather conditions, shortages in certain materials, accidents, strikes, and other more remote causes that cannot be anticipated.

CPM Calculations. The operations of adding and subtracting may be very complex on a big project, and com-

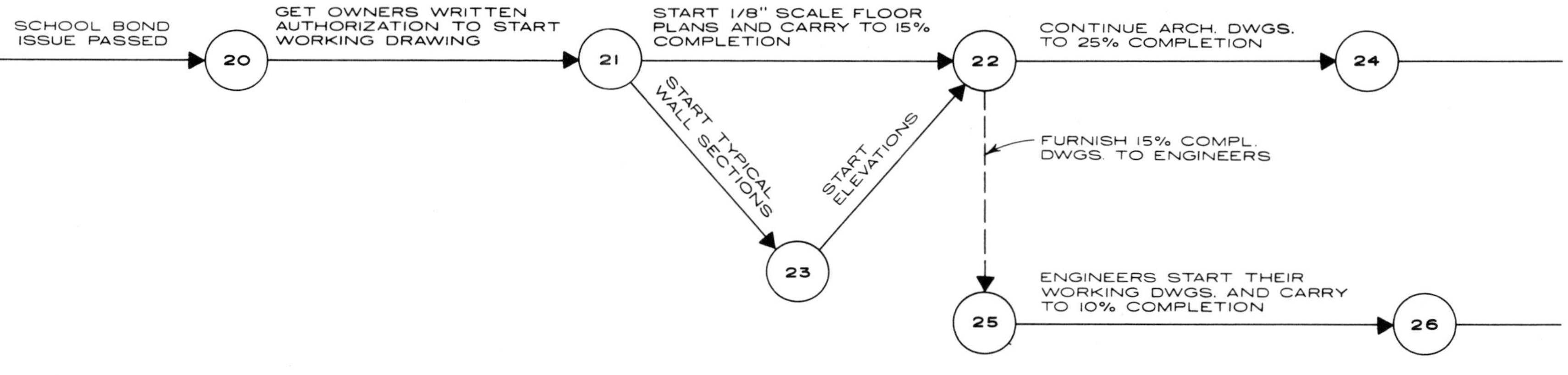

Figure 2.44 Typical CPM network diagram. Reprinted from C. G. Ramsey and H. R. Sleeper, *Architectural Graphic Standards*, 6th ed., American Institute of Architects, John Wiley & Sons, 1970.

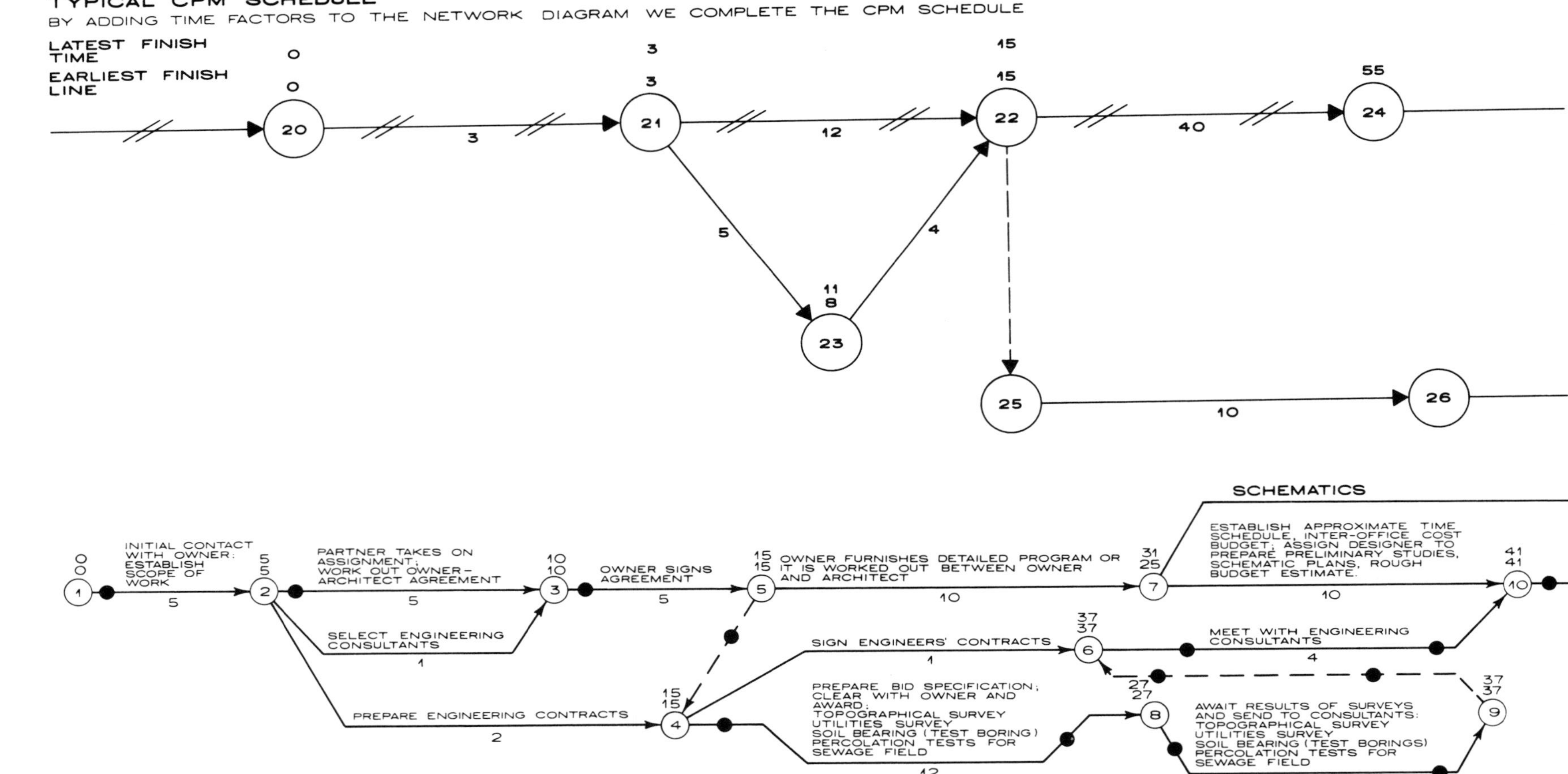

Gustave R. Keane, FAIA; Eggers and Higgins, Architects–Planners; New York, New York

Figure 2.45 (*a*) Typical CPM schedule. (*b*) Portion of CPM. Reprinted from C. G. Ramsey and H. R. Sleeper, *Architectural Graphic Standards*, 6th ed., American Institute of Architects, John Wiley & Sons, 1970.

SEASCAPE CONDOMINIUMS
San Diego County
Architects: The Landau Partnership, Inc.
Photo: Office

puter programs have been developed that are very helpful in comparing and modifying floats and dates in the planning phase and during construction.

Bar Graphs. A bar graph indicates the calendar dates for the start and finish of all major construction activities. Unlike the critical path diagram, it does not give any information regarding the interrelationship of activities. However the bar graph is very easy to read and understand; thus it remains the most widely used form of graphic presentation for construction scheduling.

Compressing the Schedule. Inflation, seasonal changes, or the start of other projects may cause the contractor to wish to compress the schedule. The CPM method is very helpful in this task because it shows how time cuts on the critical activities indicated in the diagram will affect the total schedule.

The use of additional man-hours and equipment to accelerate the pace of construction increases direct cost. The shorter schedule, however, also results in lower cost of overhead. The quality of construction is usually highest if a normal schedule is maintained, and compressing the schedule makes supervision more difficult and often reduces project quality.

Fast-Track Scheduling. This method is also referred to as *telescoped scheduling*. Instead of compressing the duration of certain construction activities, it pulls their starting date into the design period, thereby shortening the total time for project development. Thus, since the architect is only slightly ahead of the construction crews, the major structural building elements must be designed very early, and while foundations are being poured and the structure is framed, the architect is still designing the interior spaces.

For this approach the construction job is divided into many separate contracts, and stage bidding is required. Since this system eliminates the overall responsibility of the general contractor, it increases the architect's responsibility. If the architectural office is unable to assume the additional responsibilities of managing the development, it may be necessary to hire a separate construction manager (CM).

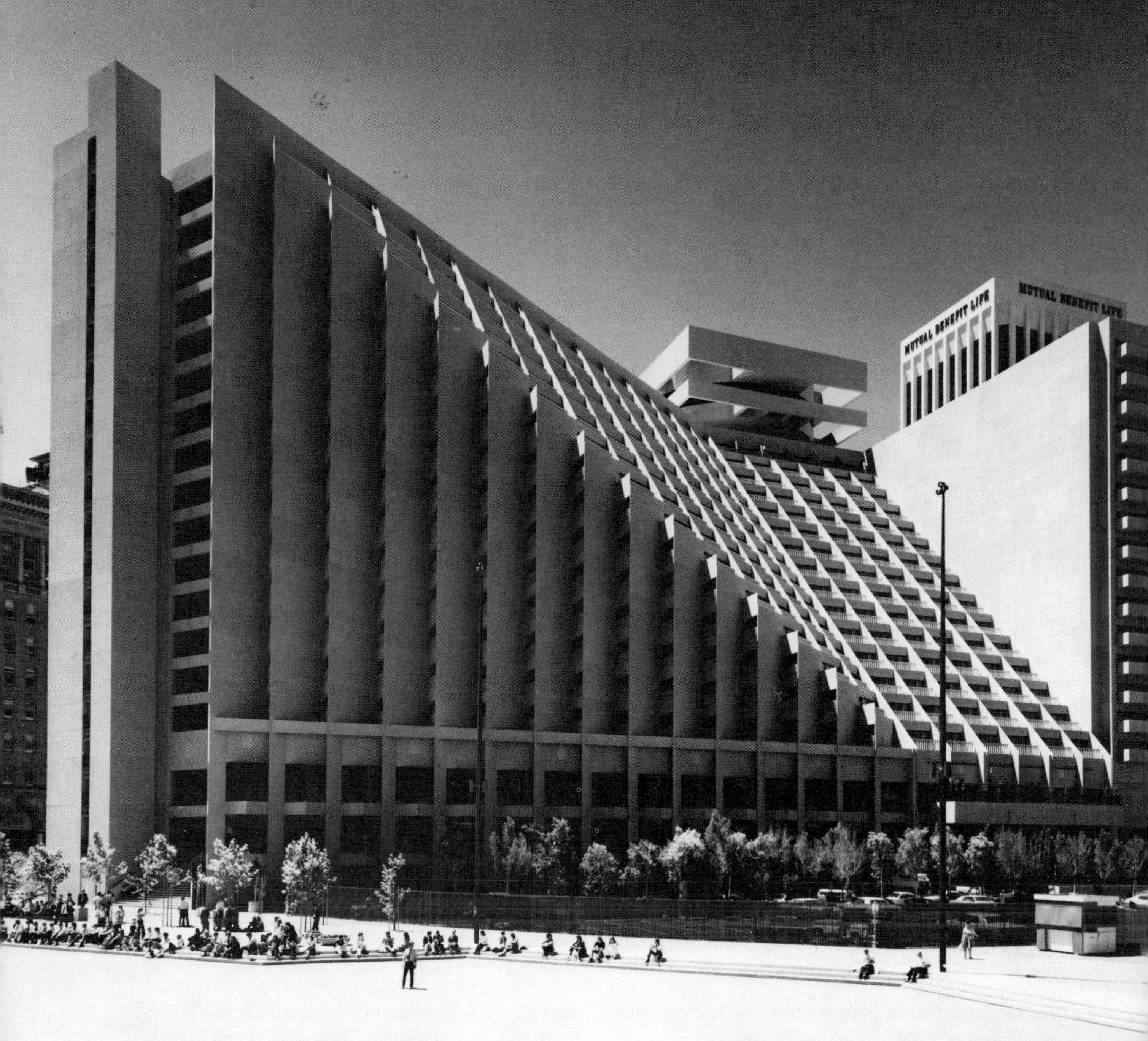

HYATT REGENCY
San Francisco, California
Architect: John Portman & Associates
Photo: A. Georges

THREE DESIGN AND TECHNOLOGY

Design is a problem-*solving* process. In Chapter 2 we found that architectural programming is a problem-*seeking* process. Yet despite its analytical, problem-solving aspects problem-seeking is in fact synthetical. Pure architectural design has always been intuitive and highly judgmental. Much too often multiple requirements are juggled simultaneously, and solutions come about by wild inspiration or quite often by accident. A clear, logical system of approach to the design process and its various stages of development usually lead to an architecturally successful solution. Even pure architectural design involves many analytical elements of the design process, especially functional requirements. Therefore in "design and technology" the architect must be aware of the functional aspects of all program requirements; this in turn calls on one's judgment with regard to priorities, one's knowledge of architectural, structural, mechanical, and material systems and their capabilities, and of course, one's sensitivity to spatial relationships.

"Design and technology" refers to the architect's ability to do the following:

1 Evaluate three-dimensional physical implications from two-dimensional programmatic requirements.
2 Analyze alternative design concepts and schemes based on specific requirements and technical constraints.
3 Evaluate schematic design decisions based on knowledge of architectural, structural, and mechanical systems and their capabilities.
4 Select design principles by evaluating advantages and disadvantages, possible problems, and conflicts of design-development decisions.

1 ORGANIZATIONAL ASPECTS OF DESIGN

Spaces in Terms of Function

The two major factors in the design of functional spaces are size and perception of size. The architect learns empirically to use spacing standards that are based on average needs for similar activities. He or she must consider the optimum space necessary for specific activities and the shape that best lends itself to these. Any space that substantially exceeds the area required to accomplish a particular activity tends to reduce the efficiency and balance of the area. There are exceptions, however. Certain spaces are deliberately designed to convey an atmosphere of grandeur. More of these exist in the Old World than in the New. Other buildings or spaces are meant to produce feelings of security, safety, and efficiency (banks), myriad, dazzling choices (warehouses), or mechanical busyness (foundries). All these varied ap-

DESIGN AND TECHNOLOGY

	ORGANIZATION	ECONOMICS	PERCEPTION
	Functional areas Circulation systems Technical systems	Initial cost Efficiency Maintenance Construction time	Aesthetics Symbolism
PHYSICAL Design Requirements	Functional Circulation Structural Mechanical Electrical Solar systems Construction	Budget Efficiency Maintenance Construction schedule Solar alternatives	Aesthetic goals Symbolic concepts Psychological and Sociological goals
ALTERNATIVE Schemes Concepts Evaluations	Functional Construction Structural Mechanical support systems	Initial cost Efficiency Maintenance Scheduling Alternative systems	Perceptional implications
SCHEMATIC Design Analyze	Functional Circulation Structural Mechanical	Maintenance Detail cost	Detail goals
DESIGN Development Evaluation	Functional Technical evaluation Support arguments	Economics Efficiency Maintenance	Details

peals to emotional response involve the human perception of space.

As varied activities within a space are identified and categorized, basic standard spaces will be applied to activities that are similar; thus maximum use will be made of available space, and standardized spaces based on function will become basic building blocks for determining traffic flow, appropriate adjacent activities, privacy, pleasant environment, and expansion.

Example. The basic clerical/secretarial work space, one of the smallest of these standard units of space, may contain more furniture than a desk and a chair. The human being assigned to this unit needs enough space to enter, depart, push the chair back without having it slam into the wall, open drawers, stretch, and so on, with minimum exertion and without experiencing claustrophobia. Optimum size is 7 × 8 feet. Smaller is too small; larger is wasted, therefore unnecessarily expensive space.

Interior Spaces. Results of a series of studies by Peter Cowan (London: University College, 1964) at four London hospitals suggest that 150 square feet of space is sufficient for 70% of human activities. Such a space

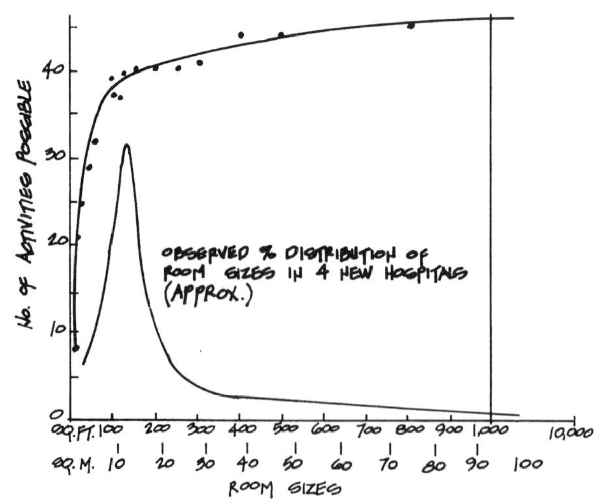

Figure 3.1 Graph by Peter Cowan, University College, London, 1964.

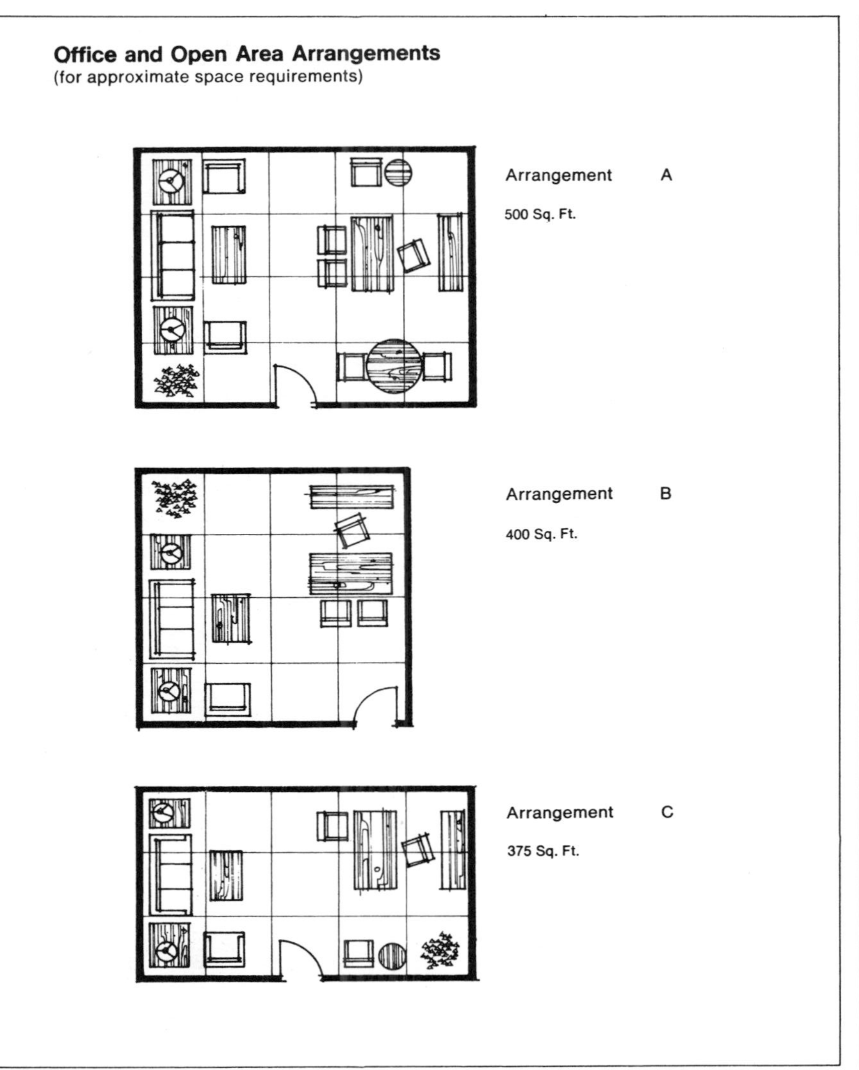

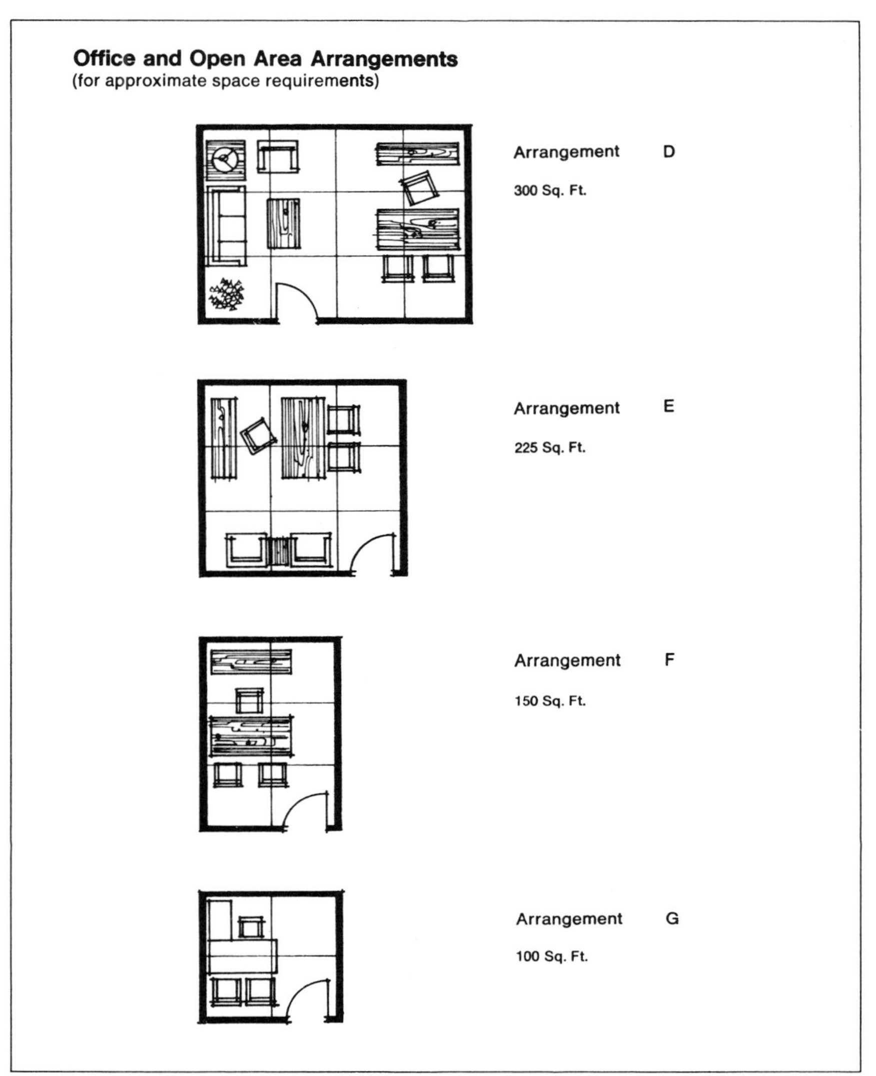

Figure 3.2 *Source*. William Dudley Hunt, Jr., *Total Design*, McGraw-Hill Book Company, 1972.

(assuming environmental controls exist) can be used as living room, dining room, bedroom, study, seminar room, small classroom, small office, waiting room, apartment house laundry facility, small shop, art gallery, lunchroom, or workshop. Buildings with flexible interior arrangements can accommodate a wide variety of functions, and knowing what these are, the designer can prescribe optimum space sizes for any type of use. Table 3.1 lists some sizes and functions frequently encountered in the design of interior spaces. Regardless of the number of activities, interior space must accommodate its users, their movements, and any needed equipment.

Design is often intuitive or judgmental. Since a change in one element affects all others, the architect must know the scope of human activity in the area being designed, as well as how to accommodate it. The architect must also be able to select shapes and sizes to satisfy economic requirements.

Example of Functional Design. An experimental laboratory with tables, benches, sinks, and movable equipment should be encompassed in a rectangle (or square) whose sides are at a ratio of 1.5:1. A 20-story building containing two such labs per floor is poorly designed; a 2-story building with 20 laboratories per floor is much better.

In designing a high school complex, the architect must visualize necessary sizes and relationships in three dimensions; merely studying the blueprints is not sufficient. If the goals are efficiency and economy he or she would group together all interior spaces calling for similar ceiling heights. Thus all spaces requiring 9-foot ceilings could be flexibly arranged in a single building. Likewise, the auditorium, "little theater," cafeteria, gymnasium, and library could be located together, as "special-use" areas. Spatial pleasure is maintained by varying levels, heights, light sources, shapes.

Table 3.1 Design of Interior Space: Typical Uses and Approximate Areas

Use of Space (Capacity)	Approximate Area (ft²)	Use of Space (Capacity)	Approximate Area (ft²)
Education		Office	
Small classroom	300–600	Private	100–300
Large classroom	800–900	Semiprivate	150–400
Lecture room (60–80)	1200–1600	Conference room	300–600
Science lab	1200–1400	Reception/information	400–600
Gymnasium	2,000–10,000	Personnel/interviews	150–200
Cafeteria (500)		Medical office	
Kitchen	2600–2800	Examination/treatment	80–140
Serving area	2600–2800	Consultation	120–180
Dining area	7200–9600	Laboratory	130–240
		X-rays	300–500
The Arts		Hotel/motel: twin-bed suite	250–350
Concert hall, no loft (2000)	45,000–55,000	Industry	
Theater, with stage (800)	20,000–25,000	Warehouse	
Health		Storage	10,000–40,000
Private suite	150–180	Office/equipment	5000–20,000
Semiprivate suite	200–240	Recreation	
Laboratories		Baseball diamond	95,000–100,000
150/200-bed hospital	1800–2200	Basketball court	6000–6500
100/150-bed hospital	1400–1800	Bowling alley	2400–2600
Small hospital	500–700	Handball court	2000–2000
Religion: church (500)	5000–6000	Volleyball court	3800–4000
		Tennis court	7200–7400
Commerce		Hockey rink	56,000–62,000
Supermarket		Football field	74,000–78,000
Customer area	20,000–25,000	Soccer field	75,000–77,000
Service section	6500–8500	Polo field	575,000–600,000

Eating Places. A "good" example avoids all undesirable cross-circulation and recognizes different spatial needs. Cafeteria customers are happy because they know where they are to go. Principal requirements are as follows:

- Serving section is easily accessible from entrance.
- Serving area opens on dining room.
- Customers return dirty dishes on their way out.
- Clean dishes are returned directly to serving section.
- Outside deliveries are made into food-storage area.
- Food-storage supplies are adjacent to serving section.
- Stored supplies are directly accessible from kitchen.
- Prepared food is handed from kitchen to serving section.
- Ceiling heights are low in support areas and high in customer dining area, to provide spaciousness and pleasant atmosphere for diners.
- The change in ceiling height allows more efficient use of natural light and acoustics.

A "bad" example entails many unnecessary (therefore wasted) motions, crossups between dirty and clean dish areas, and a cramped atmosphere, usually attributable to the following causes:

- Serving section disoriented from entrance.
- Entering customers bump into exiting customers.
- Clean dishes must be transported through busy kitchen to be returned to serving area; service people bump into one another, causing strain and frustrations.
- Deliveries are made into kitchen; delivery people must cross kitchen to get to storage area.
- Ceiling height is the same (low) throughout.

Locker Rooms. A good plan recognizes the necessity of effectively handling the spatial relationships between shower section and public sections. This involves the following considerations:

- Cross-circulation of shoe and barefoot traffic is avoided.
- Entrance opens directly into dressing and locker area, and toilet.
- Equipment can be checked out on the way to the gym.
- Towel-issue area has direct access both to outside delivery and interior distribution (people emerging from showers find towels immediately).
- Team area is immediately adjacent to but separate from showers.
- Small office and equipment and toilet rooms are grouped together.
- The main activity area (locker and dressing section) is a single, large, separate space that is different in height, natural lighting, and mechanical and electrical systems from the other spaces.
- The traffic pattern is simple and clearly defined.

A bad scheme forces crossing shoe with barefoot traffic, office and equipment checkout are widely separated, and there is no direct access to the towel area for delivery people; to enter, one must go down a hall and run into the shower area before reaching the lockers, and having two shower areas and two drying spaces is inefficient, an unnecessary waste of space. The design may have looked pretty on paper, but it does not balance three dimensionally.

Parameters for three other uses are as follows:

- *Science Facility.* The large storage area is immediately accessible to both straight labs and the classroom-laboratory. Preparation rooms open directly into labs.
- *Diagnostic X-Ray Suite.* The traffic flow of professionals from X-ray room to darkroom to viewing room to storage is completely separate from patient traffic; thus technicians can work unimpeded and without unexpected interruptions from lay persons.
- *Branch Bank.* Requires the same kind of separation of work and public space as the X-ray suite. Tellers are on one side of the public rectangle, more complex services are on the opposite side, and entrances are on the other two opposing sides—this space is extremely efficient.

Conclusion. All the examples thus far presented convey the premise of design as function; that is, a space should be evaluated in terms of the human activities that will take place in it. Furthermore, one's perception of spaces influences one's physioemotional response to them. An efficient and effective design produces a pleasant environment as well as economic benefit to the owner of that space.

Exterior Space. Exterior space can be visualized as architecture without a roof, and functional design is as essential to exterior space as it is to interior space. Projected uses of exterior space must be identified and categorized in the same manner as for interior space. Most exterior spaces must accommodate heavier (foot and vehicular) traffic volume than interior spaces.

Some passive activities (watching athletic events) need more space than some active activities (bicycling).

Nevertheless, we will categorize a few sample activities into "active" and "passive," and also human "alone" and human augmented by vehicular machinery. The terms *active* and *passive* are, of course, relative.

Human Alone—Active

- Strolling, jogging, brisk walking, skipping, running, dancing, etc.
- Participation in sports.
- Ascending and descending stairways.
- Shopping.
- Hiking, camping.
- Acting on stage or in a movie.
- Barroom brawl.

Human Augmented—Active

- Rollerskates, skateboard, bicycle, motorcycle; traveling (to a specific destination or casually).
- Automobile and its variants; traveling (freeway driving or racing).

Human Alone—Passive

- Resting, looking at scenery, reading, waiting for others or a bus, talking, etc.
- Visiting a fair or street market.
- Waiting in line.
- Using public toilet facilities.
- Being a member of an audience.
- Eating or drinking.
- Playing a musical instrument, singing.

Human Augmented—Passive

- Sitting in a parked vehicle.
- Waiting at a traffic light.
- Waiting to make a left turn.
- Riding in a bus, train, or airplane.
- Trying to start a stalled vehicle.

Use of Space. Analysis of space use determines the optimum size of exteriors as well as interiors, even though the outdoor or exterior space use is likely to be more complex or tenuous than interior use. Visual harmony and spatial relationships are also important to the design of exteriors.

The Japanese architect Yoshinobu Ashihara theorizes that in scale design of exterior space, an area 8 to 10 times larger than that of interior space will provide an environment similar to the interior one. Thus if a room 10 feet square is considered small and intimate, all exterior space that is 80 to 100 feet square would be small enough to be considered similarly intimate.

A room 30 × 60 feet is quite large, yet people can still interact informally without losing a sense of togetherness. Eight times that size (240 × 480 ft) is the largest exterior space in which people retain some sense of intimacy; this size corresponds roughly to the size of large plazas in European cities.

Ashihara further hypothesizes that an 80-foot module could be used in designing exterior spaces to avoid visual monotony; that is, a large city square measuring 300 × 600 feet might be interrupted every 80 feet or so by planters, benches, fountains, trees, sculpture, lighting fixtures, and so on, to reduce the enormity of the space to a human scale of perception. By superimposing a scale model of an 80-foot grid over the plan of any exterior space, a designer can better comprehend its size.

It is also possible to connect a series of large spaces, yet retain spatial order and scale within each, since this is essentially the same kind of design as a series of interconnected interior spaces that are visually defined without being physically partitioned (such as an airport terminal). Areas can be arbitrarily defined as exterior or interior, public or private (e.g., public and private beaches). Once the rules of design have been thoroughly learned, they can be broken.

Distance Perception. The maximum distance a person can easily walk is about 1000 feet; territorial or "personal" space perception is limited to 1500 feet. Consequently distances exceeding 1500 feet are said to be beyond architectural scale. Human perception of another human being is about 4000 feet, maximum. Exterior space exceeding 1 mile is considered too large to be perceived as "a space" unless a connecting network of vehicular transport is provided.

A Short History of Cities. Humankind's lack of a prehensile tail and our structurally induced preference for upright locomotion severely limited the ability of primitive peoples to escape other predators. Therefore humans tended to be "with" each other; thus the first cities (settlements) came into being.

Walking distances determined a human gathering's size and location—even its shape. Campkeepers had to be able to reach home on foot at the first threat of danger;

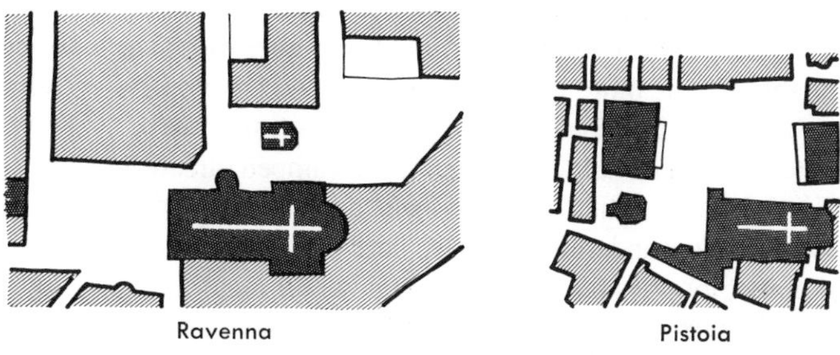

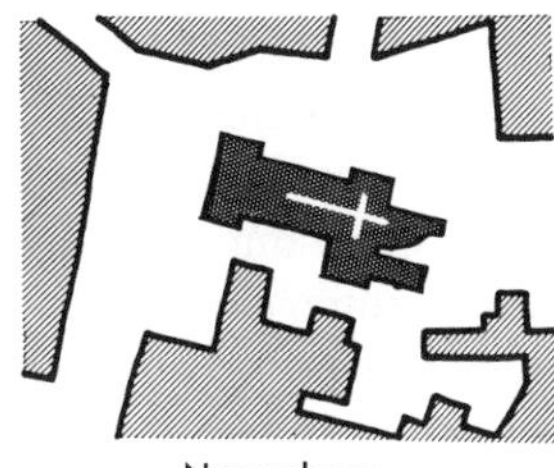

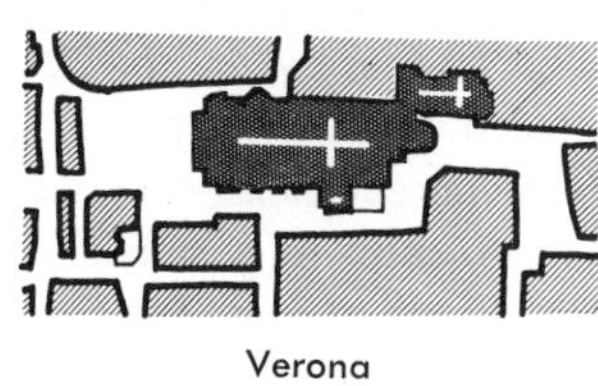

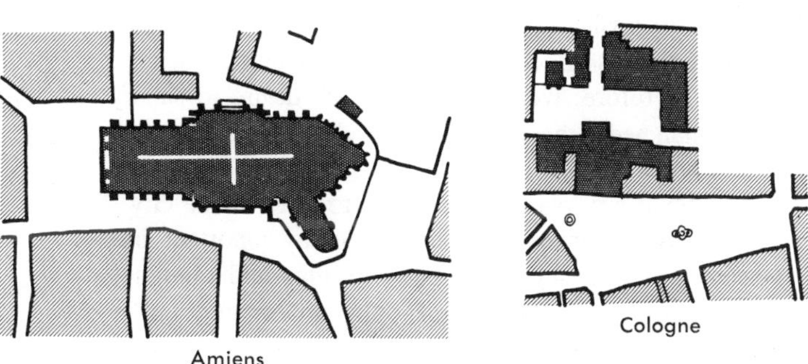

Figure 3.3 *Source*. John Ormsbee Simonds, *Landscape Architecture*, McGraw-Hill Book Company, 1961.

food-gatherers had to walk to edible wild plants and potable water; hunters could not travel excessive distances to reliable hunting grounds. The natural resources of the countryside determined the number of inhabitants that could be supported at any single location, and the daylight hours limited perimeters in any direction. The first cities were movable and needed no walls.

Archeologists have found remnants of cities 10,000 years old, but this does not mean that cities began 10,000 years ago. No one knows the true age of city life. By the time permanent cities were established, humans in several parts of the world had discovered that travel by horse, donkey, elephant, ostrich, or camel was preferable to walking. Then the wheel was invented, although undoubtedly it was considered to be too sacred to "use" for a long while. The ancient Celts, for example, used the wheel and—at the same time—regarded it as sacred at least as late as A.D. 500.

The power hierarchy of very ancient cities was probably as follows:

- God-king.
- Priests (male and/or female, but mostly male), who chose the god-king.
- Military support.
- Everybody else.

Agronomy and animal husbandry led to the expansion of city sizes because they provided the techniques to make available larger, more reliable sources of food. Temple, storehouses, palace, and military barracks came to be situated behind a wall; ordinary citizens camped outside.

Time passed. Cities gradually became bastions of defense against wandering nomadic hordes, "strangers," and other city priesthoods thirsty for power through conquest. Ordinary people were allowed to live more or less permanently inside city walls, provided they squeezed in before sunset, since their presence ensured that more bodies were available for defensive purposes. The gates of ancient cities were locked at sunset. Thus a person who has received "the key to the city" has been entrusted, symbolically, to be sure, with that city's riches.

As the ecclesiastical governments gave way to military dictatorships (e.g., those of Alexander the Great, Imperial Rome, Genghis Khan), which further entrenched themselves into dynasties of power, cities began to reflect their respective rulers' craving for grandeur, beauty, culture, or defense. The great cities of history (1000 B.C. onward) were built to serve these needs: Babylon (beauty), Alexandria (culture), El Escorial (defense), Marseilles and Rome (grandeur).

City Planning of the Past. Whatever impression ancient rulers wished to convey about the cities they caused to be built was aimed at an audience of human beings. Cities, therefore, were set up with the desire to satisfy the human needs that were considered to be of paramount importance.

Medieval city planners arranged to have at the city's heart a large square or plaza, surrounded by important, imposing structures—government buildings and churches (which were, in medieval times, also government buildings). Here the common folk could come, to be impressed by the magnificence around them. This is why many a city square is referred to as "the commons." Later, as the population grew and became more demanding and less awestruck, other, more plebian attractions were added as seasonal or special lures: markets, religious festivals, carnivals, and executions.

Rich and poor alike were protected from the elements by galleries, canopies, colonnades, and porticos. The old section of Bologna still has a 20-mile network of sidewalks covered by porticos. These covered sidewalks have been used and admired for centuries because they encourage pleasurable strolling and sociability.

Artisans of the past liked to adorn sidewalks, walls, and streets with textured materials—cobbles, tile, glass—for practical purposes and for beauty. The cobblestone streets of Milan were paved in such a way that carriage wheels were guided away from sidewalks, thus preventing vehicles from swerving and striking pedestrians.

Leonardo da Vinci, the creative genius of Renaissance Europe, planned a city with a double network of streets: one elevated (for pedestrians), the other at ground level (for vehicles). Leonardo the engineer reasoned that the most efficient traffic system for both feet and vehicles required separate, continuous networks for each. Leonardo the artist knew that aesthetic pleasure could best be achieved by setting the human perspective above the dust and noise of ground-level functions, something that the designers of the Acropolis had also known.

Nineteenth-century Viennese town planner Camillo Sitte believed that the minimum dimension of a city plaza should be the height of the principal adjacent building; its maximum dimension should not exceed twice that height unless the building is meant to convey monumentality. He was the last of the ancient city planners.

Circulation Systems

The Pedestrian Versus the Vehicle. The ancient Romans recognized the negative effect of vehicles on cities. Heavy wagons were forbidden in central Rome after dusk, and at the Forum in Pompeii large, slablike stone barriers were placed at all entrance points to prevent intrusion of vehicles.

The advent of mechanical transportation has reversed this perspective, forcing humankind into a losing competition with machines for urban space. The ubiquitous automobile demands more and more space. It is a modern nightmare pervading every part of an urban environment and causing a major dichotomy in the intended goals of city planning and design. Despite the advantages of fast travel and communication, the automobile is responsible for a great many unfortunate changes in society. It has imposed its own scale on urban design, requiring immense space for its movement and storage, and it assigns pedestrians to a peripheral, ever-narrowing, sidewalk environment, choking them with noxious fumes.

Technology Aids the Pedestrian. Even though one may be appalled at the population explosion as evidenced by tremendous masses of people milling about, filling every available nook, urban spaces can still be designed to produce orderly human movement. When contemplating the design of pedestrian space, one should consider the following human traits:

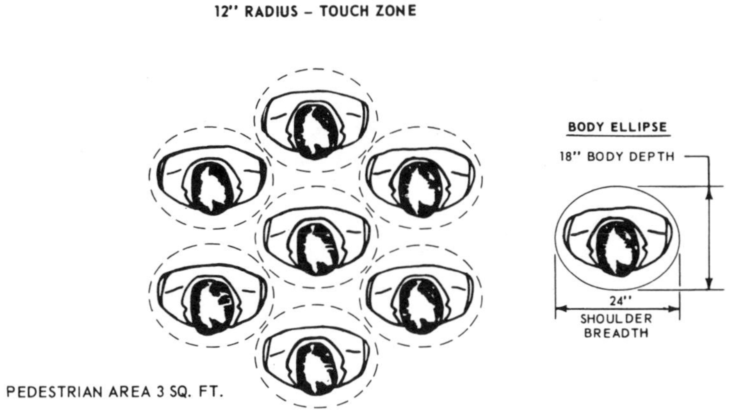

12" RADIUS – TOUCH ZONE

BODY ELLIPSE

18" BODY DEPTH

24" SHOULDER BREADTH

PEDESTRIAN AREA 3 SQ. FT.

Figure 3.4 *Source.* John J. Fruin, *Pedestrian Planning and Design,* Metropolitan Association of Urban Designers & Environmental Planners, 1971.

• There is a preference for avoiding bodily contact with others (at least among Northern Europeans).

• Human physical dimensions were the determinant of almost all existing entrances, corridors, sidewalks, and so on.

• When traffic is dense, pedestrians tend to shorten the forward stride while maintaining normal side space.

• People walking tend to internalize *only* clear, simple directions and signals. Otherwise, they stop to think about where they are going.

• We tend to maintain a distance of 18 inches from stationary objects and walls except under the most crowded conditions.

• Ascending and descending stairs require greater energy use than does travel on a level surface and involve more danger from falling.

Designing a Sidewalk. Whether a sidewalk is indoor or outdoor, the same width rules should be observed for maximum efficiency and comfort: 18 inches on either edge to account for the human avoidance pattern; 24 inches more on both sides to accommodate standing pedestrians or window shoppers; 2 feet for parking meters, utility poles, trashcans, standing ashtrays, lighting fixtures, fire hydrants, shrubbery, benches, and so on. A 15-foot sidewalk, after these allowances, will allow 4 people to walk abreast. In addition to the spatial estimates just given, good sidewalk design should provide the following:

1 Individual freedom to choose one's own normal walking pace.
2 Space to bypass slow-moving pedestrians.
3 Easy crossing and changing of direction anywhere, including traffic concentration points.

If traffic demand exceeds a walkway's capacity, the result will be crowding and delay—even panic. A favorable walking environment is created only if the walkway allows normal, unconflicted stride during all expected traffic fluctuations.

Functional components are entrances, corridors, stairs, pedmovers, waiting spaces, and directional signs. Good building design should organize these elements coherently; a building's pedestrian circulation system should be direct and uncomplicated, even for first-time or infrequent users. If the visual space is confused, pedestrians will become confused.

Building component design should contain simple, direct, logical architectural statements that visually convey direction, orientation, and purpose. A confused visual pattern cannot be adequately corrected by adding directional signs. Signs should be supplementary, confirming the design rather than allowing one to decipher it.

Stairway dimensions tend to restrict motions: pace is circumscribed according to width of stair tread and riser height, there is a need for railings, and the individual's speed of forward progress is determined by speed of pedestrian(s) ahead.

Important elements of functional stairway design are as follows:

• Stairway approaches spacious enough to avoid pedestrian lineup.

• Per person space of 3 square feet.

• Good lighting.

• Stair edges, treads, and railings designed to assist travel, especially for handicapped persons.

• Riser heights less than 7 inches, to reduce exertion and improve traffic flow (people are able to move faster on stairs as riser height is decreased).

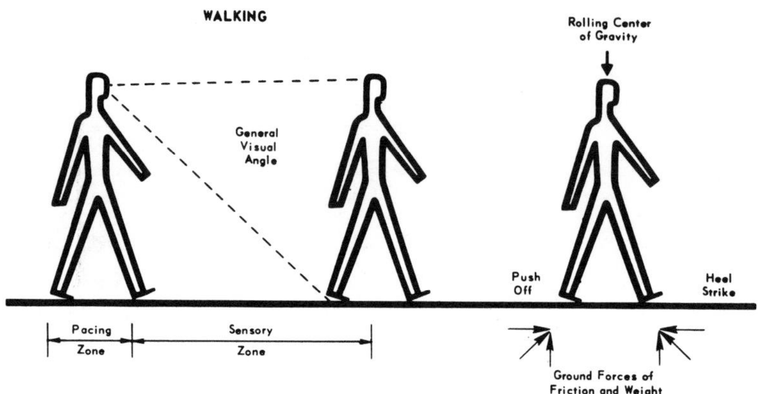

Figure 3.5 Human pacing and sensory zones. *Source*. John J. Fruin, *Pedestrian Planning and Design,* Metropolitan Association of Urban Designers & Environmental Planners, 1971.

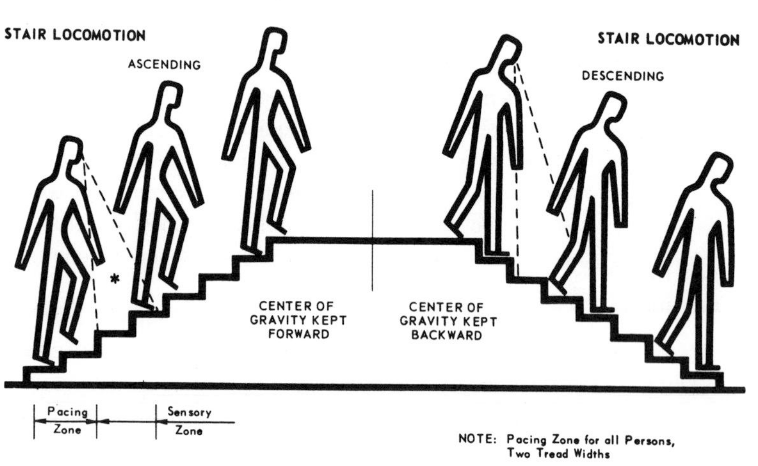

- When a stairway is placed in a corridor, the entrance to the stairs governs corridor design.
- Where minor traffic snarls occur, the width of the stair is extended a minimum of one pedestrian lane (30 inches).

Elevators. The mechanical principles of lifting and lowering people and goods have been known and used for some time. Efficient, safe elevator transportation has made skyscrapers possible, thus creating more space for urban populations by moving them up rather than out.

The elevator is the most universally accepted mechanical pedestrian mover. The functional design of elevators involves lobby and cab shapes; capacity in an elevator cab is based on an assumed requirement of about 2 square feet per person. An acceptable waiting time for elevator service is 30 seconds for commercial buildings, 60 seconds for residential.

"Sky-lobby" elevator systems divide a building into two or three units, stacked one on top of the other. Passengers going to upper floors take express elevators to an intermediate sky lobby, where they transfer to upper-floor elevators. Shafts for upper and lower building segments are used in common by two or three elevators. The sky-lobby system at the World Trade Center in New York has increased estimated rentable floor area by 13%

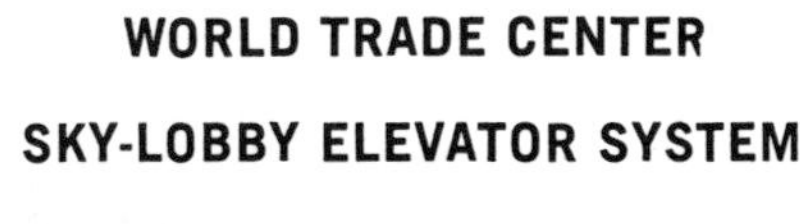

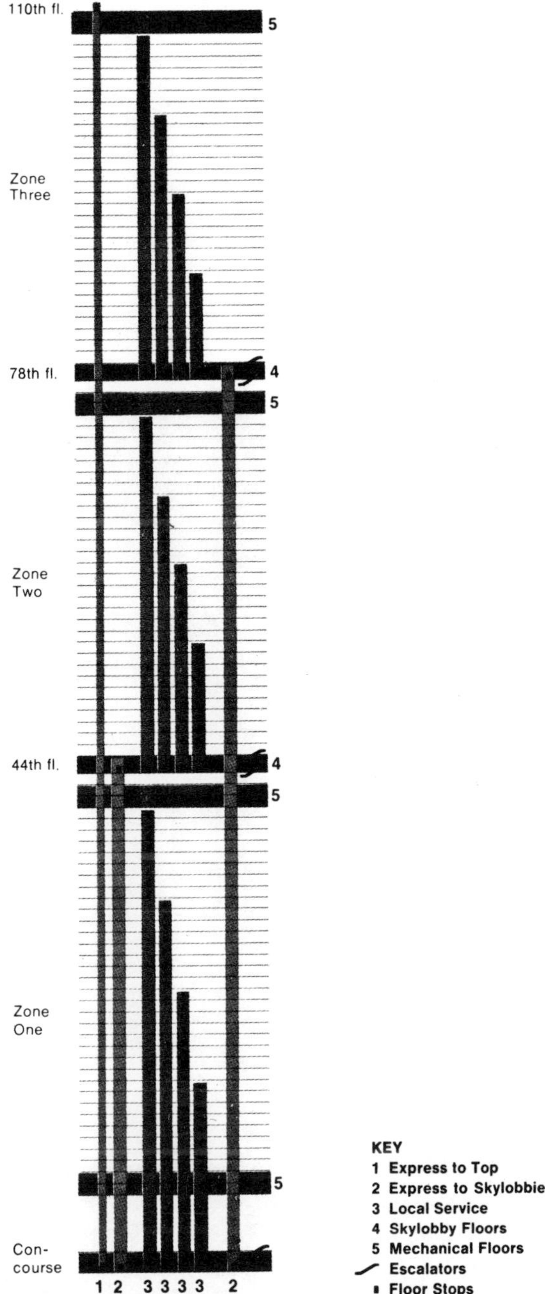

Figure 3.6 *Source.* John J. Fruin, *Pedestrian Planning and Design,* Metropolitan Association of Urban Designers & Environmental Planners, 1971.

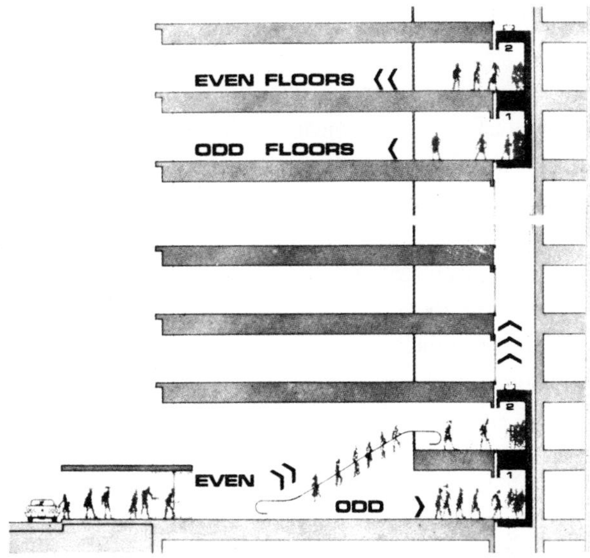

Figure 3.7 *Source.* John J. Fruin, *Pedestrian Planning and Design,* Metropolitan Association of Urban Designers & Environmental Planners, 1971.

The double-decker system is in operation in the Time-Life Building in Chicago and in the John Hancock Tower in Boston. Double-deck elevators are 2 stories high, with upper and lower compartments. Passengers enter from two entrance lobbies: a lower lobby serving odd-numbered floors, and an upper lobby or mezzanine serving even-numbered floors. Double-deckers operate in response to passenger calls in both compartments. This system, of course, increases elevator capacity by 100% without additional shaft structure. Double-deckers can also be combined with sky lobbies to produce even greater space savings.

Escalators. An escalator is a moving staircase that provides a continuous series of individual treads for standing pedestrians. Because considerable agility is necessary to step on and off, however, escalators can cause long lineups, even at low traffic levels; thus a clear area of 500 square feet should be provided at escalator approaches to accommodate pedestrian surges. The mechanical staircase automatically discharges pedestrians regardless of the space available, and outlets should be even more spacious than entrances. Supplementary, stationary stairs should be built close to escalators, for use in case of breakdown. Escalators are discussed in more detail in the section ''Vertical Travel Construction Techniques.''

Pedestrian conveniences partake of both the old, natural world and the new, technological world. People still like to stroll and talk. They also like electronic gadgetry, the magic of science. Good functional design includes such creature comforts as the following:

- Trash receptacles and mailboxes.
- Police and fire department call boxes.
- Telephones.
- Special designs for the handicapped (e.g., ramped curbs).
- Toilets, lavatories, benches for resting or waiting.
- Information booths.
- Water fountains.
- Vending machines.
- "Vest-pocket" parks. Such facilities should be designed to treat the eye—and possibly the ear and the nose—and to take maximum advantage of available sun, shade, and view. They should be conducive to conversation or to a picnic lunch, and they should be completely accessible to the handicapped.

Malls. Today's answer to the medieval plaza is the mall, usually a commercial shopping center, that admits foot traffic only, aside from maintenance vehicles and the police. Such structures may be indoor or outdoor. The following features should also be considered in designing and/or constructing a mall:

METROPOLITAN OPERA HOUSE, LINCOLN CENTER
New York, New York
Architects: Harrison & Abramovitz
Photo: B. Serating

1 At the mall's outer edges, adequate access for the above mentioned mechanical transport.
2 A street system that replaces traffic movement lost to the mall area.
3 Adequate parking.
4 Coordinated promotion for the various components of the new facility.

Santa Monica, California, and in many other cities, creation of a mall involves merely closing off streets or street sections. Aesthetic considerations and pedestrian amenities may be constructed at the outset or later, if the increased volume of business warrants such improvements.

Objectives for pedestrian design can be summarized as follows:

1 *Safety*. Reduction of foot and vehicular traffic confrontations.
2 *Security*. Unobstructed view of other pedestrians, good lighting, and conveniently placed police and fire emergency call boxes.
3 *Convenience*. Foot-traffic control systems, easily read signs, comfortable walking distances between parking lot(s) and stores or between one store and another store.
4 *Continuity*. Grade-separated pedestrian networks, above or below street level.
5 *Comfort*. An aesthetic atmosphere designed in accordance with scientific principles to be stimulating in some areas (storefronts and store entrances) and relaxing in others (benches).

Vehicular Circulation. The American way of life requires the automobile and its derivative vehicles—vans, motorcycles, snowmobiles, semis, rough-terrain vehicles, pickup trucks. These machines are widely regarded as necessary to individual well-being, like food, shelter, and a job.

Access Roads. Virtually all buildings or centers are served by access streets or roads. Large shopping complexes are often located close to an expressway; vehicles are directed to them by an access street. Even facilities that lie beyond city limits, such as colleges, manufacturing plants, feedlots/slaughterhouses, and oil refineries, are positioned adjacent to a state highway. In addition to access to property, access roads must provide easement for local drainage and sewer system, utility lines, and streetlights, and there must be allowance for pedestrians.

Driveways. Site access designers should bear in mind the necessity of accommodating left and right turns, and entrances and exits. Drivers should have enough distance to make clear turn signals before traffic lights. Driveways on both sides of a street must be coordinated for minimum or no interference with each other and to avoid an overlap of left-turn lanes.

The least desirable access location is the one close to a signal-controlled intersection. If the driveway is less than 200 feet from the intersection, access to it from the street is likely to be blocked for both left- and right-turners by traffic waiting for the light to change.

Parking. Physical, legal, and economic constraints determine amount and type of parking facilities. Where land is cheap and abundant, multilevel parking structures are not needed; in busy, downtown areas a multilevel lot is almost always justified, even if its capacity is not delineated by law. The architect must evaluate his designs according to the following variables:

- Vehicular movement within the parking lot itself.
- Entrances and exits.
- Amount of traffic generated by the lot.
- Pedestrian convenience and safety.
- Stall sizes.

Circulation within the lot must be facilitated by (1) a major two-way road to guide vehicles to each level and back down again, and to provide exit access to parked vehicles; (2) aisleways on each level—both through the lot and around its outer edge—of sufficient width to permit one-way vehicular travel in each aisleway and to handle cars maneuvering to park or leave stalls (drive-in movie theater design is similar).

Another important feature of the circulation system is adequate space at the lot's inner entrance, to prevent entering traffic from forming a backed-up obstruction on the access street. Large, easily seen and read directional signs—even a traffic signal and/or railroad crossing bar to regulate flow of traffic—are paramount.

Ramp-slope standards are as follows:

- Departure ramps, 10° maximum.
- Approach ramps, 15° maximum.
- If the exit slope (upward) rises to sidewalk level, it must have a transition slope section 16 feet long—5° maximum incline—before it intersects the sidewalk. This is to prevent the hood of a car from blocking the driver's view of pedestrian traffic.

In addition, property-line walls should not obstruct a driver's view of pedestrians. If such walls are at sidewalk's edge, the exit driveway end should be set

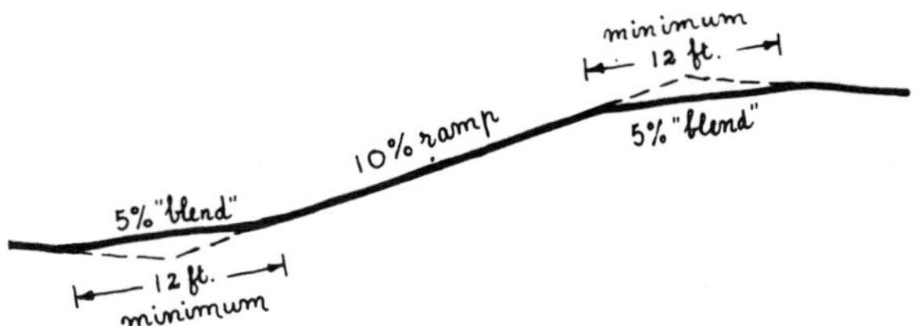

Figure 3.8 *Source.* Geoffrey Baker and Bruno Funaro, *Parking,* Reinhold Publishing Company, 1958.

back at least 6 feet from the outer wall of the structure: the further back from a sidewalk are the walls, the shorter should be the distance between driveway end and wall, foot for foot.

Pedestrians can disembark from multilevel parking lots by several means: elevators or escalators (e.g., the underground lot of Century City, California), or ramped walkways parallel to the main inside vehicular road but separate from it. In many states pedestrians have legal right-of-way, but because of the restricted area of the lot, pedestrians may find caution a better protector.

Parking stall design should observe the following guidelines:

1 Minimum stall space for average car, 9 × 18 feet.
2 Minimum space for compacts, 8 × 16 feet. Perhaps compact cars could be stored on a separate level, for compacts only, to maximize use of space and avoid confusion. A separate level for compacts could be announced at the entrance.
3 Parking for both long-term users (employee) and short-term users (visitor or shopper).
4 Attendant and self-parking.
5 Allowance for parking angles.

Well-marked oblique-angle parking stalls are easier to maneuver into and out of than are perpendicular stalls, but they require more space. Aisleways should permit a vehicle to park in a single turning movement, although unless the lot is almost empty, this goal is seldom attained. Angles stalls should be designed to reverse direction flow in alternate parking aisleways.

Vertical Travel Construction Techniques

Vertical traffic circulation in any multistory building is the key to successful design function, for normal use or for emergencies.

Stairs. The number of stairs required in any building is usually controlled by local building codes. As a rule there are restrictions on the horizontal distance from any point on a floor to a stairway, the floor area taken up by the stairway itself, and capacity; special provisions apply to public buildings.

Stairs and landings should be designed to carry a live load of 100 pounds per square foot or concentrated at maximum stress points at 300 pounds per square foot.

Treads and Risers. Treads (the horizontal distance between risers) should be 10 to 13 inches wide, exclusive of nosing (the projection beyond the riser below). The most comfortable riser height (vertical distance between treads) is 7 to 7½ inches. Treads less than 6 inches wide, or risers more than 8 inches high are unsafe. The steeper the stair slope, the greater the ratio of riser to tread (there is always one less tread than riser per flight of stairs). A step (tread plus riser above it) must measure 17 to 17½ inches. Minimum vertical headroom from riser to overhead construction should not be less than 6 feet, 8 inches.

Railings. Handrails are generally set between 2½ and 2 feet, 10 inches above the stairway walking surfaces. Along a wall, handrail clearance should be at least 1½ inches. *Balusters* are vertical posts that support a handrail. The railing support at landings or floors is called an *angle* post. The post terminating or beginning a stair railing is the *newel*.

Stair Types. *Straight* stair flights go in a single direction (up or down) per flight. Flights may be parallel, angled (usually 90°, at each landing), or scissored (a pair of straight runs in opposite directions with a fire-resistant wall between them).

Circular stairs appear to follow a large circle. *Spiral* stairs have a smaller radius (3½–8 ft) and may be supported by a center post. Winders (steps with tapered treads) should be avoided in *curved* staircases because the narrowness of the inside treads is unsafe. "Balanced" steps (tread width of straight portion equals width at line of travel) spread the change in angle over the entire flight.

Fire Stairs. Fire escapes—outside metal-grating stairs (with a "jump-down" at the bottom), and landings attached to exterior walls with unprotected openings were acceptable at one time; however these are not permitted for new construction.

Fire-exit stairs should be totally enclosed (no openings to building interior proper) by high fire-resistant walls to prevent spread of smoke and flames. Wired glass windows are permitted in exterior walls of the stair tower not exposed to fire hazard. Access should be provided on each story through fire-protected landings or balconies open on an exterior wall. Doors should be at least 40 inches wide and self-closing; the viewing area, of clear, wired glass, should be 720 square inches—or less. The top of the shaft should be openable, either thermally operated or a skylight, to let heat escape.

Public buildings require more than one smokeproof fire exit; these should be as far apart as possible. Bottom exits should lead directly to the outdoors.

Stairs outside a building are also acceptable as a fire exit if they satisfy all requirements of inside stairs. Outside stairs should be separated from the building interior by fire-resistant walls with fire doors or fixed wired glass windows protecting openings.

Steel Stairs. Pressed-sheet steel stairs are used in fire-resistant buildings. Steel sheets are formed into risers and subtreads (pans), into which stone, concrete, composition, or metal treads may be inserted and given a nonslip surface.

Concrete. Depending on support, concrete stairs may be cantilevered or inclined beams and slabs. The entire stairway may be precast or cast in place as a unit, or slabs or T-beams may be formed first and steps built later. Concrete treads should have metal nosings to protect tread edges.

Wood. Stairs constructed of wood are permitted for wood-frame and nonfireproof buildings, single-family houses, and duplexes.

Construction of a built-in-place stair (it can also be shopmade) starts with the cutting of carriages (rough timber step support) to receive the risers and treads. The lower portion of the wall stringer (inclined, finished piece), which should be cut at least one-half inch deep to house the steps, is set in place against the wall, with the cut profile fitting the stepped profile of the top of the carriage. *Headers* are horizontal pieces supporting stringers or landings. Treads and risers are then nailed to the carriage; the tongues at the bottom of the risers fit into grooves at the rear of the treads. Nosings are molded on the underside, as a finish.

If the outer stringer is an open stringer (cut to fit line of riser and tread), it should be mitered to fit corresponding miters in the ends of risers, then nailed against the outside carriage. Tread ends project beyond the open stringer. If the outer stringer is closed (parallel top and bottom) tread and riser ends should be wedged and glued into the wall stringer.

Escalators. An escalator includes a steel-trussed framework, handrails, and a conveyor belt with steps; it is an inclined bridge spanning floors. At the upper and lower ends are a pair of motor-driven sprocket wheels. A worm-gear generator is at the escalator's upper terminal. Two roller chains travel over the sprockets and pull the conveyor belt of steps around and around. The steps move on a set of tracks attached to the trusses; each step is supported on four resilient rollers. Slope of the stair is standardized at 30°. A structural frame should be installed around the stairwell to carry the floor and railing span. The stairway itself should be independent of this frame.

Installation and Arrangement. A vertical variation from the level of supporting beams of ½ inch in specified floor-to-floor height is permitted in escalator design. The escalator is "shimmed" to bring it level.

Trusses are usually brought on site in three sections, then assembled and raised into position with chain hoists through an elevator or on the outside of the building.

Escalators are usually installed in pairs—up and down. The units may be placed parallel to each other per story or crisscrossed. Crisscrossed stairs are more compact and minimize walking distance between stairs.

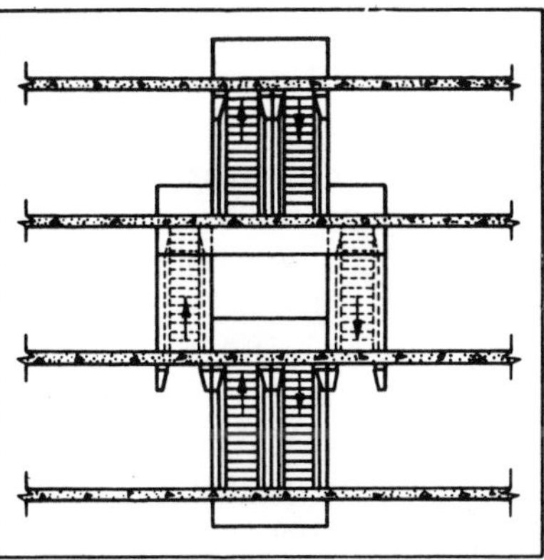

Parallel arrangement

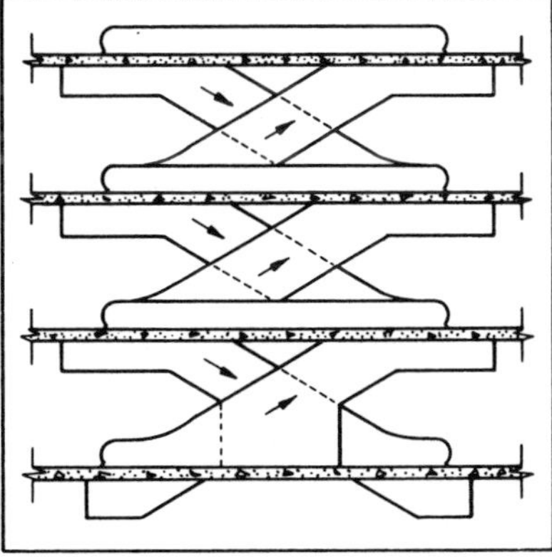

Crisscross arrangement

Figure 3.9 *Source.* Frederick S. Merritt, *Building Construction Handbook,* McGraw-Hill Book Company, 1975.

Fire Protection. Escalators may be set up as fire exits if they are enclosed in the same manner as stationary exit stairs and if they lead one way (outside) only. Ordinary escalators must have protection for top and bottom floor openings or, as an acceptable alternative, a standard, supervised sprinkler system such as one of the following.

- Sprinkler vent.
- Spray nozzle.
- Partial enclosure.
- Rolling shutter (automatically encloses the top of each escalator).
- Control and machine spaces enclosed in fire-resistant material, yet ventilated.

Ramps. Ramps slope as steep as 15% (15 ft per 100 ft), but 10% is preferred. With a 10% maximum slope and a story height of 12 feet, a ramp connecting two floors must be 120 feet long. It need not be a straight slope: curved, zigzag, or spiral ramps save more space. Level landings 44 inches long (in the direction of travel) should be added at door openings or where an abrupt change of slope or direction occurs. Landings should be as wide as the ramp. Both ramps and landings should carry a live load of 100 pounds per square foot.

Railings should take a horizontal thrust of 50 pounds per foot at the top of the rail. Minimum ramp width is 30 to 44 inches for heights between landings. All surfaces should have a nonskid finish.

In a structure geared to the needs of elderly or handicapped people—or just as a measure of the owner's thoughtfulness—ramps should be built instead of stairs. Powered ramps (moving walkways, escalators without steps) may operate on slopes up to 8° at speeds up to 180 feet per minute, and on slopes up to 15° at speeds up to 140 feet per minute.

Elevators. Two types of elevator are in general use: electric traction (for passengers) and hydraulic (freight service).

Electric. An electric traction installation has the following components:

1 A shaft to house the works.
2 A cage of light metal supported on a structural frame, which is placed inside the shaft. This is the car, or cab.
3 Hoist wire ropes attached to the cab's top, to raise and lower it in the shaft.
4 A grooved, motor-driven sheave. The ropes pass over this sheave and are fastened to counterweights, which are cast iron blocks used to lessen the amount of power necessary to raise and lower the cab, and to start and halt it.
5 An electric motor, with brakes and auxiliary equipment. All this and the sheave are mounted on a heavy frame. The machinery may be housed above the shaft (penthouse) or in the basement.
6 Separate sets of T-shaped guide rails, to control counterweight and cab paths.
7 Safety springs or buffers (see below), placed in the pit beneath the shaft to bring cab or counterweight to a safe halt if either descends past the bottom terminal (at normal speeds only).

Elevator unit stresses should not exceed 80% of the static building loads unless static stress loads exceed normal projected elevator usage. Unit stresses in a guide rail or reinforcement—calculated without disaster or failure impact allowance—should not exceed 15,000 psi; deflection should not exceed ¼ inch.

For fire protection in elevator shafts serving 3 or more stories, an adequate ventilating system for smoke and hot gases should be located in the penthouse or just below the top floor. Indirect vents should have noncombustible ducts to the outside, either open permanently or capable of opening automatically. Vent area should not be less than 2 square feet per elevator cab.

Terms used in connection with elevators include:

- *Buffer.* May be spring or oil; it absorbs and dissipates kinetic energy of cab or counterweight.
- *Door Contact.* An electrical device preventing cab movement in the shaft unless the cab or shaft door is closed.
- *Runby.* The distance a cab can travel beyond a terminal without striking a stop.
- *Emergency stop switch.* A manually operated switch located in the cab that disconnects electrical power from the motor.

Systems governing cab operation include *generator-field* (individual generator for each cab), *multivoltage* (various fixed voltages impressed on the motor armature), and *rheostatic* (varies the resistance of the armature or the field circuit).

Actuating control methods may incorporate a *cab switch* (cab is manually stopped and started), *signal buttons* (cab starts automatically but is stopped manually at the desired floors, or *full automation*.

In the *single automatic* system the cab responds to the first button pressed and ignores all other calls until it arrives at the destination. It cannot store calls.

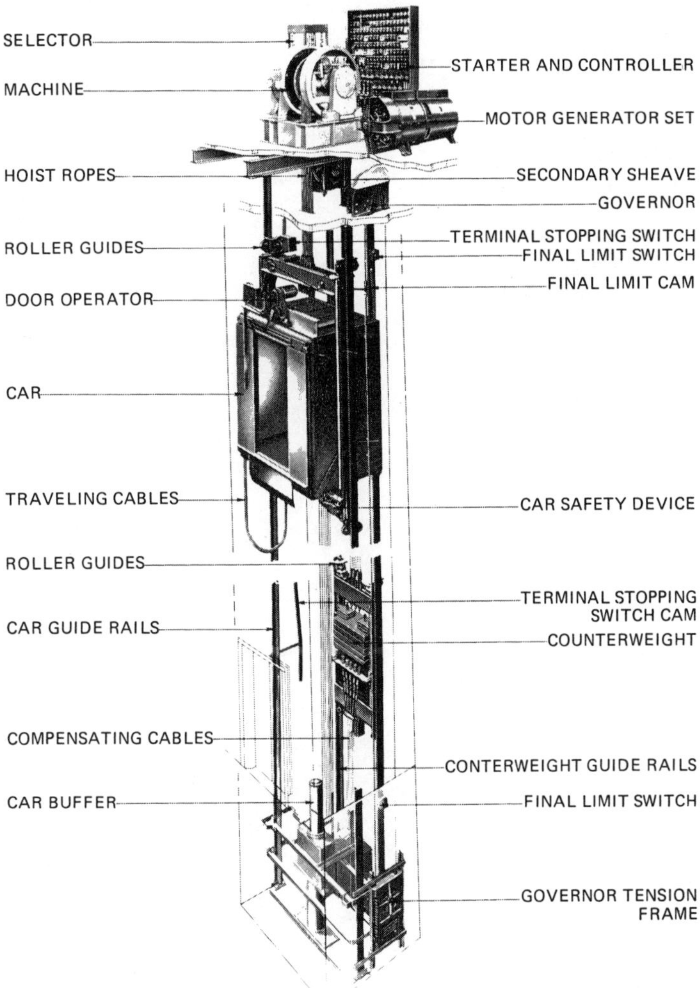

Figure 3.10 Typical passenger elevator installation. Courtesy of Otis Elevator Company.

In *selective/collective* control, calls are answered in the direction of travel; that is, when an "up" button is pushed at a landing, the elevator will stop at that point only if it is going up.

Elevators may be dispatched automatically, in that a timer signals the cabs to leave the terminal at fixed intervals, or when loaded at 80% capacity, as indicated by a device in the floor of the cab.

Several additional safety devices are incorporated into automatic elevators:

- Automatic load weigher to prevent overcrowding.
- Buttons in cab and starter system to stop doors from closing and to hold them open for heavy traffic.
- Lights to indicate floors.
- Two-way loudspeaker system for communication with starter station.
- Auxiliary power system.
- Lights and/or auditory signals to warn of repairs needed.
- Automatic speed slowdown as cab nears a stop.
- Mechanism for adjustment if cab stops short or past floor level.
- Safety devices to prevent doors from closing on a passenger standing in the doorway.

Methods of roping an elevator have a considerable effect on the loading balance of the hoisting ropes, machine bearings, and building parts. The *double-wrap* rope system uses a secondary or idler sheave. In *signal-wrap,* the ropes pass over the traction or driving sheave only once. The sheave has wedge-shaped or undercut grooves that grip the ropes by packing them between the sides of the grooves. The sheave has half the loading weight of

FIRST NATIONAL BANK BUILDING
Chicago, Illinois
Architects: Joint Venture: C. F. Murphy Associates, The Perkins & Will Partnership
Photo: Harr, Hedrich-Blessing

double-wrap. Rope life, however, may be shorter because of pinching by the sheave grooves.

When an elevator motor must be installed in a basement, the load on the overhead supports is increased, rope length is tripled, additional sheaves are needed, higher friction losses are accrued, and more rope bends are needed, requiring greater traction between ropes and sheaves for the same elevator loads and speeds. In addition, there is higher power consumption, more rope wear, and greater operating expense.

Hydraulic. A hydraulic elevator motor raises and lowers the cab with a plunger or piston moved by a liquid (usually oil) under pressure in a cylinder. A dimpled closure called a *safety bulkhead* is located at the bottom of a pressure cylinder (above its head), to control fuel loss in case of cylinder-head failure.

The cab sits on top of the plunger. To raise the cab, the pump begins discharging oil into the pressure cylinder, thus forcing the ram (jack) up. When the cab reaches the desired height, the pump stops or is stopped manually. Oil is released from the cylinder to lower the cab, and the oil returns to a storage tank.

Single-bearing cylinders operate like a hydraulic jack in elevator and sidewalk lifts where the cab is guided at top and bottom to prevent eccentric loads from exerting side stress on the cylinder bearing. A cylinder of heavy steel is sunk into the ground as far as the load will be rising. The ram is thick-walled steel tube, polished to a mirror finish and sealed at the top of the cylinder with a compression pack. Oil is admitted under pressure near the top of the cylinder, while air is removed through a bleeder.

The bearings of a *two-bearing* plunger are kept immersed in oil. The *movable bearing* type, for general industry, supports the lower end of the ram, and another bearing supports the plunger at the top of the cylinder. The *cage bearing* is supported by a secondary cylinder about 3 feet below the main cylinder head. Oil enters just below the head and descends through holes in the bearing to lift the plunger.

When the cab or platform is light, a *double-acting cylinder* may be used. To raise the plunger, oil is admitted below the piston; to lower it, oil is forced into the cylinder near the top—above the piston—and is allowed to flow out below.

Jack plunger sizes for the various types range from 2½ inches in diameter for small lifts to 18 inches in diameter for those operating at 150 to 300 psi.

Hydraulic elevators are less complex than electric ones. The cab and its frame rest on the hydraulic ram (jack, cylinder) that raises and lowers them. No wire ropes, overhead equipment, penthouse, cab safeties, or speed governors are needed. Without heavy overhead loads, hoistway columns and footings may be smaller. The cab and its load move slowly (in fact, they *cannot* fall fast); therefore the bumpers (buffers) need only be heavy springs. Capacity of standard hydraulic freight elevators ranges from 2000 to 20,000 pounds at 20 to 85 feet per minute; they can also be designed for much heavier loads.

Small Conveyors. Dumbwaiters, trays, and pneumatic tubes, usually too small for passenger use, are convenient for routing paperwork and other items (e.g., food) among departments of large commercial buildings or from floor to floor of a multistory structure.

Dumbwaiters. Dumbwaiters work like miniature elevators, with a shaft and ropes on pulleys. The trays may be operated by push-button, or they may be manually raised and lowered by pulling on appropriate ropes. Once upon a time they were used in hotels as "room service." Automatic dumbwaiters handling 100 to 500 pounds at 45 to 150 feet per minute can be mechanically loaded and unloaded or designed for floor-level loading.

Trays. A vertical conveyor shaft should be installed next to other vertical shafts to minimize space use. Vertical conveyor trays are sometimes the most economical means of providing for materials flow and distribution throughout a multistory building.

Tray installation is similar to that for escalators: a continuous roller chain is driven by an electric motor, engaging sprockets at top and bottom. The chain extends to the uppermost floor to be served. Carriers spaced at intervals along the chain transport the trays from floor to floor at about 72 feet per minute. Vertical conveyors are enclosed in fire-resistant shafts. In case of fire, vertical sliding doors, released by fusible links, snap down over the wall openings and seal off the shaft at each floor.

To operate vertical conveyor trays, the attendant sets the floor-selector dial or presses a button by the dispatch cutout. As the trays are placed on the loading station, they are automatically moved into the path of traveling carriers. Each tray rides up and around the top sprocket and is discharged on its downward trip at the preselected floor. It takes only 4½ minutes for a 26-story delivery of office memoranda; 200 pounds or more of paperwork or office supplies can be circulated per minute.

Pneumatic Tubes. The carrier is a metal cylinder into which is inserted paper, money, or other light cargo. A cap is then screwed on, the cylinder is placed in the tube, the tube opening is shut and locked, a lever is pressed, and the cylinder is whisked to its destination. Pneumatic tubes are quite noisy when in operation: the whoosh of air and the loud clang of arriving cylinders can be disconcerting and distracting.

Construction Systems and Materials

Systems. It is possible for the architect while still in school to gain a basic, generalized picture of the building construction process, to be augmented later through the actual stages of work experience (apprentice/journeyman/master are the classic steps), professional trade journals, and materials manufacturers' literature. Since, however, it is hard for the working architect to keep up with the continuous flow of new technical developments in construction, most architects select—from this enormous mass of techniques and materials—the unit systems they like best, then work with the selected few. Such selections are made over time and through trial and error.

Even so, to minimize potential difficulties arising during and after construction, professionals should try to understand basic properties of materials and construction methods. Factors involved in making these selections are (1) function, (2) site dimensions and type, (3) durability, (4) cost, (5) maintenance, (6) expected life of the building, and (7) appearance. A good deal of "comparative shopping" is necessary before such decisions can be made.

Soil. Beneath every building is soil, of many different varities and compositions. An initial step is to test the soil on the chosen building site for its weight-bearing quality. To determine the strength of its potential support, the architect must know the following:

- Soil type.
- Water table level.
- Depth and thickness of the stratum that will bear the building's weight.
- Uniformity (or lack of same) of the soil deposits.

"Test bore" is the method usually prescribed by the building code. Other methods include test pits (dug here and there on the site), and loading platforms (weighting the surface to see how well the undersoil will stand up), wash (water-flushing to bring up understratum composition), auger, and core boring. The preliminary drawings will show where on the site test borings are to be drilled. The architect consults engineering specialists to estimate placement of these points scientifically.

The resulting soil log (report) gives the architect the information needed to design the proper footings and foundations for both live and dead weight loads of the anticipated structure, as well as feasibility of basements, waterproofing, and so on. Soil-boring reports are often included in the contract documents to discourage owner outrage if unusually severe settling occurs.

Table 3.2 Allowable Soil-Bearing Values

Material	Maximum Value (lb/ft^2)
Rock	—[a]
Compact coarse sand	8000
Hard clay	8000
Compact fine sand	8000
Medium-stiff clay	6000
Compact inorganic sand	4000
Soft, sandy clay	2000
Loose inorganic sand	1000
Loose organic sand	0

[a] 20% of building's ultimate crushing strength.

All foundations settle unless they rest on bedrock (seldom found at or neat ground surface). If settling is slight, uniform, and has been previously gauged, it is a minor matter. Table 3.2 shows various types of soil and their weight-bearing capabilities (values) as established by the Uniform Building Code. The possibility of uneven settlement can be offset by footings of varying proportions and size. Depending on soil composition, settlement may occur immediately or over a period of years.

Spaces between soil particles that are filled with air and/or water are known as *soil voids*. The ratio of these spaces to the floating particles is the *volume* of the soil voids. Reduction of soil-void volume increases soil's compressibility. The more compressed the soil, the more weight it can bear.

Site Preparation. The site must be cleared of all extraneous material in preparation for receiving the new structure. General excavations are hollowed; required utilities are installed. Existing structures are torn down and the debris cleared away, including footings and foundation walls (unless such can be utilized under the new building). These terms are defined briefly as follows:

1 *Earthwork*. Includes excavation, backfilling, and rough and finish grading.
2 *Excavation*. Involves digging of basements, trenching for footings and utilities, and leveling under slabs. It is usually performed by power equipment.

3 *Backfilling*. The process of placing soil in the area around footings or walls after foundation forms have been removed. Backfill material is placed in thoroughly compacted soil layers about 6 inches thick, to avoid subsequent settlement. However backfill used over drain lines should be porous and free from debris that might cause voids to form.

Temporary support during construction will protect and keep desirable landscape features. Neighboring structures must also be shielded or supported. Temporary supports include the following:

• *Shoring*. Employs wooden posts, beams, or other timbers; it is often applied to vertical surfaces, such as in an excavation.

• *Bracing*. May be temporary or permanent. It is used to hold material firmly in place. In site work a type of bracing called *cribbing* is a framework of timbers used to keep a bank of earth in place.

• *Underpinning*. Temporarily supports existing foundations or walls that are being extended down to meet the level of a newer, deeper foundation. Two methods in common use are the *pit* and the *pile*.

• *Sheeting*. Provides a continuous sheet of timber, steel, or other material, often used below grade where very wet soil may cause a problem.

Foundations. The foundation is the substructure of a building; it supports the building's superstructure. There are two general types: *spread* and *pile*.

Spread foundations, such as walls, pilasters, columns, or piers, rest on an enlarged base called a *footing* and distribute the weight of the building. Footings are designed to carry the total building load. They are always constructed on compacted soil below the frost line to eliminate damage to the building due to the movement of freezing soil. Other spread foundations called raft and mat, or "floating" foundations, are used over low-bearing-capacity soils. They are constructed of concrete and are heavily reinforced with steel so that the entire foundation acts as a unit.

A *pile* foundation transmits buildings loads through weak soil to harder layers, either vertically or through surface friction with the ground along its length. Piles of wood, steel, or concrete are driven into the soil mechanically by heavy hammers powered by steam, air, or diesel fuel.

• *Wood Piles*. Straight, uniformly tapered, untreated tree trunks driven into the soil, small end down. Permanent wood piles are entirely embedded in soil and cut off below the lowest ground water level.

• *Precast Concrete Piles* (round, square, octagonal). Fabricated up to 40 feet long and reinforced for transport-

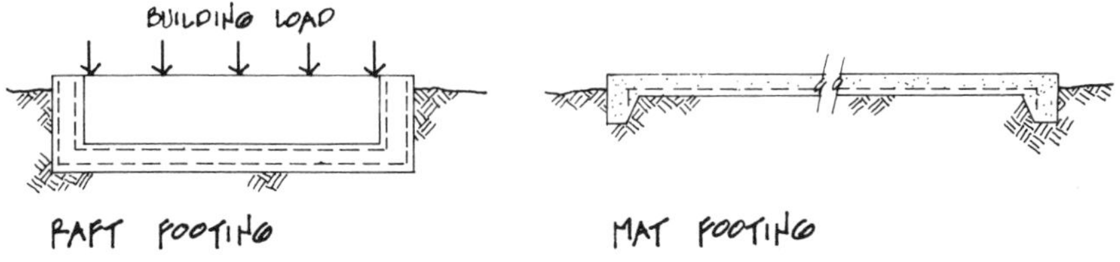

Figure 3.11 Drawings by Jeff Lee, Kemper & Associates.

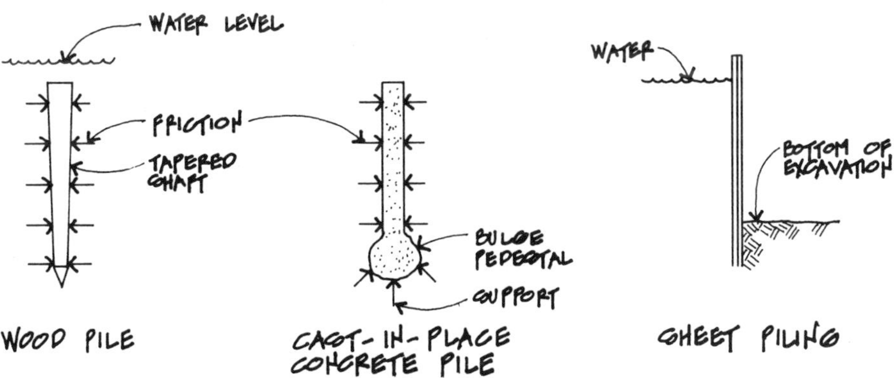

Figure 3.12 Drawings by Jeff Lee, Kemper & Associates.

ing and driving. They are most commonly used for the heavy loads encountered on large projects.

• *Cast-in-Place Concrete Piles.* A steel shell is driven into the ground by means of a heavy core called a *mandrel.* At the appropriate depth, the core is withdrawn and the shell is filled with concrete.

• *Metal Pipe Piles.* Cylindrical shells driven to appropriate depths, cleaned of all adhering soil, then filled with concrete.

• *Structural Steel Piles.* "H" or "I" steel beams, which are used in dense earth to support very heavy loads.

• *Sheet Piling.* Wood or metal sections are effective if a water dam is necessary.

Moisture Protection. Water is capable of running along structural members for a considerable horizontal distance before dropping. Capillary action may cause ground water to run uphill in certain soils. Roofs are sloped, earth is graded, and material joints are detailed principally to control water flow. Moisture leaks are not only annoying but can cause expensive damage to the structure and its contents. Condensed water vapor may cause decay, corrosion, or other harmful physical changes.

Drainage. Subsurface water is controlled by porous fills and properly placed drainage tiles; surface water is controlled by grading and shaping site topography to provide a gradually sloping transition from high to low site contours. *Gutters, flumes, berms,* and *warped paved surfaces* collect and guide water to disposal yard drains, catch basins, and underground storm drainage lines.

Drain tiles are placed in a porous bed of gravel, slightly below the lowest basement floor, to divert subsurface flow. Joints between tiles are left open but are protected from clogging by placing wire screen or building paper over the tiles, then backfilling with a porous material. Before footings or foundation walls are installed, rainwater or ground water that has collected in excavations must be pumped out. If the water table is high, continuous pumping or sheeting may be required.

Dampproofing stops ground or rain water from penetrating into areas above or below grade and is generally accomplished by asphalt-based coatings or the use of a *parging* coat of cement plaster. Liquid paraffin-base waterproofing can be used as a temporary measure.

Waterproofing prevents moisture (using hydrostatic pressure) from penetrating parts of a building that are in direct contact with the earth.

• *Integral* waterproofs are obtained by adding various compounds to the concrete mix to fill voids in the concrete, repel water, increase the chemical activity of the cement, and harden the concrete. Commonly used are hydrated lime, fatty acids, iron filings, and other metallic compounds. Integrally waterproofed concrete should be placed with a vibrator to eliminate air pockets. A mixture of cement and lime mortar called *surface coating* can be applied to the inside faces of walls and on the tops of slabs.

• *Membrane* is the commonest waterproofing system. Several layers of asphalt felt are cemented together with hot tar or asphalt pitch. The membrane is then applied to the surface in contact with the earth so that water pressure forces the membrane against the surface that has been waterproofed. Often a membrane is covered with cement plaster, which serves to protect the membrane and further waterproof the surface. *This system generally gives the best protection against unwanted moisture.*

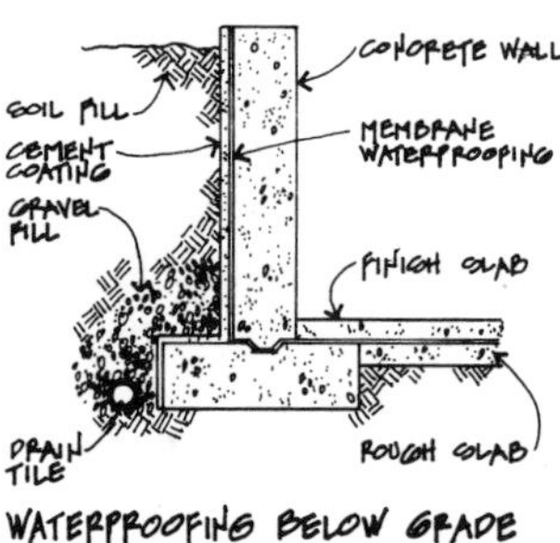

Figure 3.13 Drawing by Jeff Lee, Kemper & Associates.

• *Caulking* is a method of filling openings or joints between different materials that cannot be sealed by any other means. Caulking or sealants must be elastic and watertight, they must remain adherent, and they should not be affected by temperature extremes, nor harden or crack with age.

Roofing. Aside from considerations of overall cost, roofing should be selected according to roof slope, the expected life of the roofing, wind resistance, microclimate, and where the roof is visible, color and other appearance criteria. Most roofing materials are specified on the basis of a square equal to 100 square feet of roof surface.

• *Asphalt.* Used to saturate roofing felts, as an adhesive buildup, and as a flood surface coat in which gravel or slag is embedded (coal-tar pitch is also used). Built-up roofing alternates three- to five-ply (or more) layers of asphalt-saturated felts with hot or cold asphalt or pitch.

• *Asphalt Shingles.* Made from asphalt-saturated felt that is embedded with a permanent mineral surface and installed over solid sheathing on roofs having a slope of 3° to 12° or greater. *Asphalt roll* roofing is similar but is applied in continuous 3-foot-wide strips, which are lapped and nailed.

• *Wood Shingles*. Cedar, cypress, or redwood, available in stock sizes and many grades; they are either machine sawed or hand split (shakes). Wood shingles are used for roofing or siding over solid or spaced sheathing and are fastened with corrosion-resistant nails.

• *Metal Roofing Materials*. These include galvanized iron, *terneplate,* aluminum, and copper. Metal roofing corrodes; it also produces galvanic activity and thermal movement. Special installation details that permit expansion and contraction have been developed, however, employing compatible fasteners.

• *Tile*. Can be clay, slate, or cement; it comes in many shapes, sizes, finishes, and colors. Tiles are applied on sloping roof surfaces, lapped over preceding courses, and fastened with nails through predrilled holes.

Other roofing materials include *asbestos-cement* sheets and shingles (lightweight, fireproof, carcinogenic), *glass* (limited strength, limited use), *canvas* (temporary), and *plastic* (developed for curved shapes).

Flashing refers to both the method and the materials used to seal and protect joints formed by different parts of a structure or where different materials are brought together. Flashing covers all joints exposed to the weather as well as joints allowing expansion or contraction. Materials used for flashing include galvanized steel, copper, aluminum, and bituminous-coated fabrics.

MATTHEWS HOUSE
East Hampton, New York
Architect: Alfredo De Vido
Photo: L. Reens

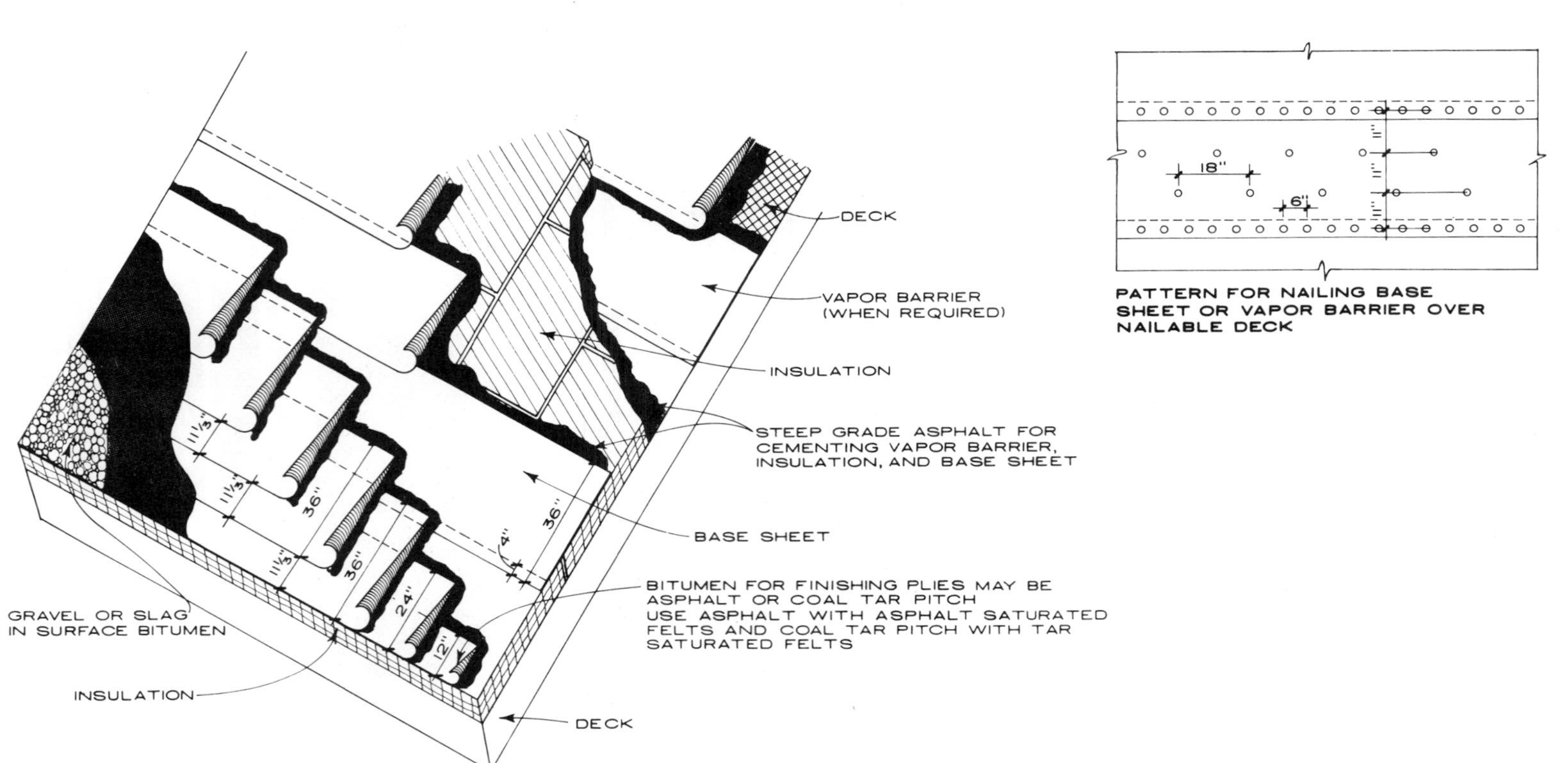

PATTERN FOR NAILING BASE SHEET OR VAPOR BARRIER OVER NAILABLE DECK

20 YEAR TYPE BUILT-UP ROOF OVER INSULATION

NOTES:

For smooth surface roofs omit gravel or slag. On slopes over 1" per foot back-nailing of all felts along top edge is usually required.

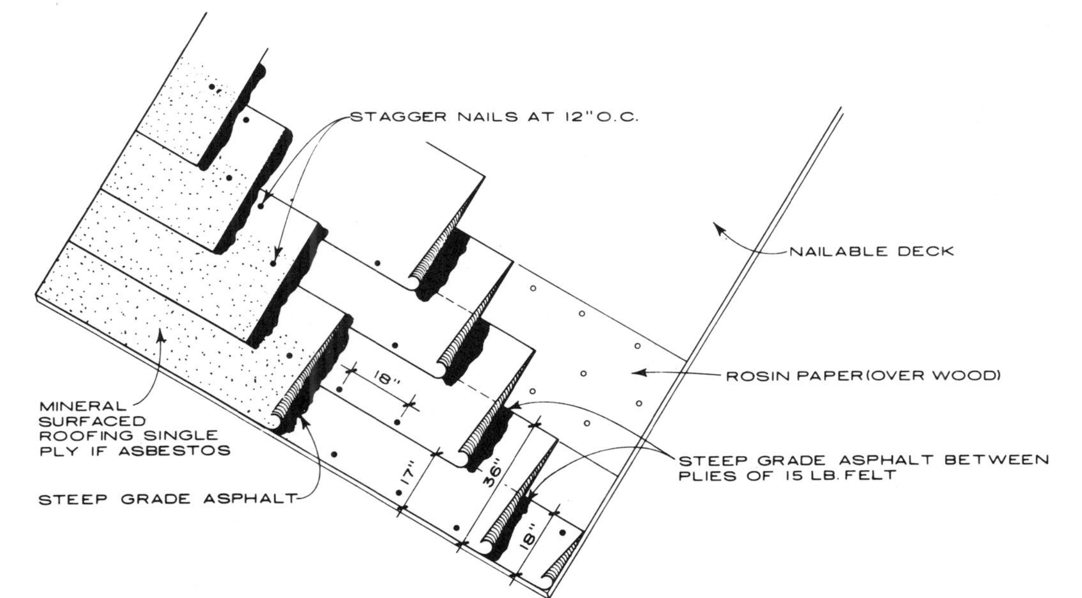

NOTES:

Over non-nailable deck or insulation omit rosin paper and cement solidly with asphalt.
Nailing strips must be provided.

Minimum slope for organic felt = 3" per ft.

Minimum slope for asbestos felt = 1/2" per ft.

MINERAL SURFACE BUILT-UP ROOF

Developed by: Angelo J. Forlidas, AIA; Charlotte, North Carolina; from data furnished by: Robert M. Stafford, P. E.; Consulting Engineer; Charlotte, North Carolina

Figure 3.14 *Source.* C. G. Ramsey and H. R. Sleeper, *Architectural Graphic Standards,* 6th ed., American Institute of Architects, John Wiley & Sons, 1970.

NOMENCLATURE

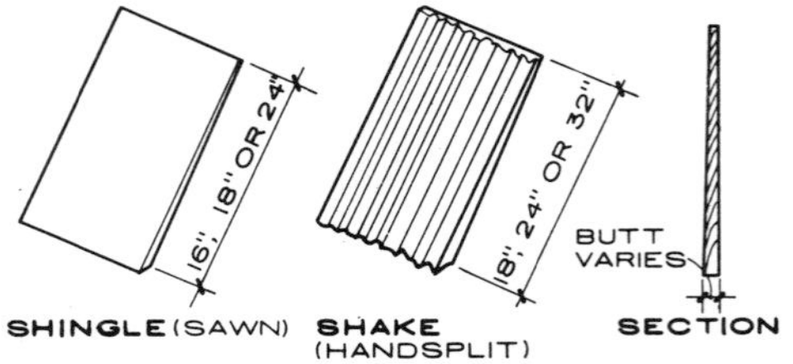

16", 18" OR 24"

18", 24" OR 32"

BUTT VARIES

SHINGLE (SAWN) SHAKE (HANDSPLIT) SECTION

Species: Shingles and shakes are available in Red cedar, Redwood and Tidewater red cypress.

SCHEDULE OF SHINGLE TYPES

GRADE*	SIZE	EXPOSURE (AT LISTED SLOPES)		
		5 IN 12 AND UP	4 IN 12	3 IN 12
1, 2 & 3	24"	7 1/2"	6 3/4"	5 3/4"
1, 2 & 3	18"	5 1/2"	5"	4 1/4"
1, 2 & 3	16"	5"	4 1/2"	3 3/4"

* Grade description:

No. 1 = Premium grade: 100% heartwood, 100% clear and 100% edge grain.

No. 2 = Intermediate grade: not less than 10" clear on 16" shingles, 11" clear on 18" shingles and 16" clear on 24" shingles. Flat grain and limited sap wood permitted.

No. 3 = Utility grade: 6" clear on 16" and 18" shingles, 10" clear on 24" shingles. (For economy applications and secondary buildings.)

SCHEDULE OF SHAKE TYPES

TYPE	SIZE LENGTH & THICKNESS	EXPOSURE* 4 IN 12 SLOPE
HANDSPLIT AND RESAWN	18" x 1/2" TO 3/4"	7 1/2"
	18" x 3/4" TO 1 1/4"	7 1/2"
	24" x 3/4" TO 1 1/4"	10"
	24" x 1/2" TO 3/4"	10"
	32" x 3/4" TO 1 1/4"	13"
TAPERSPLIT	24" x 1/2" TO 5/8"	10"
STRAIGHT-SPLIT (BARN)	18" x 3/8"	7 1/2"
	24" x 3/8"	10"

* Roof slopes less than 4 in 12 not recommended for shakes without special construction. See table of "Underlayment and sheathing."

UNDERLAYMENT AND SHEATHING

ROOFING TYPE	SHEATHING	UNDERLAY-MENT	NORMAL SLOPE		LOW SLOPE	
WOOD SHINGLES	Spaced	No underlay-ment required	5 in 12 and up	No underlay-ment required	3 in 12 to 5 in 12(2)	No underlayment required
	Solid (1)	No. 15 asphalt saturated felt.	5 in 12 and up	No underlay-ment required	3 in 12 to 5 in 12(2)	No underlayment required (3).
WOOD SHAKES	Spaced	No. 30 asphalt saturated felt (interlayment).	4 in 12 and up	Underlayment start-er course; interlay-ment over entire roof.	Shakes not recommended on slopes less than 4 in 12 with spaced sheathing.	
	Solid (1) (4)	No. 30 asphalt saturated felt (interlayment).	4 in 12 and up	Underlayment start-er course; interlay-ment over entire roof.	3 in 12 to 4 in 12 (2) (5)	Single layer under-layment over entire roof; interlayment over entire roof.

(1) May be desirable for added insulation and to minimize air infiltration.

(2) Requires reduced weather exposure.

(3) May be desirable for protection of sheathing.

(4) Recommended for areas subject to winddriven snow.

(5) Shake exposure as follows: 10" for 32" shake, 7 1/2" for 24" shake and 5 1/2" for 18" shake.

Eaves flashing: Recommended in severe climates or where design temperature is 0 degrees or colder.

A. Normal slope: Apply an additional course of underlayment. Extend from eave up to a point 12" inside interior wall line.

B. Low slope: Apply an additional course of underlayment cemented down. Extend to a point 24" inside interior wall line.

18" WIDE, 30 LB. INTERLAYMENT OVER TOP PORTION OF EACH COURSE OF SHAKES

1 1/2" MINIMUM OFFSET

RAFTERS

EXPOSURE

EXPOSURE X 2

1/4" MIN.

1 TO 1 1/2"

DOUBLE STARTER COURSE

36" WIDE 30 LB FELT STARTER STRIP

SPACED SHEATHING, 1" x 4" OR 1" x 6", SPACING EQUAL TO SHAKE EXPOSURE

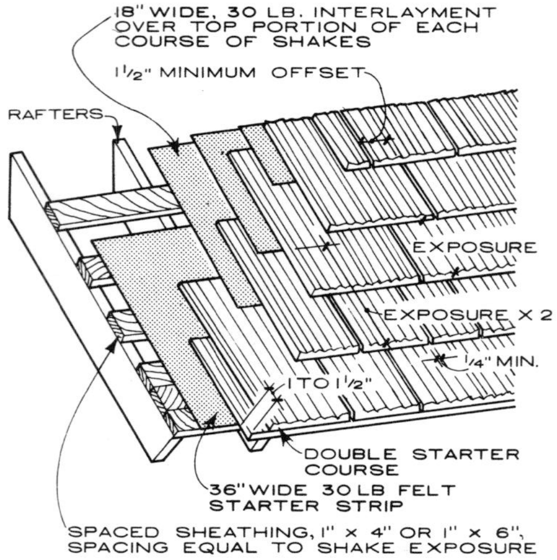

INSTALLATION OF SHAKES OVER SPACED SHEATHING (4 IN 12 MIN.)

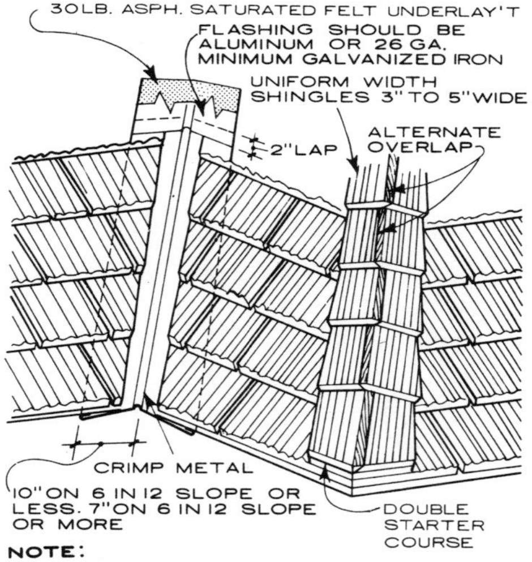

30 LB. ASPH. SATURATED FELT UNDERLAY'T

FLASHING SHOULD BE ALUMINUM OR 26 GA. MINIMUM GALVANIZED IRON

UNIFORM WIDTH SHINGLES 3" TO 5" WIDE

2" LAP

ALTERNATE OVERLAP

CRIMP METAL

10" ON 6 IN 12 SLOPE OR LESS. 7" ON 6 IN 12 SLOPE OR MORE

DOUBLE STARTER COURSE

NOTE:
Copper flashing should not be used with red cedar.

VALLEY HIP & RIDGE APPLICATION OF SHAKES & SHINGLES

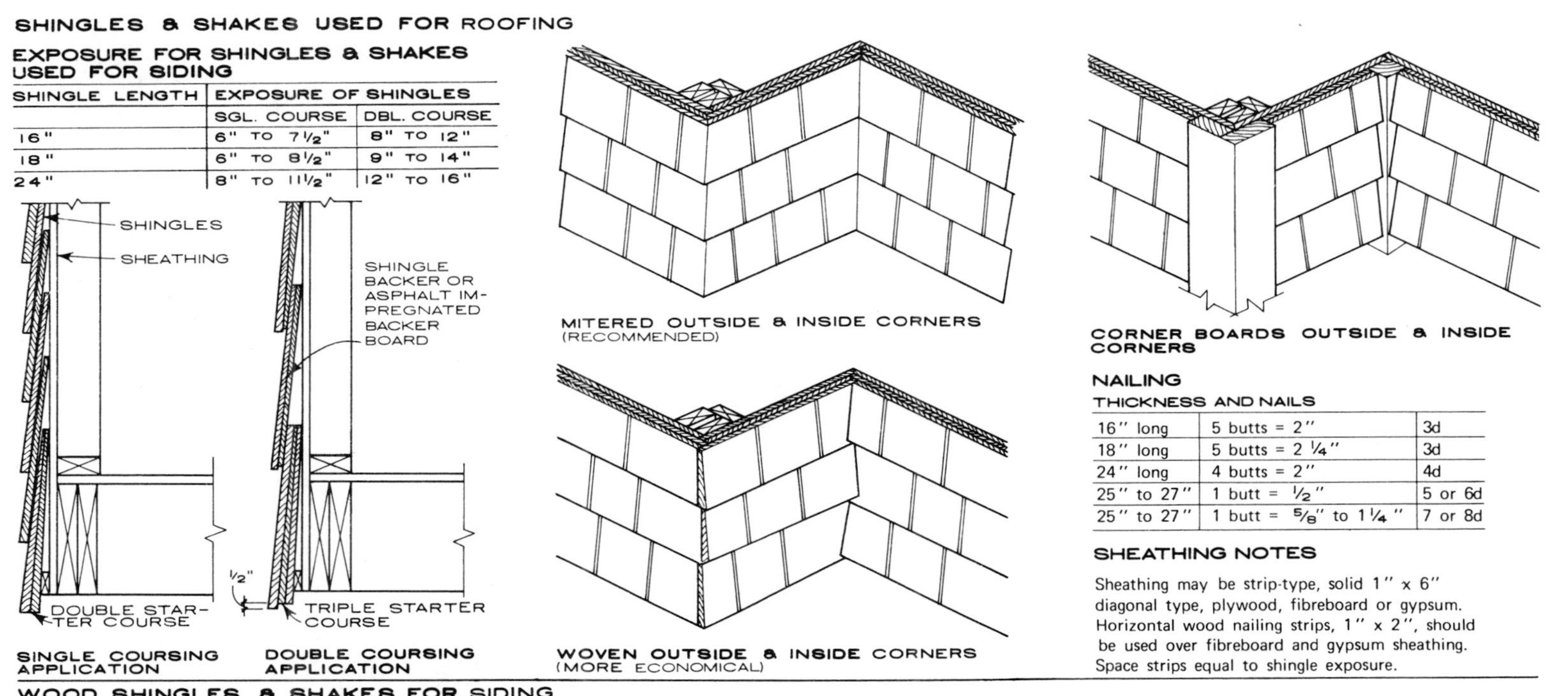

EXPOSURE FOR SHINGLES & SHAKES USED FOR SIDING

SHINGLE LENGTH	EXPOSURE OF SHINGLES	
	SGL. COURSE	DBL. COURSE
16"	6" TO 7 1/2"	8" TO 12"
18"	6" TO 8 1/2"	9" TO 14"
24"	8" TO 11 1/2"	12" TO 16"

NAILING

THICKNESS AND NAILS

16" long	5 butts = 2"	3d
18" long	5 butts = 2 1/4"	3d
24" long	4 butts = 2"	4d
25" to 27"	1 butt = 1/2"	5 or 6d
25" to 27"	1 butt = 5/8" to 1 1/4"	7 or 8d

SHEATHING NOTES

Sheathing may be strip-type, solid 1" x 6" diagonal type, plywood, fibreboard or gypsum. Horizontal wood nailing strips, 1" x 2", should be used over fibreboard and gypsum sheathing. Space strips equal to shingle exposure.

WOOD SHINGLES & SHAKES FOR SIDING

Developed by: Holroyd and Gray, Architects; Charlotte, North Carolina; from data furnished by: Robert M. Stafford, P. E.; Consulting Engineer; Charlotte, North Carolina

Figure 3.15 *Source*. C. G. Ramsey and H. R. Sleeper, *Architectural Graphic Standards*, 6th ed., American Institute of Architects, John Wiley & Sons, 1970.

Doors and Windows. Doors allow or prohibit access to a building and subdivide interior areas. They may be handsome or merely functional, such as fire doors. Methods of opening include swinging, sliding, folding, overhead, revolving, automatic (electric "eye"), and push/pull. Most doors are installed on the job, although several types are available as factory-assembled units, often prefinished.

- *Wood Doors.* Constructed of solid wood, paneled (wood or glass panels), solid wood core (plywood veneer), and hollow (solid wood frame) or grid core. Exterior doors are coated with waterproof adhesives, whereas interior doors are soundproof and water and radiation resistant.
- *Steel Doors.* Generally used in areas requiring specific fire ratings. Metal-clad or Kalamein doors are available with various cores that will not burn as long as the sheet metal prevents oxygen from reaching them. Hollow metal doors consist of sheet metal covering a metal frame. They are fire resistant and should remain rigid and permanent, under normal use, for the life of the building.
- *Aluminum Doors.* Commonly used in entrances, for storefront work, or in curtain wall construction. Lightweight, corrosion resistant, and dimensionally stable, they rarely satisfy fire code requirements.
- *Glass Doors.* Constructed partially or entirely of transparent or opaque tempered glass. They may use silvered (one-way) glass or a sun-shield tint or filter. Revolving door systems or level push/pull types (often pivoted at top and bottom) are usually glass.

Windows provide natural light and ventilation, although in recent years increased use of air conditioning systems has made natural ventilation less important. Choice of window types should reflect consideration of heat loss or gain, weather resistance, privacy, building code standards on fire resistance, and outdoor views. Windows may be purchased factory finished in varied sizes, in complete assemblies that include hardware, weatherstripping, and screens. Openable windows are identified by the way they work: double-hung, casement, sliding, pivoted, louvered, projected, and so on. Established industry standards determine the manufacture of windows and window materials.

- Wood is selected for its capability to resist shrinkage and warping due to exposure. The most common is kiln-dried Ponderosa pine, which is treated to resist fungi, insects, and moisture. Most wood-frame windows are milled as complete units, glazed and ready to install.
- The durability of steel windows depends on protection from corrosion. Most units are finished with a baked-on primer containing a rust inhibitor. Steel-frame windows are generally glazed and finish-painted on site.
- Aluminum windows are lightweight, strong, durable, anodized in several attractive finishes that provide substantial resistance to corrosion. They are available in a great many types and standard sizes. Aluminum extrusions allow the accommodation of condensation drains, weatherstripping, and glazing beads.

Storefront work involves metal support sections and glass as a package unit that includes entrance door, windows, frames, hardware, and fixed sections of metal or glass. The integrating of related elements speeds up installation.

Curtain walls are exterior building walls that support no weight other than their own. Designed to be durable, weather resistant, and maintenance free, they are generally installed in large panels, resulting in economy of fabrication and erection.

Materials

Concrete. Concrete is a mixture of sand, crushed rock, or other aggregates, and a hardened paste of cement and water. Wet, this mixture is plastic and may be cast, molded, or poured into predetermined sizes or shapes. Upon "hydration" of the water, concrete becomes hard and stony. Concrete is used in nearly every type of structure. It must possess the following essential properties:

- Strength to carry superimposed loads.
- Durability, to resist exposure to weather and wear.
- Workability, to ensure proper handling, placing, finishing, and curing.

Cement refers to any substance that unites nonadhesive materials; in the composition of concrete, the word is understood to mean "portland" cement (Table 3.3). Portland cements are composed mostly of lime and silica. This material is mixed with water; then hydration occurs, and the paste hardens.

Aggregates are inert elements mixed into the water-cement paste; they comprise roughly 75% of the volume of concrete. The quality and the cost of concrete are affected by the kind of aggregates used. Fine aggregate is material less than ¼ inch in diameter; material exceeding ¼ inch in diameter is coarse aggregate. Maximum aggregate diameter size rarely exceeds 1½ inches for most standard construction. All aggregate used should be clean, hard, and sharp edged for maximum strength.

Table 3.3 Several Different Types of Portland Cement

Portland Cement Type	Concrete Type	Principal Use
I	Standard	General, all-purpose
II	Modified	Slow-setting, less heat
III	High early strength	Quick-setting, early strength
IV	Low heat	Very slow-setting, very little heat
V	Sulfate resistant	Exposure to alkaline water or soils

Proportioning. The ratio of materials comprising concrete is called the "mix." For example, a 1:3:5 mix consists of one part portland cement, three parts fine aggregate (sand), and five parts coarse aggregate (gravel or crushed rock) by volume. Since fine aggregate is used to fill voids between the pieces of coarse aggregate, the size and grading of coarse aggregate determine the amount of sand.

Concrete strength is a function of the water-cement ratio. Excessive water reduces both strength and durability, whereas an insufficient amount produces a stiff mixture that is difficult to place and finish. Ideally, one should use the minimum amount of cement paste necessary to coat each aggregate particle and fill all voids. Admixtures (Table 3.4) are substances added to concrete to alter characteristics or achieve desired qualities.

Forms are molds into which concrete is poured or placed; they hold the concrete in the desired shape until the material has set sufficiently to perform its design function. Forms may be completely prefabricated (or job constructed) units of wood, steel, fiberboard, and so on.

Table 3.4 Ingredients and Uses of Several Types of Admixtures

Admixture Type	Ingredients	Principal Use
Accelerator	Calcium chloride	To shorten setting time
Flexible sealant	Resins, fats, oils	To withstand freezing action
Pigment	Chemical oxides	To give permanent coloring
Workability agent	Powdered silicate, lime	To improve plasticity
Retardant	Starches, sugars, acids	To slow setting time
Waterproofing	Stearate compounds	To decrease water absorption

Since they constitute a large part of the expense of concrete construction, forms should be economical to build, simple to strip down, and reusable wherever possible.

Placing. Before concrete is placed on grade, the subgrade should be cleaned of all debris and wetted down to prevent water evaporation from the concrete mix. Forms should be clean, tight, adequately braced, and wetted or oiled as required. Reinforcing steel should also be clean and held firmly in place in the forms.

Concrete should be placed close to its final position, evenly and continuously, to avoid separation of the aggregates. Any procedure that permits separation will result in honeycombing or voids throughout the mixture; therefore concrete should never be deposited at one location and allowed to flow to other areas, nor should it be allowed to drop freely more than about 4 feet. Concrete may be placed by sprouts or chutes; it may be pumped uphill or placed pneumatically (gunite); it may be deposited through water; it may be compacted by the use of vibrators, which will result in greater density, homogeneity, and durability. However no placement procedure in itself will make concrete stronger or more waterproof.

Concrete may be placed in all weathers except extreme heat or cold. Under those conditions special protective methods must be employed in addition to normal techniques.

The *finish* of concrete depends only on the limitations of the material and the architect's imagination. Some finishes may be applied while the concrete is still plastic; other finishes, such as the popular "brush-hammered" finish, are not applied until the concrete has set.

Curing affects the extent and rate of hydration, consequently the strength of the concrete. All the various methods protect against rapid moisture evaporation or temperature extremes. Curing usually takes 3 to 14 days and supplies additional moisture by spraying, covering, or sealing the surface with various materials. In cold weather, concrete is often steam-cured. The most favorable temperature is between 50° and 70°F. Colder conditions may result in cracking, while extremes of heat may produce excessive shrinkage.

Joints are necessary in concrete work to allow handling of conveniently sized areas, to allow shrinkage, and to ensure the isolation of independent elements when this is required.

- *Control Joints.* Tooled, sawed, or premolded, and installed to permit shrinkage of large areas. They create a deliberately weakened section to induce cracking at the location chosen rather than at random.

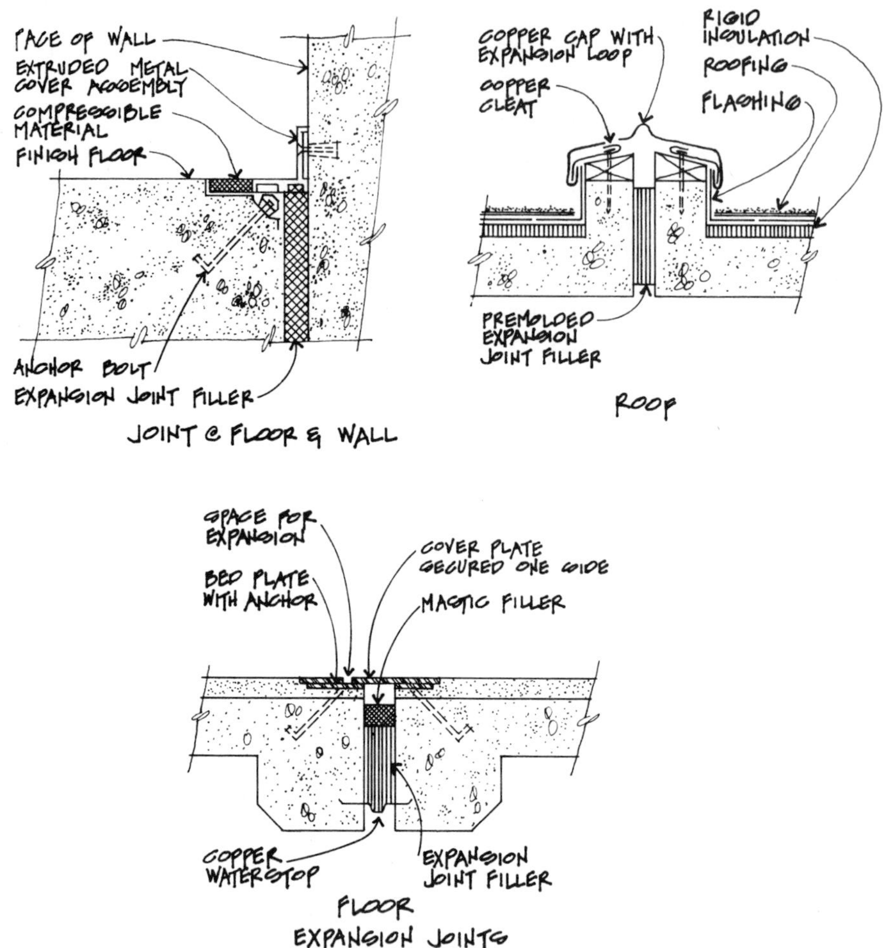

Figure 3.16 Drawings by Jeff Lee, Kemper & Associates.

- *Expansion Joints*. Designed to permit expansion or contraction due to temperature changes. The weakened plane generally extends through the structure from footings to roof. Exposed control joints should be caulked with an elastic joint filler and completely weatherproofed.
- *Construction Joints*. Seams established between two successive concrete pours in large areas that cannot be handled in one operation.
- *Isolation Joints*. Separate one concrete section from another so that each one can move independently. They are often found in floors at columns, footings, and junctures between floors and walls.

Almost all concrete used in construction is *reinforced* by the tensile strength of steel bars, rods, or mesh. One of the many advantages of reinforced concrete is that supporting beam shapes can be controlled in size and contour. Aside from conventionally reinforced flat slabs, there is the grid or pan-floor system that employs uniformly spaced metal or paper tubes around which a lightweight concrete with good insulation and fire resistance is poured.

Precast concrete is prefabricated and placed in the structure, rather than cast in place. This reduces formwork cost and gives a substantial saving of construction time. Precast floor and roof units are solid or hollow-core planks, often with tongue-and-groove edges. Such planks are provided with special clips to anchor them to supporting members. Precast reinforced concrete slabs are also used as curtain walls for buildings having steel or concrete frames.

Two other popular forms of precast concrete are tilt-up and lift-slab. In *tilt-up*, a wall is cast horizontally, then tilted up to its final, vertical position. *Lift-slab* involves casting floor and roof slabs of a multistory building one

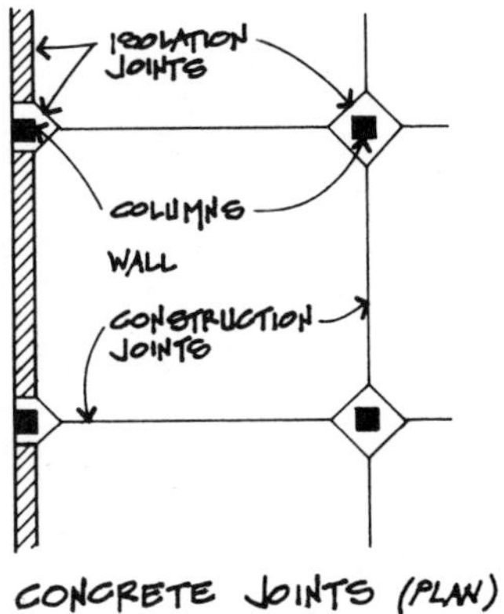

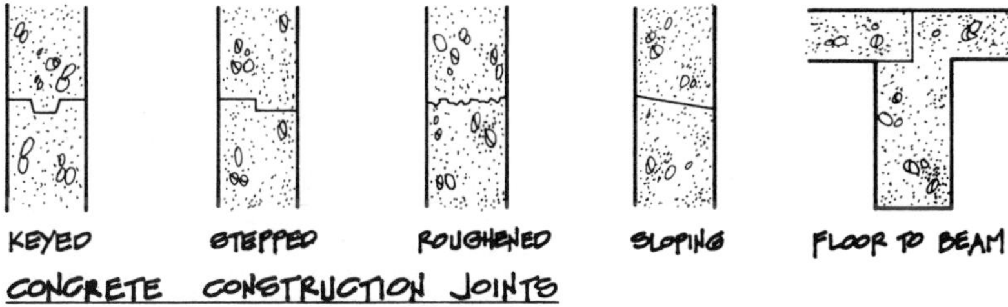

Figure 3.17 Drawings by Jeff Lee, Kemper & Associates.

upon another, then jacking or lifting the slabs to their final positions. Tilt-up and lift-slab also save on formwork expense, since wall and floor surfaces are cast horizontally at a convenient level.

Prestressed concrete counteracts tensile stresses that normally develop when concrete components are loaded, by "prestressing" or stretching the reinforcing steel, thereby compressing the concrete. Thus the size of structural members can be substantially reduced. Prestressed concrete may be pretensioned or posttensioned; that is, stretching may be induced before or after the concrete is poured. This material is generally used for long spans, for thin, strong sections, and to give fire resistance.

In addition to the systems previously described, concrete rigid frames, thin-shell construction, and many plank systems are in use.

Masonry. Masonry is one of the oldest construction methods known to man. Brick, stone, clay and porcelain tile, concrete and gypsum block, and several other materials are used in masonry. Each material has its own unique properties, limitations, and uses. The aesthetic properties of most types of masonry make this form of construction particularly well suited to a wide variety of applications: wall assemblies, floor surfacing, exterior paving, decorative screens, fireplaces (indoor and outdoor), patios and sundecks, and so on. The appearance of masonry is strongly affected by color, texture, and pattern.

Exterior masonry walls must have the following characteristics:

- *Strength.* To carry applied loads.
- *Watertightness.* To prevent water penetration.
- *Durability.* To resist weather and wear.
- *Good Insulation.* To "cool in summer and warm in winter."
- *Soundproof.*
- *Fire Resistance.*

Brick is a rectangular block that is formed, then dried and hardened by intense heat. It is usually solid but may be cored up to 25%. The most common brick material is hard-burned clay, which has a low water absorption rate and high compressive strength. Burned clays produce a wide range of natural colors from buff through a descending scale of reds to maroon and even dark purple. Bricks may also be fire glazed in any color to a satin or gloss finish. Surface textures, produced during formation, may

HOWE AVENUE NURSING HOME
New Rochelle, New York
Architects: Frost Associates
Photo: G. Amiaga

be smooth, matte, stippled, combed, rug-face, and so on. Brick is identified by its particular placement in a wall.

Brick types used in building construction are *common* and *facing* brick. Common brick is available with smooth or textured faces, in standard, oversize, and modular sizes and in the grades listed in Table 3.5. Facing brick is available in SW and MW; it is graded according to mechanical perfection, color range, and similar properties.

Table 3.5 Grades of Common Brick

Type	Application	Strength (psi)
Severe weathering (SW)	Freezing and wet locations	2500
Moderate weathering (MW)	Minor freezing, moisture	2200
No weathering (NW)	No freezing, interior	1250

To obtain good masonry work, one must be aware of the rate of absorption of the brick. This factor has an important effect on the bond between brick and mortar. If the brick absorbs water from the mortar too quickly, a poor bond will result, causing leaks or other damage. Bricks should be wetted prior to use to prevent rapid absorption. They should always be set in a full bed of mortar, with mortar filling all vertical (head) joints. Partially filled joints may result in leaky walls and substantially reduced strength; disintegration may occur in such joints when penetrating water expands and contracts in freezing and thawing cycles.

Mortar joints fall loosely into two classes: *trowled* and *tooled*. Tooling provides maximum protection against water penetration.

Bonding patterns are used to help strengthen brick walls and are selected on the basis of appearance. Some common patterns are shown in Figure 3.20.

Today very few brick walls are laid solid. Most are of a ''cavity'' type in which two tiers (wythes) of brick are

CONCAVE
V-JOINT
FLUSH JOINT
RAKED JOINT

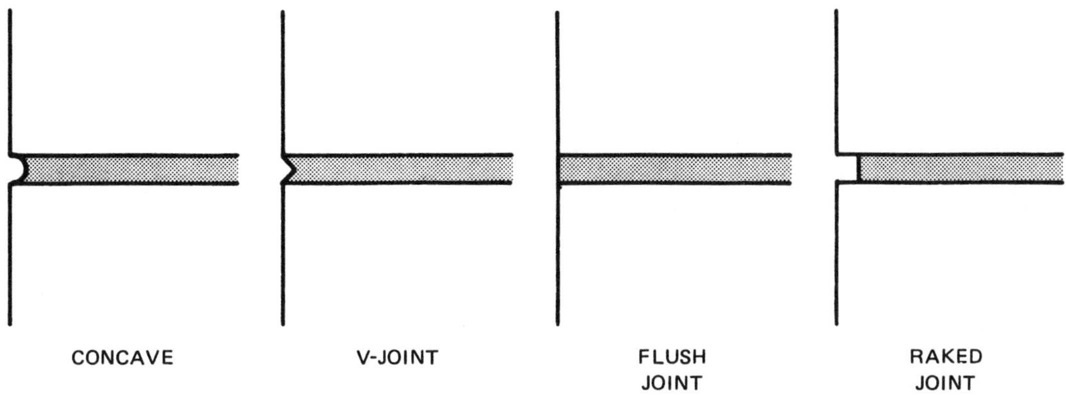

Figure 3.18 Various types of joint finish used on concrete block. *Source*. R. T. Kreh, Sr., *Masonry Skills*, Van Nostrand Reinhold, 1976.

STRETCHER
HEADER
SOLDIER
SHINER
ROWLOCK
SAILOR

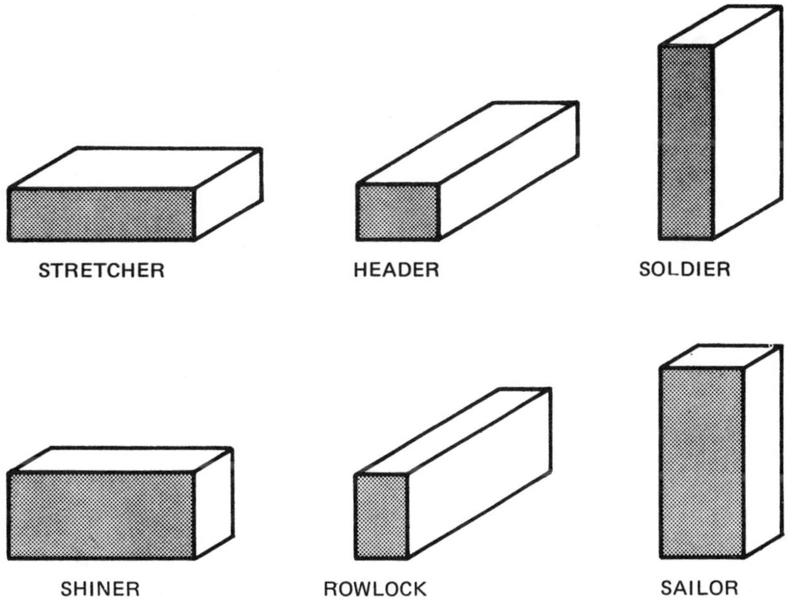

Figure 3.19 Brick positions and their trade names; shaded portions show the section of the brick that is exposed. *Source*. R. T. Kreh, Sr., *Masonry Skills*, Van Nostrand Reinhold, 1976.

TOOTHING
RACKING
RUNNING OR COMMON
1/3 BOND
STACK
FLEMISH
ENGLISH
FLEMISH CROSS
BONDING PATTERNS

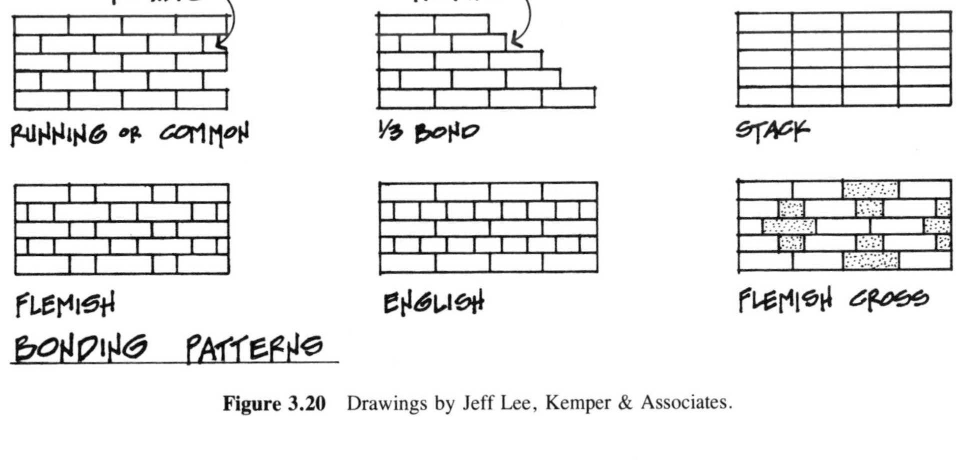

Figure 3.20 Drawings by Jeff Lee, Kemper & Associates.

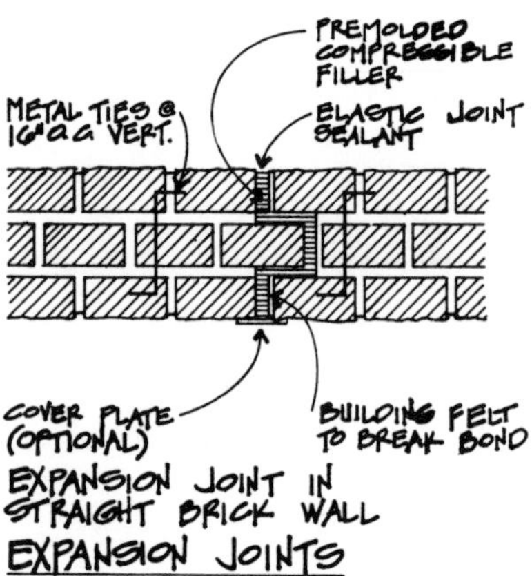

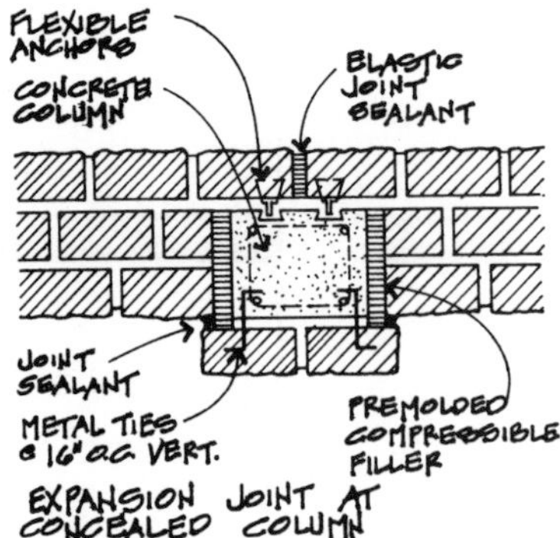

Figure 3.21 Drawings by Jeff Lee, Kemper & Associates.

separated by about 2 inches of air space. In reinforced masonry work steel pipe is set in this space and solidly grouted with a mixture of cement, sand, water, and sometimes pea-gravel.

When walls are excessively long or when a building has several wings, expansion joints may be required to isolate one part of the building from another, to prevent cracking or other failures due to movement.

Nonstructural facing (e.g., brick veneer) is the term applied to exposed masonry that is attached to its backing but is not structurally bonded to it. Units are held in place with wires, metal clips, or wire lath.

Concrete masonry is built using molded concrete units from conventional concrete mixes with normal or lightweight aggregates. Types include concrete "brick," concrete block and tile, and cast stone. The most popular is concrete block, which is manufactured solid or hollow, for load-bearing or non-load-bearing walls, in modular sizes (e.g., 8 × 8 × 16 in) and has properties very similar to those of brick.

Structural clay tile, a hollow, burned-clay unit manufactured from the same clays as brick, is used for load-bearing or non-load-bearing walls, fireproofing, backup, and furring, in nonexposed locations. Clay tiles are slowly being replaced by stronger materials for fireproofing steel and various partitions. Structural clay facing tiles, used for interior partitions, are available in a wide range of textures and natural and glazed finishes.

Gypsum blocks are solid or cored units formed from gypsum plaster, which is made of powdered gypsum crystals and water. Standard units of 12 × 30 inches are used as a plaster base for interior partitions. Because it is crystalline, gypsum is uniquely fire resistant, lightweight, and soundproof.

Stone has been used in building construction since earliest times. Today, however, it is costly and relatively scarce; thus various man-made products have largely supplanted it as a staple building material. Stone is now used almost exclusively for surface finish of limestones, granites, and marbles. Table 3.6 lists natural materials whose properties are difficult to control. Strength, porosity, permeability, and appearance are important considerations. When used as a veneer, stone must be positively anchored with special metal accessories.

Mortar is a mixture of cement, lime, sand, and water used to bind individual masonry units. It is prepared in a plastic state and later hardens into a stony mass. While plastic, the mortar must be easily workable and able to retain its water; when hardened it must be bond strong, durable, compressive, and watertight. Mortar may be tested for "slump" to ensure a proper mix. It should not be used more than 4 hours after it has been mixed, and it is impossible to "work" it. Table 3.7 presents the mortar ratios considered to give optimum mixes.

Table 3.6 Uses for Common Types of Stone

Type	Use
Rubble	Coping, sills, block walls, etc.
Dimension	Surface veneer
Crushed	Aggregates
Gravel	Driveways, landscape filler
Flagstone	Paving
Crystal finish	Monuments, gravestones, columns

Table 3.7 Mortar Ratios for Optimum Mixes

	Volume of Mortar Constituent		
Material	Cement	Lime Putty	Sand
Brick	1	1	5
Concrete block	1	½	4
Stone rubble	1	1½	6
Setting tile	1	½	3

MILLCROF INN
Alton, Ontario, Restoration
Architect: Hamilton Ridgely Bennett
Photo: Applied Photography

Wood. Wood is a renewable raw material, since trees live and grow. Because of continued research, conservation, and technology, wood remains—after a thousand years—a major resource of the construction industry. Lacking the uniform properties of a mass-produced, manufactured material, however, wood is being mechanically modified through laminating, bonding, impregnating, and other processes.

Wood is very strong relative to its weight and is easily worked with simple tools; it is a durable, warm, attractive material. Wood framing, which costs less than either steel or concrete framing, often is capable of withstanding fire damage better than unprotected steel.

Wood is either *soft* or *hard*. Softwoods come from conifers (evergreens); hardwood comes from deciduous trees (those that shed their leaves each season). Some softwoods, such as Douglas fir, are harder than some hardwoods, such as poplar or basswood.

The *grade* of a piece of lumber is established by the number, character, and location of imperfections that lower its strength, diminish durability, or affect its use. The most common imperfections are knots, checks, and pitch-pockets.

- *Softwood* grades are based on American lumber standards: yard lumber (general building purposes), structural lumber (timber graded for strength), and factory and shop lumber (finish items such as sashes and doors).
- *Hardwood* grades are based on the amount of clear, usable lumber in a timber (felled tree). Hardwood accounts for about 25% of the total board-foot production of all lumber.

GERSTEIN HOUSE
Rockport, Massachusetts
Architects: Huygens & Tappé Inc.
Photo: B. Maris

STUDEBAKER HOUSE
Mercer Island, Washington
Architect: Wendell H. Lovett
Photo: C. Staub

Moisture Content and Seasoning. Wood tends to absorb moisture and swell when humidity is high, and to lose moisture and shrink when humidity is low. Fresh-cut, "green" lumber can be seasoned by air drying (which takes several months) or kiln drying (which takes a few days). Lumber is considered to be "dry" if its moisture content is 19% or less. Seasoned lumber is lighter, less likely to warp or shrink, and less vulnerable to attack by insects or decay.

Preservatives. Wood must be protected against insects, bacteria, fungus, and fire. Wood preservatives consist of oils such as creosote, or waterborne salts such as chromated zinc chloride. Decay may be prevented if wood is kept dry and well ventilated, or if it is submerged continuously to avoid oxidation. Insect infestation can be controlled by termite shields, treating near-ground-level wood, or poisoning ground adjacent to the building. Fire-resistive treatment consists of impregnating the wood with ammonium phosphate, which deters combustion, or by coating the wood with a compound that retards the spread of fire.

Plywood is an engineered panel composed of an odd number of thin sheets or plies of wood, permanently bonded together. Outside face grains are parallel to each other; center layers are placed at right angles to adjacent plies. Plywood panels are also made with various cores: wood chips, paper pulp, sawdust, wastepaper, and fibers that have been compressed under high heat and pressure.

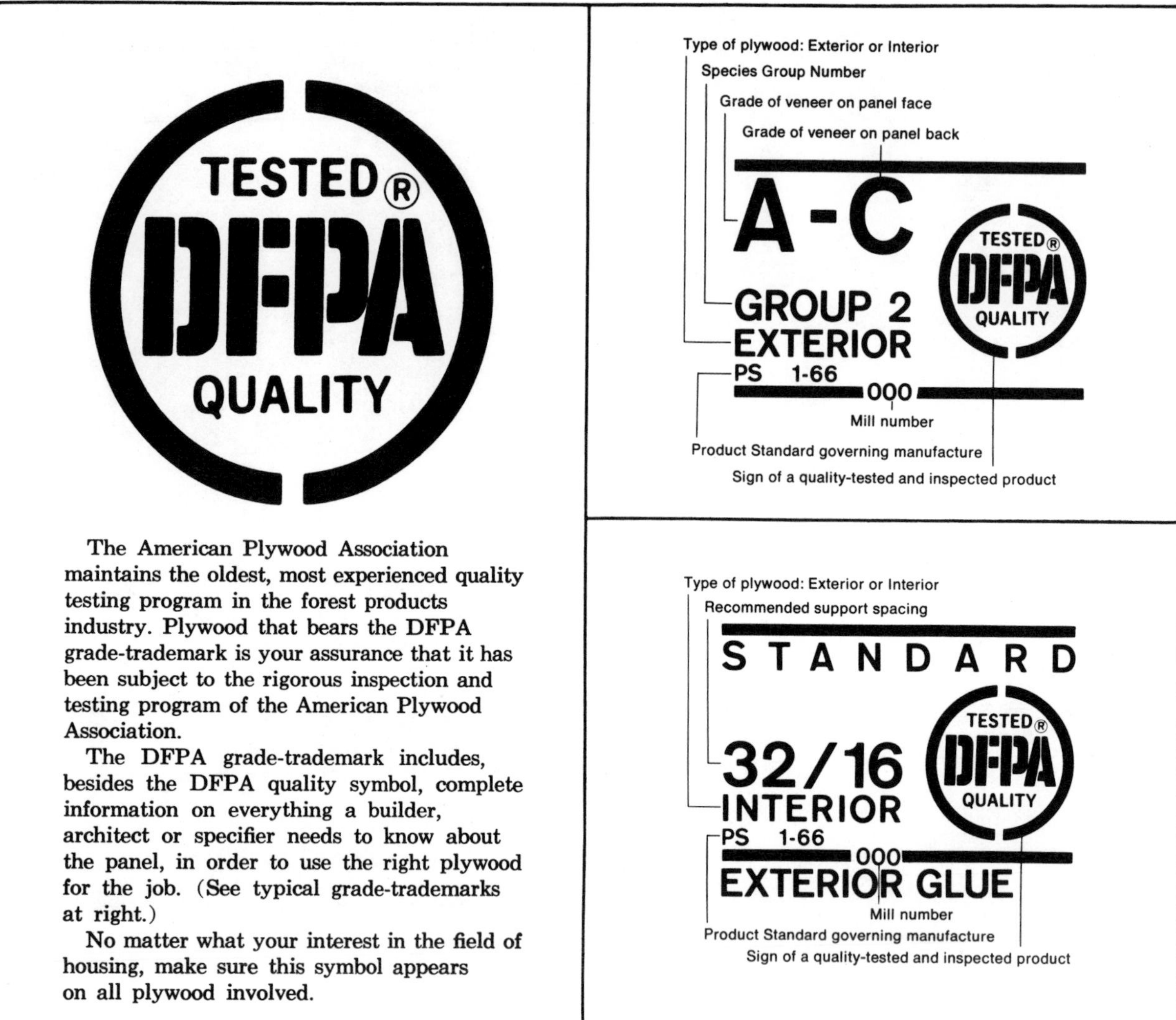

Figure 3.22 *Source*. U.S. Plywood Association.

The advantages over standard lumber of plywood (as well as hardboard, particle board, and fiberboard) are strength in both directions, greater resistance to checking and splitting, less dimensional change due to moisture, lighter weight, and good acoustical and insulating.properties.

Plywood is classified as interior or exterior, depending on the waterproof quality of the adhesive used and the quality of the plies: for example, overlaid (covered with resin-impregnated paper), marine (special glue), prefinished (stained, ready to use), patterned (grooved, rough-sawed, etc.). This material may be faced with almost any species of softwood or hardwood veneer.

Veneer. The visual effects of veneers depend on the cutting method. The "rotary out," in which the log is turned against a razor-sharp blade so that the peeled veneer unwinds, is the most widely used. Other methods include plain slicing, quarter-slicing, and rift cut. Different cuts produce different grain characteristics and appearances.

Glued, laminated lumber (glu-lam) is fabricated from layers of wood that are joined with adhesives; all the layers have the grain running parallel. It is produced under rigidly controlled conditions, resulting in strong, stable pieces that are up to one-third stronger than sawed pieces of equal size. The glu-lam process is used for decking, sandwich panels, and many structural beam and arch shapes.

If specifying glued, laminated sections, the architect must designate the type of adhesive and the required stress grade and appearance grade.

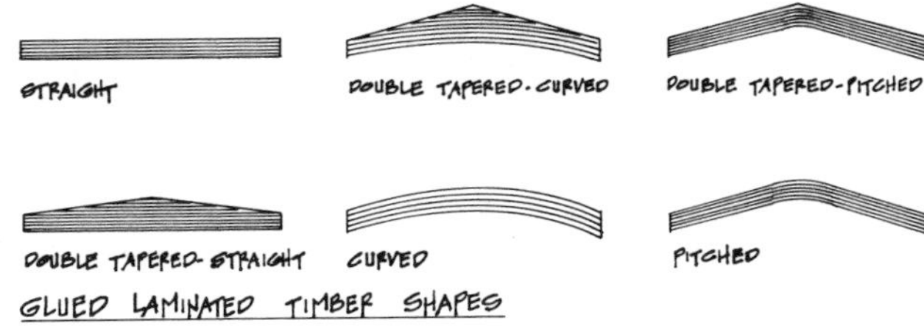

Figure 3.23 Drawings by Jeff Lee, Kemper & Associates.

• Most wood-frame structures built today utilize the 100-year-old "Western" or platform-framing method. Other systems are post-and-beam, trusses, rigid plywood frames, and domes with laminated ribs.

• Wood trim, molding, wainscoting, and ornamental work are made from good grades of soft and hardwood and are used to cover joints between materials that would otherwise crack or split along the joint.

• Milled work (frames, cabinets, shelving, etc.) is delivered to the site ready to install. Since millwork is fragile, it should be shop-primed or sealed, handled carefully, and stored in a dry, cool environment to reduce warping or other damage.

• Wood siding and panels are milled from common dimension lumber in many standard sizes and shapes; staining, painting or use of a natural finish follows. Almost all exterior siding is made of softwood; interior panels can be soft or hard. Exterior siding patterns should be weather resistant.

• Wood joints are classified as exterior and interior; each type offers numerous possible characteristics. Many different kinds of fastener can be used: nails, screws, connectors, adhesives, pins, bolts, and so on. Interior joints do not need to be weather resistant; structural joints are detailed to meet the same requirements as the larger sections they join.

POPE RESIDENCE
Newport Beach, California
Architects: Richard H. Dodd & Associates
Photo: Wayne Thom

Metals. Metals are solid, opaque, relatively hard natural substances that occur all over the earth and are mined in a form called "ore." They are good conductors of heat and electricity; some are magnetic as well. Almost all metals used in building construction are alloys, since pure metals tend to be soft and pliable. Pure gold, for example, will hold a fingerprint. Metal used in construction, is chosen on the basis of tensile strength, coefficient of expansion, corrosion resistance, and ease of handling in fabrication and structuring.

All natural metals deteriorate when exposed to oxygen, soil, water, or chemical agents. Oxidation or rust (exposure to oxygen), corrodes iron, for example. Another type of deterioration is galvanic action. When two dissimilar metals are in physical contact with each other and water is present (as in the outdoors), one metal will disintegrate while the other remains intact. For example, if aluminum siding is held in place with steel nails, the aluminum under and around the nails will crumble and the siding will eventually fall. To avoid galvanic action, different metals should not be placed in physical contact with each other; only compatible metals (e.g., aluminum fasteners for aluminum siding) should be used together.

The following metals are listed in order of galvanic activity; each metal is corroded by all those of higher number.

1 Aluminum.
2 Zinc.
3 Iron or steel.
4 Stainless steel (alloy).
5 Tin.
6 Lead.
7 Brass.
8 Copper.
9 Bronze (i.e., copper + tin).
10 Gold.

Clearly, aluminum is corroded by all the metals listed, even though it is not "biodegradable"; gold is not corroded by any metals; soft, pliable copper is number 8.

Corrosion may be prevented in several ways. Formation of an alloy is an *internal* method; *external* methods involve anodized, or galvanized, or other protective coatings. Galvanized metal is protected by a coat of zinc to iron or steel, and by a coat of paint; galvanized metals are considered to be sufficiently isolated from one another to prevent galvanic corrosion. Cor-Ten steel is an alloy that develops a protective oxide coating, ranging in natural coloration from vermilion to cobalt violet, when exposed to the atmosphere.

Ferrous (iron-bearing) metals are among the most abundant resources in the world; iron comprises about 5% of the earth's crust. Pure iron is hard, plastic, and easily magnetized; it oxidizes rapidly, is difficult to acquire and costly to isolate, and is too weak for most uses. Most commercial iron alloys contain some carbon.

• *Wrought iron* has less than 1% carbon added to the pure metal. It is hard, easily worked and welded, and resists fatigue and corrosion. It can be forged, bent, rolled into shape, and hammered, but not cast. Pipes, sheets, bars, lathes, and ornamental ironwork and furniture are made of wrought iron.

• *Cast iron* is hard and brittle. It can be cast into almost any shape, but it is too delicate for hammering, rolling, or pressing. Cast iron has the same general uses as wrought iron.

• *Steel* is non mixed with 5 to 85% carbon. It is hard, strong, tough, and malleable, and can be rolled, drawn, bent, cast, or welded. Steel is used in construction work for structural frames, concrete reinforcement, decking, curtain walls, antiburglar window bars (wrought iron serves for these, too), stair-tread guards, and a host of miscellaneous functional and ornamental items.

Nearly all *nonferrous metals* used in building construction are alloys, and all that are mentioned here resist corrosion.

• *Aluminum* is available in all fabricated forms and is lightweight, substantially reducing shipping, handling, and installation costs. It is used in minor structural framing, siding, curtain walls, window frames, doors, flashing, insulation, roofing, screens, hardware, and so on. As previously mentioned, aluminum is susceptible to galvanic action as well as to oxidation (pitting), which occurs especially in coastal or industrial areas.

• *Copper alloys* are extremely good electrical and thermal conductors. These easily worked metals are commonly used for roofing, flashing, as electrical conductors, and for screens and wire cloth. When exposed to oxygen, copper develops a greenish "patina" that halts further corrosion.

• *Brass* (or *bronze*) is an alloy of copper and zinc. Originally bronze was an alloy of copper and tin, thus distinguishing it from brass. Both alloys are superior in workability and are used for castings, finish hardware, and in plumbing, heating, and air conditioning systems.

Other commercial metals used are lead, zinc, nickel-silver, and rose-gold (10 carats).

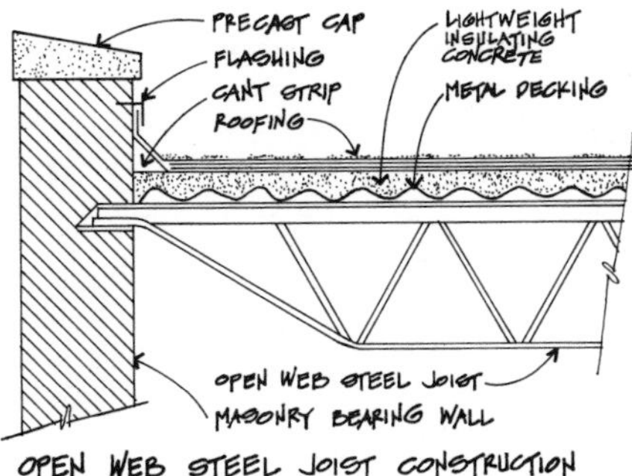

Figure 3.24 Drawing by Jeff Lee, Kemper & Associates.

Structural steel is medium carbon steel that is hot-rolled in standardized sections such as I-beams, wide flange beams and columns, angles, tees, zees, bars, and plates. Sectional combinations such as girders, trusses, and rigid bents are also important. Appropriate fasteners include rivets, solder, and bolts, which may be in the shop or cast (or worked) on site.

Open web joists are standard sized, prefabricated lightweight trusses. *Ribbed steel sheets* are used as permanent forms for concrete slabs.

Glass—and its variants, porcelain, mosaic tile, china, enamel—is made by heating a mixture of sand, soda and lime. It can be opaque, translucent, transparent, silvered (mirror), polaroid (to filter out ultraviolet light), nonglare, pigmented, or tinted. It can be shaped by blowing, casting, pressing, rolling, or baking. It can be bonded to metal (e.g., enamel onto copper, gold, or silver). Glass can be tough and hard (porcelain appliances) or brittle and fragile (window glass). It can be made to be shatterproof (automobile windshields). Table 3.8 names the types of glass that are available and gives their uses by construction industry.

Table 3.8 Types of Glass Used by the Construction Industry

Glass Type	Use
Window	Single or double strength, for glazing
Heavy sheet	Glazing in large sheets
Plate	Distortion-free applications
Tempered	Heat-treated to strengthen
Patterned	To obscure vision, reduce light transmission
Wire	Fire-retardant
Heat-absorbing	To reduce solar heat and glare
Insulating	Double glass panes
Laminated	Shatterproof, bulletproof
Structural	Exterior building facing
Corrugated	Decorative, for partitions
Mirror	Metallic reflecting surface

Glazing. Glass must be installed in a frame with clips or glazing points to keep it completely separated from the frame itself, and the glazing compound used must create a watertight seal with the frame while holding the glass firmly, without tension. Glazing materials in general use

PARK BAND SHELL
St. Petersburg, Florida
Architects: Harvard, Jolly and Associates
Photo: Office

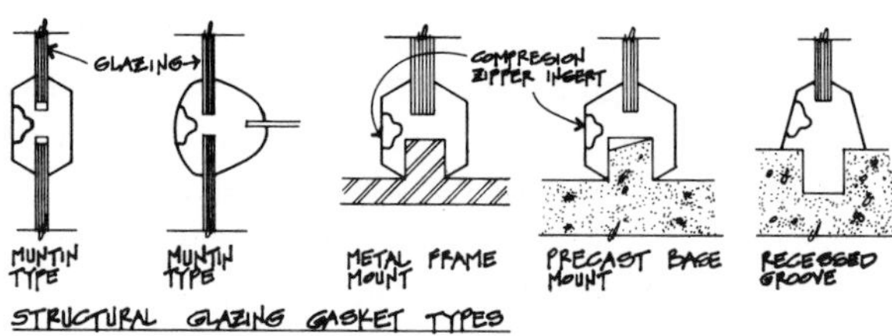

Figure 3.25 Drawings by Jeff Lee, Kemper & Associates.

include putties, elastic compounds, zipper gaskets, rubber, Neoprene, and vinyl. All surfaces to be glazed should be dry, clean, and warmer than 40°F.

Plastics. "Plastics" is a commercial nickname for several synthetic materials that can be shaped by flow. Made from resins, cellulose, and proteins, plastics can be reinforced by glass, jute, asbestos, cloth, paper, carbon and boron fibers, and sapphire whiskers.

Plastics are corroded by sunlight and water vapor; fire-resistant additives weaken the molecular structure. They suffer fatigue behavior over time and creep considerably under load, even if reinforced. They may craze, fade, hollow, or erode. Oddly enough, plastics do well when exposed to air polluted by industrial wastes, since the intensity of ultraviolet radiation is cut down in such areas and the plastics acquire a protective film of dirt. Table 3.9 gives some commercially available plastics and their uses in architecture.

In the structural use of plastics, reinforced laminates are sandwiched to a low-density core. Cores used may be plastics: rigid Polyurethane form or expanded Styrene, Vinyl, Epoxy foam. Facings take bending movements; core takes shear.

Low-cost prefabricated housing can be made in the shape of a hexagonal, folded-plate, conical dome. The air gap between the outer skin and gel coat (1/16 inch thick) and the inner skin (1/32 inch thick) is filled with slabs of rigid Polyurethane foam or foamed glass. Plastic sandwich flanges are the unit connectors.

Finish Work. Finish work involves not only workmanship but also materials, methods, and treatments used to finish a building. Finish material selection is made according to characteristics, decorative effect, cost, personal preference, experience, and taste.

Plaster, one of the oldest finish materials known, has retained its popularity over the years. It is a mixture of cement (portland cement or gypsum), aggregate (sand, vermiculite, perlite, etc.), and water. Portland cement plaster is used for exteriors; gypsum plaster is used for interiors. Hair, fibers, or Vinyl or mineral chips are sometimes added for particular effects. Chemical admixtures control the material's malleability. Since plaster comes premixed, only water must be added; it may be entirely mixed on site, however.

Plaster is applied in two coats (base and finish) or three (scratch, brown, and finish), over a base of concrete, masonry, metal lath, or various types of fiber lath. To minimize cracking, each coat of plaster must be allowed to dry adequately. Temperature extremes should be avoided while plastering to prevent freezing or excessive evaporation.

Lath of metal, plasterboard, or wood spans open spaces between frame sections to form a surface on which plaster can be applied. Metal lath is available as flat/expanded, rib lath, woven wire mesh, and in other forms. Lathing boards are rigid sheets of gypsum, covered with porous paper, available as solid or perforated

Table 3.9 Architectural Uses of Some Common Plastics

Registered Trademark[a]	Chemical Name	Uses
Vinyl[b]	Polymer vinyl chloride	Finish surfacing, prefabricated structural units, lacquers, adhesives, safety glass
Polyethylene[b]	Polymer methyl methacrylate	Finishes, prefabricated structural units, laminates
Plexiglas[c]	Polymer acrylate	Windows, finish hardware, lighting fixtures, adhesives, safety glass
Epoxy[c]	Phenol acetone, epichlorohydrin	Adhesives, caulking compounds
Bakelite[c]	Phenol formaldehyde	Paints, finish hardware, laminates
Mylar[c]	Polymer hydric alcohol	Laminates, adhesives, sun screens
Polyurethane[c]	Polyester diisocyanate	Flexible foam insulation
Silicone[c]	Polymer resin	Water-repellant paints for concrete and masonry above grade

[a] Although only one trademark is given for each material, others have been registered for these chemicals.
[b] A thermo plastic compound (i.e., it softens when heated); is used with and without reinforcements.
[c] A thermosetting compound (i.e., requires hot cures and high laminating pressures); must be reinforced.

sheets or covered with reflective aluminum foil on one side to impart vapor and thermal resistance.

The plaster is finished with paint, tile, wallpaper, or other treatment. Special plaster mixes include fire resistant, acoustic, lightweight (vermiculite), Keene's cement (water resistant), bonding (interior concrete), and tinted portland cement (exterior stucco finishes).

Drywall, used instead of interior plaster, is a panel with a gypsum plaster core that is reinforced by paper laminated to both sides. It is applied dry rather than wet and is cleaner and speedier to use. Drywall is available in many prefinished decorative patterns, with fire-resistant ratings (the ⅝ inch thickness provides a 1-hour fire-rated surface) and sheeted on one side with foil for thermal insulation.

Finish *flooring* materials range from relatively thin (Vinyl, rubber, linoleum, cork, asphalt, carpeting) to thicker materials that can withstand structural stresses, such as concrete or wood. Other floor materials are terrazzo, ceramic tile, brick, and stone.

Selection of finish flooring should be based on location, occupancy, suitability, design, maintenance, and cost. The following points should be taken into account.

- Wood floors will not tolerate moisture.
- Terrazzo must always be placed with divider strips to avoid cracking.
- A subfloor must be depressed in order to accommodate a thick finish floor. Quarry tile in a mortar bed requires at least 1½ inches depth.
- Joints where different kinds of flooring surface meet must be detailed flush or gradated.
- Final finishes (waxing, sealing, polishing) must be correct for the material. Wax for wood flooring will damage asphalt tile because the tile is petroleum based.

Paint is a protective, often decorative, coating of finely ground solids (pigment) held in suspension by a liquid vehicle. Vehicles (binder, dryers, and solvents) also supply the protective and durable qualities. When applied to a primed surface, paint forms a solid film to preserve the undermaterial. Plastic paints can cover a surface with a single coat that dries in half an hour; the finish coat can be chosen to be waterproof, antibacterial, fire resistant, or hard enough to walk on.

Pigmented paints are classified as white, colored, opaque, tints, extenders, stains, exterior, interior, enamels, lacquers, metallic, lead, Vinyl, varnish, shellac, and sealers. Most are available ready-mixed.

Bituminous coatings made from coal-tar and asphalt are used to protect submerged ferrous metal and to waterproof masonry. Other special paints include rust-preventive, fire-resistive, and insecticidal paints.

Paint should be applied under temperate conditions in an area that is clean and dry. The architect should specify how surfaces are to be prepared for pigmented finishes, the method of application (brush, air gun, roller; dipping, rubbing, etc.), and the number of coats desired. Failures such as blistering, scaling, and peeling can be minimized if the surface has been primed and is clean and dry.

Insulation. All modern buildings must be insulated, that is, protected on the inside from the unpredictable, sometimes inhospitable, vagaries of weather. Unlike a shanty, a lean-to, or a tent, a modern building is more than just shelter; it provides a comfortable, inviting environment for the human beings it serves.

Heat is lost through conduction, convection, and radiation; materials with low thermal conductivity are used in heat control. Choice of insulation depends on the materials' physical characteristics, their resistance to heat flow, and their overall cost. Table 3.10 describes common types of thermal insulation materials.

Table 3.10 Types and Uses of Common Insulation Materials

Form	Type	Use
Loose fibrous	Cork, glass, mineral wool, vermiculite, perlite	Flat air spaces (attics)
Batt or blanket	Glass or mineral wool enclosed in paper, cloth, or aluminum foil	Air spaces (between rafters, studs)
Board or sheet	Cork, glass fiber, paper pulp, foamed plastic	Sheathing for walls, rigid insulation on roofs
Reflective	Aluminum foil combined with layers of paper	Insulation plus vapor barrier
Foam	Urethane and polystyrene	Spray-on, rigid board, or sandwich panels

An insulator is any material whose thermal conductivity K is less than .5, where K is the number of British thermal units (Btu) that will flow through a substance 1 foot square and 1 inch thick per hour if there is a temperature difference of 1°F between inside and outside. Insulators are rated according to heat flow; numbers refer to heat-loss coefficients or K-factors. The lower the K-factor, the better the insulating qualities.

2 THE ECONOMIC IMPLICATIONS OF DESIGN

Construction Time and Costs

Structural concrete that is poured in place takes much longer to complete than do prefabricated steel frames. Similarly, laying a cedar-shingle roof is more time-consuming than using 4 × 8 foot plywood panels for the same purpose; and labor costs cancel out any saving of material costs. In addition to "long lead" (slow delivery) items and other ordinary construction delays, rising prices and unpredictable shortages have caused architects to consider new design approaches.

Mass-produced rather than custom-made items are steadily gaining in favor, although the building industry lacks universal standards. Architectural firms are experimenting with construction management, prepurchasing, fast-track (crash) construction phases, and negotiated contracts.

Efficient Use of Space

Subtracted from the gross area or gross square feet (GSF) of a building are the general service and circulation areas:

- Mechanical and electrical equipment rooms.
- Laundry facility.
- Toilets.
- Storage.
- Custodial areas ("broom closets").
- Corridors, aisles, lobbies, foyers, and galleries.
- Staircases, elevators, and escalators.

These areas usually comprise 25 to 50% of the GSF. Overall building efficiency or net square feet (NSF) is 50 to 75%.

Example I. If all usable areas in an office building are equal to 5000 square feet and the general service and circulation areas comprise 35,000 feet, building efficiency could be calculated as follows:

$$\frac{65{,}000 \text{ NSF}}{65{,}000 + 35{,}000 \text{ GSF}} = 0.65$$

$$0.65 \times 100 = 65\%$$

With today's construction costs, building space efficiency is of critical concern to owners and developers. The architect must understand the design and economic implications of building efficiency.

Example II. Let us design an arrangement for eight elementary school classrooms, equal in size (30 feet square) and self-contained, to make the best use of the space available. Each requires a single access point, toilets, a mechanical equipment room, identical ceiling heights, including walkways, and covered—but not necessarily enclosed—roof overhangs and aisleways between classrooms. The costs of the various types of space appear in Table 3.11. Tables 3.12 to 3.16 outline five possible approaches. In the formulas accompanying these tables, NSF is net area, in square feet and GSF is gross square feet. As in Table 3.11, "support facilities" consists of machinery, custodial, and toilet facilities.

Scheme A, which utilizes 75% of the gross area, is the most efficient. Furthermore, it is the cheapest overall to build, even though individual units cost the most because the circulation space is entirely enclosed and must be provided with a complete life-support system. The following points are axiomatic:

1 The more inefficient the design, the greater the total cost and the less the individual cost.
2 Efficiency usually results in overall economy.

Table 3.11 Cost[a] of Various Types of Spaces

Space	Percentage of Full Area	Cost per Square Foot
Interior corridor	100	$40
Exterior walkway (ground level)	50	$20
Exterior walkway (upper level)	75	$30
Stairs	75	$30
Classroom	150	$60
Support facilities (mechanical, custodial, toilets)	200	$80

[a]Other cost-influencing components (linear feet of perimeter walls, duct and pipe runs, electrical wiring, insulation, air conditioning, etc.) are to be disregarded.

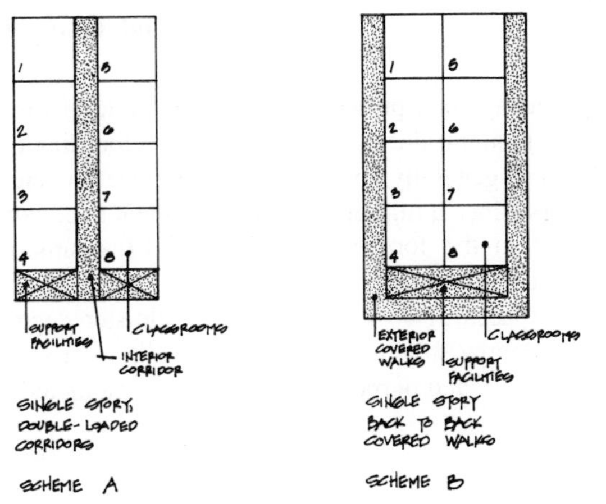

Figure 3.26 Drawings by Jeff Lee, Kemper & Associates.

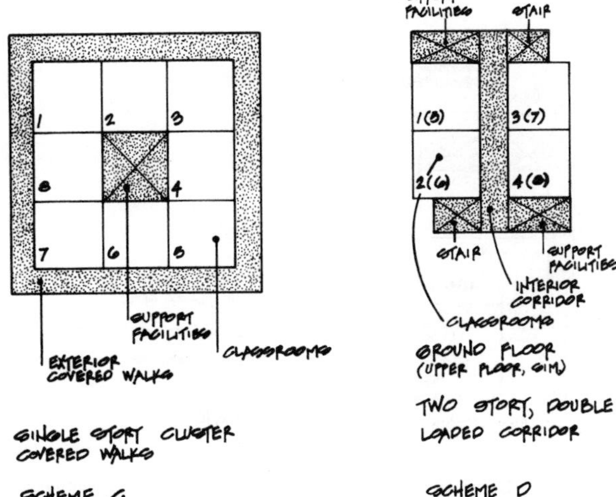

Figure 3.27 Drawings by Jeff Lee, Kemper & Associates.

Table 3.12 Scheme A: 1-Story, Double-Loaded Corridors

Spaces	Net Area, NSF (ft^2)	General Service and Circulation (ft^2)	Cost per Square Foot	Total Cost
Classrooms (8)	7200	—	$60	$432,000
Support facilities	—	900	80	72,000
Interior corridor	—	1350	40	54,000
Totals	7200	2250	—	$558,000

$$\text{Efficiency} = \frac{7200\ (\text{NSF})}{7200 + 2250\ (\text{GSF})} = \frac{7200}{9450} = 0.75\ (75\%)$$

$$\text{Unit building cost} = \frac{\text{total cost}}{\text{gross area}} = \frac{\$558{,}000}{9450} = \$59/\text{ft}^2$$

Table 3.13 Scheme B: 1-Story, Back-to-Back Covered Walls

Spaces	Net Area, NSF (ft^2)	General Service and Circulation (ft^2)	Cost per Square Foot	Total Cost
Classrooms (8)	7200	—	$60	$432,000
Support facilities	—	900	80	72,000
Exterior covered walks (ground level)	—	3500 × ½	20	70,000
Totals	7200	2650		$574,000

$$\text{Efficiency} = \frac{7200\ (\text{NSF})}{7200 + 2650\ (\text{GSF})} = \frac{7200}{9850} = 0.73\ (73\%)$$

$$\text{Unit building cost} = \frac{\text{total cost}}{\text{gross area}} = \frac{\$574{,}000}{9850} = \$58.50/\text{ft}^2$$

Table 3.14 Scheme C: 1-Story Cluster, Covered Walks

Spaces	Net Area, NSF (ft^2)	General Service and Circulation (ft^2)	Cost per Square Foot	Total Cost
Classrooms (8)	7200	—	$60	$432,000
Support facilities	—	900	80	72,000
Exterior covered walks (ground level)	—	4000 × ½	20	80,000
Total	7200	2900		$584,000

$$\text{Efficiency} = \frac{7200\ (\text{NSF})}{7200 \times 2900\ (\text{GSF})} = \frac{7200}{10{,}100} = 0.71\ (71\%)$$

$$\text{Unit building cost} = \frac{\text{total cost}}{\text{gross area}} = \frac{\$584{,}000}{10{,}100} = \$56.50/\text{ft}^2$$

Table 3.15 Scheme D: 2-Story, Double-Load Corridor

Spaces	Net Area, NSF (ft^2)	General Service and Circulation (ft^2)	Cost per Square Foot	Total Cost
Classrooms (8)	7200	—	$60	$432,000
Support facilities	—	900	80	72,000
Interior corridors	—	1800	40	72,000
Two stairs (exit requirements)	—	1200 × ¾	30	36,000
Total	7200	3600		$612,000

$$\text{Efficiency} = \frac{7200\ (\text{NSF})}{7200 + 3600\ (\text{GSF})} = \frac{7200}{10{,}800} = 0.67\ (67\%)$$

$$\text{Unit building cost} = \frac{\text{total cost}}{\text{gross area}} = \frac{\$612{,}000}{10{,}800} = \$56.50/\text{ft}^2$$

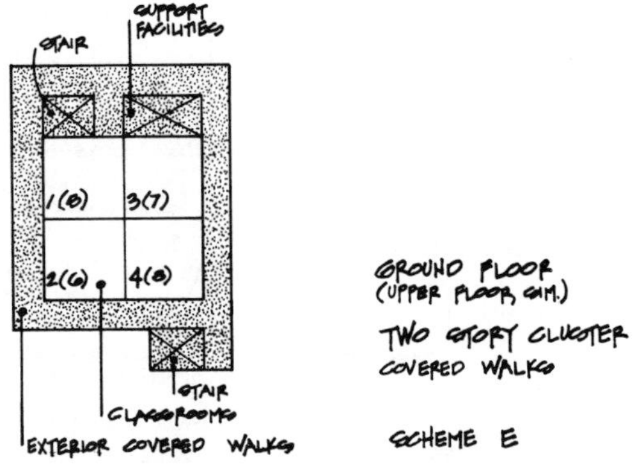

Figure 3.27 Continued Drawing by Jeff Lee, Kemper & Associates.

Table 3.16 Scheme E: 2-Story Cluster, Covered Walks

Spaces	Net Area, NSF (ft²)	General Service and Circulation (ft²)	Cost per Square Foot	Total Cost
Classrooms (8)	7200	—	\$60	\$432,000
Support facilities	—	900	80	72,000
Exterior covered walks (ground level)	—	3400 × ½	20	68,000
Exterior covered walks (upper level)	—	3400 × ¾	30	102,000
Two stairs (exit requirements)	—	1200 × ¾	30	36,000
Total	7200	6050		\$710,000

$$\text{Efficiency} = \frac{7200\ (\text{NSF})}{7200 + 6050\ (\text{GSF})} = \frac{7200}{13{,}250} = 0.54\ (54\%)$$

$$\text{Unit building cost} = \frac{\text{total cost}}{\text{gross area}} = \frac{\$710{,}000}{13{,}250} = \$53.50/\text{ft}^2$$

3 Multistory plans are more efficient in large buildings.
4 Building efficiency or lack of it greatly influence total cost.
5 Design decisions should not be based on a single element; the right balance is necessary.
6 Efficient layouts yield shorter duct and pipe runs, fewer runs, fewer walls, and other economies.

This analysis can be applied to almost all building types.

Cost of Covered Space. Covered exterior spaces, such as sidewalks, stairs, and rest and waiting areas, act as semiprotective devices against inclement weather. People using such protected spaces are grateful for the owner's thoughtfulness. Also, covered outdoor linkages, and so on, generally cost less than completely enclosed corridors, since a full, artificial environment need not be provided in the former case. Table 3.17 summarizes a rule-of-thumb approach to various types of covered exterior spaces. A wooden gazebo in the cloistered garden of a residential structure, for example, differs greatly in type, quality, and purpose from a concrete-canopied bus stop.

Table 3.17 Cost of Enclosed Covered Exterior Space

Type of Space	Percentage of Enclosed Space Cost
Roof overhang (no permanent construction below)	25%
Roof overhang (finished construction at grade level)	50%
Roof overhang (finished construction above grade)	75%
Covered space (partly environmentalized)	75%
Covered space (partly enclosed, no environmentalization)	50%

Volume Cost. The cost of a building is also influenced by the volume enclosed by its walls and roof. Ceiling height that is 1½ times that of an average room has 50% greater volume, as well as surface area, which requires exterior and interior finish work. Greater space volume requires more lighting, more air conditioning, and more heat because of the distance between the light source and the people and activities on the floor below it.

The functions of a space often determine its volume. Theaters, concert halls, hotel lobbies, airports, and convention centers require high ceilings and greater volumes to respond to the activities of large groups. The acoustics of a concert hall and the required reverberation period dictate the quantity of volume of that space. A stage loft containing wires, pulleys, above-ceiling lighting, and catwalks allow changing of sets and lighting requires from 70 to 90 feet clear height. Television studios, which must provide overhead lighting as well as space for overhead camera angles, require up to 3 times normal ceiling heights.

A very rough rule of thumb to use in estimating volume cost is: multiply anticipated unit construction cost by 1½. Large interior volumes of space are, of course, more costly than conventional spaces.

Performance, Life, and Cost

The energy crisis, shortages, and the spiraling cost of all materials and services have severely curtailed lavish use of building materials. Wall and floor facings of marble or granite, once common for banks, museums, and government buildings, now seem exotically extravagant.

Selection of building materials must be carefully weighed in terms of performance, life, and cost. Low maintenance and operating expenses are paramount. However manufacturers of construction materials are slow in responding to innovative ideas by making major changes in manufacturing processes, and the ideal (i.e., nearly maintenance free) materials are generally not available.

Design Comparison. The lifecycle of a specific building design is meaningless unless it can be compared to an alternate lifecycle. Long-term lifecycle costs include design, initial alterations, maintenance, operation, and system operational costs. Additionally, the architect may have to limit his or her analysis of alternatives to the client's ability to spend.

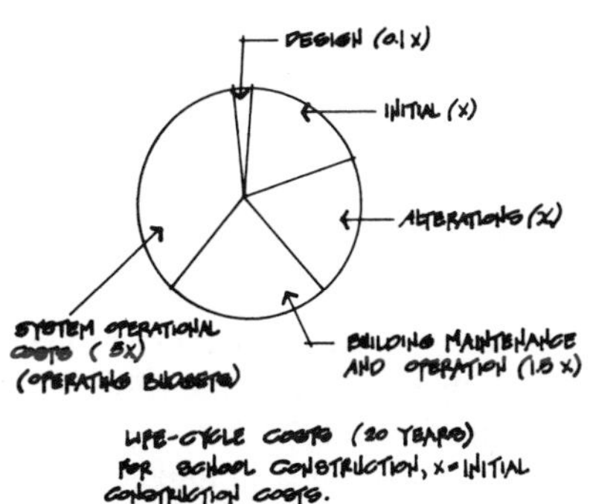

Figure 3.28 Drawing by Jeff Lee, Kemper & Associates.

Lifecycle cost estimating is a technique involving appraisal of initial costs, operating and maintenance expenses, and renovation and replacement costs of a structure, component, or material over the life of the building. Among the lifecycle alternatives might be the following:

- Construct a new building.
- Renovate an existing building.
- Build for long-term life.
- Build for temporary short-term use and plan to rebuild later.

Long-term alternate designs should be appraised (e.g., dual duct vs. terminal reheat HVAC systems, masonry wall vs. curtain wall). Cost differentials between materials or components must be evaluated, as well (e.g., concrete block vs. demountable partitions), and costs of operational systems must be analyzed (self-service vs. traditional retail sales, in-house printing vs. outside commercial service, etc.).

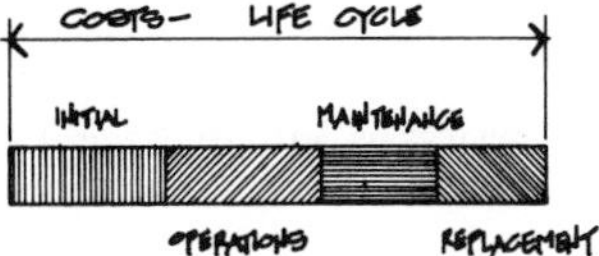

Figure 3.29 Drawing by Jeff Lee, Kemper & Associates.

Value Analysis. This method combines the cost studies just described with quality and performance values. Of course equations become difficult—a concept of value has been introduced that defies hard, precise definition. Therefore value analyses tend to compare functions on a statistically quantifiable basis, using predetermined minimum performance standards. Value analysis is most effective when used in early phases of conceptual design and to identify optimum systems, materials, and components.

Cost-Benefit Analysis. This method additionally takes into account structural, social, and other tangible transactions that may be involved in the design of a building. A balance sheet is drawn with positive costs and benefits on one side of the ledger, negative ones on the other. All factors are quantified into monetary terms or time differentials. This method can be used in evaluating major urban development and redevelopment projects, a multiparty corporate project, a new freeway location, a proposed airport expansion, and so on.

Capital Cost. In the capital cost evaluation method structural systems are compared by adding the initial cost of materials and labor per square foot. Since the structural systems chosen are the best of their type, the final decision is based on cost alone. For example, suppose that a 2-story schoolhouse is required by code to have fire-rated exterior walls. The owner has a limited budget, which in turn restricts the architect's choices with respect to functional design to load-bearing characteristics alone. There are three excellent load-bearing systems from which to choose: 8-inch poured concrete, 12-inch reinforced masonry, and 10-inch reinforced brick-faced. According to Table 3.18 the 12-inch reinforced masonry wall (Figure 3.30) is the cheapest of the three to make and build. Therefore it is the right one to select on the basis of a capital cost evaluation.

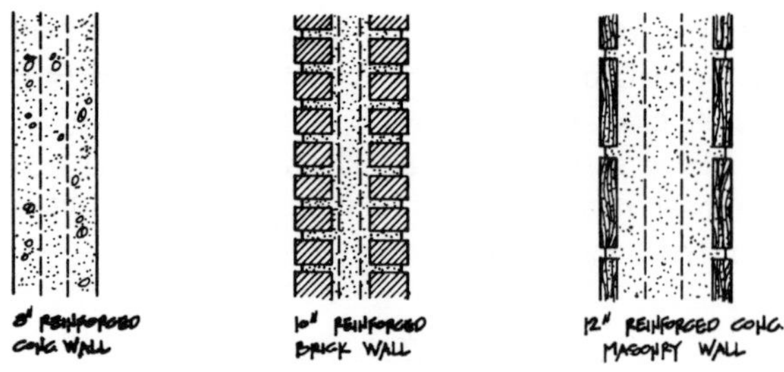

Figure 3.30 Drawings by Jeff Lee, Kemper & Associates.

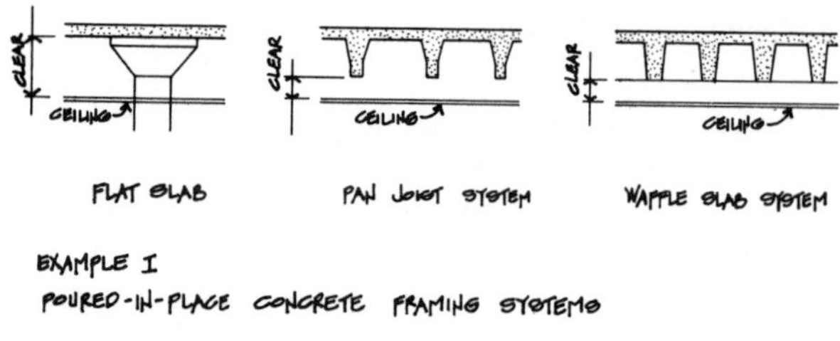

Figure 3.31 Drawings by Jeff Lee, Kemper & Associates.

Table 3.18 Costs of Types of Wall in Capital Cost Example

	Cost per Square Foot		
Type of Wall	Labor	Material	Total
8-in concrete	$3.7	$1.88	$5.61
12-in masonry	3.16	1.49	4.65
10-in brick	4.51	2.21	6.72

Table 3.19 Costs for Poured-in-Place Concrete Framing Systems

	Cost of System		
Item	Flat Slab	Pan Joist Slab	Waffle Slab
Forms	$ 831	$1001	$1019
Concrete	708	667	690
Finish	113	113	113
Reinforcement	1184	1128	1147
Total per day	$2836	$2909	$2969
Total cost per square foot	$4.54	$4.65	$4.75

Example I, Value Analysis. A proposed multistory office building, to be located in Fire Zone 1, must meet the following predetermined standards:

- Floor live load, 100 pounds per square foot.
- Column spacing, 25 feet in each direction.
- Fire-resistive construction.
- Minimum floor-to-floor dimensions.
- Suspended ceilings throughout.

There is a temporary shortage of structural steel, leaving only three basic reinforced concrete systems to be analyzed: flat slab, pan joist slab, and waffle slab. Table 3.19 breaks down the costs for each system illustrated in Figure 3.31.

The following items are to be considered in this analysis besides cost: the flat-slab system reduces floor-to-floor height by 6 inches; this saves construction time by 5 days per floor, compared to the two remaining systems. Since the flat-slab system is also the cheapest to build, it is the correct selection.

Example II, Value Analysis. Roof structural design of a single-story shopping center is to be based on cost and minimum construction time. The structure must have the following attributes:

- Fireproofing.
- Thermal insulation.
- A suspended ceiling.
- Composition roofing.

Two equally usable systems of 20-inch open web steel joints and 26-gauge metal decking (Figure 3.32) satisfy all requirements, as Tables 3.20 and 3.21 indicate. Clearly Scheme B saves 20¢ in dollars per square foot. An additional savings of 6¢ per square foot is realized by reducing the building height 4 inches for a total savings in dollars per square foot of 26¢. Therefore Scheme B is the right choice.

Limitations of Techniques. All these techniques (lifecycle, value analysis, cost-benefit, capital cost) combine annual and capital expenditures in a single figure. The accounting methods used to obtain a single figure from costs that occur throughout a year or a period of years vary:

1 Reducing all costs to present values.
2 Spreading expenses uniformly over a given period.
3 Aiming for a given return rate on one's investment.
4 Calculating interest rates.
5 Making inflation forecasts.

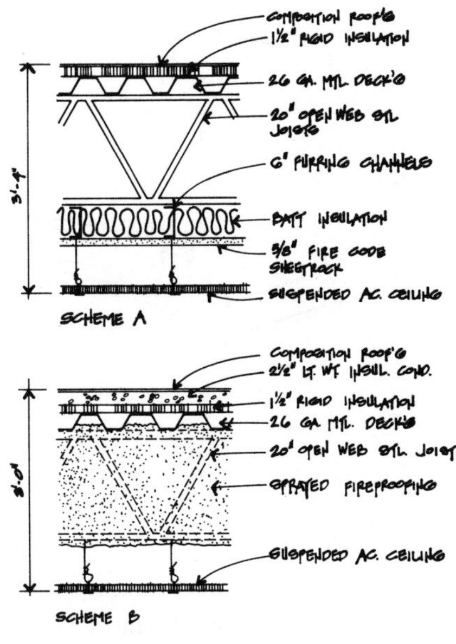

Figure 3.32 Drawings by Jeff Lee, Kemper & Associates.

Table 3.20 Scheme A: Expensive Construction

Item	Cost per Square Foot
Composition roof	$0.17
1½-in rigid insulation	0.29
26-gauge metal decking	0.39
Open web steel joist	1.57
6-in furring channels	0.37
6-in batt insulation	0.48
Fire code sheetrock	0.38
Suspended acoustical ceiling	0.70
Total	$4.35

Table 3.21 Scheme B: Less Expensive Construction[a]

Item	Cost per Square Foot
Composition roof	$0.17
1½-in rigid insulation	0.29
26-gauge metal decking	0.39
Open web steel joist	1.57
2½-in lightweight insulating concrete	0.35
Sprayed fireproofing	0.68
Suspended acoustical ceiling	0.70
Total	$4.15

[a]Eliminates unnecessary building height and the furring channels; uses a cheaper insulation material.

The lack of information on the anticipated life of building components limits the applicability of evaluation techniques to initial costs.

Maintenance Costs

Design decisions relating to the use of materials must be balanced with respect to cost, function, corrosion resistance, and anticipated building life. An owner may redecorate his or her home every few years. An institution should not have to arrange for major redecoration on the same basis, because this disrupts operations, lowers efficiency, and is extremely expensive. The decision to expose exterior concrete walls rather than paint them, for example, positively affects maintenance cost of the building because exposed concrete weathers well and requires little or no attention. On the other hand, concrete painted at the time of construction might require repainting every 5 years, since exterior finishes deteriorate from exposure to sun, rain, temperature changes, chemicals, soot, wind, and bacteria. Interior finishes are subject only to wear resulting from use, although in urban areas pollutant infiltration is a problem.

3 DESIGN AS AESTHETICS

The Evolution of Perception

The earliest "structures" were purely functional; they were shelters. Yet on the inner walls of these caves man produced the first painting—incredibly beautiful and lifelike—more than 70,000 years ago. From the picture plane, man translated what he had perceived into three dimensions, thus creating free-standing structures. With these structures, as with every other human creation, people strove to communicate with their fellow creatures and with their god(s). When the inevitability of one's own death came to be realized, structural designs took on a grander, more permanent aspect: communication with the future. The pyramids were built to last—forever. The word became form.

Architectural language, however, is not a strictly visual communication but a combination of perception, understanding, and emotional response. Architectural awareness is learned so early in life that it becomes partly intuitive. Architecture is perceived as a compressed statement of our varied external environment, and it is valued according to our internal environments.

Since almost everything man-made is used by people—especially architecture—a direct connection exists between the human body and buildings. Once measurements were based on various parts of the body and allusions to them remain in the language as idioms: rule-of-thumb, arm's length, a head taller or shorter, can't fathom it. The system of inches and feet, which assumed that the measure of the thumb's breadth was 1 inch was gauged by people with wide thumbs and big feet (1 foot = 12 inches). Thus people use their experience of body/space needs to judge dimensional acceptability in architecture.

Buildings and sculpture are perceived as being "at rest." Since the human body at rest is "balanced," an unbalanced building may appear to be moving or falling (such as the famous Leaning Tower of Pisa). Similarly, a room attuned to body measurements is perceived as a harmonious whole, and a picture hung "crooked" disturbs the mind behind the eye. Our aesthetic judgment is influenced by such fundamental perceptions as the following: the horizon is a horizontal line; the force of gravity or falling is a vertical line; the angle of these two lines is a right angle.

Space. Architecture used to be considered to be mass or form—improving on nature, as it were. A modern definition, taken from behavioral psychology, is that architecture is the manipulation of space to accommodate the movement of people (behavioral psychology itself being the manipulation of people to accommodate an existing space, an idea that is behind a large portion of building-construction economics). Our senses have learned to accurately interpret perceived space; that is, lines of perspective symbolize distance on the picture plane.

Spaces that lack ventilation or light or limit freedom of movement give rise to feelings of restriction and discomfort; yet a person can live in such confinement for many years if necessary, since survival space is much smaller than agreeable or pleasant space. Depending on individual space needs, a room with a low ceiling, no windows, narrow door frame, textured walls, and a carpeted floor may be either cozy or oppressive. A narrow, high-ceilinged room may give some the impression of being trapped in a box canyon. Twisting or curved walls may produce disorientation. The fear of restricted spaces is known as claustrophobia; fear of open spaces is called agoraphobia. Some people also fear heights or depths. Amusement park "funhouses" are deliberately designed to induce these fears.

Even spaces on a two-dimensional page can affect content comprehension. Material that is broken up into short paragraphs is more easily read and, to many, more "agreeable" to read. A 1-inch margin all around the page attracts the eye/mind to the printed matter. Addition of ½ inch of space to either top or bottom enhances the attraction. Pages that are wider than they are long can sacrifice some margin space because the shape of the page fools the eye/mind into believing that the page is shorter. Lots of space is interpreted as reflecting quality, wealth, and power. Advertisements that wish to impress the eye/mind with the high quality of products or services use extremely wide margins.

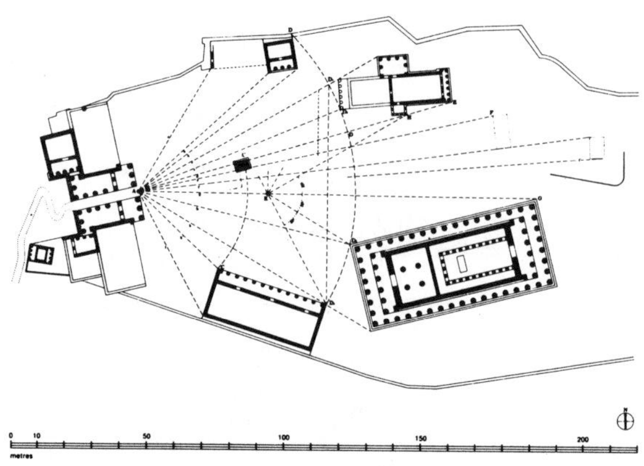

Figure 3.35 An Ionic site: the Acropolis III, Athens. *Source.* C. A. Doxiadis, *Architectural Space in Ancient Greece,* 1972, reprinted in Charles Moore and Gerald Allen, *Dimensions,* Architectural Record Books, 1976.

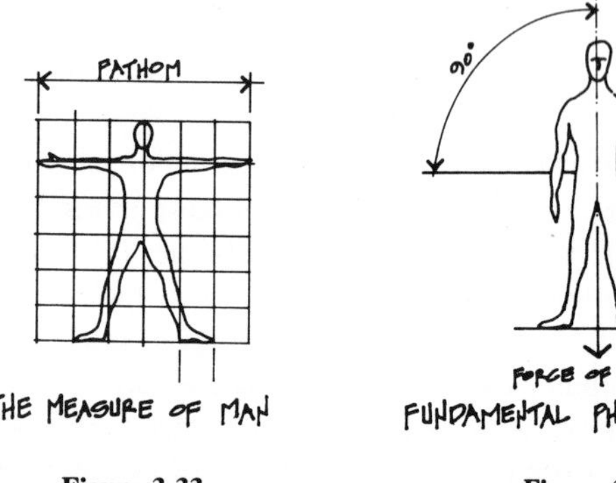

Figure 3.33

Figure 3.34

Drawings by Jeff Lee, Kemper & Associates.

Space

Space in architecture is a special category of free space, phenomenally created by the architect when he gives a part of free space shape and scale. Its first two dimensions — width and breadth — are responsive mainly to functional imperatives in the narrow sense, but the manipulation of its third dimension — height — grants the inhabitant's mind the special opportunity to develop yet other dimensions beyond.

Architects' words seem to rile people. We talk of "making" a space, and others point out that we have not made a space at all; it was there all along.[1] What we *have* done, or tried to do, when we cut a piece of space off from the continuum of all space, is to make it recognizable as a *domain*, responsive to the perceptual dimensions of its inhabitants.

Curiously, the acts the architect can most effectively perform with space appear to be opposing ones, though both seem to work. You can capture space or let it go, "define" it or "explode" it. Space is surely one of the few things that you have more of after you have "exploded" it, but it seems to thrive in captivity too. The failures come when we don't make it recognizable, when we do not distinguish a piece from the continuum.

Source. Charles Moore and Gerald Allen, *Dimensions*, Architectural Record Books, 1976.

Manipulation of Space. Expert manipulation and utilization of space can invoke every emotional reaction known to mankind. People reveal their psychology by the way they arrange space and themselves within the space. We act differently in a church and in a ballpark. The shape of space offers some indication of how one is expected to behave in that space. Behavior is usually dictated by the amount of movement permitted. Men are better oriented with respect to movement and direction in rectangular rooms, and they feel disorientation in square or round rooms. For women, the reverse is true. In this society rectangular rooms are considered to be ordinary living or working space; square or round rooms tend to be either very ancient or very modern and are associated with art, culture, and religion.

Our spatial boundaries are not our skins; rather, they extend varying distances beyond our physical selves according to our individual need for territory (i.e., personal space). Persons who invade one's personal space are perceived as potential enemies. If an invasion is accidental, as in a crowded elevator cab, we remain quiescent and avert our eyes from others to avoid provoking or seeming to exhibit aggressive or defensive attack. On the other hand, we interpret a deliberate invasion, such as an attempted sales pitch or sexual seduction, as *an actual attack on our physical selves,* and we respond according to our social conditioning. Thus we perceive our personal space as part of our physical space.

Minimum survival space produces severe emotional distress. When forced to live in refugee camps or prisons, for example, some persons become psychotic, claustrophobic, or even agoraphobic (the confined space represents the known, open space the unknown).

The Perception of Form

Congruent with the early definition of architecture as form or mass, form is the main characteristic that is seen in a structure. *Form follows function* is the modern architect's credo, which applies to ancient structures as well, although the pyramids, for example, must give one pause. According to one modern theory, the pyramids were built as they were to afford ease in construction for the purpose of achieving height. We will never know for sure.

To today's eye/mind perception, functional design (can openers, chemical processing plants) is more pleasing than apparently nonfunctional design (sculpture). The technological revolution has made many of us gadget-oriented, aesthetically.

Most shapes conform to fundamental geometries and are easily recognized as such. Cubes are perceived as hard (sharply delineated edges) and light (they could be boxes, hollow inside); spheres are perceived as soft (no edges) and heavy or solid. We learn as children that sharp edges or points discourage touching; therefore rounded objects are more touchable. Rounded contours suggest comfort and pleasure in handling. Softness (round) and lightness appear ''friendly,'' since the combination appears to be nonthreatening. A heavy, hard or harsh-lined object conveys seriousness, purpose, and austerity. Conical shapes vary in our subjective view according to angle of slope: a sharp-peaked cone thrusts; a low, squat cone sags; an equilateral cone is static. (The equilateral Great Pyramid of Giza with its sharp-edged sides is undoubtedly meant to convey timelessness.)

Scale. In architecture, ''measuring to scale'' means using the human being as the ''scale.'' The height of a brick wall, for example, is estimated in ''hands.'' Other clues are used in constructing an airplane hanger, whose size is based on the size of the airplane(s) that will occupy it.

When we want to know how big or small something is, the answer formulated must be related to our general physical size. We have learned to expect certain objects to be consistent in size; our perception of reality is built on expected consistency or predictability. An invasion of gigantic insects or, other small creatures made suddenly enormous (a recurring fantasy theme), would be un-

Figure 3.36 A 4-story street front, by M. F. Cummings and C. C. Miller. *Source. Architecture* (1865); reprinted in Charles Moore and Gerald Allen, *Dimensions*, Architectural Record Books, 1976.

Scale

As shape has to do with the meaning of individual things, scale has to do with their physical size, and therefore their importance and their meaning in relation to something else. No matter how unimportant or plain it may be, every part of every building has a size. And so scale, which involves arranging various sizes in some order, and choosing particular sizes when the option is available, is of great interest to all architects, and it is very much talked about.

But often it is nevertheless not entirely clear just what scale really is. We talk, for instance, of a large-scale housing development, and we usually mean just that it is big. In a different context, we say that an architectural drawing has a scale, meaning that so many units of measure on the drawing represent so many units of measure in the actual building. Then there are super scale, miniature scale, monumental scale, and — perhaps the most talked about of all — human scale.

People use all these terms presumably because they mean something. So the problem in talking about scale is not to exclude any of these possible meanings, but instead to find some common intent in them all. One common intent is this: whenever the word scale is used, something is being compared with something else. The large-scale housing development is large in comparison to an average housing development. The scale of the architectural drawing notes the size of the rendered building in comparison to the real thing.

Source. Charles Moore and Gerald Allen, *Dimensions*, Architectural Record Books, 1976.

SUSSEX DRIVE REDEVELOPMENT
Ottawa, Ontario, Restoration "Mile of History"
Architect: A. J. Capling
Photo: E. Richter

speakably terrifying. We learn at an early age that large is better than small ("my house is bigger than yours"). Thus large buildings imply authority and worth; small buildings (vacation homes, dollhouses) are meant to charm, that is, small is to round/soft as large is to sharp/hard.

Proportion. Proportion is the relation of a part to other parts in relation to a whole, its "balance" based on an idealized human form. The untrained eye or the "painter's eye" (which, conversely, implies a great deal of training) sees an expertly designed or natural panorama as a unified whole, its every part coordinated and integrated to achieve the entire unit. This harmonious coordination is the proportion of the scene.

The proportion of the human body as related to other forms has inspired artists and mathematicians of a philosophical bent to seek a mathematically computed, perfect proportion system that could be applied to every item in the universe and to the universe itself. ("Man is the measure of all things," said Sophocles.) Pythagoras' Golden Mean, Leonardo da Vinci's Ideal Man (of Hellenistic origin) and Le Corbusier's Modulor (from which architects have derived the word "module") exemplify this approach.

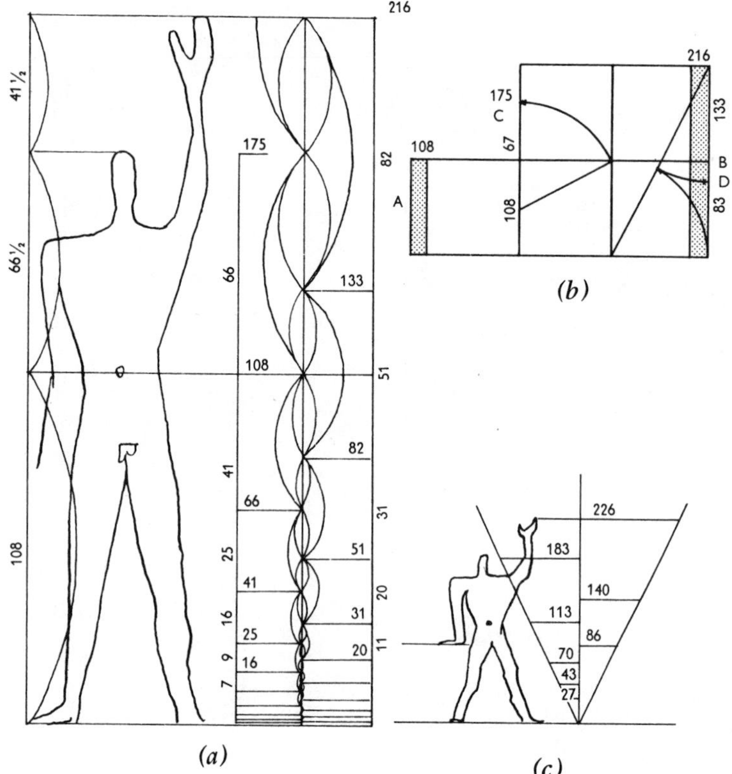

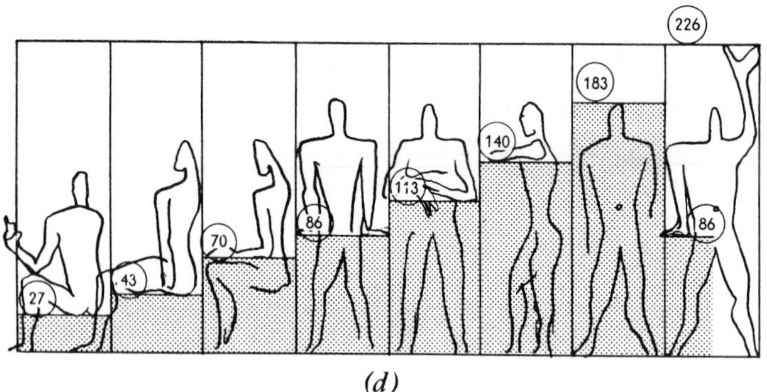

Figure 3.37 (*a*) Proportional figure. (*b*) Unit A = 108, double unit B = 216, elongation from A = C = 175, shortening from B = D = 83. (*c*) Module. (*d*) Unlimited figure indication. *Source*. Ernst Neufert, *Neufert-Bel,* Bertelsmann Fachverlag, 1970.

Third, there is scale. As pointed out in the chapter on scale, there is a close connection between scale and character expression. Thus, a room whose proportions are pleasing at, say, intimate scale, would be disastrous if the same proportions were duplicated at monumental scale. To feel the impact of the potential horror in this thought, just imagine your neighborhood Cozie Tea Shoppe, with its low ceiling and narrow doorways, blown up to the dimensions of Grand Central Station.

It is partially by means of proportion that one identifies objects. You recognize a brick, for example, not only by the material of which it consists but by its shape, which means its proportions, length to width to height. You ***know*** the size of a brick, so you immediately sense the scale of the brick wall or building at which you are looking. Therefore an outsize or undersize brick ***in the same proportions*** would be a violation of scale, misleading to the eye and damaging to character expression.

Source. Eugene Raskin, *Architecturally Speaking,* Reinhold Publishing Company, 1954.

To the three major scales—normal, intimate, and monumental—should be added a fourth, a minor one which I like to call "shock" scale. It is minor because (perhaps fortunately) its use is limited to very rare applications. Yet when well done and in the proper instance it can be tremendously effective.

We are all aware of the peculiar fascination that people feel for things that are extremely "out of scale." Why do we exclaim over the tiny locomotive, the miniature elephant, the cute little Eiffel Tower that hang from a charm bracelet?

Source. Eugene Raskin, *Architecturally Speaking,* Reinhold Publishing Company, 1954.

Rhythm. Any recurrent or cyclic theme, idea, object, or function in a time-space continuum that can be recognized and predicted is said to be rhythmic. Strict, equidistant pacing is considered to be formal and ceremonious, as in the Acropolis; accelerated pacing is exciting.

The principal use of rhythm in architecture is to aid perception of space. In designing a large space such as a mall or an airport terminal, the architect may use recurrent groupings of furniture, fountains, textures, colors, landscaping, or sculptural elements to enrich the space so that it becomes pleasurably scaled to the human eye/mind. Other architectural expressions of rhythm include windows, tract houses, columns, arches, doorways, stairs, tree-lined avenues that suggest a colonnade, and laundromats.

Light. We perceive light as contrasted to darkness: a symbol of light is space; a symbol of darkness is confinement. These cognitive interpretations are so ingrained that what is perceived becomes its symbol—the concrete and the abstract become one and the same. Therefore the light must shine in darkness.

The architect determines the admission of natural light and the placement of artificial light sources in a building. A room with a window at midwall and another room of the same physical dimensions with a window in the corner are entirely different rooms having entirely different characters. An illuminated space at night and a

Of course, the crux of the whole matter lies in the ability of the architect to choose the kind of rhythm that will express the emotion he wishes his building to convey and his capacity to feel that emotion himself in the first place. If the architect designs without the inner excitement that accompanies the truly creative act, if he is unmoved by the import of what he is doing, he will at best select his rhythms by rote; the result will inevitably be as unconvincing as the mechanical sexuality of a bored burlesque queen with a corned beef sandwich on her mind.

That is why the architect who disclaims any special interest in a particular building on the grounds that he is "just doing a job" so often fails utterly to do the job.

Source. Eugene Raskin, *Architecturally Speaking,* Reinhold Publishing Company, 1954.

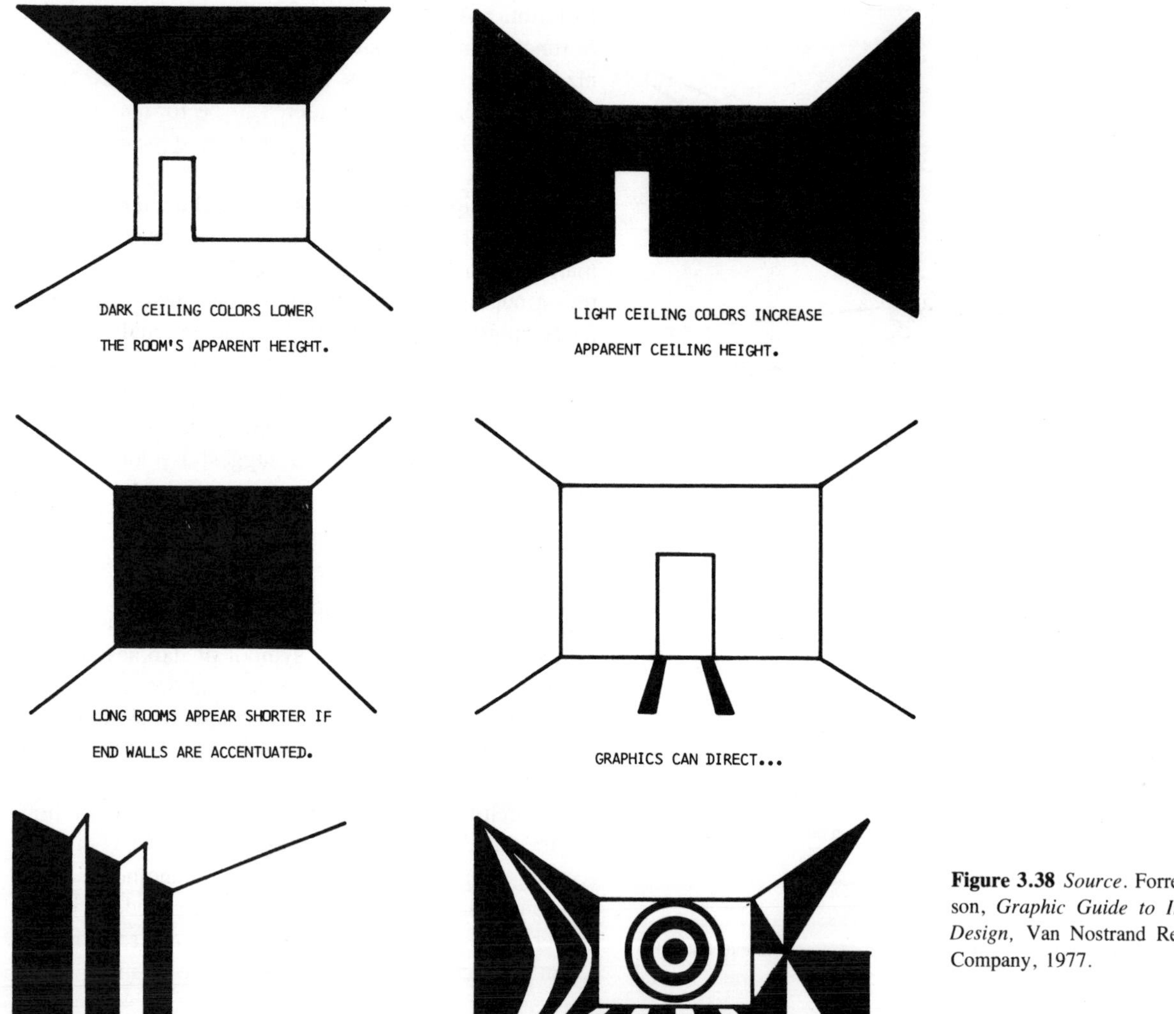

Figure 3.38 *Source.* Forrest Wilson, *Graphic Guide to Interior Design,* Van Nostrand Reinhold Company, 1977.

shady space in the daytime are magnets to the eye/mind because of the pull of contrast.

Light is associated with heat, life, clarity, activity, weightlessness, insight, and revelation; darkness with cold, obscurity, blindness, ignorance, inferiority, evil, and death. Subdued light is regarded as serene and tranquil with elements of healing, suitable for churches, parks, and hospitals.

Light can also create an enclosed space that is secure but not oppressive. People around a campfire feel safe from the unknown terrors of the night (to give an impression of spaciousness, one would not use concentrated light). Light becomes oppressive only when there is too much of it for too long: we have nowhere to hide.

Color. Color in architecture is a dependent variable, it is not autonomous. Like space manipulation, color is capable of awakening every human emotion. Architects should realize that accidental use of color (wiring, plating, wood stains) may induce reactions to a building that were not intended. Colors, which are abstract intangibles, are (like light) considered to be indistinguishable as symbols from the concrete or semiconcrete: weight, size, distance, dimension, life, death.

Certain colors and color-harmonies evoke unconscious but learned psychological reactions:

- Red is fiery and exciting; grey-green is soothing; beige is neutral.

COLOR IS SAID TO INDUCE A SENSE OF WELL-BEING, DISCOMFORT, ACTIVITY, OR PASSIVITY. IT HAS INFLUENCE IN ENLARGING OR DIMINISHING THE APPARENT SIZE AND DIMENSION OF ROOMS AND IN CREATING ROOM ATMOSPHERE.

IT IS CERTAIN THAT COLOR EXERTS AN INFLUENCE UPON ROOM OCCUPANTS. IT IS NOT AS CERTAIN THAT THESE EFFECTS CAN BE PREDICTED WITH ABSOLUTE CERTAINTY.

THE FOLLOWING OBSERVATIONS ARE TO BE USED AS GUIDES FOR THE INTERIOR DESIGNER AND CONFIRMED BY EXPERIENCE AND OBSERVATION.

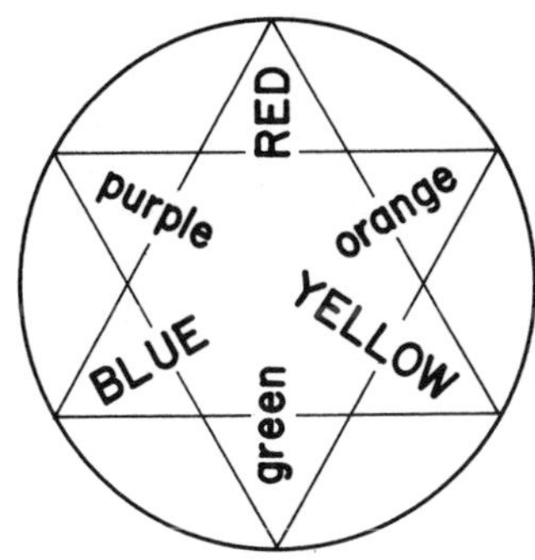

COLOR CIRCLE—MAJOR TRIANGLE OF RED, BLUE, YELLOW, WHICH ARE PRIMARY COLORS, AND OPPOSED TRIANGLE OF GREEN, ORANGE, PURPLE, WHICH ARE SECONDARY COLORS RESULTING FROM THE MIXING OF PRIMARY COLORS.

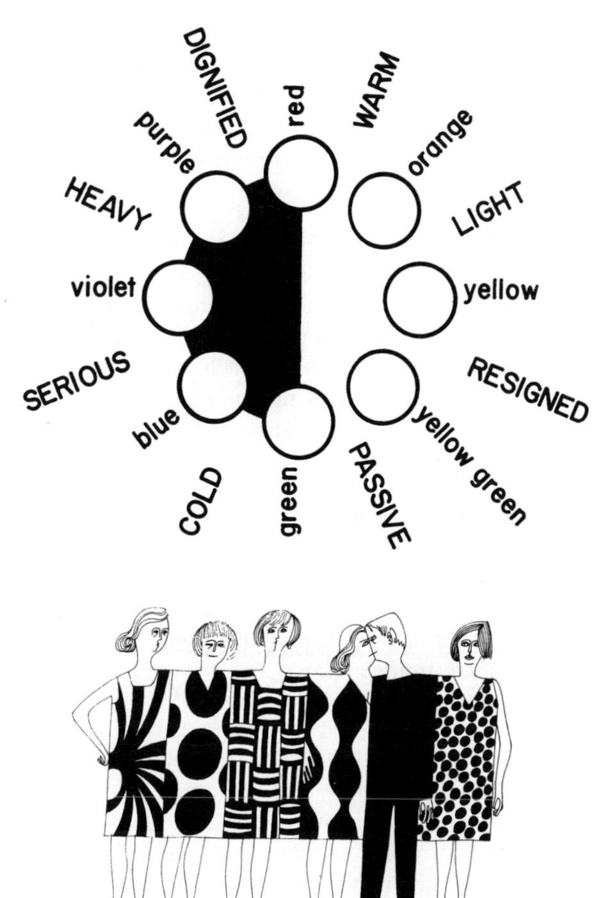

Figure 3.39 Color. *Source.* Forrest Wilson, *Graphic Guide to Interior Design,* Van Nostrand Reinhold Company, 1977.

- Earth and leather browns are masculine; pink is feminine; lavender and chartreuse are effete.
- Black is mysterious and/or oppressive; white is clear and pure.
- To an American, red/white/blue is patriotic.
- Red/orange/brown is autumn.
- Red/yellow/purple is "loud"; blues/greens/lavender is "quiet."
- Violet/blue/blue-green/salmon/pink/golden-orange is sunset.

A popular theory of room color is like sympathetic or homeopathic medicine: the quality of a space that is desired to be most prominent should be matched by a tint or shade that suggests that quality.

1 Walls should be light colored to show off a room's spaciousness, or to cause it to seem spacious when it is not.

2 Floors should be dark and solid (e.g., indoor/outdoor carpet for an illusion of ground, grass, or flowers).

3 Ceilings should appear to be weightless and distant, like the sky.

It is possible to suggest a building's function by the use of a single color (hospital-white, bordello-red) or simple color scheme (plant store, green and brown). Interior colors may be used to accentuate, divide, continue a flow, attract, repel, or camouflage. The relationship to a moving observer of three-dimensional or seemingly three-dimensional ("seemingly" because color is used to provide psychological illusion) objects in space is the basis of holography. The sense through which we make such perceptions is called *kinesthesia*. Someday use of color will be made three-dimensional through holograms.

Sound. "Acoustical" materials are commonly thought to be used to absorb or deaden sound. Yet through acoustic principles one can also strengthen sound and resonance into myriad reverberations like a tuning fork, only more coarsely, by bouncing sound waves off surfaces. An echo is a result of applied acoustics.

Touch. Architecture is particularly conducive to tactility, since all surfaces have texture. A smooth piece of wood feels good to the hand; walls of rough, unfinished stone do not. Subgrade walls where water seepage occurs with each rainfall are slimy to the touch because physical conditions permit mosses and algae to grow on the walls' surfaces. Porcelain is cold; leather is warm.

Smell. Certain buildings (hospitals, elementary school classrooms, gymnasium lockerrooms, tobacco-curing sheds, canneries, automobile garages, feedstores, and drugstores) have characteristic smells that arouse memory-associations that remind us of who we are and where we come from.

Eidetics. "Eidetic," usually teamed with memory (as in "photographic" memory), is the term applied to the sensation of experiencing all—or two or more—of the senses simultaneously: sound that conveys form, for example, such as rich, resonant organ music—and "rich" also suggests taste. Taste and smell are simultaneously experienced all the time. Vision and texture can be produced by the following architectural effects:

- Chromium-plated steel, *smooth* and shiny to the *eye,* diverts attention from its shape.
- Textures can clash and harmonize like colors.
- Mirror-faced buildings appear as formless but textured reflections of their environments.

Conclusion. Aesthetic appeal, interest, and excitement are not enough in the design of structures and spaces. Three other objectives form the major portion of architectural values:

1 *Order,* which is the basis of civilization (although in looking at the grand pattern, "organized chaos" seems to be the closest humans can come to this ideal).
2 *Quality,* describing items skillfully made from appropriate materials.
3 *Usefulness,* applying to items that are practical, based on required function.

These three precepts minus any thought of emotional appeal have resulted in a vast horde of ugly, uncomfortable, depressing, costly structures. Good design, on the other hand, must encompass everything that accommodates human use.

4 STRUCTURAL ENGINEERING

By Ajit S. Randhava

Ajit S. Randhava received his Bachelor of Science degree in civil engineering from Panjab University (India) in June 1966. He received his Master of Science degree in structural engineering from the University of California at Berkeley in December 1967. Randhava is a registered civil and structural engineer in the state of California. He is a member of the Structural Engineering Association of Southern California, the American Concrete Institute, and the Post-Tensioning Institute. Ajit Randhava has 10 years of diversified structural engineering experience.

Structure is the essence of a building; it gives the building its strength, rigidity, and form. Most architects retain a structural engineer to provide all structural calculations, drawings, details, and specifications. Despite this outcome, it is incumbent on the architect to have an understanding of the principles of structural design. The structure of a building can be divided into four major systems:

1 The framing system for the floor(s) and roof.
2 The system of walls (bearing) and/or columns.
3 The foundation(s) system, which transfers all loads to the supporting soil.
4 A bracing system, which will hold everything together and resist lateral loads from wind and/or earthquakes.

This section offers a survey of the systems just enumerated. It includes sample calculations and discussions of the advantages and disadvantages of different structural systems.

Table 3.22 Common Structure Engineering Abbreviations and Symbols

Abbreviation or Symbol[a]	Is Read as
cu ft	Cubic foot
cu in	Cubic inch
cu yd	Cubic yard
ft	Foot
in	Inch
lb	Pound
kip	Thousand pounds
ton	Two thousand pounds
ft-lb	Foot-pound
in-lb	Inch-pound
lin ft	Linear foot
lin in	Linear inch
pcf	Pounds per cubic foot
psf	Pounds per square foot
psi	Pounds per square inch
sq ft	Square foot
sq in	Square inch
cont	Continuous
bm	Beam
col	Column
dia	Diameter
M	Bending moment
R	Reaction
V	Shear
S	Section modulus
I	Moment of inertia
W	Uniform load per foot
L	Length of member
E	Modulus of elasticity
Δ	Deflection
A	Area

[a]The same abbreviation is used for both the singular and plural. Thus "ft" indicates foot or feet, as applicable.

General Section

Building Loads

Dead Load. Dead load is the vertical load due to the weight of all permanent structural and nonstructural components of a building, such as floors, roofs, walls, and fixed service equipment. The first step in the design of a building is to determine the loads to be sustained by the structure during its life span. The Uniform Building Code requires that floors in office buildings and in other buildings where partition locations are subject to change, be designed to support, in addition to all other loads, a uniformly distributed dead load equal to 20 pounds per square foot.

Live Load. Live load is the load superimposed by the use and occupancy of the building, not including the wind load, earthquake load or dead load. The UBC contains specifications for live loads, broken down by type of load and application.

All buildings must be designed in accordance with the building code in a particular locality. Also many times a client has a special loading criterion which, if more conservative, should be used for design. The basic live loads for floors given by the UBC can be reduced as follows:

1 Except for places of public assembly, and except for live loads greater than 100 pounds per square

foot, the design live load on any member supporting more than 150 square feet may be reduced at the rate of 0.08% per square foot of area supported.

2 The reduction shall not exceed 40% for horizontal members or vertical members receiving load from one level only, 60% for other vertical members, nor R as determined by the following formula:

$$R = 23.1\ (1 + D/L)$$

where R = reduction (%)
D = dead load per square foot of area supported by the member
L = unit live load per square foot of area supported by the member

Snow Loads. Snow loads, full or unbalanced, are to be considered in place of minimum roof live loads where such loading would result in larger members or connections. The weight of snow varies considerably, from about 8 pounds per cubic foot for fresh dry snow to about 20 pounds per cubic foot for wet or packed snow. The snow load to be used is to be determined by the local building official. The potential accumulation effects at parapets and other low points must be considered in design. According to the UBC, snow loads in excess of 20 pounds per square foot may be reduced for each degree of pitch over 20 degrees by a factor R_s as follows:

$$R_s = \frac{S}{40} - \frac{1}{2}$$

Where R_s = snow load reduction (psf/degree of pitch over 20°)
S = total snow load (psf)

A 2-month duration is generally recognized as the proper design level for snow loads. Although in a single year, some snow will remain on roofs for periods exceeding 2 months, such snow loads seldom approach the design load.

Wind Load. Buildings or structures shall be designed to withstand the minimum horizontal and uplift pressures set forth by the UBC, allowing for wind from any direction. In addition, extensive studies of basic wind velocities related to geographical location have resulted in the development of a detailed wind velocity map for the United States. The UBC wind pressures are minimum values and are adjusted by the appropriate building officials for areas that are subjected to higher wind pressures. The design wind load is assumed to act horizontally on the vertical projection of the building. The wind pressure in pounds per square foot increases as the square of the velocity in miles per hour, thus a wind of 80 miles per hour produces wind loads 4 times greater than a wind of 40 miles per hour.

Either wind or seismic load, whichever produces the higher stresses, is used in building design. Roofs of all enclosed and unenclosed buildings are designed to withstand pressures acting upward normal to the surface equal to some percentages of wind pressures given by the UBC. This percentage is listed in different building codes and varies from place to place. The UBC gives upward pressures of ¾ and 1¼ times for enclosed and unenclosed buildings, respectively. Sloping roofs have different inward pressure requirements normal to the surface. Most of the codes allow an increase of one-third in allowable working stresses, when considering wind or earthquake forces either acting alone or combined with vertical loads. This increase is not allowed when vertical loads act alone.

Special Loads. In addition to dead, typical live, snow, earthquake, and wind loads, there are certain other special loads, as follows:

1 Earth pressure caused by the retained earth behind walls.
2 Hydrostatic pressures when all or parts of a structure are below the ground water, or for offshore structures below the surface of the sea.
3 Impact due to moving loads, cranes, blast, and similar forces.

Roof and Floor Framing Systems. Selection of the structural form that best satisfies the various requirements and objectives of a particular project is the most important design decision. The essential features of any roof or floor framing system are deck, beams, and girders supported on columns or walls. The most common building materials for building shell construction are steel, concrete, and wood. The choice of a framing system depends on the availability of materials, as well as on design loads, building dimensions, building code restrictions, considerations of economy, construction schedule, acoustical and thermal properties, fire resistance required, environments, and other factors.

Some Typical Deck Materials

Wood

1 Plywood, 16 inch to 4 foot spans for roof, 12 to 24 inch spans for floor. For floors, a second layer of

NEW ENGLAND AQUARIUM
Boston, Massachusetts
Architects: Cambridge Seven Associates
Photo: S. Rosenthal

plywood, particle board, or lightweight fill are used on top of the structural layer of plywood.

2 Tongue and groove wood decking (2 or 3 in thick), 4 to 8 foot spans.

Steel Decking. Metal deck with insulation board or vermiculite fill is used on roofs. Lightweight or regular weight concrete is used on top of metal deck for floors. Common span sizes are between 4 and 12 feet. Sometimes fire resistance also requires restrictions on a maximum allowable span.

Concrete

1 *Reinforced Concrete Slab*: (*a*) one-way slab, economical up to 16 feet; (*b*) two-way slab, economical up to 24 feet; (*c*) higher spans (can be used with added cost).

2 *Prestressed (pre- or posttensioned) Concrete Spans.* Spans up to 30 feet long can be used; very economical for spans below 16 feet.

3 *Precast Concrete Planks.* Used with or without concrete fill for floor spans up to 32 feet. Many other precast floor systems are available; such as the single or double T for example.

Some Typical Beams, Joists and Girders

Wood Beams and Joists. Used up to 30 feet. Floor joists are more economical for spans below 20 feet. For purlins the spans between 20 and 24 feet are more economical.

1 Wood trusses closely spaced, 30 to 60 feet.
2 Large wood trusses widely spaced, 50 to 100 feet.
3 Glu-lam beams, 24 to 100 feet.

Table 3.23 Requirements of Four Building Codes on Three Subjects

Subject	Uniform Building Code	Basic Building Code	National Building Code	Southern Standard Building Code
Roof live load	Section 2305, page 128: basic live load is reduced as area increases.	Section 710, page 196: basic criteria very similar to UBC with more stress on snow loads.	Sections 902–905, page 122: basic live load of 20 psf used without any reduction.	Section 1203, page 12–3: live load criteria for roof very similar to the National Building Code.
Live load reduction	Section 2306, page 129: live load reduction applies to both roof and floor life loads except for some special structures or special loads (e.g., places of public assembly).	Section 720, page 203: basic criteria very similar to UBC.	Sections 902–908, page 123: no reduction for roof live load; floor live load reduction criterion is different from but similar to the UBC.	Section 1203.1 (e), page 12–3: no reduction for roof live load; floor live load reduction is very different from all the other three codes.
Wind loads	Section 2311, page 130: wind pressures for different structure heights given; special requirements for upward pressures are also listed.	Sections 713–717, pages 199–202: very detailed criteria on wind; somewhat different from other codes.	Section 903, page 124: criteria similar to UBC.	Section 1205, pages 12–5: different criteria for inland and costal regions; appendix gives hurricane requirements.

Reinforced Concrete

1 Conventionally reinforced concrete beam, spans 20 to 40 feet. (Uneconomical for spans beyond 40 ft.)
2 Prestressed beams; (*a*) precast beams, 20 to 60 feet; (*b*) single or double Ts, 40 to 80 feet; (*c*) Prestressed in place, 40 to 100 feet.

Structural Steel Beams.

1 Small span joists (open web), 20 to 40 feet.
2 Long span joists (open web), 40 to 144 feet.
3 Steel beams, 20 to 100 feet.

Building Codes. As Chapter 1 pointed out, there are many national, regional, state, county, and city building codes. Examples from three codes used at national level appear in Table 3.23, which also mentions another regional code used mainly in the southern and southeastern states. However some of the city, county, or regional codes cover in more detail local problems that are not always covered in national codes. Since incorporating references to all these codes would have been extremely difficult, only the UBC is used in this section. The complexity of Table 3.23 gives an idea of the varying emphases and outright differences among codes. The reader is advised to consult local building officials when dealing with the design of a building in a particular area.

Summary

1 Section modulus of rectangular cross section about its neutral axis:

$$S = \frac{bd^2}{6}$$

where S = section modulus
b = width of section
d = depth of section

2 Moment of inertia of rectangular section about its neutral axis:

$$I = \frac{bd^3}{12}$$

where I = moment of inertia
b = width of section
d = depth of section

3 Area of a rectangular cross section:

$$A = bd$$

where A = area of section
b = width of section
d = depth of section

4

$$r = \sqrt{\frac{I}{A}}$$

where r = radius of gyration
I = moment of inertia
A = area of section

For example, for a rectangular section:

$$I = \frac{bd^3}{12}, \qquad A = bd$$

$$r = \sqrt{\frac{bd^3}{12} \times \frac{1}{bd}} = \sqrt{\frac{d^2}{12}} = \frac{d}{\sqrt{12}}$$

5 Maximum moment in a simply supported beam with uniformly distributed load across the entire span:

$$M = \frac{WL^2}{8}$$

where M = maximum moment and occurs at midspan
W = uniform load per unit length
L = span length

Units of M depend on units of W and L. For example, if units of W are kips per linear foot and L is the span in feet, then the units of M will be in kip-feet.

6 Maximum moment in a simple beam with a concentrated load at the midspan:

$$M = \frac{PL}{4}$$

where M = maximum moment at midspan
P = concentrated load at midspan
L = span length

7 Maximum moment in a simple beam with two concentrated loads at third points:

$$M = \frac{PL}{3}$$

where M = maximum moment as it occurs under each concentrated load
P = concentrated load
L = span length

8 Maximum cantilever moment for cantilever beam with uniformly distributed load across the entire cantilever:

$$M_c = \frac{Wl^2}{2}$$

where M^c = maximum cantilever moment that occurs at the support
W = uniform load per linear foot
l = length of cantilever

9 Maximum deflection for simple beam with concentrated load at center of span:

$$\Delta = \frac{PL^3}{48EI}$$

where Δ = maximum deflection at midspan
P = concentrated load at midspan
L = span length
E = modulus of elasticity of the material of beam
I = moment of inertia of section

10 Maximum deflection for simple beam with uniformly distributed load across the entire span:

$$\Delta = \frac{5}{384} \times \frac{WL^4}{EI}$$

where W = uniformly distributed load per linear foot; all other variables are as defined in formula 9.

Wood Framing

Wood is a dependable, economical, available material with a high ratio of strength to weight. It is easily cut, laminated, and fastened. In recent years, technical developments and the establishment of an engineered timber fabricating and laminating industry have had a profound effect on construction. Engineered timber is widely used in such diversified construction as schools, churches, residences, industrial buildings, and commercial buildings (e.g., at shopping centers). Some disadvantages that restrict the use of this material for big buildings are its tendencies to swell and shrink, its susceptibility to rot and to insect infestation, and its poor fire resistance.

Wood differs from most other structural materials in that it is organic. The microscopic fibers of which it is composed are actually tiny tubes with closed ends, whose length parallel to the axis of the tree is many times their lateral dimension, imparting, different properties parallel and perpendicular to the wood grain. Specifically, the flexural, axial, and shear stresses are higher parallel to the grain than perpendicular to the grain. Wood shrinks and swells perpendicular to the grain and exhibits almost no dimensional change parallel to the grain. Allowance must be made for changes in dimension if amount of moisture in the air is not to be constant.

Plywood is made up of a combination of three or more thin plies, glued together with the grain of alternate plies at right angles. The strength of plywood is more or less the same along the length and width of a panel, and the material is less susceptible to warping, splitting and checking. For complete information about grades and plywood manufacturing, the designer should see the current U.S. Product Standard (PS) for softwood plywood and the U.S. Commercial Standard (CS) for hardwood plywood.

Lumber Sizes. Sawn lumber is available in standard rectangular sizes. The width varies in 1- or 2-inch increments, and the depth varies in 2-inch increments. The standard sizes are nominal, not actual. For example, a 2 × 10 board actually measures 1½ × 9¼. Properties of sections for sawn lumber and timber such as net cross-sectional area, section modulus, moment of inertia, and weight per lineal foot, are tabulated in many handbooks. The measure of the timber quantity is called the *board-foot*.

board-feet per lineal foot = nominal width (in) × nominal depth (ft)

Allowable Stresses. The allowable unit stresses for sawn lumber under normal duration of load and under continuously dry conditions, as in most covered structures, are listed in many handbooks and building codes, for different species and grades. Most of the codes give the allowable bending (flexural) stresses for single member uses and for repetitive member use. Single-member use is intended for the design of structures in which an individual member, such as a beam, girder, or post, carries its full design load. Repetitive member uses are intended for the design of members in bending, such as joists, trusses, rafters, studs, planks, or decking, that are spaced not more than 24 inches, are fewer than 3 in number, and are joined by floor, roof, or other load-distributing elements adequate to support the design load. For the same species and grades, the allowable stresses for repetitive member uses are higher than single-member use.

When the duration of the full maximum load does not exceed the period indicated, increase the allowable unit stresses as follows:

15%	for 2-months duration, as for snow loads
25%	for 7 days duration, as for roof loads
33⅓%	for wind or earthquake loading
100%	for impact

These increases are not cumulative and are incorporated in most of the building codes, including the UBC. The resultant structural members shall not be smaller than required for a longer duration of loading. These increases do not apply to modulus of elasticity that is used in the calculation of deflections. These stress increases also apply to glu-lam members.

Wood Diaphragms. Lumber and plywood diaphragms are used to resist horizontal forces in horizontal and vertical distributing or resisting elements. The most common diaphragms are planks or plywood. Plywood varies in thickness from ⅜ to 1⅛ inches. The allowable shear values for the vertical and horizontal diaphragms are given in the UBC and other building codes.

Secondary Framing Members. Rafters or joists spaced at intervals 12, 16, or 24 inches are used to support all roof or floor sheathing. The most common spans for these are 10 to 20 feet long. These members are also designed as beams and are supported by main carrying members as described later. On panelized roof construction the secondary framing is subdivided into two members. The main secondary member, called the *purlin,* is spaced at 8-foot over-center spans between main members, and rafters or subpurlins are spaced at 16- or 24-inch spans between purlins. Purlins can span up to 30 feet; they are normally 4 or 6 inches wide and 12 to 16 inches deep.

Main Members. Glu-lam beams or trusses are the most common main members used in wood construction. Wood-stud walls or masonry walls are also used to support the secondary members.

Glu-Lam Beams. Surfaced lumber, ¾ or 1½ inches before gluing, is used to laminate straight members and curved members having radii of curvature within the bending radius limitations for the species. Thus finished depths of laminated members are generally multiples of the 1½- or ¾-inch net thickness. However other lamination thicknesses may be used to meet special requirements, resulting in finished depths that are not multiples of these net thicknesses. Standard widths of glued-laminated members are 2¼, 3⅛, 5⅛, 6¾, 8¾, 12¼, and 14¼ inches. The properties of these sections can be found in various handbooks. The basic design procedure for glu-lam members is the same as for sawn lumber members. The basic stresses are modified for the following corrections, as applicable.

Curvature Factor. For the curved portion of members, the allowable unit stress in bending is to be modified by multiplication by the curvature C_c. The formula for C_c can be found in the UBC.

Slenderness Factor for Beams. Lateral support is necessary when the depth of a beam exceeds its breadth, and the basic stresses in bending are modified as required. When the slenderness factor C_s, does not exceed 10, the full allowable unit stress in bending may be used. When C_s exceeds 10, the allowable bending stress is reduced. In no case shall C_s exceed 50. The formulas for C_s and stress reduction are given in the UBC and elsewhere.

Size Factor for Beams. When a rectangular beam is deeper than 12 inches, the allowable unit stress in bending (F_b') is found by multiplying the basic bending stress F_b by size factor C_F

$$C_F = \left(\frac{12}{d}\right)^{1/9}$$

$$F_b' = C_F \times F_b$$

where d = depth of beam

The values obtained from this formula are based on a uniformly loaded beam. For other conditions of loading, the C_F values can be found in reference No. W7, Section 903. However values determined from the formula above are sufficiently accurate for most design situations. Adjustment of bending stress for size factor is not cumulative with adjustments for slenderness factor.

Trusses. Type of truss and arrangement of members may be suited to the shape of structure and the loads and stresses involved. The types most commonly built are bowstring, flat or parallel chord, and triangular or pitched. For most construction other than houses, trusses usually are spaced 12 to 20 feet apart. For houses, very light trusses are erected, generally at 16 or 24 inches, center to center. Individual truss members may be solid sawn, glued laminated, or mechanically laminated. Steel rods or other steel shapes may be used as members of timber trusses.

In the most popular form, the bowstring truss, spans of 100 to 150 feet are common. Since the top chord is nearly the shape of an ideal arch, stresses in chords are almost uniform throughout a bowstring truss span, and web stresses are low under uniformly distributed loads. Parallel chord trusses are used less often because chord stresses are not uniform along their length, and web stresses are high. However these trusses are being used as secondary members in buildings for spans from 30 to 60 feet for roofs and 20 to 40 feet for floors. Triangular trusses are used for shorter spans, as in residential construction. Economical ratios of depth of truss to length of span are usually about 1:6 to 1:8 for bowstring trusses, 1:8 to 1:10 for flat trusses, and 1:6 or more for pitched trusses.

A camber should be provided in the trusses to prevent the total load deflection from producing a sag below a straight line between points of support. In structures employing trusses, a system of bracing is required to provide resistance to lateral forces and to hold the trusses true and plumb. Erection braces are required to hold the trusses in a safe position until sufficient permanent construction is in place to provide full stability.

Wood-Bearing Walls. Wood walls are generally constructed from 2 × 4 or 2 × 6 wood studs spaced at 16 or 24 inches over center, with the wide face of the stud perpendicular to the wall. For tall walls or for heavily loaded walls, 3 × 4 or 3 × 6 studs are used.

Wood Columns. Most main members are directly supported on wood columns. Seat connections of different kinds are available for girder-to-column connections.

Although a number of factors influence the load-carrying capacity of a column, the principal ones are the laterally unsupported length l and the least lateral dimension. The least lateral dimension may be expressed as the least radius of gyration of the section r, or as the minimum width of the section d, as is done with most wood columns. Simple solid wood columns consist of a single piece or of pieces properly glued together to form a single member.

Allowable unit stresses in simple solid columns are determined from the following formula:

$$F_C = \frac{3.619E}{(l/r)^2}$$

For columns of square or rectangular cross section, this becomes

$$F_C' = \frac{0.3E}{(l/d)^2}$$

Spaced columns are formed of two or more individual members with their longitudinal axes parallel, separated at the ends and the midpoints of their length by blocking, and joined at the ends by timber connectors capable of developing the required shear resistance. End blocks with connectors and spacer blocks are required to obtain spaced column action when the individual members of a spaced column assembly have an l/d ratio greater than

$$\left(\frac{0.3E}{F_C}\right)^{1/2}$$

For an assembly of members having a lower l/d ratio, the individual members are designed as simple solid columns.

Mechanical Fasteners. Nails, spikes, screws, lags, bolts, and timber connectors, such as shear plates and split rings, are used for connections in wood construction. The factors to be considered in determining allowable loads for mechanically fastened joints are lumber species, critical section, angle of load to grain, spacing of mechanical fastenings, edge and end distances, conditions of loading, and eccentricity. The allowable design loads for fasteners of various sizes are given in handbooks.

In addition, many other hardware items such as framing anchors, joist and beam hangers, column caps, column base plates, tie-down anchors, hurricane anchors, and wood-to-steel hangers, are available from different manufacturers (e.g., "Strong Tie" by the Simpson Company).

Summary

1 The measure of wood quantity is called the board foot.
   board-feet per linear foot of a member = nominal width (in) × nominal depth (ft)
2 Sawn lumber is used primarily in rectangular shapes.
3 Most commonly used plywood thicknesses are ⅜, ½, ⅝, ¾, and 1⅛, or 1 inch tongue and groove.
4 Glu-lam beams are available in sections 2¼, 3⅛, 5⅛, 6¾, 8¾, 10¾, 12¼, and 14¼ inches wide.
5 Allowable stress in simple solid column

$$F'_C = \frac{3.619E}{(l/r)^2}$$

where: F'_C = allowable compressive stress
E = modulus of elasticity
l = unbraced length
r = radius of gyration

6 The modulus of elasticity E of most commonly used dry woods varies between 1.6×10^6 psi and 1.8×10^6 psi.
7 Most commonly used timber weighs between 35 to 40 pounds per cubic foot.
8 Refer to reference Books Nos. W1 to W7 and M1. Reference W1 and W4 are recommended for numerical problems.

Concrete

Concrete is a stonelike material obtained by permitting a carefully proportioned mixture of water and cement, sand, and gravel or other aggregate, to harden in forms of the shape and dimensions desired. The bulk of the material consists of fine and coarse aggregate. Cement and water interact chemically to bind the aggregate particles into a solid mass. The components of a concrete mix are proportioned so that the resulting material has adequate strength, proper workability for placing, and low cost. It has been customary to define the proportions of a concrete mix by the ratio, by volume or weight, of cement to sand to gravel (e.g., 1:2:4).

Admixture is a material other than portland cement, aggregate, or water that is added to concrete to modify its properties. Air-entraining, accelerator, retarder, waterproofing, cement replacement, and special-purpose admixtures are common.

The unit weight of so-called stone or regular weight concrete varies from about 145 to 152 pounds per cubic foot and can generally be assumed to be as 150 pounds per cubic foot. Lightweight concrete can be obtained by gas-forming admixtures. However, in America it is almost always produced from special lightweight aggregates. The weight of the lightweight concrete normally varies between 90 and 110 pounds per cubic foot.

Properties and Tests

Fresh Concrete. Slump is the most important test of the workability of fresh concrete. For workable concrete, there must be sufficient water to permit the plastic mass to be placed and consolidated without honeycomb or excessive water rise, or to make concrete "pumpable" if it is to be placed by pumps; in addition, the surface provided must be amenable to proper finishing. (Workability requirements vary with the job and with the placing, vibration, and the finishing equipment used.)

Slump is tested in the field very quickly. An open-ended, truncated metal cone, 12 inches high, is filled in three equal-volume increments with the concrete mixture in question, and each increment is consolidated separately, all according to standard procedures. Slump is the sag of the concrete, measured in inches, after the cone has been removed.

Hardened Concrete. The main measure of the structural quality of concrete is its compression strength. Tests for this property are made on cylindrical specimens whose height is twice their diameter—usually 6 inches diameter and 12 inches high. The compression strength obtained from such tests is represented symbolically as f_c'. Unless otherwise specified, f_c' is based on tests on cylinders 28 days old, which are made, cured, and tested in accordance with standard procedures. Sometimes cylinders are tested at 7 days. The strength at 7 days is roughly 70% of strength at 28 days. The most commonly used concretes have compressive strength varying between 2000 and 5000 psi. Compressive strength referred to here is at 28 days test strength.

Modulus of Elasticity. This property is used in all design, but it is seldom determined by test, and almost never as a regular routine test. It can be computed with reasonable accuracy from the empirical equation

$$E_c = 33(w)^{1.5} (f_c')^{1/2}$$

where E_c = modulus of elasticity (psi)
w = unit weight of the hardened concrete (pcf)
f_c' = compressive strength of concrete (psi)

Tensile Strength. The standard splitting test is a measure of almost pure uniform tension f_{ct}. The beam test measures bending tension f_n on extreme surfaces, calculated for a stress distribution that is assumed to be perfectly elastic and triangular. Concrete is very weak in tension and is reinforced in the tension zone. Other properties frequently important for particular conditions are durability (to resist freezing and thawing), color, surface hardness, impact hardness, abrasion resistance, shrinkage, behavior at high temperatures, insulation value, fire resistance, and fatigue resistance.

Reinforcement. Since concrete has very low tensile strength, most of the building codes recommend that the concrete be able to resist all the compressive stresses and the reinforcing steel be able to resist all the tensile stresses. Reinforcing steel comes in plain bars and deformed steel bars. The most commonly used steel is deformed steel bars, or *rebars*.

The ASTM specifications for billet steel (A615, A616, A617) require identification marks to be rolled into the surface of one side of the bar to denote the producer's mill designation, the bar size, the type of steel, and, for grade 60 and grade 75 bars, grade marks indicating yield strength.

The most common grades of reinforcement are ASTM 615 grade 40 and ASTM 615 grade 60, where 40 and 60 are yield strengths of the respective steels. The modulus of elasticity of reinforcement steel (E_s) is approximately 29×10^6 psi. The other form of reinforcement, used mostly in slabs on grade or topping slabs, is called welded wire fabric. This is a grid made with two kinds of cold drawn wire, smooth (plain) or deformed. The wires can be spaced in each direction of the grid as desired.

Curing. Curing of concrete consists of the natural and artificial processes that affect the extent and rate of hydration of the cement. Methods for curing are classified as:

1. Those that supply water throughout the early hydration process and tend to maintain a uniform temperature. These methods include ponding, sprinkling, and application of wet burlap or cotton mats.
2. Those designed to prevent loss of water but doing little to maintain a uniform temperature. One such method involves using waterproof paper and impermeable membranes on top of wet concrete surface.

Theories of Concrete Design. The two main theories of concrete design are presented in terms of (*a*) elastic behavior (working stresses), and (*b*) inelastic behavior (ultimate strength design).

Working Stress Method. At low stresses, up to about $f_c'/2$, the concrete is seen to behave nearly elastically as in Figure 3.40; that is, stresses and strains are quite closely proportional. The straight line d represents this range of behavior with little error for both fast and slow rates of loading. At any given load, the compression strain in the concrete is equal to the compression strain in the steel. In the equations that follow, subscripts c and s correspond to concrete and steel, respectively.

$$e_c = \frac{f_c}{E_c} = e_s = \frac{f_s}{E_s}$$

$$\text{modulus of elasticity} = E = \frac{\text{stress}}{\text{strain}} = \frac{f}{e}$$

$$\frac{f_c}{E_c} = \frac{f_s}{E_s}$$

$$f_s = \frac{E_s}{E_c} f_c = n f_c$$

where $n = E_s/E_c$ is called modular ratio.

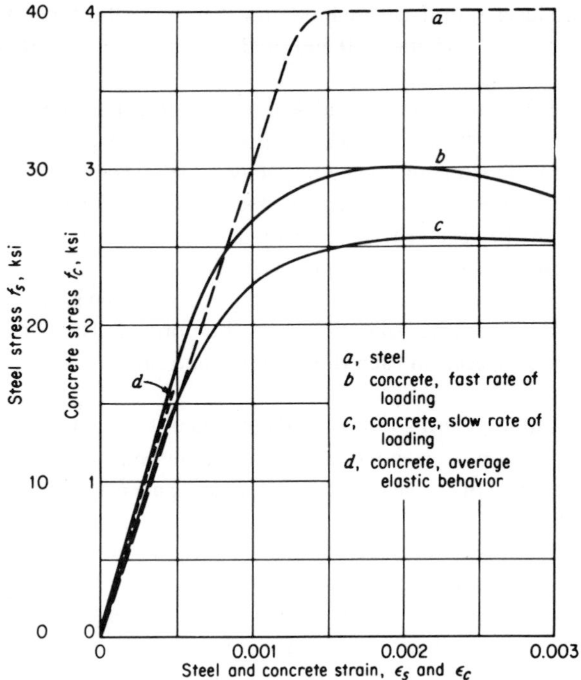

Figure 3.40 Concrete and steel stress-strain curves. *Source.* From *Design of Concrete Structures* by Winter, Urquhard, O'Rourke, and Nilson. Copyright 1964 by McGraw-Hill, Inc. Used with permission of McGraw-Hill Book Company.

Let A_c = net area of concrete (i.e., gross area minus area occupied by reinforcing bars)
A_g = gross area
A_s = area of reinforcing bars
P = axial load

Then

$$P = f_c A_c + f_s A_s \geqslant f_c A_c + n f_c A_s$$

or

$$P = f_c (A_c + nA_s) = f_c \quad [A_g + (n - 1) A_s]$$

The term $(A_c + nA_s)$ or $[A_g + (n - 1) A_s]$ is called transformed area A_t.

Ultimate Strength Method (Concrete). Structural practice often necessitates the calculation of the stresses and deformations that occur in a structure in service under design load. This can be done by the method just presented. It is equally if not more important that the structural engineer be able to predict with satisfactory accuracy the ultimate strength of a structure or structural member. In most of the current building codes, the ultimate strength design has replaced the working stress design as the standard reinforced concrete design procedure. In designing by ultimate strength methods, the possibilities of overload and understrength are treated separately. The dead load and the live load are increased by overload factors to obtain the ultimate loads to be used for design. These overload factors are called just load factors, and the values for dead load, live load, seismic, wind, earth pressure, and so on, are given in the codes. For example, the American Concrete Institute (ACI) Building Code gives the following:

$$\text{dead load factor} = 1.4$$

$$\text{live load factor} = 1.7$$

In addition to load factors, the so called ϕ factor is used in ultimate strength design. In predictions of the ultimate strength of the structure, the code recognizes that the completed structure or member may be understrength because of understrength materials, inaccuracies in workmanship, or manufacturing tolerances, or variations in the degree of supervision and control. To account for these, the code provides the use of the capacity reduction factor ϕ. Values of ϕ factor are given in codes for moment, shear, bond, compression, and so on. For example, the ACI code gives values of 0.9 and 0.85 for flexure and shear, respectively. To provide safety, the theoretical ultimate strength, reduced by the coefficient ϕ, must be adequate to resist the ultimate loads.

Singly Reinforced Rectangular Beam (U.S.D.). In working with singly reinforced rectangular beams, the following formula is used:

$$p_b = 0.85 k_1 \frac{f'_c}{f_y} \times \frac{87{,}000}{87{,}000 + f_y}$$

where p_b = balanced steel ratio, such that the steel starts to yield and reaches its ultimate strain capacity at precisely the same load
k_1 = 0.85 for f'_c = 4000 psi
= 0.80 for f'_c = 5000 psi

The ACI code requires that

$$p_{\max} = 0.75\, p_b$$

$$a = \frac{A_s F_y}{0.85 f'_c b} = \frac{p f_y d}{0.85 f'_c}$$

T Beams. With the exception of precast systems, reinforced concrete floors are almost always monolithic. It is evident, therefore, that a part of the slab will act with the upper part of the beam to resist longitudinal compression. The slab forms the beam flange, while the part of the beam projecting below the slab forms the web or stem. The ACI code recommends that the effective flange width used in the design of symmetrical T beams not exceed one-fourth of the span length of the beam, its overhanging width on either side of the web should not exceed 8 times the thickness of the slab nor one-half the clear distance to the next beam. For beams having a flange on one side only, the effective overhanging flange width shall not exceed half the span length of the beam, nor 6 times the thickness of the slab, nor half the clear distance to the next beam. The neutral axis of a T beam may be either in the flange or in the web, depending on the proportions of the cross section, the amount of tensile steel, and the strengths of the materials. If the calculated depth to the neutral axis is less than or equal to the slab thickness, the beam can be analyzed as if it were a rectangular beam of width equal to the effective flange width.

Columns. Concrete compression members whose unsupported length is more than 3 times the least dimension of the cross section are classified as columns. Concrete columns are of three main types:

1 Columns reinforced with longitudinal steel and closely spaced spirals.
2 Columns reinforced with longitudinal steel and lateral ties.
3 Steel columns encased inside concrete.

Types 1 and 2, the ones more generally used, can be square, rectangular, or round. Most codes provide the following limiting dimensions:

1 Minimum diameter of 10 inches for round columns or, for rectangular columns, a least dimension of at least 8 inches and a gross area not less than 96 square inches.
2 The longitudinal reinforcement for noncomposite compression members shall be not less than 0.01 nor more than 0.08 times the gross area of the section.
3 The minimum number of longitudinal reinforcing bars in compression members shall be six bars in a circular arrangement and four bars in a rectangular or square arrangement.
4 The radio of spiral reinforcement p_s shall be not less than the value given by

$$p_s = 0.45 \frac{(A_g - 1)}{A_c} \frac{f'_c}{fy}$$

where f_y is the specific yield strength of spiral reinforcement, but not more than 60,000 psi.

For working stress design the formula for tied column capacity is

$$P = 0.85\, A_g\, (0.25 f'_c + f_s P_g)$$

where P = allowable column load
A_g = gross area of column
f'_c = concrete ultimate strength (28 days)
f_s = allowable stress in column vertical reinforcement (40% of minimum yield but not to exceed 24,000 psi)
P_g = ratio of total vertical steel area to gross concrete area A_g

Note that the effects of slenderness and any eccentricity are not included in the relation above.

For spiral column

$$P = A_g(0.25 f'_c + f p_g)$$

Columns subjected to axial load and bending moment are designed by a standard interaction formula or by means of interaction curves. Also, tables and curves are available in ACI handbooks for working with columns of different size.

Walls. Reinforced concrete walls can be bearing or nonbearing. Bearing walls carrying reasonably concentric loads may be designed by the empirical provisions given as follows:

1 *Working Stress Design*

$$f_a = 0.225 f'_c \left[1 - \left(\frac{h}{40t}\right)^3\right]$$

where f_a = allowable compressive stress (psi)
h = clear distance between lateral supports for wall (in)
t = wall thickness (in)
f'_c = 28 days compressive strength (psi)

2 *Ultimate Compressive Strength*

$$f_{au} = 0.55\, \Phi f'_c \left[1 - \left(\frac{h}{40t}\right)^3\right]$$

where f_{au} = ultimate compressive stress for wall
ϕ = capacity reduction factor for compression

Maximum h/t ratio for bearing walls is 25.

Framing Systems. Some of the most common framing systems are outlined as follows.

Slab, Beam, and Girder System. A one-way slab spans between beams, which in turn are supported by

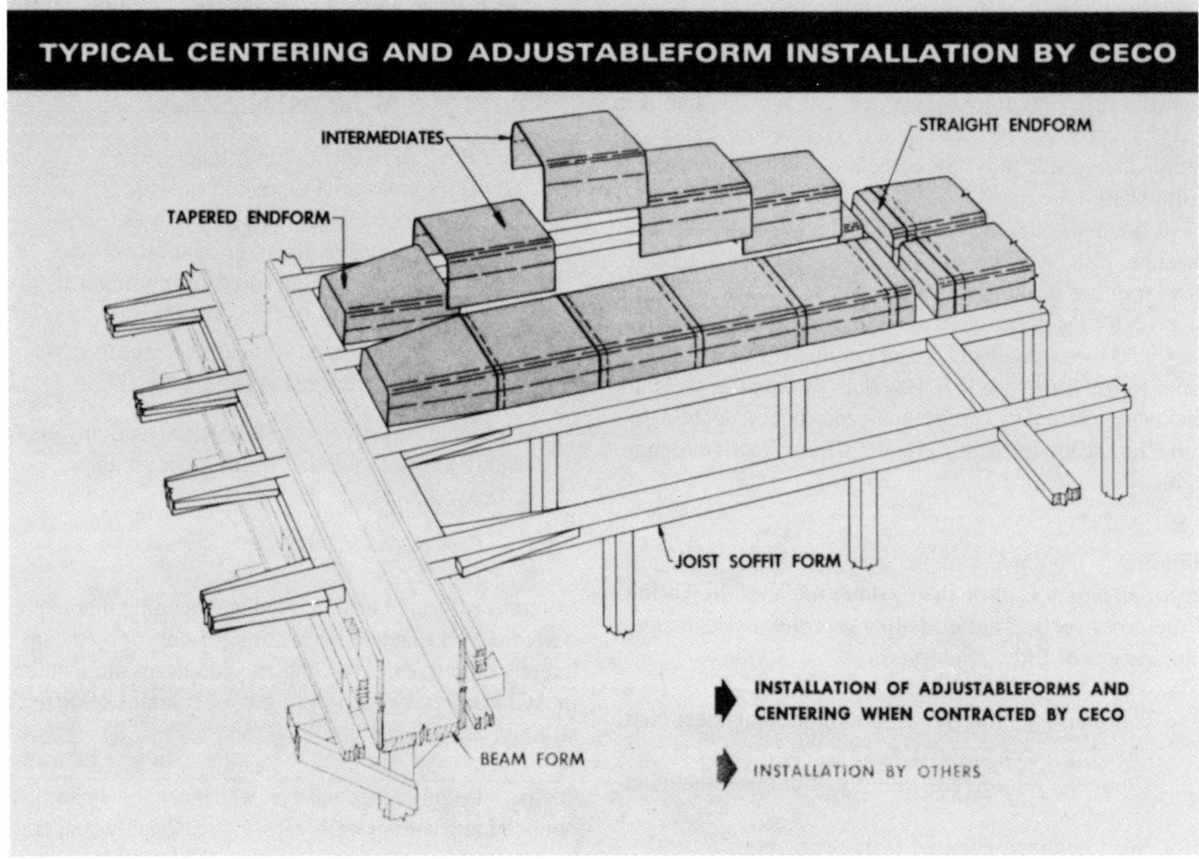

Figure 3.41 *Source*. CECO catalog, Los Angeles, California.

girders. Girders are supported by columns. Usually the bay size varies from 20 to 35 feet. Forming is the most expensive item in concrete construction, and this type framing is economical where beam and girder size dimensions and spans are repetitive. One-way solid slabs can be supported as follows:

1 Slab supported on monolithic concrete beams and girders.
2 Slab supported on steel beams and girders. Shear connectors can be used to provide for composite action.
3 Slab with light gauge steel decking, which serves as form and reinforcement for this concrete.

One-Way Ribbed Slabs or Pan Joist System. A ribbed floor consists of a series of small, closely spaced reinforced concrete T-beams, framing into the supporting columns. The T-beams, called joists, are formed by creating void spaces in what otherwise would be a solid slab. The voids are formed by using wood, steel, or fiberboard pans (Figure 3.41). The most common pan widths are 20, 30, and 40 inches.

One-way joist construction was developed to reduce dead load by providing adequate depth with less dead load than for solid slabs; the result is smaller concrete and reinforcement quantities required per square foot of floor area. Economy can be obtained by designing joists and slabs so that forms of the same size can be used throughout a project. Distribution ribs called bridging are constructed normal to the main ribs to distribute loads to more than one joist and to equalize deflections. One distribution rib is usually used at the center of spans of up to 30 feet, and two such ribs are usually placed at the third points of spans longer than 30 feet. These ribs are usually a minimum of 4 inches wide, reinforced with one no. 4 or no. 5 bar continuous top and bottom. Design of a joist is similar to that of a T-beam. The slab thickness usually varies between 2½ and 4½ inches, reinforced with mesh or reinforcement.

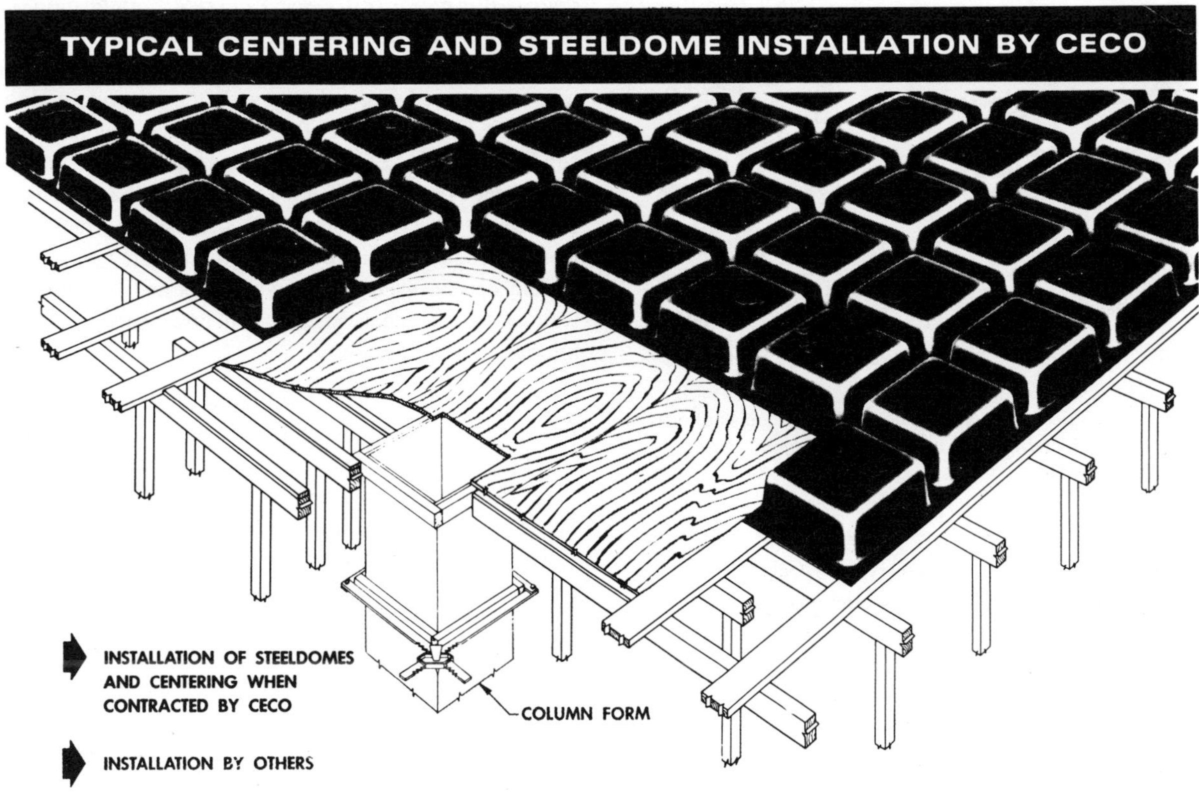

Figure 3.42 *Source.* CECO catalog, Los Angeles, California.

Two-Way-Slabs. A two-way slab is a concrete panel reinforced for flexure in more than one direction. Several types are used for floors and roofs.

Two-Way Solid Slabs. Two-way solid slabs can be supported by beams on all four sides, with main reinforcement running in two directions. The perimeter beams are concrete poured monolithically with the slab, structural steel (often encased in concrete), or bearing walls. This system is suitable for intermediate and heavy loads on spans up to about 30 feet.

Flat Slab System. For analysis, design, detailing, bar fabrication, and placing and formwork, the flat plate is the simplest form of two-way slab. A flat plate is defined as a two-way slab of uniform thickness supported by any combination of columns and walls, with or without edge beams, with and without drop panels and column capitals. Shear and deflection limit the economical length of flat plate spans to under about 30 feet for light loading and about 20 feet for heavy loading. Column capitals or drop panels are used where heavy loads cause high punching shear stresses. Simplicity and repetitive use of form work like flying forms make this a very economical concrete floor or roof system. The omission of beams and girders cuts down story height in a highrise building, resulting in cheaper construction.

Two-Way Ribbed Slab. As in one-way slab systems, the dead weight of two-way slabs can be reduced considerably by creating void spaces in what otherwise would be a solid slab. For the most part, the concrete removed is in tension and ineffective; thus the lighter floor will have virtually the same structural characteristics as the corresponding solid slab. A wafflelike appearance (Figure 3.42) is imparted to the underside of the slab, hence the name "waffle slab."

Prestressed Floors. Prestressing is the intentional creation of permanent stresses in a structure or assembly, for the purpose of improving its behavior and strength under various service conditions. The basic principle of prestressing was applied to construction perhaps centuries ago, when ropes or metal bands were wound around wooded staves to form barrels (Figure 3.43). When the bands were tightened, they underwent tensile prestress,

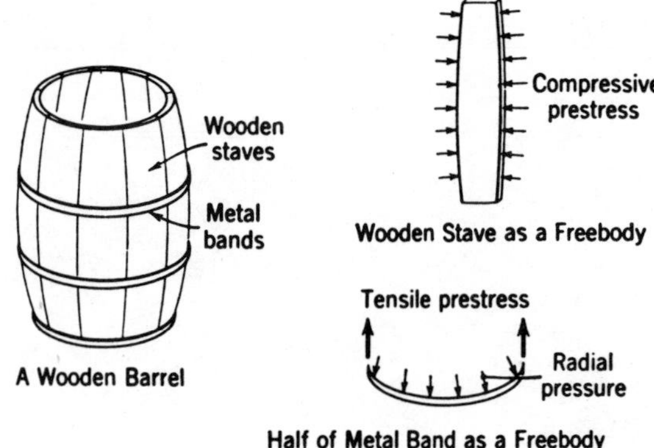

Figure 3.43 Principle of prestressing applied to barrel construction. *Source.* T. Y. Lin, *Design of Prestressed Structures,* 2nd ed., John Wiley & Sons, 1967.

which in turn created compressive prestress between the staves, enabling them to resist the hoop tension that would be produced by internal pressure when the barrels were filled with liquid. In other words, both the bands and the staves were prestressed before being subjected to any service loads.

The same principle applies to all other structures. Modern development of prestressed concrete is credited to E. Freyssinet of France, who in 1928 started using high-strength steel wires for prestressing. Such wires, with an ultimate strength as high as 270,000 psi, are used today. Wide application of prestressed concrete was not possible until reliable and economical methods of tensioning and end anchorage were devised in 1939. Future development of prestressed concrete in the United States may involve the application of post-tensioning to buildings and bridges, including this combination of pretensioning, posttensioning, and conventional reinforcing to structures and structural components. As mentioned earlier, concrete is very weak in tension, and the compressive stresses induced by the prestressing offset some or all of these tensile stresses.

In most structures the tensile stresses induced by the full or partial dead loads are balanced by the prestressing. The approach based on this concept, called the *load-balancing method*, was developed by Professor T. Y. Lin of the University of California, Berkeley. Some of the advantages of prestressing concrete are as follows: since all or a portion of the dead load is balanced by prestressing, the result is light and shallow structural members, leaving more head room and less story height; furthermore, long span concrete structures are possible only because of prestressing. Two kinds of prestressed structure are in common use: poured-in-place and precast.

Poured-in-Place Prestressed Concrete. Here the concrete can be pretensioned, in which case the wires are stressed in the forming. Next the concrete is poured or the wires are placed in conduits inside the concrete and the wires are posttensioned after the concrete has hardened and has developed enough strength as specified at the time of transfer of stresses. The wires in this case are normally bonded to the concrete, and stesses are transferred from wires to the concrete through concrete bonds. This system can be used in one-way slabs and beams, two-way slabs, or other special structures such as tanks, bridges, and domes.

Precast Prestressed Concrete. The growth in popularity of prestressed concrete in the United States has so far been along the lines of precast, pretensioned products. Some of the most commonly used are hollow-core planks and precast girders and columns. Concrete topping reinforced with wire mesh on top of plank gives more depth and acts also as the diaphragm to resist lateral stresses. Sometimes planks without the concrete fill are used; in such cases any diaphragm action desired is accomplished by the mechanical connectors. The most common plank thicknesses are 4, 6, 8, 10, and 12 inches. Sometimes bearing walls are used instead of girders and columns. Hollow-core planks are widely employed in shopping centers, hotels, apartments, parking structures, and so on. The planks are very economical for spans between 20 and 30 feet.

Single and double tees are often found in long span structures, with or without concrete topping on top.

There are many other precast products such as precast joists, precast channels, and precast slab members used just for forming the concrete.

Summary

1 The weight of regular weight concrete varies from 140 to 150 pounds per cubic foot.
2 The weight of lightweight concrete varies from 90 to 110 pounds per cubic foot.
3 The most commonly used concrete strength is between 2000 and 5000 psi.
4 Concrete does not resist tension stresses.
5 The most commonly used reinforcement steels are
ASTM A615, Grade 40 (yield stress 40 ksi)
ASTM A615, Grade 60 (yield stress 60 ksi)
6 Only high-strength wires with a strength of 270 ksi are used in prestressed concrete.
7 The slump of most commonly used concrete varies from 3 to 4 inches.

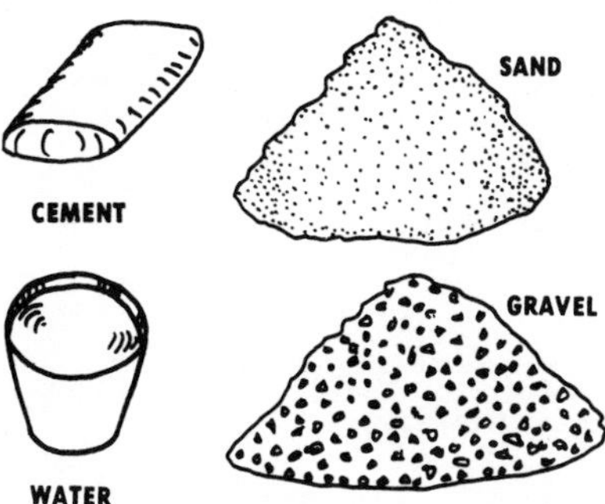

Figure 3.44 Ingredients in grout. *Source. The Masonry Society News,* Denver, Colorado.

8 The modulus of elasticity of concrete is given by

$$E_c = 33(w)^{1.5}\sqrt{f'_c}$$

where E_c = modulus of elasticity (psi)
W = weight (pcf)
f'_c = ultimate compressive strength (psi at 28 days)

9 The modular ratio n is the ratio of the modulus of elasticity of steel to the modulus of elasticity of concrete.

10 The load factors for dead and live loads are 1.4 and 1.7, respectively.

11 The ϕ factor is given as follows:

0.90	for flexural
0.85	for shear
0.75	for spirally reinforced columns
0.70	for tied columns and bearing
0.65	for bending in plain concrete

12 In balanced design, reinforcing steel starts to yield at the same time that the concrete reaches its ultimate strain.

13 Minimum reinforcement in a concrete column should be 1% of the gross area; maximum reinforcement should not exceed 8%.

14 Interaction curves give the relationship between axial load and moment in a column or in other compression members.

15 In bearing walls the minimum ratio of reinforcement to gross concrete area is 0.0015 for vertical and 0.0025 for horizontal reinforcement.

16 Height-to-thickness ratio for concrete bearing walls is 1:25.

Steel

Although iron has been used by man at least since the beginning of Egyptian pyramids, its role as a structural material was limited for centuries because of the difficulties of smelting it in large quantities. With the Industrial Revolution came both the need for iron as a structural material and the capability of smelting it in quantity. The invention of the Bessemer converter in 1856, and the subsequent development of the Siemens-Martin open hearth process for making steel, made it possible to produce structural steel and triggered the tremendous developments and accomplishments in the use of structural steel during the last hundred years.

The main components of steel are iron plus carbon, and other alloying metals (manganese, nickel, aluminum, copper, etc.) in small quantities. In carbon steels the elements carbon and manganese have a controlling influence on strength, ductility and weldability. Most structural carbon steels are more than 98% iron, roughly 0.25% carbon and 1% manganese by weight. Carbon increases the hardness or tensile strength but has adverse effects on ductility and weldability. Thus small quantities of various alloying elements are sometimes used to increase the ''hardenability'' of a steel to achieve the maximum effectiveness from a given low percentage

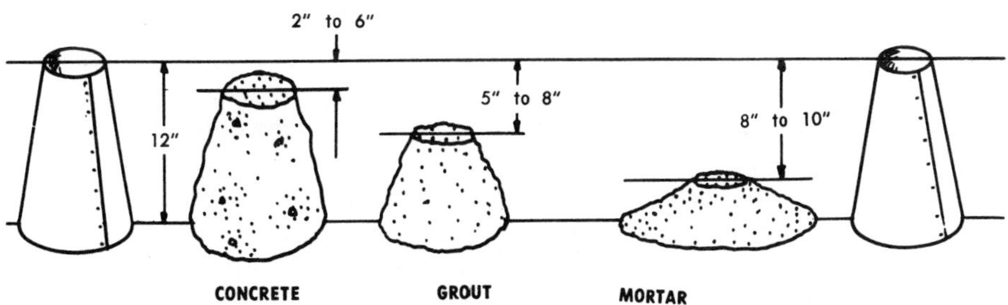

Figure 3.45 Slump tests of concrete, mortar, and grout. *Source. The Masonry Society News,* Denver, Colorado.

ATMOSPHERIC ENVIRONMENT SERVICE HEADQUARTERS
Toronto, Ontario
Architects: Boigon & Heinonen
Photo: Realisation

of carbon. Small amounts of copper increase corrosion resistance, and fractional percentages of silicon, nickel, and vanadium also have generally beneficial effects on steel behavior.

The behavior of a structural material is described mainly in terms of strength and ductility. Figure 3.46 shows the characteristic stress-strain curve of most steels with structural applications. The figure notes the four typical ranges of behavior, that is, the elastic range, the plastic range (during which the material flows at constant stress), the strain-hardening range, and the range of strain at and beyond the ultimate stress during which necking occurs. In a tensile bar, this last range terminates in fracture. Figure 3.47 shows the initial portion of Figure 3.46 to an expanded scale and in somewhat idealized form. The curve is drawn for ASTM A7 steel and is similar to A36 steel. The most serious disadvantage of steel is that it oxidizes easily and must be protected by paint or some other suitable coating. When steel is used in an enclosure where a fire could occur, the steel members must be encased by a fire-resistant enclosure made of masonry, concrete, vermiculite concrete, or other appropriate material. In addition to its high strength, structural steel has the advantage of ductility. This capacity to undergo large plastic deformations without rupture makes it an ideal material for use in structure that must be designed to resist lateral loads from wind or earthquake.

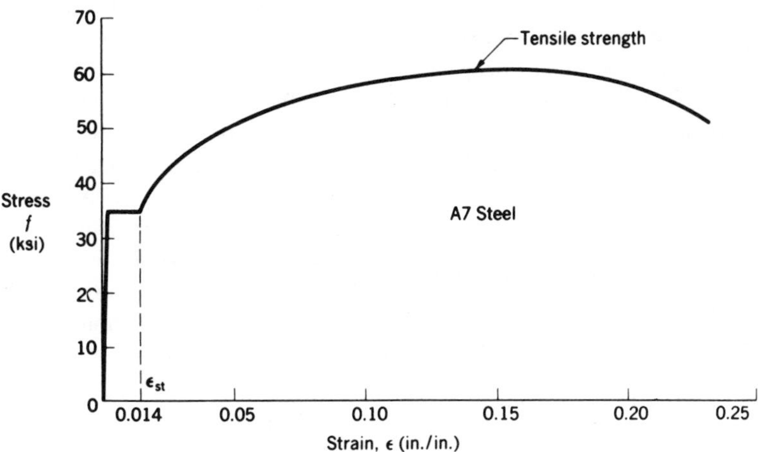

Figure 3.46 Complete tensile stress-strain diagram for structural carbon steel. *Source.* Lynn S. Beedle and T. V. Galambus, *Structural Steel Design,* Ronald Press, New York, 1964.

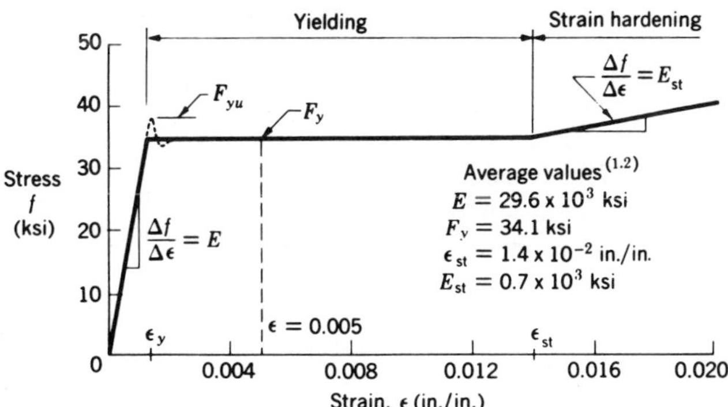

Figure 3.47 Portion of stress-strain diagram for A7 steel. *Source.* American Institute of Steel Construction.

Several types of steel are available, and these have been given standard designations by the American Society for Testing and Materials (ASTM). The structural steel in most widespread use in the United States is ASTM A36, which has a minimum yield of 36.0 ksi. Other special steels are available, with yield points as high as 100.0 ksi. Since ASTM A36 is so commonly used, all the discussion and examples that follow are based on its use.

Steel mills have a standard classification for the many products they make. Structural shapes, for example, are identified by their cross-sectional characteristics (angles, channels, wide flange beams, I-beams, tees, pipes, tubes, H-piles, etc.). For convenience, structural shapes are simply identified by letter symbols according to the following schedule:

Section	Symbol
Wide flange shape	W
Standard 1 shape	S
Bearing pile shape	H
Miscellaneous beams	M
Structural tees cut from W, S, or M shapes, respectively	WT, ST, MT
American Standard channels	C
All other channels	MC
Angles	L

Each shape has its particular functional use, but the workhorse of building construction is the wide flange W section. The standard nomenclature consists of the group symbol, the nominal depth in inches, and the weight in pounds per lineal foot. Thus "W16 × 26" indicates a wide flange member (symbol W), 16 inches deep and weighing 26 pounds per lineal foot. The production of all standard rolled shapes to final size, by punching, drilling, and assembling the components into finished members ready for shipment is called fabricating.

Design of Steel Beams. In most cases the design of a steel beam is governed either by deflection or by bending stress. In very rare cases, such as heavily loaded short span beams, shear may govern the design. The American Institute of Steel Construction (AISC) *Manual of Steel Construction* has listed the allowable stresses for bending and shear for different shapes for different conditions. The most commonly used stresses for pure bending are as follows:

$0.6\,F_y$ for noncompact members
$0.66\,F_y$ for compact shapes

The *AISC Manual* lists all the requirements a section must meet to qualify for a compact shape. The laterally unbraced length of the compression flange also affects the allowable bending stress. The *AISC Manual* gives two values of the laterally unbraced compression flange length, namely L_c and L_u. The allowable bending stress is $0.6F_y$ for values of unbraced length less than L_u.

Floor Framing Systems. Two of the most commonly used floor systems in steel buildings are described below: beams, girders, and columns, and the bar joist-girder-column system.

Beams, Girders, and Columns. The most common spans are from 20 to 32 feet in both directions.

Deck and Beams. An all concrete deck can be poured in place, or concrete can be poured on top of a metal deck. The most common beam spacing is from 6 to 12 feet. Slab thickness is generally governed by (*a*) loads on the deck, (*b*) deflection requirements, and (*c*) fire rating.

The concrete used can be lightweight or regular weight. Metal deck is normally 1½ or 3 inches thick, and the thickness of the concrete fill on top of the deck varies from 2½ to 4½ inches, reinforced with wire mesh for composite-type decks and with reinforcement for the simple forming type of deck. Depending on the loads, spacing, and span of beams, an alternate system with composite beam action can be used. The beam depth usually varies between 12 and 18 inches and is connected to the girders with stiffener plate and bolts.

Studs welded on top beams help to create shear transfer between the deck and the top of the steel beam. After the concrete has hardened, the whole system acts as a T-beam and has much more capacity to carry vertical loads than would a steel beam of the same size, alone. In long span beams carrying heavy live loads, the weight savings in steel beams utilizing the composite action more than compensate for the added cost of welding studs on top of a beam. For small spans with comparatively light live loads, however, it is not economical to use composite beams. Some of the obvious advantages of composite construction are as follows:

1 Savings in steel.
2 Reduction in the depth of members.
3 Increased stiffness of a floor system.
4 Increased overload capacity of a floor.

A weight saving in steel of 20 or even 30% is possible compared to noncomposite construction in bridges and in some buildings with long span beams.

Girders. The construction industry usually employs wide flange beams or plate girders, either composite or noncomposite. Plate girders are built up by welding flange plates to the web plate in the shop. Plate girders are used where height is restricted to prohibit the use of the deep beam, or for heavily loaded floors where there is enough space to use sections deeper than the available rolled sections, with a resulting savings in weight. Also, deep sections cut down the deflections. The weight savings achieved by using plate girders must justify the extra cost of fabrication of plate girders. Plate girders can be of uniform thickness or tapered. In many cases, the girders are part of the lateral forces resisting system and they carry both lateral and gravity load stresses.

Bar Joist, Girder, and Column System. This system is similar to the one involving beams, girders, and columns except that open web bar joists instead of steel beams are used at a comparatively close spacing of 16 to 48 inches over center. When metal deck is used, its gauge is very light, compared to the other system. The girders are as described previously, or trusses are used. Depths of short span joist varies from 8 to 12 inches, and long span joists are available in depths of 18 to 48 inches. Bridging, provided between the joists to give them lateral stability, also helps to distribute some concentrated floor loads to adjacent joists. The advantages of steel open web joists are light weight, ease in erection, and the space for electrical and mechanical piping and duct work provided by the open web. This kind of system is more common on the East Coast.

Roof Framing System. The basic elements of the roof framing are the same as for the floor. Metal deck, beams or purlins, girders, and columns are main structural elements. Metal deck of light gauges (26–18 GA) is most commonly used, depending on the following factors:

1 Vertical loads.
2 Lateral shear stresses.
3 Spacing of beams.
4 Fire-rated system.

The depth of the most commonly used roof decks varies from 1 to 1½ inches. However in certain cases for long spans, decks of 3 inches or deeper are used. Insulation board or vermiculite fill is placed on top of the metal deck. Where fire rating is required for the roof deck alone, vermiculite fill with keydeck mesh (chicken wire mesh) is usually used, and the bottom of the deck is not sprayed. Also metal deck with vermiculite fill gives higher allowable lateral shear values compared to the same deck with insulation board on top. Vermiculite is a very lightweight soft material composed of cement, sand, and water. It has a dry density of about 28 to 30 pounds per cubic foot and a compressive strength of only 140 psi.

Purlins can be classified into two span categories, long and short.

Short Spans. For spans up to 30 feet, rolled shaped beams, Z-type light gauge or open web bar joist can be used. Rolled shapes sections are as found in the *AISC Manual,* Z-shaped purlins are made in the depth range 8 to 18 inches from 12 or 10 GA sheets. The latter require bridging just like bar joists and are most commonly used in roofs of industrial or shopping-center-type commercial buildings. The open web bar joist for short spans are usually from 8 to 24 inches deep; they have a top flange or chord made up from two angles and a bottom flange or chord made up from two bars or two angles; the web is a bar bent at an angle and welded in between the top and bottom chord members. The most common spacing of purlins is between 6 and 12 feet.

Long Span. Long span purlins are used for spans up to about 144 feet. In open web bar joists, the most common shapes, both top and bottom chords are double angle or other shapes. The depths range from 30 to 72 inches, and bridging is required, just as for short spans; spacings of 4 to 12 feet are common.

Girders. Girders can be rolled in shape, built-up, tapered steel girder or trusses. Span length can vary from 20 to 100 feet. For most offices, hotels, and similar buildings, the spans are small; however for industrial buildings, shopping centers, and other structures (sports arenas, ice rinks, etc.), the spans can be very large. Wherever columns can be permitted, the shorter spans should be used because spans greater than 60 feet are very uneconomical.

Connections. Three basic types of fastener are employed in steel construction, namely: rivets, bolts, and welds. Rivets, once widely used for main connections, are now seldom specified in new construction and are not discussed here. However the basic principle of rivet design is similar to that of bolt design.

Bolts. Unfinished bolts and high-strength bolts are the two main types. Unfinished bolts (known in construction as "common," "ordinary," or "machine" bolts) are characterized chiefly by the rough appearance of the shank. Unfinished bolts are made of low carbon steel whose physical properties are designated by ASTM A307. The weekest section of any bolt is the threaded portion, and the strength of the bolt is usually computed by using the "stress area"—an approximated average area based on the nominal and root diameters. The nut is an important part of the bolt assembly. Nut dimensions and strengths are specified so that the strength of the bolt is developed before the occurrence of thread stripping or other type of nut failure. The dimensions for nuts and bolts of various sizes are given in the *AISC Manual* and other handbooks.

Bolts are used in holes 1/16 inch larger than the nominal bolt diameter. Unfinished bolts may be tightened easily, using a spud wrench or a pneumatic-powered impact wrench. The allowable shear stress for an A307 bolt is 10 ksi; allowable tensile stress is 20 ksi. The allowable shear and tension values of different size bolts appear in the *AISC Manual.* In the design of purlins, girts, struts, and so on, A307 bolts should always be considered. Unfinished bolts are ideally suited for joining low tonnage, light framework structures where slip and vibration are not important factors. Shear failure of a bolt can occur in single shear or in double shear.

The minimum distance between centers of bolt holes should be not less than 2⅔ times the nominal diameter of the bolt, but preferably not less than 3 diameters. The minimum and maximum edge distances from center of bolt hold to the nearest edge of the parts in contact are listed in the *AISC Manual* and other building codes.

High-Strength Bolts. High-strength bolt connections can be friction type or bearing type. Shear connections subjected to stress reversal or severe stress fluctuation, or where slippage would be undesirable, must be friction

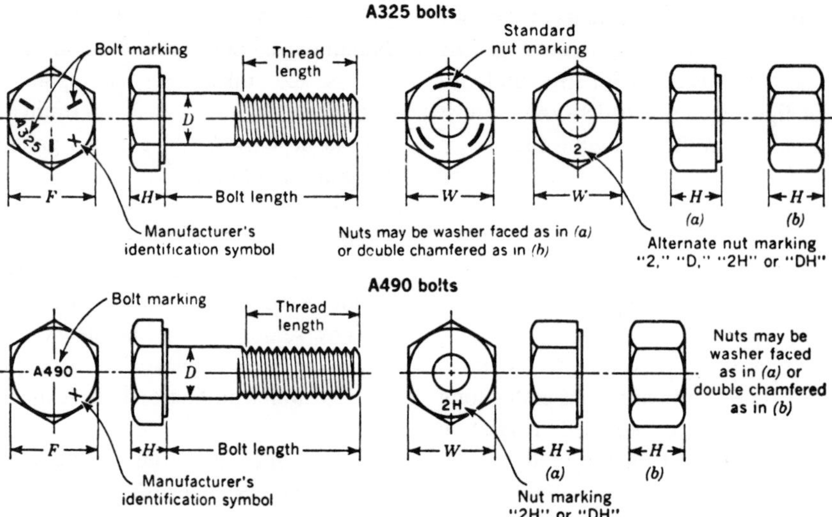

Figure 3.48 *Source*. American Institute of Steel Construction.

type. The two main types in this category are ASTM A325 high-strength carbon steel bolts and ASTM A490 high-strength alloy steel bolts. The bolts, nuts, and washers, if required, must always conform to the requirements of the current edition of the ASTM specifications for high-strength carbon steel bolts for structural steel joints (A325) or for quenched and tempered alloy steel bolts for structural joints (A490).

Identification. There is no difference in the appearance of high-strength bolts intended for friction- or bearing-type connections. To aid installers and inspectors in identifying the several available grades of steel, bolts and nuts are manufactured with permanent markings (Figure 3.48). Heavy hexagonal structural bolts manufactured to ASTM specification A325 are identified on the top of the head by three radial lines, the legend "A325," and the manufacturer's symbol; bolts manufactured to meet A490 are marked with the legend "A490" and the manufacturer's symbol. Heavy hexagonal nuts manufactured to A325 or A490 have also marks on top. as Figure 3.48 indicates.

Installation. Standard methods such as calibrated wrench tightening or turn of nut tightening, as described in the *AISC Manual,* will give the required pretension on the bolts. Washer requirements, depending on method of installation and diameter of holes are described in the *AISC Manual*.

Inspection. The inspector observes the installation and tightening of bolts to ascertain that the selected tightening procedure is being properly used and to verify that all bolts have been tightened. The inspector may use a special inspecting wrench to test whether the bolt has the required tension provided. There are other methods, as well, such as the Bethlehem load indicator washer.

If it is expedient to use A490 bolts in lieu of A325 bolts when the latter are not available, the initial tension of the A490s need not exceed that required for A325 bolts. The ASTM publishes allowable values of A325 and A490 bolts in tension and shear.

Welding. The progress made in quality welding equipment and electrodes, the advancing art and science of designing for welding, and the growth in trust and acceptance of welded structures have combined to make welding a powerful implement for the construction industry. Welding permits the architect and structural engineer complete freedom of design—freedom to develop and use modern economical design principles, and freedom to employ the most elementary or the most daring concepts of form, proportion, and balance to achieve greater aesthetic value.

The principal types of weld are fillet and butt (sometimes called groove). The basic difference between the two types is the manner in which the stress transfer takes place. Butt or groove welds normally act in direct tension or compression, whereas fillet welds normally are subjected to shear as well as tension or compression and flexure, since they are placed on the edge or side of the base metal.

Even though the butt weld possesses greater strength than the fillet weld, most structural connections are joined by fillet welding. This is due mainly because larger fit-up tolerances are permitted when fillet welds are used. The butting together of sections necessitates the cutting of members to more or less exact lengths. Welded joints may be classified as tee, edge, lap, corner, bevel, or butt. Another grouping refers to the position of the electrode during placement of a weld, such as flat, horizontal, overhead, or vertical.

Occasionally short lengths of fillet welds are distributed along the edges of a joint or along the edges of a cover plate on a girder. These *intermittent fillet welds* are used when the strength required is less than that developed by a continuous fillet weld of the smallest permitted size.

Plug or slot welds are used to provide additional strength when there is insufficient room to place the needed length of fillet weld. The effective shearing area of a plug or slot weld is considered to be the nominal cross-sectional area of the hole or slot in the plane of the faying surface.

In joints connected only by fillet welds, weld size is determined by the thicker of the two parts joined, except that the weld size need not exceed the thickness of the thinner part joined unless the calculated stress requires a larger size. In computing the stress due to direct loads on longitudinal and transverse fillet welds, it is customary to divide the force action on the weld by its throat area. The throat area is taken as the product of the weld length and its theoretical throat. Shear, flexure, and axial forces all cause shearing stresses in fillet welds. Hence the resultant of the shearing stresses is used to proportion the weld.

Summary

1 Hooke's law states that deformations or strains are directly proportional to stresses in the elastic range. This is expressed symbolically as follows:

$$E = \frac{f}{e}$$

where E = modulus of elasticity
f = stress
e = strain

2 Bending stress is equal to bending moment divided by section modulus, thus:

$$f_b = \frac{M}{S}$$

where M = bending moment
f_b = bending stress
S = section modulus

3 Allowable bending stress is found using the following relations:

$0.6\,F_y$ for noncompact shapes
$0.66\,F_y$ for compact shapes

where F_y = yield stress provided the member is laterally braced as required by the *AISC Manual*.

4 The modulus of elasticity of most steels varies between 29×10^6 and 30×10^6 psi; the latter figure is most commonly used unless a very precise calculation is required.

5 Composite beam is one in which concrete floor along with steel beam acts as a T-beam. Horizontal shear between two materials is transferred by welded studs on top of beam.

6 The most commonly used steels in building construction are A36 (yield stress of 36 ksi) and V50 (yield stress of 50 ksi).

7 Most commonly used bolts are A307 (common bolts) or A325 and A490 (high-strength bolts).

8 The minimum distance between centers of bolt holes is 2⅔ times bolt diameter. Most commonly used is 3 times diameter or 3 inches.

9 Steel weighs 490 pounds per cubic foot, approximately.

10 The most commonly used welds are the fillet weld and the butt weld.

11 Shear stress in the wide flange beam is given by the formula

$$f_v = \frac{V}{dt}$$

where f_v = shear stress
V = total shear at the section under consideration
d = depth of beam
t = web thickness

12 Compressive stress depends on the slenderness ratio of the member.

Earthquake Design

The following definitions apply only to this subsection on earthquake design.

1 *Base*. The level at which the earthquake ground motions are considered to be imparted to the structure.

2 *Lateral-Force-Resisting System*. The part of the structural system assigned to resist lateral forces such as earthquake or wind.

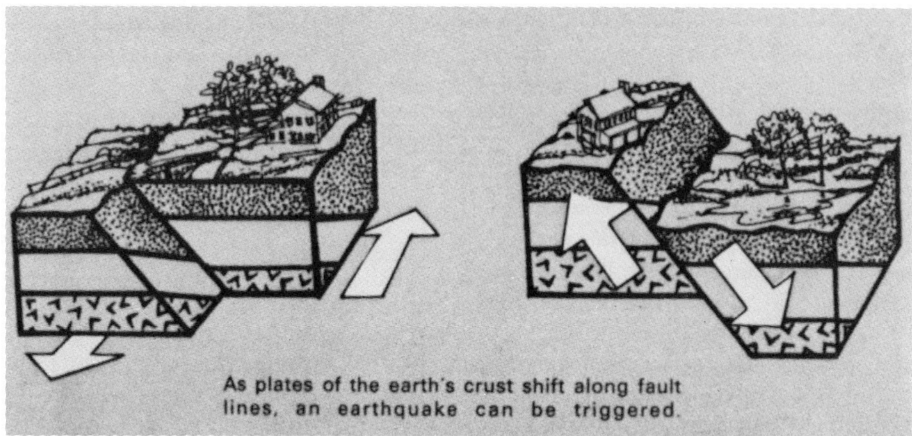

Figure 3.49 When the Earth Shudders. *Source. U.S. News & World Report,* August 9, 1976.

3 *Moment-Resisting Space Frame.* A vertical load-carrying space frame; its members and joints are capable of resisting forces primarily by flexure.

4 *Braced Frame.* A truss system or its equivalent, provided to resist lateral forces; the members are subjected primarily to axial stresses.

5 *Ductile-Moment-Resisting Space Frame.* A moment-resisting space frame complying with some special requirements to achieve more ductility and deformations.

6 *Shear Wall.* A wall designed to resist lateral forces parallel to the plane of the wall.

7 *Essential Facilities.* Structures that must be safe and usable for emergency purposes after an earthquake to preserve the health and safety of the general public. Such facilities include hospitals, fire stations, police stations, and municipal government disaster operation centers.

8 *Fault.* A fracture in the earth's crust along which two portions of the crust have slipped with respect to each other (Figure 3.49). Such movements produce various kinds of displacement (Figure 3.50).

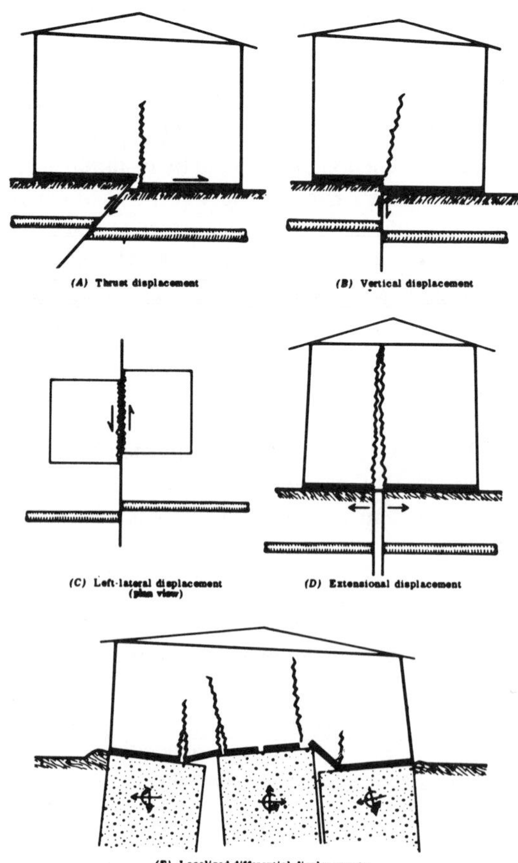

Figure 3.50 Basic types of ground rupture and associated pipeline and building damage in the northern San Fernando Valley, February 9, 1971. *Source.* U.S. Department of the Interior.

A severe earthquake is one of the most frightening and destructive phenomena of nature, usually causing loss of human life. Its terrible after effects include many collapsed buildings and much structural damage. Most earthquakes occur in areas bordering the Pacific Ocean. This circum-Pacific belt, called the "ring of fire," incorporates the Pacific coasts of North and South

America, the Aleutian Islands, Japan, Southeast Asia, and the islands surrounding Australia. Half a million people within this area have lost their lives because of earthquakes, and property valued at billions of dollars has been severely damaged or destroyed.

Seismology, the scientific study of earthquakes, is a comparatively new discipline. However we do know that an earthquake is the oscillatory and sometimes violent movement of the earth's surface that follows a release of energy in the earth's crust. When subjected to deep-seated forces, the crust may first bend; then, when the stress exceeds the strength of the surface rocks, the crust breaks and "snaps" to a new position. In the process of breaking, vibrations called seismic waves are generated. These waves travel from the source of the earthquake (hypocenter) to more distant places along the surface and through the earth at varying speeds, depending on the medium through which they move.

The United States has experienced less destruction than has been visited on other countries located in the so-called ring of fire, but millions of Americans live in potential quake areas. Large parts of the western United States in particular are known to be vulnerable. Geologists have found that earthquakes tend to recur along faults, which really reflect zones of weakness in the earth's crust. For example, the most earthquake-prone areas in the conterminous United States are those that are adjacent to the San Andreas fault system of coastal California and the fault system that separates the Sierra Nevada from the great basin (see Figure 3.51).

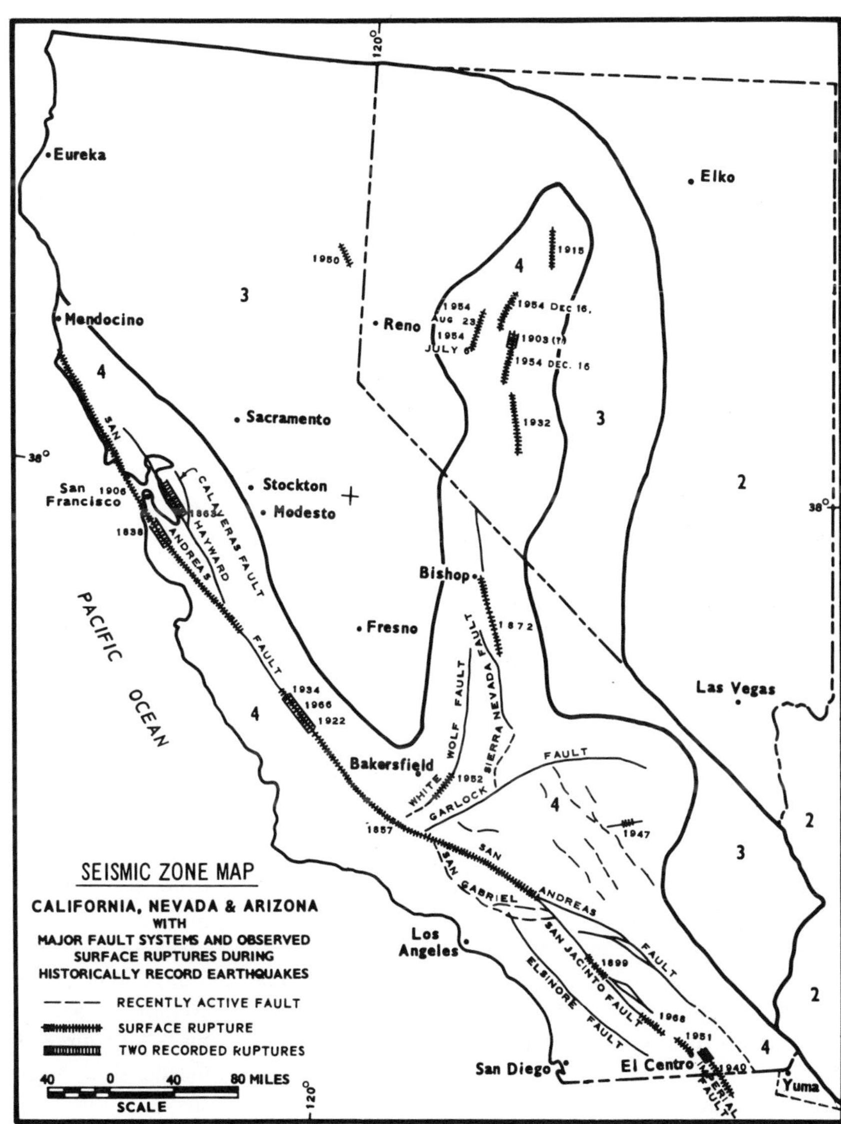

Figure 3.51 *Source. Seismic Design for Buildings,* Department of the Army, Navy, and Air Force, April 1973.

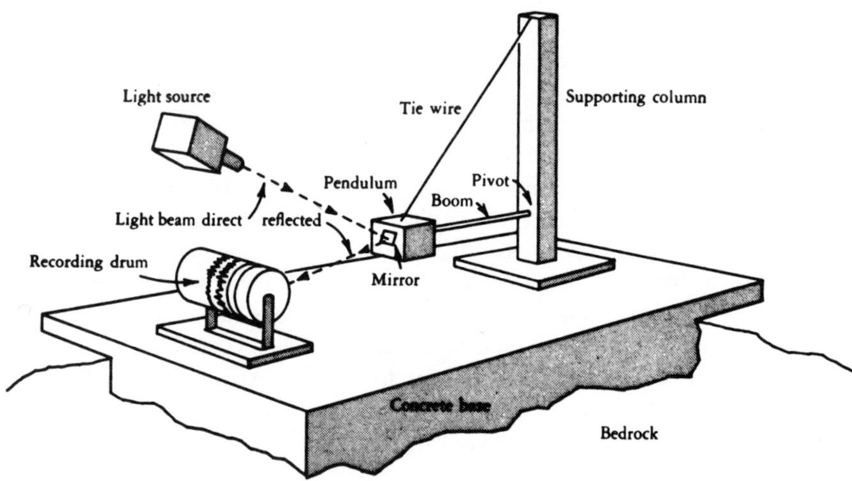

Figure 3.52 Principle of seismograph operation. *Source. Sunset Magazine,* February 1975.

Measuring Earthquakes. The vibrations produced by earthquakes are detected, recorded, and measured by instruments called seismographs (Figure 3.52). The seismograph tracking mechanism responds to the motion of the ground surface beneath the instrument and produces a zigzag line that reflects the varying amplitude of the vibrations. This record is called a seismogram, and from the data it contains, specialists can determine the time, the epicenter, and the focal depth of an earthquake, and estimates can be made of the amount of energy that was released by the quake.

The two general types of vibration produced by earthquakes are surface waves, which travel along the earth's surface, and body waves, which travel through the earth. Surface waves usually have the strongest vibrations and probably cause most of the damage done by the earthquakes.

The severity of an earthquake can be expressed in several ways. The magnitude of an earthquake on the Richter scale is a measure of the amplitude of the seismic waves and is related to the amount of energy released, which can be estimated from seismograph recordings. The intensity, as expressed by the modified Mercalli scale, is a subjective measure that describes the severity of a shock that was felt at a particular location. Damage or loss of life and property is another, ultimately the most important, measure of an earthquake's severity.

The Richter Scale, named after Dr. Charles F. Richter of the California Institute of Technology, is the best known instrument for measuring the magnitude of earthquakes. The scale is logarithmic; thus a recording of 7 signifies a disturbance with ground motion 10 times as large as a recording of 6. A quake of magnitude 2 is the smallest quake normally felt by humans. Earthquakes with a Richter value of 6 or more are commonly considered to be major in magnitude. Richter values for a few of the world's major earthquakes are as follows:

Place	Year	Richter Magnitude
India	1897	8.7*
San Francisco	1906	8.3*
Japan	1923	8.3*
Chile	1960	8.5
Alaska	1964	8.4

*Magnitudes estimated.

The modified Mercalli scale measures the intensity of an earthquake's effects in a given locality in values ranging from I to XII. The most commonly used adaptation covers the range of intensity from the condition of ''I—not felt except by very few, favorably situated,'' to ''XII—damage total, lines of sight disturbed, objects thrown into the air.'' Evaluation of earthquake intensity can be made only after eyewitness reports and results of field investigations have been studied and interpreted. The maximum intensity experienced in the Alaska quake of 1964 was X, and in the San Francisco quake of 1906, it was XI.

Earthquakes of large magnitude do not necessarily cause the most intense surface effects. The effect in a given region depends to a large degree on local surface and subsurface geologic conditions. An area underlain by unstable ground, for example, is likely to experience much more noticeable effects than an area equally distant from an earthquake's epicenter but underlain by firm ground. An earthquake's destructiveness depends on many factors in addition to magnitude. These include focal depth, distance from the epicenter, local geologic conditions, and the design of buildings and other manmade structures. The extent of damage also depends on the density of population and construction in the area shaken by the quake.

San Francisco was rebuilt after the earthquake and fire of 1906, under provisions that a wind force of 30 pounds per square foot, would be adequate for a building designed with a proper system of bracing. In the years that followed, leading structural engineers employed the concept of lateral earthquake forces proportional to masses. However this simple Newtonian concept did not find its way into codes until 1927, when it was written into the UBC, and more extensively in 1933, following the Long Beach, California, earthquake.

Earthquakes consist of horizontal and vertical ground vibrations. The horizontal motion is usually much greater than the vertical, although in a few recorded cases vertical and horizontal motions have been of approximately the same magnitude. Because of the considerably greater stiffness of buildings in the vertical direction, however, the effect of vertical ground motion has generally not been considered in design. When the ground beneath a structure moves suddenly to one side, the building tends to remain in its original position because of its inertia. As a result, the building suffers a distortion and starts vibrating with its own time period, and the accelerations produce inertia forces. The dynamic response of a structure to earthquake motions is characterized by a complex series of vibrations that have become subject to analysis only with the availability of modern electronic digital computers. Inertia forces are proportional to mass of the building times its acceleration:

$$F_i \propto M \times a$$

where F_i = inertia forces
M = mass of the building
a = acceleration induced in the building by ground motion

Figure 3.53 illustrates the behavior of buildings under inertia forces.

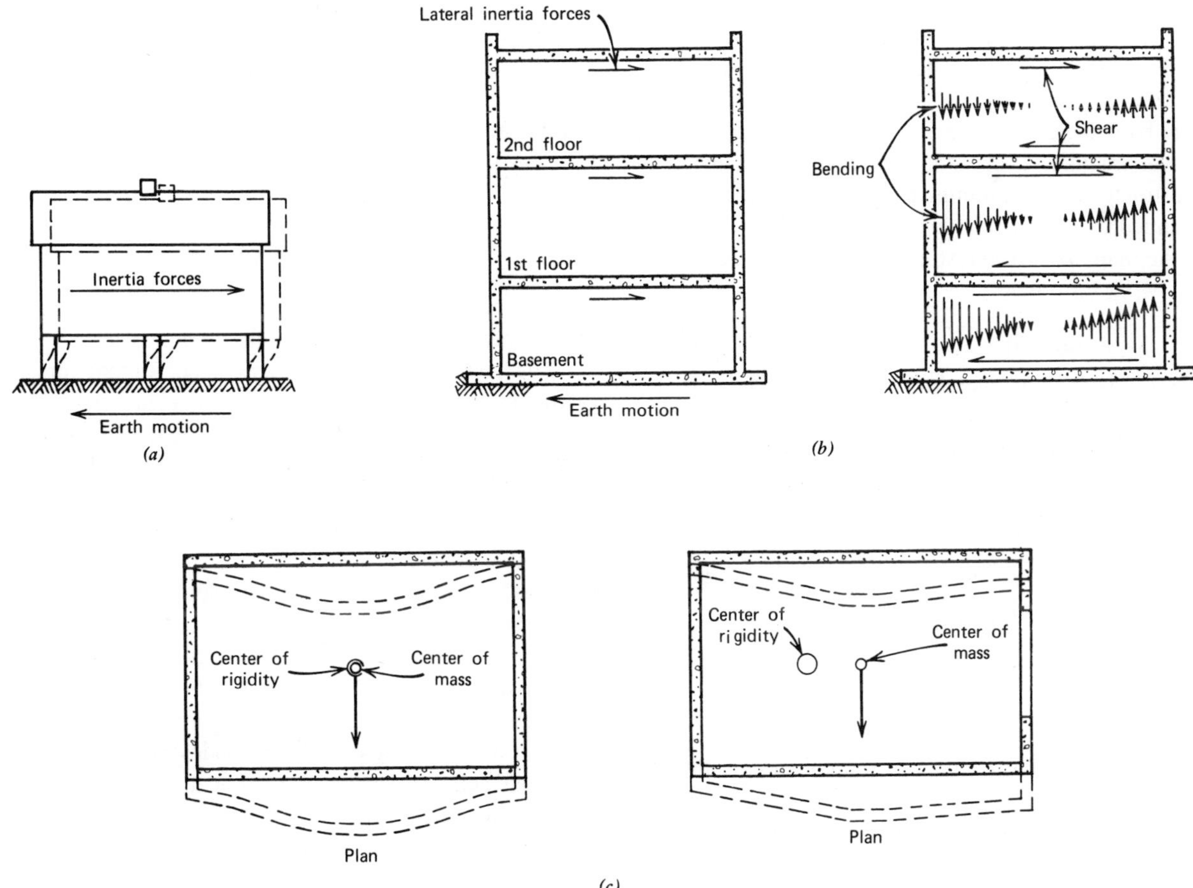

Figure 3.53 (*a*) Effect of an earthquake on a house on piers. (*b*) Forces and stresses due to earth motion. (*c*) Lateral distortions of buildings. *Source. Analysis and Design of Small Reinforced Concrete Buildings for Earthquake Forces* (A Portland Cement Association Publication).

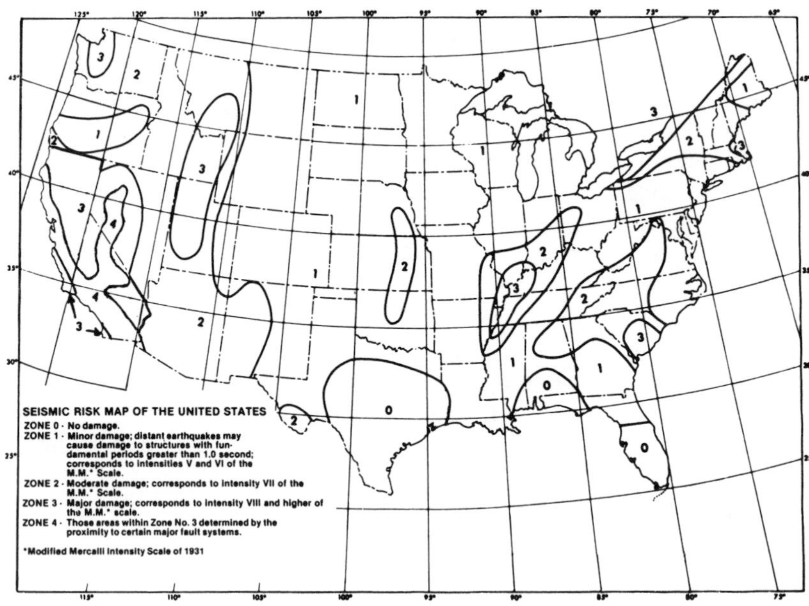

Figure 3.54 Seismic zone map of the United States. *Source*. Uniform Building Code, 1976 edition.

Based on this principle, the building codes substitute assumed equivalent design static lateral forces for the true response to ground motions. The assumed equivalent base shear is determined by the empirical formula. The design lateral force is usually specified in terms of a total base shear V, which is distributed along the height of the structure. Every structure should be designed and constructed to resist minimum total lateral seismic forces assumed to act nonconcurrently in the direction of each of the main axes of the structure in accordance with the following formula:

$$V = ZIKCSW$$

where V is the total lateral force or shear at the base, also called base shear, and

Z is a seismic zoning factor whose value depends on the location of the structure, as determined from Figure 3.54

The UBC assigns the following values for Z:

For location in zone	
1	3/16
2	3/8
3	3/4
4	1

In other words, the factor Z is an indication of the seismicity of the site.

In addition, I is the occupancy importance factor and K, a factor depending on the type of structure or structural system used, is meant to reflect differences in the ductility or energy absorption capacity, as well as the degree of structural redundancy, of various structural systems. The UBC recommends values of I and K corresponding to different types of structure.

The value of C, the coefficient related to the flexibility of the structure, has been established empirically in an attempt to recognize the effect of the period and stiffness of the structure in response to the ground motions. Thus we have

$$C = \frac{1}{15\sqrt{T}}$$

where the time period of the structure T is a function of the dimensional properties of the building.

The soil factor S, or numerical coefficient for site-structure resonance, takes into account the effect of the characteristics of the type of soil under the structure. Its value is found and recommended by the geologist and soil engineer on the project. In the absence of any soil investigation, empirical formulas are given in the UBC and other codes.

Finally, the total dead load and applicable portions of the other loads, such as partitions, permanent equipment, snow, and storage loads in warehouse occupancies, are symbolized by W. The requirements of the applicable portions of other loads vary in different building codes and in different regions. Local codes and the building officials should be consulted about this.

The total lateral force or base shear V, must be distributed over the height of the structure in accordance with the formula

$$V = F_t + \sum_{i=1}^{n} F_i$$

where V = base shear
n = number of stories
F_t = concentrated force at the top (level n) and is given by $F_t = 0.07TV$

The value of F_t need not exceed $0.25V$ and may be considered to be zero if T (time period) is 0.7 second or less. The remaining portion of the total base shear V must be distributed over the height of the structure including level n according to the following relation:

$$F_n = \frac{(V - F_t) w_x h_n}{\sum_{i=1}^{n} W_i h_i}$$

which shows that at each level designated x, the force F_x is proportional to the mass and height above ground of the level x under consideration. Buildings should be designed to resist lateral forces in any direction because an earthquake can cause ground displacements in any direction. However the horizontal components of ground motion can be replaced by two components acting parallel to the axes of the building, which are perpendicular to each other. The lateral forces, computed as a specified proportion of the vertical load, are usually assumed to act as concentrated forces applied at the different floor levels. These forces are distributed through floors or roofs, then referred to as diaphragms, to the vertical resisting elements as described later.

Diaphragms. A diaphragm is analogous to a plate girder laid in a horizontal or sloped (in case of roofs) plane, where floor or roof deck performs the function of a plate girder web, the joints or beams function as web stiffeners, and the peripheral beams or integral reinforcement in walls or other perimeter elements function as flanges. A diaphragm may be constructed of concrete, wood, or metal decks in various forms. Diaphragms can be classified as flexible and rigid.

Flexible Diaphragms. The relative stiffness of vertical elements is much greater compared to diaphragm. Thus a flexible diaphragm is considered to distribute the lateral forces to the vertical resisting elements on a tributary area load basis. A flexible diaphragm is normally not considered to be capable of distributing torsional stresses resulting from concrete or masonry masses. Wood and metal decks without concrete fill are said to be flexible diaphragms.

Rigid Diaphragms. A rigid diaphragm is assumed to distribute horizontal forces to the vertical resisting elements in proportion to their relative rigidities. Under symmetrical loading, a rigid diaphragm will cause each vertical element to deflect an equal amount, with the result that a vertical element with a high relative rigidity will resist a greater proportion of the lateral force than will an element with a lower rigidity factor. Concrete floors or metal decks with concrete fill on top are rigid diaphragms.

Torsion Moment. Torsion moment is generated whenever the center of gravity (c.g.) of the lateral forces or mass does not coincide with the center of rigidity (c.r.) of the vertical resisting elements, provided the diaphragm is sufficiently rigid to transfer torsion. Torsional moment M_t equals total lateral force F_p times eccentricity e:

$$M_t = F_p \times e$$

Most codes have a requirement for the accidental torsion requirements equivalent to the story shear acting with an eccentricity of not less than 5% of the maximum building dimension at that level.

Separation of Structures. Adjacent buildings or parts of the same building dissimilar in mass, height, or stiffness should be sufficiently separated to prevent them from pounding together if they happen to vibrate out of phase with each other during an earthquake. This can be achieved by providing special expansion joints. The width of the expansion joint or separation depends on the relative displacements of the adjacent buildings. In the absence of the actual calculated deflections for small buildings, most codes recommend an arbitrary rule of 2 inches for the first 20 feet of height above the ground plus ½ inch for each 10 feet of additional height. For higher or more flexible buildings, the seismic joint between the structures should be at least 4 times the design deflections as determined from analysis.

Drift. Drift is the relative movement between two adjacent stories. Drift should not exceed 0.005 times the story height unless it can be demonstrated that greater drifts are tolerable. Nonstructural damage during an earthquake can be considerably reduced by properly designing the building skin connection to floors at each level, and the partition connections to floors above, to accommodate drift movements.

Overturning. Every building or structure must be designed to resist the overturning effects of the wind forces or the earthquake forces specified in here. At any level, the design overturning moment in the story under consideration must be distributed to the various resisting

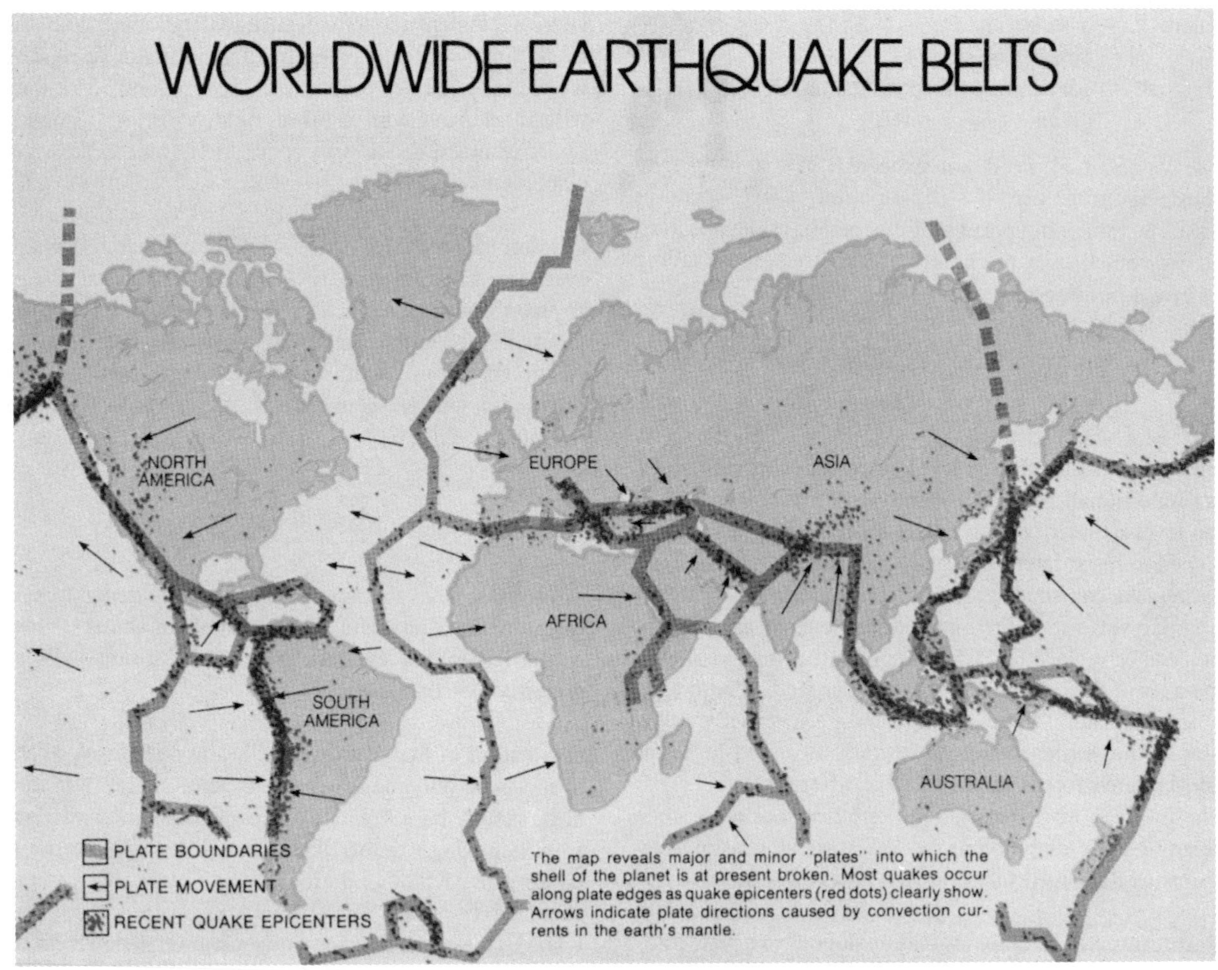

Figure 3.55 *Source. The Plain Truth Magazine,* September 1976.

elements in the same proportion as the distribution of the shears in the resisting system.

Minor Alterations. Minor structural alterations may be made in existing buildings and other structures, but the resistance to lateral forces must be not less than that which existed before such alterations were made, unless the building as altered can be shown to meet all the code requirements.

Reinforced Masonry or Concrete. All masonry or concrete elements within structures located in seismic zones 2, 3, and 4 must be reinforced to qualify as reinforced masonry.

Earthquake Prediction. Killer quakes have made the headlines with disturbing frequency in recent years. Guatemala, Italy, Iran, Russia, China, and many other countries in South America and Asia have experienced gigantic earthquakes quite recently. Even before the disaster in China, earthquakes in 1976 killed more than 24,000 people, making it the deadliest year for quakes since 1970, according to the U.S. Geological Survey.

Instinctively we do not like to think about earthquakes happening where we are. Yet hundreds of millions of people live in major earthquake belts (Figure 3.55). Failure to face the possibility of experiencing an earthquake crisis can lead to uncontrolled panic, immobilizing fear, and dangerous rumors, as well as disregard for basic safety precautions. The tragic results are unnecessary injuries, deaths, and property losses.

In recent years, scientists have found that most big earthquakes do not come like a bolt from the blue. Telltale seismic evidence usually is present to signal an impending trembler. Many seismologists now theorize that rocks in the vicinity of a future earthquake break apart slightly, under increasing pressure.

Equipment Qualification. Architect Gary L. McGavin, from the Wyle Laboratories in Los Angeles, concluded in his report on "Seismic Qualification of Equipment in Essential Facilities":

In order to adequately serve the public after a large earthquake, some building types have been defined as essential facilities. These are buildings whose functions will be necessary during an emergency and include facilities such as hospitals, communication centers, and police and fire stations. Studies reported by the American Institute of Architects Research Corporation and Public Technology, Inc. (1977) have shown that requests for the services that these facilities provide can be expected to increase by 300 to 700 percent immediately after a major earthquake in an urban area.

Recent advances in earthquake regulations and codes have resulted in buildings that are likely to remain structurally intact after an earthquake. There are, however, many types of nonstructural components (equipment not designed as a structural member) located in these facilities that are required for the successful operation of the essential facility. Very little attention has been paid to these items by building codes and earthquake regulations. Methods of seismic qualification are currently available to the design professions and have been extensively employed in the Nuclear Power Industry for safety related equipment, on the Trans-Alaskan pipeline and many military projects.

A definition for nonstructural equipment cannot be easily adapted from any of the building code sources. We can separate nonstructural equipment from structural equipment by labeling it as those items which are not an integral part of the building structural system and are not designed to accept, transmit or participate in the loading characteristics of the structure either statically or dynamically.

Wind

Wind loads are of importance, particularly in the design of large structures (tall buildings, radio towers, long span bridges, etc.), and for structures such as mill buildings and hangars, having large open interiors as well as walls in which large openings may occur. The wind velocity that should be considered in the design of a structure depends on its geographical location and on its exposure. Wind pressure per square foot is a function of the square of the wind velocity in miles per hour.

$$W_p = KV^2$$

where w_p = wind pressure (psf)
V = wind velocity (mph)
K = constant, whose value can be found in wind design handbooks

Wind Zones. The United States is divided into different wind zones and each zone has different wind pressure requirements, which are minimum values and must be adjusted by the building officials for areas subjected to higher wind pressures. For purposes of design, the wind pressures are taken on the gross area of the vertical projection of that portion of the building or structure measured above the average level of the adjoining ground. Open buildings also must be designed for upward wind pressures acting on the horizontal projected areas as described in codes.

Hurricanes. Some building codes, like the Southern Standard Building Code, have special requirements for areas subject to exceptionally high wind velocities. For example, Table 3.24 gives the Southern Standards Building Code wind pressure requirements for various height zones. Adequate anchorage of the roof to the walls and columns and of the walls and columns to the foundations is required in all cases. All primary and secondary members must be designed for uplift loads, and tiedowns are to be provided where specified.

Table 3.24 SSBC Wind Pressure Requirements

	Horizontal Loads (psf)	
Height Zone (ft)	For Southern Inland Regions	For Southern Coastal Region[a]
Less than 30	10	25
31–50	20	35
51–99	24	45
100–199	28	50
200–299	30	50
300–399	32	50
Over 400	40	50

Earthquake and Wind Summary

The following summary of important earthquake design requirements from the 1976 UBC may be used as a study aid. However the UBC material in its entirety should be used in the actual design of buildings for earthquake forces, as well as any local governing building code.

1 Forces are assumed to be applied horizontally at each floor or roof level above the foundation. Forces are assumed to act nonconcurrently in the direction of each of the main axes of the structure.
2 Total lateral seismic force $V = ZIKCSW$

3 The zone coefficient Z is based on the seismic probability map given in the UBC.

$Z = \frac{1}{16}$ in zone 1
$Z = \frac{3}{8}$ in zone 2
$Z = \frac{3}{4}$ in zone 3
$Z = 1$ in zone 4

4 The horizontal force factor K is found as follows:

Resisting Elements	*K Value*
All building framing systems except as classified below	1.00
Buildings with a box system (lateral forces resisted by shear walls)	1.33
Buildings with a dual bracing system (ductile-moment-resisting space frame and shear walls) must comply with three criteria:	.80
1. Frame and shear walls must resist total lateral force in accordance with relative rigidities.	
2. Shear walls acting alone must resist total required lateral force.	
3. Ductile-moment-resisting space frame must have capacity to resist 25% of required lateral force.	
Buildings with a ductile-moment-resisting space frame capable of resisting the entire lateral force	.67

Some special structures, such as elevator tanks, have special K values.

$C = \dfrac{1}{15\sqrt{T}}$, maximum value of $C = .12$.

6 T is the fundamental period of vibration of the structure in the direction considered, measured in seconds.

$$T = \frac{0.05h}{\sqrt{D}}$$

where h = height above the base to the top of the main part of the structure (ft)
D = dimension of the building parallel to the applied force (ft)

In multistory ductile frame buildings, $T = 0.10$ times number of stories.

7 W = total dead load (in storage and warehouse occupancies, W = total dead load + 25% of floor live load).

8 Total lateral force V is distributed in the height of the building as follows: a portion of V called F_t, is concentrated at the top of the structure; F_t varies from 0 to $0.25V$. The force at any level $x = F_n$, and

$$F_n = \frac{(V - F_t)w_x h_x}{\sum_{i=1}^{n} w_i h_i}$$

where w_x is the dead load located at or assigned to level x, h_x is the height in feet above the base to level x, and $\Sigma_{i=1}^{n} w_i h_i$ is the summation of the wh quantities for each level.

9 Where wind loads produce higher stresses, they should be used as the design parameter in lieu of earthquake loads.

10 Parts of buildings and their anchorage are designed in accordance with the following relation

$$F_p = ZIC_pSW_p$$

where F_p is the lateral force on the parts of the structure under consideration, Z is as previously defined, C_p is the coefficient as indicated below, W_p is the weight of the part of the structure, and I and S have the same meaning as for the equation for total lateral seismic force.

Parts of Building	*Value of C_p*
Interior and exterior bearing and nonbearing walls	0.20 (normal to surface)
Cantilever parapet walls	1.00 (normal to surface)
Ornamentations and appendages	1.00 (any direction)
Floors and roofs acting as diaphragms	0.12 (any direction)
Connections for exterior panels	2.00 (any direction)
Connections for prefabricated structural elements other than walls	0.30 (any horizontal direction)

11 Individual pile or caisson footings should be interconnected by ties that can carry by tension or compression a horizontal force equal to 10% of the larger pile cap loading.

12 Total shear in any horizontal plane should be distributed to the elements of the lateral-force-resisting system in proportion to their rigidities.

13 Provisions should be made for the *increase* in shear resulting from the horizontal torsion due to eccentricity between the center of mass and the center of rigidity. *Negative torsional shears are neglected.* Shear-resisting elements should be capable of resisting a minimum torsional moment equal to the story shear acting with an eccentricity of 5% of the maximum building dimension at that level.

14 Every building should be designed to resist overturning caused by wind or earthquake.

15 In all seismic zones except zone 1, buildings over 160 feet in height should have a ductile-moment-resisting space frame capable of resisting at least 25% of the required seismic force of the entire structure. All buildings designed with a K factor of .67 or .80 must have a ductile-moment-resisting space frame of structural steel or cast-

in-place reinforced concrete. If the frame is ductile, it must meet certain special requirements in the code.

16 All portions of structures should be designed and constructed to act as an integral unit in resisting horizontal forces, unless separated structurally by a distance sufficient to avoid contact under deflection from seismic or wind forces.

17 Masonry or concrete elements resisting seismic forces must be reinforced in seismic zones 2, 3, and 4.

18 Only the roof live load may be neglected when considering the effect of seismic forces in combination with vertical loads.

19 Concrete or masonry walls must be anchored to all floors and roofs providing lateral support for the wall, for a minimum force of 200 pounds per linear foot of wall.

20 Interior partitions must be designed for a minimum force of 5 pounds per square foot applied perpendicular to the partitions.

21 Lateral deflections or drift of a story relative to its adjacent stories shall not exceed 0.005 times the story height, unless it can be demonstrated that greater drift is tolerable.

22 Essential facilities are structures or buildings that must be safe and usable for emergency purposes after an earthquake, to preserve the health and safety of the general public.

23 Wind pressures, expressed in pounds per square foot, are proportional to wind velocity, given in miles per hour.

24 An epicenter is the part of the earth's surface directly above the point at which a fault slip began.

25 A fault is a fracture in the earth's crust accompanied by a displacement of one side of the fracture with respect to the other in a direction parallel to the fracture.

26 A seismograph is an instrument that plots a continuous record of the successive earth waves generated by an earthquake.

SAN FRANCISCO UNITARIAN CHURCH
San Francisco, California
Architects: Callister, Payne & Rosse
Photo: P. Molten

5 MECHANICAL SYSTEMS

By Howard N. Helfman

Howard N. Helfman graduated cum laude from the University of Southern California in 1944; he holds a Bachelor of (Electrical) Engineering degree. At USC he was elected to Eta Kappa Nu, the honorary electrical engineering society, and Tau Beta Phi, the honorary engineering society.

A Registered Mechanical and Electrical Engineer in the state of California, Helfman is also registered in the states of Washington, Florida, Texas, Arizona, Pennsylvania, Massachusetts, and Oregon. He belongs to the National Society of Professional Engineers, the American Society of Heating, Refrigerating and Air Conditioning Engineers, the American Society of Plumbing Engineers, and the Mechanical Engineers Association.

As senior extension teacher at the University of California at Los Angeles, teaching courses in air conditioning theory and design, Helfman is in private practice as a consulting mechanical engineer in the city of Los Angeles.

The mechanical systems for architectural projects fall into three main categories: plumbing; heating, ventilating, and air conditioning (HVAC); and life safety.

The plumbing systems include the potable water supply and the waste and drainage systems, as well as specialized piping such as is required for medical gases in hospitals, compressed air systems, fuel gases, and process piping. The HVAC section includes all exhaust systems, plus makeup air and air conditioning and heating systems. Life safety involves sprinkler systems, wet and dry standpipes, fire hose cabinets, and on-site hydrants.

Normally the architect is not expected to prepare original designs in these areas, but he or she must be competent to make rational choices from among alternative designs that are presented. Such factors as initial cost, suitability for the application, space limitations, energy management, maintenance factors, aesthetics, safety, and the present and future availability of different forms of energy, must be taken into account.

In comparing relative costs of alternatives, it is important to consider all cost variables, such as the impact on other trades, interest rates, inflation rates, and operating and maintenance costs. All expenses to be incurred in the future (e.g., costs of energy and maintenance) should be brought back to present value. The architect's judgment is required in estimating many of these items—particularly future fuel costs, inflation rates, and future taxes.

Plumbing

Potable Water Supply. In the great majority of instances, potable water can be obtained from a municipal or other public water system. However in special applications, water is obtained from wells, lakes, rivers, surface water runoff impounded by dams, or salt water conversion. Distillation of salt water conversion is usually prohibitively expensive. As a rule this approach is used when no other water source is available. The decision to secure a water supply from wells must include considerations of depletion and the possibility of soil subsidence.

Municipal or public water supply systems, when available, are invariably the source of choice. They are generally reliable and adequately monitored to provide a dependable source of safe, potable water.

In making a choice of potable water supply, the primary considerations should be reliability and dependability. Cost is a secondary factor.

Water Treatment. Water drawn from wells, lakes, rivers, or other natural sources should be carefully analyzed, and chlorinated or otherwise purified to render it safe for human consumption.

Municipal systems, on the other hand, generally supply water that is suitable for human consumption, and water treatment is required only in the event of unacceptable hardness. Water-softening equipment is not always cost effective, however, and the designer must exercise judgment. Water-softening equipment involves an expenditure for equipment, chemicals, and labor, and soft water is more corrosive than nonsoftened water. Water-softening equipment can be applied to the entire service to a structure (i.e., to both hot and cold water), or as an alternative, it may be used on just the hot water. The latter course requires separate piping runs and additional plumbing. There is an increased capital cost in piping, but less equipment is needed and operating costs are lower. Thus the choice of softening or not softening and the degree of application are matters for the designer's judgment, and all the variables above must be considered.

Water Distribution System. Water distribution systems for lowrise buildings are seldom uncomplicated because the variations between the minimum and maximum pressures in the structure are modest. In a highrise

APPLEWOOD HEIGHTS POOL
Mississauga, Ontario
Architect: Stark Temporale
Photo: Smith & Hicks

KONA-HILTON HOTEL
Kona, Hawaii
Architect: Wimberly, Whisenand, Allison & Tong
Photo: Walton

structure, however, the pressure variation due to the weight of the column of water equal to the height of the building may be beyond the acceptable range. In addition, the water pressure available at the street level to lift that column of water to the top of the building is frequently inadequate. (This can even occur in lowrise buildings.)

Thus there are two problems to be solved in connection with water distribution systems for highrise buildings. One is getting adequate pressure at the top of the building, and the second is maintaining within acceptable limits the pressure variations between the different levels. A number of schemes are available to boost street pressure to raise the column of water the full height of the building and leave adequate residual pressure at the top.

Pumping System. House pumps are available that will maintain a constant pressure at the pump discharge, regardless of flow rate through a combination of multiple pumps, variable speed pumps, or special controls. These systems require relatively small space, are usually self-contained, packaged devices, and are predictable and reliable in operation. If they are not installed at the ground level, at least they must be no higher in the building than is dictated by the residual pressures at the point of installation. For a typical building the street pressure might be adequate to serve the first five floors but inadequate to handle the sixth floor and above. In this case, it would be appropriate to supply a pumping unit to service the sixth and higher floors, using the street pressure to take care of the lower five floors. This would reduce the size of the pumping unit, thus the capital cost. Some additional expense is incurred in providing the second riser for the upper part of the building, but this is usually negligible compared to the savings in pump costs.

Tanks. Another possible water distribution arrangement involves the use of a house tank mounted on the roof, depending on street pressure or a small house pump that can pump during off hours as well as during hours of peak demand to maintain the water level in the tank. Water is then supplied to the structure by a downfeed system, and the natural head provides adequate water pressure to the fixtures. If there is insufficient head, this tank can be pneumatically charged with an air compressor to give the required pressure. Such house tanks are heavy and bulky and form part of the structural considerations in the design of the building, particularly for seismic loads; but being passive devices, they do not depend on pump operation or other mechanical means. A pneumatically charged house tank can be located on the lower floors or in the basement, provided enough pressure is maintained to lift the column of water to the top of the building and to leave adequate residual pressure at that point. Air-charged pneumatic pumping systems have higher levels of dissolved air in the water, however, and dissolved oxygen increases the corrosiveness of the supply water and also may be unaesthetic at tap discharge (since the issuing water may have the appearance of soda water).

The problem of variable pressures at the different levels due to the static head is most easily managed by providing pressure-regulating valves at the runoffs to the individual floors as required. There may be one valve for each level, or two or three levels may be combined on a single valve.

Piping Materials. Piping systems can be fabricated of galvanized steel, wrought iron, copper, plastic, or cement asbestos. Normally, economic considerations and code limitations dictate choice of material. Plastics are usually the most economical material, but their use is frequently prohibited by local codes, and the designer must be aware of the limitations of plastic pipe, with respect to the pressure and/or temperature of the water.

Piping material is selected on the basis of economics and suitability for the purpose. Some of the advantages and disadvantages of various materials are as follows.

1 *Copper.* Copper is durable and does not corrode readily. However, it is subject to electrolytic attack if dissimilar metals are used and dielectric separation is not provided. Copper joints are soldered, and the labor factor is relatively low. The price of copper fluctuates widely but is generally higher than that of other types of pipe material. Price varies considerably on the world market, but because of the low labor factor and the corrosion resistance of copper, copper is frequently the material of choice.
2 *Cement Asbestos.* This material is highly brittle but is completely corrosion proof. For this reason it is often used for underground service.
3 *Steel Pipe.* Steel pipe is relatively inexpensive. Joints are usually screwed in the smaller sizes and flanged or welded in larger sizes, usually 2½ inches and up. The labor factor involved in threading and/or welding the joints is greater than that required to make copper fittings, but the overall price, including labor and materials, is usually very competitive. Steel pipe to handle water systems is usually galvanized.

Other Considerations. In addition to the selection of the proper material for the potable water piping system, the designer must take into account the following factors and provide for them in the design.

Pipe Expansion and Contraction. Changes in temperature will cause pipe to expand and contract. For copper tubing, the change in length will be approximately 1.1 inches per 100 feet of pipe for 100° F change in temperature. It is slightly less than this for iron pipe. This expansion and contraction must be allowed for, in the form of expansion joints or swing joints, or the pipe must be supported in such a way that it can move without resistance from the structure. Failure to provide for expansion can cause damage to the piping system or the structure and can cause cracking and other strange sounds.

Sizing of Pipes. Factors affecting the size of the pipe are the flow rate, the velocity and noise level that can be tolerated, and the friction loss. Excessive velocities will result in erosion of the pipe and high noise levels. If the friction drop is too high, it may be impossible to maintain proper pressure levels in the structure. Undersizing of pipe can result in an excessive economic penalty. In general, the designer should specify pipe that is small enough to meet budget restrictions, but not so small that it creates excessive velocities or friction loss. Flow rates are established by the type and the number of fixtures served by the line.

Hot Water Systems. The choice of energy for heating the water depends on present and future availability and cost of the heating equipment, as well as the energy to fuel it. The energy source can be gas or other fossil fuel, electrical energy, or solar power. Heat rejected from air conditioning or refrigeration equipment may also be used.

Large structures usually have a central water heating system, to ensure that fixtures remote from the heater are supplied with a constant source of hot water. Circulating pumps are usually provided for this purpose, and the hot water is circulated from the storage tank through a loop connecting all the fixtures and back to the tank again.

For small systems or when fixtures are remote from each other, small individual water heaters, either fuel fired or electric, may be located adjacent to the fixture. Circulating pumps are not required. Fuel-burning heaters call for a source of combustion air and a means to vent the products of combustion from the structures.

Pipe Insulation. In general, domestic cold water piping is not insulated. However in special situations, where the temperature of the pipe may be below the ambient dew point temperature, it is necessary to insulate cold water pipes to prevent condensation. Hot water piping systems should be insulated to prevent heat loss from the pipes. This is particularly important for hot water systems that utilize circulating pumps.

As in most situations, economics determines the optimum thickness of insulation to reduce the energy loss in hot water pipes. Here the cost of extra insulation is balanced against the energy costs that would be saved. As fuel supplies are decreasing and the price of energy is rising, optimum insulation thickness is inevitably rising.

Plumbing Fixtures. Local plumbing codes usually prescribe the minimum number of fixtures based on the occupancy of the building. Many codes also require provision of special arrangements for handicapped persons—for example, one or more extrawide toilet stalls with handrails, one or more lavatories with sufficient clearance underneath for a wheelchair, and one or more drinking fountains that can be operated from a wheelchair.

The architect must select floor-mounted or wall-mounted urinals and water closets. Wall-mounted fixtures are more expensive and require more maintenance, but they leave unrestricted floor areas, which are easier to clean and are more sanitary. Water closets can be equipped with flush valves or with tanks. Flush valves require larger sizes of pipe to serve them, but they use less water, are not subject to vandalism, and need much less maintenance.

Sanitary Drainage Systems. These systems are designed to carry waste fluids from plumbing fixtures inside a structure. Since the flow is induced by gravity, it is important that all horizontal lines be pitched downward in the direction of flow. Rate of pitch under normal circumstances is 2% (¼ in/ft). Where inadequate vertical height is available, however 1% (⅛ in/ft) can be accommodated. Local codes vary in this respect.

The size of the waste system is based on the anticipated flow rate; thus it depends on the type and the number of fixtures being served by the particular line. Each fixture must be separated from the rest of the system by a suitable trap to prevent sewer gases from backing up through the line. Since the siphon action of water flowing to the waste system can draw the water out of the trap, breaking the trap seal, vents must be provided at the line side of the trap for each fixture to eliminate the siphon effect.

Three systems of drainage are in general use. These are (1) conventional, (2) continuous waste and vent, (3) and SOVENT. The continuous waste and vent is used where it is impractical to accommodate a vent pipe at the trap. The SOVENT system is relatively new and generally more expensive; it utilizes special copper fittings.

Materials generally used for soil waste and vent pipe above grade are cast iron, either with bell and spigot with lead and oakum joints or with compression joints; standard weight steel hubless pipe with stainless steel couplings; standard weight hubless pipe with cast iron couplings; DWV copper; type M copper; type L copper; type K copper; ABS plastic, polyvinyl chloride (PVC) plastic; schedule 40 galvanized steel with cast iron screwed fittings; and schedule 40 galvanized steel with cast iron, screwed drainage fittings.

Basic Principles. Plumbing codes are formulated based on goals of environmental sanitation worthy of accomplishment though properly designed, acceptably installed, and adequately maintained plumbing systems. Some of the details of plumbing construction must vary, but the basic sanitary and safety principles are the same. The results desired and necessary to protect the health of the people are the same everywhere, and these principles merit serious study. Furthermore, as unforeseen situations arise that are not covered in the body of the applicable code, the principles may serve to define the intent.

• *Principle no. 1.* All premises intended for human habitation, occupancy, or use shall be provided with a supply of pure and wholesome water, neither connected with unsafe water supplies nor subject to the hazards of backflow or back siphonage.

• *Principle no. 2.* Plumbing fixtures, devices, and appurtenances shall be supplied with water in sufficient volume and at pressures adequate to enable them to function satisfactorily and without undue noise under all normal conditions of use.

• *Principle no. 3.* Plumbing shall be designed and adjusted to use the minimum quantity of water consistent with proper performance and cleaning.

• *Principle no. 4.* Devices for heating and storing water shall be so designed and installed as to prevent dangers from explosion through overheating.

• *Principle no. 5.* Every building having plumbing fixtures installed and intended for human habitation, occupancy, or use on premises abutting on a street, alley, or easement in which there is a public sewer shall have a connection with the sewer.

• *Principle no. 6.* Every family dwelling unit on premises abutting on a sewer or with a private sewage-disposal system shall have, at least, one water closet and one kitchen-type sink. It is further recommended that a lavatory and bathtub or shower be installed to meet the basic requirements of sanitation and personal hygiene. All other structures for human occupancy or use on premises abutting on a sewer or with a private sewage-disposal system shall have adequate sanitary facilities, but in no case less than one water closet and one other fixture for cleaning purposes.

• *Principle no. 7.* Plumbing fixtures shall be made of smooth nonabsorbent material, shall be free from concealed fouling surfaces, and shall be located in ventilated enclosures.

• *Principle no. 8.* The drainage system shall be designed, constructed, and maintained so as to guard against fouling, deposit of solids, and clogging, and with adequate cleanouts so arranged that the pipes may be readily cleaned.

• *Principle no. 9.* The piping of the plumbing system shall be of durable material, free from defective workmanship, and so designed and constructed as to give satisfactory service for its reasonable expected life.

• *Principle no. 10.* Each fixture directly connected to the drainage system shall be equipped with a water-seal trap.

• *Principle no. 11.* The drainage system shall be designed to provide an adequate circulation of air in all pipes with no danger of siphonage, aspiration, or forcing of trap seals under conditions of ordinary use.

• *Principle no. 12.* Each vent terminal shall extend to the outer air and be so installed as to minimize the possibilities of clogging and the return of foul air to the building.

• *Principle no. 13.* The plumbing system shall be subjected to such tests as will effectively disclose all leaks and defects in the work.

• *Principle no. 14.* No substance that will clog the pipes, produce explosive mixtures, destroy the pipes or their joints, or interfere unduly with the sewage-disposal process shall be allowed to enter the building drainage system.

• *Principle no. 15.* Proper protection shall be provided to prevent contamination of food, water, sterile goods, and similar materials by backflow of sewage. When necessary, the fixture, device, or appliance shall be connected indirectly with the building drainage system.

• *Principle no. 16.* No water closet shall be located in a room or compartment that is not properly lighted and ventilated.

• *Principle no. 17.* If water closets or other plumbing fixtures are installed in buildings where there is no sewer within a reasonable distance, suitable provision shall be made for disposing of the building sewage by some accepted method of sewage treatment and disposal.

• *Principle no. 18.* Where a plumbing drainage system may be subjected to backflow of sewage, suitable provision shall be made to prevent its overflow in the building.

• *Principle no. 19.* Plumbing systems shall be maintained in a sanitary and serviceable condition.

• *Principle no. 20.* All plumbing fixtures shall be so installed with regard to spacing as to be reasonably accessible for their intended use.

• *Principle no. 21.* Plumbing shall be installed with due regard to preservation of the strength of structural members and prevention of damage to walls and other surfaces through fixture usage.

• *Principle no. 22.* Sewage or other waste from a plumbing system that may be deleterious to surface or subsurface waters shall not be discharged into the ground or into any waterway unless it has first been rendered innocuous through subjection to some acceptable form of treatment.

Fire Protection

Various strategies are employed in building construction to minimize or eliminate damage to property from fire and to protect life. These include containment of the fire to small areas, alarm systems, fire extinguishing systems, and schemes for removal of smoke, particularly from exit stairways. In highrise buildings, at least one elevator is usually connected to an emergency power supply.

Alarm Systems. Smoke sensors in commercial use include ionization-type detectors, which are sensitive to the presence of the ionization products of combustion, smoke detectors that optically measure the opacity of the air, the rate-of-change type of fire detectors, which react only to a relatively high rate of change of temperature, and fixed temperature sensors, which in effect are thermostats set to react at a predetermined temperature level. Depending on the circumstances, these sensors are employed to sound alarms either locally or at fire departments. They may activate smoke removal systems, reroute elevators, or activate fire extinguishing equipment.

Standpipes. Standpipes are vertical pipes that convey water for the extinguishment of fires. The three types of standpipe in general use are wet, dry, and combination.

Wet Standpipes. Wet standpipes are vertical lines connected to the water supply and having hose connections, frequently with fire hose cabinets tied to these lines at each floor and the roof. Wet standpipe systems are generally intended for use by tenants of the structure, not by the fire department. Fire hose cabinets must be located in such a way that all portions of the building can be reached, and the hoses must be long enough for this purpose. Wet standpipes may be left dry in cold climates where they are subject to freezing conditions; water enters the line from the service connection only in the event of a fire emergency.

Dry Standpipes. Dry standpipes are vertical pipes, provided for the use of the fire department. They are not connected to the water service, but terminate at the exterior of the building at ground level in a siamese connection. This permits two or more pumper trucks to tie into the same vertical dry standpipe. Connections are furnished at the second floor level through the roof.

Combination Standpipes. Some community codes require the use of combination standpipes for highrise buildings. These are vertical lines that are connected to the water service but also have a street connection for the fire department and can be used either by the tenants of the structure or by the fire department.

Sprinkler Systems. Sprinkler systems (i.e., piping systems intended to apply water automatically to extinguish fires) may be required by local codes, depending on the type of building, its area, and the yard and street space adjoining the structure. There are four basic types in common use.

1 The most common, least expensive sprinkler system is the fixed-temperature wet system. Water pressure fills the entire system, and water is released from individual sprinkler heads in the event of fire. The sprinkler heads are fitted with heat-sensitive fusible plugs, set to release the water at a predetermined temperature. Buildings are rated as light hazard, ordinary hazard, or extra hazard, and the spacing of the sprinkler heads is determined on the basis of these ratings.

2 In colder climates where the sprinkler systems are subject to freezing, a dry system is employed. The piping system is filled with air under pressure, and if a sprinkler head goes off, this vents the air, which opens the dry pipe valve. Water then forces the air out of the system, and the water flows through the fused sprinkler.

3 The rate-of-temperature-rise deluge system is used for some areas, particularly unheated, where a high fire hazard exists and a rapid response is required. Sprinkler heads are not fused. The fire sensors are remote. When a sensor reacts, the system fills with water and all sprinklers discharge simultaneously. In areas where a quick reaction time is desired even though a deluge of water might cause excessive damage, a rate-of-temperature-rise reaction system is employed. This is a combination dry system charged with pressurized air; however the sprinklers are fused. If a rate-of-temperature-rise sensor is activated, it will open the water valve to the system, but no water can be released unless a sprinkler head has fused as well. When this system is used, the reaction time is fast, but water is released only through the sprinkler heads that have been activated.

Smoke Removal Systems. Many larger structures employ sophisticated schemes for the removal of smoke. High structures, for example, may have smoke tower stairshafts. At each floor, the entrance to the stairshaft is protected by a vestibule. Separate supply and exhaust fans connected to the emergency power system maintain pressure differentials in the event of a fire between the stairshaft, the vestibule and the commercial floor area. These pressure differentials are intended to maintain the stairshaft free of smoke so that vertical access to and from the building can be maintained for fire fighting purposes as well as for evacuation.

In many cases the air conditioning system is tied into the fire alarm system so that exhaust fans will automatically remove smoke from the fire floor and will maintain other floors of the building at higher pressures to prevent smoke migration. Fire dampers and fire doors are extensively used to isolate fires and prevent them from spreading through shafts and ducts, and other spaces.

Gas Fire Extinguishing Systems. Carbon dioxide and other flame-extinguishing gases such as Halon can be employed to put out fires. Carbon dioxide, which is useful because it smothers fires by denying them oxygen, can be dangerous for personnel, since it denies oxygen to them as well. Carbon dioxide systems are frequently used for kitchen hoods and localized high fire hazard areas.

Halon is a gas that effectively extinguishes fires, yet does not exclude oxygen; thus people can survive in a Halon atmosphere. These systems are extremely expensive, however, and are usually reserved for the protection of high-cost critical areas (e.g., computer rooms) that would be damaged by other means of fire extinguishing.

Air Conditioning

In the process of air conditioning, heat is removed from the space to be conditioned by supplying air that is both cooler and dryer than the desired conditions. The unit of heat in the English system is the British thermal unit (Btu), which is the amount of heat required to change the temperature of one pound of water by 1°F.

Two forms of heat must be removed. The first is sensible heat, or heat that changes the temperature of a substance when it is either added or removed. The second is latent heat, which involves the addition or removal of water vapor from the air. Any type of heating or air conditioning system must include ventilation for health and comfort of the building occupants (as well as to meet local code requirements). Consideration must also be given to exhaust requirements for toilets, kitchens, storage area (particularly of hazardous materials), and other areas from which odor, dust, or heat must be removed.

The sources of heat to a space should be understood by the architect, who must design the structure to minimize the amount of energy required to maintain comfort conditions. These heat sources are as follows:

1 Solar radiation through glazing.
2 Heat conduction through the exterior envelope.
3 Metabolic heat from people.
4 Lights.
5 Heat-producing equipment.
6 Infiltration of outside air.

Solar Radiation. The amount of radiant energy that reaches the earth from the sun varies, of course, with time and with changes with the sun angle. Similarly, the amount of radiant energy that enters a structure depends on the type and areas of the glazing and its orientation, and on the degree of shading afforded. Well-designed exterior shades will reduce this solar heat gain to approximately one-quarter of the value tabulated. Light-colored inside Venetian blinds or drapes reduce it to approximately two-thirds of the value indicated. Certain heat-absorbing glasses reduce this heat gain to approximately 70%, and mirrored reflective finishes can cut it to approximately 20 to 30%.

Conduction Heat Gains. The amount of heat that flows through the building envelope will be affected by the outdoor temperature, the thermal resistance and mass of the walls, the exterior color, and the wall orientation. It is relatively easy to increase the thermal resistance by adding insulation. Lighter colors reflect some of the sun's rays rather than absorbing them, thus reducing the temperature differential. The thermal resistance of glass can be increased by using panes of double or even triple thickness. Because the sun beats down on the roofs of structures, the architect should be especially careful to have adequate thermal resistance in the roof. Light colors to reflect solar radiation are particularly desirable.

Heat Gain from People. The amount of heat given off by people depends on their age, sex, and degree of activity. This heat is both sensible and latent, for people both heat the air and give up moisture. The total amount of heat per person can vary from approximately 450 Btu per hour per person in a sedentary occupation to 1500 or 2000 Btu per hour or more from someone who is active.

Lights. All the electrical energy that is fed into the lighting system eventually decays into heat, some radiant and some convective. If lights are recessed, a portion of this heat is given to the attic, or floor above. Fluorescent lights are more efficient than incandescent lamps at converting electrical energy into light; thus, for the same lighting level, the former require less power. High-pressure sodium and HID lamps are even more efficient than fluorescents. Heat from lights constitutes a major load on the air conditioning system.

Equipment. Electric typewriters, copying machines, and other office machinery, computers, restaurant equipment, and similar devices that give up heat contribute their share to the heat buildup. When the amount of heat released is extremely high, exhaust hoods for the equipment can be beneficial.

Infiltration of Outside Air. The outside air usually has more heat energy than does the air in a conditioned space, and any outside air that leaks into the structure will contribute to the heat buildup. Most air conditioning systems depend on pressurization of the structure to prevent infiltration. However the outside air that is introduced through the apparatus to provide this pressurization and for ventilation purposes will add to the heat load. In general, the warmer the climate, the more desirable it is to minimize the energy required by limiting the amount of outside air.

Basic Refrigeration Cycles

Vapor Compression. The vapor compression cycle depends on the ability of the boiling temperature of a fluid to change with the pressure imposed on it. In general, the boiling temperature (saturation temperature) is reduced if the pressure is reduced and is increased if the pressure is increased.

A suitable fluid (the refrigerant) is placed in a heat exchanger (the evaporator), and its pressure is maintained at a relatively low value so that the saturation temperature is low, say 40 to 45°F. The air or water that is to be cooled then transfers heat to this fluid through the heat exchanger, causing the fluid to boil at the low temperature. A compressor is connected to the evaporator through its suction connection so that, as the fluid in the evaporator boils, the compressor maintains the low pressure. The compressor then discharges the vapor at a higher pressure (also at a higher saturation temperature) to another heat exchanger (the condensor). In this case the high pressure and the corresponding high saturation temperature allow the vapor to reject heat through the condenser heat exchanger, to water or to air, and to be recondensed to the liquid form. The liquid is then conveyed back to the evaporator to repeat the cycle. At the entrance of the evaporator, a restrictor, either an expansion valve or a capillary tube, separates the high-pressure liquid coming from the condenser from the low-pressure liquid boiling in the evaporator. The system can be reversed using the cycle to produce heat. Depending on the temperature of the heat sink from which heat is being drawn, the heat output can be from 2 to 4 times the heat input to the compressor.

The ton is the unit of refrigeration in the English system. One ton is equal to the amount of cooling required to freeze 1 ton of ice in 24 hours. Numerically it is equal to 12,000 Btu per hour. For air conditioning duty, the power requirements are approximately 1 to 1½ horsepower per ton of refrigeration.

Absorption Cycle. The absorption cycle is a method of refrigeration in which water is the refrigerant and heat is the driving force. The evaporator in the absorption machine is maintained at a very low pressure so that the saturation temperature of the water is in the 40°F range. A solvent, such as lithium bromide or ammonia, captures the water vapor so that the pressure in the evaporator remains low. However at some point the solvent becomes saturated and no longer can absorb water vapor. Then the solution consisting of the solvent and the water must be regenerated. Heat is added, which drives off the water vapor, the solvent is returned to the evaporator, and the water vapor is transported to a condenser where it is condensed by rejecting its heat to a second water circuit. The condensed water (refrigerant) is then returned to the evaporator to complete the cycle.

The absorption machine requires approximately 20,000 Btu per ton-hour of refrigeration, thus is considerably less efficient than the mechanical vapor compression cycle in its use of power or energy to produce refrigeration. However it provides a means of converting waste heat to refrigeration.

Types of Cooling

Evaporative Cooling. Adiabatic cooling is possible in some arid climates. Useful cooling effects can be achieved by adiabatic saturation, that is, passing air over a wetted surface. If the initial air is dry, the air emerging from the wetted surface will be moist and cool.

Direct Expansion. In the direct expansion (DX) system, the refrigerant is metered through an expansion valve or capillary tube to the evaporator and cools air directly. It has the advantage of being economical, energy efficient, and simple. However it is somewhat more difficult to achieve precise temperature control. The system is not suitable when multiple fan coil units are utilized.

Chilled Water. In the chilled water system, the refrigerant is metered either through an expansion valve or capillary tube (DX) or a float valve (flooded). Water is cooled, rather than air, and the water is transported through pipes to heat exchangers, where the air is ultimately cooled. The chilled water system is precisely controllable and permits multiple fan coil units. In addition, the fan coils can be located quite remote from the refrigeration machinery. Because of the lower refrigerant temperatures and the pumping energy required, it has a slightly lower energy efficiency than the DX system.

Air Conditioning Systems

All-Air Systems. Heating or cooling is achieved by conveying heated or cooled air to the space to be conditioned. There are several variations of the all-air system. Some of these are as follows.

Single Zone. These can be either built up or self-contained. Condensers can be cooled by either air or water. A single duct conveys heated or cooled air to the conditioned space. There is one room thermostat, and one zone of control.

Dual-Duct or Multizone. This arrangement permits simultaneous heating and cooling of different zones from the same equipment. Two separate ducts are utilized: one conveys heated air, the second carries cooled air. For each zone of control, paired mixing dampers (one from each of the two ducts) are connected to a common duct serving the zone. A zone thermostat programs the mixing dampers to apportion the relative percentages of heated and cooled air to satisfy the requirements of that particular zone. In the double-duct system, the heated and cooled ducts are run throughout the structure, and mixing dampers are located adjacent to the controlled zone. In the multizone system, all zone takeoffs are made at the unit, and the individual zone runs go from there to the zones.

The dual-duct or multizone arrangement is less energy efficient than others in that heated and cooled air can be mixed, thus wasting energy. There are a number of refinements, however, particularly in the controls, that can make this system relatively efficient. These include resetting of the duct temperatures to the minimum permissible differential, using rejected condenser heat for this first stage of heating, and using leakproof mixing dampers.

Variable Air Volume. The variable air volume system permits individual zone control from a single supply duct. Temperature control in each zone is achieved by varying the volume of air supplied to that particular zone. The variations of this system include a changeover from heating to cooling; providing separate heating systems for the skin; and providing terminal reheat at each zone. The system is very energy efficient because the fan power is reduced at light loads.

Air-Water Systems. An air-water system employs both air and water for transporting the heat and cooling functions.

Induction Air Conditioning. The induction system makes use of special terminal units containing a secondary coil. Primary air, which is dehumidified and cooled or heated as required, is supplied to these units under pressure, then is discharged through nozzles in the induction units. This induces secondary air from the room to be drawn across the secondary coil, where the temperature can be controlled to maintain the desired conditions within that space. This system is particularly useful for buildings having multiple zones of similar size and orientation, such as hospitals and highrise office buildings. The individual induction units do not require power wiring, nor do they normally require drain lines for condensates.

Variable Air Volume with Terminal Reheat. Cold air is supplied through a common duct each zone. The air volume to the zone is varied as necessary to maintain temperature. Since heating may be required, a reheat coil is available for each zone as necessary.

All-Water Systems. Water systems rely on the transportation of chilled or hot water, or both, through pipes to fan coil units, where air is heated or cooled as required. A separate fan coil is used for each zone of control. There are several variations.

Two-Pipe System. As the name implies, the two-pipe water system uses two pipes, one for supply and one for return. Either hot or cold water is fed through the pipes. The changeover can be performed manually, or it can be determined by outdoor temperature, return water, or air temperature. This system is relatively inexpensive; however the entire structure must be on either heating or cooling at one time. It is not possible to heat one space (say, the north exposure) while simultaneously cooling the southern exposure.

Three-Pipe System. The three-pipe system uses one pipe to convey cold water, the second pipe for heated water, and the third for a common return. It does have the capability of heating and cooling different zones simultaneously, and since there is one common return, the piping costs are reduced. The system is rarely used any more because heated and cooled water are ultimately mixed in the common return line, and this is very inefficient.

Four-Pipe System. This arrangement uses a chilled water supply and return pipe and a hot water supply and return. The piping costs are higher than for the three-pipe system, but operating costs are considerably lower, and the system permits complete independent zoning.

Electrohydronic. This is an arrangement of water-to-air heat pumps or reverse cycle units. A circulating water loop serves as a heat sink. Individual water-to-air heat pumps are provided for each zone of control and are connected to this heat sink. Each zone of control (i.e., each unit) can either reject heat to the sink or take heat

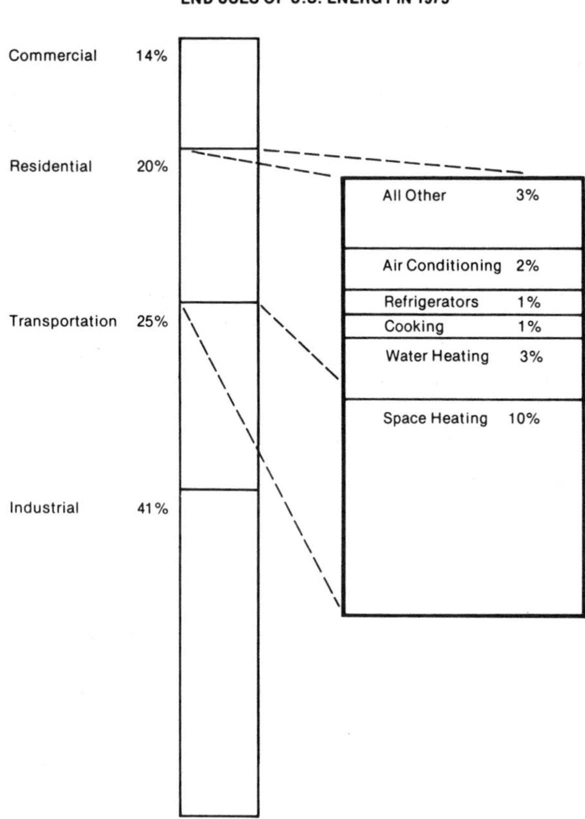

Figure 3.56 *Source.* Eugene Eccli, *Low-Cost Energy Efficient Shelter,* Rodale Press, 1976.

out of the sink, depending on its individual zone requirements. If the majority of the units are rejecting heat to the loop and the loop temperature becomes too high, a closed-circuit cooling tower comes into play to limit the high-side temperature. In the same way, if a majority of the units are taking heat out of the loop and the loop temperature gets too low, the hot water boiler limits the low-side temperature. This can be very effective from an energy standpoint in that much of the time heat is transferred from one portion of the building to another. Each zone of control requires a separate and independent water-to-air heat pump.

Energy Strategies. The current fuel crisis and the consequent emphasis on energy management demonstrate the need for the architect to be aware of some of the strategies available to minimize energy consumption within structures. Some of these approaches involve construction features, and some are chiefly mechanical.

Building Mass. In many areas of the United States, particularly in the Southwest, the summer nighttime temperature is considerably lower than the daytime temperature. Buildings with massive walls have a very important set of properties: the walls absorb heat during the day and reject it at night. Given sufficient mass, this thermal inertia, or flywheel effect, can balance the daytime heat gain against the nighttime heat loss, with the result that net heat flow through the building envelope is reduced to a very low value.

Shading and Fenestration. External or internal shading devices will reduce the solar radiation into the structure. In general, exterior shades are to be preferred over interior, since the solar radiation is stopped before it penetrates the building. As mentioned earlier, heat-absorbing glasses can reduce solar radiation by a factor of approximately one-third, and reflective glasses can reduce radiation by as much as 80%. Outside overhangs are especially effective on south-facing windows because it is possible to arrange them so that the sun's rays are blocked in the summertime, yet in the winter when heat is needed, the sun is allowed to shine into the window.

Building Orientation. Rotating a structure can often materially affect heat gains or heat losses. Generally, the long dimension should be oriented in the east-west direction rather than north-south. This rule of thumb is particularly valid because the south-facing windows can be shaded as indicated to prevent summer radiation but permit winter radiation.

Building Color. The color of a building affects the absorption or reflection of the sun's rays. To reduce the summer heat gain, a light-colored surface is preferable, and of course to increase heat gains in the winter time a dark color would be better. Type of climate and the need for heating or cooling are the determining factors in the choice of building coloration. This is particularly true of the roofs, since they are most affected by the sun's rays.

There are a number of other strategies with respect to the mechanical heating, ventilating, and air conditioning systems that can yield appreciable energy savings. The list is quite long, but a few of the major possibilities are given below.

Heat Pumps or Reverse-Cycle Units. These vapor-refrigeration cycles operate either as a cooling system or, by reversing the cycle, as a heating system. For cooling they have efficiencies comparable to those of standard air conditioning units or systems. In the heating mode, however, they will deliver from 2 to 4 times the amount of heat that can be had from electric resistance heaters. The degree of improvement depends on the temperature of the heat sink.

Heat Recovery Systems. With special condensers, the heat that would normally be rejected by the refrigeration system to the cooling tower or to the air-cooled condenser can be recovered and used to heat the portions of the structure that require heating. Alternatively, this system can be used for heating domestic water.

Economizer Cycles. This is an arrangement of dampers and controls that permits the use of outside air instead of return air during the cooling cycle, whenever the total heat content of the outside air is less than that of the conditioned space. Frequently the outside air is cool enough to eliminate the need for refrigeration entirely, and at other times its use can result in a reduced load on the refrigeration cycle.

Use of Non-depleting Energy Sources, such as the Sun's Rays. Energy radiating from the sun can be captured either by flat plate solar collectors or by concentrating collectors. Flat plate collectors without glazing are suitable for the efficient collection of solar energy at low temperatures, such as for heating swimming pools. To achieve higher temperatures (up to approximately 200°F), single- or double-glazed flat plate collectors are efficient. For temperatures above 200°F, concentrating collectors that focus the sun's rays on a small area are more efficient. At present solar heating systems are becoming economically feasible for heating swimming pools and for heating domestic water. Space heating is also feasible in many instances.

Solar cooling systems, which require the use of an absorption refrigeration machine, are relatively inefficient compared to the vapor-compression cycle, having coefficients of performance of approximately 0.6 compared to coefficients of performance of 3 or 4 for the compression cycle. Therefore solar cooling systems are not particularly economic; at best, they are marginal in this respect. Rankine cycles now being developed should be commercially available in the near future and may make solar cooling more attractive.

Solar cells for direct conversion of sunlight to electricity are now being produced with reasonable efficiencies, and it is hoped that these will become cost effective within approximately 10 years.

Air Conditioning Design Considerations

Ventilation. Outdoor or ventilation air is usually mixed with return air and supplied to the air conditioned building through the air conditioning apparatus. The minimum amount of ventilation air supplied is usually dictated by local codes, but in any event it must be at least sufficient to satisfy the maximum of any of the following requirements:

1. Supplies sufficient oxygen to sustain the human metabolic process.
2. Dilutes odors and smoke, particularly tobacco smoke.
3. Pressurizes the building to overcome infiltration of outside air.

The amount of air required to support metabolism is relatively small, being in the order of magnitude of less than 5 cubic feet of air per minute. The dilution of odors and smoke requires a minimum of 5 cubic feet per minute for a nonsmoking person and up to 50 cubic feet per minute and more for cigar smokers.

Pressurization requirements vary depending on the number of windows, the outside wind velocities, and how well the building is sealed; usually, however, they fall within the range of ½ to 2 air changes per hour. The amount of ventilation air is finally determined by studying the occupancy, construction type, building orientation, and usage of the structure.

Design Temperatures. The selection of the design conditions for both the indoor and outdoor will affect the size of the air conditioning and heating plant for any given structure. Summer indoor design temperatures are usually selected between 72 and 75°F, with a relative humidity range averaging 50%. The energy shortage is having a strong influence on a trend to raise the indoor design temperature. In many instances, 78 and even 80°F designs are being considered. For winter, indoor temperatures of 70 to 72°F are usual.

Both summer and winter outdoor design conditions are based on probabilities. It is not economically reasonable to design an air conditioning system to maintain a structure at the indoor design temperature on the warmest anticipated day. The summer outside design is usually taken as the temperature that is exceeded during approximately 1% of the daylight hours during the summer cooling season. For competitive situations and where budgets are tight, the outdoor design may be selected as one that is exceeded 2.5% during the daylight hours of the summer cooling season. Since the wet-bulb temperature is related to the total heat content of the air, it is essential that outdoor summer design conditions include a statement of the wet-bulb temperature as well as the anticipated dry-bulb temperature.

Winter design temperature is usually selected as the medium of extremes; that is, the median temperature of the extremes encountered each year during a successive period of years. For the more competitive job, 1% may be used.

Air Distribution Systems. Cooled and heated air, moved by fans or blowers through necessary heat exchangers, is distributed through ductwork to air diffusers, where it is introduced to the space to be conditioned. Centrifugal or squirrel cage fans are most commonly used, since they are efficient, quiet, and dependable. Forward curved squirrel cage fans are frequently employed because they operate at relatively low speeds and are quite quiet. Fans with the blades inclined backward or with airfoil sections are used for situations requiring higher pressures or variable pressures. These fans have nonoverloading characteristics: that is, fan motor horsepower cannot exceed a fixed value for any particular fan speed; thus there is less opportunity to overload the fan motor. Axial flow fans (propeller type) have the advantage that the airflow does not change direction in going through the fan. Axial flow fans can be constructed to provide efficiencies comparable to the squirrel cage, but in general they tend to be considerably noisier, and special precautions must be taken with respect to the sound level.

Duct systems are generally constructed of galvanized steel sheets and can be either round or rectangular. Oval ducts are also available. Although round ducts are usually less expensive than rectangular sections to fabricate and to install, space requirements and other considerations may dictate the choice of rectangular shapes. Fiberglass ducts are now available in both rigid and flexible round types. Rectangular fiberglass ductwork can be fabricated from board stock. Fiberglass ducts are competitive with sheet metal plus insulation and weigh considerably less.

The total pressure in a low-pressure air distribution duct system seldom exceeds 4 inches of water column. Medium pressure systems usually go from about 4 to 6 inches, of water column, with high pressure systems being those in excess of 6 inches of water column. The higher the total pressure of the system, the greater the fan horsepower required, and since the fan horsepower represents an appreciable fraction of the total energy used by an air conditioning system, it is desirable to maintain the total pressure of a duct system at the minimum value permissible. Low-pressure ductwork, of course, is larger, therefore requires greater clearance areas, higher building height, and more sheet-metal.

Air leakage from duct systems is a function of the static pressure within the duct. To minimize leakage, ducts should be sealed or taped at the joints. This is particularly important as the pressure becomes higher.

Air diffusers are available in a wide variety of styles, shapes, and sizes. They range from bar-type grilles for wall mounting, to round, rectangular, and slot-shaped diffusers for ceilings. There are types that come as integrated units with lights and with acoustical tile ceilings. Type and style of air diffuser depend to a large extent on the architectural effect desired. Air diffusers represent a relatively small percentage of the total capital cost of an air conditioning system and are usually the only visible portion of that system; thus cost should not be the overriding consideration in selection of the style and type of air diffuser.

System Considerations for a Particular Structure

The choice of a particular system to heat and cool a structure is influenced by many factors, including economics, design temperatures, physical space availability, the need for maintaining separate thermal temperature zones, the availability of energy (particularly of the source of energy), and aesthetics.

Air conditioning systems of certain types tend to fit certain structures. Hospitals, for example, which have similar requirements, tend to utilize similar air conditioning systems. Following is a list of typical building types, together with the usual choice of air conditioning system for each type of structure.

Office Buildings. Office buildings should be designed for a shifting tenant occupancy. There is usually a need for many independent zones of control and for great flexibility to permit rearranging of these zones as the population shifts.

Small 1- or 2-story offices can be served by roof-top, packaged, air-cooled units. These lack some flexibility, but the capital cost is very low and any other type of zoning system becomes quite expensive in small increments.

Larger structures can be very well served by double-duct or multizone units. As mentioned previously, however, great care should be exercised in the application of this type of system to minimize energy waste. Double-duct systems provide great flexibility, both in zoning and in revising the system, and have been widely applied to office structures.

Highrise buildings are frequently served by induction-type systems for the skin and either variable volume or double duct for the core. Normally the core of such a structure requires no heat. Induction systems call for a minimum of shaft space and relatively small ducts and pipes. The system is very flexible and has a great potential for zoning.

Also suitable for large office buildings are fan coil units, either two or four pipe, or the electrohydronic system. These types do not have the flexibility of the induction system or the double duct; however some of the capital cost can be deferred until tenant space is leased. This advantage is particularly noticeable with the electrohydronic system.

Theaters. Theaters do not require temperature zoning capability. They are often nighttime loads and have high latent heat loads because of the large number of people per square foot of floor area. This means that the system must have a high dehumidifying capacity. Theaters are frequently air conditioned with single-zone fan coil units using either chilled water or direct expansion refrigeration. Outside air or ventilation requirements are usually high. Special care must be taken to reduce noise levels to acceptable values.

The heating of theaters depends on available fuel and may be from natural gas or other fossil fuel, electric resistance heat, or by reverse cycle refrigeration (heat pump).

Factories. Factories are most often single-story structures. They are usually of a large, clear span height. Most factories are heated and ventilated only, although there is a continuing and growing trend toward more and more comfort cooling. Certain applications, such as textile weaving and color printing, require control of temperature and/or humidity to maintain production or quality. In many instances, the increased productivity and reduced level of errors and rejections that accompany comfort-controlled atmospheres are adding to the economic feasibility of air conditioned factories. Separate thermal zones, if they exist at all, are usually large and can be handled by independent units. Either large rooftop, self-contained package air conditioners or central chilled water plants with fan coils have been effectively applied to factories.

Hospitals. Comfort systems for hospitals are under severe regulatory code restrictions.

Surgical suites normally require 100% outside air to flush out odors and hazardous vapors. Exhaust openings are usually located near the floor of surgical suites in order to capture heavy gases, and humidity control is essential because of the presence of static electric discharges that might ignite explosive vapors.

Nurseries, delivery rooms, intensive care areas, and cardiac care areas, are all subject to special temperature and humidity control requirements.

Extreme care must be taken in hospitals to prevent cross-contamination; thus pressure differentials between different parts of the hospital must be maintained, to minimize migration of organisms from contaminated areas. This is especially important for isolation wards.

Because of the need to minimize cross-contamination between patient areas, the wards are often conditioned using induction units or individual fan coil units for each unit. Central air handling systems can be employed, provided adequate air filtration is included. Fiberglass ductwork is usually not specified for hospital air conditioning, since it provides good breeding grounds for microorganisms.

Hotels. Because of the variable occupancy loads in hotels, central systems are usually not desirable except for the public areas of these establishments. Individual hotel rooms are normally conditioned by means of induction-type air terminals or individual fan coil units for each room.

Schools. Since it is desirable that individual classrooms be separately zoned, classrooms are usually served by fan coil units located either in the room under the windows or remote. In any case adequate ventilation must be provided, and special care taken to minimize noise.

Stores and Shopping Centers. Some large shopping malls employ central water chilling and water heating systems. Individual stores are air conditioned using separate fan coil units for each store, served by chilled and/or hot water. Smaller shopping centers and individual stores that are not a part of a shopping center usually are conditioned with self-contained rooftop packages. Air distribution is less critical in commercial establishments than in office buildings, hospitals, and so on, because shoppers are moving about and are not as sensitive to drafts.

Apartment Buildings and Multiple-Residence Structures. Lowrise apartments, that is, from one to three stories, could be served from forced air furnaces located in each apartment, with cooling coming from a remote air-cooled condenser, usually mounted on the roof. Central chilled water plants have been successfully applied to such buildings with individual fan coils for each apartment. Water-to-air heat pumps (electrohydronic system) with a circulating heat sink from which the individual heat pumps can either accept or reject heat have also been successfully applied to apartments.

Highrise structures for housing are most likely to use central water chilling and water heating plants with individual fan coils for each apartment. The electrohydronic system is also a suitable choice.

With apartments, it is essential that each tenant have individual control of the hours of operation of his or her own system and also of the temperature to be obtained.

Detached Residences. A great majority of detached residences are heated with forced air furnaces, the air being directed through a direct expansion cooling coil. This coil is connected by refrigerant piping to a remote air-cooled condensing unit to furnish the cooling. In larger residences, it is often desirable to separate the house into separate zones, usually into sleeping areas and living areas.

The threatened natural gas shortage has induced many designers to apply heat pumps for heating and cooling of residences, and this trend will no doubt accelerate.

6 ELECTRICAL ENGINEERING

By FRANK J. MOREAUX

Frank J. Moreaux studied at the Detroit Institute in Detroit, as well as at the University of California, Los Angeles. He is a member of the Illuminating Engineering Society and is a Registered Engineer in the state of California. He has worked for the United States Navy, the Marquardt Aircraft Company, and the Radio Corporation of America; for the past 15 years he has been in private practice as a consulting electrical engineer in Los Angeles.

Electricity is one of the great cosmic forces that can be harnessed to man's use. The others are weak nuclear force, strong nuclear force, gravity, magnetism, and inertia. Electricity is commonly transmitted from one location to another through insulated wires; it is generated by steam and/or water turbines and, in recent years, nuclear reactors.

The eldest of the three types of generator, water turbines use controlled water pressure from dams. Steam turbines are powered by natural gas, gasoline, diesel oil, or coal (the fossil fuels). Since the supplies of these materials are dependent on nature's diminishing resources, nuclear power seems to be the best means of filling future fuel needs.

There are two types of nuclear power plant: the ordinary reactor and the breeder reactor. The latter manufactures its own fuel—synthetic plutonium—and can produce enough surplus to feed ordinary reactors. The sole difficulty of building nuclear reactor plants involves their enormous initial cost. Also, there has been some public outcry regarding possible leakage of deadly radioactive matter from existing power plants.

Electrical flow requires a continuous conductive path; at least two wires are needed: one leading to the device to be activated and another returning to the power source. This is known as a circuit.

Harnessed electricity flows in currents of two types: direct (dc) and alternating (ac). Direct current flows steadily in one direction, from positive to negative.

Alternating current reverses its direction of flow at regular intervals. Ordinary household current in the United States usually has a frequency of 60 cycles per second. This means that current flows in one direction, then in the opposite direction, repeating the entire cycle 60 times per second, reversing its direction 120 times per second. In the SI (International System) of nomenclature, the unit "cycle per second" is the hertz (Hz).

Electrical pressure between two wires is measured in volts (V) by a voltmeter. Flow of electricity (electrons) through a wire is measured in amperes (A), measured with an ammeter. Resistance to flow is measured in ohms (Ω) by an ohmmeter.

Basic Law of Electricity: Ohm's Law

Ohm's law expresses the relationship between voltage, current, resistance: volts equals amperes times ohms. The corresponding symbols are as follows:

$$V = I \times R$$

where V = voltage
I = amperes
R = ohms (of resistance)

Sample Problem. If 120 volts dc is driving current through a 60-ohm resistor, find the current, using Ohm's law.

Answer

$$I = \frac{V}{R} = \frac{120}{60} = 2 \text{ A}$$

Power

In direct current, flowing steadily in one direction from positive to negative, power is the product of volts and amperes, measured in watts (w): $W = V \times I$. Another unit, the kilowatt (kW), is equal to 1000 watts. Both watts and kilowatts are measured with a wattmeter.

Sample Problem. If 120 volts passes 2 amperes through a resistor, find the power dissipated.

Answer

$$W = V \times I$$
$$120 \times 2 = 240 \text{ W or } 0.24 \text{ kW}$$

When power is calculated for alternating current, a ratio called "power factor" (PF) enters the picture; this is the ratio of true power to apparent power ($W = V \times I \times PF$). Where apparent power is volts times amperes, PF can have values ranging from 0 to 1.0. When current flows only through a resistor, PF = 1.0.

Sample Problem. If 240 volts ac causes 10 amperes to flow into a motor whose power factor is 0.8, find the apparent power and the real power in the motor.

Answer

$$\text{Apparent power} = V \times \text{I}$$
$$240 \times 10.0 = 2400 \text{ V-A or watts}$$
$$\text{True power} = V \times I \times PF$$
$$240 \times 10.0 \times 0.8 = 1920 \text{ watts or } 19.2 \text{ kW}$$

Therefore low power factor is a loss of usable power: 2400 − 1920 = 480 watts lost in the system.

Sources of Electricity

A dc generator, battery, or rectifier can generate direct current. When a dc generator is driven by an ac motor, the combination is called a motor generator (MG) set. There are two general types of battery, primary and secondary. The recharging of a primary battery (e.g., a "pen light" battery) is difficult and unsatisfactory. Secondary batteries, such as the lead-acid type used in automobiles or emergency-generator batteries, can be recharged many times. A rectifier is a device that converts ac to dc; it also supplies direct current or recharges batteries.

Alternating current can be generated by an ac generator (called an alternator) or produced by an inverter from a dc source. Power companies generate most ac in huge alternators; the electricity is then transmitted through wires to the user.

Transformers

A transformer, which changes ac voltage up or down, consists of two (primary and secondary) separate windings of wire wrapped around an iron core. This device may be used to step voltage up to a high level for transmission over great distances. Another transformer, installed on the user's property, brakes the voltage down to a safe value for household or commercial use. The product of the voltage and the current in the primary winding must equal the product of the voltage and the current in the secondary winding.

An efficient transformer dissipates about 2% of the power flowing through it.

Phases. Alternating current systems have another property—they operate in phases. Two systems are common in commercial work, single phase and 3-phase. For example, utility companies generate and distribute only 3-phase power. A 3-phase system gives the same amount of power as three connected single-phase systems acting in unison. Single-phase power may be acquired from 3-phase systems, but not vice versa. The power formula of a 3-phase power system is $W = V \times I \times PF \times 1.73$. The factor 1.73, which is necessary in making calculations for a 3-phase system, is the square root of 3, a standard conversion factor.

AC System Connections. A single-phase system may use either two or three wires. With a transformer as a power source, two secondary wires may be brought onto the customer's property. This system will provide only 120 volts. Older buildings were so wired, but the system is inadequate for modern construction.

With three secondary wires from the transformer, including a center tap connection (called the "neutral" wire), either 120 or 240 volts may be supplied to the customer. Large loads such as water heaters and stove-oven units may be connected to the two outer wires to receive 240 volts; small loads such as lamps and small appliances may be connected between the center tap and one of the two outer wires to obtain 120 volts. The two secondary voltages have a ratio of 2:1. The center tap is connected to the earth ("grounded") by a water pipe to dissipate abnormal voltages that might flow through the secondary wires because of leakage inside the transformer. This system is a 3-wire, single-phase system, providing 120/240 volts.

A 3-phase system has either three or four wires. Its transformer consists of three single-phase transformers connected to the power system. The secondary windings may be connected in only two ways: "star/wye" or "delta."

Three secondary terminals exist in the delta connection, and voltage is the same between any two secondary wires. Usual values are 240 and 480 volts. One of the three secondary windings is often center tapped and grounded for safety; a fourth neutral wire may be brought to the user from this connection. Voltage between the neutral and either of the two adjacent wires will be half the voltage between any two corners of the delta. A 240-volt, 4-wire delta can provide any or all of the following voltages simultaneously:

240 volts	3 phase
240 volts	1 phase
120 volts	1 phase

If the line-to-line voltage were 480 volts, the voltage table would be as follows:

480 volts	3 phase
480 volts	1 phase
240 volts	1 phase

An alternate 3-phase transformer secondary connection is the star, or wye. One end of each secondary is joined to form a neutral wire that is grounded for safety. The voltage from line to line is 1.73 times the line to neutral voltage: $1.73 \times 120 = 208$ volts. A 3-phase load connected to this system is 208 rated volts line-to-line and is called a 3-phase, 4-wire, 120/208 volt system. Another standard voltage for this system is 277/480 volts ($277 \times 1.73 = 480$ V).

Table 3.25 lists the secondary connection systems in general use.

Table 3.25 Standard Secondary Connections

Number Phases	Voltage (V)	Number of Wires	Connection Name
1	120	2	2-Wire
	120/240	3	3-Wire
3	240	3	Delta
	120/240	4	Delta
	480	3	Delta
3	208	3	Star or wye
	120/208	4	Star or wye
	480	3	Star or wye
	277/480	4	Star or wye

Electric Lights

The most widely used electric lights are the incandescent and the fluorescent. The incandescent lamp is cheap but inefficient; it consists of a filament sealed in a glass envelope. When the filament is heated to a high temperature by the passage of current, it glows. The power factor is 1.0.

A fluorescent lamp is more efficient and more complex than an incandescent. An arc of electricity—the same kind that causes a weakened power system to short out—is created inside a glass tube with metal terminals sealing both ends. The arc excites minerals coating the inner walls of the glass tube, and the minerals "fluoresce," producing light. The power factor is between .80 and .95, lagging.

Lighting Fixtures

A lighting fixture includes the lamp, socket(s) for mounting it, reflectors, diffusers and, for fluorescents, starters and ballasts. The voltage rating of a fixture may not exceed 300 volts-to-ground in commercial buildings, 150 in residences. Usual ratings are 277 and 120 volts, respectively.

Motors

The type of motor to be used in a power system is determined by the nature of the power system and by the kind of load to be driven. All motors must be protected from overload by thermal overload relays.

For small loads of up to ½ horsepower, the *single-phase ac motor* predominates. It is an induction motor of not quite constant speed.

CATE SCHOOL CHAPEL
Carpinteria, California
Architect: George Vernon Russell
Photo: Office

The *3-phase induction motor,* on the other hand, is used for large loads. It runs at nearly constant speed and is rugged, simple, economical, smaller and lighter than other motor types of equal horsepower, easy to maintain, and almost trouble-free, although its power factor is only about .8 (80%).

The *3-phase synchronous ac motor* has a constant speed. It can adjust its power factor over a wide range, which sometimes offsets the lagging power factor of heavy loads. Since it is more expensive to buy and maintain than the 3-phase induction motor, it is rarely used.

Small *single-phase synchronous motors* are used in electric clocks, tape recorders, and record players, where constant speed is necessary.

The small-sized *''universal'' motor* operates on ac or dc. Its speed is not constant, decreasing as the load increases. An example of its application is the motorized bicycle.

The main advantage of *dc motors* is adjustable speed control. These are the motors used on elevators. They require more maintenance than ac motors and are also more expensive.

Electric Heaters. Electric heaters are resistors that convert electrical power into heat, which then may be transferred to air or water. Electric heaters have a power factor of 1.0 and are 100% efficient.

Receptacles. A receptacle is a wall outlet for connecting small appliances, table lamps, office machines, and so on. Receptacles in residences must be placed at approximately 12-foot (or less) intervals along walls of a room. New construction generally requires 3-wire receptacles, the third wire being a safety ground connection.

Switches. Switches for controlling lights and receptacles are mounted on walls adjacent to the doors of rooms. The "off" side of the toggle switch interrupts the hot wire to a fixture.

When there are several entries to a room, as to a hallway or a living room, and it should be possible to control the lights from more than one location, a system of 3-way and 4-way switches may be installed. For two control locations, two 3-way switches should be installed; for each additional location, a 4-way switch should be added.

Rheostats or Dimmers. A rheostat is a variable resistor placed in a circuit to permit fine control of flowing current. It is sometimes installed for adjusting incandescent lighting levels. Fluorescent lamps can be dimmed, but special rheostats and ballasts are required.

Starters and Contactors. A contactor is a magnetically operated switch connecting or disconnecting wires to various electrical devices. When used to control a motor, this switch is called a starter and includes overload relays or thermal cutouts to protect the motor from overheating.

Starters and contactors may be directly controlled by thermostats, toggle switches, pressure switches, or other sensing devices.

Wire Sizes

Wires come in various standard sizes. The smaller sizes are designated by American Wire Gauge (AWG) numbers (#14 AWG, #10 AWG, #2 AWG, etc.). Number 14 wire, for example, is the smallest size permitted for lighting and receptacle circuits.

The smaller the number, the larger the wire size. When a size larger than 1 was designed and introduced, it was called 0. Numbers 00, 000, and 0000 are still larger. The basis of numbering large building wire is the circular mill or circular area of wire (CM): 250,000 CM, 500,000 CM, and so on.

Selecting Wire Sizes. The various electrical codes include tables of current-carrying capacities for different sizes and types of wire. Since there are many variances among the numerous codes, an architect should consult only the code applicable to a particular project.

Circuits that supply power to motors must be sized to carry no more than 80% of their rated amperes. Long-period loads must also be limited to 80% of the conductor ratings. Loads should be limited to two-thirds of the rated amperes to allow load growth.

Selecting an adequate wire does not assure an acceptable design. Another factor to consider is voltage drop. Voltage drop due to wire-system resistance should not exceed 5% maximum, preferably 3%, to minimize flickering of lights when load changes occur.

Table 3.26 shows copper wire–conduit sizes and ampere capacity (not design), according to the National Electrical Code (NEC).

Table 3.26 NEC Sizes and Amperage for Copper Wire Conduits

		Trade Size (in) for Number of Wires in Conduit			
Amperage (A)	Wire Size	1	2	3	4
15	14	½	½	½	½
20	12	½	½	½	½
30	10	½	¾	½	¾
40	8	½	¾	¾	1
50	6	½	¾	1	1
70	4	½	1	1	1¼
95	2	¾	1	1¼	1¼
110	1	¾	1¼	1¼	1½
125	0	1	1¼	1½	2
145	00	1	1½	1½	2

Sample Problem. Select a wire size for a conduit feeding a continuous single-phase load of 7.5 kilowatts at 120 volts.

Answer. 7.5 kW = 7500 W,

$$\frac{7500}{120} = 62.5 \text{ A}$$

Allowing 80% load, wire must be sized for 62.5/0.8 = 78 amperes. #2 wire may be used.

Wire Materials. Copper and aluminum are widely used as electrical conductors. Copper wire, which has better conductivity than aluminum, may be used in a smaller size for a given current. However the price of copper has risen in recent years, and aluminum is an adequate substitute. Both metals are acceptable.

Wiring Methods. The oldest wiring method, the "knob-and-tube" approach, is permitted in certain rural areas, mostly in older farmhouses. It is never used in modern construction.

Nonmetallic-sheathed cable (trade name: "Romex") is allowed in some jurisdictions for residential or commercial work. It consists of two or more wires insulated by a braid or plastic sheath. No other covering is required. Where permitted by code, it may be installed

UNION BUILDING, LOUISIANA STATE UNIVERSITY
Baton Rouge, Louisiana
Architects Associated: Mathes & Bergman, Wilson-Sandifer & Associates, Desmond-Miremont & Associates
Photo: Gleason

exposed or concealed; it cannot be used in commercial garages or embedded in concrete.

Interlocked armored cable, commonly known as "BX" cable, consists of two or more conductors protected by a spiral wrap of metal armor. It is factory assembled; individual conductors cannot be removed or replaced. In accordance with local codes, it may be concealed or exposed for residential or commercial structures; it cannot be embedded in concrete, however. Because the armor must be cut back at each end to permit access to the wires, there is risk of damage to the insulation. Thus a fiber sleeve must be installed inside the armor at both ends of every piece of cable.

Electrical metallic tubing (EMT), or "thinwall," must have its own permanent duct system in which individually insulated wires are installed. It consists of thin steel tubes, protected by galvanizing and joined by clamps. Where permitted by local codes, it may be installed concealed or exposed in commercial or residential structures.

Rigid conduit is like EMT but has the same wall thickness as Schedule 40 water pipe. It may be protected by enamel or galvanizing, but enamel is permitted indoors or in dry locations only. Rigid conduit is joined by threaded couplings. Although expensive, it is the most durable and rugged of all conductor systems and may be used in any location throughout the United States.

Flexible metal conduit—often called "flex"—may be used concealed or exposed but not buried. It may have a waterproof jacket for use in damp locations.

Separation of Services

Power services of different voltages and frequencies may be mixed in a common duct system as long as the following requirements are met: all circuits in the duct must be insulated for the highest voltage present on any circuit in the duct; no circuit may carry more than 600 volts.

However some classes of electrical circuit must be kept separate from others, in accord with safety requirements. The telephone companies require a separate duct system, which they do not share with others. Since intercom circuits are sensitive to noise and other interference, they too require separate ducts.

Overcurrent Protection

When excessive current flows steadily through a wire, the wire immediately begins to overheat, creating a fire hazard. In response to this problem, two principal types of overcurrent protection have been devised: the fuse and the circuit-breaker.

A fuse consists of a small piece of wire mounted in a fiber sleeve or glass plug. When excessive current flow occurs, the wire in the fuse melts, interrupting the flow. The fuse is a one-time-only device and must be replaced when it has "blown." The glass-plug fuse is rated up to 30 amperes; the cartridge fuse goes to very large amperages. The time required for a fuse to blow is in inverse proportion to the amount of excess current passing through it. Thus a short-circuit will cause a fuse wire to melt very quickly, whereas a moderate overload may be carried for seconds, even minutes, before the fuse wire melts.

The circuit-breaker, a more complex and expensive device, contains both a fuse and a switch in one unit and can be operated manually. It disconnects a circuit automatically in case of overload on that circuit. After the trouble or weak point has been found and repaired, the circuit-breaker can be manually reset, with no new parts required.

Every conductor must be supplied at its source with overcurrent protection of a size to match its capacity.

Conduit Sizes

Conduits are designated according to their nominal inside diameters. Electrical codes limit the maximum number of wires of various sizes that can be installed in one conduit of any given diameter. Having established wire sizes adequate for the load(s) that will be placed on them, a designer selects a conduit large enough for the number and size of wires.

Underfloor Duct System

In commercial work, a cellular metal duct system is laid under the floors to provide separate channels for lighting, receptacles, telephones, intercoms, and so on. A concrete floor is poured over the system, and outlets are installed where needed along the ducts. These outlets may be removed and reinstalled at other locations as the occupants' needs change. This versatile, flexible system is widely used in modern construction.

Service Entrance

A power service entrance includes wires, the meter, and the main disconnect switch. To avoid excessive voltage drop and flicker on services of 480 volts or less, the distance from the transformer to the meter should not exceed 100 to 150 feet. If greater distances exist or are required, transformers should be relocated.

Switchboard. The main switchboard for a building receives the incoming power service. It usually contains the billing meter and the required meter transformers. Fuse switches or circuit-breakers route power through separate conductors to various motors and controls, distribution panels, and so on.

The main disconnect switch may be omitted in a small commercial service that has no more than six tenant meters per building. The NEC recommends a minimum service of 3-wire, 100 amperes, for residences.

The principal service for residences is usually located outdoors for convenient access by the fire department. In large commercial buildings, it is usually indoors, but is directly accessible to firemen and other service personnel from an exterior door.

Emergency Power. Given the need to operate at least one fire pump and/or elevator, emergency lights, and other vital loads during a power outage, most large buildings require an emergency generator. Emergency light and power must be arranged for automatic transfer and start.

Elevators may be connected for manual or automatic transfer to the emergency generator; the generator is often sized to carry only one elevator, to be used in the rescue of trapped passengers during an outage. Health-care facilities have more stringent requirements, and these are enumerated in Article 517 of the NEC.

Emergency generators may use gasoline, diesel oil, natural, or butane gas for fuel. All these fuels are adequate for general use, depending on local preference and judgment. Gasoline may be easily stored on site but has limited storage life (1 year), whereas diesel oil can be stored for several years and is much safer to keep. However diesel oil requires more expensive engine construction. Natural and liquefied petroleum gas (LPG), such as butane, can be used in gasoline engines, but since they are pressurized there is a potential hazard of leaks, especially with LPG, which is heavier than air. Natural gas cannot be conveniently stored on site, but LPG can be so stored, and it does not deteriorate with age.

Emergency Circuits. Some circuits are not tied to the main disconnect switch but have their own switches. These are circuits for emergency exit lights, fire alarms, fire pumps, and so on, as described by electrical codes. Such circuits are connected ahead of the main disconnect to permit a fire department to turn off all power except circuitry necessary for fire fighting and evacuation of building occupants.

SCOTTSDALE MEDICAL PAVILION
Scottsdale, Arizona
Architects: Michael & Kemper Goodwin
Photo: C. R. Conley

Automatic Transfer Switches. Sometimes it is necessary to provide protection from loss of power from utility lines. An automatic transfer switch can be arranged to shift critical loads (e.g., national defense installations, hospital operating rooms and life support systems) to an emergency power source when the normal source is lost.

The emergency power source might be a second feeder from another part of the power company's system, or a diesel- or gasoline-fueled generator with automatic starting controls on the customer's property. For small but vital loads such as exit lights, a battery might serve as the emergency power source.

Panels

A panel is an assembly of circuit-breakers in a closed cabinet that provides a central distribution point for branch circuits to a floor or part of a floor in a building. Each breaker of the assembly serves one branch circuit and is sized to match the wire size. There may or may not be a main switch in the panel to disconnect the main feeder coming from a switchboard or another main panel located at or near the service entrance.

Load Estimates

As a rule of thumb for estimating power required for lighting, one watt per square foot for each 10 footcandles of incandescent light may be used; with fluorescents, use ½ watt per square foot for 10 footcandles. When estimating home power needs, a calculation of 3 watts per square foot may be used. For office buildings, 5 to 8 watts per square foot will provide good lighting levels and room for growth. These figures may help to determine lighting and receptacle power needs but not those of mechanical equipment, which are constrained by specific heating and cooling loads.

Voltage Levels

Most codes do not permit voltages higher than 150 volts-to-ground in residences. Since the neutral wire of a 3-wire, single-phase, 120/240 volt service is at ground potential, neither of the other two wires can exceed 150 volts-to-ground. For industrial and commercial buildings, higher voltages may be used, such as 240- and 480-volt systems.

Watt-Hour Meters

A device called a watt-hour meter is installed on the service wires to the customer's property to measure the total energy consumed, for billing purposes. On services to buildings using large loads, a kilowatt demand attachment may be added to the watt-hour meter to allow measurement of maximum power flow at any time since the last meter reading. For such users, an electrical bill is based on energy consumed and maximum power flow. Sometimes other factors affect the billing agreement, such as power factor and time of day of maximum use.

Grounding

For safety's sake, all metal enclosures housing electrical equipment or wires must be intentionally grounded to the earth through a connection consisting of bare wire or green insulated wires. (Only the safety ground wires may be green.) The preferred method is a water pipe ground connection near the power service entrance. The neutral or "identified" wire of the system must be grounded only once, at the service entrance, by connection to the ground wire.

A portable electrical device likely to be used in damp locations (a dehumidifier, electric hedge-clippers, etc.) must have a green safety wire connected to its frame and to the large extra pin on the cord plug. This pin is connected by way of ground wires or other method to the water pipe. A green wire does not normally carry electric current except in case of an accidental ground in an appliance or a short-circuit between two wires.

A *short-circuit* occurs when two insulated, current-carrying wires accidentally come into contact. Then the fuse wire melts ("blowing" the fuse), or the circuit-breaker trips to interrupt current flow. A "ground" refers to an insulated wire having had its insulating sheath damaged, making contact with its grounded metal enclosure or some other metal part, thus permitting excess current to flow, causing a short-circuit.

Codes

Several electrical codes exist, each one legally enforceable in certain areas. Many large cities (such as Los Angeles and New York) have written and adopted their own codes. In other areas the governing authorities may adopt some or all of an existing code such as the National Electrical Code, published by the National Fire Protection Association. Alternatively, a city may adopt the NEC, then alter it and add exceptions to accommodate local conditions or preferences.

Illumination

Light is a form of energy that is produced by radiant heat energy. The three commonly used techniques for generating light involve the use of incandescent, fluorescent, and arc lamps. Incandescent lamps consist of a tungsten filament through which electric current is passed. The tungsten rises in temperature until it glows brightly. Thomas Edison developed this principle in 1879. In an arc lamp, an electric arc is caused to jump between the tips of two electrodes. Arc light is extremely intense and is used for theatrical spotlights, searchlights, and "neon" advertising signs. Fluorescent lamps are arc lamps in which the arc is confined to a glass tube whose walls are coated with minerals that "fluoresce" when struck by electrons in the arc stream. The resulting light is soft, pleasant, and of low brightness; the bulbs come in various tints, and these lamps are about 3 times as efficient as incandescent lamps.

Illumination used for residences usually entails incandescent or fluorescent lamps. Fluorescents are endemic to modern commercial buildings.

Illumination Level. Several factors influence the eye's ability to see well and comfortably: illumination level, reflection of light, contrast, and glare. Illumination level is measured in footcandles as light energy falling on a work surface.

Lumens are a measure of total light output from a bare lamp operating with rated voltage. Every standard lamp has a rated lumen output. The number of lumens per square foot reaching a work surface is the illumination level in footcandles and the basis of specific light levels. Unless otherwise stated, the measurement is made on a horizontal surface 30 inches above the floor.

Fixture design determines the shape and placement of reflectors and diffusers and greatly affects the number of lumens reaching a work surface. Size, shape, room color, and fixture height also influence a fixture's efficiency. All these factors combined represent a "coefficient of utilization" (CU), which can be regarded as a measure of a fixture's total efficiency.

Reflections. Reflections are either specular or diffuse. The specular type come from glossy surfaces, where bright light sources may be seen as images on the surfaces. Diffuse reflection is from matte surfaces and does not form images.

GHIRARDELLI SQUARE
San Fráncisco, California
Architects: Wurster Bernardi & Emmons, Inc.
Photo: R. Sturtevant

As previously mentioned, the CU of light fixtures is affected by room shape and finish. Walls absorb some of the light that strikes them. When walls are placed far apart (large room), less light loss occurs through absorption than is experienced in small rooms. Floor, wall, and ceiling finishes should be of high reflectance.

Large, uncurtained windows transmit light and have a reflectance value approaching zero. The CU of fixtures near a window is substantially reduced. Curtains, drawn after dark, will help to overcome this light loss.

Contrast. Extreme or abrupt changes in illumination level between rooms or in different parts of the same space should be avoided. A desirable ratio is 3:1, and 5:1 should not be exceeded.

Glare. Direct glare results from a lamp bulb that is directly visible to the eye. The brightness of bare incandescent lamps is greater than that of fluorescent lamps. Reflected glare results when an image of the light source is reflected from a glossy surface into a viewer's eyes.

Brightness. Light intensity reflected or emitted from a surface or lamp is measured in footlamberts by a light meter. In the case of a nonluminous, diffusely reflecting surface, brightness is the product of incidental footcandles (fc) multiplied by the reflectance of a surface. If 100 footcandles falls on a surface of 60% reflectance, the brightness of the surface will be 60 footlamberts. Typical brightness values of a light source are 2800 lumens for a 40-watt fluorescent tube, 470 lumens for a 40-watt incandescent lamp.

Lighting Levels. The Illumination Engineering Society (IES) has published standards recommending certain light intensities for specific jobs. Table 3.27 presents a few of these values.

Uniformity of Illumination. Near-uniformity of illumination level may be achieved by close spacing of fixtures. Though permitted maximum spacing varies with type of fixture and type of lighting (direct or indirect), a rule of thumb is that fixtures may be spaced a

Table 3.27 Some Light Intensities Recommended by the IES

Application	Intensity (fc)
Residential	
Hallways and general illumination	10
Work areas, such as kitchen, reading, letter-writing desks	50
Offices	
Corridors, stairways	20
Regular office work	100
Detailed drafting	200
Factories	
General illumination	50
Assembly-work area	100
Inspection	200

distance not exceeding their mounting height above the floor.

Fluorescent Versus Incandescent Lamps. Incandescent lamps require only a simple, inexpensive fixture. Fluorescent lamps cost more to buy and install, but they have several advantages.

1 Electricity-into-light conversion efficiency is far greater in fluorescent lamps: incandescent lamps are about 2.5% efficient; fluorescent lamps with ballasts are about 7.5% efficient.
2 An air conditioning or refrigeration system must be sized to include heat loss from the lighting system, and fluorescent lamps suffer considerably less heat loss than do incandescent lamps, thus cutting the energy use cost of the refrigeration system.
3 Low brightness is easily obtained with fluorescent lamps.
4 A fluorescent lamp has a rated life of approximately 10 times that of an incandescent lamp (7500 vs. 750 h).

An incandescent lamp design having improved characteristics has recently been introduced to the domestic consumers. Instead of the usual gas fill of argon and nitrogen, krypton is used. This is the "5-year" lightbulb that supposedly has a life of 1000 hours or more, with slightly improved efficiency.

Table 3.28 shows costs of lighting systems using various lamp types.

Table 3.28 Costs Associated with Various Lamp Types

Type of Lamp	Capital Cost	Operating Cost
Incandescent	Low	High
Fluorescent	High	Medium
Mercury vapor	Medium	Medium
Metal halide	Medium	Low
High-pressure sodium	High	Low

Lamp Life (Lumen Output). Incandescent lamps are very sensitive to small changes in voltage. For example, a 5% increase in voltage above the rated value will give more than 15% increase in lumen output, while simultaneously halving expected lamp life. Reducing voltage has the opposite effect; thus it is sometimes advantageous to operate an incandescent fixture at less than rated voltage. Where costs of lamp replacement are high, lower voltage will greatly extend lamp life, though with reduced output. This effect may be compensated by using larger or more numerous fixtures.

Fluorescent lamps are much less affected by changes in operating voltage. A 5% voltage increase causes a fluorescent lamp to increase its light output about 5%; with reduced voltage, the converse is true. Operating life is somewhat reduced at high or low voltages, but the strongest influence on the life of a fluorescent lamp is number of starts: frequent startings greatly reduce expected life.

Conversion Benefits. If a need arises for higher lighting intensity in an existing area equipped with incandescent fixtures, a significant increase can be obtained by changing to fluorescent fixtures. There is no increase in electrical load and no need for rewiring. The light increase is due to the greater efficiency of fluorescent lamps.

Direct Versus Indirect Lighting. An angled fixture that directs most of its light upward, reflecting it from the ceiling to the rest of the room, is an example of indirect lighting. No bright sources of glare are visible to the eye, and illumination is soft and uniform, without harsh shadows or specular reflections. However because much of the light is absorbed into the ceiling and is not reflected into the space below, the system is not as efficient as direct light. In addition, an indirect system requires fairly high ceilings (10 ft or more) to work properly. Maximum light level is also constrained by ceiling brightness, which should not exceed 400 footlamberts.

Direct fixtures may be applied in rooms with 8-foot ceilings; a good fixture design will not cause excessive glare.

Recessed fixtures (available for both incandescent and fluorescent lamps) are a form of direct lighting, adaptable to suspended ceilings or for use where fixtures must be inconspicuous. The ceiling itself is fairly dark, since it depends on light reflected from walls or floor for its illumination.

A *cove fixture* is a semienclosed bare lamp concealed from direct view. Light is directed outward and upward, as in indirect lighting; it illuminates a ceiling, leaving the remaining space dimly lighted. The viewer's gaze is thus pulled toward the ceiling. A reflector behind the lamp improves its efficiency slightly.

Luminous ceilings consist of hung or suspended ceilings made of translucent panels with bare fluorescent lamps mounted in the space between the structural ceiling and the panels. The panels serve as diffusers; illumination is uniform and shadow free and has very low glare. Luminous ceilings are not especially efficient due to loss in the translucent panels.

Eggcrate louvers are fastened to direct light fixtures to restrict the angle at which the lamp can be seen. This ploy reduces glare, but it also reduces the light output of the fixture. As Table 3.29 indicates, lighting fixtures can be divided into five categories for classification and measurement.

Selection of Fixture Types. The illumination for an air conditioned building should come from fluorescent lamps because of their higher efficiency and lower heat-loss. Where flat, uniform, shadowless light is desired, indirect or semidirect lighting, or luminous ceilings, should be selected.

Table 3.29 Light Distribution Available from Various Systems

Type of System	Light Distribution
Direct	90% or more, directed downward
Semidirect	60–90%, directed downward
Generally diffuse or direct/indirect	Approximately half upward, half downward
Semiindirect	60–90%, directed upward
Indirect	90% or more, directed upward limited to about 75 foot-candles

EASTERN AIRLINES TERMINAL BUILDING
Boston, Massachusetts
Architect: Minoru Yamasaki & Associates
Photo: B. Korab

Indirect lighting fixtures require mounting at least 18 to 24 inches below a ceiling to avoid excessive brightness near the fixture. Areas with unattractive or low-reflectance ceilings (factories, basement workrooms, etc.) may benefit from direct lighting, which is independent of ceiling reflectance. In this way, a clutter of pipes and ducts can be made less conspicuous.

Fluorescent Lamp Auxiliaries. A necessary auxiliary to a fluorescent lamp is a ''ballast,'' which is an inductance to limit current flowing through the lamp to its rated value. The ballast reduces a lamp's power factor to less than 1.0, lagging. ''Preheated'' fixtures require a ''starter'' to heat the filaments at both ends of the tube. ''Rapid start–instant start'' (Slimline) fixtures do not need starters.

Mercury-Vapor Lamps. Mercury-vapor lamps are arc lamps with the following properties: very high light output and brightness, long life (16,000 h), and a warm-up time of several minutes. The color of the light varies with the kind of phosphor contained in the tube, although not all types use phosphors. These lamps are used in high-ceilinged commercial buildings or as streetlights. Each lamp must have a ballast, placed in or adjacent to the fixture, or inside the lamp itself.

Emergency Lights. Most codes require emergency lighting for public buildings to avoid panic in case of normal power outage and to permit orderly evacuation. The system need only provide a minimum light level.

The two basic types of emergency lighting system are separate power source or battery and small lamp-and-battery units.

The everyday fixtures may be connected to the separate power source by a switch that will automatically feed current to the fixtures from the emergency power source when and if normal service fails. The lamp-and-battery units are kept charged by the normal power service and turned on manually or automatically when needed.

IBM BUILDING
Albuquerque, New Mexico
Architects: Leroy Miller
Photo: D. Kent

7 SOLAR SYSTEMS

By Roy Irving

Roy Irving is the director of the Solar Heating Technician Training Program at California State College, Sonoma. He and his students have designed, built, and tested a great variety of solar heating systems, including water and air systems of both active and passive configuration. Mr. Irving is an active promoter of passive solar heating systems and low-cost, low-technology active systems.

To many people the field of solar energy seems as mysterious and incomprehensible as the technology of nuclear reactors or putting a man on the moon. It is a common belief that solar heating is not economically feasible and cannot become so until many years of research have produced some major technological breakthroughs.

In reality, the major problem with solar heating is posed by the simplicity of its principles: most people refuse to believe that anything so simple really works. Many very expensive solar heating devices have been purchased because the buyers wrongly believed that the most complicated, technical, and costly system is surely the most efficient system. Yet people on this planet have been heating their homes with solar energy for thousands of years without the benefits of space age technology.

This section gives the architect enough background in solar energy theory to know how to choose wisely be-

Residence, Stony Point, N.Y. James Marston Fitch, architect. This house is oriented to take advantage of a panoramic east-to-south view. It is partially submerged in hillside along west-to-north perimeter, to minimize impact of summer-afternoon sun and prevailing southwest-to-northwest winter winds. 88 per cent of all glass faces southeast, south or southwest. Remainder of perimeter walls are designed to minimize transmission of light and heat – opaque and insulated.

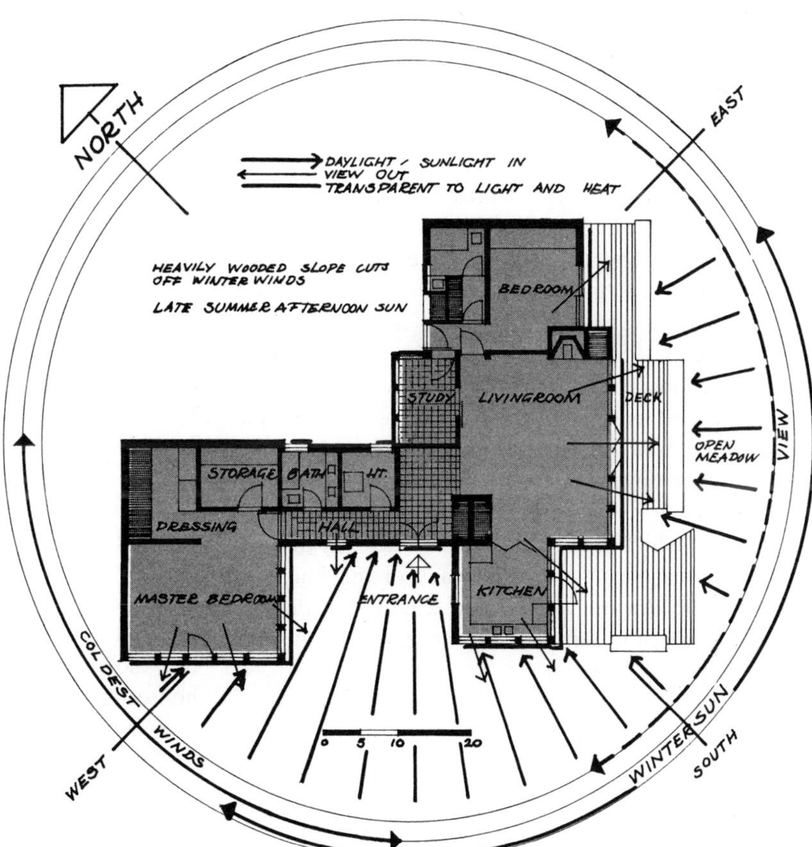

Figure 3.57 *Source.* James Marston Fitch, *American Building, The Environmental Forces That Shape It,* 2nd ed. rev., Schocken Books, New York, 1975.

Figure 3.58 Crystal House.

tween the hundreds of solar heating products now on the market and to know when the desired goal of solar heating can be achieved without the use of conventional solar collectors at all. The basic formulas for calculating collector size, storage system size, and flow rates are included.

Only since the 1930s in the United States has the sun's daily or seasonal energy budget been the subject of specific building designs that attempt to collect, store, and distribute solar energy as a principal heat source for human comfort. The Crystal House at the Chicago World's Fair of 1933 is cited as an early example of the direct "greenhouse" effect whereby glass walls or windows were used as heat collectors. George and William Keck, architects for the Crystal House, began to incorporate the ideas developed from this design into other dwellings. Their designs used large expanses of south-facing glass, which allowed the low winter sun to heat the interior masonry floors and walls of the building during the day (in much the same way as the Pueblo structures), which in turn radiated the stored heat to the spaces during the evening.

History

Now in houses with a south aspect, the sun's rays penetrate into the porticoes in winter, but in summer the path of the sun is right over our heads and above the roof, so that there is shade. If, then, this is the best arrangement, we should build the south side loftier to get the winter sun and the north side lower to keep out the cold winds. To put it shortly, the house in which the owner can find a pleasant retreat at all seasons . . . is presumably at once the pleasantest and the most beautiful.

SOCRATES
FIFTH CENTURY B.C.

The idea of heating dwellings with solar energy is not at all new. In fact, the practice of designing houses with little regard for the path of the sun or local climate is a recent development in human history and is largely confined to the United States and other "developed" countries. It was the development of inexpensive energy sources early in this century that gave us the freedom to design our homes with more attention to privacy and view than to energy conservation and solar heat gain. The placement of windows, awnings, shutters, and vegetation has become largely a matter of aesthetics. Now, as the cost of energy rises, it is clear that we must review the knowledge of the past and find ways of designing houses and communities that are energy efficient as well as beautiful.

Throughout recorded history there are references to taking advantage of the sun's path to keep our houses warm in winter and cool in summer. In Xenophon's works on Socrates we find Socrates, in relating beauty to practicality, continually returning to the example of a properly designed house. In the first century B.C. the Roman architect Vitruvius wrote, "As the position of the heavens with regard to a given tract on Earth leads naturally to different characteristics, owing to the inclination of the circle of the zodiac and the course of the sun it is obvious that designs for houses ought similarly to conform to the nature of the country and the diversities of climate."

Early residents of the Western Hemisphere also made use of the sun's energy for heating their homes more than 1000 years ago. Many American Indian settlements in the southwestern United States were designed to take advantage of the seasonal variations in the sun's path. The Acoma Pueblo near Albuquerque, New Mexico, is a high-density community consisting of rows of adobe houses positioned so that no south walls are shaded by neighboring houses. Many of the southwestern Indians clustered their houses together to reduce the ratio of surface area to volume of the structures. The small amount of surface area in combination with the high heat capacity of the thick adobe walls kept the interior of the structures at a fairly constant temperature from day to night. One such cluster of houses, Montezuma's Castle in Arizona, was built high on a cliff under a natural overhang that completely shaded the buildings during the summer months. There are many more examples of American Indian dwellings designed to fit local climatic conditions.

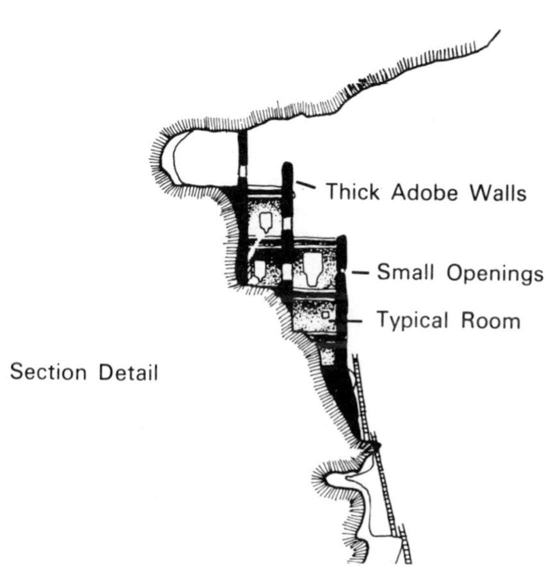

Figure 3.59 Montezuma's Castle (cliff dwelling), Camp Verde, Arizona. *Source. Solar Dwelling Design Concept,* U.S. Department of Housing and Urban Development, 1976.

Although making use of solar heat was largely a matter of common sense prior to this century, solar-heated houses recently have become conversation pieces and, unfortunately for their owners, tourist attractions. People who live in solar houses that use active solar collectors are often harassed by local civic organizations and teachers seeking to arrange tours. It is curious, however, that in this decade many people do not consider passive solar houses (i.e., houses that are heated by south windows) to be true solar-heated houses. Even early versions of federal and state tax incentives did not recognize passive solar houses as true solar-heated houses.

During the 1940s the term "solar house" generally referred to a house that received a large percentage of its heat through south windows. In 1943 the Illinois Institute of Technology started a solar house fad by publishing the results of a year-long study of its passive solar house in the Chicago suburb of Homewood. According to the report, on a January day in 1942 when the high temperature outdoors was −5°F the thermostat in the house, set at 72°F, shut off the furnace at 8:30 A.M. and did not turn it back on until 8:30 P.M. The story was published in newspapers across the country and triggered articles on solar houses in *Reader's Digest, Life, Colliers, Better Homes and Gardens,* and many other national magazines. Millions of people viewed newsreels of solar homes in motion picture theaters. A book entitled *Your Solar House,* published in 1947, contained 49 sets of plans for passive solar houses by 49 architects, one from each of the 48 states and Washington, D.C.

In all the official government figures on our national sources of energy, there is no mention of any significant contribution by solar energy. Yet the amount of energy that enters 64 square feet of south-facing window from November through March at 40° north latitude is equal to the energy in one barrel of oil. And a clothesline can save an enormous amount of energy when used in place of electric or gas clothes dryers, which are typically from 5 to 10% efficient. These passive methods of using solar energy already contribute significantly to our national energy budget and could contribute far more if we made a conscious effort to utilize them.

The first active solar heating system using flat plate collectors was built at MIT in 1939. The collector consisted of copper tubes soldered to a copper sheet at 6-inch intervals with three glass cover sheets. One unique feature of the house was that the storage tank was large enough to begin collecting heat in the summer for use during the winter months. Much of what today is considered common knowledge about flat plate collectors was learned from this house in Massachusetts.

Between 1940 and 1975, according to official government estimates, less than 200 houses were built using active solar heating systems. Since 1975 it has become impossible to keep track of the number of solar-heated houses being built. Even if the hundreds of companies now involved in the manufacture of solar products could be located and surveyed, the number of owner built systems in existence is nearly impossible to determine but is surely significant. In 1975 the U.S. Energy Research and Development Administration and the U.S. Department of Housing and Urban Development began subsidizing a small number of residential solar heating systems to demonstrate their feasibility. Fifty-three projects were funded in 1975, and a book containing detailed descriptions of the great variety of systems has been published.*

The number of solar water heaters now providing domestic hot water is far greater and is growing faster than the number of solar space heating systems. The initial cost of a solar domestic hot water system is much less than that of a space heating system and the payback period is considerably shorter, since the solar water heater reduces energy bills 12 months per year. The payback period on the materials for an owner-built solar water heater can be well under 2 years if the unit is replacing an electric water heater. Before the Depression and the national program of rural electrification, there were thousands of solar water heaters in use in Florida and California. In fact, it is estimated that in Florida alone there were approximately 50,000 solar water heaters in use prior to 1940.

In 1964 it was estimated that there were more than 500,000 solar water heaters in the world, and they were being produced in Japan and Israel at a rate of 60,000 per year. The United States has a long way to go before it catches up with the rest of the world in the use of solar energy.

Solar Heating System Components

The many different kinds of solar heating system available today can be broken down into the two broad categories: active systems and passive systems. Active systems are generally more complex and expensive than passive systems; in addition, they contain numerous moving parts, require an external energy source, and require more maintenance than passive systems. Passive systems are usually free of moving parts, require no outside energy source, and require little or no maintenance, although daily attention to manual controls may be necessary. Passive systems are not easily adaptable to existing buildings and do not maintain as constant a temperature as thermostatically controlled active systems. Passive systems, by their nature, are usually limited to storing a one-day supply of heat at a time, whereas active systems are limited only by the size of the storage compartment and the money available to build it. The efficiencies of active and passive systems are quite comparable, but passive systems are almost always more cost efficient. Though solar heating systems vary greatly in cost and complexity, they all consist of the same three basic components: collector, storage unit, and distribution system.

Solar Heating and Cooling Demonstration Program, U.S. Dep. of Housing and Urban Development, 1976.

Active Systems

Collectors. The solar collector represents by far the greatest expense of any part of a solar heating system. There are dozens of commercial collectors available, and many designs that can be assembled on the construction site by the contractor or the homeowner. Picking the right collector for a particular installation is the most important decision the designer must make.

The most commonly used type of collector for solar heating installations is the flat plate collector. A typical device consists of a thin plastic or metal panel with channels attached to it or integral in it for circulating a liquid or gas (usually water or air) to carry the heat away. The surface of the panel is given a coating that absorbs solar energy well. This can be black paint or a special chemical coating called a "selective surface." Usually some measures are taken to reduce the amount of heat the collector loses to its surroundings. Most often the absorber panel is placed in a frame with the back and sides insulated and one or more layers of glass or plastic over the panel. Glass reduces conductive and convective losses. The selective surfaces absorb solar radiation about as well as black paint but give off much less infrared heat radiation, and this can be a significant portion of the total heat loss at high temperatures.

One of the simplest and least expensive of the flat plate collectors is the trickle-type collector invented by Harry Thomason. A trickle collector consists of blackened corrugated metal panels with a perforated header pipe across the top and gutter across the bottom. The water is trickled over the corrugated panel and picks up the heat from the face of the panel. Single glazed trickle collectors at normal solar heating temperatures are comparable in efficiency to many commercial parallel pipe collectors.

Flat plate collectors are one of two general categories of solar collector that are commercially available, the other being concentrating collectors. Concentrating collectors gather the parallel rays of the sun that fall over a large area and concentrate them onto a small area. The magnifying glass is the most familiar example of a concentrating collector. More practical for large solar installations are concentrating mirrors, which are less bulky and expensive than concentrating lenses. Since most concentrating collectors collect only the parallel rays of the sun that fall perpendicular to the collector, they must be mounted so that they can track the sun as it moves across the sky. For the same reason they cannot take advantage of indirect light from the sky and clouds. Therefore concentrating collectors are most useful in areas where the sky is extremely clear and direct sunlight accounts for 90% or more of the total. Another drawback of concentrating collectors is the inefficiency of the reflective surface and the amount of maintenance required. Most inexpensive plastic reflective surfaces are only between 70 and 80% reflective and last from 5 to 7 years when constantly exposed to sunlight. In addition, if the curved surface is not enclosed in a transparent envelope, it must be cleaned periodically.

Concentrating collectors do have some advantages over flat plate collectors that may make them more desirable for certain tasks. The actual absorber area at the focal point of a concentrating collector is quite small, which results in a significant savings of expensive materials such as copper and selective surfaces. Concentrating collectors do lend themselves readily to mass production techniques, and their cost will decrease as production increases. In installations where high temperatures are necessary for generating steam or running absorption refrigeration units, concentrating collectors have a distinct advantage over flat plate collectors. Concentrating collectors are ideally suited to generating high temperatures. An accurate circular parabolic collector can achieve temperatures in excess of 6000°F at its focal point—but this does not mean that concentrating collectors are capable of collecting more energy than flat plate collectors of the same size. The amount of solar energy falling on a square foot of collector is the same, whether it is falling on a concentrating collector or a flat plate collector. A concentrating collector will heat a smaller amount of water to a higher temperature. But if a 32-square-foot flat plate collector is placed next to a 32-square-foot concentrating collector and water is pumped through them both at 1 gallon per minute, there will be little difference in the temperatures achieved by the two collectors. The difference depends on the relative efficiencies of the two collectors.

Collector Efficiency. There are virtually no government standards or consumer protection laws relating to solar collectors. Thus it is absolutely essential that the designer of a solar heating system understand thoroughly the concept of collector efficiency. Often in the field of solar heating what sounds logical is exactly the opposite of what is true. The uncertain consumer or architect may be overwhelmed by conflicting information.

The relative amounts of solar energy collected by two different collectors of the same size under similar operating conditions depend on the relative efficiencies of the two units. The term "collector efficiency" usually refers to instantaneous efficiency and is defined as the power output of the collector divided by the power input. If solar radiation is striking a collector at a rate of 300 Btu per square foot per hour and the fluid flowing through the collector is carrying away only 150 Btu per square foot per hour then the efficiency of the collector is 150/300 = 0.50 = 50%. The other half of the energy is lost by the collector to its environment. The efficiency of the collector depends on a number of factors, some in the design of the collector itself and others independent of collector design.

The efficiency of any collector, no matter what its design, will be affected by the difference between the average temperature of the absorber panel and the average ambient temperature. *The amount of energy a collector transfers to the heat storage system is equal to the amount of solar energy that strikes the collector minus the amount of energy the collector loses to its environment. The amount of energy a collector loses to its environment is directly proportional to the difference in temperature between absorber and ambient.* All collectors become less efficient as their temperature increases or as the ambient temperature decreases.

When designing a collector, certain steps are necessary to reduce the heat loss to the environment. These steps are much more important when designing a collector to operate at 200°F than when designing a collector to operate at swimming pool temperatures. A flat plate collector designed to operate at 200°F must be very well insulated, will likely have multiplate layers of glass to create insulating air spaces, and may be coated with a selective surface to minimize infrared heat radiation, which would be a significant cause of heat loss with black paint at 200°F. A collector for heating a swimming pool, on the other hand, might not incorporate any of these features. Why spend money insulating a collector that will have 75°F water circulating through it when the temperature of the surrounding air may be well above 75°F? It is quite possible for a solar swimming pool heater collector to be more than 100% efficient if the panel is receiving heat from the air as well as the sun. The aforementioned high-temperature collector, if used as a swimming pool heater, would be so well insulated that little heat would be received from the surrounding air; moreover, if it had two layers of glass, they would

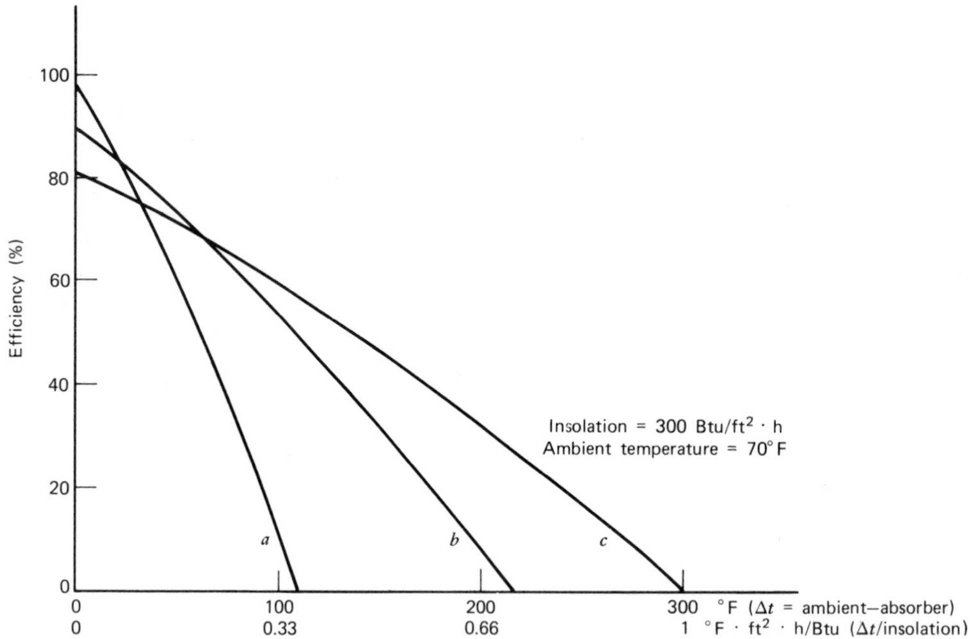

Figure 3.60 Collector efficiency: curve *a*, no glazing layers; curve *b*, 1 layer; curve *c*, 2 layers. Hypothetical.

reflect away 20% or more of the available solar energy, reducing the collector efficiency to 80% or less. Pool heating panels generally have no glazing or insulation, cost between \$3 and \$5 per square foot, and approach or surpass 100% efficiency during the summer months. The collector designed for high temperatures would cost in the neighborhood of \$15 per square foot and would be 80% efficient or less for pool heating applications.

It is obvious, then, that solar collectors are designed to operate within certain temperature ranges, and a collector that is very efficient at high temperatures may not be nearly as efficient at low temperatures as a collector that is much less expensive. If a manufacturer states that his collector is 65% efficient or 5 times more efficient than competing models, clearly he is not supplying enough information. What is really needed is an efficiency curve to show the efficiency at several differences in temperature between absorber panel and ambient. Figure 3.60 shows efficiency curves for three hypothetical collectors with 0, 1, and 2 layers of glass. The first row of numbers in the horizontal axis is the temperature difference between absorber and ambient. The NBS system for measuring efficiency, which is slightly different, is indicated in the second row of numbers. In the NBS system the temperature difference in degrees Fahrenheit in the X-axis is divided by the insolation in Btu per square foot per hour; thus the units are expressed as °F · ft² · h/Btu and the values given for most collectors range from zero to about one.

The curves in Fig. 3.60 merely provide an example and are not intended as absolutes for all collectors with the same number of glazing layers. The efficiencies of commercial collector panels vary greatly, and every attempt should be made to obtain the measured efficiency curve for each panel being considered. If the manufacturer lacks the necessary testing facilities, certain independent laboratories, universities, and a few utility companies will make the measurements free or for a low fee. By dividing the cost per square foot of each collector by the efficiency at the expected operating temperature differences, the system designer can tell exactly which collector will deliver the most energy per dollar investment.

Even though two flat plate collectors may appear identical down to the number and type of glazing layers and type of black surface used, there still may exist great differences in their relative efficiencies. This is because of the hot spots that exist on the absorber panel as a result of poor heat transfer characteristics of the panel. When the efficiency measurement is made, the average absorber temperature is taken to be $(T_{in} + T_{out})/2$, where T_{in} is the temperature of the incoming water and T_{out} is the temperature of the outgoing water. In reality, the average temperature of the collector may be much higher than this.

Figure 3.61 *Source.* Solar Heating and Cooling Demonstration Research Program, U.S. Department of Housing and Urban Development, 1976.

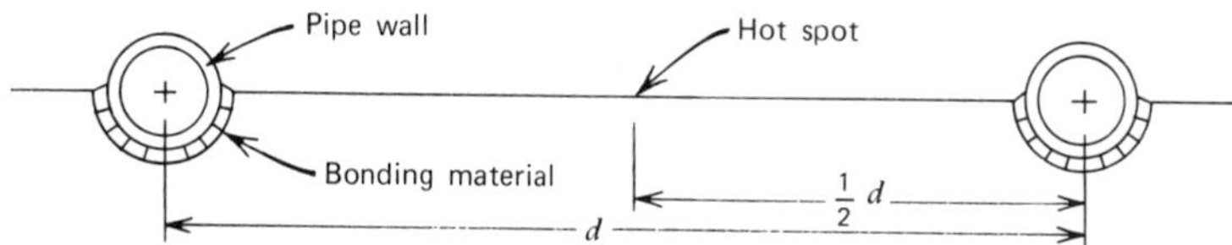

The most common type of collector available is the tube-on-plate collector, which consists of parallel pipes, usually copper, attached to a metal sheet at regular intervals. Most of the solar energy falls on the sheet and is transferred by conduction across the sheet and through the pipe into the fluid. To force the heat to flow from the point halfway between two pipes into the fluid, there must be a difference in temperature (see Figure 3.61). The size of this temperature difference depends on the thermal resistance between the water in the tube and the point halfway between the tubes. If metal pipe is used, the pipe itself contributes very little to this thermal resistance. The bond between the pipe and sheet is very important and can be the major contributor of resistance in some collectors that rely on a friction contact. The most efficient bond, formed by soldering or brazing the pipe to the sheet, contributes very little to the total resistance. Thin layers of thermally conductive adhesives are not as good as solder but usually account for only about 10% of the total resistance. The largest thermal resistance is generally in the sheet metal absorber panel itself. This resistance can be minimized by using metals with high thermal conductivities (aluminum is good, copper better), by increasing the thickness of the panel to allow more cross-sectional area for the heat to flow through, and by keeping the distance between the pipes small.

The distance between the pipes is the most critical factor. The temperature difference between hot spot and pipe is related to the square of the distance between the pipes and to the first power of the conductivity and the thickness of the panel. If the distance between the pipes were doubled, the thickness of the panel would have to be increased fourfold to keep the efficiency the same. The most efficient collectors, then, are those that have the fluid passages very close together or have the fluid in contact with the entire front or back surface of the absorber panel. Such collectors are available, with absorber panels consisting of two sheets of metal spot welded or otherwise bonded together with space between them for the fluid to circulate.

One more very important factor affecting collector efficiency is the flow rate of the fluid or gas that is circulated through the collector. This is one of the areas in which common sense gets a lot of people into trouble. Strictly in terms of collector efficiency, the faster the fluid is circulated through the collector, the more efficiently the collector will operate. Most laymen have a difficult time believing this, probably because they do not understand the difference between heat and temperature. Naturally people want to put their hand in the water at the output of their solar swimming pool heater and feel 100°F water coming out. It is sometimes difficult to explain to a client that his or her common sense is wrong. To resolve the discrepancy, it is necessary to point out the relation between the collector efficiency curve and the difference between ambient temperature and average collector temperature. *The faster the fluid is circulated through the collector, the less its temperature will increase, the lower the average collector temperature will be, and the more efficiently the collector will operate.* Of course, there is a point at which the size of the pump and motor begins to offset the gains in collector efficiency. Typically flow rates are calculated to attain a 10 to 20°F increase in fluid temperature as the fluid passes through the collector. The size of the temperature increase is a decision that must be made by the system designer by finding a balance between the maximum allowable average collector temperature and the cost and energy requirements of the pump needed to deliver the necessary flow rate.

Orientation. In most parts of the Northern Hemisphere, solar collectors should be oriented so that they face geographic south (not magnetic south) and sloped so that they are perpendicular to the sun at solar noon (not noon standard time) at the time of the year heat is most needed. If the collector will be shaded in the morning or afternoon by fog, trees, or other obstructions, it should be turned slightly east or west to face the sun halfway between actual sunrise and sunset. A collector will be perpendicular to the sun at solar noon at a given time of the year when the collector is facing geographic south and its angle with the horizontal is equal to the latitude of its location minus the solar declination for the time of year. The solar declination given for each month of the year in Table 3.30 is the same everywhere on earth. If it were desirable to have a solar collector at 40° north latitude perpendicular to the sun on January 21, the device would face geographic south at an angle of $40° - (-20°) = 60°$.

Table 3.30 Solar Declination (Approximate)

	+23.5°	June 21
July 24	+20.0°	May 21
August 23	+11.0°	April 20
September 23	00.0°	March 21
October 22	−11.0°	February 21
November 22	−20.0°	January 21
December 21	−23.5°	

Collectors that are to be used year round, as in domestic hot water heating, are usually fixed at an angle that slightly favors the winter sun to keep efficiency fairly constant at all times. The rule of thumb usually given is latitude plus 10° or latitude plus 15°. For small domestic hot water heater collectors, it is worthwhile to design an adjustable mount for the collector so that it can be tilted several times a year to take advantage of changes in solar declination. Of course, in the Southern Hemisphere the collector should face north and the slope should be latitude *plus* solar declination.

Be absolutely certain the person surveying the site for the foundation of the house or installation of collectors knows how to find geographic south. The most common mistake is facing the collectors toward magnetic south, which can be many degrees east or west of geographic south. Another common mistake that can produce even worse results is to assume that geographic south is where the sun is at noon. The sun is at geographic south at solar noon, which may occur as much as 1 hour 45 minutes before or after noon, clock time, depending on longitude and time of year.

Storage Systems. Active systems usually incorporate a heat storage device that makes it possible to solar heat a house through several days of cloudy weather. The size of the storage system depends on the duration of the cloudy spell the designer wants to prepare for. It is technically possible to build a storage system that can store enough heat during summer to heat a house through the winter. Typically, though, storage systems are designed to supply heat for 2 or 3 days of cloudy weather. A system for storing much more than a 3-day supply of heat would cost more than the collector.

Storage by Specific Heat Capacity. The storage of heat necessitates a large thermal mass. Thermal mass is specific heat capacity times weight, and water has the highest specific heat capacity of any material available for solar heat storage. The specific heat capacity of water is 1 Btu per pound · degree (Fahrenheit), which means that it takes 1 Btu of heat to increase the temperature of 1 pound of water by 1°F. If 1 pound of water were cooled down by 1°F, it would give off 1 Btu of heat. Most rock has a specific heat capacity near 0.2 Btu/lb · °F. Metals are much lower than rock, and water-antifreeze mixtures lie somewhere between water and rock. Table 3.31 gives specific heat capacities C of various materials. The thermal mass of 1000 gallons of water weighing 8330 pounds would be:

$$1 \text{ Btu/lb}\cdot°\text{F} \times 8330 \text{ lb} = 8330 \text{ Btu/°F}$$

This means that 1000 gallons of water could absorb 8330 Btu and increase in temperature by only 1°F, or, as the 1000 gallons of water cooled by 1°F, it would give off

Table 3.31 Thermal Properties of Various Materials

Material	Specific Heat Capacity, C (Btu/lb · °F)	Latent Heat Capacity, Solid-Liquid, L (Btu/lb)	Melting Point (°F)	Density, (lb/ft^3)
Water	1.0	144	32	62
Basalt	0.20	—	—	184
Steel	0.12	—	—	489
Paraffin wax	0.70	65	100 (variable)	55
Salt hydrates				
$NaSO_4 \cdot 10H_2O$	0.40	108	90	90
$Na_2S_2O_3 \cdot 5H_2O$	0.40	120	120	104
Fire brick	0.22	—	—	198
Concrete	0.16 (approx)	—	—	110–175

8330 Btu. The more thermal mass in a storage system, the more heat it can absorb for a given temperature change. A storage system that does not have enough thermal mass will undergo too large a temperature change and will cause the solar collector to operate inefficiently as the too-hot fluid is circulated through it.

The greater the thermal mass of the storage system, the less temperature change it must undergo to store the required amount of heat. Here again, common sense can cause problems. Many people expect their solar heat storage system to attain 200°F or more after a couple of sunny days. Such a high temperature system would require at least twice the *R* value of insulation and would cause the collector efficiency to drop off considerably. A 2000-gallon tank of water at 140°F has just as much capacity to heat a house as a 1000-gallon tank of water at 200°F and will perform with insulation materials and low-temperature collectors costing much less.

Although rock has only one-fifth the heat capacity of water by weight, a bin full of river rocks contains about twice as much weight per cubic foot as a tank of water. A cubic foot of water contains about 2.66 times as much thermal mass as a cubic foot of river rock. This is significant when one is considering the cost of insulating the heat storage compartment. Since a rock heat storage compartment needs to have 2.66 times the volume of a water heat storage compartment, a typical rock bin will have about twice the surface area of a water tank with the same thermal mass. With twice the surface area, it would be necessary to double the thickness of the insulation on the rock bin to keep its heat loss the same as that of the water tank. This means that a rock bin requires 4 times as much insulation as a water tank with the same thermal mass and heat loss. R-30 Urethane insulation is currently priced at about 65¢ per square foot wholesale. A 2000-gallon cylindrical water tank has about 230 square feet of surface area and would cost about $150 to insulate to R-30. A rock bin with the same thermal mass would cost about $600 to insulate equally well.

When rock bins are used to store the heat collected by air-type collectors, it is important that the rocks have sufficient surface area for good heat transfer and sufficiently large air spaces between them for good air flow. This can be accomplished by using rocks that are fairly round and fairly uniform in size. River rocks 3 to 4 inches in diameter are commonly used for heat storage. It is true that greater density, thus more thermal mass per cubic foot, can be attained by mixing rocks of different sizes, but this results in smaller passages for the air to flow through and more work for the blower.

There are fluids now available that can be used as substitutes for water in solar collectors and storage systems. The main advantage of these solar collector fluids is their very low freezing point, which makes it unlikely that they will freeze and damage collectors. However all the solar collector fluids now on the market have a lower heat capacity than water, thus they should be confined to use in the collector and avoided for heat storage. A 1000-gallon tank of solar collector fluid would have to increase in temperature much more than a 1000-gallon tank of water to store the same amount of heat. In addition, no solar collector fluid yet developed can compete with water in cost. It is a simple matter to circulate the collector fluid from the collector through a copper pipe heat exchanger immersed in the storage tank, thereby reducing the total amount of collector fluid needed to a few gallons.

Storage by Latent Heat Capacity. When solid materials are melted to form liquids, they absorb a great deal of heat while remaining at a constant temperature. As the materials return to their solid form, the abosrbed heat—that is, the latent heat of fusion, is released. This quantity, symbolized *L*, is given for certain materials in Table 3.32. Many materials have melting points within the temperature range that is useful in solar heating applications; among them are certain waxes and salt mixtures.

Table 3.32 Average Temperatures for New York, 1965–1969

	Temperature (°F)	
Year	Average Dry Bulb	Average Wet Bulb
1965	53.5	47.0
1966	54.2	47.5
1967	52.2	46.2
1968	53.3	46.5
1969	54.1	47.9
Average	53.5	47.0

Storage by latent heat capacity is especially useful in applications where constant temperatures are desirable, as in a solar-heated sauna, and it requires only a fraction of the volume of a comparable water system. The melting points of these salts and waxes are adjustable and can even be set to occur at room temperature, thus creating enormous thermal inertia when used in the floors or walls of the living space. Unfortunately, salts have a tendency to break down and lose their effectiveness after 100 or so such phase changes. Quite a bit of research is being aimed at overcoming this problem. Waxes do not break down like salts, but they are highly flammable and become very good insulators as they solidify. It is very difficult to get the heat back out of solidified waxes.

Distribution Systems. Getting the heat from the storage compartment of a solar heating system to the living space is really not much different from getting the heat from a conventional furnace to the living space. Since the working temperatures are much lower with a solar heating system, larger flow rates of air or water or larger radiators are necessary to distribute the same amount of heat.

Forced air seems to be the most popular choice for distributing solar heat. Air-type collectors with rock storage systems are obviously easy to adapt to forced-air distribution, but even the designers of water systems are leaning heavily toward forced air. It is not very difficult or expensive to place a water-to-air heat exchanger in the main forced air duct, be it in a new house or in an existing house that already has forced air heat.

Radiant distribution for solar heating systems requires much larger radiators than do conventional hydronic systems because of the lower temperatures involved. It is difficult to add solar heating to a house with existing radiant heating. It is much easier to increase the flow rate of a forced air system than to increase the size of existing radiators. Radiant distribution is much better suited to new construction, since a slab floor can be used as a low-temperature radiator.

With active systems the heat must be transported from the collector to the storage system and from the storage system to the living space, and it is preferable to accomplish all this automatically to obtain maximum efficiency from the system. All the necessary hardware is readily available, most of it from the local hardware store.

The fluid that is circulated through the collector should be drawn from the bottom of the storage compartment; then it should enter the bottom of the collector (except in trickle systems), leave the top of the collector, and return to the top of the storage compartment. In liquid systems care must be taken to ensure that the point at which the fluid leaves the collector is the highest point on the line within the collector; otherwise air may become trapped at high points in the collector, partially blocking the flow. The pump or blower should be installed at the coolest part of the line (i.e., where the water or air leaves the bottom of the storage compartment). Not only is this better for the pump or blower, but it prevents vapor lock problems, which sometimes occur in water systems when the pump is positioned so that it must remove such hot water from the collector.

Ideally, fluid should be circulated from the storage compartment to the collector whenever the collector is warmer than the bottom of the storage compartment.

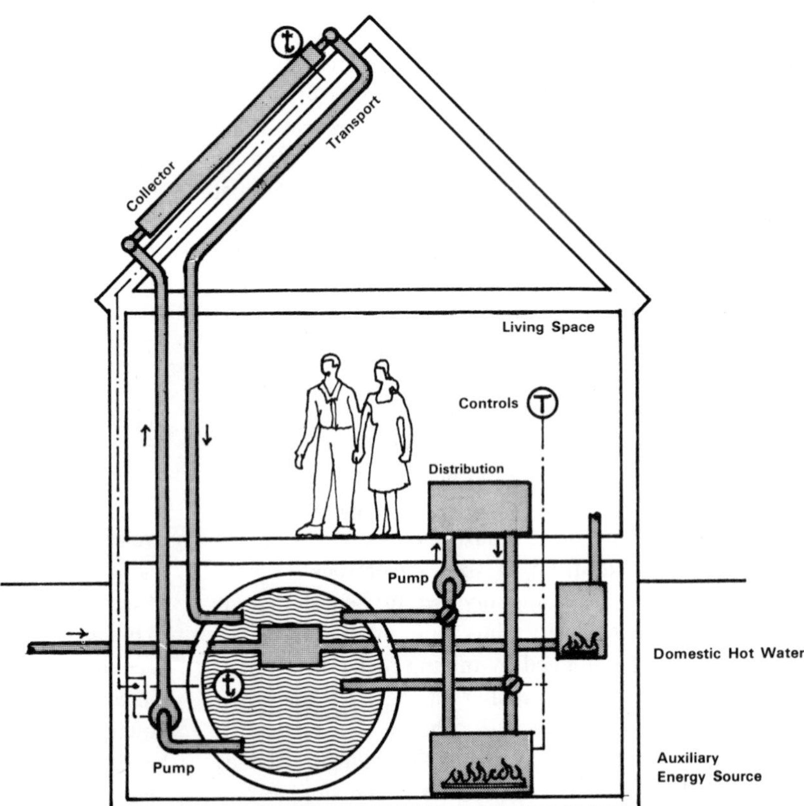

Figure 3.62 Schematic diagram of warm water, flat plate system. *Source. Solar Dwelling Design Concepts,* U.S. Department of Housing and Urban Development, 1976.

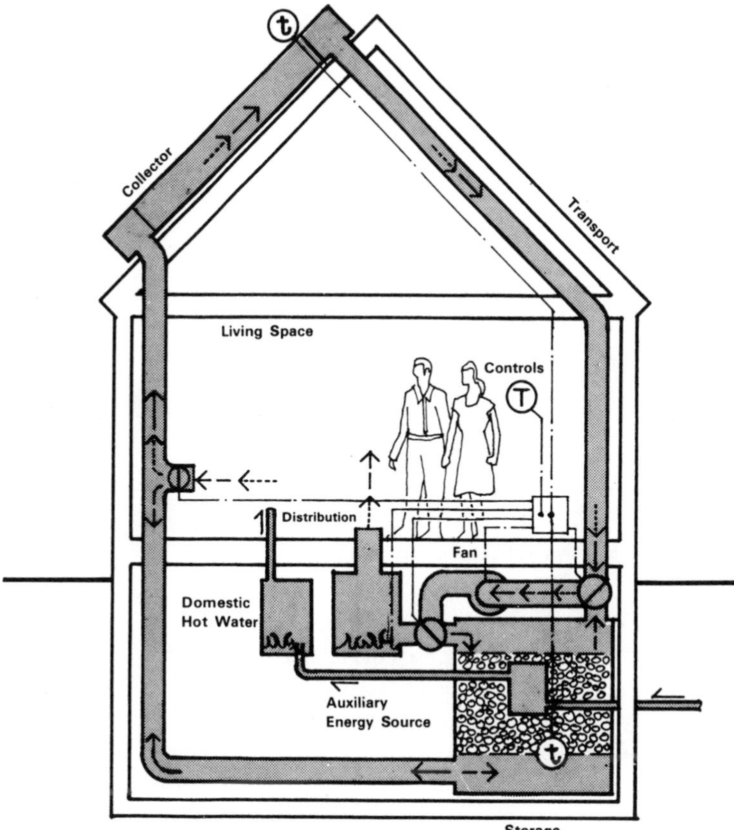

Figure 3.63 Schematic diagram of warm air, flat plate system. *Source. Solar Dwelling Design Concepts,* U.S. Department of Housing and Urban Development, 1976.

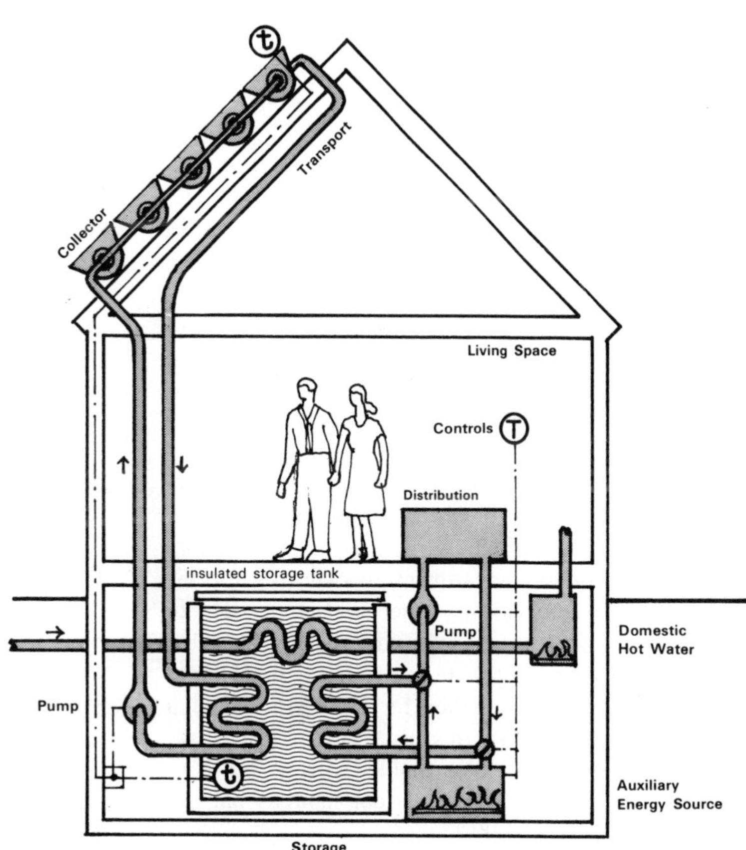

Figure 3.64 Schematic diagram of warm water concentrating system. *Source. Solar Dwelling Design Concepts,* U.S. Department of Housing and Urban Development, 1976.

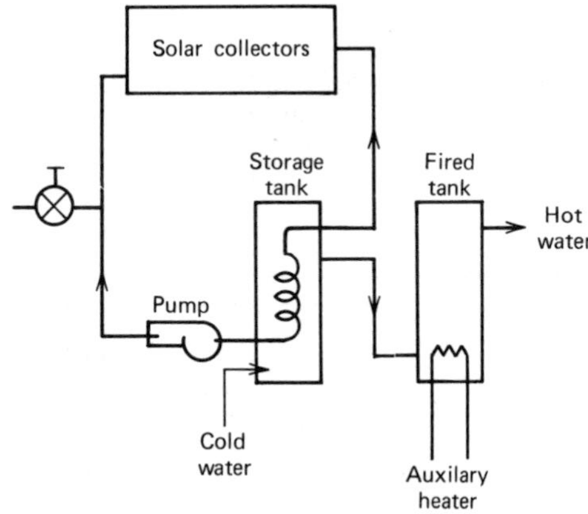

Figure 3.65 *Source. Pacific Regional Solar Heating Handbook,* U.S. Energy Research and Development Admin., 1976.

To achieve this, the pump or blower is controlled by a differential thermostat that senses the temperatures at the bottom of the tank and at the collector and activates the motor only when heat will be gained. Differential thermostats can be purchased from many sources for as little as $40 and are available with several options. The most popular option is an antifreeze circuit that activates the pump-in water systems when the collector temperature is near 32°F. A high limit option is also available to prevent system components from being damaged by extremely high temperatures. For domestic hot water heating systems there is an option to prevent the pump from running when the collector is below 70°F, in case all the hot water is used on a warm evening and the tank is full of 50°F tap water. Care must be taken in locating the collector temperature sensor to ensure that the warm water being drawn from the bottom of the tank does not affect it and "fool" the differential thermostat into letting the pump run all night.

The fluid that is circulated to the house for space heating should be drawn from the top of the tank and returned to the bottom of the tank. The pump or blower can be controlled by the same thermostat that controls the conventional heating system. A chronothermostat is a refinement that automatically sets the room temperature lower at night to help stretch the supply of solar heat. One additional device that is needed is a temperature sensor in the storage compartment, to switch over to the backup system automatically when the temperature of the storage compartment is too low to adequately heat the house. Appropriate sensors are commonly available from heating and ventilation suppliers for about $15, although they were not designed for this exact purpose. They usually consist of a single-pole, double-throw switch controlled by a mercury bulb on a 5-foot capillary and are adjustable from −10 to 90°F.

All pipes and ducts must be well insulated, and this may be very expensive with air systems. A 10 inch duct, which has 10 times the surface area of a 1 inch pipe, must have 10 times the thickness of insulation, or 100 times as much insulation, to keep the heat loss the same. If possible, pipes and ducts should be positioned so that heat is lost to the living space instead of to the outdoors.

Air Versus Water Systems. There is a good deal of controversy over the relative costs and efficiencies of air and water systems. As the solar collector market becomes more competitive and measured efficiency curves become available to the consumer, however, the controversy should come to an end. It has been the experience of this author that air systems are slightly more expensive and less efficient than water systems. Air-cooled collectors themselves are actually slightly less expensive than water-cooled collectors; but the added cost of ducts, blowers, and extra insulation more than offsets the slight savings. Air systems are quite popular in Colorado, where protection against freezes is an important consideration. The most common ways of preventing water systems from freezing are running the pump intermittently at night, using antifreeze in the collector, and using an automatic collector draindown mechanism. All these methods require some input of energy and/or money, which may make air systems more attractive in some parts of the country.

Passive Systems. Passive solar heating systems are becoming increasingly popular as more and more people become aware of their simplicity and low cost. In most passive systems the collector and storage systems are one and the same, consisting of a thick concrete wall or floor or large mass of water, which receives the solar heat

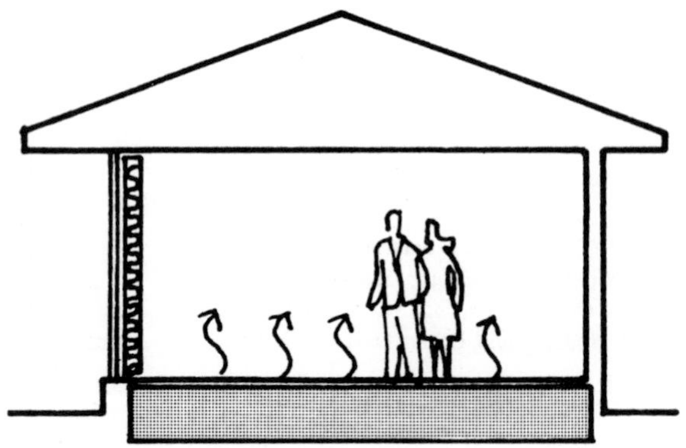

Figure 3.66 Heat storage in a massive floor. *Source. Solar Dwelling Design Concepts,* U.S. Department of Housing and Urban Development, 1976.

directly through south-facing windows. Typically, enough south-facing windows are provided to admit a 24-hour supply of heat during a sunny January day. The thermal mass of a concrete floor and/or wall in combination with the normal thermal mass of the other building materials can keep the interior temperature of the house from fluctuating more than 10°F from sunrise to sunset and through to the following sunrise.

Distribution of heat to the living space is typically radiant, direct from the storage system. Some have attempted to adapt passive systems to existing houses by using large bins or river rock and continuously running blowers to recirculate the air in the house through the rock bin to stabilize the room temperature. However most such systems suffer from serious overheating problems during winter months. The cause is most likely a combination of insufficient thermal mass and insufficient surface area of rock for transfer of heat at low temperature differences. When the storage system is a concrete slab floor or wall directly exposed to the sunlight, the air in the room typically stays about 5 to 10°F cooler than the slab, and both fluctuate by the same amount, about 10°F. When the air in the room is used to carry heat admitted by south windows to a rock bin, the air in the room must be hotter than the storage system during the day (to put heat into storage) and cooler than the storage system at night (to take heat out of storage). If this is the case, and the rock bin fluctuates by 10°F, the air in the room may fluctuate by 20°F or more. To solve this problem, the rock bin would have to be designed to undergo a much smaller temperature fluctuation than a concrete floor or wall that is directly exposed to the sunlight.

BURROUGHS–WELLCOME RESEARCH TRIANGLE
Burroughs, North Carolina
Architect: Paul Rudolph
Photo: J. W. Molitor

Since concrete and rock have about the same specific heat capacity, a passive rock bin system would need several times as much weight of river rocks as it would concrete directly exposed to the sunlight to maintain the same temperature range. Another frequent cause of overheating in passive rock bin systems is that the blower used is far too small. Flow rates for this type of system should be calculated in the same way as flow rates for active air systems; that is, the blower must provide enough flow to carry the heat away at the same rate it is coming in through the south windows.

Windows that face geographic south receive the most heat in winter and are easiest to shade in summer. East and west windows are by far the biggest source of heat gain in the summer and contribute little heat in winter. North windows can also be a significant source of excess summer heat in far northern latitudes during the early morning and late afternoon. To take advantage of these conditions, passive solar houses are generally designed with few or no east, west, and north windows, and many of them have no more total window area than the average tract home. Trees and shrubs are often used to shade the east, west, and north sides of the house.

South windows must be shaded during the hotter parts of the year. Unfortunately, in most parts of the world the hottest part of the year lags the time of year when the sun is at its highest by about 2 months. This seriously limits the amount of control over indoor temperatures that can be provided by fixed overhangs. Adjustable awnings give much finer control and can provide the maximum energy savings if properly used by the occupants of the house. Automatically controlled adjustable awnings would be the ideal solution to the shading problem. Shading south windows from the inside with curtains and blinds is better than nothing, but not nearly as good as shading from the outside. The curtains themselves and the glass will absorb quite a bit of heat and will transfer it to the air in the room. Some current research on high technology materials for passive systems involves windows that turn semireflective when the room temperature reaches a certain point, and concrete and sheet rock with salt in the pores that melts at room temperature, providing latent heat storage. Such materials would solve a lot of design problems but are not yet commercially available.

It is usually not practical to design a passive solar house to collect more than a 1-day supply of heat at a time, although this is not impossible. The problem is getting enough thermal mass in the house to stabilize the temperature when several days' heat is being accumulated and released. Certain types of construction, such as adobe and stone houses, have enough thermal mass built in to make several days of storage possible, but it is essential that the insulation be applied to the outside of the walls, so that the thermal mass remains inside the insulation envelope. Massive south walls of water are another way of providing storage for several days of heat. In Steve Baer's house near Albuquerque, New Mexico, the entire south wall consists of 55-gallon drums full of water, lying on their sides with the ends exposed to the sunlight (Figure 3.67). The resulting 30-inch-thick wall of water provides an enormous amount of thermal mass. In most cases though, passive systems should be relied on for providing heat on sunny winter days only; they should be used in conjunction with a backup system of some kind, perhaps active solar.

If the heat lost through south windows is considered as part of the normal heat loss of the house, the only major efficiency losses of the window as a collector are losses due to reflection off the glass and reflection back out through the window off objects in the house. Under these conditions the efficiency of a double-pane south glass window in collecting solar energy is about 70%. It is important, however, to calculate the heat loss per square foot of south glass and compare it to the amount of heat gained through this 70% efficient collector. In most parts of the country it is necessary to use double-pane glass and to cover the glass at night with heavy curtains or insulated shutters if the south windows are to collect more heat than they lose in sunny weather. In extremely cold northern climates or in climates with a great deal of cloud cover, even double-pane glass will lose more heat than it gains unless extreme care is taken to cover it with very well-insulated shutters whenever the sun is not out.

Backup Heat. Almost all solar heating systems are used in conjunction with a backup heating system, which can heat the living space directly or heat the storage system, which in turn heats the living space. Fast-burning smokeless wood stoves make excellent backup systems for both passive and active solar heating systems. These stoves burn with a combustion efficiency of near 100% and give off an intense heat for a rather short time. This makes them undesirable in nonsolar houses because the room is first too hot, then too cold, as the fire burns rapidly and then goes out. In solar-heated houses, however, this fast, efficiently burning fire can be used to reheat the storage system, be it a tank of water or a concrete slab floor.

Nocturnal Cooling. In many parts of the United States (including many desert areas) solar-heated houses can be cooled in the summer by taking advantage of lower nighttime temperatures to cool the storage system. With passive solar houses the means of effecting this can be as simple as opening the windows in the evening and clos-

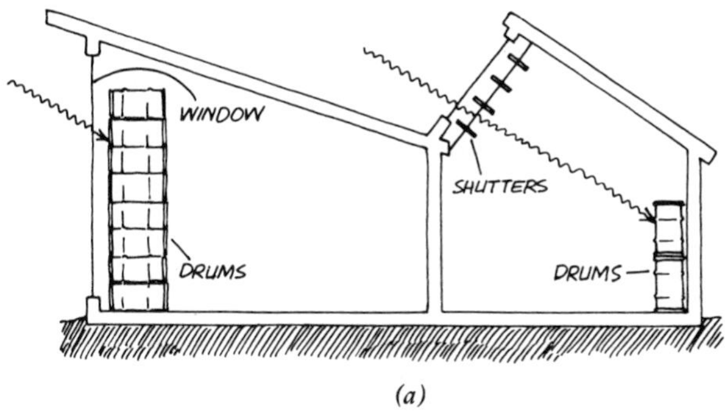

(a)

(b)

Figure 3.67 (*a*) Two possible locations for drumwalls. (*b*) Southwest view of the Baer house in Corrales, New Mexico. *Source.* Bruce Anderson, *The Solar Home Book,* Cheshire Books, 1976.

ing them in the morning. It is quite possible to keep the interior of a passive solar house below 75°F even when the outdoor temperature remains well over 100°F for several hours. All that is required is a climate with cool nighttime temperatures and a well-insulated, properly shaded house.

Thermosiphon Systems. A thermosiphon system is a hybrid of active and passive water systems. It makes use of a flat plate collector and a separate storage tank, but no outside energy is required to circulate the water, and the only moving part is the water itself. This is accomplished by placing the tank higher than the collector and connecting them together (Figure 3.68). As the water in the collector is heated by the sun, it expands and becomes lighter and is forced up by the heavy, cooler water in the bottom of the tank. The system behaves just as if it had a pump and a differential thermostat. The collector must be of the parallel pipe type rather than the series type often seen in how-to magazines and books. The series-type collector consists of one continuous piece of pipe winding through the collector and causes much resistance to flow, which in a thermosiphon system would cause a very low flow rate and inefficient collector.

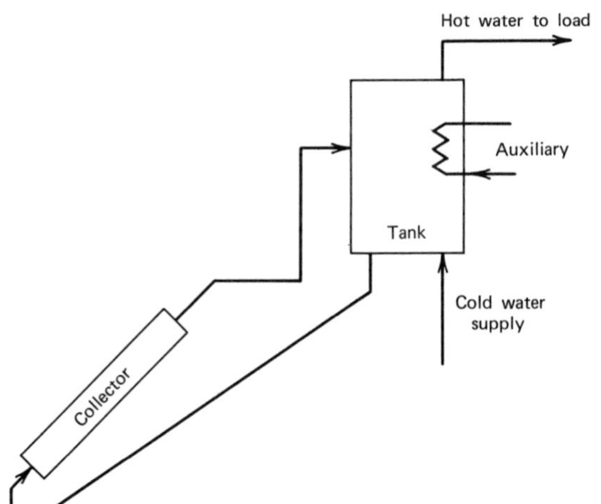

Figure 3.68 Thermosiphon domestic hot water heater. *Source.* John A. Duffie, *Solar Energy Thermal Processes,* John Wiley & Sons, 1974.

The most common problem associated with thermosiphon systems is improper installation, creating in the lines high spots that collect air bubbles and eventually stop the circulation completely. High spots should be avoided if at all possible. Expansion chambers and/or bleeder valves should be installed if it proves impossible to eliminate high spots.

Thermosiphon solar domestic water heaters can be just as efficient as pumped systems as long as resistance to flow is kept to a minimum. Thermosiphon water systems for space heating are not common because of the obvious problem of raising thousands of gallons of water above the collector. Large thermosiphon systems are ideally suited to houses on south-facing hillsides where the collector can be positioned below the house. Thermosiphon systems will work with the collector and the storage tank at the same level, but they will circulate backward at night when the collector is cooler than the tank. Mechanical check valves are of no use because the thermosiphon does not have enough force to open them. There is, however, a patented one-way valve that is effective, and complete systems are commercially available that fit between the studs on a south wall, with the collector on the outside and the storage tank inside.

Thermosiphon air systems are usually very inefficient. It takes large differences in temperature and elevation to force air through the narrow passages in solar collectors and rock bins. It is very difficult to get flow rates large enough for efficient collector operation.

Sizing System Components

The basic steps in designing a solar heating system are calculating (1) the amount of heat that is needed (heating load), (2) the size of collector needed to supply the heat, (3) the size of storage system needed to store the heat, and (4) the flow rate necessary to carry the heat away from the collector at the same rate it is coming in.

Heating load calculations for space heating systems are usually done for January, assuming that this is the coldest month of the year at the location of the system. Calculating the heating load of a house is a somewhat tedious procedure that cannot be explained briefly. However a great number of books available contain chapters on calculating heating load; thus that information is not repeated here. The one important difference between calculating heating load for a conventional furnace and for a solar heating system is that the solar heating system is usually sized for an average winter day, whereas a conventional heating system is designed to keep the house at 70°F on 97.5% of all winter days. The temperature difference between indoors and outdoors on an average day in winter equals the number of degree days in the winter months divided by the number of days. If the solar heating system were designed for the worst possible weather conditions, it would be utilized to its full capacity only a few days each year and might never pay for itself.

For a solar domestic hot water heater, the daily heating load equals the amount of heat needed to raise the temperature of the water plus the amount of heat lost through the insulation around the tank. Following are the basic formulas:

$$\text{heat to raise water temperature (Btu/day)} = 8.33\ \text{Btu/(gal}\cdot{}^\circ\text{F)} \times V \times \Delta t(^\circ\text{F})$$

$$8.33\ \text{Btu/gal}\cdot{}^\circ\text{F} = \text{heat capacity of 1 gallon of water}$$

where V = total amount of hot water used per day (which may be several times the capacity of the conventional water heater)

Δt = required temperature increase of the water, which equals desired hot water temperature minus tap water temperature

$$\text{approximate heat lost through insulation (Btu/day)} = \frac{24\ \text{h/day} \times A\ (\text{ft}^2) \times \Delta t\ (^\circ\text{F})}{R\ \text{h}\cdot\text{ft}^2\cdot{}^\circ\text{F/Btu}}$$

where A = surface area of tank = $2\pi r^2 + 2\pi rh$

r = radius (ft)

h = height (ft)

Δt = average temperature difference between water in tank and air around tank

R = R value of insulation = 3.7 per inch thickness of fiberglass

The factors that determine collector size are heating load, collector efficiency, and available solar energy. Available solar energy data can be found in a number of sources. Most commonly used are the tables in the American Society of Heating, Refrigeration, and Air Conditioning Engineers (ASHRAE) *Handbook of Fundamentals,* and these have been reprinted in numerous recent books. These tables give the maximum possible daily solar radiation for different latitudes at different times of the year on surfaces of different slopes. Other tables are useful if the local climatic conditions (number of cloudy days, sky clearness, etc.) are taken into account. Sometimes accurate solar radiation records can be found at local weather stations operated by universities, utility companies, and various county, state, and local government agencies. The U.S. Department of Energy has solar radiation data and other related meteorological data available in the form of FORTRAN-compatible computer tape. This information is from the National Oceanic and Atmospheric Administration's network of weather stations and dates back some 25 years. Following is the basic formula for calculating collector size:

$$\frac{\text{heating load (Btu/day)} \times \begin{array}{c}\text{(number of days heat to be}\\ \text{collected in one day)*(days)}\end{array}}{I\ (\text{Btu/ft}^2) \times \text{collector efficiency (\%)/100}} = \text{collector area (ft}^2\text{)}$$

*If it is sunny on the average 2 out of 5 days the collector must collect a 5-day supply of heat every 2 days or a 2½-*day* supply of heat in 1 day.

where I = total solar energy that falls on a square foot of collector on a clear day at the time of year the system is being designed for.

For passive systems using double-pane glass, the efficiency of the collector is about 70%, the number of days supply of heat to be collected is 1, and the insolation is that falling on a 90° surface.

The size of the storage system depends on the heating load, the desired number of storage days, the specific heat capacity of the storage medium,* the density of the storage medium, and the allowable temperature change of the storage medium. The basic formula for storage system size is as follows:

$$\frac{\text{heating load (Btu/day)} \times \text{desired days of storage (days)}}{\begin{array}{c}\text{specific heat capacity}\\ \text{of storage medium (Btu/lb}\cdot{}^\circ\text{F)} \times \Delta t\ ({}^\circ\text{F})\end{array}} = \text{storage system size (lb)}$$

where Δt = allowable temperature range of the storage medium, that is, the maximum temperature allowable minus the minimum temperature at which the system will still provide heat at the necessary rate.

Note that this formula yields the weight of the storage system and the result must be divided by the density of the medium to get cubic feet or gallons. The density of water is 8.33 pounds per gallon. A bin of river rock is about one-third air space, hence has only two-thirds the density of solid rock. The density of different concrete mixtures varies greatly. For passive systems the Δt should be about 10°F, and the number of days of storage is 1.†

The flow rate in active systems depends on the instantaneous solar radiation, the size and efficiency of the collector, the specific heat capacity and density of the fluid, and the allowable temperature increase of the fluid as it passes through the collector. The basic formulas for calculating collector flow rate are as follows:

$$\text{water flow rate (gal/min)} = \frac{I\ (\text{Btu/ft}^2\cdot\text{h}) \times \text{collector size (ft}^2) \times \text{collector efficiency (\%)/100}}{8.33\ (\text{Btu/gal}\cdot{}^\circ\text{F}) \times \Delta t\ ({}^\circ\text{F}) \times (60\ \text{min/h})}$$

$$\text{airflow rate (ft}^3\text{/min)} = \frac{I\ (\text{Btu/ft}^2\cdot\text{h}) \times \text{collector size (ft}^2) \times \text{collector efficiency (\%)/100}}{0.018\ (\text{Btu/ft}^3\cdot{}^\circ\text{F}) \times \Delta t\ ({}^\circ\text{F}) \times (60\ \text{min/h})}$$

where I = instantaneous solar radiation at collector surface at noon

*See Table 3.31.

†The heat capacity of water is 1. Different rocks and concrete mixtures are close to 0.2. Consult engineering handbooks for exact values.

Δt = increase in temperature of the water or air as it passes through the collector. This amount must be decided by the designer. In general, the number should be kept as small as possible. A 10°F increase works well for collectors smaller than 100 square feet, and a 20°F increase is sufficient for most collectors.

There are two rules of thumb:

1 Water flow rates should be around 0.015 to 0.030 gallon per minute per square foot of collector.
2 Airflow rates should be around 7 to 14 cubic feet per minute per square foot of collector.

Note that the collector efficiency used in the flow rate formula should be the efficiency at noon when the maximum flow rate is needed. For calculating collector size what is actually needed is the overall collector efficiency from sunrise to sunset. This can be roughly determined by estimating the collector efficiency (from the efficiency curve) for each hour of operation, then taking an average. A much more accurate method is presented by William A. Beckman in *Solar Heating Design by the F-CHART Method* (New York: John Wiley & Sons, 1977).

Definitions

1 *Absorber Panel*. The part of a solar collector that actually absorbs the electromagnetic radiation; the metal panel and its block coating.
2 *Ambient Temperature*. The temperature of the environment surrounding an object; the ambient temperature of a solar collector refers to the temperature of the air around it.
3 *Differential Thermostat*. A thermostat that senses the temperature at two different locations and makes a decision to close a switch based on these relative temperatures; a differential thermostat in a solar heating system activates the circulating pump when the collector is warmer than the stor-

BLUMENTHAL RESIDENCE
Eastern Shore, Maryland
Architect: Hugh Newell Jacobsen
Photo: R. C. Lautman

age system (i.e., when heat can be gained by the storage system).

4 *Efficiency*. Usually refers to instantaneous efficiency, defined as power out divided by power in; also, overall efficiency is total energy out divided by total energy in.
5 *Glazing*. A transparent cover or covers to protect the absorber panel and reduce the heat losses of a solar collector.
6 *Insolation*. Incoming solar radiation measured in units of energy density or power density, that is, Btu per square foot, or Btu per square foot-hour.
7 *Langley*. The metric unit of solar energy, equal to 1 calorie per square centimeter or 3.687 Btu per square foot.
8 *Selective Surface*. A surface that absorbs certain wavelengths of electromagnetic radiation and reflects others. (Most surfaces are selective surfaces.) The selective surface most commonly used in solar heating is a surface that is a good absorber of visible light and short wave infrared and a poor absorber (thus a poor emitter) of long wave infrared heat radiation.
9 *Solar Declination*. The angle of the rays of the sun that strike the earth relative to the plane of the equator. At the vernal and autumnal equinoxes the solar declination is zero; that is, the sun is directly above the equator. At the summer solstice in the Northern Hemisphere the solar declination is +23.5°, and at the winter solstice in the Northern Hemisphere it is −23.5°.
10 *Thermal Mass*. The specific heat capacity of an object times its weight, expressed in Btu per degree fahrenheit. An object with a thermal mass of 1000 Btu/°F will increase in temperature by 1°F as it absorbs 1000 Btu of heat.

8 ENVELOPE: ENERGY PROGRAM A SIMULATION PROCESS FOR BUILDING DESIGN (APRIL 16, 1976)

By ALBERT C. MARTIN & ASSOCIATES

Today we are facing more and more restrictions on the use of our traditional energy resources. Because buildings use more than 30% of our total energy resources—and waste much of that—they are a prime target for energy conservation. The responsibility of the building design professions is clear: to find new and better techniques for the design of buildings that conserve energy while preserving the qualities of function, economy, and beauty that have always been valued by building designers and owners alike. When new information or innovative techniques are found, they must be shared with the design professions to permit the rapid and widespread recognition of their value.

There has long been a professional need for techniques to evaluate and compare during the early stage of concept design the energy-using characteristics of the basic building envelope, its shape, and its skin construction. To meet this need in our own practice, we have drawn on a computer-aided design process using an "envelope:energy" base model. It provides quick, accurate results for comparing the relative costs in terms of energy of alternative building envelopes. The process is economical and is regularly applied as a working design tool. We believe that this approach should be shared with the design professions. It should become an integral part of the design process, as one step in improving the energy use efficiency of our nation's buildings.

This section is a report to the design professions, presenting the results of research on one particular representative building type, in which we studied the relative effects of alternative envelope concepts on energy consumption and costs. The "output" curves graphically explain the relative effectiveness of different envelope configurations, orientations, and skin designs. The report also shows, by example, the working of the envelope:energy analysis process and suggests the potential of this new design tool.

Issues and Purpose

Potential Energy Savings in Buildings. The potential for saving energy in buildings is tremendous. Homes and buildings now consume as much as 34% of all the energy used in the United States; as much as 30% of that amount is lost because of inefficient systems for utilizing and conserving energy in buildings. An additional 20% or more could be saved by imposing moderate limitations on the performance and operating criteria of building mechanical and electrical systems.

Neither waste nor excessive use of energy can be tolerated in a world of limited and high-priced energy resources. Already, legislation exists that imposes severe restrictions on new building design to reduce energy consumption. The design professionals must take up the cause of efficient energy use and actively seek, and apply, innovative ways to conserve energy in buildings.

Let us review the range of opportunities for conserving energy in buildings.

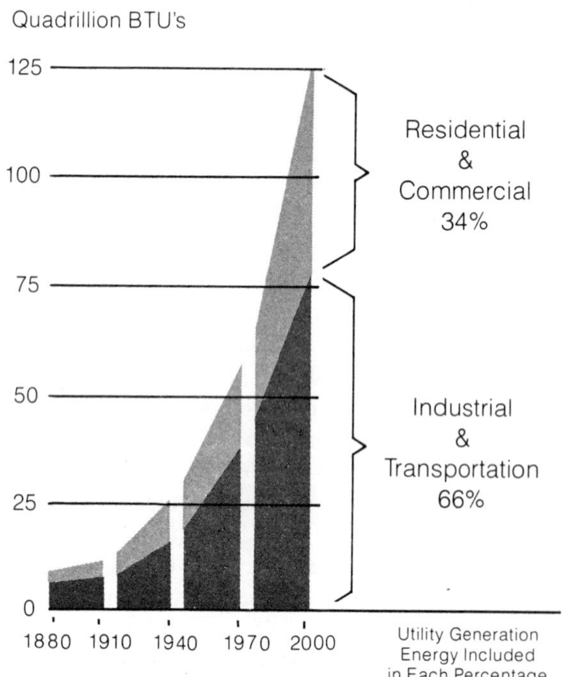

Figure 3.69

Design To Save Energy. To design a thoroughly energy-effective building, a full spectrum of energy-consumption elements must be considered. Hundreds of individual subsystems and components must be analyzed, interrelated with others, and reanalyzed before the final design decisions are made. Windows, for example, have a major effect on the heat loss or heat gain of a building; they affect the electric lighting system, as well, and the placement of furniture and partitions. But windows also play an important role in the function and comfort of the building, and in the visual appeal of the exterior. Once these factors have been interrelated, a design concept selected, and heating and cooling loads calculated, any change—such as reorienting the building or adding sun screens to the exterior wall—requires a major reanalysis of the energy-using characteristics. By traditional methods, this was possible only by calling on experienced judgment, or by spending many hours at manual computation. Quantitative comparisons of various alternative concepts were not feasible.

Many of the decisions affecting energy savings must be made by the building owner and user—because they affect the performance of the building for its intended use, or because they affect the costs of the building. Building owners, developers, and users should be aware of the importance of the design factors that can lead to energy conservation in their buildings, and they should insist on energy-saving analyses and design concepts from their design professionals.

The significant factors that affect the energy consumption of a building are listed on page 427. All are important—lighting levels, thermal comfort levels, operating schedules, air conditioning system design characteristics, as well as envelope factors. Each of these energy factors must be studied and integrated with the total design if energy savings are to be maximized. Since design of the envelope precedes decisions on most of the other factors—and because the envelope has many interfaces—design optimization decisions are highly complex. This research study on the energy and lifecycle costs of the building enveloe is just one part of the whole effort, but it is a very important part.

The Envelope and Energy. Of all the building elements with energy-saving potential, the ones that offer the greatest array of choices are those included in the building envelope. Hundreds of feasible combinations exist, and all will have an impact on energy consumption, as well as on the capital investment, the annual cost of operation, and the visual quality and functional performance of the building. Envelope design decisions are crucial to the success of the building for its entire life. Yet these decisions are made in the earliest stages of

Factors That Affect Energy Use in Buildings

Functional factors
- Building location
- Building size and function
- Floor area per person
- Efficiency of processing equipment and appliances
- Building operating schedules

Environmental factors
- Lighting levels
- Thermal comfort levels

Envelope factors
- Orientation of building
- Shape of building
- Mass of building
- Wall and roof insulation value (''*U*'' factor)
- Glass area and location
- Reflectivity of ''skin'' (walls, roof, glass)
- Skin shading or screening

Air-conditioning system factors
- Air conditioning system design characteristics
- Air conditioning equipment selection and efficiency
- Heat recovery and recycling
- Natural (outside air) ventilation provisions

Energy source factors
- Energy source selection
- Choice of fuel

Electrical system factors
- Electrical power utilization efficiencies
- Lighting system design characteristics

conceptualization, often virtually without the benefit of quantitative comparisons or alternatives.

Architects and engineers have had, for many years, both the imagination and the technology to develop building envelopes with great thermal efficiency. But the possible combinations of envelope variables are so great that it was not feasible to spend the time and money to accurately determine and analyze the energy use of all the alternatives—even of a small number of alternatives. For one design alone, a determination of air conditioning energy requirements presents a computational task of major proportions. Thus the designers of building envelopes for high thermal performance relied on experienced judgment and engineering generalizations, which yielded solutions that were workable, but sometimes inefficient, thus not optimal in energy use.

With the availability of the computer model design process for evaluating the thermal performance of building envelope factors, almost all the energy-saving variables of the envelope can be explored and evaluated, quickly and economically, as part of the design process.

Methodology

The Simulation Process. Our envelope:energy computer-aided design process works simply. Using traditional architectural and engineering design approaches to alternative concepts, together with an appropriate

Annual "Environmental Systems" Energy Distribution, Typical Office Building:

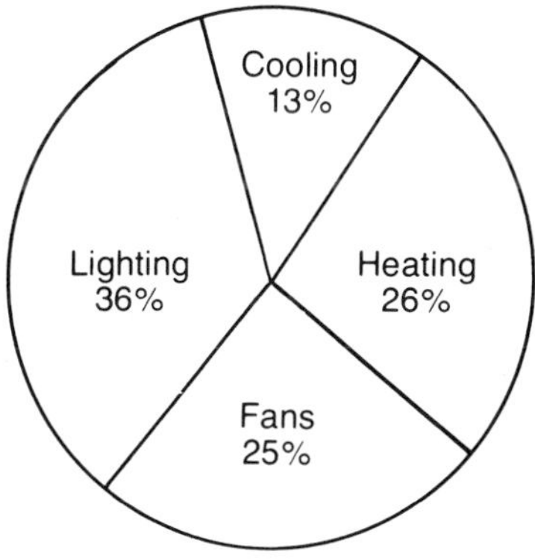

New York

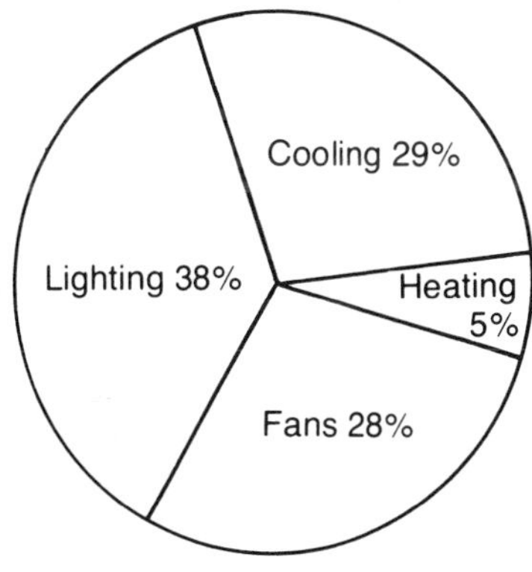

Los Angeles

Figure 3.70

computer model, evaluation criteria for each alternative concept can be established.

The process depends critically on the comprehensiveness of the computer model of the building's thermal performance. Just as a block model shows the visual effects of a building as a viewer moves around it, the envelope:energy model of a building computes the energy demands (on a simplified basis) through a full year's cycle of seasons. It finds the peak hourly energy demand and the total annual heating and cooling energy requirements (based on load calculations). Then, using the costs of buying and utilizing energy, both the initial capital investment in skin and mechanical equipment and the annual energy cost of operation are calculated.

Flexibility is important in the conceptual design stage, and to encourage the investigation of many variables, or alternative designs, simplifying assumptions were made that greatly reduced computational time and increased the economy of the model's use. For example, the impacts of varying effectiveness of different heating and air conditioning systems, of different operating schedules, or of alternative energy sources, were not included in the simulation model in the conceptual stage of design. Even though the calculations are made on a simplified basis, they are quite accurate for purposes of comparing alternative concepts.

The Computer. Only a small amount of computer time is needed; thus the use of the model is well within the range of reasonable and conventional design fees. As a consequence, the effects of a whole spectrum of envelope design variables on energy use and costs can be evaluated for most buildings now being designed. The envelope:energy computer model is tailored to help select a building envelope that minimizes energy use in balance with many nonenergy considerations. The model is not intended for air conditioning system design comparisons or for optimizing system operation. Such evaluations are later steps in the design process.

Using the programs that we have assembled or developed, the evaluation process works in the following simple way.

1 Weather data for the locale of the building are obtained, then processed by the weather package of programs for use by the computer load calculation programs, and plotted for general design guidance.
2 A "base" building concept is designed from the client's architectural program, and descriptive parameters of the building are coded for computer processing. Descriptive data include thermal and shading characteristics of wall and roof materials, as well as internal heat sources of equipment, lighting, and people.
3 From the input data, and the load calculation programs, the computer calculates the heating and cooling loads for each hour of the weather data. It determines the peak load and sums up the hourly energy demand for heating or cooling to simulate a year of operation.

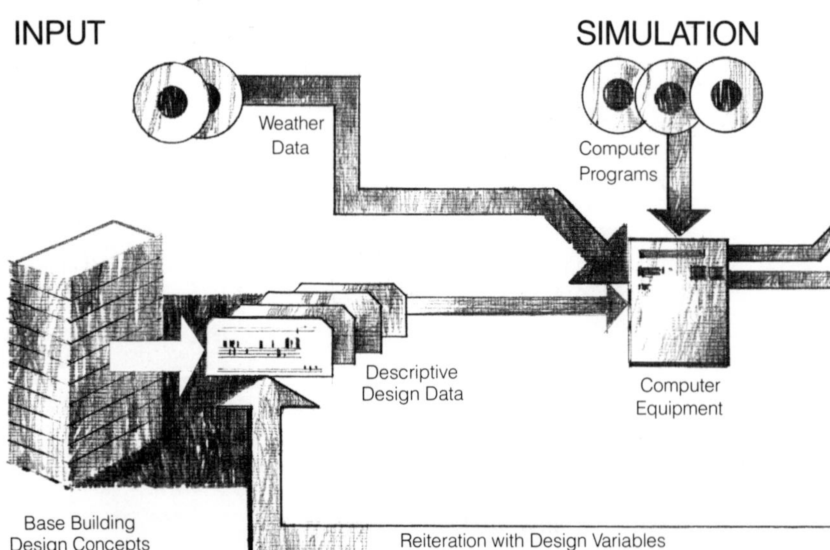

Figure 3.71

4 From cost estimates for air conditioning systems plus estimates for skin construction elements, the initial capital investment in skin and mechanical equipment is calculated. From fuel and electrical costs the approximate annual operating energy cost is calculated (system efficiencies and operating characteristics are not included in this simplified model).

5 The capital cost and the annual energy cost, as well as system peak capacities, are the evaluation criteria for comparing alternative designs. Printout gives actual numerical values for each of the following factors:

Total heating capacity Total cooling capacity	Thousand Btu per hour
Total air supply capacity	Refrigeration tons Cubic feet per minute
Building skin and mechanical system capital cost	Dollars per square foot of building
Annual operating energy cost	Dollars per year

6 The design is modified with one (or more) of the applicable envelope design variables, and the evaluation criteria are again computed for comparison with the "base" building values.

In a typical design process, this procedure can be repeated to reach an optimum combination of energy use, initial cost, operating cost, visual design, functional design, and other factors.

This section presents a detailed analysis of a representative building—a multistory office building in two distinctly different climatic locations, New York and Los Angeles—with the results for alternative envelope variables plotted for easy examination and comparison. Because of the typical characteristics of the building, the results may be extrapolated to cover a reasonably wide range of building types and locations. The results present convincing evidence of the important effect of certain envelope design decisions on the ultimate energy use and cost of the building.

Input

Weather Data. Since the envelope:energy design process considers the interaction of the building envelope with weather conditions, accurate information on weather conditions throughout the year is a necessity. Fortunately, historical weather data are readily available for all representative locations in the United States. Traditional design methods used only a fraction of the data—the "peak" conditions—for sizing the maximum capacities of the heating and cooling systems. Since the actual year-round energy consumption could be only approximated, there was substantial potential for design error. With computerized computations, energy consumption can be calculated on an hourly basis throughout the year with relative ease.

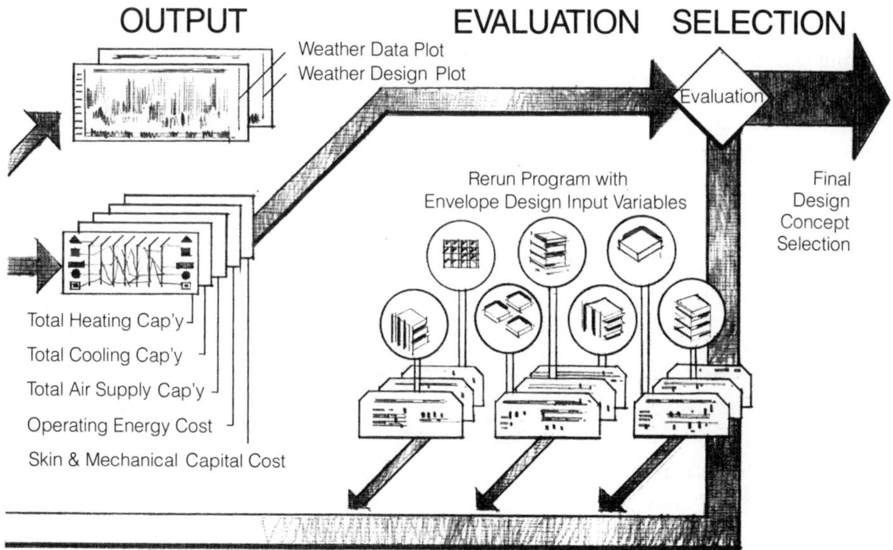

The weather data are available on magnetic tape, suitable for computer input, from the National Weather Service's National Climatic Center. Each year's tape contains surface observations taken every hour (total of 8760 per year) at meteorological stations throughout the United States. The data include dry-bulb temperature, wet-bulb temperature, wind velocity, and cloud cover (or haze) conditions. Tapes are available for all years since 1950 at most locations.

For the computer input, a tape is selected that is deemed representative of the probable weather conditions (see Appendix for further details). A sample of these data, for two locations, are shown in the top two plots of Figure 3.72.

In the envelope:energy analysis, the "weather package" program processes the raw weather data into a form suitable for input into the energy load calculation program. Even with the computer, the cost of computing energy loads for each of 8760 hours of the year is expensive. To reduce computer time, we use a statistically simplified representation of the hourly weather data that provides more than sufficient accuracy for evaluating the relative energy effects of alternative building envelope concepts, with a substantial savings in computer time and cost.

To obtain this simplification, the raw data are scanned and three representative days per month are selected for use as 24-hour design weather profiles. The high, median, and low dry-bulb temperature days are chosen. These profiles are used to calculate the hourly energy consumption for three days per month for each of the 12 months—a total of only 864 hours.

A weighted average of the 864-hour data is computed. Then simple multiplication gives an approximate energy consumption for the entire year, for much less computer time than would be needed to calculate 8760 individual hours. The accuracy of the resulting "synthesized" weather data may not be sufficient for simulation of air conditioning system operation, but it is quite adequate for the comparison of the energy-use effects of alternative envelope design concepts. The lower two plots in Figure 3.72 are the simplified high, low, and median data.

Geographic Effects. Changes in weather conditions due to location can cause major differences in the effects of different energy-saving design variables. The use of the correct weather data for the locate is important. However conclusions made from studies in one location can yield valuable guidance for other locations, if they are applied with judgment and with knowledge of local

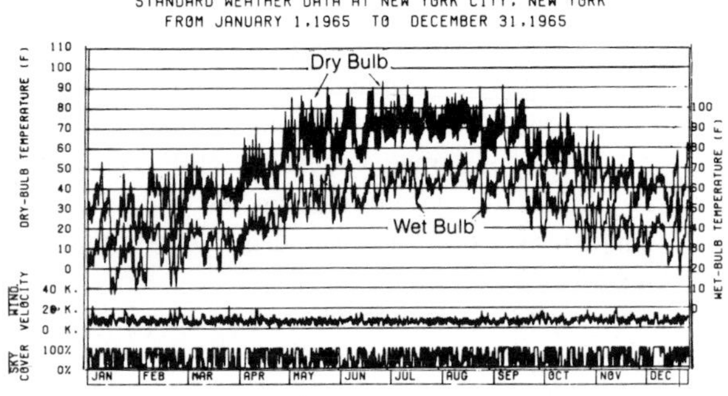

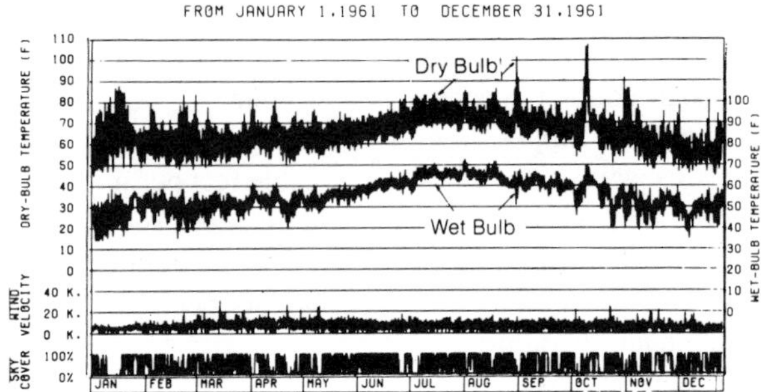

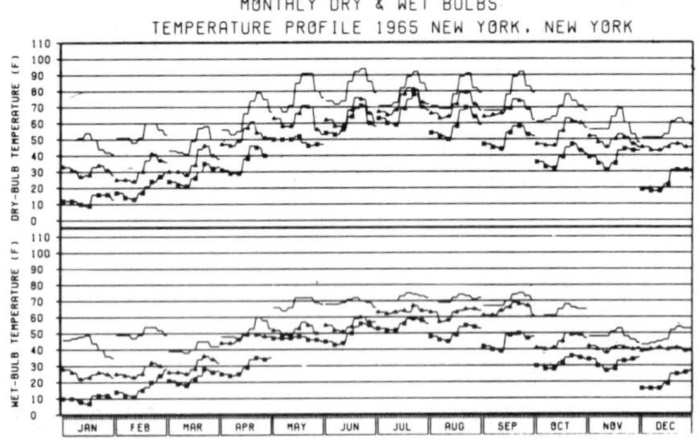

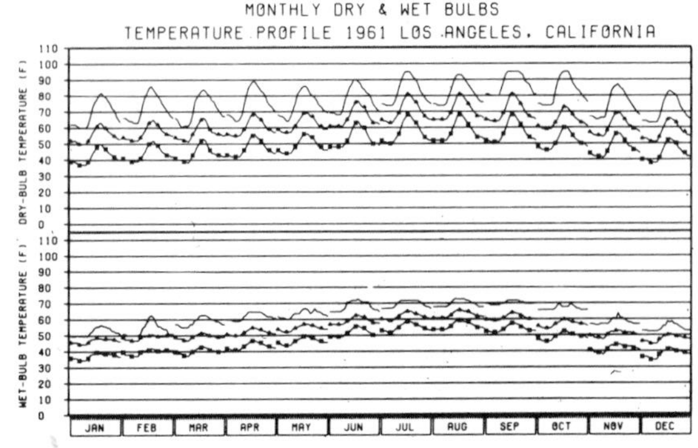

Figure 3.72

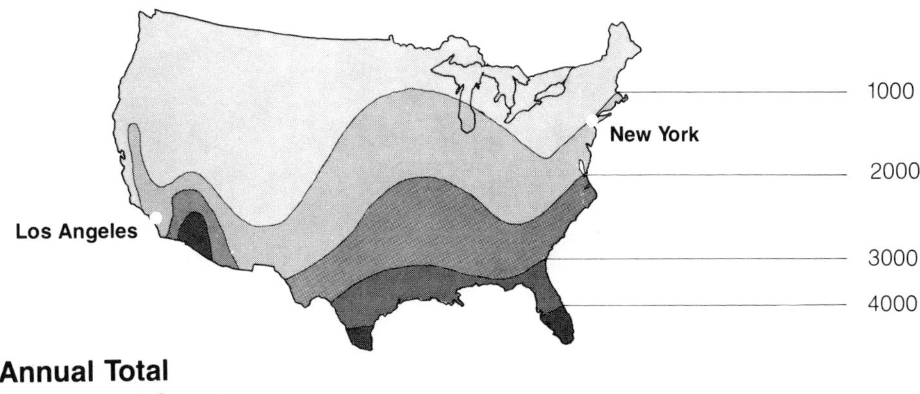

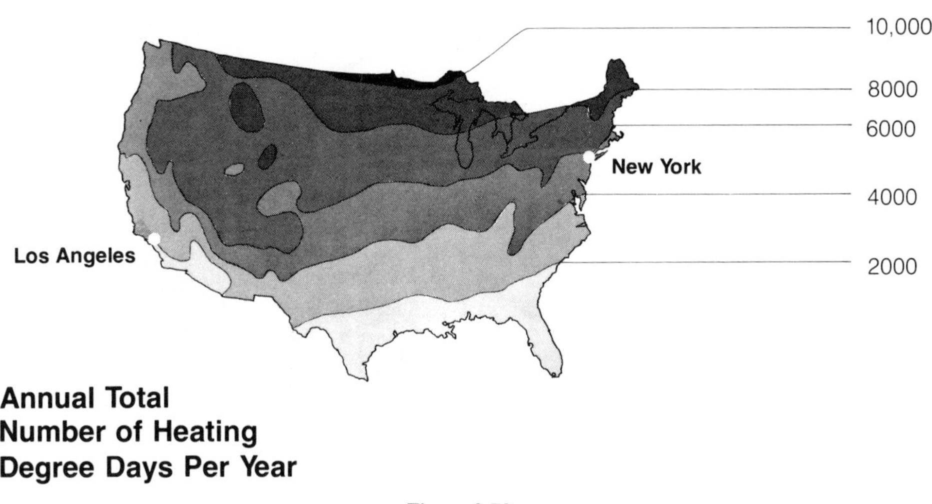

Figure 3.73

conditions. Figure 3.73 shows how some key weather parameters vary throughout the country from those at the two locations used in this study.

Base Building. For this research study, a representative office building was chosen as typical of a large range of building types and sizes. This ''base'' building is a hypothetical office building having 10 floors and a total gross floor area of 150,000 square feet. The significant characteristics of the base building design are illustrated in the section on variables. More detailed data are included in the Appendix.

The initial study of a square floor plan was augmented by four more shapes (donut, triangle, rectangle, and circle) to show the relative effects of glass to gross floor area, and other variables.

In an actual building design situation using the energy:envelope design process, any number of building shapes may be evaluated (as well as any number of orientation angles), each as a ''variation'' of the base building. As an example of this capability, among the variables considered here are changes in floor-by-floor height or in total number of floors.

The results of the study on costs and energy consumption for the base building provide a reference baseline for comparing the relative values of the alternative designs, or variables, analyzed.

Envelope Variables. A representative range of typical building envelope design choices that are important to energy consumption were analyzed. Each as evaluated as an alternative design concept or ''variable'' of the base

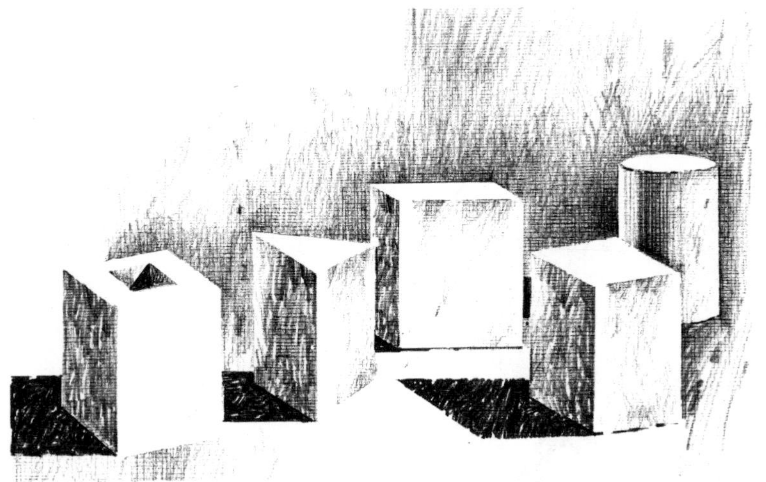

Donut
Triangle
Rectangle
Square
Circle

Figure 3.74

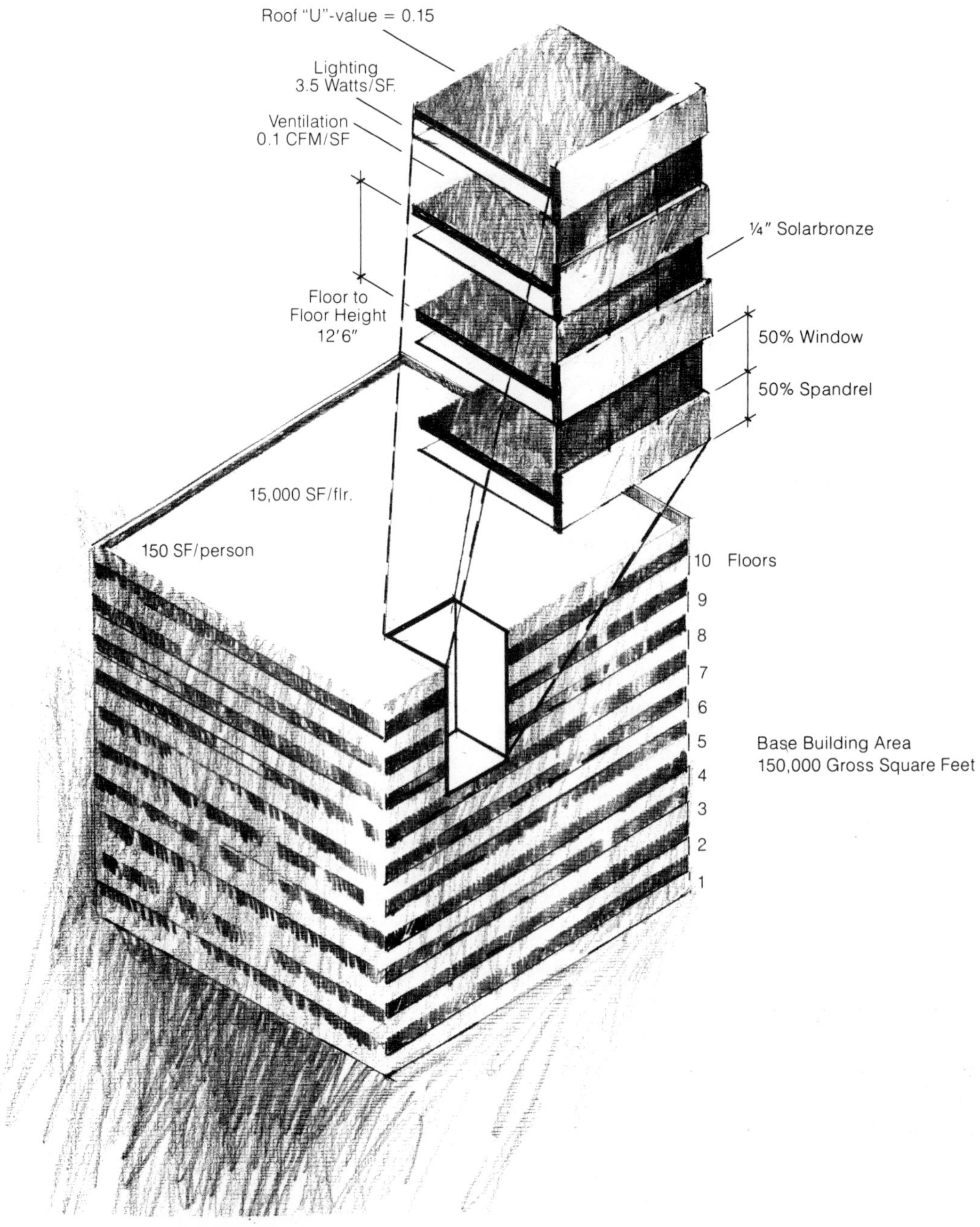
Roof "U"-value = 0.15
Lighting
3.5 Watts/SF.
Ventilation
0.1 CFM/SF
Floor to
Floor Height
12'6"
¼" Solarbronze
50% Window
50% Spandrel
15,000 SF/flr.
150 SF/person
10 Floors
9
8
7
6
5
4
3
2
1
Base Building Area
150,000 Gross Square Feet

Figure 3.75

building design. As indicated in Figure 3.71, each "variable" was treated as one change in the design concept of the base building. The output results were recomputed for each design variation. The variables are described in detail in the pages that follow. To simplify the identification of the results given in the Output section, each variable has been given a code number.

The computer-aided design process is not limited to these variables alone. For example, orientation effects can be calculated for any angle of rotation. Any building shape, height, or proportion can be analyzed, or any fin or overhang dimension. Also, the effects of any combination of transmissive or reflective skin characteristics can be calculated.

The 23 variables that were used are as follows:

1 45° rotation.
2 90° rotation.
3 11-foot, 6-inch height
4 13-foot, 6-inch height
5 75% window/25% wall.
6 25% window/75% wall.
7 75% window wall + thermopane.
8 Mirror glass.
9 Mirror thermopane units.
10 5-foot horizontal overhang.
11 5-foot vertical fins.
12 5-foot south overhang—east-west fins.
13 3-foot overhang—waffle.
14 5-foot overhang—waffle.
15 45° rotated waffle.
16 90° rotated waffle.
17 Opaque east-west walls—south overhang.
18 Canted east-west walls—south overhang.
19 One 2-story building.
20 One 2-story building with insulation.
21 Three 2-story buildings.
22 Three 2-story buildings with insulation.
23 Air exchange of 0.5 cubic foot per minute.

Rotation. Orientation of the building is changed by rotating the building plan about its vertical axis from the north-south orientation of the base building 0°; first 45°, then 90°, as indicated by positions 0 through 2 in Figure 3.76. Any degree of rotation could be studied by the process, but 45° and 90° are the most significant. Orientation, of course, is important to the heat gain effects of solar radiation on the building. In a building oriented north-south, the south side receives more direct sunlight than the north, and the east and west facades receive the rays of the sun at lower angles than the south—and at different times of day. Since all these aspects affect the heat gain of the envelope, a change of orientation will cause changes in energy consumption, especially for shading devices of certain shapes or types.

Floor Height. Decreasing or increasing the floor-to-floor dimension from the original dimension for the base building (i.e., 12½ ft) to 11½ feet, and to 13½ feet, changed the height, therefore the exterior wall area and total volume of the building (3 and 4 in Figure 3.77). The total floor area remains fixed. The total glass area also remains unchanged, but the window/wall ratio changes as the height is changed. The effect of these variables is to change the total amount of skin area, while keeping the building area constant.

We explore these variables to learn what differing building heights or ceiling heights do to energy use. At this design stage, the relative energy and cost effects of duct space needs versus floor-to-floor height costs are not taken into account.

Window/Wall Ratio. Decreasing or increasing the relative amount of glass area by changing the window/wall ratio from the base building value of 50 to 75%, and to 25%, changes the thermal characteristics of the skin in two ways (5 and 6 in Figure 3.78). First, it changes the heat transmitted by conduction, since glass has higher conductance than the spandrel wall material. Second, since glass is relatively transparent to thermal radiation, it changes the amount of radiant heat that is passed through the skin. Using mirror thermal pane glazing on the 75% window/wall ratio concept significantly improves thermal performance (7 in Figure 3.78).

Glazing. The thermal effects of glass materials on energy consumption are both significant and complex. The high U value of glass causes it to contribute to higher energy consumption because of conduction in both winter and summer. During cooling periods, cooling loads on air conditioning systems from "direct" solar radiation through glass are great. But during heating periods, solar radiation can potentially reduce the heating energy required by the building.

One way to reduce thermal losses (or possibly gains) through glass is to change its reflectivity and conductivity. Reflectivity can be changed by adding a mirror coating to the solar bronze heat-absorbing glass of the base building (8 in Figure 3.79). Both reflectivity and conductivity can be changed by using mirror thermopane, a dual glazing material with a reflective coating (9 in Figure 3.79). In evaluating alternative glazing materials, it is important to remember that although thermal effectiveness is greatly affected by the choice of glass, so are cost and appearance.

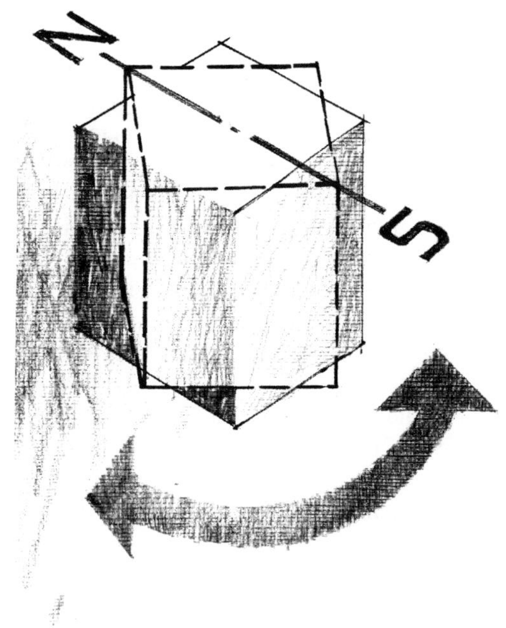
N
S

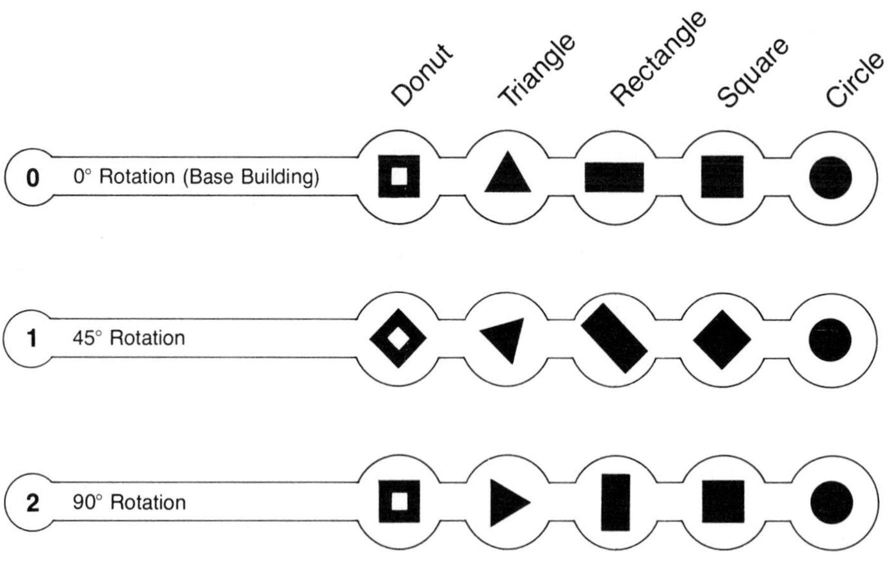
Donut
Triangle
Rectangle
Square
Circle
0 0° Rotation (Base Building)
1 45° Rotation
2 90° Rotation

Figure 3.76

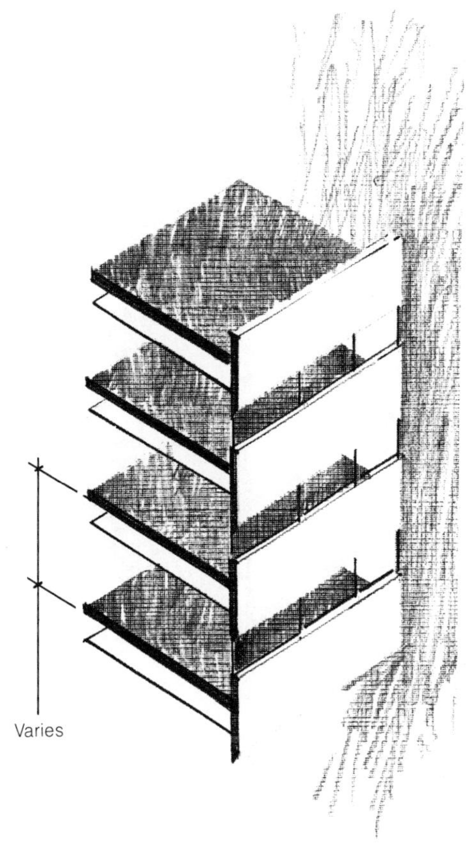
Varies

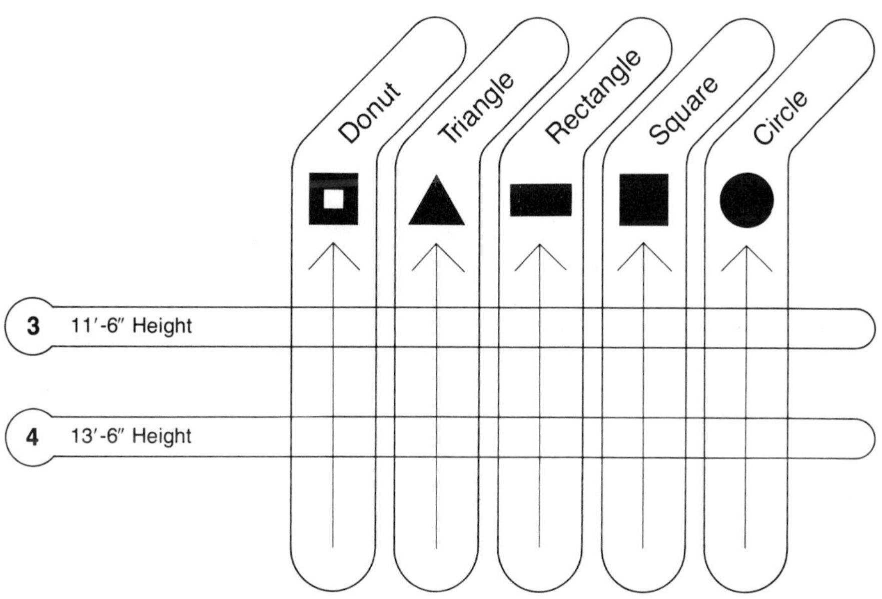
Donut
Triangle
Rectangle
Square
Circle
3 11′-6″ Height
4 13′-6″ Height

Figure 3.77

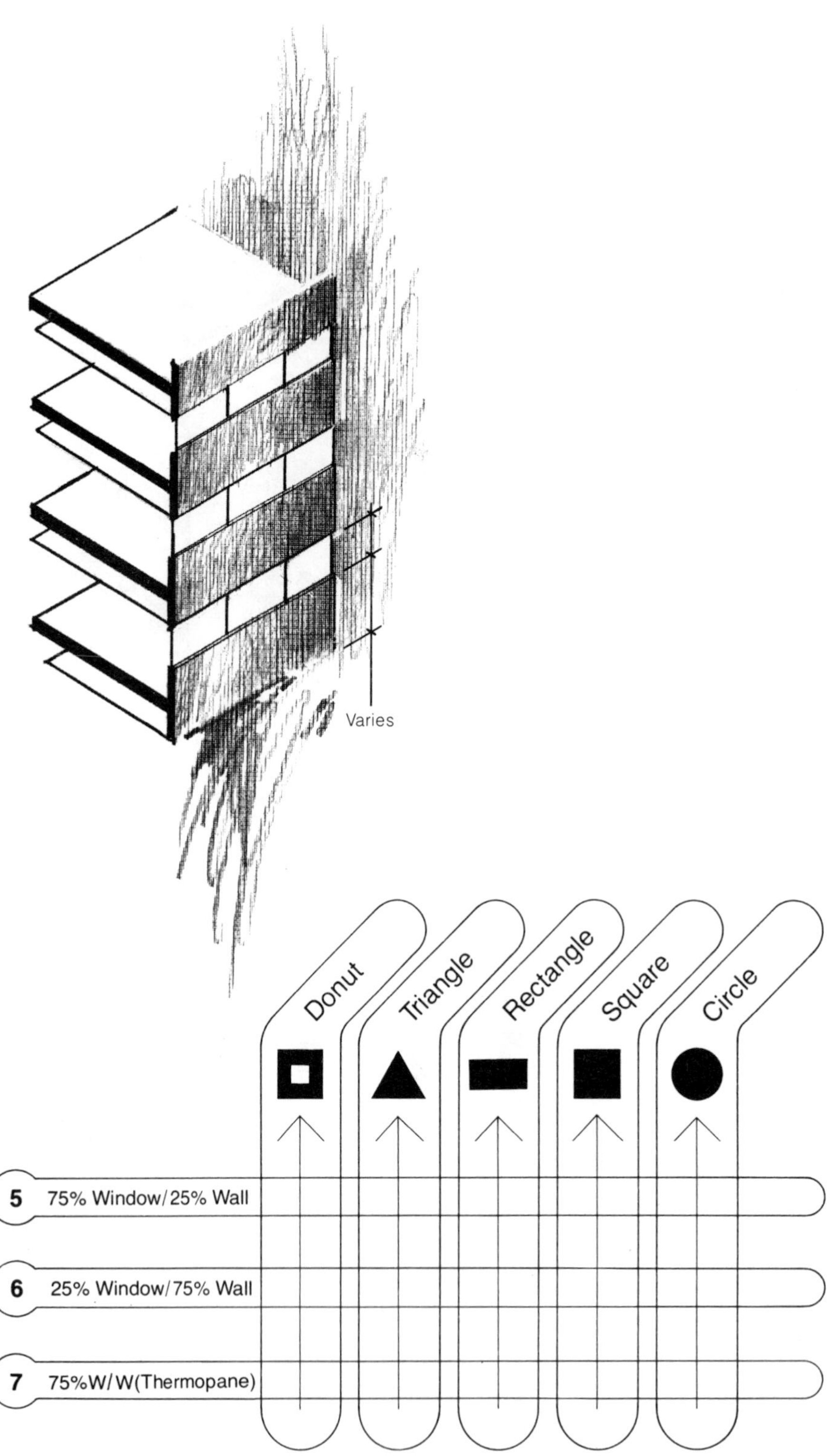
Varies
Donut
Triangle
Rectangle
Square
Circle
5 75% Window/25% Wall
6 25% Window/75% Wall
7 75%W/W(Thermopane)

Figure 3.78

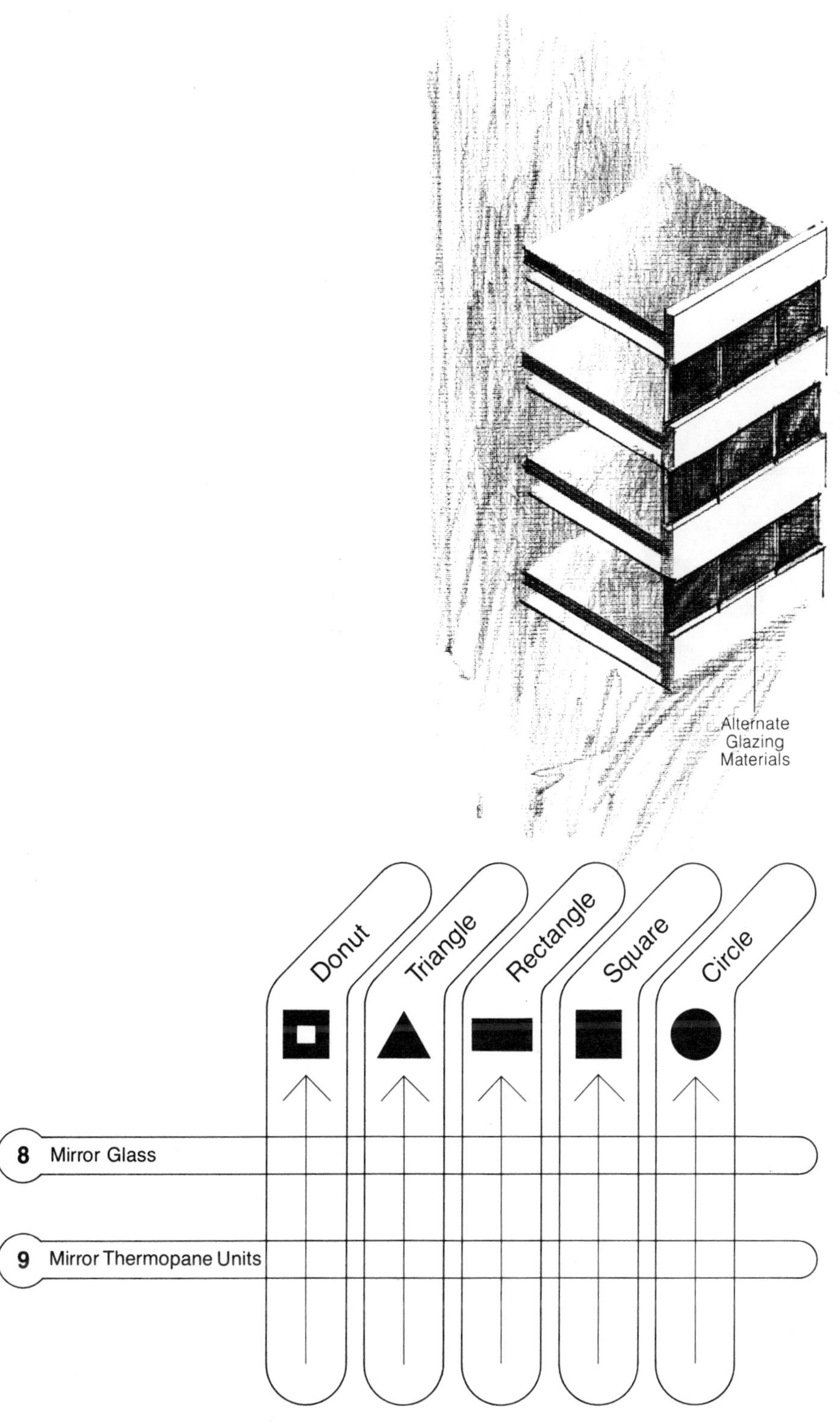
Alternate Glazing Materials
Donut
Triangle
Rectangle
Square
Circle
8 Mirror Glass
9 Mirror Thermopane Units

Figure 3.79

Overhang and Fin. External shading devices are effective ways of reducing solar heat loads on building glass and wall areas. Overhangs are most effective on south walls, since they block the high angle sun rays that strike the building in the middle of the day. Fins provide protection from the low angle rays of morning and afternoon, against which overhangs are ineffective. In this study, three combinations were examined: overhangs on all sides at each floor, vertical fins on all sides, spaced at 10 feet on center, and (except for the triangular and circular buildings) overhangs on the south wall and fins on the east and west walls (10–12 in Figure 3.80). In all cases, the overhangs and fins have a depth of 5 feet from the face of the wall to the outer edge of the device.

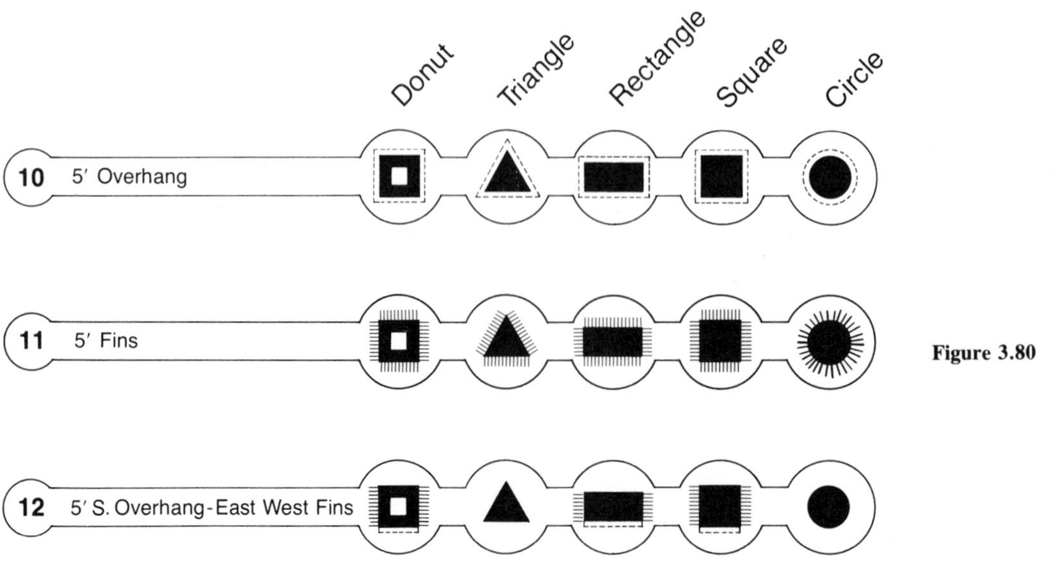

Figure 3.80

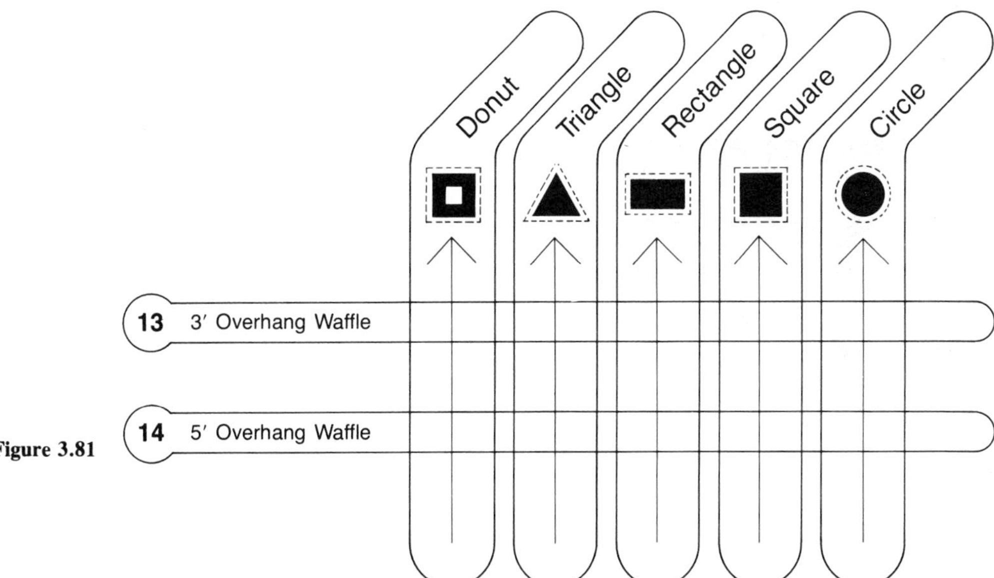

Figure 3.81

Waffle. Combining overhangs and fins creates a "waffle" effect that offers the benefits of both—although the building cost increases and the visibility from the building decreases. Two waffle systems applied to all walls of the building were explored: a 3-foot depth and a 5-foot depth (13 and 14 in Figure 3.81).

Rotated Waffle. The effectiveness of sun shading devices is especially dependent on their orientation to the solar radiation. Knowledge of the relative effects of rotating each of the building shapes, with waffle sunshades on all sides, provides further insight into the value of sunshades.

As before, the buildings using a 5-foot waffle were rotated from the base building orientation (0°) by an angle of 45°, then by an angle of 90° (15 and 16, Figure 3.82).

Combination. Other wall and sun shading combinations may have major impacts on building energy consumption. Two likely choices were selected for this study. The first (17 in Figure 3.83) has opaque east and west walls (no windows), and a 5-foot overhang on the south wall (north and south walls retain the 50% window/wall ratio of the base building). The second (18 in Figure 3.83) has a 5-foot overhang on the south wall, and the east and west walls have 10-foot fins that are angled or canted 45° toward the north—thereby providing shading from morning and afternoon sun. In addition, for the second variable the rectangular building has been rotated 90°, so that the longer walls are facing east and west. These combinations are not applicable to the triangular and circular building shapes.

An Equivalent 2-Story Building. Modifying the building shape so that wall and roof areas change in relation to the total floor area (which was kept constant in this study) may also have a major impact on building energy consumption. To examine this effect, the building height was reduced from 10 stories to 2 (75,000 ft^2 per floor; 19 in Figure 3.84) but with the identical floor-plan shape and all other building characteristics the same (see Appendix for actual dimensions). Since the total heat transfer through the larger roof is significant, its effect was analyzed by varying the roof insulation. This was done by adding insulation to decrease the U value of the roof from 0.15 (the base building value) to 0.05 (20 in Figure 3.84).

Three 2-Story Buildings. To further explore the effects of size and shape, the single 2-story building was replaced by *three* 2-story buildings that, together, have the same total floor area. Each has the same floor plan shape as the base building. The first has no other changes; the second has additional roof insulation (21 and 22 in Figure 3.85).

These variables allow us to explore the effects of buildings of different size and shape. Several small buildings have a greater envelope skin area than one compact building of the same floor area, and the effects of wall and roof differ also. These variables can exert significant effects on energy consumption of alternative building concepts.

Air Change. To determine the effect of a higher ventilation rate, the fresh air requirement of 0.1 cubic foot per minute per square foot for the base building was changed

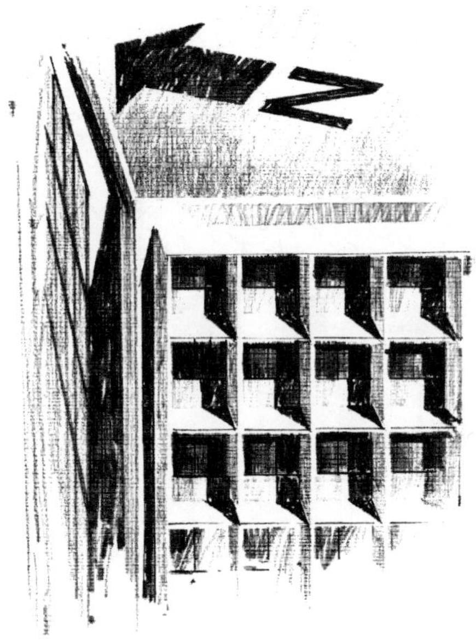

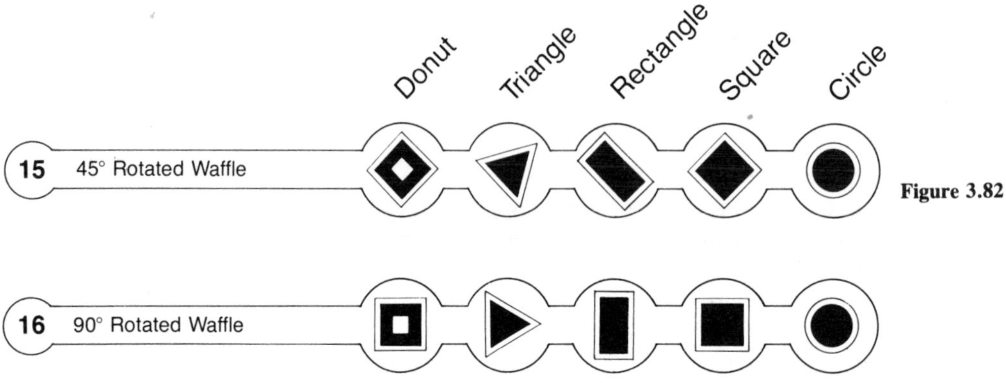

Figure 3.82

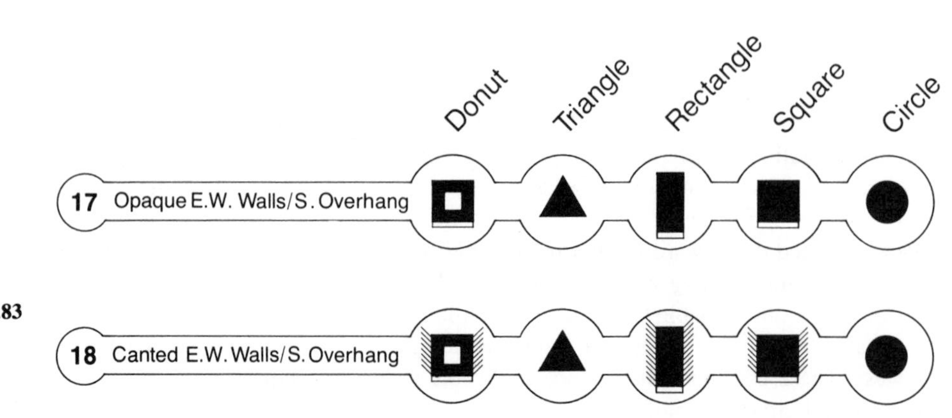

Figure 3.83

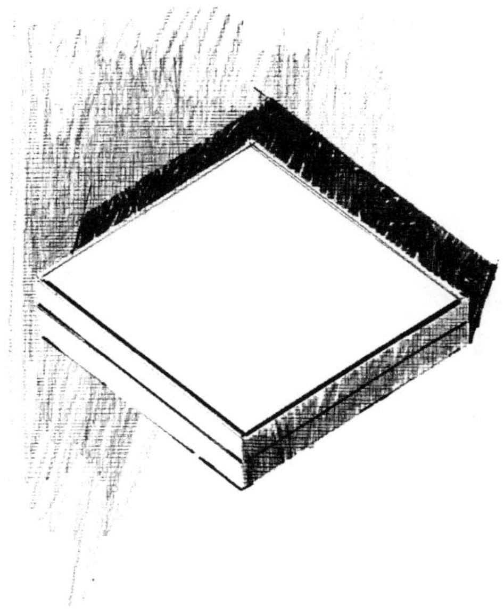

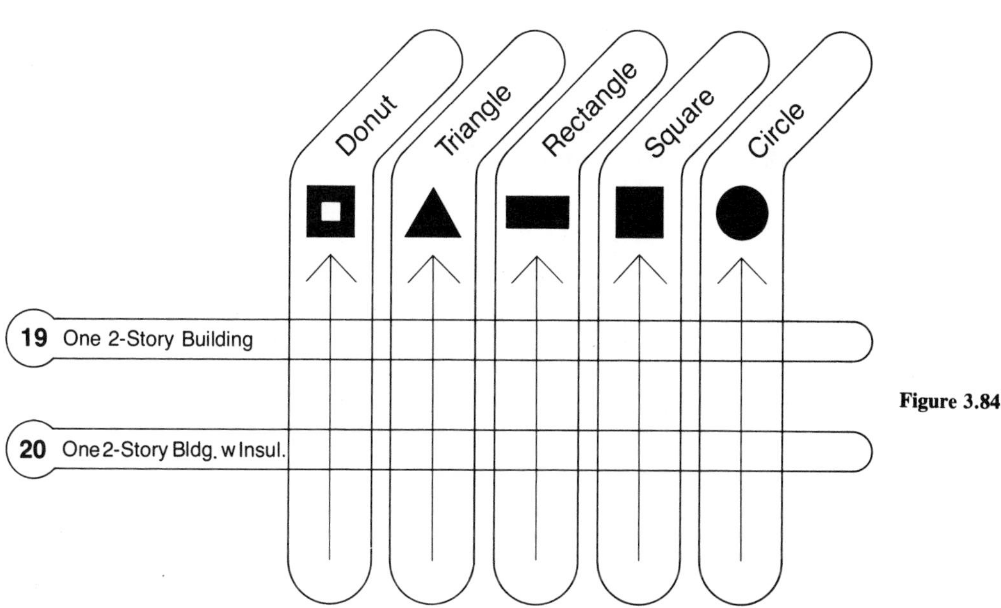

Figure 3.84

to a value of 0.5 (Figure 3.86). These values were arbitrarily chosen for this study to indicate the effects of different ventilation rates.

Natural ventilation using operable windows, an option that is not included in this report, is worthy of consideration for a select number of occupancies—primarily those that can rely on the individual occupants to ''maintain'' the desired comfort level of their spaces.

Output

Results. As discussed in the section on Simulation, the outputs of the computer analysis are the skin and mechanical equipment capital costs, and the annual operating energy cost. If desired, these two parameters can be combined into a single value of equivalent annual cost by applying an interest rate and amortization period.

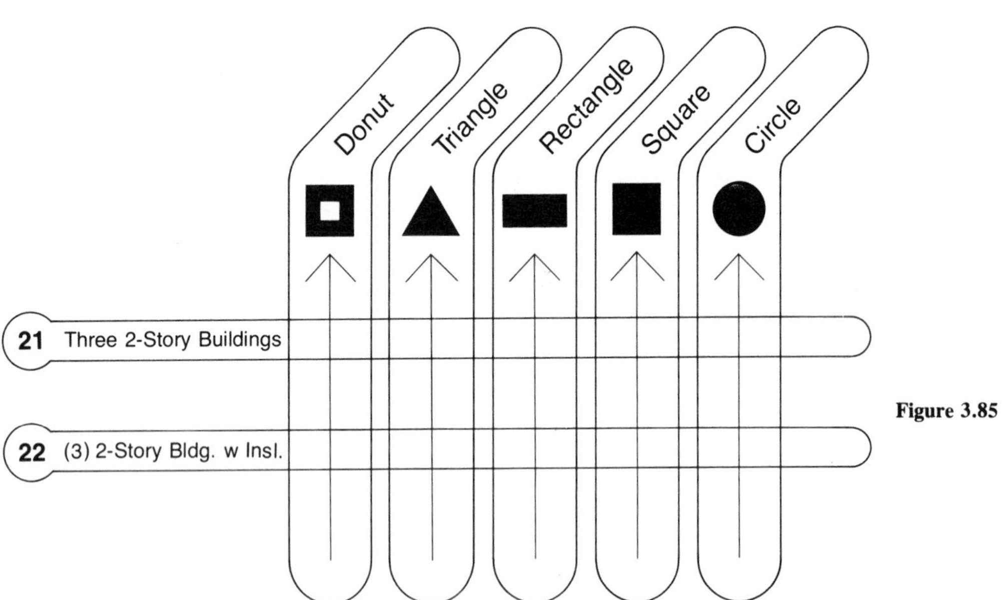

Figure 3.85

The "skin and mechanical capital cost" represents the construction cost of the elements of the building skin and of the mechanical heating and air conditioning plant and distribution system. Cost units representative of material, equipment, and installation for comparable items have been used. Peak heating and cooling demands determine the plant capacities used for computing the mechanical systems cost.

The "annual operating energy cost" is the cost of energy required for both heating and cooling for a full year. Energy consumption computed by the program is multiplied by a unit energy cost for both heating or cooling to obtain the "annual operating energy cost," which is a common base for evaluating total annual energy consumption of various design approaches. The cost factors that were used are in the Appendix. The building's operating cycle was calculated at 5 A.M. to 11 P.M., 5½ days per week.

These output parameters are presented next, as families of curves having the five shapes for the 23 en-

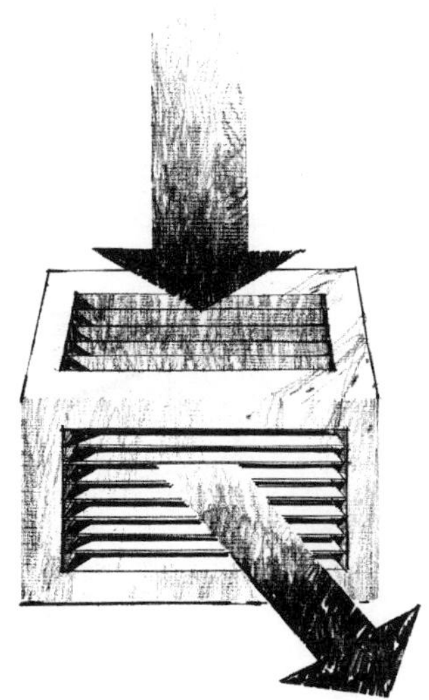

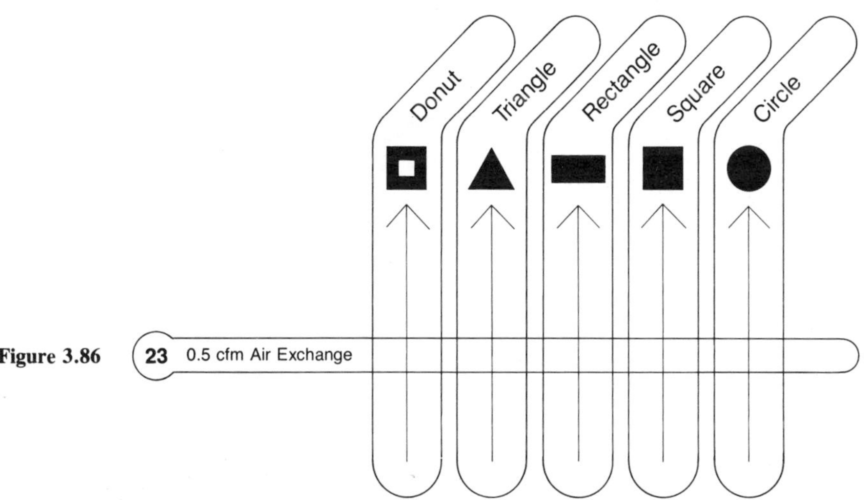

Figure 3.86

velope design variables. The relative effects of the different variables can be quickly compared. Two sets of curves are given for each location—Los Angeles and New York.

The two cost criteria, applied in conjunction with sound design judgment, provide a rational quantitative basis for quickly comparing and evaluating a wide range of alternative envelope design concepts for energy use effectiveness. Along with other design evaluation criteria, such as appearance, durability, and maintenance factors, both the building designer and the owner have a powerful evaluation tool to aid in selecting the best design alternatives for a specific project. Additional curves of peak heating and cooling capacity and of total air supply requirements are included in the Appendix.

This simulation process does not assess the impacts of different heating and air conditioning systems or operating schedules, or of alternative energy sources, which have varying degrees of effectiveness. At the early stage of designing and evaluating building envelope concepts, alternative mechanical and energy systems designs are seldom developed. Furthermore, their choice has little if any effect on the choice of an envelope design—at least within the range of the systems that are usually considered.

Construction costs have been held constant for all locations, even though some variations exist. This permits comparison of relative effects from one location to another at an earlier time than otherwise would have been possible. Because energy costs are significantly different from the West Coast to East, actual local costs have been used: when a shape is not tested with a certain variable it shows as a gap in the plot line in Figures 3.87 to 3.90.

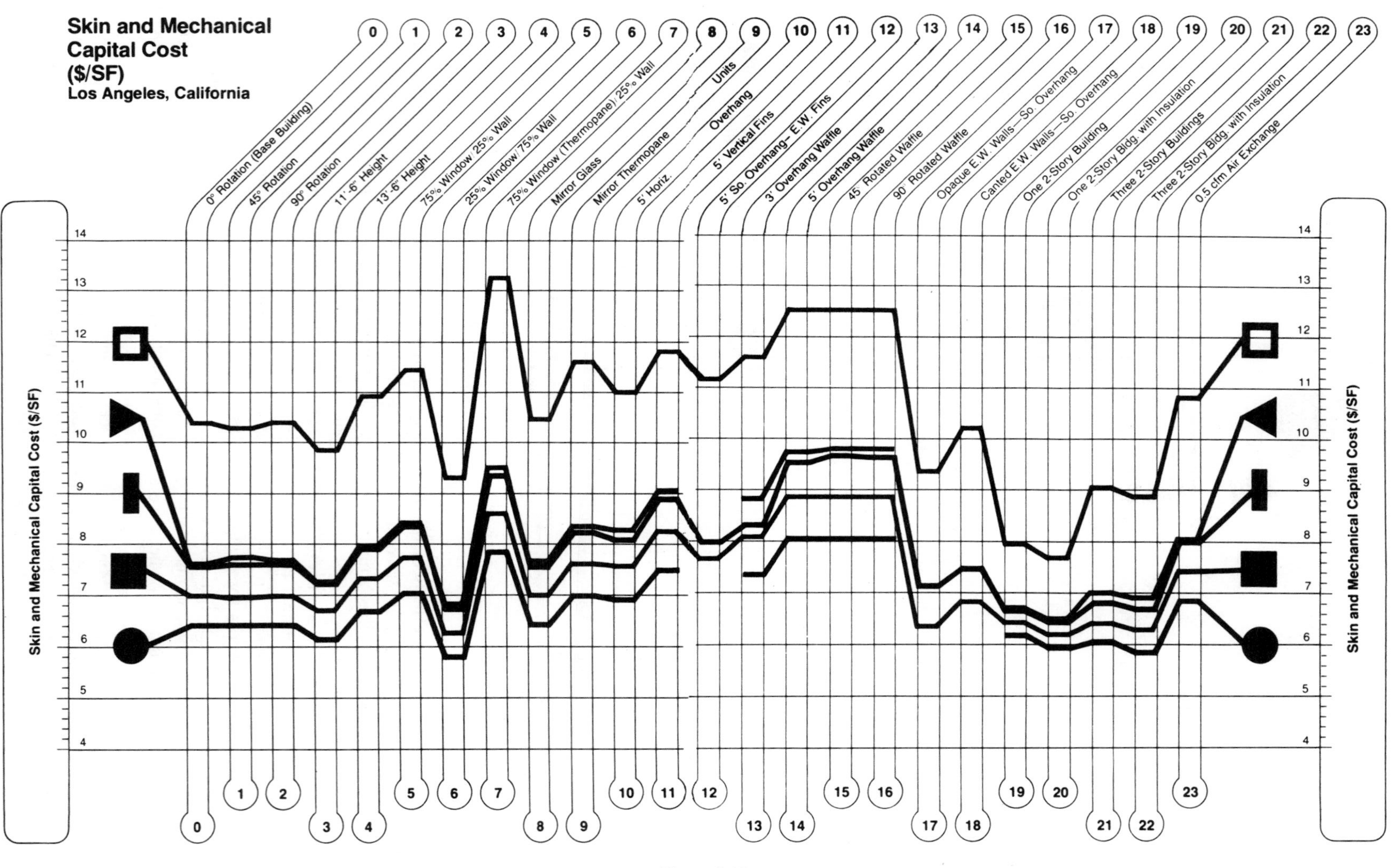

Skin and Mechanical Capital Cost ($/SF)
Los Angeles, California
0° Rotation (Base Building)
45° Rotation
90° Rotation
11'-6" Height
13'-6" Height
75% Window/25% Wall
25% Window/75% Wall
75% Window (Thermopane)/25% Wall
Mirror Glass
Mirror Thermopane
5' Horiz.
Units
Overhang
5' Vertical Fins
5' So. Overhang—E.W. Fins
3' Overhang Waffle
5' Overhang Waffle
45° Rotated Waffle
90° Rotated Waffle
Opaque E.W. Walls—So. Overhang
Canted E.W. Walls—So. Overhang
One 2-Story Building
One 2-Story Bldg. with Insulation
Three 2-Story Buildings
Three 2-Story Bldg. with Insulation
0.5 cfm Air Exchange
Skin and Mechanical Capital Cost ($/SF)

Figure 3.87

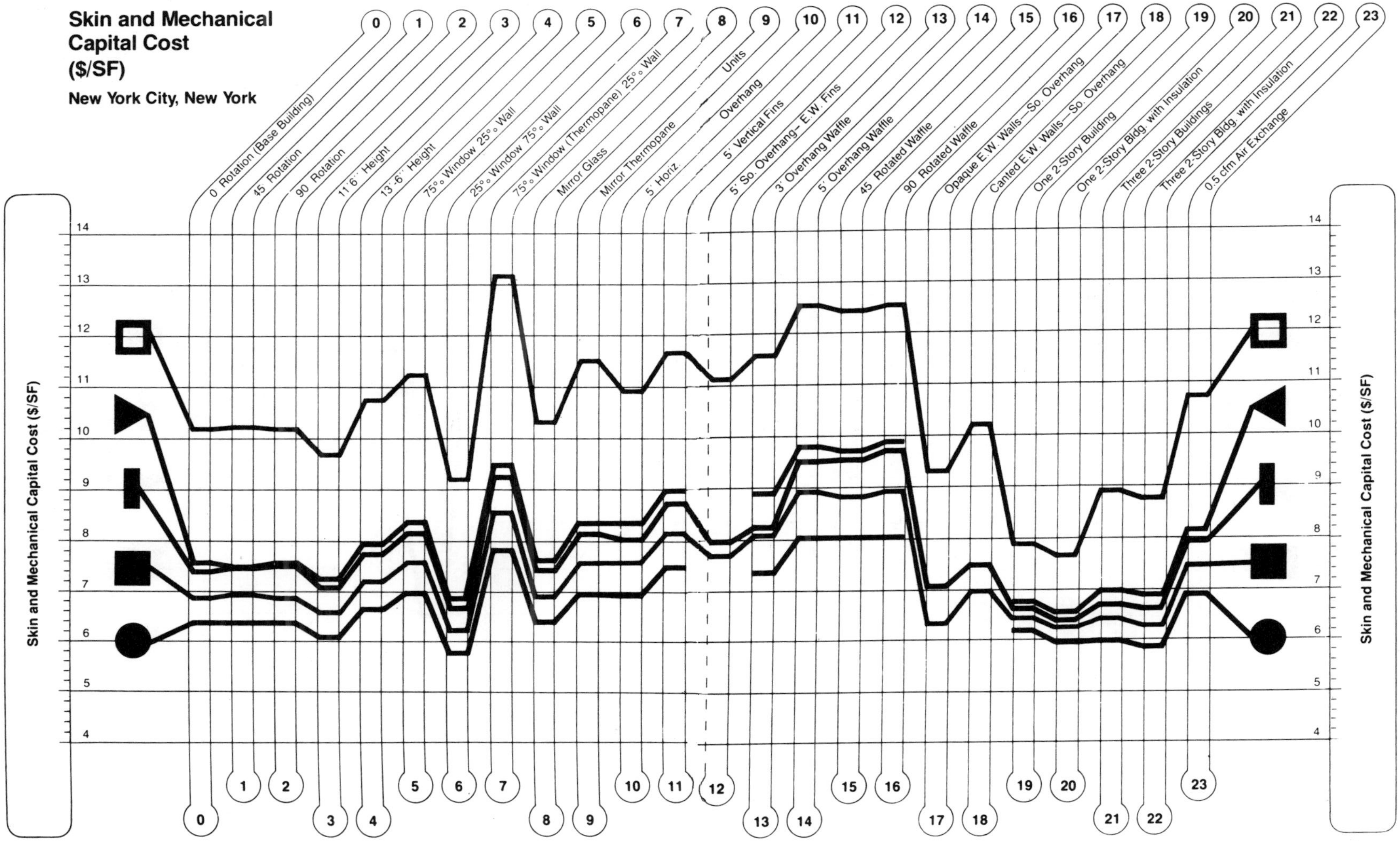

Skin and Mechanical Capital Cost ($/SF)

New York City, New York

Figure 3.88

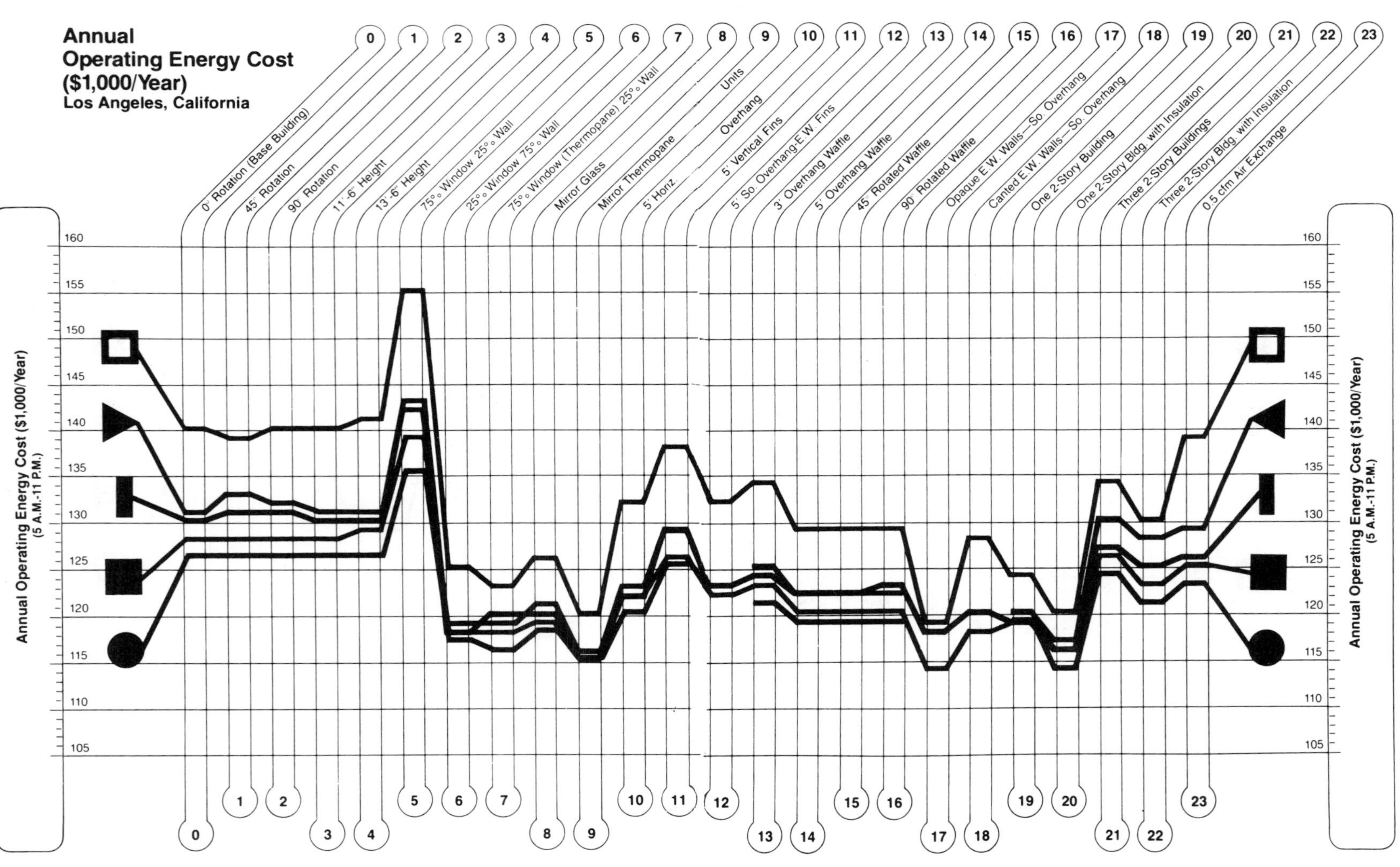
Annual
Operating Energy Cost
($1,000/Year)
Los Angeles, California
0 0° Rotation (Base Building)
1 45° Rotation
2 90° Rotation
3 11'-6" Height
4 13'-6" Height
5 75% Window 25% Wall
6 25% Window 75% Wall
7 75% Window (Thermopane) 25% Wall
8 Mirror Glass
9 Mirror Thermopane
10 5' Horiz.
Units
11 Overhang
12 5' Vertical Fins
13 5' So. Overhang-E.W. Fins
14 3' Overhang Waffle
15 5' Overhang Waffle
16 45° Rotated Waffle
17 90° Rotated Waffle
18 Opaque E.W. Walls—So. Overhang
19 Canted E.W. Walls—So. Overhang
20 One 2-Story Building
21 One 2-Story Bldg. with Insulation
22 Three 2-Story Buildings
23 Three 2-Story Bldg. with Insulation
0.5 cfm Air Exchange
Annual Operating Energy Cost ($1,000/Year)
(5 A.M.-11 P.M.)
160
155
150
145
140
135
130
125
120
115
110
105

Figure 3.89

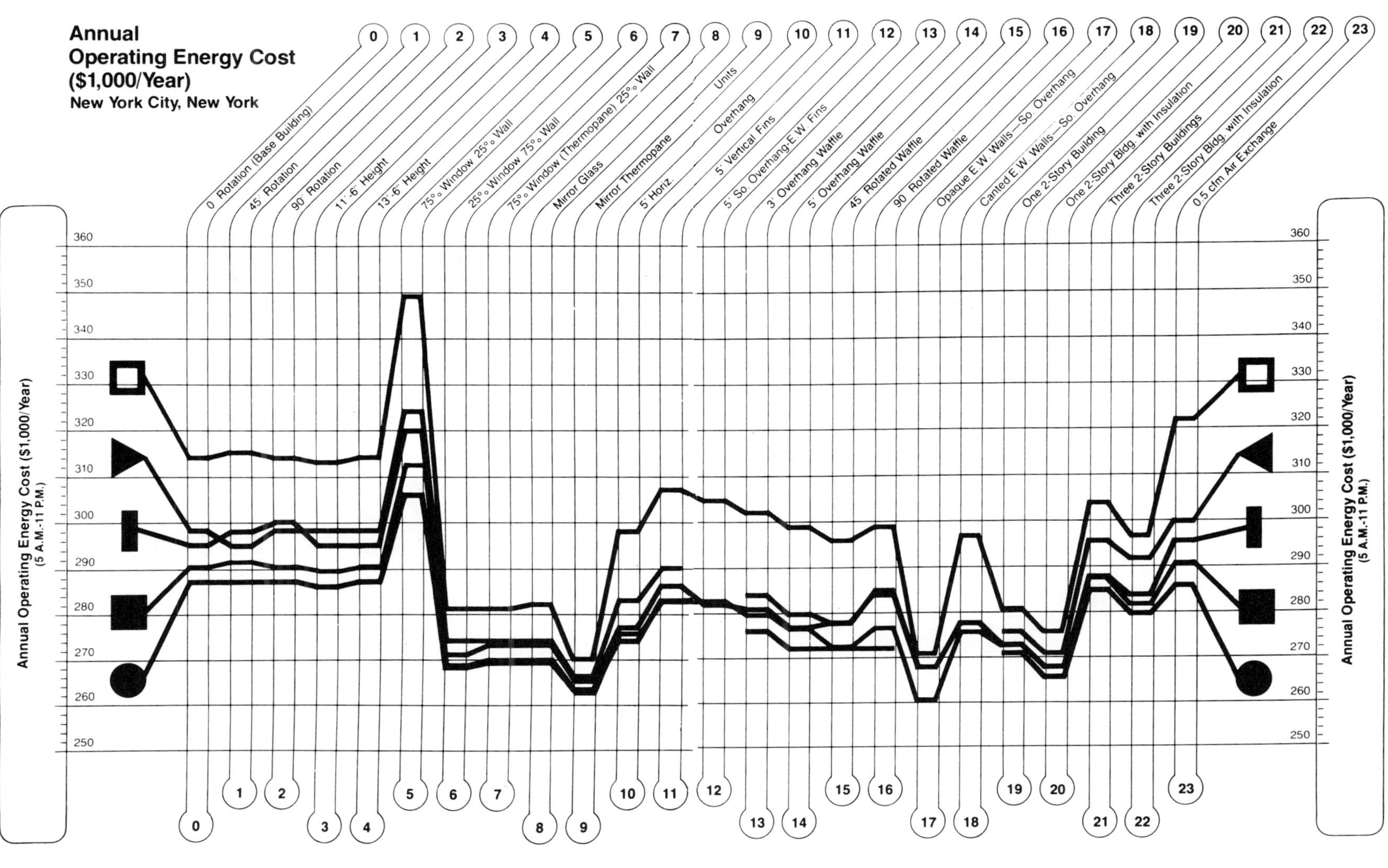

Annual
Operating Energy Cost
($1,000/Year)
New York City, New York
0 Rotation (Base Building)
45 Rotation
90 Rotation
11'-6" Height
13'-6" Height
75% Window 25% Wall
25% Window 75% Wall
75% Window (Thermopane) 25% Wall
Mirror Glass
Mirror Thermopane
5' Horiz.
Units
Overhang
5' Vertical Fins
5' So. Overhang-E.W. Fins
3' Overhang Waffle
5' Overhang Waffle
45 Rotated Waffle
90 Rotated Waffle
Opaque E.W. Walls—So. Overhang
Canted E.W. Walls—So. Overhang
One 2-Story Building
One 2-Story Bldg. with Insulation
Three 2-Story Buildings
Three 2-Story Bldg. with Insulation
0.5 cfm Air Exchange
Annual Operating Energy Cost ($1,000/Year)
(5 A.M.-11 P.M.)
360
350
340
330
320
310
300
290
280
270
260
250
0
1
2
3
4
5
6
7
8
9
10
11
12
13
14
15
16
17
18
19
20
21
22
23

Figure 3.90

Conclusions. Many conclusions can be drawn from the results of this study. Using the comparative curves, building designers and users can decide for themselves among alternative shapes, orientations, or skin designs that might be applicable to their projects. The two sets of curves on costs can be used to compare relative construction costs of alternative envelopes, as well as relative annual energy consumption costs.

As an example, consider a cylindrical building in Los Angeles having a capital cost of $6.30 per square foot ($945,000 for the full 150,000 ft² building) for the skin and mechanical equipment for air conditioning and $126,000 per year (84¢/ft² per year) operating energy cost. If mirror glass were used instead of the solar bronze glass, the capital cost would not be increased, but the operating cost would be decreased to $118,000 per year—an annual saving of $8000.

If mirror thermopane glass were used instead of plain mirror glass, the annual operating energy saving would be $11,000. However the capital cost of the building would be increased by $82,500 (55¢/ft²). If, however, 5-foot overhangs with the solar bronze glass were used instead of a reflective glass, the capital cost would again be increased by 55¢ per square foot over the base building (based, of course, on the assumptions made on the cost of overhang construction—see the Appendix). Comparatively, the annual saving would only be $6000.

From this analysis, the mirror thermopane glass would seem to be an appealing alternative for consideration—if a reflective exterior appearance were appropriate to the urban setting and to the overall design considerations.

The early decision-making process need not end with a consideration of the variables presented here. A unique application, a "new variable," may be added, which might lower even further the capital or energy consumption costs. Analytical refinements are obtainable with many computer simulation programs.

Perhaps even more valuable, though, are the generalized conclusions presented, which may confirm the intuitive judgments that designers have long been making. Now the judgments can be supported by quantitative calculations—frequently a more credible and convincing basis for decision for those responsible for building effectiveness and economy. Nationally, our foreseeable energy resources are known to be limited, and legislation directed at the conservation of energy is being enacted at all levels of government. Clearly, the need for innovation and commitment to low energy use designs has never been more necessary.

Appendix

Study Location. The analysis of comparative building envelopes and weather conditions began with the Southern California locale, for actual buildings in various stages of design. It was later extended to project locations in Seattle and Mississippi, and finally to a hypothetical project in New York—a climate representative of many eastern and central continental temperate zone cities.

1 *Los Angeles, California*
  Latitude 34°, longitude 118°, design.
  Year: 1961.
  Outside Design Conditions
    Dry-bulb temperature 95°F.
    Wet-bulb temperature 72°F.
    Wind speed 7.5 miles per hour.

2 *New York, New York*
  Latitude 41°, longitude 74°, design.
  Year: 1965.
  Outside design conditions
    Dry-bulb temperature 94°F.
    Wet-bulb temperature 77°F.
    Wind speed 7.5 miles per hour.

Weather Data. Weather data for the studies came primarily from the National Climate Center of the National Weather Service in the form of magnetic tapes (TDF 1440 format), suitable for computer input. Additional information was obtained from any local sources that had available significant data. For example, in Los Angeles, the City Department of Water and Power has complete and detailed records covering many years.

The selection of the "design year" for the computer calculations was made by comparing 10-year averages and selecting the year that most closely matched the average data—or was judgmentally determined to be most suitable as a basis for air conditioning design. For example, for New York City, the year 1965 was chosen by using the weather data for the period 1965–1969 and averaging the wet- and dry-bulb temperatures in each of those years (Table 3.32). Since the averages most closely approximated the 1965 weather data, the weather profiles of that year were used in the study. The records include the dry- and wet-bulb temperatures, the wind velocity, and the cloud cover for 8760 continuous hours. (Wind velocities are plotted in magnitude only, and directions are omitted. Sky cover shows only the amount of cloud, not the cloud types.)

Base Building Specifications

1 *Size*. 150,000 square feet gross area; 10 stories, 15,000 square feet per floor.
2 *Occupancy*. 150 square feet per person—for full gross area.
3 *Shape*. Five standard building plans (square, rectangle (1:2.5), triangle, square donut, and circle) all with the same square footage (150,000 ft^2) (see Building Shape and Orientation).
4 *Orientation*. North-south, 0° rotation.
5 *Floor-to-Floor Height*. 12 feet, 6 inches.
6 *Envelope (facade)*. 50% window/wall ratio, height of glass 6 feet, 3 inches to 2 feet, 3 inches above floor, continuous.
7 *Wall U value*. 0.16, medium color.
8 *Roof U value*. 0.15, medium color.
9 *Glass*. ¼-inch solar bronze heat-absorbing plate glass, shading coefficient, 0.67; *U*, 1.06.
10 *Drapes*. Medium color, semiopen weave. (Drapes are assumed to be closed when the solar heat gain exceeds 75 Btu/ft^2 of glass area. The two actual study conditions were (*a*) glass with open drapes, shading coefficient—0.67, *U*, 1.06, and (*b*) glass with closed drapes, shading coefficient, 0.50; *U*, 0.81.)
11 *External Sun Control Devices* (e.g., overhangs, fins). None.

UNITED NATIONS HEADQUARTERS
New York, New York
Architects: Harrison & Abramovitz
Photo: U. N.

12 *Ventilation.* 0.1 cubic foot per minute per square foot of floor area.
13 *Lighting Load.* 3.5 watts per square foot.
14 *Heat from Lights.* 50% to room, 50% to return air.
15 *Operating Hours.* 18 hours per day (5 A.M.—11 P.M.) typical day, 5½ days per week.
16 *Inside Design Condition.* Temperature, 75°F (dry bulb).
17 *Relative Humidity.* 50% (humidity ratio, 0.0093), no humidification was considered.

Base Building Shape and Orientation Details. Table 3.33 gives the building dimensions and orientation of alternative building shapes used in the studies. All shapes have the same gross floor area of 150,000 square feet.

Cost Factors. The capital and operating energy cost charts were computed using the price assumptions listed in Table 3.34. They are based on price levels prevailing in the Southern California area in 1974. Since the same values were used for all studies in all geographical locations, all comparative results were referenced to the same baseline. The only variations in results between one geographical location and another were those due to weather conditions. With this approach, absolute cost values are roughly correct, but relative values, for comparing one design variable with another, are quite accurate.

Table 3.33 Basic Building Shape and Orientation Details

Shape	Dimensions	Base Position, Rotated 0°	Rotated 45°	Rotated 90°
Square:				
base, 10 story	122′ x 122′			
2 story	273′ x 273′			
(3) -2 story	158′ x 158′			
Rectangular: 1:2.5				
base, 10 story	193′ x 77′			
2 story	433′ x 173′			
(3) -2 story	250′ x 100′			
Triangular:				
base, 10 story	186′ x 186′ x 186′			
2 story	433′ x 433′ x 433′			
(3) -2 story	240′ x 240′ x 240′			
Square Donut:				
base, 10 story	141′ x 141′ (70′ sq.)			
2 story	316′ x 316′ (158′ sq.)			
(3) -2 story	182′ x 182′ (191′ sq.)			
Circular:				
base, 10 story	138′ diameter			
2 story	309′ diameter			
(3) -2 story	178′ diameter			

Table 3.34 Breakdown of Cost Factors

Item	Cost
Skin construction costs	
Overhang	$5.25/ft^2 of overhang
Fins	$6.25/ft^2 of fin
Spandrel	$8.50/ft^2 of spandrel
Solar bronze	$9.50/ft^2 of glass (¼-in plate)
Mirror glass	$10.50/ft^2 of glass
Mirror thermopane	$14.50/ft^2 of glass
Roof	$5.00/ft^2 of roof
Roof with insulation	$5.50/ft^2 of roof
Mechanical costs	
Cooling plant	$200.00/ton of refrigeration
Heating plant	$8.00/MBH
Duct and fan	$1.50/cfm of supply air
Energy costs	
Electrical energy	
Los Angeles	$0.025/kW·h
New York	$0.060/kW·h
Heating energy	
Los Angeles	$0.092/MBH
New York	$0.0368/MBH
ENR Cost Index	2301.42

All prices are based on units of the items—not on square feet of building area. For example, total fin costs are determined by multiplying the total area of the fins (5 feet times building height times number of fins) by the unit price of $6.25 per square foot of fin area. Mechanical costs are determined by multiplying the total quantity required by the unit price. Calculations by the computer convert these total prices into costs per square foot of building floor area.

The total annual cooling energy requirement in thousands of Btu per hour (MBH) is computed by summing the positive numbers for each of the 18 operating hours for the 12 monthly high temperature profile days, the 12 median days, and the 12 low days; weighing these at 0.15 for the high, 0.73 for the median, and 0.12 for the low day total, then summing the three results. This represents the total energy requirements for 12 mothly "design days." Multiplying by 4.3 weeks per month and then by 5.5 days per week results in an approximation of one full year's cooling energy consumption of the building. Total cooling energy requirement TC is then given as follows

$$TC = ((0.15A) + (0.73B) + (0.12C)) \times (5.5 \text{ days/week} \times 4.3 \text{ weeks/month}) \text{ (MBH)}$$

where A, B, and C are the sum of all positive numbers in (18 × 12) hours of cooling loads due to the high, median, and low temperature profiles, respectively.

The total cooling electrical energy requirement TCP is as follows:

$$TCP = \frac{TC \text{ (MBH)}}{12} \times \frac{1 \text{ kW}}{\text{MBH}} = \frac{TC}{12} \text{kW·h}$$

The total light and receptable energy requirement TLP is as follows:

$$TLP = 150{,}000 \text{ ft}^2 \times 3.5 \text{ W/ft}^2 \times 5108.4 \text{ h} = 2{,}681{,}910 \text{ kW·h}$$

The total fan motor energy requirement TFP is as follows:

$$TFP = (FPS + FPR)\text{kW} \times 5108.4 \text{ h}$$

$$FPS = \frac{\text{supply air (cfm)} \times 5.5 \text{ inches of water}}{6346 \text{ cfm-in/hp}} \times \frac{0.75 \text{ kW/hp}}{0.70 \text{ efficiency}}$$

$$FPR = \frac{\text{(return + exhaust) (cfm)} \times 2.5 \text{ inches of water}}{6346 \text{ cfm-in/hp}} \times \frac{0.75 \text{ kW/hp}}{0.70 \text{ efficiency}}$$

Operating Energy Cost Calculation Method. In the envelope:energy model, energy loads are calculated by our Building System Simulation Program for each of the 24 hours in three representative days per month (days representing the high, median, and low temperature profiles for each month). Positive energy figures represent net heat gain by the building, or cooling load; negative figures represent net heat loss by the building, or heating load.

Similarly, the total heating energy requirement TH is as follows:

$$TH = (0.15D + 0.73E + 0.12F) \times (5.5 \text{ days/week} \times 4.3 \text{ weeks/month})$$

where D, E, and F are the sum of all negative numbers in (18 × 12) hours of cooling loads due to the high, median, and low temperature profiles, respectively.

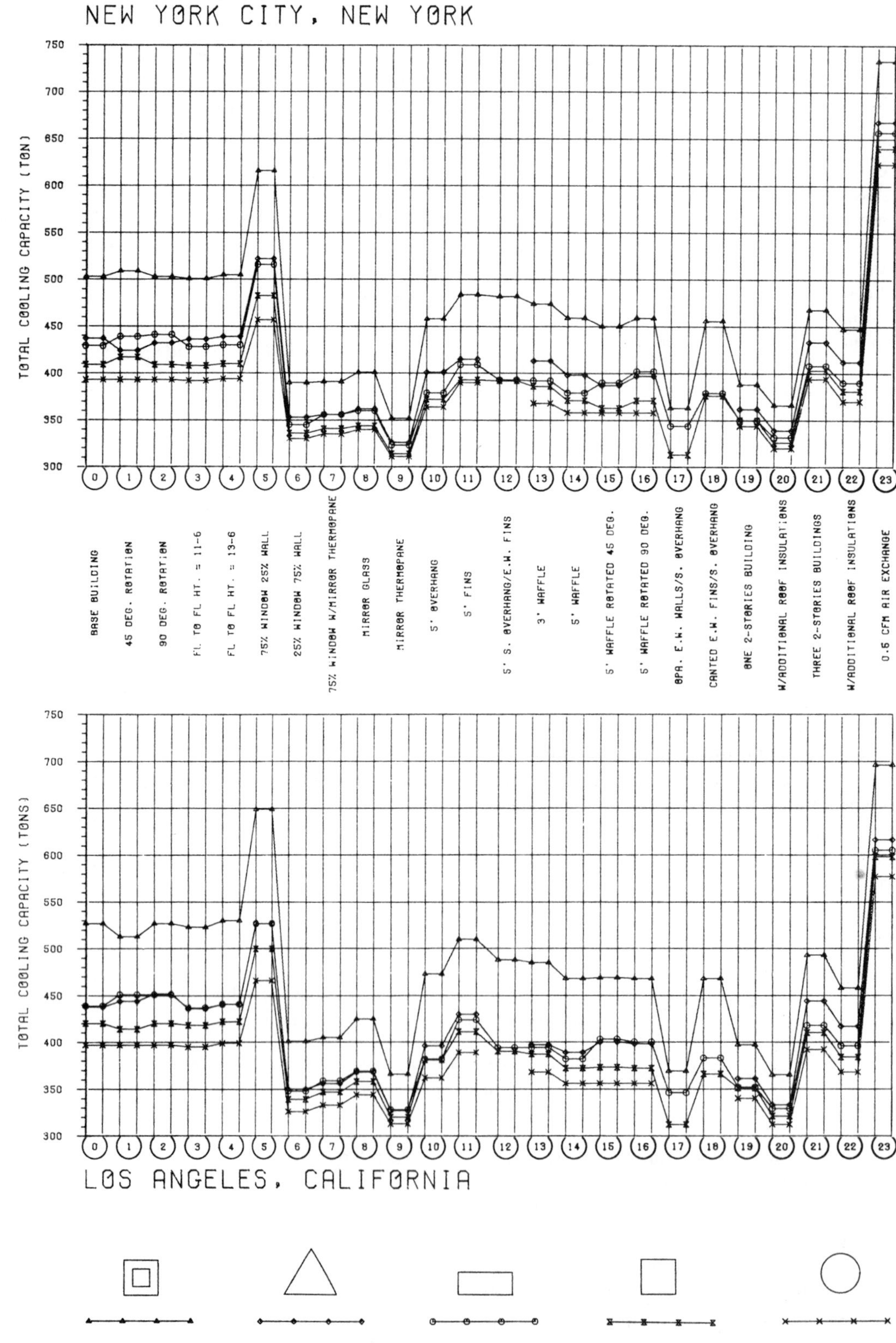

NEW YORK CITY, NEW YORK
TOTAL COOLING CAPACITY (TON)
BASE BUILDING
45 DEG. ROTATION
90 DEG. ROTATION
FL TO FL HT. = 11-6
FL TO FL HT. = 13-6
75% WINDOW 25% WALL
25% WINDOW 75% WALL
75% WINDOW W/MIRROR THERMOPANE
MIRROR GLASS
MIRROR THERMOPANE
5' OVERHANG
5' FINS
5' S. OVERHANG/E.W. FINS
3' WAFFLE
5' WAFFLE
5' WAFFLE ROTATED 45 DEG.
5' WAFFLE ROTATED 90 DEG.
OPA. E.W. WALLS/S. OVERHANG
CANTED E.W. FINS/S. OVERHANG
ONE 2-STORIES BUILDING
W/ADDITIONAL ROOF INSULATIONS
THREE 2-STORIES BUILDINGS
W/ADDITIONAL ROOF INSULATIONS
0.5 CFM AIR EXCHANGE
TOTAL COOLING CAPACITY (TONS)
LOS ANGELES, CALIFORNIA

Figure 3.91

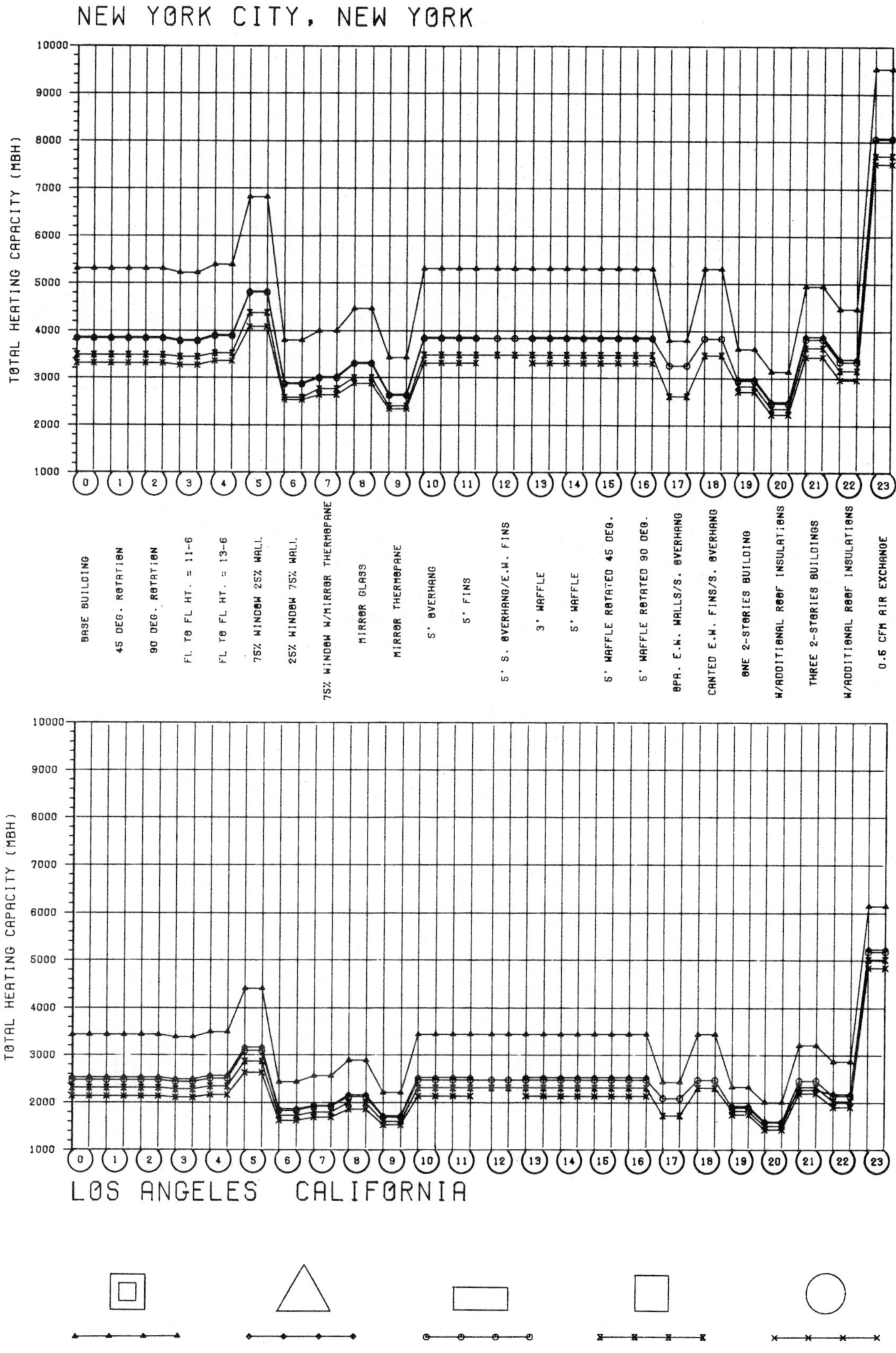
NEW YORK CITY, NEW YORK
TOTAL HEATING CAPACITY (MBH)
10000
9000
8000
7000
6000
5000
4000
3000
2000
1000
0 1 2 3 4 5 6 7 8 9 10 11 12 13 14 15 16 17 18 19 20 21 22 23
BASE BUILDING
45 DEG. ROTATION
90 DEG. ROTATION
FL TO FL HT. = 11-6
FL TO FL HT. = 13-6
75% WINDOW 25% WALL
25% WINDOW 75% WALL
75% WINDOW W/MIRROR THERMOPANE
MIRROR GLASS
MIRROR THERMOPANE
5' OVERHANG
5' FINS
5' S. OVERHANG/E.W. FINS
3' WAFFLE
5' WAFFLE
5' WAFFLE ROTATED 45 DEG.
5' WAFFLE ROTATED 90 DEG.
OPA. E.W. WALLS/S. OVERHANG
CANTED E.W. FINS/S. OVERHANG
ONE 2-STORIES BUILDING
W/ADDITIONAL ROOF INSULATIONS
THREE 2-STORIES BUILDINGS
W/ADDITIONAL ROOF INSULATIONS
0.5 CFM AIR EXCHANGE
TOTAL HEATING CAPACITY (MBH)
10000
9000
8000
7000
6000
5000
4000
3000
2000
1000
0 1 2 3 4 5 6 7 8 9 10 11 12 13 14 15 16 17 18 19 20 21 22 23
LOS ANGELES CALIFORNIA

Figure 3.92

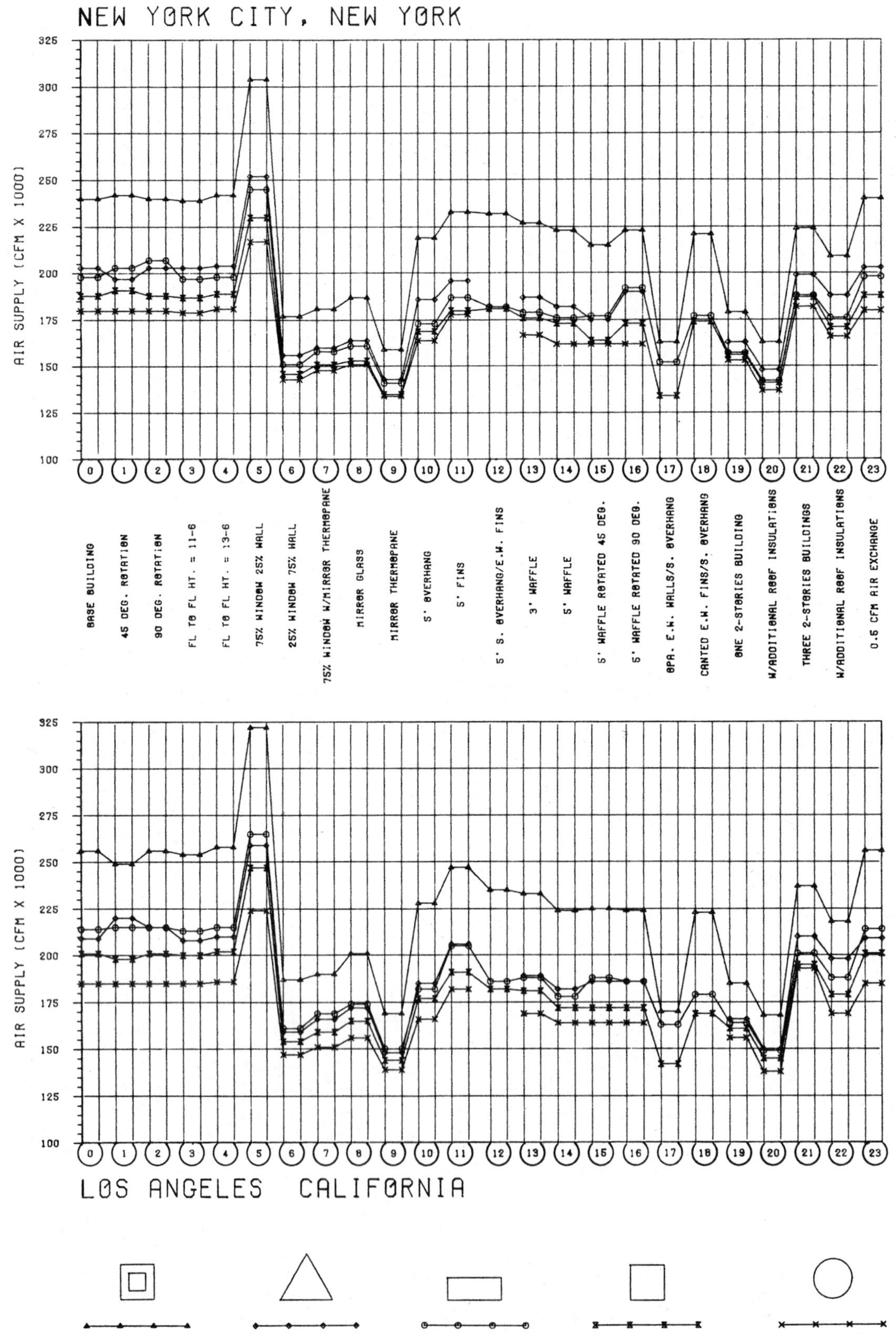
NEW YORK CITY, NEW YORK
AIR SUPPLY (CFM X 1000)
325
300
275
250
225
200
175
150
125
100
0 1 2 3 4 5 6 7 8 9 10 11 12 13 14 15 16 17 18 19 20 21 22 23
BASE BUILDING
45 DEG. ROTATION
90 DEG. ROTATION
FL TO FL HT. = 11-6
FL TO FL HT. = 13-6
75% WINDOW 25% WALL
25% WINDOW 75% WALL
75% WINDOW W/MIRROR THERMOPANE
MIRROR GLASS
MIRROR THERMOPANE
5' OVERHANG
5' FINS
5' S. OVERHANG/E.W. FINS
3' WAFFLE
5' WAFFLE
5' WAFFLE ROTATED 45 DEG.
5' WAFFLE ROTATED 90 DEG.
OPA. E.W. WALLS/S. OVERHANG
CANTED E.W. FINS/S. OVERHANG
ONE 2-STORIES BUILDING
W/ADDITIONAL ROOF INSULATIONS
THREE 2-STORIES BUILDINGS
W/ADDITIONAL ROOF INSULATIONS
0.5 CFM AIR EXCHANGE
LOS ANGELES CALIFORNIA

Figure 3.93

The operating energy costs *OEC* are as follows:
For New York:

$$OEC = (TCP + TLP + TFP)\text{kW}\cdot\text{h} \times 6¢/\text{kW}\cdot\text{h} + TH\ (\text{MBH}) \times 0.368\ ¢/\text{MBH}$$

For Los Angeles:

$$OEC = (TCP + TLP + TFP)\text{kW}\cdot\text{h} \times 2.5¢/\text{kW}\cdot\text{h} + TH\ (\text{MBH}) \times 0.092\ ¢/\text{MBH}$$

(The average heating system efficiency is assumed to be 60%.)

Program Abstract: Weather Package (WEAPKG)

Objects

1. Decodes weather data tape available from National Climatic Center, North Carolina, in TDF 1440 format. Prints hourly dry-bulb temperature, wet-bulb temperature, dew point temperature, barometric pressure, wind velocity, wind direction, cloud type, cloud amount, and cloud modifier.
2. Summarizes dry, wet, and dew point temperatures at every 2° interval and prints temperature distribution bar charts.
3. Finds yearly average of dry, wet, and dew point temperatures. Selects three sets of 24-hour profiles of dry- and wet-bulb temperatures representing high, average, and low profiles of each month for 12 months and punches out 72 cards to be used in heating and cooling load calculation programs.
4. Prepares hourly weather data tape to be used in hour by hour building simulation program.
5. Prepares data tape to plot hourly weather profiles.

Software. Fortran V and Cal-Compt Plot Routine.

REFUSE INCINERATOR
New York
Architects: I. Richmond & C. Goldberg; Engineers: Metcalf & Eddy
Photo: J. W. Molitor

CNA PARK PLACE
Los Angeles, California
Architects: Langdon & Wilson
Photo: W. Thom

Computerized Design Process for Building HVAC Systems
HVAC Load Estimation

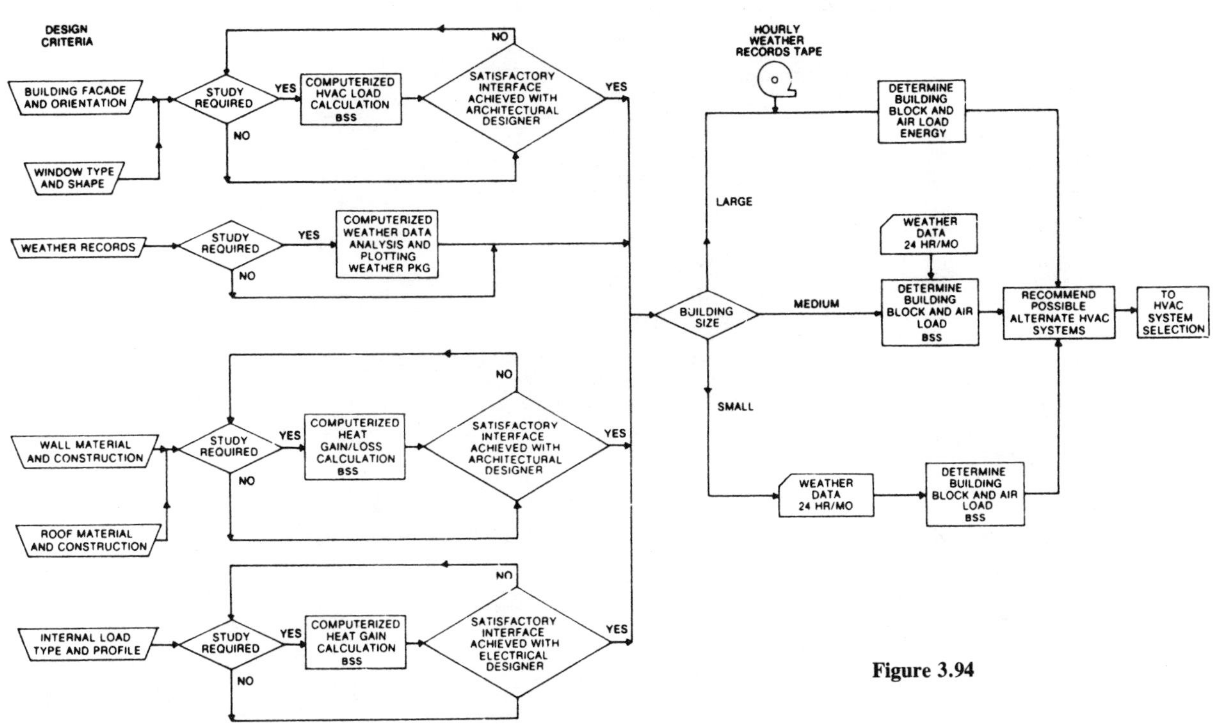

Figure 3.94

Hardware. Univac 1108 Exec 11/65k, Cal-Compt Plotter.

Limitation. Can decode up to 10 years of weather data tape in TDF 1440 format.

Execution. 180 seconds of central processing unit time for one year's record.

Program Abstract: Building System Simulation Program (BSS)

Objects

1 Calculates heating and cooling load of rooms, zones, and building based on the methodology defined in the ASHRAE 1972 Guide.
2 Calculates heating load at input outside air temperature.
3 Calculates hourly cooling loads at 24 hours per month for 12 months using the 24 hour per month temperature profiles.
4 Finds peak heating and cooling requirements of rooms, zones, and building.
5 Finds supply air requirements of rooms, zones, and building.
6 Prints one 24-hour cooling load profile per month for 12 months for zones and building.
7 Summarizes monthly and yearly cooling requirements for zones and building.
8 Punches out 24 cards for each zone and 24 cards for building for cooling load profile plot program.

Software. FORTRAN V.

Hardware. Univac 1108 Exec 11/65K.

Limitation. Capacity of the program is a maximum of 200 rooms, 10 zones, and one building.

Execution. 60 seconds of central processing unit time for 50 rooms, 3 zones, and 1 building.

FEDERAL RESERVE BANK
Minneapolis, Minnesota
Architects: Gunnar Birkerts & Associates
Photo: B. Korab

FOUR
CONSTRUCTION

Construction administration deals with various contracts and construction documents, contractual and legal relationships and responsibilities. It also encompasses construction techniques and construction management processes. To summarize, *construction administration* refers to the architect's ability in the following areas:

1 Understanding fully contracts and construction documents.

2 Being aware of contractual, ethical, and legal relationships and responsibilities.

3 Knowing and utilizing updated construction techniques, systems, and details.

4 Understanding management procedures of the construction field relative to the control of quality, cost, and time.

CONSTRUCTION ADMINISTRATION

	PREPARATION	QUALITY CONTROL	TIME	COST
DOCUMENTS	Permits	Moisture control	Site erection	Material
Working drawings	Contract components	Finishes	Shop manufacturing	Quantities
Specifications	Codes	Durability	Trade sequences	Weights
Schedules		Thermal control		Labor
		Acoustics		Fabrication
		Specification		Erection
CONTRACTS	Law agency	Conformance	Work stoppages	Strike cost
Owner-Architect	Contract language	Changes	Penalties	Certificate of payment
Consultants	Limiations of contract	Guarantees	Delays	Bidding
Contractors	Lien law	Tests	Schedule compliance	Change orders
	Bonds	Surveys		Tests
	Insurance	Errors and omissions		
	Arbitration	Insurance		
ADMINISTRATION	Field documents	Shop drawing	Fabrication time	Fabrication
Shop drawings	Techniques	Field quality	Erection time	Erection
Samples	Sequences in construction	Quality control		Cost control
Supervision		Samples		
Inspection		Corrections		
Tests				

1 PRINCIPLES OF DETAILING AND SPECIFICATION

Quality Control

Drawings and specifications consist of thousands of messages from the architect and his or her consulting engineers to the contractor, the subcontractors, and the people on the job and in the shop. This material helps translate the project design into a finished product and makes it possible to produce the project at the intended level of quality, within reasonable budgetary and time allotments. To produce a good set of drawings and specifications, the architect should always use common sense; no less necessary are good judgment and an awareness of changing technology—that is, innovation should be tempered by practicality.

Specification writing is a difficult and time-consuming activity. The technical specifications describe the project detailing every piece of material, whether concealed or exposed, and every piece of fixed equipment needed for the operation of the project; a portrayal of the physical shape and dimensions of the project is lacking, however.

The preparation of a specification is becoming more involved, more technical, and more exacting. Modern materials, innovations in construction, unorthodox designs—all call for investigation, research, and ingenuity. These factors, together with the complexities of mechanical equipment now found to be essential, weigh heavily on the architect whose task is to provide an accurate, clear, and complete legal document recording the decisions made. The pressure of time is always present: every minute counts, and the greater part of the time used in writing specifications should be allotted to the solution of unusual and complicated problems, not to the harried search for known facts and standard practice data. Such data should be easily available, and the specification form should be ready-made; then the actual work of compilation can be a simple and orderly process that can be safely and expeditiously performed under stress.

The majority of architects prepare new specifications by reference to their old ones. A few have their own standard specifications which, they admit, are not kept up to date; others have started standards but never completed them; all acknowledge the danger of following specifications for work previously completed, because of the likelihood of using phrases that do not apply, copying outmoded clauses, and being unprepared for new situations brought about by technological change.

The technical specifications cover the major types of work: civil, architectural, structural, mechanical, and electrical. Each of these types is further divided and subdivided in the specifications and given a general title that describes work performed by building tradesmen, such as plasterers, plumbers, and sheet metal workers.

The Divisions

1 *General Requirements.* Includes most requirements that apply to the job as a whole or to several of the technical sections, and especially the requirements sometimes referred to as special conditions. General conditions and supplementary conditions are not included in the divisions of the specifications.
2 *Site Work.* Includes most subjects dealing with site preparation and development. Site utilities in divisions 15 and 16 must be coordinated with these subdivisions.
3 *Concrete.* Includes most items traditionally associated with concrete work; exceptions are paving, piles, waterproofing, and terrazzo.
4 *Masonry.* Includes most materials traditionally installed by masons; exceptions are paving and interior flooring.
5 *Metals.* Includes most structural metals and metals not falling under the specific provisions of other divisions; exceptions are reinforcing steel, curtain walls, roofing, piles, doors, and windows.
6 *Wood and Plastics.* Includes most work traditionally performed by carpenters; exceptions are wood fences, concrete formwork, doors, windows, and finish hardware.
7 *Thermal and Moisture Protection.* Includes most items normally associated with insulation and preventing the passage of water or water vapor; exceptions are paint, waterstops and joints

installed in concrete or masonry, and gaskets and sealants.

8 *Doors and Windows*. Includes hardware, doors, windows, and frames; metal and glass curtain walls; transparent and translucent glazing. Exceptions are glass block and glass mosaics.

9 *Finishes*. Includes interior finishes not traditionally the work of the carpentry trade.

10 *Specialties*. Includes factory-assembled, prefinished items.

11 *Equipment*. Includes most items of specialized equipment.

12 *Furnishings*. Includes most items placed in the finished building.

13 *Special Construction*. Includes on-site construction consisting of items that normally would fall under several other divisions but require control that can be attained only by including all parts in a single section.

14 *Conveying Systems*. Includes the systems that utilize power to transport people or materials.

15 *Mechanical*. Includes most items that have been traditionally associated with the mechanical trades.

16 *Electrical*. Includes most items that have been traditionally associated with the electrical trades.

The Construction Specification Institute (CSI) format lists typical subjects for inclusion in each division. For example:

Division 9. Finishes
Lath and plaster.
Gypsum drywall.
Tile.
Terrazzo.
Veneer stone.
Acoustical treatment.

Note that the sections comprising a division are each a basic unit of work. The CSI format is based on the principle of placing sections together in related groups. The CSI system is the most widely used system. It incorporates a complete guide for short specifications and also a national computer system used by both small and large architectural offices. These basic documents set the framework for the trade sections, but completion of the technical specifications calls for the initiative and experience of the architect. Although the form of each section should be based on the work to be described, the sections are similar in structure. Here are examples taken from two separate projects.

Ceramic Tile

Special note
Work required
Work included under other sections
Samples
Manufacturers
Materials
Standard specifications
Setting methods
Mortar
Tile work—general
Application of wall tile
Application of floor tile
Protection
Completion
Extra tile for maintenance

Movable Metal Partitions

Special note
Work required
Work included under other sections
Shop drawings
Manufacturers
Types of partition
Partitions
Doors and frames
Hardware
Metal base
Metal ceilings
Hose cabinets
Glass and glazing
Finish
Protection

Each section should begin with the "special note" and "work required" paragraphs, which make the general conditions (and special conditions) part of the technical specifications, and clearly describe the scope of work, respectively.

Water and Moisture Control. The competent architect seeks to avoid problems due to water and moisture by careful design and detailing. The accumulation of water is affected by rainfall, wind, time, and the saturation of earth and building materials. The source of unwanted moisture is not always apparent, and access to areas needing repair may be difficult or impractical. In addition, even after repairs are made, many months may pass before their effectiveness can be realistically evaluated.

The four general categories of water and moisture control are as follows:

1 Roofing, roof drainage, and related details.
2 Walls, windows, doors, and other wall openings.
3 Subgrade ground water and surface drainage.
4 Miscellaneous (fixture and equipment drainage or overflow, condensation, shower and other "wet" rooms, etc.).

Roofing, Roof Drainage, and Related Details. In selecting a roofing system, one must consider slope, appearance, combustibility, permanence, walkability, and relative cost. The appropriate section of specifications describes the materials used in the system and their general application. Guarantees, tests, and clean-up requirements may also be included. The drawings illustrate limits of roofed areas, roof drainage, and details of roofing joints at other parts of the structure, such as walls, skylights, and edges. The more detailed information is at one's disposal, the better.

Roofing manufacturers can be very helpful in furnishing specification and drawing information and will often accept responsibility if their materials or installation are found to be faulty. The architect should not rely blindly on any manufacturer's information or claims, however. A roofer's guarantee may be limited to the repair of his roof, whereas water damage in other areas is very likely the architect's problem. Properly installed, good-quality roofing has adequate drainage; roofing edge conditions have been detailed.

Walls, Windows, Doors, and Other Wall Openings. In selecting masonry, concrete, or plaster, it is important to consider the prevention of direct moisture penetration to the inside. The drawings and specifications may indicate prevention in one or more of the following ways:

1 Specifying dense material that is moisture resistant.
2 Specifying mortar joints or combining units that aid in the positive shedding of water.
3 Specifying impermeable backing material that will prevent water from entering interior spaces.
4 Specifying the application of a surface sealant.
5 Providing flashing or coping to shed water at the most susceptible problem points.
6 Providing caulking.

Building codes often provide guidelines for control of moisture. However the architect should not depend entirely on them; past experience should also be considered, and personal judgment exercised.

Wall conditions must be carefully detailed to achieve practicality, good appearance, and moisture resistance. Codes and standard practice are helpful but not always sufficient. Manufactured window, door, and louver assemblies are generally designed for adequate weather protection, but the installation method called for according to the drawings or specifications must also be effective. The following questions must be answered satisfactorily.

- Do parts overlap sufficiently?
- Are joint tolerances reasonable?
- Is caulking to be used? If so, what type?
- Can breakable parts be replaced?
- What will happen if water flows horizontally? If it is windblown?
- If a window-wall system is used, it may be specified almost entirely, its details limited to considerations of external appearance. Does the specification (often supplied by the manufacturer) provide for testing or guarantees of its waterproof characteristics?

In recent years significant advances have been made in the development of dependable caulking materials that do not lose their initial effectiveness by drying out, shrinking, or cracking. The material selected should be able to withstand extremes of weather and exposure and should be capable of bridging the gaps it is expected to seal; it should flex with the relative movement of the parts it is sealing; it should withstand abrasion; its color should match surrounding materials. It is better to apply caulking as *extra* insurance against leaking than to depend on it to do the major part of the job.

Subgrade Ground Water and Surface Drainage. The control of water in and on the ground is well worth the architect's special attention. He or she should learn the characteristic action of subsurface moisture and be able to assure positive drainage of surface water.

The earth around a building may be thoroughly saturated with water for a long time. Thus construction materials must prevent water penetration. Below-grade concrete or masonry walls will not do this unless treated with a proper membrane. Certain admixtures—penetrating sealers and the like—impede moisture penetration, but more positive measures are necessary to keep subsurface moisture from interior spaces. Membrane application to the exterior of subgrade walls is recommended. Such membranes should extend from a point above grade, completely around the buried surfaces of the building, although it is usually very difficult to install a continuous membrane because of footings, penetration of pipes, rough handling during early construction stages, and so on. However the membrane should be carried to a point well below the bottom floor line.

To reduce hydrostatic pressure on the membrane and water penetration through the subgrade floor slab, a system of subsurface drains should be installed. These perforated pipes will pick up free water and allow it to flow to the outside, where it can be dispersed.

Drain pipes, which should be installed along the outside base of walls subject to ground water, should be embedded in crushed rock to discourage clogging with silt. The ground water table may rise to contact the underside of the floor slab nearer the middle of the building; therefore, if possible, water should be intercepted by drains at that location, as well.

Although paving around a building may reduce the amount of adjacent ground water, it may not prevent it, particularly in hillside areas or where the rainy-season water table is near the surface. This problem exists because paving is often subject to cracking or imperfect jointing, and substantial amounts of water can trickle through such openings.

The architect should be familiar with recommended minimum surface slopes for landscaped and paved areas and the design of area drains, gutters, trenches, culverts, and drain pipe, and great care is necessary in the establishment of floor elevations relative to the surrounding grade. Inadequate drainage design has caused severe damage and has resulted in legal actions.

Miscellaneous. Certain fixtures use or produce moisture. Thus the architect must provide for possible leakage in the drawings and specifications.

- Air conditioning units may require drain pans or sinks.
- Water heaters might be placed over drain pans as protection against failure.
- Washing machines may require drain pans.
- Some toilet rooms should have floor drains in case of overflow or to help in mopping down.

Condensation may appear as "frost" when cold surfaces are created in warmer spaces where the moisture content

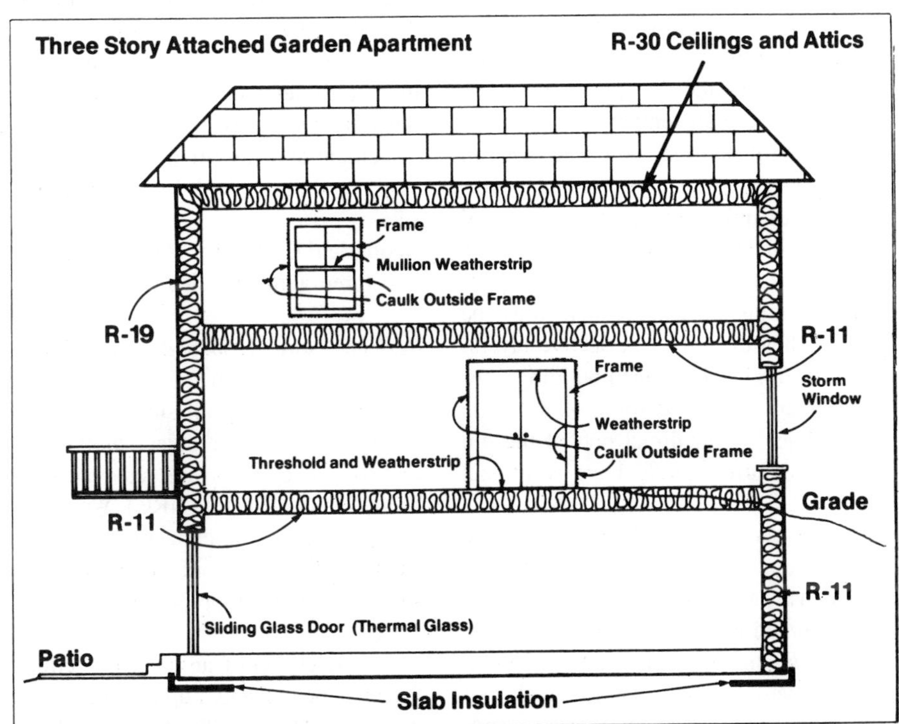

INSULATION IS THE KEY to energy conservation, according to residential products division of Johns-Manville. Recommended minimums are shown here for garden apartment construction. With rapidly increasing energy costs, even these values may have to be upped in a few years. Prevention of air infiltration is an essential partner to insulation, as indicated by suggestions for caulking and weather stripping of doors and windows. Thermal glass is a further back-up.

Figure 4.1 *Source. Construction News,* February 1978.

of the air is relatively high. A good window or skylight detail can anticipate such a condition by providing for drainage of condensed moisture before it can damage nearby finish materials. Sometimes double-layer insulating glass is specified, both to solve this problem and to provide thermal insulation.

If the insulation or ventilation is not properly detailed, condensation may occur inside roofs or walls. Smooth, cold surfaces in warm, high-humidity spaces should be avoided.

In *showers and other wet rooms*, where free water is repeatedly in contact with wall or floor surfaces, appropriate drainage is required. Exposed material must not be soluble or otherwise subject to deteriorate when wet. An impervious, protected membrane must be installed, providing a continuous, positive barrier against water penetration.

Thermal Control. There are four major points to be considered in this area.

1 Determination of the building's fenestration should reflect consideration by the architect of the requirements to control the direct radiation of the sun, which can measurably add to the occupants' comfort, and to maintain an appropriate air temperature.

2 Selection of thermal insulation should be made in conjunction with the design of air conditioning equipment, according to values indicated by the mechanical engineer's heat loss calculations. Some enclosing layers of interior spaces insulate adequately without addition of a specific thermal insulating material. Others must be supplemented by batts, boards, fill, or reflective layers. Exterior walls and roofs of air conditioned buildings, for example, as well as many walls and roofs of naturally ventilated structures subject to the direct rays of the sun or to extremes in temperature, should have additional insulation.

If the enclosing construction is *hollow,* a low-cost mineral or fibrous low-density batt or blanket may be sufficient, or a low-density fill material such as mineral wool, which can be poured into the space between framing members. If *exposed* construction is used, it is possible to apply a rigid board between roofing and roof sheathing or decking in wall construction, as a sandwich material between interior and exterior finishes. If conditions warrant, a fill (gypsum or similar material) can be poured that will harden in place as a thermally insulating layer.

The architect who is properly serving his or her client will select insulation partially on the basis of desired characteristics and partially on the basis of the material's fire-resistive qualities, in conformity to building fire codes. Table 4.1 gives one manufacturer's recommendations.

3 Pipe and duct insulation is designed to minimize heat loss of air, water, or other liquid as it is being conveyed from one place to another. A blanket material, such as Fiberglas glass fibers, is usually wrapped around the duct or pipe. Sometimes a preformed, rigid insulation is used; occasionally a hardening fill is poured around the conducting tube. This kind of insulation is selected by the mechanical engineer, but the architect should make sure there is ample space to contain the enlarged pipe or conduit and that the pipe is placed for maximum efficiency and unobtrusiveness.

4 Expansion and contraction of materials due to temperature change must be anticipated. Through proper specification of detail, such changes can be accommodated without detrimental effects. Score marks and expansion joints in concrete slabs, and expansion screeds in plaster and metal dividers in terrazzo, will help prevent cracks. Slip joints in long stretches of sheet metal will allow movement so that waterproof integrity can be maintained while resisting buckling or rupturing of solder joints. Good window-wall design detailing will also allow for some relative movement of parts. Sometimes the natural tendency of materials to expand and contract must be forcefully resisted. For example, heavy reinforcement and careful curing of a tennis court are necessary to minimize and distribute cracks.

Acoustical Control. Acoustical control can be divided into three general fields of consideration.

Reflected and Absorbed Sound Within a Space. Although spaces such as auditoriums or "quiet rooms" must be treated on all surfaces, in most cases the ceiling is the principal object of the architect's attention.

Acoustic ceilings are rated according to their noise reduction coefficient (NRC), which is determined by the composition and thickness of the material used and by its method of installation. Thick material, resilient installation, and sound-trapping pores or pits tend to increase the NRC.

The selection of an acoustic ceiling material is based on a balance of NRC, appearance, cost, and fire-resistive qualities. The specifications should call for a particular product (except in the case of public works, where specifications must be "open"), noting its NRC performance rating and the fire-resistive qualities. Samples for approval should be required. Shop drawings are sometimes helpful, especially if a grid layout or the hanging details must be described in more detail than is given in the architect's drawings and specifications.

Table 4.1 Recommended Optimum Attic Insulation for Specific Areas and Energy Costs

For Winter Heating

Type of fuel:	**Heating Cost**							
Gas (therm)	15c	18c	24c	30c	36c	54c	72c	90c
Oil (gallon)	21c	25c	34c	42c	50c	75c	$1.00	$1.25
Electric (kWh)		1c	1.3c	1.6c	2c	3c	4c	5c
Heat pump (kWh)	1.7c	2c	2.6c	3.3c	4c	6c	8c	10c
Degree Days:	**Recommended R-Values**							
0-2,000	*R-19*	*R-19*	*R-19*	*R-19*	*R-19*	*R-19*	*R-19*	*R-19*
2,000-4,000	*R-19*	*R-19*	R-19	R-19	R-30	R-30	R-38	R-38
4,000-6,000	R-19	R-19	R-30	R-30	R-33	R-38	R-44	R-49
6,000-8,000	R-30	R-30	R-33	R-33	R-38	R-49	R-49	R-57
8,000-10,000	R-30	R-30	R-38	R-38	R-44	R-49	R-60	R-66
10,000 or more	R-38	R-38	R-44	R-49	R-49	R-60	R-66	R-66

Ashrae STD 90 Criteria

For Heating and Cooling

Type air conditioner:	**Cooling cost**					
Gas (therm)	12c	15c	18c	24c	30c	36c
Electric (kWh)	2c	2.5c	3c	4c	5c	6c
Cooling hours:	**Recommended R-Values**					
Less than 500	*	*	*	*	*	*
500-1,000	*	R-33	R-38	R-44	R-44	R-49
1,000-1,500	R-30	R-30	R-33	R-38	R-44	R-44
1,500-2,000	R-30	R-30	R-30	R-33	R-38	R-38
More than 2,000	R-19	R-30	R-30	R-30	R-33	R-38

*Indicates no cooling load, with minimal air conditioning use in northern areas of the country. Use values in heating chart.

NOTE: Cooling hours indicates the number of hours that the cooling unit is expected to operate.

TRANSLATING "COST PER UNIT" ENERGY FIGURES from the National Bureau of Standards into R-values, Johns-Manville came up with these recommendations for insulation in different parts of the country. To determine recommended attic insulation, locate your heating/cooling zone and find the energy cost per unit for your locale and energy source. Recommended R-value is in the space where cost and zone intersect. Check with your local weather station for degree days and/or cooling hours in your area. If both heating and cooling are involved use the higher R-value for maximum efficiency.

Source. Construction News, February 1978.

The drawings indicate the relation of the acoustical material to adjacent construction. For example:

- What conditions exist at the intersection of an acoustic ceiling with the wall?
- Where does the acoustical material run over a partition?
- Where does it change to a different height?
- Where is a cornice trim to be used?
- Where are light fixtures recessed?

A reflected ceiling plan should be drawn, showing grids or tile intersections to be symmetrical around an element such as an entrance door or featured light fixture.

Intrusion and Attenuation of Sound into a Space from Outside Sources. To create conditions of human comfort and performance efficiency, the U.S. Department of Housing and Urban Development and many building departments require measures to reduce penetration of outside noise, especially in multi-residential structures.

The sound transmission coefficient (STC) of walls, partitions, and floors is a measure of the amount of sound that will penetrate a wall or other enclosing element. Many manufacturers of wall or floor construction materials such as gypsum wallboard, lightweight fill, or sound-deadening board, publish good data on sound attenuation. Public agencies, including HUD, also publish such useful information.

Reducing sound transmission is not successful unless sound is prevented from going under, around, and through a wall. A hollow-center, lightweight door may be a source of undesirable sound penetration, even though the wall is adequately constructed. Detailing as a method of describing general construction of a wall with

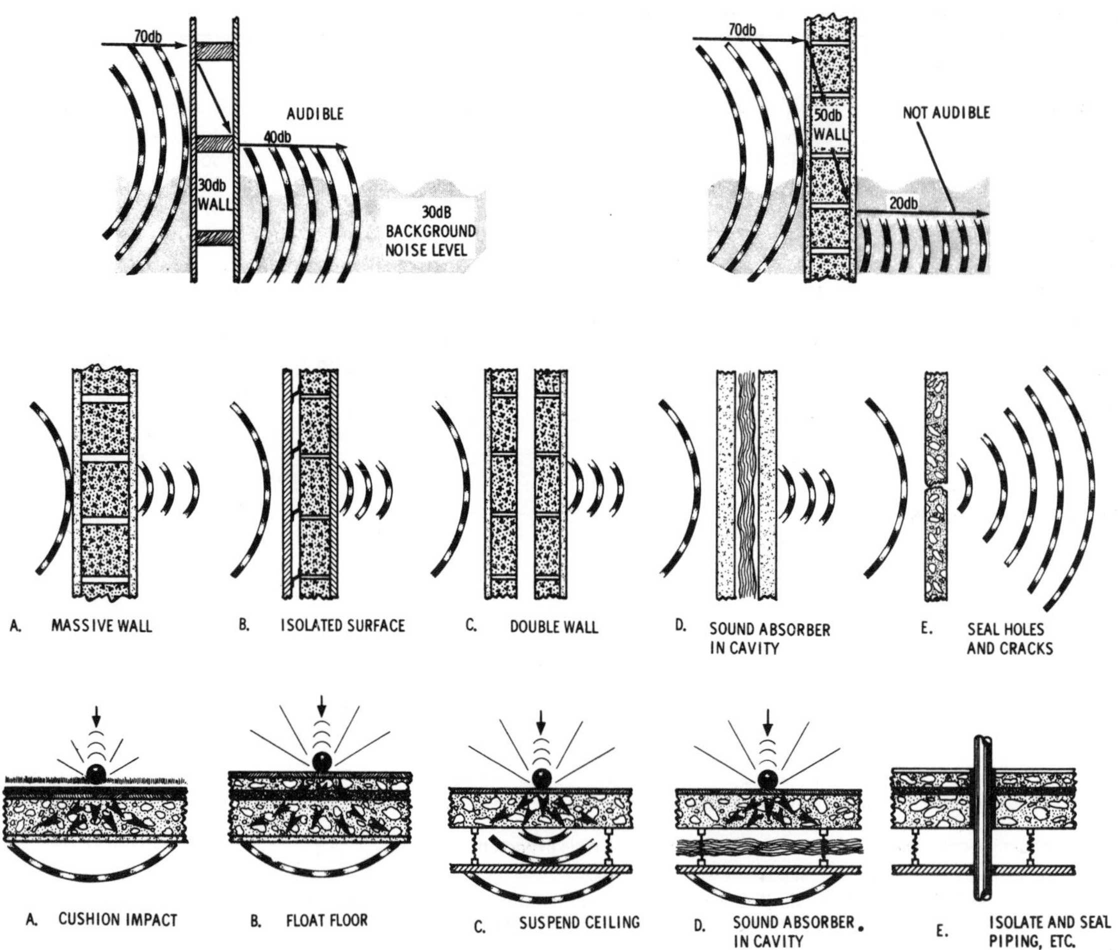

Figure 4.2 Methods of controlling airborne and impact sound transmission through walls and floors. *Source*. U.S. Government.

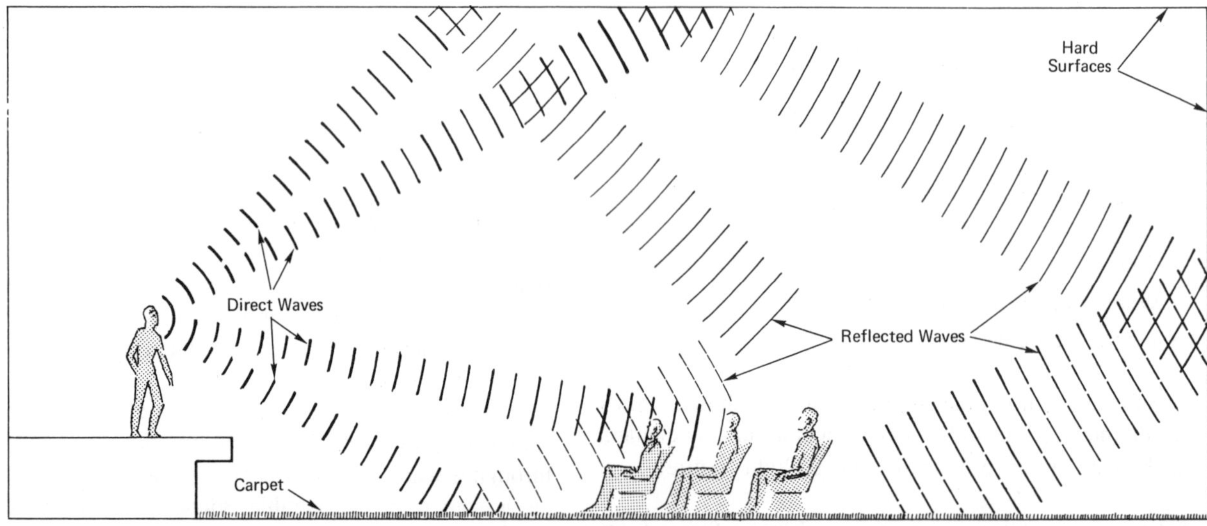

Figure 4.3 Propagation of direct and reflected sound waves in a room. *Source*. U.S. Government.

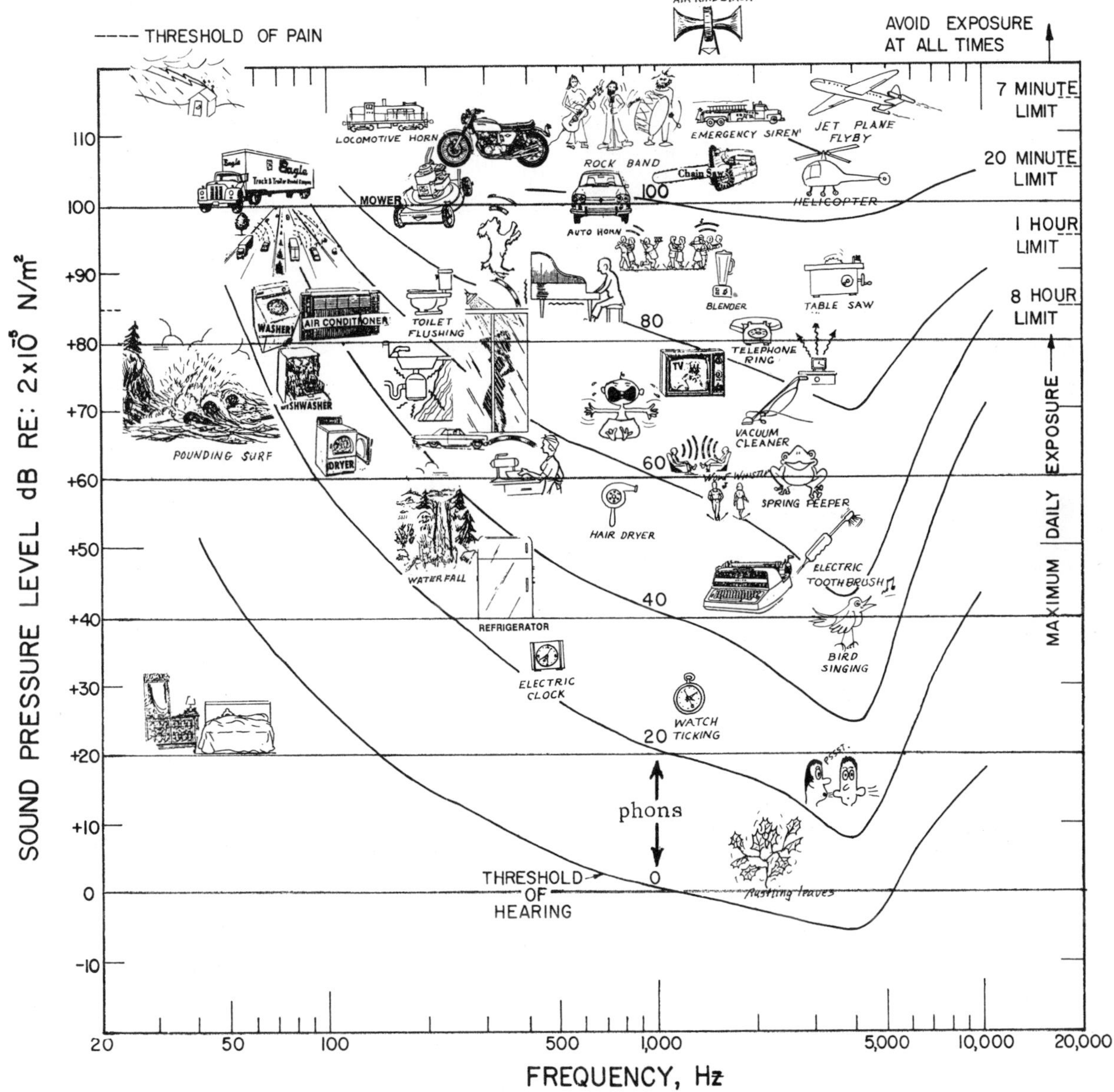

Figure 4.4 Common sound sources plotted by their dominant frequencies and levels, as typically heard. *Source.* U.S. Government.

a given STC shows how the wall terminates at the floor and ceiling—for example, gypsum board is caulked at its intersection with the floor; a partition may extend beyond a ceiling or be caulked at that joint.

The quality of a light construction, wood-frame, 2- or 3-story apartment house or office structure is conspicuously lessened if footsteps or other similar sounds are audible from below. This problem can be reduced by the following means:

- Carpeting the floor above.
- Pouring a concrete fill over the floor sheathing above.
- Insulating sound by a rigid layer of soundboard in the floor construction or a resilient suspension of the ceiling construction, or both.

The construction documents must describe such materials and the method of installation, as well as the relationship with other construction parts.

Equipment and Airflow Noises. If compressors, pumps, fans, and other machinery with rapidly moving parts are not properly isolated, vibrations are transmitted into structural parts of a building, resulting in unwanted

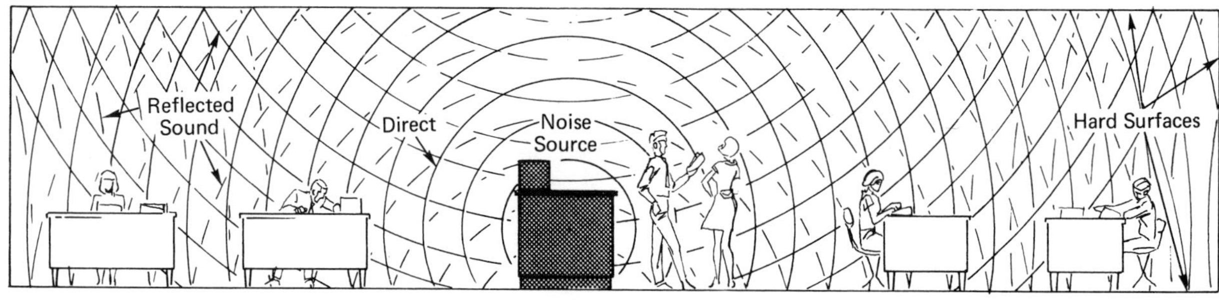

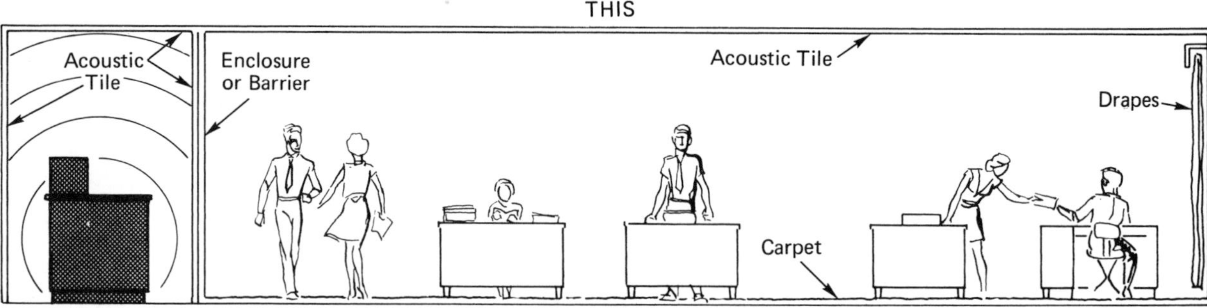

Figure 4.5 Noise control of the transmission path. *Source*. U.S. Government.

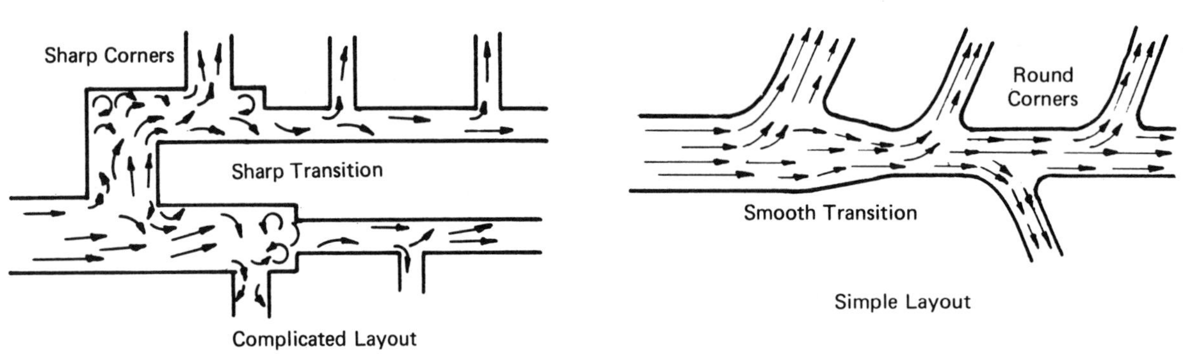

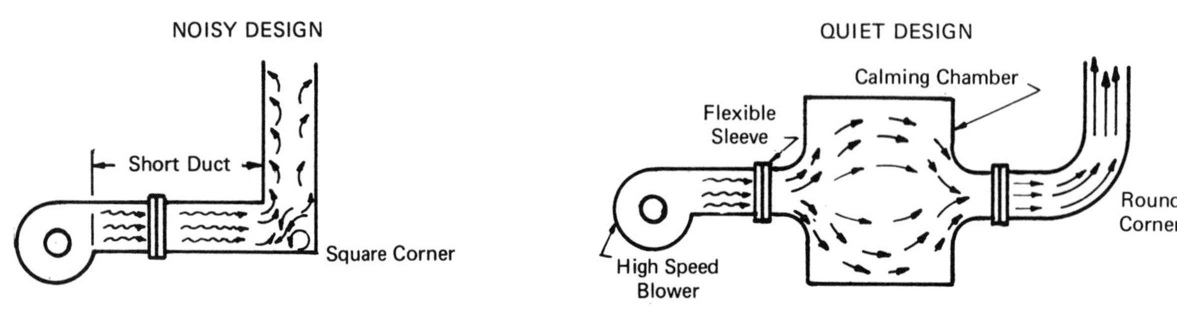

Figure 4.6 Design of quiet flow systems. *Source*. U.S. Government.

sound in nearby areas. Such equipment is usually provided with isolation mounts, but these should be supplemented by increasing the mass of the base or by adding more effective mounts. Special flexible joints near the compressor or pump can help solve the problem of sound vibrations traveling through pipes or conduits.

Often sounds of rushing air from air conditioners are often present even in the best-constructed buildings. Added acoustical comfort can be achieved in reduction of air velocity as air flows through the registers by increasing the cross-sectional area of the duct and register or by providing additional registers. Acoustical lining inside the duct may also help.

Construction designed to ensure better acoustical properties usually requires additional material, thus adding to complexity, cost, and construction time. A properly designed acoustical environment encourages better worker performance and enhances human comfort.

Quality Control in Fabrication and Erection. Some construction items are fabricated in the factory or shop; others may be made at the site, either in place or adjacent thereto. If a given item is available manufactured, or if it can be fabricated in the shop, it will be less expensive than a job-fabricated item would be, and the construction schedule will be shortened.

Mass-Produced Components. To ensure a perfect fit, the fabricated item and its future location in a building must be very carefully controlled. Compressors, light and plumbing fixtures, electrical devices, standard windows, and some modular equipment are mass produced. Manufacturers' literature indicates physical dimensions and any pertinent utility connection requirements, but previous experience with a product, independent test information, and data from performance warranties are advisable supplements.

Custom-Produced Items. Another class of building components may be shop or factory fabricated individually for a specific job: structural steel, elevators, railings, special doors or stairs, cabinets, some electrical equipment, some air conditioning equipment, and food service fixtures. The fabricator's drawings and specifications must completely describe the item, the performance of its function, and its appearance. These drawings are

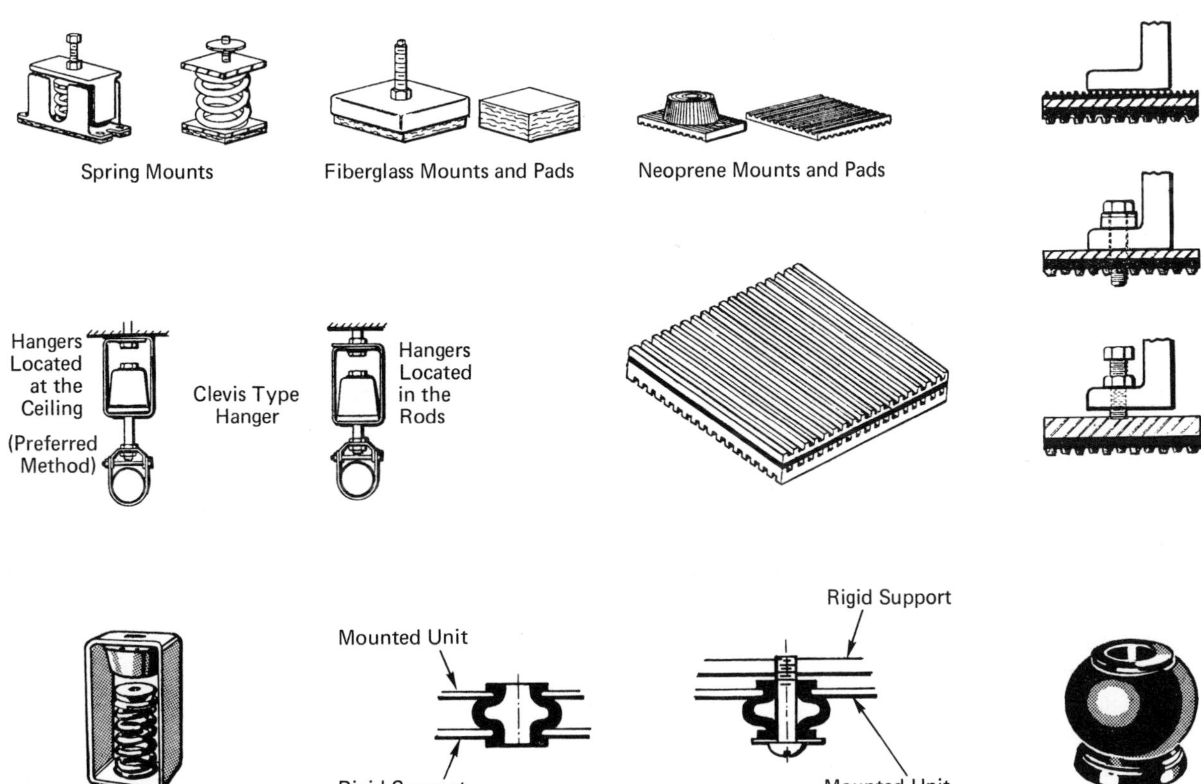

Figure 4.7 Various types of vibration isolator. *Source.* U.S. Government.

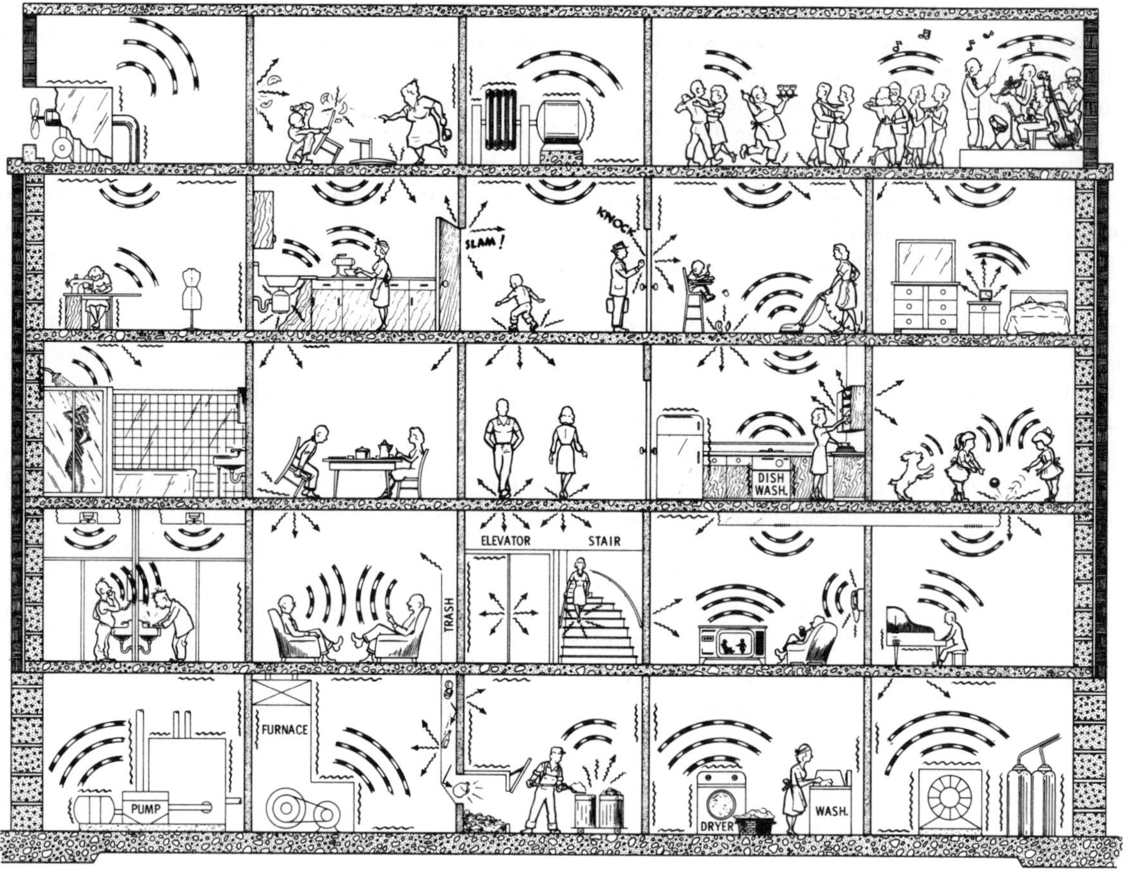

Figure 4.8 Common indoor sources of noise. *Source.* U.S. Government.

given to the general contractor and the architect for careful review to determine whether they correctly carry out the intent of the architect's construction documents and coordinate properly with other work.

The final step in controlling the quality of shop-fabricated items is to verify that the final installed product conforms to documents.

On-the-Job Production. Some portions of the construction (ductwork, storefront work, concrete, forms, most reinforcements, wood and light metal framing, sheet metal work, fencing, piping and conduit work, etc.) are fabricated and erected on the job.

Quality control depends on design and proper development of the architect's construction documents, adequate supervision of the installation, and the skill and motivation of the contractor. These factors also apply to manufactured and shop-made items.

The architect acquires orientation to various plans, using as few scales as necessary, grouping related details, and employing key plans, an easy referencing system, and the Uniform Construction Index to help the contractor's estimator, the contractor, the plan checker, and the engineers do their jobs faster, more efficiently, and with the high level of quality that is expected.

The drawings and specifications are the heart of construction quality control, conveying a set of messages to builders who must become familiar with their task as quickly as possible. The documents should be clear, logically organized, simple, and comprehensive.

Finish Control. In selecting finishes, the architect should consider the following points.

- Durability.
- Appearance.
- Cost.
- Fire resistance.
- Code acceptance.
- Ease of cleaning.
- Acoustical properties.
- Method of installation.

Lath and plaster, gypsum wallboard, tile and terrazzo, acoustical treatments, ceiling suspension systems, wood flooring and paneling, resilient flooring, carpeting, painting, wall coverings, special floorings and coatings, are the areas to which these points must be applied.

Dimensional and Finish Tolerance. Quality control begins early in the design process when the architect establishes the type of construction and materials to be used. Detailing and specification, supplied later, permit the achievement of precision and economy.

Sometimes exacting requirements must be set forth for the contractor, who is responsible for precise performance. Drawings and specifications must be produced that define beyond any doubt the limits of acceptability. For example, structures must be located within specific property limits, and these must be given; there must be adequate room for manufactured or prefabricated equipment in previously built spaces.

The architect should make sure that the contractor knows where property lines are by calling attention to bona fide monuments, or by requiring that the contractor make a precise survey to establish such limiting lines. Spaces that will contain equipment are often defined as "clear" space to assure that the equipment will fit. The contractor should be required to verify equipment dimensions.

SIMCOE MUNICIPAL BUILDING
Simcoe, Ontario, Addition and Restoration
Architect: C. A. Ventin
Photo: Office

When architectural drawings relate to existing site or structural conditions, or where fixtures, equipment, or other parts cannot be measured until a later date, certain dimensions may be imprecise. When the builder has exposed the existing structure or when the rough grading or excavation has been completed, however, the architect should be notified that specific instructions have become necessary.

Precise dimensions of a concealed footing may not be needed if at least the design dimensions have been provided. For example, pavement for a parking lot must drain without puddling, achieve minimum thickness needed, and appear reasonably flat to the eye, but the precision called for in an interior floor slab is not mandatory.

Some rules of thumb applying to tolerances in construction are as follows:

- Maximum aggregate size should not exceed three-fourths of the minimum distance between reinforcing bars.
- Concrete slabs and tile work should not exceed ⅛-inch variation along a 10-foot straight edge.
- Steel column baseplates should be true to center within $^{1}/_{16}$ inch.
- Wood doors should not be out of plane by more than ⅛ inch.
- Riser heights should not vary more than ¼ inch in any one run.

The American Institute of Steel Construction, the American Concrete Institute, the Ceramic Tile Institute, and other trade associations have set up specific criteria establishing good minimum standards.

Some of the earlier rough stages of construction can be brought to true alignment or fit by later work. Imperfect joinery in rough framing can be concealed or corrected by careful application of room finish materials. A wood base will cover an imperfect joint at the bottom of a gypsum board application on a wall. A painter can patch and touch up damage or inconsistencies in a room surface. Such measures can be taken to correct or conceal imperfections during the finishing stages of construction, to reduce unnecessarily fine tolerances. For example, each window element is usually slightly different from others, thus reducing the advantages of mass production. The forms for the openings vary slightly; the concrete deflects slightly; beams and columns are slightly out of level or thumb. Window-wall elements, however, can be designed with a variable closure trim or by casting in a lip in the concrete or in a metal frame. Almost any degree of precision can be obtained.

Durability and Permanence. If the emphasis is on minimum initial cost, the architect's options to select materials and detail for durability and permanence are reduced. However a more expensive material will be less expensive in the long run. For instance, a good seal coat over an asphaltic-concrete, paved parking lot may resist detrimental effects of dripping oil, extending the life of the lot by more than the cost of the seal. A wider overhang may reduce the need for window washing and other exterior maintenance.

A proper roofing installation is a conspicuous factor in determining the quality of a structure. When specifying a built-up or composition roof, there is a relatively small difference in cost between poor and good roofing. Better cost effectiveness is achieved with better roofing. When using roofing materials such as shingles, tile or metal, the cost of attractive appearance and permanence must be considered, as well as the weight of roofing, which affects cost because it is a determinant of the amount of supporting structure necessary.

Cost effectiveness in specifying and detailing is influenced by the life expectancy of the building. Heavy foot or vehicular traffic, anticipated weather conditions, and possibilities of soiling, vandalism, or intermittent alterations must be considered.

Access for purposes of maintenance also influences the architect's selection of durable and permanent materials. A small store building can easily be painted from the ground or from a step ladder; a highrise office structure, on the other hand, should require very little exterior maintenance beyond window washing.

Building codes must be met as a minimum standard. The architect is obliged to provide drawings and specifications that fulfill the requirements of all applicable codes.

Example: A Suspended Ceiling System. Suppose that the ceiling is high, so durability is of minimal importance. If the ceiling is to be installed in a lobby or quality restaurant, the architect may select an attractive textured board with concealed runners and splines, even a special color. The following questions arise:

- Are light fixtures going to be recessed or surface mounted?
- How will the ceiling registers and grilles be accommodated?
- Is the system to be incombustible? Is it to be fire rated?
- Are the surfaces washable?
- Is washability worth the extra cost or lessened acoustic effectiveness?
- How much acoustical absorption is desirable in a space such as a lobby? A private office? A restaurant?

Much of the installation procedure can be described in the specifications, but some conditions must be detailed: intersections with other materials, attachment or backing conditions, the pattern of grid members or unit borders.

As a rule the finishes of a building are exposed to view for the life of the structure; thus they are a critical factor in its appearance. The architect should carefully select exposed finish materials, assemble samples of them, and receive the approval of the client, as was done for design drawings or sketches. The availability of such materials should be verified and a verifying sample submitted by the contractor. Samples should be submitted of any finish material that is visually important (tile, ceiling board, plastic laminates, etc.).

If the drawings and specifications are not explicit enough, a job meeting should be arranged to review the installation with the tradesman who will perform the work. The architect should verify that the requirements of the documents are understood. He should locate grid or division lines, go over the areas to be covered, and make sure that adjacent work is protected from damage. The architect should determine that a subcontractor accepts preexisting conditions of the structure before starting work. A flooring contractor, for example, must be satisfied with the level of the subfloor surface; a painter must accept a prepainted surface as being smooth, clean, and dry.

The architect should reserve the right to reject work that does not conform to documents or fails to measure up to well-established workmanship standards.

Time Control

General Considerations. As indicated previously, fabrication and erection time can be held to a minimum if construction units can be conveniently fabricated in the shop or at a location where working conditions are favorable. Details can be worked out to facilitate installation into the final position, using suitable attachment devices. Installation of rooftop equipment, like painting and plastering, can proceed only after the roofing has been completed. Window-wall units, stairways, sales room fixtures, and so on, can be designed and detailed to minimize the trades required for their fabrication. Installation details should be as simple as possible. In addition, details and specifications should be designed to minimize the number of trades working in the same location at the same time. There should be easily defined lines of demarcation between the responsibility of one trade and another. These separations should apply also to the specifications and details.

A good set of drawings shows all necessary information and all decisions to be made at the time these documents are compiled. Often, however, certain decisions are best left until more information is available or until the structure is nearing completion. Colors for metal partitions, carpeting, paint, or elevator entrances can be selected later, giving ample time for fabrication, installation, or application. Schedules for processing by the contractor of shop drawings, lists, and architect's selections should be clearly drawn up.

In recent years, wages and material costs have risen faster than productivity. The architect can facilitate the work of the trades by specifying efficient, well-designed, easy-to-build details, as well as practical, simply catalogued, and useful requirements.

Construction Time Versus Cost. Certain construction materials and systems are more time-consuming than others in their application. For instance, poured-in-place concrete methods take much longer than a similar building framed in a structural steel system, and the application of 4 × 8 foot panels of prefinished plywood is faster, thus perhaps more economical, than the use of wood shingles. Before designing is begun, or during the process of designing a building, the architect must make decisions involving such trade offs. In fact, the availability (i.e., delivery time) of various systems and materials has become a prime concern. Raw material shortages, the dwindling sources of moderate priced energy, and worldwide political, economic, and social instability have influenced the steady supply of certain building materials. Ultimately the architect is often forced to change a design or to specify an alternate material. To avoid construction delays, architects are obliged to use mass-produced material and systems instead of custom components. In today's market it has become important to evaluate extended construction times due to inflation and also loss of revenues to the client. Consequently, designers must specify simpler materials that are readily available locally.

Given the construction industry's lack of universally applicable standards, however, it is difficult at times to make such decisions. A conscientious architect is very careful in the selection of materials (and systems) and always names specific alternates. The standard "or equal" clause is not a professional "selection." Once the architect has made a decision in regard to the material—for example, the option to use any one of three or four preselected brick types—he or she must determine their availability and their potential price differences, as these variables will affect the building budget. Problems of this type have forced many architectural offices to consider construction management, prepurchasing phased construction, fast track, scheduling, and negotiated contracts. Consequently, a number of of-

RUDOLPH JONES STUDENT CENTER, FAYETTEVILLE STATE UNIVERSITY
Fayetteville, North Carolina
Architects: MacMillan, MacMillan, Shawcroft, & Thames, partner in charge: B. Shawcroft
Photo: B. Shawcroft

fices that start by working with contractors or manufacturers in the earlier stages of design can reduce undue risks and most likely can complete a project within the intended budget, and on time. This undoubtedly means that contemporary architects should modify their office procedures by inviting earlier participation of a building design team; with time, they should gain greater knowledge and understanding of the performance and availability of the many materials in construction.

Cost Control

A major influence on project cost is the cost of the materials used. This in turn is determined by a number of variables.

Factors Influencing Cost of Materials

The Building Code. Certain minimum criteria must be met in the development of a construction project design, namely, the applicable building code(s) and standards of other governmental authorities. The code sets minimum comprehensive requirements. Depending on the project's size, location, and use, the code defines the type of construction, the kind of materials that can be used, and the permissible manner(s) of using such materials. The purpose of building codes is to guarantee the public health, safety, and general welfare.

The architect's selection of building materials in relation to their cost should be based on a thorough understanding of code requirements and restrictions, functional requirements, the owner's needs, and long-term maintenance. Then efforts to control costs are possible through knowledge and ingenuity in the use of materials.

Weights, Grades, and Thickness. Knowledge of the characteristics of material grades will aid in selecting the least expensive grade required to achieve the desired result. Unless a higher stress value or a better appearance is called for, a grade of framing lumber more expensive than the one that will do the job structurally is not necessary. The practice of using a less expensive grade of material is valid only when adequate performance can be expected.

Weights, gauges or thicknesses of material that will be adequate for the job should be specified, such as the minimum asphaltic-concrete paving thickness, minimum sheet metal gauge, and minimum glass thickness. Such minima are advisable only when they ensure adequate resistance to excessive breakage or wear.

Market Value of Materials. The cost-conscious architect must be aware of the current market, which is characterized by rapidly rising structural steel and lumber prices. However material costs vary from one locality to another. For example, wood products are usually cheaper near lumber mills, marble near quarries, and manufactured products near urban market centers.

Plumbing and light fixtures, appliances, mechanical equipment, and so on, should be investigated and analyzed before specifying, especially if many such units are required. A unit of lesser quality within the same company line may be able to perform the desired function and look as good as its more expensive counterpart.

Construction materials must be realistically appraised with respect to cost and value. The goal is to select a material in which cost, function, and appearance are appropriately balanced.

Use of Innovation. Simple, maximally effective utilization of standard components, conventional and up-to-date materials and methods (such as the easiest means of attachment or the latest code-approved assemblies), and time-saving equipment will facilitate economical construction. Experience, like consultation with experts from the trades, is very helpful.

When high-strength bolts were developed, use of more expensive welded, riveted, or bolted connections dwindled. Approval of a 1-hour stud and drywall system, with studs spaced at 2 feet on center, has helped reduce wall cost, as have new and cheaper methods of fireproofing, and better paints, adhesives, caulking compounds, and admixtures.

Consideration of the following series of questions can help the architect to use advancements and innovations and to devise ways to build a given project more easily, more quickly, and more economically:

- Can a new type of prefabricated stair unit be set into place without slowing down other phases of construction?
- If stairs are installed early, will they be able to withstand the heavy use to which they will be subjected during later work?
- Can railings be conveniently attached?
- Will the stairs hold up through the years?

Suppose that a contractor bidding a job sees that a prefabricated stair unit has been specified by the architect. Once he has verified that the stairs are durable, that they are easy and quick to install, and that they can be furnished at the job at less cost than previous methods, he is able to bid less.

Coordinated Construction. The principle of shop fabrication is sometimes brought to the job site. The plumber can take job measurements and make up assemblies of piping that can be carried to specific locations for final installation. Such assemblies can be made where supplies are conveniently stockpiled and good working conditions can be achieved. Certain concrete elements can be cast on site, cured, and later lifted into place more cheaply, more rapidly, and with better quality control than would have been possible if originally cast in place.

In the example above involving precast concrete units, the structural design of the units must permit them to withstand stresses of being lifted into place, perhaps with special lifting inserts. Dimensioning and tolerances may have to be included for various parts. Connections must also be designed for final installation. Construction procedures are best reviewed and verified with the contractor who does the work.

Very close coordination must be maintained among drawings, specifications, and industry standards, as well as liaison with the subcontractor. Structural design and accessory items are precisely drawn. Such coordination of all elements should result in better quality and saving of time and money.

Efficient shop conditions reflect a combination of good work space, proper tools, special skills, and competent supervision. Shop fabrication utilizes labor more efficiently: there is less need for workers to travel, less material transport time, and better supervision and technical assistance. With proper conception and specification of shop conditions by the architect, labor costs can be controlled. Drawings should allow for the neat segregation of a transportable part of the construction to the job site, as well as providing adequate space allocation on site and instructions for installing or making connections.

Saving on Trade Work. Occasionally the architect has the option to decide whether one trade or another will perform some work. For example, a scratch coat behind the tile work could be applied by the plasterer along with the other scratch-coat work. Irrigation and sprinkler piping might be specified in a section where trades specializing in such work would do it at less cost to the owner than plumbers would, subject to approval of the unions. Sometimes paving can be done at less cost and subject to less wear during construction if it is installed at the same time as the landscaping, by the landscaping contractor.

Crafts tend to work more efficiently if they can proceed in a convenient and systematic fashion, repeating similar or identical tasks. If window glass can be installed from the interior in a multistory building, not only will man-hours be saved during the original installation, but replacement will be greatly simplified. A suspended ceiling can be hung over an entire floor at one time, provided the partitions are detailed to terminate under the ceiling and not penetrate it. This method of installation requires very little cutting and fitting; thus working conditions will be convenient, and the movement of material will be greatly simplified.

Trade Sequencing. Where overlapping of trades is necessary, it is sometimes possible to eliminate some of the overlapping steps through logical design and detailing. When scheduling trades, a builder should strive to achieve the following features:

1 Keep the work of each trade or subcontract clearly defined and separate from the others.
2 Minimize the need for trades to move on and off the job. Continuity of personnel familiar with a job may help increase efficiency, eliminate substantial transport of equipment, and simplify clean-up. In addition, materials and supplies can be grouped into more economical shipments, and stockpiling can be reduced.
3 If one trade does not have to work around another, if one person does not have to stand idle while another completes a task in the same area, if the by-product of a messy trade does not interfere with another, problems involving the need for personal cooperation can be minimized.
4 Avoid scheduling the work of any trade early if it is likely to be damaged by subsequent activities.
5 If expensive equipment is involved (especially scaffolding, cranes, and construction hoists), try to arrange for more efficient utilization by several trades to shorten the period of usage.

The architect may facilitate desirable trade sequencing by grouping the work of what would normally be several crafts into one subcontract. An example is window-wall work. Here the miscellaneous and ornamental metal work, glazing, caulking, and similar activities, are under one subcontract trade with total and well-defined responsibility. Another example is an air conditioning contract that includes related plumbing, electrical, sheet metal, and insulation work, as well as equipment bases and supports.

Specifications can include requirements to order at an early date, according to their availability, critical materials such as fixtures or certain finish materials.

A progress schedule should be required. A larger, more complicated project calls for sophisticated scheduling methods such as the critical path method (CPM), the program evaluation review technique (PERT), or fast-track scheduling, discussed in Chapter 2.

Cost of Specifications. "Tight" specifications leave fewer unanswered questions and are more explicit in directing the builder to construct what the architect intended. Projects done for institutional or governmental clients who insist on tight specifications are usually more costly because of detailed requirements.

The contractor who wishes to be low bidder may be concerned about having to meet many specific requirements and about reductions in freedom of action. If it is feared that time-consuming supervision over subcontractors will be necessary, the result will be a higher estimate, and probably greater cost to the owner.

On the other hand, an estimator who was encouraged by a very complete set of documents might anticipate little risk of an unfavorable interpretation during construction, foreseeing little need for time-consuming clarifications or negotiations. The subcontractors might be expected to do their work efficiently and completely. They, in turn, might feel the same way about their estimates. Thus perhaps a minimum risk situation would be created, with bids kept low.

Certain specification sections are effectively tightened through code requirements or building department supervision of minimum trade standards. General structural work (e.g., timber, steel, masonry or reinforced concrete, earthwork, plumbing, electrical, work, plaster-

MUTUAL BENEFIT LIFE INSURANCE BUILDING
Philadelphia, Pennsylvania
Architects: The Eggers Partnership
Photo: G. Amiaga

ing, roofing, elevators, glass, and glazing) is closely supervised by most building department jurisdictions: requirements are spelled out in the codes, and building inspectors are active in the field. In all these codes, a portion of the specifications falls under the heading of "compliance with the code."

In writing specifications, the architect should judge each case on its own merits.

- Are the intended bidders known? Has previous experience with these contractors been successful?
- May the contract be negotiated with a single general contractor?
- Is the project large or small?
- Is the client a public entity or an institution?

Performance Specifications. Where an end result may be specified rather than equipment, as in air conditioning, a proposed contractor's design is subject to review by the architect (or the architect's engineer). Available spaces should be checked, heat loss calculations verified, and power and other utility requirements coordinated.

Or, an architect's drawings may show visible profiles and other appearance features of a window-wall, a swimming pool, or an industrial roof structure. Structural and functional criteria would also be specified, but the bidder would be left to his or her own ingenuity and particular technique to accomplish the required functions, subject to final review and approval by the architect.

WOOD FRAME RESIDENCE
Raleigh, North Carolina
Architect: George Matsumoto
Photo: Office

2 CONTRACTS, LEGAL RESPONSIBILITIES, AND ETHICS

Bidding

The two methods of selecting a contractor involve direct selection and competitive bidding.

Direct Selection. A contractor's reputation is a major factor in negotiated contracts. After the owner has selected a reputable contractor, the owner, with the architect's assistance, negotiates the terms of the construction contract. The architect must then examine the contractor's proposal to be sure that it is reasonable and is based on equitable costs of materials, labor, and equipment. The negotiated contract may be expressed in a lump sum or in the direct cost of the work plus a fee.

Competitive Bidding. The bidder is a person or an organization who submits a bid for a prime contract with an owner. The owner can better his or her chances of obtaining the lowest possible price by seeking proposals from many qualified bidders. The weakness of the competitive bidding system, however, lies in the assumption that all bidders are equally competent.

Bidding begins after the completion of the contract drawings and specifications. In private work, an *invitation to bid* is sent to a list of prequalified bidders by the architect and the owner. Several bidders should be invited, to ensure adequate price competition.

Public work contracts are nearly always made through competitive bidding. Bidders are invited to submit proposals by means of a newspaper advertisement. All interested bidders who can meet bonding requirements may submit proposals.

The *bid bond* guarantees that the chosen bidder will enter into the contract. The face amount of the bid is usually 10% of the amount of the bid. If the low bidder fails to enter into a contract, his surety must pay the owner the difference between his bid and the next higher bid. In private work, the bid bond may be used as an alternative to deposit of a certified check or bank draft.

Bid Deposit. The amount of the bid deposit is either a lump sum or a percentage of the base bid proposal, in the form of a certified check or a bank draft. This amount is included in the advertisement for bids or in the notice to bidders. A lump sum is preferable to the contractor, since it allows bidders to determine the amounts of their respective bid deposits without indirectly revealing the amount each one is proposing. Lump sum figures are the architect's estimated percentage of the construction cost.

The bid bond form is included in the specifications. If no specific form is required, bidders provide a standard form of the surety (bank or finance company) writing the bond. The bid deposit must also guarantee that the contractor will carry out the construction contract and will furnish a performance bond, if required, within the specified time. Otherwise the difference between the contractor's proposal and the next acceptable bid is forfeited, up to a maximum of the bid deposit amount.

The Bidding Process. Each bidder is furnished with sets of drawings and specifications free of charge, although a nominal deposit is usually required for each set

LABOR AND MATERIAL PAYMENT BOND

NOW, THEREFORE, THE CONDITION OF THIS OBLIGATION is such that, if Principal shall promptly make payment to all claimants as hereinafter defined, for all labor and material used or reasonably required for use in the performance of the Contract, then this obligation shall be void; otherwise it shall remain in full force and effect, subject, however, to the following conditions:

1. A claimant is defined as one having a direct contract with the Principal or with a Subcontractor of the Principal for labor, material, or both, used or reasonably required for use in the performance of the Contract, labor and material being construed to include that part of water, gas, power, light, heat, oil, gasoline, telephone service or rental of equipment directly applicable to the Contract.

2. The above named Principal and Surety hereby jointly and severally agree with the Owner that every claimant as herein defined, who has not been paid in full before the expiration of a period of ninety (90) days after the date on which the last of such claimant's work or labor was done or performed, or materials were furnished by such claimant, may sue on this bond for the use of such claimant, prosecute the suit to final judgment for such sum or sums as may be justly due claimant, and have execution thereon. The Owner shall not be liable for the payment of any costs or expenses of any such suit.

3. No suit or action shall be commenced hereunder by any claimant:

a) Unless claimant, other than one having a direct contract with the Principal, shall have given written notice to any two of the following: the Principal, the Owner, or the Surety above named, within ninety (90) days after such claimant did or performed the last of the work or labor, or furnished the last of the materials for which said claim is made, stating with substantial accuracy the amount claimed and the name of the party to whom the materials were furnished, or for whom the work or labor was done or performed. Such notice shall be served by mailing the same by registered mail or certified mail, postage prepaid, in an envelope addressed to the Principal, Owner or Surety, at any place where an office is regularly maintained for the transaction of business, or served in any manner in which legal process may be served in the state in which the aforesaid project is located, save that such service need not be made by a public officer.

b) After the expiration of one (1) year following the date on which Principal ceased Work on said Contract, it being understood, however, that if any limitation embodied in this bond is prohibited by any law controlling the construction hereof such limitation shall be deemed to be amended so as to be equal to the minimum period of limitation permitted by such law.

c) Other than in a state court of competent jurisdiction in and for the county or other political subdivision of the state in which the Project, or any part thereof, is situated, or in the United States District Court for the district in which the Project, or any part thereof, is situated, and not elsewhere.

4. The amount of this bond shall be reduced by and to the extent of any payment or payments made in good faith hereunder, inclusive of the payment by Surety of mechanics' liens which may be filed of record against said improvement, whether or not claim for the amount of such lien be presented under and against this bond.

Signed and sealed this day of 19

(Principal) (Seal)

(Witness)

(Title)

(Surety) (Seal)

(Witness)

(Title)

Figure 4.9

THE AMERICAN INSTITUTE OF ARCHITECTS

AIA Document A311

Performance Bond

KNOW ALL MEN BY THESE PRESENTS: that
(Here insert full name and address or legal title of Contractor)

as Principal, hereinafter called Contractor, and,
(Here insert full name and address or legal title of Surety)

as Surety, hereinafter called Surety, are held and firmly bound unto
(Here insert full name and address or legal title of Owner)

as Obligee, hereinafter called Owner, in the amount of

Dollars ($),

for the payment whereof Contractor and Surety bind themselves, their heirs, executors, administrators, successors and assigns, jointly and severally, firmly by these presents.

WHEREAS,

Contractor has by written agreement dated 19 , entered into a contract with Owner for
(Here insert full name, address and description of project)

in accordance with Drawings and Specifications prepared by
(Here insert full name and address or legal title of Architect)

which contract is by reference made a part hereof, and is hereinafter referred to as the Contract.

AIA DOCUMENT A311 • PERFORMANCE BOND AND LABOR AND MATERIAL PAYMENT BOND • AIA ®
FEBRUARY 1970 ED. • THE AMERICAN INSTITUTE OF ARCHITECTS, 1735 N.Y. AVE., N.W., WASHINGTON, D. C. 20006

Figure 4.10

THE AMERICAN INSTITUTE OF ARCHITECTS

AIA Document A310

Bid Bond

KNOW ALL MEN BY THESE PRESENTS, that we
(Here insert full name and address or legal title of Contractor)

as Principal, hereinafter called the Principal, and
(Here insert full name and address or legal title of Surety)

a corporation duly organized under the laws of the State of
as Surety, hereinafter called the Surety, are held and firmly bound unto
(Here insert full name and address or legal title of Owner)

as Obligee, hereinafter called the Obligee, in the sum of

Dollars ($),
for the payment of which sum well and truly to be made, the said Principal and the said Surety, bind ourselves, our heirs, executors, administrators, successors and assigns, jointly and severally, firmly by these presents.

WHEREAS, the Principal has submitted a bid for
(Here insert full name, address and description of project)

NOW, THEREFORE, if the Obligee shall accept the bid of the Principal and the Principal shall enter into a Contract with the Obligee in accordance with the terms of such bid, and give such bond or bonds as may be specified in the bidding or Contract Documents with good and sufficient surety for the faithful performance of such Contract and for the prompt payment of labor and material furnished in the prosecution thereof, or in the event of the failure of the Principal to enter such Contract and give such bond or bonds, if the Principal shall pay to the Obligee the difference not to exceed the penalty hereof between the amount specified in said bid and such larger amount for which the Obligee may in good faith contract with another party to perform the Work covered by said bid, then this obligation shall be null and void, otherwise to remain in full force and effect.

Signed and sealed this day of 19

(Principal) *(Seal)*

(Witness)

(Title)

(Surety) *(Seal)*

(Witness)

(Title)

AIA DOCUMENT A310 • BID BOND • AIA ® • FEBRUARY 1970 ED • THE AMERICAN INSTITUTE OF ARCHITECTS, 1735 N.Y. AVE., N.W., WASHINGTON, D. C. 20006

Figure 4.11

THE AMERICAN INSTITUTE OF ARCHITECTS

AIA DOCUMENT A701

INSTRUCTIONS TO BIDDERS

Table of Articles

ARTICLE 1

DEFINITIONS

1.1 Bidding Documents include the Advertisement or Invitation to Bid, Instructions to Bidders, the bid form, other sample bidding and contract forms and the proposed Contract Documents including any Addenda issued prior to receipt of bids.

1.2 All definitions set forth in the General Conditions of the Contract for Construction, AIA Document A201, or in other Contract Documents are applicable to the Bidding Documents.

1.3 Addenda are written or graphic instruments issued by the Architect prior to the execution of the Contract which modify or interpret the bidding documents by addition, deletions, clarifications or corrections.

1.4 A Bid is a complete and properly signed proposal to do the Work or designated portion thereof for the sums stiplated therein supported by data called for by the Bidding Documents.

1.5 Base Bid is the sum stated in the Bid for which the Bidder offers to perform the Work described as the base, to which Work may be added or deducted for sums stated in Alternate Bids.

1.6 An Alternate Bid (or Alternate) is an amount stated in the Bid to be added to or deducted from the amount of the Base Bid if the corresponding change in project scope or materials or methods of construction described in the Bidding Documents is accepted.

1.7 A Unit Price is an amount stated in the Bid as a price per unit of measurement for materials or services as described in the Contract Documents.

1.8 A Bidder is one who submits a Bid for a prime contract with the Owner for the Work described in the proposed Contract Documents.

1.9 A Sub-bidder is one who submits a bid to a Bidder for materials or labor for a portion of the Work.

ARTICLE 2

BIDDER'S REPRESENTATION

2.1 Each Bidder by making his bid represents that:

2.1.1 He has read and understands the Bidding Documents and his Bid is made in accordance therewith.

2.1.2 He has visited the site and has familiarized himself with the local conditions under which the Work is to be performed.

2.1.3 His Bid is based upon the materials, systems and equipment described in the Bidding Documents without exceptions.

ARTICLE 3

BIDDING DOCUMENTS

3.1 COPIES

3.1.1 Bidders may obtain from the Architect (unless another issuing office is designated in the Advertisement or Invitation to Bid) complete sets of the Bidding Documents in the number and for the deposit sum, if any, stated in the Advertisement or Invitation. The deposit will be refunded to Bidders who submit a bonafide Bid and return the Bidding Documents in good condition within 10 days after receipt of Bids. The cost of replacement of any missing or damaged documents will be deducted from the deposit. A Bidder receiving a contract award may retain the Bidding Documents and his deposit will be refunded.

3.1.2 Bidding Documents will not be issued to Sub-bidders or others unless specifically offered in the Advertisement or Invitation to Bid.

3.1.3 Complete sets of Bidding Documents shall be used in preparing bids; neither the Owner nor the Architect assume any responsibility for errors or misinterpretations resulting from the use of incomplete sets of Bidding Documents.

3.1.4 The Owner or Architect in making copies of the Bidding Documents available on the above terms, do so only for the purpose of obtaining bids on the Work and do not confer a license or grant for any other use.

3.2 INTERPRETATION OR CORRECTION OF BIDDING DOCUMENTS

3.2.1 Bidders shall promptly notify the Architect of any ambiguity, inconsistency or error which they may discover upon examination of the Bidding Documents or of the site and local conditions.

3.2.2 Bidders requiring clarification or interpretation of the Bidding Documents shall make a written

Figure 4.12

requested, and is refunded upon return of the drawings and specifications in good condition. On larger projects, sets of documents should also be on file at central trade offices or local plan rooms for inspection by contractors and subcontractors.

The bid documents prepared by the architect include the following:

- Invitation or advertisement for bids.
- Instructions to bidders.
- Bid form.
- Owner-contractor agreement form.
- Information on bid deposits, including requirements of bid bond.
- Performance and payment bond forms.
- The general conditions of the contract for construction, as well as supplementary conditions and special conditions.
- Technical specifications, including allowances, alternatives and provisions, if any, for separate contracts.
- Working drawings.
- Addenda.

The bid form describes the scope of the work, the total sum of the base bid price, unit prices, bonds covering performance, labor, and materials, and alternates. It includes addenda and identifies the bidder in legal terms. Since all bidders will compete for the same work, all bid forms are identical.

Bids are opened at the architect's office or on the owner's premises. Sealed bids may be opened in the presence of bidders. In public works, the bid opening is open to all interested parties. The decision to award a contract to the lowest "responsible" bidder is normally made within 10 days of opening of bids. If the lowest bidder is determined to be "not responsible," the contract is awarded to the next lowest bidder submitting a proposal.

TEMPLE BETH ZION
Buffalo, New York
Architects: Harrison & Abramovitz
Photo: E. Stoller Associates

Contracts

The *owner-contractor agreement* is the basic contract. It incorporates all the other documents and stipulates the contract sum. The general conditions set forth the legal and regulatory requirements of the contract. The supplementary conditions name requirements of each particular type of project and owner. The special conditions refer to a specific project condition. The drawings provide graphic representation of all work to be done: measurements, arrangements, location of materials and equipment, structure, systems, and siting. The specifications provide technical information about the quality of materials and equipment shown on the drawings and the method and quality of installation (workmanship).

Addenda and modifications are changes made, respectively, before and after the execution of the contract. Modifications that affect the cost or time of completion of the contract, called change orders, must be authorized by the owner and signed by both owner and architect. Minor modifications that do not affect cost or time completion are called field orders and may be signed by the architect without the owner's authorization.

General Description. A contract is an agreement that is enforceable by law. To be valid, a contract must contain *all* the following elements:

1 Identification and legal capacity of the parties, namely, the promisor (one who promises) and the promisee (one to whom a promise is made).
2 Signatures attesting to mutual consent.
3 Sufficient consideration, that is, any act or forbearance of an act that is of benefit to the promisor. A contract must include something of value in the form of promises exchanged.

In addition, the contract must be for a lawful purpose.

Since a contract is a voluntary relationship, its purpose must be clearly understood by both parties. One party makes an offer; the second party accepts it unconditionally. If any of the elements just enumerated is absent, or if the contract is void by statute or common law, it is considered to be "not binding."

The limitation(s) of an offer must always be stated; for example, "This offer is good until noon, August 7, 1979." A counteroffer constitutes a rejection of a previous offer made by the other party. The architect may state: "We will commence with the design of the project in accordance with decisions made at the meeting of July 4, 1976, unless we hear to the contrary." If the client offers no reply, this may be accepted as assent in establishing a contract, although it is preferable to receive a written confirmation of all decisions.

Contract documents are considered to be complementary: the requirements of any one document are as binding as if required by all.

Contracts establish certain limits of responsibility. The architect, for instance, tries to guard the owner against defects and deficiencies in the contractor's work by periodic on-site observations. However the architect is not responsible for construction methods, techniques, sequences or procedures, or safety precautions during construction work, nor is the architect responsible for any acts or omissions of the contractor, the subcontractors, their agents or employees, or any other persons performing work in connection with the project.

In furnishing a statement of probable construction cost, the architect does not guarantee that bids will not vary from any such statement or other cost estimate he prepares.

Description of Contract Documents. The contract is customarily signed by the owner and contractor in triplicate. If either does not sign any one or more of the documents, the architect must identify the unsigned pieces. In executing the contract, the contractor indicates that he or she is familiar with the conditions under which the work is to be performed according to the contract documents, which include all labor, materials, equipment, and other items necessary to properly complete the work. Copies of drawings and specifications are furnished to the contractor free of charge.

All copies of the drawings and specifications distributed and furnished by the architect are the property of the architect and must be returned to him or her on completion of the work, in accordance with the general conditions of the contract. The agreement must state that the drawings and specifications as "instruments of service" are the architect's property, not to be used on other work except by previous agreement with the architect.

The time-of-completion clause included in the construction contract consists of four basic parts: starting time, completion time, liquidated damages (if necessary), and penalty and bonus (optional).

Starting Time. The starting time date should follow the date of execution of the contract. The insertion of the words "upon receipt of a notice to proceed" in the agreement provides for issuance of such an order after all other matters relating to contract and construction operations have been resolved.

Completion Time. The completion time is expressed in terms of a specific number of days or a specific date.

GENERAL CONDITIONS OF THE CONTRACT FOR CONSTRUCTION

ARTICLE 1

CONTRACT DOCUMENTS

1.1 DEFINITIONS

1.1.1 THE CONTRACT DOCUMENTS

The Contract Documents consist of the Owner-Contractor Agreement, the Conditions of the Contract (General, Supplementary and other Conditions), the Drawings, the Specifications, and all Addenda issued prior to and all Modifications issued after execution of the Contract. A Modification is (1) a written amendment to the Contract signed by both parties, (2) a Change Order, (3) a written interpretation issued by the Architect pursuant to Subparagraph 2.2.8, or (4) a written order for a minor change in the Work issued by the Architect pursuant to Paragraph 12.3. The Contract Documents do not include Bidding Documents such as the Advertisement or Invitation to Bid, the Instructions to Bidders, sample forms, the Contractor's Bid or portions of Addenda relating to any of these, or any other documents, unless specifically enumerated in the Owner-Contractor Agreement.

1.1.2 THE CONTRACT

The Contract Documents form the Contract for Construction. This Contract represents the entire and integrated agreement between the parties hereto and supersedes all prior negotiations, representations, or agreements, either written or oral. The Contract may be amended or modified only by a Modification as defined in Subparagraph 1.1.1. The Contract Documents shall not be construed to create any contractual relationship of any kind between the Architect and the Contractor, but the Architect shall be entitled to performance of obligations intended for his benefit, and to enforcement thereof. Nothing contained in the Contract Documents shall create any contractual relationship between the Owner or the Architect and any Subcontractor or Sub-subcontractor.

1.1.3 THE WORK

The Work comprises the completed construction required by the Contract Documents and includes all labor necessary to produce such construction, and all materials and equipment incorporated or to be incorporated in such construction.

1.1.4 THE PROJECT

The Project is the total construction of which the Work performed under the Contract Documents may be the whole or a part.

1.2 EXECUTION, CORRELATION AND INTENT

1.2.1 The Contract Documents shall be signed in not less than triplicate by the Owner and Contractor. If either the Owner or the Contractor or both do not sign the Conditions of the Contract, Drawings, Specifications, or any of the other Contract Documents, the Architect shall identify such Documents.

1.2.2 By executing the Contract, the Contractor represents that he has visited the site, familiarized himself with the local conditions under which the Work is to be performed, and correlated his observations with the requirements of the Contract Documents.

1.2.3 The intent of the Contract Documents is to include all items necessary for the proper execution and completion of the Work. The Contract Documents are complementary, and what is required by any one shall be as binding as if required by all. Work not covered in the Contract Documents will not be required unless it is consistent therewith and is reasonably inferable therefrom as being necessary to produce the intended results. Words and abbreviations which have well-known technical or trade meanings are used in the Contract Documents in accordance with such recognized meanings.

1.2.4 The organization of the Specifications into divisions, sections and articles, and the arrangement of Drawings shall not control the Contractor in dividing the Work among Subcontractors or in establishing the extent of Work to be performed by any trade.

1.3 OWNERSHIP AND USE OF DOCUMENTS

1.3.1 All Drawings, Specifications and copies thereof furnished by the Architect are and shall remain his property. They are to be used only with respect to this Project and are not to be used on any other project. With the exception of one contract set for each party to the Contract, such documents are to be returned or suitably accounted for to the Architect on request at the completion of the Work. Submission or distribution to meet official regulatory requirements or for other purposes in connection with the Project is not to be construed as publication in derogation of the Architect's common law copyright or other reserved rights.

ARTICLE 2

ARCHITECT

2.1 DEFINITION

2.1.1 The Architect is the person lawfully licensed to practice architecture, or an entity lawfully practicing architecture identified as such in the Owner-Contractor Agreement, and is referred to throughout the Contract Documents as if singular in number and masculine in gender. The term Architect means the Architect or his authorized representative.

2.2 ADMINISTRATION OF THE CONTRACT

2.2.1 The Architect will provide administration of the Contract as hereinafter described.

2.2.2 The Architect will be the Owner's representative during construction and until final payment is due. The Architect will advise and consult with the Owner. The Owner's instructions to the Contractor shall be forwarded

Figure 4.13

SUPPLEMENT TO THE GENERAL CONDITIONS AND INSTRUCTIONS ON THEIR USE

The supplements shown herein are representative of those which may be required on a typical project, but are not intended to be all-inclusive. Not all of the additions or modifications shown will be necessary for every project. Those that are employed frequently are noted "Usual" while those that may be used infrequently are noted "Occasional".

SUPPLEMENTARY CONDITIONS

(Suggested Introductory Paragraph)

The following supplements modify, change, delete from or add to the "General Conditions of the Contract for Construction," AIA Document A201, Twelfth Edition, April 1970. Where any Article of the General Conditions is modified or any Paragraph, Subparagraph or Clause thereof is modified or deleted by these supplements, the unaltered provisions of that Article, Paragraph, Subparagraph or Clause shall remain in effect.

(Occasional)

Where provisions of the General Conditions relate in general to the work of the Contractor and Subcontractors, these Paragraphs are modified in Division 1 "General Requirements" of the Specifications; these include the following paragraphs:

(Here list numbers of the Paragraphs modified in Division 1)

NOTES TO THE ARCHITECT

While it is understood the Supplementary Conditions modify only those portions of the printed document specifically mentioned in the text of the supplements, it is good practice to set forth the exact status of those portions of the printed document which are not modified.

The following Paragraphs have been modified or added in the Guide:

1.1	4.13	11.1
1.3	7.5	11.3
2.2	9.2	12.1
4.4	9.3	15.1
4.7	9.4	
4.11	9.8	

If the Architect follows the recommendation of the Uniform Construction Index (AIA Document K103, AGC Document 19, CSI Document 001a) and places certain subject matter in Division 1 which also occurs in the General Conditions (i.e., Samples, Shop Drawings, Cutting and Patching, Clean-up) the "Occasional" paragraph should be used. In addition to listing the A201 provision numbers here, where modifications to the paragraphs so handled would otherwise appear in sequence in the text of the Supplementary Conditions, a reference should be included reminding the Contractor, Subcontractors and Owner that these are in Division 1. For example, after modifications to Paragraph 4.11 —if this were to be modified as suggested in this Guide—there would follow: "4.13—*Delete this Paragraph in its entirety; provi-*

Figure 4.14

1 THE OWNER HAS A RIGHT TO EXPECT

Accurate Drawings The Owner has a right to expect that the Architect has exercised due diligence, skill, and good judgment in the preparation of the Contract Documents to the end that the accepted Contractor will deliver, in full compliance with the Contract Documents, without misunderstanding or unexpected cost, a building adequate for its intended purpose.

2 THE CONTRACTOR HAS A RIGHT TO EXPECT

Contract Documents The Contractor has a right to expect that the information shown and described in the Contract Documents is sufficient to enable him to prepare complete and accurate estimates and that he will not be penalized for any deficiencies in these documents.

Local Ordinances The Contractor is entitled to assume the Architect is familiar with local ordinances pertaining to the design and construction of buildings and has described in the Specifications any unusual stipulations which would affect cost. The Contractor accepts responsibility for compliance with local administrative requirements concerning building operations. (See Paragraphs 4.6 and 4.7 of AIA Document A201, the General Conditions of the Contract for Construction.)

Permits The Architect where applicable should file as early as possible required sets of documents with the appropriate local authorities to start processing for a general building permit.

3 THE ARCHITECT HAS A RIGHT TO EXPECT

Selection of Bidders The Architect is entitled to full confidence from the Owner during the selection of the bidders and the taking of bids. The Owner should not attempt to dictate either the bidders to receive invitations to bid or the bidding procedures.

Instructions to Bidders Instructions to bidders explain the procedures to be followed in preparing and submitting bids and are used in conjunction with the proposed Contract Documents. Instructions to Bidders, AIA Document A701, should be used for this purpose.

Contractors' Responsibility Each contractor invited to bid has the responsibility to the Architect and the Owner to ascertain, prior to accepting the invitation, if he will be able to properly prepare a bid and submit same at the time and place requested. He is expected to utilize every effort to obtain the lowest possible prices within the limits of ethical construction practices and in complete conformance with the requirements of the Contract Documents. In the event a contractor cannot meet the above requirements, he should immediately notify the Architect and withdraw from the bidding. The Architect also has the right to expect that every contractor

Figure 4.15

Time requirements are fulfilled when the construction work is complete and the owner can occupy the building for its intended use. The general conditions include a provision to extend the time allotted under conditions beyond the contractor's control. Although time limits are difficult to enforce without the stipulation of liquidated damages in the agreement, they may be a basis for terminating a contract (unreasonable delay). Thus the owner may be able to deduct legally from the contract sum the amount of provable loss suffered as a result of delayed completion.

Liquidation Damages. Liquidated damages are necessary to resolve contract terminations. This refers to the amount per day in provable losses to the owner. However it does not imply the extraction of a penalty from the contractor.

The construction contract may be terminated by either party (i.e., the owner or the contractor). The contractor may terminate if the construction work is stopped for 30 days under a court order, or by a ruling of another public authority having jurisdiction, through no fault of either the contractor or any person performing work under contract to the contractor. The contractor may stop the work for 30 days if the architect fails to issue a certificate for payment or if the owner fails to make payment as provided. The contractor, upon 7 days' notice to the owner and the architect, may terminate the contract and recover from the owner payment for all completed work and for losses sustained for materials, tools, equipment, and machinery, including reasonable profit and damages. Costs incurred by the owner must be ceritified by the architect. If the unpaid balance of the contract sum is greater than the cost of completing the work, including the architect's fees for extra services, such excess is paid to the contractor. (If costs exceed the unpaid balance, the contractor must pay the difference to the owner.)

The owner may order the contractor to stop the work of any portion of it if the contractor fails to correct defective workmanship or persistently fails to supply materials or equipment in accordance with the contract documents, until the cause of the dissatisfaction has been eliminated.

The owner, after giving the contractor and his surety 7 days' notice, may terminate the contractor's employment and take possession of the site and all materials, and so on, owned by the contractor, under the following conditions: (*a*) the contractor is found to be bankrupt, (*b*) the contractor makes a general assignment for the benefit of his creditors, (*c*) a receiver is appointed on account of the contractor's insolvency, (*d*) the contractor repeatedly refuses to supply skilled workmen or materials, (*e*) the contractor fails to make payments to subcontractors, or (*f*) the contractor disregards laws or ordinances, or is guilty of violating the provisions of the contract documents. The owner may then complete the work by any expedient method, and no further payment is made to the contractor until work has been completed. Liquidated damages and penalty and bonus provisions should be specified in the supplementary conditions.

Penalty and Bonus. To encourage completion on time, a penalty and bonus provision may be incorporated in the construction contract, instead of liquidated damages. The amount of penalty or bonus should be determined on the basis of tangible values, such as a predicted profit from rentals after occupancy of an apartment building, and it should be stipulated per diem. Penalty clauses should always be accompanied by provisions of a bonus for early completion. Penalty clauses alone have been held invalid by some courts.

The date on which either penalty or bonus is to take effect should be clearly stated, referring to completion of the entire project or a portion thereof.

Compensation

Contract Modifications. The construction contracts may be modified in the supplementary conditions, instructions to bidders, or proposal forms, as follows:

1 *Notice to Proceed.* Stipulates the date the contractor is to begin work and specifies time of completion.
2 *Liquidated Damages.* States the sum per day based on provable losses.
3 *Penalty and Bonus.* Establishes sums to be paid or subcontracted from the contract sum, if any.
4 *Unit Prices.* States value per unit of measurement for materials or services for extra work or changes.
5 *Additive or Deductive Alternatives to the Construction Contract.* Calls for a lump sum for work to be added to or deducted from the contract, if acceptable.
6 *Retainage.* A sum withheld from progress payments to the contractor in accordance with the terms of the agreement.
7 *Separate Contracts Assigned.* Architect and owner select subcontractors, then place all work under a general contractor for purposes of administration and coordination.
8 *Subcontractors.* Requires the contractor to list the names of several prequalified subcontractors from which owner and architect may select most desirable.

Agreements. There are three basic forms of compensation agreement between architect and owner.

- A percentage of the construction cost of the project.
- A multiple of direct personnel expense.
- A professional fee plus expense.

Percentage of the Construction Cost of the Project Contract. The owner agrees to pay the architect's fee through a stipulated percentage ("basic rate") of the cost of the construction work, as well as payment/reimbursement for special or specified expenses.

This contract also defines the extent of the architect's services and reimbursements by the owner for such items as the following:

- Cost of transportation.
- Long-distance calls and telegrams.
- Reproduction, postage, and handling of drawings and specifications.
- Fees for permits.
- Renderings and models.
- Special consultants' fees other than normal engineering services.

Further articles define the owner's responsibilities in terms of the following:

1 Owner's accessibility to the architect's accounting records.
2 Method of terminating the agreement by either owner or architect.
3 Ownership of contract documents.
4 Limitations of assigning the contract to successors.
5 An arbitration clause.
6 Extent of agreement and limitations of architect's responsibilities.
7 Applicable law governing the contract.

This type of contract is best suited for full services on normal projects of definite scope.

Multiple of Direct Personnel Expense Agreement. Compensation for services is determined by applying a multiplier to the regular rates of pay plus benefits of the architect's personnel directly engaged in performing services, plus a multiple of the costs of consultants. This is about 2½. The multiple of costs of consultants is the consultants' established rate, including salary, overhead, and a sum for their participation and responsibility.

This type of agreement is most appropriate for projects of fluid scope involving, for instance, unusual planning and contract awarding procedures and/or partial services for specific work.

PAUL MELLON CENTER FOR THE ARTS, CHOATE SCHOOL
New York
Architects: I. M. Pei & Partners
Photo: J. Molitor

Professional Fee plus Expense Agreement. Payment to the architect is based on a combination of fixed fee for the architect's personal services and a multiple of expense for work performed by the architect's employees and consultants.

The fixed fee is predetermined on anticipated personal services and project complexity. If the architect performs considerable technical work, the estimated value of this work may be included in the fixed fee, the agreement may stipulate that technical services performed by the architect are subject to an additional hourly rate.

The personal fixed fee is proportionate to the scope of the project and is not subject to change unless a corresponding change in the project scope occurs, since this is the basis for the fixed fee. All other expenses (personnel, consultants, services, owner's responsibilities, reimbursable expenses, payments, keeping of accounts, and general provisions) are similar to those of the other two agreements.

This type of contract is best used in connection with projects of special purpose requiring the architect's close attention.

Change Orders

The owner must give prompt written notice to the architect of any defect in the project or noncomformity with contract documents that the owner may observe or become aware of, although he may accept defective or nonconforming work rather than insisting on its removal and correction. Under the latter circumstances, the architect should issue a change order to reflect an appropriate reduction to the contract sum. If this amount is determined after final payment has been made, the contractor should pay it directly to the owner.

A change order is a written instruction to the contractor from the architect, signed by the owner or his agent and the architect, authorizing a change in the scope of the work. It adjusts the contract sum and/or the contract time, and is issued after the execution of the contract. The change order must be signed by the contractor to indicate that the modification is acceptable to him.

Credit to the owner is determined by mutual acceptance of a lump sum cost by agreed-upon unit prices or plus a mutually accepted fixed or percentage fee. The amount of each approved change order is shown on the contractor's application and certificates of payment.

When the cost of a change is not agreed in advance, the contractor proceeds with the work on receipt of the change order. The architect will determine its cost, based on expenditures and savings, including an allowance for overhead and profit if the contract sum is increased. The contractor must keep an itemized accounting and supporting data. If cash allowances are provided for such work and the extra cost is determined to be more or less than the allowance, the contract sum is adjusted accordingly by change order. If application of previously agreed unit prices to work proposed in a change order would create a hardship on the owner or the contractor, applicable unit prices should be equitably adjusted to prevent such hardship.

Costs of unknown physical conditions of an unusual nature encountered below ground that differ from those indicated by the contract documents may be adjusted by a change order; for example, the discovery of utility lines not indicated on the survey may mean a requirement for relocation.

Contract time may be extended only by a change order if there are delays in the work progress as a result of any of the following causes listed in the General Conditions of the AIA contract:

> Any act or neglect of the owner or the architect, or by any employee of either, or by any separate contractor employed by the owner, or by changes ordered in the work, or by labor disputes, fire, unusual delays in transportation, unavoidable casualties or any causes beyond the contractor's control, or by delay authorized by the owner pending arbitration, or by any cause which the architect determines may justify the delay.

The contractor must make a written claim for time extension to the architect no more than 20 days after the occurrence of a delay; otherwise a claim is waived. Only one claim is necessary in the case of a continuing delay.

Field Orders

Minor changes that do not involve an adjustment in the contract sum or a time extension may be authorized by the architect with a field order. Field orders are binding on both owner and contractor.

Written interpretations or drawings may be requested from the architect by the owner or the contractor. The architect must issue them promptly in the form of a field order. The owner and the contractor should agree with the architect on a schedule for the issuance of documents, for otherwise it becomes difficult to prove any delay. If there is no agreed on schedule, a claim cannot be made as a result of failure to furnish interpretations until 15 days after a demand for them.

Compliance with Contract Documents

The owner should furnish required information (surveys, reports, etc.) as quickly as is necessary for the progress of the work. The architect is entitled to rely on the accu-

CHANGE ORDER

AIA DOCUMENT G701

OWNER ☐
ARCHITECT ☐
CONTRACTOR ☐
FIELD ☐
OTHER

PROJECT:
(name, address)

CHANGE ORDER NUMBER:

TO (Contractor)

ARCHITECT'S PROJECT NO:

CONTRACT FOR:

CONTRACT DATE:

You are directed to make the following changes in this Contract:

The original Contract Sum was . . . . $.
Net change by previous Change Orders . . . . $.
The Contract Sum prior to this Change Order was . . . . $.
The Contract Sum will be (increased) (decreased) (unchanged) by this Change Order . . . $.
The new Contract Sum including this Change Order will be . . . . $.
The Contract Time will be (increased) (decreased) (unchanged) by ( ) Days.
The Date of Completion as of the date of this Change Order therefore is .

ARCHITECT	CONTRACTOR	OWNER
Address	Address	Address
BY	BY	BY
DATE	DATE	DATE

Figure 4.16

WASSERMAN HOUSE
Weston, Connecticut
Architect: John Fowler
Photo: D. Hirsch

racy and completeness of these data and cannot be held responsible for any errors contained in contract documents.

As the owner's agent, the architect must ensure compliance with the contract documents by interpreting them, verifying changes, establishing standards of acceptability, judging degree of conformity and progress of the project as constructed (compared to the project as planned), and issuing certificates authorizing payments to the contractor for work performed and materials supplied.

One of the architect's responsibilities is to protect the owner from defects or deficiencies in the work of the contractor. The architect may reject work which, in his or her opinion, fails to conform to the contract documents. The architect's right to reject work that does not conform to the intent of the contract documents is one means of exerting pressure on the contractor to protect the owner from defective work. Safety precautions, construction techniques, procedures, and methods or sequences are solely the responsibility of the contractor.

The architect may not give direct orders to contractors' or subcontractors' employees. It is the contractor's responsibility to complete the work in accordance with the contract documents. These are the terms of the contract entered into with the owner, and the architect is not responsible if the contractor fails to meet these terms.

Observation of work progress may be done by the architect or a representative. Neither can guarantee the work of the contractor or be responsible for construction methods, nor for the contractor's failure to carry out the work in accordance with the contract documents.

Most of the decisions of the architect under the general conditions of the contract are subject to arbitration. Any rejections of materials or workmanship, for example, are subject to arbitration.

Cost Estimates and Analysis

Analyzing and making accurate estimates of probable construction costs are major responsibilities of the architect. The owner always should be kept informed of all concomitants of the cost of the project.

The architect makes a professional analysis of the probable cost of construction of the project using the best current sources of information available. The agreement between owner and architect provides that the latter will submit a statement to the owner of probable construction and cost based on area, volume, or other unit cost analyses. The owner should be informed of changes in the estimate as a result of changes in the project's scope or market conditions, without "guarantees."

The purpose of the statement of probable construction cost is to correlate the design with the owner's budget. The architect should obtain the owner's approval of the statement at the conclusion of each phase of construction, as well as approval of the drawings and specifications.

Preparation of detailed estimates entitles the architect to additional compensation. If a fixed limit of cost is stipulated in the agreement, the architect should obtain detailed estimates from a professional estimator. If the owner imposes an unconditional cost limit, the architect must be free to make adjustments in scope and quality, and in obtaining bid proposals.

Cost analysis may take two forms:

1 A series of statements of probable construction cost.
2 Detailed estimates of construction cost (prepared by the architect or by a professional construction cost estimator).

Costing Methods

Area and Volume. The number of cubic feet to be contained in the outer surfaces of the building is multiplied by an assumed cost per square foot. Accuracy depends on assigning reasonably correct prices per cubic foot and per square foot.

Unit Use. A rough rule-of-thumb calculation, unit use is based on multiplication of the known costs of units by the number of units proposed—for example, dollars per bed times the number of beds in a hospital project.

In-Place Unit. More accurate than the area-and-volume method, this approach consists of the total costs of all materials and labor, including allowances for overhead, profit, and selected unit of construction. Current unit costs can be obtained from contractors or handbooks. The following items are normally excluded from unit costs:

- Cost of the land.
- Architect's compensation.
- Cost of professional services furnished directly by the owner (surveys, tests, bonds, soil borings, etc.).
- Site improvements and landscaping.
- Utilities more than 5 feet from the building.
- Flagpoles, radio and television antennae, sculpture, murals, and signs.
- Unusual foundations.

Applicable costs from this list must be added to the unit cost to determine entire project cost.

Quantity and Cost. This is sometimes referred to as the materials-and-labor method. Required quantities of materials are estimated in material units (thousands of bricks, number of board-feet of lumber, etc.), and labor required to install materials is calculated in hours at current wage rates. The sum of labor and material costs is estimated to be the contractor's direct costs, to which is added overhead and profit.

The many variables affecting cost analysis include the following:

- Size of the project (a larger building often costs less per unit than a smaller structure).
- Shape of the building (compact configurations cost less per unit than those with extensive perimeters, complex shapes, or complicated roof forms).
- Height (buildings with unusually tall stories cost less per cubic foot than those with stories of normal height).
- Type of construction and finish.
- Unusual foundation problems.
- Project's location.
- Allowances for trade jurisdictions, utility costs, and local ordinances.

Certificates for Payment. Upon completion of each construction work phase, the contractor submits an application for payment to the architect, who determines or verifies the value of the work performed, then authorizes a certificate for payment. The contractor must show the total dollar value of the completed work to date, plus that of stored materials, retainage fee (this amount is held back until final payment), and the total of previous payments.

The amount of the payment certificate, which is decided by the architect, must be carefully established to avoid damage to the owner or to the contractor. Thus the architect must make sure that the contractor has paid all bills for materials, labor, and subcontractors' work—that is, that the amount of the contractor's request for payment is just.

If the contract provides for payment of "materials delivered to the site," quantities and storage methods should be checked. If such materials are stored off site, payment may be made on the basis of subsequent incorporation. The contractor should arrange and pay for insurance, and the stock should be checked periodically. If the contract calls for payment of "work incorporated" only, material payments should not be allowed.

If a certificate is to be issued outside the contract, that favors the contractor, the owner's consent should be obtained and noted on the certificate. If a surety bond is involved the architect may also have to obtain the surety's consent.

The architect's signature on a certificate for payment tells the owner that a payment as shown is due the contractor according to the contract between owner and contractor. It also gives an accounting of the work's present status, the total amount of change orders approved by the owner to date, previous payments approved, and amounts withheld from payments.

The contractor is required to swear that all payments have been made by way of previous certificates and amounts received.

As a project nears completion, the contractor sends the architect a statement claiming substantial completion; a semifinal inspection is then made by the architect to determine whether the construction is sufficiently completed in accordance with contract documents that the owner can use or occupy the project as intended. If the project is indeed substantially complete, the architect prepares a certificate of substantial completion for the approval and acceptance of contractor and owner.

Tests and Inspections

Inspections and tests are instrumental in determining compliance or noncompliance with the contract documents. The testing agency should be selected by the owner (subject to approval of the architect or engineer), or selected by the architect or engineer subject to approval of the owner. The owner should pay for the agency's services on certification of its invoices by the architect or engineer, or through a predetermined allowance set forth in the contractor's proposal.

Under the general conditions of the contract, the architect may reject work that does not conform to contract documents. Whenever the architect considers it advisable to implement the intent of the contract documents, he has the authority to require special test inspections.

The specifications should contain a section listing materials to be tested and describing what is required, the method of testing, and the method of reporting of results. It should also tell who furnishes material specimens to be tested and who pays for such tests. It is wise for the owner to pay directly for testing of materials: this makes the testing laboratory responsible to the owner.

If conflicts of interest are to be avoided, testing agencies must be independent of the contractor or manufacturer. Since testing costs are difficult to estimate in advance, the owner must provide a rough estimate for inclusion in the construction loan application, include the costs as a cash allowance, or pay for tests from separate funds. By employing an independent testing agency, the owner gains the advantage of using its services in preliminary structural and technical determinations and incorporating results in the early stages of design prior to final publication of the testing agency's report and analysis.

When tests are required by contract or by law, the contractor must advise the architect of the time and date of the test, so that the latter has an opportunity to observe the inspection. If the architect determines that the work has not been properly performed, he may require part of the work to be subjected to special tests after the project has begun. He should obtain written authorization from the owner instructing the contractor to order such special tests and to give notification of the date of testing. If such tests show failure of the work to comply with contract documents or to meet the standards of any ordinances, the contractor must pay the costs, including the architect's additional services, resulting from such failure. If the tests indicate conformity with the contract documents, the owner bears the costs and authorizes the architect to issue an appropriate change order.

Major test areas include the following:

- Geology.
- Soil.
- Slump, compressive strength, and aggregate tests of concrete.
- Mill analyses for steel.
- Welding and welding electrodes.
- Construction components.
- Asphalt paving.
- Roofing.
- Sealants.
- Infiltration of wind and water through windows and curtain walls.

APPLICATION AND CERTIFICATE FOR PAYMENT *AIA DOCUMENT G702*

PAGE ONE OF PAGES

PROJECT:
(name, address)

TO (Owner)

ATTN:

ARCHITECT:

ARCHITECT'S PROJECT NO:

CONTRACTOR:

CONTRACT FOR:

APPLICATION DATE: APPLICATION NO:

PERIOD FROM: TO

CHANGE ORDER SUMMARY

Change Orders approved in previous months by Owner — TOTAL		ADDITIONS $	DEDUCTIONS $
Subsequent Change Orders			
Number	Approved (date)		
TOTALS			

Net change by Change Orders $________

State of: County of:

The undersigned Contractor certifies that the Work covered by this Application for Payment has been completed in accordance with the Contract Documents, that all amounts have been paid by him for Work for which previous Certificates for Payment were issued and payments received from the Owner, and that the current payment shown herein is now due.

Contractor:

By: Date:

Application is made for Payment, as shown below, in connection with the Contract. **Continuation Sheet, AIA Document G702A**, is attached.

The present status of the account for this Contract is as follows:

ORIGINAL CONTRACT SUM ....$________

Net change by Change Orders ....$________

CONTRACT SUM TO DATE ....$________

TOTAL COMPLETED & STORED TO DATE ....$________
(Column G on G702A)

RETAINAGE ______% ....$________
or as noted in Column I on G702A

TOTAL EARNED LESS RETAINAGE ....$________

LESS PREVIOUS CERTIFICATES FOR PAYMENT ....$________

CURRENT PAYMENT DUE ....$________

Subscribed and sworn to before me this day of 19

Notary Public:

My Commission expires:

In accordance with the Contract and this Application for Payment the Contractor is entitled to payment in the amount shown above.

Architect:

By:

☐ OWNER
☐ ARCHITECT
☐ CONTRACTOR
☐
☐

This Certificate is not negotiable. It is payable only to the payee named herein and its issuance, payment and acceptance are without prejudice to any rights of the Owner or Contractor under their Contract.

AIA DOCUMENT G702 • APPLICATION AND CERTIFICATE FOR PAYMENT • MARCH 1971 EDITION • AIA®

Figure 4.17

- Acoustical materials.
- Elevators.
- Mechanical and electrical equipment.

Soil tests are always performed by an independent testing laboratory and paid for by the owner. The architect and his structural engineer base their designs on the contents of the soil report, but are not responsible for its accuracy. Testing laboratories must file copies of all reports.

Guarantees

A guarantee is a promise to substantiate (verify) actual, tangible, real things. A warranty is a promise to substantiate labor. For example, certain trade organizations stipulate methods for the installation of various materials. The contractor *warrants* that the completed installation complies with the specified grade of workmanship.

The general conditions require the contractor to warrant to the owner and the architect that all materials and equipment furnished under the contract are new unless otherwise specified, and that all work is of good quality, free of faults and defects, and in accordance with contract documents. All work not conforming to these standards may be considered to be defective.

A manufacturer pays a premium to an insurance company to guarantee its product for a specified period of time. Required guarantees must clearly defined the items to be guaranteed—to what extent, by whom, and for how long; effective dates must be given, as well.

It is good practice to date guarantees from the date of "substantial completion," although when the owner occupies a portion of the project before completion of the whole, this must be further defined according to circumstances. The preparation of specifications should include adequate guarantees based on normal practice. Appropriate and equitable guarantees should be required, their submission enforced, and their provisions applied when the occasion arises.

A general 1-year guarantee on a project is required of the contractor for all materials, workmanship, and equipment. Longer guarantees may be specified for such items as roofing, sealants, and hardware.

A guarantee is only as effective as the organization that stands behind it. The long-standing reputation of a firm is a better guarantee than pages of legal jargon in fine print.

Some architects require the contractor to sign a written guarantee at the completion of the work, covering all items to be guaranteed under the specifications. Such guarantees are prepared in triplicate, signed, and executed. They are then distributed to owner, contractor, and architect.

If any of the work is found to be defective or not according to the contract documents (within a year after the date of substantial completion or a longer period prescribed by law or the terms of any special guarantee required by the contract documents), the contractor must correct such work promptly after receipt of written notice from the owner, unless the owner has previously given the contractor written acceptance of the condition(s) in question.

An example of defective work would be clear, anodized aluminum hardware installed instead of dark bronze, anodized aluminum hardware as specified. The contractor could either put in correctly anodized hardware or negotiate with the owner to accept the present installation.

The owner may authorize the architect to conduct a thorough inspection before the guarantee period expires (especially if a defect becomes apparent) to see whether any work by the contractor is needed to make good on his guarantees. The architect should be compensated for this additional work. If defects become apparent and cannot readily be corrected, the contractor may pay the owner in lieu of correction, representing the difference between the value of the project as it exists and as it was intended.

Insurance

To satisfy insurance requirements, the architect should send a form letter to the owner, telling him of his obligations under the general conditions of the contract and advising him to request counsel from his insurance agent concerning coverage required. In this way the architect is absolved of any responsibility for the insurance of the owner or the contractor. The architect should file a copy of the reply from the insurance agent, setting forth the extent of the coverage, and should request file copies of all policies from both owner and contractor. Such coverage is concerned mainly with protection against the following claims of perils:

1 Loss by fire.
2 Claims for personal injury or death resulting from operations required for execution of the construction contract.
3 Claims for property damages.
4 Third-party claims.

Property Insurance. The owner must secure and maintain insurance against fire or other peril as prescribed by law or contract (standard extended coverage),

THE AMERICAN INSTITUTE OF ARCHITECTS

AIA DOC. A331
JAN. 1966 ED.

A331

GUARANTY FOR BITUMINOUS ROOFING

WHEREAS, , a corporation whose address is , hereinafter called the Supplier, has manufactured and sold and caused to have applied, pursuant to its specifications and inspection, the necessary roofing materials to construct

a flat roof of approximately squares, and

a steep roof of approximately squares, and

bituminous base roof flashing of approximately linear feet on the building described below:

Owner:

Building:

Location:

Date of Completion of Roofing: 19 ,

By: (roofer),

(address).

AND WHEREAS, said roof is in accordance with the Architect's final roof plan attached hereto;

AND WHEREAS, by careful examination of said roof and by cut samples taken in the presence of the Architect and the Supplier's representative, it has been determined that required quantities of roofing materials have been used and that roofing materials have been applied in conformance with contract documents;

AND WHEREAS, Supplier represents and wishes to guarantee, subject to the limits stated herein, that its roofing when so applied is effectively water tight for a period of years despite normal wear and tear by the elements, as well as guaranteeing it against defects in workmanship or materials;

NOW THEREFORE, said Supplier guarantees to the said Owner that, as set forth below, during a period of years from the date of completion of said built-up roofing described above, Supplier will at its own expense, make or cause to be made, any repairs that may be necessary, as a result of defects in workmanship or materials supplied by the Supplier or of normal wear and tear by the elements, and will maintain said roof in water tight condition free from all leaks arising from such causes. For purposes of this Guaranty, damage to the roof caused by hurricanes, lightning, tornadoes, gales, hailstorms or other unusual natural phenomena shall not be deemed to be "normal wear and tear by the elements."

AIA DOC. A331 JAN. 1966 ED.

Figure 4.18

EXCLUSIONS: This Guaranty does not cover, and Supplier shall not be liable for the following:

1. Metal work, including metal flashings and such damage as may result from application of these materials;
2. Any damage to the roof caused by structural defect in, or failure of, the building or defects in, or failure of, any roof deck, or any other material, including insulation, used as the base over which the roof is applied;
3. Any damage to the building or the contents thereof;
4. Damage to the roof due to mechanical abrasion or abuse not caused by Supplier.

INSPECTION AND REPAIRS: Upon written notice by Owner to Supplier of need of repair of roof, the Supplier shall inspect the roof. Following such inspection:

1. Supplier, at its own expense and regardless of cost, shall make such repairs as are required by the Guaranty.
2. In case Owner or his agent has notified Supplier and confirmed in writing that repairs are required and such repairs are not covered by the Guaranty (including repairs required by Owner's alteration, extension or addition to the roof) Supplier, after having obtained Owner's consent thereto, in writing, shall make or cause to be made, such repairs at Owner's expense in accordance with specifications and procedures as established by Supplier and this Guaranty shall thereupon remain in effect for the unexpired portion of its original term. If Owner fails to so consent or if repairs are made by one other than the Supplier or Supplier's designee, this Guaranty with respect to such area shall be automatically terminated.
3. In the event that (1) Owner notifies Supplier and has confirmed in writing the need of repair of roof, and (2) Supplier is unable to promptly inspect and repair same, and (3) an emergency condition exists which requires prompt repair in order to avoid substantial damage to Owner, then Owner may make such temporary repairs as may be essential and any such action shall not be a breach of the provisions of this Guaranty.

INSPECTION SERVICE: Supplier agrees to reinspect the completed roof not earlier than 24 months after completion of the roofing, and if it is determined that there are defects in the roofing, then Supplier shall make, or cause to be made at its own expense, such repairs as are necessary to remedy said defects within the scope of its responsibility under the terms of this Guaranty.

IN WITNESS WHEREOF, Supplier has caused this instrument to be signed and sealed by its duly authorized officer this day of 19

By:

Title:

Name of Corporation:

Seal:

BITUMINOUS ROOFING GUARANTY		TWO PAGES
AIA DOC. A331	JAN. 1966 ED.	PAGE 2

Figure 4.18 *(Continued)*

CERTIFICATE OF INSURANCE

AIA DOCUMENT G705

This certifies to the Addressee shown below that the following described policies, subject to their terms, conditions and exclusions, have been issued to:

NAME & ADDRESS OF INSURED

COVERING (SHOW PROJECT NAME AND/OR NUMBER AND LOCATION)

Addressee:
(Owner)

Date

KIND OF INSURANCE	POLICY NUMBER	Inception/Expiration Date	LIMITS OF LIABILITY	
1. (a) Workmen's Comp.			$//////////////	Statutory Workmen's Compensation
(b) Employers' Liability			$	One Accident and Aggregate Disease
2. Comprehensive General Liability			$	Each Occurrence—Premises and Operations
			$	Each Occurrence—Independent Contractors
			$	Each Occurrence—COMPLETED OPERATIONS AND PRODUCTS
(a) Bodily Injury			$	Each Occurrence—Contractual
			$	Aggregate—COMPLETED OPERATIONS AND PRODUCTS
(b) Personal Injury			$	Each Person Aggregate
			$	General Aggregate
(c) Property Damage			$	Each Occurrence—Premises—Operations
			$	Each Occurrence—INDEPENDENT CONTRACTOR
			$	Each Occurrence—COMPLETED OPERATIONS AND PRODUCTS
			$	Each Occurrence—Contractual
			$	Aggregate—
			$	Aggregate—OPERATIONS, INDEPENDENT CONTRACTOR, PRODUCTS AND CONTRACTUAL
3. Comprehensive Automobile Liability				
			$	Each Person—
(a) Bodily Injury			$	Each Occurrence—
(b) Property Damage			$	Each Occurrence—
4. (Other)				

UNDER GENERAL LIABILITY POLICY OR POLICIES

Yes No

1. Does Property Damage Liability Insurance shown include coverage for XC and U hazards? .... ______ ______
2. Is Occurrence Basis Coverage provided under Property Damage Liability? .... ______ ______
3. Is Broad Form Property Damage Coverage provided for this Project? .... ______ ______
4. Does Personal Injury Liability Insurance include coverage for personal injury sustained by any person as a result of an offense directly or indirectly related to the employment of such person by the Insured? .... ______ ______
5. Is coverage provided for Contractual Liability (including indemnification provision) assumed by Insured? .... ______ ______

UNDER AUTOMOBILE LIABILITY POLICY OR POLICIES

1. Does coverage above apply to non-owned and hired automobiles? .... ______ ______
2. Is Occurrence Basis Coverage provided under Property Damage Liability? .... ______ ______

CANCELLATION OR NON-RENEWAL
In the event of cancellation or non-renewal of any of the foregoing, fifteen (15) days written notice shall be given to the party to whom this certificate is addressed.

EXTENT OF CERTIFICATION
This certificate is issued as a matter of information only and confers no rights upon the holder. By its issuance the company does not alter, change, modify or extend any of the provisions of the above policies.

NAME OF INSURANCE COMPANY

ADDRESS

SIGNATURE OF AUTHORIZED REPRESENTATIVE

ONE PAGE

Figure 4.19

LAS VEGAS CONVENTION CENTER
Las Vegas, Nevada
Architects: Adrian Wilson & Associates
Photo: J. Shulman

as well as vandalism and malicious mischief endorsements on the building during the course of its construction. The coverage should be 100% of the insurable value, including materials and equipment in the project itself or stored on the construction site, and the interests of the contractors, all subcontractors, and the owner. The owner, as trustee for the insured, has the power to adjust and settle a loss with the insurers. The owner files copies of policies with the contractor for purposes of review and information. If the contractor decides that the coverage is inadequate for his or his subcontractor's needs, he may request the owner to extend the coverage and pay the owner any additional premiums. The contractor may request that other special coverage be included in the property insurance, the cost being charged to him by change order.

The owner, the contractor, and all the subcontractors must waive all rights against the other(s) for damages caused by all covered physical loss.

Any party concerned with the work of the project may require the owner as trustee to provide a bond for the correct performance of his duties. The owner must then deposit monies received and distribute funds according to agreements reached by interested parties or an award by arbitration. If no special agreements are made, the damaged work is replaced by change order.

Liability Insurance. It is the owner's responsibility to secure and maintain liability insurance coverage that will protect him against claims arising from operations under the contract. Loss of property use that delays occupancy, for example, constitutes an insurable hazard.

Each contractor must secure and maintain insurance (obtained before commencing work under the contract) necessary to cover his responsibility and liability on the project; the subcontractors should carry similar insurance. The contractor must submit to the owner, through the architect, two copies of each insurance certificate, which must contain a clause stating that the policy may not be canceled without 15 days' prior written notice to the owner, the contractor, and the architect. The owner must request that the contractor furnish copies of policies. The architect should not issue any certificates of payment until he has been advised by the owner that the contractor has provided satisfactory evidence of insurance.

The contractor should include coverage for the following conditions.

Statutory Liability Insurance. To protect the contractor from claims under Workmen's Compensation and other employee benefit acts in the statute minimum of the state in which the work is performed.

Employer's Liability Insurance. For damage and bodily injury as a result of accidents or occupational disease.

Comprehensive General Liability Insurance. This coverage protects the insured in the following cases:

1 Bodily injury to or death of persons or damage to or destruction of property, resulting from the execution of work or arising from any omission or act of negligence of the contractor, the subcontractors, and their employees or agents, including damage to adjacent property.
2 Bodily injury to or death of contractor or any subcontractor, employee, or agent, due to the condition of the premises or other property of the owner or architect in connection to work performed under the contract.
3 Loss, damage, or expense incurred because of bodily injury to or death of persons or because of damage to or destruction of property resulting from the operation of an elevator or material hoist operated in connection to work under the contract.
4 Loss, damage, or expense incurred because of injury to or destruction of tangible property, including loss of use resulting from such damage.

Automobile Liability Insurance. Laws vary from state to state. Insurance should be for not less than liability limits either specified in the contract or required by law; coverage must include contractual liability insurance against claims and expenses arising out of the performance of the work and attributable to bodily injury, sickness, disease, or death, or to injury or destruction of property that is caused by negligence of the contractor, the subcontractor, or their employees. Claims, damages, or losses attributable to defects in the architect's drawings and specifications are *excluded* from this obligation. All insurance policies should be carried in the state in which the contract is being performed.

The extent of each architect's insurance should be adequate to protect the individual from liability for errors, omissions, or negligent acts arising out of the performance of his professional services. No written agreement can be relied on to protect the architect against claims arising out of his failure to meet the prescribed standards of care in furnishing his services.

Bonds. A surety bond is an agreement under which the party called the "surety" (usually a corporation) agrees to answer to another party, called an "obligee" (the owner) for the debt, default, or failure to fulfill obligations of a third party, called the "principal" (the contractor).

As with guarantees, bonds themselves are no substitute for the qualities of integrity, financial worth, and experience, of the contractor and high standards for his equipment and personnel. However bonds do provide protection against loss resulting from the failure of others to perform.

If the amount of the contractor's bid is inadequate, he may be forced to default on the contract. Reasons may include the following:

- Deficient cost or other accounting records.
- Unforeseen price increases.
- Delays.
- Labor problems.
- Defaults by subcontractors.
- Physical disabilities of contractor or key personnel.
- Lack of adequate working capital.
- Unforeseen tax obligations.

If the owner decides against the requirements of a bond, the architect should write a letter recording that decision.

Surety bonds may be statutory (i.e., required by law). The architect should assure himself of the adequacy of the surety company to perform. The U.S. Treasury Department annually issues a list of qualified companies.

Performance. A performance bond is issued to assure the owner that the contractor will perform all terms and conditions of the construction contract and to protect the owner against loss up to the bond penalty amount, in case of default. The surety has the option of physically completing the contract or furnishing sufficient funds for completion of the work, with the owner assuming responsibility for having the work finished. A performance bond insures legal completion of a contract *without regard to quality of performance*.

No Lien. This type of performance bond is a statutory requirement in some states where the owner-contractor agreement has been filled as a "no lien" contract. Its effect is to deny the right to file a lien connected to that contract.

Labor and Material Payment. Such a bond guarantees that the surety will pay the contractor's bill for labor and materials if the latter defaults. The performance bond

WAYNESBOROUGH COUNTRY CLUB
Washington, Pennsylvania
Architects: Ewing Cole Erdman Rizzio Cherry Parsky
Photo: Office

and the labor and material payment bond should not be combined—this may create procedural difficulties in handling any claims against the bond because of the owner's competing interests on one hand and those of the laborers and material suppliers on the other. In some states this is called the *statutory bond*.

Lien. A lien bond indemnifies the owner against loss resulting from filing liens against his property.

Maintenance. This type of bond guarantees maintenance cost or quality of construction for a stipulated period after project completion; it is rarely used alone.

Errors and Omissions. The law concerned with professional liability is becoming more active each year as a result of development of new, modified principles extending previously established precedents. There is, of course, considerable ground for legal maneuvering.

Architects must take out professional liability insurance, sometimes referred to as "errors and omissions insurance." Specialization and complexity make it difficult for the professional architect to personally oversee each detail of design and contract administration. He must rely on his employees and consultants, but he remains responsible for their acts.

"Privity of contract" no longer applies to the architect. Recent court cases have held that those who design a structure can be held liable to the owner and to tenants for injuries arising out of latent defects or unknown dangers in the building design. Defense costs are very high in such suits, even if the architect is cleared.

BARBADOS HILTON
Barbados, BWI
Architects: Warner Burns Toan Lunde
Photo: Hilton International

"Ordinary care and reasonable skill" is evaluated by deciding whether negligence in the preparation of contract documents is on the same level as the "care and skill" exercised by other professionals in the same locality. The law does not permit such standards to be established below the level of the public's reasonable needs to assure health, safety, and welfare.

Professional liability insurance contains protection and coverage, including the insured's liability for errors, omissions, or negligent acts, and the legal defense of the architect and his employees, if needed. Since the statute of limitations varies from state to state, the architect should secure coverage extending beyond the period allowed for retroactive claims.

The architect can also be held liable for omissions outside his contractural obligations, such as committing unintentional "negligent acts." This includes both work performed with inadequate skill and omitted items. The architect's liability for negligence is *not covered* by the insurance of the contractor or the owner.

A wrongful act, injury or damage for which a civil action can be brought must satisfy four basic requirements:

1 A legal duty must exist.
2 There must have been a breach of that duty.
3 The breach must have been the proximate cause of damage.
4 Damage must have resulted.

In the absence of all four conditions, negligence cannot be effectively shown.

Liability for Errors. The architect's liability is governed by broadly applicable general principles of law. Some specific cases of liability for errors and/or negligence in which the architect may not be able to collect compensation or may be held liable for damages are as follows:

1 The lowest bid or actual construction cost considerably exceeds the appropriated or authorized limits.
2 In public construction work, no appropriation was made for the building or contracting officials were not so empowered.
3 The architect either was not qualified to accept public contracts or was disqualified from accepting them.
4 Charter requirements were not followed or the appropriation was void because of failure to comply with legal requirements.
5 The architect wilfully omits or departs from agreement terms, the owner's instructions, or the approved documents.
6 Contract documents are not completed within a specified time, are incomplete, or provide inadequate information for bidding purposes.
7 Plans and specifications or the project constructed therefrom do not fulfill the purpose for which they were designed or are defective in other than minor details.
8 Prepared drawings and/or specifications violate the law and do not comply with state statutes or

KAHALA HILTON HOTEL
Honolulu, Hawaii
Architects: Killingsworth, Brady & Associates
Photo: J. Shulman

city ordinances, building codes, or zoning laws. If the architect's ignorance of the law causes the owner loss, the owner may be awarded damages. Courts take the position that the architect must design and specify work that conform to all laws, rules, and regulations applicable at the place of construction.

9 The architect's administration of the construction contract is inadequate, and it is ruled that defective work could have been discovered through reasonable care and skill.

10 An owner's loss is attributable to the architect's imposition on the contractor of errors in certificates of payment or in approvals of contract changes not authorized by the owner.

If the architect fails to use care, skill, and competence in carrying out his professional responsibilities, he is ordinarily liable to all persons suffering personal injury or property damage caused by his negligence, regardless of contract, if such injury or damage was the result of his acts or failure to act.

The Occupational Safety and Health Act

With the passage in 1970 of the Williams-Steiger Occupational Safety and Health Act (OSHA), the architect became liable for work accidents occurring during the construction of a building or among the employees in his own office. Furthermore, the owner can hold the architect responsible for extra costs (an estimated 5–10%) of changes to make a building conform to OSHA standards. OSHA standards apply to existing places of employment as well as to all new ones.

The act covers workers only, but it involves every employer in a business affecting commerce who has one or more employees (exceptions do not include architects, contractors, and subcontractors on a construction site), and it specifically refers to "employment performed in a workplace."

The OSHA priority system of inspections is as follows: (1) catastrophes and fatal accidents, (2) valid employee complaints, (3) work done by the Target Industry Program (TIP) and the Target Health Hazards Program (THHP), and (4) random selection.

TIP tries to reduce hazards in industries with high injury frequency rates (longshoring, meat and meat products, roofing, sheet metal, and wood products, mining, manufacture of trailers, etc.). THHP concentrates its efforts on five toxic substances commonly encountered in industry: asbestos, lead, cotton dust, carbon monoxide, and silica.

Public Law 91-596
91st Congress, S. 2193
December 29, 1970

An Act

84 STAT. 1590

To assure safe and healthful working conditions for working men and women; by authorizing enforcement of the standards developed under the Act; by assisting and encouraging the States in their efforts to assure safe and healthful working conditions; by providing for research, information, education, and training in the field of occupational safety and health; and for other purposes.

Be it enacted by the Senate and House of Representatives of the United States of America in Congress assembled, That this Act may be cited as the "Occupational Safety and Health Act of 1970". Occupational Safety and Health Act of 1970.

CONGRESSIONAL FINDINGS AND PURPOSE

SEC. (2) The Congress finds that personal injuries and illnesses arising out of work situations impcse a substantial burden upon, and are a hindrance to, interstate commerce in terms of lost production, wage loss, medical expenses, and disability compensation payments.

(b) The Congress declares it to be its purpose and policy, through the exercise of its powers to regulate commerce among the several States and with foreign nations and to provide for the general welfare, to assure so far as possible every working man and woman in the Nation safe and healthful working conditions and to preserve our human resources—

(1) by encouraging employers and employees in their efforts to reduce the number of occupational safety and health hazards at their places of employment, and to stimulate employers and employees to institute new and to perfect existing programs for providing safe and healthful working conditions;

(2) by providing that employers and employees have separate but dependent responsibilities and rights with respect to achieving safe and healthful working conditions;

(3) by authorizing the Secretary of Labor to set mandatory occupational safety and health standards applicable to businesses affecting interstate commerce, and by creating an Occupational Safety and Health Review Commission for carrying out adjudicatory functions under the Act;

(4) by building upon advances already made through employer and employee initiative for providing safe and healthful working conditions;

(5) by providing for research in the field of occupational safety and health, including the psychological factors involved, and by developing innovative methods, techniques, and approaches for dealing with occupational safety and health problems;

(6) by exploring ways to discover latent diseases, establishing causal connections between diseases and work in environmental conditions, and conducting other research relating to health problems, in recognition of the fact that occupational health standards present problems often different from those involved in occupational safety;

(7) by providing medical criteria which will assure insofar as practicable that no employee will suffer diminished health, functional capacity, or life expectancy as a result of his work experience;

(8) by providing for training programs to increase the number and competence of personnel engaged in the field of occupational safety and health;

Figure 4.20 Opening text of the Williams-Steiger Occupational Safety and Health Act of 1970. Reprinted from Peter S. Hopf, *Designer's Guide to OSHA*, McGraw-Hill Book Company, 1975.

The enforcement of OSHA means that the architect must conduct himself not only as a creative designer but as an ethical employer looking out for his employees' health and well-being. Penalties are severe if an employer is warned beforehand that an inspector has been called to check employee complaints about unsafe conditions. No amount of hasty "sprucing up" will prevent an inspector from analyzing conditions as they existed before the tip-off.

Arbitration. Enforcement action begins with an inspector's visit to the workplace. There is a 75% probability that he or she will find at least one OSHA violation. After this visit the employer will receive (1) a citation listing specific violations and (2) notification of possible penalties imposed by the Labor Department. The employer has 15 days from receipt of these two documents to set in motion a countersuit. Otherwise, he accepts the allegations as true. In the more than 45,000 enforcement actions taken since the law's enactment, 95% of the employers cited have accepted the charges and the attendant penalties.

An employer who wishes to contest sends a letter outlining his disagreement with the inspector's conclusions to the area director of the Labor Department's Occupational Safety and Health Administration. The enforcement action is then suspended until a decision can be made following a formal hearing by OSHA's Review Commission, or until an out-of-court settlement has been reached.

If a case reaches court, the employer is allowed to be heard in the nearest suitable courtroom to his workplace. Since lawyers are not required, the defendant employer may argue his own case. At the hearing the Labor Department must produce substantial evidence to prove its charges. The defendant employer is presumed to be innocent unless proved otherwise. As in other courts, failure to substantiate charges means losing the case.

If, on the other hand, the court finds for the plaintiff, the Review Commission judge assesses the penalty. He or she then mails the decision to the involved parties, and it goes into effect 30 days after receipt, unless one of the three commission members calls for a discretionary review. This occurs perhaps 10% of the time; the decision (either way) is made by the commission. Such decisions may be taken to the United States Court of Appeals within 60 days of the lower court ruling.

Penalty Assessments. The act requires the commission to determine penalties on the basis of (1) the size of the firm, (2) the seriousness of the violation(s), (3) the defendant employer's "good faith," and (4) previous violations, if any. The commission has ruled that relatively minor violations (uncovered trash cans, dirty toilets, inadequate lunch provisions, etc.) should not necessitate corresponding penalties, lest the offending employer regard such decisions as harassment. Continued violations of this sort, however, are not leniently dealt with, nor are minor unsafe working conditions (e.g., failure to ground power tools, careless storage of flammable liquids) condoned in general. Small businesses are given every consideration, in recognition of their relatively weak financial status. The commission does not assess ruinous penalties, especially if the defendant small business is quick to bring its standards up to those of OSHA.

Further Liability. The commission is not empowered to discipline employees who violate safety standards. Instead, it holds the employer responsible for worker laxity under the theory that the employer is responsible for the actions of his workers. Thus if workers fail to use required protective equipment or clothing that has been provided for them by their employer, the employer is nevertheless liable because he failed to make sure that the equipment was put to proper use.

The employer, of course, is not expected to have an omnipresent, all-seeing eye to detect every instance of worker noncompliance, nor is he required to maintain one-to-one supervision over every employee; an occasional mistake or instance of unexpected employee exposure to hazard is tolerated.

Contractor/Subcontractor Involvement. The language of the act refers to "each employer." Although the owner employs the general contractor, the general contractor employes subcontractors who, in turn, engage workers. Therefore the general contractor and the subcontractors are considered to be *employers* under the terms of the act. An employer violates OSHA standards by exposing his own employees to work hazards, regardless of who created the hazards.

Samples of the OSHA Text

1 Trench or conduit covers must support or withstand a truck rear-axle load of 20,000 pounds, minimum.

2 Strength of a fixed stairway must carry 5 times the normal live load.

3 Fixed ladder strength must be 200 pounds live load per rung.
   - *a* Rungs, cleats, steps must be free of splinters, sharp edges, burrs, and hazardous projects.
   - *b* Rungs must be designed so that the foot *cannot* slide off.

4 Exits of a 3-story building must have a 1-hour fireproof rating; 4 stories or more require a 2-hour fireproof rating.
   - *a* Exits and access to same shall be readily available at all times.
   - *b* All exits must open directly on a space that gives safe access to a public way.
   - *c* Any door, passage or stairway that is not an exit but is likely to be taken for one must be clearly identified. Exits must also be clearly identified.

5 Airborne average concentration of *asbestos* to which any employee may be exposed per 8-hour period shall not exceed 2 fibers longer than 5 micrometers per cubic centimeter of air.

6 Protection must be provided against effects of noise when sound levels exceed 90 decibels per 8-hour period (see Table 4.2).

7 Storage tanks containing flammable material cannot be located under electric lines or near flammable liquid or

Table 4.2 Maximum Permitted Sound Level Per Period of Worktime, Per Day[a]

Duration (h)	Maximum (dB)
8	90
6	92
4	95
3	97
2	100
1½	102
1	105
½	110
¼ (or less)	115

[a]Exposure to impact noise shall not exceed 140 dB.

gas-carrying pipes unless fire walls have been provided, separating the hazards.

8 The floors of any workplace shall be free of protruding nails, splinters, loose boards, or holes. Floors shall be kept dry unless wet processes are in progress, in which case proper drainage shall be maintained and the workers provided with dry flooring on which to stand or waterproof footgear.

9 Potable water must be provided in all places of employment for drinking, washing, cooking, and food preparation.
   a Common drinking cups and other such utensils are prohibited.
   b Nonpotable water outlets must be clearly identified as "unsafe."

10 Separate toilets shall be maintained for men and women unless the facilities are lockable, occupied by only one person at a time, and provided with a water closet.
   a All toilets must be provided with toilet paper and holder. Floors and walls of toilet shall be watertight.
   b Each water closet shall be in a separate compartment with a door.

Safety Color Code for Marking Hazards and Other Environments

Red. Fire protection apparatus:

Alarm pull boxes.
Blanket boxes.
Buckets.
Exit signs.
Extinguishers.
Hose locations.
Industrial hydrants.
Pumps.
Sirens.
Sprinkler piping.
Post indicator valves for sprinkler systems.
Danger signs.
Lights at barricades and temporary obstructions.
Emergency stop buttons, switches, bars for hazardous machinery.

Orange. Dangerous parts of machines or powered equipment that may cut, crush, shock, or otherwise cause injury:

When enclosure doors are open.
When gear-belt or other guards around moving equipment are open or removed.

Yellow. Caution.

Physical hazards such as striking against, stumbling, falling, tripping, being caught in between.

Blue. Caution—limited to starting, use, and movement of equipment under repair.

Purple. Radiation hazards.

Green. Safe.
Location of first-aid equipment.

Black, White, or Combination. These shall be the basic designations of traffic and housekeeping.

OSHA Violations

Examples

1 A roof under construction has no railings or barricades and is covered with loose debris: workers could fall off the roof; the debris could be blown or pushed carelessly off the edge, striking persons below.
2 An open bucketful of sand is being hoisted by a worker who is not wearing gloves or protective headgear.
3 A stairway under construction lacks a handrail.
4 An opening for a well or utility pipes is left uncovered.
5 Pipe sections have been piled precariously askew without protective covering.
6 Rickety wood scaffolding provides insufficient protection from falling for masons or pipefitters atop it.
7 Warning signs have not been posted around a dismantled earthmover.
8 A welding area has inadequate ventilation, causing workers to become faint.

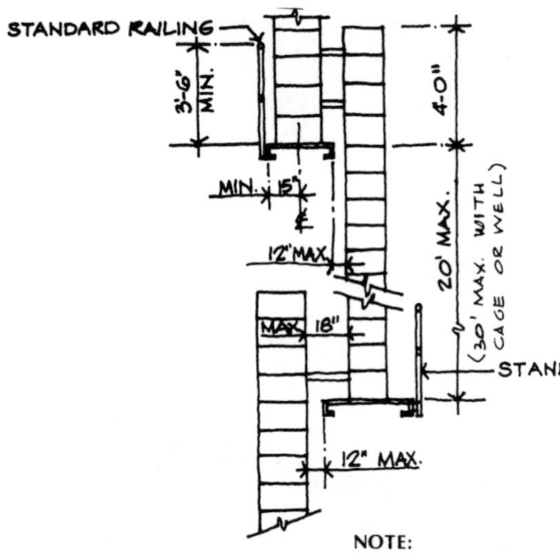

Figure 4.21 Typical OSHA requirement. Reprinted from Peter S. Hopf, *Designer's Guide to OSHA*, McGraw-Hill Book Company, 1975.

9 A wooden storage shed contains both flammable and toxic substances. The single entrance/exit door is open. Two workers are smoking cigarettes nearby.

10 Many large trucks are passing through a construction site, using very narrow access routes. They are hauling dirt away from a major excavation that is late in being made. There are no flagmen or traffic routing signs.

The Courts. In a stunning 8–0 vote, the U.S. Supreme Court recently upheld the right of OSHA to set penalties without going to court, thus dismissing a challenge of OSHA's constitutionality under the doctrine of due process.

Still to be determined is the constitutionality of OSHA's right to make inspections (i.e., to conduct a search) without a warrant. Idaho courts have found this procedure to be unconstitutional. In a related action, a Maryland circuit court found the Maryland occupational safety act, patterned after the federal act, unconstitutional to the extent that it permitted searches without warrants. The case is now before the Maryland Court of Appeals.

Inspections without warrants also have been banned by court decisions in Alaska, Georgia, Kentucky, Montana, New Mexico, Ohio, Texas, and Utah. Under present conditions, employers in other states can demand a warrant, although there is always the chance of legal action by OSHA.

Liens

A lien is a legal claim by one party against another's property for satisfaction of a debt. The owner is liable for payment to those who supply materials for the project or perform work on it. Claims for payment become liabilities of record against the property. Lien laws protect persons performing work or providing materials by giving them security for their compensation.

Since laws and procedures for perfecting a lien vary from state to state, the architect should request the owner to seek advice from his attorney regarding the completeness and adequacy of releases.

Lien laws in the construction industry are more stringent than those for other trades and industries because materials and workmanship incorporated into buildings usually cannot be repossessed and because contractors are more likely to default. An architect can successfully file a mechanics' lien on a building to secure any unpaid balance of his fee. The courts have ruled that when an architect provides drawings and construction administration, he is considered to have provided *labor* in the construction of buildings.

To protect the owner, the general conditions of the contract stipulate that neither final payment nor any portion of the retained percentage of the construction cost is to be paid until the contractor has delivered a release or waiver of liens to the owner. Before final payment becomes due, the contractor must furnish the architect with

PEPSICO WORLD HEADQUARTERS
Boston, Massachusetts
Architect: Edward Durell Stone & Associates
Photo: E. Stoller

an affidavit that all payrolls, bills for materials and equipment, or other indebtedness relative to the work (for which the owner might be responsible) have been paid or otherwise satisfied.

To ensure that the releases or waivers of liens secured from the contractor are complete, the owner should receive an affidavit from the contractor stating that all waivers and lien releases submitted are complete to the best of his knowledge, except those specifically listed. The architect should also secure written consent of the surety, if any, prior to final payment.

In lieu of a release or waiver the contractor may post a bond indemnifying the owner against liens. If a lien remains unsatisfied, the contractor must refund to the owner all monies the owner may be forced to pay in discharging such lien, including legal costs and attorney's fees.

The time limitation for filing liens is usually 30 days from date of completion. Time limits for various conditions must be met precisely for a lien to be perfected. The lien notice is filed in the office of the clerk of the county in which the property is located. (If the property is located in more than one county, the lien notice must be filed in the offices of all county clerks affected.)

The duration of a lien for private work is 1 year from date of filing the notice; for public work the duration is 6 months. The period for filing may be extended by court order.

Wage laborers have priority (seniority) over all others in filing liens concerned with the work. Liens for labor performed or materials supplied have priority over mortgages and subsequently recorded judgments. These parties are given priority according to the order in which their liens are filed.

The discharge of liens may be achieved by payment of the obligation, by forced sale of property (private work), or by payment from project appropriations (public work). Construction may be permitted to continue without satisfying the lien by the issuance of a bond for an amount fixed by the court that is not less than the amount of the lien, or by filing sufficient funds including accrued interest, with the county clerk.

CONTRACTOR'S AFFIDAVIT OF RELEASE OF LIENS

AIA DOCUMENT G706A

OWNER ☐
ARCHITECT ☐
CONTRACTOR ☐
SURETY ☐
OTHER

TO (Owner)

ARCHITECT'S PROJECT NO:

CONTRACT FOR:

CONTRACT DATE:

PROJECT:
(name, address)

State of:

County of:

The undersigned, pursuant to Article 9 of the General Conditions of the Contract for Construction, AIA Document A201, hereby certifies that to the best of his knowledge, information and belief, except as listed below, the Releases or Waivers of Lien attached hereto include the Contractor, all Subcontractors, all suppliers of materials and equipment, and all performers of Work, labor or services who have or may have liens against any property of the Owner arising in any manner out of the performance of the Contract referenced above.

EXCEPTIONS: (If none, write "None". If required by the Owner, the Contractor shall furnish bond satisfactory to the Owner for each exception.)

SUPPORTING DOCUMENTS ATTACHED HERETO:

1. Contractor's Release or Waiver of Liens, conditional upon receipt of final payment.
2. Separate Releases or Waivers of Liens from Subcontractors and material and equipment suppliers, to the extent required by the Owner, accompanied by a list thereof.

CONTRACTOR:

Address:

BY:

Subscribed and sworn to before me this
day of 19

Notary Public:

My Commission Expires:

AIA DOCUMENT G706A • CONTRACTOR'S AFFIDAVIT OF RELEASE OF LIENS • APRIL 1970 EDITION • AIA®

ONE PAGE

Figure 4.22

FORM 104-A

NOTICES TO OWNER REGARDING MECHANICS' LIEN LAW

To: OWNER **From: CONTRACTOR**

To: OWNER	From: CONTRACTOR
(Name)	(Name)
(Street Address)	(Street Address)
(City)	(City)

Re: PROPOSED WORK OF IMPROVEMENT

(Description Of Work To Be Performed)

(Location Of Jobsite)

OWNER'S COPY

In accordance with Section 7019 of the Business and Professions Code, State of California, the following official notice prescribed by the State of California Contractors State License Board is given to the owner of the above described proposed work of improvement as a pre-requisite to entering into a contract for the performance of said work of improvement by the above named contractor.*

"NOTICE TO OWNER"
(Section 7019 — Contractors License Law)

Under the Mechanics' Lien Law, any contractor, subcontractor, laborer, materialman or other person who helps to improve your property and is not paid for his labor, services or material, has a right to enforce his claim against your property.

Under the law, you may protect yourself against such claims by filing, before commencing such work of improvement, an original contract for the work of improvement or a modification thereof, in the office of the county recorder of the county where the property is situated and requiring that a contractor's payment bond be recorded in such office. Said bond shall be in an amount not less than fifty percent (50%) of the contract price and shall, in addition to any conditions for the performance of the contract, be conditioned for the payment in full of the claims of all persons furnishing labor, services, equipment or materials for the work described in said contract.

Assuming a contract will be signed with the owner for the above described work of improvement, the following official notice is tendered as a pre-requisite to presentation of the first invoice for materials and/or labor on said work of improvement, per Section 7018 of the Business and Professions Code, State of California.

"NOTICE TO OWNER"

Under the Mechanics' Lien Law any contractor, subcontractor, laborer, supplier or other person who helps to improve your property but is not paid for his work or supplies, has a right to enforce a claim against your property. This means that, after a court hearing, your property could be sold by a court officer and the proceeds of the sale used to satisfy the indebtedness. This can happen even if you have paid your own contractor in full, if the subcontractor, laborer, or supplier remains unpaid.

Method of Serving Notice: ☐ *Personal service* ☐ *First Class Mail* ☐ *First Class with Certificate of Mailing (P.O.D. Form 3817)* ☐ *Certified Mail* ☐ *Registered Mail*

Date ______________________ *Contractor or Contractor's Agent* ______________________
(Sign Here)

Acknowledgement ______________________
(Owner Sign Here)

*7019. On or before December 31, 1969, the board shall prescribe a form entitled "Notice to Owner" which shall describe provisions of the state's mechanics' lien laws relating to the filing of a contract concerning a work of improvement with the county recorder and the recording in such office of a contractor's payment bond for private work. Each contractor licensed under this chapter, prior to entering into a contract after December 31, 1969, in excess of six hundred dollars ($600) with the owner of a single-family dwelling, a duplex, or a triplex for work to be performed for the improvement of property, shall give a copy of this "Notice to Owner" to the owner. **A contractor shall not, however, be required to provide a copy of such form to the owner of property who is acting in a capacity of a licensed general building contractor for such improvement.**

➧ See Reverse Side For Information To Owner Concerning Mechanics' Lien Law ➧

(over)

Figure 4.23 *Source. Building News,* State of California.

INFORMATION ABOUT MECHANICS' LIENS

A mechanic's lien must be recorded within 90 days after the completion of the work of improvement as a whole unless the owner records a notice of completion. If a notice of completion is recorded, the mechanic's lien must be recorded within 30 days thereafter unless the claimant is a general contractor or specialty contractor who contracted directly with the owner; in which case the mechanic's lien must be recorded within 60 days after the notice of completion was recorded. A mechanic's lien expires unless a foreclosure suit is filed within 90 days after the lien was recorded. The Mechanic's Lien Law is frequently amended. If you have any question as to procedure, see your attorney.

RECORDING INFORMATION

The mechanic's lien must be recorded in the county where the job is located. The 1974 fee for recording one page is $3.00, plus $1.00 for each additional page or fraction thereof. However, this price is subject to change and should be checked with the County Recorder's office, since the recorder will not record a document unless it is accompanied by the correct fee.

INTEREST RATES

To establish the proper interest rate to be charged on the unpaid balance look to the contract provisions. If the contract does not specify the rate, or if the contract is oral, the legal rate of interest is 7% per annum.

20 DAY PRELIMINARY NOTICE

(Excerpts from Section 3097 of State of California Civil Code)

(a) Except one under direct contract with the owner or one performing actual labor for wages, every person who furnishes labor, service, equipment or material for which a lien otherwise can be claimed under this chapter, or for which a notice to withhold can otherwise be given under this chapter, shall, as a necessary prerequisite to the validity of any claim of lien and of the notice to withhold, cause to be given to the owner or reputed owner, to the original contractor or reputed contractor, and to the construction lender, if any, or to the reputed construction lender, if any, a written preliminary notice as prescribed by this section.

(b) All persons having a direct contract with the owner, except the contractor or one performing actual labor for wages, who furnish labor, service, equipment, or material for which a lien otherwise can be claimed under this chapter, or for which a notice to withhold can otherwise be given under this chapter, shall, as a necessary prerequisite to the validity of any claim of lien and of the notice to withhold, cause to be given to the construction lender, if any, or to the reputed construction lender, if any, a written preliminary notice as prescribed by subdivision (c) of this section.

(c) The preliminary notice referred to in subdivisions (a) and (b) above shall be given not later than 20 days after the claimant has first furnished labor, services, equipment, or materials to the jobsite and shall contain the following information:

The name of the person who contracted for purchase of such labor, services, equipment or materials.

A general description of the labor, service, equipment or materials furnished, or to be furnished, and if there is a construction lender, he shall be furnished with an estimate of the total price thereof in addition to the foregoing.

A statement that if bills are not paid in full for labor, services, equipment or materials furnished, or to be furnished, the improved property may be subject to mechanics' liens.

The name and address of such person furnishing such labor, services, equipment or materials.

A description of the jobsite sufficient for identification.

(Note): Copies of an efficient form to comply with the provisions of the above 20-day preliminary notice requirement may be obtained from Building News, Inc. Order Form 105-A. Cost: $5.25 for Handipak of 50 forms, plus 5% sales tax, plus 75c shipping charge. Order by mail (prepaid) from Building News, Inc., P.O. Box 3031, Terminal Annex, Los Angeles, Calif. 90051.

INSTRUCTIONS FOR SIGNING AND VERIFYING THIS FORM

Signature: If the claimant of the stop notice is a corporation, an officer or managing employee should sign. If the claimant is a partnership, a partner or managing employee should sign. If the firm is a sole proprietorship, whether or not doing business under a fictitious name, the owner of the business or a managing employee should sign. See below for example:

CORPORATION

Firm Name JOHNSON ELECTRICAL CO.,INC.

By Sid Johnson, Pres.

SOLE PROPRIETORSHIP (Fictitious Name)

Firm Name SPEEDY ELECTRICAL CO.

By Sid Johnson, owner

PARTNERSHIP

Firm Name JOHNSON ELECTRICAL CO.

By Sid Johnson, Partner

SOLE PROPRIETORSHIP (Own Name)

Firm Name SID JOHNSON ELECTRIC CO.

By Sid Johnson, owner

Verification: This is a declaration under penalty of perjury. If it is signed in the State of California, it does not have to be notarized. However, to be valid, the verification **must** contain the date, the city where signed, and the signature. See above for example:

DO NOT RECORD

FORM 106

RECORDING REQUESTED BY
JOHNSON ELECTRICAL CO.

AND WHEN RECORDED MAIL TO
JOHNSON ELECTRICAL CO.
Name
6207 Maple Blvd.
Street Address
Compton, California
City & State

LEGAL NOTICE TO CLAIM MECHANIC'S LIEN

SPACE ABOVE THIS LINE FOR RECORDER'S USE

MECHANIC'S LIEN

The undersigned, Johnson Electrical Co. (Name of person or firm claiming mechanic's lien. Contractors use name exactly as it appears on contractor's license.), claimant,* claims a mechanic's lien upon the following described real property: City of Los Angeles, County of Los Angeles, California, 1163 Sierra Road, Los Angeles, California (General description of property where the work or materials were furnished. A street address is sufficient, but if possible, use both street address and legal description.) Lot 12, Tract 1001, as shown on Map recorded in Book 12, page 10, official records of Los Angeles County;

The sum of $ 1,000.00 (Amount of claim due and unpaid.) together with interest thereon at the rate of 7% (See note on reverse) percent per annum from February 15 (Date when balance became due.), 19 67, is due claimant (after deducting all just credits and offsets) for the following work and material furnished by claimant: Install electrical wiring - labor and materials (Insert general description of the work or materials furnished.)

Claimant furnished the work and materials at the request of, or under contract, with, Smith Construction Co., Jim Smith (Name of person or firm who ordered or contracted for the work or materials.)

The owners and reputed owners of the property are: Martin Jones and Mary Jones (Insert name of owner of real property. This can be obtained from the County Recorder or by checking the building permit application at the Building Department.)

SEE REVERSE SIDE FOR COMPLETE INSTRUCTIONS

Firm Name: JOHNSON ELECTRICAL CO.
(See instructions on rear for proper signing.)
By: Sid Johnson Owner
(Signature of claimant or authorized agent.)

VERIFICATION

I, the undersigned, say: I am the Owner of ("President of", "Manager of", "A partner of", "Owner of", etc.) the claimant of the foregoing mechanic's lien; I have read said claim of mechanic's lien and know the contents thereof; the same is true of my own knowledge.

I declare under penalty of perjury that the foregoing is true and correct.

Executed on February 19 (Date of signature.), 19 67, at Los Angeles (City where signed.), California.

Sid Johnson
(Personal signature of the individual who is swearing that the contents of the claim of mechanics lien are true.)

DO NOT RECORD

Figure 4.24. *Source. Building News,* State of California.

INSTRUCTIONS For Using Legal Notice Prerequisite To Filing Claim Of Lien And/Or Stop Notice

CHART SHOWING "20-DAY PRELIMINARY NOTICE" REQUIREMENTS ON

PRIVATE JOBS

CLAIMANT STATUS	CONTRACT STATUS	NOTICE REQUIREMENT	PENALTY For Failure To Give Preliminary Notice
ORIGINAL CONTRACTOR (This term means a **prime** or general contractor only)	Direct contract with owner or owner-builder	Not required to give notice* (See Footnote)	Not applicable* (See Footnote)
SUBCONTRACTOR (This term **may include** a **"general contractor"** acting as a sub-contractor or a **"specialty contractor"** acting as a sub-contractor or a sub sub-contractor)	A. Direct contract with owner or owner-builder. B. No direct contract with owner or owner-builder.	Required to give notice to: Construction lender, (if any) ONLY under "A" status at left and if "B" status at left ALSO to owner and original contractor	(a) Loss of Stop Notice and Lien Rights **and** (b) Disciplinary action by Contractors' State License Board
MATERIALMAN or SUPPLIER ARCHITECT ENGINEER OR OTHER NON-CONTRACTOR CLAIMANTS	With **direct contract** with owner or owner-builder	Required to give notice to a. Construction lender only	Loss of Stop Notice and Lien Rights
	No direct contract with owner or owner-builder	Required to give notice to a. Owner b. Original contractor c. Construction lender, if any	Loss of Stop Notice and Lien Rights
WORKMAN DOING ACTUAL LABOR FOR WAGES	Employee	Not required to give notice	Not applicable

* In case you are not the sole prime contractor on the job, because of ambiguties in the law, it is strongly suggested that you give notice to the construction lender to protect more adequately your stop notice right.

** Section 1193(h) of the Code of Civil Procedure as amended effective November 13, 1968 states:

(h) Where the contract price to be paid to any subcontractor on a particular work of improvement exceeds four hundred dollars ($400), the failure of that contractor, licensed under Chapter 9 (commencing with Section 7000) of Division 3 of the Business and Professions Code, to give the notice provided for in this section constitutes grounds for disciplinary action by the Registrar of Contractors.

CHART SHOWING "20-DAY PRELIMINARY NOTICE" REQUIREMENTS ON

PUBLIC WORKS

CLAIMANT STATUS	CONTRACT STATUS	NOTICE REQUIREMENT	PENALTY For Failure To Give Preliminary Notice
ORIGINAL CONTRACTOR (This term means a **prime** or general contractor only)	**Direct contract** with Public Agency	Not required to give notice	Not applicable
SUBCONTRACTOR (This term **may include** a **"general contractor"** acting as a sub-contractor or a **"specialty contractor"** acting as a sub-contractor or a sub sub-contractor)	**Direct contract** with **Prime** Contractor	Not required to give notice	Not applicable
	NO direct contract with either (a) Original (prime) contractor or (b) public agency	Required to give notice to **both** (a) public agency & (b) original (prime) contractor	(a) Loss of stop notice rights on the job (but not deprived of right of action against bond*) **AND** (b) Disciplinary action by Contractors' State License Board
MATERIALMAN or SUPPLIER ARCHITECT ENGINEER OR OTHER NON-CONTRACTOR CLAIMANTS	**Direct contract** with **public agency**	Not required to give notice	Not applicable
	Direct contract with **original** (prime) **contractor**	Not required to give notice	Not applicable
	NO direct contract with either (a) original (prime) contractor or (b) public agency	**Required to give** notice to **both** (a) public agency & (b) original (prime) contractor	Loss of stop notice rights on the job (but not deprived of right of action against bond*)

***Right To Sue On Bond.** On a bonded job, failure to follow the 20-day preliminary notice procedure does not affect a claimant's right to sue on the bond, provided, however, that statutory procedures against the bond are followed. (See Government Code Section 4209, which requires a notice be given to the prime contractor within 90 days from last furnishing of labor or material before suit on the contractor's bond can be filed.)

1. **DETERMINE** who, if any, must receive notice by reference to charts **AT LEFT.**

2. **FILL IN ALL NECESSARY BLANKS** on face of form and **sign** where indicated. (Note: **Cost estimate figure** at bottom of form WILL NOT COME THROUGH on **owner's** (or) **public agency's** copy and **original contractor's** copy, due to shortened carbon paper serving these copies.

3. **SERVE white** copy on **lender,** or reputed lender, if any. Serve **pink** copy on **owner** or reputed owner. Serve **blue** copy on **original contractor** (if any). Serve these three parties in **ANY** of the following manners. Be sure to attach acknowledgement post card—see last page of this form.

A. PERSONAL DELIVERY

Service of notice may be given by delivering the same to the person to be notified personally, or by leaving it at his address of residence or place of business with some person in charge. In the event of personal delivery, it is advisable, if possible, to obtain signed acknowledgement of receipt in blanks provided below:

"I acknowledge receipt of 20-day preliminary notice, per copy on reverse side."

______________________________ Date__________
(Agent Of Lender Or Reputed Lender Sign Here)

______________________________ Date__________
(Owner, Or Reputed Owner — On Private Work)
(Designated Agent Of Public Agency Or Job Architect—On Public Work)

______________________________ Date__________
(Original (General) Contractor Or Reputed Contractor)

B. FIRST CLASS MAIL — WITH "CERTIFICATE OF MAILING"

To use this method of mailing, obtain P.O.D. Form 3817 from any postoffice, fill out form, attach 10c stamp to form and personally deliver form and envelope containing this notice to any postoffice. (Envelope should have regular 13c first class postage on it.) Postoffice will sign receipt and return to you as proof of mailing. Form MUST be used for each separate pieces of mail to be certified. This method establishes legal proof that form was mailed — but does not prove its receipt.

C. CERTIFIED MAIL

To use U.S. **CERTIFIED MAIL,** sender should (1) fill out P.O.D. Form 3800; (2) tear off sticker at end of P.O.D. Form 3800 reading "Certified Mail" and attach this sticker to **front** of envelope; (3) fill out P.O.D. Form 3811 and attach to **back** of envelope; (4) affix 60c in stamps, plus 13c regular first class postage; and (5) drop in any mailbox. (Supplies of these forms may be obtained free at any postoffice.) If return receipt is requested, add 25c to postage.

D. REGISTERED MAIL

If U.S. **REGISTERED MAIL** is used, envelope must be taken to any postoffice and registered for a fee of $2.10 plus 13c regular first class postage. If return is requested, this requires payment of an additional 25c.

NOTE: Form may be addressed to person to whom notice is to be given, at his residence or place of business address, or at the address shown by the building permit on file with the authority issuing a building permit for the work.

NOTE: On Use of CERTIFIED or REGISTERED MAIL, SERVICE IS **COMPLETE AT TIME OF DEPOSIT** of said mail. Postal fees for this service may be reduced by NOT requesting return receipt, which WILL be on file at postoffice for inspection at any time — BUT will be destroyed by postoffice after ONE YEAR has elapsed. Certificate of Mailing Form provides legal proof that item was mailed but does not prove it was received.

4. **COMPLETE** Office Records below on buff colored "FILE" (hard) copy and **RETAIN** in your files.

— — — *FOR OFFICE RECORD ONLY* — — —

DECLARATION OF SERVICE
(SECTION 3097.1 (b) CALIF. CIVIL CODE)

I, ______________________________, declare: That I served copies of the Preliminary Notice on reverse side by first class registered/certified mail, postage prepaid, on the lender, owner, and original contractor at address on reverse side, on ________________ (date).

I declare, under penalty of perjury, that the foregoing is true and correct.

Executed on ________________ (date), at ________________ California.

____
(Signature of Person Making Service)

Date of Notice of Completion Is: ________________

Date of Expiration of Lien Rights Is: ________________

If First Class Mail With Certificate Of Mailing; Or Certified Mail; Or Registered Mail Are Used, BE SURE TO STAPLE POST OFFICE RECEIPTS FOR SUCH MAILINGS HERE. Be Sure Also To Staple Return Post Card "Acknowledgement Of Receipt Forms."

WHEN MAILING IN WINDOW ENVELOPE BE SURE THIS BAND OF RED STARS
* *
IS SHOWING IN THE WINDOW OR ELSE YOU ARE MAILING TO THE WRONG PARTY!

Figure 4.25 *Source. Building News,* State of California.

Arbitration

The architect renders most of his decisions as an arbitrator when acting under the general conditions of the contract; therefore he is obligated to act with the greatest care, fairness, and deliberation, making certain that the owner understands the transition from owner's agent to impartial arbitrator between owner and contractor.

Formal arbitration is the hearing and settlement of a dispute between two or more parties through informal hearings: any disputing parties may agree to arbitrate, regardless of whether a contract exists or whether a valid contract provides for arbitration. Arbitration is quick and less expensive than judicial proceedings, and lends itself to disputes involving technical expertise. The award, binding on the parties, is entered as a judgment in the local court having jurisdiction. There is usually no appeal.

Arbitration is a combination of English common law (unwritten but set by precedent) and statutory (written) laws, consisting of hearings conducted like court trials but less formally. Arbitrators are not required to follow strict rules of evidence. They must hear all the evidence material to the issue, but they may determine for themselves what is relevant. Witnesses and documents may be subpoenaed.

Arbitration is legally enforceable under many state laws but not under all; all states, however, allow parties to agree to arbitrate a dispute. Certain states have special laws regarding arbitration. The architect should ascertain from legal counsel whether an arbitration clause should be included in the general conditions.

Construction industry arbitration is conducted according to Construction Industry Arbitration Rules. Each trade association has approved and adopted these rules; all such arbitration is administered by the American Arbitration Association (AAA).

Initiating Arbitration. An agreement to arbitrate may take the form of a "future dispute" clause in a contract or the submission of a dispute to the AAA and the defending party of the claim. Upon receipt of such documents, the AAA assigns one of its staff (official title: tribunal administrator) to the case. If the place of arbitration has not been designated in the contract or otherwise stated, the AAA will choose an address in accordance with its rules.

Selecting the Arbitrator(s). Upon receiving the demand for arbitration or the submission agreement, the tribunal administrator sends each party a copy of a list of proposed arbitrators. Parties are allowed 7 days to study the list and reject any individual. If parties request more information about proposed arbitrators, it is furnished.

The tribunal administrator composes the tribunal from indicated preferences and mutual choices of both parties. He or she is at the disposal of both parties, expediting administration and assisting both sides in all procedural matters until an award is rendered.

The litigating parties may agree to a single arbitrator in simple cases. In construction industry cases, the tribunal usually consists of three arbitrators: an architect, an attorney (acting as chairperson), and a contractor. If agreement cannot be reached, the AAA will make administrative appointments, excluding any arbitrator previously rejected.

Hearing Preparation. The tribunal administrator manages details and arrangements, relieving the arbitrator of such burdens and eliminating direct communication between the parties and the arbitrator except at the hearing. By specifically forbidding communication with the arbitrator(s), except in the presence of both parties, AAA rules make it impossible for one side to offer arguments or evidence that the other has no opportunity to rebut.

If it becomes necessary for the arbitrator(s) to visit a project site for investigation, representatives from both parties must be present the entire time; nothing may be said or presented except in the presence of all.

Presentation of the Case. The complaining party proceeds first, presenting his case in an orderly, logical manner, beginning with a statement that clearly but briefly describes the controversy and indicates what is to be proved. Then follows a discussion of possible remedies. Documents and witnesses are introduced next. Finally a statement is made summarizing the evidence, and the arguments and a rebuttal of points made by the opposition.

If a transcript of hearings is needed, the tribunal administrator makes the arrangements. The right to representation by counsel in arbitration is guaranteed by the rules of the AAA.

The arbitrators are advised by the AAA never to announce the basis for their decision in the award, since this might lead to legal argument on the decision that could be decided only in the courts.

The architect should consult a competent attorney in case one of the parties refuses to submit the dispute to arbitration or to accept an award made by the arbitrators. Legal counsel must be consulted on how the arbitration may be enforced.

IMPORTANT

When you include in your Agreements an arbitration clause naming the AAA, you rely on AAA service, and you place upon the Association the responsibility of providing that service. You will enable AAA to carry out that responsibility with maximum speed and efficiency if you advise the Association immediately whenever such a clause is used, and not wait until a dispute arises to inform it of its responsibility.

For the Arbitration of future disputes:—

The American Arbitration Association recommends the following arbitration clause for insertion in all commercial contracts:

STANDARD ARBITRATION CLAUSE

Any controversy or claim arising out of or relating to this contract, or the breach thereof, shall be settled by arbitration in accordance with the Rules of the American Arbitration Association, and judgment upon the award rendered by the Arbitrator(s) may be entered in any Court having jurisdiction thereof.

For the Submission of existing disputes:—

We, the undersigned parties, hereby agree to submit to arbitration under the Commercial Arbitration Rules of the American Arbitration Association the following controversy: (cite briefly). We further agree that the above controversy be submitted to (one) (three) Arbitrators selected from the panels of Arbitrators of the American Arbitration Association. We further agree that we will faithfully observe this agreement and the Rules and that we will abide by and perform any award rendered by the Arbitrator(s) and that a judgment of the Court having jurisdiction may be entered upon the award.

COMMERCIAL ARBITRATION RULES

Section 1. AGREEMENT OF PARTIES — The parties shall be deemed to have made these Rules a part of their arbitration agreement whenever they have provided for arbitration by the American Arbitration Association or under its Rules. These Rules and any amendment thereof shall apply in the form obtaining at the time the arbitration is initiated.

Section 2. NAME OF TRIBUNAL — Any Tribunal constituted by the parties for the settlement of their dispute under these Rules shall be called the Commercial Arbitration Tribunal.

Section 3. ADMINISTRATOR — When parties agree to arbitrate under these Rules, or when they provide for arbitration by the American Arbitration Association and an arbitration is initiated thereunder, they thereby constitute AAA the administrator of the arbitration. The authority and obligations of the administrator are prescribed in the agreement of the parties and in these Rules.

Section 4. DELEGATION OF DUTIES — The duties of the AAA under these Rules may be carried out through Tribunal Administrator, or such other officers or committees as the AAA may direct.

Section 5. NATIONAL PANEL OF ARBITRATORS — The AAA shall establish and maintain a National Panel of Arbitrators and shall appoint Arbitrators therefrom as hereinafter provided.

Section 6. OFFICE OF TRIBUNAL — The general office of a Tribunal is the headquarters of the AAA, which may, however, assign the administration of an arbitration to any of its Regional Offices.

Section 7. INITIATION UNDER AN ARBITRATION PROVISION IN A CONTRACT — Arbitration under an arbitration provision in a contract may be initiated in the following manner:

(a) The initiating party may give notice to the other party of his intention to arbitrate (Demand), which notice shall contain a statement setting forth the nature of the dispute, the amount involved, if any, the remedy sought, and

(b) By filing at any Regional Office of the AAA two (2) copies of said notice, together with two (2) copies of the arbitration provisions of the contract, together with the appropriate administrative fee as provided in the Administrative Fee Schedule.

The AAA shall give notice of such filing to the other party. If he so desires, the party upon whom the demand for arbitration is made may file an answering statement in duplicate with the AAA within seven days after notice from the AAA, in which event he shall simultaneously send a copy of his answer to the other party. If a monetary claim is made in the answer the appropriate fee provided in the Fee Schedule shall be forwarded to the AAA with the answer. If no answer is filed within the stated time, it will be assumed that the claim is denied. Failure to file an answer shall not operate to delay the arbitration.

Figure 4.26 *Source*. American Arbitration Association.

Award. The award is made by the tribunal within the limits of the arbitration agreement, and each claim submitted is ruled on. If there is more than one arbitrator, the majority decision is binding. The purpose of the award is to completely dispose of the controversy. Thus an award may not be changed by the arbitrators unless the parties agree to reopen the proceeding and restore the power of the arbitrators, or unless the law provides otherwise.

The award may be monetary or a performance award (requiring each party or both to carry out certain actions), or both. It is entered immediately in the court having jurisdiction, without appeal.

Fees. The arbitrator's fee is based on a daily rate agreed to by the parties, usually equivalent to the normal daily rate of the arbitrator's profession. Arbitrators serve the first 2 days without compensation. The AAA is paid an administrative fee equally by each party according to a schedule based on the amount in dispute. Each party pays its own attorney.

Ethical Responsibilities

Financial. Since the architect is paid for services rendered based on his knowledge, judgment, and skill, he cannot be engaged in any activity that would make his remuneration contingent on profit or loss in the building construction operation (conflict of interest). His professional judgment must be free from bias that might be caused by a financial interest in the building operation or in a particular building material.

Many owners require the architect's assistance in problems of land assembly, financing and promotional designs, and drawings, brochures, and similar exhibits. As the owner's agent, the architect can provide overall

PROJECT PROCEDURE

O Interview Architects-Engineers
O Visit Applicable Projects of Selected Firms
O Commission Architect-Engineer
A Develop Scope and Program
— A: Client's Space Needs; Interdepartmental Relationships; Space Standards; Systems and Operations; Tenant Areas; Master Plan; Project Budget; Economic Feasibility
O Review Scope and Program
A Prepare Schematics
— A: Site Plan; Set Building Module; Determine Building Height and Floor Size; Parking Layout and Traffic Plan; Special Facilities Requirements; Scale Model of Architectural Concept; Renderings of Architectural Concept; Cost Budget Based on Schematic Plans
O Review Schematics and Budget
A Prepare Preliminary Leasing Brochure
A Prepare Preliminary Plans
— A: Plans and Elevations Showing Architectural, Structural, Mechanical, and Electrical; Outline Specifications; Detailed Cost Estimate; Landscaping Plans; Mockups and Testing
O Review Preliminaries
A Prepare Working Drawings and Specifications
— A: Complete Detailed Plans; Cost Estimate Verification; Plan Checking
A Issue Bid Documents to Contractors
O Competitive or Negotiated Contract
O Segregated Contracts
— Foundations; Structural Steel; General; Etc.
A Assist in Bid Review
O Award Construction Contract
C Construction
A Construction Supervision

Prime Responsibility

O Owner A Architect- Engineer C Contractor

Figure 4.27 *Source.* William Dudley Hunt, Jr., *Total Design,* McGraw-Hill Book Company, 1972.

GALLO WINERY
Modesto, California
Architects: John S. Bolles Associates
Photo: R. Partridge

coordination of other services such as real estate, public relations, and communications. Therefore, in addition to his professional design fees, the architect may receive a developer's fee or fees for management; he also may make a profit by buying, improving, rezoning (or attempting to rezone), or holding land as equity in proceeding with a project as architect/developer. If the architect is not involved in considerations leading to the development process, he may have to design and build according to decisions previously developed by others, consequently producing construction documents that are merely adequate.

The practicing architect may wish to join an established professional group such as the American Institute of Architects (AIA) or the Society of American Registered Architects (ARA), or in Canada, the Royal Architectural Institute of Canada. Membership is open to licensed architects through local chapters of these organizations. In the United States the AIA is the larger of the two professional groups.

Various subgroups have been established to serve interest of specific groups. Excellent documents are available through these organizations. For example, the California Council of the American Institute of Architects (CCAIA) has published (among many other such documents) a "List of Services," as CCAIA Document 100-72-A. this material assists clients in understanding the full scope of effort and time that may be required of the architect and his or her consultants. Part 2 of this document is quoted below.

2.1.1 Phase I. Predesign Services

1 Project development scheduling.
2 Project programming.
3 Internal function, flow studies, and space planning.
4 Existing building surveys.
5 Governmental agency consultation.
6 Initial concept and budget reviews.
7 Economic feasibility analysis and reports.
8 Promotional materials for fund raising and project financing services.
9 Administrative services and conferences.
10 Other services as needed.

2.1.2 Phase II. Site Development Services

1 Site analysis and selection.
2 Site master planning.
3 Detailed site improvement studies.
4 On-site utility studies.
5 Off-site utility studies.
6 Zoning analysis and processing.
7 Administrative services and conferences.
8 Other services as needed.

2.1.3 Phase III. Design Services

1 Architectural schematic design.
2 Engineering systems analysis.
3 Architectural design development.
4 Statement of probable construction cost.
5 Special design.
6 Landscape design.
7 Interior design.
8 Graphics design.
9 Furniture and special fixture design.
10 Renderings, models, and mock-ups.
11 Governmental and regulatory agency review.
12 Administrative services and conferences.
13 Other services as needed.

2.1.4 Phase IV. Construction Document Services

1 Architectural working drawings.
2 Structural working drawings.
3 Civil working drawings.
4 Mechanical working drawings.
5 Electrical working drawings.
6 Specifications and general conditions.
7 Governmental and regulatory agency approvals.
8 Special bid documents (alternate, segregated, or advanced bids).
9 Final statement of probable construction cost.
10 Administrative services and conferences.
11 Other services as needed.

2.1.5 Phase V. Services During Bidding and Negotiation

1 General bidding documents.
2 General construction bidding.
3 Negotiated construction bidding.
4 Segregated construction bidding.
5 Addenda and drawings revisions.
6 Construction agreement.
7 Administrative services and conferences.
8 Other services as needed.

2.1.6 Phase VI. Services During Construction

1 Construction contract administration and conferences.
2 Construction job cost accounting.
3 Quotation requests, review, and change orders.
4 Shop drawings and submittal review.
5 Clarifications.
6 Construction observation and certification.
7 Testing and inspection coordination.
8 Full-time project representation.
9 Final acceptance.
10 Other services as needed.

2.1.7 Phase VII. Postconstruction Services

1 Maintenance and operational programming.
2 As-built drawings.
3 Warranty reviews.
4 Client conferences.
5 Other services as needed.

2.1.8 Phase VIII. Special Services

1 Special studies.
2 Computer applications.
3 Expert witness.
4 Architectural competition advisor.
5 Fine arts and crafts.
6 Other services as needed.

Ethical Standards. The AIA is widely known to the public and to government agencies, and the courts have recognized it as symbolic of professional merit. The AIA "Standards of Ethical Practice" form the basis for any disciplinary action that may be taken as a result of noncompliance by a corporate member. The standards reflect recognition of certain obligations to the public, the client, the profession, and to related professionals. The ARA has similar documents and rules regarding ethical practices.

The Public. Architects should above all serve and promote the public interest in the effort to improve the human environment and to bring honor and dignity to the profession of architecture. They should conform to the registration laws governing the practice of architecture in any jurisdiction in which they practice. Architects should support the human rights of all mankind and should not discriminate against any employee or applicant because of sex, race, creed, or national origin. Architects should not use paid advertising; indulge in self-laudatory, exaggerated, misleading, or false publicity; or solicit or permit others to solicit in their name, advertisements for any publication presenting their work.

PRE-CONTRACTUAL

Refer to AIA Handbook Chapters 9, 10 and 11, and B-Series Documents

Upon receipt of notification from the prospective client (Owner) that you are being considered as the Architect for his project, the following tasks should be completed prior to execution of an Agreement.

	Dates	Initials	Item	Remarks
1.			Determine (preferably prior to initial interview) if the Owner is financially sound.	
2.			Verify your ability to meet the professional liability insurance and licensing requirements in the project locality. (HBC 4)	
3.			Determine scope and type of project.	
4.			Determine viability of project: How will it be financed? Will there be special considerations with ☐ economics ☐ social or community groups ☐ zoning or others	
5.			Determine what constitutes Basic Services.	
6.			Determine what constitutes Additional Services. (See list in B-Series Documents)	
7.			Ascertain method contemplated for award of construction contract: ☐ direct selection ☐ competitive bidding (open or closed) ☐ single prime ☐ separate prime contracts ☐ construction manager. (HBC 16)	
8.			Review Owner's program of requirements for completeness and suitability.	
9.			Determine Owner's time schedule for bidding and occupancy.	
10.			Review Owner's budget and determine its basis (e.g., cost estimate, available funds, etc.).	

Figure 4.28

TERMS AND CONDITIONS OF AGREEMENT BETWEEN OWNER AND ARCHITECT

ARTICLE 1

ARCHITECT'S SERVICES

1.1 CONSTRUCTION PHASE—ADMINISTRATION OF THE CONTRACT FOR CONSTRUCTION

1.1.1 The Construction Phase will commence with the award of the Contract for Construction and will terminate when final payment to the Contractor is due, and in the absence of a final Certificate for Payment or of such due date, sixty days after the Date of Substantial Completion of the Work.

1.1.2 The Contract Documents shall consist of the Owner-Contractor Agreement, the Conditions of the Contract (General, Supplementary and other Conditions), the Drawings, the Specifications, and all Addenda issued prior to and all Modifications issued after execution of the Contract. Unless the context indicates clearly to the contrary, terms employed in this Amendment shall have the same meaning as those defined in the 1976 Edition of AIA Document A201, General Conditions of the Contract for Construction. An enumeration of the Contract Documents appears in Article 2.

1.1.3 Unless otherwise provided in Article 2 of this Amendment, and incorporated in the Contract Documents, the Architect shall provide administration of the Contract for Construction as set forth in the 1976 Edition of AIA Document A201, General Conditions of the Contract for Construction. Unless otherwise provided in this Amendment, the Architect's duties and responsibilities during construction shall be as set forth in the following Subparagraphs 1.1.4 through 1.1.17.

1.1.4 The Architect shall be a representative of the Owner during the Construction Phase, and shall advise and consult with the Owner. Instructions to the Contractor shall be forwarded through the Architect. The Architect shall have authority to act on behalf of the Owner only to the extent provided in the Contract Documents unless otherwise modified by written instrument in accordance with Subparagraph 1.1.17.

1.1.5 The Architect shall visit the site at intervals appropriate to the stage of construction or as otherwise agreed by the Architect in writing to become generally familiar with the progress and quality of the Work and to determine in general if the Work is proceeding in accordance with the Contract Documents. However, the Architect shall not be required to make exhaustive or continuous on-site inspections to check the quality or quantity of the Work. On the basis of such on-site observations as an architect, the Architect shall keep the Owner informed of the progress of the Work, and shall endeavor to guard the Owner against defects and deficiencies in the Work of the Contractor.

1.1.6 The Architect shall not be responsible for and shall not have control or charge of construction means, methods, techniques, sequences or procedures, or for safety precautions and programs in connection with the Work. The Architect shall not be responsible for or have control or charge over the acts or omissions of the Contractor, Subcontractors, or any of their agents or employees, or any other persons performing any of the Work, and shall not be responsible for the failure of any of them to carry out the Work in accordance with the Contract Documents.

1.1.7 The Architect shall at all times have access to the Work wherever it is in preparation or progress.

1.1.8 The Architect shall determine the amounts owing to the Contractor based on on-site observations and on evaluations of the Contractor's Applications for Payment, and shall issue Certificates for Payment in such amounts, as provided in the Contract Documents. The accuracy of each Application for Payment shall remain the primary responsibility of the Contractor, and the Architect may presume it to be accurate.

1.1.9 The issuance of a Certificate for Payment shall constitute a representation by the Architect to the Owner, based on the Architect's observations at the site as provided in Subparagraph 1.1.5 and the data comprising the Contractor's Application for Payment, that the Work has progressed to the point indicated; that, to the best of the Architect's knowledge, information and belief, the quality of the Work is in accordance with the Contract Documents (subject to an evaluation of the Work for conformance with the Contract Documents upon Substantial Completion, to the results of any subsequent tests required by or performed under the Contract Documents, to minor deviations from the Contract Documents correctable prior to completion, and to any specific qualifications stated in the Certificate for Payment); and that the Contractor is entitled to payment in the amount certified. However, the issuance of a Certificate for Payment shall not be a representation that the Architect has made exhaustive or continuous on-site inspections to check the quality or quantity of the Work, has reviewed the construction means, methods, techniques, sequences or procedures, or has made any examination to ascertain how and for what purpose the Contractor has used the moneys paid on account of the Contract Sum.

1.1.10 The Architect shall be the interpreter of the requirements of the Contract Documents and the judge of the performance thereunder by both the Owner and Contractor. The Architect shall render interpretations necessary for the proper execution or progress of the Work with reasonable promptness on written request of either the Owner or the Contractor, and shall render written decisions, within a reasonable time, on all claims, disputes and other matters in question between the Owner and the Contractor relating to the execution or progress of the Work or the interpretation of the Contract Documents.

Figure 4.29

Architects should not publicly endorse a product, system, or service, or permit the use of their name or photograph to imply such endorsement. However an individual may be identified with any product, system, or service designed or developed by him or her.

The Client. Architects should preserve the confidences of their clients or employers. Architects should represent truthfully and clearly to prospective clients or employers their qualifications and capabilities to perform services. After being selected for their professional qualifications, architects should agree with the client or employer about the nature and extent of the services to be provided and the compensation.

An architect should not undertake any activity or employment, have any significant financial or other interest, or accept any contribution if it would reasonably appear that such activity, employment, interest, or contribution could compromise the individual's professional judgment or prevent him or her from serving the best interest of the client or employer.

Architects may make contributions of service or anything of value to endeavors they deem to be worthy, but not for the purpose of securing a commission or influencing personal engagement or employment.

The Profession and Building Industry. An architect should not attempt to obtain, offer to undertake, or accept a commission for which he knows another legally qualified individual or firm has been selected until he has evidence that the latter's agreement has been terminated and he gives the latter written notice that he is making such an attempt.

An architect should recognize the contribution of others engaged in the design and construction of the physical environment and should not knowingly make false statements about the professional work of those so engaged, nor maliciously injure or attempt to injure their prospects, practice, or employment positions.

An architect should not offer his or her services in a design competition except as provided in the Competition Code of the AIA.

Office Management

Employees. The main objective of office management is the control of procedures and staff to make a profit. There must be adequate incentive, communication, and leadership. Employees should know at the outset what kind of firm they are joining, what the individual's role will be, and what kind of future each can anticipate. Management should also promote an atmosphere of harmony and pride. Each member of the technical staff should have responsibilities equal to his or her capacities and potential. Promotion and responsibilities should be based solely on the employee's ability to perform.

A personnel policy manual outlining policies, benefits, and practices of the firm and an office procedure manual explaining filing systems, use of office forms, correspondence formats, and drafting standards should be prepared and maintained.

The two main organizational concepts (horizontal and vertical) have areas of overlap and may be combined, as the following definitions suggest.

1 *Horizontal Staff Organization.* The staff is composed of specialists, and each project passes from one specialist to another. This Type of organization lends itself to a large office doing substantial volumes of work.
2 *Vertical Staff Organization.* Each project is assigned to a team headed by a project architect, who is a generalist. Programming, design, and production of working drawings, structural, electrical, and mechanical specifications, and construction contract administration are handled cooperatively by the team.

Legal Structure. An architect may elect to assume one of several legal entities. Those usually chosen are as follows:

1 Sole proprietorship.
2 Partnership.
3 Corporation.
4 Joint ventures.

1 Sole Proprietorship. Legal responsibility remains with the architect. If he or she wishes to remain a sole proprietor, it is necessary to decide whether to maintain a small practice in which the individual is totally responsible or to hire employees and delegate responsibility.

Advantages. The architect maintains control of the design philosophy, the method of production, and the type of practice. He is responsible for the total performance of his office and is subject to income tax as an individual.

Disadvantages. It is more difficult to reorganize into a team. There is no continuity of ownership. The sole proprietor is personally liable for debts and liabilities incurred.

2 Partnership. The law relating to partnerships is extremely complex and varies from state to state. A partnership is formed by voluntary agreement between

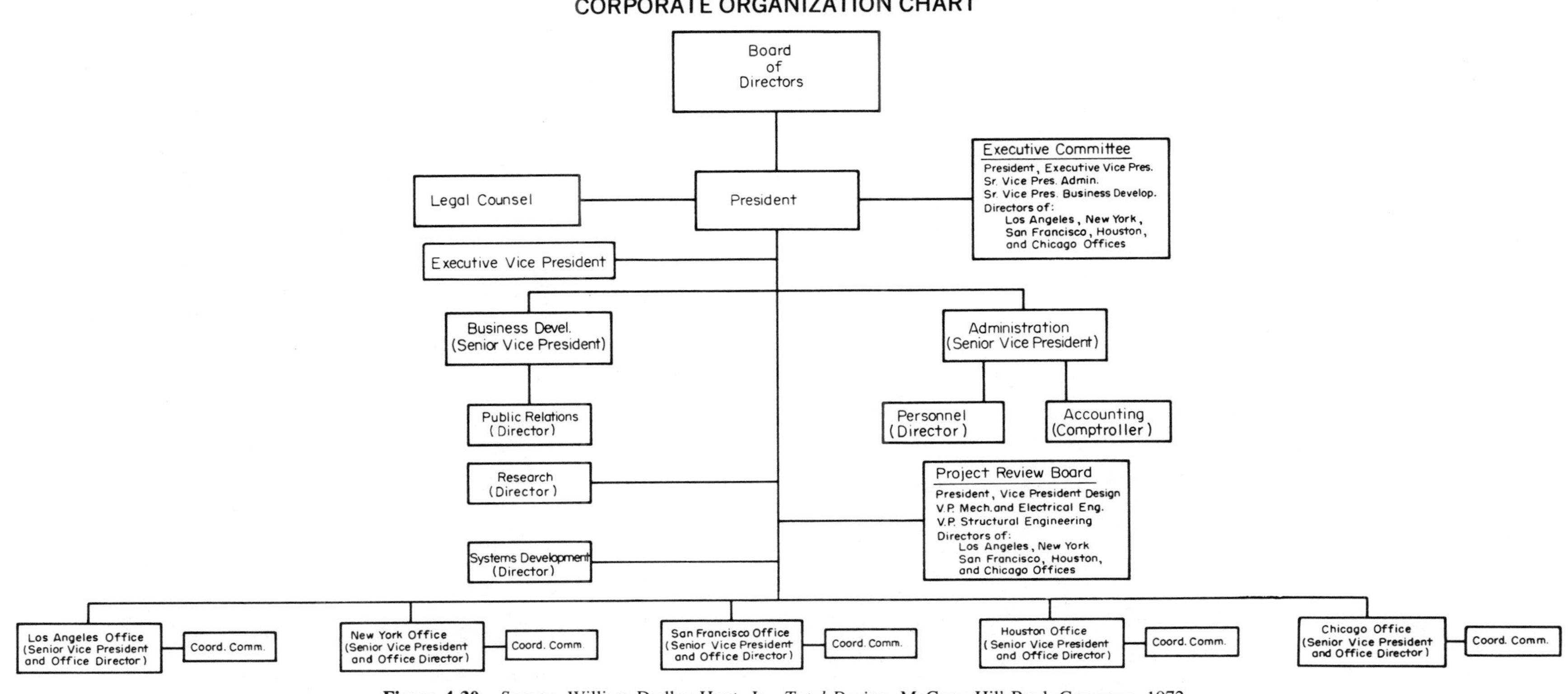

Figure 4.30 *Source*. William Dudley Hunt, Jr., *Total Design*, McGraw-Hill Book Company, 1972.

IRVINE COMPANY HEADQUARTERS
Newport Beach, California
Architect: William L. Pereira Associates
Photo: J. Shulman

the partners to share profits, to be liable jointly for debts and obligations, and to contribute a share of the capital of the partnership. Among the many variations possible in such agreements are the following: (*a*) a limited partner contributes capital but does not participate in management and is liable only for his or her own acts, and (*b*) junior partners have a smaller share of the profits, restricted authority in management, make little or no contribution to the capital, and often are not liable for partnership losses.

Advantages. An association of principals having various skills may develop a larger and more diverse organization than is possible under a sole proprietorship. Continuity of practice is more feasible.

Disadvantages. Partners are personally liable for all debts and liabilities, including liability of a partner for acts of other partners. Decisions of one partner are binding on the partners.

3 Corporation. These firms are controlled by the general business corporation law of the state of incorporation. Architects and other professionals may either be officers or employers of a corporation.

In a few states general business corporation law has allowed architects to incorporate as ordinary business corporations. The architect-shareholders are still personally liable for their own professional errors and omissions, although they may be immune to liability for professional projects with which they are not concerned.

Professional corporations allow incorporation by architects, engineers, and other professionals. In addition, professional associations have characteristics similar to those of corporations, thus are treated similarly for tax purposes.

Advantages. Incorporation offers a means of ownership in an organization for staff architects, better tax and retirement benefits, and continuity of practice. The corporation is able to obtain working capital through issuance of stock rather than by borrowing, and organizational efficiency is encouraged.

Disadvantages. Tax benefits are dubious in some states. A corporation is a more inviting target for lawsuits. Practicing as a corporation outside the state of incorporation may be more difficult. Relationships with clients may be less personal.

4 Joint Ventures. Usually a joint venture is formed for a specific project and terminated on its completion. The joint venture agreement must clearly describe limitations of activity of each party to the agreement.

3 CONSTRUCTION MANAGEMENT

The success of a project during construction depends on the general contractor and his employees, the subcontractors and their employees, the materials suppliers, the shop fabricators, the building inspectors, and all the others who must cooperate and provide their particular expertise. All activities must be carried out expediently, and instructions and decisions must be documented to provide a clear, full understanding for all participants.

No two construction projects are exactly alike. A basic understanding of field construction processes, construction management, project administration, and job procedures is essential in dealing with the situations encountered during construction. Numerous attempts have been made to establish rational standards to be applied in resolving problems that affect quality, time, and cost during construction. Each situation that arises is slightly but distinctly different from others, and many rulings thought to have established precedents have been reversed by higher court decisions. Furthermore, differing individual state statutes have resulted in a lack of uniformity among court decisions on similar matters in different states. An architect must simply follow the general conditions of the construction contract according to local laws, AIA or ARA ethics, and common sense.

Details and Instructions

The general conditions stipulate that the architect must furnish written interpretations in the form of drawings or other documents for proper work execution. This information must be supplied promptly to avoid contractor claims for delay of work completion. Such instructions and clarifications are commonly transmitted to the contractor as field sketches and do not result in either additions or deductions to the contract sum or time. Frequently these interpretations are relatively minor, being given in the field through conversation with the contractor or the superintendent. Important interpretations should always be given or confirmed in writing. A considerable addition or deduction to the contract sum or time must be authorized by a written change order and approved by the owner.

The architect can use a standardized field order form to issue minor interpretations or changes (not involving a change in contract sum or time) published by the AIA. This document can be expanded to authorize the contractor to proceed immediately, even though a change in the contract sum may result, by deleting ''approvals required.'' A subsequent change order covering the work in question must also be issued.

All field sketches, orders, bulletins, revisions, and so on, constitute amendments to the working drawings, the specifications, or both. They must be recorded upon implementation and incorporated into the final record drawings.

Drawings

A project is seldom completed exactly as shown on the original contract documents. Hence drawings are required for purposes of instruction and to indicate changes agreed to during construction.

Record Drawings. Record drawings (once called ''as-built'') are revised construction drawings showing major changes made during the construction process; these are furnished by the contractor to the architect.

It is the contractor's responsibility to maintain at the site copies of all contract documents, marked to record all changes made during construction. The architect may provide the owner with a set of reproducible record drawings showing all significant changes made during construction. Such record drawings are particularly useful if future alterations or additions to the project are contemplated.

AIA documents recognize that the only parties thoroughly familiar with the actual construction are the contractor, the contractor's employees, and the subcontractors. Therefore its general conditions document requires that the contractor deliver to the architect (for the owner) a complete set of marked-up drawings. The drawings are also the owner's record of construction, including modifications reported by the contractor's field information and notes.

Shop Drawings. Preparation of shop drawings, showing specific items in detail with exact dimensions of every component including finishes, is left to the contractor, subcontractor, manufacturers, suppliers, or distributors. ''Shop drawings'' may be drawings, diagrams, illustrations, schedules, performance charts, brochures, or similar forms of data.

Submission. When shop drawings are required by the contract documents or during the course of construction, the contractor must review them, stamp them with his or her approval, and submit them promptly to the architect in proper sequence to prevent delay in the work of the general contract or the subcontractor. Shop drawings must contain the following information:

1 Date.
2 Name of project.
3 Architect.
4 Contractor.
5 Originating subcontractor.
6 Manufacturer or supplier.
7 Work for which the submission is being made.
8 Specification section.
9 Locations at which the materials or equipment are to be installed.
10 A space for the architect's review stamp.

Processing is simplified if shop drawings are submitted to the architect as reproducible transparencies, printed at any state of review, approval, or change. This procedure eliminates redrawing, as well as possible errors of omission through failure to record comments or revisions on all copies of submitted drawings.

Manufacturer's descriptive data on catalog sheets for materials, equipment, and fixtures should be submitted in multiple copies; some are returned to the contractor, and some retained by the architect. Such data must include dimensions, performance characteristics and capacities, wiring diagrams and controls, and schedules. If more than one product or model is described on the sheet, the contractor should clearly identify the item that is desired.

The contractor must obtain and distribute required prints of shop drawings from and to the subcontractors and material suppliers before and after final approval.

The architect should maintain an office log indicating dates of receipt of shop drawings, return of approved drawings to the contractor, and ultimate delivery of materials to the project.

WEINSTEIN RESIDENCE
Old Westbury, New York
Architects: Richard Meier & Associates
Photo: E. Stoller ESTO

Approval. The architect must ensure that changes are not made on reproducibles that have been stamped with his or her approval.

The contractor approves and submits the shop drawings to the architect, thereby signifying that all field measurements, field construction criteria, materials, catalog numbers, and similar data of each shop drawing, with the requirements of the work and the contract documents, have been or will be determined, verified, and coordinated by the architect.

It is the architect's responsibility to promptly review shop drawings submitted by the contractor. It is easier for the architect to review the drawings if the contractor draws a heavy line around proposed deviations or adds a note specifically requesting approval of these items.

The architect approves shop drawings only for conformity with the design concept of the project and the information in the contract documents. Approval of a separate or specific item does not necessarily mean approval of an entire assembly of which the approved item is a part. At no time should the architect approve shop drawings for correctness of measurements, field construction, criteria, and so on, since that is the contractor's task.

When time is critical, "promptness" must be defined in terms of the number of working days necessary to complete the work in question. A loose definition may lead to disputes.

After making necessary revisions, the contractor must resubmit the required number of corrected shop drawings until approval has been secured. To avoid confusion, the contractor must direct special attention (in writing or as drawings) to revisions other than those based on corrections requested by the architect in previous submissions.

Approval of shop drawings by the architect does not relieve the contractor of responsibility for any deviation from the contract documents or for errors or omissions unless the contractor has informed the architect in writing of such deviations at the time of submission and the architect has given written approval. The architect's approval must be obtained before any work requiring a shop drawing submission is begun.

JOHN DEERE LIMITED
Grimsby, Ontario
Architects: Neigh Owen Rowland & Roy
Photo: Panda

Changes in Contract Sum or Time

The general conditions require that a change in the work or adjustments in the contract sum or time be authorized by a change order, which may be initiated by the owner, the contractor, or the architect. The document itself has space for a complete description of the change, modifications in the contract sum, time for completion, if any, and a summary of the contract to date. The change order summary itemizes change orders previously approved by the owner, as well as additions, deductions, and net change in the total contract sum. The amounts of approved change orders should be shown on the contractor's application for payment.

If the contract contains a provision for cash allowances, the contract sum will be adjusted accordingly by change orders. The amount will include handling costs on the site, labor, installation costs, overhead, profit, and any other expenses incurred by the contractor that effect increases to the original allowance.

Change orders originating with the owner are usually to increase the contract through addition of an item or items not previously considered. The architect is asked to provide detailed design drawings and specifications for this item, and he is paid an extra fee for the work. When the owner has approved the drawings, the architect advises the owner to accept the contractor's proposal and promptly issues a change order describing the work, and the amount and time to be added to the contract. The change order, having been reviewed, checked, and signed by the architect, is then routed to the contractor for signature. The final, legal authorization requires the owner's signature. Subsequently the change order is returned to the contractor for implementation.

Even the most expert professional cannot anticipate and describe every item required in contemporary building construction. Developments making possible improvements in design aspects, construction details, or use of materials are almost certain to occur as the work proceeds. The owner, as previously stated, may wish to

"EXTRA WORK" DEFINED

For the purpose of this extra work order only, the term "cost" is defined to include the actual cost, less any discounts allowed, of all subcontracts, material, and direct labor used on the extra work, including payroll taxes, health and welfare and vacation fund contributions, workmen's compensation and other insurance premiums which are measured by payroll, sales taxes, cartage, equipment rental, and other direct costs incurred in performing the extra work. The term "cost", however, excludes supervisory work (other than working foremen), rent, utilities, and transportation provided by vehicles owned by us.

FORM 111

EXTRA WORK CONFIRMATION

TO: Smith Construction Co.
(Contractor's Name)
6207 Maple Blvd.
(Contractor's Address)
Compton, California 90261
(City, State and Zip)

PROJECT: Jones Residence
(Name)
1163 Sierra Blvd.
(Address)
Los Angeles, Calif.
(City, State And Zip)

FROM: Martin Jones
(Name)
1101 Logan Drive, Apt. 1
(Address)
Los Angeles, California 90064
(City, State and Zip)

This memorandum confirms the conversation of 5-12-67 (date) between Martin Jones (owner or his agent) and Smith Construction Co. (contractor or his agent) wherein we were instructed to perform the following work on the above described project which is not included in our basic contract and is an "extra": Change living room window to (Describe Work Requested To Be Done)
6^{0} x 7^{0} sliding door

IT IS UNDERSTOOD THAT THE METHOD OF COMPUTING PAYMENT WILL BE:
[INITIAL ONE ONLY]

_______ **LUMP SUM:** $_______ (Total amount to be added to the contract price for the cost of the extra work)

_______ **COST, PLUS PERCENTAGE:** In addition to all other amounts payable under the contract, we shall be paid the cost of the extra work (as defined on reverse) plus 10 (Percent for overhead) % overhead plus 10 (Percent for profit) % profit.

_______ **COST, PLUS FIXED FEE:** The price to be paid us for the extra work will be the cost of the extra work (as defined on reverse) plus a fixed fee of $_______ (Amount of fixed fee)

_______ **IN ACCORDANCE WITH BASIC CONTRACT:** The price to be paid us for performing the extra work shall be determined in accordance with the provisions of our basic contract.

IT IS UNDERSTOOD THAT THE TIME FOR PAYMENT WILL BE:
[INITIAL ONE ONLY]

_______ **PRIOR TO START OF EXTRA WORK:** Extra work to be done when payment actually received by contractor.

_______ **UPON COMPLETION OF EXTRA WORK:** Payment will be made in full when the extra work has been satisfactorily completed.

_______ **PROGRESSIVELY:** Payments will be made as the work is done and will be made concurrently with payment dates under the basic contract payment schedule.

_______ **IN ACCORDANCE WITH THE BASIC CONTRACT:** The time of payment for the extra work shall be as provided for in the basic contract.

Please advise immediately if this memorandum fails, in any way, to confirm your understanding of the conversation.

DATE: May 12, 1967
(Date Confirmation Signed)

FIRM NAME: SMITH CONSTRUCTION CO.
(Name of Contractor)

By Jim Smith
(Signature of Contractor or Authorized Agent)

Figure 4.31 *Source. Building News,* State of California.

include features that had not been considered before the contract was executed. During construction, for example, the architect might be advised by the engineer that a change from one type of air handling unit to another that is immediately available would improve the quality of the air conditioning system and reduce construction time appreciably. The architect would request the owner's authorization to issue a change order to increase the contract sum while reducing contract time. The owner would comply willingly because he stands to receive a direct benefit from the change.

If the change were required because of an oversight (error or omission to the contract documents) by the architect's or his consultants, the architect might be liable for the added cost.

If the contractor were unable to secure an air handling unit named in the contract within time alloted for completion, he could request a change order to substitute a more expensive unit, possibly incurring liability for the extra cost. A change order would be issued reflecting change in work but no change to contract time.

SEVEN CONTINENTS RESTAURANT
O'Hare International Airport, Chicago
Architect: Gertrude Lempp Kerbis for the Office of C. F. Murphy & Associates
Photo: Office

Hardware

Hardware covers a wide variety of fastenings, fittings, and equipment made from various metals and plastics and finished in various ways.

Selection. Hardware selection is one of the earliest decisions to be made, particularly when metal doors and windows are specified, even though finish hardware may not be applied until the latter stages of construction. The prime considerations are operating characteristics and particular requirements. The selection of material and finish depends on architectural treatment, decorative scheme, weathering, and product durability.

Hardware Consultant. The architect may wish to hire a hardware consultant or to seek advise from a manufacturer's representative before writing these specifications. A good consultant is usually able to obtain desired results simply, economically, satisfactorily, avoiding unnecessary delays and complications and remaining independent of pressures from manufacturers to promote their products. He or she is familiar with new products and modifications, manufacturing and warehousing facilities in various parts of the country, availability of materials, and delivery times. A consultant can also obtain feedback from previous jobs about performance characteristics of different brands.

A manufacturer's representative can point out definite savings that can be achieved by making slight changes in the specifications. In many instances, these changes may have no effect on the design and operation of the project and may be acceptable to both architect and owner. Additionally, they may speed up the work, contributing to lower ultimate cost.

Hardware List. The contract specification requires the contractor to submit a hardware list to the architect for approval, identifying the manufacturer's name and catalog number for each item. It is generally submitted within 30 days of award of contract.

When the architect has reviewed the list and has made necessary changes, the hardware is assembled and packaged, with each package distinctly marked for intended use and the locations indicated on the hardware schedule.

Upon delivery of the items, the supplier must furnish a complete duplicate list for checking, clearly marked to correspond to the marking on each package and giving locations of openings and catalog numbers. The contractor is responsible for the delivery of all required hardware to the site, regardless of any omissions over which he had no control.

Hardware Schedule. This is an itemized schedule on a contract drawing showing for each assembly the quantity and type of hardware (e.g., ''BB'' = ball-bearing hinges, ''NRP'' = nonremovable pin). ''Assembly'' refers to all the items required to install, for example, a single door—hinges, door pulls, closers, threshold, lockset, doorstop, and door closer. A number corresponding to the hardware schedule number on the drawings is assigned to each assembly, and when the manufacturer packages all items, the assembly number appears on the outside.

Rough Hardware. This category includes utility items not finished for appearance but mill-fastened or galvanized, such as items used in wood framing, fastenings, and hangers of many types, shapes, sizes. Examples are casement and special window hardware, sliding and folding door supports, fastenings for screens, storm sashes, shades, venetian blinds, and awnings.

Template Hardware. Items that are to be fastened to metal parts, such as jambs or doors, are called template hardware. Sizes, shapes, location, and size of holes are made to conform accurately to the prepared drawings, to ensure the ultimate fit of all associated parts.

Finish Hardware. This usually refers to cabinet hardware, knobs, catches, closers, window fastenings, casement sash adjusters, door holders, automatic exit devices, and lock-operating trim such as escutcheon plates, strike plates, knob rosettes, push-bars, kickplates, hinges, door pulls, locks, and locksets, that are exposed to view. Most such hardware has a finish added to the parent metal: enameling or lacquering, highly polished or medium polished, satin or matte, or oxidized or anodized plating in metals such as chrome, brass, copper, and aluminum. Wrought, cast, and stamped parts are available for different items.

Government standards define finishes, characteristics, sizes, dimensions, spacing of holes, and materials for many items; these publications are useful in identifying and ensuring proper fit of hardware items to the parts to which they will be mounted.

Correspondence

Months of planning and preparation of contract documents receive the final test during the construction phase. A good way to establish effective lines of communication is to schedule a meeting directly after execution of the owner/contractor agreement, to be attended by the owner, the general contractor, the project architect(s),

HAMPTON COLISEUM
Hampton, Virginia
Architects: Odell Associates Inc.
Photo: G. H. Schenck, Jr.

the structural, mechanical, and electrical engineers, the architect's field representative, and the owner's on-site representative (''clerk-of-works'') if any, to acquaint all parties with administrative procedures to be followed during project construction.

The architect is responsible for documenting all decisions reached at meetings with the owner and for transmitting all conference notes, project records, project statistics, cost information, and so on, to the owner and the consultants affected.

Conference notes (resulting in a project record or confirmation notice) should be taken at all meetings, noting date, location, names, and a brief summary of key decisions. A conference should always be based on a written agenda or on a clear understanding by all parties of what is to be decided. Ideally, conferences should end in conclusions.

Communication and recording of basic decisions is imperative if misunderstandings are to be avoided during this stage of development. All documents leaving the architect's office should be accompanied by a transmittal letter describing the material and giving the reason for transmittal.

Field Change Authorization. A *field change authorization* is issued by the project architect when a field condition requires immediate resolution. If possible, a reasonable maximum cost for such changes, which may not be exceeded by any field change authorization, should be agreed on at the outset. If the cost appears to exceed the established maximum, the architect should request an estimate of cost and should issue subsequently an instruction bulletin.

TRANSMITTAL LETTER

AIA DOCUMENT G810

PROJECT:
(name, address)

ARCHITECT'S PROJECT NO:

DATE:

TO:

ATTN:

If enclosures are not as noted, please inform us immediately.

If checked below, please:

( ) Acknowledge receipt of enclosures.
( ) Return enclosures to us.

WE TRANSMIT:

( ) herewith ( ) under separate cover via ____________
( ) in accordance with your request ____________

FOR YOUR:

( ) approval ( ) distribution to parties ( ) information
( ) review & comment ( ) record
( ) use ( ) ____________

THE FOLLOWING:

( ) Drawings ( ) Shop Drawing Prints ( ) Samples
( ) Specifications ( ) Shop Drawing Reproducibles ( ) Product Literature
( ) Change Order ( ) ____________

COPIES	DATE	REV. NO.	DESCRIPTION	ACTION CODE

ACTION CODE
A. Action indicated on item transmitted
B. No action required
C. For signature and return to this office
D. For signature and forwarding as noted below under REMARKS
E. See REMARKS below

REMARKS ____________

COPIES TO: (with enclosures)
☐
☐
☐
☐
☐

BY:

AIA DOCUMENT G810 • TRANSMITTAL LETTER • APRIL 1970 EDITION • AIA® •
THE AMERICAN INSTITUTE OF ARCHITECTS, 1785 MASSACHUSETTS AVENUE, N.W., WASHINGTON, D.C. 20036

ONE PAGE

Figure 4.32

ARCHITECT'S FIELD ORDER

AIA DOCUMENT G708

OWNER ☐
ARCHITECT ☐
CONSULTANTS ☐
CONTRACTOR ☐
FIELD ☐
OTHER ☐

PROJECT:
(name, address)

FIELD ORDER NO:

OWNER:

DATE:

TO (Contractor)

ARCHITECT'S PROJECT NO:
CONTRACT FOR:

CONTRACT DATE:

You are hereby directed to execute promptly this Field Order which interprets the Contract Documents or orders minor changes in the Work without change in Contract Sum or Contract Time.

If you consider that a change in Contract Sum or Contract Time is required, please submit your itemized proposal to the Architect immediately and before proceeding with this Work. If your proposal is found to be satisfactory and in proper order, this Field Order will in that event be superseded by a Change Order.

Description: (Here insert a written description of the interpretation or change)

Attachments: (Here insert listing of attached documents that support description)

ARCHITECT:

BY:

AIA DOCUMENT G708 • ARCHITECT'S FIELD ORDER • APRIL 1970 EDITION • AIA® • © 1970
THE AMERICAN INSTITUTE OF ARCHITECTS, 1735 NEW YORK AVE., NW, WASHINGTON, D.C. 20006

ONE PAGE

Figure 4.33

FORM 112

CONVERSATION CONFIRMER

FROM: ____________________ (Name)

____________________ (Address)

____________________ (City, State and Zip)

PROJECT: ____________________ (Name)

____________________ (Address)

____________________ (City, State and Zip)

TO: ____________________ (Name)

____________________ (Address)

____________________ (City, State and Zip)

This memorandum confirms the conversation of ______ (date of conversation) between ______ (insert name)

and ______ (insert name) in which it was said:

____________________ (Describe The Conversation)

____

____

____

Date: ______ (Date Memo Written)

Firm Name: ____________________

By: ____________________ (Signature of person sending confirmer)

FORM 112 — Published By **BUILDING NEWS, INC.**, 3055 Overland Ave., Los Angeles, Calif. 90034 — (213) 870-9871 © 1967

Figure 4.34

Price Quotations and Instruction Bulletins. This material is approved by the client and issued by the project architect. The bulletin is a direct authorization for the contractor to proceed with the work. It must be followed by a change order reflecting the adjustment in contract sum and time. Often, several bulletins are covered by a single change order.

A request for estimate (price quotations) is used when necessary to make a revision that will add to or subtract from the contract price. It should be supported by drawings, revised specifications, or a written description of the proposed change, indicating precisely its extent and scope.

A request for estimate is *not* a directive to proceed with the change.

The project architect issues a request for estimate to the contractor, who promptly returns estimated price quotations for the work in question. The architect then recommends either acceptance or rejection of the estimate to the client. Upon the client's approval of the quotation(s), the architect issues a bulletin for execution of the work.

Notice of Clarification. This document is issued and used by the project architect to make substitutions in the specifications and/or drawings and modifications when no increase or decrease in construction cost results.

Project Field Report. On a major project, a field representative attends all field meetings in the architect's

METRO TORONTO WEST REGIONAL DETENTION CENTER
Etobicoke, Ontario
Architect: Moffat, Moffat & Kinoshita
Photo: Karl Sliva

place. As agent, the field representative makes periodic visits to the site, receives and analyzes field tests and reports, checks the progress of record drawings, interprets drawings and specifications for the general contractor, prepares punch lists containing items to be corrected, and maintains a log of project activities (results and findings) during his or her visits in a project field report.

Project Record Notice. If a change in scope, budget, or schedule is documented in a project record notice, the architect must direct a copy, as confirmation of the change, to the client, the consultant, the contractor, and other parties affected. All project record notices should be numbered consecutively to simplify checking for completeness.

Filing System. The project architect is responsible for maintaining a complete file of the project record notices (and their proper distribution). The ideal filing system is subject oriented: each subject or activity, from air conditioning equipment to final inspections, is filed separately. An efficient retrieval format is essential. Such a system is difficult to set up and maintain because of the number of subjects involved in construction projects; it is impossible to predetermine the subjects that will require individual files because numerous letters, memos, and reports dealing with more than one subject will be filed. Under "Construction," for example, go all correspondence and other information pertaining to the construction phase, shop drawings, inspection reports, and project records.

The filing designation should be shown on all documents, letters, memoranda, and so on, since this facilitates filing of office copies and may encourage respondents to use the correct filing number.

Payments

Application for Payment. Under the AIA general conditions, upon completion of each phase of the work the contractor must submit to the architect an application for payment, as well as receipts or other vouchers showing payments made for materials and labor, including payments to subcontractors. Submission must be made at least 10 days before each payment date.

The contractor must also submit a schedule of values for various portions of completed work, attached to the first application for payment. The schedule of values represents the total contract sum, broken down into categories to facilitate payments to subcontractors, supported by all verification data, and prepared in a format requested by the architect or agreed to by architect and contractor. Each item should include its proper share of overhead and profit.

The contractor is required to show the total dollar amount of work completed to date, the dollar value of stored materials, the amount of retainage, the total of all previous payments (if any), and the amount of current payment requested, giving dollar payments and percentages for each portion. Such a submission, if accurate, greatly aids the architect in deciding work value. Submission of both application for payment and schedule of values reduces the possibility of errors. The architect then transmits these documents to the owner for acceptance and payment.

The amount of the payment accords with the value of the work performed, with the amount of retained percentage deducted. For example, suppose that the total value of earthwork is $80,000 and the contractor claims 50% completion of that section of work. If the agreed-upon retainage is 10%, the contractor is eligible for half of $80,000 less 10%, or $36,000. These amounts must be carefully established to avoid possible loss to the owner or the contractor. The architect may be held liable if his failure to determine accurately the value of work completed results in a loss to the owner, the contractor, or both.

Certificate for Payment. Having made an application for payment, the architect issues a certificate for payment in the amount due, less retainage. Acceptance of work or materials not in accordance with the contract documents is not implied by certificates issued, payments made to the contractor, nor use or occupancy by the owner. Certificates of payment issued on a basis other than contract stipulation must bear a notation of the owner's consent. If a surety bond is in effect, the architect must determine whether the surety's consent is necessary, as well.

The architect's signature on the application and certificate for payment tells the owner that the architect has approved payments to the contractor in the amount indicated, according to the construction contract. In turn, the contractor must swear that all payments (for which previous certificates were issued and monies received) to subcontractors and materials suppliers have been made.

If payments to be made are for materials delivered that are stored on or off site but not incorporated in the work, the architect may require the contractor to submit bills of sale establishing owner's title to such material to protect the owner's interest. (Such payments are not made if the contract calls only for payments of "work-incorporated" materials.) Payments for stored materials should not exceed 75% of actual value. Furthermore, the contractor must acquire and pay for insurance, and the materials should be periodically checked.

Payments to subcontractors must be made after the contractor receives payment from the owner. The contractor must pay each subcontractor an amount equal to percentage of completion, less percentage retained from payments to the contractor. Subcontractors must make similar payments to their respective subcontractors and workers.

Work-Completion Application. When a project nears completion, the contractor sends the architect a statement claiming substantial completion. Then the architect makes a semifinal inspection to determine whether the construction is indeed sufficiently completed in accordance with the contract documents, so that the owner can occupy or use the project as intended. The architect prepares a certificate of substantial completion for approval and acceptance by both contractor and owner, attaching a

CERTIFICATE OF SUBSTANTIAL COMPLETION

AIA DOCUMENT G704

OWNER ☐
ARCHITECT ☐
CONTRACTOR ☐
FIELD ☐
OTHER

PROJECT:
(name, address)

ARCHITECT:

ARCHITECT'S PROJECT NUMBER:

TO (Owner)

CONTRACTOR:
CONTRACT FOR:

CONTRACT DATE:

DATE OF ISSUANCE:

PROJECT OR DESIGNATED AREA SHALL INCLUDE:

The Work performed under this Contract has been reviewed and found to be substantially complete. The Date of Substantial Completion is hereby established as
which is also the date of commencement of all warranties and guarantees required by the Contract Documents.

DEFINITION OF DATE OF SUBSTANTIAL COMPLETION

The Date of Substantial Completion of the Work or designated portion thereof is the Date certified by the Architect when construction is sufficiently complete, in accordance with the Contract Documents, so the Owner may occupy the Work or designated portion thereof for the use for which it is intended.

A list of items to be completed or corrected, prepared by the Contractor and verified and amended by the Architect, is appended hereto. The failure to include any items on such list does not alter the responsibility of the Contractor to complete all Work in accordance with the Contract Documents.

ARCHITECT BY DATE

The Contractor will complete or correct the Work on the list of items appended hereto within days from the above Date of Substantial Completion.

CONTRACTOR BY DATE

The Owner accepts the Work or designated portion thereof as substantially complete and will assume full possession thereof at (time) on (date).

OWNER BY DATE

The responsibilities of the Owner and the Contractor for maintenance, heat, utilities and insurance shall be as follows:
(NOTE — Owner's and Contractor's legal and insurance counsel should determine and review insurance requirements and coverage)

AIA DOCUMENT G704 • CERTIFICATE OF SUBSTANTIAL COMPLETION • APRIL 1970 EDITION • AIA® ONE PAGE

Figure 4.35

CONTRACTOR'S AFFIDAVIT OF PAYMENT OF DEBTS AND CLAIMS

AIA Document G706

OWNER ☐
ARCHITECT ☐
CONTRACTOR ☐
SURETY ☐
OTHER

TO (Owner)

ARCHITECT'S PROJECT NO:

CONTRACT FOR:

CONTRACT DATE:

PROJECT:
(name, address)

State of:

County of:

The undersigned, pursuant to Article 9 of the General Conditions of the Contract for Construction, AIA Document A201, hereby certifies that, except as listed below, he has paid in full or has otherwise satisfied all obligations for all materials and equipment furnished, for all work, labor, and services performed, and for all known indebtedness and claims against the Contractor for damages arising in any manner in connection with the performance of the Contract referenced above for which the Owner or his property might in any way be held responsible.

EXCEPTIONS: (If none, write "None". If required by the Owner, the Contractor shall furnish bond satisfactory to the Owner for each exception.)

SUPPORTING DOCUMENTS ATTACHED HERETO:

1. Consent of Surety to Final Payment. Whenever Surety is involved, Consent of Surety is required. AIA DOCUMENT G707, CONSENT OF SURETY, may be used for this purpose.
   Indicate attachment: (yes) (no).

The following supporting documents should be attached hereto if required by the Owner:

1. Contractor's Release or Waiver of Liens, conditional upon receipt of final payment.
2. Separate Releases or Waivers of Liens from Subcontractors and material and equipment suppliers, to the extent required by the Owner, accompanied by a list thereof.
3. Contractor's Affidavit of Release of Liens (AIA DOCUMENT G706A).

CONTRACTOR:

Address:

BY:

Subscribed and sworn to before me this
day of 19

Notary Public:

My Commission Expires:

AIA DOCUMENT G706 • CONTRACTOR'S AFFIDAVIT OF PAYMENT OF DEBTS AND CLAIMS • APRIL 1970 EDITION — ONE PAGE

Figure 4.36

list of items that the contractor must complete or correct. (If the architect's inspection discloses that the project is not, in fact, substantially completed, he notifies the contractor. A subsequent inspection is scheduled, for which the contractor prepares a revised list of items to be completed or corrected.)

Caution must be exercised to ascertain that the work conforms with the definition of substantial completion in the contract documents before a substantial completion certificate is issued.

Final Payment. The contractor's application for final payment is made on the same form used for the progress payments. Additional requirements include the submission to the architect of the following material:

1 An affidavit that all payrolls, bills for materials and equipment, and other indebtedness connected with the work for which the owner might be responsible, have been paid or otherwise satisfied.
2 A document indicating that consent of surety to final payment has been secured.

After the contractor has submitted the final application for payment, supported by all required documents called for in the general conditions, the architect issues the final certificate for payment. Before doing this, the architect should make a final check to determine that the following conditions have been fulfilled:

1 The degree of work completion required by the contract has been reached.
2 The owner's interests have been protected by the filing of liens provided in the general condition.
3 Accounts between owner and contractor have been adjusted to reflect all additions and deductions to the original contract sum.
4 Written guarantees and certificates of inspection have been delivered to the owner.

Failure To Pay. If the architect fails to issue a certificate for payment for any reason attributable to the contractor but not to a particular subcontractor, the contractor must pay the subcontractor immediately following normal issuance date of the certificate for payment, for the subcontractor's completed work, less retainage.

The architect may furnish to any subcontractor information regarding percentages of completion certified to the contractor for work completed by such subcontractor. For example, if the contractor refuses to comply with certain aspects of the contract relating to concrete work, the architect may refuse to issue a certificate for payment until the work is corrected. However the plumbing contractor is entitled to be paid for his completed work.

4 THE METRIC SYSTEM

Weights and measures may be ranked among the necessaries of life to every individual of human society. They enter into the economical arrangements and daily concerns of every family. They are necessary to every occupation of human industry; to the distribution and security of every species of property; to every transaction of trade and commerce; to the labors of the husbandman; to the ingenuity of the artificer; to the studies of the philosopher; to the researches of the antiquarian, to the navigation of the mariner, and the marches of the soldier; to all the exchanges of peace, and all the operations of war. The knowledge of them, as in established use, is among the first elements of education, and is often learned by those who learn nothing else, not even to read and write. This knowledge is riveted in the memory by the habitual application of it to the employments of men throughout life.

JOHN QUINCY ADAMS
Report to the Congress, 1821

How Our Customary System Grew

Most people do not think of a system of weights and measures as a language. Yet the words and symbols for length, mass, time, temperature, and so forth, allow individuals to communicate with one another in terms of quantity. This knowledge is so vital that it is often learned by people who never even learn to read or write.

The customary system of measurement used today in the United States dates back to colonial times, when measuring standards differed from country to country, and sometimes from town to town and from trade to trade. There was great confusion, promoted by a jumble of poorly defined units.

The measuring standards we inherited from the British stemmed from a hodgepodge of Anglo-Saxon, Roman, and Norman weights and measures, based largely on folkways. For instance, early records indicate that an inch was once defined as "three barleycorns, round and dry" when laid together, and a yard was roughly the

TRAMWAY TERMINAL
Squaw Valley, California
Architects: Shepley Bulfinch Richardson & Abbott
Photo: J. Shulman

length of a man's arm. But the English had started trying to set up certain uniform standards as far back as the twelfth century. The yard of Henry II differs from the one we use today by only about one part in a thousand.

In his first message in 1790, President Washington told Congress that it was time for America to set its own standards of weights and measures. Secretary of State Thomas Jefferson submitted two plans, but neither was adopted despite prodding by the president.

About this time, the French statesman Tallyrand persuaded his government to adopt a new system of weights and measures. The result was the decimal-based ''metric'' system. Its concept had been developed in 1670 by a vicar named Gabriel Mouton, who defined the meter as a specific fraction of the earth's circumference. The scheme was radically different from any of the commonly used measurement methods of the day. This metric system is wholly rational, quite simple, and internally consistent. It is the system that most of the world has come to recognize and adopt.

While France, followed by other nations, adopted the metric system, the debate about standards continued in the United States. In 1816 President Madison reminded Congress that the lack of uniformity in weights and measures represented unfinished business, and John Quincy Adams submitted a comprehensive report on the desirability of the metric system in 1821. No action was taken, however. In 1866 Congress passed an act making lawful the use of metric in the United States, but a national changeover was not implemented. Nevertheless, ever since 1893, our customary fundamental standards of length and mass have been defined as fractions of metric units, the meter and the kilogram, respectively. For example, an inch is officially 25.4 millimeters.

The most important influence on the attitude of Americans toward the metric system has been the spread of this system of measurement throughout the world. By 1921, when Japan began converting to the metric system, it had been adopted by about half the countries of the world. Almost all the other nonmetric countries have since followed suit. England switched in 1965 to the metric system, Canada and Australia converted in 1970. Now more than 90% of the world population lives in nations that are metric or committed to the metric system.

The metric system is more extensively used in the United States than most people realize. Doctors, druggists, and scientists use it for virtually all their measurements. In 1957, the year of the launching of Sputnik, the U.S. Army adopted the metric system for its weaponry. Then in 1970 the National Aeronautics and Space Administration became the first federal agency to adopt the system. In addition, metric measurements and practices have been increasingly used in certain manufacturing industries.

The Logical Metric System

Today the metric system is known as the SI system (for *Système International d'Unités*). It is simpler than any other scheme of measurement that has been used. There are only seven base units for different types of measurement.

1 The unit of *length* is the meter.
2 The unit of *mass* is the kilogram.
3 The unit of *temperature* is the kelvin.
4 The unit of *time* is the second.
5 The unit of *electric current* is the ampere.
6 The unit of *light intensity* is the candela.
7 The unit of *amount of substance* is the mole.

All other SI units are derived from these seven. For example, a newton, the unit of *force,* is expressed in terms of meters, kilograms, and seconds. A pascal, the unit of *pressure,* is one newton per square meter. And so on. Although the metric system was designed to fill all the needs of scientists and engineers, laymen need know and use only a few simple parts of it. In any event, four of the SI base units (second, ampere, candela, and mole) are already used in our customary system.

The SI is based on the decimal system and follows a consistent name scheme. This makes for easier and more accurate calculation. Multiples and submultiples are always related to powers of 10. Thus SI uses the prefixes "deka" (10 times), "hecto" (100 times), "kilo" (1000 times), "mega" (a million times), and so on; going in the other direction, we have "deci" ($^1/_{10}$), "centi" ($^1/_{100}$), "milli" ($^1/_{1000}$), "micro" ($^1/_{1,000,000}$), and so on.

It is plain that SI is easier to learn than the system of inches and pounds. Schools could well use the time now spent in teaching this system, with all the associated fractions and complicated calculations, for other subjects. Also, because metric is easier to use, it saves time and errors. Computations are much simpler. There is only one unit for each quantity, and the relationship between the units is simple. If everyone used a common measurement language, scientists, engineers, businessmen, educators, and government officials throughout the world would be able to communicate more freely and with less misunderstanding.

Definitions of Units

The meter was the original fundamental unit of the metric system, and all units of length and capacity were to be derived directly from the meter, which was intended to be equal to one ten-millionth of the earth's quadrant. Furthermore, it was originally planned that the unit of mass, the kilogram, was to be identical with the mass of a cubic decimeter of water at its maximum density. The units of length and mass are now defined independently of these conceptions.

In October 1960 the Eleventh General (International) Conference on Weights and Measures redefined the meter as 1,650,763.73 wavelengths of the orange-red radiation in vacuum of krypton-86 corresponding to the unperturbed transition between the $2p_{10}$ and $5d_5$ levels.

The kilogram is independently defined as the mass of a particular platinum-iridium standard, the International Prototype Kilogram, which is kept at the International Bureau of Weights and Measures in Sevres, France.

The liter has been defined as a cubic decimeter since October 1964.

Thus all metric standards and measurements of length, area, and volume are based on the meter.

Length. A *meter* (m) is a unit of length equal to 1,650,763.73 wavelengths in a vacuum of the orange-red radiation, corresponding to the transition between levels $2p_{10}$ and $5d_5$ of the krypton-86 atom.

Area. A *square meter* (m^2) is a unit of area equal to the area of a square, the sides of which are 1 meter.

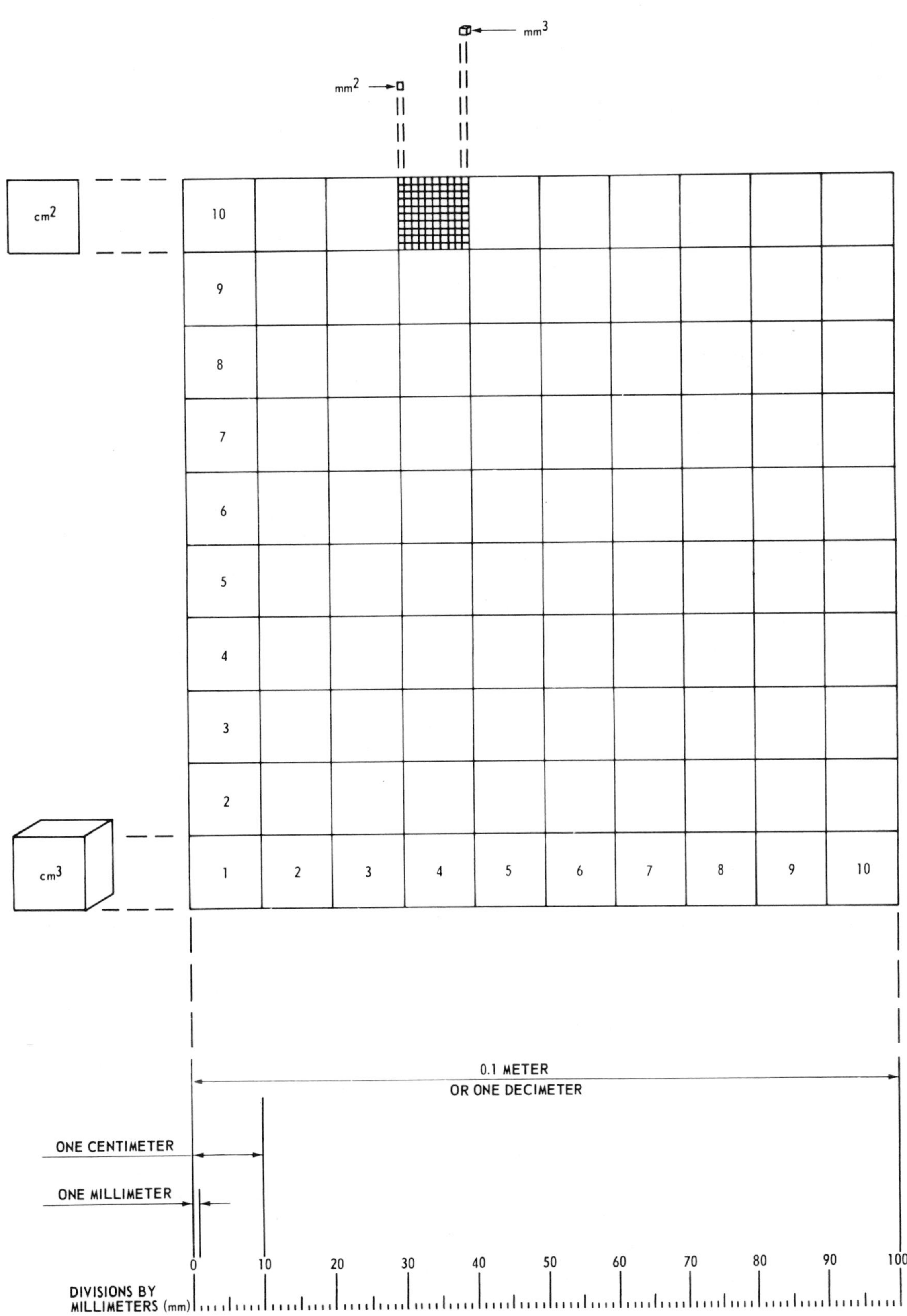

Figure 4.37 The meter. *Source*. U.S. Government.

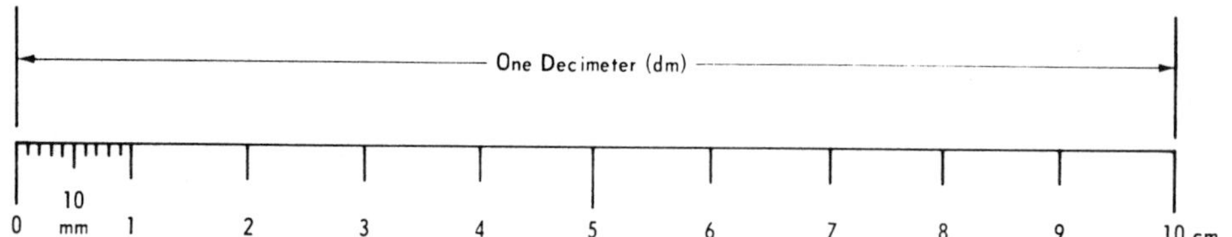

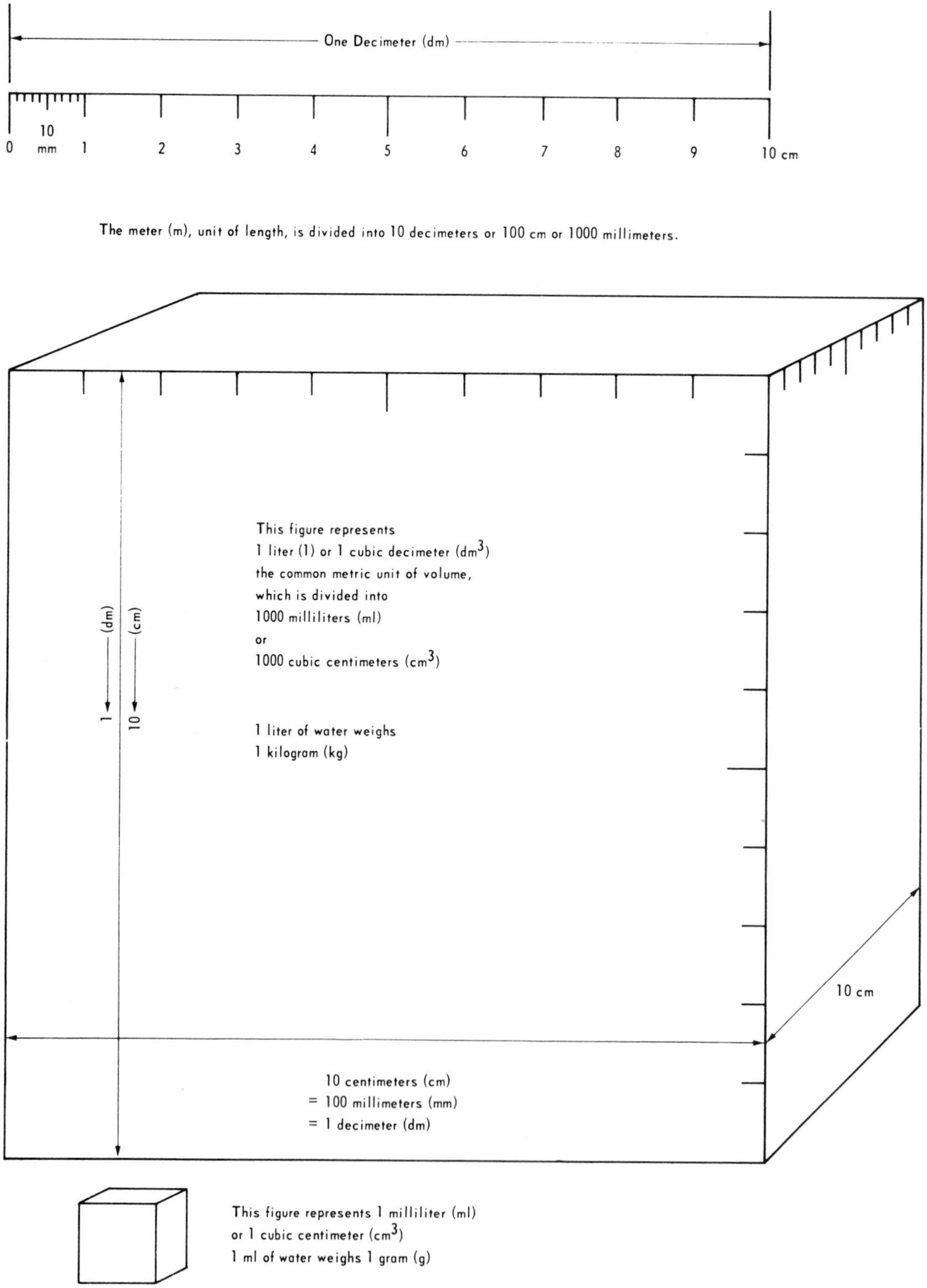

One Decimeter (dm)
10
0
mm
1
2
3
4
5
6
7
8
9
10 cm
The meter (m), unit of length, is divided into 10 decimeters or 100 cm or 1000 millimeters.
This figure represents
1 liter (l) or 1 cubic decimeter (dm3)
the common metric unit of volume,
which is divided into
1000 milliliters (ml)
or
1000 cubic centimeters (cm3)
1 liter of water weighs
1 kilogram (kg)
1 (dm)
10 (cm)
10 cm
10 centimeters (cm)
= 100 millimeters (mm)
= 1 decimeter (dm)
This figure represents 1 milliliter (ml)
or 1 cubic centimeter (cm3)
1 ml of water weighs 1 gram (g)

Figure 4.38 The liter. *Source*. U.S. Government.

Volume. A *cubic meter* (m^3) is a unit of volume equal to a cube, the edges of which are 1 meter. (A *liter* (l) is a unit of volume equal to a cubic decimeter.)

Mass. A *kilogram* (kg) is a unit of mass equal to the mass of the International Prototype Kilogram, which is a particular cylinder of platinum-iridium alloy, preserved in a vault in Sevres, France, by the International Bureau of Weights and Measures.

Electricity. Principal definitions are as follows:

The *ampere* (A) is that constant current which, if maintained in two straight parallel conductors of infinite length, of negligible circular cross section, and placed 1 meter apart in vacuum, would produce between these conductors a force equal to 2×10^{-7} newton per meter of length.

The *coulomb* (C) is the quantity of electricity transported in 1 second by a current of 1 ampere.

The *ohm* (Ω) is the electric resistance between two points of a conductor when a constant difference of potential of 1 volt, applied between these two points, produces a current of 1 ampere in this conductor, which is not the source of any electromotive force.

The *volt* (V) is the difference of electric potential between two points of a conducting wire carrying a constant current of 1 ampere, when the power dissipated between these points is 1 watt.

The *watt* (W) is the power that gives rise to the production of energy at the rate of 1 joule per second.

Light. The *candela* (cd) is the luminous intensity, in the perpendicular direction, of a surface of 1/600,000 square meter of a blackbody at the temperature of freezing platinum under a pressure of 101,325 newtons per square meter.

The *lumen* (lm) is the luminous flux emitted in a solid angle of 1 steradian by a uniform point source having an intensity of 1 candela.

Temperature. The *kelvin* (K) is the unit of thermodynamic temperature; it is the fraction 1/273.16 of the thermodynamic temperature of the triple point of water.

Force. The *newton* (N) is the force that gives to a mass of 1 kilogram an acceleration of 1 meter per second per second.

Angles. The *radian* (rad) is the plane angle between two radii of a circle that cut off on the circumference of an arc equal in length to the radius.

Time. The *second* (s) is the duration of 9,192,631,770 periods of the radiation corresponding to the transition between the two hyperfine levels of the ground state of the cesium-133 atom.

Special Considerations: The Use of SI Units in Building Design and Construction

Linear Measurement (Length)

1 The preferred units for measurement of length in building design, construction, and production are the millimeter (mm) and the meter (m).

2 In special applications, the kilometer (km) is used for the measurement of long distances, and the micrometer (μm) is used for precision measurements.

3 The *centimeter (cm) is to be avoided* in all building design and construction applications.

4 The arguments for the deletion of the centimeter are as follows:

   a The centimeter is not consistent with the preferred use of multiples, which represents ternary powers of 10.

   b The order of magnitude between the millimeter and centimeter is only 10, and the use of both units would lead to confusion.

   c The millimeter provides integers within appropriate tolerances for all building dimensions and nearly all building product dimensions, so that decimal fractions are almost entirely eliminated from documents. In contrast, acceptance of the centimeter would inevitably lead to extensive use of decimal fractions, which is undesirable.

5 On drawings, unit symbols may be deleted if the following rules are applied:

   a The drawing is designated "all dimensions shown in millimeters," or "all dimensions shown in meters."

   b Whole numbers always indicate millimeters (e.g., 3600, 300, 25). In addition

   - Any length up to 328 feet can be shown by a simple five-digit number; for example: 327 feet, 10 11/16 inches equals 99,941.
   - Similarly, any length up to 32 feet, 9 inches can be shown by a four-digit number.
   - Any length up to 3 feet, 3 5/16 inches can be shown by a three-digit number.

   c Decimalized expressions, taken to three decimal places, always indicate "meters" (e.g., 3.600, 0.300, 0.025).

Table 4.3 Units for Volume and Fluid Capacity and Their Relationships

Preferred Units			
All Volumes	Fluid Volume Only	Limited Application	Relationships
Cubic meters	—	—	$1\ m^3 = 1000\ l = 1000\ dm^3$
—	Liters	Cubic decimeters	$1\ l = 1\ dm^3 = 10^{-3}\ m^3$ $10^6\ mm^3$ $= 1000\ ml$
—	Milliliters	Cubic centimeters	$10^{-6}\ m^3$ $10^3\ mm^3$
Cubic millimeters	—	—	$1\ mm^3 = 10^{-9}\ m^3$

6 The use of millimeters and meters, as recommended, saves space and time in drawing, typing, and computer applications. It also improves clarity in drawings with many dimensions.

7 *Survey Measurement.* The change to SI units will also eliminate the discrepancies between the units "international foot" and "U.S. survey foot," "international mile" and "U.S. survey mile" (the survey mile is approximately 3 mm longer), and corresponding derived units for area measurement.*

Area

1 The preferred unit for area measurement is the square meter (m^2). Very large areas can be expressed in square kilometers (km^2), and small areas will be expressed in square millimeters (mm^2), or in square meters using exponential notation (e.g., $10^{-6}\ m^2$).

2 The hectare (ha) is used for surface measurement of land and water *only*:
$1\ ha = (100\ m)^2 = 10{,}000\ m^2 = 10^4\ m^2 = 0.01\ km^2$.

3 The *square centimeter (cm^2) is to be avoided,* to minimize confusion. Any measurement of area given in square centimeters should be converted to square millimeters or square meters ($1\ cm^2 = 100\ mm^2 = 10^{-4}\ m^2$).

*Since 1893, the basis of length measurement in the United States has been derived from metric standards. In 1959 the definition of length of the "foot" was changed from *1200/3937 meter* to *0.3048 meter exactly,* which resulted in the new value being shorter by two parts in a million. At the same time it was decided that any data derived from and published as a result of geodetic surveys within the United States would remain with the old standard. Thus all land measurements in U.S. customary units are based on the "U.S. survey foot," which converts to *0.3048006 meter* (1200/3937 m). The change to SI will eliminate this dual standard.

4 At times, it is more appropriate to indicate the surface or cross-sectional area of building products by linear dimensions (e.g., 40 mm × 90 mm, 300 × 600). It is preferred practice to indicate the width dimension first and height second.

Volume and Fluid Capacity

1 The preferred unit for measurement of volume in construction and for large storage tank capacities is the cubic meter (m^3).

2 The preferred units for measurement of fluid capacity (liquid volume) are the liter (l) and the milliliter (ml).

3 By international definition established in 1964, the liter is equal to one-thousandth of a cubic meter or one cubic decimeter (dm^3).

4 Because the cubic meter contains one billion (10^9) cubic millimeters, the cubic decimeter (dm^3) and the cubic centimeter (cm^3) may find limited application in some industries, particularly since they represent preferred steps of 1000 in volume measurement. However it is recommended that any such cases be converted to the preferred units for volume measurement in building design and construction applications (Table 4.3).

Geometrical Cross-Sectional Properties

1 The expression of geometrical cross-sectional properties of structural sections involves raising the unit of length to the third, fourth, or sixth power. Values can be shown either in mm^3, mm^4, or mm^6, with exponential notation, or in m^3, m^4, or m^6, with exponential notation.

2 The following measurement units are suitable:

a Modulus of section
mm^3 or m^3
($1\ mm^3 = 10^{-9}\ m^3$)

SHELL RESEARCH CENTER
Oakville, Ontario
Architects: Shore, Tilbe, Henschel, Irwin
Photo: Edward Jones

b Second moment of area
Torsional constant
mm^4 or m^4
($1\ mm^4 = 10^{-12}\ m^4$)

c Warping constant
mm^6 or m^6
($1\ mm^6 = 10^{-18}\ m^6$)

3 Thus the cross-sectional properties of a wide flange beam, 460 mm deep, and 82 kg/m mass per unit length, could be expressed as follows:

a Plastic modulus Z_x
$= 1.835 \times 10^6\ mm^3$
or $1.835 \times 10^{-3}\ m^3$

b Second moment of area I_{x-x}
$= 0.371 \times 10^9\ mm^4$
or $0.371 \times 10^{-3}\ m^4$

c Torsional constant J
$= 0.691 \times 10^6\ mm^4$
or $0.691 \times 10^{-6}\ m^4$

d Warping constant C_w
$= 0.924 \times 10^{12}\ mm^6$
or $0.924 \times 10^{-6}\ m^6$

Plane Angle

1 Although the SI unit for plane angle, the radian (rad), should be used in calculations for reasons of its coherence, the customary units of angular measure, degree (°), minute (′), and second (″) of arc will continue to be used in many applications in cartography and surveying.

2 The degree (°), with parts denoted by decimals (as in 27.25°), will continue to be utilized in engineering and in construction.

Time Interval

1. In general applications, the day (d), hour (h), and minute (min) are permitted non-SI alternatives to the SI base unit for time, the second (s).
2. It is recommended that the minute (min) be avoided as far as possible to minimize the number of units in which time is a dimension.
3. For instance, *flow rates* should be expressed in cubic meters per second, liters per second, or cubic meters per hour, rather than in cubic meters per minute or in liters per minute, to reduce the variety of units is reduced. For example:
   1 m³/s = 1000 1/s (DO NOT USE 60 m³/min)
   1 1/s = 3.6 m³/h (DO NOT USE 60 1/min)
   1 m³/h = 1000 1/h (DO NOT USE 16.67 1/min)
4. Because of the various lengths of the months, this unit should not be used to indicate a time dimension, unless a specific calendar month is referred to.
5. Where the calendar year (symbol "a" for annum) is used as a measurement for time interval, it represents 365 days, or 31,536,000 seconds.

Temperature and Temperature Interval

1. The SI base unit of (thermodynamic) temperature is the kelvin (K), and this unit is used for expressing both thermodynamic temperature and temperature interval.
2. Wide use is also made of the degree Celsius (°C), for the expression of ambient temperature levels in Celsius temperature, and for temperature intervals.
3. The temperature interval of one kelvin equals exactly one degree Celsius. Therefore the degree Celsius may be used in lieu of kelvin in calculations involving temperature interval, although the kelvin (K) is preferred.
4. A temperature expressed in degrees Celsius is equal to the temperature expressed in kelvins less 273.15. There are no negative (minus) temperature values in the kelvin scale.
5. It is recommended that the kelvin (K) be used in compound units involving temperature or temperature interval.

Mass, Weight, and Force

1. The significant difference between SI and traditional metric or other measurement systems is the use of explicit and distinctly separate units for "mass" and for "force."
2. The SI base unit *kilogram (kg) denotes the base unit of mass* (the quantity of matter of an object that is constant and independent of gravitational attraction).
3. The derived SI unit *newton (N) denotes the absolute derived unit of force* (mass times acceleration: kg·m/s²).
4. The general use of *the term "weight" should be avoided* in technical practice for two reasons: (*a*) in common parlance "weight" is confused with "mass"; and (*b*) weights describes *only a particular force* that is related solely to gravitational acceleration, which varies on the surface of the earth.
5. Although the customary gravitational system may seem to be serviceable in the area of "statics," the absolute and more universally useful concepts of the clear SI distinction between "mass" and "force" will grow increasingly significant as engineering and construction become more and more involved in "dynamic" considerations.
6. In dynamic calculations, the value of a mass in kilograms (kg) is used directly with the appropriate acceleration. Thus the customary (frequently mystifying) expression $m = W/g$ is *not* applicable, and is indeed inconsistent with SI. Hence SI simplifies and clarifies dynamics.
7. For engineering design purposes, in United States locations (except perhaps Alaska), the following value is recommended for acceleration of gravity; g = 9.8 m/s². (The standard international value is 9.80665 m/s²).
8. The use of the factor 9.8 (m/s²) is recommended for g because it
   - *a* Provides adequate accuracy in nearly all instances.
   - *b* Gives fewer decimal places than the use of 9.81, or even 9.80665, which was advocated in Britain.
   - *c* Provides a number in the product different from the number obtained with the use of a factor of 10 (advocated by some), which may be easily overlooked, thus causing errors as well as introducing overdesign by 2%.
9. The newton (N) extends through to derived quantities for pressure and stress; energy, work, and quantity of heat; power; and many of the electrical units.
10. The unit kilogram-force (kgf) is inconsistent with SI, and traditionally metric countries are now dropping it in favor of the newton. *The kilogram-force (kgf) should not be used in the United States.*

Pressure, Stress, and Elastic Modulus

1 The SI unit for both pressure and stress (force per unit area) is the pascal (Pa), which replaces a large number of customary units and also supersedes a few traditional but non-SI metric units.
2 Although it may be useful in some applications to read out test results in newtons per square millimeter (which is identical with MN/mp^2), or in kilonewtons per square millimeter, it is preferable and recommended to always show computations and results in megapascals (MPa) or kilopascals (kPa).
3 The non-SI units *the "bar"* (which is 100 kPa or 0.1 MPa) *and the "millibar"* (which is 100 Pa or 0.1 kPa), *should not be used* with SI in design or construction applications.

Energy, Work, and Quantity of Heat

1 The SI unit of energy, work, and quantity of heat is the joule (J), which is equal to a newton-meter (N·m) and to a watt-second (W·s).
2 The joule provides *one* coherent unit to supersede a large number of traditional units: Btu, therm, calorie, kilocalorie, foot pound-force, and so on.
3 For many years, and long before the joule was named, the kilowatt-hour* was used extensively as the unit of energy in electrical energy consumption. Most existing electricity meters show kilowatt-hours, and recalibration in the SI unit megajoule (MJ) would be needlessly costly. Therefore the kilowatt-hour will be permitted as an alternative unit in electrical applications, but it should not be introduced in new areas.
4 The joule should *never* be used for torque, which is widely designated as newton meter (N·m).

Rotational Dynamics. For dimensional consistency in calculations involving rotational dynamics, the units shown in Table 4.4 are recommended because they contain the SI unit for angular displacement, the radian (rad), which provides dimensional integrity in equations.

Power and Heat Flow Rate

1 The SI unit for power and heat flow rate is the watt (W), which is already in worldwide use as the general unit for electrical power.

*The accepted symbol for this unit in the United States is "kWh"; the correct SI symbol is *kW·h*.

Table 4.4 Units Recommended for Rotational Dynamics

Quantity	Recommended SI Unit	Alternative Unit That Disregards Angular Displacement
Torque	N·m/rad	N·m
Moment of inertia	$kg·m^2/rad^2$	$kg·m^2$
Moment of momentum	$kg·m^2/rad·s$	$kg·m^2/s$

2 The watt and its multiples will now replace a number of traditional units of power and heat flow rate:

For general power	the horsepower (electric, boiler), and the foot pound-force per hour (or minute or second)
For heat flow rate	the Btu per hour, the calorie per minute (or second), the kilocalorie per minute (or second), and the ton of refrigeration

Electrical Units. The only changes in units used in electrical engineering are as follows: the renaming of the unit of conductance to siemens (S) from "mho," and the use of the SI unit for frequency, hertz (Hz), in lieu of cycles per second (cps).

Lighting Units

1 Already in common use are the SI units for luminous intensity, the candela (cd), and for luminous flux, the lumen (lm).
2 The candela (cd) directly replaces "candle" and "candlepower."
3 Illuminance will be expressed in the SI unit lux (lx), which is equal to the lumen per square meter (lm/m^2) and replaces the lumen per square foot and the footcandle.
4 Luminance will be expressed in the SI unit "candela per square meter" (cd/m^2), which replaces candela per square foot, footlambert, and lambert.

Dimensionless Quantities. Dimensionless quantities, or ratios, such as relative humidity, specific gravity, decibel (dB), and pH, remain unchanged when converting to SI.

Table 4.5 Design Constants: Name, Symbol, Value, and Unit

Name	Symbol	Value	Unit
Standard atmosphere pressure (international value)	P_0	101.325	kPa
Absolute (zero) temperature	T	0.0 (−273.15)	K (°C)
Velocity of sound in air (P_0, 20°C, 50% relative humidity)	M	344	m/s
Specific volume of perfect gas (P_0, 20°C)	V_0	22.414	m^3/kmol (l/mol)
Characteristic gas constant for air	R_a	287.045	J/kg·K
Characteristic gas constant for water vapor	R_v	461.52	J/kg·K
Natural logarithms	e	2.71828	
Pi (π)	π	3.14159	

Constants for Use in Building Design Calculations. Table 4.5 presents a selection of internationally agreed values and empirical constants for use in design calculations.

Conclusion

The popular acceptance of the metric system in the United States is a matter of great importance, and the near future should bring many related proposals. The most recent proposal is the 100-millimeter basic unit. Although the "100-mm unit" is in line with current trends, we should learn from the experience of England and Canada in converting to the metric system. Much of Europe, for example, has been working toward a higher degree of standardization with a so-called 3M system (where M = 100 mm and 3M = 300 mm, or about 1 ft). The basic multiple module is thus 1200 mm, which approximates the familiar 4-foot module, used extensively in the United States. The reason for adopting the 3M system is simply that it already exists. Moreover, the system is relatively easy to work with. The superior numerical workability of a 12-based system over a 10-based system is generally accepted. In fact, this has been the beauty of the otherwise very awkward English system. For example, 12 can be divided evenly by 1, 2, 3, 4, 6, and 12; whereas 10 can be divided evenly by only 1, 2, 5, and 10. For architectural purposes, 1200 divides rather nicely into usable dimensions in the 3M system. For instance, 1200 mm defines a sheet of standard building material, plywood, drywall, and so on; 300 mm defines a brick (more or less) 600 mm in closet depth, and so on. In contrast, 200 or 500 mm and their multiples have limited practical value. However the most important point is that the existing sizes of building materials and components in the English system have developed naturally (e.g., 1200 mm = 47.25 in or the 4-ft plywood sheet). Thus they have a certain validity, and the change would be less drastic. The changeover to metric need not be as traumatic in regard to retooling, quantities of material, or production systems. It is unlikely that the 3M system would meet every dimensional requirement, but it does provide the most practical point of departure in applying the metric system to architecture.

5 BUILDING VALUE: ENERGY DESIGN GUIDELINES FOR BUILDINGS*

Foreword to the California State Guidelines

By Sim van Der Ryn

The relatively long life of buildings places a unique demand on architects to consider the future wisely both in design and construction. Building practices commit us to patterns of living and energy use for decades to come. We expect the costs of energy to rise dramatically, and conservation of our limited resources is essential to ease our path into the future.

The design of our buildings must reflect our wisest and our most conservative sense of future possibilities. "Marketplace economics," which has been allowed to determine our recent building patterns, is not adequate, as it reflects only some of the present values and costs of things and cannot encompass the conditions that will develop through the lifetime of those buildings. Thus we must develop performance and evaluative criteria that reserve for us the greatest economy and options for qual-

*This section has been adopted from the state guidelines with permission of the authors. The original guidelines (1976) were prepared by Bender IdeMoll of Portland, Oregon.

SEATTLE CENTER COLISEUM
Seattle, Washington
Architect: Paul Thiry
Photo: H. N. Stratford

ity of life through and beyond the lives of our buildings, not for the present moment alone.

These guidelines have been prepared to assist state construction in California to fulfill these fundamental responsibilities in a manner consistent with sound fiscal, engineering, and architectural practices.

Valuation

Price by itself is no measure of value or effectiveness. First cost of buildings is an inadequate basis for their design and evaluation, and we have established structural, health, fire, earthquake, and other performance standards that must precede cost analysis and form the framework for it.

Rising energy costs are increasing the significance of operating costs of a building over its lifecycle. The inability of our normal costing systems to reflect and account for such conditions has led to the development of new valuation techniques such as lifecycle costing and energy analysis. It has also led, implicitly, to a realization of the need for a range of different valuation techniques for different purposes and situations.

A particularly significant factor in any attempt at valuation is our lack of knowledge about many aspects of the future, including the following:

- Inflation and interest rates are likely to fluctuate more than the difference in return of present options. This may turn potentially profitable investments into losses, or it may make unlikely options profitable.

• Unpredictable technological successes or failures and future energy and tax policies make energy prices during the lifetime of a building impossible to predict within an order of magnitude.

• Various energy options—such as dependence on foreign oil, rapid consumption of our own remaining reserves, and implementing policies of energy conservation—have important social and political implications that overshadow the present cost of such options but are not reflected in this amount.

• In recent years the useful life of buildings has been based on their rate of functional obsolescence from technological or social change rather than on their physical condition. Since future rates of such changes cannot be predicted, the useful lifecycle of buildings also cannot be known in advance. Nor do we know whether we will be wealthier or poorer in the future. Thus our ability to afford certain performance standards, activities, and patterns of living cannot be determined, nor the return on alternative investment options.

• Because of inflation, labor contract changes, material shortages, and so on, even present construction costs of buildings often can be predicted within only 50% at the design stage.

Since normal real estate investment analysis is based on precise numerical analysis, the analysts' uncertainty of the underlying assumptions about the future is often obscured. Such uncertainties are frequently of greater magnitude and importance than the accuracy of the numerical accounting, and evaluations based on such procedures cannot provide a very sound basis for building decisions. Under these circumstances, there has been a change in the nature and number of dimensions that are useful for evaluating the economic performance of a building. Four of these are as follows:

1 *As a Real Estate Investment*. The costs of constructing, owning, and operating the building over its lifetime.
2 *As an Energy Structure*. The physical quantities of energy supplied, as well as the efficiency of using that energy to light, heat, cool, and ventilate the building over its lifetime.
3 *As a Total Operating Entity*. The building's effect on the performance and well-being of the people who will occupy it, as well as the costs and energy used in constructing and operating the building itself.
4 *As a Public Investment*. The contribution and costs to public systems and the "common good."

Each of these viewpoints represents a valid way of comparing alternative building program and designs, depending on the priorities of the analyst. Each corresponds to different horizons of responsibility for real costs that result from our activities. Together they suggest areas in which both public and private builders should be more accountable for the costs they generate.

As a Real Estate Investment. The traditional separation of construction and operating costs often results in higher total costs of owning a building due to excessive maintenance and operating costs incurred because of cheap construction. Unwary owners are frequently left with big fuel bills for poorly insulated and constructed buildings. Recent rapid increases in construction and operating costs—particularly energy costs—have combined with high maintenance costs to bring closer attention to the total costs of constructing, owning, and operating a building over its entire lifetime, including expected real price increases for energy.

This "lifecycle cost" (Table 4.6) provides much more comprehensive and quantitative information for decision making than was available through past practices of examining only construction and financing costs. Its real value lies in its use in program and design decisions concerning the following:

• Levels of performance required to respond to user needs.

• Selection among alternative modes, physical configurations, and mechanical components of the building design being developed, when these options have different first costs and operating costs.

• Tradeoffs between "best" subsystem values and the integrated values of the whole building.

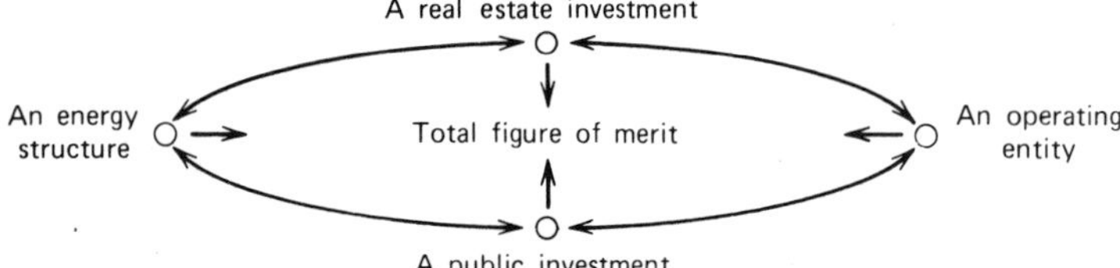

Figure 4.39 *Source*. State of California, Office of the Architect. *Building Value*, 1977, OSA (72).

Table 4.6 Lifecycle Costing

	Proposed Building	Average of Comparable State Buildings	Hypothetical Conventional New Energy Code Bldg.
Total Initial Costs:	$ 12,347,500	$ 13,473,600	$ 13,147,000
Total Operating and Maintenance Costs Over 50 Years:	$107,253,000	$147,258,000	$107,686,690
Total Lifecycle Costs:	$119,600,500	$160,731,600	$120,833,690

Lifecycle Costing permits comparison of the total costs of owning and operating a building over its entire lifetime.

Source. State of California, Office of the Architect. *Building Value*, 1977, OSA (72).

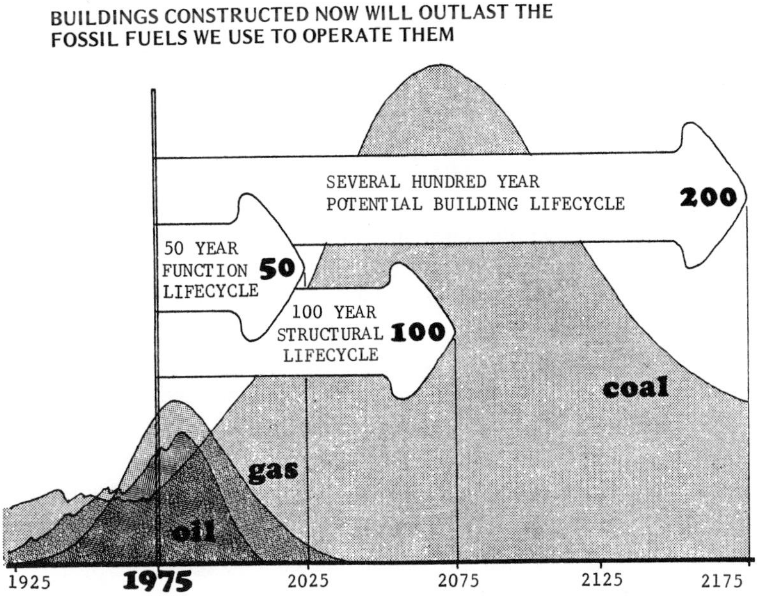

BUILDINGS CONSTRUCTED NOW WILL OUTLAST THE FOSSIL FUELS WE USE TO OPERATE THEM

Figure 4.40 *Source*. State of California, Office of the Architect. *Building Value*, 1977.

As an Energy Structure. Buildings constructed now must reflect anticipation of what will be done when energy produced from fossil fuels cannot be purchased at any price. The economic, social, and political implications of that situation require us to examine energy use directly in energy terms rather than through economics that deals only with present costs. Energy analysis requires measurement of the total amount of fuels used per unit of area, as well as the efficiency of the building systems singly and together, to obtain the best performance from the energy used. It is important also to investigate the energy needs for the operation of supply and waste systems outside the building, and the different implications of using different sources of energy.

As an Operating Entity. The construction and operating of office buildings account for only about 8% of the total cost of the activities sheltered by these structures. More than 90% of the overall cost goes for the salaries of the personnel using the building and their supplies and equipment. The effects of the building on the effective operation of its occupants, and the effects of the occup-

OPERATING COSTS

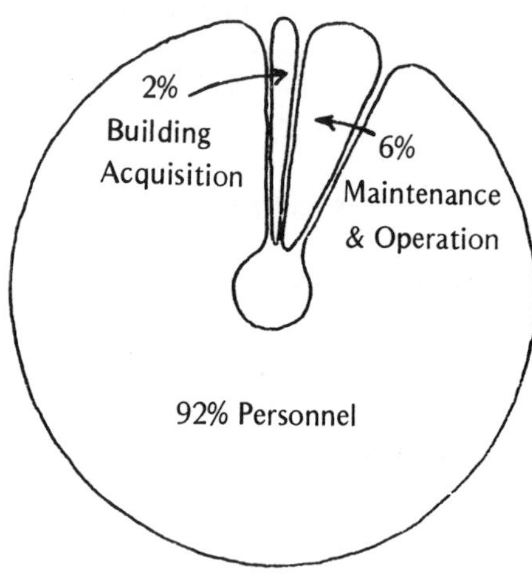

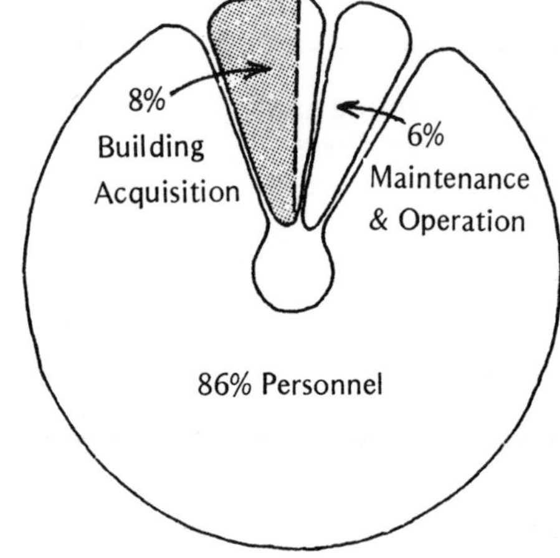

CONVENTIONAL BUILDING
1965 figures from National Bureau of Standards Study of Federal Office Buildings

A BETTER WORKING ENVIRONMENT THAT IMPROVED WORKER EFFECTIVENESS BY ONLY 6½% WOULD BE COST-EFFECTIVE EVEN IF IT QUADRUPLED BUILDING COST!

Figure 4.41 *Source*. State of California, Office of the Architect. *Building Value,* 1977.

ants on the effective operation of the building, can substantially influence total costs of the whole operation. Valuation as an operating entity calls for examination of the following factors:

- Different institutional options (i.e., avoiding the need for some building space or personnel).
- Effects of building design on health, morale, and working conditions.
- Effective relationships to support services for the building's activities and occupants—recreation, food, copying services, drug stores, and bars.
- Effectiveness of operating procedures for the building (i.e., how users interact with building operation).

It is often difficult to quantify the effects of buildings and people on each other, yet a better working environment that improved the effectiveness of workers by only 6½% would be cost effective even if it *quadrupled* the cost of the building.

As a Public Investment. Whereas the private builder does not bear the costs of energy supply, transportation, water and waste treatment, health, and other support services associated with use of the finished structure, in the case of state buildings both building and other costs come out of the same pocket. Thus it is appropriate to examine and evaluate these systems together, to minimize total costs. The concept of valuating building projects as public investments addresses reduction of the impacts on utility, transportation, safety service, and other public services. In light of this kind of accounting, the future value of increased self-sufficiency in buildings is clear, particularly if it is acquired by the use or reuse of energy or other resources acquired or retained on site (e.g., solar energy and heat recovery).

Externalized costs that could be reduced by evaluation of buildings as public investments include the following:

- *Energy Supply and Cost.* The expected fuel savings of California's proposed Site One Office Building avoids the need for $1 million worth of new electric generating plant capacity, in addition to saving energy resources.
- *Transportation.* Building siting and transport policy that would permit one-third of the state employees in Sacramento to live within walking or bicycling distance and another third to use public transit would provide direct savings of 800,000 gallons of gasoline and

$480,000 per year, in addition to reducing air pollution and noise.

• *Agricultural Land Costs.* A study of irrigating desert land in eastern Washington to replace urbanized prime agricultural land found the additional cost to electrical ratepayers in the Northwest to be in excess of $80 million per year.

• *Climate Control.* Studies in Davis, California, found that a proper landscaping and street tree planting program could lower summer temperatures in the city by more than 10°F, substantially eliminating the need for air conditioning.

Structural, fire, earthquake, health, and other codes have already been based on the public savings of making small additional investments in building construction to prevent large costs of preventable problems.

Other closely related costs that should be examined are as follows:

• Water supply.
• Sewage.
• Health costs of sedentary work.
• Public safety (police and security).
• Employment and unemployment.
• Materials recycling and reuse.

Comparative Analysis

The primary purpose of any building value analysis is to determine the following:

• Whether the proposed project is affordable (i.e., its costs).
• Selection of alternatives during design.
• Assessing a particular design relative to the state of the art—comparing it to existing projects to ascertain whether the proposed design is more or less effective and costly.

FIRST BAPTIST CHURCH
Columbus, Indiana
Architect: Harry Weese & Associates
Photo: B. Korab

Table 4.7 **Building Valuation Analysis**

	Proposed Building	Average of Existing State Buildings	Hypothetical Energy Code Building
Real Estate Investment			
First Costs	$ 12,347,500	$ 13,473,600	$ 13,147,000
Op. & Maint./Year	507,800*	531,000*	440,000*
Lifecycle Costs:			
A. 50 years	$119,600,500	$160,731,600	$120,833,690
B. 100 years	*cost projections presently unreliable*		
Energy Structure			
Construction Energy Cost	5,852 bbl	5,852 bbl	5,852 bbl
Bbl. Oil/Year	777	5,852	1,901
Lifecycle Energy Cost			
A. 50 years	44,702	298,452	100,902
B. 100 years	83,552 bbl	591,052 bbl	195,952 bbl
Operating Entity:			
Annualized Building Cost			
Personnel Costs	*data presently unavailable*		
Total Costs			
Public Investment:			
Annualized Operating Entity Costs			
Reducation of External Costs			
Energy	$1 million reduction in energy plant costs	None	$800,000 reduction in energy plant costs
Transportation Comparative Value	None	None	Not Located

*Using annual inflation rates of 7% for energy and 5% for general costs.

Source. State of California, Office of the Architect. *Building Value*, 1977, OSA (72).

Table 4.7 summarizes a sample ''cross-network analysis'' comparing expected performance and costs of a proposed office building to an existing building and a hypothetical building designed to meet new energy efficiency standards.

Evaluation. As already indicated, design budgets should incorporate an evaluation of building performance as a real estate investment, as an energy structure, as an operating entity, and as a public investment. Monetary valuation of a building should include as much of the total costs of construction, owning, operating, and maintaining a building over its entire lifetime as possible.

The items chosen for inclusion in such an analysis reflect the values of the analyst. Such choices dramatically influence what is built and how, which in turn has a significant impact on our future living conditions. These choices represent major ethical decisions about our future. Some of these variables are as follows:

- Whether operating as well as owning costs are considered.
- How the length of the building's lifecycle is considered (functional vs. structural life).
- The way costs are assigned to future energy uses.

BUILDING SHELL LIFE-COST WORKSHEET

PROJECT NEW CONSTRUCTION PROJECT (BASE) HEATING ZONE I COOLING ZONE I
CONSTRUCTION DATA WALLS: VENEER CONSTRUCTION LIGHT COLOR DARK U-FACTOR 0.10
ROOF: STEEL FRAME & DECK CONSTRUCTION LIGHT COLOR DARK U-FACTOR 0.10
GLASS: TYPE SINGLE GLASS SHADING NONE

	NORTH/~~NORTHEAST~~ WALL	GLASS	EAST/~~SOUTHEAST~~ WALL	GLASS	SOUTH/~~SOUTHWEST~~ WALL	GLASS	WEST/~~NORTHWEST~~ WALL	GLASS	ROOF	TOTAL
1. ELEMENT AREA	3042	338	2048	227	3042	338	2048	227	45500	
2. ELEMENT FIRST COST/SQ FT	$3.00	2.90	3.00	2.90	3.00	2.90	3.00	2.90	2.90	A
3. ELEMENT FIRST COST (Line 1 × Line 2)	$9126	980	6144	658	9126	980	6144	658	131950	165766
4. HEATING EQUIPMENT COST/100 SQ FT	$18.80	212.00	18.80	212.00	8.80	212.00	8.80	212.00	18.80	
5. COOLING EQUIPMENT COST/100 SQ FT	$6.70	260.00	11.40	260.00	13.50	723.00	17.80	1241.00	47.20	
6. Line 4 + Line 5	$25.50		30.20		32.30		36.60		66.00	
7. U-FACTOR / 0.10	1		1		1		1		1	
8. EQUIPMENT COST/100 SQ FT (Line 6 × Line 7)	$25.50	472.00	30.20	472.00	32.30	935.00	36.60	1433.00	66.00	
9. ELEMENT AREA ÷ 100 SQ FT	30.4	3.38	20.5	2.27	30.4	3.38	20.5	2.27	455.0	B
10. EQUIPMENT FIRST COST (Line 8 × Line 9)	$775	1595	619	1071	982	3160	750	3253	30030	42235
11. HEATING FUEL COST/100 SQ FT	$2.40	24.10	2.40	20.30	2.40	13.40	2.40	20.30	1.50	
12. COOLING FUEL COST/100 SQ FT	$0.11	4.70	0.24	12.30	0.18	12.60	0.27	12.30	0.67	
13. Line 11 + Line 12	$2.51		2.64		2.58		2.67		2.17	
14. U-FACTOR / 0.10	1		1		1		1		1	
15. ANNUAL FUEL COST/100 SQ FT (Line 13 × Line 14)	$2.51	28.80	2.64	32.60	2.58	26.00	2.67	32.60	2.17	
16. ELEMENT AREA ÷ 100 SQ FT	30.4	3.38	20.5	2.27	30.4	3.38	20.5	2.27	455.0	
17. ANNUAL FUEL COST (Line 15 × Line 16)	$76.30	97.34	54.12	74.00	78.88	123.34	56.79	74.00	987.35	

18. LIFE-CYCLE FUEL COST MULTIPLIER:
- [x] New Construction, Life-Cycle = 40 years, Fuel Cost Multiplier = 40
- [ ] Modernization, Life-Cycle = 20 years, Fuel Cost Multiplier = 20
- [ ] Escalating Fuel Costs, ____ years, ____% annual escalation; from Table II; Fuel Cost Multiplier = ____

C 1622 → D × 40

19. LIFE-CYCLE FUEL COST (Line 17 × Line 18) E 64880

20. ESTIMATED LIFE-CYCLE OWNING COSTS (BOX A + BOX B + BOX E) F 272881

Figure 4.42 *Source*. State of California, Office of the Architect. *Building Value,* 1977, Educational Facilities Laboratory (26).

• Attitudes toward the residual value of buildings at the end of their ''functional'' lifecycle.

• Inclusion or exclusion of interest and interest rates in lifecycle costs.

Calculating Lifecycle Costs

• Monetary analysis of construction should be based on lifecycle costs rather than initial construction costs.

That is, economic evaluation must include lifecycle cost evaluation of solar systems, cash flows, discounting of costs, lifecycle models, treatment of taxes, insurance, and governmental incentives, as well as comparison of alternatives and inclusion of an uncertainty factor in cost evaluations. The last item is crucial, since it is hard to justify four-decimal precision accounting based on conditions that make order-of-magnitude estimates of doubtful accuracy.

Energy Lifecycle Costs. Lifecycle costs should be calculated in various forms:

1 In terms of both dollars and energy.
2 For both 50-year and 100-year lifecycles for the buildings.
3 Based on a 7% per year increase in the real cost of fossil fuels through the year 2000.
4 With zero interest and inflation rates for money as well as with currently projected rates.

Lifecycle costs, calculated in dollars and in terms of energy use, assist design for low cost over the lifetime of a building rather than for initial low cost with consequent high operating costs. Dollar lifecycle costing gives best current guesses of costs, whereas energy lifecycle costing makes visible areas of uncertainties and the proportion of costs that involve energy, as well as facilitating new cost information.

LIFESPAN ENERGY BUDGETS
FOR RECENT CONVENTIONAL CONSTRUCTION

RESIDENTIAL COMMERCIAL OFFICE BUILDINGS

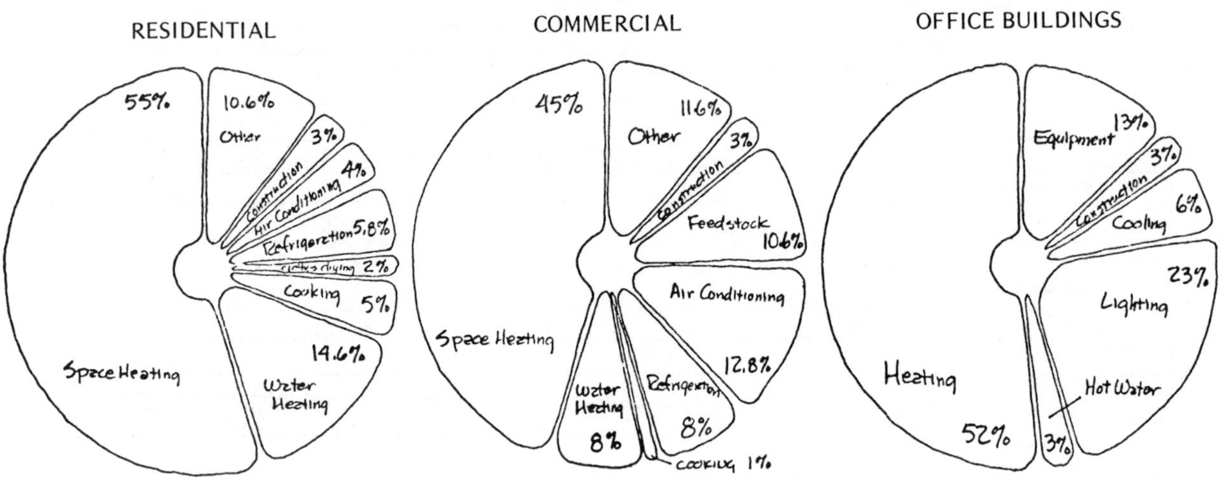

Based upon data from the American Institute of Architects

Figure 4.43 *Source*. State of California, Office of the Architect. *Building Value*, 1977, AIA (4).

Energy lifecycle costs of buildings are usually expressed as yearly prorated energy use. This can be calculated by adding costs of initial material and construction energy use to costs of expected operation, maintenance, and demolition energy use throughout the life of the building, then dividing by the number of years of operation. It is best to express energy use as primary resource use rather than energy use at the building site, to prevent energy waste in production and delivery. Inflation, too, must be taken into account in determining the form of energy use (see Table 4.8).

The energy necessary to produce building materials and to construct a conventional building is equal to 1 to 1.5 times the energy normally used each year for its operation and maintenance. Andrew MacKillop, in *Low-Energy Housing*, gives figures of 53,700 kW·h for construction energy for a standard British house and an average yearly energy resource use of 34,250 kW·h for operating the home. These figures are substantially lower than figures for housing in the United States and lower yet than those for so-called energy-intensive office buildings. Richard Stein calculates that on an all-electric

Table 4.8 Fuel Cost Multipliers for Inflating Fuel Costs

	Annual Inflation Rate				
Years	*2%*	*4%*	*6%*	*8%*	*10%*
5	5.3	5.6	6.0	6.3	6.7
10	11.2	12.5	14.0	15.6	17.5
15	17.6	20.8	25.7	29.3	35.0
20	24.8	31.0	40.0	49.4	63.0
25	32.7	43.3	59.2	79.0	108.0
30	41.4	58.4	84.8	122.0	181.0
40	61.6	98.8	165.0	280.0	487.0
50	86.3	159.0	309.0	620.0	1280.0

Source: Educational Facilities Laboratory (26)

Source. State of California, Office of the Architect. *Building Value*, 1977, Educational Facilities Laboratory (26).

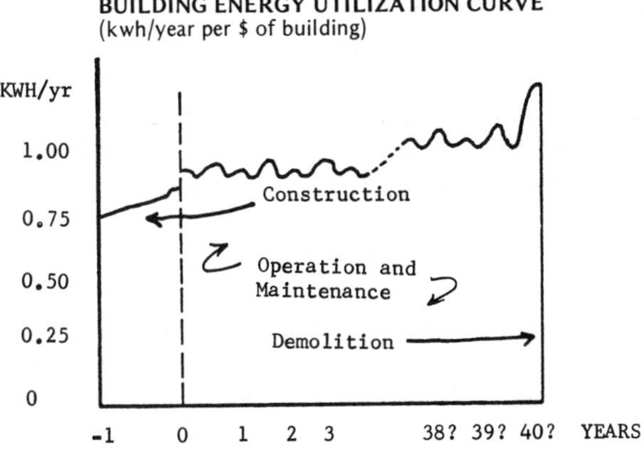

Figure 4.44 *Source.* State of California, Office of the Architect, *Building Value,* 1977, Richard Stein (90).

basis, 1.28 kW·h is required for construction of every $1 of new office buildings, with operation and maintenance requiring 1 kW·h per year per $1 of building value, rising to 1.13 kW·h per year as maintenance requirements increase.

Building Lifecycles. Buildings have several lifecycles; some of these are as follows:

• Financing lifecycles are shortest and are dependent on finance regulations and profit patterns rather than on any real connection to functional lifecycles. Tax depreciation regulations frequently result in shortening other lifecycles to fit the financial cycles. Depreciation should be based on initial cost of a building, less residual value when the structure is sold or demolished.

• Functional lifecycles (a building may have several) are the timespan over which the building is expected to accommodate an initial use. Buildings usually still have value at the end of a functional lifecycle. Such residual values are rarely incorporated into tax laws, however, allowing building owners to write the buildings off and demolish them to reuse the sites. If demolition takes place, the residual value of the building, when destroyed, is equal to the price of equivalent space.

• Mechanical equipment lifecycles are about 15 years—ending when the equipment wears out or becomes obsolete. Thus a building may be refitted several times as well as reused.

• Structural lifecycles include the whole period over which a building is useful. Its total value is measured in a sequence of lumps, since the value changes when sold, rehabilitated, or used for different purposes.

Because of financing customs, we generally associate the lifespan of a building with "functional obsolescence" cycles or financial depreciation cycles. Correctly built structures can and do last for many centuries. Planning for longer lifecycles frequently can minimize the effort to rebuild, replace, or adapt our buildings. Designs based on structural lifecycles of at least 100 to 200 years reflect the real potentials of the structures more than do current practices. Valuation based on both 50- and 100-year lifecycles allows examination of the full value of a building separated from its value relative to a single and initial functional use.

Borrowed Money

• "Present value" accounting hides long-term effects of actions.

Most funding for state building comes from current tax revenues rather than from market borrowing. Thus it reflects the real setting aside of current work/income by taxpayers for shared public activities and also parallels the real pattern of building construction and operation costs.

Whereas taxes allocate present effort, borrowed money negotiates an allocation of present *and* future effort. For public building (except in case of specific benefactor repayment) the latter allocation is inappropriate, since taking in taxes in the future to repay loans from taxpayers is merely a transfer—it does not affect the real allocation of effort already made. In principle, the use of borrowed money represents only the exchange of present work for future work, and the interest, or return on investment, represents either a transfer payment or an increase in real wealth generated by the investment.

The use of interest accounting has the effect of discounting the *real* future—both costs and benefits—associated with a project. Higher interest rates, by discounting the present value of the future, reflect a push for short-term profits and toward the immediate use of our resources. To sustain our society, we must ensure that we will continue to have the resources to support us tomorrow, and we must reconsider measures that cause us to discount our future.

Investment alternatives generate more wealth only if a multiplier effect exists in the investment (such as an oil well), if it puts to work nonrecurring resources (such as solar energy or people's time) that would otherwise be idle, or if they produce more social wealth (producing lasting rather than disposable goods, immediate and extended use of a product or activity rather than a postponed benefit, etc.).

In any case, "opportunity costs," or the investment of money now to generate more wealth or share of future wealth, implies that any current interest rate will be sustainable and/or that increase in wealth is expectable. The future variability of many conditions makes those assumptions questionable. In addition, it must be asked whether alternative investments actually increase wealth or merely cause transfer of wealth to the state, whether certain investments yield high returns because they are exploitive of people's work, natural resources, the future, or the self-reliance and political power of individuals, and if so, whether investment in such areas is beneficial to the citizens.

These real opportunity costs cannot be evaluated on a monetary basis. Only a case-by-case political evaluation can determine their real value and costs. Combined with the previously mentioned limited ability of financial accounting to deal with future uncertainties, this suggests that valuation should include accounting based on real costs and real work as accrued (excluding interest and inflation rates of money), as well as accounting incorporating monetary interest and inflation rates.

The uncertainties of alternative opportunity costs of investments, money costs, inflation, real growth of wealth, and so on, suggest the wisdom of building incrementally—in recognition of the realities of current supplies of work and money—rather than committing ourselves to operating financial policies that are unable to reflect real conditions.

Fuel Costs

- Future energy price increases should be reflected in cost estimates and should be based on average or local price levels, whichever is greater.

Energy costs and prices are expected to increase dramatically over the coming decades as we deplete our rich reserves of fossil fuels and become less able to afford to subsidize more expensive energy sources. Such increases should be reflected in cost estimates and should be based on average or local price levels, whichever is greater.

Energy costs that are lower than average will act as incentives for energy users to move into an area. Such in-migration will necessitate new and more costly energy sources, eliminating any temporary price advantages. The real value of low cost energy is equal to the market value of the higher cost of energy that must replace it. Since the low cost energy can be sold elsewhere at market value, conservation based on a higher price has added economic value, and the use of lower than average prices appears to be unjustified.

- The monetary value of fossil fuels used in construction and operation should be based on their expected scarcity value 50 years hence.
- The cost of any fossil fuels used to substitute for usable solar energy falling on the building site should be calculated at the same future scarcity value.

In the absence of conclusive evidence that immediate use of our reserves of fossil fuels can provide multiplier leverage toward better, sustainable energy sources, such use should be minimized, reserving these reserves for a time when their worth and quality is more valued, and the use of income energy—which is lost if not used—substituted for them.

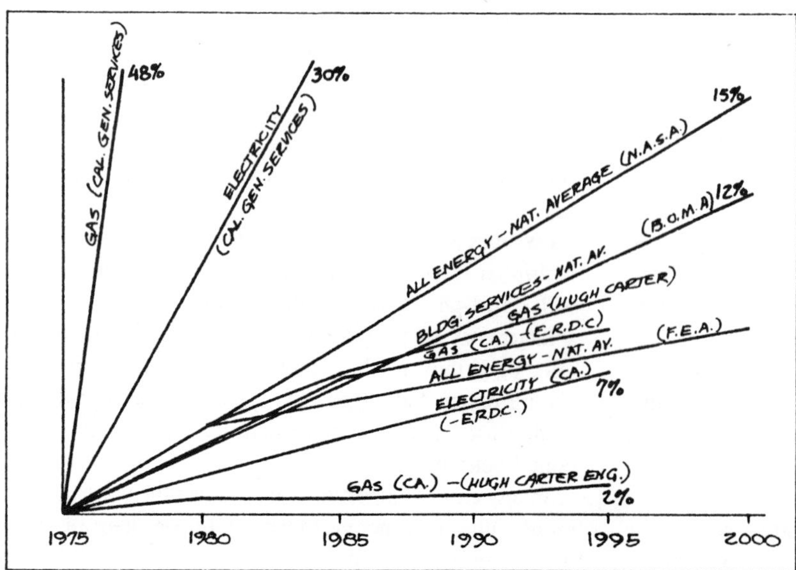

Figure 4.45 Fuel price projections for California. *Source.* State of California, Office of the Architect, *Building Value,* 1977, OSA (72).

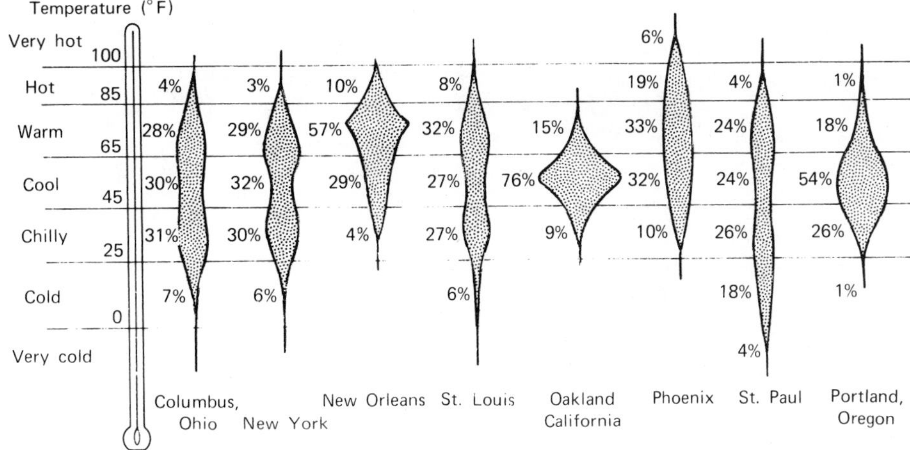

Figure 4.46 Temperature portraits of American climates. *Source*. State of California, Office of the Architect, *Building Value,* 1977, Regional Climate Analysis (5).

Unused solar energy falling on a building site represents an unrealized income potential of the site. The loss of that income should be reflected in the financial evaluation of the building.

Future Value

• The expected residual value at the end of the functional life of a building should be included in its cost analysis.
• New buildings (specifically all new parking structures) should be designed for conversion to other uses.

Parking structures are expensive solutions to the parking problem. The cost of building stalls for cars in a building ranges from 5 to 10 times that of providing a space on the ground. Considered as a structure, however, the parking is cheap, with building costs only 25 to 30% of those for dwelling houses and office buildings. This is because of the very limited amount of additional framework and installations required in a parking structure. About 75% of the construction cost is accounted for by the structure's load-carrying frame alone.

Parking structures are becoming increasingly common as a solution to parking problems, especially in central business districts. Such structures are sometimes planned with uncertain future profitability. Urban planning is dynamic: the site that is proper today for a parking garage may be inappropriate in the future, when plans for rerouting traffic have been implemented.

The relatively long life of buildings frequently results in several major changes in their use as urban patterns and neighborhood and user needs change. Some spaces have housed office buildings, parking lots, and apartments over the last 40 years, and the uncertainty of future institutional and land use patterns makes design for adaptability a wise protection of building investment. Sweden has developed perceptive criteria for parking garages and their future conversion to other uses.

Energy Systems

Climate and Building Design

Avoiding the need for nonrenewable energy is usually easier than obtaining it.

• Natural energy flows occurring on a building site, such as sunlight and night sky cooling, should be used to advantage by building design to reduce heating, cooling, and ventilating loads.
• The contribution of plant materials to building climate control should be included in lifecycle energy costing and in the sizing and design of mechanical equipment.

Climate Design Resources

Building Site. Taking careful advantage of specific microclimatic conditions (air movement and temperature, ground temperature, shading by vegetation, thermal and cloud cover conditions, underground temperatures, etc.) can strongly affect conditions in a building, reducing the need for mechanical climate control.

Orientation. Analysis has indicated that substantial benefits are possible from careful consideration of building configuration and orientation in relation to surface area, prevailing winds, summer shading, and winter heat gain.

DUNEHOUSE
Atlantic Beach, Florida
Architect: William Morgan P.A.
Photo: Office

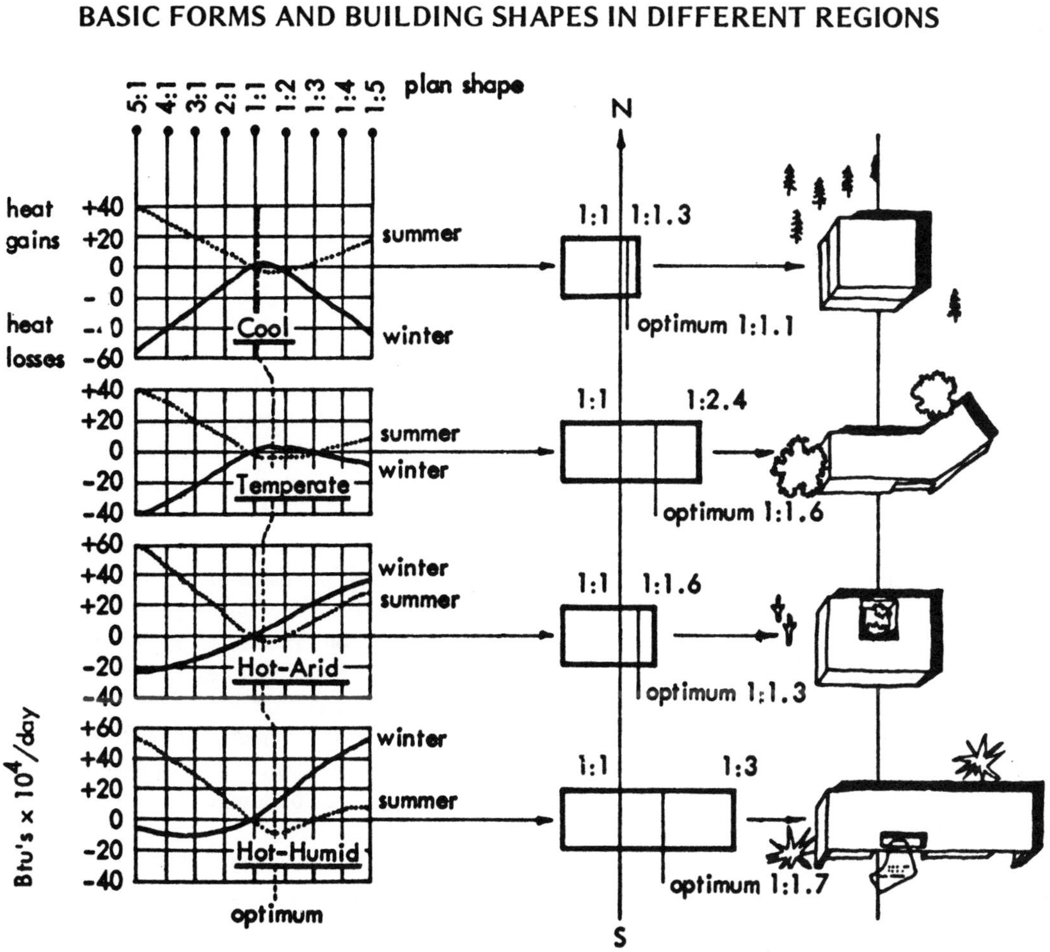

BASIC FORMS AND BUILDING SHAPES IN DIFFERENT REGIONS

Figure 4.47 *Source.* State of California, Office of the Architect, *Building Value,* 1977, OLGYAY (74).

Building Configuration. The results of many studies on building configuration, structure, and shading in response to such environmental forces as solar conditions and gravity are available to the responsible architect who wants to explore optimum configurations for various specific conditions.

Window Placement and Shading. Window placement, orientation, and size are important factors in the thermal and psychological performance of a building. Properly designed, shaded, and insulated, windows can become an excellent and inexpensive source of solar heating rather than an additional load for heating and cooling equipment.

Air Movement. A study by the American Society of Landscape Architects Foundation reprinted in *House and Home* (April 1975) demonstrated a number of site planning measures to take advantage of wind and thermal conditions. Some of these are summarized below.

Storing Heat in Building Materials. We often ignore the potential of daytime solar heat, stored in building materials themselves, to warm spaces at night. When materials that are inside the building (e.g., a concrete floor or an adobe wall) are heated by sunlight coming through windows, their thermal capacity and the speed with which they can transfer heat determine how much heat can be stored. With uninsulated outside walls, heat from outside is transferred slowly through the wall, determining some time later the temperature of the inside surface of the wall and its ability to emit heat to the room or absorb heat from it. Wall thicknesses can be designed so that this "thermal lag time" is useful—that is, the afternoon heat arrives inside in the evening to warm the room, or the cold nighttime temperatures arrive at the inside surface of the wall in the daytime to cool and absorb heat from the room.

Underground Construction. The thermal, ecological, and cost benefits of building underground are bringing the long tradition of underground architecture to new prominence. Legal, economic, insurance, structural, psychological, and energy considerations are new in this field and must be carefully studied. Lifecycle costs show underground building to be increasingly feasible as energy costs increase.

Natural Daylighting

• Natural daylighting should be maximized in satisfying lighting needs.

Electrical lighting is usually the greatest air conditioning load on an office building, and its replacement by well-designed daylighting can have a major effect on energy use for space conditioning as well as lighting. Addition of heavy curtains or insulating panels to windows of buildings used for many hours and in cold climates can convert an energy drain into an energy gain.

Mechanical Solar Systems

• Solar or other renewable energy sources should be used wherever possible to meet energy demand for cooling and heating of all new construction.

• Solar energy or waste heat from other uses should be used for hot water heating in all new buildings.

The technology associated with the use of solar energy has progressed to the point of making available commercial systems, either for direct use or for augmentation of systems with solar/mechanical energy collection and storage or solar/heat pump systems.

Solar Equipment Manufacturers. Solar energy equipment is now available commercially on a scale large enough to provide easy access for designers.

Various solar-oriented periodicals that contain advertising and reader service cards and cover technical and economic developments are also useful in keeping track of manufacturers and their products.

Fuel Conservation

• Elimination of unnecessary need for nonrenewable energy and improvement efficiency of its use should be stressed in all new construction to the degree justified by costing procedures outlined here.

Fossil fuels are in limited supply, but they do a lot of work for very little cost. Reduction of their unnecessary use can stretch out their supply and help slow the increase in energy costs. *A nation of energy-efficient buildings by 1990,* by the American Institute of Architects, provides a good analysis of the economic benefits of conserving fuels through more efficient buildings. In addition, many energy conservation manuals suggesting various fuel conservation measures are now available.

Conservation Potentials. The General Services Administration has published *Energy Conservation Design Guidelines for Office Buildings,* which discusses the relative energy conservation potentials in relation to various aspects of a building's design, construction and operation. This material indicates areas in which a designer's effort can have the greatest impact on fuel conservation. Table 4.9 gives a simple list of energy conservation potentials in office buildings.

Conservation Guidelines. The ''Envelope:Energy Program'' of Albert C. Martin & Associates, which appears in Chapter 3, is a valuable aid in establishing building criteria that will foster the conservation of energy.

Coefficient of Building Performance. In most large buildings different systems are simultaneously heating and cooling and generating heat and needing heat—each doing its specific task efficiently, yet working at cross-purposes with other systems or not operating cooperatively to improve the performance of the building as a whole. Calculation of the coefficient of performance of the mechanical systems of a building as a whole rather than as separate parts can assist creative design and inte-

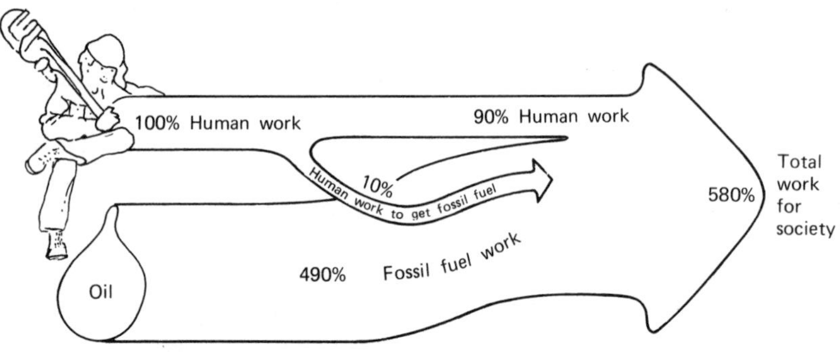

Figure 4.48 Expensive fossil fuels multiply the work available from our own effort; stretching out reserves of fossil fuels keeps them available to do difficult work in the future. *Source.* State of California, Office of the Architect, *Building Value,* 1977.

Table 4.9 Estimated Energy Conservation Potentials in Office Buildings: Listed in Order of Potential Savings

Category	Item	Potential
HEAT GAIN		58
	transmission	8
	infiltration	6
	cfm ventilation	8
	temp. differential ventilation	8
	power	5
	artificial lighting	10
	solar radiation	9
	people	2
	business machines	2
HEAT LOSS		42
	transmission	10
	infiltration	7
	cfm ventilation	9
	temp. differential ventilation	9
	solar radiation effects	7
BUILDING DESIGN		31
	site	4
	orientation	3
	plan	5
	configuration	5
	envelope	9
	structure	1
	codes and standards	4
EQUIPMENT		23
	heating system	9
	cooling system	9
	ventilation system	3
	power system	2
CLIMATE		19
	temperature	10
	sun	7
	wind	2
LIGHTING		11
	artificial lighting system	8
	natural lighting system	3
VENTILATION		10
	infiltration amount	7
	natural ventilation	3
GEOGRAPHIC LOCATION		10
PHYSIOLOGICAL NEEDS		10
DOMESTIC HOT WATER		2
SOLID WASTE MANAGEMENT		1

Source. State of California, Office of the Architect, *Building Value,* 1977, GSA/Dugin (36).

gration of the various systems. Emphasis should be placed in improvement in operating procedures, which can be of equal or greater importance than the effectiveness of equipment design.

Energy Cascading

• Uses of energy should be cascaded wherever possible to make multiple and fullest use of remaining energy quality of waste energy from each application.

Energy cascading is the careful use of the energy quality remaining after a use of high quality energy. Both the waste heat from generating electricity to operate our lights and the heat released from the lamps themselves can be used to heat buildings. The heated or cooled air then can be used to preheat or cool the incoming ventilation air. Heat exhausted by air conditioners can be used to preheat hot water.

Total energy plants employ energy cascading for the generation of both electrical and thermal energy from fossil fuels at a building site. With such an arrangement it is possible to use the waste heat from the electrical generation for space heating, water heating, and air conditioning—nearly doubling overall efficiency and cutting fuel consumption in half.

Probably the most difficult problem is that of balancing electrical and thermal loads, particularly since they change daily and seasonally. Even during a period when the only thermal load is for hot water, the efficiency of total energy plants can equal that of a central power plant. If adjacent office buildings and apartment houses are served, the day and evening needs are more balanced. Such plants, which are used to a considerable extent in Scandinavia and West Germany, provide a good means of improving effectiveness of use of fossil fuels in energy generation.

Institutional Performance

Institutional Options

• Alternative institutional arrangements should be explored prior to the construction and operation of any new building. Such alternatives should include noninstitutional performance of policy objectives, rehabilitation of existing buildings, leasing, decentralized space procurement, and reimbursement for individual procurement of working space.

More effective institutional structures requiring fewer buildings—home rather than hospital treatment, community homes rather than minimum security prisons, campus-free colleges—can result in substantial savings where their performance is acceptable. Use and adaptation of existing facilities rather than new construction can often offer savings in time as well as dollars, and more effective use of space can frequently develop when individuals have incentive to be imaginative.

LA CITÉ
Montreal, Quebec
Architects: Eva Velsei & Dan Hangunu
Photo: W. Dagenais

Employee Effectiveness

• All buildings should be programmed for specific user needs.

Involving users in building programming and design can be as productive in terms of morale and work effectiveness as in creating effective working conditions.

• A contingency fund should be included in all new construction for occupant changes.

Even the most careful design process cannot anticipate the improvements in building use that emerge through actual occupancy and use. Changing personnel and functions require gradual, almost continuing adaptation of building layout and interior details.

• Construction processes should be broken down to facilitate successful performance by the majority of contractors in the locale where construction is to occur.

Effective local involvement is important to the cost and execution of building construction as well as to operation.

• In buildings of four levels or less, elevators should be provided only for handicapped persons and freight. Stair and ramp circulation should be emphasized in building design and layout.

For many holders of sedentary jobs, going to and from work and lunch form the only opportunity for the minimal exercise necessary to maintain good health.

• All new construction should allow for user-operable natural ventilation.

Different people and different activities and different moods require different temperature conditions, and this is the source of one of the most consistent disagreements in a working environment. We provide individual air control on airplanes, why not in buildings?

• Recreational facilities should be available and accessible to employees from where they work.

Morale in offices is often improved when relationships between people have an opportunity to develop beyond work functions. Recreation and exercise on lunch hours and breaks can also contribute to the health and performance of employees.

• New buildings should not exceed four stories in height except where required by special environmental and social planning priorities.

Design decisions on factors such as building configuration and height need to be addressed from the standpoint of the combined effects of health and exercise considerations, construction cost increases in taller buildings, elevator costs, fire protection, impacts on land prices, social effects, and costs of public services such as transportation and police protection. Traditional decision factors, of course, should not be ignored.

Performance Standards

• Lighting levels should not exceed the maximums listed in Table 4.10: 20 to 30 footcandles should be provided in work areas, with provision for individuals to augment light levels at work stations as needed.

Lighting levels in most new buildings are considerably in excess of task needs. Recommended school lighting levels in the United States have shot up from 30 footcandles in 1930 to between 70 and 150 footcandles, although other countries do not use such high levels. There is enough light from 30 footcandles to come within 7% of the theoretical limit of our visual apparatus, an increase to 150 footcandles would yield a further increase of only 3 to 4%.

Variation is necessary to accommodate individual tasks and individual eyesight problems, but such situations should be handled on an individual basis rather than raising overall light levels and lighting costs, with the major resultant impacts on air conditioning costs.

The development of new high efficiency incandescent lamps in response to increased energy costs, and energy-saving (19%) dc "ballast" in combination with cathode-shielded fixtures and full-spectrum fluorescent

Table 4.10 Recommended Maximum Lighting Levels

Task or area	Footcandle levels	How measured
Hallways or corridors -----	10 ± 5	Measured average, minimum 1 footcandle.
Work and circulation areas surrounding work stations -----	30 ± 5	Measured average.
Normal office work, such as reading and writing (on task only), store shelves, and general display areas ------------	50 ± 10	Measured at work station.
Prolonged office work which is somewhat difficult visually (on task only) ----------	75 ± 15	Measured at work station.
Prolonged office work which is visually difficult and critical in nature (on task only)------	100 ± 20	Measured at work station.
Industrial tasks --------	ANSI-A11.1-1973	As maximum.

Source. State of California, Office of the Architect, *Building Value,* 1977.

lamps, is expected to help in achieving needed performance levels. The Energy Resources Development Administration and Phillips are among those attempting to improve the efficiency of incandescent lamps, and John Ott's research has led to changes in fluorescent lamps aimed at avoiding health problems attributed to the present design.

• Structural codes should be reviewed to eliminate unnecessary pyramiding of safety factors.

Performance requirements for building systems frequently are excessive, contributing to the costs of institutional operation. Richard Stein's inquiries into unnecessary performance requirements, in *Spotlight on the Energy Crisis*, have shown a number of areas in which costs can be reduced.

Support Services

• Street level space in new buildings should be available for convenience services.

Urban areas occupied by government offices or large corporations frequently fail to provide for the many support services necessary for both institutional operation and personal needs. Restaurants, grocery stores, print shops, office equipment supply and repair, bars, and drugstores are often totally absent over a large area. As a result, the primary institutions do not operate with maximum effectiveness, and urban space and facilities are ineffectively used.

Operating Procedures

• Operation of building systems should be congruent with function: general area lighting and comfort control systems should be separately controlled for each work area, by means of controls easily accessible to workers.

Symbolic factors play a significant role in the formation of people's attitudes. Being able to work at night without turning on the lights in a whole building, and being able to decide when artificial lighting is and is not needed are examples of important, though small, factors in people's effectiveness.

• Building design, location, and site planning should encourage user involvement in responsibility for private and public spaces, as well as their operation and maintenance.

Design patterns can encourage or impede user development with the physical and social operation of buildings and surrounding areas. Certain building patterns support people's ability to take responsibility for shared spaces and maintain security and social control.

Externalized Costs

Land Use

• New construction should not take place on prime agricultural land.

Population and resource trends point to greater dependence on agricultural productivity in the future. When urban areas are unnecessarily expanded into prime agricultural land, the latter must be replaced with marginal land entailing considerable ongoing energy and capital subsidies—an increasing and unnecessary burden on scarce resources. Urban sprawl also can double a community's capital and operating costs.

Transportation. Building locations should be chosen that do the following:

• Permit one-third of the employees to live within walking or bicycling distance of work.
• Minimize commuting needs and permit such needs to be fulfilled by public transit.
• Minimize impacts on city services and infrastructure.

Building location policies that preserve our options of reducing energy consumption in the future by choosing more efficient commuting patterns, or individually choosing more efficient commuting patterns, eliminating some forms of communication, can reduce that increasing economic burden.

Parking

• Bicycle and motorcycle parking should be provided for the occupants of all new and existing buildings.

• Whenever public transit service is available, automobile parking should be provided only for the handicapped and for nonlocal visitors. Where automobile parking must be provided, the full costs should be charged to the users.

Climate

• Adverse microclimatic conditions should not be imposed upon surrounding buildings and public or private

Table 4.11 Resource Multipliers

Multiply delivered energy by the following multipliers to obtain estimated total nonrenewable energy resources required by each delivery system.

Non-Electric		Electric	
Solar Space Heat	.19	Hydro-Electric	.03
Geothermal—Hot Water Heating (Exist. Flows)	.25	Geothermal Steam Electric (Exist. Flows)	.06
Domestic Natural Gas	1.19	Coal Fired Electric (Strip Mined)	4.06
Liquefied Natural Gas from North Slope	1.34	Shale Oil Electric	5.05
Domestic On-Shore Petroleum	1.34	Coal Gasification Electric (Strip Mined)	6.64
Alaska North Slope Petroleum	1.45	Nuclear Fission Electric (LWR)	7.88
High Grade Oil Shale	1.65		
Coal Gasification (Strip Mined)	2.19		

Source. State of California, Office of the Architect, *Building Value,* 1977.

outdoor spaces through heat rejection, light reflection, shading, or undesirable impacts created by other means.

Shadows cast by buildings can prevent proper operation of solar heating systems in nearby buildings. Reflective window glazing, unshaded asphalt paving, and heat rejected from air conditioners cause major discomfort in nearby spaces.

• Paved areas, including streets adjacent to new construction, should be shaded by plant materials or other means during cooling seasons.

• Plant materials or other shading should be selected and located to shade a minimum of 85% of the surface at maturity.

• Low-maintenance, drought-resistant plants native to the area of construction should be used where possible, except where substantial nuisance factors exist.

Temperatures of unshaded asphalt streets often rise more than 50°F above the ambient air temperature because these surfaces absorb sunlight. Lack of summer shading increases outside air temperatures by 10°F and temperatures inside buildings by up to 20°F. This frequently means more mechanical cooling, which in turn discharges more heat into the outside air, again increasing the cooling load on buildings and the discomfort of people.

Shade Factors. Shade factors are useful in calculating the effect of trees in reducing solar heat gain in the summer and available solar energy in the winter.

Shade Patterns and Rates of Growth and Plant Selection. No rate of growth holds good for any species of tree under all circumstances. A tree's performance is governed very much by the area in which it is planted: climate and soil are all-important. Soils vary considerably in depth, moisture content, and nutrient supply. These factors in turn depend on temperature and rainfall. Trees of different species, however, have characteristic patterns of growth.

Energy Supply and Costs. The resource multipliers listed in Table 4.11 are useful in determining the type(s) of energy to be used.

• A source stream analysis of all energy supplies for new construction should be made to minimize total costs and stretch availability of nonrenewable fuels.

Source Stream Analysis. Although energy may be used very efficiently within a building, the choice of whether to burn different fuels directly in the building, to use them somewhere else to make steam or electricity (which is then used in the building), or to take various other options, may result in significantly more or less use of irreplaceable fuel resources. Source stream analysis is the calculation of the amount of our energy reserves that would be used up under various options of supplying the same end demand in a building. The goal is to lessen total resource use. The rules are fairly simple, and they are not dissimilar to the laws of thermodynamics; the deeper you dig and the more you change energy forms, the more you lose.

Energy Quality

• Energy quality should be matched to particular applications, and energy of unnecessarily high quality should not be used in any application.

Table 4.12 Evaluation of Energy Quality Relative to Coal, Expressed as Calories of Coal Necessary to Obtain Energy with Qualities Equivalent to the Sources Listed

Energy Type	Energy Quality
Solar heating	0.00009
Uranium^{235} as mined	0.0003
Solar energy in photons	0.045
Photosynthetic products, uncollected	0.05
Geothermal steam (volcanic area)	0.625
Gulf of Mexico oil	0.7
Alaskan oil	0.7
Western coal before mining	0.9
Coal already mined	1.0
Tidal energy, 20 ft. tide	1.66
Heating gas	1.8
Elevated water	3.125
Electricity	3.7
Food at supermarket	24.
Average human service in United States	126.
College educated service	312.
Doctor's service	1,250.

Source. State of California, Office of the Architect, *Building Value,* 1977.

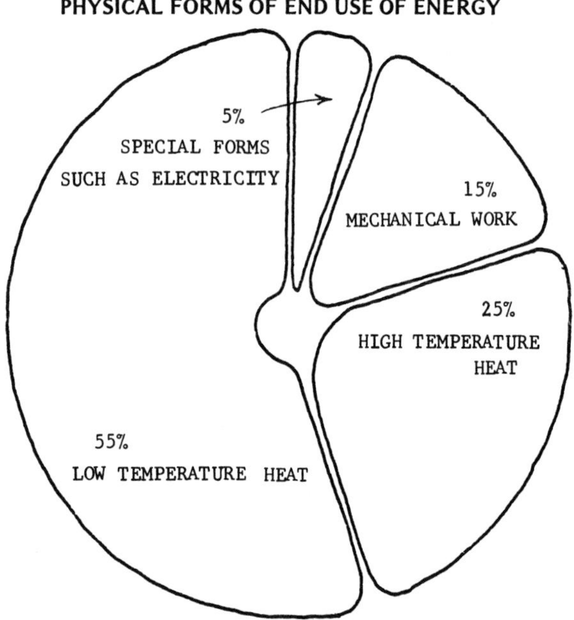

Figure 4.49 *Source.* State of California, Office of the Architect, *Building Value,* 1977, Amory Levins (56).

Different kinds of energy have different capabilities and different qualities (Table 4.12). Some are more concentrated (a gallon of gasoline vs. a cord of wool), some are more easily transported, some cannot be stored. Some are variable and some reliable (solar heat vs. natural gas), some necessitate a lot of work to get a relatively small amount of energy, while others furnish a lot of energy for a little work. Some are limited in supply, some renewable. Different kinds of energy can do different kinds of work (mechanical, electrical, heat) and all vary in how easily they can be transformed to do different kinds of work.

Only a small portion of our energy use requires high quality. We can use less expensive and less severely limited renewable energy sources for many applications, allowing us to save our limited high-quality energy for special needs.

The use of expensive and limited high-quality energy sources for jobs that do not require their special properties wastes resources and dollars. Space heating and hot water can be achieved with waste heat from electrical generation, direct solar or mechanized solar heating. Liquid fuels for transportation and mobile applications can be produced by fermentation of plant wastes; it is not necessary to squander electricity. Coal, natural gas, petroleum, and hydroelectricity can be reserved for the high-temperature processes, special applications, and future use, rather than for operating hot water heaters.

Employment

• Where costs are comparable, processes should be chosen that favor employment over capital or energy expenditures.

Higher energy costs make employment-intensive processes more competitive. A movement to increase the

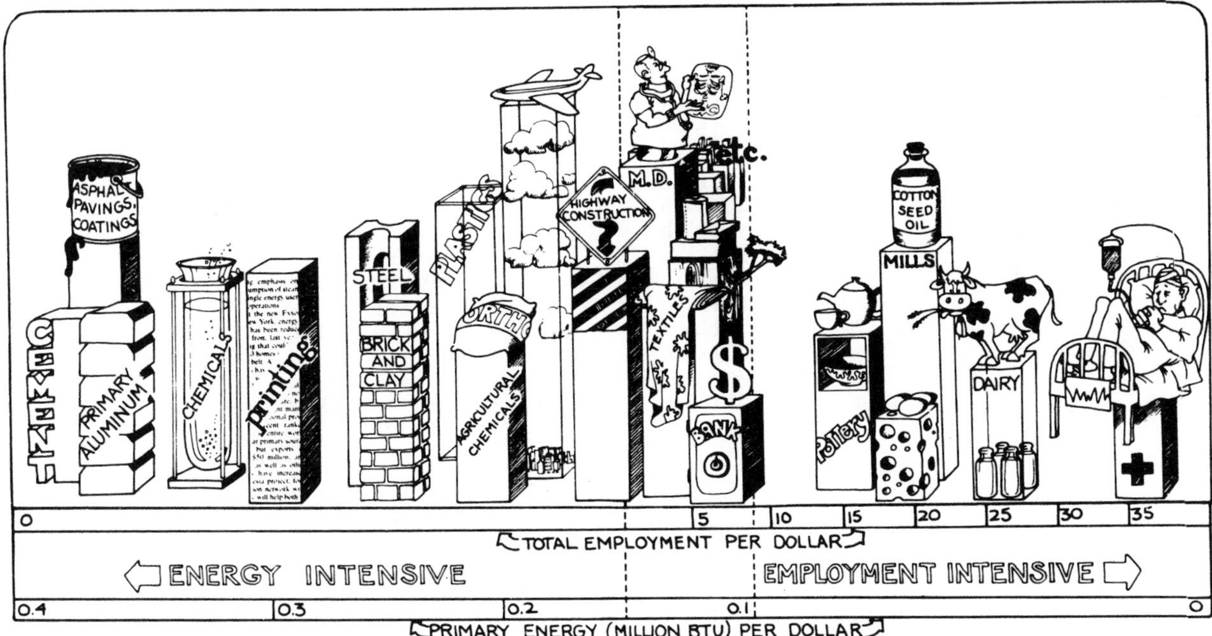

Figure 4.50 Energy and employment intensity of various activities. *Source*. State of California, Office of the Architect, *Building Value,* 1977, drawing by Diane Schatz. Data by Bruce Hannon (39).

use of such processes simultaneously resolves employment problems and reduces energy use. Most energy-intensive industries are fairly recent developments, made possible by inexpensive energy; unfortunately they have replaced more traditional services and goods that can be produced in ways that use less energy and offer more employment.

Full accounting of unemployment costs, alternative investment options, and implications of emerging capital, energy, and employment cost trends suggest the value of employment-intensive processes.

The potentials for employment-providing and energy-saving changes is particularly great in regard to construction materials and processes (Table 4.13). In *Low-Energy Housing,* MacKillop documents the potential for a 90% reduction in construction energy use in British housing through changing to employment-intensive material specifications. Similar but less radical changes in specified materials and processes in building design can generate significant changes in energy and employment in construction. Many traditional, but seldom used, building processes conserve energy and materials, are low in cost, and provide more rewarding work for the builders.

In *Architecture for the Poor,* Hassan Fathey reports on the construction of a whole village by traditional techniques. Using sun-dried bricks, the author was able to create comfortable homes for less than 20% of what our cheapest, barren, "low-cost" housing would have cost. Such techniques work as well for larger buildings, indeed, they have been employed for centuries in elegant and beautiful mosques, shopping arcades, and public buildings throughout West Asia.

Many of these techniques allow opportunities for rewarding work for the tradespeople using them—expression of design and building skill through creation of individual brick patterns in each dome of a building, or design of special lighting fixtures for a building, as frequently practiced by Alvar Aalto in Finland.

Materials

- Where costs are comparable, preference should be given to building materials and to material suppliers who demonstrate the highest levels of reuse and recycling.
- All new construction should be designed and constructed to permit maximum future recovery of materials.
- All structural materials and members should be permanently marked with their designed load capacity and configuration.
- Where costs and performance are comparable, preference should be given to construction materials that (*a*)

Table 4.13 Typical Materials and Energy Inputs for Standard Housing Units (Parker-Morris standard 3-bed semidetached, 100 m² floorspace)

Materials	*Energy Inputs*	*Materials Transport*	
Bricks: 16,000	3200 kWh	Bricks 60 miles at 1.5 kWh/ton mile:	3200 kWh
Steel: 1.2 tons	9200 kWh	Timber 250 miles at 1kWh/ton mile:	1100 kWh
Glass : 320 ft²	2000 kWh	Cement 40 miles at 1.5 kWh/ton mile:	400 kWh
Concrete : 10 tons	5000 kWh		
Cement: 2 tons	3600 kWh		4700 kWh
Plaster: 3 tons	900 kWh		
Timber: 4.3 cu. m.	310 kWh	*Site Preparation*	
Plastics: 250 lbs	300 kWh	Excavation/Handling: 2000 cu. ft =	6000 kWh
Paint: 4700 sq. ft.	500 kWh	Cement mixing and Miscellaneous	
Copper & Brass: 500 lbs	2300 kWh	machinery: 100 gals fuel =	4200 kWh
Others: —	4000 kWh		10,200 kWh
	31,510 kWh	Total inputs 31,500 + 10,200 + 4700	
			TOTAL 53,700 kwh

Alternative 1: 10% soil-cement blocks	
8 cu. yds. cement and handling:	12,500 kWh
Soil: 50 tons (hand labour):	50 kWh
Localised wood supply:	150 kWh
Glass:	2000 kWh
In situ rendering materials:	100 kWh
Metals:	1500 kWh
Others	2500 kWh
	TOTAL 18,800 kwh

Alternative 2: Rammed earth	
80 cu. yds earth, 70 men days:	100 kWh
160 cu. yds. earth invert:	150 kWh
Glass:	1500 kWh
Timber:	150 kWh
Rendering:	50 kWh
Metals	1000 kWh
Others:	2000 kWh
	TOTAL 4450 kwh

Source. State of California, Office of the Architect, *Building Value,* 1977.

minimize energy use and depletion of scarce resources, (*b*) provide greater employment, and (*c*) minimize health hazards in their manufacture and installation.

• Site materials such as topsoil and construction debris should be kept segregated into appropriate categories for reuse and recycling.

The dependence of modern architecture on expensive, exotic, or depleting resources is much greater than is apparent at first glance. For example, the following materials are in frequent use today: high-strength steels with rare metal alloys; concrete, with high-energy portland cement; energy-expensive aluminum; synthetic petroleum-based plastic and composite materials for wall coverings, fixtures, roofing, roads, and sealants; titanium and other scarce metal-based paint pigments; and heat-reflecting glass coated with gold and silver. Yet we must make major reductions in the use of them all as our resource limits become felt in building construction.

Our rates of use of renewable resources such as timber and agriculturally produced oils and chemicals are far above their rates of renewal; this is the result of depleting growth that has been stored for hundreds of years. As such existing stands are depleted, we face substantial shortage of even our renewable resources before sustainable yields can be reestablished. These prospects underscore the importance of wise use and reuse of our remaining resources.

Resource Limits. Failure to reuse and recycle our rapidly depleting resources causes a major loss of wealth to us and to future generations. A great deal of work and energy are necessary to replace or substitute for them, and we experience increasing political and economic dependency on the suppliers of our remaining reserves of those materials. More metal was removed from the earth in the first third of this century alone than had been mined in the entire span of human history—enough, if wisely conserved, to operate any sane society for generations without further need for new resources.

Energy Cost of Materials. Building materials differ widely in the energy requirements associated with mining, processing, and fabricating them. Cement, aluminum, and asphalt coatings are produced in some of our most energy-intensive industries, whereas wood

GALLERY OF MODERN ART
New York, New York
Architects: Edward Durell Stone & Associates
Photo: E. Stoller Associates

Table 4.14 Production Energy Saved by Recycling

Material	Point of Impact	Virgin Material	Recycled Material	Percent Saved	Ease of recycling
Steel	Molten Steel	46.7	22.6	52	Present technology limited by impurities, separation and collection.
Aluminum	Molten Aluminum	224.5	8.2	96	Present technology limited by separation and collection.
Plastics	Molten	45.2	2.0	96	Extremely difficult; no satisfactory technology known.
Paperboard	Pulp	6.6	3.3	50	Present technology for separated waste; no satisfactory technology for mixed waste.
Glass	Transportation	7.8	7.8	0	Difficult and costly.

Source. State of California, Office of the Architect, *Building Value,* 1977.

products use relatively little energy. "Energy per pound" means little until specific uses are compared. For example, a shed might be roofed in aluminum, slate, or tile; the metal would be an expensive choice, but less weight of it would be required to do the job. In addition to different resource depletion, energy use, and employment potentials, different materials have different social impacts—asbestiosis, polychlorinated biphenyl poisoning, transportation demands, and so on.

Recycling Benefits. As Table 4.14 indicates, the recycling of materials also offers major potentials for energy savings—eliminating the expenditures for mining, concentrating, and processing the ores or other materials. Such savings will become even more pronounced as it becomes necessary to use lower grade sources for new materials. Reuse of fabricated materials and products provides obvious additional savings by avoiding the need to refabricate or manufacture replacements.

Numerous examples can be given: designing wood buildings, which usually can be easily disassembled; use of bolted collections in steel and prefabricated concrete construction; specification of reusable concrete planks and beams, or posttensioned assemblies rather than poured-in-place concrete; use of mortar with lower strength than the masonry in masonry construction; selection of European-style precast concrete paving stones for sidewalks. These fabrication procedures can immensely increase the recovery of materials and improve the residual value of buildings at the end of their useful life. Recycling of materials provides additional benefits to local and regional economies through development of employment within the region and retention of wages, profits, and secondary employment within the area.

Water Supply. Water use in new construction should be minimized through the following measures:

- Use of water-conserving fixtures in all sinks, showers, and wash basins.
- Use of native drought-resistant plant materials in landscaping.
- Reuse of water for appropriate applications such as vehicle washing or landscape irrigation.
- Conservation of water use in air conditioning.
- Analysis of supply sources in terms of basic conservation policy and measures.

Our use of increasingly scarce water is generally excessive. Topping the list are flush toilets, which consume 100 gallons per day per household. A 75% reduction in water use is easily possible with proper equipment choice and system design.

Sewage Systems

- Toilets using more than 2 quarts of water per flush should not be installed in any new construction. Preference should be given to various waterless toilet systems and on-site sewage treatment wherever feasible, particularly for small buildings and remote sites.

Conventional toilet systems involve dilution of our sewage 100 times with water, which more than doubles our domestic water requirements, necessitates sewage treatment of 100 times the volume of materials, and causes soluble nutrients in our sewage to contaminate our rivers and lakes instead of returning to the fields to grow more food. Increased fertilizer needs, expensive tertiary sewage treatment, massive sewer and sewage treatment

WATER USE IN CALIFORNIA

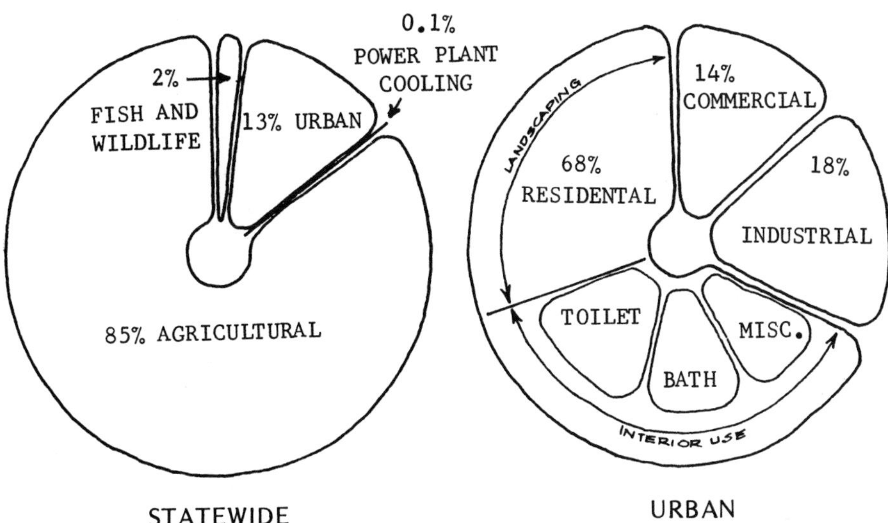

Figure 4.51 *Source.* State of California, Office of the Architect, *Building Value,* 1977.

facilities, and vast water supply and purification systems are major and avoidable costs resulting from such systems. Development of tested low-flush toilets, vacuum and compressed air toilets, and grey water reuse techniques provide desirable options to traditional toilet systems for a wide variety of specific situations.

Vacuum systems are ideally suited for multistory office buildings. Installation and operating costs result in considerable savings over conventional units. Since office buildings seldom have extensive bathing and laundry facilities, most of the water usage is for toilets. In a 20-story building, 2000 people use 26 gallons per person (24 gallons for toilets, 2 for sinks). A vacuum toilet uses only 4 gallons per person daily—8000 gallons compared to 52,000 gallons. A vacuum toilet saves water by using only 3 pints for each flush, compared to up to 6 gallons in conventional systems. Thus savings in water costs and treatment costs result from a 90% reduction in volume.

• Control and absorption of storm water should be accomplished on site wherever possible.

Most cities have combined sanitary and storm sewers, which cause release of raw sewage into rivers and streams during every major storm in addition to requiring processing of much larger volumes of sewage. On-site detention of storm water runoff can be an effective economical method of storm water management. It can serve to control local flooding and sewer overflows, supplement water supplies, assist in aquifer recharge, and reduce the large costs of centralized underground sewage systems.

Community Value

• Building location, size, configuration, and architectural design should be chosen to harmonize with surrounding neighborhoods.

In closing I would like to quote the past national president of the AIA, John McGinty:

> A future of limited resources does not need to be a future of limited options. Recycled buildings can possess a warmth, a touch of humanity that is difficult to achieve in new structures. Rebuilt inner cities can provide convenience, maturity and relationships to neighbors and to people and a variety of uses that is seldom found in new suburbs. Energy conservation does not need to mean caves and candles, dark and cold. It also does not mean substituting a solar collector on the roof for a boiler in the basement. It should mean a beauty that comes from the natural harmony between the built and the natural environment, between man and his natural origins. The response to this issue alone will be as significant an architectural design determinant as was the industrial revolution. If we can succeed in meeting this design challenge, the future of our profession is secure.

I hope this book will give my fellow architects and all future architects a little help to think in these terms.

—A. M. KEMPER

BIBLIOGRAPHY

Anderson, Bruce and Michael Riordan, *The Solar Home Book,* Cheshire Books, Wellington, New Zealand, 1976.

Architect's Handbook of Professional Practice, American Institute of Architects, Washington, DC, 1972 edition.

Babcock, Richard F., *The Zoning Game,* University of Wisconsin Press, Madison, WI, 1973.

Baker, Geoffrey and Bruno Funaro, *Parking,* Reinhold Publishing Co., Stamford, CN, 1958.

Berelson, Bernard and Gary A. Steiner, *Human Behavior,* shorter edition, Harcourt, Brace and World, New York, 1967.

Berendt, Raymond D. and Edith L. R. Corliss, *NBS Handbook 119,* U.S. Department of Commerce, Washington DC, 1976.

BOCA Basic Building Code, 6th edition, Building Officials, Chicago, 1975.

Brenchley, F. G., *Practical Building Acoustics,* Wiley-Interscience, New York, 1976.

Callender, John Hancock, *Time-Saver Standards,* 5th edition, McGraw-Hill Book Co., New York, 1974.

Caudill, William Wayne, *Architecture By Team,* Van Nostrand Reinhold Co., New York, 1971.

Clough, Richard H., *Construction Project Management,* John Wiley & Sons, Inc., New York, 1972.

The Community, Time-Life Books, Alexandria, VA, 1976.

The Community Builders Handbook, 1954 Members Edition, Urban Land Institute, Washington DC, 1954.

Cullen, Gordon, *Townscape,* Reinhold Book Corp., New York, 1968.

Deasy, C. M., *Design For Human Affairs,* Schenkman Publishing Co., Cambridge, MA, 1974.

De Chiara, Joseph and Lee Koppelman, *Planning Design Criteria,* Van Nostrand Reinhold Co., New York, 1968.

De Chiara, Joseph and John Hancock Callender, *Time-Saver Standards For Building Types,* McGraw-Hill Book Co., New York, 1973.

Doxiadis, C. A., *Action For Human Settlements,* W. W. Norton & Co., New York, 1976.

Eccli, Eugene, *Low-Cost, Energy Efficient Shelter,* Rodale Press, Emmaus, PA, 1976.

Egan, M. David, *Concepts in Architectural Acoustics,* McGraw-Hill Book Co., New York, 1972.

Feld, Jacob, *Construction Failure,* Wiley-Interscience, New York, 1976.

FHA Minimum Property Standards, U.S. Department of Housing, Washington DC, 1965.

Fire Protection Handbook, 14th edition, National Fire Protection Association, Boston, MA, 1976.

Fitch, James Marston, *American Building, The Environment Forces that Shape It,* 2nd edition, Schocken Books, New York, 1972.

Fruin, John J., *Pedestrian Planning & Design,* Metropolitan Association of Urban Designers & Environmental Planners, New York, 1971.

Goldsmith, Selwyn, *Designing for the Disabled,* 2nd edition, McGraw-Hill Book Co., New York, 1967.

Goodman, Paul and Percival Goodman, *Communitas,* Vintage Books, 1960.

Green, Isaac, Bernard E. Fedewa, Charles A. Johnston, William M. Jackson, and Howard L. Deardorff, *Housing for the Elderly,* Van Nostrand Reinhold Co., New York, 1974.

Hall, Edward T., *The Hidden Dimension,* Doubleday Anchor Books, New York, 1966.

Heimsath, Clovis, *Behavioral Architecture,* McGraw-Hill Book Co., New York, 1977.

Hopf, Peter S., *Designers Guide to OSHA,* McGraw-Hill Book Co., New York, 1975.

Hornbostel, Caleb, *Material for Architects,* Reinhold Publishing Co., Stamford, CN, 1965.

Hosken, Fran P., *The Functions of Cities,* Schenkman Publishing Co., Cambridge, MA, 1973.

Hosken, Fran P., *The Language of Cities,* Schenkman Publishing Co., Cambridge, MA, 1972.

Hunt, William Dudley, Jr., *Total Design,* McGraw-Hill Book Co., New York, 1972.

Jellicoe, Geoffrey and Susan Jellicoe, *The Landscape of Man,* Viking Press-Studio Book, New York, 1975.

Kira, Alexander, *The Bathroom,* Viking Compass Books, New York, 1976.

Kreh, R. T., Sr., *Masonry Skills,* Van Nostrand Reinhold Co., New York, 1976.

Leckie, Jim, Gil Masters, Harry Whitehouse, and Lily Young, *Other Homes and Garbage,* Sierra Club Books, San Francisco, CA, 1975.

Liebing, Ralph W. and Mimi Ford Paul, *Architectural Working Drawings,* Wiley-Interscience, New York, 1977.

Lynch, Kevin, *Site Planning,* 2nd edition, MIT Press, Cambridge, MA, 1971.

Marks, Harold, *Traffic Circulation Planning for Communities,* Gruen Associates, Los Angeles, CA, 1974.

McGuinness, William J. and Benjamin Stein, *Mechanical and Electrical Equipment for Buildings,* 5th edition, John Wiley & Sons, Inc., New York, 1971.

Merritt, Frederick S., *Building Construction Handbook,* 3rd edition, McGraw-Hill Book Co., New York, 1975.

Moore, Charles and Gerald Allen, *Dimensions,* Architectural Record Books, New York, 1976.

Moreland, Frank L., Editor, "The Use of Earth Covered Buildings," report (1975), National Science Foundation, Washington, DC, 1975.

Munson, Albe E., *Construction Design for Landscape Architects,* McGraw-Hill Book Co., New York, 1974.

O'Brien, James J., *Construction Inspection Handbook,* Van Nostrand Reinhold Co., New York, 1974.

Parker, H., *Simplified Engineering for Architects and Builders,* 5th edition, John Wiley & Sons, Inc., New York, 1975.

Rabb, Judith and Bernard Rabb, *Good Shelter,* New York Times Book Co., New York, 1975.

Ramsey, C. G., and H. R. Sleeper, *Architectural Graphic Standards,* 6th edition, The American Institute of Architects, John Wiley & Sons, Inc., New York, 1970.

Raskin, Eugene, *Architecturally Speaking,* Reinhold Publishing Co., Stamford, CN, 1954.

Raskin, Eugene, *Sequel To Cities,* Bloch Publishing Co., New York, 1969.

Rosen, Harold J., *Construction Specification Writing,* Wiley-Interscience, New York, 1974.

Rutledge, Albert J., *Anatomy of a Park,* McGraw-Hill Book Co., New York, 1971.

Salvadori, Mario, *Mathematics in Architecture,* Prentice-Hall, Englewood Cliffs, NJ, 1974.

Salvadori, Mario and Robert Heller, *Structure in Architecture, The Building of Buildings,* Prentice-Hall, Englewood Cliffs, NJ, 1975.

Schmidt, John L., Harold Bennett Olin, and Walter H. Lewis, *Construction Principles, Materials and Methods,* American Savings & Loan Institute, Chicago, 1972.

Simonds, John Ormsbee, *Landscape Architecture,* McGraw-Hill Book Co., New York, 1961.

Smith, Craig B., *Efficient Electricity Use,* Pergamon Press, Elmsford, NY, 1976.

Solar Dwelling Design Concepts, AIA Research Corporation, U.S. Department of Housing, Washington, DC, 1976.

Sommer, Robert, *Personal Space,* Prentice-Hall, Engelwood Cliffs, NJ, 1969.

Spreiregen, Paul D., *Urban Design: The Architecture of Towns and Cities,* McGraw-Hill Book Co., New York, 1965.

Szokolay, S. V., *Solar Energy and Building,* 2nd edition, Wiley-Interscience, New York, 1977.

UBC Uniform Building Code, 1976 edition, Whittier, CA, 1976.

Von Hertzen, Heikki and Paul D. Spreiregen, *Building a New Town,* MIT Press, Cambridge, MA, 1973.

Wade, John, Architecture, *Architecture Problems and Purposes,* Wiley-Interscience, New York, 1977.

Wagner, Richard H., *Environment & Man,* 2nd edition, W. W. Norton & Co., New York, 1974.

Walker, Les and Jeff Milstein, *Designing Houses,* Overlook Press, Woodstock, New York, 1976.

Wass, Alonzo, *Manual of Structural Details for Building Construction,* Prentice-Hall, Englewood Cliffs, NJ, 1968.

White, Edward T., *Introduction to Architectural Programming,* Architectural Media, Tucson, AZ, 1972.

Whittick, Arnold, *Encyclopedia of Urban Planning,* McGraw-Hill Book Co., New York, 1974.

Wilson, Forrest, *Graphic Guide to Interior Design,* Van Nostrand Reinhold Co., New York, 1977.

INDEX